Safe Boating Remains Our Objective

Jeff Jones, Publisher

Getting you safely and enjoyably to your next boating destination.

This has been Waterway Guide's main objective for many years. And well it should be, as it offers a simple rationale for our commitment to the excellence of our content and the Waterway Guide brand. Our team has been espousing this mantra for several years now in our own publications and through our relationships with other marine media outlets.

This year we find ourselves in a pandemic situation of historical significance. It has rocked our boats like nothing since World War II (IMHO). Our lives and lifestyles have been upended. Yet, we continue to seek fun and adventure on the water while abiding by the same time-honored maritime rules that have been guiding us for generations. On the other hand, there are a whole bunch of new and confusing regulations at almost every port of call. Your Waterway Guide team was quick to respond to this changing environment even before the pandemic storm hit us full force.

In February 2020, our staff developed the **COVID-19 Marina/Service Reports and Access** that became the go-to source for changing regulations and marina access across this country. Over 8,000 marinas across the world are in our database and displayed in our various media channels. The monumental task of keeping their information updated became a focused effort led by newcomer Ethan Jett, who worked diligently to keep the facts in order and coordinate the postings. Using our **Hurricane Damage Reports** as the model, we worked with NOAA, USCG, communities, our cruising editors and marinas to verify the facts and report them on the website at www.waterwayguide.com. Hundreds of thousands of boaters were seeking information about how to get access to their vessels and whether marinas were open or closed. Our reporting became a vital pipeline of information. Kudos to the staff for that effort.

For regular users of our printed *Waterway Guides*, you may notice a few changes with this edition. There are new chart excerpts from Aqua Map based on NOAA cartography, revised marina tables and updated aerial images.

By the time you read this you are no doubt aware that many boat shows in 2020 were cancelled due to the pandemic. Instead of picking up your Guide(s) at a boat show, you may want to order your Waterway Guide(s) through our website or one of our resellers. We are pleased to report that the revised, 2nd edition of our *Florida Keys* guide is now available, which is our latest offering along with the *Western Gulf Coast* edition. With 20 publications in our lineup, including the *Skipper Bob* series, we have you covered in most of America's most spectacular waterways in addition to the Bahamas and Cuba.

The pandemic and the effects it is having on small businesses everywhere impacts our company's decisions on a daily basis. Our printing schedules, attendance at boat shows, relationships with on-the-water cruising editors and the thousands of destinations we promote have all been altered. But our commitment to accuracy and safe boating has not.

Finally, we are dedicated to offering more and easier access to Waterway Guide content on our diverse digital platforms. I believe you will be impressed with the amount of information you can now access on your laptop or mobile devices. Our Waterway Guide Explorer website continues to be the industry gold standard for boaters and cruisers. In 2019 we offered exceptional enhancements online through a subscription model that provides both digital and print options for planning your travel and destinations. The Waterway Guide Marinas mobile app is still going strong after 5 years and there is a new and robust WG App that will offer even more options for boaters who want up-to-date and accurate information at their fingertips.

Whether cruising the Great Lakes; exploring the out islands of the Bahamas; motoring lazily along the ICW; fishing Chesapeake Bay, or splashing about the Florida Keys on a fun-filled weekend, take Waterway Guide along and safely enjoy your time on America's waterways.

Best,

Jeff Jones, Publisher

WATERWAY GUIDE OFFICES

Corporate/Production Office
16273 General Puller Hwy.
P.O. Box 1125
Deltaville, VA 23043
804-776-8999
804-776-6111 (fax)
www.waterwayguide.com

BOOK SALES

waterwayguide.com/shipstore

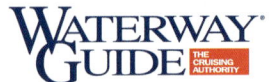

FOUNDED IN 1947

Publisher	**JEFF JONES** jjones@waterwayguide.com
President	**GRAHAM JONES** graham@waterwayguide.com
General Manager/ Editor-in-Chief	**ED TILLETT** etillett@waterwayguide.com
Managing Editor	**JANI PARKER** jparker@waterwayguide.com
Graphic Design/ Production Manager	**SCOTT MCCONNELL** scott@waterwayguide.com
Operations Manager	**HEATHER SADEG** heather@waterwayguide.com
Marketing & Advertising Traffic Manager	**ETHAN JETT** ethan@waterwayguide.com
Book Sales Manager	**LINDA JERNIGAN** linda@waterwayguide.com
Sales & Marketing Manager	**KELLY CROCKETT** kelly@waterwayguide.com
Senior Advisor/ Skipper Bob Editor	**TED STEHLE** tstehle@waterwayguide.com
News Editor	**LISA SUHAY** lisa@waterwayguide.com
Web Master	**MIKE SCHWEFLER**
Office Assistant	**LEON HOLZMAN**

NATIONAL SALES

GRAHAM JONES   graham@waterwayguide.com

REGIONAL MARKETING REPRESENTATIVES

KELLY CROCKETT   kelly@waterwayguide.com

PETE HUNGERFORD   pete@waterwayguide.com

REGIONAL CRUISING EDITORS

MARK BAKER
SCOTT RICHARD BERG
MICHAEL CAMERATA
MATT & LUCY CLAIBORNE
TOM DOVE
CAPT. DENA HANKINS & JAMES LANE
CAPT. GEORGE & PAT HOSPODAR
DEB & DENNIS JANSMA
CAPT. JOHN JOHNSTON
MICHAEL O'REILLY & ANN PHILLIPS
MARY & THERON RODRIGUEZ
BOB SHERER (CONTRIBUTING EDITOR)

CUBA CRUISING EDITORS

ADDISON CHAN
NIGEL CALDER (CONTRIBUTING EDITOR)

 @WaterwayGuide    @waterway_guide

Printed in Canada

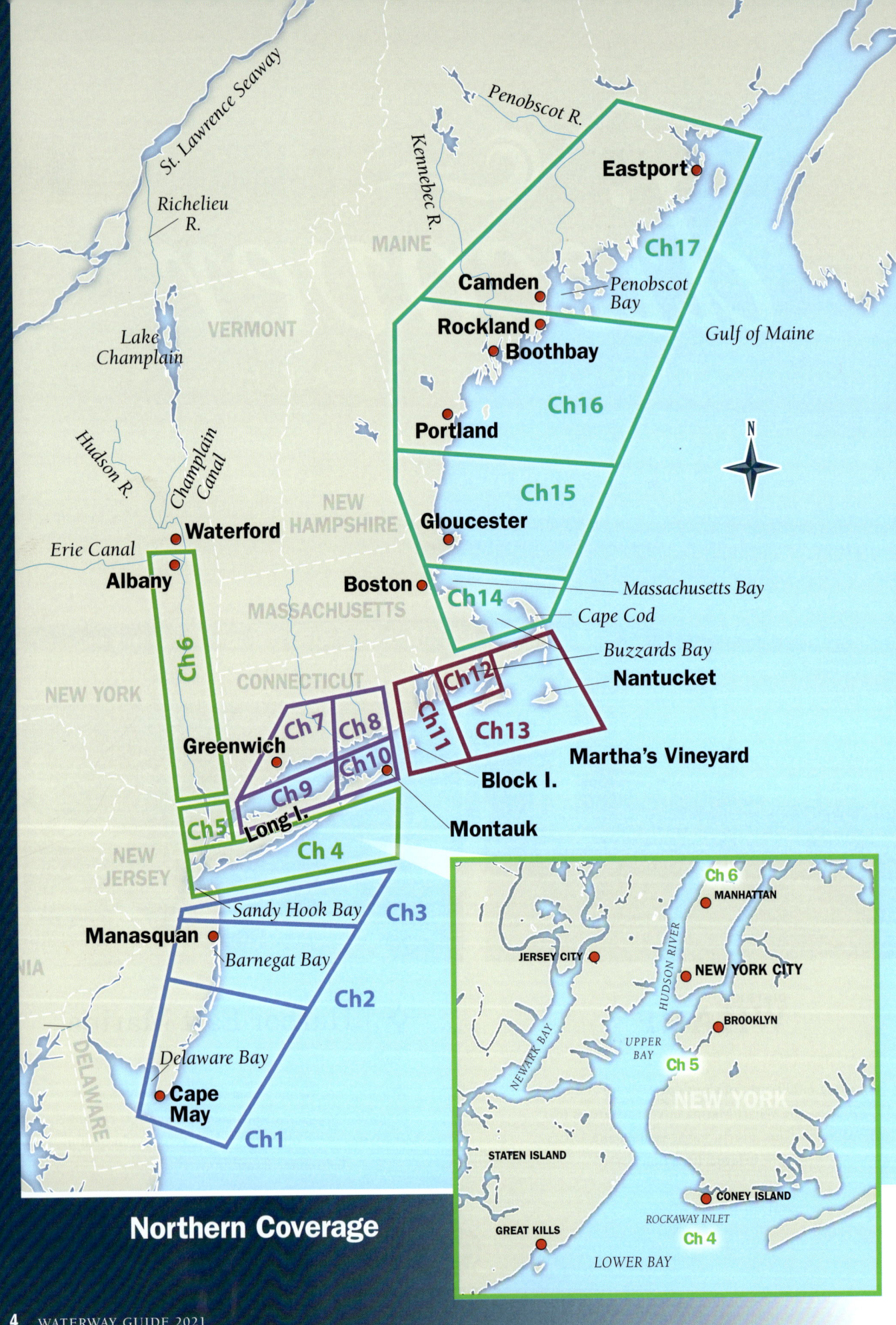

Northern Coverage

Ch17

Ch16

Ch15

Ch14

Ch12

Ch11

Ch13

Ch7

Ch8

Ch9

Ch10

Ch6

Ch5

Ch4

Ch3

Ch2

Ch1

Eastport

Camden
Penobscot Bay

Rockland
Boothbay

Portland

Gloucester

Boston

Massachusetts Bay

Cape Cod

Buzzards Bay

Nantucket

Martha's Vineyard

Block I.

Montauk

Greenwich

Long I.

Waterford

Albany

Erie Canal

Hudson R.

Champlain Canal

Lake Champlain

Richelieu R.

St. Lawrence Seaway

Kennebec R.

Penobscot R.

Gulf of Maine

MAINE

VERMONT

NEW HAMPSHIRE

MASSACHUSETTS

CONNECTICUT

NEW YORK

NEW JERSEY

DELAWARE

Sandy Hook Bay

Manasquan

Barnegat Bay

Delaware Bay

Cape May

N

Inset: New York City area

Ch 6

MANHATTAN

JERSEY CITY

NEW YORK CITY

BROOKLYN

HUDSON RIVER

NEWARK BAY

UPPER BAY

Ch 5

NEW YORK

STATEN ISLAND

GREAT KILLS

CONEY ISLAND

ROCKAWAY INLET

Ch 4

LOWER BAY

Contents

2021 Northern Edition, Vol. 74, No. 5

New Jersey offers the mariner a diverse mix of both open water and protected cruising grounds. The Jersey coast, while open ocean, offers all-weather inlets spaced close enough to be convenient for even slower craft seeking protection, with full amenities just inside the jetties. In comparison, the New Jersey Intracoastal Waterway is protected and offers a plethora of intriguing and convenient ports to visit for those able to navigate its shallow depths. At Sandy Hook, the skipper can turn the helm in any direction and head for a wide choice of destinations. To the west across Raritan Bay are the sheltered industrial canals of Arthur Kill and Perth Amboy, seldom visited by yachts going north or south.

The magnificent South Shore of Long Island stretches 115 nm from Coney Island to Montauk Point. A long set of barrier islands runs between most of Long Island's mainland and the Atlantic Ocean allowing cruisers to come in and out of the numerous inlets. Back at the Lower Bay, a trip under the Verrazo-Narrows Bridge takes you through The Narrows into New York Harbor and onwards to the East River. A side trip on the Hudson River to the Troy Lock is included for those continuing north on the Great Loop.

Long Island Sound, a popular inland sea, lies between New York City and Block Island, RI. It is 90 nautical miles long, up to 20 miles wide and narrower at both ends. "The Sound," as it is commonly called, is a major commercial artery, an important fishing and lobstering ground and one of the great cruising areas in the United States. Many mariners based on Long Island Sound never leave the Sound, even though they cruise all season long, year after year. Crisscrossing between Connecticut's rocky shore and Long Island's sandy beaches, they cruise the summer away, anchoring in isolated coves, visiting luxurious marina cities, racing under sail, fishing, taking long side trips up navigable rivers and exploring big bays.

TABLE OF CONTENTS

BLOCK ISLAND TO NANTUCKET SOUND

After exiting Long Island Sound through the current-washed Race, mariners enter the varied cruising grounds of southern New England-Block Island Sound, the Atlantic coast of Rhode Island and the justly famous waters of Narragansett Bay, including Newport. The big, crooked arm of Cape Cod and its island neighbors represent some of the most famous and beloved summer communities in the United States. Much of the charm of the whole area—bound by Buzzards Bay on the west, Vineyard and Nantucket sounds on the south, the Atlantic Ocean on the east and Cape Cod Bay on the north—comes from the dominating influence of the Atlantic Ocean, always nearby in one form or another.

ABOVE CAPE COD

The passage through or around the crooked elbow of Cape Cod marks a major step for most coastal cruising plans and the entrance into an endless mariner's paradise. Waterway Guide covers the waters from Cape Cod Bay to Eastern Maine in the final chapters of this edition.

INDEXES

TABLE OF CONTENTS

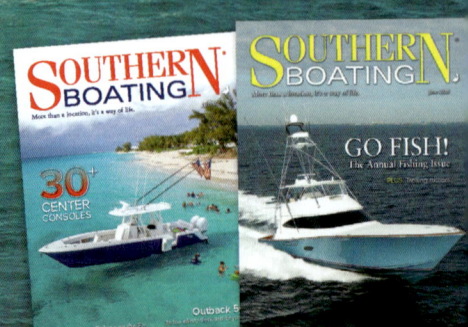

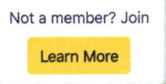

Meet Our Crew

Waterway Guide's on-the-water Cruising Editors bring us firsthand information about the navigation, news and trends along the waterways we cover. In addition to contributing to the annual guide, they provide daily updates on the Waterway Explorer at www.waterwayguide.com. We are pleased to introduce you to our crew.

Cruising Editors

Mark Baker and his partner Ann have been avid "part-time liveaboards" since purchasing their 37-foot, shoal-draft, racer/cruiser 10 years ago. Since that time they have put over 4,000 nautical miles under the keel and have personally made all repairs and upgrades to their sailboat. They enjoy meeting new folks in the towns and cities along the way and also seeking out secluded spots to enjoy the natural world and to experience some good ol' gunkholing. Ann is a talented birdwatcher and Mark enjoys underwater photography and the study of geology. Both being former teachers, they are practitioners of life-long learning..

Scott Richard Berg is a lifelong boater and full-time cruiser with five decades of experience on a range of vessels from el Toro prams to a 135-foot Baltic Trader. He operated Chardonnay Boatworks, a full-service marine repair company, for many years from a series of cruising sailboats (all named *Chardonnay*). He is the immediate past president of the SSCA, an ABYC-Certified Master Technician and holds an Amateur Extra Class radio license. Scott is Waterway Guide's on-the-water Cruising Editor for the Potomac River.

Michael Camarata started his sailing/boating life in the early 1970s when he decided to buy a Sunfish-type sailboat with his future wife, Carol Zipke. A few years later they bought a larger sailing dinghy with TWO sails. This was to set a pattern of larger and more complicated sailing vessels that continued to the vessel they now own and live aboard, a 44-foot sailing catamaran, *Infinite Improbability*, which Michael says is their last upgrade. Michael and Carol's cruising area originally ranged from New York City to Nantucket and north of the Cape Cod Canal. Now, having sold all of their "dirt-based property" the couple roams from southern New England to the Florida Keys and the Bahamas. They live in Mystic, CT, in the summer and Marathon, FL, in the winter.

Matt and Lucy Claiborne currently cruise the U.S. East Coast and the Bahamas full time on their 38-foot sailboat *Dulcinea*. Starting in South Florida and the Keys, they've owned boats ranging from a 38-foot sailing catamaran and 19-foot runabouts to kayaks and paddleboards. Matt and Lucy both hold SCUBA certifications, FAA pilot certificates and USCG Master licenses. They love everything about the cruising lifestyle from sailing the Sea of Abaco to sundowners with friends on the Chesapeake Bay.

Tom Dove began sailing in 1955, created popular programs for Annapolis Sailing School in the 1960s (including the world's first flotilla cruises), and has cruised on a variety of sailboats in the U.S. and various other parts of the world. He has been writing about boating for books, national and regional magazines and television for the past 30 years. In 2017, he chose a more "age appropriate" vessel and now ambles happily along the Atlantic coast with his wife, Kathy, on *SNOWBIRD*, a renovated 1977 Grand Banks 32 trawler.

Capt. Dena Hankins and James Lane moved aboard their first boat in Seattle, WA, in 1999 and their travels since under sail have spanned two oceans and countless sounds, bays, rivers, and waterways. After starting aboard a 48-foot wooden Seawolf ketch, they've been struck by two-foot-itis in reverse several times, downsizing for the ease and freedom of a smaller boat. Since seaworthiness is key, they currently live on and sail a Baba 30 named *Cetacea*. Since independence is another non-negotiable requirement, *Cetacea* is outfitted with an off-the-grid electrical system and a composting head. Dena and James have contributed to the Northern, Chesapeake, ICW, and Southern *Waterway Guides* and have been covering Maine since 2015. Dena is a multi-published novelist and short-story author who writes best in quiet anchorages. James is an inspired photographer and storyteller who finds grist for both mills in his everyday life aboard.

Capt. George and Patricia Hospodar have been boaters for over 40 years and have cruised more than 43,000 miles together aboard two sailboats and their 48-foot Symbol motor yacht, *Reflection*. Since 2008 they have traveled up and down the Atlantic ICW numerous times between their home on Barnegat Bay in Brick, NJ, and their "adopted" home at Banana Bay Marina in Marathon, FL, and have completed the America's Great Loop journey twice through the waterways of the U.S. and Canada. George and Pat are Platinum lifetime members of the America's Great Loop Cruisers' Association, as well as members of the Marine Trawler Owners Association and the Marathon Yacht Club. Together they have authored two popular boating books: *Reflection on America's Great Loop* and *The Great Loop Experience from Concept to Completion*, and they are often featured speakers at boat shows, TrawlerFests and other nautical events.

Captain John "JJ" Johnston is our expert on the Erie Canal and the New York State Canal System. He is originally from Pittsburgh, PA, but calls Fairport, NY, his home canal town. Capt. JJ retired from Kodak's motion picture division in 2007 and became a captain on *Sam Patch*, a popular Erie Canal tour boat. He also served as Executive Director of CANAL NY, a destination marketing organization, traveling on his 29-foot diesel inboard C Dory, *Penguin*, across the State of New York, promoting the waterway and learning about its history, operation and navigation. He's motored all 524 miles of the NY State Canal System, been up and down all 57 locks, overnighted in 45 canal communities.

Michael O'Reilly and Ann Phillips came to sailing by first messing about with canoes and kayaks while living on the Canadian shore of Lake Superior. Sailing replaced the smaller boats, and over the last 15-plus years they have enjoyed many extended summer cruises. Most recently they completed a cruise through four of the five Great Lakes, and currently plan on exploring Lake Ontario, the St. Lawrence Seaway down to Newfoundland, and beyond. Mike is a long-time freelance journalist, writing mostly about the sciences. With the transition to this new watery life, Mike now spends most of his work time writing about traveling, destinations and cruising. Ann is an accomplished photographer. Together they are chronicling their life afloat.

Mary and Tharon Rodriguez enjoy cruising the Great Lakes in Michigan Summers and Florida Keys/Bahamas the remainder of the year. Their fleet includes *Fuzz*, an S2 7.3, located on the Great Lakes, and *Tipsy Gypsy*, 36-foot Hinterhoeller Nonsuch, located in Florida. They are both digital nomads working and cruising full-time and sharing their adventures through writing blog posts, taking pictures for Instagram, and uploading videos on YouTube. They are fun-loving, adventure-seeking, mid-westerners with a whole lot to offer our team. Learn more about them by visiting www.maryandtharon.com.

Long-time skipper **Bob Sherer** is a contributing editor at Waterway Guide. Bob (better known in cruising circles as "Bob 423") focuses on navigational alerts along the Atlantic ICW. Bob and his wife, Ann, just completed their eighth trip down the ICW from Poughkeepsie, NY, to Key West. Bob is best known for his activity on numerous cruising forums and the couple has a popular blog at www.fleetwing.blogspot.com. Bob and Ann spend 9 months of the year aboard *Fleetwing*, a Beneteau 423, with four-legged crew member, Hoolie, a Brittany.

Cuba Cruising Editor

Addison Chan is the Cruising Editor for the Cuba edition of *Waterway Guide*. He and his wife, Pat, have cruised from the U.S. to Cuba and The Bahamas multiple times aboard their 42-foot sailboat, *Threepenny Opera*. Addison has a popular Facebook group called *Cuba, Land and Sea*, which is a clearinghouse of current information about cruising and traveling in Cuba. The Cuba cruising guide addresses questions posed there that encompass not only the boating aspects of Cuba but the other aspects of experiencing Cuba as well. Addison's world travel, seamanship, navigation skills and spirit for adventure all combined to offer what we consider to be the most experienced view of Cuba's culture, its people and insight for anyone taking their boat there.

Other Contributors

Waterway Guide gathers information and photos from a variety of sources, including boaters, marinas, communities and tourism divisions. We would like to thank everyone who contributed to this edition and especially Gary Tisdale (photo contributor).

The adventure of a lifetime
America's Great Loop

2+ Countries • 14+ States and Provinces • 100+ Locks • 5,250+ Miles...
...all aboard your own boat!

America's Great Loop Cruisers' Association

AGLCA is a group of over 6,000 people who share a passion for the Great Loop. We provide information and inspiration that help our members move the Great Loop from their bucket list to reality. Whether you're brand new to the idea of the Great Loop, you're actively planning for it, or you're ready to drop the dock lines and head out now, AGLCA offers something for you!

Membership includes:

- Events
- Discounts
- Newsletters
- Podcasts
- Camaraderie
- Blogs
- Cost Calculators
- and so much more!

Visit our website:
www.GreatLoop.org

500 Oakbrook Lane,
Summerville, SC 29485
Tel: 877-GR8-LOOP

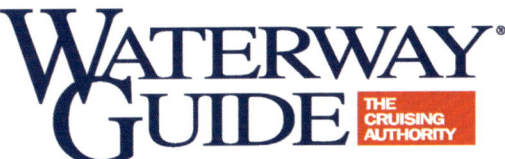

Be Prepared for Cold Weather Boating

While a hunter or angler may not think of themselves as a boater, any time you're on the water, a life jacket should be part of your essential gear and worn at all times. Often a hunter or angler will set out on their trip alone, and neglect to wear a life jacket or file a float plan with the details of their trip.

A person who falls into the water experiences increased danger with water temperature that is below normal body temperature (98.6 degrees F). You have one minute to adjust to the cold shock of being in the water, 10 minutes of meaningful movement to get help and get out of the water, and one hour before he/she becomes unconscious from hypothermia.

Here are some tips to keep in mind before you go cold weather boating this winter and early spring.

• Do make sure everyone is wearing a life jacket. Even experienced swimmers can experience shock within one minute in the frigid water and may lose muscle control within 10 minutes.

• Do file a float plan with someone you trust that includes details about the trip, boat, passengers, towing or trailer vehicle, communication equipment, and emergency contacts. Download a free float plan template at www.FloatPlanCentral.org.

• Do dress properly for the weather, always wearing layers, and bring an extra set of clothes in case you get wet. Remember, dress for the water temperature, not the air temperature.

• Do catch your breath. A sudden unexpected fall into cold water causes an involuntary gasp (or torso) reflex. It takes less than ½ cup of water in your lungs to drown. If you remain calm, you have a greater chance of self-rescue.

• Do look for ways to increase your buoyancy. If you're in the water with others, huddle together with everyone facing inwards to help everyone stay afloat and keep warm.

• Don't panic if you fall into the water. Stay afloat with the help of your life jacket, regain control of your breathing, and keep your head above water in vision of rescuers. Stay with the boat if possible.

• Don't apply heat to extremities like arms and legs of a rescued victim. This sudden change in temperature may cause cardiac arrest.

Recreational water activities during the cold months are a lot of fun, but always remember safety first….You never know when wearing your life jacket will save your life.

Source: The National Boating Safety Council (www. safeboatingcampaign.com)

Port Security

In the U.S., the U.S. Coast Guard and Customs and Border Patrol–both components of the Department of Homeland Security–handle port security. Local law enforcement agencies and the FBI also have a role in port security at the local and regional level. Each year, more than 11 million maritime containers arrive at our seaports. At land borders, another 11 million arrive by truck and 2.7 million by rail. Homeland Security is responsible for knowing what is inside those containers, whether it poses a risk to the American people and ensuring that all proper revenues are collected.

As an example, one in five food items is now imported. American consumers demand fresh limes and blueberries all year round and, as a result, during the winter months in the U.S., nearly 80 percent of the fresh fruits and vegetables on our tables come from other countries. With the ever-increasing amount of trade, the agricultural risks to the United States grow. The threat to crops and livestock is real.

In response to this threat and others, the U.S. Coast Guard has established "protection zones" around all U.S. Navy vessels, tank vessels, and large-capacity cruise vessels, even when underway. U.S. Navy bases, U.S. Coast Guard bases and some shoreside facilities, such as nuclear power plants, are also in protection zones. Non-military vessels (this means YOU) are not allowed within 100 yards of these protection zones. To do so can rack up serious civil penalties and even imprisonment. These protection zones vary from port to port and from facility to facility, but ignorance of the protection zones is not a viable excuse. Having said that, law-abiding boaters sometimes find themselves unable to comply with the letter of the law without hitting a jetty, for example. In such cases, common sense and good communication should prevail.

America's Waterway Watch Program

Government officials view the recreational boating community as an ally. We can do our part (and perhaps stave off more stringent regulations and surveillance measures) by becoming familiar with the Coast Guard's America's Waterway Watch program. Think of it as a neighborhood watch program for the waterways.

It is not the intent of America's Waterway Watch to spread paranoia or to encourage spying on one another, and it is not a surveillance program; instead, it is a simple deterrent to potential terrorist activity. The purpose of the program is to allow boaters and others who spend time along the water to help the authorities counter crime and terrorism. To report suspicious behavior, call the National Response Center at 877-249-2824 (877-24WATCH). For immediate danger to life or property, call 911, or call the Coast Guard on Marine VHF-FM Channel 16.

This section includes a list of ports and places that require a little forethought and vigilance on your part. Following the steps in the action plan below will help ensure a trouble-free journey and keep you and your crew out of the headlines.

Prepare:

- Before you leave, check the current charts for the area in which you will be traveling and identify any security areas. Security zones are highlighted and outlined in magenta with special notes regarding the specific regulations pertaining to that area.

- Check the latest *Local Notice to Mariners* (available online at www.navcen.uscg and posted at some marinas) and identify any potential security areas that may not be shown on the chart.

- Listen to VHF Channel 16 for any Sécurité alerts from the Coast Guard (departing cruise ships, U.S. Navy vessels, fuel tankers, etc.) for the area you will be cruising prior to your departure.

- Talk to other boaters in your anchorage or marina about the areas where you will be traveling. They may have tips and suggestions on any potential security zones or special areas they may have encountered on their way.

Stay Alert While Underway:

- Mind the outlined magenta security areas noted on your charts.

- Look for vessels with blue or red warning lights in port areas and, if approached, listen carefully and strictly obey all instructions given to you.

- Keep your VHF radio switched to VHF Channel 16 and keep your ears tuned for bulletins, updates and possible requests for communication.

- Avoid commercial port operation areas, especially those that involve military, cruise line or petroleum facilities. Observe and avoid other restricted areas near power plants, national monuments, etc.

- If you need to pass within 100 yards of a U.S. Navy vessel for safe passage, you must contact the U.S. Navy vessel or the Coast Guard escort vessel on VHF Channel 16 to let them know your intentions.

- If government security or the U.S. Coast Guard hails you, do exactly what they say, regardless of whether or not you feel their instructions have merit.

Additional Resources

America's Waterway Watch:
www.americaswaterwaywatch.org

Department of Homeland Security:
www.dhs.gov

U.S. Customs and Border Protection:
www.cbp.gov

SKIPPER'S HANDBOOK

Customs Reporting Procedures

Operators of small pleasure vessels, arriving in the U.S. from a foreign port are required to report their arrival to Customs and Border Patrol (CBP) immediately. The master of the vessel reports their arrival at the nearest Customs facility or other designated location. These reports are tracked in the Pleasure Boat Reporting System. An application to lawfully enter the U.S. must be made in person to a CBP officer at a U.S. port-of-entry when the port is open for inspection.

CBP has designated specific reporting locations within the Field Offices that are staffed during boating season for pleasure boats to report their arrival and be inspected by CBP. The master of the boat must report to CBP telephonically and be directed to the nearest Port of Entry to satisfy the face-to-face requirement, or report to the nearest designated reporting location, along with the boat's passengers for inspection.

You may be required to rent a car or take a cab to the nearest airport or federal office several miles away for the inspection. These offices are often closed on weekends. If your arrival is after working hours, you are required to stay on board and clear in the next morning. You must, however, clear in within 24 hours of your arrival. Everyone on board, regardless of nationality, has to report in person. U.S. nationals must take their passports or passport cards. All non-U.S. Nationals should take their passports with valid visas and a Green Card, if held. Take your boat papers, either U.S. documentation or state registration with state decal number. You should also present a list of firearms and ammunition on board.

Clearing In with the ROAM App

Travelers arriving by boat into many popular U.S. ports can check into the country on their phones or tablets. The Reporting Offsite Arrival–Mobile (ROAM) app is the official replacement for the Local Boater Option (LBO) and Small Vessel Reporting System (SVRS) programs that have been used over the years. These programs required an initial interview to get in but usually resulted in a quick phone call instead of a face-to-face meeting to re-enter the U.S.

If you have a www.Login.gov account, you can log into the app immediately. If you need a password, the app directs you to the website. Then it walks you through the steps, including entering the specifics for each person on board and for your vessel. Once you've entered all of the details and submitted it for a review, an officer may initiate a video call to discuss the trip or to ask any necessary questions. All of this happens directly inside the app. Of course, there are still instances where in-person reporting is required. If you require an I-94, need to pay customs fees or duties, or need to obtain a cruising permit, you will still need to check in in-person. Boaters are still required to have a current fee decal onboard.

Now that the app has been implemented on a larger scale, travelers entering by boat in the Great Lakes; most of the East Coast (Delaware to Florida); Texas and San Diego, CA; and the U.S. territories in the Caribbean can use the app. New locations are continually being added, and because the program is new, it's probably a good idea to call your port of arrival to ensure they are using the ROAM app.

To download the ROAM app, just search the Apple App Store or the Google Play Store on your device. For more information, visit the CBP website or contact the CBP office at your port of arrival.

Additional Resource

U.S. Customs and Border Control:
www.cbp.gov/travel/pleasure-boats-private-flyers

Float Plan

BoatU.S.

1. Phone Numbers

Coast Guard:_____

Marine Police:_____

Local TowBoatU.S. Company:_____

2. Description of the Boat

Boat Name:_____ Hailing Port:_____

Type:_____ Model Year:_____

Make:_____ Length:_____ Beam:_____ Draft:_____

Color, Hull:_____ Cabin:_____ Deck:_____ Trim:_____ Dodger:_____

Other Colors:_____ # of Masts:_____

Distinguishing Features:_____

Registration No:_____ Sail No:_____

Engine(s) Type:_____ Horsepower:_____ Cruising Speed:_____

Fuel Capacity, Gallons:_____ Cruising Range:_____

Electronics/Safety Equipment Aboard

VHF Radio:_____ Cell Phone:_____ CB:_____ SSB:_____

Frequency Monitored:_____ Loran:_____ SatNav:_____

Depth Sounder:_____ Radar:_____ GPS:_____

Raft:_____ Dinghy:_____ EPIRB:_____ A/B/C/406M
(Indicate Type)

3. Trip Details

Owner/Skipper (Filing Report):_____

Phone:_____ Age:_____

Address:_____

Additional Persons Aboard, Total:_____

Name:_____ Age:_____

Address:_____ Phone:_____

Boating Experience:_____

Name:_____ Age:_____

Address:_____ Phone:_____

Boating Experience:_____

Name:_____ Age:_____

Address:_____ Phone:_____

Boating Experience:_____

Name:_____ Age:_____

Address:_____ Phone:_____

Boating Experience:_____

Name:_____ Age:_____

Address:_____ Phone:_____

Boating Experience:_____

Departure Date/Time:_____ Return No Later Than:_____

Depart From:_____

Marina (Home Port):_____ Phone:_____

Auto Parked At:_____

Model/color:_____ Lic. #_____

Destination Port: _____

_____ ETA:_____ No Later Than:_____

Phone:_____

Anticipated Stopover Ports:_____

_____ ETA:_____ No Later Than:_____

Phone:_____

_____ ETA:_____ No Later Than:_____

Phone:_____

_____ ETA:_____ No Later Than:_____

Phone:_____

_____ ETA:_____ No Later Than:_____

Phone:_____

_____ ETA:_____ No Later Than:_____

Phone:_____

Plan Filed With:_____

Name:_____ Phone:_____

Get in the habit of filing a Float Plan. It can assure quicker rescue in the event of a breakdown, stranding or weather delay. Fill out the permanent data in Sections 1 and 2. Then, make enough copies to last for the season. If you file a Float Plan with someone not at your home, such as a harbormaster or boating friend, be sure to notify them as soon as you return. Don't burden friends or authorities with unnecessary worry and responsibility if you are safe.

Check your *BoatU.S. Towing Guide*. Some listed companies will accept a verbal Float Plan via telephone or VHF.

VHF Communications

Skippers traveling the U.S. inland waterways use their VHF radios almost every day to contact other vessels and bridgetenders, make reservations at marinas, arrange to pass other vessels safely and conduct other business. Waterway Guide has put together the following information to help remove any confusion as to what frequency should be dialed in to call bridges, marinas, commercial ships, or your friend anchored down the creek. Remember to use low power (1 watt) for your radio transmission whenever possible. If you are within a couple of miles of the responding station (bridge, marina or other craft) there is no need to broadcast at 25 watts and disturb the transmissions of others 25 miles away.

Channel Usage Tips

- VHF Channel 16 (156.8 MHz) is by far the most important frequency on the VHF-FM band. VHF Channel 16 is the international distress, safety and calling frequency.

- If you have a VHF radio on your boat, FCC regulations require that you to maintain a watch on either VHF Channel 09 or 16 whenever you are underway and the radio is not being used to communicate on another channel. Since the Coast Guard does not have the capability of announcing an urgent marine information broadcast or weather warning on VHF Channel 09, it recommends that boaters normally keep tuned to and use VHF Channel 16, but no conversations of any length should take place there; its primary function is for emergencies only.

- The Coast Guard's main working VHF Channel is 22A, and both emergency and non-emergency calls generally are switched to it in order to keep VHF Channel 16 clear. Calling the Coast Guard for a radio check on VHF Channel 16 is prohibited.

- Radio-equipped bridges in FL use VHF Channel 09, with a few exceptions.

- Recreational craft typically communicate on VHF Channels 68, 69, 71, 72 or 78A. Whenever possible, avoid calling on VHF Channel 16 altogether by prearranging initial contact directly on one of these channels. No transmissions should last longer than 3 minutes.

- The Bridge-to-Bridge Radio Telephone Act requires many commercial vessels, including dredges and tugboats, to monitor VHF Channel 13. VHF Channel 13 is also the frequency used by bridges in several states.

Distress Calls

MAYDAY: The distress signal "MAYDAY" is used to indicate that a vessel is threatened by grave and imminent danger and requests immediate assistance.

PAN PAN: The urgency signal "PAN PAN" is used when the safety of the ship or person is in jeopardy.

SÉCURITÉ: The safety signal "SÉCURITÉ" is used for messages about the safety of navigation or important weather warnings.

VHF Channel 16 is the distress call frequency. The codeword "MAYDAY" is the international alert signal of a life-threatening situation at sea. After a MAYDAY message is broadcast, VHF Channel 16 must be kept free of all traffic, other than those directly involved in the rescue situation, until the rescue has been completed. If you hear a MAYDAY message and no one else is responding, it is your duty to step in to answer the call, relay it to the nearest rescue organization and get to the scene to help. Remember, a MAYDAY distress call can only be used when life is threatened. For example, if you have run on the rocks but no one is going to lose their life, that is NOT a MAYDAY situation.

> Note: The Coast Guard has asked the FCC to eliminate provisions for using VHF Channel 09 as an alternative calling frequency to VHF Channel 16 when it eliminates watch-keeping on VHF Channel 16 by compulsory-equipped vessels. Stay tuned for updates.

How to Make a Distress Call

MAYDAY! MAYDAY! MAYDAY!

This is: Give your vessel name and call sign.

Our position is: Read it off the GPS, or give it as something like "two miles southwest of Royal Island." (Your rescuers must be able to find you!)

We are: Describe what's happening (e.g., on fire/hit a reef/sinking).

We have: Report how many people are on board.

At this time we are: Say what you're doing about the crisis (e.g., standing by/abandoning ship).

For identification we are: Describe your boat: type, length, color, etc. (so your rescuers can more readily identify you).

We have: List safety equipment you have (e.g., flares/smoke/ocean dye markers/EPIRB).

We will keep watch on Channel 16 as long as we can.

VHF Channels	
09	Used for radio checks and hailing other stations (boats, shoreside operations). Also used to communicate with drawbridges in Florida.
13	Used to contact and communicate with commercial vessels, military ships and drawbridges. Bridges in several states monitor VHF Channel 13.
16	***Emergency use only.*** May be used to hail other vessels, but once contact is made, conversation should be immediately switched to a working (68, 69, 71, 72, 78A) VHF channel.
22	Used for U.S. Coast Guard safety, navigation and Sécurité communications.
68 **69** **71** **72** **78A**	Used primarily for recreational ship-to-ship and ship-to-shore communications.

Rules of the Road

Anyone planning to cruise our waterways should make themselves familiar with the rules of the road. *Chapman Piloting: Seamanship and Small Boat Handling* and *The Annapolis Book of Seamanship* are both excellent on-the-water references with plentiful information on navigation rules. For those with a penchant for the exact regulatory language, the Coast Guard publication *Navigation Rules: International–Inland* covers both international and U.S. inland rules. (Boats over 39.4 feet are required to carry a copy of the U.S. Inland Rules at all times.)

The following is a list of common situations you will likely encounter on the waterways. Make yourself familiar with them, and if you ever have a question as to which of you has the right-of-way, let the other vessel go first. Sailors need to remember that a boat under sail with its engine running is considered a motorboat.

Passing or being passed:

■ If you intend to pass a slower vessel, try to hail them on your VHF radio to let them know you are coming.

■ In close quarters, BOTH vessels should slow down. Slowing down normally allows the faster vessel to pass quickly without throwing a large wake onto the slower boat.

■ Slower boats being passed have the right-of-way and passing vessels must keep clear of these slower vessels.

■ As you pass a slower boat, take a look back to see how they were affected by your wake. Remember: YOU are responsible for your wake. It is the law to slow down, and it is common courtesy.

At opening bridges:

■ During an opening, boats traveling with the current go first and generally have the right-of-way.

■ Boats constrained by their draft, size or maneuverability (e.g., dredges, tugs and barges) also take priority.

■ Standard rules of the road apply while circling or waiting for a bridge opening.

Tugs, freighters, dredges and naval vessels:

■ These vessels are usually constrained by draft or their inability to easily maneuver. For this reason, you will almost always need to give them the right-of-way and keep out of their path.

■ You must keep at least 100 yards away from any Navy vessel. If you cannot safely navigate without coming closer than this, you must notify the ship of your intentions over VHF Channel 16.

■ Keep a close watch for freighters, tugs with tows and other large vessels while offshore or in crowded ports. They often come up very quickly, despite their large size.

■ It is always a good practice to radio larger vessels (VHF Channel 13 or 16) to notify them of your location and your intentions. The skippers of these boats are generally appreciative of efforts to communicate with them. This is especially true with dredge boats on all the waterways.

In a crossing situation:

- When two vessels under power are crossing and a risk of collision exists, the vessel that has the other on her starboard side must keep clear and avoid crossing ahead of the other vessel.

- When a vessel under sail and a vessel under power are crossing, the boat under power is usually burdened and must keep clear. The same exceptions apply as per head-on meetings.

- On the Great Lakes and western rivers (e.g., the Mississippi River system), a power-driven vessel crossing a river shall keep clear of a power-driven vessel ascending or descending the river.

Power vessels meeting any other vessel:

- When two vessels under power (either sailboats or powerboats) meet "head-to-head," both are obliged to alter course to starboard.

- Generally, when a vessel under power meets a vessel under sail (i.e., not using any mechanical power), the powered vessel must alter course accordingly.

- Exceptions are vessels not under command, vessels restricted in ability to maneuver, vessels engaged in commercial fishing or those under International Rules, such as a vessel constrained by draft.

Two sailboats meeting under sail:

- When each has the wind on a different side, the boat with the wind on the port side must keep clear of the boat with the wind on the starboard side.

- When both have the wind on the same side, the vessel closest to the wind (windward) will keep clear of the leeward boat.

- A vessel with wind to port that sees a vessel to windward but cannot determine whether the windward vessel has wind to port or starboard will assume that windward vessel is on starboard tack and keep clear.

Keep watch for crab pots!

While it is against the law to place crab pots with marker buoys inside navigational channels, they sometimes break loose and find their way there. The terms "pot" refers to the enclosed traps (usually a framework of wire) used to catch crabs in shallow waters. The attached retrieval markers can range from colorful buoys to empty milk jugs (or anything else that floats). Most buoys are painted in a color that contrasts the water surface, but some are black or even dark blue, which are especially difficult to see in the best of conditions. You do NOT want to get a line wrapped around your prop, so it is advisable to have a spotter on the foredeck when traversing fields of pots.

Coast Guard Requirements

The Coast Guard stands watch at all times to aid vessels of all sizes and the persons on board. In some areas, you can quickly reach the Coast Guard by dialing *CG on a cellular phone. If you have a question of a non-emergency nature, the Coast Guard prefers that you telephone the nearest station. As always, if there is an emergency, initiate a "MAY DAY" call on VHF Channel 16.

In addition to aiding boaters in distress, the Coast Guard also enforces maritime law and conducts safety inspections. While a Coast Guard boarding can be unnerving, if you are responsible and prepared, it will only take 15 to 30 minutes and will be a non-event. First, have your boat in order. This includes having your vessel documentation, registration and insurance documents on hand, as well as your passport. Organize this in a binder and keep it in the nav station so you don't have to fumble around looking for documents and paperwork. You will need to acknowledge the location of any weapons on board and show a permit (when required by state law).

The officers will likely focus on areas with the largest safety concerns, including the following.

Life Jackets: One Type I, II, II, or V per person plus one Type IV throwable device is required. PFDs must be U.S. Coast Guard-approved, wearable by the intended user and readily accessible. The Type IV throwable device must be located such that it is immediately available.

Visual Distress Signals: All vessels 16 feet and over must be equipped with minimum of 3 day-use and 3 night-use or 3 day/night combination pyrotechnic devices. Non-pyrotechnic substitutes: orange flag (for day use) and electric S-O-S signal light (for night use). Flares must be up to date (e.g., not expired).

Sound Producing Devices: A whistle, horn, siren, etc. capable of a 4-second blast audible for 0.5 mile must be on board for use during periods of reduced visibility. Boats 65 feet and over must have a bell and one whistle or horn required to signal intentions.

Navigation Lights: All boats over 16 feet must have working navigational lights and an independent all-around anchor light. Sailboats under power are considered powerboats and must follow "power" rules.

Fire Extinguisher: U.S. Coast Guard-approved, marine-type fire extinguishers are required on any boat with enclosed fuel or engine spaces, enclosed living spaces, or permanent (not movable by one person) fuel tanks. They must be in good working condition and readily accessible. (Number of units required depends on vessel length.)

Ventilation: Boats built after August 1, 1980, with enclosed gasoline engines must have a powered ventilation system with one or more exhaust blowers.

Backfire Flame Arrester: All gasoline-powered inboard/outboard or inboard motor boats must be equipped with an approved backfire flame arrester.

Pollution Placard: It is illegal to discharge oil or oily waste into any navigable waters of the U.S. Boats over 26 feet must display a durable oily waste pollution placard of at least 5 by 8 inches in a prominent location.

MARPOL Trash Placard: It is illegal to dump plastic trash anywhere in the ocean or navigable waters of the U.S. Boats over 26 feet must display a durable trash placard at least 4 by 9 inches in a prominent location.

Navigation Rules: Boats 39.4 feet and over must have a copy of current Navigation Rules on board. You can download a copy at uscgboating org.

Marine Sanitation Devices: The discharge of treated sewage is allowed within 3 nm of shore except in designated "No Discharge Zone" areas. The Coast Guard will check that overboard discharge outlets can be sealed (and are sealed, if within 3 nm of shore).

These requirements are detailed in a **downloadable boater's guide** at www.uscgboating.org/images/420. PDF. State and local requirements are also considered. If there is a minor violation, they may give you a written warning explaining what needs to be fixed to be in compliance. If you are found with a small violation and correct it quickly, then this will merely be a chance to interact with those whose goal is to keep you as safe as possible on the water.

Reference Materials

USCG *Local Notice to Mariners*

The U.S. Coast Guard provides timely marine safety information for the correction of all U.S. Government navigation charts and publications from a wide variety of sources, both foreign and domestic. These are divided by district, updated weekly and available as a PDF at www. navcen.uscg.gov. (Select LNMs tab at top of page.)

NOAA Charts & Corrections

Electronic Nautical Charts (ENCs)/ Booklet Charts: Updated weekly with *Notice to Mariner* corrections..

1. Go to Chart Locator at: www. charts.noaa.gov/InteractiveCatalog/nrnc.shtml.
2. Click on Paper Charts (RNC&PDF) tab.
3. Pan and Zoom and select the chart of interest. It will be highlighted in yellow.
4. On the right, under "Available Products" click on the appropriate link for the product you need.
5. Download to your local computer.

Navigation

- *NAVIGATION RULES, INTERNATIONAL— INLAND*, U.S. Dept. of Homeland Security. The U.S. Coast Guard requires all vessels over 12 meters [39 feet] carry this book of the national and international rules of the road. Can be downloaded as a PDF at www.navcen.uscg.gov.

- *U.S. Coast Pilot (1-5)*, NOAA. Includes piloting information for coasts, bays, creeks and harbors. Also includes tide tables and highlights restricted areas. Updated weekly and can be downloaded as a PDF at www. nauticalcharts.noaa.gov/nsd/cpdownload.htm.

- *U.S. Chart No 1. (Chart Symbols)* describes the symbols, abbreviations and terms used on NOAA nautical charts. Available online at www. nauticalcharts.noaa.gov/publications/us-chart-1.html.

- U.S. Aids to Navigation System is a downloadable guide from the U.S. Coast Guard with basic information on the recognition of U.S. Aids to Navigation System (ATONS). Find it at www.uscgboating.org/images/486.PDF.

Maintenance

- *Boatowner's Mechanical & Electrical Manual* (4th Edition), Nigel Calder

- *Boatowner's Illustrated Electrical Handbook*, Charlie Wing

- *Boat Mechanical Systems Handbook*, David Gerr

Seamanship

- *The Annapolis Book of Seamanship* (4th Edition), John Rousmaniere

- *The Art of Seamanship*, Ralph Naranjo

- *Boater's Pocket Reference*, Thomas McEwen

- *Chapman Piloting & Seamanship* (68th Edition), Charles B. Husick

- *Eldridge Tide and Pilot Book* (annual), Robert E. and Linda White

- *Heavy Weather Sailing* (7th Edition), Peter Bruce

- *Nigel Calder's Cruising Handbook*, Nigel Calder

- *Offshore Cruising Encyclopedia*, Steve and Linda Dashew

- *World Cruising Essentials*, Jimmy Cornell

- *Anchoring: A Ground Tackler's Apprentice*, Rudy and Jill Sechez

First Aid & Medical

- *Advanced First Aid Afloat* (5th Edition), Dr. Peter F. Eastman

- *DAN Pocket Guide to First Aid for Scuba Diving*, Dan Orr & Bill Clendenden

- *First Aid at Sea*, Douglas Justin and Colin Berry

- *Marine Medicine: A Comprehensive Guide* (2nd Edition), Eric Weiss and Michael Jacobs

- *On-Board Medical Emergency Handbook: First Aid at Sea*, Spike Briggs and Campbell Mackenzie

About the Weather

Every day on the water can't entail balmy breezes, abundant sunshine and consistently warm weather; however, staying out of bad weather is relatively easy if you plan ahead. The National Weather Service (NWS) provides mariners with continuous broadcasts of weather warnings, forecasts, radar reports and buoy reports over VHF-FM and Single Side Band (SSB) radio. There are almost no areas on the Keys where a good quality, fixed-mount VHF cannot pick up one or more coastal VHF broadcasts. Also, there is no substitute for simply looking at the sky, and either stay put or seek shelter if you don't like what you see.

SSB Offshore Weather

SSB reports are broadcast from station NMN in Chesapeake, VA, and from station NMG in New Orleans, LA. The broadcasts are not continuous, so refer to the frequency lists below. SSB reports provide the best source of voice offshore weather information. Two major broadcasts alternate throughout the day. The High Seas Forecast provides information for mariners well offshore, including those crossing the North Atlantic Ocean. Coastal cruisers will be more interested in the Offshore Forecast, which includes information on waters more than 50 miles from shore.

Weather Apps

Weather Apps
Boating Weather (FREE)
Buoy Weather (FREE)
Marine Weather by AccuWeather (FREE)
NOAA SuperRes Radar HD ($3.99)
PredictWind (FREE)
Storm Radar with NOAA Weather (FREE)
Weather Underground (FREE)
Windfinder (FREE)
Windy (FREE)

Weather Online

Weather Online
Accuweather (www.accuweather.com)
Windfinder (www.windfinder.com)
Buoy Weather (www.buoyweather.com)
National Hurricane Center (www.nhc.noaa.gov)
National Weather Service (www.weather.gov)
NOAA Marine Forecasts (www.nws.noaa.gov/om/marine)
Passage Weather (www.passageweather.com)
Predict Wind (www.predictwind.com)
Sailflow (www.sailflow.com)
The Weather Channel (www.weather.com)
Weather Underground (www.wunderground.com)

SSB Weather Frequencies

UTC	Chesapeake, VA NMN Frequencies (kHz)	New Orleans, LA NMG Frequencies (kHz)
0330 (Offshore)	4426.0, 6501.0, 8764.0	4316.0, 8502.0, 12788.0
0515 (High Seas)	4426.0, 6501.0, 8764.0	4316.0, 8502.0, 12788.0
0930 (Offshore)	4426.0, 6501.0, 8764.0	4316.0, 8502.0, 12788.0
1115 (High Seas)	6501.0, 8764.0, 13089.0	4316.0, 8502.0, 12788.0
1530 (Offshore)	6501.0, 8764.0, 13089.0	4316.0, 8502.0, 12788.0
1715 (High Seas)	8764.0, 13089.0, 17314.0	4316.0, 8502.0, 12788.0
2130 (Offshore)	6501.0, 8764.0, 13089.0	4316.0, 8502.0, 12788.0
2315 (High Seas)	6501.0, 8764.0, 13089.0	4316.0, 8502.0, 12788.0
(UTC, or Coordinated Universal Time, is equivalent to Greenwich Mean Time)		

VHF-FM/NOAA Weather Frequencies

WX1	162.550 MHz
WX2	162.400 MHz
WX3	162.475 MHz
WX4	162.425 MHz
WX5	162.450 MHz
WX6	162.500 MHz
WX7	162.525 MHz

Reading the Skies

Water and metal are excellent conductors of electricity, making boating in a thunderstorm a risky prospect. While the odds of a given boat being hit are small, the consequences are severe and deadly. Do not try and play the odds! The best advice if you are out on the water and skies are threatening is get back to land and seek safe shelter, but that's not always practical for cruisers who live aboard or are not near land. Thunderstorms occur when air masses of different temperatures meet over inland or coastal waters. An example of this would be when air with a high humidity that is warm near the ground rises and meets cooler air, which condenses and creates water droplets. This releases energy, which charges the atmosphere and creates lightning. This is why thunderstorms are a daily occurrence between March and October near southern waterways.

A tell-tale sign of a thunderstorm is cumulonimbus clouds: those tall clouds with an anvil-shaped (flat) top. Thunderstorms can also precede even a minor cold front. Keep in mind that thunderstorms generally move in an easterly direction so if you see a storm to the south or southwest of you, start preparing.

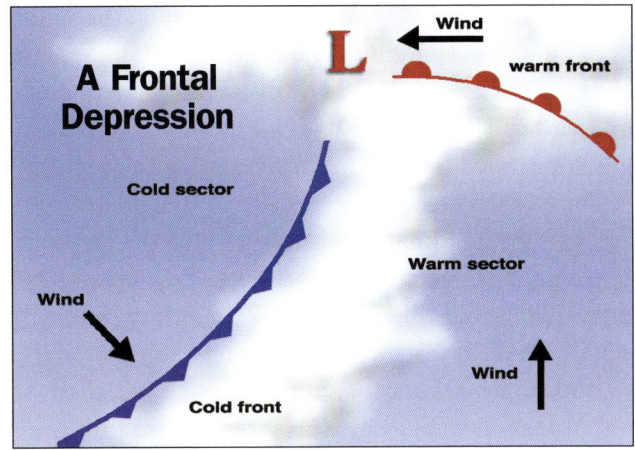

The trigger of change is a depression. Here, in a cold front, a counterclockwise flow of cold air comes in from the northwest. Warm air is sucked in from the south, which rises above the cold air, causing wind sheer and rain. The wind veers. A falling barometer is one of the warnings of a developing front.

Don't wait Until It's Too Late!

Almost all lightning will occur within 10 miles of its parent thunderstorm, but it can strike much farther than that. Also, the current from a single flash will easily travel for long distances. Because of this, if you see lightning or hear thunder, you CAN get struck!

The ability to see lightning will depend on the time of day, weather conditions and obstructions, but on a clear night it is possible to see a strike more than 10 miles away. Thunder can also be heard for about 10 miles, provided there is no background noise, such as traffic, wind or rain.

If you see lightning, you can determine the distance by timing how long it takes for you to hear the thunder. The old rule that every 5 seconds of time equals 1 mile of distance works well. So if it takes 20 seconds to hear thunder after you see lighting, then the storm is 4 miles away. This is the time to drop anchor and "hunker down."

Lightning Safety Tips

Lightning tends to strike the tallest object and boats on the open water fit this profile to a tee. The lightning will try to take the most direct path to the water, which is usually down the mast on a sailboat or the VHF antenna on a powerboat. However, both sailboats and powerboats with cabins–especially those with lightning protection systems properly installed– are relatively safe, provided you keep a few things in mind:

■ Before the storm strikes, lower, remove or tie down all antennas, fishing rods and flag poles.

■ Stay down below and in the center of the cabin. Avoid keel-stepped masts and chain plates (on sailboats) and large metal appliances, such as microwaves or TVs. Remove any metal jewelry.

If You Are Struck

1. Check people first. Many individuals struck by lightning or exposed to excessive electrical current can be saved with prompt and proper cardiopulmonary resuscitation (CPR). Contrary to popular belief, there is no danger in touching persons after they have been struck by lightning.

2. Check the bilge as strikes can rupture through-hull fittings and punch holes in hulls. Props and rudders are natural exit points on power boats.

3. Check electronics and the compasses. Typically everything in the path of the lightning is destroyed on the way down to the water, including instruments, computers and stereos.

4. Consider a short haul to check the bottom thoroughly. Lightning strikes sometimes leave traces of damage that may only be seen when the boat is out of the water.

■ Disconnect the power and antenna leads to all electronics, including radios. Do not use the VHF radio unless absolutely necessary.

■ If you are stuck on deck, stay away from metal railings, the wheel, the mast and stays (on sailboats) or other metal fittings. Do not stand between the mast and stays as lightning can "side-flash" from one to the other.

■ Stay out of the water. Don't fish or dangle your feet overboard. Salt water conducts electricity, which means that it can easily travel through the water toward you.

■ Don't think your rubber-soled deck shoes will save you; while rubber is an electric insulator, it's only effective to a certain point. The average lightning bolt carries about 30,000 amps of charge, has 100 million volts of electric potential and is about 50,000°F.

Don't Rush Back Out

Because electrical charges can linger in clouds after a thunderstorm has passed, experts agree that you should wait at least 30 minutes after a storm before resuming activities. And remember: If you can hear thunder, you can still be struck by lightning!

Natural Seasickness Remedies

■ *Take slow, deep breaths*. This helps with upset stomach and dizziness.

■ *Focus on the horizon.* Keep your body still and head facing forward and watch a stationary object. Taking the helm always helps.

■ *Ginger can help.* Eat ginger snaps, drink ginger tea or ginger ale or digest ginger in capsule form ahead of time.

■ *Peppermint works too.* Sucking on a peppermint candy, drinking peppermint tea or breathing in peppermint oil dabbed on a cloth can help with stomach issues.

■ *Try acupuncture wristbands.* They apply pressure to specific points on your wrist and can reduce nausea.

Ditch Bag Checklist

Rescue Items

- [ ] Functioning, registered EPIRB
- [ ] Handheld VHF radio (waterproof or in sealed pouch, with extra batteries)
- [ ] Sea anchor, drogue and line
- [ ] Manual inflation pump
- [ ] Selection of flares (parachute and handheld) and smoke signals
- [ ] Strobe light (may be present in inflatable PFD)
- [ ] Flashlight & batteries (headlamp is ideal)
- [ ] Whistle (may be present in inflatable PFD)
- [ ] Signal mirror
- [ ] Handheld GPS or compass (for position)
- [ ] Small pair of binoculars (to confirm a boat or plane spotting before using flares)

Survival Items

- [ ] Sponges and bailer (with handle)
- [ ] Patch kit for inflatable dinghy or life raft (or emergency clamps)
- [ ] Water (individually sealed or in collapsible containers)–at least 2 gallons per person
- [ ] Emergency food rations and can opener (if needed)
- [ ] Power Bars
- [ ] Prescription medications
- [ ] Seasickness medications/remedies
- [ ] First aid kit
- [ ] Multipurpose tool or sailor's knife
- [ ] Waterproof matches

Other Items

- [ ] Solar blanket
- [ ] Heavy-duty coated gloves
- [ ] Duct tape
- [ ] Sewing kit
- [ ] Simple fishing gear (line, jigs, hooks, etc.)
- [ ] Polypropylene line
- [ ] Waterproof sunscreen and zinc oxide
- [ ] Bug repellent
- [ ] Ziploc bags (gallon size)
- [ ] Paper and pen in Ziploc bag
- [ ] Spare prescription glasses and sunglasses (polarized to reduce glare)
- [ ] Laminated copies of passports or license
- [ ] Cash ($50 in small bills)
- [ ] Copy of the yacht's papers (including insurance)

Severe Weather & Hurricanes

While all coastal areas of the country are vulnerable to the effects of a hurricane (especially from June through November), the Gulf Coast, Southern and Mid-Atlantic states typically have been the hardest hit. But northern locales aren't immune; several destructive hurricanes have dealt a blow to areas in New England over the last 100 years, including Hurricane Sandy in 2012 and Matthew in 2016. While hurricanes can create vast swaths of devastation, ample preparation can help increase your boat's chances of surviving the storm.

According to the National Weather Service, a mature hurricane may be 10 miles high with a great spiral several hundred miles in diameter. Winds are often well above the 74 mph required to classify as hurricane strength, especially during gusts. Hurricane damage is produced by four elements: tidal surge, wind, wave action and rain.

- Tidal surge is an increase in ocean depth prior to the storm. This effect, amplified in coastal areas, may cause tidal heights in excess of 15 to 20 feet above normal. Additionally, hurricanes can produce a significant negative tidal effect as water rushes out of

Distance from Eye	Force Level	Wind Speed
150 miles	Force 8	34–40 knots
100 miles	Force 11	56–63 knots
75 miles	Force 12	over 64 knots

the waterways after a storm.

- Wind gusts can exceed reported sustained winds by 25 to 50 percent. So, for example, a storm with winds of 150 mph might have gusts of more than 200 mph, according to the National Weather Service.

- Wave action is usually the most damaging element of a hurricane for boaters. The wind speed, water depth and the amount of open water determine the amount of wave action created. Storm surges can transform narrow bodies of water into larger, deeper waters capable of generating extreme wave action.

- Rainfall varies but hurricanes can generate anywhere from 5 to 20 inches or more of rain.

Hurricane Categorization

CATEGORY	PRESSURE	WIND SPEED	SURGE
1	Above 980 mb (Above 28.91 in.)	64–82 knots (74–95 mph)	4–5 ft. (1–1.5 m)
	Visibility much reduced. Maneuvering under engines just possible. Open anchorages untenable. Danger of poorly secured boats torn loose in protected anchorages.		
2	965-979 mb (28.50-28.91 in.)	83-95 knots (96–110 mph)	6–8 ft. (1.5–2.5 m)
	Visibility close to zero. Boats in protected anchorages at risk, particularly from boats torn loose. Severe damage to unprotected boats and boats poorly secured and prepared.		
3	945-964 mb (27.91-28.50 in.)	96-113 knots (111–130 mph)	9–12 ft. (2.5–3.5 m)
	Deck fittings at risk and may tear loose, anchor links can fail and unprotected lines will chafe through. Extensive severe damage.		
4	920-944 mb (27.17-27.91 in.)	114-135 knots (131–155 mph)	13–18 ft. (3.5–5.4 m)
	Very severe damage and loss of life.		
5	Below 920 mb (Below 27.17 in.)	Above 135 knots (131–155 mph)	Above 18 ft. (Above 5.4 m)
	Catastrophic conditions with catastrophic damage.		

If your boat is in a slip, you have three options: Leave it where it is (if it is in a safe place); move it to a refuge area; or haul it and put it on a trailer or cradle. Some marinas require mandatory evacuations during hurricane alerts. Check your lease agreement, and talk to your dockmaster before a hurricane if you are uncertain. Keep in mind that many municipalities close public mooring fields in advance of the storm. In some localities, boaters may be held liable for any damage that their boat inflicts to marina piers or property; check locally for details. Because of this, rivers, canals, coves and other areas away from large stretches of open water are best selected as refuges.

Consult your insurance agent if you have questions about coverage. Many insurance agencies have restricted or canceled policies for boats that travel or are berthed in certain hurricane-prone areas. Review your policy and check your coverage, as many insurance companies will not cover boats in hurricane-prone areas during the June through November hurricane season. Riders for this type of coverage are notoriously expensive.

Preparing Your Boat

■ Have a hurricane plan made up ahead of time to maximize what you can get done in amount of time you will have to prepare (no more than 12 hours in some cases). You won't want to be deciding how to tie up the boat or where to anchor when a hurricane is barreling down on you. Make these decisions in advance!

■ Buy hurricane gear in advance (even if there is no imminent storm). When word of a hurricane spreads, local ship stores run out of storm supplies (anchors and line, especially) very quickly.

■ Strip everything that isn't bolted down off the deck of the boat (canvas, sails, antennas, bimini tops, dodgers, dinghies, dinghy motors, cushions, unneeded control lines on sailboats), as this will help reduce windage and damage to your boat. Remove electronics and valuables and move them ashore.

■ Any potentially leaky ports or hatches should be taped up. Dorades (cowls) should be removed and sealed with deck caps.

■ Make sure all systems on board are in tip-top shape in case you have to move quickly. Fuel and water tanks should be filled, bilge pumps should be in top operating condition and batteries should be fully charged.

■ You will need many lengths of line to secure the boat; make certain it is good stretchy nylon (not Dacron). It is not unusual to string 600 to 800 feet of dock line on a 40-foot-long boat in preparation for a hurricane. If you can, double up your lines (two for each cleat), as lines can and will break during the storm. Have fenders and fender boards out and make sure all of your lines are protected from chafe.

■ If you are anchored out, use multiple large anchors; there is no such thing as an anchor that is too big. If you can, tie to trees with a good root system, such as mangroves or live oaks. Mangroves are particularly good because their canopy can have a cushioning effect. Be sure mooring lines include ample scope to compensate for tides 10 to 20 feet above normal.

■ Lastly, do not stay aboard to weather out the storm. Many people have been seriously injured (or worse) trying to save their boats during a hurricane. Take photos of the condition in which you left your boat and take your insurance papers with you.

Returning Safely After the Storm

■ Before hitting the road, make sure the roads back to your boat are open and safe for travel. Beware of dangling wires, weakened docks, bulkheads, bridges and other structures.

■ Check your boat thoroughly before attempting to move it. If returning to your home slip, watch the waters for debris and obstructions. Navigate carefully as markers may be misplaced or missing.

■ If your boat is sunk, arrange for engine repairs before floating it, but only if it is not impeding traffic. Otherwise, you will need to remove it immediately. Contact your insurance company right away to make a claim.

Additional Resources

National Hurricane Center:
www.nhc.noaa.gov

BoatU.S. Hurricane Tracking & Resource Center:
www.boatus.com/hurricanes

Overview of a Mooring System

A mooring refers to any permanent structure to which a vessel may be secured. A "mooring system" refers to the various components–an anchor, a rode (typically a rope, chain, or cable), a buoy and a pennant. An anchor is used to fix a vessel to a point on the bottom of the seafloor without connecting it to land.

There are four basic types of anchors used in moorings: deadweight anchors, mushroom anchors, pyramid anchors and helix anchors. The table below describes the types of anchors and their characteristics.

Table 1. Anchor Summary Table

	HOLDING POWER	ADVANTAGES	DISADVANTAGES	NOTES
	An 8,000-lb. concrete mooring has approximately 4,000 lb. of holding power	• Simple design • Good for most bottom types • Holds position even if dragged during storm	• Heavy and bulky • Requires assistance for installation	• Better suited for rock bottoms • Deadweight moorings made from concrete can lose over one-half of their weight when submerged in water • Deadweight moorings made from granite can lose over one-third of their weight when submerged in water • Fault lines in stone anchors can crack when putting in staples
	A 500-lb. mushroom anchor has approximately 1,200 lb. of holding power	• High holding power-to-weight ratio	• Limited success in rocky areas • Prone to spin-out and chain wrap	• Better suited for muddy bottom conditions • Weight of mushroom anchors generally would be 10 to 20 lbs per foot of boat in mud bottom • Proper installation is important to assure it is buried
	A 650-lb. pyramid anchor has approximately 6,500 lb. of holding power	• High holding power-to-weight ratio • Simple design	• Limited success in rocky areas • Higher cost	• Better suited for muddy bottom conditions • Size and shape help penetrate the bottom more rapidly • Weight of pyramid anchors generally would be 10 to 20 lbs per foot of boat in mud bottom
	A 10-inch screw Helix anchor has approximately 10,000 lb. of holding power	• High holding power-to-weight ratio • Small size • Longevity • More environmentally sensitive	• Heavy and bulky • Requires specialized installer • Difficult in rock • More difficult to move	• Better suited for softer bottom conditions • Don't perform as well in rocky bottoms • Type of helix used might differ with condition of bottom • Requires diver to set and maintain

Source: *A Preliminary Guide to Mooring Systems, Mooring Choices and Mooring Selection.* Maine Coastal Program (www.maine.gov/dmr/mcp/downloads/access/moorings.pdf. For other helpful publications visit www.maine.gov/dmr/mcp/publications/index.html).

Anchoring Fundamentals (Excerpt)

In order to enjoy the rewards of that secluded anchorage, or to experience a drag-free night of squalls, maybe a storm, you must first be prepared. Preparation means that you have onboard, and have the ability to use the appropriate ground tackle, which is properly sized to handle all of the conditions that Mother Nature might toss your way.

Seabeds and Anchors

Sand, mud, and weeds are the types of bottoms most likely to be encountered by cruising folks; and, as there won't always be a choice, cruisers need to be outfit with anchors that will enable them to anchor securely in all three.

SuperMax, Spade, Delta, Bruce, Fortress, and other general-purpose anchors, in addition to the Fisherman-style anchors, all work well in sand. However, anchors with a 45 degree fluke angle—'navy-type' anchors—and those adjustable shank anchors that are set to the 45 degree angle, do not do well in sand. If they do set, once the wind picks up, they usually won't hold.

With anchors, size matters. For "sand", unless the manufacturer suggests differently, for wind speeds from zero to around 25 knots, the anchor sizes listed in the manufacturer's sizing chart are usually adequate; gale force winds usually require an increase of one size, and for storm force winds, whether a storm, or just a squall, go up two sizes. These are minimums; it is always better to go bigger, especially for long duration winds.

Any anchor that works in sand will most likely work in mud, but the holding power of the anchor will be less in mud than in sand–anywhere from one third to one sixth. Therefore, an anchor used in mud, even with a 45 degree fluke angle–the optimum angle for mud–will need to be bigger than that used in sand, at the very least one size bigger than that mentioned above, and two sizes is better.

In weeds, general-purpose anchors, if they grab, usually just hook into the weeds, often pulling out once the wind picks up. For an anchor to hold well in a weedy bottom, it must have the weight to crush down to the seabed, and have palms or flukes long enough to dig below the weeds, into the seabed itself. The anchors that can do this reliably are the "fisherman-style" anchors. Having one of these anchors onboard, such as a Luke take-apart anchor, not only broadens your choices of anchorages, if sized appropriately (two pounds per foot of boat) it also makes for a great storm anchor.

A fourth type of bottom is the "solid bottom", either rock or coral. Bottoms like this often have a covering of soil, too thin for good holding, but thick enough to fool the folks anchoring. If you're suspicious that you're in a 'rock' or 'coral' bottom, double check by backing down on the anchor, eventually using high RPMs if the bottom is solid rock or coral, the anchor will usually just drag along the bottom, maybe catch and release. If the wind is going to pick up while 'anchored' in a bottom like this, a wise captain will seek another anchorage, one with better holding.

Scope

It is Mother Nature that dictates the amount of rode that must be deployed, and as the wind rises, a scope of at least 10:1 may be needed. When calculating for scope, add together the depth of water, height of the freeboard, and any rise in the tide. But if the wind is expected to rise, also include the: depth that the anchor buries (1-2 feet in sand, 4-15 feet in soft bottoms), height of waves (1-6 feet), and the height of any storm surge (3-25 feet).

Adequate scope is critical, so when high winds are expected, don't skimp, letting out extra will pay more dividends than will trying to get by with as little as possible.

Multiple Anchors

here are times when more than one anchor may be required. Multiple anchors are not an opportunity to use just any little old anchor. Any anchor deployed, whether singularly or in concert with others, must be sized appropriately for the conditions, be of a design that is compatible with the type of seabed in which it is used, and have adequate scope.

If your current ground tackle does not conform to the above recommendations, upgrade it, and do so sooner, rather than later. And also remember to follow Rule 30-day shapes and lights for anchored vessels.

Rudy and Jill Sechez are the authors of "ANCHORING–A Ground Tackler's Apprentice." To read more, order a copy at www.waterwayguide.com or call 800-233-3359. Rudy and Jill are Trawler Training and Anchoring Consultants, providing one-on-one onboard sessions, consultations, and group seminars. They are also available to talk to groups and clubs. To arrange to have them speak to your organization, contact them at rudyandjill@yahoo.com.

Dealing With Onboard Waste

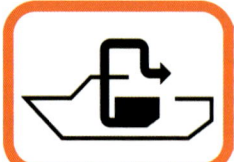

Up until the late 1980s, many boaters simply discharged their untreated sewage overboard into the water. After a revision to the Clean Water Act was passed in 1987, the discharge of untreated sewage into U.S. waters within the three-mile limit was prohibited. Shortly thereafter, pump-out stations became a regular feature at marinas and fuel docks throughout the U.S. waterways.

Simply stated, if you have a marine head installed on your vessel and are operating in coastal waters within the U.S. three-mile limit (basically all of the waters covered in the guide you are now holding), you need to have a holding tank, and you will obviously need to arrange to have that tank pumped out from time to time.

Government regulation aside, properly disposing of your waste is good environmental stewardship. While your overboard contribution to the waterways may seem small in the grand scheme of things, similar attitudes among fellow boaters can quickly produce unsavory conditions in anchorages and small creeks. The widespread availability of holding tank gear and shoreside pump-out facilities leaves few excuses for not doing the right thing.

No-Discharge Zones

- No-Discharge means exactly what the name suggests: No waste, even waste treated by an onboard Type I marine sanitation device (MSD), may be discharged overboard. All waste must be collected in a holding tank and pumped out at an appropriate facility.

- Keep in mind that there are some areas that forbid overboard discharge of any waste, including gray water from showers or sinks. Familiarize yourself with local regulations before entering new areas to ensure you don't get hit with a fine.

- No-Discharge Zones in Florida include Destin Harbor, the Florida Keys National Marine Sanctuary and the City of Key West.

The Law

- If you have a marine head onboard and are operating on coastal waters within the U.S. three-mile limit (basically all of the waters covered in this Guide), you need to have an approved holding tank or Type I MSD. In a No-Discharge area even a Type I MSD system must have a holding tank.

- All valves connected to your holding tank or marine head that lead to the outside (both Y-valves AND seacocks) must be wire-tied, padlocked or absent of the valve handle and in the closed position. Simply having them closed without the (non-releasable) wire ties will not save you from a fine if you are boarded.

- You may discharge waste overboard from a Type I MSD in all areas except those designated as No-Discharge Zones. A Type I MSD treats waste by reducing bacteria and visible solids to an acceptable level before discharge overboard.

- While small and inconvenient for most cruisers, "Port-A-Potties" meet all the requirements for a Type III MSD, as the holding tank is incorporated into the toilet itself.

Pump-Out Station and Holding Tank Basics

- Some marinas are equipped with pump-out facilities, normally located at the marina's fuel dock. Note that some marinas charge a fee for the service.

- Several municipalities and local governments have purchased and staffed pump-out boats that are equipped to visit boats on request, especially those at anchor. Radio the local harbormaster to see if this service is available in the area you are visiting. There is normally a small fee involved.

- You will want to keep an eye out on your holding tank level while you are cruising, especially if you are getting ready to enter an area where you many not have access to proper pump-out services for a few days. Plan a fuel stop or marina stay to top off the fuel and water tanks and empty the other tank before you set out into the wild.

Marine Sanitation Devices

Florida Statute 327.53 requires that vessels 26 feet or longer with an enclosed cabin and berth facilities must have one of the three types of MSDs described below on board when in state waters.

■ Type I MSD: Treats sewage before discharging it into the water using maceration. The treated discharge must not show any visible floating solids and must meet specified standards for bacteria content. Raritan's Electro Scan and Groco's Thermopure systems are examples of Type I MSDs. Not permitted in No-Discharge Zones.

■ Type II MSD: Type II MSDs provide a higher level of waste treatment than Type I units and are larger as a result. They employ biological treatment and disinfection. These units are usually found on larger vessels due to their higher power requirements. These may not be discharged in No-Discharge Zones.

■ Type III MSD: Regular holding tanks store sewage until the holding tank can either be pumped out to an onshore facility or at sea beyond the U.S. boundary waters (i.e., three miles offshore).

Penalties and Fines

■ Misuse or failure to equip a vessel with a Marine Sanitation Device may result in a non-criminal infraction with a $56 penalty.

■ Illegal dumping/discharge of a Marine Sanitation Device may fresult in a non-criminal infraction with a $250 penalty.

Additional Resource

BoatU.S. Guide to Overboard Discharge:
www.boatus.com/foundation/guide/environment_7.html

EPA Listing of No-Discharge Zones:
www.epa.gov/vessels-marinas-and-ports/no-discharge-zones-ndzs-state

 **BoatU.S.®**
MARINE INSURANCE PROGRAM

WINTERIZING CHECKLIST

Boat's Name: _____ Length: _____ Model: _____

Name: _____

Address: _____

City: _____ State: _____ Zip: _____

Phone: _____ Email: _____

ENGINE ROOM

ENGINE(S)

☐ Fill fuel tanks and add stabilizer to gasoline

☐ Change oil and filter

☐ Change fuel filters/separators in engine(s)

☐ Check coolant level in freshwater-cooling system and add coolant if necessary

☐ Run antifreeze through raw-water-cooling system

☐ Make sure water strainers are filled with antifreeze

☐ Fog cylinders in gasoline engines

☐ Top up battery electrolyte level and put batteries on marine charger

INSTALLED GENERATOR

☐ Change oil and filter

☐ Change fuel filters/separators

☐ Check coolant level in freshwater-cooling system and add coolant if necessary

☐ Run antifreeze through raw-water-cooling system

☐ Make sure water strainers are filled with antifreeze

OTHER SYSTEMS

☐ Flush and fill air conditioning system with antifreeze

☐ Run antifreeze through watermaker and pickle as per owner's manual

OUTBOARDS

☐ Fill installed fuel tanks and add stabilizer

☐ Turn off fuel supply and fog while running

☐ Drain gear case and add fresh lubricant

☐ Flush engine with muffs and fresh water

☐ Store unit in lowest position

☐ Inspect/replace anodes

☐ Empty fuel from portable tanks into car tank and take them home for storage

8 The Boater's Guide to Winterizing

www.BoatUS.com/insurance

 **WINTERIZING CHECKLIST**

OUTDRIVES

- ☐ If water intake is in lower unit, flush and run antifreeze through using muffs
- ☐ Drain gear oil and add fresh lubricant
- ☐ Inspect/replace anodes

BELOWDECKS

- ☐ Pump out holding tank and add antifreeze to head
- ☐ Drain water heater and bypass it
- ☐ Drain freshwater system and run antifreeze through it
- ☐ Run antifreeze through refrigeration, deck washdown pump, etc., per owner's manual
- ☐ Drain shower sump and other places where water pools
- ☐ Remove food
- ☐ Open lockers to air
- ☐ Take home cushions or store on their sides
- ☐ Take home portable electronics
- ☐ Close propane valves and take home portable canisters
- ☐ Verify bilge pump and switch operate properly
- ☐ Clean and dry bilges
- ☐ Secure all ports and hatches
- ☐ Turn off all circuit breakers

IN THE WATER

- ☐ Close all seacocks except for cockpit drains
- ☐ Plug exhaust ports
- ☐ Check docklines and chafe guards – center boat in slip
- ☐ Add or adjust fenders for proper placement

BEFORE YOU GO

- ☐ Tie off tiller/steering wheel
- ☐ Cover/shrinkwrap boat
- ☐ Lock cabin and leave spare key with marina manager

Distance: Outside (Coastwise) Route–New York, NY to Chesapeake Bay Entrance, VA

Coastwise Distances – New York, NY to Chesapeake Bay entrance, VA
(nautical miles)

	Chesapeake Bay Entrance	Chincoteague, VA	Ocean City, MD	Indian River Inlet, DE	Trenton, NJ	Former U.S. Steel Basin, PA	Philadelphia, PA	Chester, PA	Marcus Hook, PA	Wilmington, DE	C & D Canal, East Entrance	Harbor of Refuge, DE	Delaware Bay Entrance	Cape May Harbor, NJ	Atlantic City, NJ	Barnegat Inlet, NJ	Manasquan Inlet, NJ	New York, NY	Montauk Point, NY	Nantucket Shoals
Nantucket Shoals 40°30.0'N., 69°25.0'W.	381	328	295	285	400	395	372	356	353	347	336	285	285	271	242	221	212	223	113	-
Montauk Point, NY 41°01.7'N., 71°47.3'W.	322	262	227	209	327	322	299	283	280	274	263	212	212	192	157	131	117	122	-	
New York, NY 40°42.0'N., 74°01.0'W.	267	201	161	145	268	263	240	224	221	215	204	153	153	128	94	63	40	-		
Manasquan Inlet, NJ 40°06.9'N., 72°30.3'W.	291	161	121	105	212	207	184	169	165	159	148	98	97	85	52	22	-			
Barnegat Inlet, NJ 39°46.0'N., 74°06.3'W.	199	141	101	86	193	188	165	150	146	140	129	79	78	65	32	-				
Atlantic City, NJ 39°22.6'N., 74°24.9'W.	171	113	73	57	164	159	136	121	117	111	100	50	49	37	-					
Cape May Harbor, NJ 38°57.1'N., 74°52.6'W.	141	80	40	24	131	126	103	88	84	78	67	17	16	-						
Delaware Bay Entrance 38°50.5'N., 75°03.3'W.	136	72	32	15	115	110	87	72	68	62	51	2	-							
Harbor of Refuge, DE 38°49.0'N., 75°05.2'W.	136	71	31	14	116	111	88	73	69	63	52	-								
C & D Canal, East Entrance 39°33.8'N., 75°32.8'W.	206	123	83	66	64	59	36	21	17	11	-									
Wilmington, DE 39°43.2'N., 75°31.5'W.	218	134	95	77	54	49	26	11	8	-										
Marcus Hook, PA 39°48.2'N., 75°25.2'W.	224	140	101	83	46	41	18	3	-											
Chester, PA 39°50.0'N., 75°22.0'W.	227	144	104	86	43	38	15	-												
Philadelphia, PA 39°56.8'N., 75°08.3'W.	242	159	119	101	28	23	-													
Former U.S. Steel Basin, PA 40°08.2'N., 74°45.3'W.	265	182	142	124	5	-														
Trenton, NJ 40°37.6'N., 73°34.9'W.	270	187	147	129	-															
Indian River Inlet, DE 38°36.5'N., 75°03.6'W.	118	60	20	-																
Ocean City, MD 38°19.6'N., 75°05.6'W.	100	41	-																	
Chincoteague, VA 37°56.1'N., 75°22.8'W.	69	-																		
Chesapeake Bay Entrance 36°56.3'N., 75°58.6'W.	-																			

Five Fathom Bank Lighted Buoy F (38°46.8'N., 74°34.5'W.) to Philadelphia, 111 miles
Delaware Lighted Buoy D (38°27.3'N., 74°41.8'W.) to Philadelphia, 116 miles
Chesapeake Light (36°54.3'N., 75°42.8'W.) to Norfolk, 42 miles; to Baltimore, 165 miles

Distances: Hudson River, NY

Distances on the Hudson River – New York, NY to Troy Lock, NY
(nautical miles)

	Troy Lock	Watervliet	Troy	Rensselaer	Albany	Coeymans	Coxsackie	Athens	Hudson	Catskill	Saugerties	Kingston	Hyde Park	Poughkeepsie	Newburgh	West Point	Peekskill	Haverstraw	Ossining	Nyak	Tarrytown	Yonkers	New York (The Battery)
New York (The Battery) 40°42.0'N., 74°01.0'W.	134	132	132	126	126	115	108	102	102	99	89	80	71	66	53	45	38	33	29	25	24	16	-
Yonkers 40°56.1'N., 73°54.3'W.	118	116	116	110	110	100	93	86	86	83	74	64	55	50	37	29	23	18	14	10	9	-	
Tarrytown 41°04.7'N., 73°52.2'W.	110	108	108	102	102	92	85	78	78	75	66	56	47	42	29	21	15	9	6	2	-		
Nyack 41°05.4'N., 73°54.9'W.	110	108	108	102	102	92	85	78	78	75	66	57	48	43	29	22	15	10	6	-			
Ossining 41°09.6'N., 73°52.3'W.	106	104	104	98	98	88	80	74	74	71	62	52	43	38	25	17	11	5	-				
Haverstraw 41°11.8'N., 73°57.5'W.	102	100	100	94	94	84	76	70	70	67	58	48	39	34	21	13	6	-					
Peekskill 41°17.3'N., 73°56.0'W.	96	94	94	88	88	78	71	64	64	61	52	43	34	29	15	8	-						
West Point 41°23.1'N., 73°57.3'W	89	87	87	81	81	70	63	57	57	54	45	35	26	21	8	-							
Newburgh 41°30.1'N., 74°00.3'W.	81	79	79	73	73	62	55	49	49	46	37	27	18	13	-								
Poughkeepsie 41°42.3'N., 73°56.5'W.	68	66	66	60	60	49	42	36	36	33	24	14	5	-									
Hyde Park 41°47.3'N., 73°56.9'W.	63	61	61	55	55	44	37	31	31	28	19	9	-										
Kingston 41°55.1'N., 73°59.0'W.	56	54	54	48	48	38	30	24	24	21	12	-											
Saugerties 42°04.4'N., 73°56.7'W.	46	44	44	38	38	28	21	14	14	11	-												
Catskill 42°13.0'N., 73°52.1'W.	37	35	35	29	29	19	11	5	5	-													
Hudson 42°15.3'N., 73°48.1'W.	32	30	30	24	24	14	7	1	-														
Athens 42°15.6'N., 73°48.5'W.	32	30	30	24	24	14	6	-															
Coxsackie 42°21.0'N., 73°47.6'W.	26	24	24	18	18	7	-																
Coeymans 42°28.5'N., 73°47.4'W.	18	16	16	10	10	-																	
Albany 42°37.9'N., 73°45.3'W.	8	6	6	0	-																		
Rensselaer 42°37.9'N., 73°45.1'W.	8	6	6	-																			
Troy 42°43.7'N., 73°41.8'W.	2	0	-																				
Watervliet 42°43.7'N., 73°41.9'W.	2	-																					
Troy Lock 41°45.1'N., 73°41.1'W.	-																						

Distance: Inside (NJ ICW) Route–Manasquan Inlet, NJ to Cape May Canal, NJ

Distances by Intracoastal Waterway – Manasquan Inlet, NJ to Cape May Canal, NJ
(nautical miles)

	C & D Canal (east entrance)	Cape May Canal (west entrance)	Cape May Harbor	Wildwood	Stone Harbor	Avalon	Sea Isle City	Ocean City	Mays Landing	Atlantic City	Beach Haven	Barnegat Inlet	Forked River (town)	Seaside Park	Toms River (town)	Mantoloking	Bay Head	Manasquan Inlet	Shark River Inlet*	New York, NY (The Battery)
New York, NY (The Battery) 40°42.0'N., 74°01.0'W.	190	142	138	133	128	123	119	108	124	97	79	66	63	54	58	46	44	40	34	-
Shark River Inlet* 40°11.2'N., 74°00.5'W.	156	108	103	99	94	89	85	74	90	62	45	32	29	20	23	11	9	6	-	
Manasquan Inlet 40°06.1'N., 74°01.9'W.	150	102	98	93	88	83	79	68	84	57	39	26	23	14	18	6	4	-		
Bay Head 40°03.8'N., 74°03.1'W.	146	98	94	89	85	79	76	64	80	53	35	22	19	10	14	2	-			
Mantoloking 40°02.2'N., 74°03.4'W.	144	96	92	88	83	77	74	63	79	51	33	20	17	9	12	-				
Toms River (town) 39°56.9'N., 74°11.8'W.	142	94	90	86	81	75	72	60	77	49	31	18	15	7	-					
Seaside Park 39°55.3'N., 74°05.0'W.	137	89	85	80	75	70	66	55	71	44	26	13	10	-						
Forked River (town) 39°50.1'N., 74°11.7'W.	132	84	80	75	70	65	61	50	66	39	21	8	-							
Barnegat Inlet 39°46.0'N., 74°06.3'W.	131	83	79	74	69	64	60	49	65	38	20	-								
Beach Haven 39°34.0'N., 74°14.8'W.	111	63	59	54	49	44	40	29	45	18	-									
Atlantic City 39°22.6'N., 74°24.9'W.	95	47	43	39	34	28	25	13	30	-										
Mays Landing 39°26.9'N., 74°43.4'W.	100	52	47	43	38	33	29	18	-											
Ocean City 39°17.3'N., 74°34.4'W.	82	34	30	25	20	15	11	-												
Sea Isle City 39°09.4'N., 74°42.0'W.	71	23	18	14	9	4	-													
Avalon 39°06.6'N., 74°44.0'W.	67	19	15	10	5	-														
Stone Harbor 39°03.4'N., 74°46.0'W.	62	14	9	5	-															
Wildwood 39°00.5'N., 74°49.8'W.	57	9	5	-																
Cape May Harbor 38°57.1'N., 74°52.6'W.	52	4	-																	
Cape May Canal (west entrance) 38°58.0'N., 74°58.0'W.	48	-																		
C & D Canal (east entrance) 39°33.8'N., 75°32.8'W.	-																			

*Outside distances between New York and Manesquan Inlet

Distances: Long Island Sound–Greenport, NY to East Rockaway Inlet, NY

Inside Route Distances – South Side of Long Island Sound
Greenport, New York to East Rockaway Inlet, New York
(nautical miles)

	*Manasquan Inlet, NJ	*New York (The Battery)	*Rockaway Point	East Rockaway Inlet	Long Beach	Freeport	Jones Inlet	Jones Beach	Amityville	Babylon	Fire Island Inlet	Bay Shore	Patchogue	Bellport	Moriches Inlet	Westhampton Beach	Shinnecock Inlet	Shinnecock Canal (north end)	Riverside	Sag Harbor	Greenport
Greenport 41°06.0'N., 72°21.5'W.	116	107	94	85	80	77	76	72	66	61	62	57	48	42	34	28	21	16	21	11	-
Sag Harbor 41°00.2'N., 72°17.7'W.	117	108	95	86	81	78	77	73	67	62	63	58	49	43	35	29	22	17	22	-	
Riverside 40°55.0'N., 72°39.4'W.	108	99	86	77	72	69	68	64	58	53	54	49	40	34	26	20	13	8	-		
Shinnecock Canal 40°53.9'N., 72°30.3'W.	100	91	78	69	64	61	60	56	50	45	46	41	32	26	18	12	5	-			
Shinnecock Inlet 40°50.3'N., 72°28.6'W.	97	88	75	66	61	58	58	54	47	42	44	39	29	23	15	9	-				
Westhampton Beach 40°48.2'N., 72°38.4'W.	89	80	67	58	53	49	49	45	39	34	35	30	21	15	7	-					
Moriches Inlet 40°45.8'N., 72°45.3'W.	85	76	63	54	49	46	45	42	35	30	32	27	17	11	-						
Bellport 40°45.1'N., 72°56.0'W	75	66	53	44	38	35	35	31	24	19	21	16	6	-							
Patchogue 40°45.5'N., 73°01.2'W.	72	63	50	41	36	32	32	28	22	17	18	13	-								
Bay Shore 40°42.8'N., 73°14.2'W.	60	51	38	29	24	21	21	17	10	5	9	-									
Fire Island Inlet 40°37.8'N., 73°18.6'W.	60	51	38	29	24	21	20	16	12	8	-										
Babylon 40°41.2'N., 73°18.9'W.	57	48	35	26	21	18	17	13	6	-											
Amityville 40°39.6'N., 73°24.8'W.	51	42	29	20	15	12	11	7	-												
Jones Beach 40°36.2'N., 73°30.8'W.	44	35	22	13	8	4	4	-													
Jones Inlet 40°34.4'N., 73°34.9'W.	41	32	19	10	5	4	-														
Freeport 40°37.6'N., 73°34.9'W.	42	33	20	11	6	-															
Long Beach 40°35.7'N., 73°39.4'W.	36	27	14	5	-																
East Rockaway 40°34.9'N., 73°45.4'W.	31	22	9	-																	
*Rockaway Point 40°32.4'N., 73°56.5'W.	27	13	-																		
*New York (The Battery) 40°42.0'N., 74°01.0'W.	40	-																			
*Manasquan Inlet, New Jersey 40°06.1'N., 74°01.9'W.	-																				

* Outside distances westward of East Rockaway Inlet

Distances: Outside (Coastwise) Route–Cape Cod, MA to New York, NY

Coastwise Distances – Cape Cod, Massachusetts to New York, New York
(nautical miles)

	Port Newark, NJ	Elizabethport, NJ	Perth Amboy, NJ	New York City, NY	Montauk Point, NY	Port Jefferson, NY	Greenport, NY	Sag Harbor, NY	Montauk, NY	Stamford, CT	South Norwalk, CT	Bridgeport, CT	Stratford, CT	New Haven, CT	Hartford, CT	New London, CT	Stonington, CT	Great Salt Pond, RI	Providence, RI	Fall River, MA	Newport, RI	New Bedford, MA	Woods Hole, MA	Vineyard Haven, MA	Nantucket, MA	Nantucket Shoals, MA	Cape Cod Canal (E. Ent.)
Cape Cod Canal (E. Ent.) 41°46.8'N., 70°29.0'W.	193	191	202	182	76	134	99	100	85	152	151	138	132	127	140	89	77	66	74	69	54	31	22	43	69	144	-
Nantucket Shoals, MA 40°30.0'N., 69°25.0'W.	227	225	223	223	113	178	142	143	127	196	195	182	176	171	187	136	126	114	131	126	111	111	92	88	85	-	
Nantucket, MA 41°17.2'N., 70°05.7'W.	208	206	216	196	89	149	113	114	99	167	166	153	147	140	155	103	92	80	91	77	71	53	33	29	-		
Vineyard Haven, MA 41°27.3'N., 70°35.8'W.	183	181	191	171	63	123	87	88	74	141	140	127	121	114	129	77	67	54	65	51	45	28	7	-			
Woods Hole, MA 41°31.4'N., 70°40.4'W.	178	176	186	166	59	118	82	83	69	136	135	123	117	109	125	72	61	50	57	44	38	15	-				
New Bedford, MA 41°38.1'N., 70°55.1'W.	178	176	186	166	60	118	80	81	66	136	135	122	113	111	124	74	58	48	58	54	38	-					
Newport, RI 41°29.8'N., 71°19.8'W.	151	149	159	139	35	91	56	57	42	109	108	95	90	84	98	48	34	23	21	16	-						
Fall River, MA 41°42.4'N., 71°09.8'W.	166	164	174	154	51	107	71	72	58	125	124	110	105	100	113	63	49	38	21	-							
Providence, RI 41°48.5'N., 71°24.0'W.	171	169	179	159	56	112	76	77	72	130	129	115	110	105	118	68	55	43	-								
Great Salt Pond, RI 41°11.1'N., 71°34.9'W.	133	131	141	121	15	74	37	39	23	92	91	78	72	65	80	29	19	-									
Stonington, CT 41°19.9'N., 71°54.6'W.	121	119	129	109	19	61	28	29	18	79	77	64	59	52	66	12	-										
New London, CT 41°21.4'N., 72°05.4'W.	116	114	124	104	28	56	25	27	20	74	73	60	54	49	62	-											
Hartford, CT 41°45.0'N., 72°39.0'W.	143	141	151	131	75	84	62	64	66	102	101	86	81	74	-												
New Haven, CT 41°17.4'N., 72°54.5'W.	80	78	88	68	62	23	47	49	51	37	36	25	15	-													
Stratford, CT 41°11.3'N., 73°07.3'W.	69	67	77	57	65	15	52	54	56	27	26	10	-														
Bridgeport, CT 41°10.3'N., 73°10.8'W.	64	62	72	52	74	15	58	60	62	22	21	-															
South Norwalk, CT 41°05.7'N., 73°24.7'W.	52	50	60	40	84	23	71	73	75	11	-																
Stamford, CT 41°01.8'N., 73°32.3'W.	45	43	53	33	85	24	72	74	76	-																	
Montauk, NY 41°02.8'N., 71°57.5'W.	117	115	125	105	16	58	22	21	-																		
Sag Harbor, NY 41°00.2'N., 72°17.7'W.	115	113	123	103	32	56	11	-																			
Greenport, NY 41°06.0'N., 72°21.5'W.	114	112	122	102	30	54	-																				
Port Jefferson, NY 40°57.0'N., 73°04.5'W.	64	62	72	52	68	-																					
Montauk Point, NY 41°01.7'N., 71°47.3'W.	126	124	123	20	-																						
New York City, NY 40°42.0'N., 74°01.0'W.	12	10	20	-																							
Perth Amboy, NJ 40°30.3'N., 74°15.7'W.	15	10	-																								
Elizabethport, NJ 40°38.8'N., 74°11.2'W.	5	-																									
Port Newark, NJ 40°41.8'N., 74°09.0'W.	-																										

Distances: Gulf of Maine–Calais, ME to Cape Cod, MA

Gulf of Maine Distances – Calais, Maine to Cape Cod, Massachusetts
(nautical miles)

	Nantucket Shoals	Provincetown, MA	Cape Cod Canal	Plymouth, MA	Scituate, MA	Boston, MA	Lynn, MA	Marblehead, MA	Salem, MA	Gloucester, MA	Rockport, MA	Newburyport, MA	Portsmouth, NH	York Harbor, ME	Portland, ME	Augusta, ME	Bath, ME	Wiscasset, ME	Boothbay Harbor, ME	Bangor, ME	Bucksport, ME	Searsport, ME	Rockland, ME	Stonington, ME	Buck Harbor, ME	Bar Harbor, ME	Jonesport, ME	Machiasport, ME	Lubec, ME	Eastport, ME	Calais, ME
Calais, ME 45°11.4'N, 67°16.7'W	312	258	270	268	259	265	261	251	252	245	236	241	230	222	198	214	187	189	168	176	159	152	145	118	125	98	66	61	26	24	-
Eastport, ME 44°54.3'N., 66°59.0'W.	297	243	255	253	244	250	246	236	237	230	221	226	216	208	183	200	173	175	153	162	145	137	130	102	109	83	42	46	3	-	
Lubec, ME 44°51.7'N., 66°59.0'W.	286	232	244	242	233	239	235	225	226	219	210	215	204	196	172	188	161	162	142	150	133	126	118	91	98	72	40	35	-		
Machiasport, ME 44°41.9'N., 67°23.6'W.	271	214	226	224	215	221	217	207	208	200	192	197	186	178	153	169	142	144	123	132	115	107	100	73	80	52	20	-			
Jonesport, ME 44°31.6'N., 67°37.0'W.	257	197	209	206	196	203	198	188	189	182	173	178	167	159	135	149	122	124	105	113	96	89	82	53	60	34	-				
Bar Harbor, ME 44°23.5'N., 68°12.0'W.	243	179	190	188	177	184	179	169	170	163	154	159	148	140	115	130	103	105	86	94	77	70	62	33	39	-					
Buck Harbor, ME 44°20.3'N., 68°44.2'W.	237	165	176	174	159	162	157	148	149	138	131	137	123	114	85	94	67	68	57	39	22	16	22	16	-						
Stonington, ME 44°09.2'N., 68°39.8'W.	226	155	165	163	155	158	153	143	145	133	126	132	119	109	81	90	63	64	53	47	30	24	20	-							
Rockland, ME 44°06.0'N., 69°05.5'W.	223	148	160	155	142	147	142	132	133	126	115	118	107	99	71	86	59	62	42	50	33	23	-								
Searsport, ME 44°27.0'N., 68°54.0'W.	242	166	178	174	161	166	161	151	152	145	134	137	127	118	90	105	78	80	61	30	13	-									
Bucksport, ME 44°34.3'N., 68°48.0'W.	250	175	187	182	169	174	169	159	160	153	143	145	135	126	98	113	86	89	70	17	-										
Bangor, ME 44°47.7'N., 68°46.3'W.	267	192	204	199	186	191	186	176	177	170	160	162	151	144	115	131	104	106	87	-											
Boothbay Harbor, ME 43°51.0'N., 69°37.6'W.	207	119	130	125	112	115	110	101	102	95	84	86	74	64	36	50	23	21	-												
Wiscasset, ME 43°59.5'N., 69°40.1'W.	217	127	139	133	120	123	118	109	110	103	92	94	82	72	44	57	30	-													
Bath, ME 43°54.5'N., 69°48.7'W.	213	123	137	129	115	119	114	104	105	98	88	89	78	67	40	27	-														
Augusta, ME 44°10.0'N., 69°46.4'W.	240	150	164	156	142	146	141	131	132	125	115	116	104	94	66	-															
Portland, ME 43°39.4'N., 70°14.7'W.	203	107	118	112	97	100	95	86	87	79	66	67	56	43	-																
York Harbor, ME 43°07.9'N., 70°38.6'W.	182	75	83	75	60	63	58	48	49	42	29	25	11	-																	
Portsmouth, NH 43°04.6'N., 70°44.5'W.	180	73	81	73	58	61	56	46	47	40	27	22	-																		
Newburyport, MA 42°48.8'N., 70°52.4'W.	171	63	72	64	48	51	47	37	38	31	16	-																			
Rockport, MA 42°40.0'N., 70°36.5'W.	157	49	58	50	34	37	33	23	24	17	-																				
Gloucester, MA 42°36.6'N., 70°39.6'W.	155	45	52	43	26	26	22	11	12	-																					
Salem, MA 42°31.3'N., 70°52.5'W.	159	49	53	45	24	27	18	5	-																						
Marblehead, MA 42°30.2'N., 70°50.7'W.	156	45	48	39	22	19	14	-																							
Lynn, MA 42°27.3'N., 70°56.6'W.	159	47	48	40	22	13	-																								
Boston, MA 42°22.0'N., 71°03.0'W.	163	49	52	40	21	-																									
Scituate, MA 42°11.9'N., 70°43.5'W.	143	29	29	20	-																										
Plymouth, MA 41°57.6'N., 70°39.8'W.	144	26	20	-																											
Cape Cod Canal 41°46.8'N., 70°29.0'W.	144	22	-																												
Provincetown, MA 42°02.5'N., 70°10.0'W.	132	-																													
Nantucket Shoals 40°30.0'N., 69°25.0'W.	-																														

Each distance is by the shortest route that safe navigation permits between the two ports concerned. Vessels standing along the coast must make their own adjustments for non-direct routes. For example the table shows a distance of 214 miles by direct route from Machiasport to Provincetown; the distance via Matinicus Rock and Cape Ann is 235 miles. Distances from Eastport to Machiasport and other ports southward are via the deep Head Harbour Passage, which is 8 miles farther than via the shallower Lubec Channel.

GPS Waypoints

The following list provides selected waypoints for the waters covered in this book. The latitude/longitude readings are taken from government light lists and must be checked against the appropriate chart and light list for accuracy. Some waypoints listed here are lighthouses and should not be approached too closely as they may be on land, in shallow water or on top of a reef. Many buoys must be approached with caution, as they are often located near shallows or obstructions. The positions of every aid to navigation should be updated using the Coast Guard's *Local Notice to Mariners*, which is available online at: www.navcen.uscg.gov/lnm.

The U.S. Coast Guard will continue to provide Differential GPS (DGPS) correction signals for those who need accuracy of 10 meters or less, even though most GPS receivers now come with an internal capability for receiving differential signals.

Prudent mariners will not rely solely on these waypoints to navigate. Every available navigational tool should be used at all times to determine your vessel's position.

C&D Canal to Cape May

LOCATION	LATITUDE	LONGITUDE
Junction Lighted Bell Buoy CD	N 39°33.867'	W 075°33.300'
Ship John Shoal Light (on shoal)	N 39°18.317'	W 075°22.600'
Elbow of Cross Ledge Light	N 39°10.933'	W 075°16.100'
Miah Maull Shoal Light (on shoal)	N 39°07.600'	W 075°12.600'
Fourteen Foot Bank Light	N 39°02.900'	W 075°10.933'
Brandywine Shoal Light (on shoal)	N 38°59.167'	W 075°06.783'
Brown Shoal Light	N 38°55.333'	W 075°06.050'
Cape May Canal W. Ent. S. Jetty Light 10	N 38°57.967'	W 074°58.033'

Cape May to Sandy Hook

LOCATION	LATITUDE	LONGITUDE
Cape May Inlet West Jetty Light 5	N°38 56.200'	W 074°51.917'
Great Egg Harbor Inlet Otr. Lgtd. Whst. B. GE	N°39 16.233'	W 074°31.933'
Absecon Inlet Breakwater Light 7	N°39 21.833'	W 074°24.433'
Little Egg Inlet Outer Lighted Whistle B. LE	N°39 26.800'	W 074°17.367'
Barnegat Lighted Whistle Buoy B1	N°39 44.483'	W 074°03.850'
Manasquan Inlet Light 3	N°40 00.170'	W 074°01.917'

New York Harbor

LOCATION	LATITUDE	LONGITUDE
Ambrose Light	N 40°27.000'	W 073°48.000'
Junction Lighted Buoy TC	N 40°28.400'	W 074°02.300'
Atlantic Highlands Breakwater Light	N 40°25.117'	W 074°01.167'
Great Kills Light	N 40°31.300'	W 074°07.900'
Coney Island Light	N 40°34.600'	W 074°00.700'
Romer Shoal Light	N 40°30.800'	W 074°00.800'

South Shore of Long Island

LOCATION	LATITUDE	LONGITUDE
Rockaway Inlet Lighted Bell Buoy 2	N 40°31.767'	W 073°56.383'
Jones Inlet Light	N 40°34.383'	W 073°34.533'
Fire Island Light	N 40°37.950'	W 073°13.117'
Moriches Inlet Approach Breakwater Light 2	N 40°45.800'	W 072°45.183'
Shinnecock Inlet Approach Lgtd. Whst. B. SH	N 40°49.000'	W 072°28.600'
Montauk Point Lighted Whistle Buoy MP	N 41°01.800'	W 071°45.700'

Long Island Sound, North Shore

LOCATION	LATITUDE	LONGITUDE
Chimney Sweeps Lighted Buoy 1	N 40°51.750'	W 073°46.783'
Hen and Chickens South Lighted Buoy 2	N 40°54.200'	W 073°44.400'
Great Captain Rocks Lighted Buoy 2	N 40°58.950'	W 073°39.067'
Great Captain Island Light	N 40°58.900'	W 073°37.400'
Twenty-Six Foot Spot Lighted Bell Buoy 32A	N 40°58.100'	W 073°32.800'
Stamford Harbor West Breakwater Light 3	N 41°00.900'	W 073°32.800'
Greens Ledge Light 4	N 44°17.417'	W 068°49.700'
Cable and Anchor Reef Lighted Bell B. 28C	N 41°00.550'	W 073°25.133'
Bridgeport Harbor Ch. Appr. Lgtd. Whst. B. BH	N 41°06.233'	W 073°11.733'
Middle Ground Light	N 41°03.583'	W 073°06.083'
Stratford Point Light	N 41°09.117'	W 073°06.200'
New Haven Harbor Lighted Whistle B. NH	N 41°12.100'	W 072°53.800'
Branford Reef Light	N 41°13.300'	W 072°48.300'
Goose Island Lighted Bell Buoy 10GI	N 41°12.100'	W 072°40.500'
Guilford Harbor Lighted Bell Buoy 4	N 41°15.000'	W 072°39.200'
Long Sand Shoal W. End Ltd. Gong B. W	N 41°13.583'	W 072°27.600'
Saybrook Breakwater Light	N 41°15.800'	W 072°20.567'
Long Sand Shoal East End Buoy E	N 41°15.800'	W 072°19.350'
Bartlett Reef Light	N 41°16.467'	W 072°08.233'
New London Channel Lighted Buoy 1	N 41°17.600'	W 072°04.800'
Seaflower Reef Light	N 41°17.767'	W 072°01.983'
North Dumpling Light	N 41°17.300'	W 072°01.200'
Latimer Reef Light	N 41°18.300'	W 071°56.000'
Inner Reef North Buoy 5	N 41°14.533'	W 072°46.050'

Long Island Sound, South Shore

LOCATION	LATITUDE	LONGITUDE
Stepping Stones Light	N 40°49.467'	W 073°46.483'
Hart Island Light 46	N 40°50.700'	W 073°46.000'
Plum Point Lighted Buoy 1	N 40°49.933'	W 073°43.717'
Gangway Rock Light 27A	N 40°51.483'	W 073°44.750'
Execution Rocks Light	N 40°52.683'	W 073°44.267'
Glen Cove Breakwater Light 5	N 40°51.700'	W 073°39.600'
Cold Spring Harbor Light	N 40°54.800'	W 073°29.600
Eaton's Neck Light	N 40°57.233'	W 073°23.717'
Port Jefferson Appr. Lighted Whistle Buoy PJ	N 40°59.300'	W 073°06.400'
Mattituck Inlet Breakwater Light MI	N 41°00.917'	W 072°33.667'
Orient Point Light	N 41°09.800'	W 072°13.400'
Valiant Rock Lighted Whistle Buoy 11	N 41°13.767'	W 072°04.000'
Race Rock Light	N 41°14.617'	W 072°02.817'
Gardiners Island Lighted Gong Buoy 1GI	N 41°09.000'	W 072°08.900'
Gardiners Bay S. Ent. Lighted Bell Buoy S	N 41°02.200'	W 072°03.100'
Threemile Harbor Ent. Lighted Bell Buoy TM	N 41°02.700'	W 072°11.300'
Montauk Harbor Ent. Lighted Bell Buoy M	N 41°05.100'	W 071°56.400'

Rhode Island

LOCATION	LATITUDE	LONGITUDE
Watch Hill Lighted Bell Buoy 2	N 41°17.983'	W 071°51.667'
Great Salt Pond Entrance Bell Buoy 2	N 41°12.100'	W 071°35.700'
Block Island N. Reef Lighted Bell Buoy 1BI	N 41°15.500'	W 071°34.600'
Point Judith Lighted Whistle Buoy 2	N 41°18.500'	W 071°28.300'
Narragansett Bay Ent. Lighted Whistle B. NB	N 41°23.000'	W 071°23.400'
Beavertail Light	N 41°26.967'	W 071°23.983'
Brenton Point Lighted Whistle Buoy 2	N 41°25.900'	W 071°21.800'
Sakonnet River Ent. Lighted Whistle B. SR	N 41°25.700'	W 071°13.400'

Buzzards Bay

LOCATION	LATITUDE	LONGITUDE
Buzzards Bay Entrance Light	N 41°23.800'	W 071°02.017'
Westport Harbor Entrance Light 7	N 41°30.400'	W 071°05.300'
Padanaram Breakwater Light 8	N 41°34.450'	W 070°56.350'
Phinney Rock Lighted Buoy DP	N 41°33.100'	W 070°53.000'
Butler Flats Light	N 41°36.200'	W 070°53.700'
New Bedford West Barrier Light	N 41°37.617'	W 070°54.367'
Dumpling Rocks Light 7	N 41°32.300'	W 070°55.283'
Ned Point Light	N 41°39.050'	W 070°47.733'
Sippican Harbor Lighted Buoy 2	N 41°39.700'	W 070°43.600'
Cleveland East Ledge Light	N 41°37.850'	W 070°41.650'
Quisset Harbor Entrance Lighted Buoy 2	N 41°32.600'	W 070°40.000'
Lone Rock Lighted Buoy	N 41°27.650'	W 070°51.150'
Cuttyhunk East Ent. Lighted Bell Buoy CH	N 41°26.600'	W 070°53.400'
Cuttyhunk West Entrance Buoy 1W	N 41°26.700'	W 070°55.500'

Cape Cod's South Shore, Vineyard Sound, Nantucket Sound

LOCATION	LATITUDE	LONGITUDE
Coffin Rock Lighted Buoy 1	N 41°30.700'	W 070°39.700'
Falmouth Inner Harbor Light 1	N 41°32.517'	W 070°36.500'
Hyannis Harbor Appr. Lighted Bell Buoy HH	N 41°36.000'	W 070°17.200'
4. Chatham Roads Bell Buoy 3	N 41°38.300'	W 070°02.900'
Vineyard Sound Ent. Ltd. Whistle Buoy 32	N 41°22.100'	W 070°57.400'
Quicks Hole Entrance Ltd. Bell Buoy 1	N 41°25.800'	W 070°50.400'
Tarpaulin Cove Light	N 41°28.133'	W 070°45.450'
West Chop Light	N 41°28.850'	W 070°35.983'
East Chop Light	N 41°28.217'	W 070°34.050'
Edgartown Light	N 41°23.450'	W 070°30.183'
Cape Poge Light	N 41°25.167'	W 070°27.133'
Nantucket Bar Lighted Bell Buoy NB	N 41°19.000'	W 070°06.200'
Brant Point Light	N 41°17.400'	W 070°05.417'

Cape Cod Bay to Boston

LOCATION	LATITUDE	LONGITUDE
Cape Cod Canal Appr. Lighted Bell Buoy CC	N 41°48.900'	W 070°27.600'
Billingsgate Shoal Lighted Bell Buoy 1	N 41°48.800'	W 070°05.417'
Long Point Shoal Lighted Bell Buoy 3	N 42°02.000'	W 070°09.700'
Plymouth Bay Channel Lighted Buoy 3	N 41°59.700'	W 070°36.100'
Scituate Approach Lighted Gong Buoy SA	N 42°12.100'	W 070°41.900'
Nantasket Roads Channel Lighted Bell B. 3	N 42°19.100'	W 070°52.800'
Boston Lighted Whistle Buoy B	N 42°22.700'	W 070°47.000'
Boston South Channel Entrance Buoy 1	N 42°21.900'	W 070°53.800'
Boston North Chan. Ent. Lighted Whistle B. NC	N 42°22.500'	W 070°54.300'

Massachusetts Bay to Portsmouth

LOCATION	LATITUDE	LONGITUDE
Tinkers Rock Gong Buoy TR	N 42°28.900'	W 070°48.900'
Marblehead Harbor Buoy 1MH	N 42°30.500'	W 070°50.000'
Salem Channel Buoy 3	N 42°31.100'	W 070°45.100'
Eastern Point Lighted Whistle Buoy 2	N 42°34.200'	W 070°39.800'
Annisquam River Ent. Lighted Bell Buoy AR	N 42°40.400'	W 070°41.000'
Essex Bay Entrance Lighted Bell Buoy 1	N 42°40.800'	W 070°42.300'
Merrimack River Ent. Lighted Whistle B. MR	N 42°48.600'	W 070°47.100'
Rye Harbor Ent. Lighted Whistle Buoy RH	N 42°59.633'	W 070°43.750'
Wood Island Lighted Buoy 2	N 43°27.400'	W 070°19.700'
Isles of Shoals Bell Buoy IS	N 42°58.867'	W 070°37.267'

Kittery to Portland

LOCATION	LATITUDE	LONGITUDE
York Harbor Lighted Bell Buoy YH	N 43°07.800'	W 070°37.000'
Perkins Cove Lighted Bell Buoy PC	N 43°14.400'	W 070°34.200'
Cape Porpoise Lighted Whistle Buoy CP	N 43°20.300'	W 070°23.600'
Wood Island Light	N 43°27.400'	W 070°19.700'
Portland Lighted Horn Buoy P	N 43°31.600'	W 070°05.500'
Portland Head Light	N 43°37.400'	W 070°12.500'

Casco Bay to Penobscot Bay

LOCATION	LATITUDE	LONGITUDE
Halfway Rock Light	N 43°39.350'	W 070°02.200'
Little Mark Island Monument Light	N 43°42.533'	W 070°01.867'
Fuller Rock Light	N 43°41.750'	W 069°50.017'
Pond Island Light	N 43°44.400'	W 069°46.200'
Sheepscot River Ent. Lighted Bell Buoy 2SR	N 43°45.600'	W 069°41.200'
Seguin Light	N 43°42.500'	W 069°45.500'
Burnt Island Light	N 43°49.500'	W 069°38.400'
The Cuckolds Light	N 43°46.800'	W 069°39.000'
Ram Island Light	N 43°48.233'	W 069°35.950'
Manana Island Lighted Whistle Buoy 14M	N 43°45.300'	W 069°22.500'
Pemaquid Point Light	N 43°50.200'	W 069°30.350'
Marshall Point Lighted Whistle Duoy MP	N 43°55.300'	W 069°10.900'
Two Bush Ledge Lighted Bell Buoy 5TB	N 43°56.783'	W 069°04.917'
Tenants Harbor App. Lighted Bell Buoy 1	N 43°57.700'	W 069°10.900'
Whitehead Light	N 43°58.717'	W 069°07.450'
W. Penobscot Bay Ent. Lighted Gong B. PA	N 44°01.100'	W 069°00.300'
Matinicus Island Lighted Bell Buoy 9MI	N 43°53.100'	W 068°52.867'

Penobscot Bay to West Quoddy Head

LOCATION	LATITUDE	LONGITUDE
Brown Cow Ledge Whistle Buoy 2BC	N 44°06.733'	W 068°43.850'
Isle Au Haut Light	N 44°03.900'	W 068°39.100'
Saddleback Ledge Light	N 44°00.900'	W 068°43.600'
Burnt Coat Harbor Ent. Whistle Buoy BC	N 44°05.017'	W 068°26.233'
Long Island Lighted Gong Buoy LI	N 44°08.300'	W 068°20.500'
Long Ledge Lighted Gong Buoy 1	N 44°13.267'	W 068°17.783'
Frenchman Bay S. App. Lighted Whistle B. FBS	N 44°09.600'	W 068°08.800'
Great Duck Island Light	N 44°08.500'	W 068°14.700'
Mount Desert Rock Light	N 43°58.100'	W 068°07.700'
Schoodic Lighted Bell Buoy 2S	N 44°19.100'	W 068°02.100'
Southeast Rock Lighted Whistle Buoy 6A	N 44°19.800'	W 067°48.600'
Seahorse Lighted Bell Buoy 2SR	N 44°25.700'	W 067°38.500'
Moose Peak Light	N 44°28.500'	W 067°31.900'
Libby Island Light	N 44°34.100'	W 067°22.000'
Little River Daybeacon 1	N 44°39.050'	W 067°11.533'
West Quoddy Head Bell Buoy WQ	N 44°48.900'	W 066°57.000'

Bridge Basics

Bridges have to be factored in when planning a trip. Depending on where you cruise, you may be dependent on bridge openings; a particular bridge's schedule can often decide where you tie up for the evening or when you wake up and get underway the next day. While many are high (over 65 feet), and some usually remain open (such as railroad bridges), others are restricted for different hours in specific months, closed during rush hours and/or open on the quarter-hour, half-hour or even at 20 minutes and 40 minutes past the hour. To add to the confusion, the restrictions are constantly changing. Just because a bridge opened on a certain schedule last season does not mean it is still on that same schedule. (See "Bridges Schedules" in the next section of this guide or www.waterwayguide.com for the most current schedules.) Changes are posted in the Coast Guard's *Local Notice to Mariners* reports, which can be found online at www.navcen.uscg.gov. It is also a good idea to check locally to verify bridge schedules before your transit.

Most bridges monitor VHF Channel 09, designated by the Federal Communications Commission as the "bridgetender channel." Bridges in NC and VA still answer on VHF Channel 13, as do the locks in the Okeechobee. In any waters, it is a good idea to monitor both the bridge channel and VHF Channel 16–one on your ship's radio and one on a handheld radio, if your main set doesn't have a dual-watch capability–to monitor oncoming commercial traffic and communications with the bridgetender.

When using VHF, always call bridges by name and identify your vessel by name and type (such as sailing vessel or trawler) and whether you are traveling north or south. If you are unable to raise the bridge using VHF radio, use a horn signal. (For further information, see the *Coast Pilot 4, Chapter Two: Title 33, Navigation Regulations, Part 117, Drawbridge Regulations*.) If the gates do not come down and the bridge does not open after repeated use of the radio and the horn, call the Coast Guard and ask them to call the bridgetender on the land telephone line, or you may be able to call the bridge directly. Phone numbers for many bridges are given in the following Bridges & Locks section, although some of the numbers are not for the actual bridgetender, but for a central office that manages that bridge. Some bridges are not required to open in high winds. If you encounter a bridge that won't open, it is

Swing Bridges:
Swing bridges have an opening section that pivots horizontally on a central hub, allowing boats to pass on one side or the other when it is open.

Lift Bridges:
Lift bridges normally have two towers on each end of the opening section that are equipped with cables that lift the road or railway vertically into the air.

prudent to drop the hook in a safe spot until the situation is resolved.

Most bridges carry a tide board to register vertical clearance at the center of the span. (Note that in Florida waters the tide board figure–and the one noted on the chart–is generally for a point that is 5 feet toward the channel from the bridge fender.) In the case of arched bridges, center channel clearance is frequently higher than the tide gauge registers. So check your chart and the tide boards and, unless it specifically notes that vertical clearance is given "at center," you may be able to count on a little extra height at mid-channel, under the arch of the bridge. Some bridges may bear signs noting extra height at center in feet.

Pontoon Bridges:

A pontoon bridge consists of an opening section that must be floated out of the way with a cable to allow boats to pass. Do not proceed until the cables have had time to sink to the bottom.

Bascule Bridges:

This is the most common type of opening bridge you will encounter. The opening section of a bascule bridge has one or two leaves that tilt vertically on a hinge like doors being opened skyward.

Because many bridges restrict their openings during morning and evening rush hours, to minimize inconvenience to vehicular traffic, you may need to plan an early start or late stop to avoid getting stuck waiting for a bridge opening.

Bridge Procedures:

■ First, decide if it is necessary to have the drawbridge opened. You will need to know your boat's clearance height above the waterline before you start. Drawbridges have "clearance gauges" that show the closed vertical clearance with changing water levels, but a bascule bridge typically has 3 to 5 feet more clearance than what is indicated on the gauge at the center of its arch at mean low tide. Bridge clearances are also shown on NOAA charts.

■ Contact the bridgetender well in advance (even if you can't see the bridge around the bend) by VHF radio or phone. Alternatively, the proper horn signal for a bridge opening is one prolonged blast (four to six seconds) and one short blast (approximately one second). Bridge operators sound this signal when ready to open the bridge, and then usually the danger signal–five short blasts–when they are closing the bridge. The operator of each vessel is required by law to signal the bridgetender for an opening, even if another vessel has already signaled. Tugs with tows and U.S. government vessels may go through bridges at any time, usually signaling with five short blasts. A restricted bridge may open in an emergency with the same signal. Keep in mind bridgetenders will not know your intentions unless you tell them.

■ If two or more vessels are in sight of one another, the bridgetender may elect to delay opening the bridge until all boats can go through together.

■ Approach at slow speed and be prepared to wait, as the bridge cannot open until the traffic gates are closed. Many ICW bridges, for example, are more than 40 years old and the aged machinery functions slowly.

■ Once the bridge is open, proceed at no-wake speed. Keep a safe distance between you and other craft, as currents and turbulence around bridge supports can be tricky.

■ There is technically no legal right-of-way (except on the Mississippi and some other inland rivers), but boats running with the current should always be given the right-of-way out of courtesy. As always, if you are not sure, let the other boat go first.

■ When making the same opening as a commercial craft, it is a good idea to contact the vessel's captain (usually on VHF Channel 13), ascertain his intentions and state yours to avoid any misunderstanding in tight quarters.

Bridge Schedules

KEY:

Statute Mile Marker
Vertical Clearance

Drawbridge clearances are vertical, in feet, when closed and at mean high water in tidal areas. Bridge schedules are subject to schedule changes due to repairs, maintenance, events, etc. Check Waterway Explorer at www.waterwayguide.com for the latest shedules or call ahead.

NEW JERSEY BRIDGES MONITOR (VHF) CHANNEL 13

New Jersey ICW

112.2 / 23' **Two Mile Bridge:** Opens on signal, except from 9:15 a.m. to 10:30 a.m. on the fourth Sunday in March, when the draw need not open. If the fourth Sunday falls on a religious holiday, the draw need not open from 9:15 a.m. to 10:30 a.m. on the third Sunday of Mar. From 10:30 p.m. on Dec. 24 until 10:30 p.m. on Dec. 26, the draw will open on signal only if at least 2-hour notice is given.

108.9 / 25' **Wildwood (Rio Grande/NJ) Bridge:** Opens on signal.

105.2 / 55' **North Wildwood Blvd. (NJ 147) Bridge:** Fixed

102.0 / 10' **Stone Harbor Blvd. Bridge:** Also known as **96th St. Bridge**. Opens on signal, except from 10:00 p.m. to 6:00 a.m. between Oct. 1 through Mar. 31, when the draw will only open on signal if at least 8-hour notice is given. From 6:00 a.m. to 6:00 p.m. on Sat., Sun. and federal holidays from Memorial Day through Labor Day, the draw will open only on the hour, 20 min. after the hour, and 20 min. before the hour. From 10:00 p.m. on Dec. 24 until 6:00 a.m. on Dec. 26, the draw will open on signal only if at least 2-hour notice is given.

98.5 / 35' **Avalon Blvd. (601) Bridge:** Fixed

96.0 / 23' **Townsend Inlet Bridge (exit to ocean):** Opens on signal, except from 9:15 a.m. to 2:30 p.m. on the fourth Sunday in Mar., when the draw will not open. If the fourth Sunday falls on a religious holiday, the draw will not open from 9:15 a.m. to 2:30 p.m. on the third Sunday of Mar. From 11:00 p.m. on Dec. 24 until 11:00 p.m. on Dec. 25, the draw will open on signal only if at least 2-hour notice is given.

93.2 / 35' **Sea Isle Blvd. (625) Bridge:** Fixed

84.5 / 35' **34th St. (Roosevelt Blvd.) Bridge:** Fixed

80.1 / 55' **Stainton Memorial (NJ 52) Bridge:** Fixed

77.0 / 65' **Ocean City–Longport Bridge (exit to ocean):** Fixed

76.0 / 56' **NJ 152 Bridge:** Fixed

75.0 / 25' **JFK Memorial Bridge (exit to ocean):** Fixed

74.0 / 14' **Margate City Bridge:** Opens on signal

71.2 / 9' **Dorset Ave. Bridge:** Opens on signal except from Jun. 1 through Sept. 30 from 9:15 a.m. to 9:15 p.m., when the draw need only open at 15 and 45 minutes after the hour.

70.0 / 10' **Albany Ave. Bridge:** Opens on signal except from 11:00 p.m. to 7:00 a.m. and from Nov. 1 through Mar. 31 from 3:00 p.m. to 11:00 p.m., when the draw need only open if at least 4 hours notice is given. From Jun. 1 through Sept. 30, the draw need only open on the hour and half hour from 9:00 a.m. to 4:00 p.m. and from 6:00 p.m. to 9:00 p.m.; from 4:00 p.m. to 6:00 p.m. the draw need not open. Opening schedule can vary with annual events. Call ahead.

68.0 / 35' **Atlantic City Expressway Bridge:** Fixed

68.9 / 5' **AMTRAK Bridge:** Usually open unless a train is approaching.

67.2 / 20' **Absecon Blvd. (US 30) Bridge:** Opens on signal if at least 4 hours of notice is given, except from Apr. 1 through Oct. 31, from 7:00 a.m. to 11:00 p.m., when the draw need only open on the hour. Opening schedule can vary with annual events. Call ahead.

65.1 / 60' **Brigantine Blvd. Bridge (exit to ocean):** Fixed

37.0 / 60' **Manahawkin Bay (NJ 72) Bridge:** Fixed

14.1 / 30' — **Thomas A. Mathis (NJ 37) Bridge:** Opens on signal, except from Memorial Day through Labor Day from 8:00 a.m. to 8:00 p.m., when the draw need only open on the hour and half-hour; from Dec. 1 through Mar. 31, when the draw need only open if at least a 4-hour notice is given; and from Apr. 1 through Nov. 30 from 11:00 p.m. to 8:00 a.m., when the draw need only open if at least a 4-hour notice is given.

14.0 / 60' — **J. Stanley Tunney Bridge:** Fixed

6.3 / 30' — **Mantoloking Bridge:** Opens on signal, except from 9:00 a.m. to 6:00 p.m., from Memorial Day through Labor Day on Sat., Sun. and federal holidays, when the draw need only open on the hour, 20 min. after the hour and 40 min. after the hour.

3.6 / 30' — **SR 632 (Bridge Avenue) Bridge:** Opens on signal. Note: Vertical clearance of 65 feet when open.

3.0 / 31' — **Point Pleasant Bridge:** Opens on signal. Note: Vertical clearance of 66 feet when open.

1.1 / 30' — **NJ 35 Bridge:** Opens on signal, except (1) from 8:00 a.m. to 10:00 p.m. between May 15 and September 30 on Saturdays, Sundays and federal holidays, when the draw need only open 15 minutes before the hour and 15 minutes after the hour; and (2) from 4:00 p.m. to 7:00 p.m on Mondays through Thursdays and from 12:00 p.m. to 7:00 p.m. on Fridays (except federal holidays), when the draw need only open 15 minutes before the hour and 15 minutes after the hour. Year-round from 11:00 p.m. to 8:00 a.m., the draw need only open if at least a 4-hour notice is given.

0.9 / 3' — **Brielle Railroad Bridge (exit to ocean):** Usually open. Note: Draw is at 45-degree angle in open position so favor north side of channel.

Shark River Inlet, NJ

0.0 / 15' — **Shark River Inlet (Ocean Ave.) Bridge (exit to ocean):** Opens on signal.

0.8 / 13' — **Main Street (NJ 71) Bridge:** Use South Channel. Operates as one unit with Shark River Railroad Bridge. Opens on signal, except from 4:00 p.m. to 7:00 p.m., Monday through Friday (except federal holidays) and from 9:00 a.m. to 9:00 p.m. Saturdays, Sundays and federal holidays from May 15 through September 30, when the draw need only open on the hour and half hour if a vessel is waiting to pass.

0.9 / 8' — **Shark River Railroad Bridge:** Operates as one unit with Main St. Bridge. Opens on signal, except from 4:00 p.m. to 7:00 p.m., Monday through Friday (except federal holidays) and from 9:00 a.m. to 9:00 p.m. Saturdays, Sundays and federal holidays from May 15 through September 30, when the draw need only open on the hour and half hour if a vessel is waiting to pass.

0.9 / 50' — **NJ 35 Bridge:** Fixed

Sandy Hook, NJ

5.0 / 65' — **Highlands Bridge:** Fixed

4.5 / 22' — **Oceanic Bridge:** Opens on signal, except from Dec. 1 through Mar. 31, when the draw need only open on signal if at least 24-hour notice.

4.0 / 20' — **Sea Bright Bridge:** Opens on signal, except between 9:00 a.m. and 7:00 p.m. from the Fri. before Memorial Day through Labor Day, on Fri., Sat., Sun. and holidays, when the draw need only open on the hour. The draw need not open at any time for a sailboat unless it is operating under auxiliary power or is being towed by a powered vessel. (Note: This is a new schedule as of 2018.)

Raritan Bay, NJ

8' — **NJ Transit Railroad Bridge:** Opens on signal, except from 6:00 a.m. to 9:30 a.m. and from 4:30 p.m. to 7:30 p.m., Mon. through Fri. (except holidays), when the bridge need not open.

110' — **Victory Bridge:** Fixed

110' — **Edison (US 9) Bridge:** Fixed

134' — **Garden State Parkway Bridge:** Fixed

The Narrrows, NY

215' — **Verrazzano–Narrows Bridge:** Fixed

Alternate Arthur Kill Route, NY

143' **Outerbridge Crossing Bridge:** Fixed

140' **Goethals Bridge:** Fixed

31' **Arthur Kill Railroad Bridge:** Usually open.

150' **Bayonne Bridge:** Fixed

Side Trip: Hudson River, NY

213' **George Washington Bridge**: Fixed

139' **Tappan Zee Bridge:** Fixed

155' **Bear Mountain Bridge:** Fixed

172' **Newburgh-Beacon Bridges:** Fixed

134' **Mid-Hudson Suspension Bridge:** Fixed

167' **Walkway Bridge Over the Hudson:** Fixed

135' **Kingston-Rhinecliff Bridge:** Fixed

142' **Rip Van Winkle Bridge:** Fixed

139' **Alfred H. Smith Railroad Bridge:** Fixed

135' **Castleton-on-Hudson Bridge:** Fixed

60' **Dunn Memorial Bridge:** Fixed

25' **CSX Transportation Railroad Bridge:** Swing bridge that opens on signal, except from Dec. 16 through Mar. 31, when the draw opens on signal if at least 24-hour notice is given.

60' **Patroon Island Bridge:** Fixed

61' **Troy-Menandes Bridge:** Fixed

55' **Congress Street Bridge:** Fixed

29' **Federal Street Bridge:** Opens on signal from Apr. 1 through Dec. 15 if at least 24-hour advance notice is given. From Dec. 16 through Mar. 31, the draw need not open.

61' **Collar City (NY 7) Bridge:** Fixed

150' **Troy Federal Lock & Dam:** Schedule varies with season. Monitors VHF Channel 13. Operational hours in 2019 were from 7:00 a.m. to 5:00 p.m., May 17 to Oct. 16. Vessels are required to arrive at a lock at least 15 minutes prior to closing to ensure being locked through, and at a bridge at least 5 minutes prior to ensure an opening. Refer to the Waterway Explorer at waterwayguide.com for the most up-to-date schedule.

East River, NY

127' **Brooklyn Bridge**: Fixed

134' **Manhattan Bridge:** Fixed

133' **Williamsburg Bridge:** Fixed

131' **Queensboro Bridge:** Fixed

40' **Roosevelt Island Bridge:** Opens on signal if at least 2-hour advance notice is given to the draw tender at the Grand Ave. Bridge, the New York Department of Transportation (NYCDOT) Radio Hotline (311) or NYCDOT Bridge Operations Office (718-361-9217). Openings may be delayed up to one-half hour.

Side Trip: Harlem River, NY

25'-55' All Harlem River non-fixed bridges from Wards Island Foot Bridge (Mile 0) to Harry Hudson Bridge (11 total) open on signal if at least 4-hour advance notice is given to the New York Department of Transportation (NYCDOT) Radio Hotline (311) and the Triborough Bridge and Tunnel Authority (TBTA). The draws need not open from 6:00 a.m. to 9:00 a.m. and 5:00 p.m. to 7:00 p.m., Mon. through Fri. (except federal holidays).

5' **Spuyten Duyvil Railroad Swing Bridge:** Opens on signal.

Upper East River, NY

138' **Robert F. Kennedy (Triborough) Bridge:** Fixed

134' **Hell Gate Railroad Bridge:** Fixed

130' **Bronx-Whitestone Bridge:** Fixed

152' **Throgs Neck Bridge:** Fixed

Long Island South Shore, NY

30' **Atlantic Beach Bridge (exit to ocean):** Opens on signal from Oct. 1 through May 14. From May 15 through Sep. 30, the draw need only open on the hour and half-hour from 4:00 p.m. to 7:00 p.m. on weekdays and from 11:00 a.m. to 9:00 p.m. on Sat., Sun., Memorial Day, Independence Day, and Labor Day. During the same time period, the draw need only open from 2 hours before to 1 hour after predicted high tide. Predicted high tide occurs 10 min. earlier than that predicted for Sandy Hook.

14' **Reynolds Channel Railroad Bridge:** Opens on signal.

20' **Long Beach Twin Bridges:** Opens on signal, except (1) from midnight to 8:00 a.m. (year-round), when the draw opens on signal if at least 4-hour notice is given; and (2) from May 15 through Sep. 30 from 3:00 p.m. to 8:00 p.m. on Sat., Sun., and federal holidays, when the draw only open on the hour and half-hour. From 10:00 p.m. to midnight on July 3 the draw need not open.

20' **Loop Parkway Bridge (West):** Fixed

21' **Loop Parkway-Long Creek Bridge:** Opens on signal every other hour on the even hour, except from Apr. 1 through Oct. 31 on Sat., Sun., and federal holidays, when the draw opens on signal every 3 hours beginning at 3:00 a.m.

20' **Loop Parkway Bridge (East):** Fixed

21' **Meadowbrook State Parkway Bridge:** Opens on signal if at least a one-half hour notice is given to the New York State Department of Transportation, as follows:
(1) every other hour on the even hour; (2) from Apr. 1 through Oct. 31, on Sat., Sun., and federal holidays, every 3 hours beginning at 1:30 a.m. (Notice may be given from the phone located at the moorings on each side of the bridge or by marine radio.) From 9:00 p.m. to midnight on July 4 the draw need not open.

20' **Wantagh State Parkway (Sloop Channel) Bridge:** Opens on signal after at least a one-half hour advance notice is given by calling the number posted at the bridge. From 6:30 a.m. through 12 noon and from 12:15 p.m. through 4:00 p.m., Mon. through Fri., one bascule lift span may remain in the closed position. A full two-lift span opening will be given between 12 noon and 12:15 p.m., provided at least a 1-hour advance notice is given by calling the number posted at the bridge. From 7:30 a.m. through 8:30 p.m. on Sat., Sun. and federal holidays, the draw will open on the hour and half-hour, provided at least a half-hour advance notice is given by calling the number posted at the bridge. 631-952-6777

24' **Wantagh State Parkway (Goose Creek Channel) Bridge:** Fixed

60' **Robert Moses Causeway Bridge:** Fixed.

29' **Captree State Parkway Bridge:** Opens on signal every other hour on the even hour if at least a one-half hour advance notice is given by calling the number posted at the bridge. From Apr. 1 through Oct. 31, on Sat., Sun., and federal holidays, draw opens every 3 hours beginning at 3:00 a.m.

65' **Robert Moses Bridge (exit to ocean):** Fixed

18' **Smith Point Bridge:** Opens on signal from 8:00 a.m. to 4:00 p.m. from Oct. 1 through Apr. 30 and from from 6:00 a.m. to 10:00 p.m. from May 1 through Sep. 30. At all other times during these periods, the draw will open as soon as possible but no more than 1 hour after a request to open.

10' **West Bay Bridge:** Opens on signal from 8:00 a.m. to 4:00 p.m. from Oct. 1 through Apr. 30 and from from 6:00 a.m. to 10:00 p.m. from May 1 through Sep. 30. At all other times during these periods, the draw will open as soon as possible but no more than 1 hour after a request to open.

14' **Beach Lane Bridge:** Opens on signal from 8:00 a.m. to 4:00 p.m. from Oct. 1 through Apr. 30 and from from 6:00 a.m. to 10:00 p.m. from May 1 through Sep. 30. At all other times during these periods, the draw will open as soon as possible but no more than 1 hour after a request to open.

15' **Quogue (Post Lane) Bridge:** Opens on signal from 8:00 a.m. to 4:00 p.m. from Oct. 1 through Apr. 30 and from from 6:00 a.m. to 10:00 p.m. from May 1 through Sep. 30. At all other times during these periods, the draw will open as soon as possible but no more than 1 hour after a request to open.

55' **Ponquogue Bridge:** Fixed

Shinnecock Canal, NY

25' **CR 80 Bridge:** Fixed

22' **Shinnecock Canal Railroad Bridge:** Fixed

Shinnecock Lock: Operates 24 hours a day. Opens on signal (three short blasts on the horn or whistle). 631-852-8299

23' **Sunrise Highway (NY 27) Bridge:** Fixed

Cape Cod Canal, MA

0.7 **7'** **ConRail Railroad Bridge:** Usually open, except for the passage of trains or for maintenance. If the draw is not in the fully open position, the opening signal is one prolonged and one short blast.

2.0 **135'** **Bourne Bridge:** Fixed

4.5 **135'** **Sagamore Bridge:** Fixed

SKIPPER'S HANDBOOK

Cape May to Raritan Bay, NJ

■ Cape May to Little Egg Harbor, NJ ■ Barnegat Bay to Sandy Hook, NJ ■ Sandy Hook & Raritan Bay, NJ

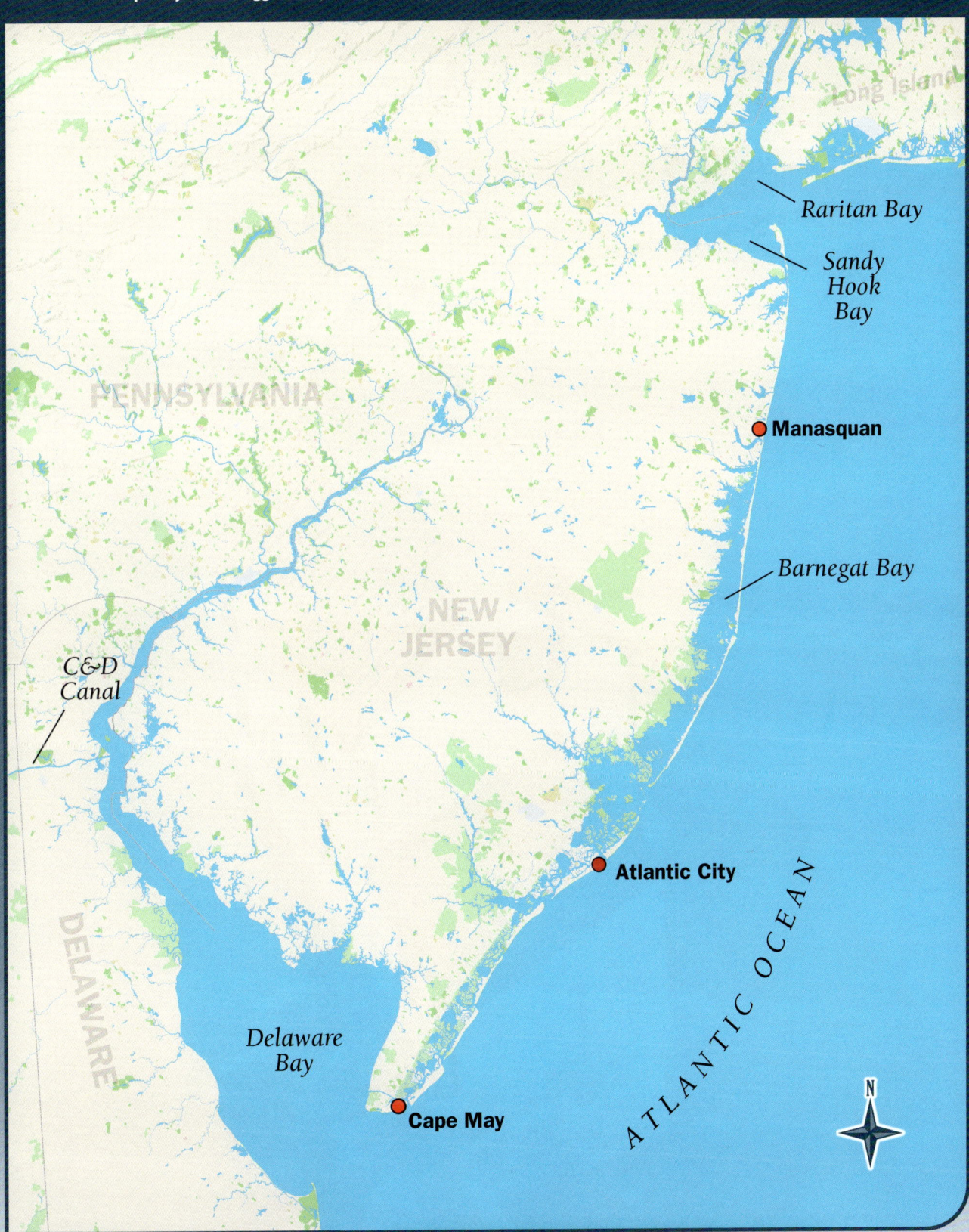

Long Island

Raritan Bay

Sandy Hook Bay

PENNSYLVANIA

● **Manasquan**

Barnegat Bay

NEW JERSEY

C&D Canal

DELAWARE

● **Atlantic City**

ATLANTIC OCEAN

Delaware Bay

● **Cape May**

N

Visit Waterway Explorer at www.waterwayguide.com

Cape May to Little Egg Harbor, NJ

■ NAVIGATING THE NJ ICW

The New Jersey Intracoastal Waterway (NJ ICW) provides something for every taste, beginning with serious birdwatching in Cape May and including the amazing estuaries and pinelands. The south Jersey shore towns along the NJ ICW offer fresh seafood, beautiful sunrises and sunsets, deep water inlets, fishing opportunities galore, kayaking, swimming and dockage at marinas along the way.

Cape May, Atlantic City and Atlantic Highlands/ Highlands are the more well-known stops along this route but Ocean City, Toms River, Point Pleasant/ Brielle and Manasquan are also noteworthy stops. On the ocean route from Manasquan Inlet it is just 24 nm to Sandy Hook, which opens up to an enclosed, single body of water that comprises three separately charted bays: Sandy Hook Bay to the southeast, Raritan Bay to the west and Lower Bay to the north, which is largest of the three and sometimes referred to as Lower New York Harbor.

At Sandy Hook you can set a course in almost any direction and head for any one of many destinations. To the south on the ocean side are the beaches and inlets of the New Jersey coast, while to the south on the inside of Sandy Hook is the popular harbor of Atlantic Highlands and two rivers: Shrewsbury and Navesink. To the west through Raritan Bay are the harbors of Keyport, NJ; Perth Amboy, NJ; and Great Kills, NY. To the north you will find New York City and Jersey City.

Cruising Conditions

The NJ ICW follows the same marking as the Atlantic Intracoastal Waterway (ICW) with red markers inland and green markers seaward. Where inlet channels cross the NJ ICW marker colors will reverse sides. Boaters are encouraged to pay very careful attention at all times and are advised to generally follow the outside radius of curves; however, do honor the markers because the navigation channel itself is very narrow.

> Remember: Wind dictates the water levels in the NJ ICW and supersedes tidal considerations.

The NJ ICW can be challenging for a couple of reasons: First, the channel has not been dredged in many years and as a result there is shoaling along the route, some of which is severe especially between Cape May and Atlantic City. Second, the NJ ICW is one of the most congested waterways in the country so it is not uncommon, especially on weekends, to find fishing boats blocking the channel.

The entire length of the NJ ICW from Cape May to Manasquan Inlet is subject to rapid change. Channels deepen and shoals form without warning. In general cruising boaters report a clear passage for the entire 118-mile statute mile (102.3-nm) length of the NJ ICW with MLW depths typically ranging anywhere from 4 to 6 feet MLW on the route. Depths of 3.5 feet MLW (and sometimes less) do exist; therefore, whenever possible, cruisers should seek local knowledge to get the latest on current channel conditions. You may also wish to review the Coast Guard's *Local Notice to Mariners District 5* (www.navcen. uscg.gov) for the latest conditions on the NJ ICW.

Barnegat Bay — Barnegat Inlet
Long Beach
Tuckerton — North Beach Haven
Little Egg Harbor
Great Bay — Little Egg Inlet
Abescon Bay
Atlantic City — Absecon Inlet
Ocean City — Great Egg Inlet
Cape May — Wildwood
N

Cape May, NJ

CAPE MAY HARBOR AREA		Largest Vessel Accommodated	VHF Channel Monitored / Working	Transient Slips / Total Slips	Approach / Dockside Depth (reported)	Floating Docks	Gas / Diesel	Groceries, Ice, Marine Supplies, Snacks	Repairs: Hull, Engine, Propeller	Lift (tonnage), Crane, Rail	Min / Max Amps	Courtesy Car, Laundry, Pool, Showers	Pump-Out Station	Nearby: Grocery Store, Motel, Restaurant
		Dockage					Supplies		Services					
1. Corinthian Yacht Club of Cape May MM 113.5	(609) 884-8000	50	/	3/	7.0/5.0	F		I			30	S		R
2. South Jersey Marina ⌨ WiFi MM 114.0	(800) 754-0622	140	16/9	25/70	10.0/10.0	F	GD	IMS			30/100	LS		GMR
3. Utsch's Marina ⌨ WiFi MM 114.0	(609) 884-2051	75	16/9	25/350	8.0/7.0	F	GD	IMS	HEP	L55	30/50	LS	P	GR
4. Miss Chris Marina MM 114.5	(609) 884-3351	100	16/	2/13	8.0/6.0	F	GD	IS			30/50			GMR
5. Roseman's Boat Yard MM 114.5	(609) 884-3370	60	/	1/20	4.0/11.0	F	GD	IMS	HEP	L75	30/50		P	GMR
6. Cape May Marina, LLC ⌨ WiFi MM 114.5	(609) 435-5757	70	73/73	30/210	10.0/10.0	F	GD	IS		L70	30/50	PS		GMR
7. Canyon Club Resort Marina ⌨ WiFi MM 114.0	(844) 384-6353	125	16/9	40/260	8.0/8.0	F	GD	IMS	HEP	L80	30/100	LPS	P	GMR
8. Snug Harbor Marina MM 113.0	(609) 884-4217	32	/	/124	5.0/5.0	F	GD	IMS	EP	L15	30	S	P	R
9. Harbor View Marina MM 113.0	(609) 884-0808	50	16/66	10/200	7.0/20.0	F	GD	IMS			30/50	S	P	R
10. Bree-Zee-Lee Yacht Basin MM 112.8	(609) 884-4849	46	/	10/1100	4.0/6.0	F	GD	IM	HEP	L35	30	LS		MR
11. Hinch Marina WiFi MM 112.5	(609) 884-7289	33	16/68	10/116	10.0/5.0	F		IMS		L25	30/50	S		R
12. Two Mile Landing Marina WiFi MM 112.5	(609) 425-9800	125	16/69	10/60	20.0/20.0	F		I			30/50	S		GMR

⌨ Internet Access WiFi Wireless Internet Access onSpot Dockside WiFi Facility

See WaterwayGuide.com for current rates, fuel prices, website addresses, and other up-to-the-minute information. (Information in the table is provided by the facilities.)

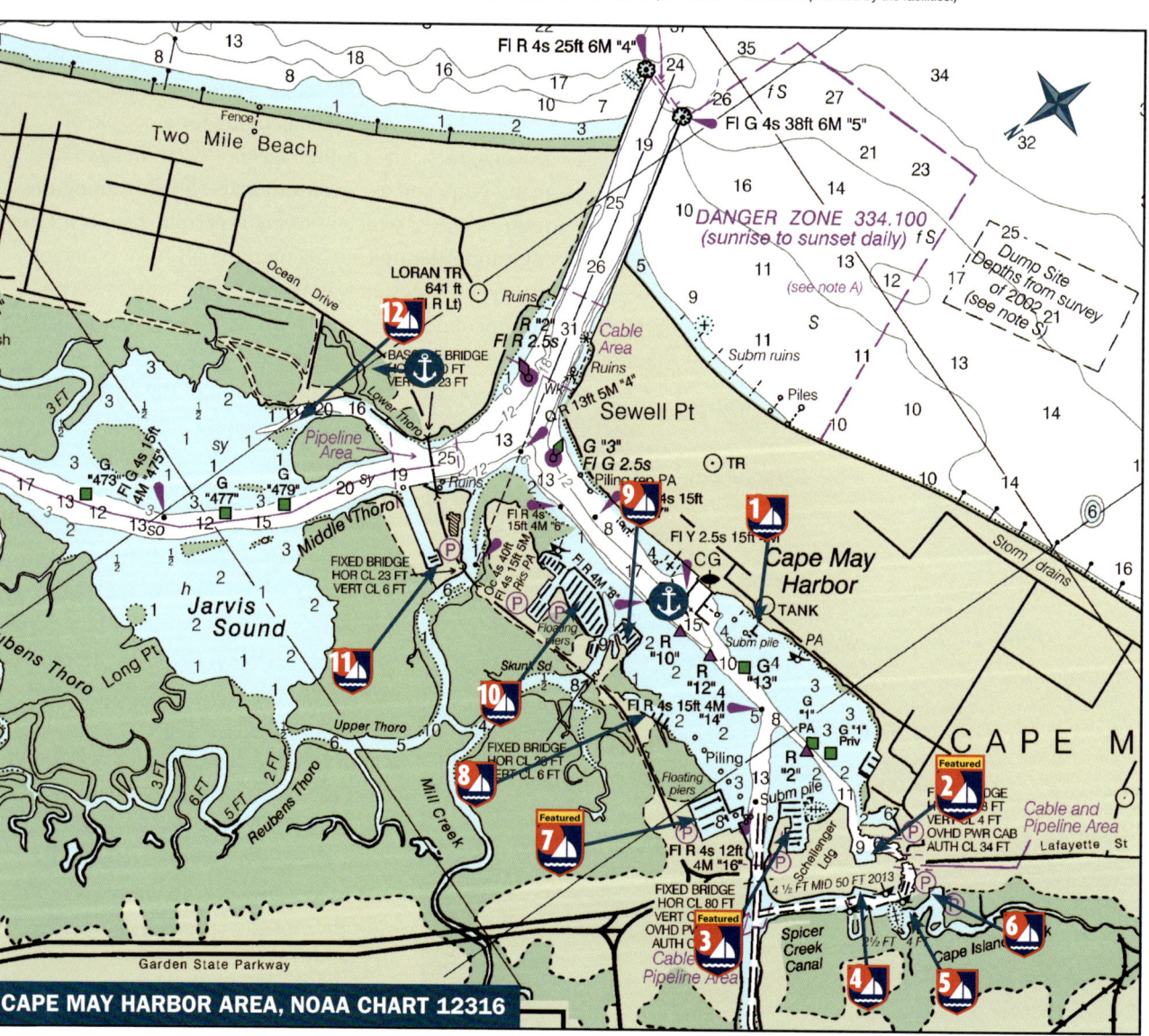

CAPE MAY HARBOR AREA, NOAA CHART 12316

The following are some suggestions for safely traveling the NJ ICW:

- Do not travel on weekends when the traffic on the waterway can be overwhelming.

- Pay strict attention to the state of the tide if you draw more than 3 feet.

- Boats drawing between 3 and 3.5 feet should leave Cape May 2 to 3 hours after low tide in Cape May Harbor to ensure sufficient water to Atlantic City.

- Boats drawing more than 3.5 feet should consider the ocean route to Atlantic City.

- Between Cape May and Atlantic City (Mile 65) the controlling vertical clearance on the waterway is 35 feet.

Boaters traveling in early spring or late fall should not assume that all charted aids to navigation will be present. Some of the floating aids to navigation between Cape May Inlet and Manasquan Inlet are removed each fall to avoid damage from ice during winter months. Coast Guard Group Cape May (609-898-6900, ext. 8) attempts to service and re-establish all aids to navigation by Memorial Day each spring. Also, the Coast Guard frequently moves floating aids to mark the best channel; therefore, your charts may not agree with the aids you see.

■ CAPE MAY TO STONE HARBOR

Cape May

Cape May is a safe, all-weather entrance from the Atlantic Ocean into Cape May Harbor at the southern terminus of the NJ ICW (Mile 114). The well-protected harbor makes it a popular layover for skippers waiting out bad weather before heading north along the New Jersey coast or for those headed to the Delaware Bay or the C&D Canal farther north.

Cape May was settled by whalers and fishermen in colonial times and is reputed to be "the nation's oldest seashore resort." Its heritage dates from at least 1812, peaking architecturally in the late 19th century. The entire town has been proclaimed a National Historic Landmark. Cape May likely has the largest collection

LOBSTER HOUSE
(609) 884-8296
Fisherman's Wharf | Cape May, NJ 08204
Exit No. 0 Garden State Parkway
Cocktails • Luncheons • Dinners

SINCE UTSCH'S MARINA 1951

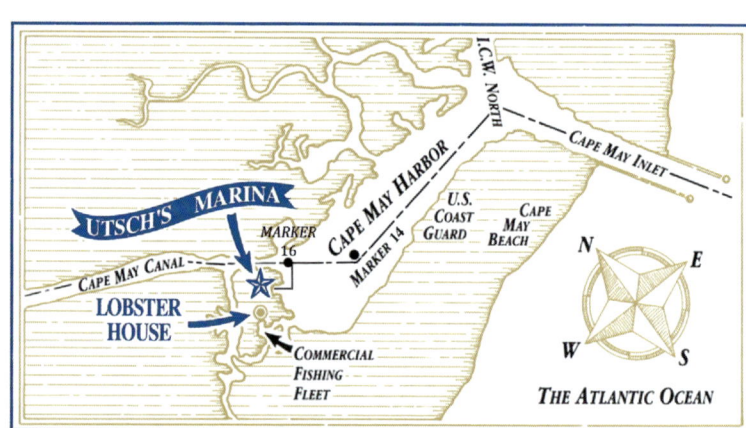

Nearby & On-Site Attractions:

- Historic City of Cape May
- MAC for the Arts
- Cape May Point Lighthouse
- Charter Boat Fleet
- On-site Chapel: Non-denominational Christian Services every Sunday
- East Coast Parasailing–Jet Boat–Jet Skis
- Adjacent to Lobster House Restaurant

- Bait & Tackle Shop
- Ship's Store
- Transient & Seasonal Slips
- Deluxe Showers, Restrooms & Lounges
- Laundry Facilities
- Wireless Internet Access
- Picnic tables & Gazebos
- Bike Rentals
- 25 & 55 ton open end Travel lifts
- Engine Franchises:

COMPLETE MARINE FACILITIES

Located in Cape May Harbor on the south side of the Cape May Canal, we are a 300 slip, family owned & operated marina. Since 1951, an Utsch family member is always on hand to greet you. Ernie III or Charles and staff will do their best to make your stay a memorable experience.

WE MONITOR CHANNEL 16 VHF
Discounts Available for Volume Fuel Purchases

UTSCH'S MARINA
SHIP'S STORE–BAIT & TACKLE SHOP
BROKERAGE–STORAGE–SERVICE & REPAIRS

(609) 884-2051
www.capemayharbor.com
utschm@comcast.net

LOCATED BETWEEN CANAL AND SCHELLENGER'S LANDING

CANYON CLUB MARINA

Cape May's Full Service Marina

- Transient dockage to 125
- Monitor VHF-CH 9 & 16
- Clean restrooms & showers
- Free cable TV & wireless internet
- Floating docks
- Swimming Pool
- Ship's store
- Courtesy Shuttle
- 30/50/100 amp electric service
- High-speed, in-slip fueling

- Full service department featuring:
Complete outfitting, Travel lifts to 80 tons, Parts & electronics departments, A/C & refrigeration repair, Hull & prop repairs, Winter storage, Fiberglass & paint shop, Diesel & gas engine repairs

Canyon Club
RESORT MARINA

900 Ocean Drive • Cape May, NJ 08204
844-384-6353
reservations@canyonclubmarina.com
www.CanyonClubMarina.com

CELEBRATING 66 YEARS AS CAPE MAY'S PREMIER MARINA!

UTSCH'S
MARINA

Schellenger's Landing, 1958

Utsch's Marina, 1956

The historical "era" of Schellenger's Landing, Cape May Harbor and the nation's oldest seashore resort are rich in history! Schellenger's Landing was originally a shipbuilding center for not only commercial fishing boats, but for tugs commissioned by the US Government. UTSCH'S MARINA, founded in 1951 caters to the "old ways and times." We now have a 300 plus slip marina, with a Bait & Tackle Shop, a Ship's Store to accommodate any part needed to keep your boat in "Ship Shape!" Locals and visitors alike today can still enjoy all kinds of activities in this unique area just before entering Cape May proper.

609-884-2051 | 1121 Route 109, Cape May
CapeMayHarbor.com

SOUTH JERSEY MARINA

UTSCH'S MARINA

CANYON CLUB RESORT MARINA

Cape May Inlet

Coming from Chesapeake City

Eastbound vessels, particularly slower vessels, departing Chesapeake City to Cape May should give some consideration to the tidal current in the C & D Canal and at the head of the Delaware Bay. Obviously, a slow boat will have a better time with the tide if it is going out when you transit this section. Departing Chesapeake City at low tide will give you a favorable current for most of the trip. For a 5-to 7-knot vessel this will take between 10 and 11 hours.

of Victorian period houses in the country. Small gingerbread cottages nestle beside grand showpieces, all preserved and restored, with many tastefully pressed into commercial service. Curlicue porches and steeply peaked, lovingly rebuilt dormers adorn many houses within walking distance of the western harbor's marine facilities. Cape May's beaches are legendary, its dunes are still nearly pristine and the harbor is a secure storm anchorage.

NAVIGATION: Use NOAA Charts 12314, 12316 and 12317. Approaching Cape May Inlet from either the NJ ICW or the Atlantic Ocean, your landmark is a charted 641-foot tall LORAN tower, which is located on the east side of the inlet. The tower is nearly four times the height of the 165-foot tall Cape May Lighthouse at the southwestern tip of the Cape and it is topped

by a flashing red light. Additionally, an onshore Ferris wheel north of Cape May is prominent and easily seen up to 5 miles offshore. Cape May Inlet is deep and visibly protected by substantial rock jetties on either side making it one of the safest and best-marked inlets on the East Coast.

Cape May Inlet is always extremely busy and you can expect to meet every type of vessel at every speed imaginable. The inlet is also popular with the fishing crowd and the mouth is often congested with small recreational fishing boats. The commercial fishing fleet generally has its outriggers extended while traversing the inlet, making them very beamy. The outriggers are not lighted and can be very difficult to see in poor light.

Entering Cape May Harbor is easy from every approach–from Delaware Bay through the jettied entrance to the Cape May Canal, from the NJ ICW itself on the north or through Cape May Inlet on the east. Ebb tides run east, both in the canal and in the inlet. NOAA Chart 12316 will be helpful in sorting out the buoys and depths for all three approaches.

During periods of reduced visibility you can activate the Mariner Radio Activated Sound Signal (MRASS) at Cape May Canal West Entrance North Jetty Light 11 (LLNR 1675). Use VHF-FM Channel 83A / 157.175MHz and key the microphone five times when within a range of 1 nm of the light. Following activation, the MRASS will provide a sound signal for approximately 30 minutes and then automatically secure.

During the peak travel season when the weather and tide turn favorable, you can expect an armada of yachts to pour out of Cape May Harbor in both directions to take advantage of an opportunity for a smooth passage. On the other hand, it is also not uncommon to see yachts, even high-powered ones, return to Cape May after taking a pounding from the elements at work in both Delaware Bay and the Atlantic Ocean. Any attempt to challenge the opposition of both wind and tide along the axis of the bay is not recommended.

Dockage: Cape May has many large, accommodating marinas with transient slips available, although be aware that space may be severely limited during fishing tournaments. Proceeding around the harbor in a clockwise direction from the south the first facility you will encounter is the Corinthian Yacht Club of Cape May, located just west of the Coast Guard station. This club is very popular with sailors and fills up quickly during the heavily traveled seasons. You may contact the club commodore for permission to dock and dine there.

Just inside the mouth of Schellenger Creek is the full-service South Jersey Marina, reached by a straight-ahead course into the creek between green daybeacon "1" and red daybeacon "2" (instead of turning northwest toward Cape May Canal at flashing red "12"). The marina lies just beyond the commercial dock and the highly visible Lobster House Restaurant. Turning room is at a premium here but there is plenty of depth and the marina's dock staff skillfully maneuvers large craft into position to match various skippers' plans for time and tide. They provide in-slip fueling and an exceptionally clean restroom and shower complex and on-site laundry. Vessels up to 140 feet long and requiring depths up to 9 feet can be accommodated. Dockside services include local weather and fishing reports and the coordination of boat repairs through their sister facility, Canyon Club Resort Marina, also located on Cape May Harbor. The marina also offers a shuttle service to town.

Near the west end of Cape May Harbor and adjacent to the Cape May Canal entrance, Utsch's Marina (immediately west of the canal entrance) is a full-service facility that can accommodate deep-draft vessels on approach and at berth. Utsch's offers all the usual amenities plus slips on floating docks, WiFi and a well-stocked marine store. This cruiser-friendly marina has been family-owned and -operated since 1951. Be sure to contact the marina for instructions on how to best approach it.

Just east of the Cape May Canal entrance, Canyon Club Resort Marina's wide docks are canopied by hundreds of outriggers extending from the hulls of sportfishing boats dedicated to searching offshore canyons. There is usually ample transient space on floating cement docks with in-slip fueling. It also has a large in-ground pool in a well-landscaped setting, coin-operated laundry facilities, a complete repair facility and a ship store with fishing tackle, sportswear, charts, artwork and gifts. The marina also offers shuttle service to town.

Snug Harbor Marina is located in the protected Cedar Creek off the channel with gas and diesel fuel and repairs. Call ahead for approach slip availability, depths and directions. The turn north from the channel into Harbor View Marina and Bree-Zee-Lee Yacht Basin should be made just after flashing green "7" adjacent to the Coast Guard's northernmost docks. Head toward the middle entrance of the seawall and then stay adjacent to the wall to the westernmost entrance toward the fuel docks. Both facilities offer fuel and transient slips. (Call ahead for depths.)

North of the bascule bridge over Middle Thoroughfare on the western side is Hinch Marina, a family-run facility accommodating smaller vessels (up to 35 feet). They also have a lift, a Ship Store and an on-site bait and tackle shop. Behind Thoroughfare Island are the floating docks of Two Mile Landing Marina, which has transient space and offers an on-site restaurant and a gift store.

If approaching from the Cape May Canal, marine facilities are available on Spicer Creek Canal. Miss Chris Marina has limited space and few amenities but offers paddleboard and kayak rentals for bird watching and is home to several charter boats. Roseman's Boat Yard is a full-service yard (no transient slips) with gas and diesel. Note that they report 4-foot MLW approach depths. The 210-slip Cape May Marina is located on Cape Island Creek and caters to transients in an attractive environment. Access to these facilities directly from Cape May Harbor is limited by the **Lafayette Street Bridge** (4-foot fixed vertical clearance).

Anchorage: Although marina slips are generally available (even during the peak of fall migration), all bets are off during Cape May's frequent fishing tournaments. There is ample room for shallow-draft vessels west of the Coast Guard station, outside (or even in) the mooring field.

GOIN' ASHORE

CAPE MAY, NJ

Cape May has been a booming summer tourist destination for nearly two centuries and is the oldest seashore resort in the United States. The town has the largest collection of Victorian architecture in the nation has been a National Historic Landmark since 1976. The main attraction of Cape May is the Victorian town itself with its quaint houses and interesting shops, its pedestrian mall and seaside vistas from the boardwalk, not to mention its dozens of eager-to-please restaurants. Cape May is also known for its many fine bed and breakfast inns.

Should you choose to go to the beach, be aware that in season, you must have a beach tag to use Cape May's beaches. Tags are required between the hours of 10:00 a.m. and 5:00 p.m., from Memorial Day weekend in May through Labor Day in September. Beach tags can be purchased at any beach entrance. The cost is $6 daily, $15 for three days, $20 for a week.

SERVICES

1. **Cape May County Library**
   110 Ocean St. (609-884-9568)

2. **Cape May Post Office**
   700 Washington St. (609-884-3578)

3. **Cape May Welcome Center**
   609 Lafayette St. (609-884-5508)

ATTRACTIONS

4. **Cape May Trolley Tours**
   Purchase tickets at the Washington Street Mall Information Booth at Ocean St. where most tours start (unless otherwise noted) or call 609-884-5404.

5. **Greater Cape May Historical Colonial House Museum**
   Originally a tavern and the family house of Revolutionary War Patriot Memucan Hughes (circa 1730). Open seasonally (June 15 to September 15) on Wednesdays through Saturdays (1:00 p.m. to 4:00 p.m.) at 653 ½ Washington St. (609-884-9100).

6. **Miss Chris Marina and Kayaks**
   Located behind Captains Cove Restaurant with kayak rentals as well as whale watching, bird watching and charter fishing trips (609-884-3351).

SHOPPING

7. **Acme Groceries**
   315 Ocean St. (609-884-7217)

8. **SeaGear Marine Supply**
   Offers a full complement of supplies for cruising or commercial boats at 1144 Rt. 109 (609-884-2711).

9. Swain's Hardware

Full-service, family-owned hardware store at 305 Jackson St. (609-884-8578).

MARINAS

10. Canyon Club Resort Marina
900 Ocean Dr. (844-384-6353)

11. Cape May Marina LLC
124 Rosemans Ln. (609-435-5757)

12. Roseman's Boat Yard
5 Rosemans Ln. (609-884-3370)

13. South Jersey Marina
1231 Route 109 (800-754-0622)

14. Utsch's Marina
1121 Rt. 109 Schellengers' Landing (609-884-2051)

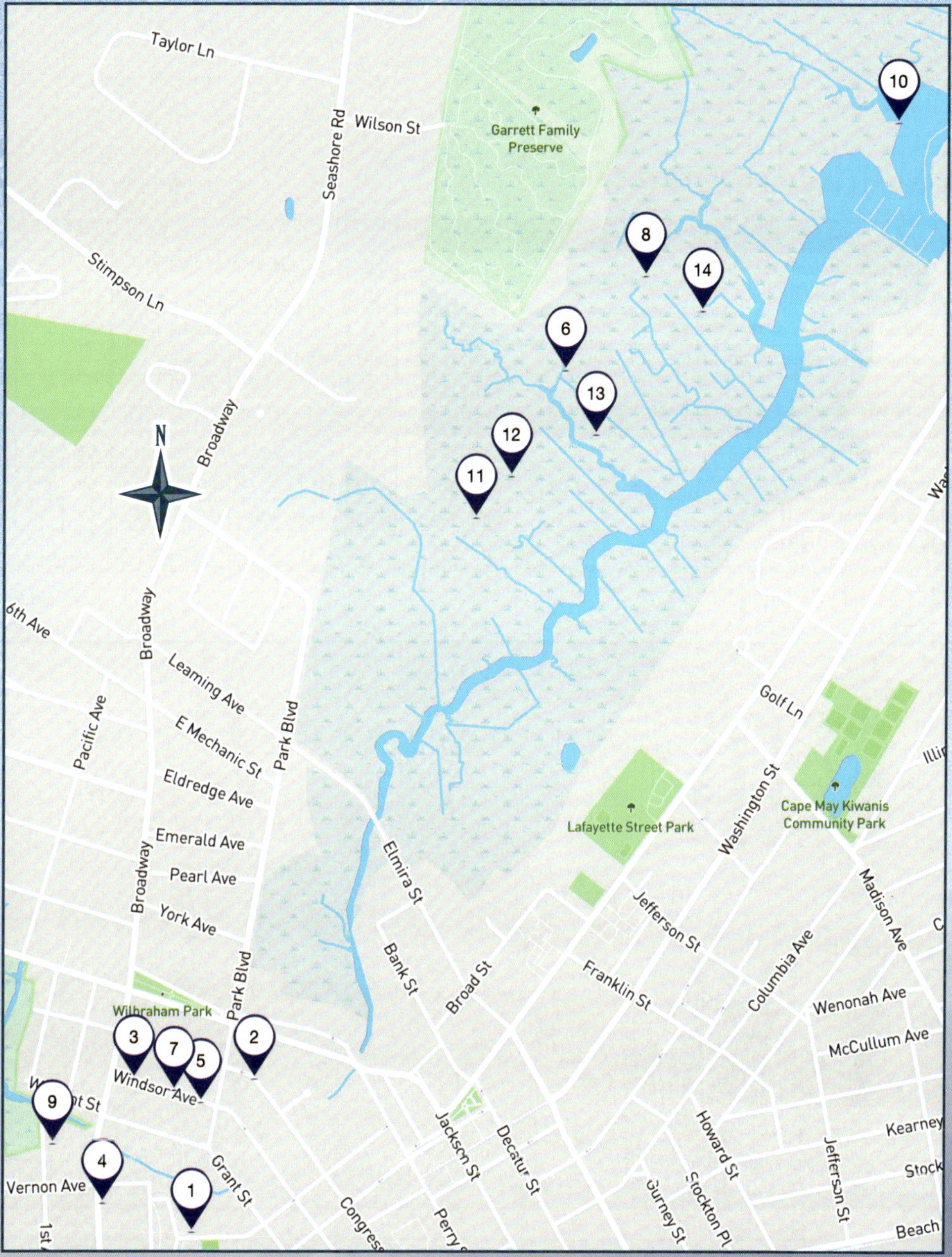

Wildwood Area, NJ

			Dockage			Supplies		Services					
WILDWOOD	Largest Vessel Accomodated	VHF Channel Monitored / Working	Approach / Dockside Depth (reported)	Transient Slips / Total Slips	Floating Docks	Gas / Diesel	Groceries, Ice, Marine Supplies, Snacks	Repairs: Hull, Engine, Propeller	Lift (tonnage), Crane, Rail	Min / Max Amps	Courtesy Car, Laundry, Pool, Showers	Pump-Out Station	Nearby: Grocery Store, Motel, Restaurant
1. Grassy Sound Marina MM 105.5 (609) 846-1400	40	/	16.0/6.0	8/90	F	G	IMS	HEP	L5	30/100		P	GMR
2. B & E Marine ⌨ MM 108.5 (609) 522-6440	35	/	5.0/5.0	/60	F	G	M	HEP		30			GMR
3. Schooner Island Marina ⌨ WiFi MM 109.0 (609) 729-8900	110	16/9	12.0/8.0	30/320	F	GD	GIMS	HEP	L60	30/50	LPS	P	GMR
4. Lighthouse Pointe Marina ⌨ WiFi MM 109.5 (609) 729-2229	40	16/10	12.0/7.0	15/160	F		I			30/50	LS	P	GMR
5. Pier 47 Marina MM 109.5 (609) 729-4774	40	/	6.0/6.0	5/140	F	G	IMS	HEP		15/50		P	GMR
STONE HARBOR													
6. Stone Harbor Marina MM 102.5 (609) 368-1141	55	9/	4.0/4.0	12/260	F	GD	IM	HEP	L40	30/50	S		GMR
7. Smugglers Cove MM 102.0 (609) 368-1700	60	68/	6.0/6.0	/	F	GD	IMS			30			GMR
8. Camp Marine Services ⌨ MM 101.0 (609) 368-1777	45	/	4.0/8.0	2/30	F		M	HEP	L30,C		C	P	3

⌨ Internet Access   WiFi Wireless Internet Access   onSpot Dockside WiFi Facility

See WaterwayGuide.com for current rates, fuel prices, website addresses, and other up-to-the-minute information. (Information in the table is provided by the facilities.)

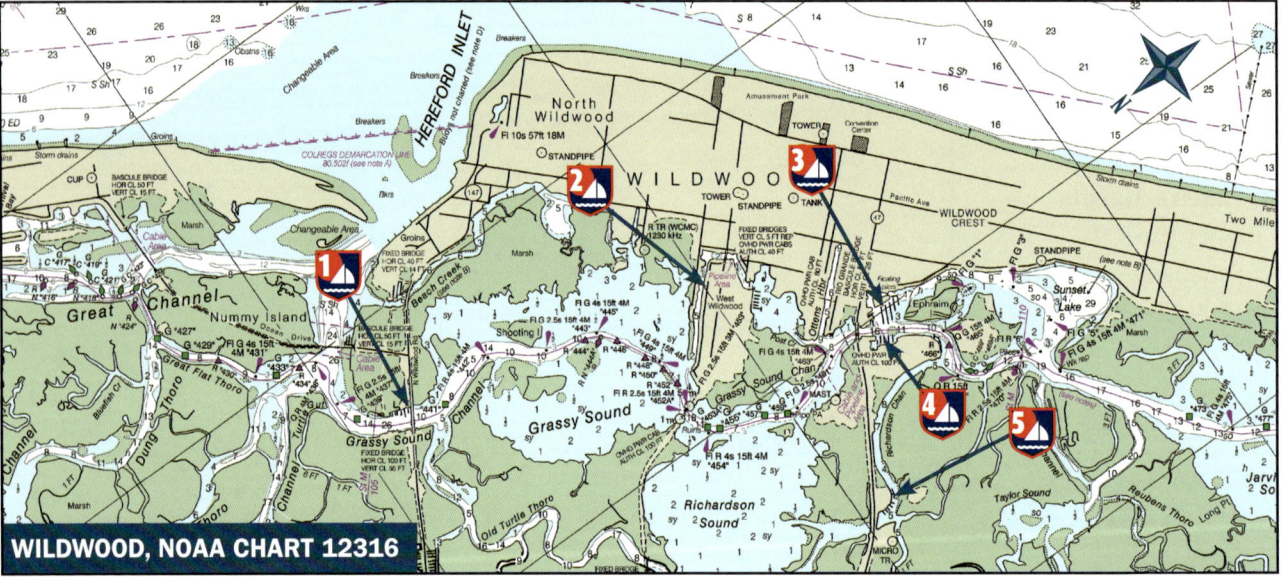

WILDWOOD, NOAA CHART 12316

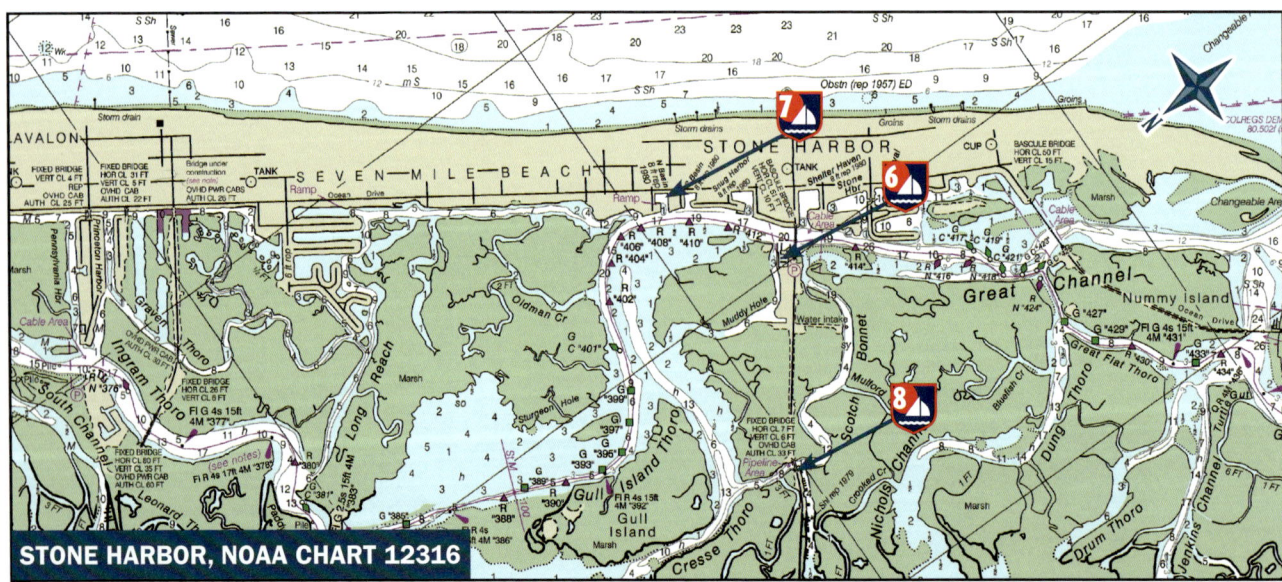

STONE HARBOR, NOAA CHART 12316

You can also anchor east of the Coast Guard Station with good holding and protection from wind and seas. This is a good spot for an overnight during a coastal transit; however, there is a lot of boat traffic transiting the channel and creating wakes at all hours of the day and night. Anchor at least 100 yards off the Coast Guard pier or you may be told to move. Also be aware that you may experience early-morning reveilles and cadence calls as new recruits go through their paces at the base.

⚠ At press time (winter 2020-2021) a submerged sailboat (with only its mast above water at high tide) was reported in the east anchorage near shore between green daybeacon "7A" and green daybeacon "7."

When the anchorage is crowded, particularly during the passage of cold fronts during fall and spring, two anchors may well be advisable. No launch service is available and the ride to facilities and restaurants to the west is a long row and can be difficult by strong currents. Plan carefully. Utsch's Marina, however, offers a courtesy dinghy dock for those at anchor, as do some of the shoreside restaurants.

Wildwood–NJ ICW Mile 110

The NJ ICW route is easily followed to Wildwood, a beachfront resort town with a variety of attractions including a beach boardwalk and several amusement parks. The Wildwood boardwalk is 2 miles long and 5 blocks from the marinas. There are beautiful, wide, white sandy beaches a little farther on. With over 2 miles of arcade games, carousels, water parks and restaurants, Wildwood is a great family destination. There is a tram service that runs along the boardwalk from sunrise to sunset during the summer and several trolley companies conduct tours that run all year through different routes around town. Visit www.wildwoodsnj.com for a monthly calendar of events.

NAVIGATION: Use NOAA Chart 12316. Heading north up the NJ ICW (inside route) you will pass the Coast Guard installation to starboard, then Sewell Point, where the Cape May (Cold Spring) Inlet channel branches off to starboard and the NJ ICW heads to port. An onshore Ferris wheel is prominent and can easily be seen up to 5 miles offshore.

The first bridge you will encounter upon leaving Cape May is the Two Mile Bridge across Middle Thorofare in Wildwood Crest (Mile 112.2). The bascule bridge has a closed vertical clearance of 23 feet and opens on signal with exceptions for Easter and Christmas. See details at Waterway Explorer (www.waterwayguide.com)

North Wildwood

The next bridge when northbound is the **Wildwood (Rio Grande/NJ 47) Bridge** at Mile 108.9 in Stone Harbor. The bascule bridge has a 25-foot vertical clearance and opens on signal.

At Mile 107.1 you will pass an old railroad bridge of which the center span has been removed.

⚠️ The channel is shoaling on the south side of the channel from flashing green "453" to flashing green "449." Keep a sharp eye on the depth sounder when making the turn after clearing the the old railroad bridge, even though the chart shows 5- to 7-foot MLW depths in this area.

The North Wildwood Blvd. (NJ 147) Bridge

at Mile 105.2 is a fixed high-rise bridge with a 55-foot vertical clearance. Continuing north, the **Ocean Drive Bridge** between Stone Harbor and Nummy Island at Mile 104 (15-foot closed vertical clearance) leads to Hereford Inlet and opens on signal during the season. (During the off-season, October 15 to May 15, a 24-hour notice is required for an opening.)

⚠️ Do not attempt to travel from this bridge to the Atlantic Ocean through Hereford Inlet. Despite dredging in 2020, Hereford Inlet remains closed and all aids to navigation have been removed. At low tide a sandbar known locally as "Champagne Island" has formed across the inlet.

North of Wildwood the NJ ICW heads away from Hereford Inlet. Expect shoaling between red nun buoy "424" and green can buoy "417" at NJ ICW Mile 102. Proceed with caution.

Dockage: There are numerous marinas in the Wildwood and Stone Harbor areas between Mile 108 and Mile 109.5. Pier 47 on Richardson Channel before the Wildwood Bridge is primarily a dry storage facility with boat rentals. They offer some repairs for vessels to 40 feet.

There is a cluster of marine facilities just before the Wildwood Bridge.

Lighthouse Pointe Marina is part of a condominium association and has 30- and 40-foot slips and basic amenities. Schooner Island Marina has slips with in-slip pump-out service, a large swimming pool and a Ship Store.

B&E Marine is a full-service marina and boat yard located on a channel to the south just after the old railroad bridge. To the north just past the North Wildwood Blvd (NJ 147) Bridge is Grassy Sound Marina, which caters mostly to sportfishing vessels to 40 feet. Both facilities sell gas (no diesel).

Anchorage: Wildwood has a good anchorage at Sunset Lake (Mile 110), which carries 5-foot MLW depths at the entrance and holds deeper water inside. Enter Sunset Lake from the ICW by turning between flashing red "470" and flashing green "471" and following the NJ channel markers. The first set of NJ markers are flashing red "6"and flashing green "5." (Leave the green on the right and the red on the left as you exit the ICW.) Turn right (south) to enter Sunset Lake. While heavily used, the well-protected anchorage affords privacy and easy access to nearby ocean beaches.

Stone Harbor–NJ ICW Mile 102

Stone Harbor has its own bird sanctuary, the only heron rookery located within a city. Both herons and egrets nest here and bird watchers come in late summer and early fall to watch these and other species that stop off during their migrations. The nearby Wetlands Institute (609-368-1211) features exhibits on local marine life in their natural habitat, dune walks and kayaking. Check their website (www. wetlandsinstitute.org) for detailed event information.

NAVIGATION: Use NOAA Chart 12316. The NJ ICW route runs behind the barrier beach of this popular resort area. The depths at Stone Harbor are generally good and cruising boat amenities are more than adequate.

The **Stone Harbor Blvd. Bridge** (also known as the **96th St. Bridge**) at Mile 102 has a 10-foot closed vertical clearance and opens on signal except (1) from October 1 through March 31 from 10:00 p.m. to 6:00 a.m. when the draw need only open if at least 8 hours notice is given; (2) from Memorial Day through Labor Day from 6:00 a.m. to 6:00 p.m. on Saturdays, Sundays and federal holidays, when the draw need open only on the hour, 20 minutes after the hour and 20 minutes before the hour; and (3) from 10:00 p.m. on December 24 until 6:00 a.m. on December 26, when the draw need open only if at least 2 hours notice is given. The bridge periodically undergoes repairs and can be very slow so use caution as you pass. Bridges in this area monitor VHF Channel 13.

⚠ Shoaling has been reported in the main navigation channel of the NJ ICW between green daybeacon "399" and flashing green daybeacon "383." Exercise caution in this area.

Dockage: Just north of the bridge, Stone Harbor Marina is home to a large yacht brokerage and offers slips to 55 feet, installations and repairs and gas and diesel fuel. The Yacht Club of Stone Harbor (609-368-1201) offers courtesy dockage to members of reciprocal yacht clubs.

Anchorage: You can anchor south of the Stone Harbor Blvd. Bridge at Mile 102.1 in at least 15 feet MLW. The entrance carries at least 6 feet at mid-tide. Restaurants and several dinghy docks are nearby. The next place to drop the hook is about 10 miles north at Whale Creek. For current information about Stone Harbor, visit www.stone-harbor.nj.us or www.stoneharborbeach.com.

◼ GULL ISLAND THOROFARE TO ATLANTIC CITY

Gull Island Thorofare to Great Egg Harbor–NJ Mile 102 to Mile 80

The NJ ICW route swings away from the barrier beach through Gull Island Thorofare (beginning at Mile 101) and then crosses Great Sound and wiggles its way through Ingram Thorofare.

NAVIGATION: Use NOAA Chart 12316. The fixed **Avalon Blvd. (601) Bridge** (35-foot fixed vertical clearance) crosses the channel at Mile 98.5. The bridge is being rehabilitated with scaffolding hanging below the bridge roadway reducing its vertical clearance to 33 feet. The work is scheduled to be completed by May 25, 2021.

The **Townsend Inlet Bridge** (23-foot vertical clearance) at Mile 97 opens on signal except at Easter and Christmas. See the restricted schedule at Waterway Explorer (www.waterwayguide.com).

After passing Townsend Inlet the route runs through twists and turns before crossing Ludlam Bay. At Mile 93.5 is the fixed **Sea Isle Blvd. (625) Bridge** (35-foot vertical clearance). Great Sound and Ludlam Bay are extremely shallow outside the narrow channel, especially on a falling tide. Several shoal areas deserve increased attention including:

- At the junction of Ben Hands Thorofare and Main Channel at green "329" through green "311" in the Devils Island Passage.
- In Peck Bay between daybeacon "282" and daybeacon "272."
- In Beach Thorofare near daybeacon "262" (reported depths near 5 feet MLW).

Be sure to proceed on a rising tide and use caution in these areas! It is best to check the NOAA charts online for the latest updates before transiting this area, as well as the *Local Notice to Mariners* (www.navcen.uscg.gov).

 Do not attempt to travel to the Atlantic Ocean through Corson Inlet, which is closed to navigation.

Dockage: Avalon Marine Center (near red nun buoy "376") is a full-service facility that welcomes transients and offers gas and diesel fuel. The Ingram Thorofare current, which sluices through the marina, is wicked and most transients are docked on the T-heads. Make sure you have help docking. The Avalon Yacht Club (609-967-4444) also offers courtesy dockage to members of reciprocal yacht clubs. Well-kept Sunrise Marina is located in an upscale neighborhood (The Marina at Avalon Anchorage) and can accommodate vessels to 65 feet. Commodore Bay Marina is located in a quiet protected lagoon off Cornell Harbor at red nun buoy "374" south of the Townsends Inlet Bridge. They have slips to 105 feet with full amenities.

Farther north at Ludlam Thorofare is Minmar Marine & Boat Sales. This is a boat brokerage with sales, boat and jet ski rentals, engine services, dry storage and some transient slips. Call ahead to make reservations at any of these marinas on summer weekends as docks can be especially crowded.

Anchorage: There is room to anchor on the Main Channel on Whale Creek at Mile 89.8. While somewhat exposed to the east, there is excellent holding here in 7- to 14-foot MLW depths with a mud and sand bottom.

Ocean City Area–NJ ICW Mile 80 to Mile 77

The resort town of Ocean City is set between the Atlantic Ocean, Great Egg Harbor Inlet and Great Egg Harbor Bay, with elegant homes and a splendid beach. Docks run side-by-side along the NJ ICW route on the city waterfront and also across the harbor in Somers Point. Ocean City is a good take-off point for

Great Egg Harbor River, NJ

W|G

		Dockage					Supplies		Services					
	Largest Vessel Accommodated	VHF Channel Monitored / Working	Approach / Dockside Depth (reported)	Transient Slips / Total Slips	Floating Docks	Gas / Diesel	Groceries, Ice, Marine Supplies, Snacks	Repairs: Hull, Engine, Propeller	Lift (tonnage), Crane, Rail	Min / Max Amps	Courtesy Car, Laundry, Pool, Showers	Pump-Out Station	Nearby: Grocery Store, Motel, Restaurant
AVALON, SEA ISLE CITY													
1. Avalon Marine Center WiFi MM 97.0	(609) 967-4100	100	/9	15/106	10.0/10.0	F	GD	IMS	HEP	L70,C	30/50	S	P	GM
2. The Marina at Avalon Anchorage MM 97.0	(609) 967-3592	41	/	/31	5.0/4.0	F	G	IMS	HEP		30			R
3. Commodore Bay Marina ▫ WiFi MM 96.5	(609) 967-4448	105	16/72	10/110	6.0/10.0	F					30/100	LS		GMR
4. Minmar Marine & Boat Sales ▫ MM 93.5	(609) 263-2201	40	16/68	3/115	5.0/4.0	F	G	IMS	HEP	L35	30	S	P	GMR
PECK BEACH													
5. All Seasons Marina MM 84.5	(609) 390-1850	50	16/	/300	12.0/5.0	F	GD	MS	HEP	L35	30/50	S	P	GMR
OCEAN CITY AREA													
6. Bay Club Marina-Ocean City MM 79.5	(609) 398-4100	50	/	5/37	12.0/5.0	F					30/50			GMR
SHIP CHANNEL													
7. Somers Point Marina 1.0 mi. NW of MM 79.0	(609) 927-5900	28	16/68	2/80	18.0/4.0	F		IMS	HEP	L6		S		GMR
8. Harbour Cove Marina 1.0 mi. NW of MM 79.0	(609) 927-9600	55	/	/415	4.0/4.0	F	GD		HEP	L35	30/50	PS	P	GMR
9. Graef Boat Yard 1.0 mi. NW of MM 79.0	(609) 927-2205	40	/	/60	6.0/6.0	F		IM	HEP	L40	30/50			GMR
POWELL CREEK													
10. Thompson Marine & Engine	(609) 927-2415	50	16/68	/6	7.0/7.0	F	G	M	HEP	L25	30		P	
11. Seaport Marina ▫ MM 56.0	(732) 939-2841	42	/	8/47	4.0/3.6	F	G	IMS	HEP	L20	30			5
LONGPORT													
12. Seaview Harbor Marina ▫ WiFi MM 76.0	(609) 823-2626	125	/	150/300	10.0/7.0	F	GD	IMS			30/100	LPS	P	GMR
RISLEY CHANNEL													
13. Sea Village Marina-Temporarily Closed 2.0 mi. NW of MM 76.0	(609) 641-2699	42	/	1/75	5.0/3.0	F			HEP		30/50	LPS	P	M

▫ Internet Access   WiFi Wireless Internet Access   onSpot Dockside WiFi Facility

See WaterwayGuide.com for current rates, fuel prices, website addresses, and other up-to-the-minute information. (Information in the table is provided by the facilities.)

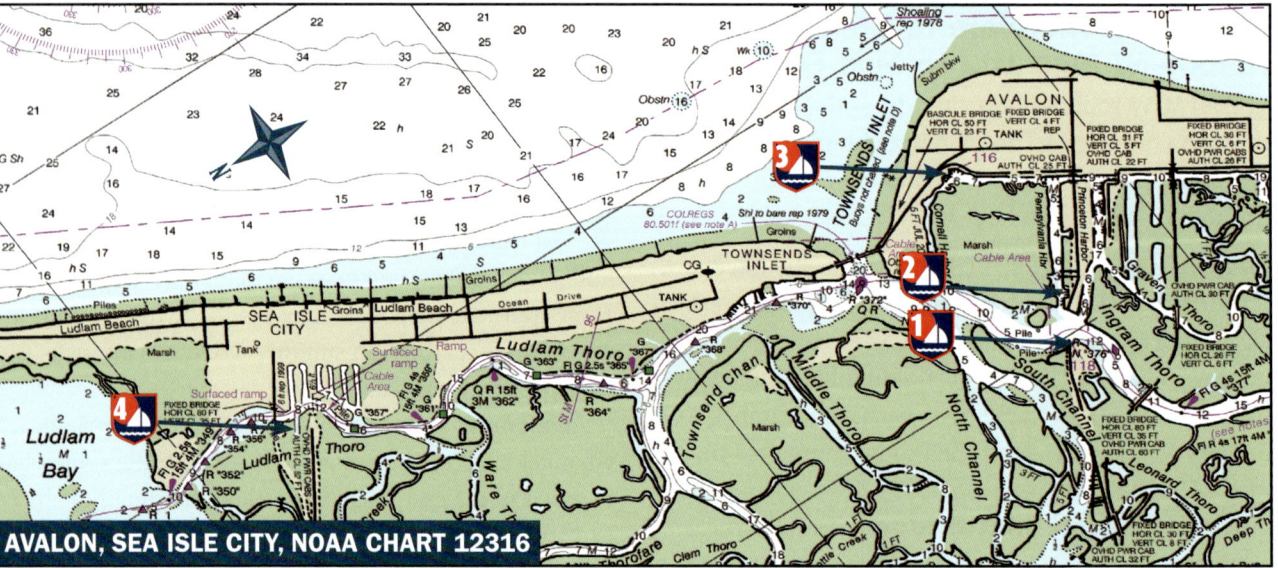

AVALON, SEA ISLE CITY, NOAA CHART 12316

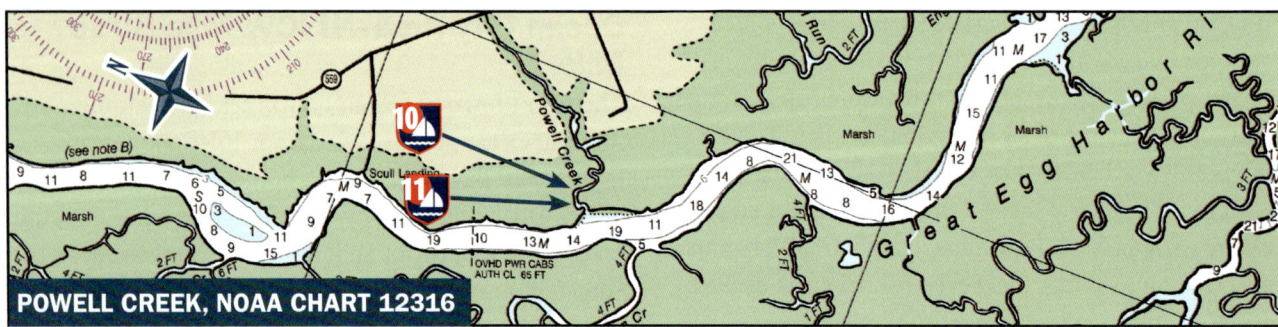

POWELL CREEK, NOAA CHART 12316

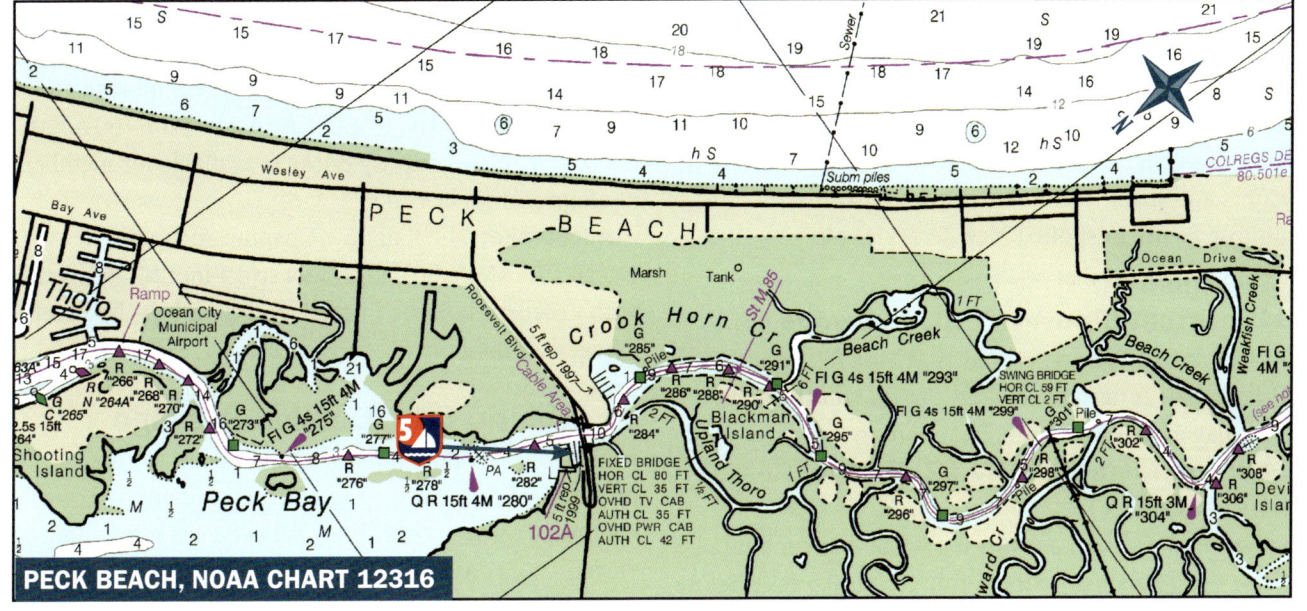

PECK BEACH, NOAA CHART 12316

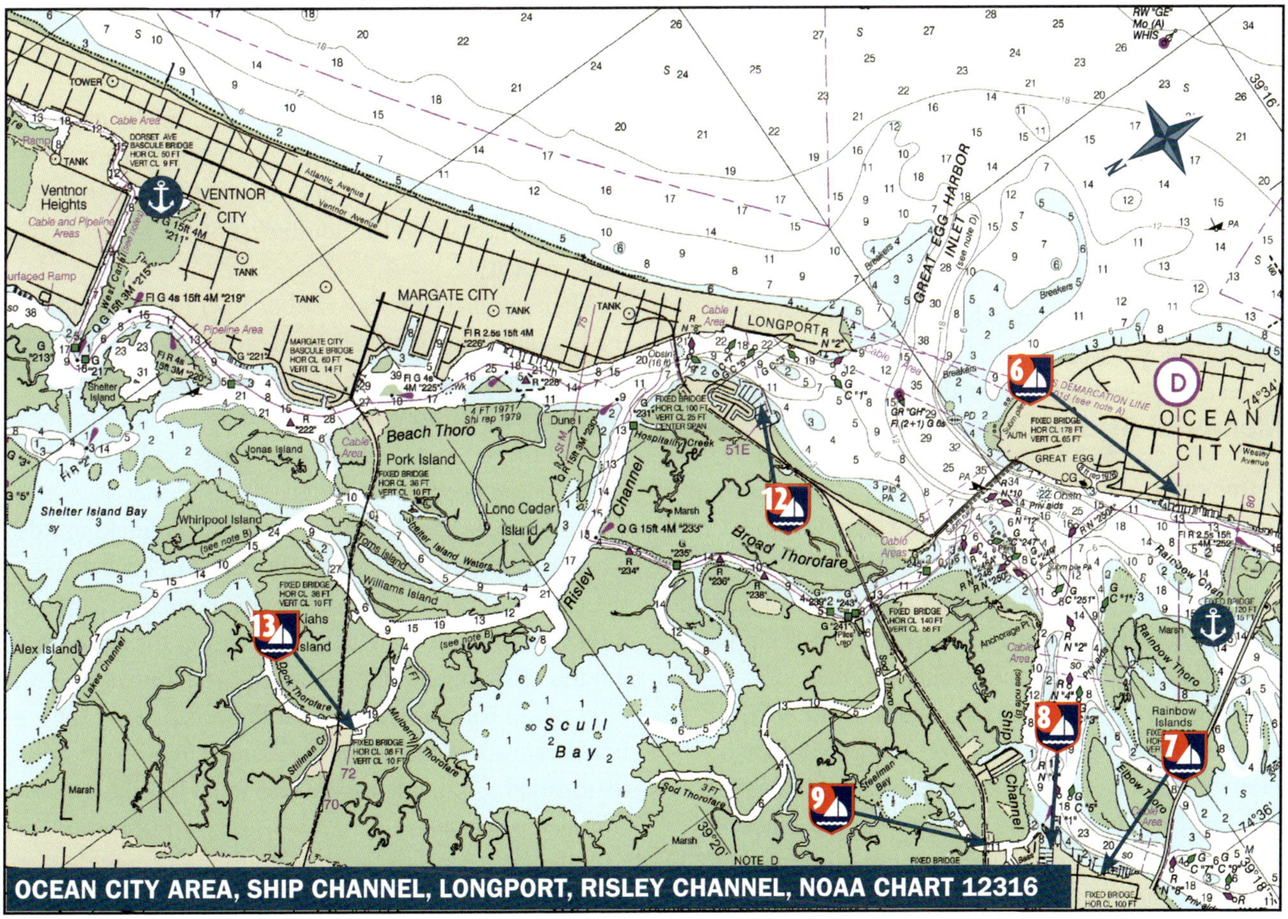

OCEAN CITY AREA, SHIP CHANNEL, LONGPORT, RISLEY CHANNEL, NOAA CHART 12316

Garden State Parkway Bridge

one of the NJ ICW's most attractive side cruises. The route runs along an unspoiled wilderness river that is unknown even to many resident mariners. Meandering west from Great Egg Harbor Bay, Great Egg Harbor River is safe and well-marked with deep cedar-stained waters and marshy pine-lined banks that offer a glimpse of the unspoiled New Jersey of old.

NAVIGATION: Use NOAA Chart 12316. The fixed **34th Street (Roosevelt Blvd.) Bridge** has 35-foot vertical clearance and is at Mile 84.5 south of Peck Bay. A narrow channel carries you through Peck Bay and along Beach Thorofare to the fixed **Stainton Memorial (NJ 52) Bridge** (55-foot vertical clearance).

The markers can be confusing when approaching Great Egg Harbor from the south. About 0.5 mile before you reach the fixed 65-foot **Ocean City–Longport Bridge**, the NJ ICW turns to port through Broad Thorofare at the fixed **NJ 152 Bridge** (56-foot vertical clearance).

⚠️ Following Broad Thorofare is not recommended due to extreme shoaling between green daybeacon "243" and green daybeacon "233." Instead, pass under the Ocean City–Longport Bridge, keeping the red aids to port until passing buoy red-green "GH" where the aid colors reverse until you pass under the fixed 25-foot **JFK Memorial Bridge** and re-enter the NJ ICW.

Dockage: Several marinas are located just north of the 34th Street (Roosevelt Blvd.) Bridge, which spans the lower end of Peck Bay at Crook Horn Creek. At Mile 84.5 you will find the large (300-slip) All Seasons Marina, which offers slips, storage and service plus a Ship Store with tackle and fishing supplies.

There is a channel after red daybeacon "254" at the Stainton Memorial (NJ 52) Bridge (55-foot vertical clearance) that leads to Bay Club Marina in Margate City, which offers limited transient space (to 50 feet). Mariners are urged to use caution when transiting the area.

Numerous marinas are located to the north of the fixed **Ship Channel Bridge** (with 60-foot vertical clearance) just 1 nm northwest of Mile 79 of the NJ ICW. Located at picturesque Somers Point are Graef Boat Yard, Harbour Cove Marina and Somers Point Marina. Harbour Cove has deep-water slips and a fuel dock, while Graef Boat Yard is a full-service working

yard that offers repairs. They will even come to you for some jobs. Somers Point Marina has a brokerage, engine sales and service, a Parts Department, boat storage and slips (to 30 feet). The Ocean City Yacht Club (609-399-6600) may have courtesy dockage available for members of reciprocal yacht clubs.

Anchorage: The Rainbow Channel anchorage at Ocean City (Mile 80) has 6-foot to 15-foot MLW depths with excellent holding in mud and sand. It is, however, exposed to the northeast and west.

To Atlantic City: Outside Passage

In pleasant weather, most skippers prefer to run outside from Ocean City to its companion resort, Atlantic City. It is only 8 nm between sea buoys and Ocean City's Great Egg Harbor Inlet is generally safe for passage in reasonable weather.

NAVIGATION: Use NOAA Chart 12316. Depths in Great Egg Harbor Inlet shift frequently and buoys are moved accordingly so reliable local information is a must if you plan to try the inlet. The Ocean City–Longport Bridge (65-foot charted fixed vertical clearance) crosses to the southwest of the inlet at Ocean City.

When taking Great Egg Harbor Inlet to the ocean, the best approach is to follow the red-and-white center-channel buoys to green-red flashing (2+1) buoy "GH." Breakers may be prevalent due to frequent shoaling near "GH." Proceed to red-and-white Morse (A) buoy "GE."

The ocean approach through Absecon Inlet at Atlantic City is easy, although it can be a rollicking ride when a southerly wind is up. Hundreds of boats make the passage daily in all but the worst conditions and weekends are especially busy. Enter from the sea buoy 2 miles offshore and honor the approach buoys to stay clear of the bar reaching toward the ocean along the northerly side of the channel. Channel depths are well maintained to provide easy access to all but the largest commercial vessels.

Follow the seaward buoy line into the very wide channel. As with all inlets, the buoys and markers are moved often to reflect changing conditions making an up-to-date NOAA Chart 12316 and *Local Notice to Mariners* (www.navcen.uscg.gov) navigation alerts a must when entering any of the inlets along the New Jersey coast.

To Atlantic City: Inside Passage– NJ ICW Mile 77 to Mile 67

Protected from gales and free of the small-boat fishing fleets, the inside passage is the preferred route to take in heavy weather.

If you stop in Margate City, check out Lucy the Elephant, a local landmark with a colorful past. The 65-foot-high structure was built in 1881 as a tavern and inn. Today, the huge belly of the elephant houses a museum of local memorabilia. An impressive movie about Lucy is available on the exhibit website at www.lucytheelephant.org.

NAVIGATION: Use NOAA Chart 12316. Easterly winds in the summer raise tides for better channel depths but spring and fall northwesterlies blow the water out to sea, making the NJ ICW channel even more shallow.

⚠ Attempt this passage only on a rising tide and try to get local advice as depths as low as 4 feet MLW have been reported in some spots including in the vicinity of green daybeacon "221" (Mile 73).

North of Ocean City the channel runs along Broad Thorofare, then makes a right-angle turn into Risley Channel, and then takes a turn to port of about 120° on Beach Thorofare, where it passes the resort of Margate City and the **Margate City Bridge** (14-foot closed vertical clearance; opens on signal). The channel between Margate and Ventnor is generally deep and clear but mind the strong currents that flow in this area between Great Egg Harbor and Absecon Inlets.

Turning into or out of the West Canal at Ventnor City be sure to honor the three green buoys ("217," "215" and "213") that lead you around the south point at the canal entrance. There is no water inside those buoys!

Our Cruising Editor has observed less than 6 feet at three-quarter tide near the **Dorset Ave. Bridge** at Mile 71.2. The 9-foot vertical clearance bascule bridge crosses the channel at Ventnor City. The bridge opens on signal except from June 1 through September 30, from 9:15 a.m. to 9:15 p.m., when the draw need only open at 15 and 45 minutes after the hour.

The next bridge is just over 1 mile away. **The Albany Ave. Bridge** crosses at Mile 70 has 10-foot vertical clearance and a seasonal schedule. The bridge opens on signal except: (1) year-round from 11:00 p.m. to 7:00 a.m., and from November 1 through March 31 from 3:00 p.m. to 11:00 p.m. when the draw need only open unless at least a 4-hour notice is given; and (2) from June 1 through September 30: from 9:00 a.m. to 4:00 p.m. and from 6:00 p.m. to 9:00 p.m. when the draw need only open on the hour and half hour; from 4:00 p.m. to 6:00 p.m. the draw need not open. The schedule of annual events also affects bridge openings. Call ahead or see detail at Waterway Explorer (www.waterwayguide.com).

Atlantic City Area, NJ

WG

ATLANTIC CITY		Largest Vessel Accommodated	VHF Channel Monitored / Working	Transient Slips / Total Slips	Approach / Dockside Depth (reported)	Floating Docks	Gas / Diesel	Groceries, Ice Marine Supplies, Snacks	Repairs: Hull, Engine, Propeller	Lift (tonnage), Crane, Rail	Min / Max Amps	Courtesy Car, Laundry, Pool, Showers	Pump-Out Station	Nearby: Grocery Store, Motel, Restaurant
		Dockage					**Supplies**		**Services**					
1. All Marine Center of Atlantic City [wifi] MM 69.0	(609) 347-7050	55	16/9	/	7.0/7.0	F	G	IMS	HEP	L35				5MR
2. Farley State Marina at Golden Nugget Casino & Hotel ▢ [wifi]	(800) 876-4386	300	65/65	150/640	12.0/8.0	F	GD	GIMS			30/100	LPS	P	GMR
3. Kammerman's Marina ▢ [wifi] 1.0 mi. S of MM 65.0	(609) 348-8418	180	16/	12/19	9.0/8.0	F	GD	IMS			30/100	LS	P	GMR
4. Historic Gardner's Basin ▢ [wifi] 1.0 mi. S of MM 65.0	(609) 348-2880	50	9/	8/35	12.0/4.5	F		IS			30			GR

▢ Internet Access   [wifi] Wireless Internet Access   ◉ onSpot Dockside WiFi Facility

See WaterwayGuide.com for current rates, fuel prices, website addresses, and other up-to-the-minute information. (Information in the table is provided by the facilities.)

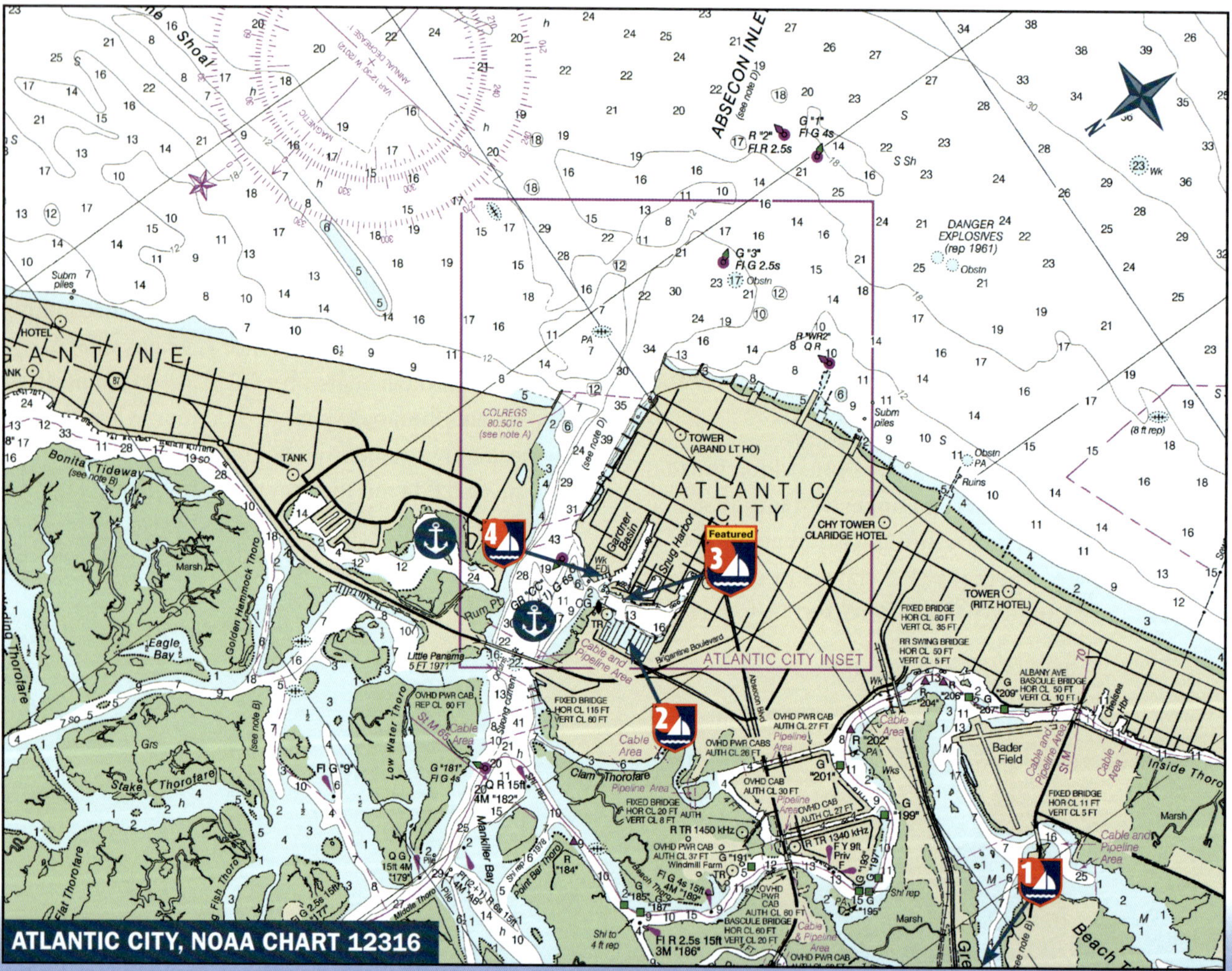

ATLANTIC CITY, NOAA CHART 12316

GOIN' ASHORE

ATLANTIC CITY, NJ

Atlantic City is one of the best cruising destinations on the New Jersey coast. Its blazing skyline has become the east coast's most impressive, all night beacon for offshore cruisers. Whether you are planning a several-day stop or you need a place to get out of the weather, look no farther than this robust port with some of the most beautiful beaches on the New Jersey coast. The original 7-mile-long Atlantic City Boardwalk, built in 1870, was the first of its kind in the world and was the inspiration for the board game, Monopoly. Today's boardwalk, which has been rebuilt over the years, stretches from Absecon Inlet southwest along 4 miles of spectacular beach and is the longest in the world.

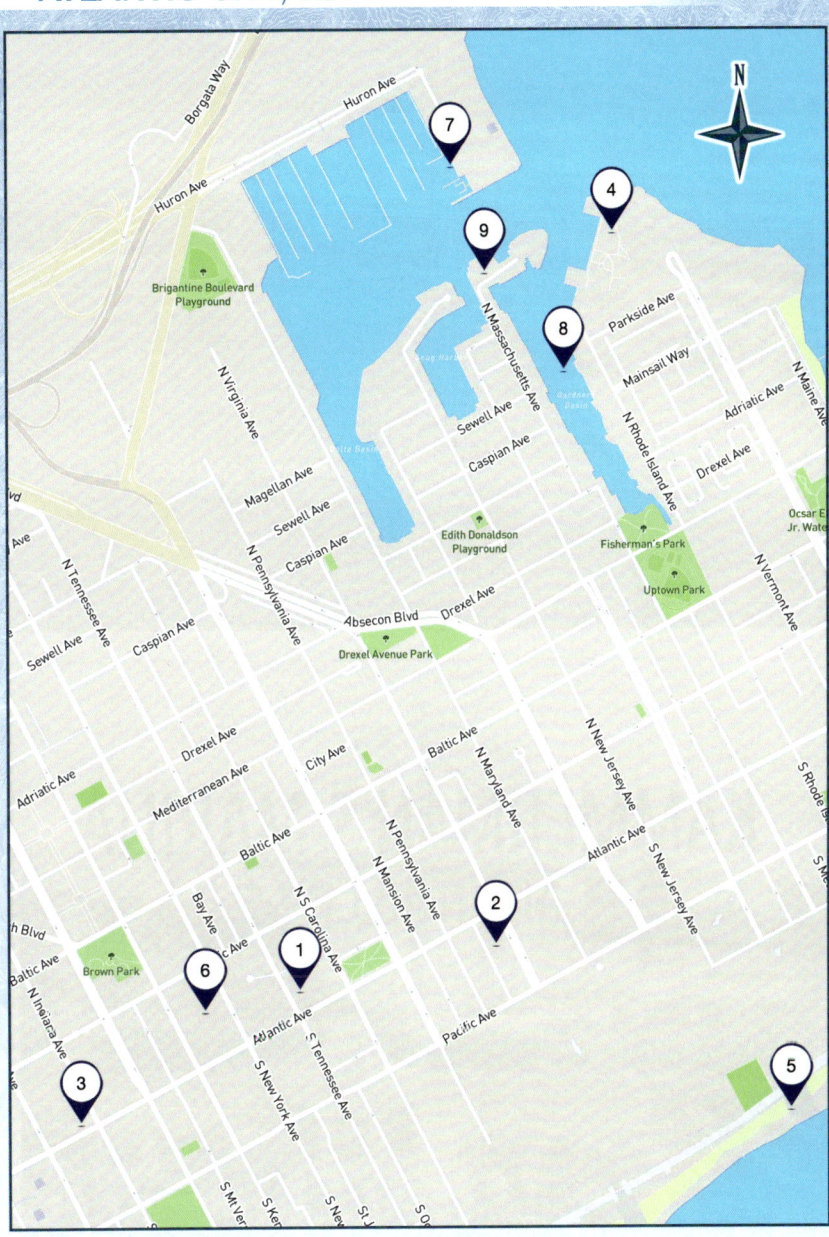

SERVICES

1. Atlantic City Free Public Library
1 N. Tennessee Ave.
(609-345-2269)

2. Atlantic City Information Center
12 Virginia Ave. (609-345-5600)

3. Atlantic City Post Office
1801 Atlantic Ave., Ste. 101
(609-348-2940)

ATTRACTIONS

4. Atlantic City Aquarium
Large aquarium featuring underwater exhibits plus an exotic animal show and other rotating events. Open daily 10:00 a.m. to 5:00 p.m. at Historic Gardner's Basin (800 N. New Hampshire Ave., 609-348-2880).

5. Atlantic City Historical Museum
Open Sunday through Saturday from 9:00 a.m. to 5:00 p.m. at Garden Pier (609-347-5839).

SHOPPING

6. Save A Lot
Discount supermarket chain at 1501 Atlantic Ave. (609-344-0872).

MARINAS

7. Farley State Marina at Golden Nugget Casino & Hotel
600 Huron Ave. (800-876-4386)

8. Historic Gardner's Basin
800 N. New Hampshire Ave.
(609-348-2880)

9. Kammerman's Marina
447 Carson Ave. (609-348-8418)

Atlantic City

KAMMERMAN'S MARINA

⚠ Shoaling has been reported between red daybeacon "206" and green daybeacon "209" at Mile 69.5 in the vicinity of Bader Field.

At Mile 68 on Great Thorofare, the fixed **Atlantic City Expressway Bridge** (35-foot vertical clearance) is followed immediately by the **New Jersey Transit Railroad Bridge**, a swing bridge with 5-foot closed vertical clearance. The railroad bridge operates remotely will open on signal from 11:00 p.m. to 6:00 a.m. At all other times, the draw will open on signal from 20 minutes to 30 minutes after each hour and remain open for all waiting vessels. When the draw is opening and closing or is closed, yellow flashing lights located on the ends of the center piers are displayed continuously until the bridge is returned to the fully open position.

Dockage: Seaview Marina is located near the Egg Harbor Inlet with 300 deep-water slips and resort-like amenities. (Note that Sea Village Marina to the north up Risley Channel was closed at press time in winter 2020-2021.)

Anchorage: At Mile 71.5 in Ventnor City, boaters can anchor in the basin (accessible by West Canal) in 6 to 8 feet MLW with good all-around protection and excellent holding in mud and sand.

Atlantic City–NJ ICW Mile 65

Atlantic City is renowned for its classic boardwalk, wide sandy beaches, imposing piers, elegant beach front hotels and gambling casinos; however, the city should also be known for its all-weather inlet from the Atlantic Ocean and its secure harbor along a considerable and relatively uninterrupted stretch of New Jersey coastline.

NAVIGATION: Use NOAA Charts 12316 and 12318. Atlantic City is easily approached from either the NJ ICW or the Atlantic Ocean, via Absecon Inlet. From the south, the NJ ICW channel leaves Inside Thorofare and enters Beach Thorofare to swing in a wide semicircle behind the city, under the fixed **Absecon Blvd. (U.S. 30) Bridge** (20-foot vertical clearance) at Mile 67.2. This bascule bridge opens on signal on the hour and half hour from April 1 through October 31, from 7:00 a.m. to 11:00 p.m. At all other times, a 4-hour notice is required. Openings also vary due to annual events; call ahead on VHF Channel 13.

To reach most of the local marinas, repair yards, and other marine facilities, you must head toward the ocean, under the fixed **Brigantine Blvd. Bridge** (60-foot vertical clearance). Then, enter Clam Creek in front of the U.S. Coast Guard Station. Favor the ocean side of the channel as you make your way through the entrance, especially rounding red nun buoy "2," which marks a 5-foot (or less) shoal.

The lights of Atlantic City are visible for 20 miles north or south on an offshore approach. Pay attention to the position of the entrance buoys if approaching in the dark as they can be obscured in the background lighting of the casinos. As previously noted, the onshore Ferris wheel here is prominent and is easily seen up to 5 miles off shore.

As an interesting side note, the lighted backdrop of the city proved to be particularly hazardous to commercial shipping during World War II. German U-Boats would lay offshore at night and fire torpedoes at freighter traffic, which was conveniently (and fatally) silhouetted against the bright shoreline.

Dockage: Cruisers arriving in Atlantic City have several marina choices. First is All Marine Center of Atlantic City (formerly Atlantic City Boatyard) at Mile 69 off the main channel on Great Thorofare. They offer fast and easy fueling and great service.

The largest marina in the area is the 640-slip Farley State Marina situated on the west side of Clam Creek Basin adjacent to the Golden Nugget Casino. This is a full-service marina with dockage for a variety of crafts up to 300 feet in length. Spend a day on the water, then head on over to enjoy the award-winning restaurants, shows, casino games and nightlife at Golden Nugget. Reservations are a good idea as the marina is often busy.

Kammerman's Atlantic City Marina is at the entrance to the second inlet from Clam Creek Basin across from the Coast Guard station. Family-owned and -operated since 1961, they offer fair fuel prices, bulk fuel pricing, transient and seasonal dockage, marine mechanics on call, a helpful staff and all the expected amenities. Kammerman's has the largest fuel dock in the city (with high-speed pumps).

Historic Gardner Basin is situated on the easterly side of Clam Creek Basin and is essentially an aquarium with some slips. The restrooms are public (without locks) and WiFi only reaches the porch of the aquarium. On the plus side there are nearby restaurants and it is bicycling distance to the boardwalk. Past the aquarium in Gardiner Basin is Albert C. Westcoat Co. with repairs for vessels to 60 feet.

Anchorage: The Coast Guard does not permit anchoring in Clam Creek Basin; however, there is a substantial anchorage area south of the highway bridge in 8- to 22-foot MLW depths with good holding in sand. Take care to honor flashing green "CC" at the mouth to Clam Creek Basin, as there is a shoal to the west of the line joining them. Expect challenging currents and a 5-foot tidal range in calculating appropriate scope. You will share this space with scores of local boats on weekends as well as traffic, noise and loads of lights from land. From here it will be a dinghy ride of about 0.5 mile to the basin, where a dinghy landing is available at the city marina in Gardner Basin. There is a 4-hour time limit on the public dock.

There is also an anchorage at Rum Point Basin (Mile 65.1) on the opposite side of the inlet with excellent holding and all-around protection in 6- to 15-foot MLW depths. Stay to green grass side (not beach side) when entering. There is deeper water coming in than what is shown on the NOAA chart.

■ ABESCON INLET TO BARNEGAT BAY

Absecon Inlet to Great Bay–NJ ICW Mile 65 to Mile 56

NAVIGATION: Use NOAA Chart 12316. The NJ ICW shoals easily in the stretch between Absecon Inlet and Great Bay and you may see birds strolling on the sandbars building out into the channel. Many daybeacons along this route have been replaced by buoys, which may not be indicated on the chart. If you draw more than 4 feet, be sure to go through on a rising tide (half tide or better).

At Mile 64 a 7-mile alternate route for shoal-draft boats parallels the barrier beach at Brigantine then rejoins the ICW at Mile 60. Brigantine offers some services but the controlling depth for this route is only 3 feet MLW.

Back on the main route of the NJ ICW, exercise extra caution between flashing red "160" and red buoy "156A" at Mile 60. This section is very narrow and the current is strong and sets across the channel.

From just past Shad Island through Main Marsh Thorofare, the NJ ICW runs through the middle of the Brigantine National Wildlife Refuge. If the magenta line

goes on the wrong side of a buoy, do honor the buoy since the shoals are close on both sides. The best way to observe the amazing variety of bird life in the refuge is by taking a small boat or dinghy to explore the creeks and passages away from the ICW. The fall migrations are spectacular but it can be extremely buggy in this area during the summer months.

Great Bay & Mullica River–NJ ICW Mile 56 to Mile 50

NAVIGATION: Use NOAA Chart 12316. Stick dead on course when crossing Great Bay, which is extremely shallow. The bottom builds up every spring from the continuous sweep of inlet waters so you should try to run this area on a rising tide. This stretch of the NJ ICW will always suffer from shifting sands and uncertain depths.

At the northwest corner of Great Bay, the deep, winding Mullica River snakes its way west into the Pine Barrens. Three miles up the Mullica River, 14-foot-deep Blood Ditch Cut bypasses a nearly 2.5-mile-long loop in the river. Just beyond is the entrance to the deep Bass River, which leads north and is navigable to the town of New Gretna, home of many marinas and marine services and a good hurricane hole.

⚠️ Shoaling has been reported in the NJ ICW between Manasquan Inlet and Cape May Inlet. Mariners are advised to use extreme caution when transiting the area. Specific areas of concern are described below.

There is no magenta line on the chart between red daybeacon "132" and red daybeacon "130" at Mile 53. Follow the buoys staying on the green side of the channel as extreme shoaling has been reported extending out from the red side between red daybeacons "130" and "130A." Underpowered vessels with deep drafts should transit this area on a rising tide. Stay in mid-channel when passing to the west of Tow Island (Mile 53). Shoaling has been reported on the green side at daybeacon "129." Despite constant dredging, this area has a continuous shoaling problem.

Prudence must prevail where the NJ ICW route crosses the twin inlets: Beach Haven and Little Egg, between Mile 55 and Mile 50. The ocean swells carry inside to break on shoal spots but with care you can make the crossing in all but the worst weather conditions.

Sandy trail leading to Great Bay

Little Egg inlet is occasionally dredged but the inlet buoys are not charted and it should only be transited with local knowledge. Nearby Beach Haven Inlet may be shown on the NOAA chart but it is closed and all buoys have been removed. There are currently no plans to dredge or to replace the buoys there.

After rounding quick flashing red buoy "120" to port, watch very carefully for the next pair of daybeacons and favor the red side due to shoaling from Tuckers Island to the east. Prepare in advance to sort out the confusion of inlet and side-channel markers near Mile 50. The buoyed Marshelder Channel, which leads into Little Egg Harbor, can easily be mistaken for the NJ ICW. Check the buoy numbers before committing to a course. Buoy numbering will generally conform to an up-to-date NOAA chart but the location might be quite different as the Coast Guard is constantly moving buoys to keep up with the changing conditions.

Be especially vigilant at flashing red "116" (Mile 50) where the magenta line denoting the NJ ICW leads directly across a shoal area. Depths here can be as low as 3 to 4 feet MLW.

Dockage: The tributaries of the Mullica River are home to Viking Yachting Center, Chestnut Neck Boat Yard and Nacote Creek Marina. Great Bay Marina is on the north shore of Great Bay with all fuels and repairs. There is limited transient space here so call ahead for slip availability.

Anchorage: Storm waves and day-to-day currents along the shore and through the inlets make and unmake anchorages, and those you knew previously should be approached carefully before trying them again. Shoal-draft boats will find good holding and shelter from southerly and westerly winds in Great Bay at Landing Creek at Mile 55.5 with 4- to 12-foot MLW depths with holding in thick mud.

For all-around protection, there are two anchorages on the Mullica River. The first is at Blood Point and the second is after the second bend at Moss Point. Both have good holding in thick mud and at least 10 feet MLW. Note the charted 4-foot MLW spot off the southwest end of Blood Point.

Side Trip: Tuckerton–NJ ICW Mile 50

NAVIGATION: Use NOAA Charts 12316 and 12324.

⚠️ Just after Mile 50 a channel heads off to the northwest across Little Egg Harbor toward the village of Tuckerton. Shoaling has been reported between flashing green "109" and junction light flashing red "LB" off Mordecai Island.

Marshelder Channel leads to the village from Mile 50 and is somewhat better marked. The Tuckerton Seaport & Baymen's Museum is also there at 120 West Main St. and is open daily (609-296-8868). Visit www.tuckertonseaport.org for details.

Mullica River Area, NJ

		Largest Vessel Accommodated	VHF Channel Monitored / Working	Approach / Dockside Depth (reported)	Transient Slips / Total Slips	Floating Docks	Gas / Diesel	Groceries, Ice, Marine Supplies, Snacks	Repairs: Hull, Engine, Propeller	Lift (tonnage), Crane, Rail	Min / Max Amps	Courtesy Car, Laundry, Pool, Showers	Pump-Out Station	Nearby: Grocery Store, Motel, Restaurant
MULLICA RIVER			**Dockage**					**Supplies**		**Services**				
1. Viking Yachting Center	(609) 296-2388	50	16/72	14/250	10.0/10.0	F	GD	I	HEP	L60	30	PS	P	GMR
2. Chestnut Neck Boat Yard Off MM 55.0	(609) 652-1119	25	/	5/40	30.0/35.0	F	GD	IMS	HEP	L25	30		P	GMR
3. Nacote Creek Marina	(609) 652-9070	50	/	2/60	10.0/7.0	F		IM	HEP	L30	30		P	3R
GREAT BAY														
4. Great Bay Marina	(609) 296-2392	43	/	/139	4.0/4.5	F	GD	IMS	HEP	L20	30	S	P	R

🖳 Internet Access   📶 Wireless Internet Access   🌐 onSpot Dockside WiFi Facility

See WaterwayGuide.com for current rates, fuel prices, website addresses, and other up-to-the-minute information. (Information in the table is provided by the facilities.)

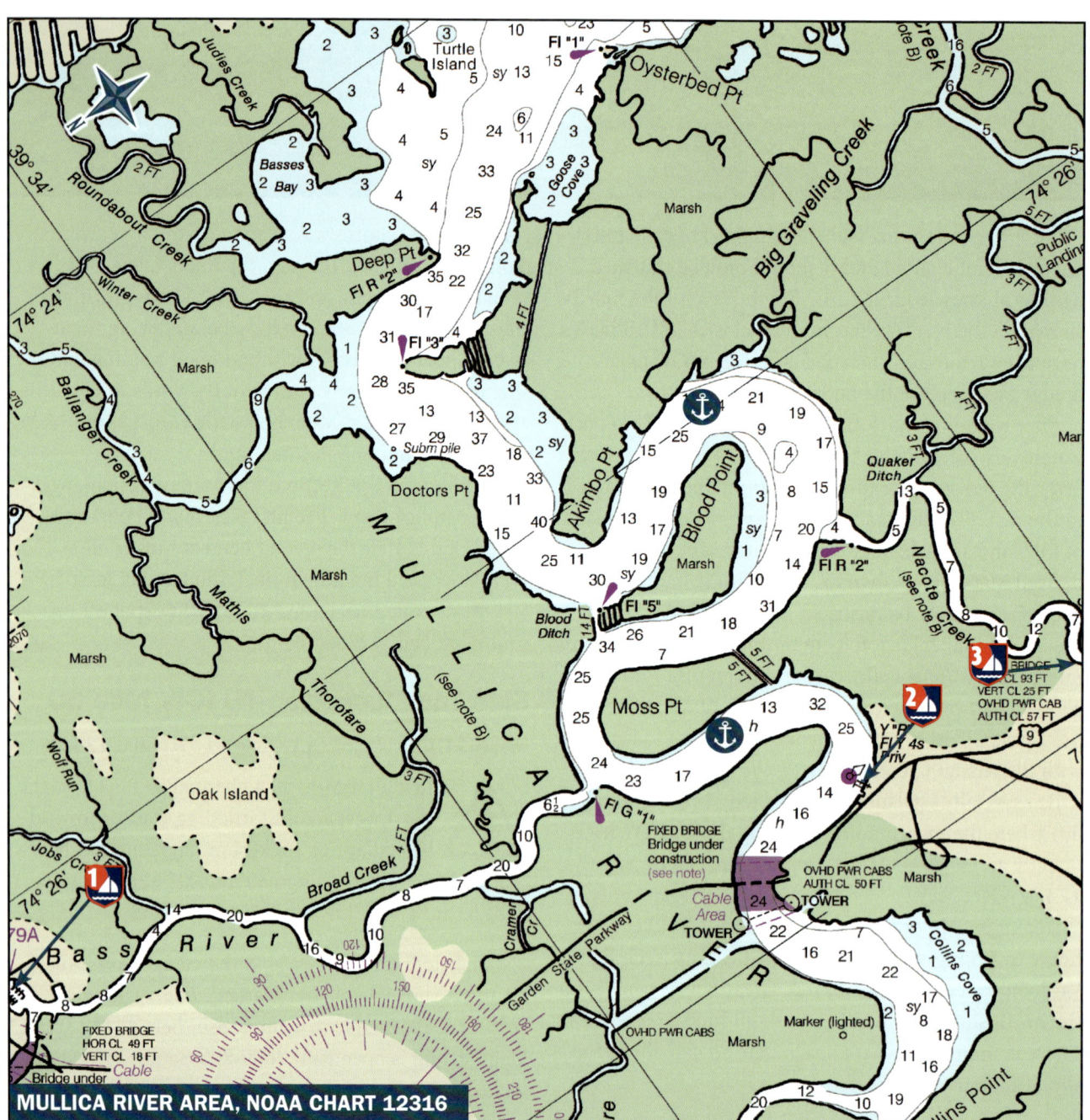

MULLICA RIVER AREA, NOAA CHART 12316

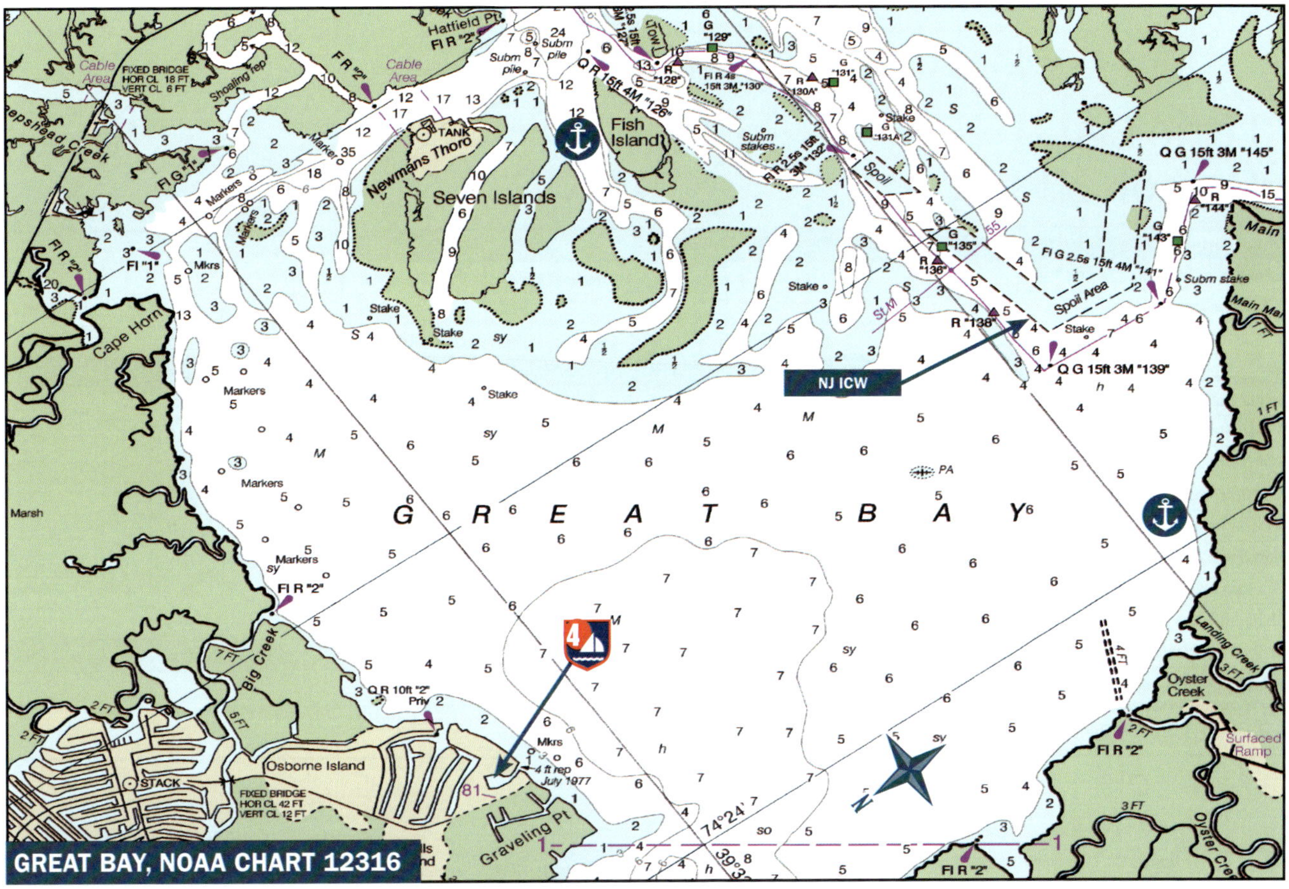

GREAT BAY, NOAA CHART 12316

Dockage: The 250-slip Sheltered Cove Marina welcomes transients (to 50 feet) on their floating docks with reported 5-foot approach depths. Tuckerton Marine is a marine service center and yacht brokerage with long-term slips and RV sites. Farther upriver is Phil Keeney & Sons, Inc., a storage and service yard specializing in engine, fiberglass and wooden boat repairs and services.

Long Beach Island–NJ ICW Mile 50 to Mile 37

North of Little Egg Inlet the NJ ICW passes behind aptly-named Long Beach Island. You can bypass Little Egg Harbor by sticking to the NJ ICW channel running close along Long Beach. Beach Haven, Spray Beach, Ship Bottom and Surf City are a few of the communities you pass in this section, all with marinas and hundreds of boats.

NAVIGATION: Use NOAA Charts 12316 Just before Mile 40 at flashing red "78" a channel branches off to starboard from the NJ ICW. Boats with less than the 15 feet overhead clearance needed for the fixed bridge noted as "under construction" on the NOAA chart can leave the NJ ICW here and follow this shorter channel

Little Egg Harbor, NJ

		Largest Vessel Accommodated	VHF Channel Monitored / Working	Transient Slips / Total Slips	Approach / Dockside Depth (reported)	Floating Docks	Gas / Diesel	Groceries, Ice, Marine Supplies, Snacks	Repairs: Hull, Engine Propeller	Lift (tonnage), Crane, Rail	Min / Max Amps	Courtesy Car, Laundry, Pool, Showers	Pump-Out Station	Nearby: Grocery Store, Motel, Restaurant
TUCKERTON				**Dockage**			**Supplies**		**Services**					
1. Phil Keeney & Sons INC., Keeneys Marina	(609) 296-9525		/	3/25	6.0/6.0	F		I	HEP			S		GMR
2. Tuckerton Marine	(609) 296-1820	40	16/	5/60	5.0/8.0	F		IM	HE		30	S		MR
3. Sheltered Cove Marina WiFi MM 126.0	(609) 296-9400	50	9/9	35/250	5.0/8.0	F	GD	IMS	HEP	L20,C	15/50	S	P	GMR
LONG BEACH														
4. Little Egg Harbor Yacht Club - PRIVATE MM 45.5	(609) 492-2529	40	/	/	8.0/4.0						30	S		R
5. Beach Haven Yacht Club Marina ▢ WiFi MM 45.5	(609) 492-9101	80	16/68	7/55	8.0/8.0		GD	IS			30/50	LS	P	GMR
6. Morrison's Beach Haven Marina ▢ WiFi MM 45.4	(609) 492-2150	60	/	10/150	5.0/5.0	F	GD	IM	HEP	L35	30/50	S	P	GMR
7. Shelter Harbor Marina WiFi MM 44.8	(609) 492-8645	55	16/	5/206	5.0/5.0	F		I	EP		30/50	LPS	P	GMR
8. Escape Harbor Marina WiFi MM 44.0	(609) 492-9108	45	/	/60	4.0/5.5	F					30/50	LS		GMR
9. Southwick's Marina MM 44.0	(609) 492-5191	30	9/	/90	3.0/5.0		G	IM	HEP	L6,C	30		P	GMR
10. Hagler's Marina MM 40.0	(609) 494-4509	30	/	10/66	3.0/4.0	F	G	IM	HEP		30	S		MR
11. Hochstrasser's Marina 2.0 mi. NE of MM 40.0	(609) 494-5340	30	/	3/65	17.0/10.0			M	HEP	C	20			GMR
12. Duck Cove Marina MM 40.0	(609) 361-1400	50	67/	5/100	4.0/4.0		GD	IMS	E	L25	30	S	P	GMR

▢ Internet Access WiFi Wireless Internet Access onSpot Dockside WiFi Facility

See WaterwayGuide.com for current rates, fuel prices, website addresses, and other up-to-the-minute information. (Information in the table is provided by the facilities.)

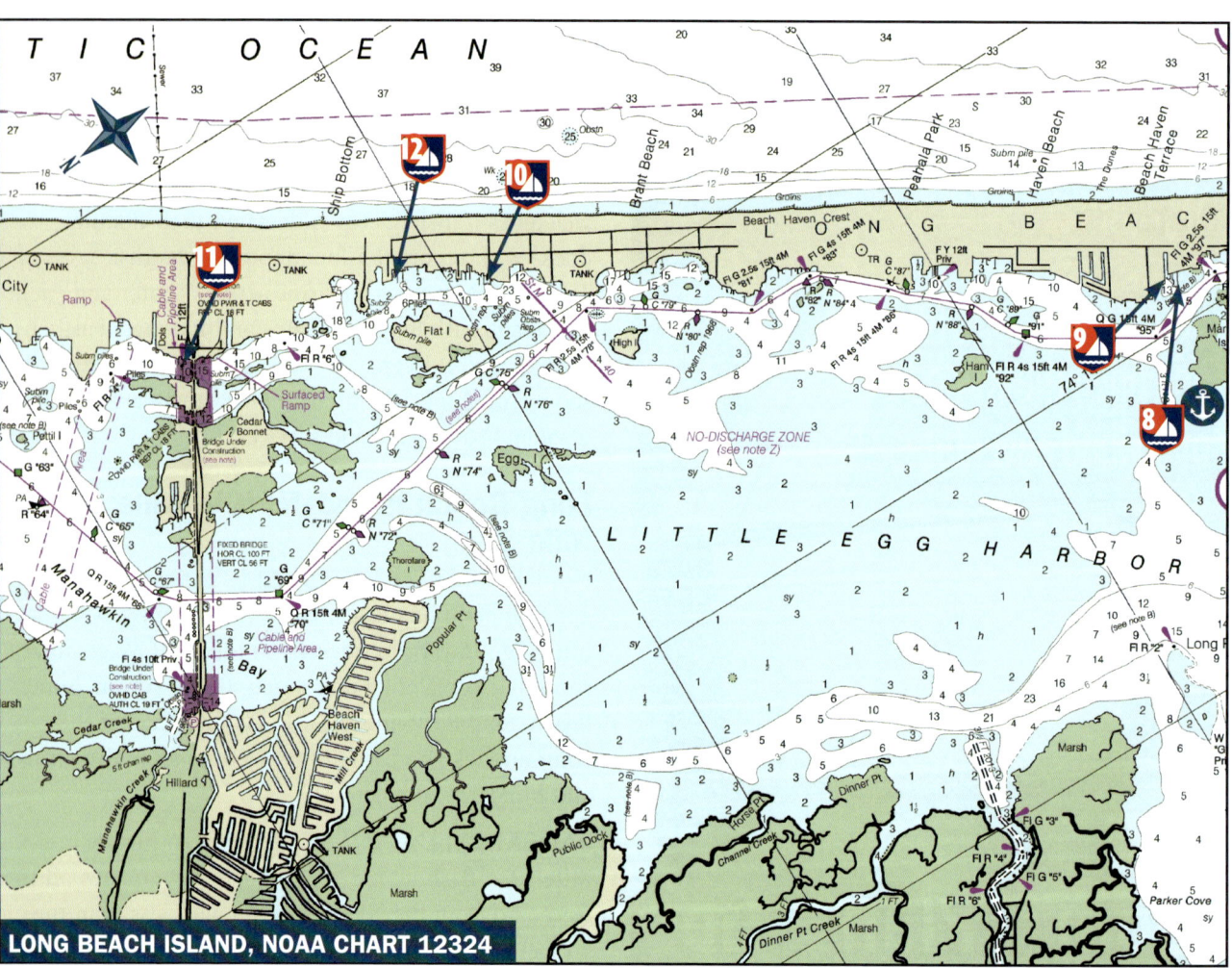

LONG BEACH ISLAND, NOAA CHART 12324

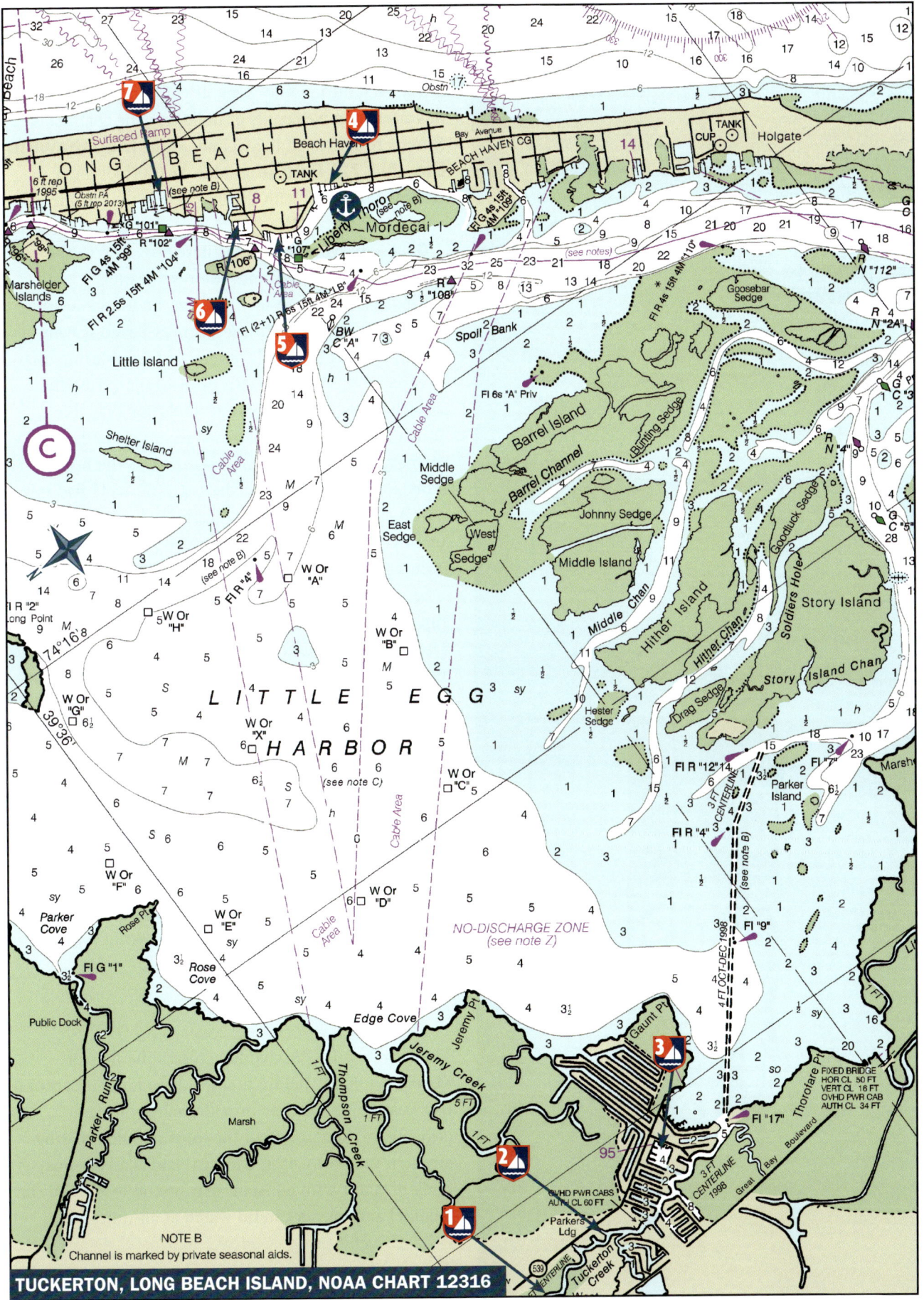

NOTE B
Channel is marked by private seasonal aids.

TUCKERTON, LONG BEACH ISLAND, NOAA CHART 12316

Where's the Buoy?

Boaters traveling in early spring or late fall should not assume that all charted aids to navigation will be present in the waterways north of Cape May (including larger rivers). Some floating buoys are taken out of service during the winter months due to decreased vessel traffic and to minimize damage from ice and severe weather. If left in place they could sustain damage from the sheets of ice that move in every winter. In some cases, the ice could pull the buoy under, which causes damage to both the buoy hull and the light. The Coast Guard attempts to service and re-establish all aids to navigation by Memorial Day each spring. The Coast Guard also frequently moves floating aids to mark the best channel, therefore your charts may not always agree with the aids you see. For the latest information on the status of aids along the NJ ICW and the Atlantic Coast, call Coast Guard Station Cape May at 609-898-6900, ext. 8.

along Long Beach Island, rejoining the NJ ICW at quick flashing red "62."

Boat traffic from this point north on the NJ ICW is heavy even during mid-week. If you can avoid traveling this stretch on weekends or holidays. The channel is extremely narrow in the vicinity of the **Manahawkin Bay (NJ 72) Bridge** at Mile 37 (60-foot fixed vertical clearance) with depths outside the channel of only 1 to 2 feet MLW.

Dockage: All the marinas here are close to the beach, market, shops and fine restaurants.

The first cluster of facilities can be found starting at NJ ICW Mile 45.5 in the heart of Beach Haven. Family-owned Beach Haven Yacht Club Marina offers a relaxing atmosphere with professional, friendly service. Slips, laundry and all fuels are available. Transient visitors can borrow beach tags and enjoy the beautiful Beach Haven area. Just to the north Morrison's welcomes transients (to 60 feet) and has a well-stocked Ship Store. Nearby Little Egg Harbor Yacht Club is private but may recognize reciprocity from other clubs. Call ahead.

Several facilities in this area are filled with seasonal slip rentals but may be able to make room for you. These include Shelter Harbor Marina (Mile 44.8) and at Mile 44, Escape Harbor Marina and Southwick's Marina. There are several small-boat facilities to the north with marine supplies. Call ahead for depths and slip availability.

Anchorage: There is an anchorage behind Mordecai Island at Liberty Thorofare (Mile 46) with 5 to 9 feet MLW with good holding in sand and mud. It is exposed to the north. At Mile 40 on the beach side there is a cove with charted depths of 12 to 25 feet MLW with room for four to six cruising boats.

■ NEXT STOP

The narrow NJ ICW channel crosses the flats of Manahawkin Bay before it enters broad, open Barnegat Bay at Mile 30. The bay provides miles of scenic cruising, making it one of the most popular boating areas on the East Coast. Barnegat Bay is a very busy body of water with constant marine traffic. Stay in the channel and keep a careful watch at all times.

Barnegat Bay to Sandy Hook, NJ

Barnegat Bay is very popular with both power boaters and sailors. The Bay was designated as a national estuary with lovely scenery, superb beaches, plenty of shoreside attractions and inviting sailing conditions. When cruising this magnificent body of water, you will find a number of resorts preserving either the grand socialite splendor of an earlier day or a more modest and casual flavor. Piney rivers make excellent hurricane holes and historical New Jersey water traditions survive in many of the mainland towns.

■ NAVIGATING BARNEGAT BAY

The entire length of the NJ ICW in Barnegat Bay is safe and sheltered with little more than a stiff chop during strong winds that normally occur in the afternoon. In the spring and early summer when a front of warm, humid air moves up from the south, be prepared for dense advection fogs when transiting the NJ ICW along the bay. The tidal range of the entire bay is less than 6 inches; however, strong southwest winds can increase height of the tide and, conversely, strong northeasts can lower it. This is especially true in the northern bay.

North of Toms River, Barnegat Bay is shoal but well marked with depths ranging from 6 to 8 feet MLW. Make certain to follow the markers with the familiar yellow logo of the ICW as you transit the bay. Do not be misled by side-channel markers and entrances to rivers that do not show the yellow logo of the ICW.

The southern portion of the bay ranges from 8 to 10 feet MLW in the channel and dependable winds help make it one of the coast's most popular sailing centers. The diurnal wind pattern in this part of Barnegat Bay is for the sea breeze to begin at about 11:00 a.m. and then increase by mid-afternoon to a velocity usually greater than that predicted. A windless day on Barnegat Bay is rare.

A good rule to remember when cruising Barnegat Bay is that the deepest water is to the west near the mainland, and the shallowest is on the east next to the barrier island. Although crab trap buoys and eel trap buoys are often scattered throughout the bay, few are near the channel.

■ BARNEGAT BAY INLET TO TOMS RIVER

Barnegat Inlet & Barnegat Light

At the northern tip of Long Beach Island next to Barnegat Inlet is Barnegat Lighthouse, which is located in the town of Barnegat Light.

With fair weather and seas, the town of Barnegat Light can be a fine overnight stop for those traveling the coastline. Because it is about halfway between New York City and Cape May, a boat capable of 6-knot speeds can make the trip down the entire New Jersey coast in two daytime hops. (The three-day alternative for slower boats consists of overnight stops at Manasquan and Atlantic City.)

The familiar red and white tower was commissioned into service in 1859 and served faithfully until 1944 when it was decommissioned. The light was relit on January 1, 2009, and now flashes a white light every 10 seconds. A private group maintains the lighthouse, which is open daily from 10:00 a.m. to 4:30 p.m. (weather permitting).

NAVIGATION: Use NOAA Chart 12324. Three channels branch off at the charted green and red junction buoy "B" next to the Coast Guard Station at Barnegat Inlet. The channel to the south enters the harbor at Barnegat Light. To the north is Oyster Creek Channel, which leads to the NJ ICW on the west side of Barnegat Bay. Be sure not to bear southeast off the main channel into Double Creek Channel, which is closed periodically due to shoaling and in the best conditions has just 3 feet MLW depths in portions of the channel. It eventually leads back to the NJ ICW but seek local knowledge before attempting to enter.

Barnegat Inlet is straight forward and easy to navigate. There is 20 feet MLW in the entrance and 12 to 15 feet MLW all the way back to the anchorage. Note that there can be large waves and breakers in if there is an outgoing tide that is opposed by a strong easterly wind, as is the case with many of the New Jersey inlets. An inquiry on VHF Channel 16 will usually bring a response of good local knowledge of the inlet conditions. Call for advice and also trust your own prudence and judgment.

The south jetty of Barnegat Inlet is marked with a 35-foot-high tower made of black steel, which is 8 feet in diameter and topped with a green light and horn. Look for the square green "7" daybeacon portion during daylight hours. The north jetty is marked with a 40-foot-high tower topped with a red light and a triangular red "6" daybeacon.

Although the inlet channel between the jetties has been straightened, widened and deepened, potentially dangerous shoals continually develop just outside the mouth of Barnegat Inlet. Shoaling on the ocean side of the inlet is most treacherous with a strong northeast wind and an outgoing tide, which can build 6-foot to 8-foot breaking seas capable of dropping you on the bottom in the troughs. These are extreme conditions, not the norm, but prudence suggests that you be aware of the possibility and consider an alternative entrance in such conditions. Also, be aware that the first 0.10 mile of the jetty behind red daybeacon "6" submerges at high tide so use caution transiting this inlet.

Dredges work on Barnegat Inlet three times a year, for a month at a time. During these periods transiting the narrow passage past the dredge equipment can be difficult.

Dockage: Aids to navigation in the inlet area are privately maintained and frequently moved due to shifting shoals, but the channel leading to Barnegat Harbor is generally well marked. Here you will find gas and diesel fuel, repairs and transient berths.

Marinas located south of the inlet entrance at Barnegat Harbor include Lighthouse Marina and the Marina at Barnegat Light. Lighthouse Marina is a commercial dock and can be a bit bouncy but they have a well-stocked Ship Store and there are grocery stores and restaurants nearby. Both The Marina at Barnegat Bay and Bayview Harbor Marina offer transient slips (to 80 feet) on floating docks with the usual amenities. Bayview also sells all fuels.

Anchorage: Coming from the inlet bear south as you pass the lighthouse toward the town of Barnegat Light and anchor west of the Coast Guard building. Anchor well away from the channel; large commercial fishing boats are berthed at the end of the harbor. There is a small dinghy dock at the boat ramp.

To Oyster Creek Channel Junction– NJ ICW Mile 26

NAVIGATION: Use NOAA Chart 12324. West of the Barnegat Lighthouse, Oyster Creek Channel joins Barnegat Inlet with Barnegat Bay. Buoys on this channel are uncharted and moved frequently and the passage should never be attempted at night by a newcomer. Even in daylight, sharp doglegs of nearly 90° can be easily overlooked and wide scans for the next set of buoys are mandatory, since missing a set will probably put you aground.

The channel can be very congested on summer weekends with fishing boats drifting in the channel and blocking your views of the navigational markers. Boats with a draft of 5 feet or more should only attempt to transit the Oyster Creek Channel on a rising tide. Shoals do shift frequently so caution is advised.

WG

Barnegat Bay, NJ

Facility	Dockage						Supplies	Services					
	Largest Vessel Accommodated	VHF Channel Monitored/Working	Transient Slips/Total Slips	Approach/Dockside Depth (reported)	Floating Docks	Gas/Diesel	Groceries, Ice, Marine Supplies, Snacks	Repairs: Hull, Engine, Propeller	Lift (tonnage), Crane, Rail	Min/Max Amps	Courtesy Car, Laundry, Pool, Showers	Pump-Out Station	Nearby: Grocery Store, Motel, Restaurant
BARNEGAT LIGHT													
1. Lighthouse Marina MM 26.0 (609) 494-2305	70	16/	4/50	7.0/8.0		GD	GIMS		L35	30	S		GMR
2. The Marina at Barnegat Light MM 26.0 (609) 494-6611	80	/	/77	8.0/8.0	F		GIS	HEP		30/50	S		GR
WARETOWN AREA													
3. Toni G's Marina MM 28.0 (609) 698-8581	34	/	15/15	6.0/6.0			IM	EP	L	30			GR
4. Mariner's Marina MM 28.0 (609) 698-1222	40	/	/200	6.0/6.0	F		M	HEP	L25	30	S		GMR
5. Key Harbor Marina (WiFi) (609) 693-9355	70	/	4/278	6.0/6.0		GD	IMS	HEP	L50	30/50	LPS	P	3R
6. Leamings Marina (609) 971-1514	26	/	/76	/8.0	F	G	IMS	EP	L9		S		R
7. Bakers Basin Marina (732) 994-8988	50	/	/130	/						30	S		R
8. Long Key Marina MM 26.0 (609) 693-9444	45	16/	/142	6.0/6.0	F	GD	IM	EP	L15	30	S	P	GMR
9. Spencer's Bayside Marina (Internet)(WiFi) MM 26.0 (609) 693-0100	55	16/	2/22	5.0/6.0	F		IM	E	L30	30/100	LS		GR
10. Holiday Harbor Marina (WiFi) MM 26.0 (609) 693-2217	65	/	4/240	6.0/6.0	F	GD	IM	HEP	L50	30/50	LPS	P	GR
FORKED RIVER													
11. Marina at Southwinds (Internet)(WiFi) MM 23.5 (609) 693-6288	60	17/	6/174	8.0/6.0		GD	IS	HEP	L25	30/50	LS	P	GMR
12. Captain's Inn MM 23.5 (609) 693-3351	70	/	30/45	7.0/6.0			IS			30	S		GMR
13. Townsend's Marina (WiFi) MM 23.5 (609) 693-6100	50	/	5/96	6.0/6.0	F		IM	HEP	L25	30	S		GR
14. Mermaid's Cove Marina (609) 756-4296	42	16/	3/46	6.0/6.0	F		IMS	HEP	C	30/50			GMR
15. Ted & Sons Forked River Marina MM 23.5 (609) 693-2185	40	/	/	6.0/6.0		G	M	HEP	L	30	S		GMR
16. The Marina at Tall Oaks MM 23.5 (609) 693-2145	65	/	10/125	8.0/6.0		GD	IM	HEP	L50	30/50	LPS	P	GMR
17. Silver Cloud Harbor Marina (Internet) MM 23.5 (609) 693-2145	**75**	**16/**	**13/240**	**10.0/9.0**		**GD**	**IM**	**HEP**	**L50**	**30/50**	**PS**	**P**	**GMR**
18. Wilbert's Marina (Internet)(WiFi) MM 23.5 (609) 693-2145	65	16/	1/17	8.0/6.0		GD	IM	HEP	L50	30/50	LPS	P	MR
19. Forked River State Marina MM 23.5 (609) 693-5045	50	16/	2/125	6.0/6.0						30	L		GMR
20. Grant Boat Works MM 23.5 (609) 971-1075	55	/	7/50	10.0/10.0			M	HEP	L25,R	30	PS		MR
21. Tide's End Marina MM 23.5 (609) 693-9423	44	/	2/35	10.0/6.0	F	G	IM	HEP	L40	30	S	P	GMR
22. Ricks Marina MM 23.5 (609) 693-2134	60	9/	10/76	10.0/10.0			IMS	HEP	L30	30/50	S	P	GMR

⌨ Internet Access   (WiFi) Wireless Internet Access   onSpot Dockside WiFi Facility

See WaterwayGuide.com for current rates, fuel prices, website addresses, and other up-to-the-minute information. (Information in the table is provided by the facilities.)

WARETOWN AREA, BARNEGAT LIGHT, NOAA CHART 12324

Flashing red-and-white 17-foot Morse (A) light "BI" marks the junction of Oyster Creek Channel and the NJ ICW on Barnegat Bay. This aid to navigation has a white light, which flashes Morse (A) (one short, one long). If heading to Forked River or other destinations to the north, do not cut this buoy! Leave it well to starboard before turning north. There is extensive shoaling inside the buoy off the Sedge Islands to the east.

Barnegat Beach & Waretown

NAVIGATION: Use NOAA Chart 12324. On the west side of Barnegat Bay, across from the town of Barnegat Light, well-marked channels lead into Barnegat Beach and Waretown with marine services and repairs.

Dockage: The 200-slip Mariner's Marina is located west of Conklin Island on Double Creek. The family-owned and -operated marina caters to both sailboats and power boats to 40 feet and advertises comprehensive service offerings. Toni G's Marina on Double Creek specializes in boating, fishing and crabbing. They have a marina store and tackle shop and offer repairs. Both of these have limited slip space so call ahead.

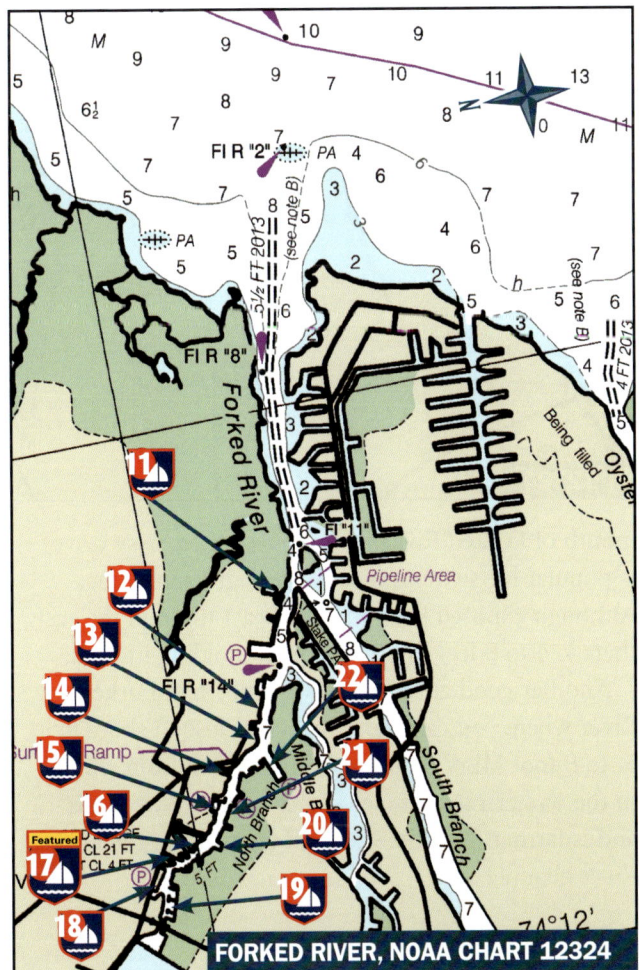

FORKED RIVER, NOAA CHART 12324

Key Harbor Marina at Barnegat Beach is a brokerage with slips and some amenities. At Waretown, Bakers Basin Marina caters to sportfishing vessels to 50 feet in a protected harbor. Call ahead.

Spencer's Bayside Marina on Waretown Creek in Barnegat has an extensive parts inventory with engine parts, general boating and safety supplies, electronics and anchors. They may be able to provide you a berth in a pinch.

To the north in a protected harbor is Holiday Harbor Marina, a deep-water facility that caters to sportfishing vessels to 65 feet. They also sell all fuels.

Anchorage: Just off the mainland town of Barnegat Beach, anchor just north of Conklin Island for protection from the prevailing south and southwest winds in 4 to 8 feet MLW with good holding in soft mud. This is exposed from the north through the east and it can be "buggy" on hot summer days.

Forked River–NJ ICW Mile 24

NAVIGATION: Use NOAA Chart 12324. Flashing red "2" just west of Morse (A) marker "BB" at Mile 24 marks the entrance to the Forked (pronounced "Fork'id") River. Stay in the channel when navigating the river as shoaling is present on both sides. Three branches of the river run back into the mainland. The two south forks are residential, while the north branch has all the facilities of interest to the cruiser including numerous boatyards and marinas, waterfront restaurants and easy access to grocery stores, drugstores and bus service to New York and Atlantic City.

Dockage: Transient dockage can be found at Marina at Southwinds, the first marina to starboard on the river. This is a full-service marina offering marine gasoline and diesel fuel that can accommodate boats to 58 feet. The marina also has top-notch marine mechanics. Next is the Townsend's Marina with slips to 50 feet and ample parts and services. The on-site Captain's Inn offers dockage (white pilings) to diners for a modest fee. Directly across the river is family-friendly Rick's Marina with deep-water slips (to 60 feet) for those who need marine services.

Continuing upriver are boat sales, storage and repair yards (but few transient slips) at Tides Inn Marina, Ted & Sons Forked River and Grant Boat Works.

The marina complex of Silver Cloud Harbor Marina features 230 seasonal slips including some reserved transient space. Amenities include a Ship Store, fuel dock, pool with cabanas, picnic areas and all types of

Barnegat Bay, NJ

			Dockage				Supplies		Services					
LAUREL HARBOR														
1. Laurel Harbor Marina ⬥ MM 20.5	(609) 693-6112	50	/	5/156	4.0/4.0		G	IMS	HP	L25	30	LS	P	GR
CEDAR CREEK														
2. Ocean Beach Marine Center MM 20.0	(609) 242-2200	40	68/	/110	5.0/5.0		GD	IM	HEP	L25	50	LS	P	
3. Lanoka Harbor Marina MM 20.0	(609) 693-2674	60	/	15/200	5.0/5.0		GD	IMS	HEP	L35	30/50	S	P	G
4. Cedar Creek Sailing Center/Marina ⬥ MM 20.0	(732) 269-1351	45	78/	2/60	6.0/5.5			IMS	HEP	L50,C	30	LS	P	GMR
GLEN COVE														
5. Berkeley Island Marine	(732) 269-1186	30	/	/	/		G	IMS	HEP	L		S		

◻ Internet Access ⬥ Wireless Internet Access ⬥ onSpot Dockside WiFi Facility

See WaterwayGuide.com for current rates, fuel prices, website addresses, and other up-to-the-minute information. (Information in the table is provided by the facilities.)

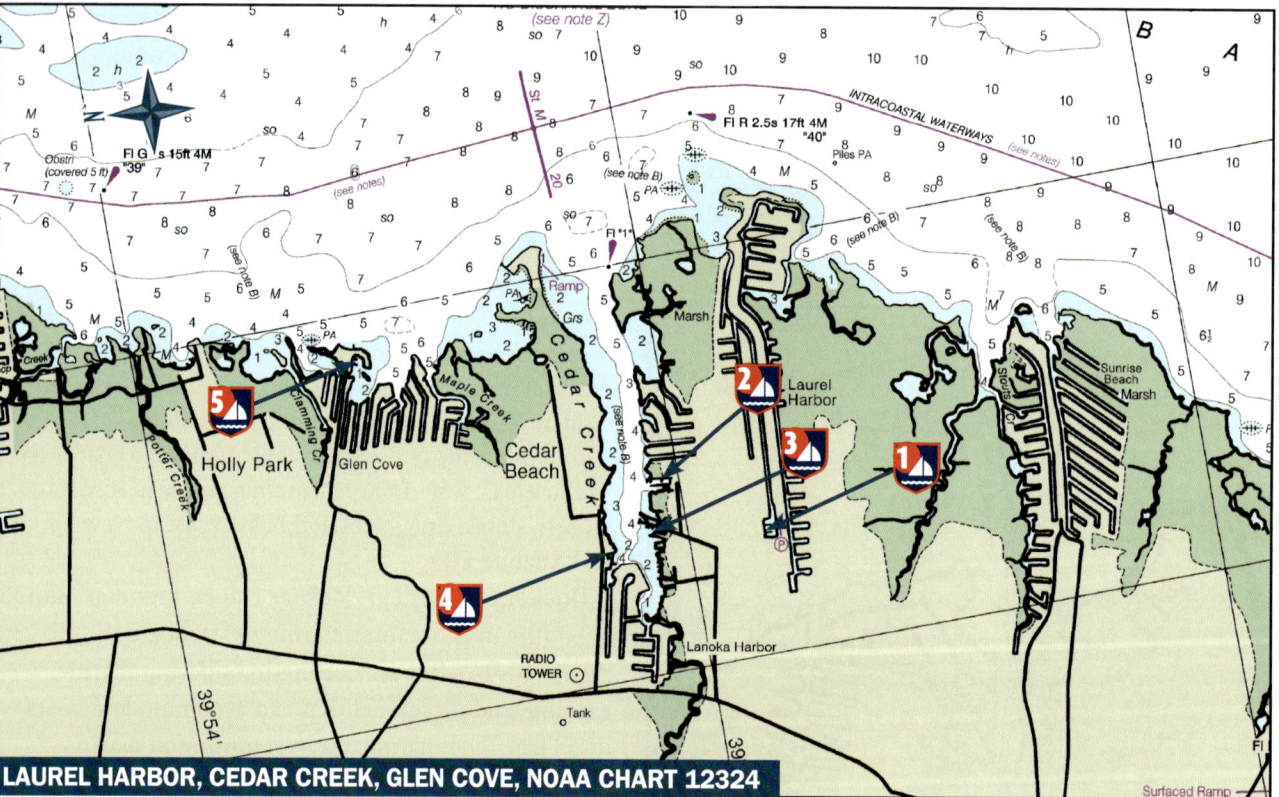

LAUREL HARBOR, CEDAR CREEK, GLEN COVE, NOAA CHART 12324

services and repairs (including emergency repairs). Their sister facilities are Marina at Tall Oaks and Wilbert's Marina.

At the head of the river is the 125-slip Forked River State Marina with limited transient space and the usual amenities.

Anchorage: Although it can be somewhat buggy and hot on breathless summer nights, Forked River is one of the best hurricane holes on the coast. It has proven nearly impervious to even the worst blows. The charted bight on the south side of the channel at the mouth of Forked River (commonly called Sissy Cove) is popular for swimming and overnight anchoring. Although exposed from the northeast through the east, there is 4 to 8 feet MLW with good holding in mud.

Another good anchorage area is north of Forked River where you can drop the hook close to shore in 5- to 8-foot MLW depths with protection from winds in the western semicircle. This is next to a wetlands and is farther from the wakes of boats using the Forked River channel.

Side Trip: Island Beach State Park

Island Beach State Park, a 10-mile-long strip of pristine barrier island, lies on the east side of the NJ ICW between Mile 27 and Mile 15. To this day it is undeveloped and preserved in its natural condition.

Anchorage: About 200 yards after passing flashing white Morse (A) "BB" at NJ ICW Mile 22, you may see boats anchored close to shore at Island Beach State Park. This area is known as Tices Shoal. You can anchor here in 4-to 10-foot MLW depths with a hard sand bottom and dinghy to shore to explore. There is a small sandy beach on the bay side and a walking path through the rolling dunes to the ocean beach about 0.25 mile across the barrier island. A $3.00 fee is collected from those boaters who dinghy ashore here to visit the ocean beach, which is a popular spot for local boaters on summer weekends.

Cedar Creek–NJ ICW Mile 20

NAVIGATION: Use NOAA Chart 12324. North of Forked River, the west side of Barnegat Bay shows the hand of the dredge and the developer with most of the channels leading to residential subdivisions. Cedar Creek, however, retains the "Down-Jersey" pine-and-cedar appeal and has emerged as a sailing center that is worth a visit. Pay close attention to channel markers as shoaling is present on both sides of the channel.

Dockage: Laurel Harbor Marina is up a protected channel with slips, gas and repair services. On Cedar Creek to the north, Ocean Beach Marine Center (Lanoka Harbor) and Lanoka Harbor Marina both offer repairs and sell all fuels and may have slip space. Cedar Creek Sailing Center/Marina is a sailboat facility with slips to 45 feet. They may be able to accommodate you as well. Transient space is limited here; do call ahead.

Toms River–NJ ICW Mile 15

This picturesque river, lined with houses and high banks, opens to the west and a number of its attractive coves provide excellent anchorages. There are delightful possibilities for exploring and several marinas accept transients including a few of complete resorts with swimming pools, on-site restaurants and shore accommodations.

The City of Toms River is an historic port dating to 1624 located at the head of the river. The Toms River Yacht Club, founded in 1871, is the second oldest in the country. Traditional captains' houses line the street and the town is working to preserve its maritime history. The Toms River Seaport Society (www.tomsriverseaport.org) has acquired several historic boats and other artifacts for its maritime museum and waterfront display, and there is an annual Wooden Boat festival usually during July. Call the Society at 732-349-9209 for details.

NAVIGATION: Use NOAA Chart 12324. Shoaling has been reported in the NJ ICW near red daybeacon "38." When entering Toms River, stand off of Goodluck Point to avoid shoaling. There is also shoaling off Long Point so do not cut inside flashing red "10" on the Tom's River.

Dockage/Moorings: There are many boat yards, marinas and yacht clubs on the Toms River. Near the mouth of the river around Goodluck Point is Good Luck Point Marina. They offer boat hauling and detailing, storage and service and have a fuel dock. Ocean Gate Yacht Basin has services from engine repairs to full fiberglass rebuilds and slips to 45 feet.

Shore Point Marina & Yacht Sales is located in an enclosed, well-protected basin at the mouth of Mill Creek on the south side of the Toms River. This is a boat brokerage that offers some maintenance services and can accommodate transient vessels up to 57 feet.

The 240-slip Lighthouse Point Marina and Yacht Club is set on 14 acres at the head of the Toms River with amenities that include deep-water slips to 75 feet, a pool and an array of services.

Marinas on the north side of the river include the private Toms River Yacht Club (the second oldest club in America) and Island Heights Yacht Club. Both offer courtesy dockage for members of reciprocal yacht clubs.

Nelson Marine Basin has slips and moorings (to 40 feet) and is home to Nelson Sailing Center. Cozy Cove Marina is snug to enter because it is so protected and has just two reserved transient slips to 40 feet. The well-regarded Dillon's Creek Marina has just two reserved transient slips (to 45 feet) and offers mechanical and other services.

Anchorage: Cocktail Cove (on the south side at Mill Creek) is particularly popular with 5 to 8 feet MLW and holding in mud with open exposure to the north. Another popular anchorage is just east of Money Island on the north side of the river with good holding in 5 to 6 feet MLW with open exposure to the south. The Pine Beach anchorage to the west on the Toms River (south shore) is the most protected with excellent holding and wind protection.

Toms River, Island Beach, NJ

TOMS RIVER AREA		Largest Vessel Accomodated	VHF Channel Monitored / Working	Transient Slips / Total Slips	Approach / Dockside Depth (reported)	Floating Docks	Gas / Diesel	Groceries, Ice, Marine Supplies, Snacks	Repairs: Hull, Engine, Propeller	Lift (tonnage), Crane, Rail	Min / Max Amps	Courtesy Car, Laundry, Pool, Showers	Pump-Out Station	Nearby: Grocery Store, Motel, Restaurant
		Dockage					**Supplies**		**Services**					
1. Good Luck Point Marina Inc. WiFi MM 37.0	(732) 269-3700		/	/115	5.0/5.0	F	GD	IMS	EP	L25	30	LS	P	GR
2. Ocean Gate Yacht Basin ⌨ MM 15.0	(732) 269-2565	45	/	/180	6.0/6.0		GD	IMS	HEP	L35	50	S	P	GR
3. Shore Point Marina & Yacht Sales ⌨ WiFi MM 15.0	(732) 244-2106	57	/	5/205	6.0/6.0	F	GD	IMS	HEP	L20	30/50	LPS	P	GR
4. Lighthouse Point Marina and Yacht Club MM 15.0	(732) 341-1105	75	/	/240	6.0/5.0			IMS	HEP	L30	30/100	LPS	P	GMR
5. Miller Yacht Sales Inc. ⌨	(732) 349-6800	62	77/	/30	5.0/4.0				HEP	L50,C	50	S		
6. Tom's River Yacht Club -PRIVATE ⌨ WiFi	(732) 929-0888		/	5/90	/			IS				PS	P	GMR
7. Island Heights Yacht Club-PRIVATE MM 15.0	(732) 929-9813		/	/	/			IS				S		R
8. Nelson Marine Basin WiFi MM 15.0	(732) 270-0022	40	79/	/100	5.0/5.0			M	HEP	L	30/50	LPS	P	GMR
9. Cozy Cove Marina MM 15.0	(732) 929-1171	40	/	2/85	6.0/6.0		G	IMS	P	L15	30	S		GR
10. Dillon's Creek Marina ⌨ WiFi MM 15.0	(732) 270-8541	46	/	10/210	6.0/6.0			IM	HEP	L25,C	30/50	LPS	P	GMR
11. Horizon Marina	(732) 929-1700	40	/	15/180	5.0/5.0			IMS	EP	L15	30	S	P	GMR
12. Pier One Motel & Marina WiFi MM 14.0	(732) 270-9090	45	9/	17/65	7.0/7.0			IMS			30/50	S		GMR
13. Hobby Lobby Marine MM 12.5	(732) 929-1711	35	/	/80	10.0/6.0	F		IM	E	L15,C	15/30	S	P	GMR
ISLAND BEACH														
14. Seaside Park Yacht Club MM 15.5	(732) 793-9611	60	/	1/41	/			IS				S		MR
15. Lavallette Yacht Club-PRIVATE 1.5 mi. SE of MM 10.0	(732) 793-8747		/	/	/			IS				S		R
16. Ocean Beach Marina 1.5 mi. SE of MM 10.0	(732) 793-7460	45	/	/250	5.0/7.0		G	IM	HEP	L	30	S	P	R
17. Chadwick Island Marina WiFi	(732) 965-8563	42	/	6/202	/		G	IMS	HEP	L	30/50	LS	P	GR

⌨ Internet Access   WiFi Wireless Internet Access   onSpot Dockside WiFi Facility

See WaterwayGuide.com for current rates, fuel prices, website addresses, and other up-to-the-minute information. (Information in the table is provided by the facilities.)

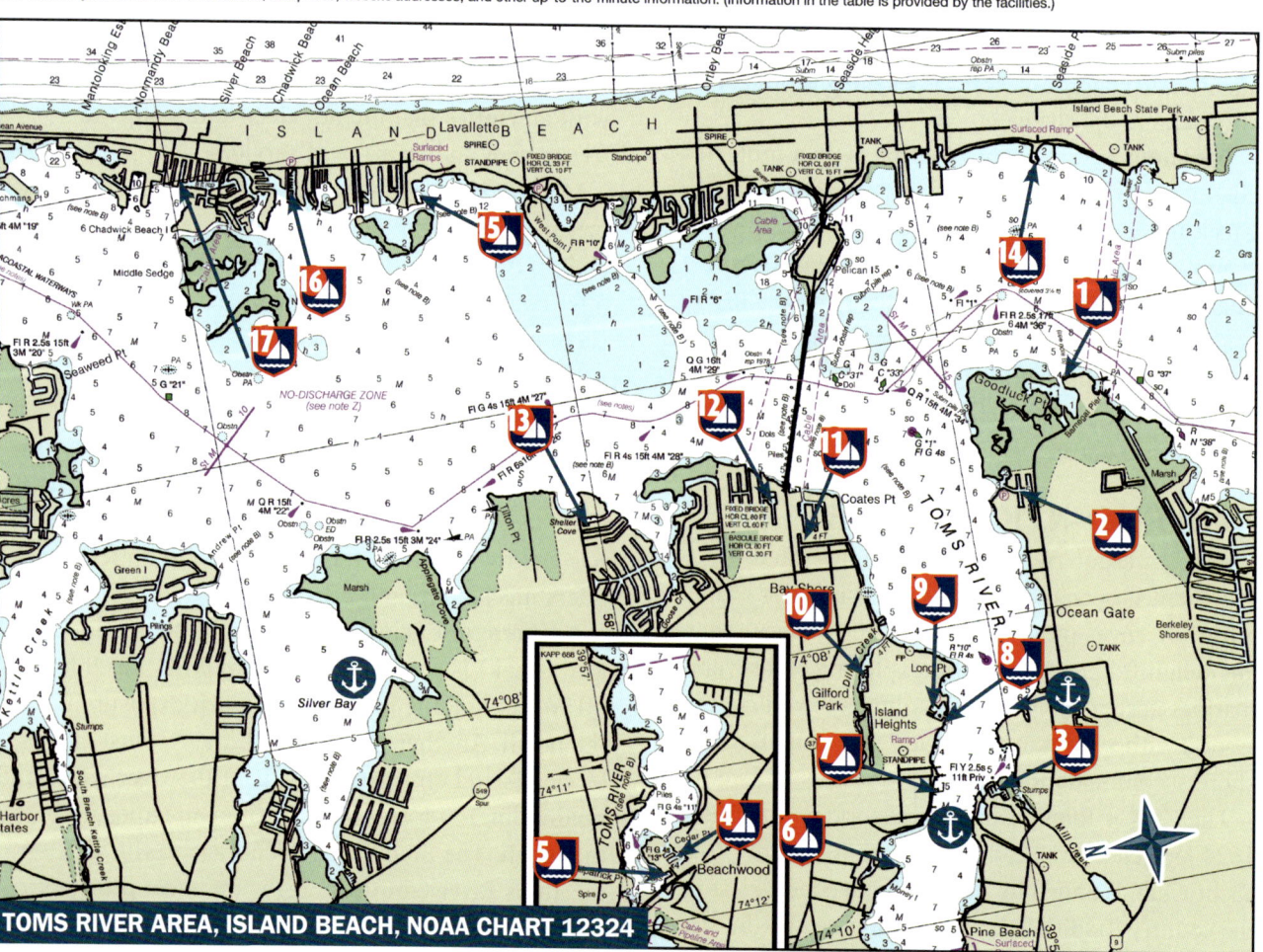

TOMS RIVER AREA, ISLAND BEACH, NOAA CHART 12324

■ TWIN BRIDGES TO POINT PLEASANT CANAL

Island Beach–NJ ICW Mile 15 to Mile 10

Heading north from Toms River, heed all marks since there is shoaling on both sides of the NJ ICW, especially just beyond the two bridges at about Mile 14 that cross from the mainland to the resort town of Seaside Heights on the barrier beach. At Seaside Heights, a 1-mile-long amusement park and a water park are worth a stop, especially if you have young (or young at heart) ones aboard.

NAVIGATION: Use NOAA Chart 12324. The northernmost of the twin bridges **(J. Stanley Tunney Bridge)** is fixed with a 60-foot vertical clearance. **Thomas A. Mathis (NJ 37) Bridge** (30-foot closed vertical clearance) will open on signal from Memorial Day through Labor Day except from 8:00 a.m. to 8:00 p.m., when the draw need only open on the hour and half hour. From April 1 through November 30 from 11:00 p.m. to 8:00 a.m. and at all times from December 1 through March 31, the draw need only open if at least four hours notice is given.

Be careful as you approach the bridges from the south. The channel is well marked but outside the magenta line there are charted submerged objects and light pilings leveled by winter ice. They constitute a hazard until they are removed when new pilings are set out (usually in June). Just north of the bridges pay close attention to the daybeacons because shallow flats crowd in on both sides and sandbars often move into the edges of the channel. Through the rest of this section deep water is to the west with shallow flats to the east.

Dockage: Pier One Motel & Marina, just north of the twin bridges, has slips to 45 feet and the opportunity to host friends or get off the boat for a night or two. Hobby Lobby in a dredged channel to the north is a boat brokerage with a few slips to 35 feet.

The towns of Seaside Heights, Lavallette and Normandy Beach string along the east side of the NJ ICW route and all have marinas that can be reached through marked channels across the flats. Both Seaside Park Yacht Club (south of the bridges at Mile 15.5) and Lavallette Yacht Club (north of the bridges) offer limited courtesy dockage for members of reciprocal yacht clubs.

Ocean Beach Marine Center (Lavallette) has a full-time staff of certified marine technicians as well as a full-time dockmaster and sells gas. Chadwick Island Marina at Island Beach has slips to 42 feet and also offers some repairs and sells gas (no diesel).

Anchorage: At Seaside Park (Mile 15.8) there is an anchorage with excellent holding in sand with 4 to 5 feet MLW. It is exposed to the west and south. A public dock is near theSeaside Park Yacht Club for dinghy landings.There are communities on Silver Bay

Mantoloking

Barnegat Bay, NJ

	Phone	Largest Vessel Accommodated	VHF Channel Monitored / Working	Transient Slips / Total Slips	Approach / Dockside Depth (reported)	Floating Docks	Gas / Diesel	Groceries, Ice, Marine Supplies, Snacks	Repairs: Hull, Engine, Propeller	Lift (tonnage), Crane, Rail	Min / Max Amps	Courtesy Car, Laundry, Pool, Showers	Pump-Out Station	Nearby: Grocery Store, Motel, Restaurant
BARNEGAT BAY				**Dockage**				**Supplies**			**Services**			
1. Baywood Marina WiFi MM 8.0	(732) 477-3322	40	/	6/200	4.0/4.0		G	IM	HEP	L10	30	PS	P	GMR
2. David Beaton & Sons, Inc. Boatyard MM 6.0	(732) 477-0259	42	68/	12/65	4.0/4.0			M	HEP	L15	30	S	P	GMR
3. Barnegat Bay Marina ⌨ WiFi MM 6.0	(732) 477-7700	65	16/68	15/110	6.0/6.5		GD	IMS	HEP	L70	30/50	LS	P	4R
4. Mantoloking Yacht Club-PRIVATE MM 6.0	(732) 892-6281		/	/52	4.0/4.0						30			
5. Traders Cove Marina ⌨	(732) 644-7618		/	15/120	6.0/6.0	F		I			15/30	LS	P	MR
METEDECONK RIVER														
6. Metedeconk River Yacht Club	(732) 477-9781	36	/	1/64	4.0/4.0			IS			30	S		R
7. Cassidy's Breton Woods Marina	(732) 477-1111	35	/	/185	6.0/4.0	F				L20	30	S		GMR
8. The Marina at Beacon 70 (formerly Forge Landing Marina) WiFi	(732) 477-0404	65	/	/200	6.0/6.0		G	I	HEP	L20	30	LS	P	GMR
9. Brennan Boat Company & Marina WiFi	(732) 840-1100	50	16/	/80	4.0/4.0	F			HEP	L25	30	PS	P	
10. Jersey Shore Marina	(732) 840-9530	50	/	/175	4.0/5.0		G	IM	HEP	L20	30	LPS	P	GMR
11. Green Cove Marina ⌨ WiFi	(732) 840-9090	50	/	15/255	5.0/3.5		GD	M	HEP	L20	30/50	PS	P	GMR
12. Wehrlen Bros Marina	(732) 899-3505	57	/	/200	5.0/4.0				HEP	L40	30	PS		MR
13. Pier 281 Marina WiFi	(732) 714-2061	75	/	/100	/			S	HEP	L37		S	P	R
BEAVERDAM CREEK														
14. Comstock Yacht Sales & Marina	(732) 899-2500	65	9/	10/71	6.0/5.0		GD	IMS	HEP	L40	30/50	S	P	GMR
15. Arnold's Yacht Basin ⌨ WiFi	(732) 892-3000	45	/	/190	6.0/5.0	F		M	HEP	L50	15/50	S	P	R
16. Forsberg's Boat Works WiFi	(732) 892-4246	45	/	/60	4.0/4.0				HEP	L20	30	S		GMR
POINT PLEASANT CANAL														
17. Johnson Brothers Boat Works ⌨ MM 1.0	(732) 892-0222	100	16/9	3/70	6.0/6.0			GIM	HEP	L35,R	15/50	LPS	P	GMR
18. Carver Boat Works, LLC ⌨ MM 4.0	(732) 892-0328	45	/	/16	4.0/6.0				HEP	L30,R	15/100		P	MR
POINT PLEASANT														
19. Clarks Landing Marina ⌨ WiFi MM 2.0	(732) 899-5559	65	5/	/105	5.0/6.0		GD	GIMS	HEP	L	30/50	S		GMR
20. Garden State Yacht Sales & Marina MM 1.5	(732) 892-4222	70	16/9	/70	6.0/6.0	F		GIMS	HEP	L50	30/50	S		GMR
21. Captain Bill's Landing	(848) 232-2880	110	15/	3/	/6.0		GD	IM						R
BRIELLE														
22. Hoffman's Marina ⌨ WiFi MM 2.0	(732) 528-6200	130	16/68	20/150	14.0/16.0	F	GD	IM	HEP	L70	30/100	LPS	P	GMR
23. Hoffman's Marina West ⌨ WiFi MM 1.0	(732) 528-6200	120	16/9	10/125	16.0/20.0		GD	IMS	HEP	L70,C	30/100	LPS	P	GMR
24. Brielle Yacht Club Marina & Sandbar Restaurant ⌨ WiFi MM 1.0	(732) 528-6250	100	16/19	10/125	8.0/6.0	F	GD	IS	E		30/50	S		GMR
BRICK TOWNSHIP														
25. Safe Harbor Crystal Point 1.0 mi. NW of MM 2.5	(732) 892-2300	90	/	3/200	8.0/8.0	F	GD	IMS			30/50	S	P	MR
26. River Rock Restaurant & Marina Bar WiFi 1.0 mi. NW of MM 2.5	(732) 840-1110	26	/	/	5.0/3.0			IS			30	S		GMR
27. MarineMax Brick WiFi 1.0 mi. NW of MM 2.5	(732) 840-2100	70	/	/160	6.0/4.0	F		M	HEP	L20	30/50	LS		MR
28. Safe Harbor Manasquan River	(732) 840-0300		/	/200	/	F					30	LPS	P	MR

⌨ Internet Access WiFi Wireless Internet Access onSpot Dockside WiFi Facility

See WaterwayGuide.com for current rates, fuel prices, website addresses, and other up-to-the-minute information. (Information in the table is provided by the facilities.)

Barnegat Bay

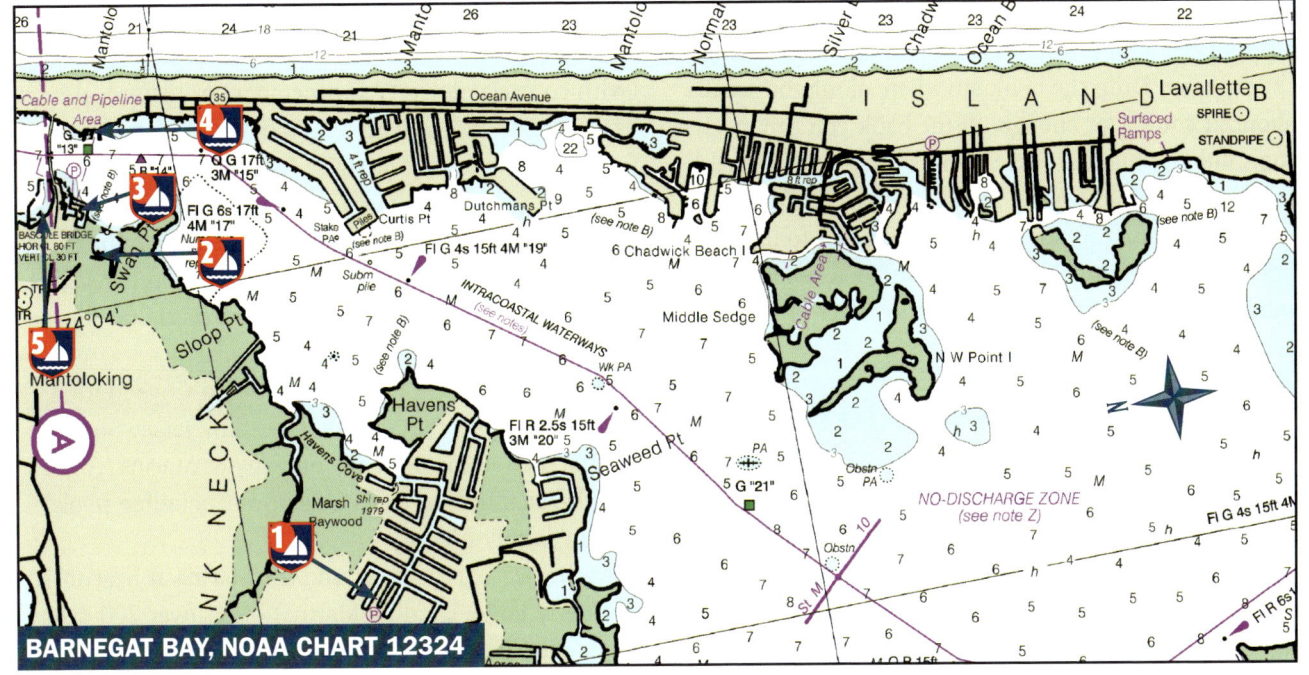

BARNEGAT BAY, NOAA CHART 12324

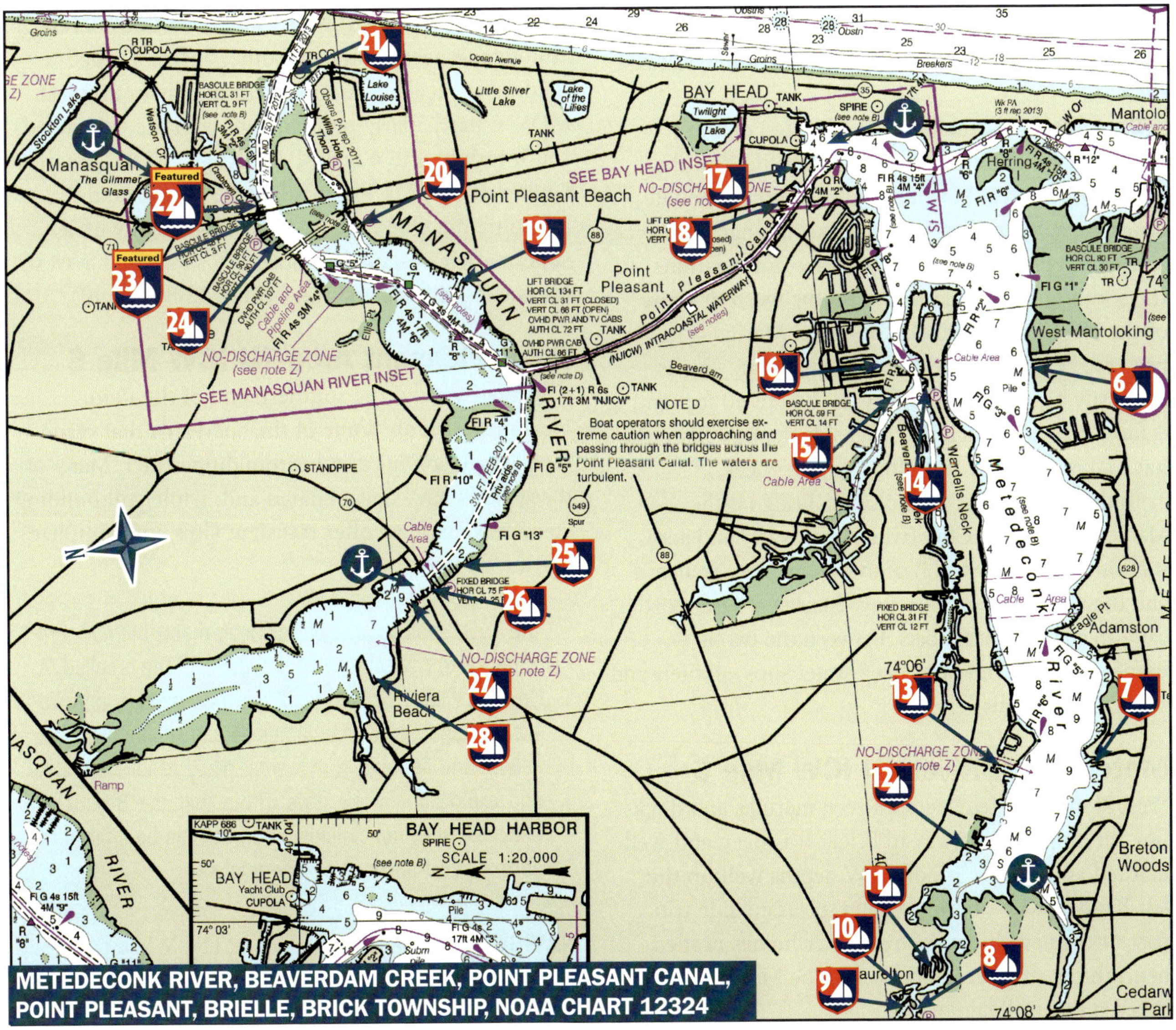

METEDECONK RIVER, BEAVERDAM CREEK, POINT PLEASANT CANAL, POINT PLEASANT, BRIELLE, BRICK TOWNSHIP, NOAA CHART 12324

on the west side of Barnegat Bay near Mile 10. This is a prime anchorage area but it is often crowded during the summer. Drop the hook anywhere along the south shore. If you go far enough off the bank you can catch the southerly breeze be free of pesky insects. Charted depths are only 5 to 6 feet MLW in Silver Bay, which has good holding in mud. It is also possible to drop the hook in Kettle Creek (Mile 9.5) with good holding in mud but charted depths are only 4 to 5 feet MLW and it is somewhat exposed to the southeast.

Mantoloking–NJ ICW Mile 10 to Mile 6

NAVIGATION: Use NOAA Chart 12324. At Mantoloking (Mile 6.3) the NJ ICW is crossed by the **Mantoloking Bridge** (30-foot closed vertical clearance) and leaves Barnegat Bay as it swings east to run close inside of the barrier beach. The bridge opens on signal except Memorial Day through Labor Day when on Saturdays, Sundays and federal holidays from 9:00 a.m. to 6:00 p.m. the draw need only open on the hour, 20 minutes after the hour, and 40 minutes after the hour.

Dockage: Yacht amenities are located on both the mainland and the beach on the NJ ICW in the Mantoloking area. Most marinas will accommodate cruising yachts and several offer a full range of services along with restaurants and shore accommodations. To the south of Mantoloking and on the western shore of the NJ ICW the 200-slip Baywood Marina is in a protected channel near near Havens Point. This is primarily a yacht brokerage with slips to 40 feet and 4-foot MLW approach and dockside depths. They also have a marina store and offer some services.

To the south of the Mantoloking Bridge is the Mantoloking Yacht Club (which is private) and across the waterway are David Beaton & Sons, Inc. Boatyard and the municipal Traders Cove Marina. These mostly cater to smaller, local boats. Between the two is Barnegat Bay Marina with deep-water slips, all fuels and services and repairs.

Metedeconk River–NJ ICW Mile 5

West along the Metedeconk River, marinas and docks line the shore all the way to Brick. It is deep and well marked and carries 5-foot MLW depths well up the left-hand branch offering a calm, pleasant side trip past pine-lined shores with summer homes nestled beneath the trees. A fall cruise on the Metedeconk River is especially enjoyable.

Dockage: On the south shore of the Metedeconk River are the private Metedeconk River Yacht Club (with courtesy dockage for members of reciprocal yacht clubs) and Cassidy's Breton Woods Marina (which caters to vessels to 35 feet).

Pier 281 is across the river with more than 100 slips that can accommodate vessels to 75 feet (including sailboats). Call ahead for slip availability. On the same (north) shore is Wehrlen Bros. Marina with 200 slips, a pool and some services.

Heading north is the first-class Green Cove Marina, nestled in a protected cove, followed by Jersey Shore Marina then Brennan Boat Company & Marina. All of of these facilities have full amenities (including pools) and are family-friendly.

At the head of the river, and the Marina at Beacon 70 (formerly Forge Landing Marina) offers over 200 deep water slips. They also have a self-serve fuel dock that is open 24 hours for your convenience.

Anchorage: The entire river makes a fine anchorage, although seaweed can be a bother at times. The holding is excellent in mud with depths from 5 feet MLW. A particularly popular spot is in the (unnamed) south fork in 4 to 6 feet MLW. Dinghy to the American Legion dock, or to Mermaids Cove Marina and ask to tie up. One mile west is a large mall with a supermarket, restaurants, specialty shops and a West Marine (51 Chambersbridge Rd., 732-864-8140).

Point Pleasant Area–NJ ICW Mile 6

Clustered around the southern end of the Point Pleasant Canal are some of the boatyards that made New Jersey famous as a boatbuilding center. Many of these yards have consolidated and, while still building custom boats, now offer transient slips and complete marina services.

The lovely seaside area of Bay Head marks the northern entrance to (or exit from) Barnegat Bay. Often called "A Country Village by the Sea," this has been a popular vacation spot since Victorian times and still treasures its culture and heritage. It is a great place to take a break and explore for a few days. (Note that the Bay Head beaches, while not considered private can be difficult to access.) Visit bayhead.org for details.

NAVIGATION: Use NOAA Chart 12324. When transiting this area through Bay Head to the Point Pleasant Canal be aware that the NJ ICW runs through a complex of

Hoffman's Marina West

Brielle

Hoffman's Marina

Manasquan

Manasquan River

Atlantic Ocean

marinas and boatyards with rigid speed regulations and the entire area is actively policed. Note that shoaling has been reported in this area so proceed with caution.

On the west side of Barnegat Bay the long, narrow Wardells Neck separates the Metedeconk River and Beaverdam Creek. The river and the creek are entered from the northwest side of Herring Island. Only boats drawing less than 4 feet should attempt to enter from the southwest side of Herring Island as depths are reported as between 2 and 3 feet MLW.

Dockage: This boating area is extremely popular, as evidenced by the number of yacht clubs and marinas with a concentration at Bay Head and along Beaverdam Creek. On the north side of Wardells Neck (western shore of bay) is Arnold's Yacht Basin with on-site boat mechanics, a fiberglass shop, canvas shop and vinyl craft shop; Forsberg's Boat Works with repairs; and Comstock Yacht Sales & Marina, a yacht brokerage and repair facility.

On the south end of the Point Pleasant Canal are Johnson Brothers Boat Works and Carver Boat Works, LLC. These are full-service boat yards with no transient slips.

Anchorage: Bay Head Harbor has at least 4-foot MLW depths with excellent holding in mud and sand. It is somewhat exposed from the south and boat wakes along the NJ ICW. Anchor near Dale Yacht Basin East for best depths (6 feet MLW).

Point Pleasant Canal–NJ ICW Mile 4.5 to Mile 2.5

NAVIGATION: Use NOAA Chart 12324. The only way out of the bay on the northeast end is to transit the Point Pleasant Canal to the Manasquan Inlet via the Manasquan River. The 2-mile-long canal connects Bay Head with the Manasquan River. Two bridges cross the canal: the **SR 632 (Bridge Ave.) Bridge** with a closed vertical clearance of 30 feet (65 feet when open) and the **Point Pleasant Bridge**, which has a 31-foot closed vertical clearance (66-foot open vertical clearance). Both bridges open on signal.

Before entering the canal, it is possible to make detailed checks with the bridgetender at the **Point Pleasant (Rte. 88) Bridge** regarding the condition of the current. (Contact the tender on VHF Channel 13 and be sure to refer to this specific bridge.) If you are without adequate power, the trip can be challenging because of the great difference between the 4-foot tidal range at Manasquan Inlet and that of less than 1

foot at the Barnegat Bay end of the canal. Try to plan your transit through the canal to coincide with slack water. Underpowered sailboats (those able to make no more than 4 or 5 knots at full throttle) should limit themselves to an hour on either side of slack water.

The entire canal is a "No Wake" zone. Take extra care on the weekends and holidays when canal traffic is heaviest. The channel between the Point Pleasant Canal and flashing red "6" is extremely narrow with shoaling on both sides. Make sure that the current does not sweep you out of the channel. If you must go through with the current during heavy traffic times be aware that not all of the vessels going through the canal will be able to give way in the case of problems.

⚠ There is a swift current through the Point Pleasant Canal approaching 4 knots on the ebb and flood. If you require the bridges to open, make arrangements with the bridgetender before you enter the canal. The canal is very narrow and there is little room to maneuver if the bridge is not open when you arrive. Do not follow another boat too closely, particularly around the bridges, and allow adequate time for the bridges to open completely before moving through the opening. Predicted slack water in Point Pleasant Canal is 2 to 3 hours after high or low tides in the Atlantic Ocean, and this time can vary greatly, depending on the direction, strength and duration of the wind. The safest time to make the passage is at slack high water, when current is at a minimum. (Slack low water averages 0.2 knot faster.) See up-to-date tide tables at tidesandcurrents.noaa.gov.

■ MANASQUAN RIVER TO SHARK RIVER INLET

West on the Manasquan River– NJ ICW Mile 2.5

NAVIGATION: Use NOAA Chart 12324. After passing through the Point Pleasant Canal, you can turn west into the Manasquan River or east towards the inlet. (There is no inside route north from here.) Severe shoaling lines both sides of the Manasquan River so make certain to stay within the channel. You will find dockage all along the Manasquan River including at several good restaurants along the river. To access marine facilities on the west end of the river you must be able to negotiate the fixed **NJ 70 Bridge** with 25-foot vertical clearance.

Dockage: On the west end of the river south of the bridge is Safe Harbor Crystal Point in a setting of riverfront mansions and magnificent sunrises and sunsets and amenities include an automated 24/7 fuel dock. Safe Harbor Manasquan River is north of the bridge with full amenities (including a pool). Call ahead for slip availability. River Rock Restaurant & Marina Bar has slips to 26 feet and MarineMax Brick is a yacht brokerage and service facility (with slips to 70 feet).

Anchorage: Manasquan anchorages are severely limited because space is lacking and the heavy boat traffic creates considerable wake. On the west end of the river there's space to anchor beyond the bridge and across from the marinas. Holding is fair in mud with 4 to 8 feet MLW.

To Manasquan Inlet

The splendid beach at Point Pleasant is privately owned but you can pay a fee to access it. The mile-long boardwalk at Point Pleasant–with the usual arcades, rides, and bars–terminates at the mouth of Manasquan Inlet. Manasquan Inlet is said to be one of the widest and safest inlets on the New Jersey coast due to well-maintained jetties and depths.

The towns of Point Pleasant and Brielle face each other across the Manasquan River at Mile 0 on the NJ ICW and the resort towns of Point Pleasant Beach and Manasquan face each other at the Manasquan Inlet. The waters in this area form one of the busiest ports on the NJ ICW with hundreds of berths, restaurants, chandleries, marinas, boat builders, repair yards and boat brokerages. Droves of charter captains are ready to take you deep-sea fishing and reservations are a must, especially on summer weekends.

 Caution: Boat traffic can be extremely congested on summer weekends in both the inlet and the river.

NAVIGATION: Use NOAA Chart 12324. The opening under the bridge is 47 feet wide and the current can be challenging at times. Traffic can be extremely heavy, particularly on weekends after the **Brielle Railroad Bridge** has been closed for a while. Choose your time carefully through the railroad bridge. When approaching the **NJ 35 Bridge**, use enough power to control your boat as the current tries to push you towards the sides

of the opening. The wind going against the tide dictates extreme caution.

The NJ 35 Bascule Bridge (30-foot closed vertical clearance) across the Manasquan River at Mile 1.1. The draw will open on signal, except (1) from 8:00 a.m. to 10:00 p.m. between May 15 and September 30 on Saturdays, Sundays and federal holidays, when the draw need only open 15 minutes before the hour and 15 minutes after the hour; and (2) from 4:00 p.m. to 7:00 p.m. on Mondays through Thursdays and from 12:00 p.m. to 7:00 p.m. on Fridays (except federal holidays), when the draw need only open 15 minutes before the hour and 15 minutes after the hour. Year-round from 11:00 p.m. to 8:00 a.m. the draw need only open if at least a 4-hour notice is given.

The Brielle Railroad Bridge follows at Mile 0.9 with 3-foot closed vertical clearance. When in the open position the draw is at a 45-degree angle so favor the north side of the channel. Proceed carefully; should the railroad bridge close, you do not want to become caught in the current between it and the NJ 35 Bridge.

Channel depths in the Manasquan Inlet vary greatly. If you must enter the inlet under adverse conditions and your boat is fast, synchronize your speed with the speed of the seas and ride through on the back of a wave, keeping well aft of the crest. In a slow boat, throttle way down so that the waves will pass under your boat. If you are cruising in a moderate-sized sailboat and the wind is against the tide, turning around after committing to either enter or exit the inlet will probably not be an option. Be prepared for a bit of discomfort and very slow progress if you attempt to exit the inlet in a westerly wind against an incoming tide.

Slow down in the inlet. An incredible amount of commercial, charter and recreational boat traffic goes in and out of Manasquan Inlet. Exercise caution, be sure to control your speed and wake and remember that you are responsible for any damage caused by your wake. The Coast Guard monitors inlet traffic closely and enforces safe boating practices

Dockage: At the east end of the river are Clark's Landing Ma rina and Garden State Yacht Sales & Marina. Both are yacht brokerages and Clarks' has slips to 65 feet and may be able to accommodate you. The well-regarded Captain Bill's Landing offers transient slips with easy in and out as well as all fuels. It is convenient to restaurants and the boardwalk.

Across the river is Brielle, where marine provisions and groceries are just a short car ride from the

WG

Shark River, NJ

SHARK RIVER		Largest Vessel Accomodated	VHF Channel Monitored / Working	Approach / Dockside Depth (reported)	Transient Slips / Total Slips	Floating Docks	Gas / Diesel	Groceries, Ice, Marine Supplies, Snacks	Repairs: Hull, Engine, Propeller	Lift (tonnage), Crane, Rail	Min / Max Amps	Courtesy Car, Laundry, Pool, Showers	Pump-Out Station	Nearby: Grocery Store, Motel, Restaurant
				Dockage				**Supplies**			**Services**			
1. Seaport Inlet Marina WIFI	(732) 681-3303	40	/	1/100	14.0/6.0	F	D	GIMS	HEP	L10	30	S		G
2. Total Marine at Seaview Inc.	(732) 775-7842	45	65/	/155	12.0/5.0	F	GD	IM	HP		30	S	P	GMR
3. Belmar Marina WIFI	(732) 681-2266	100	16/9	70/294	7.0/7.0	F	GD	I			30/100	LS	P	MR
4. Shark River Municipal Marina WIFI	(732) 775-7400	40	/16	12/155	6.0/6.0	F				L15	30/50	LS		GMR
5. Bry's Marine LLC	(732) 775-7364	40	/	1/20	4.0/8.0	F		IM	HEP	L25	30			GMR
6. Shark River Yacht Club Inc.	(732) 502-0094	65	/	6/160	6.0/6.0	F		IMS	HEP	L35	30/50	LS	P	GMR

⌨ Internet Access   WIFI Wireless Internet Access   onSpot Dockside WiFi Facility

See WaterwayGuide.com for current rates, fuel prices, website addresses, and other up-to-the-minute information. (Information in the table is provided by the facilities.)

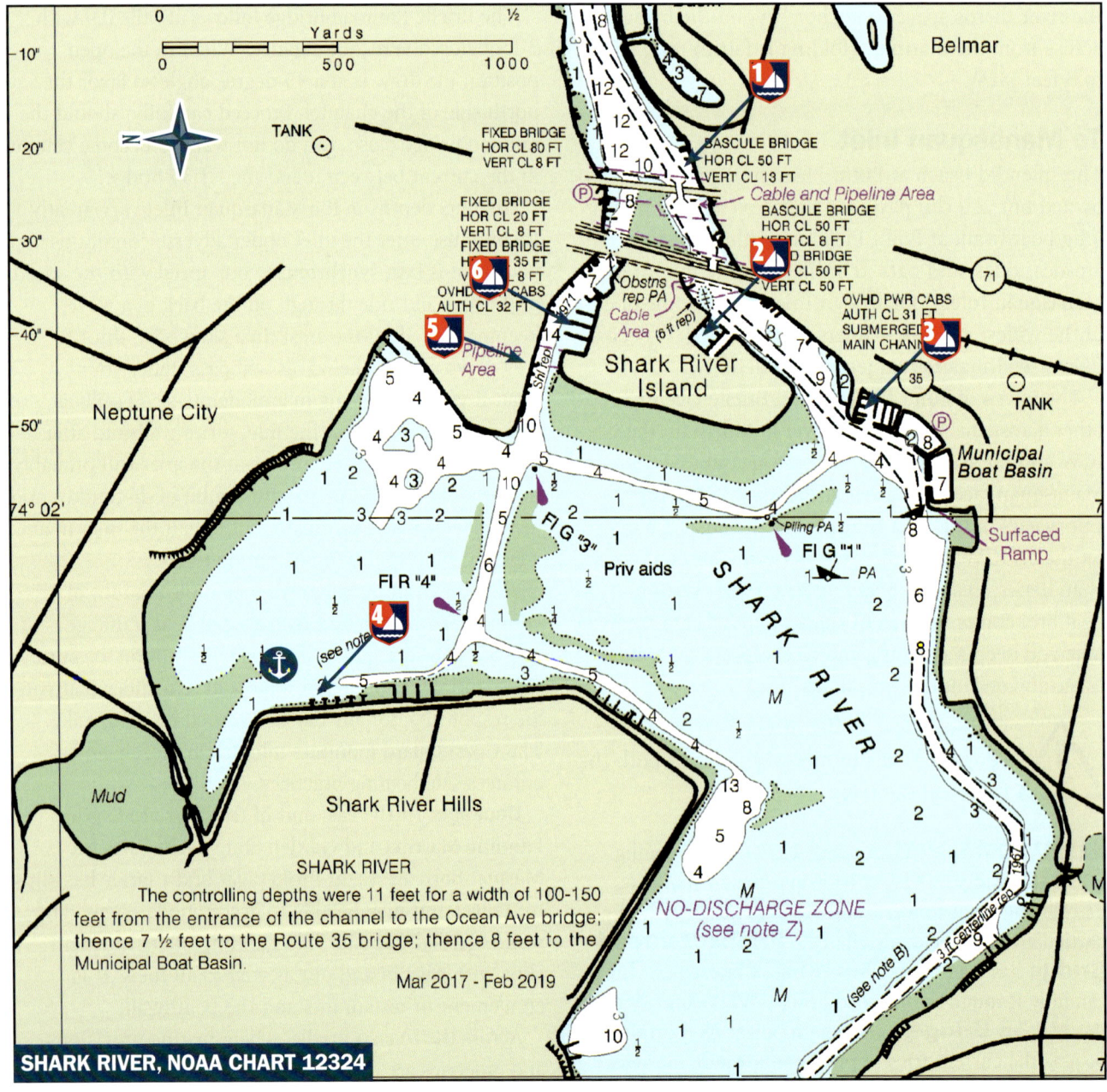

SHARK RIVER, NOAA CHART 12324

Shark River Inlet

waterfront. Hoffman's Marina and Hoffman's Marina West have transient slips to 120 feet with resort amenities including an infinity pool, private showers, a laundry room and access to several on-site restaurant. The Brielle Yacht Club Marina & Sandbar Restaurant has slips and sells all fuel and is home to South Jersey Yacht Sales. It is a short walk to shopping in Brielle from any of these marinas.

Anchorage: Some boaters anchor in the Glimmer Glass up Crabtown Creek for all-around protection in and good holding in 5-to 7-foot MLW depths. The historic **Glimmer Glass (Brielle Rd.) Bridge** (9-foot vertical clearance) opens on signal, Memorial to Labor Day on the hour and half-hour from 7:00 a.m. to 8:00 p.m.

Shark River Inlet

After exiting the Manasquan Inlet, Shark River Inlet is just 5 miles north and there is no inside route. Don't rely on the landmarks named on the chart for fixing your position on the trip north or south. Multi-story buildings, which obscure the charted landmarks, are all along the Jersey shore. Just north of Manasquan Inlet the charted danger area is an onshore military

firing range. Red flags on the beach mean that firing is underway, or scheduled shortly, and that you should stay outside the privately maintained charted buoys.

NAVIGATION: Use NOAA Chart 12324. You can count on the Shark River Inlet as a storm haven along the stretch of coast between Manasquan and Sandy Hook. It has 12-foot MLW depths and is considered safe for even those not familiar with the area as well as a worthwhile cruising stop. You will find ample accommodations, a busy charter fleet and fine beaches. **The Shark River Inlet (Ocean Ave.) Bridge** (15-foot closed vertical clearance) crosses Shark River Inlet near its opening to the ocean. The bridge opens on request.

⚠️ On an incoming tide do not enter the channel between the breakwaters until you are sure the bridge is going to open! Maneuvering room is very limited and a strong flood tide can sweep you down into it quickly.

Local fishing party boats know to wait outside in all conditions until the bridge opens. Even in benign conditions do not commit to passage until the span rises. Bridgetenders, aware of the hazard, are quick to open but heavy auto traffic sometimes causes delays, especially on summer weekends.

Charted depth at the main docks in the Municipal Boat Basin is 6 feet MLW. Dredging operations took place in the channel running south of Shark River Island in the past few years.

Three bridges cross the main (south) channel of the Shark River: the **Main Street (NJ 71) Bridg**e (use south channel with 13-foot closed vertical clearance), the **Shark River Railroad Bridge** (8-foot closed vertical clearance) and the NJ 35 Bridge (50-foot fixed vertical clearance). The two bascule bridges operate as one unit and open on signal, except from May 15 through September 30 from 4:00 p.m. to 7:00 p.m. Monday through Friday and from 9:00 a.m. to 9:00 p.m. Saturdays, Sundays and holidays, when the draw need only open on the hour and half hour if a vessel is waiting to pass.

Dockage: Seaport Inlet Marina is on the south side of Shark Island before the first bascule bridge with slips, dry and wet storage and an on-site marine retail store.

Total Marine at Seaview Inc. is a boat brokerage that sells all fuels. Belmar (Manutti Municipal) is less than 0.5 mile from the ocean with concrete floating docks with ample transient space to 100 feet, full security and marine services. The Shark River Municipal Marina on the northwest side of the Shark River is at the Neptune township and has transient slips to 40 feet on floating docks.

On the north side of Shark River Island is Bry's Marine LLC (a yacht brokerage with parts and services) and across the channel on the island is the full-service Shark River Yacht Club with slips and repairs. Fine dining, café-style restaurants and water taxi service are all available in the marina area.

Anchorage: It is possible to anchor in the charted 6-foot area east of the Shark River Municipal Marina. Here you will find at least 6 feet MLW with good holding and protection from all but southerly winds.

■ NEXT STOP

Our next chapter details the Twin Rivers and Sandy Hook Bay. The charming and unpretentious villages of Atlantic Highlands and Highlands are two distinct boroughs in Monmouth County, NJ. They are great stops for cruisers transiting the coast and looking for a safe harbor to spend a night, a few days or even longer.

Manasquan Inlet

Sandy Hook, Raritan Bay & Lower Bay

■ SANDY HOOK

Sandy Hook opens up to an enclosed, single body of water that comprises three separately charted bays: Sandy Hook Bay to the southeast, Raritan Bay to the west and Lower Bay to the north, which is the largest of the three and referred to as Lower New York Harbor.

NAVIGATION: Use NOAA Chart 12324. The Atlantic Ocean is the only navigable route to Sandy Hook, which is 17 miles north of the Shark River Inlet (should you choose the skip the Twin Rivers). There is no inside route. Except in heavy weather, you can stay fairly close to shore (keeping far enough off to clear rocks along the beach).

⚠️ As you approach Sandy Hook head offshore to Sandy Hook Channel; do not go through False Hook Channel near shore. Shoaling has been reported in False Hook Channel. The current close to the hook is quite strong at maximum flood and ebb: east on the ebb and west on the flood.

The preferred passage to follow is the main Sandy Hook Channel, which is well offshore. The Ambrose Light Tower is eastward and clearly visible. Its flashing strobe light is so intense that it is often mistaken for lightning.

Seas break on the long bar eastward from the point on Sandy Hook (note the 5-foot-MLW lump). This bar sets up the famed "Sandy Hook rip," in which the turbulent, tide-tumbled waters produce some of the best

fishing (striped bass and bluefish) found anywhere on the Atlantic coast.

Inside of Sandy Hook and south beyond the fixed-span **Highlands Bridge** (65-foot vertical clearance over the Shrewsbury River), the Navesink and Shrewsbury Rivers lace the northeastern corner of New Jersey with well-protected cruising waters. This chapter will present highlights of these lovely cruising grounds that are complete with excellent beaches, deep sea fishing opportunities and convenient dockage near ferry transportation into New York City.

The current runs swiftly here so watch out for turbulence under the bridge at full current. The rivers pass high, green banks, marshy islands and attractive residential areas. Yacht clubs, marinas and boatyards, waterfront restaurants with docks, scenic anchorages and old, established communities line the shores. In many places the Atlantic Ocean is only a short walk away across the barrier strip.

Sandy Hook Bay

Sandy Hook, NJ, a 9-mile, 1,665-acre barrier peninsula, is part of the National Gateway Recreation Area that includes ocean and bay beaches, excellent surf fishing, miles of bike and nature trails, a spectacular holly forest, Fort Hancock (a former military base) and Sandy Hook Lighthouse, the oldest working lighthouse in the country, which is now a National Historic Landmark. The active Sandy Hook Coast Guard complex dominates the narrow peninsula inside the northern tip of the hook. From there the sandy dunes stretch several miles south before rejoining the mainland in Sea Bright, NJ.

If you have access to a car or bike, be sure to stop at the Sandy Hook Visitors Center (732-872-5970) at the former Spermaceti Cove Lifesaving Station near the entrance to Sandy Hook State Park (about 3.5 miles south-southeast of Sandy Hook Point Light). They have maps and brochures for a self-guided tour. Sandy Hook is a protected wildlife preserve and many areas of the dunes are closed to foot traffic to protect several species of birds. When entering Sandy Hook by car there is a per-vehicle daily charge from Memorial Day to Labor Day. Note that the parking lots on Sandy Hook fill up early on weekends and the gates are then closed.

NAVIGATION: Use NOAA Chart 12327. Sandy Hook Bay is easily approached by well-buoyed thoroughfares–Sandy Hook Channel from the Atlantic Ocean, Chapel Hill Channel from New York Harbor and Raritan Bay East Reach from Raritan Bay–but multiple navigational aids on the intersecting channels and side channels can be confusing, especially in poor light.

If approaching Sandy Hook from the Atlantic Ocean, follow the Sandy Hook Channel around the hook into Sandy Hook Bay or, if continuing north into New York Harbor, deviate from the Sandy Hook Channel through the Swash Channel and then join the Chapel Hill Channel at red and green nun buoy "CH." This route allows smaller vessels to avoid traveling in the Ambrose Channel, which usually has a significant amount of large ship traffic.

⚠️ The tip of Sandy Hook is in an area that was originally part of the old False Hook Channel. Depths can go from 40 feet MLW to dry sand in a manner of 20 yards.

The Swash Channel is simple to navigate by following a course from Sandy Hook Channel (starting at the lighted front and back range markers for the eastbound channel) and then leaving the 54-foot-high flashing white "2" Romer Shoal Horn to starboard. If heading into Sandy Hook Bay, note that inside the tip of the "hook" green can buoys mark the shallows near shore; otherwise, depths of 15 to 20 feet MLW prevail on the route south to Atlantic Highlands. Keep a sharp lookout for the fish weirs (stakes) in this area, particularly when visibility is poor. They are rarely lighted and hard to see, even in daylight.

A vigorously enforced security zone exists in the vicinity of Naval Weapons Station Earle, about 1.25 nm southwest of Sandy Hook Point Light in Sandy Hook Bay. Marine Police patrol the area around Naval Weapons Station Earle and you will be stopped if you venture within the security area that is clearly marked by white buoys. The pier is used for loading and off-loading explosives. Pleasure boaters should stay well clear of this and other military installations. Hefty fines are given for the first offense. Any boater who finds it impossible to stay clear should immediately contact the U.S. Coast Guard by VHF radio or some other means.

Dockage: Leonardo has an almost landlocked harbor that, while extremely protected, can get hot in summer. A 5-foot-deep MLW channel leads to a basin with 7-foot MLW depths. The Leonardo State Marina has some slips for transients (to 50 feet) and sells all fuels. Maneuvering room is very tight here and no anchoring space is available. The marina reports 3-foot

Highlands

MLW approach depths so a call ahead concerning depths and other conditions would be warranted.

Anchorage: About 2 nm south inside the Sandy Hook northern tip, is the pretty and always-popular anchorage at Horseshoe Cove, where you will find deep water (10 feet MLW) fairly close to shore. This area is more shoal than charts indicate so use caution. Unfortunately, severe winter storms over the past decade have also submerged the once-visible sand spit that protected the cove and you will be subject to passing wakes from ferries; nevertheless, Horseshoe Cove remains a desirable anchorage. Ashore, drums for garbage and recyclables are near the footbridge at the north end of Horseshoe Cove. You can dinghy ashore and explore ruins of World War II bunkers north of the cove, or walk the boardwalk into the marshes to view the protected species of birds. You can walk to the beach on the island's eastern shore from here as well.

In settled weather or during an east wind, there is decent anchorage to the north off the charted Coast Guard station behind Sandy Hook with at least 7-foot MLW depths at low tide. This anchorage offers excellent holding but is exposed northwest through south. Don't forget that you must stay at least 500 feet away from all Coast Guard vessels. There are lots of wakes here from all types of vessels.

Pump-out service in Sandy Hook Bay or Raritan Bay is available by calling the Baykeeper Boat, *Head Mistress,* at 732-888-9870 or by hailing her on VHF Channel 9.

Atlantic Highlands & Highlands

South of Sandy Hook and east of Leonardo, the very hospitable Atlantic Highlands harbor is an excellent storm haven and a great place to stop for a couple of days. Atlantic Highlands offers a great alternative to New York City dockage with the SeaStreak high-speed ferry running several times daily to Manhattan and back from the Atlantic Highlands harbor. (See the full schedule at www.seastreak.com.) You can stay here and still enjoy the sights of New York City, and if you must wait for better weather before continuing north, east, or south, this is a perfect port. During severe storms from the north, however, incoming waves build to considerable heights over the long fetch across the bay from the NY side. Some waves even make their way over the town's substantial breakwater.

NAVIGATION: Use NOAA Chart 12327. The protected harbor of Atlantic Highlands is situated 3 miles south of green can buoy "1," which marks the western end of Sandy Hook Point. A 33-foot-high flashing white light at the eastern end marks the 0.75-mile-long breakwater

GOIN' ASHORE

ATLANTIC HIGHLANDS, NJ

The charming and unpretentious village of Atlantic Highlands is a great stop for cruisers transiting the coast and looking for a safe harbor to spend a night, a few days or even longer. The shoreside town has everything one might want or need in the way of dockage, anchorage, fuel, provisions, transportation and restaurants within a short walk from the harbor.

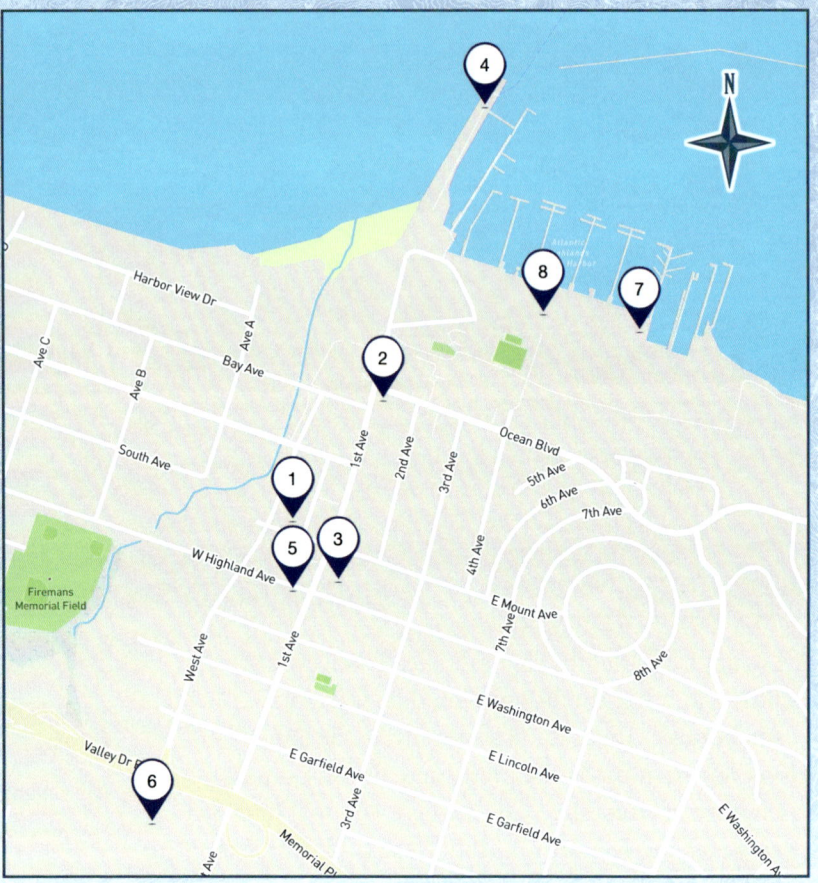

SERVICES

1. **Atlantic Highlands Post Office**
   25 Railroad Ave. (732-291-0740)
2. **Atlantic Laundromat**
   28 First Ave. (732-291-8707)
3. **Monmouth County Library**
   100 First Ave. (732-291-1444)

ATTRACTIONS

4. **SeaStreak Ferry**
   2 First Ave. (800-262-8743)

SHOPPING

5. **Jaspan Brothers Hardware**
   Chain hardware store at 117 First Ave. (732-291-1500).
6. **Super Foodtown**
   Supermarket at 3 Bayshore Plaza (732-291-4079).

MARINAS

7. **Atlantic Highlands Municipal Marina**
   2 Simon Lake Dr.
   (732-291-1670)
8. **Atlantic Highlands Yacht Club**
   6 Simon Lake Dr.
   (732-291-1118)

GOIN' ASHORE

HIGHLANDS, NJ

The side-by-side villages of Atlantic Highlands and Highlands are two distinct boroughs in Monmouth County. Both are equally attractive to cruisers and offer many amenities from services to attractions and top-notch marine facilities. Highlands is the first stop on the New Jersey Shore and cruisers come to experience the area's long tradition of maritime heritage, as illustrated by the lighthouses and many coastal heritage trails. Plan to spend several days exploring this waterfront retreat with sweeping views of the Atlantic Ocean and New York City skyline.

SERVICES

1. Highlands Post Office
170 Bay Ave. (732-872-0622)

ATTRACTIONS

2. SeaStreak Ferry
326 Shore Dr. (800-262-8743)

3. Twin Lights State Historic Site
Self-guided and guided tours are available of the former lighthouse featuring two beacons with tower climbs, exhibits and panoramic ocean and harbor views. Operated by the Twin Lights Historical Society at 2 Lighthouse Rd. (732-872-1814).

SHOPPING

4. Lusty Lobster
Carries fresh and frozen seafood, fillets and steaks, and soups and salads at 88 Bay Ave. (732-291-1548).

MARINAS

5. Bahrs Landing Marina
2 Bay Ave. (732-872-1245)

6. Bakers Marina on the Bay
1 Marina Bay Ct. (732-872-9300)

7. Captain's Cove Marina
2 Washington Ave. (732-872-1479)

8. Gateway Marina
34 Bay Ave. (732-291-4440)

9. Sandy Hook Bay Marina
1 Willow St. (732-872-1511)

Sandy Hook Bay, NJ

		Largest Vessel Accommodated	VHF Channel Monitored / Working	Transient Slips / Total Slips	Approach / Dockside Depth (reported)	Floating Docks	Gas / Diesel	Groceries, Ice, Marine Supplies, Snacks	Repairs: Hull, Engine, Propeller	Lift (tonnage), Crane, Rail	Min / Max Amps	Courtesy Car, Laundry, Pool, Showers	Pump-Out Station	Nearby: Grocery Store, Motel, Restaurant
LEONARDO				**Dockage**			**Supplies**				**Services**			
1. Leonardo State Marina	(732) 291-1333	50	16/	4/176	3.0/6.0	F	GD	GIMS			30	S	P	G
ATLANTIC HIGHLANDS														
2. Atlantic Highlands Yacht Club	(732) 291-1118	130	9/	/	10.0/10.0	F	GD	GIS			30/50	LS	P	GMR
3. Atlantic Highlands Municipal Harbor ☐ WiFi	(732) 291-1670	140	9/	15/480	10.0/6.0	F	GD	IS		L50	30/50	S	P	GR
HIGHLANDS														
4. Sandy Hook Bay Marina ☐	(732) 872-1511	65	7/7	15/130	8.0/6.0	F		IS			30/100	LPS		R
5. Captain's Cove Marina	(732) 290-1000	38	13/	2/92	15.0/6.0	F		GIS			30	S		GR
6. Bakers Marina on the Bay ☐ WiFi	(732) 872-9300	50	/	6/150	12.0/10.0	F		IS	HEP	L35	30	S		GR
7. Gateway Marina	(732) 291-4440	40	/10	/35	10.0/8.0	F	GD	GIMS	HEP	L15	30	S		GR
8. Bahrs Landing Marina WiFi	(732) 291-9554	130	9/	/30	18.0/12.0	F	GD	IS			50			GMR

☐ Internet Access WiFi Wireless Internet Access onSpot Dockside WiFi Facility

See WaterwayGuide.com for current rates, fuel prices, website addresses, and other up-to-the-minute information. (Information in the table is provided by the facilities.)

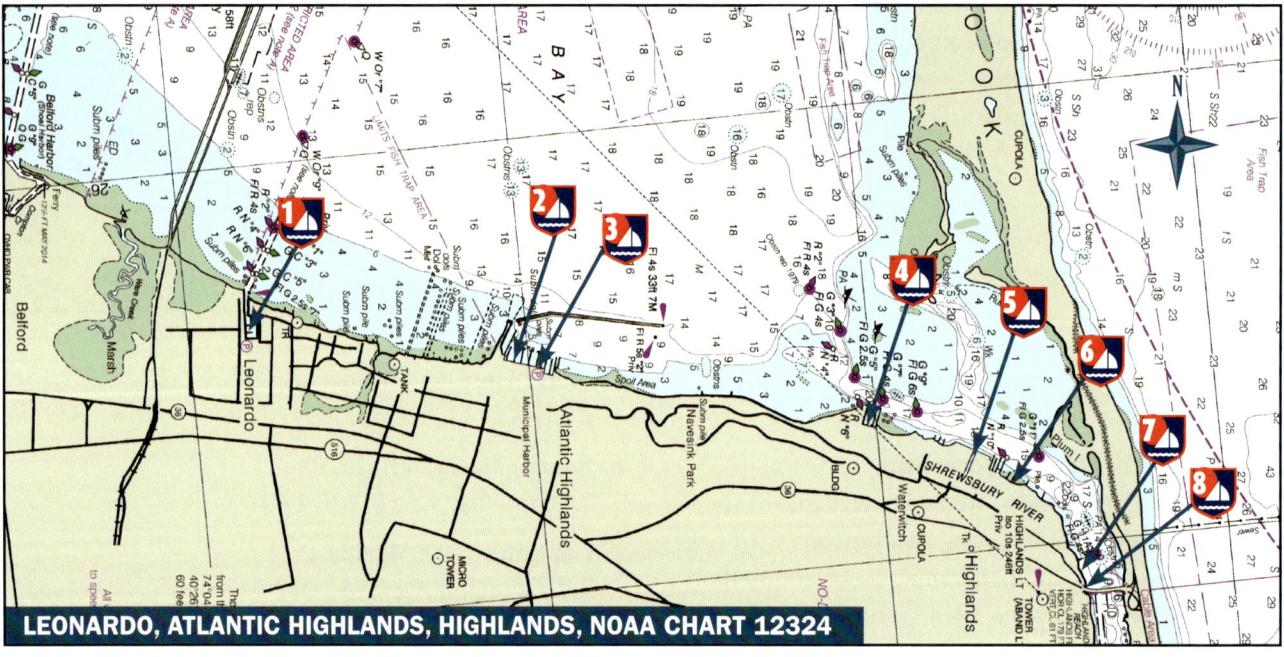

LEONARDO, ATLANTIC HIGHLANDS, HIGHLANDS, NOAA CHART 12324

A commuter boat service (SeaStreak) operates from Connors Ferry Landing in Highlands, NJ, and also from Pier One at the west end of the Atlantic Highlands harbor to New York City. Both boats go to The Battery Maritime building and to East 35th St. in Manhattan, which is close to midtown shopping. During the week several boats cruise to New York City in the morning and offer several return trips in the afternoon and evening until 6:30 p.m. (weekdays) and 8:45 p.m. (weekends). The run takes about 1 hour and is a great way to go into New York City for the day. Daily schedules are available online at www.seastreak.com.

across Atlantic Highlands harbor. Both the light and the eastern end of the breakwater are sometimes difficult to spot from a distance so set a waypoint or compass course for an efficient passage across Sandy Hook Bay. Commercial vessels also regularly enter the harbor at the western end of the breakwater but this is not recommended without local knowledge.

Dockage/Moorings: Atlantic Highlands Municipal Harbor has extensive facilities, diesel and gasoline, transient docks, services, tennis courts and a recreation area for children. Daily moorings and launch services are available May through October. (Note that power boats are not permitted on the moorings.) The Atlantic

Highlands Yacht Club (with limited courtesy dockage for members of reciprocal yacht clubs) is located here.

There are several more marine facilities to the south in Highlands. Sandy Hook Bay Marina offers wave-protected slips on floating docks with full-length finger piers and resort amenities. Bakers Marina on the Bay has transient dockage up to 110 feet and offers repairs and services. Gateway Marina has limited transient space for vessels to 40 feet and offers some repairs. Bahrs Landing Marina is a dock and dine with floating transient dockage to 130 feet.

Anchorage: There is usually plenty of anchorage room just inside the eastern end of the Atlantic Highlands breakwater and outside the mooring field, or on the south side of the eastern end of the mooring field along the shore. Depths are 8 to 10 feet MLW but 4 to 5 feet MLW close to shore. Holding is good in mud but the breakwater protects the harbor from all except east-northeast to east winds. It is quite a distance to get to shoreside facilities but there are ample dinghy landings. A dock is located immediately to the east of the harbormaster's office and floats are at the head of each aisle past the fuel dock.

■ SIDE TRIP: THE TWIN RIVERS

Navigating the Twin Rivers

NAVIGATION: Use NOAA Charts 12327 and 12324. Between Atlantic Highlands and Sandy Hook at the town of Highlands pick up flashing red buoy "2" marking the shared entrance of the Navesink and Shrewsbury Rivers (also known as the Twin Rivers), which is charted as the Shrewsbury River. Because the low intensity light can be lost among shore lights at night, a daylight approach is strongly recommended. Obtain the latest information on depths before heading in since navigation on ebb tides can be tricky.

Many marinas line this 1-mile-plus stretch to the mouth of the Navesink River, which bears off westward to the town of Red Bank, NJ. Whether you turn into the Navesink River or stay straight on the Shrewsbury River be careful of three (charted) orange-striped white can buoys that mark a submerged rock wall extending northeasterly from the south side of the mouth of the Navesink River. Stick to the channel even if you see a local boat head over the line.

The Twin Lights

The Twin Lights, situated 200 feet above sea level atop the Navesink Highlands, overlook the Shrewsbury River, Sandy Hook, Raritan Bay, the New York skyline and the Atlantic Ocean. The Two Lights, a pair of beacons built in 1862 and dedicated by President Lincoln, are the latest in a long line of lighthouses built on this promontory, which is one of the highest points of land on the Atlantic coast. The first light on this spot was erected by New York merchants in 1765, and a light has shone here continuously ever since.

Today a state-maintained occulting white light shines from the north tower during the boating season. The Twin Lights now house a state-run nautical museum displaying marine artifacts and the original building of the old Life Saving Service. The museum is a short car ride from Atlantic Highlands Harbor. Contact the museum at 732-872-1814.

Shrewsbury River, Navesink River, NJ

		Largest Vessel Accommodated	VHF Channel Monitored / Working	Transient Slips / Total Slips	Approach / Dockside Depth (reported)	Floating Docks	Gas / Diesel	Groceries, Ice, Marine Supplies, Snacks	Repairs: Hull, Engine, Propeller	Lift (tonnage), Crane, Rail	Min / Max Amps	Courtesy Car, Laundry, Pool, Showers	Pump-Out Station	Nearby: Grocery Store, Motel, Restaurant
NAVESINK RIVER AREA				**Dockage**				**Supplies**			**Services**			
1. Oceanic Marina	(732) 842-1194	50	/	/85	6.0/5.0	F		GIMS	HEP	L20	30	S	P	GR
2. Shrewsbury River Yacht Club-PRIVATE	(732) 747-9873	50	9/	2/60	8.0/6.0	F		IMS			30	S		GMR
3. Fair Haven Yacht Works 🖥 WiFi	(732) 747-3010	55	9/9	2/82	6.0/6.0	F		IM	HEP	L15,C	30/50	S	P	GMR
4. Irwin Marine #1 🖥 WiFi	(732) 741-0003	100	/	5/154	8.0/6.0	F		IM	HEP	L25	30/50	PS	P	GMR
5. Irwin Marine #2 WiFi	(732) 741-0003	50	/	4/44	8.0/6.0	F		IM	HEP	L25	30/50	PS		GMR
6. Molly Pitcher Inn/Marina 🖥 WiFi	(732) 747-2500	65	9/10	12/70	6.0/6.0	F		I			30/50	PS	P	GMR
7. Oyster Point Hotel/Marina WiFi	(732) 747-2500	60	9/10	4/34	5.0/4.0	F		I			30	S	P	GMR
SEA BRIGHT														
8. Carriage House Marina 🖥 WiFi	(732) 741-8113	50	/	6/37	10.0/10.0			GIM	HEP	L25,C	30	S	P	GMR
9. Cove Sail Marina	(732) 842-5319	50	/	6/46	10.0/13.0			IS	HEP	L	30	S	P	GMR
10. Surfside Marina	(732) 842-0844	60	/	1/52	6.0/4.0	F		M	EP	L	30	S		GMR
11. Navesink Marina 🖥 WiFi	(732) 842-3700	80	16/72	5/115	15.0/8.0	F		I	HEP	L35	30/50	LS	P	GMR
MONMOUTH BEACH														
12. Atlantis Yacht Club - PRIVATE 🖥 WiFi	(732) 222-9693	70	69/	4/55	6.0/6.0			I			30/50	LPS	P	GMR
13. Channel Club Marina WiFi	(732) 222-7717	100	9/	10/144	8.0/6.0	F	GD	IMS	HEP	L60	30/50	CPS	P	GR
LONG BRANCH														
14. Patten Point Yacht Club - PRIVATE WiFi	(732) 229-2882	50	/	3/63	4.0/3.5	F		I			15/50	PS	P	GMR
15. Kelly's Landing Marina	(732) 544-1243	55	/	/86	4.0/4.0	F					30	S	P	GR
16. Pleasure Bay Yacht Basin	(732) 222-8563	50	/	/70	5.0/4.0			IM	HEP	L35	30	LS		
17. Oceanport Landing	(732) 229-4466	60	/	4/85	6.0/5.0	F		MS	HEP	L30	30/50	S		3R

🖥 Internet Access   WiFi Wireless Internet Access   🔵onSpot Dockside WiFi Facility

See WaterwayGuide.com for current rates, fuel prices, website addresses, and other up-to-the-minute information. (Information in the table is provided by the facilities.)

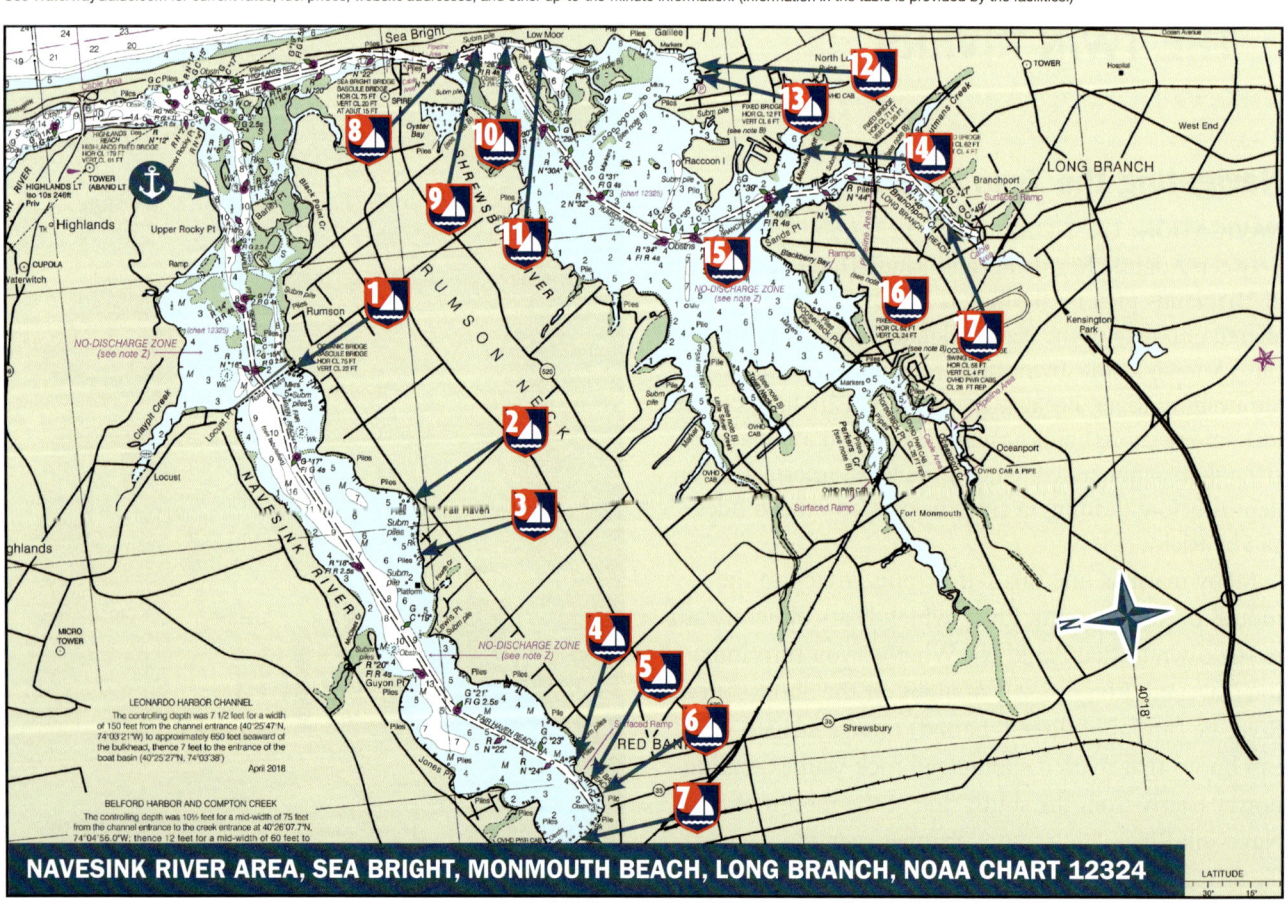

NAVESINK RIVER AREA, SEA BRIGHT, MONMOUTH BEACH, LONG BRANCH, NOAA CHART 12324

Note that the flashing red-and-green buoy "NS" marking the Navesink/Shrewsbury River junction appears to be all red until you are close by. This makes sorting out the proper channels confusing. Once the mid-channel marker is positively identified the approach then becomes straightforward.

Navesink River

The historic, harborside town of Red Bank, NJ, is at the head of navigation on the Navesink River. It is named for the color of its riverbanks. In the 1800s, Red Bank was a thriving shipping center and popular Victorian resort. Even though it is still a commercial center, it retains its rural beauty and Victorian charm.

Red Bank offers many restaurants, full-service marinas, shopping and a main-line train station all within walking distance of any dockage or anchorage. Over the past decade, Red Bank has grown in popularity with gourmet diners and those seeking a lively environment. Visit www.rueevents.com for details on events and attractions.

NAVIGATION: Use NOAA Chart 12324. Transiting the Navesink River can be tricky and local knowledge can be helpful. Pay close attention to depths. There are rocky ledges to the north and shoals on both sides of the narrow channel. The area between the junction of the Twin Rivers and the **Oceanic Bridge** is very tricky. At the opening to the Navesink River pass between red and green junction buoy "NS" and red nun buoy "2" and then continue to follow the curving channel past red nun buoys "4" and "6," watching for shoaling in the vicinity of red nun buoy "6."

About 1 mile upriver from the mouth of the Navesink River, Barley Point Reach passes between sandbars that are bare at low tide. Controlling depth is only 2.5 feet MLW so be sure to stay in mid-channel well past the Oceanic Bridge (22-foot closed vertical clearance). The bridge opens on signal at all times except from the Friday before Memorial Day through Labor Day, on Friday, Saturday, Sunday and holidays, between 9:00 a.m. and 7:00 pm., when the draw need only open on the hour. The draw need not open at any time for a sail boat unless it is operating under auxiliary power or is being towed by a powered vessel.

Dockage: On the south shore of the river just below the Oceanic Bridge at Locust Pt. is Oceanic Marina with slips (to 50 feet), parts and services. The Shrewsbury River Yacht Club is private but has some courtesy dockage for members of reciprocal yacht

clubs. The well-maintained Fair Haven Yacht Works has limited transient space and offers full mechanical, electronic, fiberglass and woodwork repairs.

Closer to Red Bank are the family-owned Irwin Marine #1 and #2, Molly Pitcher Inn/Marina and the Oyster Point Hotel/Marina. The Irwin facilities offer summer dockage, summer and winter land storage and winter storage inside. The historic Molly Pitcher Inn/Marina has ample transient space on their state-of-the-art floating docks for vessels to 65 feet and resort amenities including a fitness center and swimming pool. Oyster Point Hotel/Marina is a full-service hotel facility with transient slips on floating docks. They have 34 overnight or dock and dine slips that can accommodate vessels up to 60 feet. Buses and trains provide quick transportation to New York City and a large hospital is nearby.

Anchorage: A fine anchorage lays 1 mile upriver at Upper Rocky Point. Just past the point, turn to starboard and head back east up the old channel of the Navesink River. Make the turn well to the west of red nun buoy "10" to clear the shoal and then favor the north shore. You can stop in 4- to 10-foot MLW depths under a high bluff. A small island protects you from wakes without stopping the breeze. If you plan to swim trail a line overboard as the current is strong at maximum flood and ebb.

Shrewsbury River

The Shrewsbury River continues southward from its junction with the Navesink River, passing low and marshy shores with the channel cutting through shoal water on either side. Ashore on Rumson Neck (between the two rivers) the countryside still maintains a somewhat rural appearance.

NAVIGATION: Use NOAA Chart 12325. The **Sea Bright Bridge** (20-foot closed vertical clearance) at Mile 4 opens on signal at all times, except from the Friday before Memorial Day through Labor Day on Friday, Saturday, Sunday and holidays, between 9:00 a.m. and 7:00 pm., when the draw need only open on the hour. The draw need not open at any time for a sail boat unless it is operating under auxiliary power or is being towed by a powered vessel.

Strong currents and congestion on the approach channel to the bridge make this an area for caution and requires a firm grip on the helm. The bridge is under development with an undetermined completion date. Use caution transiting this area.

The route forks south of Sea Bright. The main channel branches west along Long Branch Reach and the narrow paths crook through shoals. A well-buoyed side route (which is privately marked) leads southward to Galilee and then swings northwest to rejoin the main channel west of Sedge Island. Numerous lighted markers on the side route to Galilee and west of Long Branch Reach have been replaced with unlit buoys, although the most recent charts do not reflect this change. This triangular side passage was created as a turnaround channel for big steam-powered boats.

The rest of the Shrewsbury River is shallow but there are several creeks to explore. The fixed **Gooseneck (Parkers Creek) Bridge** has a 24-foot vertical clearance, while the **Oceanport Creek Swing Bridge** (4-foot closed vertical clearance) has rush hour closings weekdays from May 15 to September 15. See details on Waterway Explorer (www.waterwayguide.com).

Dockage: North on the Shrewsbury River in the Sea Bright area, just past the sea Bright Bridge, are Surfside Marina (with repairs and services) and the full-service Navesink Marina, which welcomes transients and offers repairs.

In the area of Galilee, the residential shore is sealed from the Atlantic Ocean by a massive sea wall. Numerous marinas and boatyards can be found here including the private Atlantis Yacht Club (which recognizes reciprocity) and the 144-slip Channel Club Marina, which can accommodate vessels to 100 feet, has an on-site heated pool and sells all fuels. This 4-acre property is within walking distance of the beach.

Patten Point Yacht Club on Manahassett Creek at North Long Point is private but may have space on their floating docks for members of reciprocal yacht clubs. They are located before a low fixed bridge with a 6-foot fixed vertical clearance. On Branchport Creek are Kelly's Landing Marina (eastern shore) and Pleasure Bay Yacht Basin (western shore). These facilities report as low as 4-foot MLW dockside depths so call ahead. They offer repairs for vessels to 50 feet.

Boats that can clear the **Hwy. 33 (Pleasure Bay) Bridge** (25-foot fixed vertical clearance) can find dockage (to 60 feet) and repairs at Oceanport Landing (on the western shore). As in days past when Long Branch was the queen resort of the New Jersey shore, swimming in the area remains the great summer attraction here. The commuter railroad to Bay Head is still called the New York and Long Branch, and the once-fashionable Jockey Club, with its gambling casino and race track, is now lush Monmouth Park, where thoroughbreds race (June to August) within 1 mile of the marina.

■ RARITAN BAY

After rounding Sandy Hook, NJ, you can access the Kill Van Kull (an alternate route around Staten Island to New York Harbor) and the Raritan River from Raritan Bay. A number of harbors that sit along the South Shore of Raritan Bay and on the North Shore of Lower Bay (Great Kills Harbor) provide protection for cruising mariners.

To the north through The Narrows lies New York Harbor, where a skipper can head north up the Hudson River, east through the East River to Long Island Sound or west through the Kill Van Kull. East along the south shore of Long Island leads to Rockaway Inlet and the entrance to the inside passage along the South Shore or the outside run up the coast toward Montauk, Long Island.

Keansburg & Keyport Harbor

NAVIGATION: Use NOAA Chart 12327. West of Point Comfort at Keansburg the marina is on Waackaack Creek, which is protected by tidal gates. There are no channel markers on entry and there is shoaling across the entrance. You can also continue west to Keyport Harbor, which is easily entered through a well-marked, deep water channel into Matawan Creek. There is shoaling on both sides of the channel on entry so be sure to stay in the channel.

Dockage/Moorings: The 125-slip Lentze Marina Inc. at Keansburg has transient dockage to 45 feet and has a complete marine service shop. Keyport Yacht Club to the south has courtesy moorings for members of reciprocal yacht clubs. Hans Pedersen and Sons Marina has been located in Keyport since 1934. They offer boat repairs and restoration with a speciality in wooden boats.

Cheesequake (Morgan) Creek

NAVIGATION: Use NOAA Chart 12327. Farther west on Raritan Bay is Cheesequake Creek (also known as Morgan Creek). It is entered through jetties, although the east jetty might be submerged at high water. Flashing green "1" and flashing red "2" mark the entrance. **The Cheesequake Creek Bridge** (25-foot closed vertical clearance) and the adjacent **NJ Transit**

Rail Operations Bridge (3-foot closed vertical clearance) have restricted hours: (1) From April 1 through November 30 from 7:00 a.m. to 8:00 p.m., the draw at the Cheesquake Bridge need only open on the hour. From 8:00 p.m. to 11:00 p.m. the draw will open on signal. From 11:00 p.m. to 7:00 a.m. the draw will only open after at least a two-hour advance notice is given by calling the number posted at the bridge. (2) From December 1 through March 31, the draw opens on signal after at least a two-hour advance notice is given by calling the number posted at the bridge. The railroad bridge opens on signal except (1) from January 1 through March 31 from 6:00 p.m. to 6:00 a.m.; (2) from April 1 through April 30 and November 1 through November 30 from 10:00 p.m. to 6:00 a.m. Monday through Thursday, and midnight Sunday through 6:00 a.m. Monday; and (3) from December 1 through December 31 from 10 p.m. to 6 a.m. At least four-hour notice is required at the times listed above.

When leaving Cheesequake (Morgan) Creek make sure to be inside the NJ Transit Rail Operations Bridge before it closes or you may stand the chance of missing the hourly opening of the Cheesequake Creek Bridge. Both bridges crossing Cheesequake (Morgan) Creek monitor VHF Channel 13. There are no channel markers inside the creek.

Dockage: Raritan Marina is located in Stump Creek, on the port side immediately after you enter Cheesequake Creek. The well-respected facility has transient slips on floating docks to 75 feet, sells ValvTect fuel and offers repairs. They are known for quick turnaround on all service, even emergency situations.

When traveling up Cheesequake Creek, favor the west side to avoid mud flats and transit on a rising tide. There are several full-service marinas in the creek including the family-owned Lockwood Boat Works, which services powerboats and sailboats and can accommodate vessels up to 50 feet on floating docks. Their ship store provides an exceptionally well-stocked line of marine hardware, engine parts, painting and repair supplies, as well as a host of other items for all types of boats.

Perth Amboy

The historic town of Perth Amboy is located at the intersection of the Raritan River, Arthur Kill and Raritan Bay. Recreational boaters rarely transit the Raritan River north from Perth Amboy because facilities are limited.

NAVIGATION: Use NOAA Charts 12332 and 12327. Pay attention to all channel markers in this area to avoid shipping traffic as the ships must remain in the channels. There is plenty of water for pleasure craft outside of the channels except off of Ward Point at the

Perth Amboy

Raritan Bay, NJ

		Dockage						Supplies		Services				
		Largest Vessel Accomodated	VHF Channel Monitored / Working	Transient Slips / Total Slips	Approach / Dockside Depth (reported)	Floating Docks	Gas / Diesel	Groceries, Ice, Marine Supplies, Snacks	Repairs: Hull, Engine, Propeller	Lift (tonnage), Crane, Rail	Min / Max Amps	Courtesy Car, Laundry, Pool, Showers	Pump-Out Station	Nearby: Grocery Store, Motel, Restaurant
KEANSBURG														
1. Lentze Marina Inc.	(732) 787-2139	45	16/	5/125	7.0/7.0	F		GIMS	HEP	L12	30/50	LS	P	GMR
KEYPORT HARBOR														
2. Keyport Yacht Club - PRIVATE	(732) 739-0727		/9	/	8.0/6.0			IMS					S	GMR
3. Keyport Marine Basin 🖥 📶	(732) 264-9421	32	/	6/275	6.0/5.0	F	G	IMS	HEP	L10	30		S	3MR
4. Seaboard Marine 🖥 📶	(732) 264-8910	32	/	6/42	5.0/5.0	F		IM	HEP	L12	30		S	GMR
CHEESEQUAKE CREEK														
5. Raritan Marina 📶	(732) 566-5961	75	69/	15/210	6.5/6.5	F	GD	IMS	HEP	L55,C	30/100		P	GMR
6. Lockwood Boat Works 📶	(732) 721-1605	50	72/72	6/185	5.0/5.0	F	GD	M	HEP	L35	30/50	S	P	GMR
7. Brown's Boat Yard	(732) 721-6480	35	/	/	/	F	GD	M	HEP	L	30	S	P	
8. Morgan Marina 🖥 📶	(732) 727-2289	45	/	20/280	15.0/10.0	F	GD	IMS	HEP	L25,C	30/50	S	P	GR
PERTH AMBOY														
9. Raritan Yacht Club - PRIVATE 📶	(732) 826-2277	55	9/	/				IS					S	P	R
10. Perth Amboy Harborside Marina	(732) 442-1596	40		/137		F		IS			30		S	P	R

🖥 Internet Access   📶 Wireless Internet Access   onSpot Dockside WiFi Facility

See WaterwayGuide.com for current rates, fuel prices, website addresses, and other up-to-the-minute information. (Information in the table is provided by the facilities.)

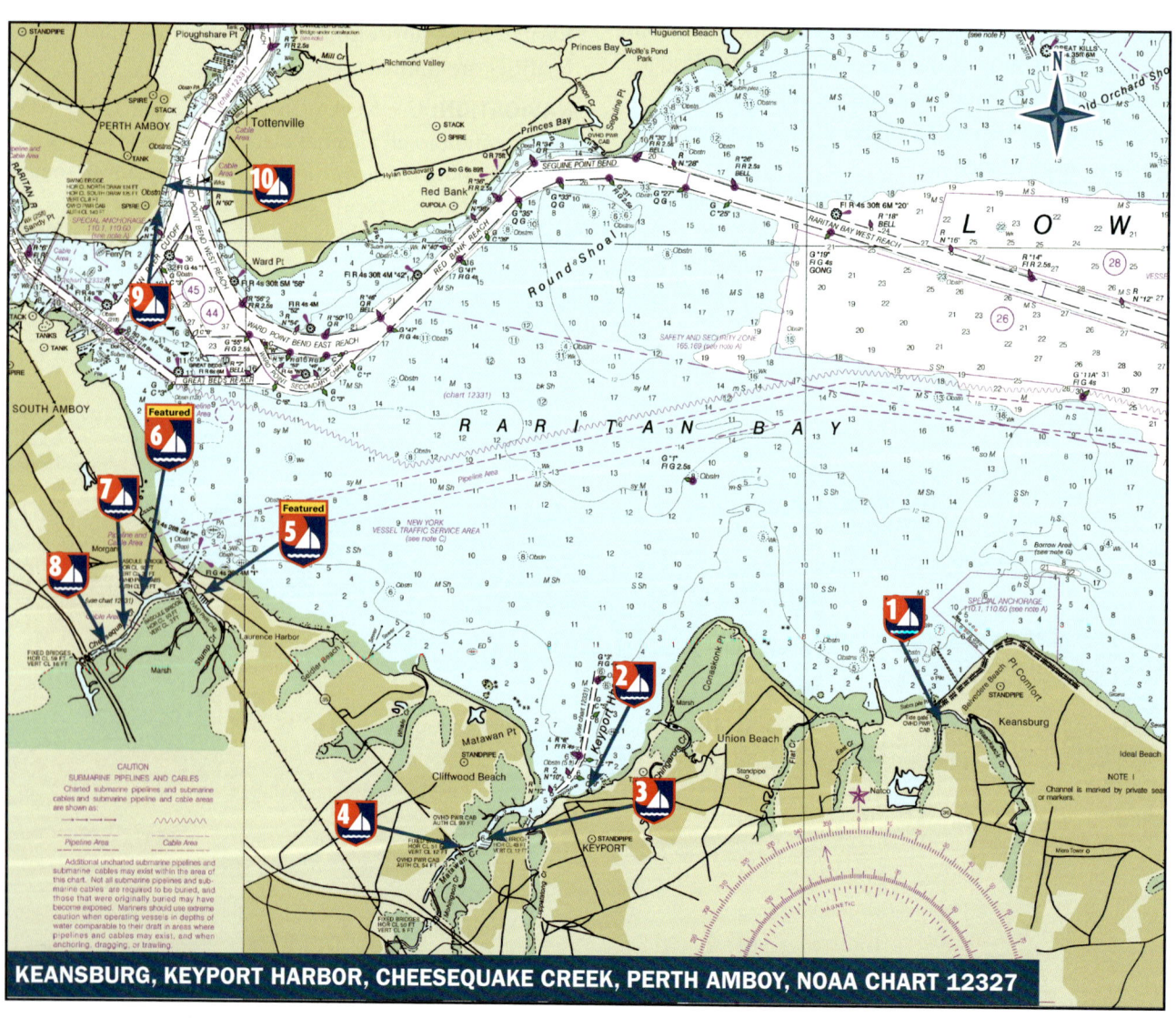

KEANSBURG, KEYPORT HARBOR, CHEESEQUAKE CREEK, PERTH AMBOY, NOAA CHART 12327

tip of Staten Island, where it is not advisable to cut inside the red aids to navigation.

Should you choose to explore upriver, the **NJ Transit Railroad Bridge** (8-foot closed vertical clearance) between Perth Amboy and South Amboy carries heavy commuter traffic. It opens on signal, except from 6:00 a.m. to 9:30 a.m. and from 4:30 p.m. to 7:30 p.m., Monday through Friday (except federal holidays), when the lift need not open. **The Victory Bridge**, just beyond the railroad bascule, has a fixed vertical clearance of 110 feet. The highway bridges farther upriver are the **Edison (U.S. 9) Twin Bridges** and the **Garden State Parkway Bridge**, with 110- and 134-foot fixed vertical clearances, respectively.

From the bridges, the Raritan River is navigable 11 miles upriver to New Brunswick through a crooked but well-marked channel and carries a fair amount of industrial traffic and flotsam through the salt marshes. Depths diminish to about 4 feet MLW in its upper reaches.

About 6 miles north of the bridges, the South River curves off to port. The Raritan River continues to starboard with shallow depths and limited facilities. Beyond a 45-foot fixed vertical clearance bridge, you come to New Brunswick, the head of navigation for the river and the home of Rutgers University. Depths abruptly shoal from 10 to 4 feet MLW at the remains of the entrance to the Delaware and Raritan Canal, which closed in 1933. This canal once linked New Brunswick to Trenton on the Delaware River.

Dockage/Moorings: Perth Amboy is home to the friendly Raritan Yacht Club, which offers guest moorings to reciprocal yacht club members. The yacht club launch can be hailed on VHF Channel 9. Also located here is Perth Amboy Harborside Marina with 137 slips on floating docks (to 40 feet) plus a mooring field. Hail the harbormaster on VHF Channel 9 to ask if a mooring is available. Provisions are only a short walk up the street. The North Jersey Coast train station is an easy 0.5-mile walk from the harbor up Market Street.

Note that there is no fuel available in Perth Amboy. Pump-out services can be obtained by calling the Baykeeper Boat on VHF Channel 9.

Coney Island Area, NY

		Dockage					Supplies		Services					
	Phone	Largest Vessel Accommodated	VHF Channel Monitored / Working	Transient Slips / Total Slips	Approach / Dockside Depth (reported)	Floating Docks	Gas / Diesel	Groceries, Ice, Marine Supplies, Snacks	Repairs: Hull, Engine, Propeller	Lift (tonnage), Crane, Rail	Min / Max Amps	Courtesy Car, Laundry, Pool, Showers	Pump-Out Station	Nearby: Grocery Store, Motel, Restaurant
SHEEPSHEAD BAY														
1. Sheepshead Bay Yacht Club - PRIVATE 🖥	(718) 891-0991	50	68/	/	45.0/15.0	F		IS			30	PS		GMR
2. Moonbeam Gateway Marina (WiFi)	(718) 252-8761	150	16/6	20/500	15.0/25.0	F		GIMS	HEP	L35	30/100	CS	P	G
GRAVESEND BAY														
3. Marine Basin Marina Inc.	(718) 372-5700	110	16/69	3/200	6.0/20.0	F		IM	HEP		30/50	S		GMR
BERGEN BEACH														
4. Kings Plaza Marina	(718) 253-5434	50	16/	20/150	50.0/21.0	F	G	IMS	HEP	L15	30/50	LS		GMR

🖥 Internet Access   (WiFi) Wireless Internet Access   📶 onSpot Dockside WiFi Facility

See WaterwayGuide.com for current rates, fuel prices, website addresses, and other up-to-the-minute information. (Information in the table is provided by the facilities.)

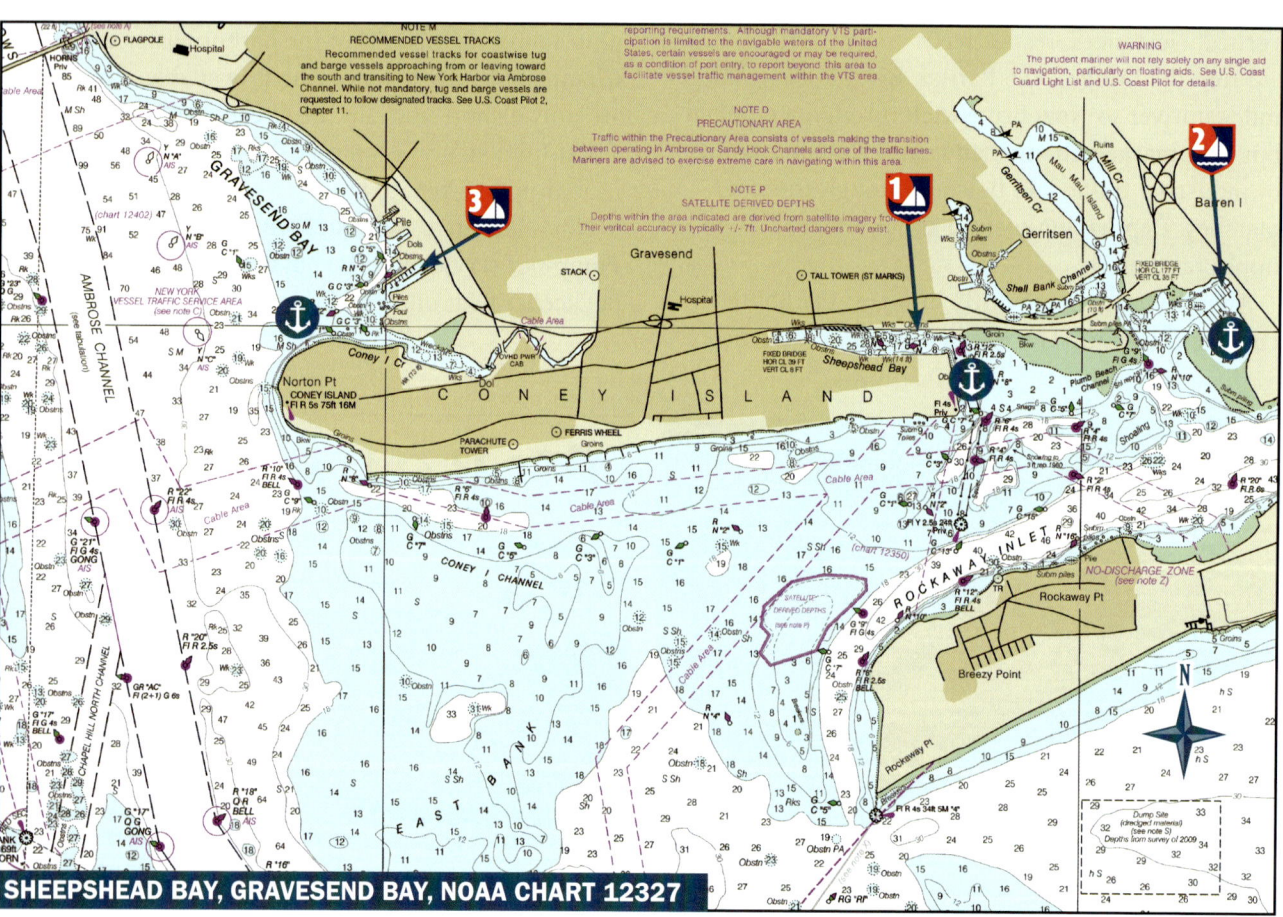

SHEEPSHEAD BAY, GRAVESEND BAY, NOAA CHART 12327

■ LOWER BAY, NY

NAVIGATION: Use NOAA Charts 12327 and 12332. The run from Sandy Hook across Lower Bay to The Narrows into New York Harbor is 8 nm almost due north. On this course pass west of Romer Shoal Light to avoid the breaking seas across a shallow spot southeast of the light and the shoal itself that runs 2 nm farther on. Leave the West Bank Light to port. Maintain a course well east of Swinburne and Hoffman Islands, which lie due west of Coney Island's Norton Point. Do not attempt to explore these small islets lying off the Staten Island shore by boat, as the water around them is extremely shallow.

Time your transit in the Lower Bay with a favorable current to shorten your cruising time. Currents in this area run up to 2 knots. Depths are good almost everywhere. If the visibility is poor, it is advisable to run GPS or compass courses. Channels are almost too well marked and the profusion of buoys, lights and lighthouses can be overwhelming at times.

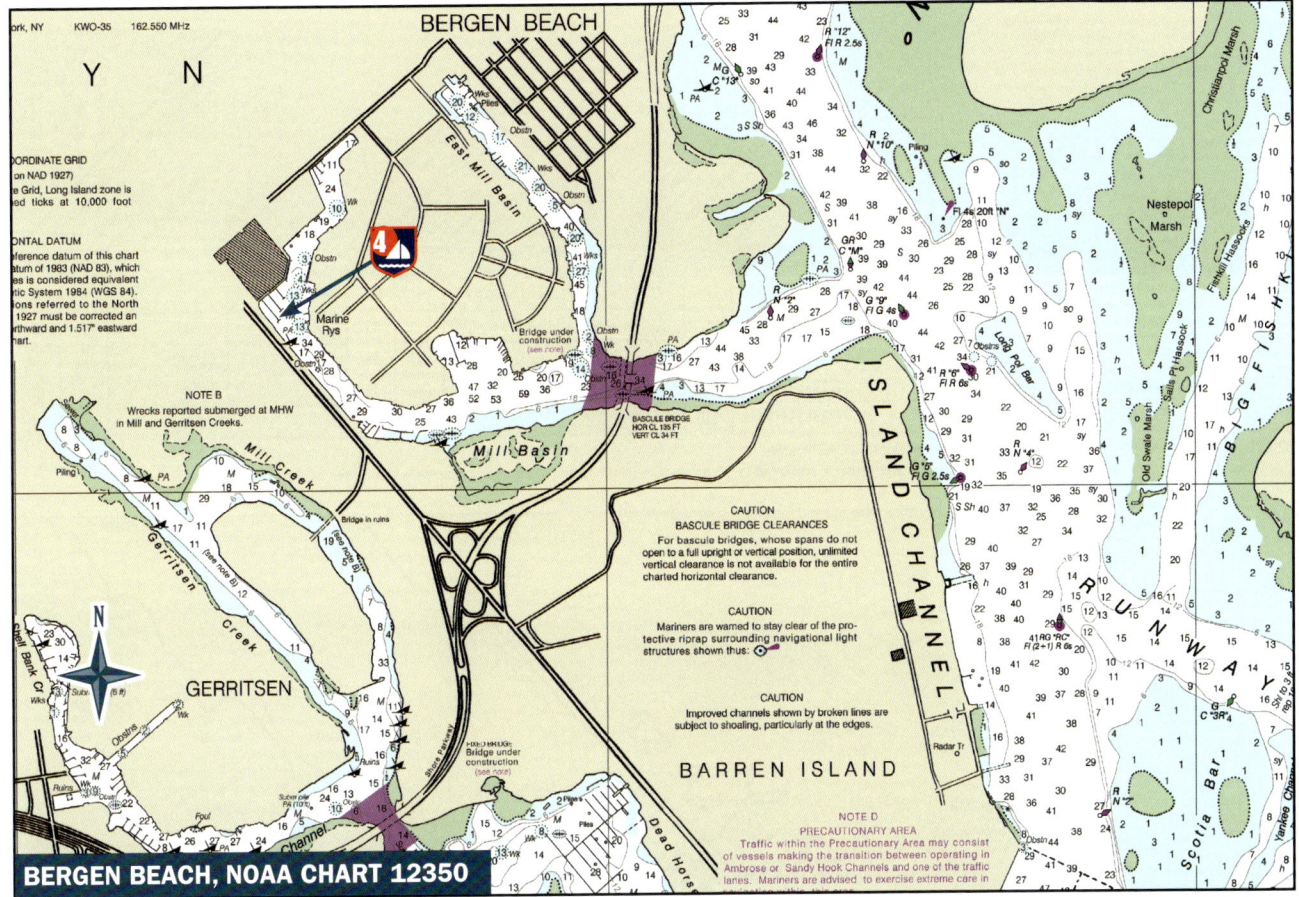

BERGEN BEACH, NOAA CHART 12350

Another option is to run outside the main shipping lanes where there is usually plenty of water. Stay close enough to follow the buoys but off-channel enough to stay clear of big ships. All commercial traffic monitors VHF Channel 13 in New York waters. It is advisable to hail approaching vessels to agree on a passing strategy. The tugboat captains and pilots will respond and they usually appreciate a call from even the smallest pleasure boat. There is great security in your knowing exactly where a 1,000-foot-long car carrier is headed and that the captain acknowledges your existence!

Great Kills Harbor

NAVIGATION: Use NOAA Charts 12327 and 12332. Great Kills Harbor, the first storm haven on the northward route through Lower Bay before reaching The Narrows, is a harbor of refuge and a charming place to visit. Located on the east side of Staten Island about 7 nm northwest of Sandy Hook and 12 nm south of The Battery (Manhattan), it is almost completely landlocked. The entry into Great Kills Harbor is easy with a well-marked channel leading from the Lower Bay past Crookes Point into the harbor. A forward range is available to assist in keeping you on course through the inshore shoals.

The Old Orchard Shoal Lighthouse was replaced by a 12-foot-high LED light in 2014. The original lighthouse will be recreated at the National Lighthouse Museum as tribute to being the "first victim of Sandy." Red nun buoy "2" notes the beginning of the channel into Great Kills Harbor.

Great Kills Harbor is a port of refuge, making a good layover port for boats heading north or south and the entrance can be run in almost any weather. Keep well to the east side when entering the basin to avoid shoaling to the west outside green marker "9" and "11." Once in the harbor be careful of the shallow area in the middle of the mooring field. It is best to follow the channel around the perimeter of the harbor.

Dockage/Moorings: Atlantis Marina & Yacht Club is located on the western side of the harbor and may be able to offer slips but call first. The private Richmond County Yacht Club controls the majority of the moorings in the basin and can usually offer space to those from other reciprocal yacht clubs. A small service fee includes use of the launch and shoreside facilities including showers and a bar and grill. Great Kills Yacht Club is also private and offers limited courtesy dockage at two docks and has moorings for members of reciprocal yacht clubs.

Great Kills Harbor, NY

GREAT KILLS		Largest Vessel Accommodated	VHF Channel Monitored / Working	Transient Slips / Total Slips	Approach / Dockside Depth (reported)	Floating Docks	Gas / Diesel	Groceries, Ice, Marine Supplies, Snacks	Repairs: Hull, Engine, Propeller	Lift (tonnage), Crane, Rail	Min / Max Amps	Courtesy Car, Laundry, Pool, Showers	Pump-Out Station	Nearby: Grocery Store, Motel, Restaurant
		Dockage						**Supplies**		**Services**				
1. Atlantis Marina & Yacht Club	(718) 966-9700	100	/	/140	12.0/5.0	F		IMS	HEP	L38		S	P	R
2. Richmond County Yacht Club - PRIVATE	(718) 356-4120		9/	/40	12.0/5.0	F		IS			30	S		R
3. Mansion Marina ⌑	(718) 984-6611	70	/	5/217	12.0/5.0	F	GD	IS	HEP	L15	30/200+	S	P	GR
4. Great Kills Yacht Club - PRIVATE ⌑	(718) 948-9615	70	/	/105	12.0/8.0	F		IS			30	S		GR
5. Moonbeam Great Kills Park Marina	(718) 351-8476	150	/	8/250	15.0/15.0	F		IMS		L35	30/50	S	P	GR

⌑ Internet Access   **WiFi** Wireless Internet Access   onSpot Dockside WiFi Facility

See WaterwayGuide.com for current rates, fuel prices, website addresses, and other up-to-the-minute information. (Information in the table is provided by the facilities.)

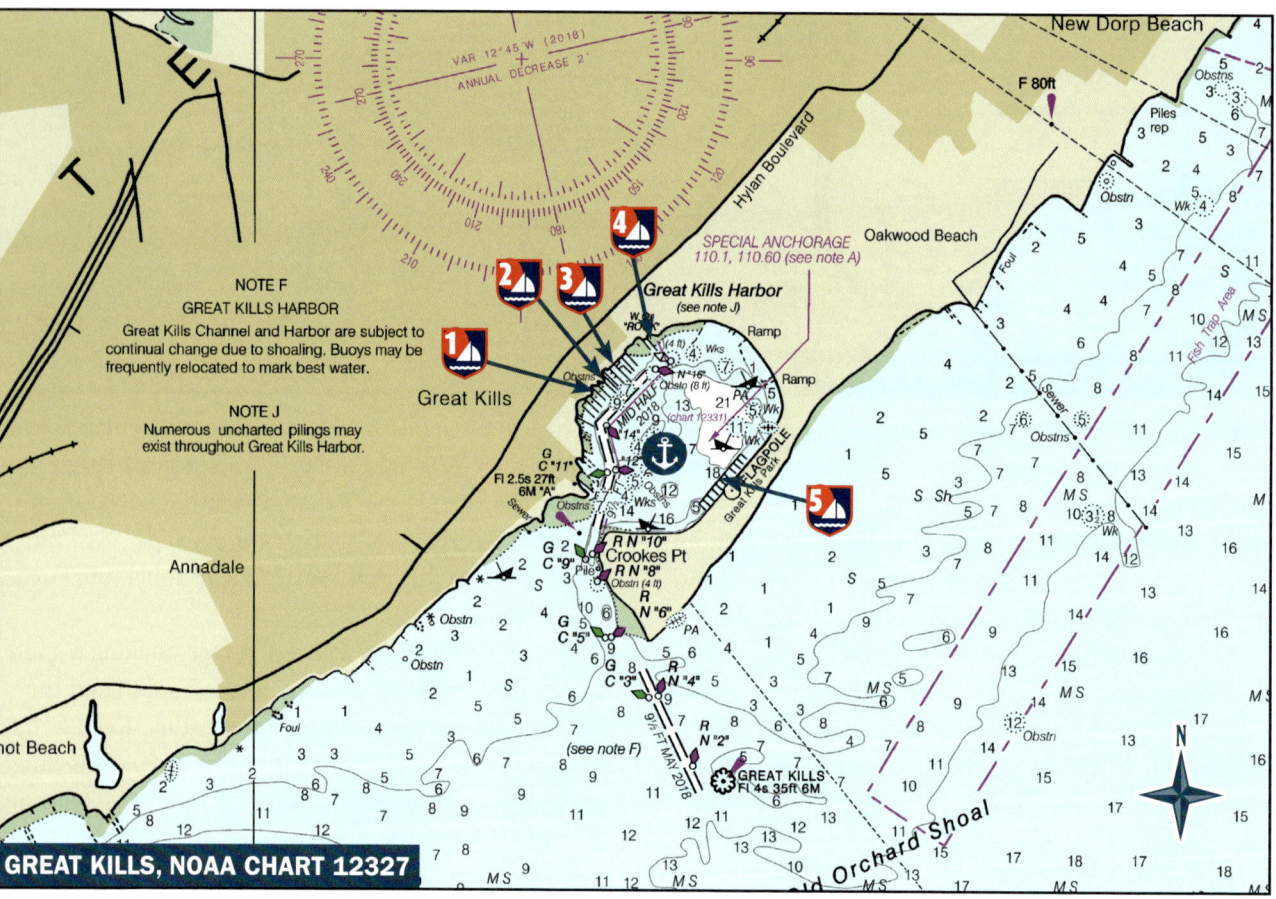

GREAT KILLS, NOAA CHART 12327

Mansion Marina is nearby with gas and diesel fuel and welcomes transients on their floating docks. Moonbeams leasing company took over management of Great Kills Park Marina in 2019. Located on the eastern side of the harbor, the recently expanded floating docks of the marina can accommodate vessels to 150 feet.

Anchorage: This harbor is very crowded with moorings so you may have difficulty finding room to anchor. If you do find room, you will have 15 to 20 feet MLW with good holding in mud and all-around protection. Anchor near the north corner, where you can take a dinghy to a boat ramp or use the launch service provided by the Richmond County Yacht Club, which also offers dinghy tie-up. There is a small market/convenience store nearby and two marine stores within a one-block walk.

GOIN' ASHORE

GREAT KILLS, NY

Entering Great Kills Harbor immediately reminds you of a picturesque, New England harbor. Its deep water and almost completely landlocked basin is very secure, offering an ideal spot to plan your visit to New York City. The harbor is 3.5 square miles in area and is surrounded by marinas to the north, marsh to the east, the Gateway National Recreation Area to the south and beach to the west. Great Kills offers excellent, efficient, public transportation to the "City," with both express buses and the Staten Island Ferry leading to the New York City subway system.

SERVICES

1. Great Kills Library
56 Giffords Ln. 9 (718-984-6670)

2. Kills Post Office
1 Nelson Ave. (718-984-2063)

ATTRACTIONS

3. Great Kills Park
Gateway National Recreation area located at the eastern end of Great Kills Harbor with a beautiful swimming beach, bathhouse and snack bar. You will also find nature trails, great fishing and multi-use paths for walking and jogging on the 523 acres. Kayak lessons and guided tours are offered during July and August at Gateway National Recreational Area (718-980-6130).

SHOPPING

4. CVS Pharmacy
Drug store chain at 4055 Hylan Blvd. (718-966-9285).

5. Stop and Shop Groceries
Located at 4343 Amboy Rd. (718-608-8950) in Eltingville Shopping Center.

MARINAS

6. Atlantis Marina & Yacht Club
180 Mansion Ave #8 (718-966-9700)

7. Great Kills Yacht Club–PRIVATE
37 Mansion Ave. (718-948-9615)

8. Mansion Marina
112 Mansion Ave. (718-984-6611)

9. Moonbeam Great Kills Park Marina
3270 Hylan Blvd. (718-351-8476)

10. Richmond County Yacht Club–PRIVATE
142 Mansion Ave. (718-356-4120)

Side Trips: Rockaway Inlet & Gravesend Bay

Jettied Rockaway Inlet, southeast of Coney Island, is wide, easy to enter, protected from north and east weather and makes an excellent port in a storm. Its only drawback is that it is a virtual dead end. Boats bound farther east on Long Island and wishing to take the inside route on the New York ICW must bypass Rockaway Inlet and head 9 miles east along the coast for East Rockaway Inlet.

Once inside Rockaway Inlet, Sheepshead Bay is to port, Dead Horse Bay is farther along and to port and Jamaica Bay is dead ahead. All three offer protection from the weather and interesting sightseeing. Because many of the harbors in this area accommodate a large number of local boats, it is often difficult to find a guest mooring or transient dockage.

Long, narrow and crowded with recreational and commercial craft, Sheepshead Bay offers the closest dockage to Coney Island. Although little dockage is available for transients, there are bait and fuel barges. On the west side of Barren Island, Dead Horse Bay is a large, deep, protected bight with dockage and anchoring possibilities.

Jamaica Bay, 7 miles long and 3.5 miles wide, is the homeport for thousands of boats. It is protected from the Atlantic Ocean by barrier beaches, dotted with marshy islands and shallows and has well-marked channels with 10-foot MLW depths throughout. Once a favored hunting area, much of the bay is now included in the Gateway National Recreation Area. Jamaica Bay is surrounded by noisy John F. Kennedy International Airport, as well as the more serene Jamaica Bay Wildlife Sanctuary, Rockaway Beach and Jacob Riis Beach.

NAVIGATION: Use NOAA Chart 12350. Heading east from Rockaway Inlet, the channel passes under the **Marine Parkway (Gil Hodges Memorial) Bridge** (55-foot closed vertical clearance) and then branches north and east. The bridge monitors VHF Channels 13 and 16 and opens on signal between 8:00 a.m. and 4:00 p.m., Monday through Friday. An 8-hour notice is required at all other times. The eastern channel runs along Rockaway Beach. A charted measured mile parallels a steel bulkhead along the south shore of the channel, south-southwest of Nova Scotia Bar.

You can make a circuit of Jamaica Bay by following the channel through the **Cross Bay Memorial Bridge** (52-foot fixed vertical clearance) and the **Beach Channel Bridge** (26-foot closed vertical clearance) along the beach. The bridge opens on signal except from 6:45 a.m. to 8:20 a.m. and 5:00 p.m. to 6:45 p.m. (commuting hours), Monday through Friday (except federal holidays).

Continuing a circumnavigation of Jamaica Bay, after passing under the swing bridge run north through Winhole Channel between the marshy islands to Grassy Bay. Submerged pilings line both sides of the channel to Howard Beach just west beyond the fixed Railroad Bridge at Grassy Bay (26-foot vertical clearance). Leaving Howard Beach to head back to the inlet, pass under the **North Channel Bridge** (26-foot fixed vertical clearance) and follow North Channel to the Marine Parkway (Gil Hodges Memorial) Bridge.

Dockage: The private Sheepshead Bay Yacht Club offers courtesy dockage for members of reciprocal yacht clubs. Dead Horse Bay features the 500-slip Moonbeam Gateway Marina, which is part of the Gateway National Recreation Area. They welcome transients to 150 feet on their floating docks.

Anchorage: Sheepshead Bay has fair holding with 8- to 20-foot MLW depths in mud and is exposed south through east. Dead Horse Bay also offers an anchorage with 10- to 20-foot MLW depths with fair holding in mud. It is open and exposed from the west through the south. Choose your anchorage based on wind direction.

Gravesend Bay is a good storm harbor and is directly on course from Sandy Hook to The Narrows. Gravesend Bay is located just before the high-rise **Verrazano Narrows Bridge** about 7 nm north of Sandy Hook. (Coney Island, while an interesting side trip, has no dockage.) Gravesend Bay is protected from every direction but the west. Anchor off the New York Sports Clubs Complex.

Another anchoring possibility is to the south near the mouth of Coney Island Creek in 9 to 12 feet MLW with good holding in mud; however, there are wrecks farther up. It is protected from all but west winds. From here you can dinghy to a park beach to walk your four-legged crew.

◼ NEXT STOP

....

Ahead lies New York Harbor, one of the world's busiest and most exciting ports. From there you can choose to transit the East River to explore Long Island Sound or continue north up the Hudson River to the U.S.–Canada line.

New York Waters

■ Long Island South Shore   ■ New York Harbor & the East River   ■ Side Trip: The Hudson River to Troy Lock

Long Island South Shore

The magnificent South Shore of Long Island stretches 115 nm from Coney Island to Montauk Point. A long set of barrier islands runs between most of Long Island's mainland and the Atlantic Ocean. Inside the barrier islands are shallow bays, islands, marshes and canals connecting numerous waterside communities. Dredged channels run from bay to bay, making a protected (albeit shallow) route similar to an inland waterway passage.

Charming bayfront villages line Long Island's South Shore. Farther east the scenery becomes more rural but summer resorts dot both mainland and barrier beaches. Those beaches closest to New York are dense with swimmers and sunbathers in the summer months, while the more remote stretches are all but deserted. There are also many parks (some with boat basins), nature trails and lots of birdwatching for enthusiasts. Buses or trains to New York are readily available from almost any South Shore community.

■ INLAND ROUTE: TO FIRE ISLAND INLET

NAVIGATION: Use NOAA Chart 12352. The inside route of the south shore runs about 75 nm from East Rockaway Inlet to the Shinnecock Canal, where you can cross to Great Peconic Bay then to the Long Island Twin Forks cruising waters that lead to Long Island Sound.

⚠ The main channels of the inside route are well marked but the project depth for dredged channels is 5 feet MLW and the battle against shoaling is constant. At the western end depths tend to be more stable but, as the route passes east, shoal spots increase and boats with more than a 3-foot draft must monitor the depth sounder continuously.

Many of the bridges that cross the channels have restricted openings as well as limited hours of operation. The controlling vertical clearance on the inside passage is low but there are alternate channels you can take to avoid the lower fixed bridges.

Predicted high tide occurs 10 minutes earlier than that predicted for Sandy Hook as given in the NOAA tide table (www.tidesandcurrents.noaa.gov/tide_predictions.html).

East Rockaway Inlet

On Reynolds Channel you will see private docks and waterfront cottages and–except for a few full-service marinas off-channel on the mainland–most of the boat facilities are fuel and fishing stations until you reach the Hempstead Town marinas. It is inadvisable to anchor along Reynolds Channel due to the crowded conditions and the off-channel shallow water through this stretch.

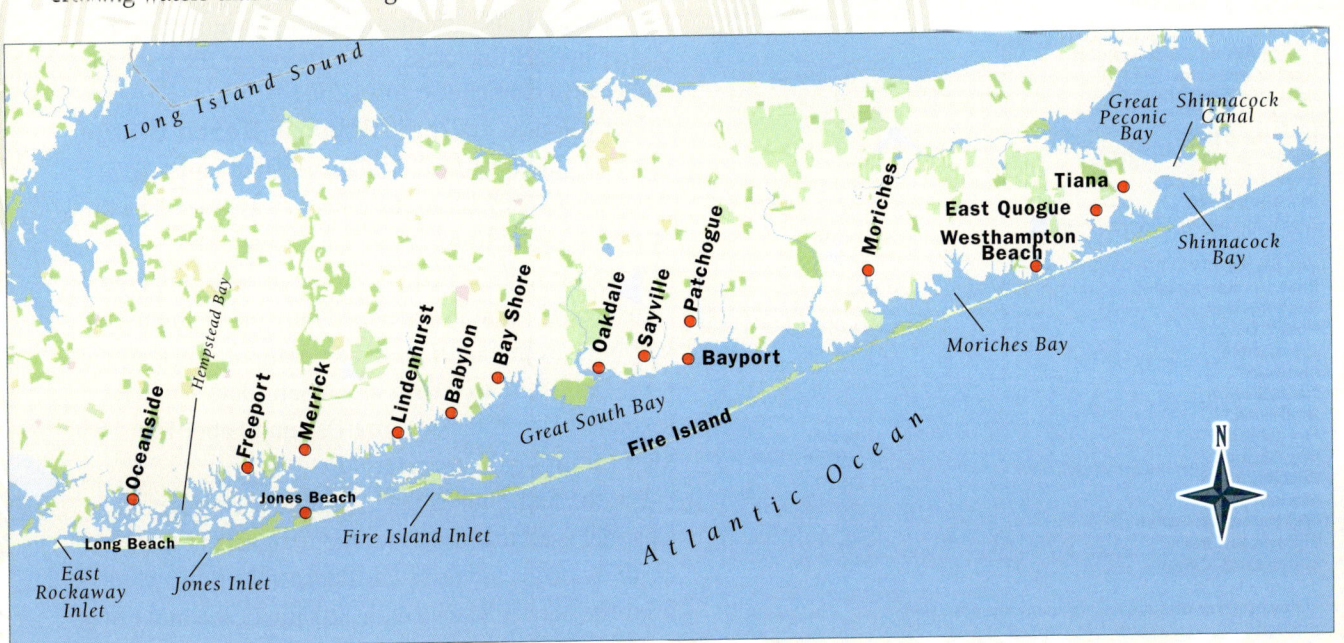

East Rockaway Inlet, NY

EAST ROCKAWAY		VHF Channel Monitored / Working	Largest Vessel Accomodated	Approach / Dockside Depth (reported)	Transient Slips / Total Slips	Floating Docks	Gas / Diesel	Groceries, Ice, Marine Supplies, Snacks	Repairs: Hull, Engine, Propeller	Lift (tonnage), Crane, Rail	Min / Max Amps	Courtesy Car, Laundry, Pool, Showers	Pump-Out Station	Nearby: Grocery Store, Motel, Restaurant
		Dockage						**Supplies**				**Services**		
1. All Island Marine	(516) 764-3300	50	68/	8/250	8.0/6.0	F	GD	GIMS	HEP	L35	30	S		GR
2. Crow's Nest Marina	(516) 766-2020	50	/	6/120	15.0/12.0	F		IMS	HEP	L40	30	S	P	GMR

▢ Internet Access   📶 Wireless Internet Access   🔵 onSpot Dockside WiFi Facility

See WaterwayGuide.com for current rates, fuel prices, website addresses, and other up-to-the-minute information. (Information in the table is provided by the facilities.)

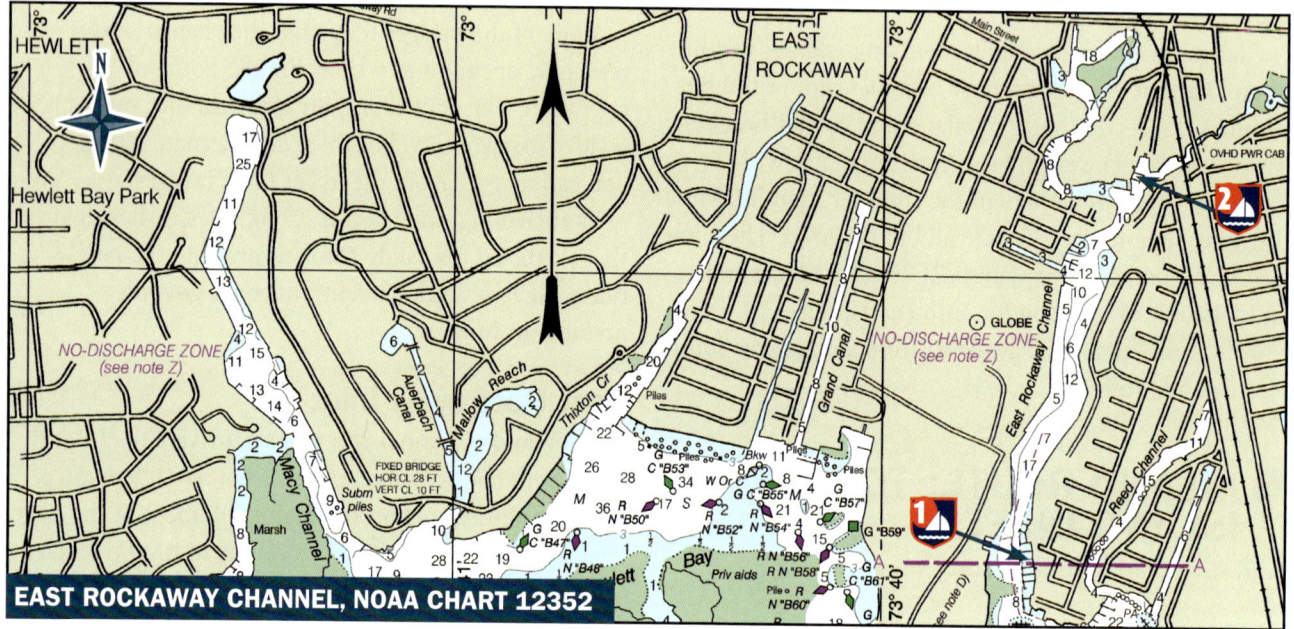

EAST ROCKAWAY CHANNEL, NOAA CHART 12352

South Shore Distances

This table gives mileage along the South Shore of Long Island. All distances are measured in approximate nautical miles.

LOCATION	BETWEEN POINTS	CUMULATIVE
VIA ATLANTIC OCEAN		
Coney Island, Norton Point	0	0
Rockaway Point	4	4
East Rockaway Inlet	8.9	13
Jones Inlet	8.3	21
Fire Island Inlet	12.6	34
Moriches Inlet	27	61
Shinnecock Inlet	13.5	74
Montauk Point	31	105
Block Island, Southwest Point	15	120
VIA INLAND WATERWAY		
East Rockaway Inlet	0	0
East Rockaway*	7	
Point Lookout	9	9
Jones Inlet	1	10
Freeport*	4	
Jones Beach	4	14
Amityville*	11	
Fire Island	12	26
Bay Shore	9	35
Patchogue	13	48
Moriches Inlet	17	65
Westhampton Beach	7	72
Shinnecock Inlet	9	81
Shinnecock Canal	3	84

*Off-waterway distance from main channel port

NAVIGATION: Use NOAA Chart 12352. Reynolds Channel is the west to east inside route from East Rockaway Inlet for the 8 nm to Jones Inlet. This route is well buoyed with 7-foot MLW depths but shoals border the channel at its eastern end. Currents run strong near all five bridges that cross the route and at the western end of the channel near Jones Inlet.

You will pass under the **Atlantic Beach Bridge** (30-foot closed vertical clearance) when entering Reynolds Channel from East Rockaway Inlet. The draw opens on signal from October 1 through May 14. From May 15 through September 30 the draw will open on signal, except that it need open only on the hour and half-hour from 4:00 p.m. to 7:00 p.m. on weekdays and from 11:00 a.m. to 9:00 p.m. on Saturdays, Sundays, Memorial Day, Independence Day and Labor Day. From May 15 through September 30.

For the first 3 miles the 0.25-mile-wide Reynolds Channel is all that separates the Long Island mainland (with its major towns of Far Rockaway and Lawrence) from the barrier beach (with Atlantic Beach and Long

East Atlantic Beach

Beach). Strung along the barrier strip are the seaside resorts of Long Beach, Lido Beach and Point Lookout.

The towns of Woodmere, Woodsburgh, East Rockaway and Oceanside are on the mainland side and are reached via several marked passages twisting through the marshes and islands of Hempstead Bay north of Reynolds Channel. For vessels over 30 feet, Hog Island Channel, about 4 nm east of East Rockaway Inlet and west of the Reynolds Channel Railroad Bridge, is the only entrance. Turn into Hog Island Channel between flashing green "C1" located off the tip of Simmons Hassock and flashing red buoy "C2" off the tip of Island Park (a double island). Stay well clear of a series of green cans in Hog Island Channel; the better depths are on the eastern (red) side of the channel.

Just past the junction of Hog Island Channel and Reynolds Channel are two bridges joining Island Park to Long Beach: the **Reynolds Channel Railroad Bridge** (14-foot closed vertical clearance, opens on signal) and the **Long Beach Twin Bridges** (20-foot closed vertical clearances). The draw of the Long Beach Bridges will open on signal from midnight to 8:00 a.m. year-round (if at least four-hour notice is given), except from 3:00 p.m. to 8:00 p.m. on Saturdays, Sundays and holidays, from May 15 through September 30, when the draw need open only on the hour and half hour.

About 0.75 mile east of the highway bridges on the south side of Reynolds Channel is a dock of the Long Beach Hospital, marked by a square white sign with a red cross (in case of a medical emergency).

Dockage: Three-quarters of a mile up Hog Island Channel, East Rockaway Channel branches off to port. Full-service marina facilities line both sides of the channel. Hotels, restaurants and amenities are within easy reach of the waterfront.

Anchorage: Although there is too much traffic to anchor along the shores of Reynold's Channel, a turn north into Bannister Creek just past the **Atlantic Beach Bridge** will bring you to the well-protected Bannister Bay. You can anchor just past the Village of Lawrence marina in 10 to 25 feet MLW with good holding in mud. The surrounding area is residential and bounded by a golf course and no amenities within easy reach but it makes for a very sheltered anchorage in inclement weather.

Jones Inlet Area

Just west of Jones Inlet, Reynolds Channel passes under the 20-foot fixed vertical clearance **Loop Parkway Bridge (West)** between Alder Island and Point Lookout. If you can pass under the bridge, you can continue to follow Reynolds

Jones Inlet, NY

		VHF Channel Monitored / Working	Largest Vessel Accomodated	Approach / Dockside Depth (reported)	Transient Slips / Total Slips	Floating Docks	Gas / Diesel	Groceries, Ice, Marine Supplies, Snacks	Repairs: Hull, Engine, Propeller	Lift (tonnage), Crane, Rail	Min / Max Amps	Courtesy Car, Laundry, Pool, Showers	Pump-Out Station	Nearby: Grocery Store, Motel, Restaurant
POINT LOOKOUT AREA				**Dockage**				**Supplies**				**Services**		
1. Angie M. Cullin East Marina	(516) 431-9200	50	/	40/184	10.0/5.0	F					30	S	P	R
2. Curtis E. Fisher West Marina	(516) 431-9200	40	/	4/152	8.0/6.0	F					30	S		GR

🖥 Internet Access   📶 Wireless Internet Access   📶 Dockside WiFi Facility

See WaterwayGuide.com for current rates, fuel prices, website addresses, and other up-to-the-minute information. (Information in the table is provided by the facilities.)

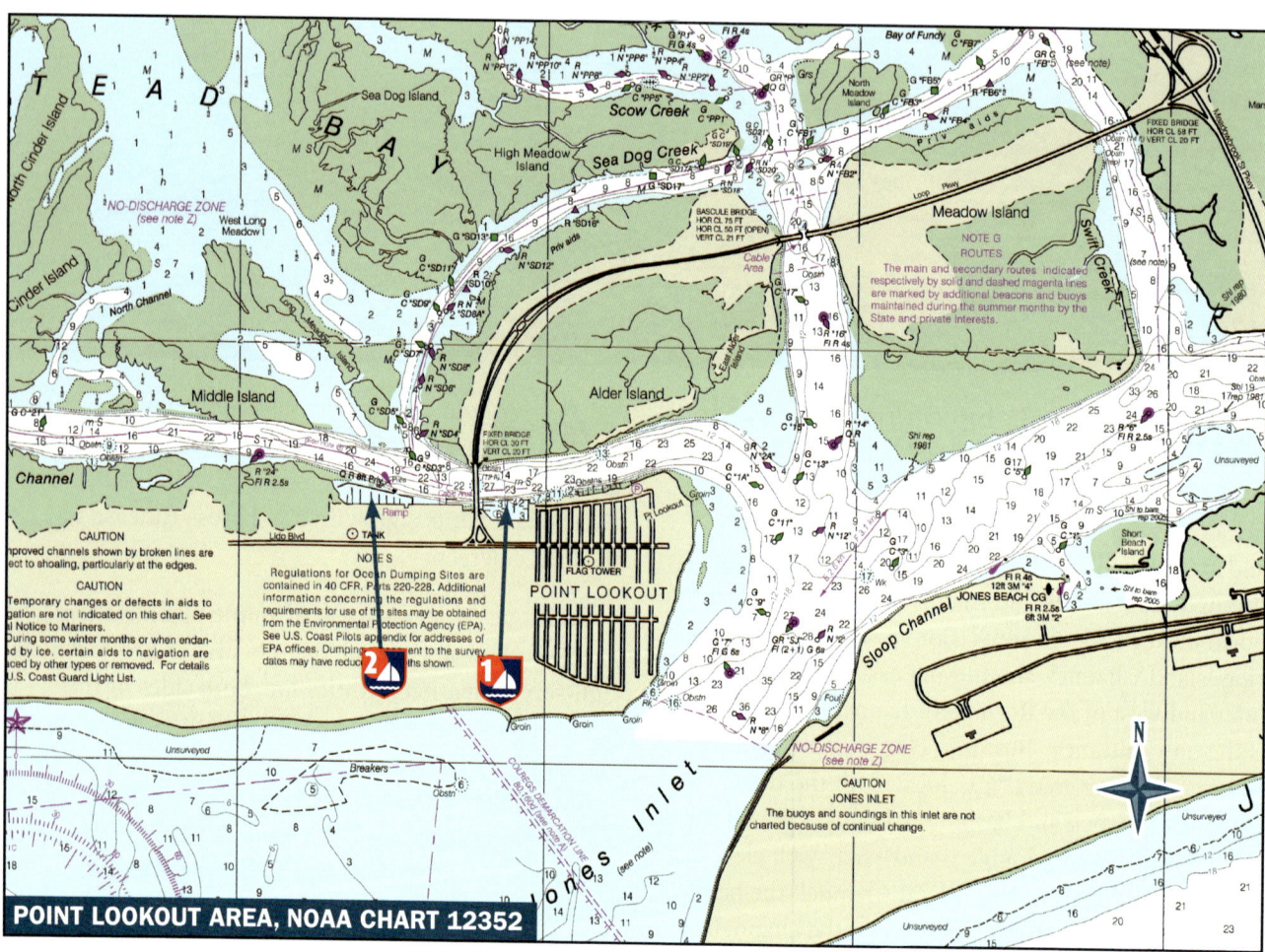

POINT LOOKOUT AREA, NOAA CHART 12352

Channel, cross Jones Inlet with its strong currents and enter Sloop Channel between Short Beach and Jones Beach and the islands and marshes to the north.

If you cannot pass under the fixed bridge, an alternate route is to turn north 0.25 mile west into Sea Dog Creek, which curves around Alder Island. Swing wide around green can "3" entering the creek. (Shoaling to 2 feet MLW has been reported near the buoy.) In a little more than 1 mile turn south on Long Creek, go through the **Loop Parkway–Long Creek Bridge** (21-foot closed vertical clearance) connecting Meadow Island and Alder Island and then turn east into Sloop Channel.

The draw of the Loop Parkway–Long Creek Bridge will open on signal every other hour on the even hour except from April 1 through October 31 on Saturdays, Sundays and federal holidays, when the draw opens on signal every three hours beginning at 3:00 a.m. Mooring platforms with flashing lights and phone numbers to call the tender for information are above and below the bascule bridge. If an opening is desired at other than a scheduled time, notice may be given from the telephone located on either side of the bridge or via VHF.

If you can negotiate the 20-foot restricted vertical clearance, there is a third route to Sloop Channel.

Proceed on Sea Dog Creek, cross Long Creek and about 1 mile farther turn south on Swift Creek and pass through the fixed Loop Parkway Bridge (East) with 20-foot fixed vertical clearance. This is best accomplished on a rising tide as the creek is very shallow.

North of Jones Inlet, a string of interesting communities stretches east on Hampstead Bay's northern shore from Baldwin through Freeport, the main yachting center for the area, and then to Amityville and the beginning of Great South Bay. Interlocking secondary channels (some natural, some dredged and most well marked) twist under bridges, through marshes, sand flats and tiny islands, past man-made canals and fingers of reclaimed land. Watch depths carefully as many channels are shoal or have silted in. With local information on prevailing depths the crew of a shallow-draft vessel can enjoy several days of leisurely cruising in the maze of canals, sloughs and waterways in this area.

Small-boat marine facilities are located on Parsonage Creek and on Milburn Creek at the head of Baldwin Bay but these are generally not set up for transients. The town of Freeport, a short bus or taxi ride from the waterfront, is the major boating and fishing center in the area. It offers many services and repair yards and several waterfronts that are all crowded with local and commercial boats. Freeport is reached via Long Creek or via Little Swift Creek, which cuts through Pine Marsh and Petit Marsh. There are three main waterways in Freeport: Woodcleft Canal (better known as the "Nautical Mile"), the straight and busy Hudson Channel to the east and winding Freeport Creek beyond that.

> To learn more about this area visit the Freeport Historical Society and Museum (350 S. Main St., 516-623-9632), where you will find a fascinating display of Freeport artifacts and information. See more at www.freeporthistorymuseum.org.

Dockage: Large town marinas are on both sides of the Loop Parkway Bridge before Point Lookout. The Hempstead Town Marina East (officially the Angie M. Cullin East Marina) is near an oceanfront park where the swimming is good and welcomes transients on floating docks. Hempstead Town Marina West (Curtis E. Fisher West Marina) has less transient space (just four spaces) so call ahead.

The waterfront along Woodcleft Canal at Freeport has the ambiance of a seafaring village. Amenities such

Jones Beach

World-famous Jones Beach State Park (1 Ocean Pkwy., 516-785-1600) opened August 4, 1929, and includes 2,500 acres of the cleanest, finest ocean beaches anywhere. Miles of well-guarded swimming areas can absorb astounding throngs of people without seeming overcrowded. Jones Beach begins at Jones Inlet and extends east along the barrier beach for about 5 miles. Jones Beach has a broad 2-mile-long boardwalk, refreshment stands, restaurants, a huge swimming pool, abundant fishing and attractive anchorages. There is a flat-rate boat docking fee ($10 in 2019). A 200-foot high red brick tower, visible for 25 miles when lit at night, serves as a striking landmark. From June through September, the Jones Beach Boardwalk Bandshell has music events every night. Nature walks are also available at the Theodore Roosevelt Nature Center (516-780-3295), which is open between Memorial Day and Labor Day, Wednesday through Sunday from 10:00 a.m. to 4:00 p.m. See details and interactive webcam at www.jonesbeach.com.

Middle Bay, NY

		VHF Channel Monitored / Working	Largest Vessel Accomodated	Approach / Dockside Depth (reported)	Transient Slips / Total Slips	Dockage		Floating Docks	Gas / Diesel	Supplies	Groceries, Ice, Marine Supplies, Snacks	Repairs: Hull, Engine, Propeller	Lift (tonnage), Crane, Rail	Services	Courtesy Car, Laundry, Pool, Showers	Min / Max Amps	Pump-Out Station	Nearby: Grocery Store, Motel, Restaurant
BARNUMS CHANNEL						**Dockage**				**Supplies**				**Services**				
1. Empire Point Marina 💻 📶	(516) 889-1067		60	9/	4/65	15.0/8.0	F			G	GIMS	HEP	L55		30/50	C	P	GMR
BALDWIN																		
2. The Mooring Marina	(516) 766-0080		27	/	/57	4.0/4.0	F				M	HEP			30			G
FREEPORT																		
3. Outboard Service of Al Grovers	(516) 379-7212		26	/	/60	20.0/8.0	F				M	HEP	L		30	S		GR
4. Hempstead Town Marina Guy Lombardo	(516) 378-3417		50	/	10/252	7.0/5.0	F								30	S	P	GR
5. Travelers Marine Service	(516) 868-1193		36	/	/14	4.0/3.0	F					HEP	L		30/50			GMR
6. Mako Marine 💻	(516) 378-7331		75	10/	2/30	10.0/12.0	F		GD	IS		HEP	L50		30/50	S		GMR
7. Yachtsmens Cove Marina 📶	(516) 546-6026		60	/	20/160	10.0/6.0	F				I	HEP	L60		30/50			GMR
8. Al Grovers High & Dry Marina	(516) 546-8880		50	/	/150	6.0/6.0	F				IM	HEP	L		30/50	S	P	GMR
9. Atlantic Yacht Haven	(516) 377-7720		46	/	/45	6.0/8.0	F				I	HEP	L35			S		GMR

💻 Internet Access 📶 Wireless Internet Access 📶 onSpot Dockside WiFi Facility

See WaterwayGuide.com for current rates, fuel prices, website addresses, and other up-to-the-minute information. (Information in the table is provided by the facilities.)

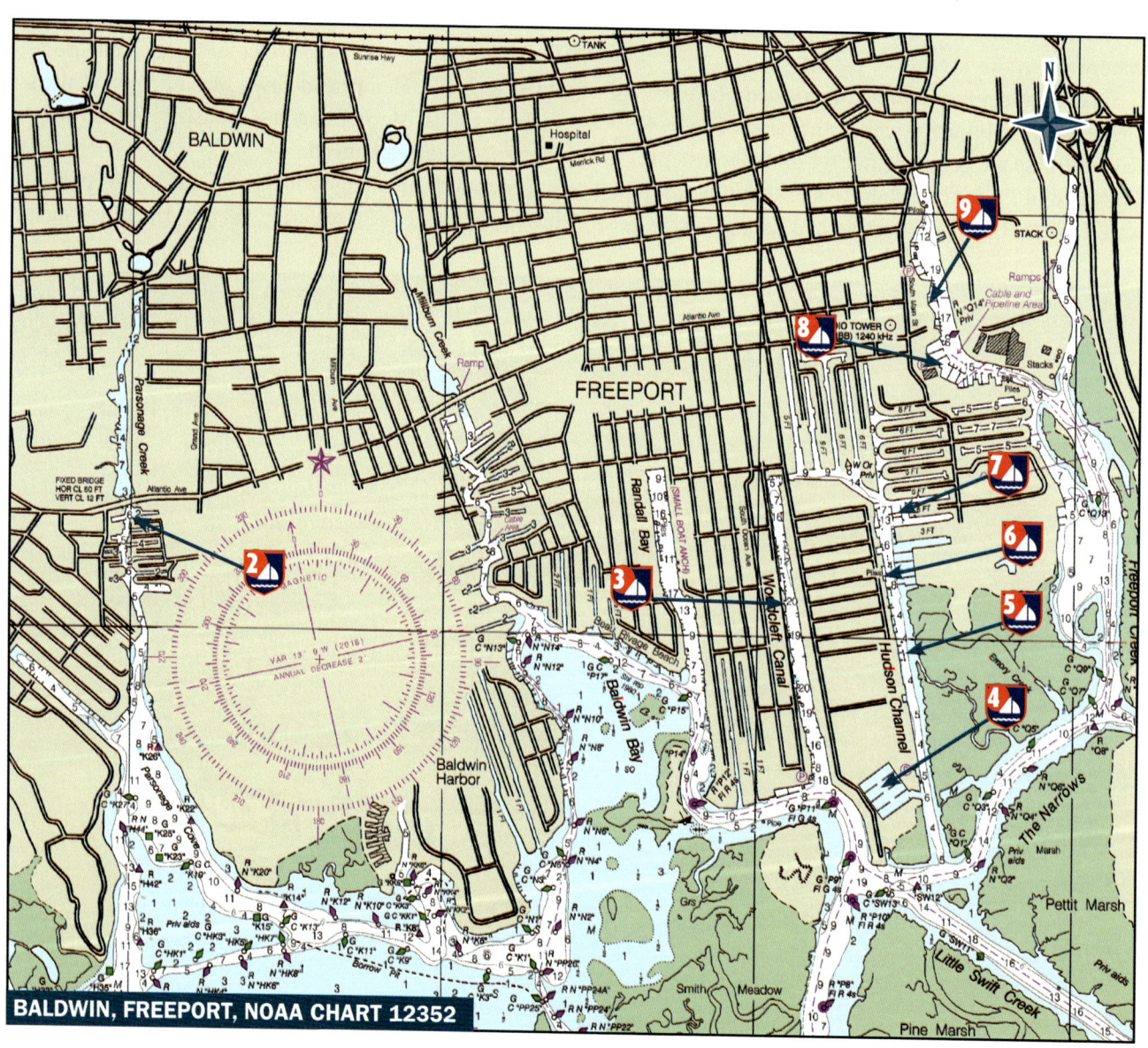

BALDWIN, FREEPORT, NOAA CHART 12352

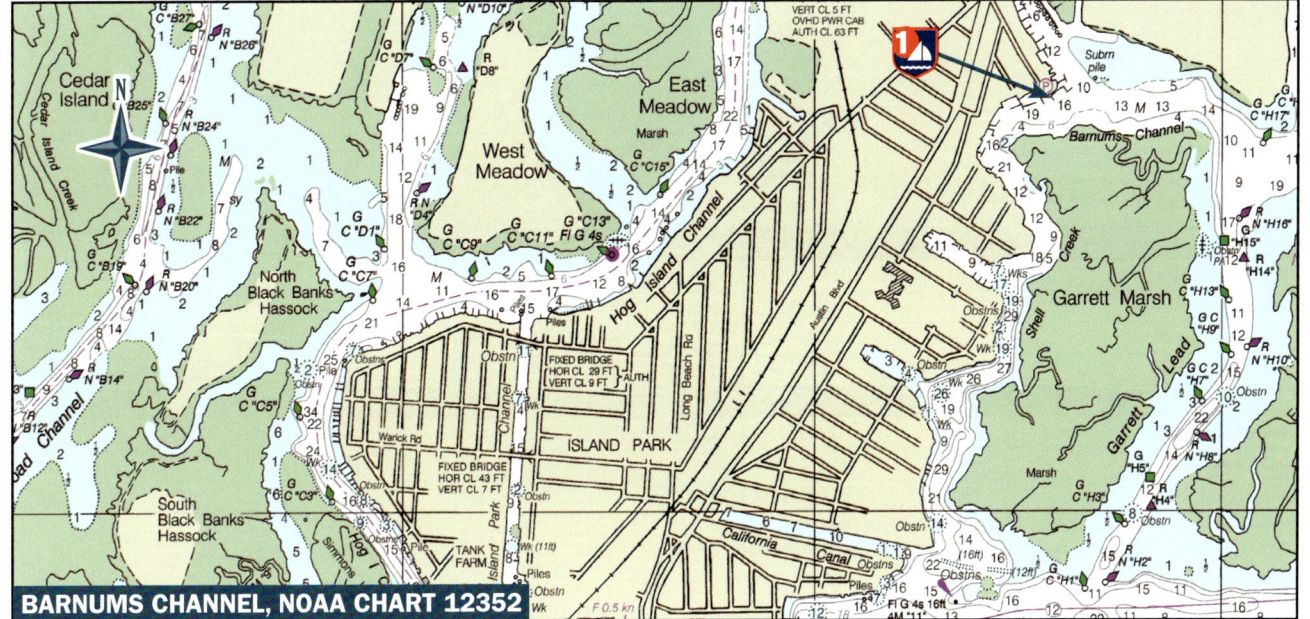

BARNUMS CHANNEL, NOAA CHART 12352

as seafood restaurants (many with outdoor dining and music), open-air bars, fish markets and boutiques are all a short walk from the docks. In season this area is crowded with fishers, recreational boaters, diners and sightseers. Most establishments here will take care of cruising craft when possible. (See marina table for details.)

Anchorage: Anchoring is available on the west side of Freeport Creek, just before the abandoned Freeport Marina at Cow Meadow Park. Although the entrance is slightly shoaled, inside depths are 9 or more feet MLW with a 6-foot tidal range.

To Fire Island Inlet

NAVIGATION: Use NOAA Chart 12352. If continuing to Fire Island on Sloop Channel, pass through the **Meadowbrook State Parkway Bridge** (21-foot closed vertical clearance) and into Sloop Channel. The bridge opens on signal every other hour on the even hour (with 30 minute notice). From April 1 through October 31, on Saturdays, Sundays and federal holidays, the draw opens every three hours beginning at 1:30 a.m. Notice may be given from the telephone located at the moorings on each side of the bridge or by marine radio.

Abeam of the mammoth water tower, the channel veers northeast under the **Wantagh Parkway (Sloop Channel) Bridge** (20-foot closed vertical clearance) and around a marshy area. A shortage of drawtenders makes for uncertain openings. If you absolutely must have an opening, give at least a half-hour advance notice by calling the number posted at the

bridge or 631-952-6777. From 6:30 a.m. through 12:00 noon and from 12:15 p.m. through 4:00 p.m., Monday through Friday, one bascule lift span may remain in the closed position. The draw will open fully between 12:00 noon and 12:15 p.m. provided at least a 1-hour advance notice is given by calling the number posted at the bridge. From 7:30 a.m. through 8:30 p.m. on Saturday, Sunday and federal holidays, the draw will open on the hour and half-hour if at least a half-hour advance notice is given by calling the number posted at the bridge.

Boats that can handle 24-foot fixed vertical clearance and don't want to wait for an opening should swing north around Green Island through the fixed Wantagh Parkway (Goose Creek Channel) Bridge, southeast down Stone Creek and then back to Sloop Channel. When turning back south down Stone Creek from the bridge, give the northeastern point of Green Island a wide berth; shoals extend from this point. As you turn south, leave green daybeacon "1" to port and follow the channel. Use caution as you proceed as shoals are encroaching from both Green Island and South Line Island.

Running the inside length of Jones Beach (and its sister beaches beyond) to Fire Island Inlet is narrow, well-maintained State Boat Channel. The channel is marked like a street with white-capped black poles with arrows that point inward to indicate deeper water. (This is in addition to the standard green and red daybeacons.) This channel is usually swarming with fishing boats anchored in mid-channel. The channel has an enforced speed limit of 12 mph. To the north are

Hempstead Bay, NY

		Largest Vessel Accommodated	VHF Channel Monitored / Working	Transient Slips / Total Slips	Approach / Dockside Depth (reported)	Floating Docks	Gas / Diesel	Groceries, Ice, Marine Supplies, Snacks	Repairs: Hull, Engine, Propeller	Lift (tonnage), Crane, Rail	Min / Max Amps	Courtesy Car, Laundry, Pool, Showers	Pump-Out Station	Nearby: Grocery Store, Motel, Restaurant
EAST BAY					**Dockage**			**Supplies**			**Services**			
1. Blue Water Yacht Club	(516) 623-5757	55	18/	20/270	5.0/5.0	F	G	IS	HEP	L25	30	LPS	P	R
2. Whaleneck Harbor Marina	(516) 378-8025	55	/	/200	5.0/9.0	F		S	HEP	L40	30	PS		GR
3. Ocean Bay Marina WIFI	(516) 378-6400	55	/	/30	15.0/10.0	F		IM	HEP	L40	50	S	P	R
4. Wantagh Park Marina	(516) 571-7460	45	/	/248	6.0/6.0	F					30	PS		GMR
SOUTH OYSTER BAY														
5. Treasure Island Marina	(516) 221-7156	40	/	/363	8.0/6.0	F		IMS	HEP	L14	30	S	P	R
6. DelMarine Inc.	(631) 598-2946	50	/	3/40	4.0/6.0			M	HEP	L20	30		P	R
7. Yacht Service Ltd.	(631) 264-2267	50	/	1/24	/	F		IM	HEP	L30	30			GR

 Internet Access   WIFI Wireless Internet Access   onSpot Dockside WiFi Facility
See WaterwayGuide.com for current rates, fuel prices, website addresses, and other up-to-the-minute information. (Information in the table is provided by the facilities.)

marsh-bordered islets with circuitous channels leading through them to more mainland communities. South of State Boat Channel is Jones Beach, followed by a string of county and town beaches and summer colonies.

Dockage: To access marine facilities on Merrick Creek from Sloop Channel, turn north into Haunts Creek across from Jones Beach State Park and then head to the northwest along Broad Creek Channel to East Bay. Note when entering Merrick Creek that green can buoy "23" marks a large shoal area with depths of no more than 3 feet or less MLW. On Merrick Creek you will find the large (250-slip) Blue Water Yacht Club, which can accommodate vessels up to 55 feet with full amenities.

Marked channels of varying depths connect the densely populated communities of Bellmore, Wantagh & Seaford, where facilities tend to be occupied by local boats. Most facilities, however, will make every effort to accommodate transients. For cruisers, Seaford is the most important of the three communities. Its marinas, which are liberally sprinkled along Island Creek, Seamans Creek and Seaford Creek, offer many services.

Massapequa, Biltmore Shores and Nassau Shores to the east can be reached via privately marked and maintained channels from Seaford. These towns offer some services but few are geared toward cruising boats. The area is crowded with private docks and attractive houses. Scores of canals are interconnected and are variously marked; however, do not attempt without local knowledge. These communities can also be reached from Amityville.

Anchorage: The wide part of East Bay between Whale Neck Point and White Point is one of the few anchorage opportunities in this area. Here you will find depths of 10 to 12 feet MLW with good holding in mud. Try to avoid anchoring in the obvious routes leading to and from the creeks.

Back on the Sate Boat Channel, Gilgo Beach presents one of the South Shore's most attractive anchorages at Gilgo Heading with at least 7-foot MLW depths. This sheltered bight almost always catches an ocean breeze across the narrow spit of land. Gilgo Beach also has a state park just as nice as Jones Beach and rarely as crowded. Both anchorages offer excellent holding in mud and sand and all-around protection.

To the east on the State Boat Channel is the Cedar Beach anchorage with 10-foot MLW depths and excellent holding and protection. Finally, the Oak Beach anchorage at the east end of Jones Beach Island offers excellent holding as well in 10 to 12 feet at MLW.

Fire Island Inlet

Fire Island is a beautiful, windswept barrier island, 32 nm long and connected to the mainland by a series of marked channels through the sand flats and shoals of Great South Bay. Fishing around the Fire Island Inlet is excellent and fishermen often crowd the approaches in any kind of weather.

Across Great South Bay from Babylon and connected by the **Robert Moses Causeway Bridge** (60-foot fixed vertical clearance) is Captree Island, a 300-acre state park devoted almost exclusively to fishing, with a bird sanctuary at the eastern end. Fishing piers, fuel and bait stations, along with charter and head boats for fishing, are located within the park. Call 631-669-0449 for details.

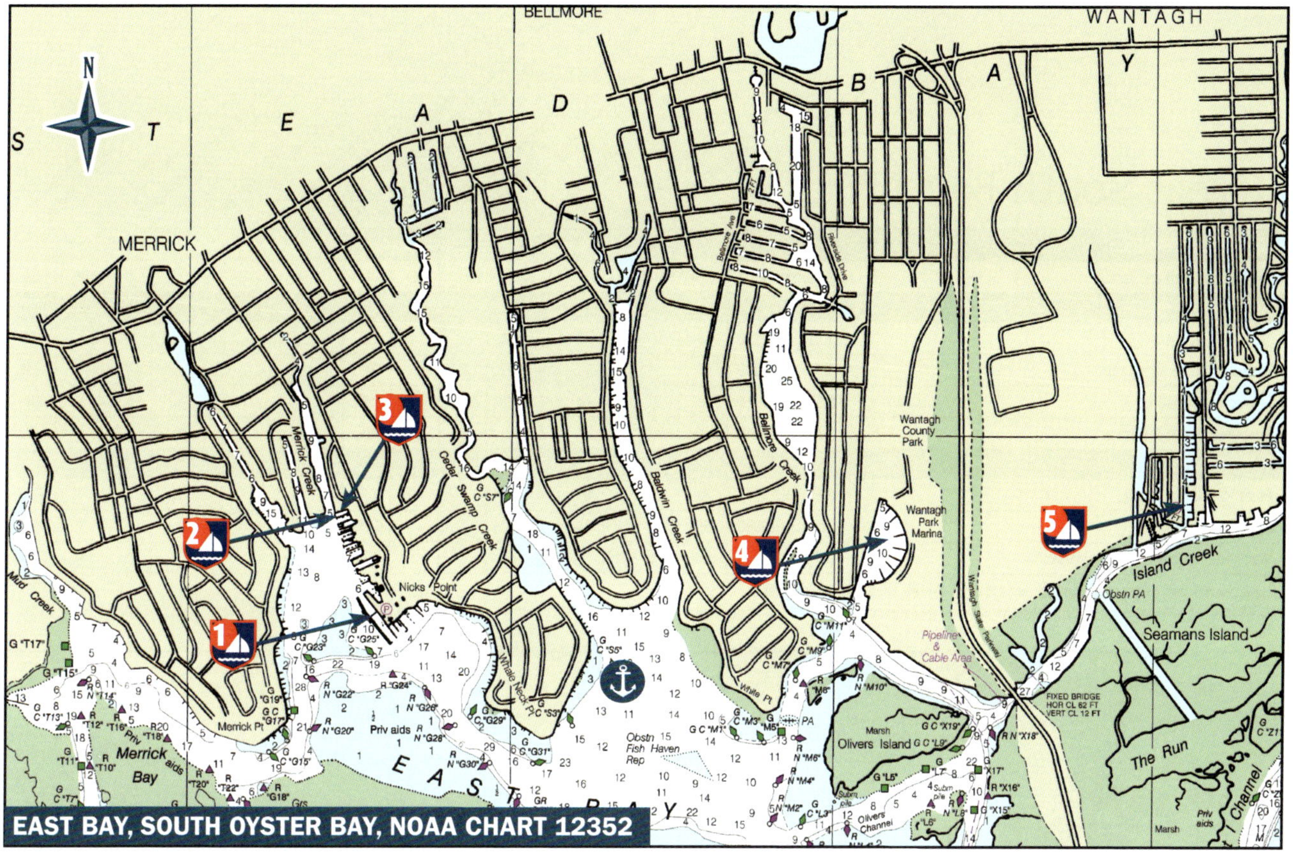

EAST BAY, SOUTH OYSTER BAY, NOAA CHART 12352

BELLMORE

WANTAGH

B · A · Y

S · T · E · A · D

MERRICK

Merrick Creek

Cedar Swamp Creek

Baldwin Creek

Bellmore Creek

Wantagh County Park

Wantagh Park Marina

Wantagh State Parkway

Nicks Point

Mill Creek

Island Creek

Seamans Island

Pipeline & Cable Area

FIXED BRIDGE
HOR CL 82 FT
VERT CL 12 FT

Merrick Pt.

Merrick Bay

E · A · S · T · B · A · Y

Obstn Fish Haven Rep

Olivers Island

Olivers Channel

Marsh

The Run

Channel

SOUTH OYSTER BAY, NOAA CHART 12352

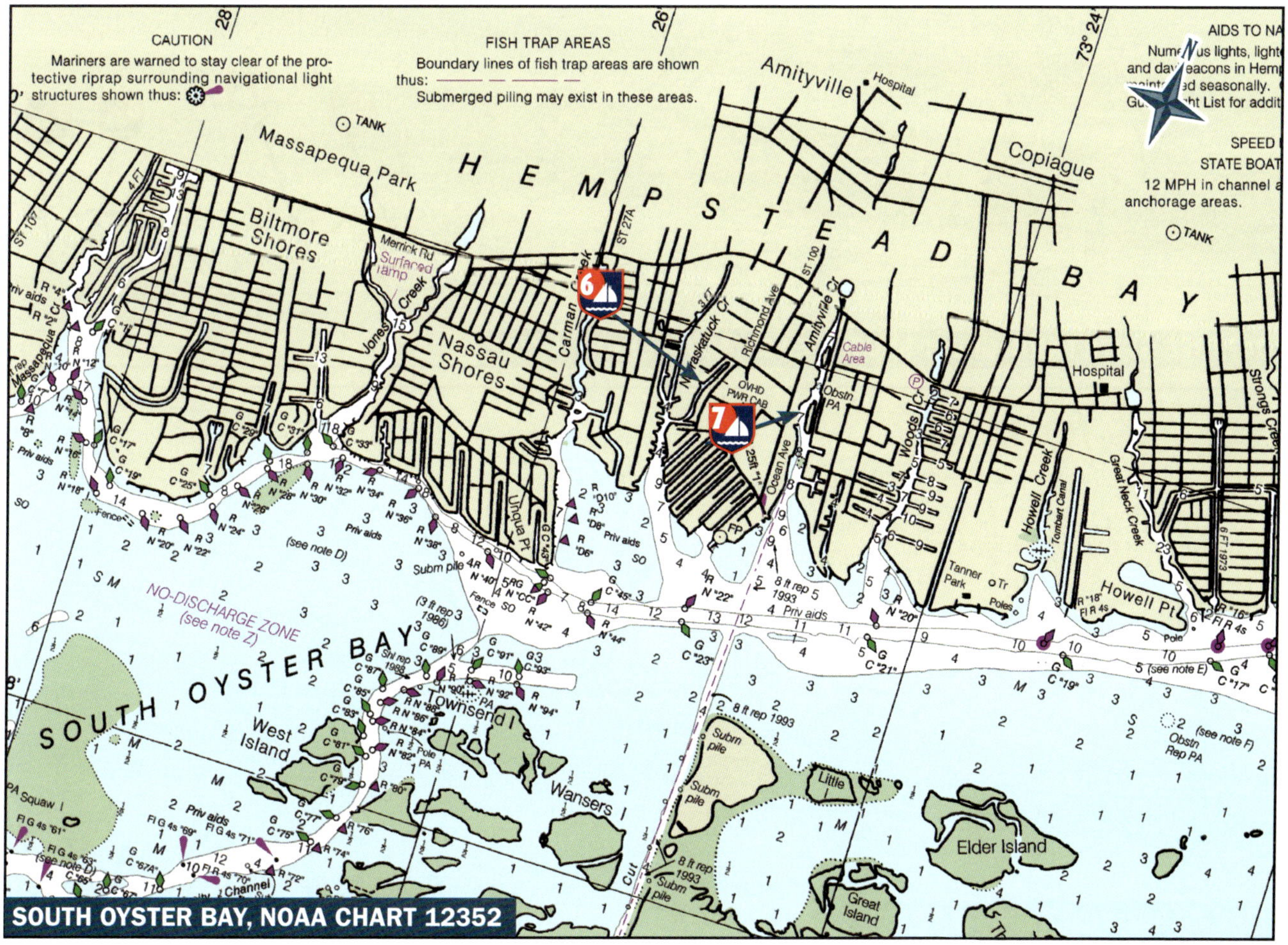

CAUTION
Mariners are warned to stay clear of the protective riprap surrounding navigational light structures shown thus:

FISH TRAP AREAS
Boundary lines of fish trap areas are shown thus:
Submerged piling may exist in these areas.

AIDS TO NA
Numerous lights, light and day beacons in Hemp maintained seasonally.
Guide ght List for additi

SPEED
STATE BOAT
12 MPH in channel a anchorage areas.

TANK

TANK

Amityville

Hospital

Copiague

H · E · M · P · S · T · E · A · D · B · A · Y

Massapequa Park

Biltmore Shores

Merrick Rd
Surfaced ramp

Jones Creek

Nassau Shores

Carman Ck

Narraskatuck Ck

Richmond Ave

Amityville Cr

Ocean Ave

OVHD PWR CB

Obstn PA

Cable Area

Hospital

Woods Creek

Tomball Canal

Howell Creek

Great Neck Creek

Strongs Creek

Howell Pt.

Tanner Park

NO-DISCHARGE ZONE
(see note Z)

S · O · U · T · H · O · Y · S · T · E · R · B · A · Y

West Island

Townsend

Wansers I

Little I

Elder Island

Great Island

Squaw I

WG

Great South Bay, NY

		Dockage					Supplies		Services				
	Largest Vessel Accommodated	VHF Channel Monitored / Working	Transient Slips / Total Slips	Approach / Dockside Depth (reported)	Floating Docks	Gas / Diesel	Groceries, Ice, Marine Supplies, Snacks	Repairs: Hull, Engine, Propeller	Lift (tonnage), Crane, Rail	Courtesy Car, Laundry, Pool, Showers	Min / Max Amps	Pump-Out Station	Nearby: Grocery Store, Motel, Restaurant
CAPTREE STATE PARK													
1. Captree Fuel, Bait and Tackle — (631) 587-3430	150	69/69	/	15.0/10.0	F	GD	GIMS			S		P	GR
GREAT SOUTH BEACH													
2. Seaview Boat Basin — (631) 583-9380	58	/	30/53	7.0/7.0			GIS				30	P	GR
3. Flynn's Marina & Restaurant — (631) 583-5000	50	/	36/50	9.0/9.0	F		GIMS				30		GMR
4. Sailors Haven Marina — (631) 597-6014	65	9/	45/48	8.0/8.0			IMS			S	30/50	P	MR
5. Atlantique Beach & Marina — (631) 583-8610		/9	/150	9.0/3.0			GS			S	30	P	GMR
FIRE ISLAND													
6. Pines Marina Fire Island — (631) 597-9581	85	9/	/70	4.0/6.0			GIS				30/50	P	GMR
7. Davis Park Marina — (631) 597-9090	50	73/	256/256	8.0/6.0	F		GIMS			S	30	P	GR
8. Watch Hill National Seashore Marina — (631) 597-6073	50	9/	180/195	6.0/4.0			GIS			S	50	P	GR

🖥 Internet Access   📶 Wireless Internet Access   onSpot Dockside WiFi Facility

See WaterwayGuide.com for current rates, fuel prices, website addresses, and other up-to-the-minute information. (Information in the table is provided by the facilities.)

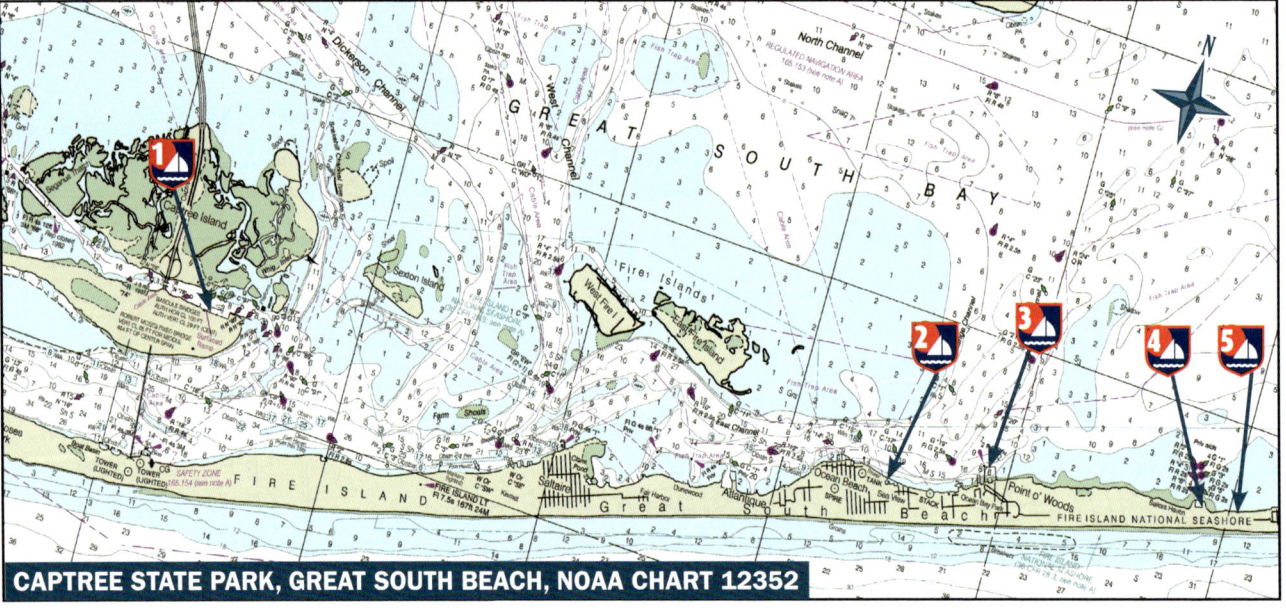

CAPTREE STATE PARK, GREAT SOUTH BEACH, NOAA CHART 12352

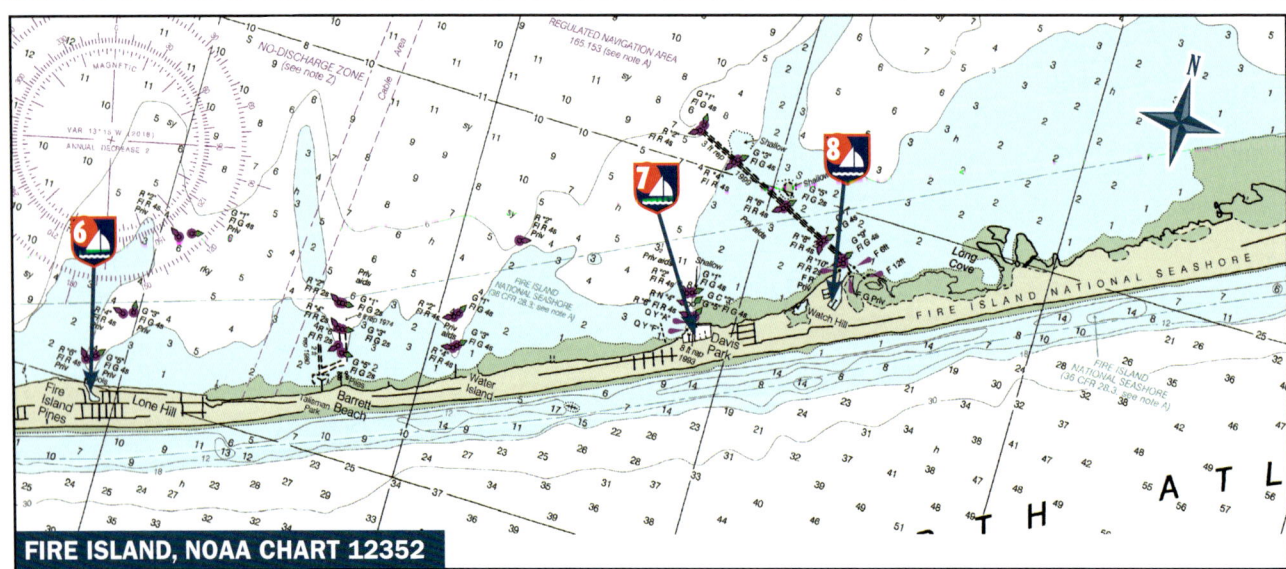

FIRE ISLAND, NOAA CHART 12352

NAVIGATION: Use NOAA Chart 12352. Next the channel enters Great South Bay and passes Captree Island, Fire Island Inlet and Fire Island. Channels lead to Captree State Park from east and west of the Robert Moses Causeway, linking it to the mainland. The State Channel cuts just south of it through the **Captree State Parkway Bridge** with 29-foot closed vertical clearance. The draw will open on signal every other hour on the even hour if at least a one-half hour advance notice is given by calling the number posted at the bridge. From April 1 through October 31, on Saturday, Sunday and federal holidays the draw opens every 3 hours beginning at 3:00 a.m.

Dockage: Captree Fuel, Bait and Tackle sells all fuels and some supplies and can accommodate vessels to 150 feet. The western end of Fire Island is occupied by Robert Moses State Park, with day-use-only slips for boats up to 43 feet, carrying up to 5-foot drafts.

Past Ocean Beach on Fire Island are Seaview Boat Basin and Flynn's Marina & Restaurant (at Ocean Bay Park). Both offer transient space, as well as some groceries and snacks. Sailor's Haven Marina is a National Seashore Park marina with 45 transient slips with a 14-day limit on stays. Nearby Atlantique Beach & Marina has slips for shoal draft (3-foot or less) vessels.

At Fire Island, Pines Marina Fire Island can accommodate vessels to 85 feet; call ahead. Davis Park Marina is a town marina for residents and nonresidents with slips offered on a first-come, first-served basis. The 256-slip marina is located in an enclosed basin. Watch Hill National Seashore Marina has slips for boats to 50 feet. None of the facilities here sell fuel or offer repairs. See the marina table for details.

Anchorage: There are numerous spots to anchor in 7- to 25-foot MLW depths between Fire Island and Captree Island, either east or west of the Robert Moses Causeway. Use the Waterway Explorer (waterwayguide.com) or the NOAA online charts for the most up-to-date information and stay clear of the main channel. Watch especially for the shoal area marked with flashing red buoy "18" just east of the bridge near the Fire Island shore. Note also the cable area east of the bridge; no anchoring is permitted here.

■ GREAT SOUTH BAY

Great South Bay begins with a narrow channel through the shoals off Amityville on the mainland and widens out to provide much of the shore's deepest water and prime sailing grounds. Mid-bay depths run from 7 to 10 feet MLW with some holes even deeper but with shallower spots as well. The Great South Bay is 25 nm long and 5 nm at its widest point near the western end, the largest of the Long Island South Shore bays.

A number of creeks reach up from Great South Bay to Amityville itself, located about 2 nm inland. Along the creeks are marinas and boatyards, most of which are for residents. A town wharf is on the bay but it dries at low water. The area has several yacht clubs and a town beach for swimming. This route affords the opportunity to drop anchor and dinghy to shallows where you can jump out and gather clams in abundance.

Lindenhurst & Babylon

Lindenhurst is the fourth largest incorporated village in the State of New York and dates back to a treaty signed with Native Americans in 1657, after which German immigrants settled it. Lindenhurst

Fire Island Light

The Fire Island lighthouse, originally completed in 1858, is on the western part of Fire Island National Seashore and is adjacent to Robert Moses State Park. The lighthouse has a focal plane of 168 feet above sea level and can be seen more than 20 miles away. The light is maintained as a private aid to navigation. The lighthouse is operated by the Fire Island Lighthouse Preservation Society and offers exhibits and a nature trail. Access to the lighthouse beach is by walking, and there are no lifeguards. The lighthouse is open from May 25 through Labor Day from 9:30 a.m. to 5:30 p.m. daily. Call 631-661-4876 for details.

Great South Bay, NY

WG

		Dockage					Supplies		Services					
		Largest Vessel Accommodated	VHF Channel Monitored / Working	Transient Slips / Total Slips	Approach / Dockside Depth (reported)	Floating Docks	Gas / Diesel	Groceries, Ice, Marine Supplies, Snacks	Repairs: Hull, Engine, Propeller	Lift (tonnage), Crane, Rail	Min / Max Amps	Courtesy Car, Laundry, Pool, Showers	Pump-Out Station	Nearby: Grocery Store, Motel, Restaurant
AMITY HARBOR AREA														
1. Amity Harbor Marine	(631) 842-1280	45	/	2/76	7.0/7.0	F	G	GM	HEP	L30	30	S		G
2. La Sala Boat Yard	(631) 842-3222	45	16/9	2/58	10.0/5.0			M	HP	L25,C	30/50	LS	P	GMR
LINDENHURST														
3. MarineMax Long Island and Lindenhurst Marina	(631) 957-5900	60	69/	20/220	10.0/5.0	F	GD	GIMS	HEP	L	30/50	PS	P	GR
4. Karl Tank Shipyard	(631) 957-5050	48	/	/15	10.0/8.0			GIMS	HEP	L15	30			GMR
5. Anchorage Yacht Club WIFI	(631) 226-2760	60	16/	/460	4.0/4.0	F	GD	GIS	HEP	L40	30	PS		GMR
BABYLON AREA														
6. Bergen Point Yacht Basin	(631) 669-3990	47	/	/100	6.0/6.0			IMS	HEP	L35,C	30		P	GMR
7. Long Island Yacht Club-PRIVATE ☐ WIFI	(631) 669-3270	52	72/	/73	5.0/4.0			IS			30/50	PS		GMR
8. Outboard Barn ☐	(631) 669-6060	30	/	6/38	12.0/15.0		GD	M	HEP	L25	30	S		GR
9. DeGarmo's Boat Yard Marina	(631) 669-0789		/	2/20	/		GD	IM	HEP	L25		LS	P	R
10. Suffolk Marine Center	(631) 669-0907	55	/	/16	7.0/5.0			M	HEP	L35	30			GR

☐ Internet Access   WIFI Wireless Internet Access   onSpot Dockside WiFi Facility

See WaterwayGuide.com for current rates, fuel prices, website addresses, and other up-to-the-minute information. (Information in the table is provided by the facilities.)

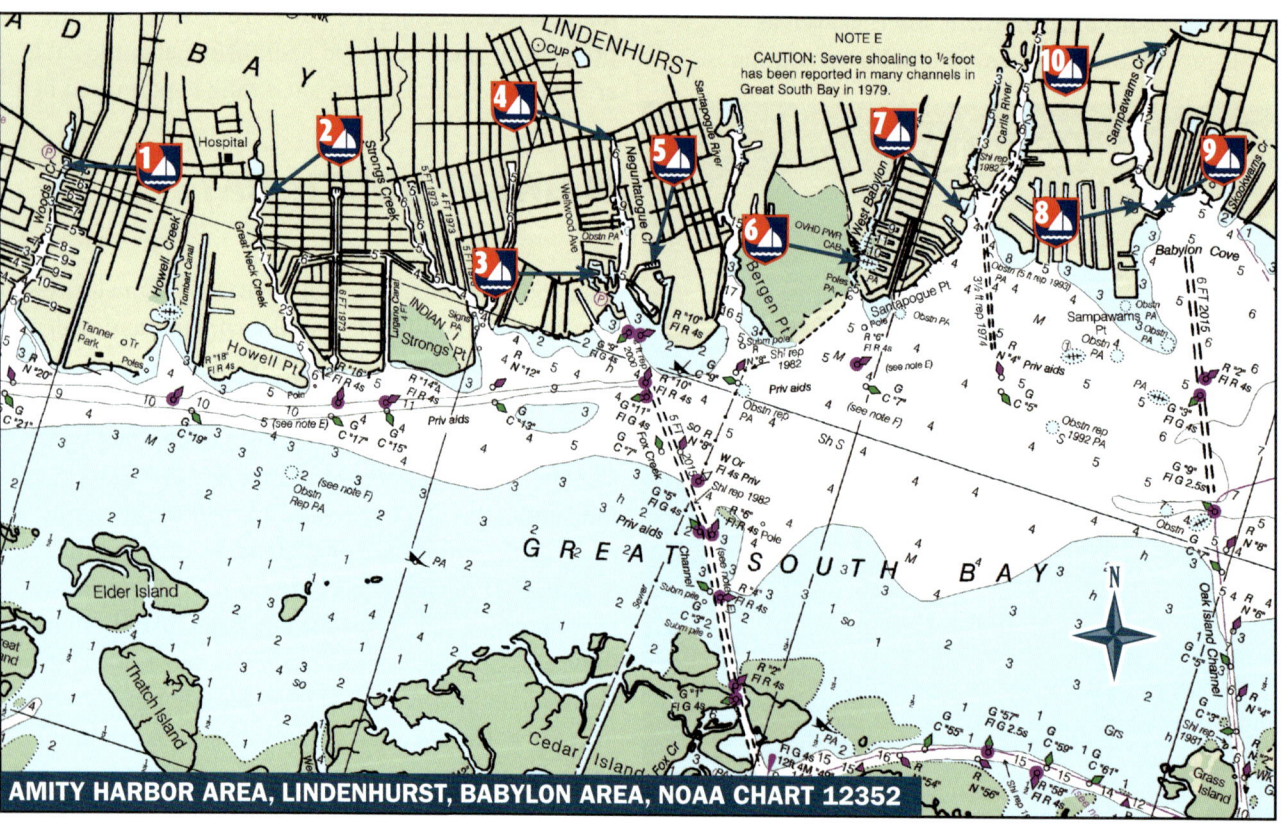

AMITY HARBOR AREA, LINDENHURST, BABYLON AREA, NOAA CHART 12352

is a pleasant village and home to around 27,000 people. If you have a chance to go ashore here, take a walk around Feller's Pond, a shady, relaxing spot. Babylon is the next mainland town to the east and offers many marinas along its creeks, including a municipal dock (for locals only), which is a long walk from the center of town. Nearby is Belmont Lake State Park (631-667-5055), with hiking trails, picnic tables, playing fields and a lake with boat rentals and bridle paths. All South Shore waters are teeming with fish, and both sport and commercial fishing are prevalent here.

NAVIGATION: Use NOAA Chart 12352. Fox Creek Channel is 2-nm long, 5-feet MLW deep and a

Great South Bay

well-marked passage that joins Lindenhurst to the State Channel farther south. There are facilities with limited transient slip space on most of the smaller creeks in this area. The 6-foot-deep Oak Island Channel connects the waterfront of Babylon with the State Channel east of Grass Island and Oak Island. Carefully observe the marked channel as you pass between Grass Island and the small, unnamed island to the east.

Dockage: Lindenhurst has full-service marinas (including repairs), a yacht club with privately-owned slips for rent and a large ship yard with marine supplies. Some supplies are also available in town, a short walk from the docks. Slips, yard services and all fuels are available in Babylon.

Bay Shore

On the mainland the big, bustling town of Bay Shore is the shopping and trading center for the surrounding area. It has all the necessary components of a good port of call: ample yacht services, good repair installations, a town pier, a yacht club, waterfront restaurants and hotels, and a well-stocked shopping center within walking range of the harbor.

Bay Shore's artificial canals are lined with handsome homes and two main boating areas, Watchogue Creek and Penataquit Creek, where marinas are plentiful. While not all marinas can handle transient boats, most will try. Great Cove and the surrounding creeks are

well protected. Marinas on the harbor offer everything from charts to electronic repair and activity is constant, with ferries running to Fire Island, fishermen coming and going, diners tying up to restaurants and sightseers walking along shore.

NAVIGATION: Use NOAA Chart 12352. One-half mile east of the entrance to Bay Shore Harbor at Brightwaters is Orowoc Creek. On the big jutting peninsula that ends at Nicoll Point is enormous Heckscher State Park (631-581-2100) with its bay beach, picnic areas, games and play areas, bridle paths and hiking trails. With a state-operated launching ramp in a small, protected harbor, this is an ideal place of refuge and a lovely anchorage, but overnight parking and docking are prohibited. Flashing red "2" marks the entry to the creek. There is an unmarked shoal on the eastern side of the creek, so be sure to stay close to flashing red "2."

Dockage: Marine facilities, supplies and yacht sales can be found at Brightwaters, Watchogue Creek and Orowoc Creek. Your best bet for a slips is at 75-slip Seaborn Marina with transient slips and an on-site inn. Call ahead for slip availability and refer to our marina table for details.

Anchorage: The shoreline in this section of Great South Bay has many inviting opportunities to anchor including Great Cove, which has 7 to 9 feet MLW with good holding in sand and mud and is protected from the northeast through northwest. Watch for boat traffic

Great South Bay, NY

BAY SHORE AREA		Largest Vessel Accomodated	VHF Channel Monitored / Working	Approach / Dockside Depth (reported)	Transient Slips / Total Slips	Floating Docks	Gas / Diesel	Groceries, Ice, Marine Supplies, Snacks	Repairs: Hull, Engine, Propeller	Lift (tonnage), Crane, Rail	Courtesy Car, Laundry, Pool, Showers	Min / Max Amps	Pump-Out Station	Nearby: Grocery Store, Motel, Restaurant
				Dockage				**Supplies**			**Services**			
1. Bay Shore Yacht Club	(631) 665-9518	50	/	/	6.0/6.0			IS					S	R
2. Burnett's Marina	(631) 665-9050	40	68/	/155	5.0/5.0	F		I				30	S	GR
3. Seaborn Marina	(631) 665-0037		/	20/75	6.0/7.0		GD	IM	HEP	L75	30/50		PS	GMR
4. Coastal Yachting Center & Marina	(631) 665-5144	42	/	3/60	6.0/6.0			GM	HEP	L,C	30		S	GMR
OAKDALE														
5. Vanderbilt Wharf Marina	(631) 567-1231	40	/	/100	5.0/4.0			IM	HEP	L	30			R
6. Oakdale Yacht Service [WiFi] ⊕onSpot	(631) 589-1087	100	16/11	/290	4.0/4.0		GD	IMS	HEP	L75	30/50	LPS		MR
7. Nicoll's Point Marina	(631) 589-8282	48	/	/64	5.0/3.5			IMS	HEP	L6	30			R

⌨ Internet Access   [WiFi] Wireless Internet Access   ⊕onSpot Dockside WiFi Facility
See WaterwayGuide.com for current rates, fuel prices, website addresses, and other up-to-the-minute information. (Information in the table is provided by the facilities.)

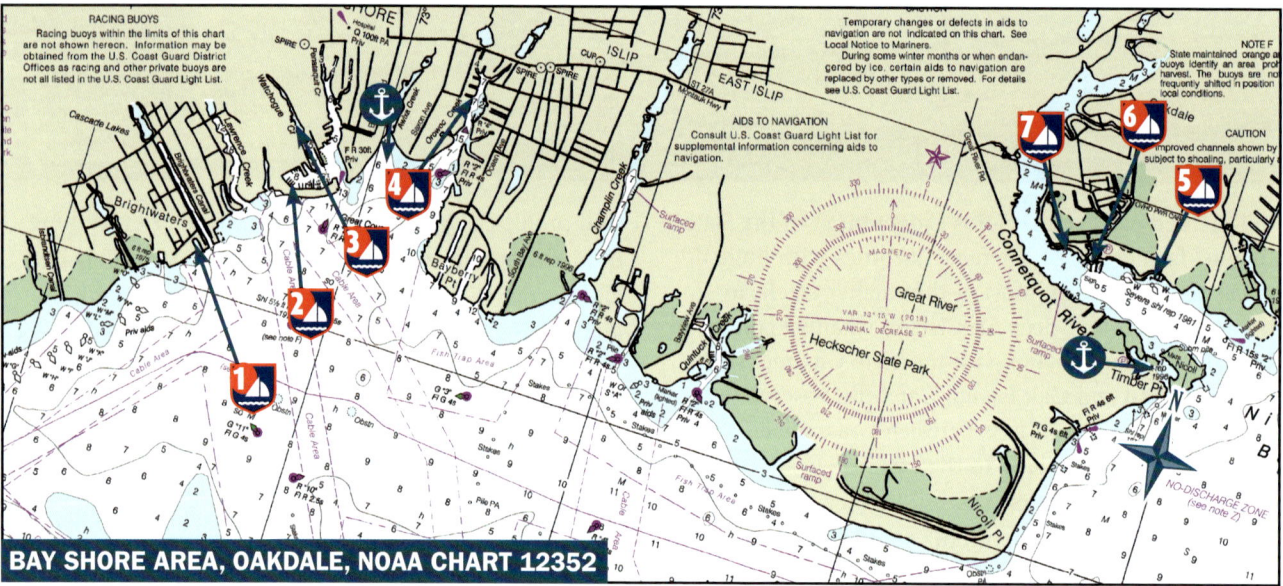

BAY SHORE AREA, OAKDALE, NOAA CHART 12352

out of the creek to avoid wakes of numerous small boats launched at the park facility. Note that this area has many underwater cable crossings.

Connetquot River to Blue Point

Around Nicoll and Timber Points, the Connetquot River empties into Nicoll Bay. The Connetquot River is a charming, secluded body of water with lovely wooded banks that offers good anchorage but not much in the way of depths. Favor the eastern shore when entering. This area is the widest part of Great South Bay. Depths hold better, mid-bay shoals are fewer and sailing is deservedly popular. Fleets of centerboard sailing craft gather in various harbors. A marked channel connecting the inland route that parallels Fire Island with the route through Great South Bay runs across the bay south of Nicoll Point.

Sayville is a residential town with tree-lined streets, well-kept houses and two waterfronts: Green Harbor in West Sayville and Brown Creek, locally known as Browns River. The latter is easy to enter between the jetties at Brown Point. The blue-and-white ferryboats coming from Fire Island can be seen shuttling in and out of Brown's River and can easily be followed in Nearby Bayport and Blue Point are typical eastern Long Island hamlets that can accommodate cruisers in slips or at anchor.

Dockage: There are several marine facilities on the east side of the Connetquot River, all reporting 3.5- to 4-foot dockside depths. Call ahead for slip availability and actual depths. The dock-lined creek at Sayville has a town pier for residents only and major repair yards serving the Great South Bay fishing fleets.

The full-service West Sayville Boat Basin boosts

Patchogue

200-feet of beachfront on 7.5 acres. They maintain transient slips to 50 feet. Bay Point Marina has slip rentals and marine service for vessels to 45 feet and their is a residents-only town dock in Bayport. Blue Point Marina on Corey Creek may have space for you but call ahead. See our marina table for details.

Anchorage: There is an anchorage behind Nicoll Island at Timber Point with 5 to 6 feet MLW with good holding. This spot offers all-around protection. You can anchor at Blue Point with good holding ground in 4 to 6 feet at MLW. This is well protected from all but a rare southeasterly. Only the surge of the Patchogue ferries disturbs the calm.

Patchogue to Brookhaven

Patchogue is the shopping and industrial town for much of eastern Long Island, and the town's waterfront takes care of hundreds of boats each season. Howells Point, on the mainland about 3 nm miles east of Patchogue, marks the start of Bellport Bay.

The villages of Bellport and Brookhaven are on its north shore, offering a scattering of marinas;

however, the bay does become increasingly shallow here. Bellport Town Dock, which lies between Howells Point and Beaver Dam Creek, provides ample room for visitors to tie up on the outside for the day. (No overnight dockage.) The town is just a 1 mile walk up a tree-shaded street, has all the charm of a New England village and boasts a chic pub and a couple of fine restaurants.

Dockage: Deep Patchogue River is entered between breakwaters from Patchogue Bay, a bight of Great South Bay. Marinas here range from fishing stations to complete repair operations. Gas and diesel fuel are also available. More marine services and facilities are to the east on Swan River, Mud Creek, Abets Creek and Beaverdam Creek. See our marina table for details.

Anchorage: A delightful anchorage just north of the Bellport Town Dock is secluded and protected. However, boats carrying a draft greater than 5 feet should approach cautiously and check the state of tide before anchoring. This area is exposed to the southwest.

Great South Bay, NY

		Largest Vessel Accomodated	VHF Channel Monitored / Working	Transient Slips / Total Slips	Approach / Dockside Depth (reported)	Floating Docks	Gas / Diesel	Groceries, Ice, Marine Supplies, Snacks	Repairs: Hull, Engine, Propeller	Lift (tonnage), Crane, Rail	Min / Max Amps	Courtesy Car, Laundry, Pool, Showers	Pump-Out Station	Nearby: Grocery Store, Motel, Restaurant
		Dockage					**Supplies**		**Services**					
SAYVILLE														
1. West Sayville Boat Basin	(631) 589-4141	50	/	20/150	6.0/6.0	F	GD	M	HEP	L	30/50	S	P	R
2. Land's End Motel & Marina	(631) 589-2040	42	/	3/38	5.0/5.0			I			30	PS		GMR
BAY POINT														
3. Bay Point Marina	(631) 363-6503	45	/	6/90	4.0/4.0		G	IM	HP		30			
BLUE POINT														
4. Blue Point Marina	(631) 363-2000	40	/	/130	6.0/5.0		G	IM	HEP	L	30			R
PATCHOGUE AREA														
5. Island View Marina & Fuel WiFi	(631) 447-1234	50	/	/44	10.0/5.0		GD	IM	HEP	L20	30	S	P	GMR
6. Leeward Cove South	(631) 654-3106	55	/	4/230	5.0/5.0	F		IM	HEP	L25	30	S	P	R
7. Frank M. Weeks Yacht Yard	(631) 475-1675	60	/	/70	7.0/7.0			M	HEP	L40	30/50	S		GR
8. White Water Marine Service	(631) 475-5000	30	/	/	5.0/5.0	F		M	EP		30			MR
9. Dickson Marine East	(631) 475-1445		16/9	/	5.0/4.0		GD	IMS	HEP	L80				
10. Aquamarina Sunset Harbour ☐ WiFi	(631) 289-3800	65	/	/332	6.0/3.0			IS	HEP	L50	30/50	LPS	P	GMR
11. Patchogue Shores Marina	(631) 475-0790		16/36	/100	6.0/6.0		G	M	EP	L30	30/50	LS	P	R
BEAVERDAM														
12. Beaver Dam Boat Basin WiFi	(631) 286-7816	53	16/68	10/70	10.0/7.0	F		M	HP	L30	30	S		GMR

☐ Internet Access   WiFi Wireless Internet Access   onSpot Dockside WiFi Facility

See WaterwayGuide.com for current rates, fuel prices, website addresses, and other up-to-the-minute information. (Information in the table is provided by the facilities.)

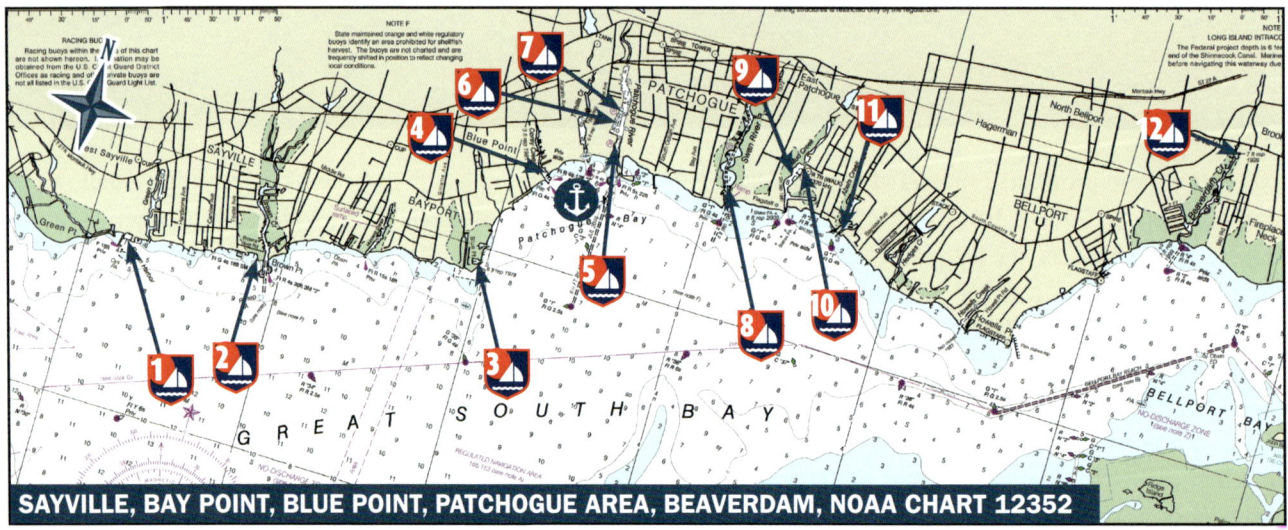

SAYVILLE, BAY POINT, BLUE POINT, PATCHOGUE AREA, BEAVERDAM, NOAA CHART 12352

Robert Moses Causeway, Great South Bay

MORICHES BAY TO SHINNECOCK INLET

Moriches Bay

Moriches Bay is about 8 nm long with central depths of 3 to 6 feet MLW, sizable shoals in its southern reaches and many coves and creeks that tend to shoal despite dredging. The towns of Moriches, East Moriches and Center Moriches rim the bay.

Seatuck Creek leads to the pretty, small village of Eastport, which has the feel of old Long Island. The main street (Montauk Highway) is lined with sunshine-bathed buildings that house shops and eateries.

South of Remsenburg on the barrier beach is the site of Pike's Inlet for the time it existed. It was created during the Halloween 1992 nor'easter, when the ocean overran this narrow strip. Subsequent storms enlarged the breach until it was several hundred feet wide. Less than a year later the Army Corps of Engineers later put a metal wall across it and poured sand into the breach to seal it.

Near the eastern tip of the inlet, there is a little-known park accessible only by foot or boat. Great Gunn Beach is a town-run park about 0.75 mile west of the inlet. Because eastern Fire Island is a national seashore, it is nearly undeveloped. Docks, restrooms and a narrow boardwalk to the beach are all the facilities here. At night, Great Gunn is nothing but the sweep of stars, the ocean and the inlet.

NAVIGATION: Use NOAA Chart 12352. Continuing east, the course doglegs into a dredged channel where markers must be observed. The **Smith Point Bridge** (18-foot closed vertical clearance) connects mainland Shirley with eastern Fire Island. The draw opens on signal from October 1 through April 30 from 8:00 a.m. to 4:00 p.m. and from May 1 through September 30 from 6:00 a.m. to 10:00 p.m. At all other times during these periods, the draw will open as soon as possible but no more than 1 hour after a request to open is received.

The channel continues about 3 nm through Narrow Bay, past Mastic Beach into the western approach to Moriches Bay. Note that the shoal-bordered channel is only a few hundred feet wide.

Narrow Bay connects Bellport Bay and Moriches Bay. The shifting shoals of Moriches Bay change so rapidly that mariners often find it difficult to maneuver without running aground. The Army Corps of Engineers cautions that shoals of 1 to 5 feet MLW are located in the vicinity of Tuthill Point and 3 to 6 feet MLW in Moriches Bay. Ongoing dredging does occur; however, the area is very prone to shoaling.

Tree stakes will guide you through the deepest sections of the bay. You are advised to leave the stakes to the south going east. These makeshift markers follow a zigzag pattern north to Harts Cove, east to Seatuck Cove and south to the marked channel. They are an enormous boon to cruising boats that would otherwise need to call the Coast Guard or local marinas to get information on the shoaling.

Dockage: Marinas are located on most of the creeks, but they are almost exclusively for local boats. The 140-slip Atlantic Cove Marina has full-service dockage facilities including valet docking as well as hauling and launching. All of these facilities report shallow depths; refer to our marina table for details.

Side Trip: Great Gunn

NAVIGATION: Use NOAA Chart 12352. On the south shore of Moriches Bay, an interesting route east from Great Gunn is through a small channel known locally as "Old Cut." It is a narrow, unmarked channel through the shallows running 10° (true) from Great Gunn. It intersects another channel that is dredged but not buoyed. This channel leads you into the relatively deep water just inside Moriches Inlet. These are unstable channels so slow and easy is the way.

From the inner mouth of Moriches Inlet, a curving channel leads back to the State Channel in Moriches Bay. Hug the southern and eastern banks of this channel until you are dead east (true) of the unnamed island inside the inlet, then you can move to center channel. That unnamed island has become a home to the growing seal population of the South Shore bays. You will see them basking on the beach but they will take to the safety of the water if a boat comes too close.

Anchorage: To do some basking of your own, beach the boat along the curving channel. (There is a steep drop-off.) It is a quick walk to the ocean beach, but do not swim in the channel. Fast-moving boats hug the shore, making it dangerous.

On weekend days Great Gunn attracts a small crowd of boats. It is also easy to anchor just off the docks and wade in; just allow for the tide. The restrooms are locked at about 5:00 p.m. There is more room to anchor east of the channel than west. Great Gunn Beach is unmarked on the chart but you will see the buoyed channel to it through the shallows of Moriches Bay.

Moriches Bay, NY

W G

			Dockage				Supplies		Services					
		Largest Vessel Accomodated	VHF Channel Monitored / Working	Transient Slips / Total Slips	Approach / Dockside Depth (reported)	Floating Docks	Groceries, Ice, Marine Supplies, Snacks	Gas / Diesel	Repairs: Hull, Engine, Propeller	Lift (tonnage) Crane, Rail	Courtesy Car, Laundry, Pool, Showers	Min / Max Amps	Pump-Out Station	Nearby: Grocery Store, Motel, Restaurant
EAST MORICHES														
1. Atlantic Cove Marina (formerly Windswept Marina)	(631) 878-2100	40	68/	10/140	4.0/4.0	F	GD	IMS	HEP	L		30	S	P	GMR
2. Remsenburg Marina WIFI	(631) 325-1677	45	/	/125	4.0/6.0	F	GD	IM	HEP	L25		30		P	G
WESTHAMPTON BEACH														
3. Ocean Resort at Bath and Tennis WIFI	(631) 288-2500	50	9/	6/65	9.0/7.0			I			30/50	LPS	P	GMR
4. Westhampton Beach Municipal Yacht Basin WIFI	(631) 288-9496	55	68/	12/125	4.0/4.0			I				S	P	GMR

💻 Internet Access   WIFI Wireless Internet Access   onSpot Dockside WiFi Facility

See WaterwayGuide.com for current rates, fuel prices, website addresses, and other up-to-the-minute information. (Information in the table is provided by the facilities.)

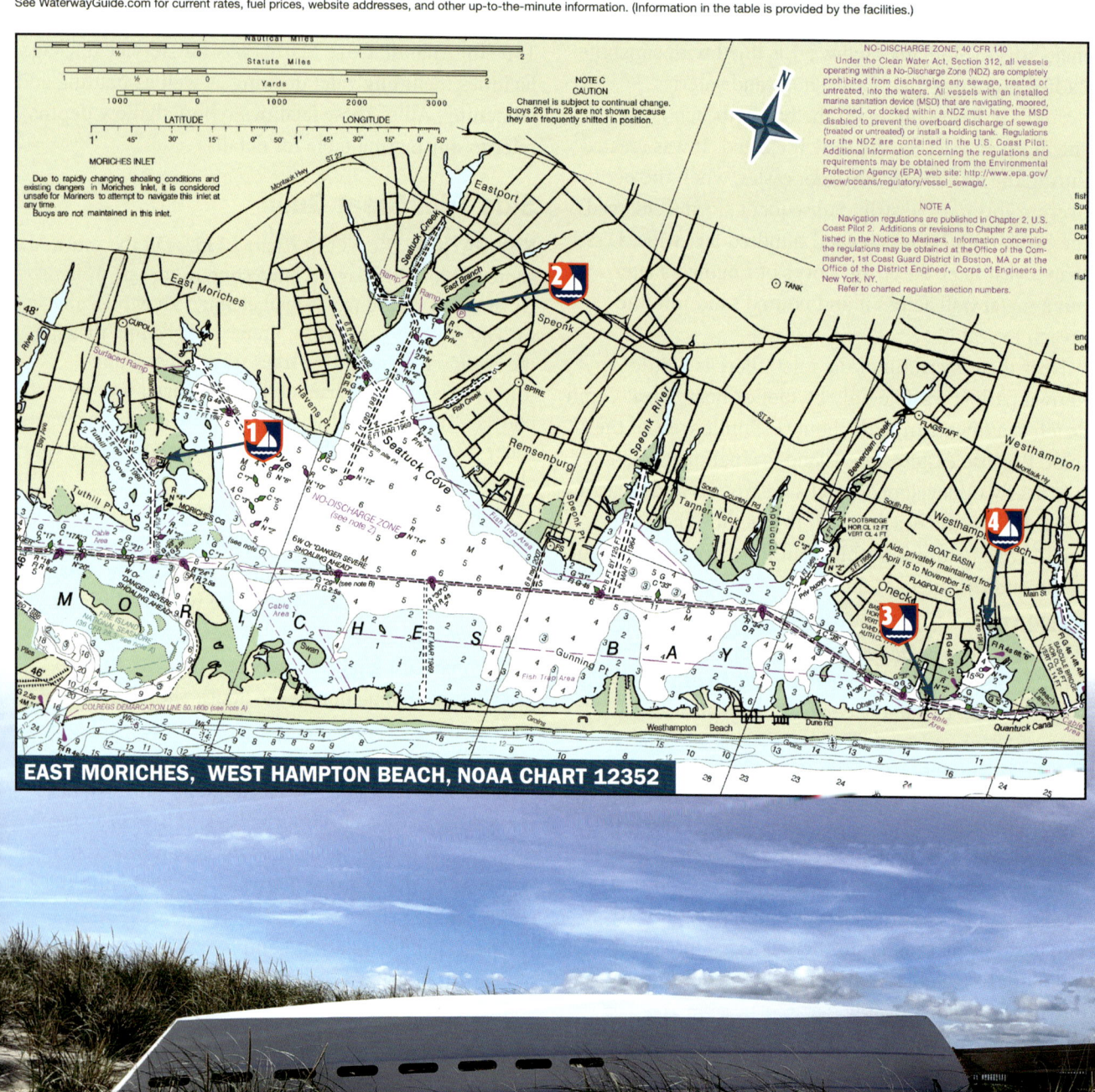

EAST MORICHES, WEST HAMPTON BEACH, NOAA CHART 12352

Quantuck Bay

NAVIGATION: Use NOAA Chart 12352. South of Speonk Point a large shoal with 2-to 3-foot MLW charted depths extends north from Gunning Point and may encroach on the channel. About 4 nm east of Moriches Inlet, transient accommodations are available along both sides of the channel at Westhampton Beach. The channel angles into Quantuck Canal in this area with two bascule bridges just 1 mile apart.

The **West Bay Bridge** has a 10-foot closed vertical clearance and is followed by the **Beach Lane Bridge** with a 14-foot closed vertical clearance. The schedule for both bridges is the same: The draw will open on signal from October 1 through April 30 from 8:00 a.m. to 4:00 p.m. and from May 1 through September 30 from 6:00 a.m. to 10:00 p.m. At all other times during these periods the draws will open as soon as possible but no more than 1 hour after a request to open is received. Just north of this area on the mainland side is Westhampton, one of Long Island's most popular summer colonies.

The channel leaves Quantuck Canal for a straight, dredged course across Quantuck Bay and then enters Quogue (rhymes with "fog") Canal. A little more than 1 mile long, the canal bends as shoals push out from the village of Quogue, an old summer resort with big homes (but few marinas). The **Quogue (Post Lane) Bridge** (15-foot closed vertical clearance) is near the western end of the canal. The draw follows the same schedule as the West Bay and Beach Lane Bridges. Just beyond the bridge Quogue Canal enters Shinnecock Bay.

Dockage: Ocean Resort at Bath and Tennis operates seasonally with memberships offered to those who rent a marina slip, cabana or cabin. Members have access to all of the resort amenities and services. Westhampton Beach Municipal Yacht Basin is nearby with transient space to 50 feet.

Shinnecock Bay

Shinnecock Bay, last of the important South Shore bays, is a pivotal point for cruising boats. The inland passage along Long Island's South Shore ends here and to the north Shinnecock Canal gives direct access to Great Peconic Bay, the Long Island North and South Fork areas and the north shore of Long Island.

The bay is about 7 nm long and closed off north and east by the Long Island mainland and is divided by long, sandy Ponquogue Point. Access from the mainland to the barrier island is via the 55-foot fixed vertical clearance Ponquogue Bridge.

Shinnecock's port houses the second largest fishing fleet in New York State with three commercial docks. The area also provides a habitat for piping plovers, least terns and other endangered species of birds.

NAVIGATION: Use NOAA Chart 12352. Shinnecock Bay starts unremarkable enough at the eastern end of narrow Quogue Canal where the channel turns north. It follows a relatively straight course through 1- to 2-foot MLW shoals past a series of private, dredged creeks (Penniman, Stone and Phillips) with attractive shores but no public marinas. Just off Phillips Point the channel crooks to the east and transient boats have a choice of marinas.

Tiana Bay lies east of Pine Neck, which is lined with several shallow finger canals. The bay is open and has fairly stable 5-foot MLW depths instead of the bars, marshes and dredged cuts of most of the eastern portion of the South Shore. According to local reports, shoals extend from Pine Neck Point nearly to the channel.

From Tiana Bay, the route passes the long finger of East Point, headland of Smith Creek, with shoals all about. Stick to the buoys. The narrow channel forks beyond the 55-foot fixed vertical clearance **Ponquogue Bridge**, where the Shinnecock Coast Guard station is located. The southeast branch runs toward Shinnecock Inlet and the northeast branch to Shinnecock Canal. Both branches go through bars and marshes. The southeast channel toward Shinnecock Inlet passes between two of the three mud flats that are known as the Warner Islands. The smallest, westernmost of the islands has been locally renamed Seal Island. This has become another seal population center of the south bays.

Dockage: Limited dockage is available at East Quogue, in the Tiana Bay area and west of the Ponquogue fixed bridge. There is limited transient space so call ahead for slip availability.

Oaklands Restaurant & Marina is a waterfront destination on the barrier island that has been a summer staple for 29 years with a full-service restaurant, bar and marina located adjacent to the Shinnecock Inlet.

Sherry & Joe Corr's Best Boat Works is across the bay in Old Fort Pond. They have just three transient slips on their floating docks, offer repairs and sell gas.

Shinnecock Canal & Lock Shinnecock Canal is located in the northwestern corner of Shinnecock Bay above Cormorant Point. The canal is the gateway to the Peconic Bays and Long Island's north shore. West of the

Shinnecock Bay, NY

		Dockage					Supplies		Services					
Facility	**Phone**	Largest Vessel Accomodated	VHF Channel Monitored / Working	Approach / Dockside Depth (reported)	Transient Slips / Total Slips	Floating Docks	Groceries, Ice, Marine Supplies, Snacks	Gas / Diesel	Repairs: Hull, Engine, Propeller	Lift (tonnage), Crane, Rail	Min / Max Amps	Courtesy Car, Laundry, Pool, Showers	Pump-Out Station	Nearby: Grocery Store, Motel, Restaurant
EAST QUOGUE														
1. Aldrich Boat Yard & Marina	(631) 653-5300	45	/	6.0/6.0	/60	F			HEP	L32	30			R
2. Hampton Marine Center	(631) 653-0687	65	/	6.0/6.0	/35		M		HEP	L20	50			R
SHINNECOCK INLET														
3. Oakland's Restaurant & Marina	(516) 523-1435	60	68/	5.0/6.0	/72		IS	GD			50	S		GMR
TIANA AREA														
4. Ponquoge Marina [WIFI]	(631) 728-2264	45	/	3.5/6.0	2/50	F			HEP	L30,C	30	S		GMR
5. Hampton Boat Works [WIFI]	(631) 728-1114	50	/	6.0/5.0	4/40	F	I		HEP	L30	30/50	S		GMR
6. Colonial Shores Cottages & Marina	(631) 728-0011	23	/	6.0/4.0	10/28	F	I					LPS		GMR
SHINNECOCK HILLS														
7. Sherry & Joe Corr's Best Boat Works	(631) 283-7359	38	68/	4.0/4.0	3/44	F	IM	G	HEP	L12	30	S	P	MR
SHINNECOCK CANAL														
8. Prime Marina Southampton [WIFI]	(631) 728-4220	90	68/	8.0/6.0	5/200		IMS	GD	HEP	L75	50	S	P	GMR
9. Mariner's Cove Marine	(631) 728-0286	52	/	9.0/5.0	6/182	F	IMS		HEP	L35	30	S	P	GMR
10. Spellman's Marine	(631) 728-9200	36	/	5.0/5.0	5/80		M		HEP	L35	50	S		GMR
11. Modern Yachts Inc	(631) 728-2266	60	/	10.0/6.0	/46		IMS	GD	HEP	L40,C	50	PS	P	GMR
12. Hampton Watercraft & Marine ☐ [WIFI]	(631) 728-8200	80	/	12.0/8.0	5/100	F	IMS	GD	HEP	L16	30/50	S		GMR
13. Shinnecock Canal Marina	(631) 852-8291	47	/	10.0/6.0	20/50	F		GD			30	S	P	GMR

☐ Internet Access   [WIFI] Wireless Internet Access   onSpot Dockside WiFi Facility

See WaterwayGuide.com for current rates, fuel prices, website addresses, and other up-to-the-minute information. (Information in the table is provided by the facilities.)

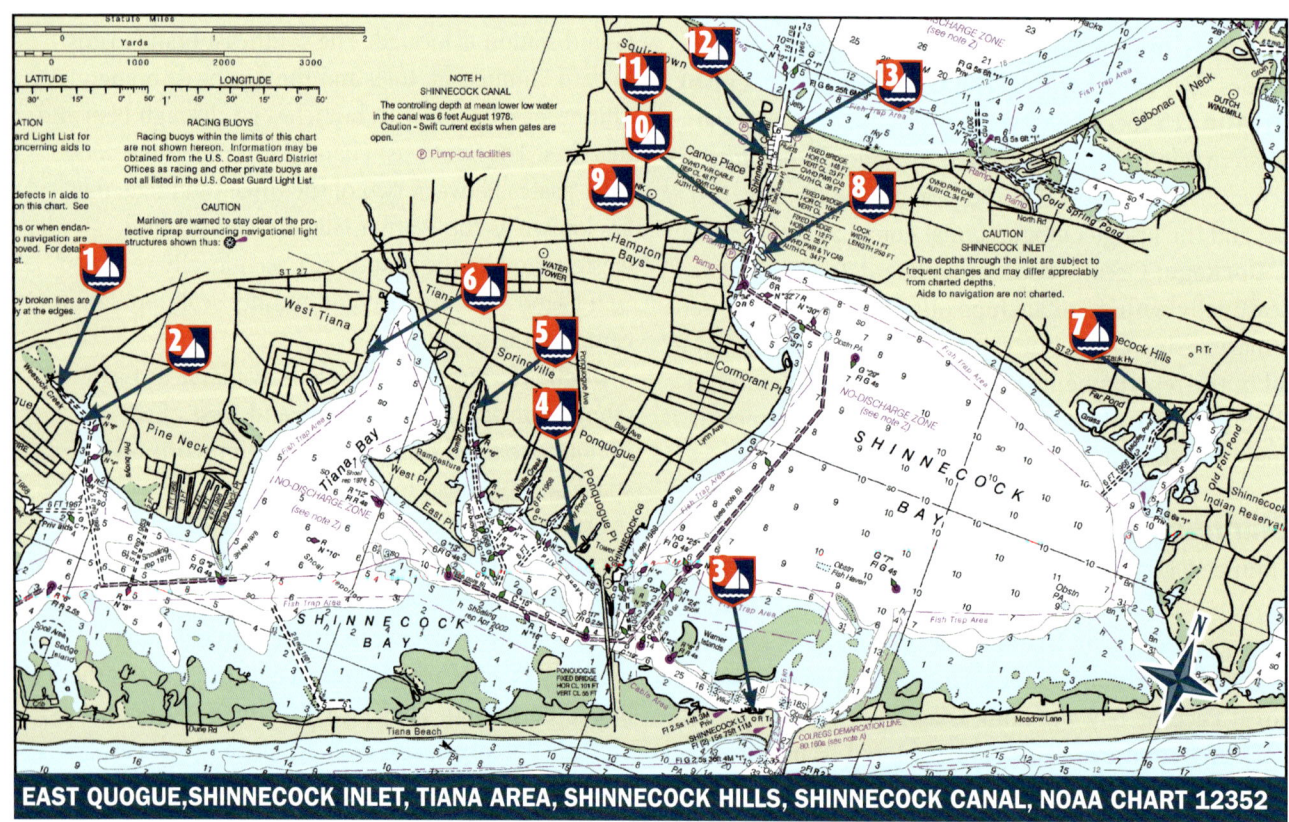

EAST QUOGUE, SHINNECOCK INLET, TIANA AREA, SHINNECOCK HILLS, SHINNECOCK CANAL, NOAA CHART 12352

Great Peconic Bay

Shinnecock Canal

canal is the lively community of Hampton Bays with motels and good restaurants.

> The part of Hampton Bays along the canal was called Canoe Place until the end World War I, perpetuating the legend that a Montauk chief dug the first canal to eliminate a canoe portage. It is still charted as Canoe Place.

NAVIGATION: Use NOAA Chart 12352. The 1-mile-long canal is wide and deep for the steady passage of boats in both directions. The **Shinnecock Canal Railroad Bridge** has a fixed overhead clearance of 22 feet, setting the clearance restriction for the canal. The 25-foot fixed vertical clearance **CR 80 Bridge** is prior to the railroad bridge. The county maintains free, unattended DIY ginpoles for un-stepping and re-stepping sailboat masts at each end of the canal.

A 250-foot-long and 41-foot-wide lock with 12 feet over the sills is located about midway through the canal. The tide running southward opens the Shinnecock Lock and Dam and parallel 27-foot tidal gates. Southbound boats usually use the tidal gates; however, larger boats are put through the lock whenever possible. Traffic lights control passage through the lock.

The locks are operated 24 hours a day and the operator controls all movement of boats through the lock by light signals. Communicate with the operator on VHF Channel 13 or by calling 631-852-8299. More information is also available at www.snark.dhs.org/shin.html). When approaching the lock, boaters should stop at a safe distance and follow specified signals. Boaters should give three short blasts on the horn or whistle. Lock operators will reply with lights in the following manner:

- Green: Lock is ready, craft may advance.

- Red: Craft must wait.

- No Light: Craft must wait or tie up to approach wall.

- Six flashes of red or green: Craft must remain stopped and await further instructions.

It is important to note that when the gates are open and the locks are not in use, you can pilot right through the canal. The current normally flows to the south when the gates are open (at up to 6 knots). When the gates are closed, you can still lock through. The current is relatively tame within 1 hour of the gate opening or closing. At other times it can be woolly. The

Sunrise Highway (NY 27) Bridge has 23-foot fixed vertical clearance and is located after the lock and before the marinas.

> ⚠️ Avoid going south with the current when it is raging. It will be a fast ride through the narrow passage. Going north in these conditions also requires slow speed and no wake to maintain control. Northbound boats without strong engines can have a hard time and should negotiate the canal at slack water. When traveling in either direction, watch for the eddies on the south side by the bridge.

Dockage: Marinas inside along the barrier strip of Shinnecock Inlet mostly cater to sportfishers. The banks of the canal are lined with marinas, boatyards, boat brokerages and fishing stations–one after another–except near the lock. The municipal Shinnecock Canal Marina at the north end of the canal offers a fully equipped facility that includes free pump-out stations, restrooms and showers, and water and electric hookups. Meschutt Beach County Park is adjacent to the marina with lifeguard-protected swimming and a full-service concession stand.

■ OUTSIDE (OCEAN) ROUTE TO SHINNECOCK INLET

If you are in a hurry, you can run the coast of Long Island offshore. It is a pleasant trip in good weather if you have the skill and the proper boat. In bad weather, however, the outside passage can be unpleasant and potentially hazardous.

Long barrier beaches run between most of the island's mainland and the Atlantic Ocean on the south shore of Long island. Thirty-foot depths are only 1 nm from shore for most of the outside run but there is considerable distance between inlets that are safe to enter, especially in poor conditions.

There are six inlets along the south shore. All can be shoal-prone and continually shifting. Weather systems moving along the east coast of the U.S. frequently assault the shore, sometimes creating new ingress and sometimes shoaling in existing ones. You can try to follow a local boat into one of these inlets; otherwise, you have no choice but to make the long trek around Montauk Point.

Rockaway Inlet

NAVIGATION: Use NOAA Charts 12350 and 12352. Rockaway Inlet is the first inlet along the South Shore, 5 miles northeast of Sandy Hook. The inlet enters through Dead Horse Bay into Sheepshead Bay and further into Jamaica Bay via the **Marine Parkway (Gill Hodges Memorial) Bridge** (55-foot vertical clearance when down, 152-foot clearance when raised). Although the inlet does not connect with the inside waterways, there are several areas of interest within the inlet itself.

There is a well-marked channel along the northern shore along Coney Island and Brighton Beach and another along the southern shore on the inside of Rockaway Point. Except in a dead-on west wind, this can afford a secure place to wait for weather to go around the point and continue along Long Island South Shore.

East Rockaway Inlet

NAVIGATION: Use NOAA Charts 12350 and 12352. The East Rockaway Inlet is the next inlet encountered proceeding along the South Shore on the outside. It is the preferable inlet to access the inside run of the South Shore because it is wide and easy to navigate. This inlet (known locally as Debs Inlet) is 10 nm from Coney Island and 13 nm from Sandy Hook. The U.S. Army Corps of Engineers tries to maintain 12-foot MLW depths in East Rockaway Inlet but as with all inlets, use caution and good common sense when you enter.

You will find the inlet easy to enter in good weather. A flashing white (every four seconds) 33-foot-high tower marks the inlet's eastern jetty extending from Silver Point. Shoaling from 1-to 5-foot MLW depths builds out from the jetty toward the west. If approaching from the east or south, give the jetty and Silver Point a wide berth.

You will pass under the **Atlantic Beach Bridge** (30-foot closed vertical clearance) when entering Reynolds Channel. The draw opens on signal from October 1 through May 14. From May 15 through September 30 the draw will open on signal, except that it need open only on the hour and half-hour from 4:00 p.m. to 7:00 p.m. on weekdays and from 11:00 a.m. to 9:00 p.m. on Saturdays, Sundays, Memorial Day, Independence Day and Labor Day. From May 15 through September 30. Once inside the inlet, you can cruise comfortably while seas build outside or you can transit the inside Reynolds Channel route and head back out at Jones Inlet.

Jones Inlet

NAVIGATION: Use NOAA Chart 12352. Jones Inlet, almost 9 nm east of East Rockaway Inlet, is dredged periodically when bottom conditions warrant. It is well marked but the buoys are uncharted and frequently moved. The inlet has been holding at a depth of 9 feet MLW but the current chart calls for cautious navigation. The western (shoal) bar should be avoided. A VHF radio request for local knowledge is always a prudent move to avoid shoal areas that might have developed since the last buoy relocation. If navigating from Jones Inlet to Fire Island Inlet on the inside route (13 miles), you will encounter several bridges with restricted openings. These are described in detail in the "Inside Route" section.

Fire Island Inlet

NAVIGATION: Use NOAA Chart 12352. Fire Island Inlet is the only pass between the Atlantic Ocean and Great South Bay but it should not be attempted without local knowledge. The U.S. Army Corps of Engineers dredges here periodically but also indicates that conditions will not be dependable until an extensive stabilization program is begun. Powerful storms have played havoc with the shifting shoals and submerged buoys. About 2 miles in from the mouth, the **Robert Moses Bridge** crosses the inlet. (Note that although the bridge is posted with 65-foot clearance, it is recommended that you pass at low tide as actual clearance seems to be closer to 60 feet.)

Fire Island Inlet is about 13 nm beyond Jones Inlet. In fair weather, you can use Fire Island Inlet to get to the open waters of Great South Bay while avoiding the tediously slow and crowded channel inside from Jones Inlet. Its buoy system is excellent but not charted because of the continuously shifting shoals. The entrance is difficult without local knowledge, even in good weather, and it is unsafe to enter when wind and tide oppose. In heavy weather breakers bar the entrance. Do not attempt entry in these conditions or with poor visibility. The local Coast Guard (Station Fire Island) will give information to those unfamiliar with the area.

Once inside the inlet, depths improve along the southern edge of the channel. Watch for flashing red buoy "10" and a series of green and red navigational aids, which will guide you toward the Robert Moses Bridge (65-foot fixed vertical clearance).

Moriches Inlet

NAVIGATION: Use NOAA Chart 12352. Fire Island Inlet and Jones Inlet are comparatively new, as they were broken through by storms in the 1930s. Moriches Inlet, however, remains the most untamed of the five South Shore inlets. The area around the inlet is also somewhat wild. To the east is a section of Westhampton Beach that the ocean is intent on reclaiming. To the west is the undeveloped eastern tip of Fire Island. Moriches Inlet was dredged in 2018 but is still recommended for small local boats and not cruisers.

At press time in winter 2020-2021 erratic Moriches Inlet had privately maintained lights at the seaward end but was not buoyed because of the inlet's rapidly changing, dangerous conditions. We recommend heading east to Shinnecock Inlet (15 nm) or west to Fire Island Inlet (27 nm) for safer passages.

Shinnecock Inlet

NAVIGATION: Use NOAA Chart 12352. Shinnecock Inlet was created by the great hurricane of 1938. It mostly maintains 20-foot MLW depths (with the exception of one charted 17-foot-MLW section at the entrance) and has stone breakwaters. When entering the inlet from the ocean, proceed carefully and slightly favor the west side of the channel. Enter the inlet between the flashing green 36-foot tower "1A" on the west jetty and the flashing red 36-foot tower "2A" on the east jetty. Shinnecock Light (75-foot flashing red every 15 seconds) will appear to the west as you enter. Many small fishing boats use the inlet so be on the lookout during your approach.

Beyond Shinnecock Inlet are the prestigious Hamptons: Southampton, East Hampton and Bridgehampton. The Hamptons retain much of their Colonial charm with trendy shops, gourmet restaurants, pleasant parks and beaches, which continue to draw the rich and famous as visitors and seasonal residents. No trip to the area would be complete without an excursion to any or all of them.

■ NEXT STOP

At the northern end of the canal, you will pass between the jetties into Great Peconic Bay and its satellite bays. This is an easy run to avoid the long, open passage around Montauk Point to Block Island Sound.

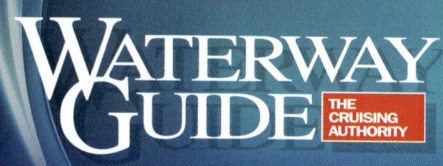

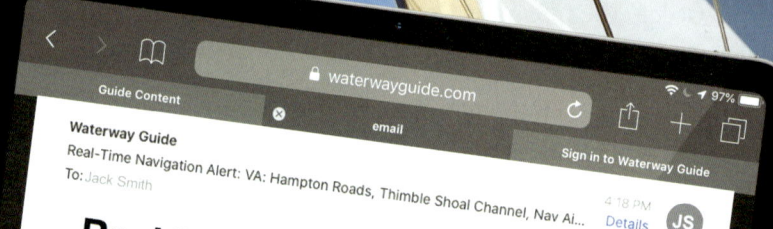

New York Harbor & The East River

■ NAVIGATING NEW YORK WATERS

North through The Narrows into New York Harbor–one of the world's finest natural harbors–is the great city of New York, with its five boroughs and 8.5 million residents. Many superlatives apply to New York City and it is not lacking in boating amenities. While there are a few possibilities in Manhattan, most of the marinas are found on the New Jersey side of New York Harbor in Jersey City, Weehawkin and Hoboken. Ferries and water taxis make the trip on a regular basis back and forth to Manhattan. These large, full-service marinas in New Jersey are close to dining, provisioning, transportation and waterfront events.

Directly alongside the skyscrapers of Manhattan runs the magnificent, scenic East River, twisting its way past the South Street Seaport, beautiful east-side buildings with penthouse gardens and Gracie Mansion, New York's mayoral home. The East River also leads to the cruising Mecca of Long Island Sound.

Also covered in this section is the Hudson River, located west of of Manhattan, connecting the Erie Canal and Lake Erie or the Champlain Canal and Lake Champlain. (Waterway Guide's Great Lakes Vol. 1 contains details on these routes.)

Cruising Conditions

New York Harbor is one of the world's busiest harbors. Ships and barges are always on the move in and out of the harbor, anchoring and docking at piers along the Hudson River, the East River and heading to ports in New Jersey. You will be accompanied by tankers, freighters of all flags, cruise ships, naval vessels, a myriad of tugs and tows and recreational boat traffic, along with continual ferry service to and from Staten Island, New Jersey ports on the Hudson and through The Narrows to ports south. Full attention is required of even the most experienced skippers. Always give big ships the right-of-way; they have limited maneuvering room. Shipping traffic monitors VHF Channel 13 and do not hesitate to contact any ship or barge if you need clarification on their intention.

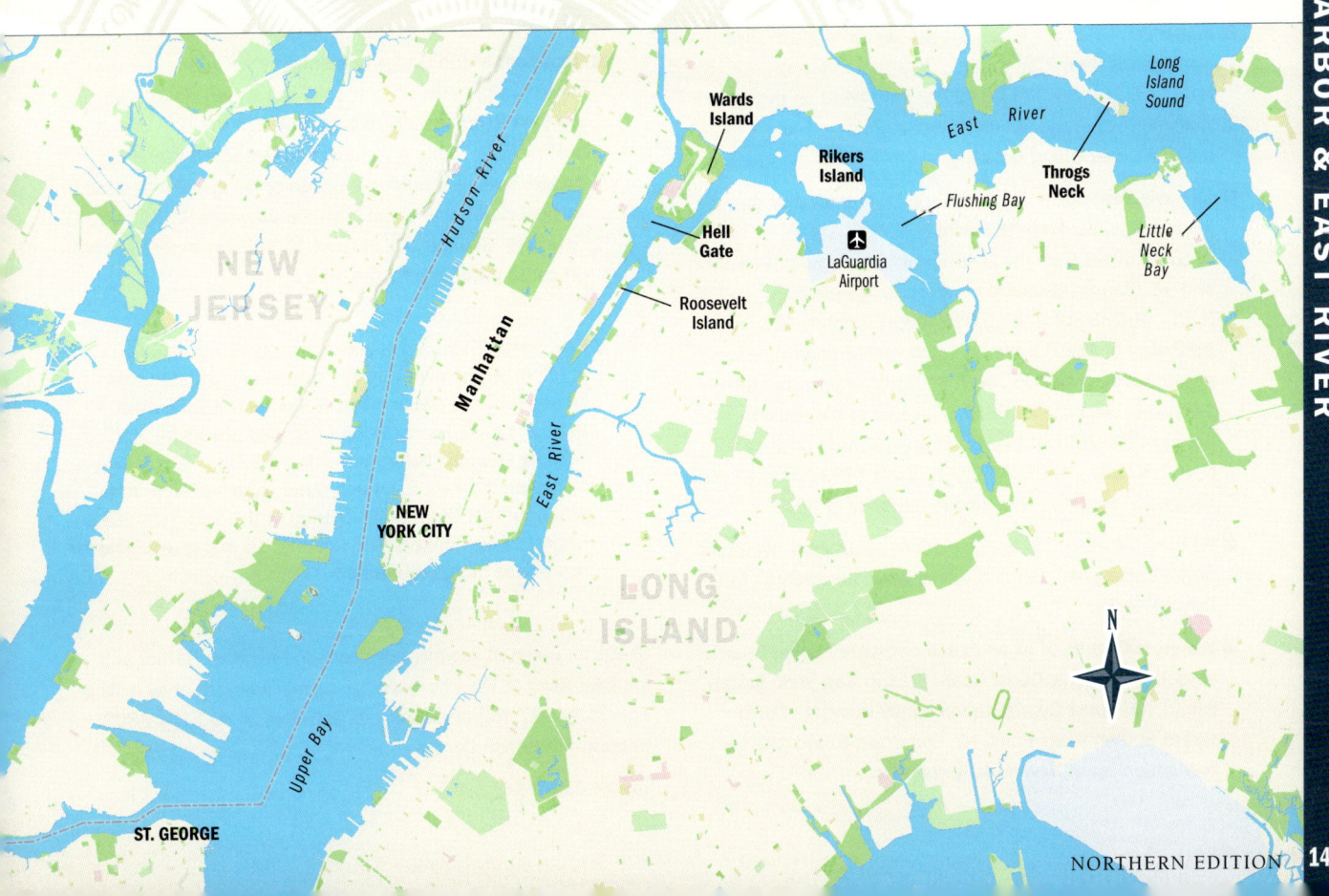

NEW YORK AREA SECURITY ZONES

The Coast Guard reports that the following security zones apply to all vessels:

- Upper New York Bay, around Liberty Island and Ellis Island: No vessels are allowed within 150 yards of either island or the bridge between the two.

- Indian Point Nuclear Power Station on the Hudson River: No vessel is permitted within a 300-yard radius of N 41° 16.207'/W 073° 57.270'. Any vessel on the Hudson River in the vicinity of Indian Point is subject to random Coast Guard boarding.

- All navigable waters of the Hudson River bound by the following points: From the point N 40° 46.150'/ W 073° 59.812' on the seawall midway between Pier 92 and 94, thence northwest to approximate position N 40° 46.233'/W 074° 0.015', approximately 125 yards northwest of Pier 92, thence southwest to approximate position N 40° 45.945'/W 074° 0.255', approximately 150 yards west of Pier 86, thence east to the seawall between Pier 84 and Pier 86 at approximate position N 40° 45.827'/W 073° 59.968' (NAD 1983), thence northeast along the shoreline to the point of origin.

- Within 25 yards of all bridge piers or abutments, overhead power cables, and pier and tunnel ventilators south of the Troy, NY, locks.

- Within 100 yards of all anchored or moored Coast Guard vessels or stations; Coast Guard Station New York, Staten Island, NY; Coast Guard Station Sandy Hook, NJ; Coast Guard Station Kings Point, NY; and Coast Guard Aids to Navigation Team New York, Bayonne, NJ.

- Additional restricted areas exist in Port Newark/Port Elizabeth in Newark Bay and around New York City, including near heliports, cruise ships, liquified hazardous gas (LHG) vessels, marine terminals and airports. For details, consult the Coast Guard *Local Notice to Mariners* for District 1.

- Roosevelt Island Bridge openings: When special security zones are put into place around the United Nations in the East River, vessels must go through the east channel of Roosevelt Island and under the Roosevelt Island Lift Bridge. Vessels requiring a bridge opening (40-foot closed vertical clearance) should call the tender at 718-361-9217 or on VHF Channel 13, at least 15 minutes before you plan on passing through the lift bridge.

- East River: There are significant security regulations in effect on the river that are continually updated and changed by the Department of Homeland Security and the U.S. Coast Guard. Skippers should always be alert to security changes before transiting the East River. While transiting the East River and other waters of New York City, note that the marine division of the New York Police Department monitors VHF Channel 16 and is available for assistance in an emergency.

Check for updated security advisories in New York Harbor and the East River at www.homeport.uscg.mil/newyork or by calling 718-354-4037. Report suspicious activities at 800-424-8802, National Response Center.

Source: 33CFR 165.169

New York Harbor waters are deep and well marked. In fog or rain follow the main channel buoys closely but you can also run just outside of the channel itself in plenty of water and steer clear of big-ship traffic. Compass or GPS courses might be needed to sort out one buoy from another and take extra time at night to be certain of the lights.

Watch for debris throughout the entire New York Harbor area, especially on the outgoing tide. Because of the waterways converging in the Harbor, debris is carried in and out from many areas. Powerboats should slow down to reduce the chance of hitting such objects. Uncertain winds generally require that sailboats use their auxiliary engines when transiting the Harbor; this is definitely the case in the East River. All vessels should monitor VHF Channel 16 and stay alert to traffic that might be just around the corner.

⚠ Laws in New York prohibit the carrying of handguns on vessels in state waters without a permit. Permits must be applied for in person. Jail sentences and stiff fines are possible.

◼ NEW YORK HARBOR

As you pass by the northern tip of Staten Island, the entire panorama of New York City is spread before you. On the New Jersey side is a condominium complex, Port Liberté, which is reminiscent of French canals and countryside. A well-marked channel leads into the canals. Ahead, rising ever higher on the New York side, are the densely packed skyscrapers of the Lower Manhattan financial district. To the west is the Statue of Liberty, looking serene and lovely at 300-feet tall on her pedestal on Liberty Island. In the past it was possible to run fairly close to the copper-green landmark, but you now must now stay at least 150 yards from either Liberty or Ellis Islands.

Ellis Island, through which millions of immigrants entered the U.S. to build new lives, lies just north of the Statue of Liberty. From a distance, its Moorish towers and minarets still have the look of a fairytale castle. There is no dockage on either island for recreational vessels. Ferry service runs to Liberty Island from The Battery in New York and from Liberty State Park in Jersey City.

Lower Hudson River, NY

		Largest Vessel Accomodated	VHF Channel Monitored / Working	Transient Slips / Total Slips	Approach / Dockside Depth (reported)	Floating Docks	Gas / Diesel	Groceries, Ice, Marine Supplies, Snacks	Repairs: Hull, Engine, Propeller	Lift (tonnage), Crane, Rail	Min / Max Amps	Courtesy Car, Laundry, Pool, Showers	Pump-Out Station	Nearby: Grocery Store, Motel, Restaurant
				Dockage			**Supplies**		**Services**					
JERSEY CITY														
1. Liberty Landing Marina ▢ WiFi MM 0.46 RDB	(201) 985-8000	200	72/72	60/520	22.0/12.0	F	GD	IMS	HEP	L60,C	30/200+	LS	P	GMR
2. Liberty Harbor Marina ▢ WiFi MM 0.46 RDB	(800) 646-2066	60	68/	/180	20.0/18.0	F	GD	IM	HEP	L60	30/50	LS	P	GMR
HOBOKEN														
3. The Shipyard Marina WiFi MM 3.45 RDB	(201) 798-8080		78/78	/50	12.0/10.0	F		S			30/50			GMR
4. Lincoln Harbor Yacht Club ▢ WiFi MM 4.0 RDB	(201) 319-5100	220	74/	50/250	12.0/5.0	F	GD	IM	P		30/100	LS		GMR
BROOKLYN														
5. ONE°15 Brooklyn Marina ▢ WiFi	(718) 490-7136	275	71/	/100	39.0/45.0	F		IMS			30/200+	S	P	GR
MANHATTAN														
6. North Cove Marina (IGY) WiFi MM 0.80 LDB	(917) 677-7680	175	69/69	20/32	25.0/16.0	F		M			30/100		P	GMR
7. Marina at Chelsea Pier ▢ WiFi MM 3.10 LDB	(212) 336-7873	300	68/	15/70	19.0/8.0	F		IS			30/100			GMR
8. 79th Street Boat Basin WiFi MM 6.30 LDB	(212) 496-2105	210	9/9	/116	20.0/3.0	F		I			30/100	LS	P	GMR

▢ Internet Access   WiFi Wireless Internet Access   onSpot Dockside WiFi Facility

See WaterwayGuide.com for current rates, fuel prices, website addresses, and other up-to-the-minute information. (Information in the table is provided by the facilities.)

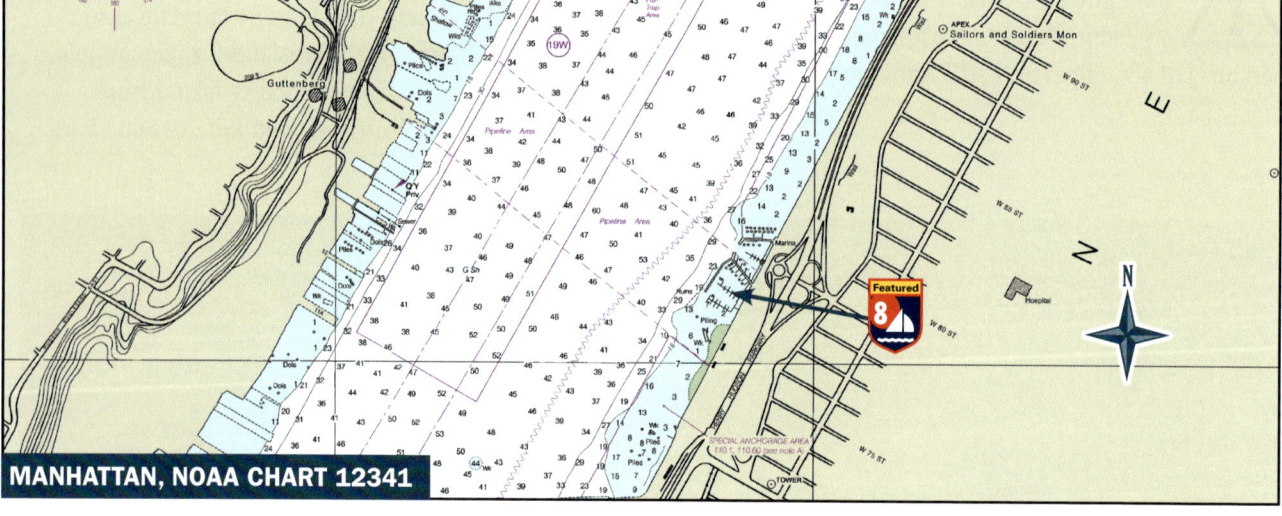

MANHATTAN, NOAA CHART 12341

Across the harbor, 0.5 mile south of The Battery, is Governors Island, formerly the headquarters of the Coast Guard's Third District. Coast Guard operations specifically for New York Harbor are now headquartered in Bayonne, NJ, and Staten Island, NY. Governors Island is open to the public every Friday through Sunday and is accessible by ferry or water taxi only. (Private boats not allowed.)

The Narrows to The Battery

The **Verrazano–Narrows Bridge** (a fixed high-rise bridge with a 215-foot vertical clearance) is eighth among the world's largest suspension bridges and is located about 8 nm north of Sandy Hook, NJ. When the bridge opened on November 21, 1962, it was the longest suspension bridge in the world. Because of this extreme length, the bridge engineers had to take the curvature of the planet into account in its design. As a result, the tops of the towers are slightly farther apart then the bases. The bridge links Staten Island to Brooklyn and serves as the dividing line between Upper Bay and Lower Bay. Fort Wadsworth on Staten Island and Fort Hamilton in Brooklyn, both still standing, once guarded this 1-mile-wide keyhole to New York Harbor.

Beyond the Verrazano Narrows Bridge on the Staten Island side is a quarantine station where ships anchor for clearance. The usual course into and out of the Upper Bay (New York Harbor) is either in the center of the channel or along the Brooklyn shore. Big freight terminals with ships loading and discharging are in the slips of Staten Island and Bayonne to the west and

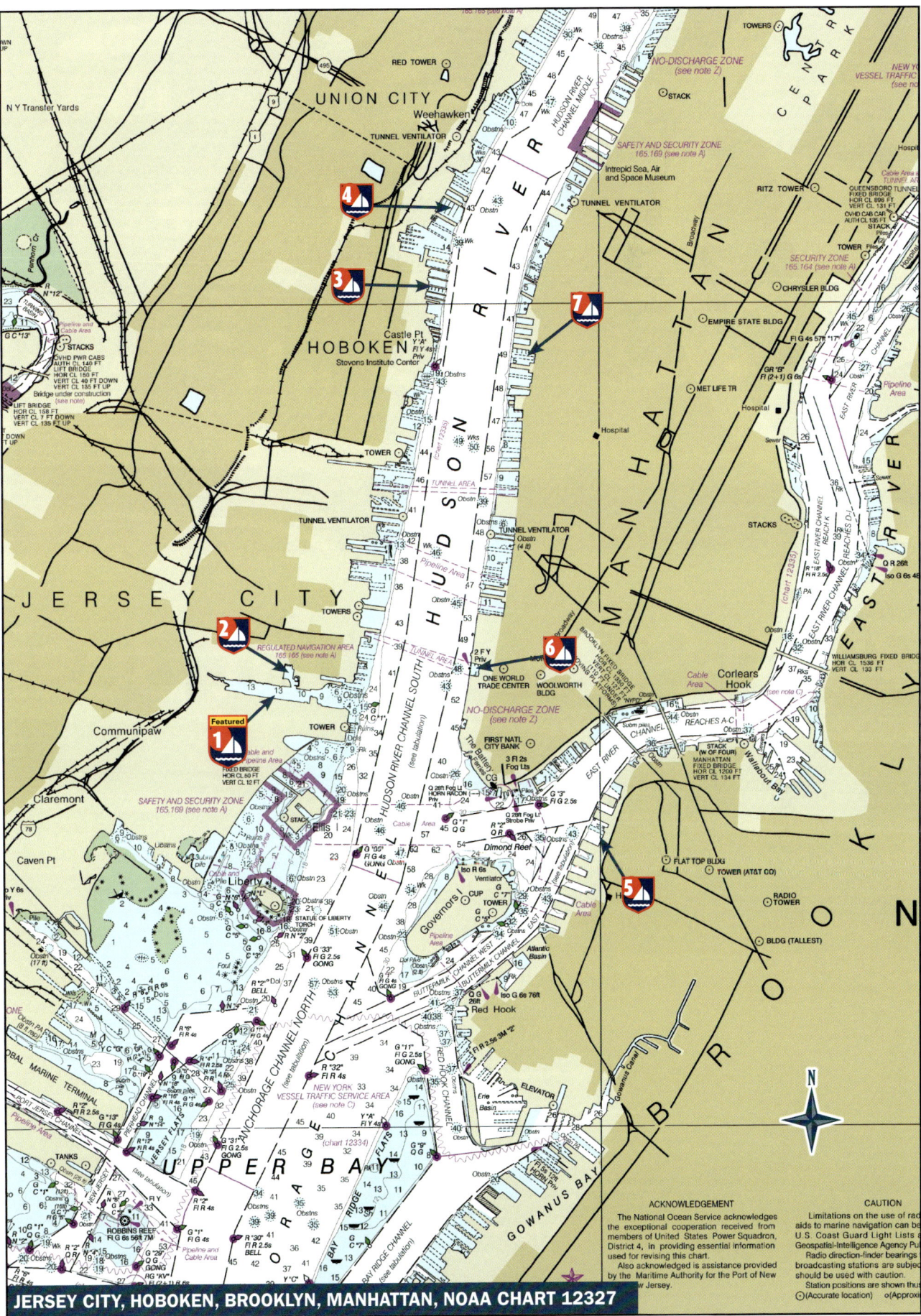

JERSEY CITY, HOBOKEN, BROOKLYN, MANHATTAN, NOAA CHART 12327

79th Street Boat Basin
The Recreational Boating Gateway to New York City

**West 79th Street
and the Hudson River
New York, NY 10024
(212) 496-2105**

**nyc.gov/parks
juana.garcia@parks.nyc.gov**

- Located at river mile 1.9, just north of the Intrepid Sea, Air & Space Museum on the Upper West Side of Manhattan
- Within walking distance of many museums and Central Park
- Close to the subway
- Restaurants
- Dedicated transient dock and moorings

- Free ice, laundry, and showers
- Free wireless internet
- Free MSD pumpout station
- Loading dock for guests and provisions
- Kayak storage
- 24-hour security
- Monitor VHF Ch. 9

NYC Parks

City of New York Parks & Recreation
Bill de Blasio, Mayor
Mitchell J. Silver, FAICP, Commissioner

Our sister marina, World's Fair Marina, is located in Flushing Bay. For information, call (718) 478-0480.

For New York City government information, call (212) NEW-YORK.

Brooklyn to the east.

The Staten Island ferries run almost continuously between Staten Island and terminals on the east side of The Battery in Lower Manhattan. The Staten Island Ferries are large orange vessels and these, along with a host of other ferries and sightseeing boats, create a busy marine traffic situation. Be certain of your course if you cross the bow of one of these vessels, especially when taking into account the effect of currents on your progress.

Currents in The Narrows build up to 2.5 knots on the ebb and up to 2 knots during the flood so skippers heading up the East River to Long Island Sound might want to base the times of their passage on Hell Gate currents. The strongest currents in New York Harbor (up to 5 knots) are found here, at the northeastern end of Manhattan. Passage through Hell Gate should be timed to carry a fair current as a visible "slack water" is rare.

An optional passage to reach the East River from the Verrazano Narrows Bridge is to hug the Brooklyn (east) shore of Upper Bay, stay east of Bay Ridge Flats through the Bay Ridge Channel and then travel east of Governors Island through the Buttermilk Channel. Currents run hard in this channel but this route avoids the large ships, Staten Island ferries and strong currents that can be found in the Upper Bay.

Anchorage: Anchoring in New York Harbor is only allowed in designated anchorages. These anchorages, however, are designed for large ships and are located in the middle of the harbor. The use of these areas requires permission from the Coast Guard.

There is an anchorage channel at Liberty State Park with 9 to 13 feet MLW with good holding in mud. Entrance to this designated anchorage is obtained by entering the channel just south of Liberty Island at green buoy "33." Anchor close to the Liberty State Park bulkhead. Avoid the area near the breakwater on the south side of this anchorage as it is shallow. This anchorage provides sufficient protection from all but southeast winds.

Alternate Route: Kill Van Kull

If you have traveled the normal route through New York Harbor more than once and are looking for something different, or if the weather is deteriorating and a trip through the Narrows to Sandy Hook does not seem inviting, think about using the protected waters of Kill Van Kull to the west of Staten Island as

a new route. Although the trip is twice as long, the channel is well marked, there are no bridge delays and depths are excellent.

Kill Van Kull to the north and the Arthur Kill to the north and west join to separate Staten Island from New Jersey. Along Kill Van Kull are a myriad of kills, rivers, streams and bays that are seldom on the itinerary of recreational boaters. ("Kill" comes from the Dutch settlers and refers to a channel, stream, creek or river.)

NAVIGATION: Use NOAA Chart 12327. Near the south end of the Arthur Kill, expensive homes line the shoreline on Staten Island to the east, Perth Amboy to the west and South Amboy to the south on the New Jersey side. Keep in the channel when rounding Ward Point at the southerly tip of Staten Island. On the Staten Island shore, just below the cantilevered **Outerbridge Crossing Bridge** (143-foot fixed vertical clearance) are small marinas offering some dockage and restaurants.

 Note that the actual velocities and directions of tidal currents in Arthur Kill may deviate significantly from those shown in tidal current tables.

Arthur Kill leads north around Staten Island in a well-marked, protected channel. Proceed north in the channel keeping west of Pralls Island (a protected bird sanctuary) to **Goethals Bridge**. The fixed high-rise bridge with a 140-foot vertical clearance is followed by the 31-foot vertical clearance **Arthur Kill Railroad Bridge** (usually open).

Just past Shooters Island, a wildlife sanctuary between Shooters Reach north and south branches, a large channel branches off to the north. Charted as Newark Bay South Reach, this is the route for container ships bound for Port Elizabeth and Port Newark.

Straight ahead on the charted Bergen Pt. West Reach is the 215-foot fixed vertical clearance **Bayonne Bridge**.

It is important to note that if you are entering Kill Van Kull from New York Harbor (i.e., headed south), you will be heading inland and buoys would be "red-right-returning" as expected, but when you head out under the Goethals Bridge (leading to Bayway on the New Jersey side and Gulfport on the Staten Island side), you are technically heading out to sea and the buoys are suddenly reversed (red to port and green to starboard).

Lower Hudson River

When you head north on the Hudson River, you will leave to the east the old commercial and cruise ship wharves, which are slowly being demolished and rebuilt. World-famous private and charter yachts are sometimes seen moored here. The Maritime Center at Chelsea Piers Marina (www.chelseapiers.com) is part of a 30-acre sports and entertainment complex housed in historic pier buildings that includes a bowling alley, skating rink, golf driving range, day spa and a 1.2-mile-long esplanade, all overlooking the river. Many private yacht groups, dinner cruises and sightseeing tours operate out of Chelsea Piers. Nearby is the Intrepid Sea, Air, and Space Museum (www.intrepidmuseum.org) at Pier 86, where the aircraft carrier *Intrepid* houses the museum.

On the opposite side of Manhatten is the 11-block complex of the Seaport Museum (212-748-8725), which includes a fleet of 19th-century clipper ships, four galleries, a working re-creation of a 19th-century print shop, a boatbuilding shop, a maritime craft center and museum shop. See details at www.oldseaportny.com. This is a great place to view the ship and pleasure traffic on the East River. Water taxis run from New Jersey and points along the Hudson to the South Street Seaport district.

Ferries and water taxis to Manhattan offer expanded nighttime services during the summer months to New York and back and the NJ Transit light-rail line (973-275-5555), located several blocks away, permits passenger service through Liberty Park and along the New Jersey shoreline to Bayonne, Hoboken and north. From the historic Central Railroad of New Jersey Terminal located at the north end of Liberty State Park, Circle Line offers multiple boat tours daily to both the Statue of Liberty National Monument and Ellis Island. (Visit www.circleline42.com for schedules and ticket information.)

> The upper Hudson River is discussed in "Side Trip: Hudson River to Troy Lock" (Chapter 6) of this guide.

NAVIGATION: Use NOAA Chart 12327.

Dockage/Moorings: On the New Jersey side of the Hudson River in Jersey City, the 520-slip Liberty Landing Marina in Liberty State Park dominates the southerly side of the Morris Canal. The marina monitors VHF Channel 72 and has a well-equipped marine center with slips (to 200 feet), supplies and marine services. The location is stunning with a picture-perfect view of lower Manhattan. Water taxi service into New York City is available. The decommissioned light ship *Winter Station* serves as the marina office. Nearby Liberty Harbor Marina offers boat storage and sells all fuels. Call ahead for slip availability.

At Pier 13 in Hoboken is The Shipyard Marina, which caters to smaller boats but maintains a few larger slips for boats up to 60 feet. Lincoln Harbor Yacht Club provides quiet transient dockage courtesy of a 700-foot wave suppression system. They can accommodate vessels to 220 feet.

Farther north is 79th Street Boat Basin, which houses the New York City Municipal Marina. The marina has transient slips for vessels up to 210 feet and mooring balls for visiting yachts up to 43 feet in length. Launch service is from 10:00 a.m. to 8:00 p.m. The north mooring field is for sailboats and the south is for power boats. (Catamarans are generally discouraged from mooring.) You must provide your own line for the mooring balls. There is a place to land your dinghy with reasonable security. This is close to public transportation and offers easy access to both uptown and downtown locations.

Continuing south on the New York (east) side of the Hudson River the Marina at Chelsea Pier can accommodate vessels up to 300 feet on floating docks and has a wave attenuator. Located in the Chelsea Piers Sports and Entertainment Complex right in the heart of the Big Apple, the marina offers easy access to all the sites and attractions that New York has to offer.

North Cove Marina (an IGY Marina) occupies a prime location in the heart of the financial district and can accommodate vessels to 175 feet on floating docks. They offer concierge service and restaurants and shopping are just steps away.

NYC's first new marina in over 50 years opened in 2019. One° 15 Brooklyn Marina with over 100 berths for vessels up to 250 feet. Call ahead for availability.

Anchorage: The anchorage is north of the mooring balls at 79th Street Boat Basin. It's over a mile north of the marina, which charges a fairly steep daily rate to park your dinghy. This area is wide open to the river's surge and holding is poor in 14 to 16 feet MLW. A mooring is a better alternative.

Why no **Goin' Ashore** for New York City? There are over 24,000 eating establishments in New York City if you count takeaways, delis and cafés. That doesn't include the Bronx, Brooklyn, Queens or Staten Island, by the way. How could we ever decide what to include? (We can't and won't even try.)

East River, NY

FLUSHING BAY		VHF Channel Monitored / Working / Largest Vessel Accomodated	Dockage				Supplies		Services				
			Approach / Dockside Depth (reported)	Transient Slips / Total Slips	Floating Docks	Gas / Diesel	Groceries, Ice, Marine Supplies, Snacks	Repairs: Hull, Engine, Propeller	Lift (tonnage), Crane, Rail	Courtesy Car, Laundry, Pool, Showers	Min / Max Amps	Pump-Out Station	Nearby: Grocery Store, Motel, Restaurant
1. Williamsburgh Yacht Club-PRIVATE (WiFi)	(718) 359-2090	39	/	/	5.0/5.0					30			GR
2. Arrow Yacht Club-PRIVATE	(718) 359-9229	33	18/	/	5.0/4.0	F	IS			S			GR
WESTCHESTER CREEK													
3. Metro Marine	(718) 823-0300	50	/	/40	15.0/5.0	F	IM	L	30	S	P	GR
LITTLE NECK BAY													
4. Bayside Marina	(718) 229-0097		/	/46	7.0/4.0	F	IS					R

☐ Internet Access (WiFi) Wireless Internet Access onSpot Dockside WiFi Facility
See WaterwayGuide.com for current rates, fuel prices, website addresses, and other up-to-the-minute information. (Information in the table is provided by the facilities.)

FLUSHING BAY, WESTCHESTER CREEK, LITTLE NECK BAY NOAA CHART 12363

■ THE EAST RIVER

The magnificent East River of New York is a 14-nm-long body of water that separates the boroughs of Manhattan and the Bronx from Brooklyn and Queens. The river passes under eight high-level bridges that are set against the spectacular backdrop of the Manhattan skyline. Each of the bridges is an architectural beauty and well worth photographing.

Winding its way from the Battery in New York Harbor to Long Island Sound, the East River is one of only two rivers in the world with two mouths and no source, according to local lore. The other river is the Harlem River, at the north end of Manhattan, which is also described in this chapter.

NAVIGATION: Use NOAA Charts 12327, 12335, 12339, 12342 and 12366. Transiting the East River from the Battery in New York City to Long Island Sound or from Long Island Sound to the Battery in New York City can be a wonderful, exciting experience. The river is deep, well marked and easy to follow.

Recreational boats can follow the main channel or take one of two shortcuts, if desired. One shortcut is between North and South Brother Islands near Rikers Island and the other is through the east side of Roosevelt Island. The latter is only for those vessels that are able to maneuver in the swift current and can transit under the restricted 40-foot vertical clearance **Roosevelt Island Bridge**. Some care must be given to avoid following navigational aids that mark some of the small rivers that empty into the East River instead of the East River markers themselves.

The key to transiting the East River, either eastward or westward, is to time the currents correctly by consulting tide and tidal current charts. Opposing currents in the river can reach over 5 knots and will seriously hinder the progress of low-powered, full displacement vessels if the transit is not properly timed. Wind-driven chop, heavy traffic and inconsistent depths can further exacerbate these contrary currents. No wonder the common name for the mid-point of the East River is "Hell Gate."

Be watchful of floating debris on the East River, especially on the outgoing tide.

The East River is heavily traveled by commercial traffic including tugs with tows, deep-draft ships, sightseeing vessels and large power boats that kick up great wakes. In its lower reaches near New York Harbor, the East River is dominated by large commercial ships heading to and from the docks on the Brooklyn shore. These ships maneuver awkwardly, hook up with tugs, and are troubled by the strong current so you must stay out of their way! Ships in these waters monitor VHF Channel 13 and you should definitely contact them if you have questions or concerns about their course.

Staten Island and Governors Island ferries can also be particularly troublesome as they cross the river frequently and at high speeds. Cross their wakes just after they have crossed the channel. Do not cut close to a docked ferry. If its powerful propellers are not throwing a monstrous wash into the channel, the ferry might be about to leave its slip and enter the channel with remarkable speed. In either case, you do not want to be nearby. There are also many small high-speed yellow water taxis and the well-known Circle Line tourist boats to negotiate. The safest course of action is to be aware of all traffic since these commercial vessels are working on a schedule. If you wish to communicate with any commercial traffic in the East River, use VHF Channel 13.

The buildings of Lower Manhattan rise to the west and Wall Street runs right down to the water below Pier 15. Fulton Ferry Landing is a wonderful park under the magnificent **Brooklyn Bridge**. This is the site of Bargemusic, which presents music year-round (www.bargemusic.org). There is no dockage here but the yellow ferries that run across the East River are accessible from the New York side.

The Brooklyn Bridge, built in 1883, has 127-foot fixed vertical clearance. Two other high-rise bridges cross the East River here: the **Manhattan Bridge** (134-foot fixed vertical clearance) and the **Williamsburg Bridge** (133-foot fixed vertical clearance). There is no dockage at South Street Seaport; however, there are many marinas in the harbor area that offer ferry access via the NY Waterway Ferries.

Roosevelt Island splits the East River at the United Nations, about 5 miles above The Battery. Boats can take either channel east or west of the island, except during security alerts, when recreational vessels must keep to the east of Roosevelt Island via East Channel. The western channel is larger with more spectacular views and fewer shoaling edges. If you have to travel the East Channel for security reasons, stay closer to the shore of Roosevelt Island as shoals extend from the Long Island side of the channel.

The **Queensboro Bridge** (131-foot vertical clearance) crosses the East River about halfway up the length of Roosevelt Island, roughly opposite New York Hospital and the Cornell Medical Center. A tramway passes overhead. The Roosevelt Island Bridge (40-foot closed vertical clearance) crosses the East Channel. If you require a bridge opening, contact the bridgetender at the **Grand Street/Avenue Bridge** on VHF Channel 13, the New York Department of Transportation (NYCDOT) Radio Hotline (311) or NYCDOT Bridge Operations Office (718-361-9217). The bridge will open on signal if at least 2-hour advance notice is provided. Openings may be delayed up to one-half hour.

Side Trip: Harlem River

The Harlem River, not heavily traveled by recreational boats, flows between the East River and the Hudson River 8 miles away at the north end of Manhattan. At Wards Island, you will proceed under a graceful, arching, green **Wards Island Pedestrian Bridge** (55-foot closed vertical clearance), one of the highest and longest footbridges anywhere. This end of the Harlem River is commercial, with railroad switching yards and sprawling housing projects.

A series of small boathouses appear as you approach the Hudson River. These are the headquarters of rowing and sculling clubs founded more than a century ago. Columbia University's athletic field and crew house are to the east, followed by residential Inwood Hill Park and Riverdale.

NAVIGATION: Use NOAA Chart 12342 Fifteen bridges cross the Harlem River. A vessel that can manage the controlling 24-foot vertical clearance will only require one bridge opening–the **Spuyten Duyvil Railroad Bridge** (5-foot closed vertical clearance), where the Harlem River meets the Hudson River. The bridgetender can be hailed on VHF Channel 13. All Harlem River non-fixed bridges open on signal if at least 4-hour advance notice is given to the New York Department of Transportation (NYCDOT) Radio Hotline (311) and the **Triborough Bridge** and Tunnel Authority (TBTA).

Hell Gate Bridge

The draws need not open from 6:00 a.m. to 9:00 a.m. and 5:00 p.m. to 7:00 p.m., Monday through Friday (except federal holidays). See up to date bridge schedules on Waterway Explorer (www.waterwayguide.com)

⚠ Current around the bridge's abutments can be very strong. Do not approach the bridge until it is completely open or you can be swept sideways into the abutments.

Anchorage: The closest anchorage is on the Hudson River. North of the **George Washington Bridge** there is an anchorage on the east side of the river in front of the Cloisters Museum in 9 to 12 feet MLW with good holding in mud.

Hell Gate

Proper timing for moving eastward or westward is based on getting through Hell Gate, which is about mid-point of the 14-mile-long East River between the Battery on the southwestern tip of Manhattan and the **Throgs Neck Bridge** (138-foot fixed vertical clearance) on the eastern end of the river at the entrance into Long Island Sound.

The East River current is the exact opposite of Long Island Sound current in that it ebbs west and floods east, while Long Island Sound current ebbs east and floods west. The divide between these two systems is near the Throgs Neck Bridge. If timed properly, a recreational boat heading upriver can catch a good ride with the flood tide up the East River and the ebb eastward into Long Island Sound.

NAVIGATION: Use NOAA Charts 12339,12363 and 12366. Upon reaching Hell Gate, stay south and east of Mill Rock and round the 33-foot flashing green daybeacon at Hallets Point. This is Hell Gate proper and the flow of water will indeed be spectacular if you arrive at maximum current. Ebb tide runs up to 5.2 knots to the southwest and floods at 4 knots to the northeast. This creates eddies and standing waves that are only dangerous to small, open boats but deserve respect and a firm hand on the helm as even large boats can be shoved around. It is much safer to transit Hell Gate at slack water, if possible. The only real danger is meeting a large commercial vessel or tug with a barge and getting in the way. Avoid this by using VHF Channel 13 to communicate with the vessel and keeping your eyes open ahead and astern.

Information needed to transit the East River is often incorporated in electronic charting software as tide and tidal current tables. Traditionally, mariners have relied on the *Eldridge Tide and Pilot Book* (www. tidesandcurrents.noaa.gov).

The object of the westward passage through the East River is to arrive at Hell Gate no less than 2 hours but up to 3 hours after high water at The Battery. The westward-bound recreational boat heading down the East River toward The Battery should try to pass under the Throgs Neck Bridge at or slightly before high tide at the bridge. By arriving at the Throgs Neck Bridge at this time, mariners can time their passage under the bridge to hit the current as it begins to ebb westward. Smaller (and slower) vessels may wish to arrive at the Battery 1 hour after low tide when traveling eastward and up to 1 hour before high tide at the Throgs Neck Bridge when traveling westward. The relatively modest adverse current at the eastern end of the East River at that time should result in a slower but more subdued ride through Hell Gate.

Don't worry if your depth sounder jumps erratically at Hell Gate since the bottom ranges from 34 feet to 107 feet to 59 feet within a few hundred yards, creating whirlpools on the surface. Pass under the high-level **Robert F. Kennedy Bridge** (138-foot fixed vertical clearance) and an adjacent **Hell Gate Railroad Bridge** (134-foot fixed vertical clearance) and leave Wards Island and Randalls Island to port. When you reach Lawrence Point, you have passed safely through Hell Gate.

The main ship channel goes north of North Brother Island but yachts can easily pass through the shorter, more direct channel between it and South Brother Island (minimum depth 25 feet MLW). Just stay clear of off-channel shoals, rocks and ledges and observe the buoys, keeping green markers to starboard, red to port. Channels leading south from here have their own buoy systems so do not confuse these with those on the East River's west-east route to Long Island Sound.

Across the East River from College Point is the mouth of the commercial Bronx River, with Clason Point separating it from the mouth of Westchester Creek. The latter has a dredged and marked channel with sales and repair available at the mouth and small-craft service upstream. From Old Ferry Point, the

high-level **Bronx-Whitestone Bridge** (130-foot fixed vertical clearance) crosses overhead. The long sweep of the Throgs Neck Bridge (152-foot fixed vertical clearance), generally accepted as the demarcation line between the East River and Long Island Sound, runs from the peninsula to just above Willets Point. At this point, the shoreline begins to look less urban and Long Island Sound lies ahead.

Side Trip: Flushing Bay

Flushing Bay is an excellent base from which to visit the city or to change crews arriving or departing from New York's two major airports. The proximity of LaGuardia Airport on the west side of Flushing Bay will make itself immediately evident to boat-borne visitors and John F. Kennedy International Airport (also in the borough of Queens) is not far. A subway stop is also nearby for an inexpensive and inevitably colorful transit to Manhattan. Closer at hand, the Flushing shopping district is a cab ride away, where a full range of shopping and restaurant possibilities are available within a few blocks. Shea Stadium, home of the Mets, is about a 15-minute walk.

On a historical note, both Throgs Neck and Willets Point are strategic locations where fortifications were built in the early 19th century to protect New York City from attack. Granite-walled Fort Totten is at Willets Point. Fort Schuyler on Throgs Neck now houses the New York State Maritime Academy. The academy's school ship, a converted Navy transport usually berthed nearby when not underway, is where cadets learn merchant service skills.

You will also pass 413.17-acre Rikers Island on the way to Flushing Bay. The island is home to one of the world's largest correctional institutions and mental institutions and New York's most famous jail. This is an inhospitable place for those without official business so observe from a distance.

NAVIGATION: Use NOAA Chart 12339. Flushing Bay offers good protection, a deep (14.5 feet at MLW) well-marked channel and, for those drawing 5 feet or less, ample anchorage room. Several marinas and two yacht clubs are situated just inside College Point. Prevailing water depths of 4 to 5 feet MLW, however, will discourage vessels with deeper keels.

⚠️ En route to Flushing Bay, you will pass LaGuardia Airport. Remember that you may not travel within 100 yards of any shore adjacent to the airport.

When headed south, Flushing Bay is a good place to wait out the slack tide, just before the southerly flow at Hell Gate and the East River.

Dockage: There are a couple of private yacht clubs in Flushing Bay and the 300-slip municipal World's Fair Marina. This facility was under construction at press time in winter 2020 -2021 so call ahead for slip availability.

Anchorage: Boats anchor in Flushing Bay in 4 to 5 feet MLW with good holding in mud. You can pick a spot anywhere in the bay for the best protection.

■ NEXT STOP

Long Island Sound awaits exploration. One of the most popular cruising grounds on the east coast, the sound has much to offer both sailors and power boaters.

Side Trip: The Hudson River to Troy Lock

■ NAVIGATING THE HUDSON RIVER

The Hudson River Valley is emerging as a haven for city refugees who want the culture without the noise and crowds of the city. Many of the riverside towns are being transformed from industrial centers to New York City suburbs. On the upper river, creeks (both natural and dredged) make protected layovers.

Cruising Conditions

Cruising the Hudson River is generally straightforward. Aids to navigation are plentiful, mid-channel depths range from 15 feet to 175 feet and marinas and hospitable yacht clubs are numerous north of Manhattan. Overnight berths should be selected for maximum protection from the river's natural chop and

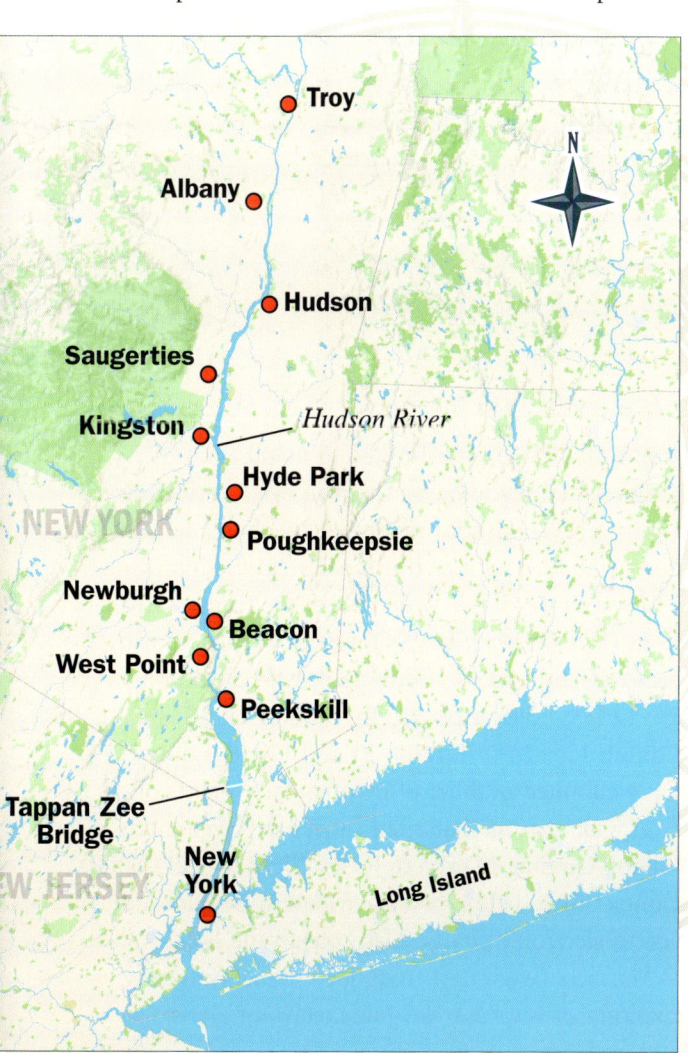

the wake from passing recreational and commercial traffic. On the upper river, creeks (both natural and dredged) can make for good, protected layover spots.

The route upriver is easily navigated for 91 miles to Kingston but extensive middle grounds and steep-to shoals must be given a wide berth after this point. In the lower Hudson River, rocky shoals are common off the channel and departure from the marked route must be made with caution and local knowledge. Above Kingston the bottom is mostly sandy with some mud and grass and few rocks.

The few hazards consist mainly of debris–both floating and submerged—and fish traps (in the spring). In the Albany/Troy area, just as in New York Harbor, drifting debris calls for an endless watch, particularly at a tide change and during the spring run-off. The wind usually blows up or down the Hudson River, but near shore it tends to sweep toward the banks. Watch for summer squalls with sudden winds of up to 30 knots. Your only warning might be black clouds along the high west-bank bluffs. Get to the weather side of the river whenever you see indications of rough conditions ahead.

Commercial traffic can be heavy at times with barge activity and should be given full right-of-way, especially in periods of poor visibility. It is generally best to communicate with any commercial vessels on VHF Channel 13.

Tidal Currents

Tidal water extends to Troy, where the mean tidal range varies from 3 to 5 feet and currents can be strong (an average of 1.5 knots as far north as Albany). When you are northbound, you will be going away from the tidal current change so you can hold a fair current longer than you will when southbound. The 153-mile Hudson estuary has two high and two low tides in 24 hours. With the rise and fall come changes in the direction of the flow. A rising tide is accompanied by a flood current flowing north towards Troy, and a falling tide by an ebb current flowing seaward. Tidal waters extend to Troy, the mean tidal range varies from 3 to 5 feet, and currents can be strong (e.g., 2 knots at The Battery with an average of 1.5 knots as far north as Albany). When you are northbound, heading away from the tidal current change, you will hold a fair current longer

Hudson River, NJ

	VHF Channel Monitored / Working	Largest Vessel Accomodated	Approach / Dockside Depth (reported)	Transient Slips / Total Slips	Floating Docks	Groceries, Ice, Marine Supplies, Snacks	Gas / Diesel	Repairs: Hull, Engine, Propeller	Lift (tonnage), Crane, Rail	Min / Max Amps	Courtesy Car, Laundry, Pool, Showers	Pump-Out Station	Nearby: Grocery Store, Motel, Restaurant

EDGEWATER			Dockage				Supplies			Services			
1. Edgewater Marina	(201) 944-2628	60	16/9	4/85	20.0/6.0	F			HP	L	30/50	S		GMR
ALPINE AREA													
2. JM Englewood Marina ▢ WIFI	(201) 568-1328	75	9/	/112	8.0/8.0	F	GD	IMS	HEP	L50	30/100	S	P	5R
3. Monte's Marine Service ▢ WIFI	(201) 568-1984	75	9/	/	8.0/8.0	F	GD	IMS	HEP	L50	30/100	S	P	5R
4. Alpine Marina	(201) 985-6580	150	9/9	10/125	20.0/12.0	F	GD	IMS			30/100	LS	P	GR

▢ Internet Access WIFI Wireless Internet Access onSpot Dockside WiFi Facility
See WaterwayGuide.com for current rates, fuel prices, website addresses, and other up-to-the-minute information. (Information in the table is provided by the facilities.)

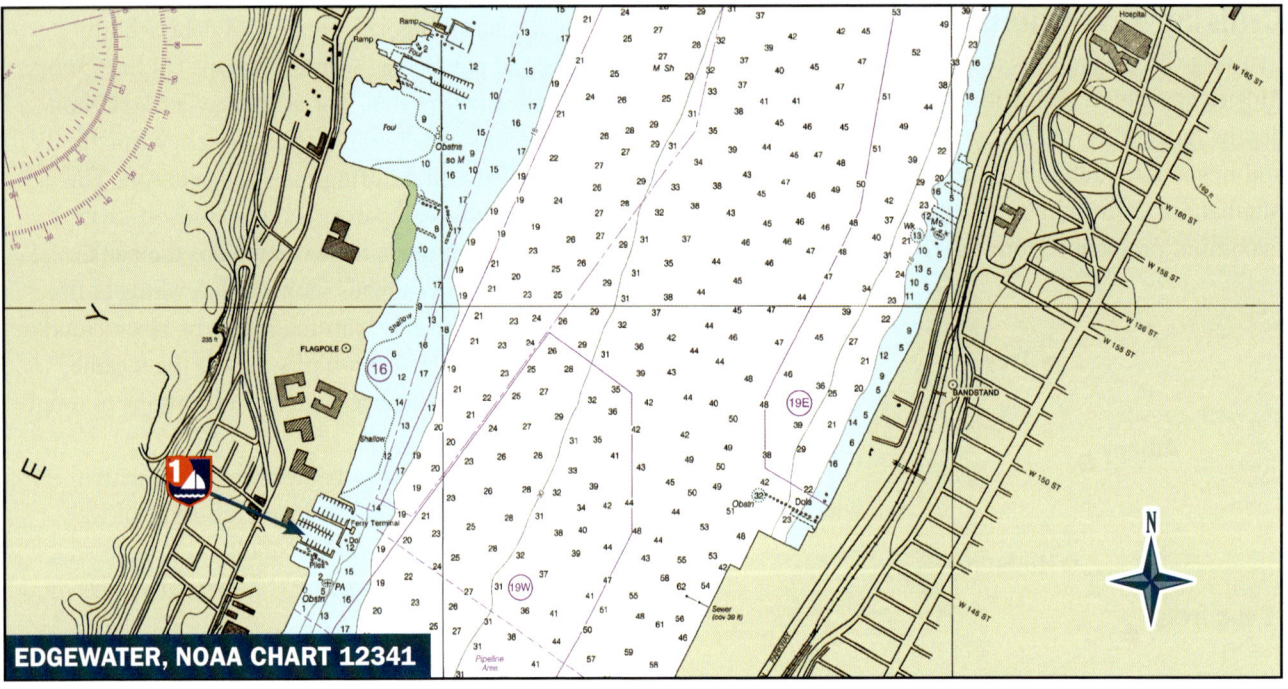

EDGEWATER, NOAA CHART 12341

than when southbound. For this passage, skippers should have a copy of the latest tide and tidal current tables aboard.

In the tidal portion of the Hudson River, select your marina slip with great care. You will want to avoid slips that are in the cross current, since maneuvering into or out of the slip may be difficult. You will also want to ensure that the marina is equipped with proper fendering to minimize damage to your boat.

Navigation

Charts might not accurately show some privately maintained markers and some markers have been discontinued, while others might not have been replaced after winter ice. It should also be noted that many public marinas list or advertise themselves as clubs and are perfectly acceptable stopovers that are not limited to members.

We do not recommend that you head upriver on the Hudson River without the necessary charts. Be sure to download into your navigation system the following Hudson River charts, which cover the Hudson River from Days Point to Troy, NY, before making your trip: NOAA Charts 12341, Edition 28; 12342, Edition 24; 12343, Edition 20; 12345, Edition 11; 12346, Edition 12; 12347, Edition 31 and 12348, Edition 34. Only a limited number of marinas carry charts of the river. One marina that often carries the river charts is Liberty Landing Marina in Jersey City (201-985-8000). Contact them before you leave New York Harbor or access electronic charts. Also consult the *Local Notice to Mariners* (www.navcen.uscg.gov) and Waterway Explorer (www.waterwayguide.com) for alerts and updates.

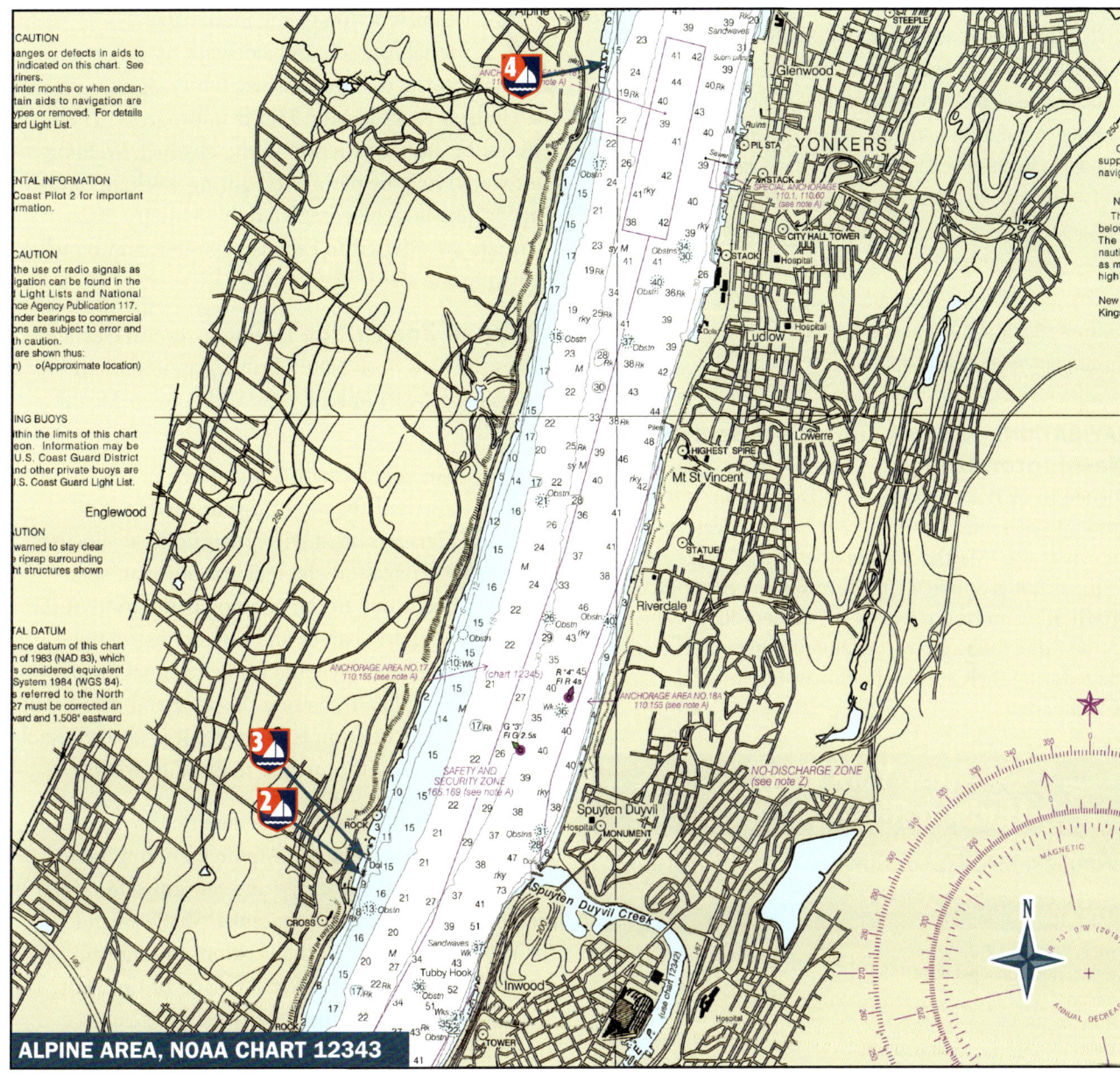

ALPINE AREA, NOAA CHART 12343

GEORGE WASHINGTON BRIDGE TO KINGSTON

George Washington Bridge to Tappan Zee Bridge–Mile 11.5 to Mile 27

The aura of the New York metropolis quickly dissipates beyond the George Washington Bridge. The tall backdrop contrasts sharply with the 300- to 500-foot thickly wooded Palisades. This striking series of cliffs, composed of columnar basalt, is named for its visual similarity to old, wooden, barrier fortifications. Opposite Hastings-on-Hudson is the New Jersey–New York border. From this point to its headwaters in the Adirondack Mountains, the Hudson River flows entirely within New York State.

Piermont Pier, the prominent 1-mile-long point just north of the state border, was the terminus of the Erie Railroad tracks until 1850. During that era, this spot was a major rail and ship cargo transfer point. Piermont is a delightful waterfront village with a marina, waterfront restaurants and an upscale shopping plaza. Unfortunately, the shallow approach is not marked and access requires local knowledge. Pete Seegar's famous replica of a North River sloop, *Clearwater,* can frequently be spotted at the end of the pier.

In 1966, folk music legend Pete Seeger announced plans to "build a boat to save the river." Seeger believed that a replica of the sloops that sailed the Hudson River in the 18th and 19th centuries would encourage people to preserve the integrity of the river. In 1969, the 106-foot sloop *Clearwater* was launched at Harvey Gamage shipyard in South Bristol, Maine. On her maiden voyage she sailed to South Street Seaport in New York City, and then ultimately made her home on the Hudson River where she has made a remarkable impact in the environmental movement.

NAVIGATION: Use NOAA Chart 12343. **George Washington Bridge** (213-foot vertical clearance) opened in 1931 during the Great Depression. It was not until 30 years later that the lower, second deck (fondly known as the "Martha Washington Bridge") was added. To the north is Spuyten Duyvil (pronounced "spite-en die-vil"), the northern part of the Harlem River. This is on the route followed by the famous Circle Line cruise boats during their scenic circumnavigations of the island of Manhattan.

New York Bay/ Hudson River Distances

Nautical Miles (approximate) from Sandy Hook

LOCATION	MILE
NEW YORK BAY	
Sandy Hook Channel Light "15"	0
Ambrose	8.6
Rockaway Point	5.2
Great Kills Harbor, Crookes Point	6.5
Coney Island, Norton Point	6.0
Verrazano Narrows Bridge	7.8
The Battery	14.0
HUDSON RIVER	
George Washington Bridge	24
Harlem River	26
Tarrytown	39
Grassy Point	49
EAST RIVER	
Brooklyn Bridge	14.5
Hell Gate, Hallets Point	20
Whitestone Bridge	25
Throgs Neck Bridge	26
Execution Rocks	31

⚠️ Construction to the main cable rehabilitation and sidewalk modification at the George Washington Bridge across the Hudson River at Mile 11.5 is in progress. There will not be any obstruction in the channel. Welding (hot work) may be performed during working hours. This project is to be completed by February 2026. Mariners are advised to exercise extreme caution when transiting the area.

Tappan Zee Bridge (139-foot vertical clearance) carries the New York State Thruway, an important interstate highway linking New York City to Albany and Buffalo.

⚠️ The replacement Tappan Zee Bridge to the north of the old bridge opened in 2018. Mariners are advised that periodic closures of the main navigation channel and adjacent span areas will occur due to the ongoing demolition of the old bridge. Cranes, barges and other construction equipment will occupy parts of the channel during this time. Be alert when transiting this area and give a wide berth to all construction equipment. It is also advisable to avoid transiting this area at night, if possible.

Dockage/Moorings: Marine facilities are in Edgewater, Englewood and Alpine including yacht clubs with courtesy dockage and moorings for members of reciprocal yacht clubs. Shallows and the ruins of old piers in the Hastings-on-Hudson and Dobbs Ferry areas can make parts of this shore difficult to approach closely. Any facilities you see are small local operations. Tappan Zee Marina to the north at Piermont can accommodate boats to 40 feet. Call ahead for directions due to the shallow approach depths.

Anchorage: North of the George Washington Bridge, there is an anchorage in front of the Cloisters Museum on the east side of the river. Here you will find 9 to 12 feet MLW at MLW with good holding in mud. If the wind is right, you can find a number of suitable anchorages close to shore at the base of the cliffs on the west side of the Hudson River. If you anchor here, prepare to be rolled during the night by some large wakes from an occasional tugboat. You might want to consider lashing gear down securely before retiring for the evening.

Tappan Zee Bridge to Bear Mountain– Mile 27 to Mile 46.7

Just north of the Tappan Zee Bridge on the east bank is Tarrytown. Tarrytown offers easy access and good provisioning. The quaint, pretty Main Street has emerged as a minor nightlife center. The restored Tarrytown Music Hall is a centerpiece to this activity. This area is about a 20-minute uphill walk from the water.

Across the river (west side) is labeled as Nyack on the NOAA chart but the center of town is about 1 mile away. This vibrant small town, known as the "Gem of the Hudson," is a center for the arts. In addition to its grand Victorian homes and many antiques shops, it offers a number of fine restaurants and a thriving nightlife. Groceries and one of the nation's largest malls (Palisades Center, off Hwy. 87) are only a short cab ride away.

Ossining on the eastern bank of the Hudson River was originally named Sing Sing, the same as the famous, sprawling hillside prison located here. A boycott of prison-made goods at the turn of the century led the town to change its name to Ossining so buyers could distinguish between goods made in the town from those made at the prison.

From Hook Mountain to Haverstraw, the west bank of the Hudson River rises more than 800 feet. Haverstraw Bay, northwest of Croton Point, is the widest part of the Hudson River at 3 nm across. The town of Haverstraw is nestled between the cliffs of High Tor to the west and the Hudson River.

Around the bend of the river on the east side is the Indian Point Nuclear Power Plant. Dockage is not allowed here. A mile beyond the southern part of the U-shaped channel of Peekskill is marked with buoys and a light. The National Maritime Historical Society (914-737-7878) is located next to the Charles Point Marina in Peekskill. The maritime art gallery and an extensive information center of maritime history are open daily including weekends. For more information, visit www.seahistory.org.

Across the Hudson River is densely forested Dunderberg Mountain, which marks the southern limit of the Highland section of the river. For the next 10

Bear Mountain Bridge

Hudson River, NY

		Largest Vessel Accommodated	VHF Channel Monitored / Working	Transient Slips / Total Slips	Approach / Dockside Depth (reported)	Floating Docks	Gas / Diesel	Groceries, Ice, Marine Supplies, Snacks	Repairs: Hull, Engine, Propeller	Lift (tonnage) Crane, Rail	Min / Max Amps	Courtesy Car, Laundry, Pool, Showers	Pump-Out Station	Nearby: Grocery Store, Motel, Restaurant
					Dockage		**Supplies**		**Services**					
TAPPAN ZEE AREA														
1. Tappan Zee Marina	(845) 359-5522	40	/	/75	/	F	G	IS	E	L25	30	S		GR
2. Washington Irving Boat Club-PRIVATE	(914) 332-0517	32	/	3/100	6.0/3.0	F		I		L		S		R
3. Tarrytown Boat & Yacht Club-PRIVATE WiFi	(914) 631-1300	70	16/9	/100	6.0/4.0	F		GI		L25	30	S		GR
4. Nyack Marina	(845) 358-3851		/	4/40	/3.0	F					30	S		GR
5. Nyack Boat Club	(845) 353-0395		/	/	10.0/12.0			IS		L5		S		GMR
6. North River Shipyard	(845) 358-2100	200	16/66	4/10	13.0/10.0	F		IM	HEP	L460,C	30/50	S	P	GMR
OSSINING														
7. **Westerly Marina**	**(914) 941-2203**	100	68/	10/180	8.0/6.0	F	GD	IM	HEP	L40	30	S	P	2.5R
8. Shattemuc Yacht Club WiFi	(914) 941-8777	65	16/	7/125	6.0/7.5	F		IS		L	30	PS	P	GMR

🖳 Internet Access   WiFi Wireless Internet Access   onSpot Dockside WiFi Facility

See WaterwayGuide.com for current rates, fuel prices, website addresses, and other up-to-the-minute information. (Information in the table is provided by the facilities.)

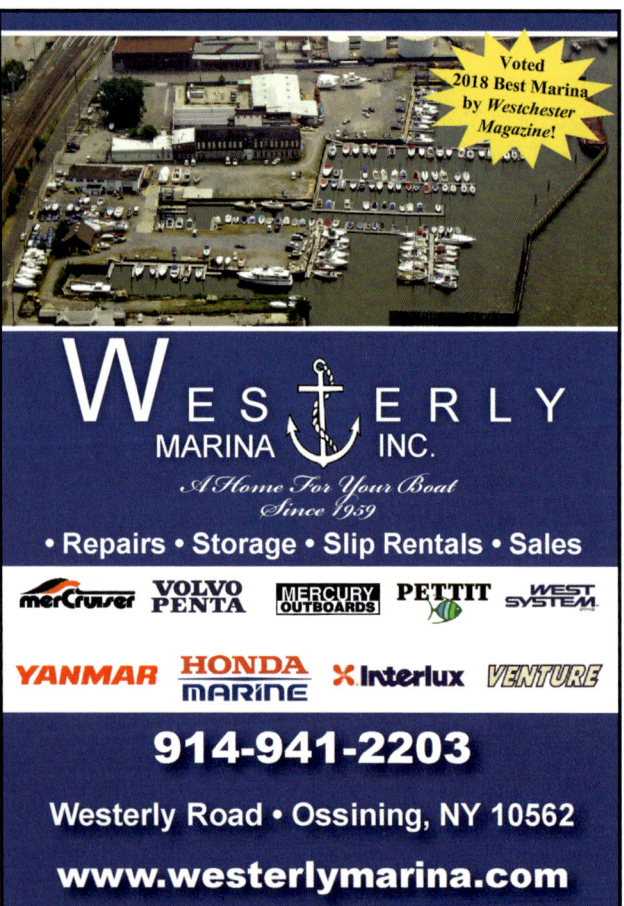

miles, the river cuts through the Appalachian mountain chain and is one of the most beautiful stretches of river scenery in the country.

> The 1,000-foot-tall Dunderberg Mountain is the legendary dwelling of the Dutch goblin held responsible for summer storms.

Between Dunderberg and Bear Mountain is Iona Island, a former Navy Depot. There is a conspicuous skeleton tower on the north side of the island. The narrow section of the river between Iona Island and the eastern shore is known as The Race. The swiftest current on the Hudson River runs here. The island was the site of a navy arsenal from 1900 until after World War II and some fences and buildings still remain. Beginning as early as March, this stretch of the river is one of the most prolific striped bass fisheries on the East Coast.

A mile or two north of Dunderberg Mountain is Bear Mountain, the site of the huge Bear Mountain State Park. All but the tour boat dock is hidden from view by the dense mountain foliage so most boaters cruising this way are unaware of the park's existence. Now that you know about it, do not pass it by. The path from the dinghy dock leads past an immense public swimming pool nestled in a mountain gully. Farther on is a trailway museum and a zoo, home of a fine collection of Hudson Valley animals and birds. Beyond is a mountain lake with scores of rental boats. Finally, you will arrive at the wonderful old Bear Mountain Inn. This area

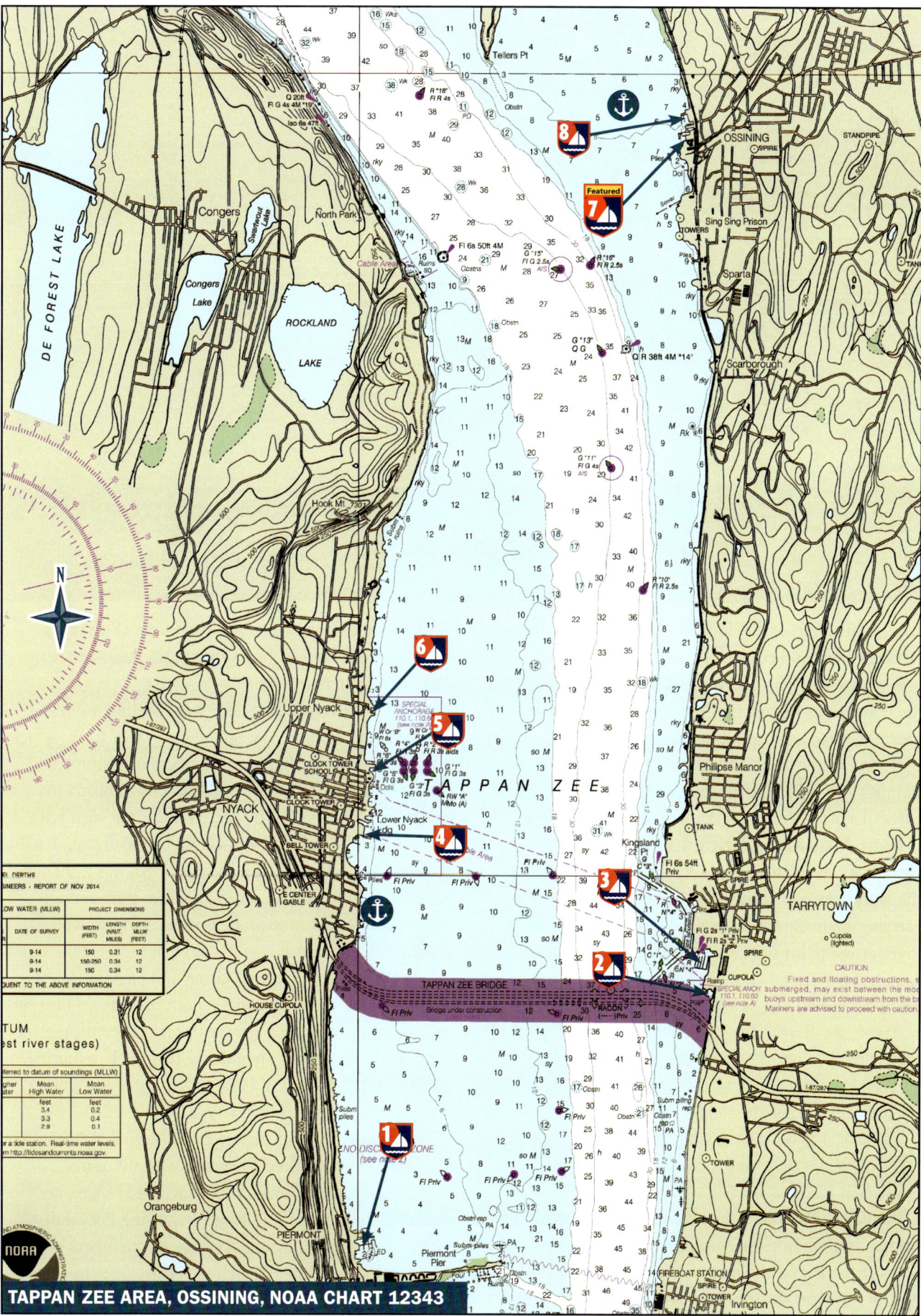

TAPPAN ZEE AREA, OSSINING, NOAA CHART 12343

West Point

attracts busloads of city folk on weekends. See www.visitbearmountain.com for more information.

It is here that you and your crew may first encounter the white swans, known as mute swans (an introduced species), often seen paddling leisurely around the river coves as far north as Catskill. Keeping a count of the number you have spotted can be a challenging pastime, particularly for the younger members of the crew.

Bear Mountain Bridge (155-foot vertical clearance), at the time of its completion in 1924, was the world's largest suspension bridge. In addition to carrying highway traffic, it also serves as the Hudson River crossing for the famous Maine-to-Georgia Appalachian Trail.

> During the Revolutionary War, the Americans stretched a huge chain across the Hudson River just north of the Bear Mountain Bridge site to prevent British warships from passing. Unfortunately, the British seized the chain (sending it to Gibraltar to protect their own harbor) and then sailed up the river and burned the town of Kingston.

Dockage/Moorings: Just north of the Tappan Zee Bridge, two private boat clubs are on the Tarrytown (eastern) side and the channel is well marked. Across the river, North River Shipyard in Nyack is

a full-service boat yard and Nyack Boat Club has a mooring field for 150 boats including guest moorings and offer launch service.

Back on the river's east side, you will find a full-service boat yard and The Shattemuc Yacht Club, which offers courtesy moorings for members of reciprocal yacht clubs. The 173-slip Half Moon Bay Marina in Croton-on-Hudson has protected, transient slips with 10-foot MLW depths for vessels up to 165 feet and sells all fuels. The adjacent Croton Point Park has a sheltered cove for swimming and sandy beaches, train service to and from Manhattan and car rentals within walking distance of the marina.

Safe Harbor Haverstraw Marina and Samalot Marine at Haverstraw Marina, located south of Grassy Point on the western shore, are both repair facilities with marine supplies. To the north are a diesel fuel dock, a marina and a yacht club in Stony Point Bay. There is more dockage across the river in Green's Cove.

The channel to the Charles Point Marina at Peekskill is marked but is limited to vessels with no more than 3-foot drafts. Transient dockage and repairs are available. To the north at Travis Point, the Peekskill Yacht Club offers courtesy dockage for members of reciprocal yacht clubs, as well as repairs. See the marina table for more details.

Anchorage: There is an anchorage at Nyack, northeast of the mooring field near the western shore. Here you will find 9 to 12 feet MLW and excellent holding in mud. It is open to all but the western quadrant. There is a public dock just south of the mooring field and north of a condo development. (Do not enter the private condo marina.) Shopping and restaurants are nearby.

Croton Point juts out into the river just north of Ossining and except in west to north winds, it is one of the best anchorages on the river and is certainly the best between here and New York City. Do not shortcut the point when going in or you will find out that a shoal really does exist here. There are 8-foot MLW depths near Ossining and 4 to 6-foot MLW depths farther up into Croton Bay abeam of Tellers Point. On the north side of Croton Point there is southerly protection in front of Croton Point Park in 6 to 9 feet MLW. There is a dinghy dock located at nearby Half Moon Bay Marina.

The anchorage across the river at Haverstraw offers 360-degree protection and is surrounded by either high hills or trees. Hug the south side of the narrow entrance channel. Cruising boats anchor on the north side of Stony Point in 14 to 19 feet MLW in south to west winds. Note that there are charted wrecks here so anchor with care.

You can anchor at Dunderberg Mountain in 13 to 20 feet MLW with excellent holding in mud. This provides protection from the west and north. Be certain to stay 300 yards off the Indian Point Nuclear Power Plant. There is lots of train noise here.

To explore the striking mountainside park at Bear Mountain, anchor either in the bight between Iona Island and the tour boat dock or, in most weather, north of the dock and before the Bear Mountain Bridge. Both have good depths and a mud bottom. The dinghy dock is behind the tour boat dock. Walk through the tunnel that passes under the railroad tracks and follow the path up the mountain. The view of your boat at anchor in the river below makes a great photo.

Bear Mountain to Newburgh-Beacon Bridges–Mile 46.7 to Mile 62.1

The narrow section of the river just north of the West Point Academy, designated as World's End, is the deepest section of the entire river (one spot charted at 175 feet deep). During the Revolutionary War, the Americans stretched another chain across the river at World's End but this was yet another vain effort.

Visiting West Point

The historical Military Academy at West Point (circa 1802) is open for bus tours for a nominal fee. Tour hours are generally between 9:00 a.m. to 3:30 p.m. daily. The 1-hour tour makes stops at the Cadet Chapel, Trophy Point, Battle Monument and the Plain. You are off the bus approximately 50 minutes with minimal walking. Requests for tours should be made through www.westpointtours.com.

The Frederic V. Malek West Point Visitors Center and Museum are open to the general public on a daily basis. The building is home to West Point Tours, the Visitors Control Center (VCC) and the Army West Point Gift Shop. All visitors need to process through the visitors center. Hours change so call first (845-938-0390/-0392)or see www.westpoint.edu/visiting-west-point.

Dockage: Transient boaters are no longer allowed on West Point's docks due to security measures. Boaters are allowed to access South Dock for football games, where full security checks are required but dock space is limited (no overnight stays). Requests for football game dockage or passenger drop-off must be made in advance. Cornwall Yacht Club, approximately 5 miles away, is the closest west bank dockage.

Hudson River, NY

		Dockage				Supplies		Services					
	Largest Vessel Accommodated	VHF Channel Monitored / Working	Transient Slips / Total Slips	Approach / Dockside Depth (reported)	Floating Docks	Gas / Diesel	Groceries, Ice, Marine Supplies, Snacks	Repairs: Hull, Engine, Propeller	Lift (tonnage) Crane, Rail	Min / Max Amps	Courtesy Car, Laundry, Pool, Showers	Pump-Out Station	Nearby: Grocery Store, Motel, Restaurant
CROTON-ON-HUDSON													
1. Half Moon Bay Marina 💻 (WiFi) (914) 271-5400	165	9/9	35/173	10.0/10.0	F		GIMS	EP		30/50	LS	P	GMR
STONY POINT AREA													
2. Haverstraw Marina 💻 (WiFi) red buoy 26 (845) 429-2001	150	16/9	/900	8.0/8.0	F	GD	GIMS	HEP	L38	30/50	LPS	P	GMR
3. Samalot Marine at Haverstraw Marina 💻 (WiFi) (845) 429-0404	150	16/9	/	26.0/8.0	F	GD	GIMS	HEP	C	30	LPS	P	GMR
4. Panco Petroleum Stony Point Terminal (800) 477-4645		/	/	/		D							
5. Penny Bridge Marina (WiFi) (845) 786-5100	40	/	/120	5.0/4.0	F		IM	HEP	L35	30	S	P	
6. Minisceongo Yacht Club 💻 (WiFi) (845) 786-8781	50	9/	5/140	7.0/10.0	F		I		L35	30/50	LS	P	R
STONY POINT BAY													
7. Patsy's Bay Marina 💻 (845) 786-5270	50	12/	15/200	5.0/6.0	F		IMS	HEP	L30	30	LPS		
8. USA Marina (WiFi) (845) 429-0100	65	16/9	5/400	4.0/4.0	F		IMS	HEP	L	30/50	LPS	P	GR
9. Seaweed Yacht Club (845) 786-8731	40	/	/	8.0/8.0	F		I			30	S	P	GMR
GREENS COVE													
10. Cortlandt Yacht Club (914) 739-3011	52	16/	6/175	3.0/3.0	F		IS		L20,C	30	PS	P	GR
11. Viking Boatyard (WiFi) (914) 739-5090	50	9/	4/180	5.0/5.0	F		IMS	HEP	L60,C	30	S	P	GMR
PEEKSKILL													
12. Charles Point Marina 💻 (WiFi) (914) 736-6942	48	/	10/80	5.0/3.0	F		IS		L35	30/50	S	P	GMR
13. Peekskill Yacht Club (914) 737-9515	48	9/	2/85	5.0/5.0			I		L25,C	30	S		G

💻 Internet Access   (WiFi) Wireless Internet Access   onSpot Dockside WiFi Facility

See WaterwayGuide.com for current rates, fuel prices, website addresses, and other up-to-the-minute information. (Information in the table is provided by the facilities.)

Across the river is Foundry Cove, where foundries cast cannon and shot during the Civil War. This is where the first American iron warship (a revenue cutter) was built in the 1850s.

Pollepel Island, widely known as Bannerman's Island, is 4 nm north of West Point on the eastern shore. Between 1900 and 1918, munitions dealer Frank Bannerman built a replica of a medieval castle here as a summer resort and storehouse. In 1967, the state obtained the property and tours were conducted until the castle burned in 1969. Today, because of the deteriorating condition of the building, landing on the island is no longer permitted.

Four nautical miles north of Pollepel Island are the twin cities of Newburgh and Beacon. (Newburgh is on the west shore, and Beacon is on the east shore.) Despite being situated more than 60 miles inland, Newburgh was a 19th-century seaport and the home of whaling ships. George Washington's 1782 to 1783 headquarters, the Hasbrough House, still stands and is open to the public. Substantial waterfront development has sprung up in Newburgh during the last several years, mostly to accommodate local small craft.

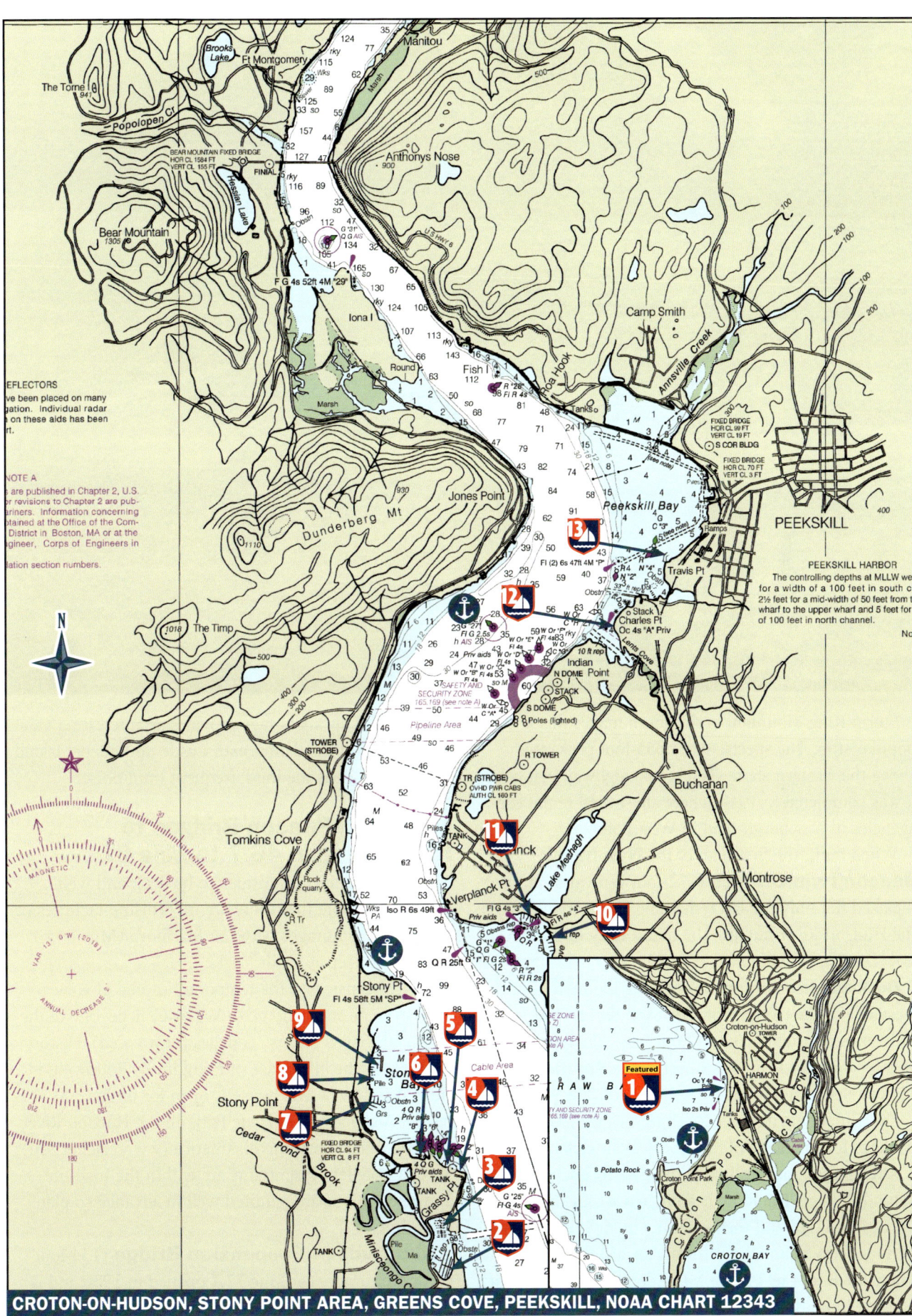

CROTON-ON-HUDSON, STONY POINT AREA, GREENS COVE, PEEKSKILL, NOAA CHART 12343

Storm King Mountain to the south makes this a popular stop. The spectacular 1,355-foot peak rises above the western shore. The scenic highway that girds it was completed in 1940. There are several rental car agencies in Newburgh (and in West Point).

When built, the first span of the **Newburgh-Beacon Twin Bridges** (172-foot vertical clearance) replaced not only the last remaining ferry service across the Hudson River but also the oldest ferry in the U.S. It now consists of two fixed spanned highway bridges.

Dockage: Just north of Storm King Mountain, on the west side of the river, is the Cornwall Yacht Club, which welcomes transient boats and sells gas. The next closest area for dockage is in Newburgh where Riverfront Marina Newburgh has slips and services. The Newburgh Yacht Club offers dockage for diners, as well as courtesy dockage for members of reciprocal yacht clubs.

Anchorage: You can find an interesting anchorage behind Pollepel Island by heading close into shore at Breakneck Point and then carefully following the 7- to 10-foot MLW channel northward toward the island. There are 8-foot to 11-foot MLW depths with excellent holding in mud. It is exposed, however, from the north

and south. This anchorage provides an interesting view of the ruins of the Bannerman Castle on Pollepel Island. The down side is the loud, frequent train noise.

Newburgh-Beacon Bridges to Kingston–Mile 46.7 to Mile 91

The Hudson River continues to be deep and well marked but note that there are no cruising facilities or protected anchorages between Marlboro (Mile 84.6) and Poughkeepsie (Mile 78.1).

Poughkeepsie was the temporary capital of New York in 1777 and is home to Vassar College, one of the so-called "Seven Sisters" colleges (now co-ed). Historic Hyde Park, the birthplace of Franklin D. Roosevelt, is a short drive away. The house is open for tours (800-337-8474). Also located in Hyde Park on the Hudson River is the Culinary Institute of America (www.ciachef.edu). Several excellent restaurants are within the Institute and reservations are required well in advance so plan accordingly.

Mid-Hudson Suspension Bridge (134-foot vertical clearance) at Mile 77.1 opened in 1930 and is one of the oldest bridges spanning the Hudson River.

Bear Moumtain

The massive 212-foot-high former railroad bridge has been in place for more than 100 years and once made Poughkeepsie an important railroad center. It is now a 1.28-mile pedestrian Walkway Bridge Over the Hudson.

A light on the south end marks Esopus Island at Mile 84. Beware of the ledge that is partly bare at low water and extends out about 300 yards from the north end. The Esopus Lighthouse, the southernmost of several old lighthouses built along the river, marks the shoals of Esopus Meadows. This one, knocked askew by winter ice, was built in 1872.

Dockage/Moorings: Marine facilities at New Hamburg are convenient to grocery stores for provisioning. Across the river on the west shore at Marlboro is the full-service West Shore Marine with slips for vessels to 60 feet.

Even though Poughkeepsie was once an active river port, it has few marinas. The well-regarded Shadows Marina to the south of the bridges has slips and services for vessels to 100 feet. Note that this facility is exposed to wakes and current. Transients are always welcome at The Hyde Park Marina where slips

are usually available inside the protected cove and if not, there are also outside docks.

The Poughkeepsie Yacht Club is not located at Poughkeepsie; instead, it is 7 nm north of the city, just southeast of Esopus Island. This friendly club welcomes all transient vessels on their floating dock or moorings.

Anchorage: We have observed boats anchored east of Esopus Island at Mile 84. The bottom is hard in 20-foot depths and depths drop off fast. This, in addition to a 4-foot tide, makes this a marginal anchorage.

For those ready to stop for the night before exploring Roundout Creek in Kingston, an anchorage can be found along the river's west shore just south of Port Ewen. Here you will find 6 to 18 feet MLW with good holding in mud. This anchorage is exposed from the northeast through southeast so plan accordingly. Be aware of the submerged dolphins shown on the NOAA chart.

Hudson River, NY

	Phone	Largest Vessel Accommodated	VHF Channel Monitored / Working	Transient Slips / Total Slips	Approach / Dockside Depth (reported)	Floating Docks	Gas / Diesel	Groceries, Ice, Marine Supplies, Snacks	Repairs: Hull, Engine, Propeller	Lift (tonnage), Crane, Rail	Min / Max Amps	Courtesy Car, Laundry, Pool, Showers	Pump-Out Station	Nearby: Grocery Store, Motel, Restaurant
STORM KING MOUNTAIN					**Dockage**			**Supplies**			**Services**			
1. Cornwall Yacht Club WiFi		50	16/	10/105	10.0/3.0	F		IS		L25	30/50	S	P	GMR
NEWBURGH														
2. Riverfront Marina Newburgh WiFi	(845) 661-4914	200	16/68	20/120	8.0/7.0	F		I	HEP		50	S	P	GMR
3. Newburgh Yacht Club 💻 WiFi	(845) 565-3920	50	/	12/120	5.5/4.0	F	GD	I		L25	30/50	PS	P	GR
NEW HAMBURG AREA														
4. White's Hudson River Marina	(845) 297-8520	40	/	2/300	20.0/20.0	F	GD	IM	HEP	L25	30	S	P	G
5. New Hamburg Yacht Club	(845) 298-1707	42	/	7/86	25.0/60.0			GIM			20			G
6. West Shore Marine	(845) 236-4486	60	16/9	6/180	12.0/12.0	F	GD	IM	HEP	L25	30/50	S		GMR
POUGHKEEPSIE AREA														
7. Shadows Marina WiFi	(845) 518-4459	100	/	30/70	12.0/12.0			S			15/50	S		MR
8. Hyde Park Marina 💻 WiFi	(845) 473-8283	150	16/	20/150	40.0/11.0	F	G	IM	HEP		30/50	S		GMR
9. Rogers Point Boating Association-PRIVATE	(845) 229-2236		/	/30	/	F	GD				30	S	P	R
10. Poughkeepsie Yacht Club 💻 WiFi	(845) 889-4742	50	/	3/75	60.0/22.0	F		I		L25	30/50	LS		R
KINGSTON AREA														
11. Hudson River Maritime Museum WiFi	(845) 706-8881	250	16/13	20/	30.0/16.0			IS			30/50	S		GMR
12. Kingston City Marina 💻 WiFi	(845) 331-6940	150	16/71	42/85	11.0/8.0	F		I			30/100	S	P	GMR
13. Hideaway Marina 💻	(845) 331-4565	55	16/9	4/100	7.0/7.0	F		IMS	P	L35	30	LS	P	GMR
14. Rondout Yacht Basin WiFi	(845) 331-7061	72	16/9	30/150	12.0/12.0	F	GD	IMS	HEP	L45	30/50	LPS	P	3R
15. Jeff's Yacht Haven	(845) 331-9248	65	16/	6/30	20.0/12.0	F		IM	HEP	L35,C,R	30	LS	P	MR
16. Certified Marina LLC 💻 WiFi	(845) 339-3060	45	16/9	5/110	15.0/12.0	F	G	IMS	HEP	L25,C	30/50	S	P	5MR
17. Lou's Boat Basin WiFi	(845) 331-4670	42	79/	/50	11.0/10.0		GD	IM			30			GR

💻 Internet Access WiFi Wireless Internet Access onSpot Dockside WiFi Facility

See WaterwayGuide.com for current rates, fuel prices, website addresses, and other up-to-the-minute information. (Information in the table is provided by the facilities.)

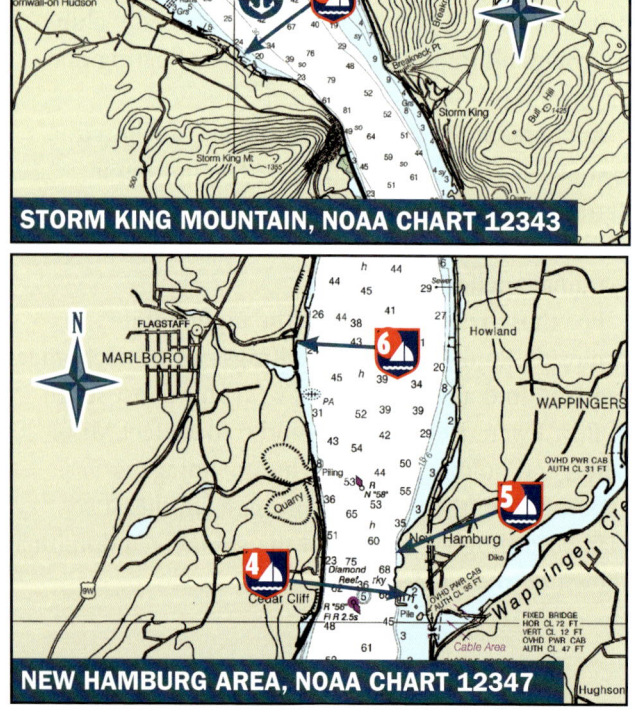

STORM KING MOUNTAIN, NOAA CHART 12343

NEW HAMBURG AREA, NOAA CHART 12347

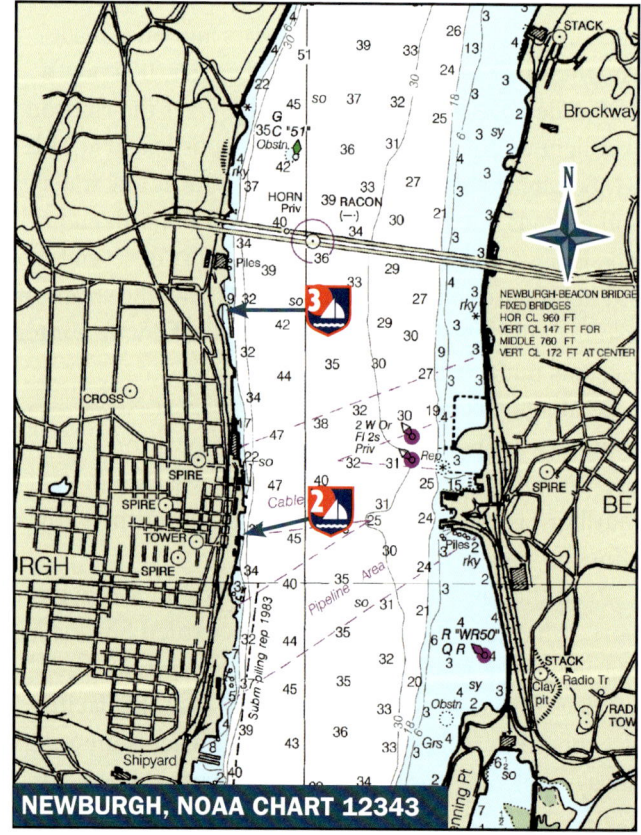

NEWBURGH, NOAA CHART 12343

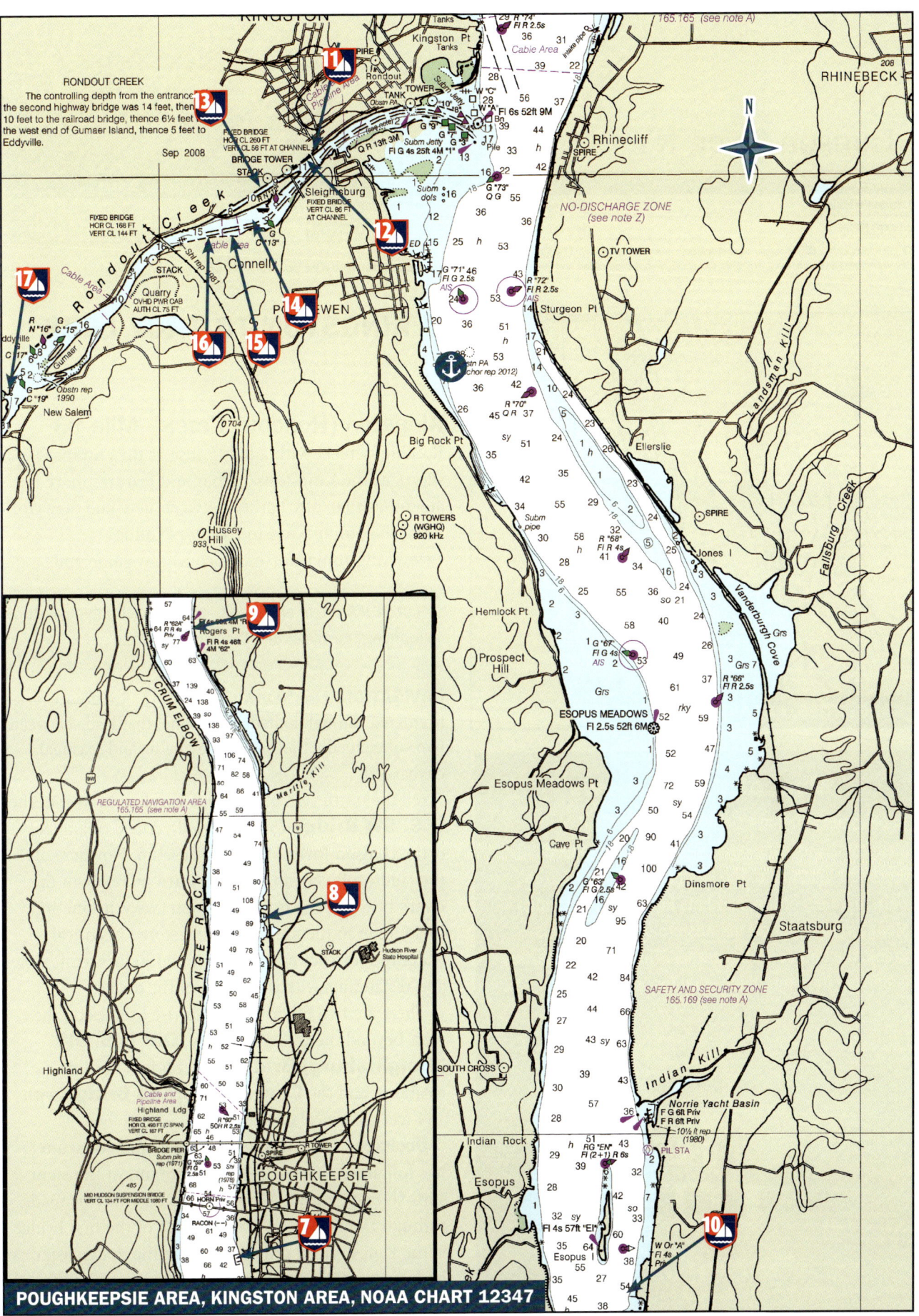

RONDOUT CREEK

The controlling depth from the entrance to the second highway bridge was 14 feet, then 10 feet to the railroad bridge, thence 6½ feet to the west end of Gumaer Island, thence 5 feet to Eddyville.

Sep 2008

POUGHKEEPSIE AREA, KINGSTON AREA, NOAA CHART 12347

Hudson River, NY

SAUGERTIES		Largest Vessel Accommodated	VHF Channel Monitored / Working	Transient Slips / Total Slips	Approach / Dockside Depth (reported)	Floating Docks	Gas / Diesel	Groceries, Ice, Marine Supplies, Snacks	Repairs: Hull, Engine, Propeller	Lift (tonnage), Crane, Rail	Courtesy Car, Laundry, Pool, Showers	Min / Max Amps	Pump-Out Station	Nearby: Grocery Store, Motel, Restaurant
				Dockage				**Supplies**			**Services**			
1. Saugerties Marina	(845) 246-7533	65	/	3/35	15.0/15.0	F	GD	IMS	HEP		CS	30		GMR
2. Lynch's Marina	(845) 247-0995	50	/	4/50	12.0/12.0			IM			S	30		GMR

🖳 Internet Access   📶 Wireless Internet Access   ⌘onSpot Dockside WiFi Facility
See WaterwayGuide.com for current rates, fuel prices, website addresses, and other up-to-the-minute information. (Information in the table is provided by the facilities.)

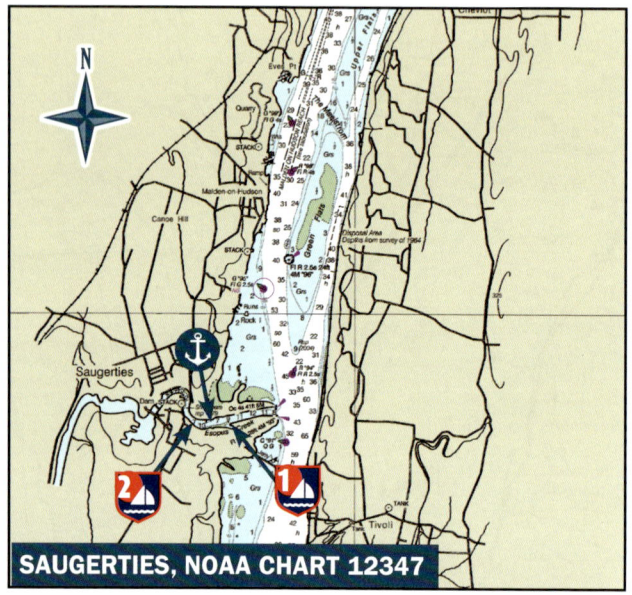

SAUGERTIES, NOAA CHART 12347

Maid of the Meadows

The Esopus Meadows Lighthouse, "The Maid of the Meadows," was completed in 1871 and replaced the 1839 lighthouse. The lighthouse was erected to warn mariners of the mud flats known as the Esopus Meadows, located off the western shore of Esopus Creek, the harbor for Saugerties. The name Saugerties is derived from the Dutch word for "sawmills."

■ KINGSTON TO TROY LOCK

Kingston (Rondout Creek)–Mile 93

Rondout Creek, with a lighthouse at the entrance, serves as the Kingston's harbor and features more amenities than any harbor between here and New York City. The online Kingston Visitors Guide (www.kingstonvisitorsguide.com) can guide you.

For NOAA weather reports, pay special attention to warnings for Ulster and Dutchess Counties.

NAVIGATION: Use NOAA Chart 12347. Rondout Creek is entered through a dredged channel that leads between two submerged jetties marked by lights and seasonal daybeacons.

On the north side of Rondout Creek, just west of the **U.S. 9W Bridge** (56-foot fixed vertical clearance) is the Hudson River Maritime Museum. Nowhere on the Hudson River can travelers learn more about the river's history than at this museum (www.hrmm.org). In addition to the museum, the restored historical waterfront district has an array of boutiques, craft stores and restaurants within 500 feet of the docks.

There are two other fixed high-rise bridges on the river beyond the U.S. 9W Bridge: **Old U.S. 9W (Sleightsburg) Bridge** with 86-foot vertical clearance and the **Conrail Railroad Bridge** with 144 feet of vertical clearance.

Dockage: The Hudson River Maritime Museum has full amenities but a limited amount of transient slips so book ahead. (Reservations can only be made through Dockwa). On the west side of the first bridge is the Kingston City Marina, where the dockmaster can be found in the small octagonal building at dockside.

They welcome transients on their floating docks with deep water slips and can accommodate vessels to 150 feet. An inexpensive trolley makes regular stops near the city docks on weekends. See the dockmaster for its schedule.

On the south side of the creek, past the second bridge, are a cluster of marinas. The full-service Rondout Yacht Basin has an on-site canvas shop. More marine facilities and all fuels are available upriver.

Anchorage: You can drop the hook 3.6 miles up Rondout Creek. Caution: You will pass under 3 fixed bridges and the first one is only 56 feet. Proceed past Gumaer Island and anchor south of the channel just before the low fixed bridge in 8 to 10 feet MLW. Mooring balls take up a lot of the anchorage and is usually very busy on weekends and holidays. There is a dinghy dock at Lou's Boat Basin (small fee).

Saugerties–Mile 101.8

Kingston-Rhinecliff Bridge (135-foot vertical clearance), 3 miles north of Kingston, was completed in 1957. Be aware that well-marked shoals to the north require large ship traffic to crisscross the river here.

> Heading north from Saugerties, you may be able to see the lovely old estate of Clermont at the top of a hillside lawn on the east bank opposite daybeacon "96." This is the oldest of the Hudson River estates and the home of seven generations of Livingstons including Chancellor Robert Livingston, the negotiator of the Louisiana Purchase as well as the co-inventor of the first practical steamboat. The British burned the original building (as well as the City of Kingston) in 1777. Clermont is now a state historic site and is open year-round until sunset Call 518-537-6622 for information or visit www.friendsofclermont.org.

Dockage: Although smaller than Kingston to the south, or Catskill to the north, this harbor is the home of two marinas: Saugerties Marina and Lynch's Marina. Both offer limited reserved transient space.

Anchorage: The depth in Esopus Creek between the marinas is 7 to 11 feet MLW with all-around protection and good holding in mud. You can dinghy to the marinas and then cross the bridge and follow the road into town (about 1.25 miles).

You can also follow Esopus Creek back to the rock face on the northern side of the creek, past Lynch's

Marina. Avoid the southern side of the creek as there is a sand bar built up there. (Do not go beyond this point as the creek gets shallow fast and has a rock bottom.) Use of a fore and aft anchor allows 3 or 4 vessels room to anchor in this protected spot in 12-foot MLW depths.

Catskill Creek–Mile 112.2

There are several plants and factories along the river between Saugerties and the mouth of Catskill Creek. It is not unusual to find river debris (logs, tree branches, etc.) in this area, especially after a heavy rain.

 The charted Maelstrom is a dangerous whirlpool on the east side of the main channel north of Saugerties.

Immediately north of Catskill is the **Rip Van Winkle Bridge** (vertical clearance 142 feet), which opened in 1935. When approaching the bridge from the south cast your gaze toward the top of Church Hill (marked on the chart) to the east to see the outline of Olana, the spectacular 19th-century building that was home to Frederic Church, one of the best known of the Hudson River School landscape artists. The house museum and property is now a state historic site.

Dockage: There are marinas and a yacht club in Catskill. A free dock at Catskill Point Park at the mouth of Catskill Creek has 7-foot MLW depths and no amenities. It is a little less than a 1 mile walk to town.

The minimum clearances of overhead structures (bridges, guard gates and utilities) range from 15.5 to 21 feet along the New York Canal System so sailors planning to exit the Hudson River and pick up the Erie Canal at Waterford need to de-mast prior to entering the system. Riverview Marine Services and Hop-O-Nose Marina both have mast-stepping and storage capabilities.

Anchorage: Duck Cove is on the west side of the river at Mile 108.3 across from Germantown. You can anchor in 6 to 8 feet MLW below the jetty. Come in from the south below the green daymarker "109" and stay at least 100 feet from the end of the jetty. We do not recommend anchoring in the narrow channel at Catskill Creek as it would impede the navigation of vessels coming and going.

Hudson River, NY

		Dockage					Supplies		Services				
	Largest Vessel Accomodated	VHF Channel Monitored / Working	Transient Slips / Total Slips	Approach / Dockside Depth (reported)	Floating Docks	Gas / Diesel	Groceries, Ice, Marine Supplies, Snacks	Repairs: Hull, Engine, Propeller	Lift (tonnage), Crane, Rail	Min / Max Amps	Courtesy Car, Laundry, Pool, Showers	Pump-Out Station	Nearby: Grocery Store, Motel, Restaurant
CATSKILL													
1. Riverview Marine Services Inc. 💻 WiFi (518) 943-5311	60	16/68	8/22	10.0/8.0	F	GD	IM	HEP	L20,C	30/50	LS	P	2.5R
2. Catskill Marina 💻 WiFi (518) 943-4170	130	16/9	15/85	10.0/10.0	F	GD	IS			30/50	LPS	P	GR
3. Hop-O-Nose Marina WiFi (518) 943-4640	100	16/	30/40	10.0/15.0	F	GD	IM	HEP	L15	30/50	LPS	P	GR
4. Catskill Yacht Club 💻 WiFi (518) 943-6459	40	16/	3/40	20.0/10.0	F	G	I	E		30	S	P	GMR
MIDDLE GROUND FLATS													
5. Hudson Power Boat Assoc. WiFi (518) 965-6761	40	16/9	4/60	30.0/10.0	F	G	I			30	S	P	GR
COEYMANS AREA													
6. Donovan's Shady Harbor Marina 💻 WiFi (518) 756-8001	180	16/68	20/120	15.0/12.0	F	GD	GIMS	HEP	L35,C	30/50	CLPS	P	GR
7. Coeymans Landing Marina 💻 WiFi 189 (518) 756-6111	60	16/9	8/85	8.0/10.0	F	GD	IMS	HEP	L38	30/50	LS	P	GR

💻 Internet Access WiFi Wireless Internet Access onSpot Dockside WiFi Facility

See WaterwayGuide.com for current rates, fuel prices, website addresses, and other up-to-the-minute information. (Information in the table is provided by the facilities.)

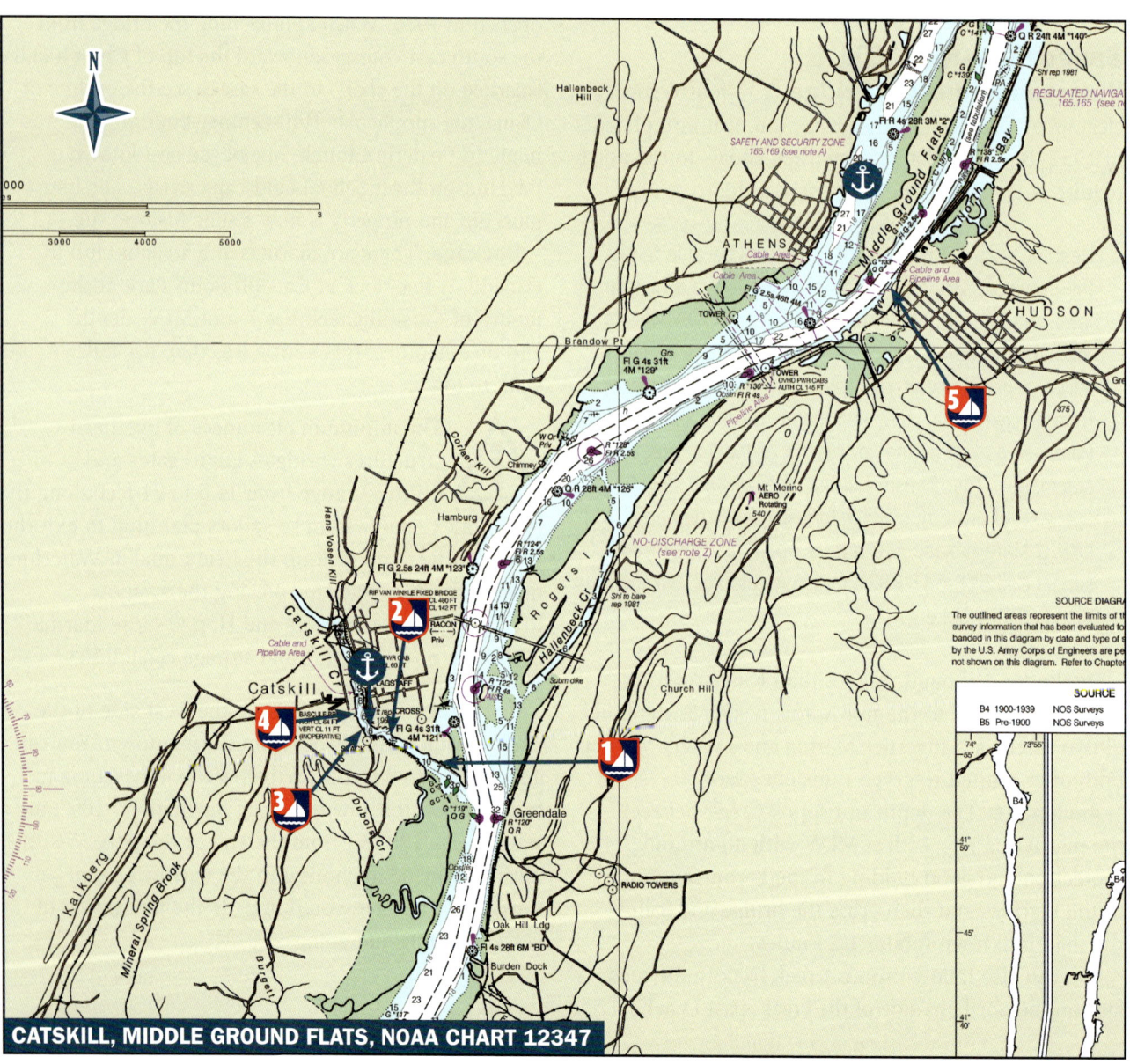

CATSKILL, MIDDLE GROUND FLATS, NOAA CHART 12347

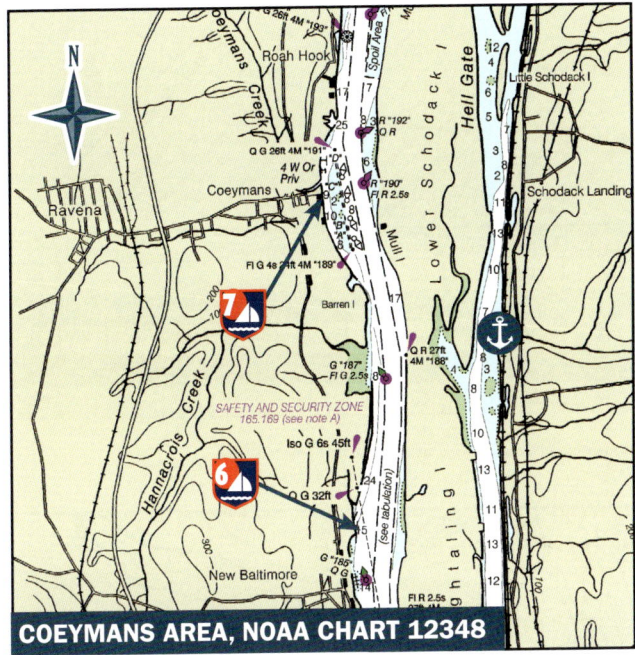

COEYMANS AREA, NOAA CHART 12348

Albany–Mile 145.5

The main ship channel passes east of Middle Ground Flats at Mile 117.5 but recreational craft frequently use the shorter route to the west, which has less current. Follow the channel to Houghtaling Island. Dockage is off the main channel, which runs to the west of the island or you can anchor on the east side of the island (entering from the south). Castleton-on-Hudson is located just north of the **Alfred H. Smith Railroad Bridge** (139-foot vertical clearance) and the high-rise **Castleton-on-Hudson Bridge** (135-foot fixed vertical clearance).

Some 10 miles to the north, you will emerge from the serenity of the upper Hudson River into the sometimes-hectic activity of seagoing ships unloading their cargoes of imported automobiles, bananas, fuel and molasses at the Port of Albany. In 1851, 15,000 Erie Canal boats and 500 sailing ships cleared this port.

> Albany has a 4-foot to 5-foot tidal range, even though it is 144 nm from the ocean.

North of the high-rise **Dunn Memorial Bridge** is a restored 19th-century building that once housed the headquarters of the Delaware and Hudson Railroad and is now part of the New York State University system. About 1 mile north of the Dunn Memorial Bridge is the **CSX Railroad Bridge** (25-foot closed vertical clearance), which opens on signal except from April 1 through December 15, from 11:00 p.m. to 7:00 a.m., when the draw will open on signal if at least 4

hours notice is given, and from December 16 through March 31, when the draw will open with at least a 24-hour notice.

Dockage/Moorings: There is a free day dock at Athens (Mile 117.4) with 10-foot MLW depths that is somewhat exposed to the southwest and northeast. You can walk to town from here for limited shopping. The Hudson Power Boat Association across the river is home base for the Columbia County Sheriffs Department, the Greenport Rescue Squad and the Hudson Fire Department. They accept transients but suggest you call ahead.

The well-regarded Donovan's Shady Harbor Marina is located in New Baltimore (Mile 187) and is an ideal transient stop for provisioning. The active marina is owned by a boating couple and hosts numerous events, such as Full Moon parties.

To the north in Coeymans, transient space and fuel can be found at another popular, full-service facility. Before leaving the river channel to head for Coeymans Landing Marina be sure to locate the position of the very long and very low north-south silt control dike. It is frequently underwater with only a few warning signs visible.

The Castleton Boat Club, located 1.5 miles north of the Castleton-on-Hudson Bridge offers transient dockage as well as a large crane for DIY mast stepping. The Boat Club's rental moorings, located across the river, include use of club facilities (showers, restrooms and bar).

The Albany Yacht Club, located on the east bank just before the Dunn Memorial Bridge (Mile 135.7), will go out of their way to make room for you. This is a fine base from which to visit the impressive Empire State Plaza & New York State Capitol (often referred to as the South Mall). Built in the 1960s, this complex is a magnificent showplace of modern granite architecture. In addition to the state government office buildings, the complex is home to one of the country's great modern museums and an acoustically superb auditorium. Affectionately called "The Egg," this bowl-shaped structure can be seen amid the 10 other buildings of the mall from the Hudson River. A tour of this complex might just be a highlight of your Hudson River cruise. Visit www.empirestateplaza.ny.gov for more details.

Anchorage: The west side of Middle Ground Flats (Mile 118) can be used as an anchorage but take special care to stay well out of the way of passing vessels. Enter the west side of Middle Ground Flats

Hudson River, NY

		Largest Vessel Accomodated	VHF Channel Monitored / Working	Approach / Dockside Depth (reported)	Transient Slips / Total Slips	Floating Docks	Gas / Diesel	Repairs: Hull, Engine, Propeller	Groceries, Ice, Marine Supplies, Snacks	Lift (tonnage), Crane, Rail	Min / Max Amps	Courtesy Car, Laundry, Pool, Showers	Pump-Out Station	Nearby: Grocery Store, Motel Restaurant
CASTLETON-ON-HUDSON				**Dockage**				**Supplies**			**Services**			
1. Castleton Boat Club WiFi 136.9	(518) 732-7077	80	16/9	5/55	12.0/8.0	F	GD	IS			30/50	S	P	GR
ALBANY														
2. Albany Yacht Club 💻 WiFi	(518) 445-9587	150	16/68	/80	25.0/18.0	F	GD	I			30/50	LS	P	GMR
TROY														
3. Troy Downtown Marina	(518) 764-0716		16/13	/	16.0/16.0	F	GD	M						GMR

💻 Internet Access   WiFi Wireless Internet Access   onSpot Dockside WiFi Facility

See WaterwayGuide.com for current rates, fuel prices, website addresses, and other up-to-the-minute information. (Information in the table is provided by the facilities.)

CASTLETON-ON-HUDSON, NOAA CHART 12348

ALBANY, NOAA CHART 12348

TROY, NOAA CHART 12348

from either the north or south. Depths are generally 15 feet MLW. From here, you can dinghy over to the town of Athens for provisioning.

You will find a better anchorage behind Stockport Middle Ground above red daybeacon "150" at Mile 122. Enter from the south side of the island and follow the deep water indicated on the chart until north of Judson Point. The entrance and channel are narrower than appears on the chart and the sides shoal abruptly. Two anchors are recommended to control swinging. There is a commuter train track on the eastern shore. Depths of 7 to 10 feet MLW can be found up to and near Gays Point. A depth sounder is essential here.

Just north of the town of Coxsackie (pronounced "Cook-sacky") is another protected anchorage (Mile 125). Note that it has been reported that the bar at the south end of the island extends significantly farther to the south than the chart indicates so if approaching from the south, favor the western shore. Control your wake when passing the nearby yacht club and private docks. Anchor in 10- to 15-foot MLW depths with excellent holding in mud.

Although the anchorage marked by white buoys just north of flashing red "170" is for big-ship use, recreational craft can find many attractive spots on the east side of Houghtaling Island (Mile 131.2) north of 30-foot, flashing red "180" in at least 8-foot MLW depths. This is the last good anchorage when heading north.

To Troy Federal Lock (Lock 1)– Mile 153.9

NAVIGATION: Use NOAA Chart 12348. North of Albany, on the west side of the river past the **Patroon Island Bridge** (60-foot fixed vertical clearance) and **Troy-Menands Bridge** (61-foot fixed vertical clearance), is the Watervliet Arsenal. Arms for U.S. military forces have been manufactured here since the arsenal's establishment in 1813. North of Watervliet, you will pass under the **Congress Street Bridge** (55-foot fixed vertical clearance) and the **Federal Street Bridge** (29-foot closed vertical clearance) between Troy and Green Islands.

The Federal Street Bridge is a lift bridge with a restricted schedule: From April 1 through December 15 the draw opens on signal with a 24-hour advance notice, given by calling the number posted at the bridge. From December 16 through March 31, the draw need not open for the passage of vessel traffic. The final bridge before the lock is **Collar City (NY 7) Bridge** (61-foot fixed vertical clearance) between Adams Island and Stormy Island at Mile 152.9.

Did You Know? In 1609 a longboat from Henry Hudson's ship, *Half Moon,* explored as far north on the Hudson River as the present city of Troy in search of a route to the Orient.

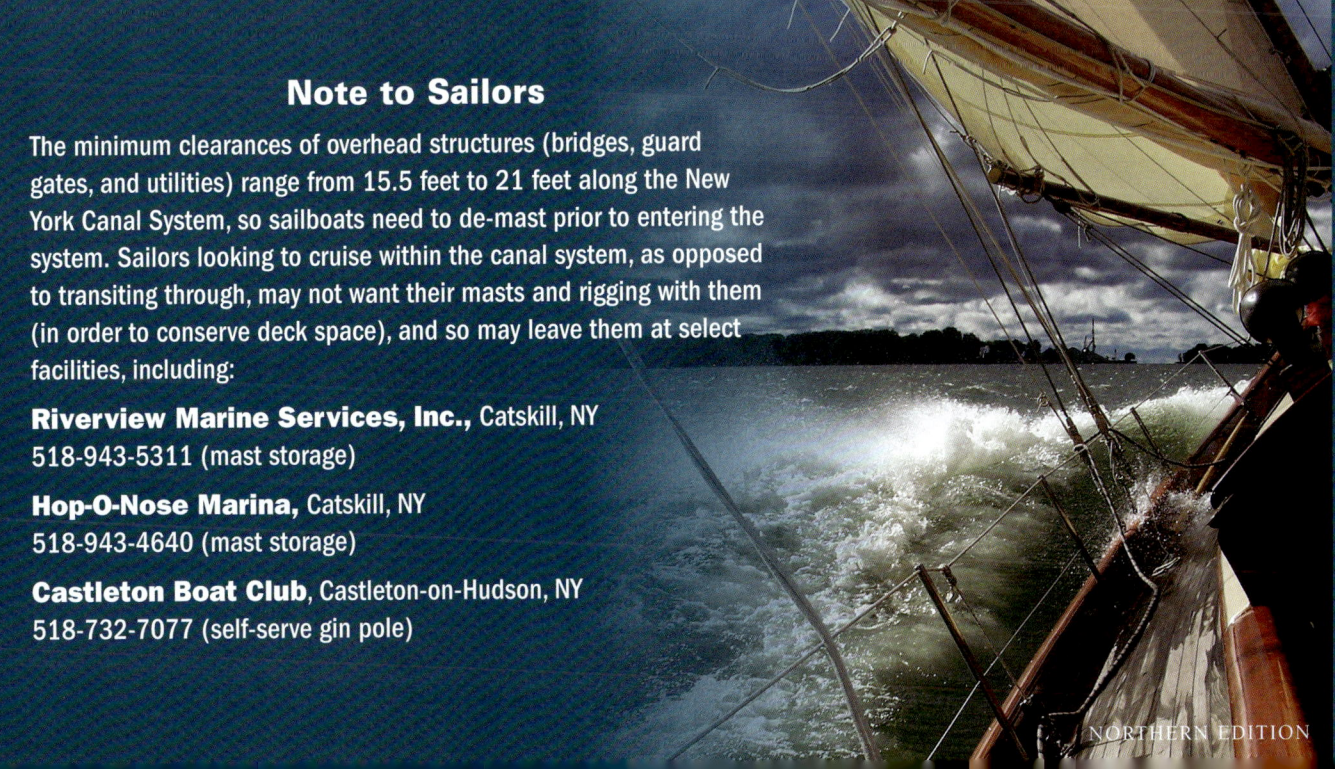

Note to Sailors

The minimum clearances of overhead structures (bridges, guard gates, and utilities) range from 15.5 feet to 21 feet along the New York Canal System, so sailboats need to de-mast prior to entering the system. Sailors looking to cruise within the canal system, as opposed to transiting through, may not want their masts and rigging with them (in order to conserve deck space), and so may leave them at select facilities, including:

Riverview Marine Services, Inc., Catskill, NY
518-943-5311 (mast storage)

Hop-O-Nose Marina, Catskill, NY
518-943-4640 (mast storage)

Castleton Boat Club, Castleton-on-Hudson, NY
518-732-7077 (self-serve gin pole)

Continuing on the New York Canal System

If you plan to continue on the NY Canal System, be sure to sign up for Canal Alerts to Mariners for up-to-the-minute information on water levels, closures or restrictions on docking due to events at www.canals.ny.gov/boating/index.html. On the NY Canal System Corp. website you will also find:

· Hours of operation
· Tolls, passes and permits
· Canal map
· Speed limits
· Navigation information
· Lock, lift and guard gate listings
· Marinas and public docks
· Lodging options

The NY Canal Corporation recommends that boaters carry the latest edition of NOAA Chart 14786. This charts may be downloaded from NOAA (www.charts.noaa.gov/OnLineViewer/14786.shtml). There are no NOAA charts available between Mile 222 and 337 of the Erie Canal (including the Genesee River).

Along with this guide, there are two other resources we recommend you keep on hand:
- *Cruising The New York Canal System* (a Skipper Bob publication)
- *Cruising Guide to the New York State Canal System* (published by the NY State Canal Corp.))

Another "must have" is the online Waterway Explorer, a free interactive reference for navigating the canal system. Specific marina and anchorage information can be found as well as details on bridges and locks. The site provides the ability to make updates, report hazards and read or write reviews on facilities. To help other boaters, please take a moment to enter a rating and add any updates when you visit a marina or anchorage. You can also sign up for weekly news and navigation updates, delivered directly to your inbox. Visit the Explorer at www.waterwayguide.com.

Lock 1, the **Troy Federal Lock**, is 153 miles from The Battery in New York City. This lock is the first of a long series that can take you to Buffalo on Lake Erie, Oswego on Lake Ontario, or Whitehall on Lake Champlain. Secure your boat to the lock using the recessed pipes or cables that run from the bottom of the lock wall to the top. The lock has a 16-foot lift and the schedule varies with season. In 2020 the lock opened on request from 7:00 a.m. to 5:00 p.m., May 18 to October 14. Vessels are required to arrive at a lock at least 15 minutes prior to closing to ensure being locked through, and at a bridge at least 5 minutes prior to ensure an opening. The lock monitors VHF Channel 13. Refer to the Waterway Explorer at www.waterwayguide.com for the most up-to-date schedule.

Dockage: Troy Downtown Marina is where the Loopers meet the locals. Overnight transient docking and two-hour complimentary docking are both available here and its convenient location makes this marina a popular provisioning stop. Be sure to call ahead if you are planning to have your mast un-stepped here.

◼ NEXT STOP

After exiting the Troy Lock you enter the quiet, non-tidal waters of the Lower Champlain Canal. From here, the cruiser has several choices:

- Option 1: Continue north up the Champlain Canal to Lake Champlain.

- Option 2: Head west on the Erie Canal to Buffalo and Lake Erie.

- Option 3: Head west on the Erie Canal and Oswego Canal to Oswego and Lake Ontario.

- Option 4: Follow Option 3, but when returning to Troy, cross Lake Ontario and return via the St. Lawrence and Richelieu Rivers, Lake Champlain and the Champlain Canal. This route is referred to as the "Triangle Loop."

All of these options are detailed in Waterway Guide's Great Lakes Vol. 1 edition, which can be purchased at www.waterwayguide.com. Regardless of what route or option you choose, you are in for an excellent adventure.

Long Island Sound

- **North Shore: To Milford Harbor, CT**
- **North Shore: New Haven, CT to Watch Hill, RI**
- **South Shore: To Mattituck Inlet, NY**
- **Long Island Twin Forks, NY**

North Shore Distances

Nautical Miles (approximate)

LOCATION	BETWEEN POINTS	CUMULATIVE
Throgs Neck Bridge	0	
City Island	3	3
New Rochelle	5	8
Mamaroneck	4	12
Greenwich	8	20
Stamford	6	26
South Norwalk	11	37
Stratford	6	43
New Haven	15	58
Guilford	17	75
Connecticut River:		
Saybrook	17	92
Essex	8	100
New London	14	114
Fishers Island	5	119
Mystic	5	124

South Shore Distances

Nautical Miles (approximate)

LOCATION	BETWEEN POINTS	CUMULATIVE
Throgs Neck Bridge	0	
Little Neck Bay	1	1
Manhasset Bay	4	5
Port Washington	2	7
Hempstead Harbor	6	13
Glen Cove	1	14
Oyster Bay Harbor	11	25
Huntington Bay	6	31
Huntington Harbor	2	33
Northport Harbor	4	37
Stony Brook	14	51
Port Jefferson	8	59
Mount Sinai	5	64
Mattituck	22	86
Orient Point	18	104
Montauk Point	24	128
Block Island	13	141

North Shore: To Milford Harbor, CT

NAVIGATING LONG ISLAND SOUND

Long Island Sound packs history, high-tech boating and fun in an estuary that stretches 90 nm between New York City and Block Island, RI. Long and slim-looking on the chart, it is actually up to 20 nm wide in the middle. Much as New York is just "the City," Long Island Sound requires no further name than "the Sound" in local conversation. It's a major commercial artery, an important fishing and lobstering ground and one of the famed cruising areas of the U.S.

Along the northern shore of Long Island Sound you'll find a string of coastal cities extending from New York to Rhode Island. While many of these cities began as industrial centers because of easy access to shipping and are now populated and diverse urban centers, there are still numerous smaller towns with harbors along the shoreline.

On weekends the Sound is a wonderland of sailboats producing a spectacular sight. In addition to the parade of cruising boats transiting the Sound, yacht clubs hold organized regattas on a regular basis. These fleets are especially common near City Island, Bridgeport, New Haven and New London under the north shore.

When cruising the Sound under sail or power, pull out your camera but detour around the racers to avoid interfering. Then dawdle a bit to catch the downwind run. A photo full of spinnakers impresses any viewer.

The local mariner need never leave the Sound from year after year. Crisscrossing between Connecticut's rocky shore and Long Island's sandy beaches, mariners cruise the summer away, anchoring in isolated coves, visiting luxurious marinas, racing under sail, fishing, taking long side trips up navigable rivers and exploring big bays.

Cruising Conditions

The weather on Long Island Sound is generally hospitable with the predictable summer thunderstorms. Thunderstorms, of course, bring strong, gusty winds. The occasional nor'easter, often lasting as long as 3 days, delivers winds, steep seas, low temperatures and torrents of rain. One shore or the other generally offers a lee but a nasty chop is the norm in these conditions. These seas will often continue for a couple days after the sky has cleared and while much reduced, they are still no fun to battle. Heavy fog, which might greet the mariner

Cross-Sound Distances

The table below is a selection of major cruising stops on Long Island Sound and the distances between them. It is not a complete list of ports and is intended solely as a guide to cruise planning. All distances have been figured along the most direct course consistent with safe, normal navigation. All figures are approximate. Actual mileage will depend on variations of course, speed, boat, weather, currents and other cruising conditions.

FROM	MILES TO:	NAUTICAL	STATUTE
CITY ISLAND (off Belden Pt.)	Stamford	17	19
	Stratford	40	46
	Clinton	64	73
	Saybrook Point	79	91
	New London	85	98
	Mystic	89	102
	Oyster Bay Harbor	17	19
	Huntington Bay	20	23
	Port Jefferson	33	38
	Mattituck Inlet	54	62
	Orient Point	75	86
STAMFORD (East Branch, past hurricane barrier)	City Island	17	19
	Stratford	27	31
	Clinton	54	62
	Saybrook Point	56	64
	New London	75	86
	Mystic	73	84
	Oyster Bay Harbor	9	10
	Huntington Bay	10	11
	Port Jefferson	24	28
	Mattituck Inlet	45	52
	Orient Point	61	70
STRATFORD (2 miles up from outer breakwater light)	City Island	40	46
	Stamford	27	31
	Clinton	31	36
	Saybrook Point	39	45
	New London	53	61
	Mystic	57	66
	Oyster Bay Harbor	30	34
	Huntington Bay	25	28
	Port Jefferson	15	17
	Mattituck Inlet	28	32
	Orient Point	42	48
CLINTON (Cedar Island)	City Island	64	73
	Stamford	54	62
	Stratford	31	36
	Saybrook Point	11	13
	New London	25	29
	Mystic	30	34
	Oyster Bay Harbor	51	59
	Huntington Bay	47	54
	Port Jefferson	32	37
	Mattituck Inlet	15	17
SAYBROOK POINT	City Island	79	91
	Stamford	56	64
	Stratford	39	45
	Clinton	11	13
	New London	17	19
	Mystic	20	23
	Oyster Bay Harbor	61	70
	Huntington Bay	56	64
	Port Jefferson	40	46
	Mattituck Inlet	20	23
	Orient Point	9	10
NEW LONDON (abeam of Shaw Cove)	City Island	85	98
	Stamford	75	86
	Stratford	53	61
	Clinton	25	29
	Saybrook Point	17	19
	Mystic	12	14
	Oyster Bay Harbor	74	85
	Huntington Bay	70	81
	Port Jefferson	59	68
	Mattituck Inlet	34	39
	Orient Point	15	17

FROM	MILES TO:	NAUTICAL	STATUTE
MYSTIC (abeam of Shaw Cove)	City Island	89	102
	Stamford	73	84
	Stratford	57	66
	Clinton	30	34
	Saybrook Point	20	23
	New London	12	14
	Oyster Bay Harbor	78	90
	Huntington Bay	75	86
	Port Jefferson	58	67
	Mattituck Inlet	35	40
	Orient Point	16	18
OYSTER BAY HARBOR (off Plum Point)	City Island	17	19
	Stamford	9	10
	Stratford	30	34
	Clinton	51	59
	Saybrook Point	61	70
	New London	74	85
	Mystic	78	90
	Huntington Bay	9	10
	Port Jefferson	25	29
	Mattituck Inlet	48	55
	Orient Point	64	73
HUNTINGTON BAY (Lloyd Harbor Light)	City Island	20	23
	Stamford	10	11
	Stratford	25	29
	Clinton	47	54
	Saybrook Point	56	64
	New London	70	80
	Mystic	75	86
	Oyster Bay Harbor	9	10
	Port Jefferson	20	23
	Mattituck Inlet	41	47
	Orient Point	58	67
PORT JEFFERSON (2 miles in from jetty light)	City Island	33	38
	Stamford	24	28
	Stratford	15	17
	Clinton	32	37
	Saybrook Point	40	46
	New London	59	68
	Mystic	58	67
	Oyster Bay Harbor	25	29
	Huntington Bay	20	23
	Mattituck Inlet	27	31
	Orient Point	44	51
MATTITUCK INLET (Mattituck Creek)	City Island	54	62
	Stamford	45	52
	Stratford	28	32
	Clinton	15	17
	Saybrook Point	20	23
	New London	34	39
	Mystic	35	40
	Oyster Bay Harbor	48	55
	Huntington Bay	41	47
	Port Jefferson	27	31
	Orient Point	20	23
ORIENT POINT (abeam of light)	City Island	75	86
	Stamford	61	70
	Stratford	42	48
	Clinton	15	17
	Saybrook Point	9	10
	New London	15	17
	Mystic	16	18
	Oyster Bay Harbor	64	73
	Huntington Bay	58	67
	Port Jefferson	44	51
	Mattituck Inlet	20	23

several mornings a year, can be thick enough to be dangerous, even to experienced mariners. The Sound has an excellent overlapping system of fog signals and it is well charted.

> Continuous weather reports are broadcast on VHF-FM WX-1 from New York City and New London, CT. Most commercial radio stations broadcast boating forecasts during the season.

As a rule in summer months winds pick up in early afternoon and get progressively stronger as the day wears on. Most powerboats wanting to make time get an early morning start or they travel at night when winds tend to die, using the chain of lights that defines a clear path down the center of the Sound. Sailboats may choose to get underway in the light winds of morning, especially if heading south from a river anchorage, before making good time under sail during the breezy afternoons. Check the current tide charts (www.tidesandcurrents.noaa.gov) and avoid situations of wind countering current if you want to avoid stiff chop.

Sailors can also set out when the wind is easing and use auxiliary power, if necessary, to run the usually placid night waters. When underway at night, stay well clear of areas where there might be lobster pots, oyster beds and fish traps; all are, at best, difficult to spot. In addition, keep a sharp lookout for tugs with tows, which often run the Sound at night. The tows are often on very long lines and can be difficult to spot. Especially around the busy port of Bridgeport, tugs can behave rather unpredictably, circling as they bring in or let out their tows in preparation for docking. A radio call on VHF Channel 16 or 13 is advisable to clarify each vessel's intentions. It is not advisable to attempt to enter an unfamiliar harbor after dark.

Tides & Currents

At the western end of Long Island Sound, an 8-foot to 10-foot rise and fall is to be expected; mean tidal range is about 7.5 feet. The tidal range drops to less than 3 feet as you travel east.

Currents on Long Island Sound are not to be taken lightly. The currents run strongest at the narrow ends of the Sound, reaching maximum velocity (up to 4 knots) at The Race and Plum Gut on the eastern end between Fishers Island and the North Fork of Long Island. Currents taper off to 0.5 knot in mid-Sound but run hard around points and shoals. In general, the flood sets

westerly and the ebb sets easterly. Riding a fair current can improve your cruising time substantially and make the trip more comfortable, especially if you can also arrange a broad or strong following wind. It's worth an early morning to ensure the current is in your favor.

Navigation

Markers on Long Island Sound are frequent with many lighthouses, both mid-channel and ashore, offering easy-to-locate reference points. Most rocks and reefs are well charted and marked. Make sure to account for current in all courses.

For the hurried transient boater passing through the Sound, the navigation is straightforward. From the Throgs Neck Bridge at the sound's western entrance, a GPS or compass course will lead you roughly northeast past the Sound's first important aid to navigation, Stepping Stones Light (pass on the north side), near City Island. Execution Rocks Lighthouse, which appears next, can be left on either side. At Execution Rocks, the course changes to almost due east (magnetic), straight down the Sound to the midpoint of Stratford Shoal Lighthouse, about 30 nm away. The course remains due east through the widest part of the Sound, almost 20 nm across. A smooth non-stop trip through the Sound to Newport will include planning for the currents mentioned above but can be done with ease.

On the other hand, there are many reasons to stop along the way. On the south side of Long Island Sound (the North Shore of Long Island), you will find large natural harbors with ample facilities and room to anchor. Hempstead Harbor, Oyster Bay and Huntington Harbor offer complete cruising grounds for small boats that never have to leave the mouth of the harbor.

On the Connecticut shore frequent small harbors cover the coast along with numerous islands, rock outcroppings and river entrances. The harbors of the western end are more complicated to enter and more tightly packed. Marinas are ample but are normally crowded with local boats. Advance reservations are necessary for dockside space. Many harbors are dominated by large elaborate yacht clubs, such as Larchmont, Indian Harbor in Greenwich and Pequot in Southport. Docking at these clubs requires reciprocal privileges from the skipper's home club. As you continue along, the rivers get bigger and the bays at their mouths more inviting. Similarly, the facilities are a bit more spread out and tend to have more space available.

Long Island Sound, NY

CITY ISLAND		Largest Vessel Accomodated	VHF Channel Monitored / Working	Transient Slips / Total Slips	Approach / Dockside Depth (reported)	Floating Docks	Gas / Diesel	Groceries, Ice, Marine Supplies, Snacks	Repairs: Hull, Engine, Propeller	Lift (tonnage), Crane, Rail	Min / Max Amps	Courtesy Car, Laundry, Pool, Showers	Pump-Out Station	Nearby: Grocery Store, Motel, Restaurant
				Dockage				Supplies	Services					
1. Minneford Marina 💻 WiFi	(718) 885-2000	125	77/77	15/164	17.0/10.0	F		GIM	HEP	L55	30/100	LS		GR
2. South Minneford Yacht Club 💻 WiFi	(718) 885-3113	57	69/	20/120	14.0/10.0	F		GIMS	HP	L80	30/50	LS		GMR
3. Consolidated Yachts NY Inc.	(718) 885-1900	150	/	5/64	14.0/14.0			IM	HEP	L60,C	30/50	S		G
4. City Island Yacht Club WiFi	(718) 885-2487		72/	/	9.0/6.0							S		R
5. Harlem Yacht Club 💻 WiFi	(718) 885-3078	45	72/72	/	8.0/4.0	F		I				LS		GR
6. Stelter Marine Sales	(718) 885-1300	28	/	/40	4.0/4.0			M	HEP		30			GR
7. City Island Yacht Sales & Marina WiFi	(718) 885-2300	70	9/	4/45	12.0/8.0	F	GD	IM	HEP	L30	30/50		P	GMR
NEW ROCHELLE AREA														
8. NYAC Yacht Club	(914) 738-2700	74	9/9	5/168	15.0/10.0	F	GD	I		L50,C	30/50	PS		R
9. Glen Island Yacht Club / West Harbor Yacht Service WiFi	(914) 636-1524	65	/	2/30	8.0/6.0	F		IM	HEP	L15,C	30	LS		GR
10. Huguenot Yacht Club	(914) 636-6300	65	73/	5/60	16.0/8.0	F		I	P	L,C	30/50	LPS		GMR
11. Wright Island Marina WiFi	(914) 235-8013	65	/	5/100	11.0/9.0	F	GD	I	HEP	L50	30/50	LPS	P	GMR
12. Imperial Yacht Club Inc.-PRIVATE 💻 WiFi	(914) 636-1122	65	/	/100	14.0/7.0			I	HEP	L70	30/50	LPS	P	GMR
13. Castaways Yacht Club 💻 WiFi	(914) 636-8444	75	/	2/120	14.0/9.0	F	GD	IS	HEP	L75	30/50	PS	P	MR
14. Polychron Marina	(914) 632-4088	35	/	/85	5.0/3.0	F		I	HEP	C	30			GR
15. New Rochelle Municipal Marina WiFi	(914) 235-6930	50	16/9	3/350	10.0/10.0	F	GD	IMS	HEP	L25	30/100	LS	P	GMR

💻 Internet Access   WiFi Wireless Internet Access   onSpot Dockside WiFi Facility

See WaterwayGuide.com for current rates, fuel prices, website addresses, and other up-to-the-minute information. (Information in the table is provided by the facilities.)

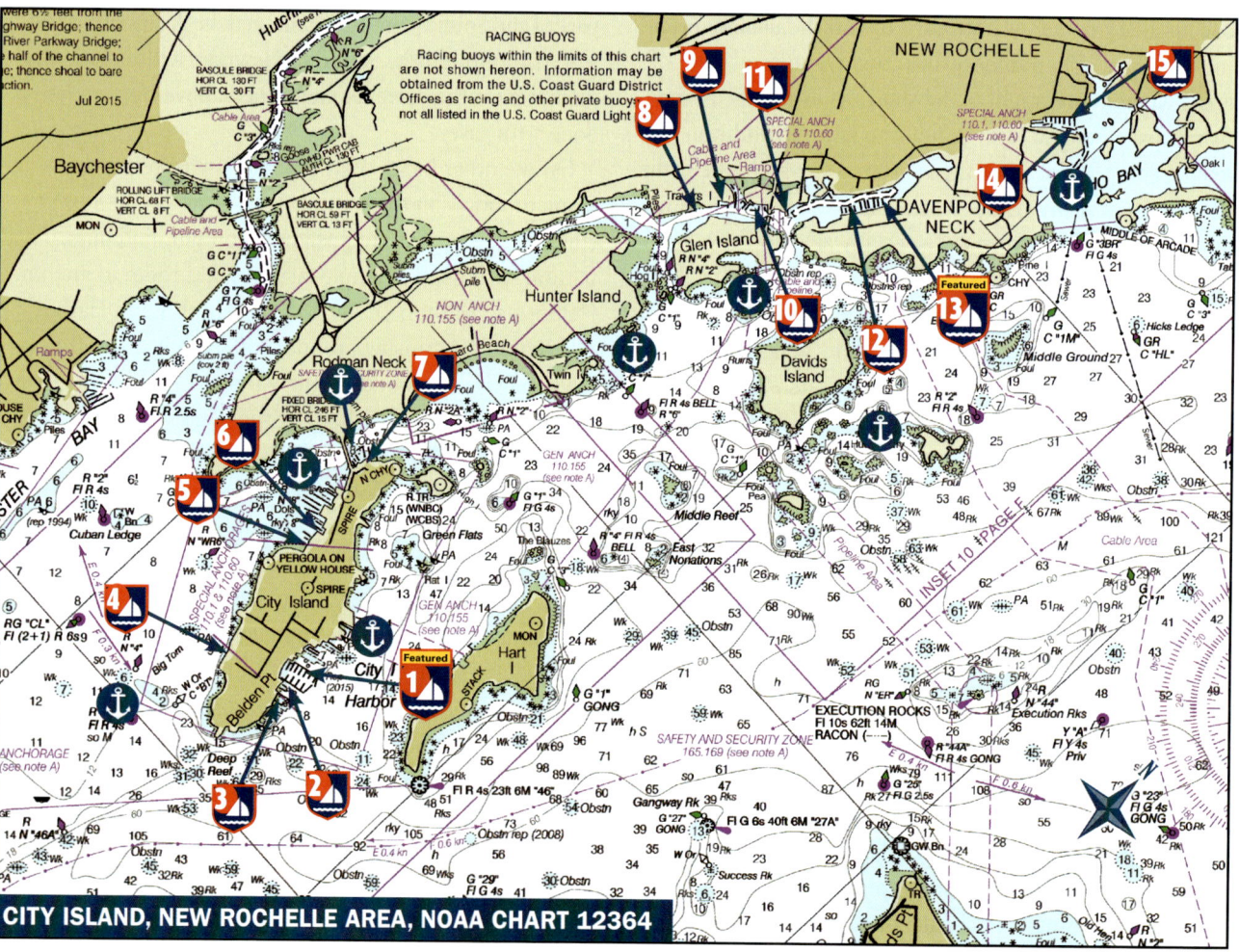

CITY ISLAND, NEW ROCHELLE AREA, NOAA CHART 12364

12-Foot Fixed Bridge

MINNEFORD MARINA

City Island

East Norwalk Blue Pumpout Program operates a mobile pump-out service for boaters along the North Shore of western Long Island Sound from Throgs Neck, NY to Bridgeport, CT from May to October. Choose your vessel's location from the drop down list online (www.pumpout.eastnorwalkblue.org/pumpout.asp) and they will empty your waste tank.

■ CITY ISLAND TO MAMARONECK HARBOR, NY

Entering Long Island Sound

Throgs Neck Bridge (152-foot fixed vertical clearance) on the East River marks the entrance to Long Island Sound. After crossing under the bridge, turn sharply north around flashing red bell buoy "48," off the point of Throgs Neck.

The Stepping Stones lighthouse, a brownstone house perched on a stone foundation, is located to the northeast, and is the first of the many distinctive lighthouses on the Sound. The eponymous "Stepping Stones" (jagged rocks, dry at low water) project southeast toward the Long Island shore of the sound and are marked by an unnumbered 4-second occulting

GOIN' ASHORE

CITY ISLAND, NY

City Island is only 1.5 miles long and one-half miles wide but it's a vibrant nautical community with copious seafood restaurants, yacht clubs (all on Eastchester Bay), several university sailing teams, many maritime historic landmarks and numerous yacht yards and marine centers. See www.cityisland.com for an extensive list of businesses.

SERVICES

1. City Island Laundromat
310 City Island Ave. (718-885-1840)

2. City Island Library
320 City Island Ave. (718-885-1703)

3. City Island Post Office
199 City Island Ave. (718-885-3153)

ATTRACTIONS

4. City Island Nautical Museum
Chronicles the island's colorful maritime and shipbuilding traditions and includes collections of maritime-themed watercolors and books. Open on Saturdays and Sundays from 1:00 p.m. to 5:00 p.m. for a small fee (190 Fordham St., 718-885-0008).

SHOPPING

5. J.J. Burke Hardware & Marine Supply
A chandlery at 526 City Island Ave. (718-885-1559).

MARINAS

6. City Island Yacht Club
63 Pilot St. (718-885-2487)

7. City Island Yacht Sales & Marina
673 City Island Ave. (718-885-2300). Bridge Marine Supply located on site.

8. Consolidated Yachts Inc.
157 Pilot St. (718-885-1900)

9. Harlem Yacht Club
417 Hunter Ave. (718-885-3078)

10. Minneford Marina
150 City Island Ave. (718-885-2000)

11. South Minneford Yacht Club
148 City Island Ave. (718-885-3113)

12. Stelter Marine Sales
495 City Island Ave. (718-885-1300)

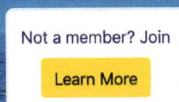

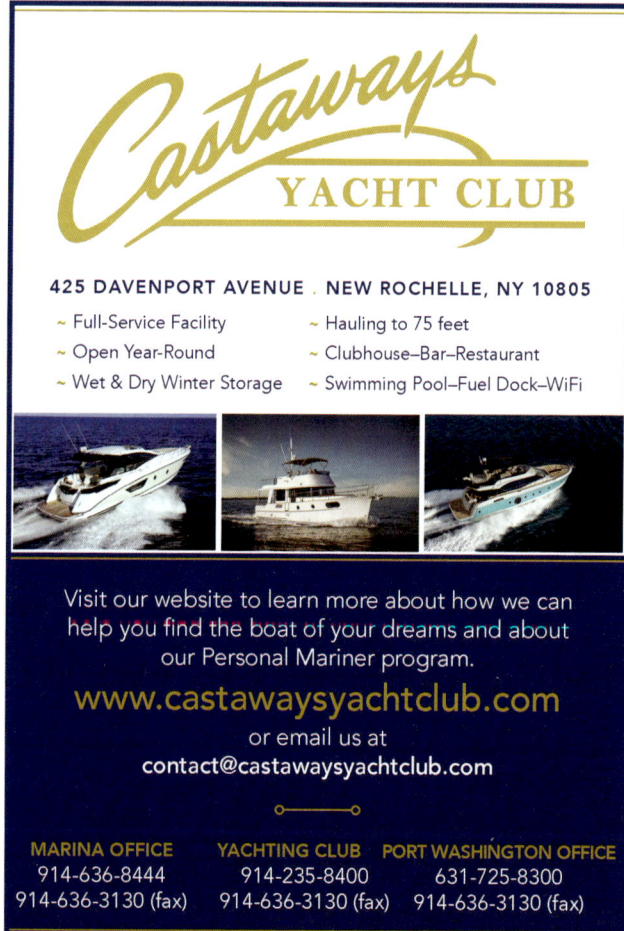

Photo labels: New Rochelle · CASTAWAYS YACHT CLUB · Davenport Neck · Glen Island

green light. Leave Stepping Stones to starboard (west) and continue north.

Eastchester Bay to the northwest has a few shoals and rocks, all of which are well marked. Along the western side of the bay is an almost landlocked cove and the entrance to protected Hammond Creek. To reach the cove, enter from the east under the Throgs Neck Bridge (North Span) (123-foot fixed vertical clearance), to the narrow entry, which has 5-foot MLW depths. If traveling straight there from the East River, this means passing under the main span of the bridge (east bound), rounding SUNY Maritime College at the tip of Throgs Neck and then passing under the North Span (west bound). Several marine facilities and a yacht club are here and you can anchor in the cove, if you can find depth and room. Consult your charts.

City Island, NY

City Island is only 1.5 miles long and 0.5 miles wide but it's remarkable boating complexes contain the first great concentration of yachts on the trip out of the East River to Long Island Sound. City Island is part of the New York City's Bronx borough and is devoted to boating services as well as boating history. Yacht clubs, marinas, shipyards, sailmakers, electrical and electronics technicians, engine mechanics and marine supply houses abound. City Island also boasts a long legacy of America's Cup fame. The 110-year string of 24 successful campaigns to defend the Cup began with *Magic*, completely rebuilt on City Island in 1870, and ended with Freedom, built on City Island in 1980. (In 1983, when City Island had no connection with the defender, America suffered her first Cup loss.) A visit to the City Island Nautical Museum is a must, although it is only open on weekends. See details at www.cityislandmuseum.org.

NAVIGATION: Use NOAA Charts 12363 and 12364. City Island is almost a self-contained community, connected to the mainland by the fixed **City Island Bridge** (12-foot vertical clearance) on the northwest side of the island. The island's "nautical village" character has been preserved over the years and City Island can serve as a great stopover to refuel, time your transit through the East River and Hell Gate or stop before cruising east through Long Island Sound. Many boats will be unable to circumnavigate City Island because of the fixed bridge at Rodman Neck. Even though most shoals and rocks are buoyed and charted, do not get too close to the dock-lined, rock-strewn shores.

Even local mariners sometimes go astray on the large, menacing rock called Big Tom, west of the island's southern tip. The clearly marked rock is the center of a triangle created by flashing red "2" to the south, red nun buoy "4" to the west and white and orange can "BT" to the east. Boats staying outside the marked triangle will have no problem but periodically someone attempts a shortcut or becomes confused by the welter of small fishing vessels obscuring the buoys and Big Tom claims yet another victim.

City Island Harbor, on the island's east side between City Island and Hart Island, is easily approached from the west on the main channel. Approaching from the east, the eastern side of City Island may be accessed by rounding Hart Island in either direction, although most skippers will find the route around the southern end more straightforward, especially in poor visibility. The northern passage around Hart Island is generally well marked, although it has its share of obstructions. If attempting the north passage, watch carefully for Pea Island, East Nonations and Middle Reef, which are all south of David's Island and not marked. Next proceed from flashing red bell buoy "4" to flashing green "1" without drifting south toward The Blauzes, which look

like two small islands at high tide but extend a small distance all around.

Dockage/Moorings: Yacht clubs, boat yards and marinas ring City Island and a number of them offer accommodations to transient cruisers. On the west side of City Island, City Island Yacht Club and Harlem Yacht Club have mooring space for transients and members of other clubs for a modest facilities fee. This includes 24-hour launch service (call on VHF Channel 72) and use of the club's restaurant, restrooms and showers. At north end of the island City Island Yacht Sales & Marina sells gas and diesel fuel and offers repairs and services.

On the east side of the island a cluster of marine facilities are available in City Island Harbor offering slip rentals, winter storage and transient dockage. South Minneford Yacht Club here has a storied past. It occupies the site of the old Minneford Shipyard, established in 1926, which produced palatial yachts for millionaires. It also built many of the great America's Cup racers, including Constellation, Intrepid, Courageous, Freedom and Enterprise, and during World War II it built torpedo boats, mine sweepers and seagoing tugs. The yard was closed around 1980 and became the current marina in 1985.

Anchorage: You can usually find room to anchor with acceptable depths and holding on either side of City Island with the caveat that both are exposed to the weather and frequent wakes of passing craft, some of which are tugs and barges or other serious water-moving machines. It is important to note there is no easy access ashore for dinghies as most of the yacht clubs are private. Some may allow a tie up if you dine with them or take a mooring. The best protection is at the island's northeastern tip in 7 to 14 feet MLW where High Island (with a tall radio transmission tower) gives shelter from the north and two small rocky outcroppings give partial protection from southerly winds across the sound. It's a designated Special Anchorage so boats at anchor need not turn on their anchor lights. Use a spotlight (pointed down at the water to protect the vision of other boaters) if coming in after dark. On still nights with no wind to stabilize the boat you might experience some uncomfortable wallowing.

The anchorage off the northwest corner of City Island, between the bridge and the northerly end of a mooring field, is protected from all directions but the south. There is 11 to 17 feet MLW with good holding in mud. On the east side of the island the City Island Harbor anchorage offers 14 feet MLW with good holding in mud. It is exposed northeast through southeast.

Note that anchoring is prohibited north of City Island off Orchard Beach, which has been carved out of the rocky shore and filled with imported sand for beach goers.

There are two overnight anchorages close to the Throgs Neck Bridge that provide protection from all but north and northeast winds. Both anchorages are convenient for those boats emerging from the East River late in the day or getting in position to catch an early morning tidal current down the East River. Little Bay and Little Neck Bay, on the southeast side of the Throgs Neck Bridge, share these features: 7 to 9 feet at MLW, no protection from tug and barge traffic wakes, open to north winds and no shore access.

New Rochelle Area, NY

The first city on the Westchester shore has two yacht harbors: New Rochelle Harbor and Echo Bay (formerly known as Lower Harbor and Upper Harbor, respectively). Both of New Rochelle's harbors are confined, busy and interesting for their constant activity. They are crowded with clubs, parks, marinas and moorings for thousands of widely assorted craft.

New Rochelle features more than 270 acres of parkland. Five Islands Park features pedestrian bridges linking various islands as well as fishing docks, beaches, barbecue facilities and an outdoor amphitheater. Neptune Park includes a fishing pier, bocce courts and horseshoe facilities. Glen Island Park comprises 105-acres of the parkland and offers a small, calm beach with plenty of surrounding grassland and several children's play areas.

NAVIGATION: Use NOAA Chart 12364. The entry to New Rochelle from Long Island Sound can be confusing to newcomers. Those without local knowledge should arrive before dark. The approach to any of New Rochelle's three entries should be made with the chart close at hand. The westernmost approach to New Rochelle's lower harbor is the least used.

The eastbound cruiser rounding City Island can choose to approach either west (the shorter and more direct route) or east of Hart Island marked with a 23-foot-high flashing red "46" off its southern tip. A series of green can buoys mark the western edge of the deep water leading to the entrance between Davids Island and Glen Island, where the 24-foot flashing red "10" marking Aunt Phoebe Rock shows where to turn northwest for the harbor channel.

The westbound cruiser is likely to enter from the northeast between Davenport Neck and Davids Island. South of Hen and Chickens and north of Execution Rocks, turn west for the deep water between Huckleberry Island and flashing red "2." Pick up the channel between flashing green "5" and red nun "4" and proceed as usual, making sure not to miss green can "9," which marks Spindle Rock.

The two channels meet at quick-flashing red buoy "14," which marks the normally well-maintained channel serving New Rochelle Harbor. Controlling depth is 8 feet MLW as far as the head of the harbor, where shoals tend to develop. The **Glen Island Bridge** (13-foot closed vertical clearance) separates the west end of the harbor from the east and opens on signal during the day. A 2-hour advance notice is required for openings between 12 midnight and 6:00 a.m. from May 1 through October 31 by calling the number posted at the bridge. A 24-hour advance notice is required for all openings from 8:00 p.m. to 8:00 a.m. from November 1 through April 30.

Crowded Echo Bay is northeast of New Rochelle Harbor. It has an outer harbor open to the southwest and an inner harbor protected from all directions. The approach to Echo Bay is north of Huckleberry Island between Middle Ground marked by green can "1M" and 6-foot MLW Hicks Ledge, marked by green-over-red can buoy "HL." During the summer, a private green light on a prominent flagstaff on the point midway between Beaufort Point and Duck Point is on a range with the green flashing buoy "3BR" for Bailey Rock. This will help you between Hicks Ledge and Middle Ground into Echo Bay.

Once in Echo Bay pass between red nun buoy "6" to the east and green can "5" to the west at Duck Point and then proceed to Beaufort Point, where you will turn west around the point inside red nun buoy "8" and "10" to avoid the 2-foot MLW depths outside the channel. There are beaches near Duck Point and around Beaufort Point is the narrow, sheltered and slip-lined inner harbor.

Dockage: New Rochelle Harbor is an excellent hurricane hole as it is protected by Davenport Neck and a cluster of islands. Varied marine facilities for power and sail, including several yacht clubs, are located north of Glen Island and in New Rochelle Harbor. The eastern branch, inside Davenport Neck, is crowded and narrow but well protected. While many of the marinas are restricted to local craft, several welcome transients. More options are available in nearby Echo Bay. Call ahead.

Anchorage: The southern branch of New Rochelle Harbor, below the Glen Island Bridge, is cluttered with permanent moorings, so there is no room to anchor.

New Rochelle

However, there is room in 14 feet at MLW just outside the harbor between the large white abandoned casino building on Glen Island's northeast corner and to the northwest of Goose Island. Turn west into the anchorage after passing north of green can buoy "9," taking care to stay clear of the rocky shoal on the northeast corner of Goose Island. This anchorage is protected from all but north to northeast winds. A second option is to stay south of Glen Island and hug the shore southwest of red nun buoy "6" near Twin Island, though rocks, foul bottom, and limited protection make it rarely attractive. In a storm situation, anchor west of the New York Athletic Club's main clubhouse in the Olympic Rowing Lagoon with 12 feet at MLW in mud.

Holding is good in In Echo Bay around the two-pronged point from the marinas. This is well protected from all but northeast to southeast in 9- to 15-foot MLW depths. Pick a spot just south of the line between flashing green "3BR" and green can "5."

On hot evenings a cool, breezy (although exposed) anchorage can be found far from shore services off Huckleberry Island's northern shore, between flashing red "2" and a log house on the shore. Here you will find 22 feet MLW in excellent holding in mud. This is exposed to the northeast and is exposed to wind and waves.

Larchmont Harbor, NY

NAVIGATION: Use NOAA Chart 12364. Larchmont Harbor is protected from the east by a stone breakwater but it is open to the south and southwest. To enter, pass either side of Hen and Chickens Ledge. If you pass to the north, stay south of Umbrella Rock, which is marked by green can buoy "7." You can also go between the breakwater's 26-foot-tall flashing red "2" and the string of marked rocks and reefs to the west. Do not approach the launch dock. A marked reef lies in front of it. Skirt the shoals along Satans Toe inside the breakwater. Keep clear of North Ledge as well. It is bare at half tide and has unmarked rocks in the center, although private navigation aids mark its north and south extremes. East of Larchmont, the shore along Satans Toe and Delancey Point is rocky and shoal. Handsome estates line the shore.

Dockage/Moorings: Larchmont Harbor is a small cove with a big yacht club and ample yachting history. The Larchmont Yacht Club is headquarters for Larchmont Race Week in mid-July, drawing hundreds of competing sailboats. Larchmont welcomes accredited members of other yacht clubs for overnight stays or for meals on its big porch overlooking the fleet. The harbor is typically crowded but guest moorings are usually available.

Anchorage: On a calm night, you can drop the hook near Horseshoe Harbor, off Umbrella Point, in 17 feet at MLW with good holding in mud. This puts you about a mile from the Larchmont Yacht Club. If

Long Island Sound, NY

W G

		Largest Vessel Accommodated	VHF Channel Monitored / Working	Dockage				Supplies		Services				
				Transient Slips / Total Slips	Approach / Dockside Depth (reported)	Floating Docks	Gas / Diesel	Groceries, Ice, Marine Supplies, Snacks	Repairs: Hull, Engine, Propeller	Lift (tonnage), Crane, Rail	Min / Max Amps	Courtesy Car, Laundry, Pool, Showers	Pump-Out Station	Nearby: Grocery Store, Motel, Restaurant
LARCHMONT														
1. Larchmont Yacht Club	(914) 834-2440	55	72/	/	12.0/7.0	F		I		L	30/50	PS	P	GMR
MAMARONECK														
2. Nichols Yacht Yard Inc. 🖥 WiFi	(914) 698-6065	90	/	/165	10.0/10.0	F		M	HEP	L50,C	30/50	S		GR
3. Harbor Island Municipal Marina WiFi	(914) 777-7744	120	16/8	2/450	8.0/8.0	F		GIMS				L	P	GMR
4. Sheldrake Yacht Club	(914) 490-5295	40	16/	/	15.0/								P	GMR
5. Safe Harbor Post Road 🖥 WiFi	(914) 698-0295	55	19/	1/50	10.0/8.0	F	GD	IM	HEP	L50,C	30/50	S		GR
6. Derecktor Shipyards 🖥	**(914) 698-5020**	**150**	**/**	**5/**	**12.0/12.0**	**F**	**GD**	**M**	**HEP**	**C**	**100/200+**		**P**	**GMR**
7. McMichael Yacht Yard #1 Inc WiFi	(914) 698-4957	50	72/72	/15	10.0/10.0	F			HEP	C	30/50			GMR
8. Mamaroneck Beach and Yacht Club WiFi	(914) 698-1130	90	10/	10/60	6.0/7.0	F		IS		C	30/50	PS		GMR
MILTON HARBOR														
9. American Yacht Club - PRIVATE	(914) 967-4800			/71	7.0/7.0	F	GD	IS			30	PS		R
10. Shongut Marine	(914) 967-3842	38	/	1/22	6.0/10.0	F			HP		30			GR
11. Rye City Boat Basin	(914) 967-2011	37	/	/425	6.0/10.0	F			HEP		30		P	GMR

🖥 Internet Access   WiFi Wireless Internet Access   ⊙onSpot Dockside WiFi Facility

See WaterwayGuide.com for current rates, fuel prices, website addresses, and other up-to-the-minute information. (Information in the table is provided by the facilities.)

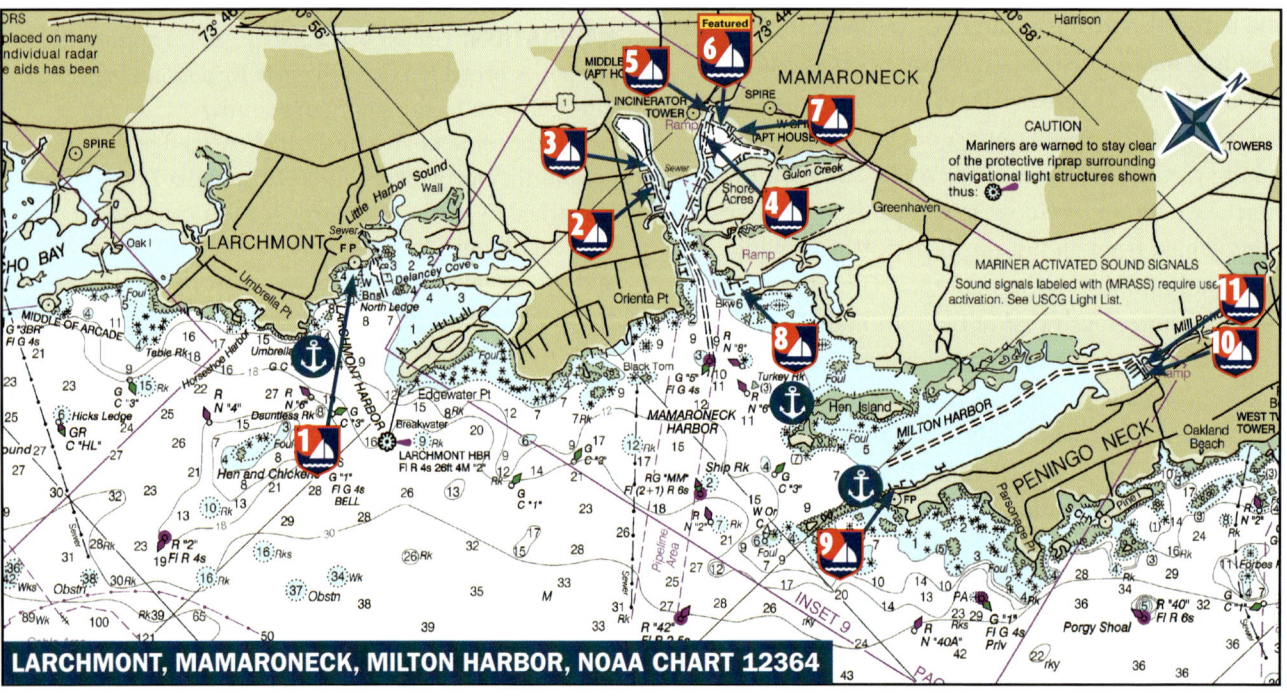

LARCHMONT, MAMARONECK, MILTON HARBOR, NOAA CHART 12364

CAUTION
Mariners are warned to stay clear of the protective riprap surrounding navigational light structures shown thus: ⊛

MARINER ACTIVATED SOUND SIGNALS
Sound signals labeled with (MRASS) require use activation. See USCG Light List.

DERECKTOR SHIPYARDS

Mamaroneck Harbor

you'd like to get closer so you can go ashore, you may find space on the edge of the mooring field behind the breakwater in 9 feet at MLW with good holding in sand and mud. Both anchorages are exposed from the southeast through the west.

Mamaroneck Harbor, NY

Mamaroneck is a most hospitable harbor for transient boaters. In addition to the outer harbor, there are two inner basins (West Basin and East Basin) separated by a park. The busy main street in the village ends at the East Basin so services and entertainment are only a short walk away. At the end of the East Basin close to the center of town is a long floating dock adjacent to a launching ramp. Brief tie-ups are allowed here when ramp conditions permit for a walk into town. Call the Harbormaster on VHF Channel 16 or 914-777-7744. The West Basin is more business-like and less visitor-oriented. A laundry, pharmacy and other shopping is all within walking distance.

NAVIGATION: Use NOAA Chart 12364. Make your entrance from Long Island Sound at flashing red bell buoy "42" (locally known as 42nd Street). Head northwest about 1 mile for flashing green "5" at Outer Steamboat Rock, leaving Ship Rock's red-flashing red-over-green buoy "MM" to the northeast. The channel to the inner harbors narrows between green can "7" and flashing red "10." The 4-mph speed limit is strictly enforced. At the green-over-red can junction buoy "A" channels lead to either side of Harbor Island, which is no longer an island.

Shoaling of the entrance channel has made Milton Harbor difficult to reach for most traveling boaters. The City of Rye Boat Basin confirms that there is less than 2 feet at MLW in some places. The 7-foot tidal range brings the harbor within reach for those willing to come and go on a schedule. As of 2019, there have been some discussion of dredging, but no plan has yet been approved.

Those with very shallow drafts or an eye on their tide charts can enter by starting at the flashing red bell buoy "42," known as 42nd Street. Just east of Ship Rock, marked by flashing red (2+1), red-over-green buoy "MM," head north-northeast between green can buoy "5" and red nun buoy "6," which mark the start of the harbor channel. Leave West Rock and Scotch Caps, a line of reefs, well to the east without running west of the line created by green can buoy "3" and green can buoy "5." The harbor is exposed to the southwest.

Dockage/Moorings: Marine facilities in the West Basin include the Harbor Island Municipal Marina, which accommodates transients on a first-come, first-served basis and Nichols Yacht Yard Inc. offering a full range of services.

The East Basin holds a yacht club with moorings, a full-service marina and several boat yards including the headquarters for Derecktor Shipyards. The famous yacht builder can service, maintain and refit all types of power and sailing yachts up to 150 feet long with up to 40-foot beam.

American Yacht Club on Peningo Neck has guest moorings available for members of reciprocal yacht clubs. The yacht club launch monitors VHF Channel 71. The City of Rye operates the George W. DePauw Municipal Boat Basin with 350 slips. This facility is usually full but will try to accommodate transients. Provision opportunities are within a short walk.

Anchorage: There are 7- to 11-foot MLW depths on the west side of Hen Island with excellent holding in mud and sand. It's a little over a mile from the anchorage to shore access at the Harbor Island Park.

You can also anchor about 1.5 nm from the town marina at Rye in 7 feet MLW with good holding in mud. You can dinghy to the town marina but there may be a time limit on how long you can stay tied up.

■ PORT CHESTER, NY TO MILFORD HARBOR, CT

Port Chester, NY

Port Chester Harbor lies east of N. Manursing Island and its wildlife preserve, beach clubs and estates. The towns of Rye and Port Chester enclose the quiet harbor, which is lined with handsome homes. The downtown area boasts a restaurant row and many retailers including a hardware store, pharmacy and grocery. Most of these are more than a mile away up the Byram River. Although the marinas along the river do not allow transient dinghy tie-up, if you dine at BarTaco (914-937-8226), they will usually allow a short trip to the provisioning along Westchester Ave.

The lower Byram River is tree-lined and scenic prior to the **I-95 (Byram River) Bridge** (60-foot fixed vertical clearance). Some of the structures at Tide Mill Yacht Basin date back to 1770 and have been photographed and painted numerous times. It is located just under 2 miles from any shopping or the downtown area.

NAVIGATION: Use NOAA Chart 12364. On approaching the harbor watch for two large barge moorings between the Fourfoot Rocks green-over-red can buoy "F" and the Bluefish Shoal. One of the barge moorings is an easy-to-spot large white cylinder. The other is a dark-colored sphere, low in the water and hard to see, with colored lines streaming from it. It is about midway between the white mooring and the Fourfoot Rocks buoy. The buoy and the moorings are not lighted so approach after sunset or at high speed is not advised without a spotlight or at high speed. Do not cut the buoys marking Great Captain Rocks, marked by flashing red "2," and Manursing Island Reef, at green can "3," just outside the breakwater.

Dockage: A privately marked channel leads south from the harbor entrance to Tide Mill Yacht Basin, a small (55-slip), well-maintained marina that welcomes transients. They have the only available fuel in the area but larger vessels may have difficulty accessing their fuel dock due to the narrow, tricky entrance.

Anchorage: You can anchor at the edge of the mooring field in Port Chester south of the 25-foot flashing green "5" in 7 to 8 feet MLW with good holding in mud.

Port Chester

Side Trip: Calf & Captain Islands, CT

The Calf Islands are just to the south of Byram Harbor. The west side of the larger Calf Island is a bird sanctuary and off-limits to visitors. Calf Island is owned by the U.S. Fish and Wildlife Service (860-399-2513) and is open throughout the year from one-half hour before sunrise to one-half hour after sunset for wildlife observation and hiking. Portions of Calf Island are also open for overnight stays by permit for those who anchor in the vicinity.

A sandbar connects the two islands that make up the Calf Islands at low tide. Little Calf Island (also known as Shell Island) is differentiated from the larger one by an imposing granite tower modeled after the Summerfield Methodist Church in Port Chester. The tower belfry is visible above the treetops of the overgrown island. It is owned by the Greenwich Land Trust and is no longer open to the public. It is also overgrown with poison ivy.

The three Captain Islands, originally claimed by both NY and CT, are less than 2 nm offshore south of Greenwich Harbor and mark the southern edge of Captain Harbor. They are the remnants of a glacial moraine and there are two theories on how they came

by their name. Some say Captain Kidd buried treasure here at one time, while another legend identifies the namesake as Captain Daniel Patrick, a partner in the first recorded real estate transaction and the town's first military commander.

Great Captain Island is 0.5-mile long and has a popular beach with picnic tables, grills, restrooms and showers, a couple of semi-protected anchorages and Great Captain Island light, a 19th-century restored stone lighthouse. Visitors to the beach are required to have a day pass but short visits are typically allowed. You can anchor or grab a mooring off the beach then land by dinghy. The Greenwich Ferry, serving Great Captain Island and Little Captain Island, runs from June to September. The schedule is based on the tide. Wee Captain Island, the last of the three, is private.

Anchoring opportunities are available on the southwest of Calf as well as on the north and northwest side near Shell Island. Or you can anchor by the Captains amid moorings only 1 to 1.5 nm from Greenwich Harbor. The north anchorage of Calf and the anchorage north of the Captains are one of the few places along this section of shoreline that are protected from winds out of the south. Base your selection on the

Captain Harbor, NY/CT

		Largest Vessel Accommodated	VHF Channel Monitored / Working	Transient Slips / Total Slips	Approach / Dockside Depth (reported)	Floating Docks	Gas / Diesel	Groceries, Ice, Marine Supplies, Snacks	Repairs: Hull, Engine, Propeller	Lift (tonnage), Crane, Rail	Min / Max Amps	Courtesy Car, Laundry, Pool, Showers	Pump-Out Station	Nearby: Grocery Store, Motel, Restaurant
				Dockage			**Supplies**		**Services**					
PORT CHESTER HARBOR														
1. Tide Mill Yacht Basin	(914) 967-2995	70	68/	2/55	7.0/8.0	F	GD	M	HEP	L35,C	30/50	S		
GREENWICH														
2. Delamar Greenwich Harbor 🖥 📶	(203) 733-5320	180	9/78	15/15	9.0/8.0	F		S			30/100	CS		GMR
3. Indian Harbor Yacht Club-PRIVATE	(203) 869-2484		/	/	9.0/8.0	F		IS			30	S		GMR
MIANUS RIVER														
4. Riverside Yacht Club - PRIVATE	(203) 637-1706	60	/74	/162	10.0/8.0	F	GD	IS		L3	30	PS	P	R
5. Palmer Point Marina and Ship's Store	(203) 661-1243	55	16/68	5/140	6.0/6.0	F	GD	GIMS	HEP	L35	30/50	S		GMR
6. Beacon Point Marine 📶	(203) 661-4033	60	/	10/250	12.0/2.0	F	GD	IM	HEP	L,C	30/50	PS	P	GMR
STAMFORD														
7. Stamford Yacht Club	(203) 323-3161		/	/40	10.0/8.0			IS			30	PS		R
8. Safe Harbor Yacht Haven 🖥 📶	(203) 359-4500	118	9/	30/366	10.0/13.0	F		IM	EP		30/50	LS		GMR
9. Harbor Point East Marina	(203) 965-6045	70	9/	/32	/	F		I	HEP	C	30/100	S		GMR
10. TGM Anchor Point Marina 🖥	(203) 363-0733	90	68/	5/72	12.0/11.0	F		I			30/50	LPS		GMR
11. Harbor Landing Marina	(203) 965-0065	50	16/9	10/130	12.0/8.0	F		I			30/50	LS	P	GMR
12. Hinckley Yacht Services - Stamford	(203) 274-8340		9/	/25	/		GD		HEP	L80			P	GMR
13. Harbor Point North Marina	(203) 965-6045	120	9/	20/32	/	F	GD	I		C	30/100	LS	P	GR
14. Seaview House Marina 🖥 📶	(203) 219-4693	120	9/	10/44	7.0/7.0	F	GD	IMS	HEP	L10	30/50	S		GMR
15. Harbour Square Marina	(203) 324-3331	170	9/	20/75	12.0/12.0	F	GD	GI	HEP		30/100	S	P	GMR

🖥 Internet Access 📶 Wireless Internet Access onSpot Dockside WiFi Facility

See WaterwayGuide.com for current rates, fuel prices, website addresses, and other up-to-the-minute information. (Information in the table is provided by the facilities.)

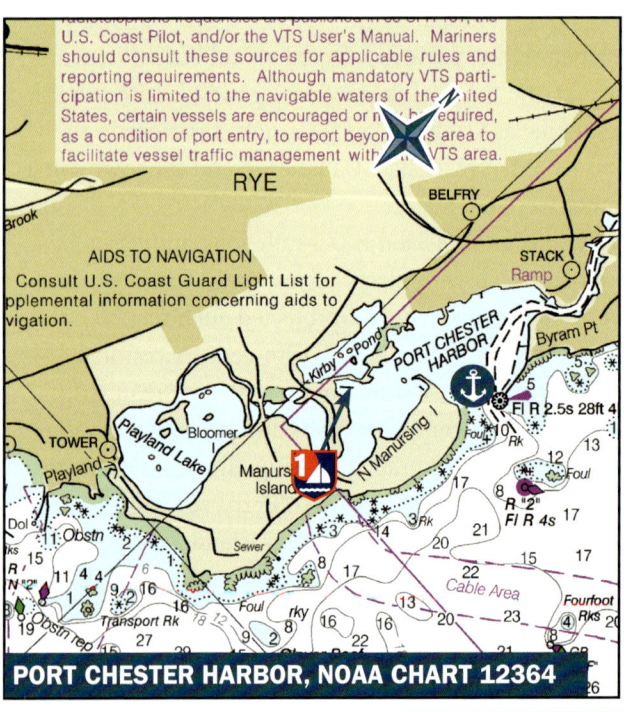

PORT CHESTER HARBOR, NOAA CHART 12364

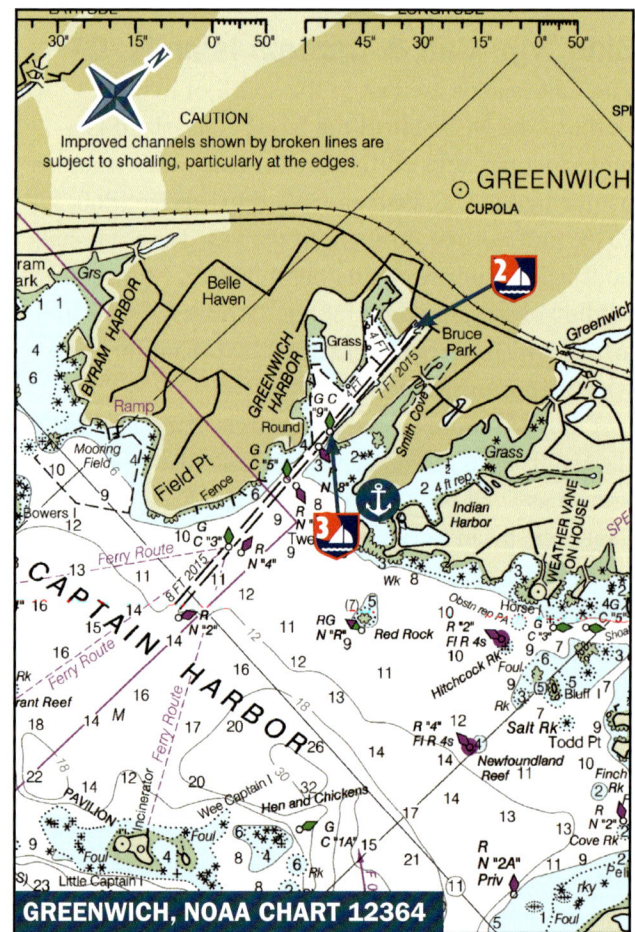

GREENWICH, NOAA CHART 12364

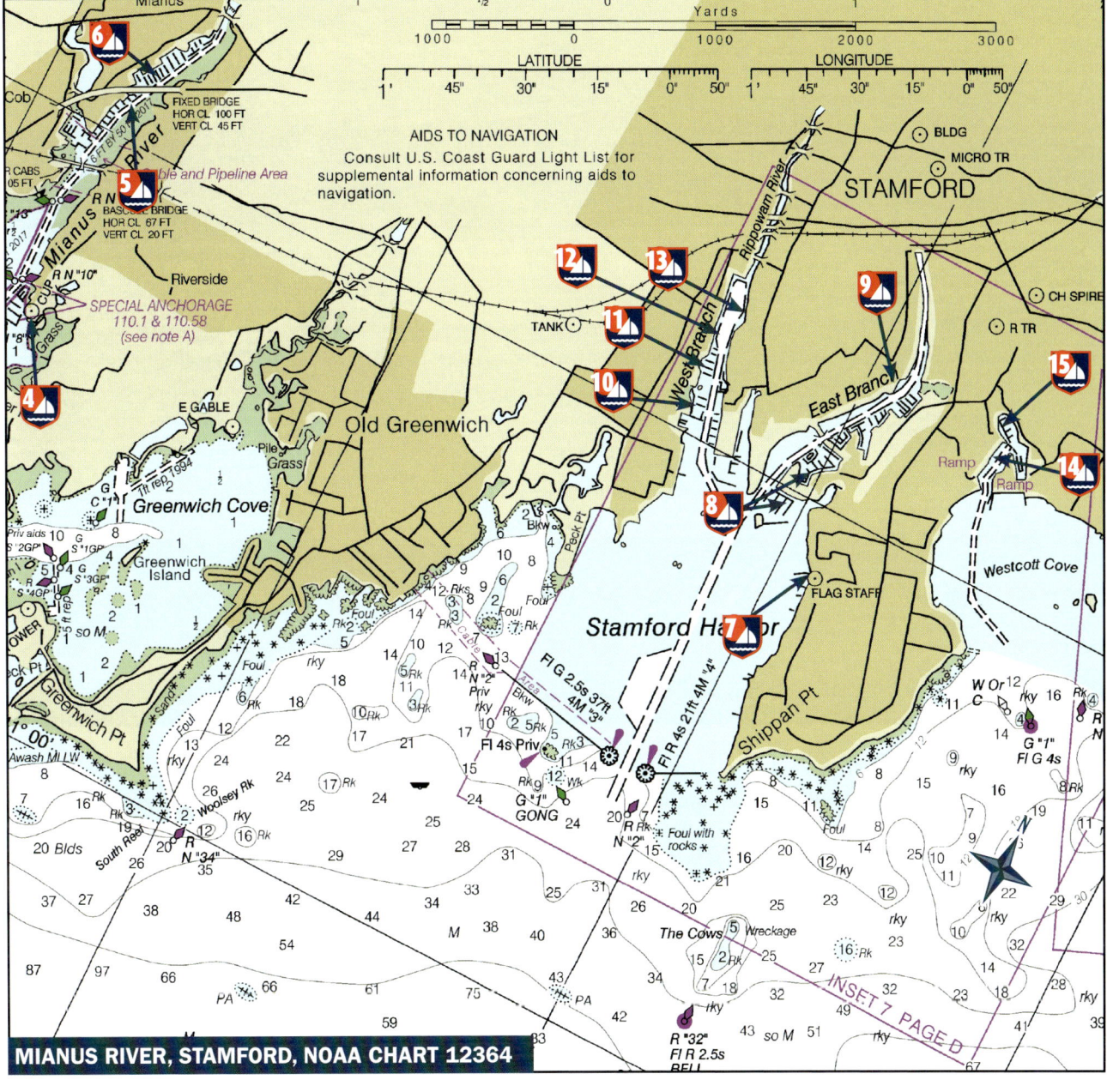

MIANUS RIVER, STAMFORD, NOAA CHART 12364

wind and wave direction forecast, and do not forget the 6- to 7-foot tidal range when choosing a spot. Stay clear of a diamond-shaped marker over a sunken wreck 40 feet off the beach at Great Captain Island.

Captain Harbor (Greenwich Area, CT)

Known today as one of the wealthiest towns in the U.S., the town of Greenwich was settled in 1640. A good place to start your exploration of this historical area is at the Bruce Museum in downtown Greenwich, which boasts both art and natural history exhibition space. Of special interest is the Seaside Center, dedicated to educating visitors about the ecology of Long Island Sound and features. Visit www.

brucemuseaum.org for more information.

For many years, Greenwich Point (locally termed "Tod's Point") was open only to town residents and their guests. Today all four beaches are open to the public.

NAVIGATION: Use NOAA Chart 12364. Enter Greenwich Harbor from Long Island Sound via Captain Harbor. Newcomers to this area should use the eastern approach through water comparatively free of rocks and shoals. Honor both the flashing green gong buoy "1" and green can "1A" marking Hen and Chickens. Byram Harbor is the westernmost of the Greenwich harbors and offers moorings, a pretty park and beach and a municipal boat club, but proof of residency is required and there are few amenities for the transient mariner.

Greenwich Harbor

Indian Harbor Point

Cos Cob Harbor is the entrance to the Mianus River and is also accessed via Captain Harbor. Coming in from Long Island Sound between Flat Neck Point and the Captain Islands, pass south or west of Newfoundland Reef's flashing red "4" and south or east of Red Rock's red-over-green nun buoy "R." After heading west around Hitchcock Rock's flashing red "2" turn northeast to green can buoy "3" and the dredged, marked entrance.

Keep strictly to the center of the channel to get the most depth. Six-foot depths are reported as far as the Riverside Yacht Club but between it and the **Metro North (Cos RR) Bridge** careful piloting is required at low tide. The Metro North Bridge (Cob RR Bridge) has a 20-foot closed vertical clearance opens on signal (as soon as practicable but no later than 20 minutes) between 5:00 a.m. to 9:00 p.m. unless a train is approaching. The draw opens on signal from April 1 through October 31, from 9:00 p.m. to 5:00 a.m. with a 4-hour advance notice and from November 1 through March 30, with at least a 24-hour notice is given by calling the number posted at the bridge. It is followed by the **I-95 (Connecticut Turnpike) Bridge** (45-foot fixed vertical clearance).

Dockage/Moorings: There are many moorings scattered throughout the harbors and neighboring islands, most of which are private or belong to the various yacht clubs. It is acceptable to use them for a day-stay or an overnight on a weekday but you must be prepared to leave if the owner shows up! The Town of Greenwich operates several small-boat marinas (www.greenwichct.gov/566/Boating-Marinas). Some allow dinghy tie-up and offer pump-out service.

On the point between Greenwich Harbor and Smith Cove the private Indian Harbor Yacht Club is open to reciprocal yacht club members only. Stay in the channel to Greenwich Harbor and the yacht club moorings are to the west. If you are from a reciprocal yacht club and plan to obtain a guest mooring, be advised that the dining room requires jackets.

Another private club (Riverside Yacht Club) is on the Mianus River to the south. To the north between the bridges is a marina (Palmer Point Marina and Ship's Store and above the I-95 bridge (45-foot fixed vertical clearance) is a power boat facility (Beacon Point Marina) with a dedicated yard crew, service teams and certified technicians. A 0.50-mile walk from either marina brings you to businesses along the highway. The village of Cos Cob lies beyond.

Anchorage: Work your way in slowly and carefully pick a spot along the channel, westward of Tweed Island. At the northwest end of Tweed Island there is 5 to 7 feet MLW with good holding in mud. This is open to the southwest.

Greenwich Cove's south of the Mianus River has some deeper protected sections but these are are chock full of moored boats. Elias Point at the channel into the cove has a somewhat exposed anchorage in 9 to 13 feet MLW in good holding in mud. Be sure not to block the channel and if anchoring fore-and-aft stay on the channel's edge. Be sure to consider the swing room of the nearest boats.

Stamford Harbor, CT

The yachting facilities in Stamford are extensive and shore diversions are numerous, making this an ideal yachting destination for long or short layovers. Stamford History Center (www.stamfordhistory.org) should be your first stop on any tour of Stamford's historic sites. The Stamford Museum and Nature Center (www.stamfordmuseum.org) has a kid-oriented nature center with trails, a small museum, farm animals and an otter pond. Every year Stamford offers a world-class sculpture exhibit throughout the summer months. Art in Public Place (www.stamford-downtown.com) features sculptures that line the sidewalks and parks in downtown Stamford.

Stamford has three harbors: Stamford Harbor, Westcott Cove east around Shippan Point, and Cove Harbor farther east beyond the Cove Rocks. Breakwaters protect the large outer basin of Stamford Harbor and the two branches at its head: West Branch and East Branch.

NAVIGATION: Use NOAA Chart 12364. Stamford Harbor is easy to enter from Long Island Sound through the two well-marked and lighted breakwaters at the entrance. The city's tall stacks and high-rise buildings are easy to spot from Long Island Sound. The 80-foot-tall lighthouse on Harbor Ledge, next to the west breakwater, can help a boater with the breakwater entrance, even though it's now privately owned and operated. The entrance through the breakwater at Stamford Harbor is 0.25 mile east of the lighthouse and can be found by using the 26-foot tall quick-flashing tower and the 45-foot, 6-second flashing red marker as range lights. When approaching, keep to the west of Shippan Point and The Cows, marked by flashing red bell buoy "32." Follow the chart carefully as you proceed; rocks and foul areas abound outside the entrance channel.

If approaching from the west and heading for the anchorage rather than into one of the two branches, the line between Greenwich Point's red nun buoy "34" and the lighthouse will bring a large industrial buoy into sight. Turn north and track between that buoy and the western breakwater's red nun buoy "2" to stay safely east of the shallow rocks (3- and 5-foot MLW depths).

To reach Westcott Cove, enter around Shippan Point (east of Stamford Harbor) and leave flashing green "1" to the west on approach. Westcott Cove is pleasant and easy to enter if you stay to mid-channel for 7-foot MLW approach depths. Cove Harbor to the northeast has a difficult entry requiring local knowledge and is devoted entirely to local boats.

Dockage/Moorings: West of the Stamford Harbor channel is a large mooring buoy used by barges along with a number of yacht club moorings. To the east of the main channel is the stately Stamford Yacht Club (established in 1890), which sponsors the famous Labor Day Weekend Vineyard Race. Stamford Yacht Club welcomes members of reciprocating yacht clubs. Beyond the club, the channel forks into the East and West branches.

The channel into the East Branch is straightforward. It offers 10 to 11-foot MLW depths and carries all the way to Stamford. Follow the channel north to the Safe Harbor Yacht Haven. It was dredged in 2016 and recognizable by the large brick buildings that surround it. Yacht Haven has 366 slips in a modern facility with a family atmosphere. They have transient slips available with cable TV and WiFi and offer repairs.

Farther north along the East Branch, above the hurricane barrier, is Harbor Point East Marina, which may have transient space. Call ahead. There are several private condominium marinas above the barrier as well. However, short-term transient slips are not available.

On the West Branch, TGM Anchor Point Marina has slips on floating docks with resort-style amenities. Harbor Landing Marina, Hinckley Yacht Services–Stamford and Harbor Point North Marina are also located on the West Branch with transient space and cruiser amenities. Harbor Point North also sells fuel.

The Stamford Municipal Marina is designated for local boats only, but you can tie up long enough for loading and unloading. Be aware, though, that the security gates at each dock allow you to leave with no

NORWALK COVE MARINA

key, but require keys to get back in.

In Westcott Cove, Seaview House Marina welcomes transient boats and offers high-speed diesel fueling. Within walking distance boaters will find a supermarket, West Marine, banks, restaurants, salon and shopping. There is also a public park with a sandy beach adjacent to the property. Just to the north is Harbour Square Marina with slips to 170 feet and all fuels and repairs. Call for channel depths, as shoaling had brought the channel entrance down to a charted depth of 4.5 feet MLW.

Anchorage: The large outer harbor can kick up a chop in strong winds but reasonable anchorage can be found just behind the western breakwater. Proceed around (private) red nun buoy "2" on the west end of the breakwater and tuck in tight behind the breakwater in about 10 feet MLW with good holding in mud. Watch for protruding rocks at low tide.

Even though the outer cove at Westcott Cove is open to the south, a small, landlocked inner lagoon offers good depths and total protection.

Darien & Norwalk Area, CT

Darien covers the entire area between Stamford and Fivemile River. The Gut (better known as Darien Harbor), Goodwives River and the town of Noroton lie within the western section of this area. Fivemile River is to the east. On the western bank, Darien is lined with houses, while the village of Rowayton is nestled on the east side. Along Rowayton's waterfront you will find a Post Office, a small grocery, numerous eating establishments, a hardware store and various small shops. You can buy local steamers and lobsters as well as most marine supplies here.

A 6-mile chain of 16 islands make up the Norwalk Islands and protect Norwalk Harbor itself. The islands were used during the Revolutionary War by Continental Army whaleboat crews who ran out into Long Island Sound to harass the British ships and then retreat to the shelter of the islands' rocks.

Norwalk, settled in 1649, was a major oystering and manufacturing center as far back as the 1700s. The working maritime heritage of the area lives on at Tallmadge Brothers, the largest oyster producer in the state of Connecticut. The company has over 22,000 acres of oyster beds and has been in business in Norwalk for over 130 years.

Nicknamed "Oyster Town," this a cruising favorite, especially for mariners zigzagging Long Island Sound

and crossing over from Huntington Bay on the Long Island shore. The four primary maritime areas of Norwalk offer anything you are likely to want: good protection, marinas, repairs, yacht clubs, restaurants, beaches and good anchorage. The scenery includes hundreds of local boats, bow-to-stern weekend traffic amid the oyster stakes and crowds of people fishing, swimming, picnicking and clamming.

A short walk over the bridge in Norwalk Harbor puts the visitor in the center of SoNo, South Norwalk's sophisticated nightlife and tourism district, anchored by the Maritime Aquarium (www.maritimeaquarium.org). This is a fabulous outing for families and features more than 1,000 marine animals native to Long Island Sound and its watershed. History buffs should take a ferry from Water St. to the Sheffield Lighthouse (www.seaport. org) built in 1827 to mark the dangerous ledges at the entrance to the city's harbor. The stone and Victorian style lighthouse still stands today on the 57-acre Sheffield Island; however, the light was replaced in 1902 by the new Greens Ledge Light farther west. Call 800-838-3006 for tour details.

NAVIGATION: Use NOAA Chart 12364. The entrance to Fivemile River can be seen only from the south but it is easy to enter. The channel is dredged through shoals on both sides and starts at flashing green gong buoy "3," a mile north of Greens Ledge Light. Watch for lobster buoys. Fivemile River is actually only 1 nm long. It is narrow but protected with good depths throughout.

The entrance to Norwalk Harbor and Norwalk River is through Sheffield Island Harbor, north of the Norwalk Islands. The high-intensity softball field lights can be seen from as far away as Bridgeport throughout the boating season. A 350-foot-tall orange-and-white power plant stack on Manresa Island on the western side of the harbor mouth provides another landmark. Go west around Greens Ledge and give the reef west of Sheffield Island (known locally as Smith Island) a wide berth. Follow the well-marked Sheffield Island Harbor channel past Manresa Island into Norwalk Harbor. Watch for barge traffic coming out of the power plant basin. As you move upstream the river changes, flowing through marshes filled with waterfowl. It is worth exploring but do so in the dinghy. The channel winds through shallow flats.

Cockenoe Harbor is the eastern route to and from Norwalk Harbor. The buoyed channel (red right returning from the Sound to Norwalk Harbor) threads through islands and shoals between 61-foot Peck Ledge

Sheffield Harbor, CT

		Dockage					Supplies		Services					
		Largest Vessel Accommodated	VHF Channel Monitored / Working	Transient Slips / Total Slips	Approach / Dockside Depth (reported)	Floating Docks	Gas / Diesel	Groceries, Ice, Marine Supplies, Snacks	Repairs: Hull, Engine, Propeller	Lift (tonnage), Crane, Rail	Min / Max Amps	Courtesy Car, Laundry, Pool, Showers	Pump-Out Station	Nearby: Grocery Store, Motel, Restaurant
WILSON COVE														
1. Rowayton Yacht Club	(203) 854-0807	30	68/	/	10.0/2.0			I				S		G
2. Wilson Cove Yacht Club	(203) 866-7020	50	78/	/100	6.0/6.0	F		I	HEP	L35,C	30/50	S		3
3. Norwalk Yacht Club	(203) 866-0941	50	78/	6/130	7.0/8.0		GD	I		L4		S		R
NORWALK AREA														
4. Total Marine of Norwalk	(203) 838-3210	80	/	10/90	15.0/9.0	F		M	HEP	L35,C	30/50	S		R
5. Rex Marine Center Inc 🖥 WiFi	(203) 866-5555	50	/	2/70	12.0/6.0	F	G	IMS	HEP	L30	30/50	S	P	GMR
6. MarineMax Norwalk	(203) 831-6311	48	/	/65	12.0/8.0	F	GD	I	HEP	L				
7. David S. Dunavan Visitors Dock	(203) 829-8892	200	9/9	20/20	12.0/8.0	F		I			30/50	LS	P	GMR
8. St. Ann Club Marina	(203) 853-8777		/	/40	12.0/8.0	F						S		MR
GREGORY POINT														
9. Norwalk Cove Marina 🖥 WiFi	(203) 838-5899	130	9/72	/400	10.0/9.0	F	GD	IMS	HEP	L160,C	30/200+	LS	P	GMR
10. Sprite Island Yacht Club	(203) 295-8466	33	12/	/	8.0/4.5	F		S				S		R
SAUGATUCK RIVER														
11. Cedar Point Yacht Club 🖥 WiFi	(203) 226-7411	50	78/	5/130	10.0/8.0	F		IS		C	30/50	S		G
12. Saugatuck Harbor Yacht Club	(203) 810-9094	53	71/	/160	8.0/	F					30/50	PS		

🖥 Internet Access   WiFi Wireless Internet Access   onSpot Dockside WiFi Facility

See WaterwayGuide.com for current rates, fuel prices, website addresses, and other up-to-the-minute information. (Information in the table is provided by the facilities.)

Lighthouse and quick flashing red "14" that marks the change between the two channels. The channel makes a hard turn around the lighthouse to keep off Cockenoe Island's southern and eastern shoals. East of Peck's Ledge be sure pass between green can buoy "5" and red nun buoy "4," which keeps the boat from meeting the Channel Rock, which is just 1.5 feet deep at MLW.

Most boating services are located before the bridges. Anyone wanting to head through them will be stymied during rush hours. The first bridge you will encounter is the **Washington Street (136) Bridge** with an 8-foot closed vertical clearance. The draw will open on signal except from 7:00 a.m. to 8:45 a.m., 11:45 a.m. to 1:15 p.m. and 4:00 p.m. to 6 p.m., Monday through Friday (except holidays), when the draw need not be open for the passage of vessels.

Farther upstream is the **Metro-North WALK Bridge** with a 16-foot closed vertical clearance. This bridge will open on signal from 5:00 a.m. to 9:00 p.m., except from Monday through Friday (excluding holidays), when the draw need not open from 7:00 a.m. to 8:45 a.m. and from 4:00 p.m. to 6:00 p.m., unless an emergency exists. Also, it will open only once in any 60-minute period from 5:45 a.m. to 7:00 a.m. and 6:00 p.m. to 7:45 p.m. Finally, from 9:00 p.m. to 5:00 a.m., a 4-hour notice is required for the bridge to open. (A delay of up to 20 minutes may be expected

if a train is approaching so closely that it may not be safely stopped.) There are more bridges farther up the Norwalk River. You can call any of the bridgetenders here on VHF Channel 13 for clarification if the above schedule leaves you mystified.

Dockage/Moorings: Moorings are everywhere on Fivemile River and a few boatyards offer services, supplies and a place to tie up. The westernmost Norwalk harbor is Wilson Cove, just past Roton Point from Fivemile River. Although many yachts moor here permanently, it can be rough even in a moderate southwesterly wind. Here you will find Rowayton Yacht Club and Norwalk Yacht Club (on opposite sides of the cove at the mouth), as well as Wilson Cove Yacht Club to the north in the cove. All have transient space (or moorings) and fuel and repairs are available.

Several more marine facilities are located on the Norwalk River with with gas and diesel fuel, repairs and reserved transient slips. Across the river and before the Washington St. Bridge is the municipal David S. Dunavan Visitors Dock with 20 slips for vessels to 200 feet. Reservations are suggested at any of these facilities especially on weekends.

The 400-slip, full-service Norwalk Cove Marina, Inc. is located in East Norwalk at Gregory Point and offers transient dockage, plus all fuels and boat repairs. It is located inside the mouth of the Norwalk River and

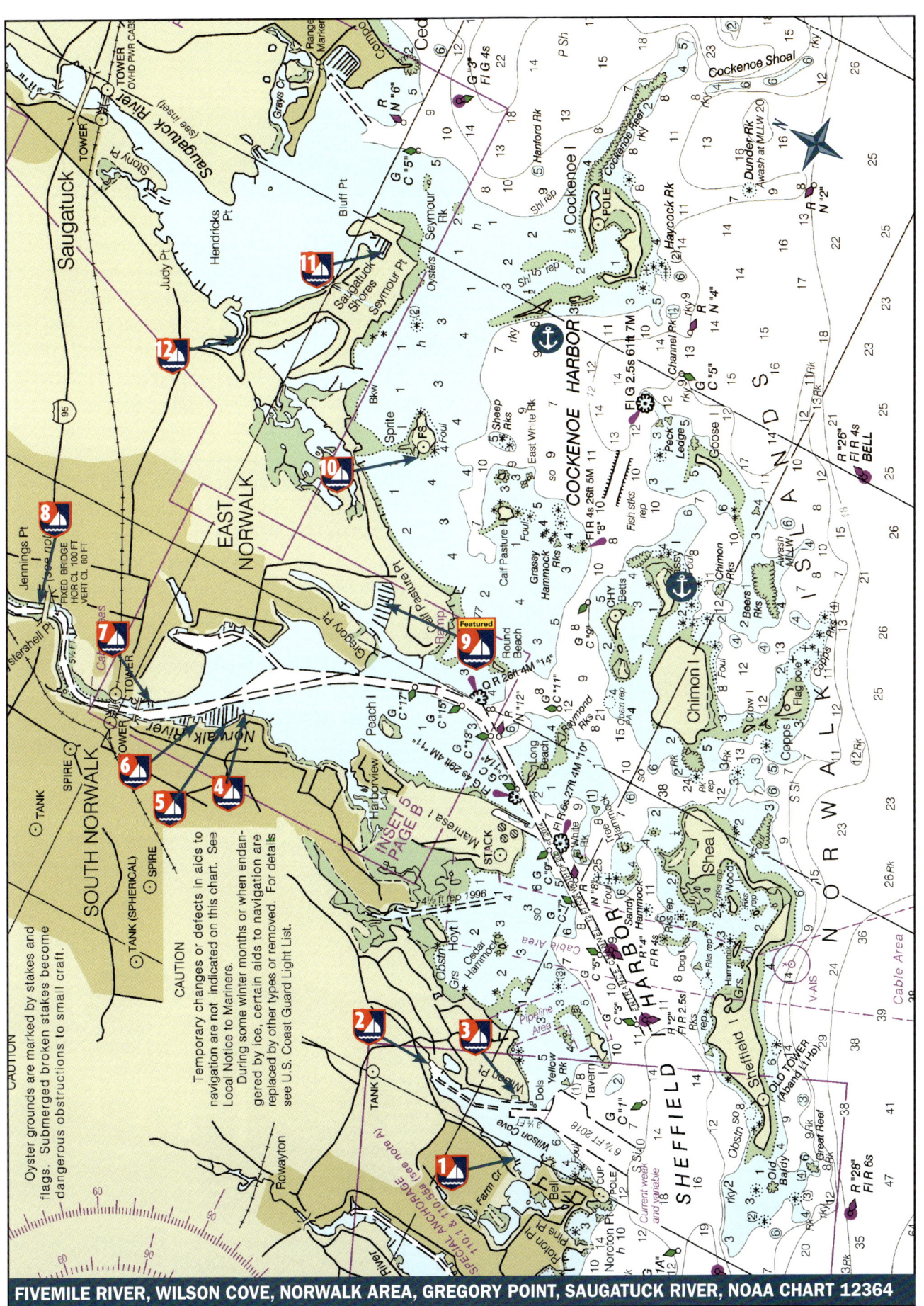

FIVEMILE RIVER, WILSON COVE, NORWALK AREA, GREGORY POINT, SAUGATUCK RIVER, NOAA CHART 12364

GOIN' ASHORE

Norwalk, CT

Norwalk, settled in 1649, was a major oystering and manufacturing center as far back as the 1700s. The working maritime heritage of the area lives on at Tallmadge Brothers, the largest oyster producer in the state of Connecticut. The company has over 22,000 acres of oyster beds and has been in business in Norwalk for over 130 years.

ATTRACTIONS

The Maritime Aquarium at Norwalk (10 N. Water St., 203-852-0700) features more than 1,000 marine animals native to Long Island Sound and its watershed; it makes a fabulous outing for families. History buffs should visit 19th-century buildings in Mill Hill Historic Park (2 East Wall St., 203-846-0525), open to the public June 22 through November 16. Or take a ferry from Water St. to the Sheffield Lighthouse, built in 1827 on the 57-acre Sheffield Island to mark the dangerous ledges at the entrance to the city's harbor. The stone and Victorian style lighthouse, built in 1868, still stands today; however the light was replaced in 1902 by the new Greens Ledge Light farther west. Call 203-838-9444 for tour details.

The Lockwood-Mathews Mansion Museum makes another fascinating stop; it is regarded as one of the earliest and finest surviving Second Empire Style country houses ever built in the U.S. It is a cultural gem that highlights the lives, styles and technology of the Victorian Era. Tours are offered early April through early January, from Wednesday through Sunday. Tours are conducted on the hour at 12:00 noon, 1:00 p.m., 2:00 p.m. and 3:00 p.m. for a fee. During the Christmas season it is beautifully decorated in true Victorian style.

The area's many art studios inspired the popular SoNo Arts Celebration, held the first weekend in August. A giant puppet parade and over 150 fine artists and craftsmen amplify an atmosphere of music and dance. The Norwalk Seaport Association (132 Water St., 203-838-9444) holds an annual Oyster Festival the weekend after Labor Day, which helps fund restoration of Sheffield Island's historic lighthouse and many other non-profit organizations.

SoNo, the historic waterfront neighborhood of South Norwalk, features turn-of-the-century architecture and a quaint gas-lit shopping and restaurant district. Also in the neighborhood are coffee shops, theaters and art galleries. There are several small supermarkets and a Walmart grocery (transportation required). There are many restaurants to please every palate in Norwalk.

can accommodate vessels up to 130 feet. They have a well-stocked ship store, a popular restaurant for lunch or dinner and are pet friendly. The Yacht Club on little Sprite Island is private.

Anchorage: There is no place to anchor in the river. Just finding room to turn around can be a problem. (The best advice is to go to the end and turn around carefully in 6-foot MLW depths.) However, just west of the mouth of Fivemile River at Butlers Island there is a great spot for anchoring in any breeze except from the east. Depths are around 8 to 11 feet MLW with good holding. Cruisers have reported a quiet night at anchor here within 100 yards of shore while northwest winds are gusting up to 30 knots. To reach this spot proceed on a course of 355° magnetic from Greens Ledge Light, pass east of green can buoy "1" and then proceed into the unnamed cove between Contentment Island and Butlers Island. Holding here is good in thick mud.

Many popular spots to drop the hook are available in the lee of the Norwalk Islands–in particular, the large area east of Chimon Island. Enter from the north, and proceed slowly over the 6-foot MLW bar to anchor in 10-foot MLW depths just east of Chimon Rocks. The northwestern shore of Cockenoe Island is also a popular anchorage. You can go ashore to swim, hike or camp; on weekends, it seems like everyone does. There is fair holding here in rocks and thick mud in at least 7 feet at MLW.

Saugatuck River (Westport, CT)

The Saugatuck River leading to Westport is interesting to explore but take care to factor the racing current in your plans, as it can be fierce. The shores of the river are lined with attractive houses, restaurants, shops, yacht clubs, a public recreational complex and a summer theater.

NAVIGATION: Use NOAA Chart 12364. Entrance to the Saugatuck River from Long Island Sound should be made east of flashing green buoy "1," which marks Georges Rock. Head northwest on either side of flashing green buoy "3" to the entrance to the marked channel in the river, between Cedar Point and Seymour Rock. A well-marked channel winds up and around Bluff Point, hugging the western shore. Depths outside the markers are as shallow as 1 foot MLW.

Dockage: Cedar Point Yacht Club, while hospitable, is often crowded. Saugatuck Harbor Yacht Club in nearby Duck Creek may have space on their floating docks. Call ahead for availability at either of these

facilities. The large (470-slip) Compo Yacht Basin, across the river at Cedar Point, sells gas and may have transient space.

Anchorage: Anchorages in the vicinity of the town are extremely limited, swing room is minimal and the channel winds are tortuous. Because of one shallow spot downriver, this area is best not approached near dead-low water. The 7-foot tidal range, though, will give you good water most of the time. One popular spot is by Kitts Island (south of Hendricks Point) in 11- to 15-foot MLW depths with good holding in soft mud.

Southport, CT

NAVIGATION: Use NOAA Chart 12364. Southport is a Colonial town, with a tiny crowded harbor and a narrow, dredged channel through shoals (some with only 0.5 foot MLW). There are no facilities for cruising boats. Shoal-draft boats can enter the harbor west of Sasco Hill Beach on the chart. Follow the buoyed channel, keeping away from the riprap around the base of the flashing green "7." Watch for a shallow spot (5.5 feet MLW) between the breakwater and the outer buoy. It is a difficult harbor to keep dredged but it can be navigated slowly and cautiously on a rising or high tide. Once inside the harbor, do not go beyond the moorings to reach the shallow, open water beyond the yacht club. The town dock, located on the northwestern shore as the channel widens, allows complimentary 30-minute tie-ups.

Bridgeport, CT Area

Bridgeport, the most populous city in Connecticut, was first settled in 1659 but not chartered as a town until 1856. Shipbuilding and whaling in the mid-19th century were made possible by the deep Black Rock Harbor.

The first bridge across the Pequannock River was financed by a lottery in 1800 and became known as Bridgeport. Shortly afterward, P.T. Barnum, founder of the "Greatest Show on Earth," was drawn to the area because of its rapid growth. The Barnum Museum (www.barnum-museum.org) at 820 Main St. (203-331-1104) is dedicated to the life and times of P.T. Barnum and Bridgeport's industrial heritage.

Black Rock is a pleasant neighborhood of west Bridgeport. Fairfield Avenue, a 10-minute walk from the marinas, has interesting restaurants and shops.

NAVIGATION: Use NOAA Chart 12364. Black Rock Harbor, almost 2 miles west of Bridgeport, is the

Black Rock Harbor, CT

WG

	Phone	Largest Vessel Accommodated	VHF Channel Monitored (Dockage)	Transient / Total Slips	Approach / Dockside Depth (reported)	Floating Docks	Gas / Diesel (Supplies)	Groceries, Ice, Marine Supplies, Snacks	Repairs: Hull, Engine, Propeller (Services)	Lift (tonnage), Crane, Rail	Min / Max Amps	Courtesy Car, Laundry, Pool, Showers	Pump-Out Station	Nearby: Grocery Store, Motel, Restaurant
FAIRFIELD														
1. South Benson Marina	(203) 256-3002	36	/	/600	/		G	IS			30			MR
CEDAR CREEK														
2. Black Rock Yacht Club (WiFi)	(203) 335-0587	50	14/14	/	8.0/5.0			IS				PS		GR
3. Fayerweather Yacht Club (☐ WiFi)	(203) 576-8860	50	14/	/	7.0/5.0	F	G	IS			30	S	P	GR
4. Fayerweather Boat Yard	(203) 334-4403	45	/	/	/			M	HEP	L,C				GMR
5. Captain's Cove Seaport (WiFi)	(203) 335-1433	200	18/	30/350	18.0/13.0	F	GD	IM	HEP	L85,C	50	LS	P	GMR
6. Cedar Marina Inc. (WiFi)	(203) 335-6262	70	/	8/140	20.0/7.0	F		IS	HEP	L15	30	S	P	R
BRIDGEPORT														
7. Bridgeport Harbor Marina (☐ WiFi onSpot)	(203) 330-8787	250	9/9	/200	30.0/12.0	F			HEP	L200	30/100	LS	P	GMR
8. Bridgeport Boatworks	(860) 536-9651	200	/	/	/				HEP	L200				MR
9. Dolphin's Cove Restaurant & Marina	(203) 335-3301	45	/	/40	/	F		IS			30	S		GR
10. Miamogue Yacht Club	(203) 334-9882	50	/	/173	15.0/8.0	F	G	IS			30/50		P	R
11. East End Yacht Club	(203) 366-3330	40	9/	/200	10.0/10.0	F	G	I			30	S		MR

☐ Internet Access (WiFi) Wireless Internet Access onSpot Dockside WiFi Facility

See WaterwayGuide.com for current rates, fuel prices, website addresses, and other up-to-the-minute information. (Information in the table is provided by the facilities.)

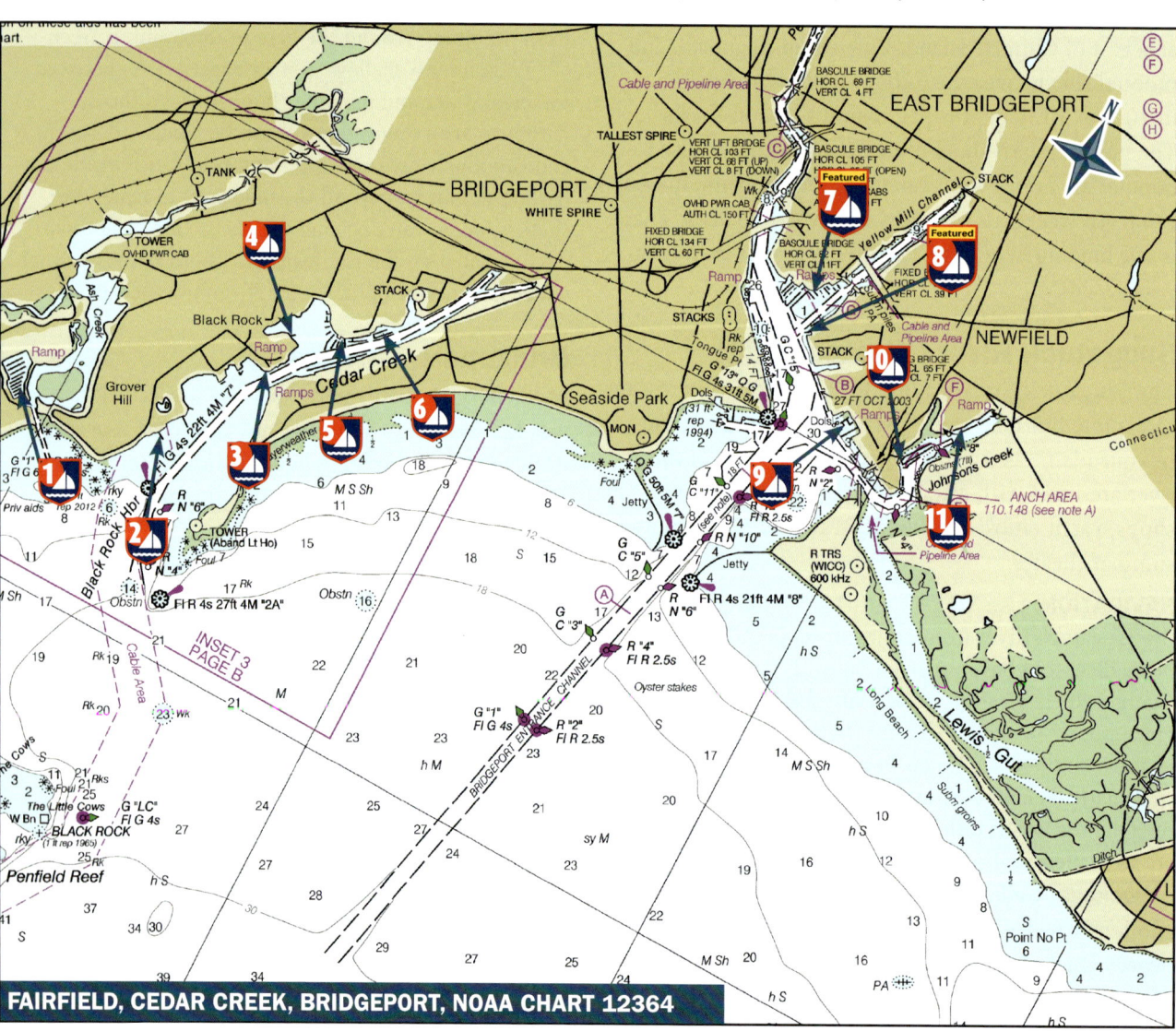

FAIRFIELD, CEDAR CREEK, BRIDGEPORT, NOAA CHART 12364

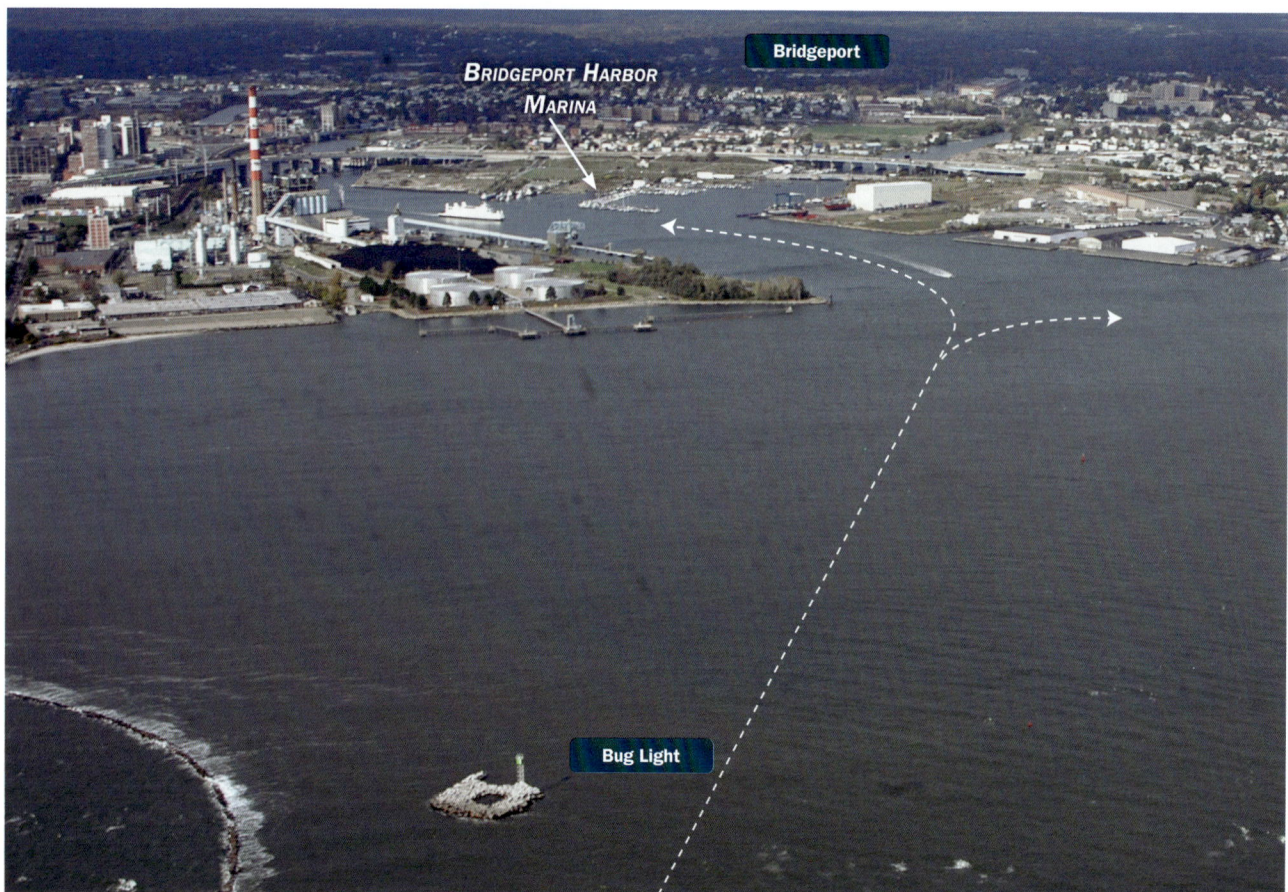

main harbor for recreational boats. It has a deep, well-marked channel, is easy to enter and has ample transient facilities. The harbor is sheltered to the east by Fayerweather Island, part of Bridgeport's big Seaside Park, with an abandoned lighthouse at the tip. Heading from Southport toward Black Rock Harbor, give the end of Penfield Reef a wide berth to keep clear of the numerous smaller rocks and Black Rock itself. Be sure that the flashing light you see is at the end of the reef and then head for flashing red gong buoy "2" marking the Bridgeport Harbor entrance about 1.5 miles away. Do not make your turn for Black Rock Harbor until you are midway between those markers, following a course of about 330° magnetic.

Bridgeport is easy to spot because of its tall stacks, factories, oil tanks and power plants, which are all visible from Long Island Sound. The large tankers, ferries and freighters traveling its big, well-marked channel are equally evident. It has a well-marked entrance and deep water that accommodates the tremendous traffic.

The Bridgeport-to-Port Jefferson ferry service transports passengers and vehicles across Long Island Sound several times a day. Contact ferries on VHF Channel 13 if you anticipate a close encounter. Be

prepared to give way, as the ferries require room to turn and maneuver.

Dockage/Moorings: Guest moorings may be available from the two yacht clubs in Black Rock Harbor, Black Rock Yacht Club and Fayerweather Yacht Club. Both monitor VHF Channel 16. The 350-slip Captain's Cove Seaport is a family-owned and operated marina, restaurant, bar, and boardwalk. Captain's Cove is home to charter fishing boats and an extensive collection of nautical memorabilia.

Most of the marinas at East Bridgeport able to handle cruising boats are on the main channel including the new (in 2019) Bridgeport Harbor Marina. The full-service, first-class marina can accommodate vessels to 250 feet with a complete menu of marine services including dockage, vessel repairs, provisioning and winter storage. It also offers 24-hour security, concierge service and an on-site restaurant.

There are also a few facilities inside Johnsons Creek (the first marked channel to the east inside the breakwaters). Call ahead. Be aware that all of Bridgeport's marinas are located adjacent to industrial areas. It is best to take a slip here.

Stratford & Devon, CT

Stratford is famous for two very diverse things: shipbuilding and helicopters. The English settled this historic city and named it for Shakespeare's Stratford-on-Avon in 1639. Shipbuilding was an important industry along the Housatonic River dating back to the 1700s. In the 1800s, large schooners were built here, most notably the 280-ton *Helen Mar*.

Over 100 years later the city made a name for itself in aviation. Igor Sikorsky flew the first helicopter at his Stratford manufacturing plant in 1939 and, to this day, the company manufactures helicopters for both the military and civilian markets. Aeronautics buffs can visit the Connecticut Air & Space Museum at 550 Main St. (www.ctairandspace.org, 203-380-1400) and the smaller but equally interesting National Helicopter Museum at 2480 Main St. (203-375-8857).

The Housatonic River's upriver stretches are scenic with green hills coming right down to the water. Devon, a small business section of Milford, is on the east bank about 2 miles north of Stratford. The river carries only 4-foot MLW depths above Devon but it is navigable and marked for 8 miles to Shelton. It is a pretty side trip for shallow-draft boats.

NAVIGATION: Use NOAA Chart 12364. To reach Stratford you can approach the Housatonic River through open, obstruction-free water. The river is about 5 miles north of Stratford Shoal Lighthouse and opposite Port Jefferson on Long Island. Tall chimneys at Devon are a good offshore landmark for the entrance between Milford Point's long, lighted breakwater (inner end submerges at three-quarter high tide) and Stratford Point. Stratford Point has shoals on all sides, an early 19th-century lighthouse and well-staked oyster beds to the east. Currents in the narrow channel of the Housatonic River run swiftly so try to hit it at the beginning of the flood when entering. Mean tidal range at Stratford is 5.5 feet and lessens as you move upriver. The flood sets to the west and can push you toward the flats along the channel if you get caught off guard.

There are three bridges: **U.S. 1 Bridge** (with 32-foot fixed vertical clearance with a restricted schedule), **Connecticut Turnpike (I-95) Bridge** (with 65-foot fixed vertical clearance) and the **Metro North (Devon) Bridge** (with 19-foot vertical clearance and a restricted schedule).

The draw of the U.S. 1 Bridge opens on signal except from 7:00 a.m. to 9:00 a.m., Monday through Friday, and 4:00 p.m. to 5:45 p.m. daily, when the draw need not open for the passage of vessels. From December 1 through March 31, from 8:00 p.m. to 4:00 a.m., the draw will open on signal if at least a 6-hour notice is given by calling the number posted at the bridge.

The Devon Railroad Bridge follows a similar schedule with a few exceptions. It will open on signal, except from 7:00 a.m. to 9:00 a.m. and from 4:00 p.m. to 5:45 p.m., Monday through Friday. From 5:30 a.m. to 7:00 a.m. and from 5:45 p.m. to 8:15 p.m. (except Saturdays, Sundays and federal holidays, the bridge need not open more than once in any 60-minute period so it can be worthwhile to hurry a little to catch an opening. From 9:00 p.m. to 5:00 a.m., the draw will open on signal if notice is given to the chief dispatcher of the railroad before 4:00 p.m. on the day of the intended passage. A delay in opening the draw will not exceed 20 minutes for the passage of approaching trains from the time of the request.

Dockage: There are numerous dockage options on the Housatonic River. A yacht club and full-service marina are along the west side of the channel across from Nells Island. Safe Harbor Stratford is a popular marina so call ahead for reservations. More facilities are to the north beyond the U.S. 1 Bridge. Call ahead for slip availability at these facilities.

Anchorage: At Nells Island in the bend across from Stratford the Housatonic River opens up with good water in the marina area. You can anchor off the northern tip of Nells Island south of green can "21" in 17 feet MLW with good holding in mud but be aware that the current is swift. Consider setting two anchors as a single anchor might break out during the current change. If you go ashore by dinghy, an outboard is a must. A second option is to anchor on the west side of the river just north of the highway and railway bridges where the current is not as strong and there is still 9 to 10 feet MLW with a mud bottom.

Milford Harbor, CT

Milford, approximately 4 miles east of Stratford, is an attractive summer resort and yachting center located at the mouth of the Wepawaug River. Milford has an easy-to-enter, well-protected but crowded harbor with good marinas that cater to transient mariners. Captain Kidd and other pirates are purported to have once roamed these waters and to have left behind buried treasure.

NAVIGATION: Use NOAA Chart 12364. Entry to the Wepawaug Riveris is through The Gulf, past low, rocky,

Long Island Sound, CT

WG

		Largest Vessel Accomodated	VHF Channel Monitored / Working	Transient Slips / Total Slips	Approach / Dockside Depth (reported)	Floating Docks	Gas / Diesel	Groceries, Ice, Marine Supplies, Snacks	Repairs: Hull, Engine, Propeller	Lift (tonnage), Crane, Rail	Min / Max Amps	Courtesy Car, Laundry, Pool, Showers	Pump-Out Station	Nearby: Grocery Store, Motel, Restaurant
STRATFORD				**Dockage**			**Supplies**				**Services**			
1. Safe Harbor Stratford WiFi Red 18	(203) 377-4477	85	9/10	6/200	15.0/12.0	F	GD	IM	HEP	L35,C	30/100	CLPS	P	GMR
2. Pootatuck Yacht Club	(203) 377-9068	70	71/	/69	/			IS				S		R
3. Village Marina	(203) 913-3105	35	/	/86	10.0/6.0	F		M	HEP		30	S		MR
4. Boardwalk Marina	(203) 378-9300	100	9/	10/165	13.0/12.0	F	G	GIS	HEP	L50	30/50	LS		GMR
MILFORD														
5. Milford Yacht Club WiFi	(203) 783-0065	75	68/68	10/80	10.0/7.0	F		IS		L2	50	PS		GR
6. Port Milford Marina ▢ WiFi	(203) 301-2222	50	9/72	10/100	8.0/8.0	F		GIM	HEP	L35	30	S	P	GMR
7. Milford Boat Works ▢ WiFi	(203) 877-1475	50	68/	10/194	9.0/8.0	F	GD	IM	HE	L35,C	30/50	LS	P	GMR
8. Milford Lisman Landing Marina ▢ WiFi	(203) 874-1610	65	9/	35/35	9.0/7.0	F		I			30/50	LS	P	MR
9. Spencer's Marina	(203) 874-4173	45	9/	/140	7.0/6.0	F	G	IMS	HEP	L25	30/50	S	P	GMR

▢ Internet Access　WiFi Wireless Internet Access　onSpot Dockside WiFi Facility

See WaterwayGuide.com for current rates, fuel prices, website addresses, and other up-to-the-minute information. (Information in the table is provided by the facilities.)

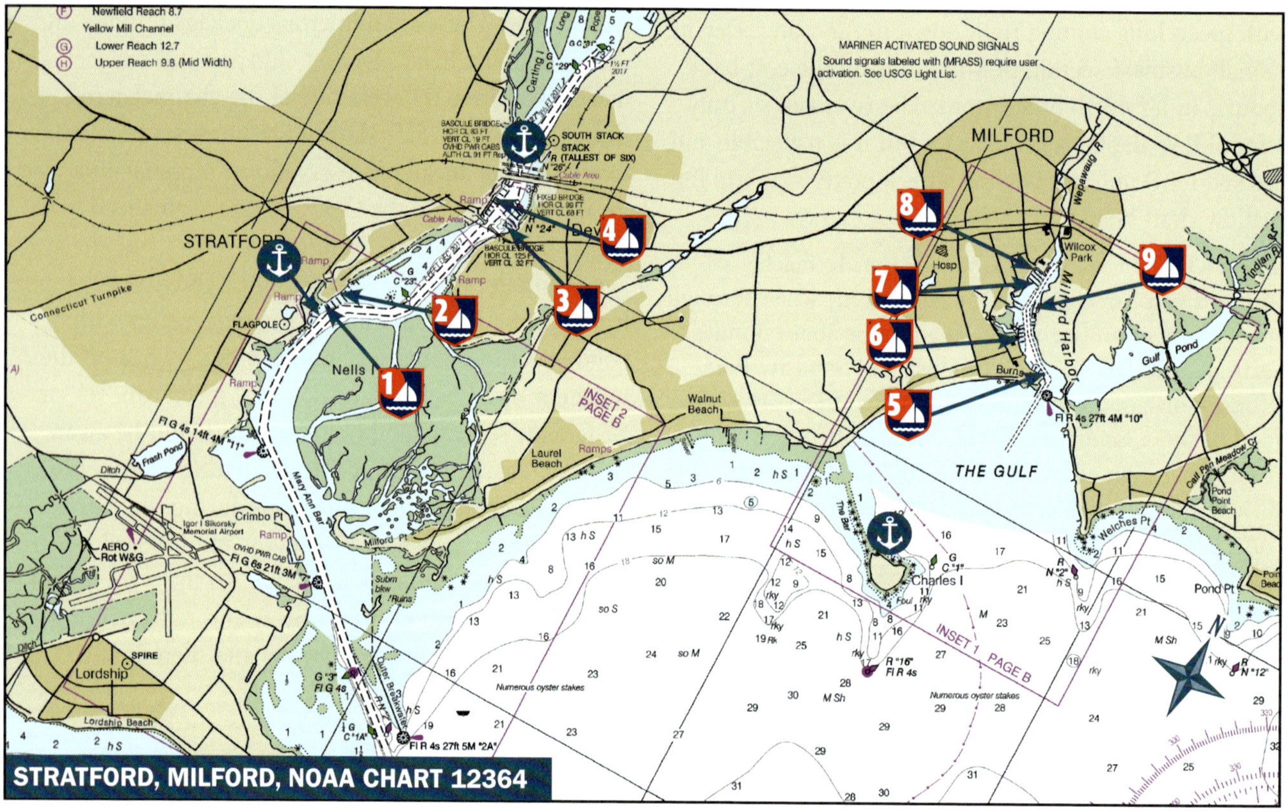

STRATFORD, MILFORD, NOAA CHART 12364

partly wooded Charles Island. Keep the island and green can "1" to the west. The channel into Milford is well marked. It is best to stay inside the buoys as the water is very shallow on both sides as you approach the harbor. The U.S. Army Corps of Engineers tries to maintain 8- to 10-foot MLW depths throughout the channel but local tow boat companies may have the most current information.

Dockage/Moorings: In the mooring-cluttered Milford Harbor, a seemingly endless flotilla of small sailing craft is constantly on the move. Most of the facilities here cater to smaller vessels. The Milford Yacht Club at the mouth of the river will berth any cruising boat (up to 75 feet) but note that club privileges are reserved for members of reciprocating yacht clubs.

Another option for cruising vessels is upriver at Milford Lisman Landing Marina, a very welcoming municipal marina located in town located just steps from beautiful historic downtown Milford. This is an all-transient marina with 35 slips that can accommodate vessels up to 65 feet.

Anchorage: You can slowly work your way in west of the Milford Harbor Channel north of Burns Point, just inside the mouth of the river, where there are 6.5-foot MLW depths.

If you want to be in a more secluded site, drop the hook behind Charles Island in 9 to 13 feet MLW. At low tide, it is protected from all directions but the east and holding is good. Note that the narrow isthmus connecting the island with the mainland disappears at high tide and the swell can make the basin uncomfortable in the prevailing southwest wind. Go right up to the north side of the island for best protection. On still nights with nothing to hold your bow to the wind you might wallow in the slight surge from the Sound.

■ NEXT STOP

New Haven begins the second half of the Long Island Sound's north shore and is the end of the Metro-North rail line from New York City. From there, the coastal towns change character, slowing down and gaining a more rural feel while natural beauty reigns.

Milford Harbor

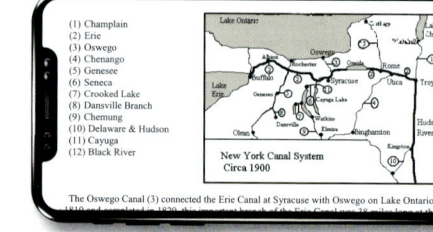

North Shore: New Haven, CT to Watch Hill, RI

■ NEW HAVEN TO WEST BROOK, CT

New Haven, CT

New Haven, Connecticut's second largest city, is situated almost 70 nm northeast of New York City. It is the home of Yale University but, as a mostly commercial port, New Haven is one of Long Island Sound's most important harbors of refuge for commercial shipping. The harbor is industrial and busy but there are two marinas away from the hubbub of the inner harbor that cater to visiting yachts. Downtown New Haven is only a short taxi or bus ride away from the harbor marinas.

New Haven has all the attractions of a major American city in a small, quite walkable package. For sightseeing, a stroll among Yale University's classic gargoyle halls and ivy walls, juxtaposed modern architecture, windowless secret societies and spacious college walks is worth the trip to town.

Yale's Beinecke Rare Book & Manuscript Library (121 Wall St., 203-432-2977) is one of the best of its kind in the world. You can see Portuguese charts from the Age of Exploration and an original copy of the Gutenberg Bible among other treasures. See details at www.beinecke.library.yale.edu. The Yale Peabody Museum of Natural History (170 Whitney Ave., 203-432-5050) is one of the oldest and largest history museums in the country. The dinosaur collection is an impressive treat for kids under age 99 or so (www.peabody.yale.edu).

NAVIGATION: Use NOAA Charts 12372 and 12371. The 2-mile-wide harbor at New Haven is protected in part by breakwaters. The channel is deep, well-marked and able to handle virtually any vessel short of a supertanker. The West River channel, west of the shipping channel after entry, is also well marked. It's narrower but deep enough to accommodate almost any recreational vessel. Outside the channels the harbor is shoal and not navigable (with the exception of Morris Cove). There are no marine facilities in the inner harbor ("New Haven Reach") for cruising yachts.

New Haven
Harbor, CT

		Largest Vessel Accomodated	VHF Channel Monitored / Working	Transient Slips / Total Slips	Approach / Dockside Depth (reported)	Floating Docks	Gas / Diesel	Groceries, Ice, Marine Supplies, Snacks	Repairs: Hull, Engine, Propeller	Lift (tonnage), Crane, Rail	Min / Max Amps	Courtesy Car, Laundry, Pool, Showers	Pump-Out Station	Nearby: Grocery Store, Motel, Restaurant
EAST HAVEN					**Dockage**			**Supplies**				**Services**		
1. New Haven Yacht Club	(203) 469-9608	40	68/	/	8.0/2.0	F							S	G
NEW HAVEN														
2. Pequonnock Yacht Club 🖥 (WiFi)	(203) 773-9460	50	9/	6/130	10.0/8.0	F		GIMS	HE	L	30/50	LS	P	GMR
3. City Point Yacht Club	(203) 789-9301	40	9/	/182	7.0/6.0	F	G	I			30	PS	P	GMR

🖥 Internet Access   (WiFi) Wireless Internet Access   onSpot Dockside WiFi Facility

See WaterwayGuide.com for current rates, fuel prices, website addresses, and other up-to-the-minute information. (Information in the table is provided by the facilities.)

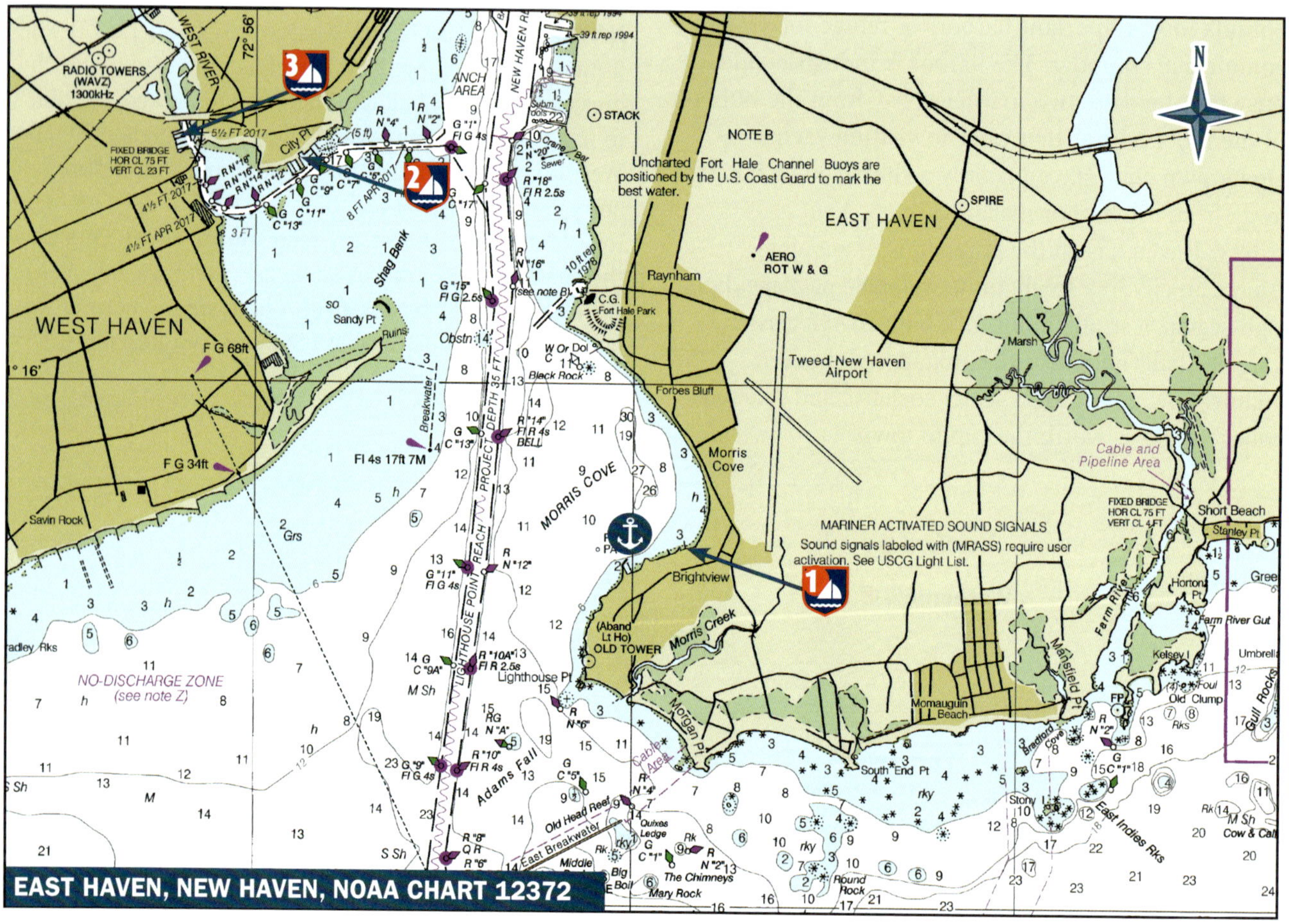

EAST HAVEN, NEW HAVEN, NOAA CHART 12372

Dockage/Moorings: New Haven Yacht Club in Morris Cove is a co-operative of sailors and sailing-oriented folks. About 0.5 miles into the West River channel, boaters are welcome on the moorings at the Pequonnock Yacht Club.

Anchorage: Inside the breakwaters and to the east, Morris Cove (near New Haven Yacht Club) provides good holding in 8 to 10 feet MLW and an easy route in and out of Long Island Sound. However, smaller vessels may find the cove to be less than adequately protected and open to unwelcome surge and current. Just inside the central breakwater west of the main channel you can find a decent spot to anchor in settled weather with the same current and surge conditions. This can be a respite if heading east or west on Long Island Sound as quickly as possible.

Branford, CT

Branford is the best port of refuge and easiest harbor entry in the almost 20 miles stretching between New Haven and Clinton. There are many restored homes dating from the Colonial days when it had important salt works (meat for Revolutionary War troops was preserved in Branford salt) and granite quarries. It also was a Yankee trading center and the original home of Yale University. Today, Branford is a vibrant community of about 28,000 residents, some of whom are affiliated with Yale and other New Haven-area universities.

NAVIGATION: Use NOAA Chart 12372. When entering Branford from Long Island Sound, you must thread a series of rocks guarding the entrance to the Branford River but they are well charted, buoyed and relatively easy to make out. They offer little challenge when visibility is good. The clearest route in is to turn northward between the Cow and Calf Rocks and Five Foot Rock, traveling east of flashing red bell buoy "34" and west of red nun buoy "32." Pass west of Blyn Rock's flashing red "2" and Bird Rock's red nun buoy "4" and pick up the channel's turn slightly east at green can "5." Another slight eastward bend between Big Mermaid (marked by flashing green "7") and Little Mermaid (marked by red nun buoy "6") sends the channel through moderate shallows into the Branford River.

The Branford River, like many Long Island Sound tributaries, has strong currents. Be aware of the direction and strength of the current when docking at any of the marinas listed. Call for docking assistance if the current is running strong.

Dockage/Moorings: Visiting cruisers can almost always find a berth in the Branford Harbor or River. Immediately to the north on entering the river, Branford Yacht Club has limited provisions for transient docking that must be arranged by contacting the dockmaster at 203-488-9798. Two Safe Harbor facilities are here as well and may be able to accommodate you. They have 675 slips total and both offer a full range of repairs and services, supported by a parts department and marine supply store. Farther upriver, the well-regarded Dutch Wharf Boat Yard offers repairs as does Branford Landing Marina. There is no protected anchorage here.

The Thimbles, CT

For the next 8 miles east of Branford, the intervening shore is wild, marshy and dotted with summer communities and granite quarries. It is rocky and challenging for those unfamiliar with the area. It should be approached with caution and careful study of the chart. All of the harbors here are packed with local boats and require local knowledge. Proceed with caution.

The Thimble Islands and nearby Stony Creek have been a popular summer community since the days of Captain Kidd, who used to hide his ships among the rocky cliffs within High Island. He may have hidden treasure here, too, although none has been found to date. (It is not a good idea to start searching on private property.)

NAVIGATION: Use NOAA Chart 12372. The Thimbles consist of 25 (private) inhabited islands and hundreds of pink granite rock formations that scatter into Long Island Sound off the unique coastal village of Stony Creek. The Thimbles are the largest group of islands on Long Island Sound and are just west of Sachem Head, off the Connecticut shore between Branford and Guilford. These clumps of rock form a narrow alley of deep water down the middle.

The Thimbles were created more than 10,000 years ago when glacial action exposed ancient granite bedrock. As the glacier moved, it picked up loose soil and stone and pried loose blocks of granite, leaving the islands after the glacier melted. This cluster of islands resembles the endless islands off the coast of Maine in miniature.

Stony Creek serves as the shore side access to the Thimbles and is well worth a dinghy ride from the anchorages. There are several dinghy docks available and a public dock for small craft. This is a busy spot occupied by a plethora of small boats, ferries, an oyster

Long Island Sound, CT

		Largest Vessel Accommodated	VHF Channel Monitored / Working	Transient Slips / Total Slips	Approach / Dockside Depth (reported)	Floating Docks	Gas / Diesel	Groceries, Ice, Marine Supplies, Snacks	Repairs: Hull, Engine, Propeller	Lift (tonnage), Crane, Rail	Min / Max Amps	Courtesy Car, Laundry, Pool, Showers	Pump-Out Station	Nearby: Grocery Store, Motel, Restaurant
				Dockage			**Supplies**		**Services**					
BRANFORD														
1. Branford Yacht Club 🖥 WIFI	(203) 488-9798	60	/	5/250	10.0/10.0	F	GD	I		L50	30/50	S	P	GR
2. Safe Harbor Bruce & Johnsons - West WIFI	(203) 488-8329	60	9/9	25/350	7.0/7.0	F	GD	IM	HEP	L50	50	S	P	GR
3. Safe Harbor Bruce & Johnsons WIFI	(203) 488-8329	60	9/65	25/650	7.0/7.5	F	GD	IM	HEP	L50	30/50	LPS	P	GMR
4. Indian Neck Yacht Club	(203) 488-9276	40	/	/90	8.0/8.0		G	I			30	S		
5. Dutch Wharf Boat Yard and Marina Inc.	(203) 488-9000	55	/	/65	10.0/10.0	F		M	HEP		50	S		R
6. Branford Landing Marina	(203) 483-6544	55	/	4/30	8.0/8.0	F	GD	IMS	HEP	L50,C	30	S		GR
GUILFORD														
7. Brown's Boat Yard 🖥 WIFI	(203) 453-6283	40	/	/25	6.0/5.0	F	GD	M	HEP	L25,C	30			3
8. Guilford Yacht Club 🖥 WIFI	(203) 415-3427	50	71/	10/158	6.0/8.0	F		I			30/50	PS	P	GMR
9. Guilford Boat Yards and Marine LLC	(203) 453-5031	30	/	2/8	1.0/6.0	F		M	HEP	L10	15			GR

🖥 Internet Access   WIFI Wireless Internet Access   onSpot Dockside WiFi Facility
See WaterwayGuide.com for current rates, fuel prices, website addresses, and other up-to-the-minute information. (Information in the table is provided by the facilities.)

fleet and lobster and fishing vessels. Excursion boats, departing hourly May through October, run to the Thimble Islands from Stony Creek. Activity starts early and carries well into the evening. A water taxi runs on the hour and is on-call for those wishing to get to Stony Creek. Proceed cautiously in this area. Swimmers are usually diving off the cliffs or paddling between boats. No services or facilities are available on the islands.

Anchorage: You can anchor practically anywhere with appropriate depth outside the harbor in Stony Creek and even on crowded summer weekends, you can usually find some protection and deep water. Take particular care to observe the underwater cable areas servicing the islands.

Crowded Pine Orchard to the west of Stony Creek is a summer community with fine homes, lots of rocks and a yacht club unexpectedly large and ambitious for a harbor this size. You can anchor outside in good weather, when there are no winds out of the east or south.

In the Thimble Islands, private mooring buoys have erased a formerly favored anchorage between High and Pot Islands and leave far too little room for proper scope in 10 to 20 feet MLW. Some gamble on shorter scope in settled weather with decent holding in the mud. Although not recommended, some cruisers have been known to pick up one of the private moorings for a night (especially during the week) with no adverse consequences.

East of Pot Island, you will find 8 to 13 feet MLW, although rock ledges and mooring balls may push you into 15-foot MLW areas. This anchorage is approached from the south by leaving red nun buoy "2CR" to the west. Although exposed to westerly and southwesterly winds, the area to the north of West Crib Island is a good option as well with 11 to 12 feet MLW.

Guilford, CT

The Village of Guilford provides a glimpse of New England architectural history at its best. Many structures dating back to the 17th century have survived and a walk through the harborside area is memorable. Guilford boasts five historic house museums. The Henry Whitfield State Museum (www.portal.ct.gov/ECD-HenryWhitfieldStateMuseum) remains the oldest stone house in New England and contains many artifacts of 17th-century Guilford and the Puritan life of the period. The shopping area and services are also available within a short walk of the harbor.

NAVIGATION: Use NOAA Charts 12372 and 12373. Guilford is located between the West and East Rivers about 3 miles north of uninhabited Falkner Island. Although the entrance to West River is buoyed, it is rather shallow.

The East River entry is easier but requires sharp attention and good visibility for the newcomer. The entrance channel into the East River has anywhere from 3.5 to 8 feet MLW in the main channel, the shallowest part being in the approach to Guilford Point, especially between green can buoy "9" and red nun buoy "10." Upriver, the National Audubon Society maintains a 150-acre reserve (Guilford Salt Meadows Sanctuary) protecting the tidal estuary and providing a panorama of scenic views.

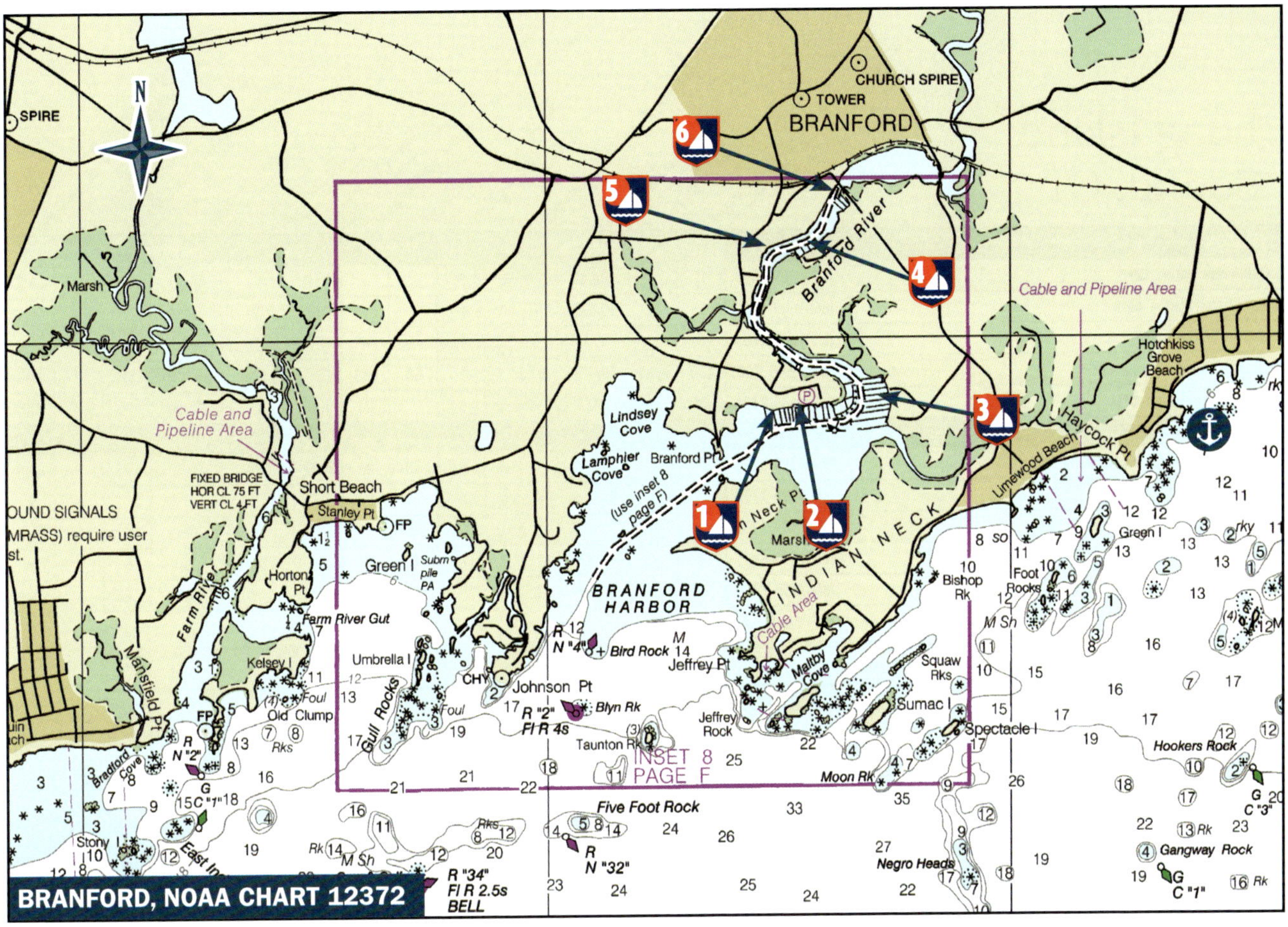

BRANFORD, NOAA CHART 12372

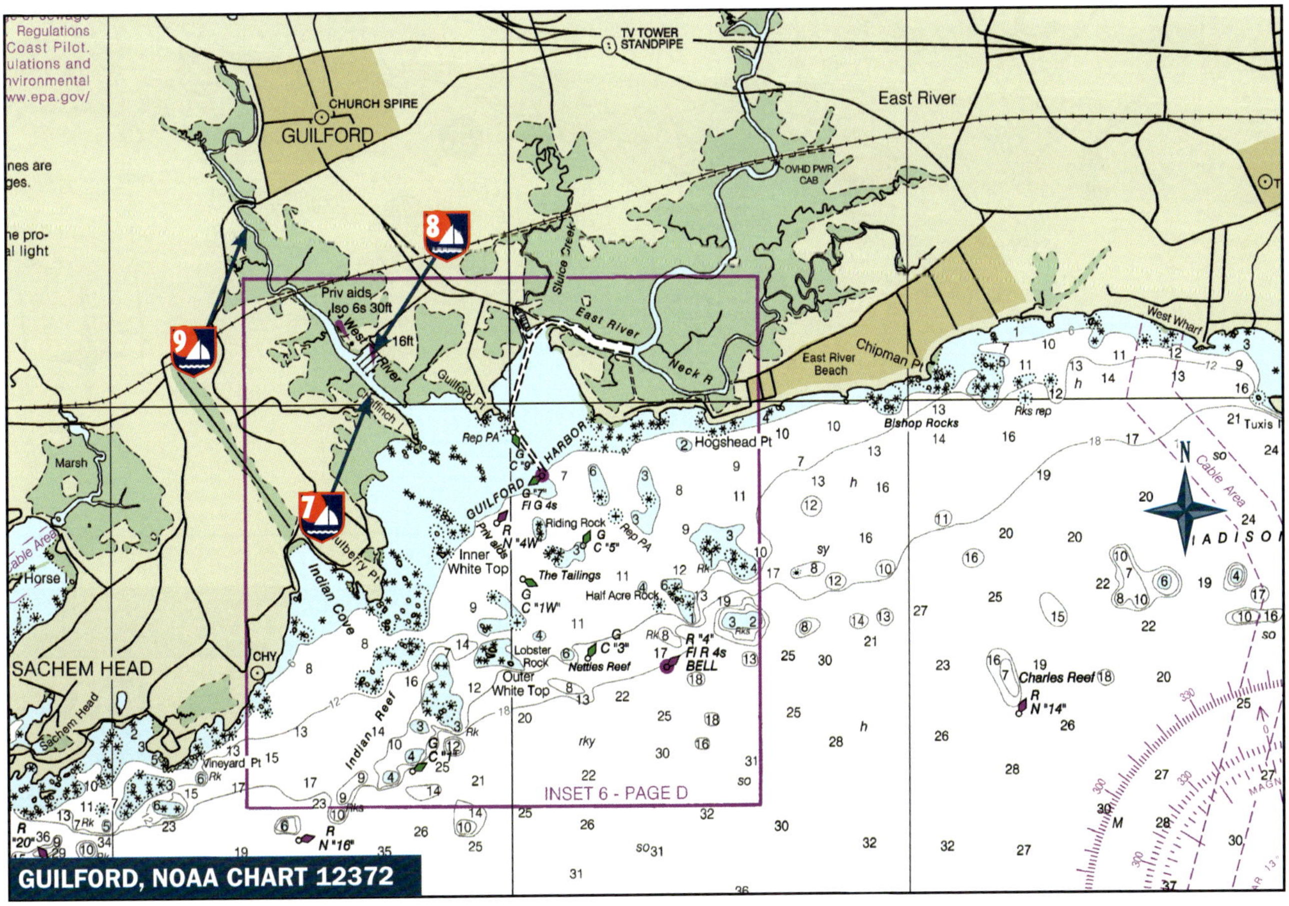

CHURCH SPIRE
TOWER
BRANFORD
SPIRE
N
Marsh
Branford River
Cable and Pipeline Area
Hotchkiss Grove Beach
Cable and Pipeline Area
FIXED BRIDGE
HOR CL 75 FT
VERT CL 4 FT
SOUND SIGNALS
(MRASS) require user
request.
Short Beach
Stanley Pt
FP
Lindsey Cove
Lamphier Cove
Branford Pt
(use inset 8 page F)
Limewood Beach
Haycock Pt
Green I
Submpile PA
Horton Pt
Farm River Gut
BRANFORD HARBOR
INDIAN NECK
Bishop Rk
Foot Rocks
M Sh
Marsh
Kelsey I
Green I
CHY
Johnson Pt
R "2"
Fl R 4s
Old Clump
Foul
Foul
Rks
Umbrella I
R "4"
N "4"
Bird Rock
Jeffrey Pt
Maltby Cove
Cable Area
Squaw Rks
Jeffrey Rock
Sumac I
Spectacle I
Hookers Rock
Taunton Rk
INSET 8 PAGE F
Moon Rk
G "3"
C "3"
Five Foot Rock
Negro Heads
Gangway Rock
R "34"
Fl R 2.5s
BELL
R "32"
N "32"
G "1"
C "1"
Stony
East I
Marshfield Pt
Bradford Cove
R "2"
N "2"
FP

GUILFORD, NOAA CHART 12372

TV TOWER
STANDPIPE
East River
CHURCH SPIRE
GUILFORD
Regulations
Coast Pilot.
ulations and
nvironmental
ww.epa.gov/
nes are ges.
he pro-
al light
OVHD PWR CAB
East River
Sluice Creek
Neck R
Priv aids
Iso 6s 30ft
West Wharf
Chipman Pt
East River Beach
West River
16ft
Guilford Pt
Clinch
HARBOR
Rep PA
Hogshead Pt
Bishop Rocks
Tuxis
N
MADISON
Cable Area
Marsh
Horse I
GUILFORD
G "7"
Fl G 4s
N "4W"
Riding Rock
Rep PA
G "5"
C "5"
Inner White Top
The Tailings
Half Acre Rock
sy
SACHEM HEAD
Mulberry Pt
CHY
Indian Cove
G "1W"
C "1W"
Lobster Rock
G "3"
C "3"
Nettles Reef
R "4"
Fl R 4s
BELL
Charles Reef
R "14"
N "14"
Outer White Top
Vineyard Pt
Indian Reef
rky
so
INSET 6 - PAGE D
R "16"
N "16"
R "20"
N "20"

Long Island Sound, CT

		Dockage					Supplies		Services					
		Largest Vessel Accomodated	VHF Channel Monitored / Working	Transient Slips / Total Slips	Approach / Dockside Depth (reported)	Floating Docks	Gas / Diesel	Groceries, Ice, Marine Supplies, Snacks	Repairs: Hull, Engine, Propeller	Lift (tonnage), Crane, Rail	Min / Max Amps	Courtesy Car, Laundry, Pool, Showers	Pump-Out Station	Nearby: Grocery Store, Motel, Restaurant
CLINTON														
1. Old Harbor Marina WiFi	(860) 669-3500	45	/	10/130	7.0/5.0	F		I	HEP	L	30/50	S		GMR
2. Port Clinton Marina WiFi	(860) 669-4563	40	9/	10/140	9.0/9.0	F			HEP	L50	30/50	LS	P	GMR
3. Harborside Marina WiFi	(860) 669-1705	180	/	/75	20.0/9.0	F		IMS	HEP	L20	30	S		GMR
4. Cedar Island Marina ▫ WiFi	**(860) 669-8681**	130	9/68	70/400	8.0/8.5	F	GD	IMS	HEP	L35,C	15/100	CLPS	P	GMR
5. Clinton Yacht Haven WiFi	(860) 669-7254	50	/	3/130	5.0/6.0	F		IM	HEP	L	30/50	LPS	P	GR
WESTBROOK														
6. Safe Harbor Pilots Point-North ▫ WiFi	(860) 399-5128	100	9/	40/250	10.0/6.0	F	GD	IM	HEP	L70	30/50	CPS	P	GMR
7. Pier 76 Marina ▫	(860) 399-7122	25	/	80/256	6.0/3.0	F		IM	EP					R
8. Safe Harbor Pilots Point-East ▫ WiFi	(860) 399-7906	100	9/	/80	10.0/9.0	F	GD		HEP	L70	30/50	S	P	GMR
9. Harry's Marine Repair	(860) 399-6165	38	/	3/76	8.0/8.0	F	G	IM	EP	L10,C	30	S	P	GMR
10. Safe Harbor Pilots Point- South ▫ WiFi	(860) 399-7906	100	9/	40/540	10.0/9.0	F	GD	IMS	HEP	L70	30/50	CPS	P	3.7MR

▫ Internet Access WiFi Wireless Internet Access ◉onSpot Dockside WiFi Facility

See WaterwayGuide.com for current rates, fuel prices, website addresses, and other up-to-the-minute information. (Information in the table is provided by the facilities.)

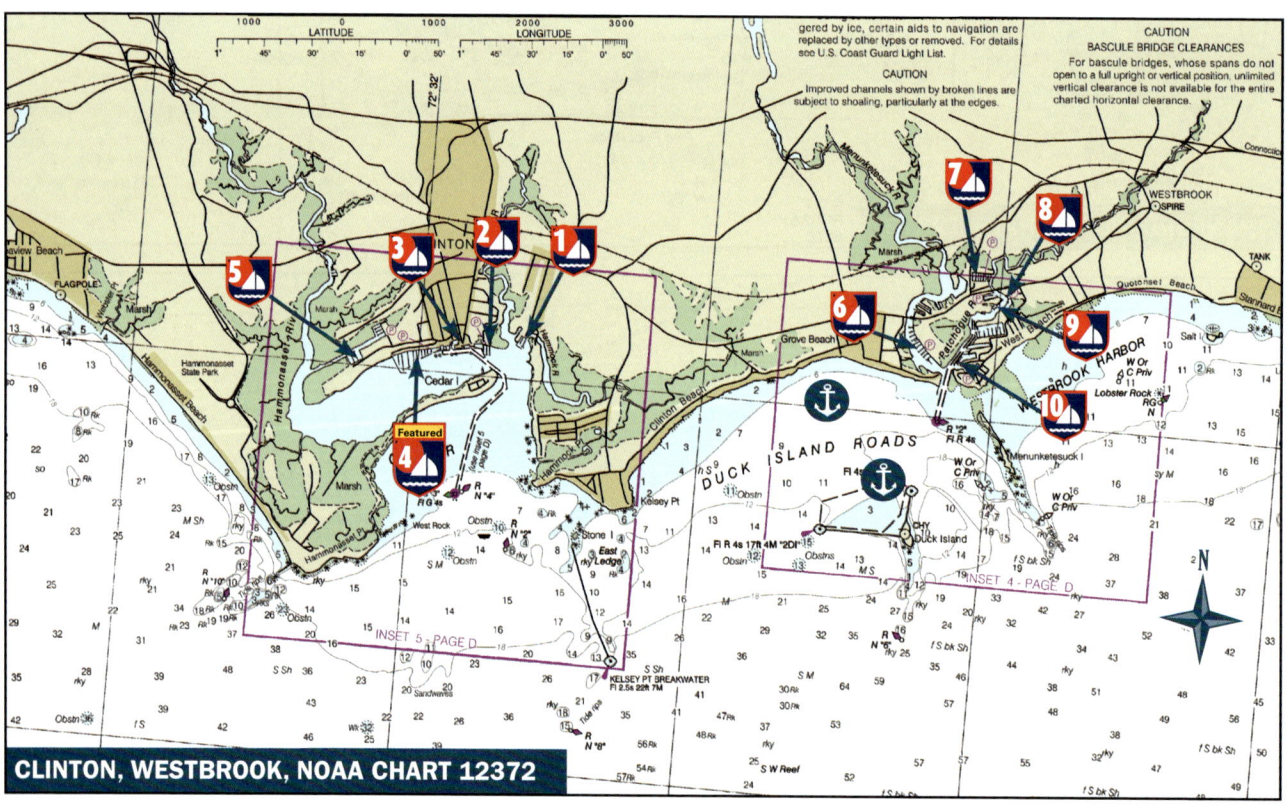

CLINTON, WESTBROOK, NOAA CHART 12372

see our interactive charts

MARINAS | SERVICES | ANCHORAGES | FREE DOCK | BRIDGES | LOCKS | NAV ALERTS | FUEL

waterwayguide.com

GOIN' ASHORE

CLINTON, CT

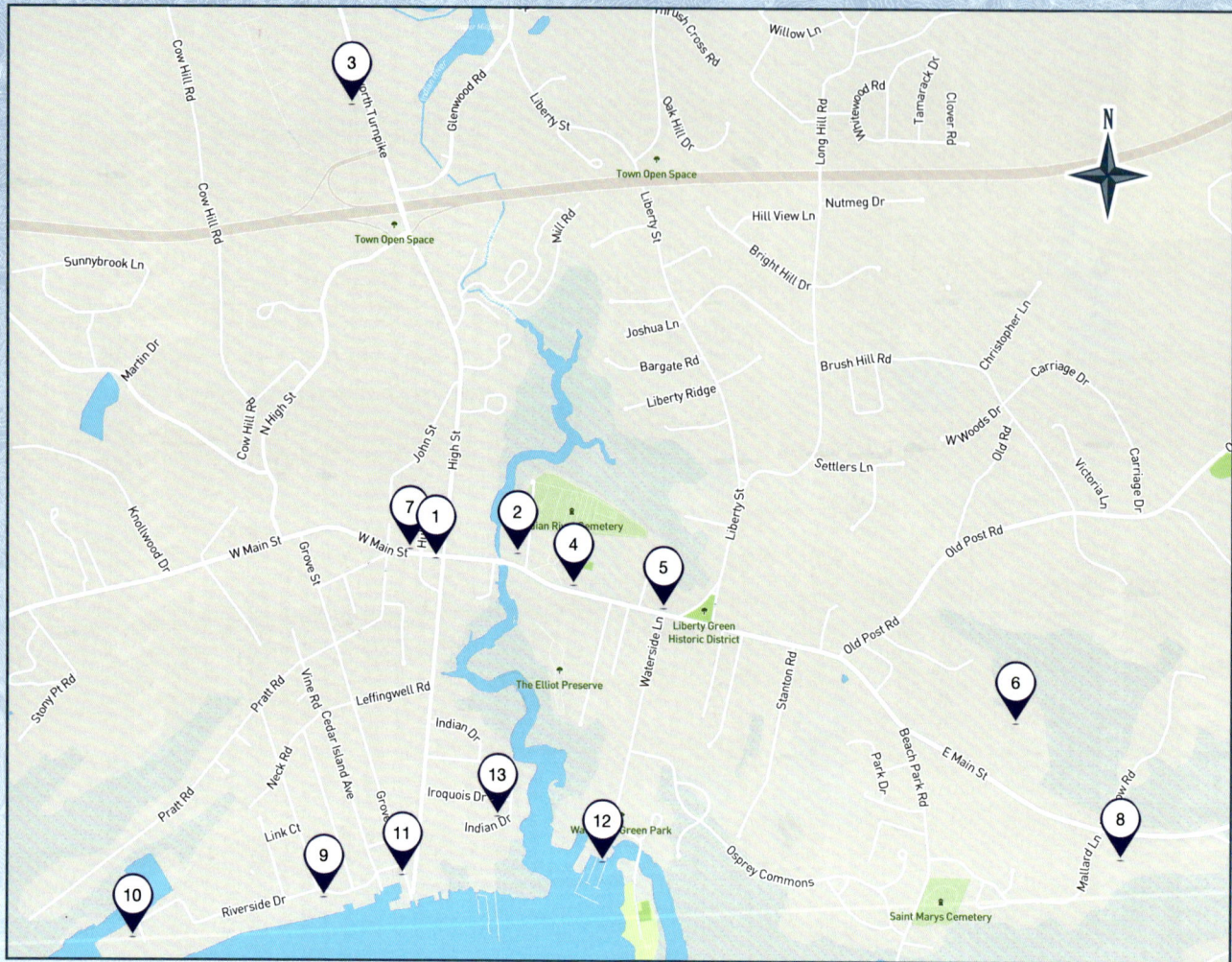

From the beginning, life in Clinton centered around the essentials of survival: fishing, farming and the all-important local industry of shipbuilding. Clinton became the home of the Collegiate School in 1701, with the Rev. Abraham Pierson selected to teach the first class of undergraduates. He continued teaching until his death in 1707, at which point students scattered for a period of time to other locations. Eventually, the Collegiate School was relocated to New Haven, where it became what it is today: Yale University.

SERVICES

1. Clinton Post Office
2 W. Main St. (860-669-4155)

2. Clinton Tourist Information Center
42-4 Church Rd.

3. Henry Carter Hull Library
10 Killingworth Turnpike (860-669-2342)

ATTRACTIONS

4. Adam Stanton House and General Store
Antique house museum with attached general store (63 E. Main St., 860-669-2132).

5. Elisha White House
Museum within an 18th-century house (also known as "Old Brick") containing portraits, period furniture and domestic tools. Open for tours by appointment at 103 E. Main St. (860-669-2148).

SHOPPING

6. Clinton Plaza Shopping Center
215 E. Main St. (860-669-2228)

7. CVS Pharmacy
Drug store chain at 17 W. Main St. (860-664-9337).

8. Shop Rite
Grocery store at 266 E. Main St. (860-669-0197)

MARINAS

Sachem Head is the harbor just west of Guilford. It is pretty, rock-lined, small and dominated by a friendly yacht club of the same name located immediately to the south upon entering. The approach is relatively straightforward. Using flashing red bell buoy "22" as a guide to avoid Goose Rocks Shoals, progress can be made in good depths to the 3-second flashing red light at the end of the harbor breakwater, which is maintained by Sachem Yacht Club from June to September.

Dockage/Moorings: About 1 mile inland of the West River entrance is Brown's Boat Yard, a full-service working yard offering marine services and all fuels. A transient slip (to 40 feet) can likely be arranged on the yard's floating docks along the river.

Transients may also find space at Guilford Yacht Club, a short distance farther upriver on the east side. The village of Guilford is about 0.5 mile away and a pleasant walk (or easily-obtained ride) from the clubhouse.

Guilford Town Marina has 122 slips and 14 moorings for transients to 38 feet. Transient slips are very limited. Boaters should call ahead to check availability.

Anchorage: Vessels can anchor just north of Sachem Head in Joshua Cove as long as care is taken to avoid unmarked ledges, Goose Rocks, and any weather out of the south. Here you will find 7- to 9-foot MLW depths in good holding with soft mud up to the area around Foskett Island.

In Sachem Head Harbor proper there is 8 to 10 feet MLW with good holding in mud with protection from all but the west. The downside is that most of the space is full of moorings. Note that there are no recommended anchorages between here and Duck Island Roads, east of Clinton Harbor.

Clinton, CT

Clinton Harbor is a good day's run for faster boats transiting to or from ports east such as Block Island, Newport or Mystic. It is also close to the Connecticut River for cruisers on their way to Essex and slower boats that make more stops. This harbor has just about everything: ease of entry, excellent protection, accommodating marinas, eye-popping views of sea and sand and good dining and provisioning. The marinas here are the way to go as there is no adequate anchorage.

NAVIGATION: Use NOAA Chart 12372. The approach is unencumbered south and west of Kelsey Point Breakwater except for a shoal marked by red nun buoy "2" at the shore end of the rock jetty. Moderate currents run in the channel here on both tides. The channel is maintained to 8.5 feet MLW and 100 feet wide; however, shoaling does occur around the entrance and the channel curves so it is very important to stay in the channel.

⚠ Clinton Harbor has a tight entrance at low tide when depths are lower than the charted 9-foot MLW depths. Dredging from 2019 may have improved the situation. We recommend waiting for outgoing traffic to exit and favor the Cedar Island (west) side upon entering. Do not, however, cut the point of Cedar Island close as there is shoaling immediately around the point.

Upon entry, round to the west around the moored boats and follow the channel along the northern shore to the marinas.

Dockage: Old Harbor Marina, Port Clinton Marina and Harborside Marina appear to the north on the channel immediately after leaving Cedar Island to the south. Here you will find boat slips, full service boat maintenance, boat repair and boat storage. Call ahead.

The 400-slip Cedar Island Marina operates a full-service, resort-type facility with all fuels and pump-out service (both on the fuel dock and with a boat). It is a deep-water facility with floating docks that can accommodate large yacht clubs and vessels up to 130 feet. They have numerous amenities including a large heated pool, fitness center and on-site restaurant. A private shuttle bus transports marina patrons to Clinton and the Clinton Crossing Outlets.

Westbrook, CT

What began as a farming community and later a shipbuilding center during the American Revolution is today a fun stopover port for cruising boaters on Long Island Sound. Good protection and a full range of amenities are available just to the north of Duck Island in the waters of the Menunketesuck and Patchogue Rivers at Westbrook. These rivers merge just before they exit into Duck Island Roads and Long Island Sound west of the Town of Westbrook. The channel is visible as you enter Duck Island Roads from the south or west.

Duck Island is a wildlife sanctuary and the summer home of gulls, cormorants, ducks, snowy egrets, glossy ibises, great blue herons and green and black-crowned night herons. If you are a nature lover, stay alert for this beautiful bird life but remember you are not allowed ashore.

NAVIGATION: Use NOAA Charts 12372 and 12374. Enter through a dredged channel beginning at flashing red buoy "2," which must be left to the east. The can and nun buoys marking this passage must be carefully observed or grounding is a near certainty. Note that green can buoy "5" is situated approximately 25 yards south of the navigable channel to the Menunketesuck River so a sharp westward turn at green can buoy "5" will provide unfortunate results. Wait and make the turn west just before green-red can "M."

In addition, the Menunketesuck River has shoaled along its western side. Deeper water is found along the dock faces located to the east. Depths here are charted at 5 feet MLW. The Patchogue River bears slightly to the east from the dredged channel and offers a 7-foot-deep MLW, 125-foot-wide alternative to the Menunketesuck. Both rivers are busy passageways but, unfortunately, anchoring is not permitted in either river.

Dockage: The eastern side of the Patchogue River is almost wholly taken over by Safe Harbor Pilots Point (South and East) Marina, while Safe Harbor Pilots Point-North dominates the east shore of the Menunketesuck River. Together, these represent one of the largest (870 total slips) and best-equipped facilities on Long Island Sound. They also have a well-stocked parts department, which will match marine discount store prices. Marine repairs are available at these and several other facilities on the Patchogue River.

Anchorage: The area outside of Westbrook in Duck Island Roads, just west of the breakwater and close in to Grove Beach, is a wake-active anchorage that is protected from the east through north. Distant breakwaters provide some protection from other directions. This is an extremely popular anchorage in summer months but landing on Duck Island is not allowed.

A better location is to tuck in behind the breakwaters extending north and west from Duck Island for 5 to 7 feet MLW with good holding in sand. This is exposed to the west but the distant Kelsey Point breakwater gives some relief from any stormy seas.

■ SIDE TRIP: CONNECTICUT RIVER

First-time visitors to the Connecticut River are surprised to discover the unspoiled natural beauty of the lower river, much of it seemingly unchanged since the days of the Colonial traders and boat builders. The vibrant entrance of the river quickly gives way to pastoral undulations, lined by quiet marshes and occasional intriguing coves and creeks.

The Connecticut River flows southward for 417 nm from New Hampshire near the Canadian border into Long Island Sound and is the largest and longest river in New England. The Mohegan Indians, who dominated the upper reaches around present-day Hartford, called it Quinetucket, meaning "beside the long, tidal river." It is the only major river in Connecticut with no city at its mouth due to depth restrictions from Long Sand Shoal and the entrance bar. The entire series of upriver valleys offered rich soil, easy transport and a central location for the Puritans who set up new towns under strict religious control while maintaining an ability to trade with others in both Massachusetts and what was then called New Holland, now called New York.

Today protected and secluded anchorages are accessible via a number of inlets and off-channel backwaters. Not far up the river are marinas, restaurants, anchorages and waterside activities, as well as the historic villages of Old Saybrook and Essex.

Long Sand Shoal

NAVIGATION: Use NOAA Chart 12372. Two miles southeast of Duck Island Roads is the beginning of Long Sand Shoal. Well-buoyed and charted, it extends about 6 miles east to the entrance of the Connecticut River. Boats heading for the Connecticut River from Duck Island Roads should go north of the shoal. For others, the choice depends on the current, which runs up to 2 knots and is generally stronger south of the shoal.

If you are riding a fair current heading along Long Island Sound, stay to the south and get the extra lift. If you are bucking the current, stay to the north where it is weaker and be sure to keep south of the charted rocks off Cornfield Point on the Connecticut coast. Be especially conscious of Hen and Chickens, which are rocks just west of Cornfield Point. While well-charted and well-marked, it is easy to go astray in this area in poor visibility....Many have.

Connecticut River Entry

NAVIGATION: Use NOAA Charts 12372, 12375 and 12377. Two handsome lighthouses distinguish the entry into the Connecticut River from Long Island Sound. Both are on the western breakwater (Saybrook side). The Saybrook Breakwater Light, also known as the Outer Light, was first lighted on June 15, 1886. It's about 3,000 feet out from Lynde Point Light. The Lynde Point Lighthouse, sometimes called the Inner Light, was built around 1800 and abuts a gabled house. When entering the harbor be sure to head for the southernmost Saybrook Light marking the entrance along the western breakwater.

Connecticut River Entrance

Connecticut River, CT

SAYBROOK POINT		Largest Vessel Accomodated	VHF Channel Monitored / Working	Approach / Dockside Depth (reported)	Transient Slips / Total Slips	Groceries, Ice, Marine Supplies, Snacks	Gas / Diesel	Floating Docks	Repairs: Hull, Engine, Propeller	Lift (tonnage), Crane, Rail	Min / Max Amps	Courtesy Car, Laundry, Pool, Showers	Pump-Out Station	Nearby: Grocery Store, Motel, Restaurant
				Dockage					Supplies			Services		
1. Harbor One Marina 🖥 📶	(860) 388-9208	150	9/	/86	20.0/8.0		GD		IM	HP	30/200+	LPS		GMR
2. Saybrook Point Resort & Marina 🖥 📶	(860) 395-3080	220	9/11	25/120	10.0/7.0	F	GD		IMS		30/100	CLPS	P	GMR
3. North Cove Yacht Club 📶	(860) 388-9132		78/	/4	7.0/7.0	F			IS			S		R

🖥 Internet Access   📶 Wireless Internet Access   onSpot Dockside WiFi Facility

See WaterwayGuide.com for current rates, fuel prices, website addresses, and other up-to-the-minute information. (Information in the table is provided by the facilities.)

SAYBROOK POINT, NOAA CHART 12372

 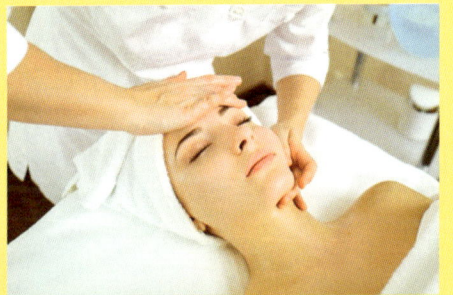 

GOIN' ASHORE

OLD SAYBROOK, CT

Old Saybrook has traditionally been important for coastal trade. The existing ship captains' homes in North Cove were adjacent to the warehouses and wharfs that handled the ships and their cargoes.

ATTRACTIONS

The village of Old Saybrook is one of the earliest settlements in Connecticut. Walking tours of the town are not to be missed or you can take advantage of the free-to-borrow local bicycles. The 17-acre Fort Saybrook Monument Park is adjacent to Saybrook Point Inn and Marina and houses the remains of the original Fort Saybrook, founded in 1635 (open daily).

Actress Katharine Hepburn maintained her main home in Fenwick for many years. The Katharine Hepburn Cultural Arts Center (The Kate) offers music events and is a museum (300 Main St., 860-510-0453). Call to schedule a tour.

The Shoreline East commuter railroad has a stop in Old Saybrook, making this a very desirable port for transients to meet guests. Once here, you can rent a car from Enterprise Car Rental (860-395-0758) or call Essex Taxi (860-767-7433). There is also a free shuttle to town.

In mid-August to mid-October, join dozens of boats for the swallow migration at Goose Island off the Old Lyme shore (opposite Old Saybrook). Every year, half a million of the small birds fly in from all directions and gather on the island at dusk. There they coalesce into a funnel and spiral down into the reeds, where they bed down for the night. It is one of Connecticut's most spectacular natural phenomena.

SHOPPING

The local Super Stop & Shop grocery at Old Saybrook Shopping Center (860-388-0850) is open for late-night provisioning. There is also a Walmart nearby. West Marine (1667 Boston Post Rd., 860-399-0080) has a large store located well to the west on Route 1 (transportation required). There's a local Farmers' Market (210 Main St., 860-833-0095) every Saturday and Wednesday (seasonal). Saybrook Hardware, 132 N. Main St. (860-388-3706), has nearly any (including marine) item you might need.

Saybrook Light

SAYBROOK POINT INN
& MARINA

Entry between the breakwaters is easy but if wind and tide are opposing, conditions can be a bit choppy. Allow for current set at all times and stay clear of off-channel shoals inside the eastern breakwater. As with any inlet keep a sharp lookout for other vessels. Although the inlet can be busy and may feel narrow after unfettered running in Long Island Sound, ruins of old shad fishing piers make the approach east of the eastern breakwater hazardous and best for local shoal-draft vessels.

The river is well marked, deep and easy to transit; however, currents periodically run swiftly near the mouth. Farther upstream, the channel narrows and demands a more vigilant watch. Large commercial vessels (including sightseeing boats) use the Connecticut River and need extra maneuvering room, particularly when currents are at their peak. (Contact these vessels on VHF Channel 13 to ascertain their intentions.) Keep in mind that vessels going with the current have the right-of-way unless other vessels are encumbered by draft or other circumstances. About 10 miles upstream near the town of Deep River the salt water of the estuary changes to fresh river water.

⚠️ Note: All No Wake Zones on the Connecticut River are strictly enforced by Connecticut Marine Police. Watch for the speed restriction buoys.

Saybrook Point & Old Saybrook, CT

Old Saybrook has traditionally been important for coastal trade. The existing ship captain homes in North Cove were adjacent to the warehouses and wharfs that handled the ships and their cargoes.

The village of Old Saybrook is one of the earliest settlements in Connecticut. Walking tours of the town are not to be missed or you can take advantage of the free-to-borrow local bicycles. The 17-acre Fort Saybrook Monument Park is adjacent to Saybrook Point Inn and Marina and houses the remains of the original Fort Saybrook, founded in 1635 (open daily).

NAVIGATION: Use NOAA Chart 12375. About 1 mile inside the entrance on the west bank of the Connecticut River is Saybrook Point. South Cove, south of Saybrook Point, is home to beautiful wildlife but is not navigable. North Cove, north of the point, is regularly dredged and has 10 feet MLW. The entrance is straightforward with a channel marked by a series of green can buoys. In poor

Connecticut River, CT

WG

OLD LYME AREA		Largest Vessel Accomodated	VHF Channel Monitored / Working	Dockage			Supplies		Services					
				Transient Slips / Total Slips	Approach / Dockside Depth (reported)	Floating Docks	Gas / Diesel	Groceries, Ice, Marine Supplies, Snacks	Repairs: Hull, Engine, Propeller	Lift (tonnage), Crane, Rail	Min / Max Amps	Courtesy Car, Laundry, Pool, Showers	Pump-Out Station	Nearby: Grocery Store, Motel, Restaurant
1. Ragged Rock Marina WiFi	(860) 388-1049	45	9/	2/243	5.0/6.0	F		IMS		L25	30	LS	P	MR
2. Between the Bridges South	(860) 388-3614	100	9/	/100	/6.0	F		I	HEP	L25	30/50	S		MR
3. Old Lyme Dock	**(860) 434-2267**	**200**	**9/**	**3/21**	**13.0/13.0**	**F**	**GD**	**I**			**30/100**	**S**		**GMR**
4. Between the Bridges North	(860) 388-1431	120	9/	6/300	14.0/7.0	F	GD	IMS	HEP	L60	30/50	PS		GMR
5. Oak Leaf Marina Inc.	(860) 388-9817	100	9/	10/100	24.0/18.0	F		IM	HEP	L35,C	30/100	LS		GMR
6. Old Lyme Marina Inc.	(860) 434-1272	60	9/	10/34	15.0/20.0			IM	HEP	L	50	S		GMR
7. Island Cove Marina, LLC WiFi	(860) 388-0029	45	/	/100	7.0/7.0	F		IM		L25	30	LS		MR
8. Safe Harbor Ferry Point WiFi	(860) 388-3260	65	9/	10/130	8.0/6.0	F		IM	HEP	L35,C	30/50	LPS		GMR
ESSEX														
9. Essex Yacht Club	(860) 767-8121	100	68/	4/43	12.0/9.0	F		I			30/50	S		GMR
10. Dauntless Marina WiFi	(860) 767-8267	125	68/	2/40	12.0/10.0	F	GD	IMS			30/100	LS	P	GMR
11. Essex Boat Works (EBW) WiFi	(860) 767-8276	80	9/68	5/20	10.0/10.0	F			HEP	L100,C	30/50			GM
12. Safe Harbor Dauntless Shipyard WiFi	(860) 767-0001	115	9/	15/110	10.0/12.0	F		IMS	HEP	L35,C	30/50	CLPS	P	GMR
13. Safe Harbor Essex Island WiFi	(860) 767-2483	200	9/68	60/125	9.0/5.0	F	GD	IS	EP	L30	30/100	LPS	P	GMR

⌨ Internet Access   WiFi Wireless Internet Access   onSpot Dockside WiFi Facility

See WaterwayGuide.com for current rates, fuel prices, website addresses, and other up-to-the-minute information. (Information in the table is provided by the facilities.)

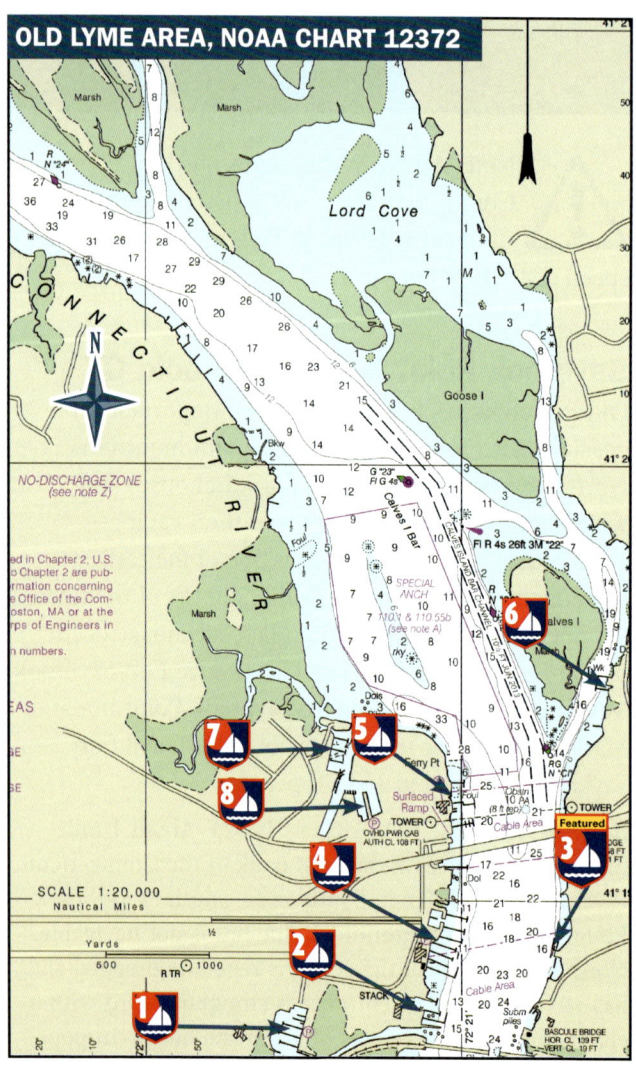

OLD LYME AREA, NOAA CHART 12372

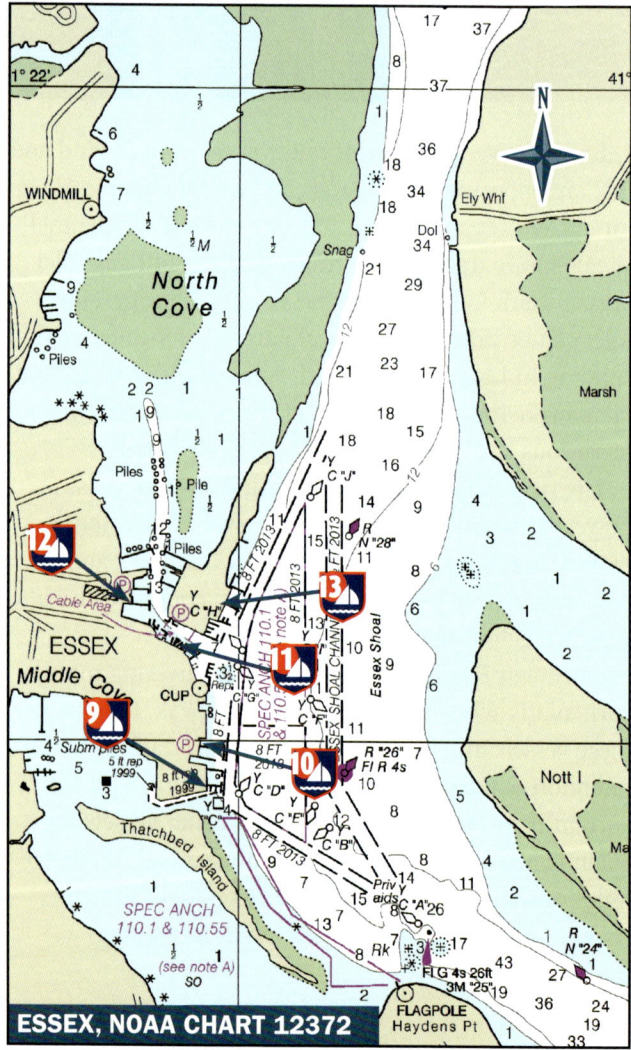

ESSEX, NOAA CHART 12372

visibility leave flashing red buoy "14" behind to the east and then look north and west for green can buoy "15" leading the way into the cove. Don't confuse these North and South coves with the ones of the same names at Essex, located farther north on the river.

Dockage/Moorings: Saybrook Point is home to Saybrook Point Inn & Marina with world-class amenities and high-quality service for yachts of all sizes (including mega-yachts). On site you will find friendly concierge service, dining and an award-winning hotel and spa. The marina has 120 slips on floating docks and a fixed fuel dock with room for 220-foot boats on the breakwater wall. They also offer 480-volt power.

North Cove is protected and attractive with an 11-foot MLW approach depth but it shallows to 6 feet MLW or less inside. More than 100 permanent moorings have been placed here, mostly in use by locals. Three complimentary transient moorings are provided by the town of Old Saybrook for up to 72 hours. You may tie up at the town dock for 20 minutes to top off water. Contact the Old Saybrook Harbormaster (860-662-0385) for availability of moorings and depth information. A transient may pick up any mooring with a yellow ribbon (indicating it's available) for up to 3 nights. It is always possible the owner will return and ask you to vacate. Nearby North Cove Yacht Club has a launch and amenities for transients for a daily fee.

Anchorage: In northerly or light winds, the area outside of Saybrook just west of the breakwater and close in to the beach is a popular swimming and picnicking anchorage for local daytrips. There are depths of 7 to 10 feet MLW with good holding in sand. This is protected from the east through north but any south or west swell will make for a lumpy night. Never anchor here in strong southerly or southwesterly winds. It becomes a dangerous lee shore. Heavy fog can develop quickly, even when the weather is clear in Old Saybrook.

A Coast Guard-designated Special Anchorage exists across from the entrance to North Cove north of Saybrook Point and east of the river channel. No anchor light is required but is highly recommended due to its open location.

GOIN' ASHORE

ESSEX, CT

The largest ship ever constructed in the Connecticut River Valley, Oliver Cromwell, established Essex Village as the place to build wooden sailing ships, and between the Revolutionary and Civil Wars over 600 vessels of many types were produced in Essex. For this reason, and others, British forces burned 27 vessels in Essex in 1814 and took or destroyed stored rigging materials and a lot of rum. Sailor's priorities haven't changed much over the years. Today Essex is a relatively small New England town with traditional Colonial and Federal style homes, sedate clapboard shops, galleries featuring local artists and several very good restaurants.

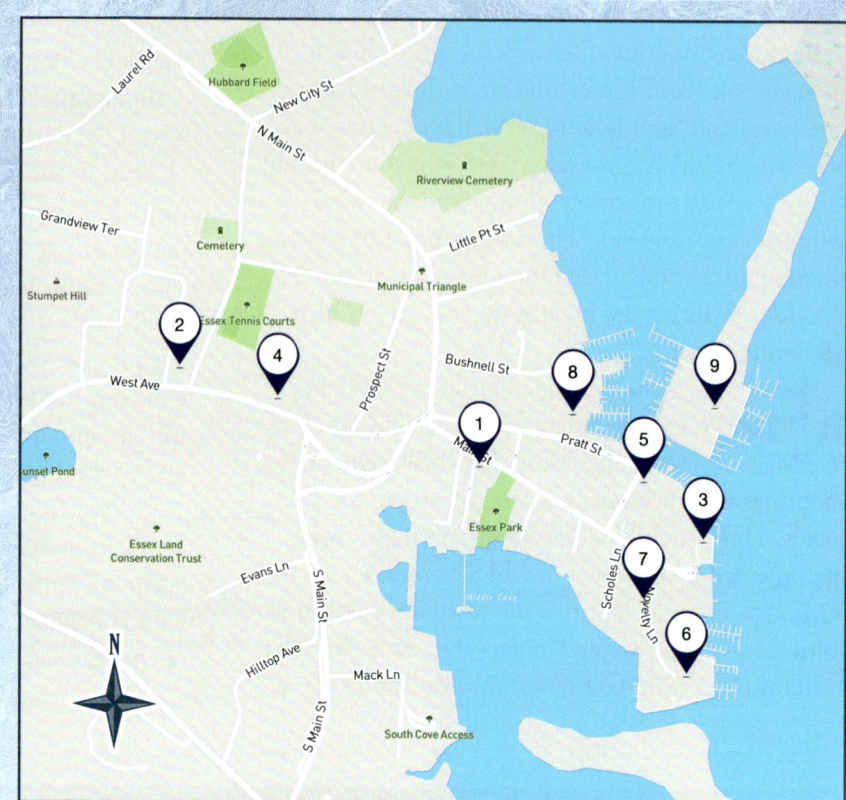

SERVICES

1. Essex Post Office
   12 Main St. (860-767-8476)

2. Essex Public Library
   33 West Ave. (860-767-1560)

ATTRACTIONS

3. Connecticut River Museum
   Located on the Steamboat Dock at the foot of Main Street (67 Main St., 860-767-8269) with a rich collection of memorabilia. Exhibits rotate on the first-floor gallery and permanent collections are stored upstairs. A replica of Bushnell's Turtle, America's first submersible vessel, is on display.

4. Pratt House Museum
   Mid-17th century house museum and one of Connecticut's oldest surviving buildings at 19 West Ave. (860-767-0681).

MARINAS

5. Essex Boat Works
   9 Ferry St. (860-767-8276)

6. Essex Yacht Club
   13 Novelty Ln. (860-767-8121)

7. Safe Harbor Dauntless
   9 Novelty Ln. (860-767-8267)

8. Safe Harbor Dauntless Shipyard
   37 Pratt St. (860-767-0001)

9. Safe Harbor Essex Island
   11 Ferry St. (860-767-2483)

Ferry Point & Old Lyme, CT

Huntley Street, which leads directly to the shopping center on U.S. Route 1, offers a grocery store, several banks, a liquor store and a Post Office. The large, well-stocked Christiansen Hardware (860-434-7053) is at 54 Halls Road should you need them.

NAVIGATION: Use NOAA Charts 12372 and 12375. Almost 2 miles north of Saybrook Point, the **Old Saybrook–Old Lyme Bridge** (19-foot closed vertical clearance, monitors VHF Channel 13) is usually open but it carries the busy Amtrak line and other train traffic and closes whenever a train approaches. On the VHF radio they will only respond to "Old Lyme Draw." The bridgetenders communicate with their counterparts in Niantic (and the controllers in Boston) to keep the bridge open as long as possible but they will not delay a closing for an approaching boat. A countdown board that indicates the length of time until an opening cannot be trusted so be wary of tight timing on a down-current approach. **The Raymond E. Baldwin Bridge** is just north with an 81-foot fixed vertical clearance.

Dockage: Marinas and boatyards are located on both sides of the Connecticut River. All of these have some reserved slips for transients and all fuels and services and repairs are available. The full-service Old Lyme Dock has the most frontage of any other local fuel dock and offers a bulk fuel discount. They also have a well-stocked Ship Store.

Beyond the high-rise bridge are more marine facilities with slips and repairs. The northern route to Old Lyme Marina, around flashing red "22," is rocky at the entrance and shallower than the NOAA chart indicates, masking obstacles lurking in the bottom mud. Marina personnel discourage even shallow-draft runabouts from this area. Enter from the south. All of the facilities here are very busy, and reservations are advisable.

Anchorage: A Coast Guard-designated anchorage is located upstream of the Raymond E. Baldwin Bridge between Ferry Point and Calves Island. Vessels less than 65 feet in length are not required to exhibit anchor lights when at anchor here but it is nevertheless highly recommended due to the amount of traffic.

Essex, CT

Essex, a favorite port of many cruisers, is situated 2.5 miles above the Connecticut River bridges. This town is compact and its attractions are easily accessible by foot from the marinas and town dock at the western edge of the Connecticut River. First settled in 1648, Essex rapidly established itself as a Colonial boatbuilding center. Over the centuries hundreds of boats have been built here including the first American Man-o-War ship. Even though the lofting sheds are gone, enough flavor of the town's maritime past remains to make it a magnet for visitors touring by land and water.

NAVIGATION: Use NOAA Chart 12375. North of Old Saybrook the well-marked main Connecticut River channel skirts the western shore of Calves Island and its marshy bar and then winds gently for several miles to Essex. There are no markers for slightly more than 2 miles but the river is wide and deep. Be sure to honor red nun buoy "24" to avoid the shoal water off Nott Island.

Dockage/Moorings: On the Connecticut River proper Safe Harbor Dauntless Marina has easy-access slips and more than 50 moorings, which will are usually open to incoming transients. Services and the facilities at Safe Harbor Dauntless Shipyard and Marina (separate from the river-side Dauntless) are available to marina customers and are a short walk away.

Somewhat better protection from the Connecticut River wash is found at the entrance to North Cove (not to be confused with the North Cove at Old Saybrook). Safe Harbor Essex Island and Safe Harbor Dauntless both offer deep-water floating slips. The Dauntless Shipyard has an extensive parts department and offers major repair services.

Anchorage: Anchorage is not a good prospect in Essex itself due to the strong reversing tides and the crowding of the mooring fields outside the channel. Many boaters do drop the hook across from Essex on either side of Nott Island. Currents are quite strong here but the holding is excellent in 8 to 12 feet MLW with a firm mud bottom. The east side of Nott Island is more protected but smaller and shallower. Obtaining local knowledge of the mud flats is a good idea.

Hamburg Cove, CT

Hamburg Cove, a favorite spot of cruising mariners, is about 1 mile upriver from Essex on the eastern side. It is landlocked and almost round offering total protection and quiet, natural surroundings during the week. Hamburg Cove is often crowded on the weekends and frequently hot during the summer months. The cove is deep almost to its green banks and on the fresher side of upriver brackish.

Connecticut
River, CT

HAMBURG		Dockage					Supplies		Services					
1. Hamburg Cove Yacht Club-PRIVATE	(860) 434-0215		/	/	/	F		I						
2. Cove Landing Marine (WiFi)	(860) 434-5240	80	/	/60	6.0/8.5	F		I	HEP	L35	30/50	LS	P	G

Column headers (diagonal): Largest Vessel Accomodated · VHF Channel Monitored / Working · Transient Slips / Total Slips · Approach / Dockside Depth (reported) · Floating Docks · Gas / Diesel · Groceries, Ice, Marine Supplies, Snacks · Repairs: Hull, Engine, Propeller · Lift (tonnage) Crane, Rail · Min / Max Amps · Courtesy Car, Laundry, Pool, Showers · Pump-Out Station · Nearby: Grocery Store Motel Restaurant

☐ Internet Access (WiFi) Wireless Internet Access ⊕onSpot Dockside WiFi Facility

See WaterwayGuide.com for current rates, fuel prices, website addresses, and other up-to-the-minute information. (Information in the table is provided by the facilities.)

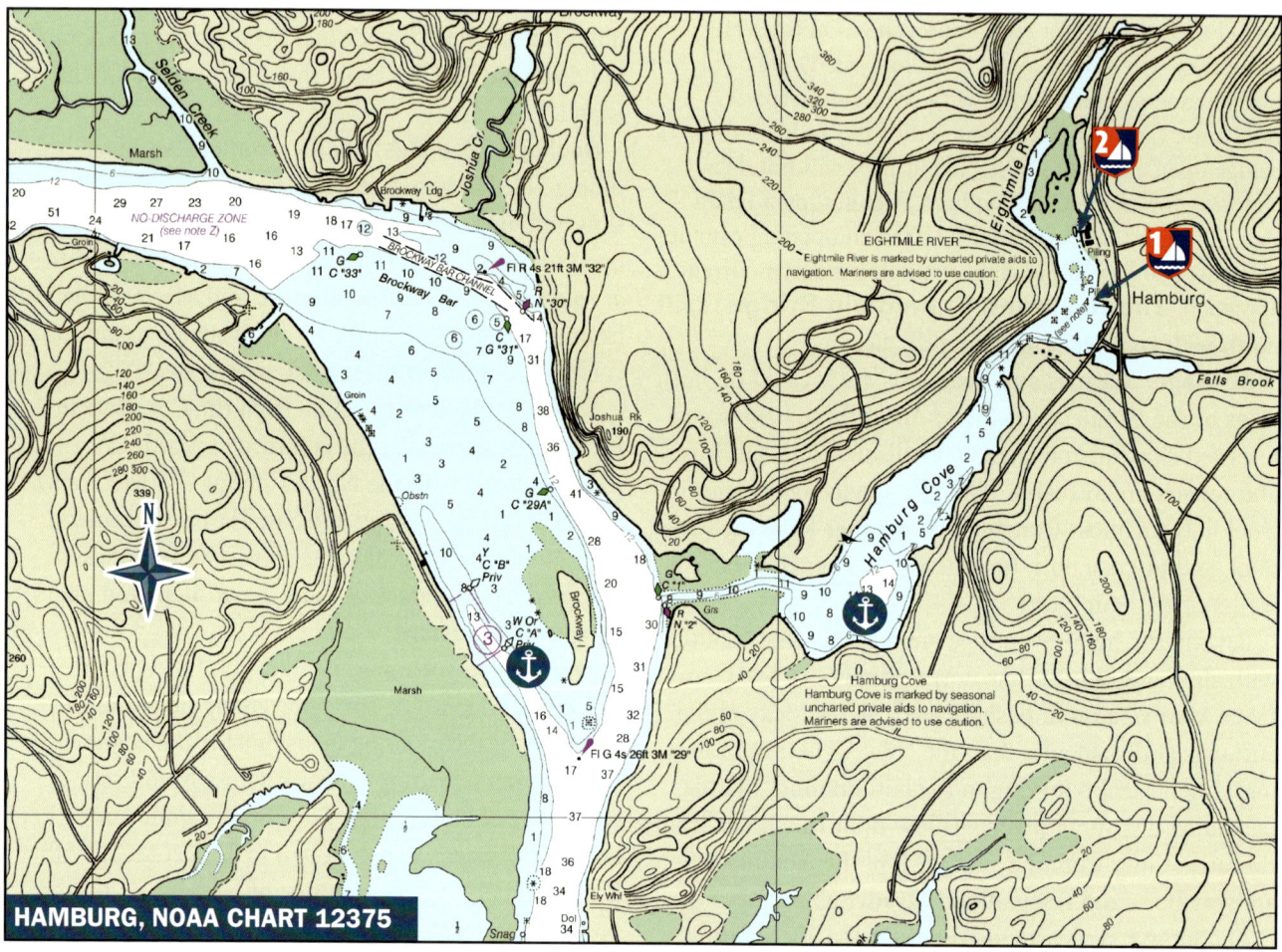

HAMBURG, NOAA CHART 12375

NAVIGATION: Use NOAA Chart 12372 or 12375. Some navigation markers have been discontinued but may still show on older charts do refer to the Waterway Guide Explorer (www.waterwayguide.com) and NOAA online charts for the most up-to-date information. The narrow entrance east of Brockway Island (with 8-foot MLW depths) is marked with privately maintained buoys that must be followed exactly. Do not cut any of the buoys. Vessels as large as 50 feet can be seen far up the creek in the town of Hamburg but the channel is narrow and challenging with little turning room or dock space in the inner harbor.

Dockage/Moorings: Cove Landing Marina may have a few rental moorings available amongst the private moorings. The marina generally specializes in the restoration and overhaul of wooden boats but virtually any repair can be arranged here. It is decades-long tradition for transients to pick up any appropriate private mooring for a night or two. Should the owner appear, they will not be upset but simply politely ask you to move off. This is more likely to occur on busy summer weekends.

Anchorage: Hamburg Cove is filled with moorings and there is no room to anchor properly. If you can find a small spot to tuck in, you will have all-around protection in 9 to 10 feet MLW with good holding in mud. A dinghy dock is available at Cove Landing Marina. More room to anchor is west of Brockway Island in 13 feet MLW with good holding in sand and mud. Enter and exit only from the south as the north side is shoal. This is slightly exposed to the north and southeast.

Deep River to East Haddam, CT

Between Essex and Haddam, the river traveler can spend happy days seeing lovely towns, marshlands and side creeks. Deep River is home to Pratt Cove and Selden Neck State Park, which both offer an opportunity for viewing wildlife. If you have a kayak this is the perfect place to use it or you can take your dinghy across to the surrounding marshlands and wonderful creeks. Please be a gentle presence in these preserved areas.

In Chester's intimate and walkable village center you will find an adequate selection of shops, galleries and locally made goods. Above Chester is East Haddam, where the riverside Goodspeed Opera House (www.goodspeed.org) performs lively, full-production Broadway musicals year-round. Check on schedules and restrictions. For more information about East Haddam, visit easthaddam.org.

NAVIGATION: Use NOAA Chart 12372 or 12375.The Connecticut River gives the boater a chance to practice river navigation. Watch the charts as you go and remember that a flowing river is no place to cut corners. A river will deposit silt as the water slows on the inside of a curve and it will eat deeper channels on the outside.

At Deep River tidal waters from Long Island Sound cease to influence the freshwater drainage from the north. Here the channel briefly divides around Eustasia Island. There are good depths to either side, although the main channel is marked to the east. If you venture into the western channel, keep an eye on your sonar readings in the area of Chester Creek Bar. The best depths are found near the eastern shore of the river.

Three miles above Chester, the village of East Haddam is unmistakably marked by the more than 100-year-old **Route 82 Bridge** (locally known as the **East Haddam Bridge**) with 22-foot closed vertical clearance. The lift bridge opens on signal open on signal except from 15 May to 31 October, between 9:00 a.m. and 9:00 p.m., when the draw need only open for recreational vessels on the hour and half-hour. Contact the draw tender on VHF Channel 13.

Dockage/Moorings: For convenient dockage or ready access to the special anchorage at the north end of Chester Creek Bar, take the fork west of Eustasia Island (leave flashing green "35" on the rock pile just south of the island on the east). The floating docks of Safe Harbor Deep River visibly line the banks to the west. Transient dock space is never a problem in this protected and tranquil setting, and from here, it is a relatively easy dinghy ride to Selden Neck State Park (accessible only by water).

Chester Creek, immediately to the north (also on the west side of the river), is home to several smaller facilities with dockage for vessels to 50 feet and gas and diesel fuel. About 0.5 mile above the Chester-Hadley ferry landing (beneath Fort Hill), the venerable Chisholm Marina is on a deep channel cut into the west bank.

At East Haddam, Goodspeed Opera House maintains a 120-foot deepwater dock (no other facilities) just south of the bridge for its waterborne visitors. A town dock south of the Goodspeed will accommodate two boats. North of the Route 82 (East Haddam) Bridge on the west side of the river, Andrews Marina at Harpers Landing almost always has slips and moorings available for transients. Farther north the full-service Midway Marina in Haddam offers slips, repairs and a yacht brokerage.

Anchorage: Beyond Brockway Island is the unmarked entrance to primitive Selden Creek. It is an excellent gunkhole where American boats hid from British raiders during the Revolutionary War. The narrow creek, with a marsh-bordered entrance and no aids to navigation, lies amid cliffs and high hills. Large boats have little room here. Depths, however, run from 9 to 13 feet MLW in the lower reaches and 3 to 4 feet MLW in the upper. The creek runs into Selden Cove with a shallow channel back to the Connecticut River. A cruise up Selden Creek is marvelous in a dinghy or small boat. Watch out for tree stumps as you go.

Another anchoring option is north of Eustasia Island on the west side of the river between Deep River and Chester. While somewhat exposed to the north, holding is good in mud in 15-foot MLW depths.

In East Haddam you can anchor south of Goodspeed Landing in 17 feet MLW. There is plenty of room, good holding in mud and protection from all but the north and south. Be aware, however, that the Goodspeed Airport runway is nearby and give it some serious thought when anchoring.

Connecticut River, CT

		Largest Vessel Accomodated	VHF Channel Monitored / Working	Approach / Dockside Depth (reported)	Transient Slips / Total Slips	Floating Docks	Gas / Diesel	Groceries, Ice, Marine Supplies, Snacks	Repairs: Hull, Engine, Propeller	Lift (tonnage), Crane, Rail	Min / Max Amps	Courtesy Car, Laundry, Pool, Showers	Pump-Out Station	Nearby: Grocery Store, Motel, Restaurant
				Dockage				**Supplies**			**Services**			
DEEP RIVER AREA														
1. Safe Harbor Deep River (WiFi)	(860) 526-5560	65	9/	5/283	15.0/5.0	F	GD	IM	HEP	L25	30/50	PS	P	GMR
2. Chester Point Marina ▢ WiFi	(860) 526-1661	60	9/9	5/135	6.0/6.0	F		IMS	HEP	L70,C	30/50	LPS		3R
3. Hays Haven Marina Inc. ▢ WiFi	(860) 526-9366	46	/	4/220	6.0/6.0	F	GD	IMS	HEP	L30	30	S	P	GR
4. Chrisholm Marina ▢ WiFi	(860) 526-5147	45	9/	4/137	8.0/6.0	F	G	IMS	HEP	L35,C	30/50	S	P	GMR
5. Middlesex Yacht Club - PRIVATE	(860) 526-5634	50	79/	/	10.0/9.0	F		I			30	PS		R
EAST HADDAM														
6. Andrews Marina ▢ WiFi	(860) 345-2286	45	68/	/76	6.0/6.0	F		GI	E		30/50	S	P	GMR
7. Midway Marina in Haddam WiFi	(860) 345-4330	60	13/	5/65	12.0/7.0	F			HEP	L12,C	30	S	P	3R
COBALT														
8. St. Clements Castle & Marina ▢ WiFi	(860) 342-0593	160	/	/22	9.0/10.0	F		M	HP		30/100	S		MR
PORTLAND AREA														
9. Portland Boat Works	(860) 342-1085	68	/	/40	10.0/10.0	F	G	IM	HEP	L60	30			GMR
10. Yankee Boatyard and Marina, Inc. ▢ WiFi	(860) 342-4735	50	68/	6/80	20.0/10.0	F	GD	MS	HEP	L20,C	50	S	P	GMR
11. Portland Riverside Marina	(860) 342-1911	50	/	10/74	20.0/15.0	F	GD	IMS	HP	L35,C	30	S		GMR
GILDERSLEEVE ISLAND														
12. Petzold's Marine Center	(860) 342-1196	63	9/	6/40	15.0/10.0	F	G	M	HEP	L55	30			
WETHERSFIELD														
13. Wethersfield Cove Yacht Club	(860) 563-8780	30	/	4/28	4.0/15.0	F	G	M			30	S		GR
14. Wethersfield Cove Marina	(860) 721-2890	34	/	7/7	15.0/								P	GR

▢ Internet Access WiFi Wireless Internet Access ⌐onSpot Dockside WiFi Facility

See WaterwayGuide.com for current rates, fuel prices, website addresses, and other up-to-the-minute information. (Information in the table is provided by the facilities.)

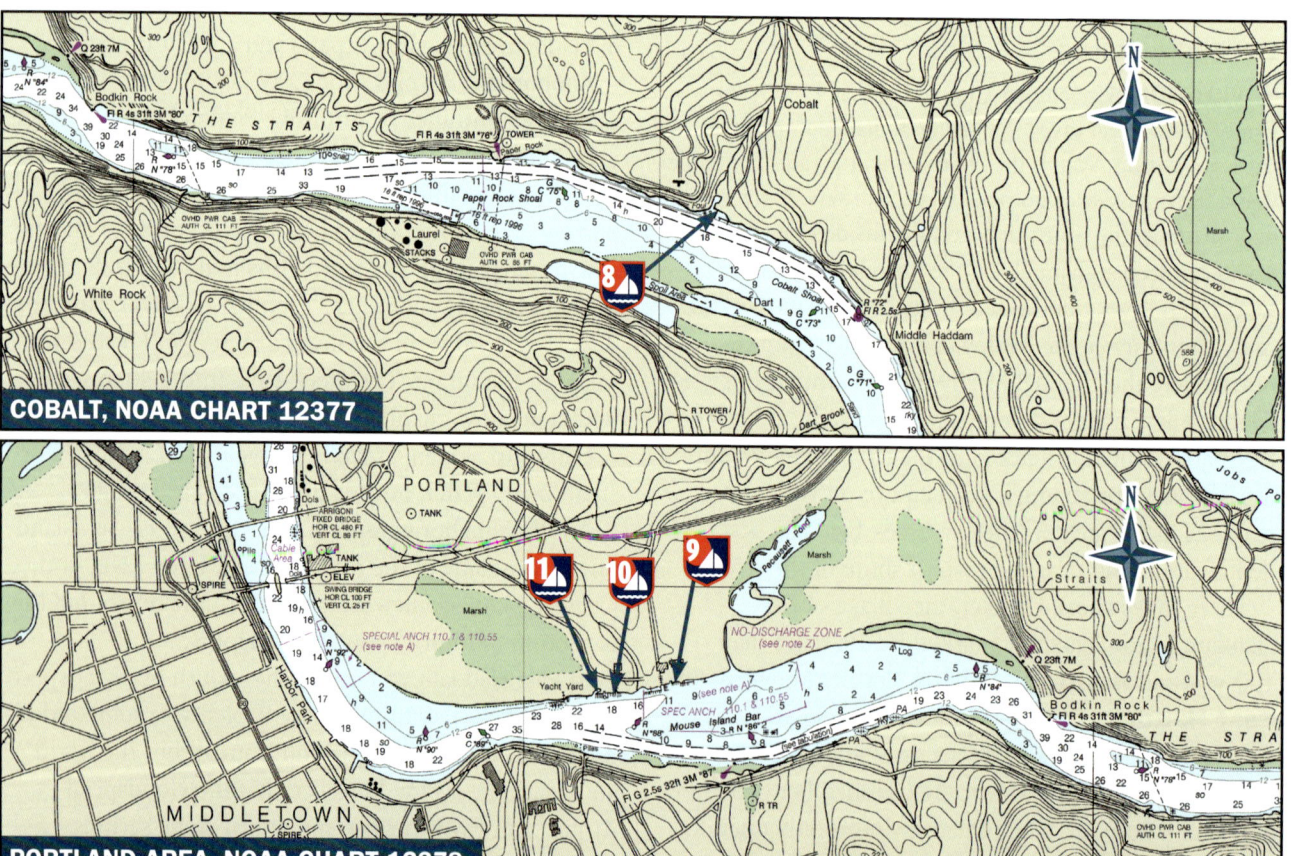

COBALT, NOAA CHART 12377

PORTLAND AREA, NOAA CHART 12378

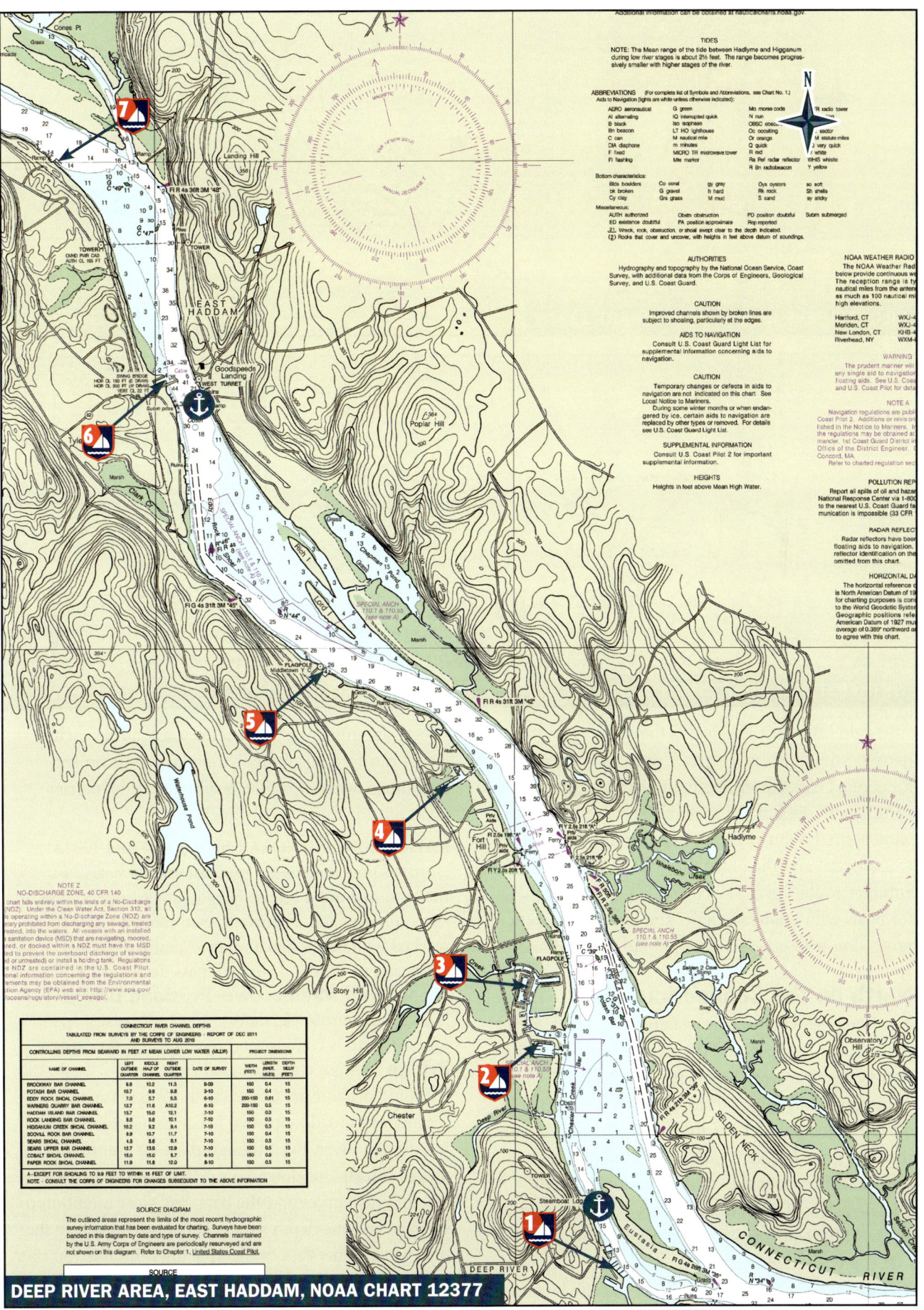

DEEP RIVER AREA, EAST HADDAM, NOAA CHART 12377

GILDERSLEEVE ISLAND, NOAA CHART 12378

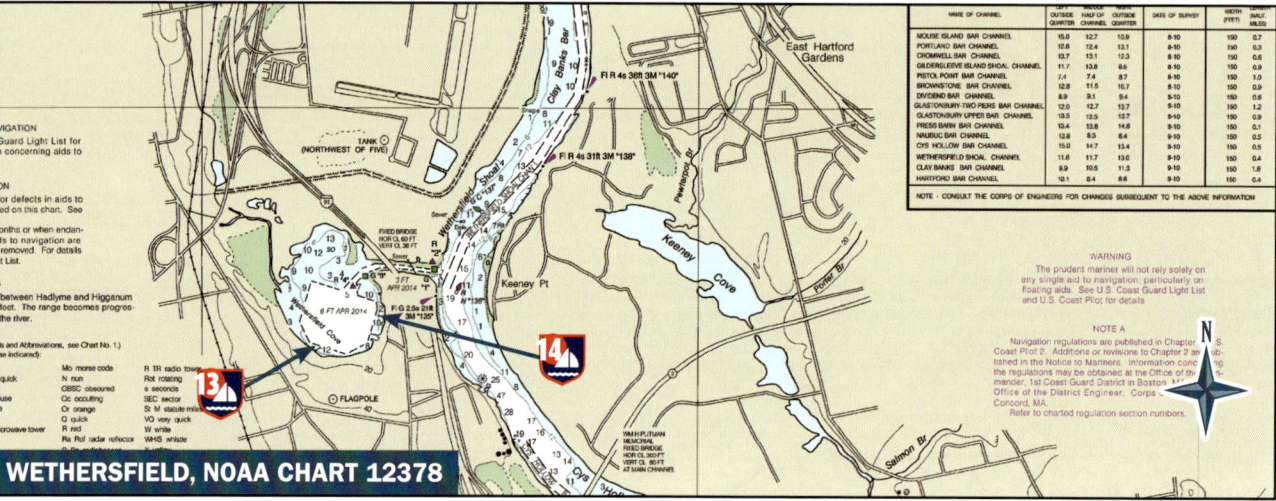

NAME OF CHANNEL	LEFT OUTSIDE QUARTER	MIDDLE HALF OF CHANNEL	RIGHT OUTSIDE QUARTER	DATE OF SURVEY	WIDTH (FEET)	NAUT. MILES
MOUSE ISLAND BAR CHANNEL	15.0	12.7	10.9	8-10	150	0.7
PORTLAND BAR CHANNEL	12.6	12.4	13.1	8-10	150	0.3
CROMWELL BAR CHANNEL	13.7	13.1	12.3	8-10	150	0.8
GILDERSLEEVE ISLAND SHOAL CHANNEL	11.7	13.8	8.6	8-10	150	0.9
PISTOL POINT BAR CHANNEL	7.4	7.4	8.7	8-10	150	1.0
BROWNSTONE BAR CHANNEL	12.8	11.5	16.7	8-10	150	0.9
DIVIDEND BAR CHANNEL	8.9	9.1	9.4	8-10	150	0.6
GLASTONBURY TWO PIERS BAR CHANNEL	12.6	12.7	13.7	8-10	150	1.2
GLASTONBURY UPPER BAR CHANNEL	13.5	13.5	13.7	8-10	150	0.9
PRESS BARN BAR CHANNEL	13.4	13.8	14.8	9-10	150	0.1
NAUBUC BAR CHANNEL	13.8	8.3	8.4	9-10	150	0.5
CYS HOLLOW BAR CHANNEL	15.0	14.7	13.4	9-10	150	0.5
WETHERSFIELD SHOAL CHANNEL	11.6	11.7	13.6	9-10	150	0.4
CLAY BANKS BAR CHANNEL	9.9	10.5	11.3	9-10	150	1.8
HARTFORD BAR CHANNEL	10.1	8.4	8.6	9-10	150	0.4

NOTE - CONSULT THE CORPS OF ENGINEERS FOR CHANGES SUBSEQUENT TO THE ABOVE INFORMATION

WETHERSFIELD, NOAA CHART 12378

Just up from East Haddam is the entrance to the narrow Salmon River. The river carries good depths for about 1 mile up into Salmon Cove and then shoals considerably. Be wary of snags and give Cones Point a wide berth. Follow the deep water on the west side of Grass Island and then turn east and then north to the entrance to the cove. The cove is a quiet overnight spot for boats with moderate drafts and offers all-around protection with good holding in mud.

North on the Connecticut River

The home of Wesleyan University is in Middletown, past Middle Haddam and through the scenic Straits. Across the river from Middletown is Portland, once an important quarrying and shipbuilding port. The old quarries, flooded and inactive now, produced much of the sandstone for New York City's famous brownstone houses. Dinosaur tracks were often found on the quarried slabs. Dinosaur State Park is farther north in Rocky Hill, requiring inland transportation.

If you wish to visit Hartford, it is best to dock at Wethersfield Cove and proceed into the city by taxi.

(There are numerous taxi services; ask at the yacht club.) Hartford has virtually no place to tie up and anchorage, while possible, is difficult in the narrow areas outside the main channel.

NAVIGATION: Use NOAA Charts 12377 and 12378. North of East Haddam, a good number of boats kiss the bottom around Mouse Island Bar east of Portland, especially heading downriver, even though it is well-marked with buoys and a range. Attentiveness is necessary. At Portland you will pass under two bridges: The **Conrail Middletown–Portland Bridge** (25-foot closed vertical clearance), which is usually open unless a train is coming, and the high-rise **Arrigoni Bridge** (89-foot closed vertical clearance).

From Portland the Connecticut River starts to meander in broad loops that are reminiscent of the Mississippi River. Even though there are quite a few ranges (mostly for downriver craft) to guide boaters through the curves and the bars, pay close attention to steerage and the depth sounder. The stretch above the bridges to Gildersleeves Island is uneventful if you don't try to pass to the west of the island, where there is a submerged dike.

Rocky Hill to the north is a quiet village with a town park with a boat launch, fishing pier and floating docks. Pull into the courtesy dock, have a hot dog and watch the Rocky Hill Ferry, the oldest continuously operating river-crossing ferry in the country. As at all ferry crossing, proceed with care.

Just past Rocky Hill, the Glastonbury Two Piers Bar Channel has an upriver range (most are downriver) marked by fixed red over flashing red (2.5 seconds). The shallows extend in a curve within the buoys so if you were to try a straight shot from inner buoy to inner buoy (especially between green cans "123" and "121"), you might go aground.

Stay to the southwestern third of the river for about 0.25 nm on either side of the **William H. Putman Memorial Bridge** (80-foot fixed vertical clearance). The only hazard left, midway between the bridge and Wethersfield Cove, is an unmarked rock off the west bank, almost blocked by a charted but unmarked point.

Above Hartford, the Connecticut River is unimproved, navigable only for boats with less than 3-foot drafts and 8-foot vertical clearances. The channel shifts constantly, with bars and other obstructions. Local knowledge is necessary.

Dockage/Moorings: St. Clements Castle & Marina is in Middle Haddam (on the north shore of the river, east of the Straits) and has transient space on floating docks for vessels to 160 feet. There are several marinas in a row on the east bank south of Portland, east of Middletown, with slips and repairs. Fuel can be found here as well.

South of Hartford, the hospitable Wethersfield Cove Yacht Club may have dock space available. The municipal Wethersfield Cove Marina is in the same basin with moorings, a dinghy dock and slips for vessels up to 34 feet in length. The channel from the river is privately marked. Enter slowly. There is 6 feet MLW in the basin but shoaling at the entrance. Pump-out service is available at the dock on weekends from 6:00 a.m. to 8:00 p m. The facility is open from Memorial Day through Columbus Day.

Anchorage: You can anchor in Wethersfield Cove in 6 feet MLW with good holding and all-around protection but you must be able to get under the 38-foot fixed vertical clearance **I-91 Bridge** to access the cove.

■ NIANTIC, CT TO WATCH HILL, RI

Niantic Area, CT

Niantic is a harbor of refuge and a commodious layover for cruisers in search of rest and provisions. Ample dock space and quiet anchorages with good holding are within walking/cycling distance of boat repairs, marine services, provisioning, restaurants, a classic movie theatre and one of the best book collections in all of New England. The Book Barn has an ever-changing collection of over 500,000 books spread out between four locations (www.bookbarnniantic.com).

The history of this area dates back to the 1600s when the Dutch traders discovered this area and began to expand beyond the Hudson River. The Thomas Lee House and the Smith-Harris House are two historic sites in Niantic Village that tell much of the history of this area.

NAVIGATION: Use NOAA Charts 12372 and 13211. Niantic Bay, 6 nm east of the Connecticut River, is big and open with Black Point on the western headland and a prominent power plant on the eastern shore, noted on the chart simply as "STACK 389 ft." The only hazard along the way is the well-marked and well-charted Hatchett Reef, and the only shelter between the Connecticut River and Niantic Bay is in the Giants Neck area in the lee of Long Rock and Griswold Island. This area should be entered with caution, the rocks are charted but numerous.

Two closely spaced bridges cross the curving entrance channel of the Niantic River. With little maneuvering room in the narrow (50-foot-wide) dogleg channel, and tidal currents approaching 4 knots on either tide, full attention is recommended on this passage.

The first bridge, **Amtrak (Niantic River) Railroad Bridge (**16-foot closed vertical clearance), opens on signal as long as oncoming trains are not within range. It is best to contact the bridgetender on VHF Channel 13 before you approach. The second is the **SR 156 Bridge** (32-foot closed vertical clearance), which opens on request except between 7:00 a.m. and 8:00 a.m., and between 4:00 p.m. and 5:00 p.m., Monday through Friday (except federal holidays). From November 1 through April 31, from 8:00 p.m. to 4:00 a.m., the draw opens on signal only if at least

Niantic Bay, CT

NIANTIC		VHF Channel Monitored / Working	Largest Vessel Accomodated	Dockage					Supplies			Services					
				Approach / Dockside Depth (reported)	Transient Slips / Total Slips	Floating Docks	Gas / Diesel		Groceries, Ice, Marine Supplies, Snacks	Repairs: Hull, Engine, Propeller	Lift (tonnage), Crane, Rail	Courtesy Car, Laundry, Pool, Showers	Min / Max Amps	Pump-Out Station	Nearby: Grocery Store, Motel, Restaurant		
1. Boats Incorporated ⌨ WiFi	(860) 739-6251	36	71/	10/186	8.0/6.0	F		G	IM	HEP	L8	30	PS	P	GMR
2. Harbor Hill Marina ⌨ WiFi	(860) 739-0331	40	/	2/70	8.0/6.0	F						30	S	P	GMR
3. Port Niantic Inc WiFi	(860) 739-2155	58	13/	/81	8.0/6.0	F			IM	HEP	L30	30/50	S	P	GR
4. Three Belles Marina WiFi	(860) 739-6264	50	9/	2/150	6.0/7.0	F		GD	IMS	HEP	L	30/50	PS	P	GMR

⌨ Internet Access WiFi Wireless Internet Access onSpot Dockside WiFi Facility

See WaterwayGuide.com for current rates, fuel prices, website addresses, and other up-to-the-minute information. (Information in the table is provided by the facilities.)

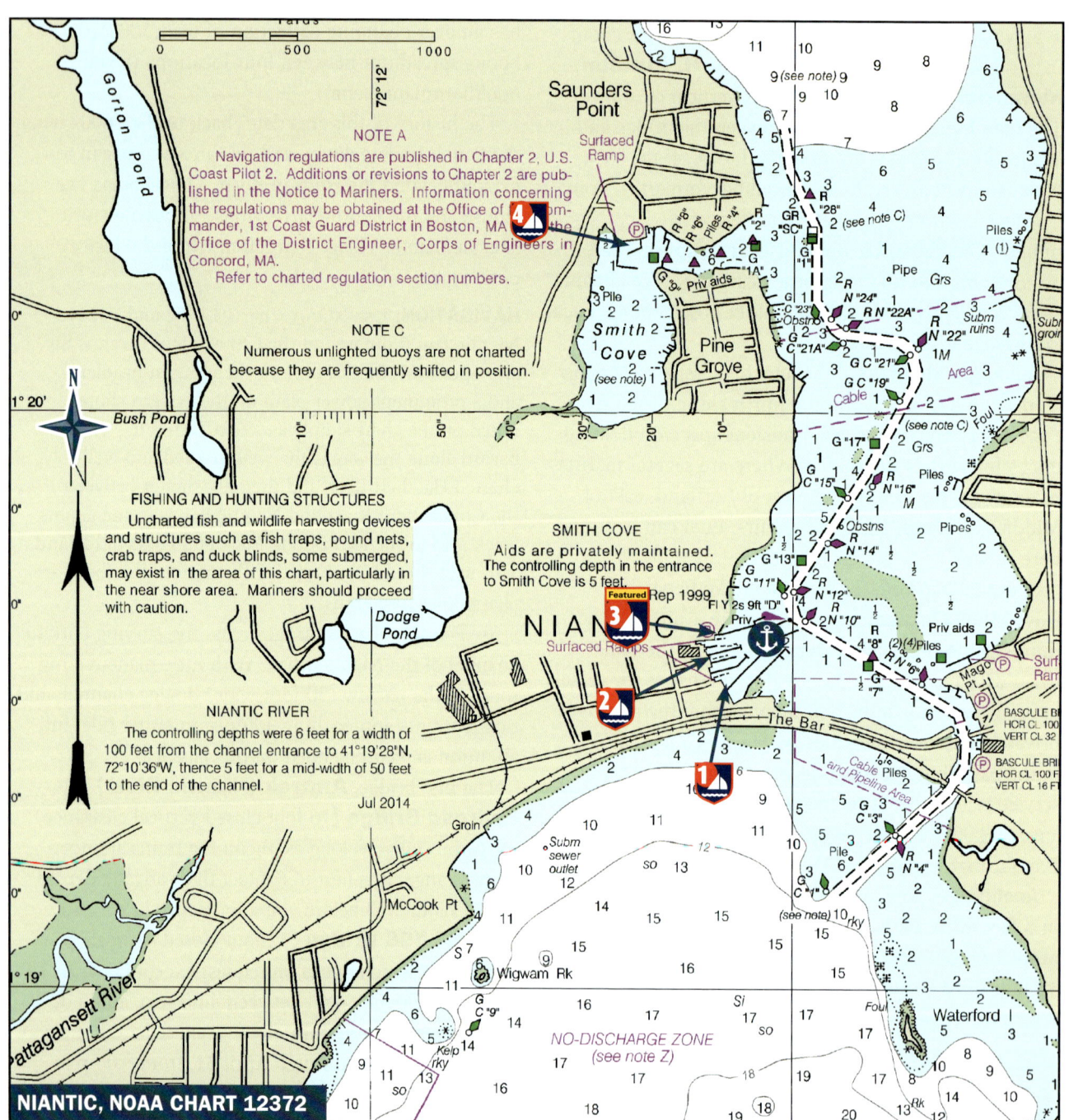

a 6-hour notice is given. For boats with high vertical clearance requirements approach only when your signal is acknowledged. It is best to coordinate your passage with the tenders of both bridges via VHF Channel 13. It is advisable to make this passage close to slack water on either tide.

The beauty of the Niantic River and the amenities available make this transit well worth the modest effort required. Current charts refer to all Niantic River markers as "private aids" because they are frequently moved. The channel is only 4 to 5 feet MLW with "knee-deep" water just outside the channel. Past the bridges the channel is well marked and easy to negotiate but the numerical sequence of the buoys and daybeacons must be strictly followed.

At the end of the first dogleg above the bridges it is possible for boats drawing 6 feet or less to approach the dock T-ends and fuel docks of the marinas on the western shore. Even this may be challenging, however, due to substantial shoals just beyond the dredged areas surrounding the docks. The center of the village of Niantic is a 2-block walk from the western shore waterfront.

Dockage: At the first channel bend back to north inside the river bridges, Boats Incorporated may have room on the seaward docks for transients. Harbor Hill Marina can also accommodate transients (to 40 feet) on floating docks with full amenities, as can Port Niantic Inc., immediately to the north. Port Niantic can accommodate vessels to 58 feet in deep water slips and provides a full array of marine parts, repairs and installations.

Upriver, the well-marked, deep channel winds past the community of Pine Grove to the entrance of pretty and protected Smith Cove and Three Belles Marina. To enter Smith Cove turn left into the marked channel at green and red daybeacon "SC." The town-dredged, 5-foot-MLW channel (with 2.5-foot tidal range) is reasonably well marked by daybeacons and naked poles for 0.2 mile. The village is about 1.5-miles away but a ride to town can usually be arranged.

Anchorage: In settled weather you may be able to anchor in 10-feet MLW on the western shore of Niantic Bay at Crescent Beach. This is open and exposed to the south through east and residual swell can make it uncomfortable. This makes a better day anchorage than an overnight one. There is a dinghy

Niantic Wetlands

dock in Niantic or you can call for a launch ride for the price of a tip to the driver.

Upriver, the Niantic River widens, becomes deeper and provides some lovely anchorages with good holding and attractive surroundings. Sandy Point and Keeny Cove both have 9- to 11-foot MLW depths with good holding in mud. The scenery and quiet atmosphere are reminiscent more of a New England freshwater lake than those of a surfside recreational community.

Do not be tempted by Smith Cove behind Three Belles Marina, which is too shallow for all but the most shoal-draft vessels (2 feet MLW).

New London, CT

The seaport of New London was established in 1646. The town has a long maritime history as a ship building center and very profitable trade center. New London is located on the western side of the Thames River, with its smaller sister port of Groton on the eastern side. Having emerged as a thriving whaling port, rivaling even New Bedford, MA, during the 19th century, New London is the largest and busiest commercial port in eastern Connecticut. It is also an important harbor of refuge, home to major U.S. Navy and Coast Guard facilities, and, in recent times, a leading recreational yachting center with excellent marinas, reliable restaurants and adequate provisioning.

If time permits, stroll the Heritage Trail of 30 bronze plaques set in the downtown district sidewalks or visit the U.S. Custom House & Maritime Museum to learn about the New London whaling history. Whale Row features restored 19th-century houses that are open to the public. The renovated 1888-vintage train station is not only interesting to look at; it also offers convenient Amtrak rail transportation to Boston and New York City.

Beyond the **Thames River Bridges**, the U.S. Coast Guard Academy (31 Mohegan Ave., 860-444-8444) dominates the bluff along the west side of the river, with its Georgian brick buildings and white clock tower. The Academy Visitors Center is open from 9:00 a.m. to 4:30 p.m. daily. The public can attend movies, tours, sporting events and the occasional band concert, but dockage is not available for visitors. If you are lucky, the 295-foot fully rigged *Barque Eagle*, America's maritime ambassador, will be in port.

NAVIGATION: Use NOAA Charts 12372, 13212 and 13213. When departing Niantic Bay eastbound mariners should give a wide berth to flashing red bell buoy "6" to avoid the rocky shoals in the vicinity of White and Little Rocks. South of Bartlett Reef (clearly marked by a 35-foot-high lattice tower with two international orange diamonds on its face) strong currents funneling through The Race (farther south) begin to make themselves evident on either tide.

Currents south of Bartlett Reef are the strongest in Long Island Sound and the waters are also the deepest (more than 300 feet in spots). Opposing winds and current can create sloppy conditions here. In a southwest breeze an eastbound cruiser with local knowledge can stay in the lee of Two Tree Island and Bartlett Reef by running the Two Tree Island Channel to Goshen Point. Reefs and rocks are adequately marked but be aware of your location at all times because visibility can drop suddenly on the sound and currents can set you far from your intended course. If entering New London Harbor leave green can buoys "3," "5" and "7" to port.

⚠ Be on the lookout for frequent ferry crossings in this area, as it bisects a major route between Orient Point and New London. Be especially cautious in reduced visibility.

The New London/Groton Harbor is located a short distance up the busy, heavily traveled Thames River. Except for water traffic, the harbor entrance is uncomplicated and well buoyed. Two distinctive lighthouses flank the entrance channel. New London Harbor Lighthouse is a classic white tower off Osprey Beach, while New London Ledge Light is a two-story, red brick building that stands on a harbor rock. Most recreational boating facilities are on the New London side of the Thames River, south of the bridges in Green Harbor and Shaw Cove.

Entry from the south is clearly marked. Pick up flashing green "1" and flashing red "2" and then follow the channel between the lighthouses into the Thames River. If entering from the east through Pine Island Channel, be aware of the many rocks in this area. While the channel is marked don't stray to port on entry. Gain familiarity with the area before using this short cut.

⚠ In addition to the Navy's rigorous monitoring of security zones around its ships and facilities, the U.S. Coast Guard is strict in enforcing a 6-mph speed limit within 200 feet of all docks and piers in the harbor. Photography of facilities and/or vessels is prohibited. Vessels underway, however, may be photographed.

The Amtrak Railroad Bridge (29-foot closed vertical clearance) and the **Gold Star Memorial (I-95/US 1) Bridges** (135-foot fixed vertical clearance) cross the Thames River a little more than 3 miles north of the harbor lights. Boats requiring a clearance of over 29 feet should alert the railroad bridgetender on VHF Channel 13. Keep in mind that railroad bridges are locked down well in advance of oncoming trains on this coastal Amtrak route. Similarly, be sure to consider the maneuverability and security requirements of large commercial and military vessels in this active port and shipping lane. The draw will open on signal to 75 feet

THAMESPORT MARINA

New London

river wakes. A better choice is outside of Shaw Cove in 15-foot MLW depths. This is closer to Waterfront Park and the shore access there.

Groton, CT

Revolutionary War buffs may want to visit Fort Griswold, the site of the 1781 massacre of American defenders by British troops led by Benedict Arnold. Today the site includes ramparts, battlements and buildings dating from the Revolution as well as a 134-foot granite monument to the defenders you can climb. Visit the Monument House Museum located in the state park for the full story of the battle. Admission is free. The Fort is located south of the bridges in Groton.

A Navy Yard was established on the Thames River in 1868 and officially commissioned as a submarine base during World War I. Groton became known as the Submarine Capital of the World when the Electric Boat division of General Dynamics delivered 74 diesel submarines to the Navy in World War II. This was followed in 1954 with the launch of the *U.S.S. Nautilus*, the world's first nuclear-powered submarine, now permanently berthed at Goss Cove as part of the U.S. Navy Submarine Force Museum. Located adjacent to the base, the museum is open during the summer and admission is free (800-343-0079).

About 1 mile north of the Navy Base, just below Gales Ferry, are the Yale (blue) and Harvard (crimson) boathouses and training quarters for the annual spring rowing regatta, the nation's oldest intercollegiate sporting event. During Race Week, New London is like Louisville during Kentucky Derby week. Boats come in from all over the northeast and anyone expecting accommodations should make reservations well in advance. Special trains are scheduled and the shores are full of spectators and the river full of boats.

Norwich, about 11 miles upriver from New London, is at the head of the Thames River. The trip upriver is pleasant, river traffic is light and the channel is well

above mean high water for all vessel traffic unless a full bridge opening to 135.3 feet above mean high water is requested.

Dockage/Moorings: Excellent yachting facilities, nautical services and supplies are located in two adjacent bights on the New London side of the Thames River. Green Harbor, approximately 1 nm inside the harbor entrance, features two marinas offering transient slips and services. Thamesport can accommodate vessels to 200 feet and has a full-service fuel dock. It is about 3 miles to downtown New London from Green's Harbor.

Shaw Cove, just 1 nm north of Greens Harbor, is totally protected and offers dockage at the full-service Crocker's Boatyard Inc., where cruisers will find deep-water slips on floating docks (for vessels up to 170 feet) and substantial repair capabilities. A short walk up Bank St. from Shaw Cove will put you in the heart of New London shopping where there are many interesting galleries, boutiques and food markets. **The Shaw's Cove Bridge** (vertical clearance: 6 feet MLW) opens on request (VHF Channel 13) to give access to the cove if there is no nearby train traffic but it is as busy as all the other Amtrak bridges in the area.

A short distance farther north, the New London Waterfront Park has a 0.5-mile promenade plus five piers with transient slips on floating docks.

Anchorage:Anchoring is possible in Greens Harbor in 6 to 10 feet MLW, although it is mostly filled with moorings and is exposed to wind and waves as well as

New London Harbor, CT

NEW LONDON		Largest Vessel Accomodated	VHF Channel Monitored / Working	Approach / Dockside Depth (reported)	Transient Slips / Total Slips	Floating Docks	Groceries Ice, Marine Supplies, Snacks	Gas / Diesel	Repairs: Hull, Engine Propeller	Lift (tonnage), Crane, Rail	Courtesy Car, Laundry, Pool, Showers	Min / Max Amps	Pump-Out Station	Nearby: Grocery Store, Motel, Restaurant
				Dockage			**Supplies**				**Services**			
1. Thamesport Marina 💻 WiFi	(860) 442-1151	200	9/68	50/150	20.0/14.0	F	GD	IS			30/100	S	P	3R
2. Burr's Marina WiFi	(860) 443-8457	120	/	25/150	12.0/9.0		GD	IMS	HEP	L20	30/50	LPS	P	GR
3. Crocker's Boatyard Inc. 💻 WiFi	(860) 443-6304	170	9/13	25/230	12.0/12.0	F	GD	IMS	HEP	L75,C	30/50	LPS	P	GMR
4. New London Waterfront Park	(860) 443-3786	295	9/	35/35	15.0/15.0	F		I				LS		GMR
GROTON														
5. Thames Harbor Inn and Marina	(860) 445-8111	55	/	12/20	50.0/50.0	F		GI				LS		GMR
6. Pine Island Marina WiFi	(860) 445-9729	42	68/	/110	7.0/5.0	F		IM	HEP	L35,C	30	LS		GMR
7. Shennecossett Yacht Club 💻 WiFi	(860) 445-8211	50	68/68	3/240	7.0/6.0	F	GD	I		L35	30/50	S	P	GM
GALES FERRY														
8. Gales Ferry Marina	(860) 464-2146	38	12/	5/85	6.0/5.0	F	GD	IM		L35	30	LS		GMR
NORWICH														
9. The Marina at American Wharf 💻 WiFi	(860) 886-6363	200	68/68	75/175	30.0/10.0	F		I	E		30/100	LPS	P	GMR

💻 Internet Access WiFi Wireless Internet Access onSpot Dockside WiFi Facility

See WaterwayGuide.com for current rates, fuel prices, website addresses, and other up-to-the-minute information. (Information in the table is provided by the facilities.)

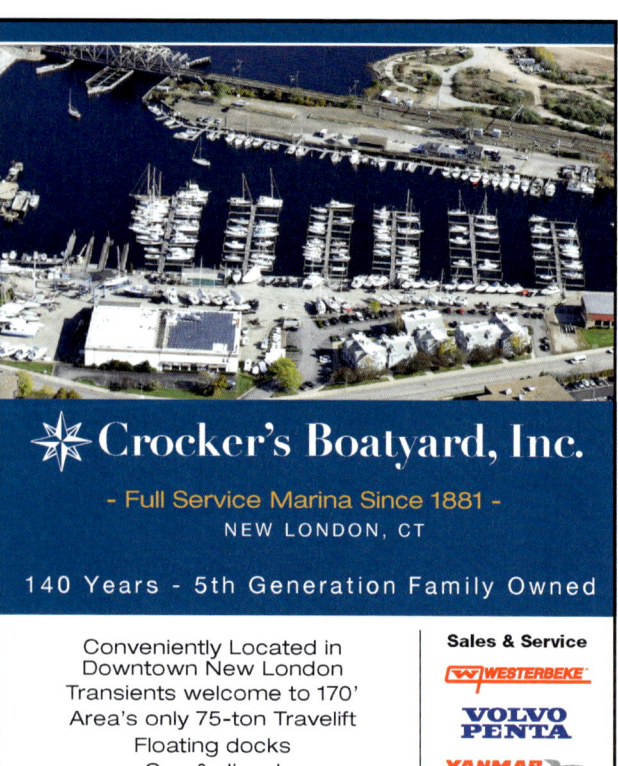

Crocker's Boatyard, Inc.

- Full Service Marina Since 1881 -
NEW LONDON, CT

140 Years - 5th Generation Family Owned

Conveniently Located in
Downtown New London
Transients welcome to 170'
Area's only 75-ton Travelift
Floating docks
Gas & diesel
Pool, laundry, free WiFi

860-443-6304   VHF CH.9
www.crockersboatyardinc.com

Sales & Service
WESTERBEKE
VOLVO PENTA
YANMAR marine
MERCURY MerCruiser
EVINRUDE

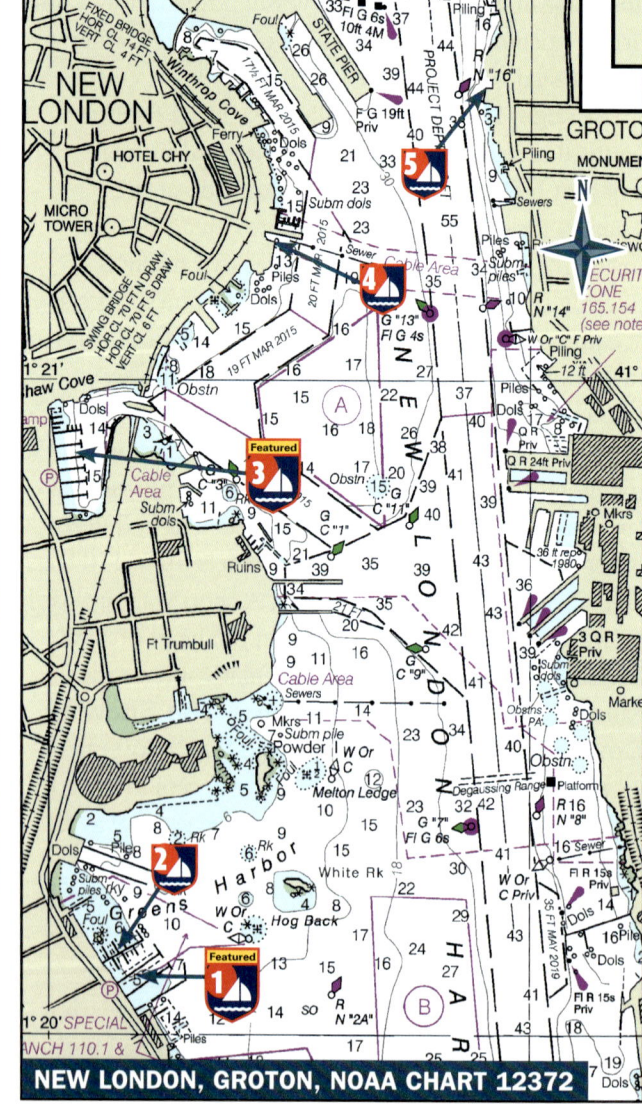

NEW LONDON, GROTON, NOAA CHART 12372

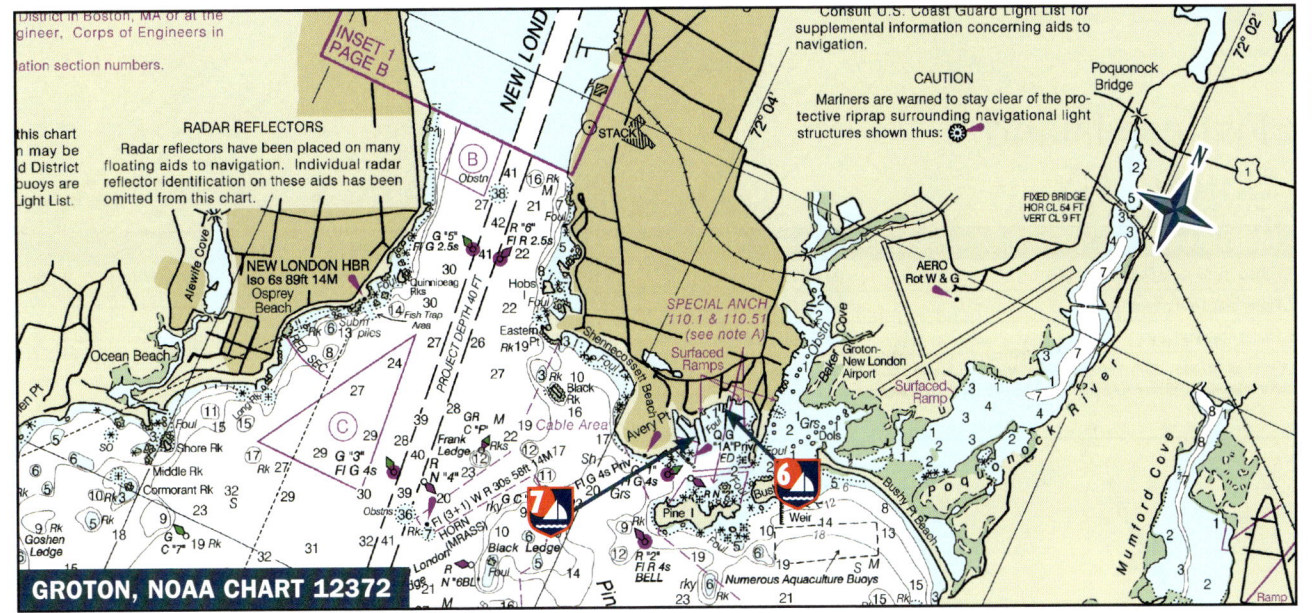

GROTON, NOAA CHART 12372

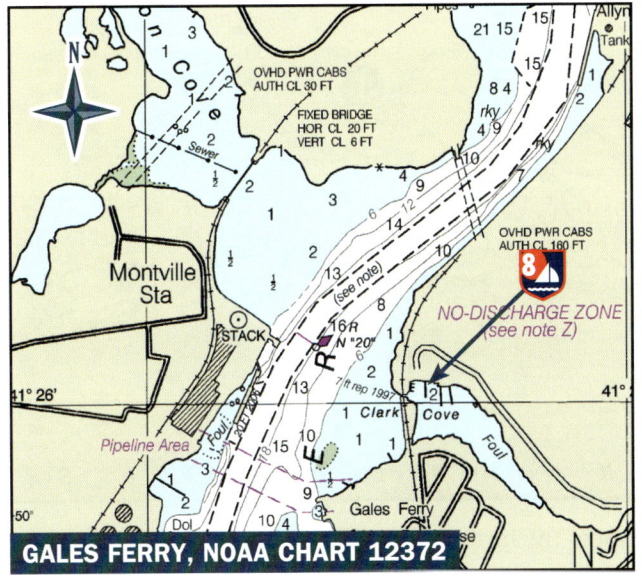

GALES FERRY, NOAA CHART 12372

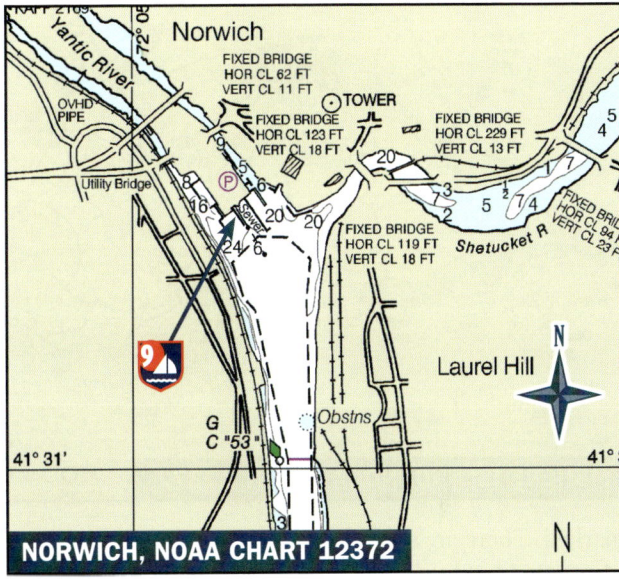

NORWICH, NOAA CHART 12372

Groton

Fishers Island Sound, NY

W G

FISHERS ISLAND		Largest Vessel Accommodated	VHF Channel Monitored / Working	Transient Slips / Total Slips	Approach / Dockside Depth (reported)	Floating Docks	Groceries, Ice, Marine Supplies, Snacks	Gas / Diesel	Repairs: Hull, Engine, Propeller	Lift (tonnage), Crane, Rail	Courtesy Car, Laundry, Pool, Showers	Min / Max Amps	Pump-Out Station	Nearby: Grocery Store, Motel, Restaurant
		Dockage					**Supplies**		**Services**					
1. Fishers Island Yacht Club Marina [WiFi]	(631) 788-7036	150	10/10	15/50	9.0/8.0		I					30/50	S	GR
2. Fisher Island Marina and Gas	(631) 788-7311		/	/	/		I	GD	HEP			30		
3. Pirates Cove Marine Inc.	(631) 788-7528	45	9/	/15	10.0/6.0	F	M		HEP	L20,C		30		3R

☐ Internet Access   [WiFi] Wireless Internet Access   ⊙onSpot Dockside WiFi Facility

See WaterwayGuide.com for current rates, fuel prices, website addresses, and other up-to-the-minute information. (Information in the table is provided by the facilities.)

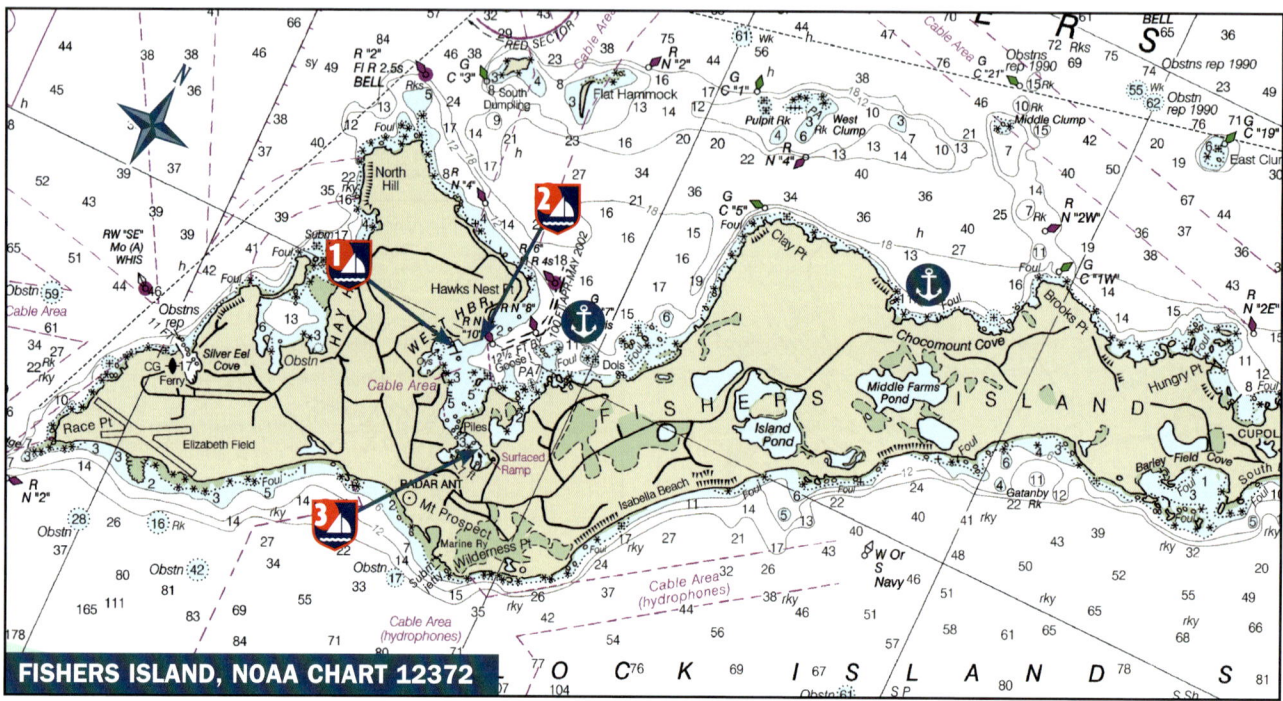

FISHERS ISLAND, NOAA CHART 12372

marked. There are several dikes above Easter Point, most notably Mohegan Dike near the **Mohegan Pequot Bridge**, which are submerged at half tide.

Dockage: Dockage in Groton can be found south of the bridges (Thames Harbor Inn and Marina) and about 4.5 miles north of the bridges at Gales Ferry Marina. Farther north is The Marina at American Wharf, located at the head of the Thames River in Norwich. Back to the south at the mouth of the river are more facilities with slips, fuel and repairs.

Side Trip: Fishers Island

Nine-mile-long Fishers Island is only 2 nm off the southeastern coast of Connecticut but belongs to New York. It is very private and the entire eastern end of the island is gated. At the western end of the island, however, there is a small village with a museum (Henry L. Ferguson Museum, 631-788-7239) that

traces the history of Fishers Island from the time of the American Indians to present day. The findings from a number of archaeological digs are also on display.

For birdwatchers, Great Gull Island to the southwest of Fisher Island has the largest nesting populations of common and roseate terns on the East Coast.

The east side of Flat Hammock, an island to the north of West Harbor on Fishers Island, is a pleasant afternoon spot to anchor for a swim.

NAVIGATION: Use NOAA Charts 12372 and 13214. The shoreline of Fishers Island has several small harbors suitable for anchoring but only West Harbor has facilities for cruising boats. The westernmost Fishers Island harbor is Silver Eel Cove, where the New London ferry docks. Visiting boats are not allowed to enter as maneuvering room for the ferry is limited. The next harbor to the east is Hay Harbor, which is shoal, rocky and crowded with sailing dinghies.

The best approach to West Harbor from the west is south of North Dumpling Lighthouse between flashing red bell buoy "2" off the tip of Fishers Island and the green can buoy "3" marking South Dumpling. Follow the red-lighted buoys along the shore to the West Harbor entrance channel. Note that the rebuilt North Dumpling Lighthouse is a private home.

Dockage/Moorings: You will find dockage, fuel and repairs in West Harbor. It is peaceful if you want to escape the heavy fog often found in the Watch Hill passage but is exposed to the north. The friendly Fishers Island Yacht Club Marina offers moorings to 150 feet and launch service. Hail them on VHF Channel 10.

Anchorage: West Harbor will accommodate a good number of boats at anchor. The holding ground is good in sand and it is well protected except in northerly and northeasterly winds.

Farther east beyond West Harbor you can drop the hook in Chocomount Cove in 7 to 11 feet MLW with good holding. This is very peaceful if the wind is moderate and blowing out of the south. East Harbor also has excellent holding in 10 to 14 feet MLW. This is a great spot in any wind except those with a northerly component. Excellent swimming, paddleboarding and snorkeling (for golf balls from the course ashore) is possible here. Smaller vessels can go quite a bit further in. You can take the dinghy ashore for a pleasant walk but no services are available.

Mystic River, CT

The seafaring village of Noank, dating back to the 1820s, all but fills the small peninsula guarding the entrance to the Mystic River. Noank is quiet and noncommercial, a place for pensive walks with classic seascape vistas. The village is small and tightly knit. It is a good place to stop for a good meal out and, given the major yards in the immediate vicinity, virtually any boat part or service needed. Noank also makes a great stop for those running the sound and looking for a quick overnight mooring. From the very start of the Mystic River there are several dock and dine opportunities (or dinghy and dine if you prefer) all the way up to the Amtrak Railroad Bridge, located about 2.5 miles from the entrance.

To the north on the Mystic River, the village of Mystic has several faces. The east side of the river is

part of Stonington, while the west side of the river is part of Groton. If you desire to soak up maritime history, Mystic is the place for you. This scenic hamlet is a family-friendly destination you may never want to leave. Within reasonable walking distance from most of the Mystic River marinas, the village is picturesque, compact and quite busy in season. This is a prime summer weekend destination for many Connecticut residents and tourists from beyond.

The village's shops and dining spots are strung out along Main Street (U.S. Rte. 1) on either side of the unique counter-weight bascule bridge at the hub of activity. West of the bridge, boutiques, galleries and gift shops with a marine theme crowd both sides of the street. There are several banks (with ATMs) and the Post Office is about one block east of the bridge. There are also small markets within a short walk of the marinas and numerous first-rate dining options. (Full provisioning requires transportation.) More restaurants can be found on the eastern side of the bridge.

Although connected to Mystic Village by a small bridge, Mason Island has long held itself somewhat apart from the mainland, largely retaining its rural-residential character. Still, there are marinas and marine services that are easily accessed from the river dotting the island's northern perimeter.

NAVIGATION: Use NOAA Charts 12372 and 13214. You can enter the Mystic area by proceeding south of Groton Long Point leaving both red nun buoy "24" and red nun buoy "22" to port (north). From Groton Long Point take a course of 066° magnetic to Whale Rock, leaving it to the east and Mouse Island to the west. This leads past the protective breakwater into Noank's West Cove (on the west side of Noank). Be sure to give Mouse Island's sloping western rock ledges ample room to east while staying within the green daybeacons to west. The channel is periodically dredged but you should expect no more than 6-foot MLW depths (and some of it is hard ledge).

Note: If traveling straight to Mystic Harbor and skipping Noank, a safer approach is to locate green can buoy "1" and follow the channel in.

On the easterly side of the Noank peninsula, the Mystic River channel runs offshore of Morgan Point and its dormer lighthouse and then begins its winding, well-marked path just beyond flashing green daybeacon "5." The channel follows the Noank shore closely, hugging

Mystic River, CT

		Largest Vessel Accommodated	VHF Channel Monitored / Working	Approach / Dockside Depth (reported)	Transient Slips / Total Slips	Floating Docks	Gas / Diesel	Groceries, Ice, Marine Supplies, Snacks	Repairs: Hull, Engine, Propeller	Lift (tonnage), Crane, Rail	Min / Max Amps	Courtesy Car, Laundry, Pool, Showers	Pump-Out Station	Nearby: Grocery Store, Motel, Restaurant
NOANK				**Dockage**				**Supplies**			**Services**			
1. Spicer's Noank Marina (WiFi)	(860) 536-4978	52	68/	20/444	7.0/7.0	F		IMS	HEP	L38,C	30/50	LS	P	GR
2. Noank Shipyard ⌨ (WiFi)	(860) 536-9651	300	9/	/158	14.0/12.0	F	GD	IMS	HEP	L70	30/50	LS	P	GR
3. Harings Marine Marina	(860) 536-2842		16/9	1/	/		GD	IMS			30			GR
4. Noank Village Boatyard ⌨ (WiFi)	(860) 536-1770	125	72/	15/55	15.0/10.0	F		I	HEP	L35,C	30/100	LS	P	GMR
MYSTIC														
5. **Mystic Shipyard** ⌨ (WiFi)	**(860) 536-6588**	150	9/68	50/270	15.0/12.0			I	HEP	L50,C	30/50	LPS	P	GMR
6. Fort Rachel Marina ⌨ (WiFi)	(860) 536-6647	60	9/	3/110	/	F		I	HEP	L35	30/50	LS		R
7. Mystic Downtown Marina (WiFi)	(860) 572-5942	55	8/	5/29	10.0/8.0	F		I			30	LS	P	GMR
8. Steamboat Inn (WiFi)	(860) 536-8300	100	/	/	12.0/12.0			I			30/50		P	GMR
9. Mystic Seaport Marina (WiFi)	(860) 572-5391	200	68/	40/40	12.0/11.0			I			30/100	LS	P	GMR
10. Seaport Marine (WiFi)	(860) 536-9651	150	/	10/115	12.0/12.0	F		M	HEP	L	30/100	LS		GMR
11. Gwenmor Marina ⌨ (WiFi)	(860) 536-0281	48	13/	4/110	6.0/6.0	F		IMS	HP	L50	30/50	S		GMR
12. Safe Harbor Mystic (WiFi)	(860) 536-2293	80	9/11	10/242	15.0/11.0		GD	IM	HEP	L35	30/100	LPS	P	GMR
MASON ISLAND														
13. Mystic Point Marina (WiFi)	(860) 669-3500	40	/	5/120	5.0/5.0	F					30	LS		GMR
14. Mason's Island Marina (WiFi)	(860) 536-2608	50	9/	6/120	6.0/5.5	F		IMS	HEP	L25,C	30	S		GMR
15. Mystic River Marina ⌨ (WiFi)	(860) 536-3123	150	9/	25/155	14.0/14.0	F	GD	IM	HEP	L35	30/200+	LPS	P	GMR

⌨ Internet Access   (WiFi) Wireless Internet Access   onSpot Dockside WiFi Facility

See WaterwayGuide.com for current rates, fuel prices, website addresses, and other up-to-the-minute information. (Information in the table is provided by the facilities.)

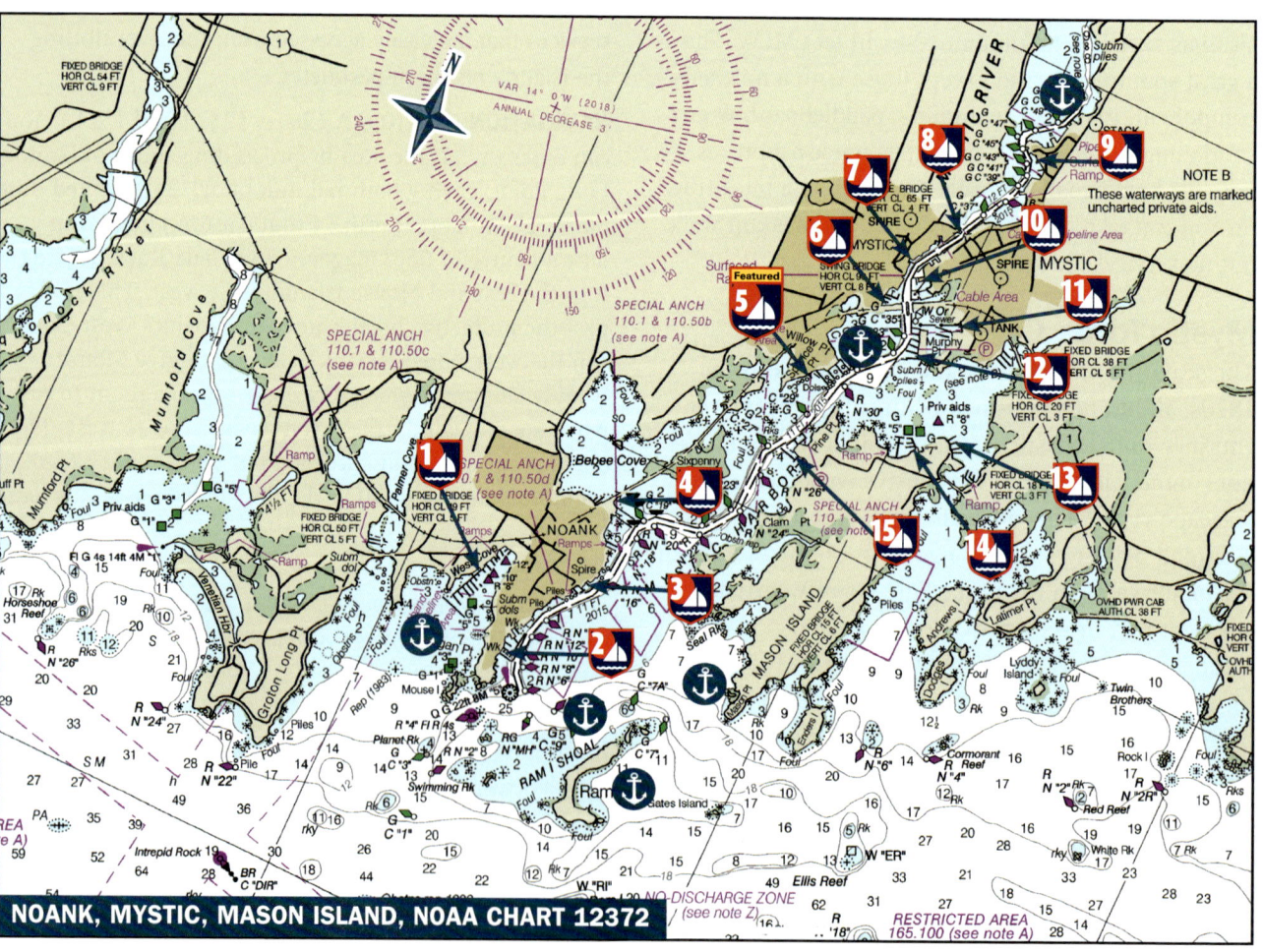

NOANK, MYSTIC, MASON ISLAND, NOAA CHART 12372

its projecting piers. The easterly side of the channel tends to shoal so give the nuns a fair berth to starboard as you pass.

Inside the harbor the channel curves, zigzags and loops among shoals and flats in a generally northerly direction for the 1.5 miles between Ram Point (east of red nun "20") and Willow Point (west of green can "31"). Continue to follow the numbered buoys consecutively. They do not follow a straight-line course so it is easy to miss some. Be aware of current and wind affecting your course upriver so as not to be set outside the channel.

If continuing to Mystic from Willow Point, the channel doglegs right for a distance of just over 0.5 mile to Murphy Point, where it curves sharply to port (toward the northwest) to the Amtrak Railroad Bridge. The bridge (with 8-foot closed vertical clearance) opens on signal from April 1 to October 31 if there is no train traffic. From November 1 to March 31, the bridge opens on signal from 5:00 a.m. to 9:00 p.m. At all other times at least an 8-hour notice is required.

The next bridge to the north is the **US 1 (Mystic Highway) Bridge** (with 4-foot closed vertical clearance), which opens on signal except from May 1 through October 31, from 7:40 a.m. to 6:40 p.m.,

when the draw need only open hourly at 20 minutes before the hour. From November 1 through April 30, from 8:00 p.m. to 4:00 a.m., the draw will open on signal if at least a 6-hour notice is given by calling the number posted at the bridge. The wait for a closed railroad bridge can be up to 20 minutes but the scenery is pleasant, the current is moderate and there is room to maneuver. Note: Boats moving with the tide have the right-of-way when the bridge opens. Both bridges monitor VHF Channels 13.

The channel curves to starboard beyond the bridge and narrows as it deepens. Stick with the channel marked by a series of green cans. Outside the channel it is quite shallow and unsuitable for either navigation or anchorage.

Dockage/Moorings: Spicer's Noank Marina in West Cove is usually filled to capacity with seasonal rentals, however sometimes there is transient space available while local tenants are off cruising. Spicer's also maintains a large mooring field on both sides of the breakwater. On the Mystic River side of the peninsula, boat slips and moorings (with launch service), full-service boat maintenance, repair and storage are available at the marine facilities strung along the channel.

Mystic

MYSTIC SHIPYARD

Mystic Harbor

Side Trip: Mystic Seaport Museum

Mystic Seaport Museum is located north of Mystic Village and the Mystic River Bascule Bridge. It is a re-created 19th-century coastal village that opens a window to America's maritime history. By re-created they mean many of the buildings were brought in from other locations in New England to preserve them but they are very authentic. Also on site is the DuPont Preservation Shipyard, where vessels are constructed or reconstructed using traditional methods of the 1800s including the *Charles W. Morgan*, the *Amistad*, the *Mayflower II* and *Sabino*.

There is so much to see and do at Mystic Seaport that it's best to dedicate more than one day to it. It is a great advantage to arrive by boat and stay at the marina docks. Admission is Included in the docking fee. You may also arrive by dinghy, paying the regular admission fee per person. Visitors wander along the quays and cobbled harbor lanes, stopping at ancient houses and shops while boarding classic wooden boats including some restored to pristine condition. Climb aboard the only remaining wooden whaling ship in the world, the *Charles W. Morgan*; one the last of the dory-laden Grand Banks fishing schooners, the *L.A. Dunton*; and the training ship *Joseph Conrad*. If you are lucky, you may meet players in period costume who are steeped in their characters' lives, trades and viewpoints.

Other attractions include one of the finest nautical libraries in existence, a planetarium, masthead carvers, classic boat and model builders, chantey singers, hoop rollers, a rope-walk, a printing shop, a ship smith shop and much more. Courses and lectures on all manner of nautical subjects are offered throughout the year, and there is a veritable kaleidoscope of priceless maritime treasures on display. The nation's last coal-fired steamer, the *Sabino*, may be available for river cruises (weather and state passenger restrictions permitting). It is being converting to solar power for its shorter river cruises in 2021. Check on the current status on arrival. There are several other charters available here.

The annual Wooden Boat Show is usually the last weekend of June and is an excellent opportunity to see (or purchase) classic wooden vessels of all ages and sizes or to buy anything you might need to maintain or upgrade your own wooden gem. There are many other special events scattered throughout the year.

For general museum information and hours call 860-572-0711 or visit www.mysticseaport.org.

Mystic Harbor

On the both sides of the river at Willow Point (West side and East side) the 270-slip Mystic Shipyard welcomes vessels up to 150 feet with full amenities, as well as repair, rigging and mechanical services to match. Farther north, between the bridges on the same side of the river are additional facilities (many family-owned and -operated) with transient dockage.

The main transient marina on Mason's Island is Mystic River Marina, on the east side of the channel and just south of Pine Point, well before the railroad swing bridge. Mystic River Marina has 14-foot MLW approach depths and can accommodate vessels to 150 feet. They also sell gas and diesel.

The Mystic Seaport Museum Marina can accommodate between 40 and 45 boats per night (more when clubs and groups are prepared to raft up). Admission to the museum is included in the fee for all aboard if you stay overnight. Holiday weekends and events such as the Wooden Boat Show and the Antique and Classic Boat Rendezvous draw substantial crowds, often taking up all possible dock spaces. Because no moorings are available and anchorage is limited outside the Seaport's relatively narrow channel, boaters intending to visit should call ahead for reservations.

At Murphy Point on the easterly side of the river the 242-slip Safe Harbor Mystic has extensive floating docks on the river and in a protected cove and can handle virtually any repair requirement. Given its proximity to Mystic Village, this is a popular place in season. Reservations are highly recommended.

Anchorage: There may be an anchorage spot or two left outside the increasingly filled mooring field at West Cove in Noank, although this area is relatively shallow (4 to 5 feet MLW) and quite exposed to winds and wakes from the south. Similarly, the three "Special Anchorage" areas charted east of the Noank peninsula will support drafts of no more than 5 feet MLW and are also mostly filled with local mooring floats.

A better bet is to anchor just east of Ram Island in depths of 7 to 11 feet MLW with good holding in firm mud. It is protected from the south through northwest. Wind or waves from the northeast through the southeast can make it uncomfortable. The island is private and the owners do not welcome uninvited guests so you may not leave the beach area.

Those with determination, experience and drafts less than 6 feet may still find anchorage possibilities to the southwest of Mason's Island. The holding is good in sand and grass but there is no protection to the south. Be sure to avoid the rocks marked by red nun buoy "6" and red nun buoy "4." There is a small beach at the causeway to Ender's Island and the peaceful monastery grounds at St. Edmund's Retreat are open to the public.

Another possibility is to the north of Mason Island, where the Mystic Harbor Management Commission has placed seasonal buoys outlining the perimeter of a shallow transient anchorage area. The fairway to the boatyards to the east is north of this anchorage. The buoys are white with the letter "A" in a circle and the word "Transient" in black letters. The southeast area has a depth of 3 feet MLW and tapers to 5 feet MLW toward the northwest. From here you can take your dinghy into the downtown Mystic area and tie up at a municipal dinghy dock located between Seaport Marine and the drawbridge. This is smack-dab in the middle of town and gives you great access to the many restaurants and shops.

A second transient anchorage area is upriver north of the federal channel, just north of Mystic Seaport Museum and south of the **I-95 highway Bridge**. This offers 8 to 9 feet MLW with good holding in sand and grass. A sign at the northern end of the museum refers to the last federal marker (green can "53") and requests that the channel beyond not be obstructed. The time limit for anchoring for all transients is 7 days. This anchorage is No-Discharge Zone. A dinghy dock is available if you wish to visit the museum grounds. The fee is the regular cost of admission.

Stonington, CT

Stonington is Connecticut's easternmost cruising port and the only one with some Atlantic Ocean exposure. Locals claim (with some justice) to have the most beautiful harbor on the East Coast. This village peninsula (called the Borough) is home to Connecticut's only remaining full-time, year-round fishing fleet. Stonington Borough boasts the third largest collection of historic houses and sites in CT. Many date from the mid-18th century and include former homes of notable patriots, shipwrights and ship captains.

NAVIGATION: Use NOAA Charts 12372 and 13214. Stonington is most directly approached from Mystic Harbor via the well-buoyed passage north of Ram Island and south of Mason Point and Enders Island. Continuing eastward, passage should be between the white "ER" beacon marking Ellis Reef to north and red nun buoys "6" and "4" (marking rocks) to the south.

Skippers of deep-draft vessels should favor the red nun buoys to avoid the rock at 5-foot MLW depths just north of Ellis Reef.

 Watch for the charted but unmarked White Rock, a 5-foot MLW spot south of red nun buoy "2," which marks Red Reef. A course favoring the red nun buoys should leave you well clear of White Rock. Take care in this area, which, like the rest of Fishers Island Sound, is well known for its bottom-jarring shoals. Daybeacons with the warning ROCK are to be taken at their word.

The approach to Stonington Harbor and to the Little Narragansett Bay channel leading to Watch Hill, is straightforward and plainly marked by the widely spaced green-and-red four-second flashing lights situated on towers atop the ends of the two breakwaters protecting the harbor. The horn sounding from 46-foot red flashing "4" to starboard can be heard from a considerable distance. The breakwater restricts visibility of outbound vessels from this approach, making a wide rounding of the green beacon and allowance for ample reaction time advisable in this relatively busy channel. Shallow-draft boats may also make entrance at the shore side of the breakwater just to the south of Wamphassuc Point. There are submerged rocks at the point, however, and the passage is narrow. It is best left to those with local knowledge.

Dockage/Moorings: Stonington Harbor Yacht Club and Dodson Boatyard at the head of the harbor have slips and dock space for visitors, although most will likely be directed to one of the yard's numerous rental moorings.

Anchorage: Unfortunately, there is little anchorage room left behind Stonington's breakwater (west side of the channel) as moorings have gradually filled in this traditional harbor of refuge. During all but the calmest weather, rollers sneaking around the edges of the breakwaters can turn an evening here into "a moving experience." The inner anchorages (noted on the chart as "Special Anchorage") at Stonington are equally crowded with moorings.

For launch service throughout the harbor call "Dodson Boatyard Launch" (VHF Channel 78) for a pick-up (for a small fee). Free pump-out service is available with a call to "Westerly Pump-out Boat" on VHF Channel 09. (Ask at Dodson's about the pump-out boat's schedule.)

Little Narragansett Bay, CT/RI

		VHF Channel Monitored / Working	Largest Vessel Accommodated	Approach / Dockside Depth (reported)	Transient Slips / Total Slips	Floating Docks	Groceries, Ice, Marine Supplies, Snacks	Gas / Diesel	Repairs: Hull, Engine, Propeller	Lift (tonnage), Crane, Rail	Courtesy Car, Laundry, Pool, Showers	Min / Max Amps	Pump-Out Station	Nearby: Grocery Store, Motel, Restaurant
STONINGTON, CT				**Dockage**				**Supplies**			**Services**			
1. Stonington Harbor Yacht Club	(860) 535-0112		78/	/	9.0/	F			I			30	LS		GMR
2. Dodson Boatyard	(860) 535-1507	130	78/	20/52	15.0/9.0	F	GD	IMS	HEP	L55,C	15/50	LS	P	GMR
WATCH HILL, RI 📶														
3. Watch Hill Yacht Club 📶	(401) 596-4986		/10	/	7.0/8.0	F		S				S		R
4. Watch Hill Docks/Frank Hall Boat Yard 📶	(401) 596-7807	100	9/16	20/23	7.0/8.0	F		I	HEP	C	30/100		P	4R

☐ Internet Access   📶 Wireless Internet Access   📶 onSpot Dockside WiFi Facility
See WaterwayGuide.com for current rates, fuel prices, website addresses, and other up-to-the-minute information. (Information in the table is provided by the facilities.)

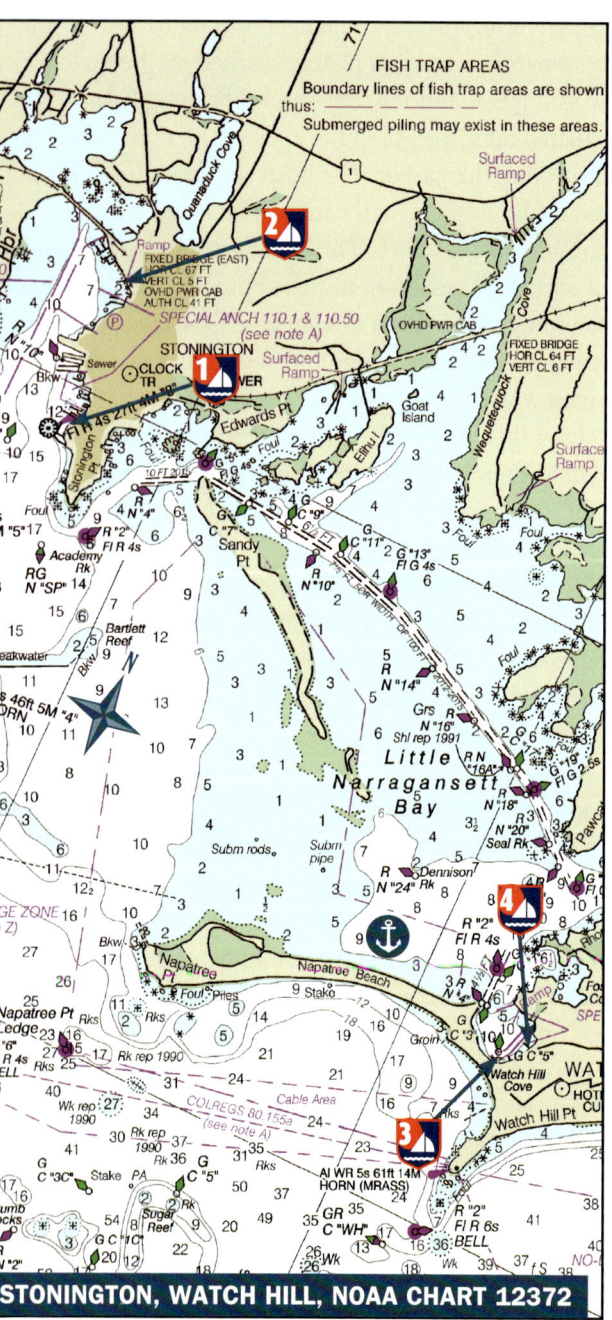

STONINGTON, WATCH HILL, NOAA CHART 12372

Watch Hill, RI

Just over the Connecticut/Rhode Island State line, at the Pawcatuck River, is the village of Watch Hill, RI, featuring long-established seaside estates, an attractive and relatively uncrowded town beach, two sprawling clapboard-sided inns, numerous shops and boutiques oriented to the summer tourist trade. The harbor is large, protected and swim friendly.

The 61-foot lighthouse on Watch Hill has been restored and includes a well-maintained museum (www.watchhilllighthousekeepers.org). The lighthouse can be accessed by foot via a private road and is open from 8:00 a.m. to sunset throughout the year.

NAVIGATION: Use NOAA Charts 12372 and 13214. After clearing the breakwaters protecting Stonington Harbor, the entrance to Little Narragansett Bay is marked by a red-over-green nun buoy marked "SP" located several hundred yards off Stonington Point. From there hold a tight course to flashing red buoy "2," which marks Academy Rock (6 feet MLW). Then keep a sharp watch to stay within the nuns and cans marking the narrow channel, which has silted in spots to depths of 6 feet MLW or less.

Take particular care in rounding north of Sandy Point at the entrance to the bay and honor flashing green buoy "5," where the water runs swiftly and deep, despite how narrow the channel appears. Many local boaters find the northern shore of Sandy Point appropriately named and an appealing stop for lunch or swimming. Occasionally, you will find one of them encroaching on the channel between flashing green buoy "5" green can buoy "9." It is unsafe to cut across the bay to starboard before coming abeam of flashing green buoy "23." The entry into Watch Hill is well marked and well charted.

Pawcatuck River, CT/RI

		Dockage					Supplies		Services						
Name	Phone	Largest Vessel Accommodated	VHF Channel Monitored/Working	Transient Slips/Total Slips	Approach/Dockside Depth (reported)	Floating Docks	Groceries, Ice, Marine Supplies, Snacks	Gas/Diesel	Repairs: Hull, Engine, Propeller	Lift (tonnage), Crane, Rail	Min/Max Amps	Courtesy Car, Laundry, Pool, Showers	Pump-Out Station	Nearby: Grocery Store, Motel, Restaurant
AVONDALE														
1. Watch Hill Boat Yard	(401) 348-8148	50	9/	2/81	5.0/5.0	F	I		EP	C	30	S		3R
2. Avondale Boat Yard 💻 WIFI	(401) 348-8187	75	9/	3/96	10.0/8.0	F	IM	GD	HEP	C,R	15/50	S	P	5
3. Greenhaven Marina	(860) 599-1049	32	/	4/65	9.0/6.0	F	IMS				30			
4. Frank Hall Boat Yard	(401) 348-8005	46	9/18	/110	6.0/6.0	F	IM		HEP	L25	50	S	P	R
5. Cove's Edge Marina	(401) 348-8689	30	/	/100	/	F			HEP	L	30			
6. Westerly Yacht Club 💻 WIFI	(401) 596-5792	35	9/	2/18	12.0/5.0	F	I	G			30	LPS	P	3
WESTERLY														
7. Pier 65 Marina	(401) 348-8154	60	9/	2/22	8.0/7.0	F	M		HEP	L30	30	S		GMR
8. Norwest Marine Inc. WIFI	(860) 599-2442	42	68/	/140	7.0/10.0	F	IMS	G	EP	L35	30/50	LS	P	R
9. Connors and O'Brien Marina	(860) 599-5567	27	/	/75	5.0/8.0	F	M		HP		30			MR
10. Viking Marina	(401) 348-8148	45	/	/50	6.0/6.0	F	I		HEP	L15	30	S		GR

💻 Internet Access WIFI Wireless Internet Access onSpot Dockside WiFi Facility

See WaterwayGuide.com for current rates, fuel prices, website addresses, and other up-to-the-minute information. (Information in the table is provided by the facilities.)

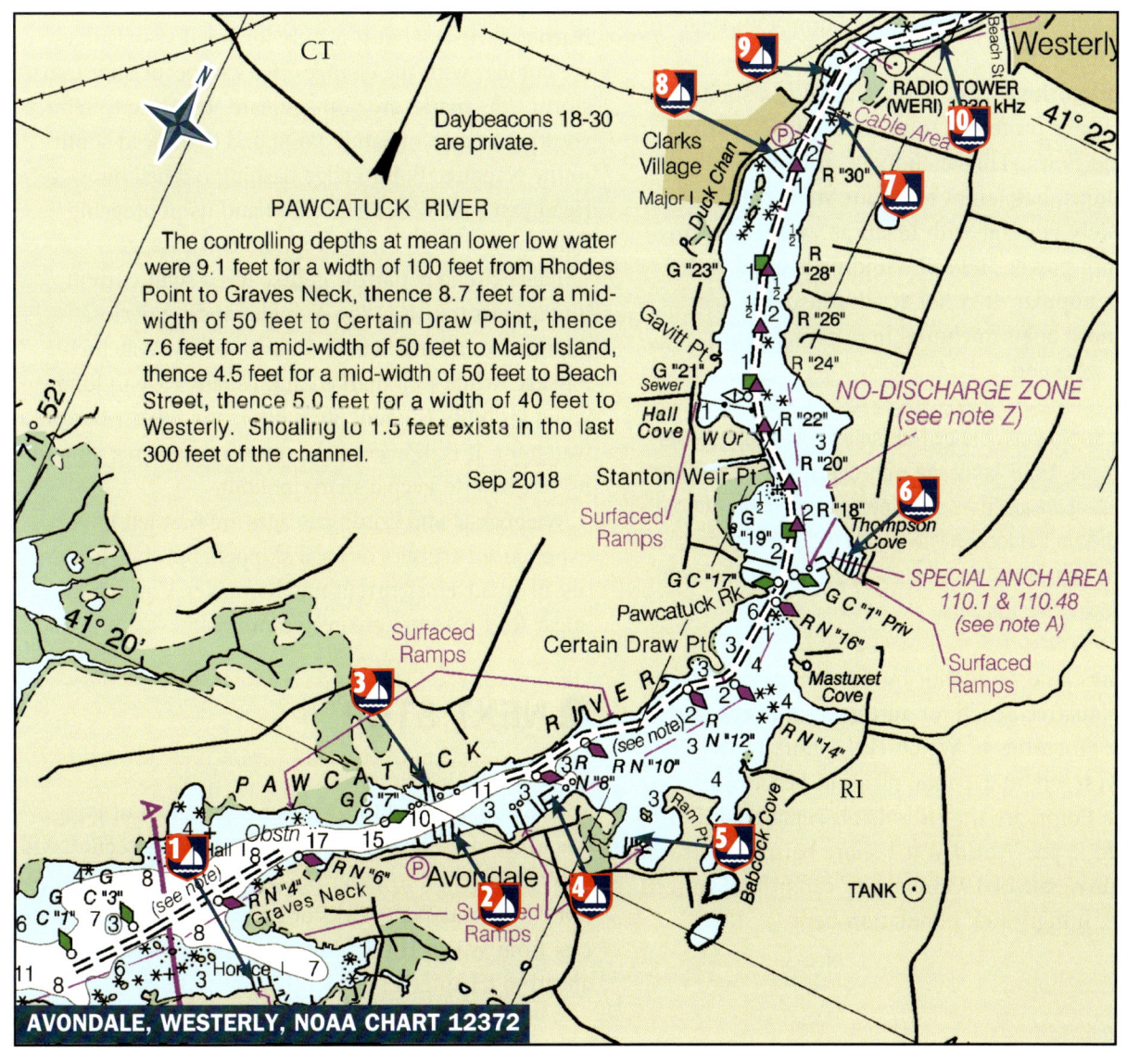

AVONDALE, WESTERLY, NOAA CHART 12372

Watch Hill Cove should be entered only via the marked 100-foot-wide channel, which carries 6.5 feet MLW. The cove is small, attractive and noncommercial with many local boats, including classic wooden tenders and motor cruisers.

Dockage/Moorings: Immediately shoreside on entering Watch Hill Cove, Watch Hill Yacht Club monitors VHF Channel 10 and maintains rental moorings, available on a first-come, first-served basis. They include launch service and use of the club's facilities and showers. Immediately to port of the yacht club on approach, Watch Hill Docks/Frank Hall Boat Yard has slips for transients and a free dinghy dock for those at anchor. This is a popular spot on summer weekends; call in advance for a reservation.

Note that Little Narragansett Bay, like the rest of Rhode Island waters, is a No-Discharge Zone (prohibiting the discharge of any sewage even if it has been treated). This prohibition is easily honored with a call to "Westerly Pump-Out Boat" on VHF Channel 09.

Anchorage:Just west of Watch Hill is a sheltered body of water protected to the south by Napatree Beach and Point. This anchorage, known locally as the Kitchens, has 7-foot to 9-foot MLW depths. It is extremely popular with locals as well as cruising boats, both power and sail. Holding is good and rafting is popular. It is not at all unusual to see 200 or more boats anchored here over a sunny summer weekend.

The cottages that were on Napatree were swept into Bay during the 1938 hurricane with much loss of life. The remains of the iceboxes and stoves sank into the bottom sand hence the local name "Kitchens." Don't worry, the kitchen appliances have long ago settled well beneath the reach of your anchor.

Dinghies land or anchor by the dozens on the bay side of Napatree Beach for an easy trek to the surf or to the amenities of Watch Hill ashore to the east. To the west, about a 1-mile pleasant beach walk to Napatree Point, are the still-visible remains of Fort Mansfield, a pre-World War I shore battery destroyed by the hurricane of 1938. Be very careful not to feed the large, hungry tick population here.

North on the Pawcatuck River

From Watch Hill the well-buoyed Pawcatuck River wends its way northward through the towns of Avondale and Westerly (RI) to Pawcatuck (CT). Depths outside the narrow channel do not encourage anchoring and marinas upriver cater primarily to the local boating community.

Dockage/Moorings: There are numerous marinas, yacht clubs and boat yards on the Pawcatuck River. There are several marine facilities close to Avondale with slips, repairs and gas and diesel fuel. Farther north is Westerly Yacht Club in protected Thompson Cove, which welcomes transients on a first-come, first-served basis. The next group of facilities is at the town of Westerly. Call ahead for slip availability.

Heading East

NAVIGATION: Use NOAA Charts 12372 and 13205. There is an exit from the southwestern side of Little Narragansett Bay but it is only for small vessels that are familiar with the changes that can occur after every storm. Any marks are non-standard. It is best to retrace your path north of Sandy Point and then head south to the Napatree Point Ledge flashing red bell buoy "6." Head east past Watch Hill Point and its photogenic lighthouse and go through Watch Hill Passage.

This extremely narrow course has a swift current; if you must transit in fog or high winds, pay close attention to all markers and travel slowly. Watch Hill Passage, while well marked and usually easy to follow when visibility is good, often has many lobster buoys to watch for. It is, however, the route a newcomer should use. Be sure to keep a sharp lookout.

Wicopesset and Lord's passages are best left to very experienced cruisers or local skippers but they get you out of an adverse current much quicker. Catumb and Sugar Reef passages are even more risky.

■ NEXT STOP

You've now traveled to the most eastern exit of Long Island Sound. The next two chapters of this section will "backtrack" a bit to cover the cruising territory on the north side and Twin Forks of Long Island. If continuing east from Watch Hill Passage, you may choose to skip ahead to Chapter 11, which begins at Block Island.

South Shore: To Mattituck Inlet, NY

The North Shore of Long Island from Little Neck Bay to Plum Gut is called the "South Shore" (of Long Island Sound) by New York and Connecticut boaters. This is not to be confused with the south shore of Long Island itself.

Long Island Sound begins at the **Throgs Neck Bridge** and Little Neck Bay. This is the start of a cruiser's paradise, the western sound. This area of Long Island Sound is generally easy to navigate, well-marked and well charted. It has mostly deep water, extensive facilities, anchorages, convenient land transportation and a seemingly unlimited number of recreational boats. The harbors of Manhasset Bay (Port Washington), Glen Cove, Oyster Bay, Cold Spring Harbor, Huntington Harbor and Port Jefferson are favorites among the cruising community. Because the rise and fall of the tide on portions of the western Long Island Sound's "South Shore" is substantial (6 to 8 feet), most marinas have floating docks.

The western end of the Sound is the narrow part, making it easy to crisscross back and forth between Long Island harbors and the "North Shore" harbors of New York and Connecticut. The eastern end of Long Island Sound's south shore is quite different from the Connecticut shore. The beach is mostly unbroken. There are high bluffs (sandy or rocky) and the shore is sparsely settled with only two substantial harbors in almost 60 miles.

■ LITTLE NECK BAY TO COLD SPRING HARBOR

Little Neck Bay

Little Neck Bay is the first harbor on the Long Island shore after you leave the East River. It is a large-mouthed bay with thickly settled shores and some of the best anchorages in the crowded New York City area. The 65-acre campus of the U.S. Merchant Maritime Academy was once the estate of Walter P. Chrysler, the automobile manufacturer. He used to commute to New York City by boat. The mansion's interior is now divided into small offices but the grounds are open to the public on weekend afternoons and during Saturday morning reviews. The Academy has quite a sailing fleet at Kings Point.

The American Merchant Marine Museum (516-726-6047) is located on campus in the Barstow House, the home of the National Maritime Hall of Fame. William Barstow invented the electric meter and was also responsible for lighting the **Brooklyn Bridge**.

On the eastern shore at Udall's Mill Pond just to the south of the charted dam is the Saddle Rock Grist Mill (516-571-7900), a 16th-century water mill that still operates, depending on the tide. It is open to the public on Sundays (1:00 p.m. to 5:00 p.m.) from May through

Manhasset Bay, NY

MANHASSET NECK		Largest Vessel Accomodated	VHF Channel Monitored / Working	Approach / Dockside Depth (reported)	Transient Slips / Total Slips	Floating Docks	Gas / Diesel	Groceries, Ice, Marine Supplies, Snacks	Repairs: Hull, Engine, Propeller	Lift (tonnage), Crane, Rail	Min / Max Amps	Courtesy Car, Laundry, Pool, Showers	Pump-Out Station	Nearby: Grocery Store, Motel, Restaurant
			Dockage					**Supplies**		**Services**				
1. Safe Harbor Capri- West 🖥 📶	(516) 883-7800	175	9/71	20/215	7.0/6.5	F	GD	IMS	HEP	L75	30/100	LPS	P	GMR
2. North Shore Yacht Club	(516) 883-9823	65	78/	/	15.0/5.0	F		I				S		GR
3. Safe Harbor Capri-East 🖥 📶	(516) 883-7800	175	9/71	20/115	7.0/6.5	F		IMS	HEP	L75	30/100	LPS	P	GMR
4. Toms Point Marina	(516) 883-6630	36	/	10/110	5.0/5.0	F		I	HE	L15,C	30/50	LS	P	GR
5. Manhasset Bay Marina/La Motta's Restaurant 🖥 📶	**(516) 883-8411**	**110**	**9/**	**20/300**	**8.0/6.0**	**F**	**GD**	**IMS**	**HEP**	**L75,C**	**30/100**	**LS**	**P**	**GR**
6. Gulfway Marine Service	(516) 767-0113	30	/	/	12.0/12.0			GIMS	HEP	C				GR
PORT WASHINGTON														
7. North Hempstead Town Dock 📶	(516) 869-6311	100	9/16	/	12.0/6.0	F		GIM	HEP				P	GR
8. Marina at Inspiration Wharf	(516) 767-2215	30	9/71	2/30	8.0/8.0	F	D	IMS	HP		30/50		P	GMR
9. Manhasset Bay Yacht Club	(516) 767-2150	100	73/	/	7.0/6.0	F		IS			30	PS		GMR
10. Port Washington Yacht Club 📶	(516) 767-1614	100	74/	/	7.0/6.0	F		IS	HEP		30	PS		GMR

🖥 Internet Access   📶 Wireless Internet Access   ⦿onSpot Dockside WiFi Facility

See WaterwayGuide.com for current rates, fuel prices, website addresses, and other up-to-the-minute information. (Information in the table is provided by the facilities.)

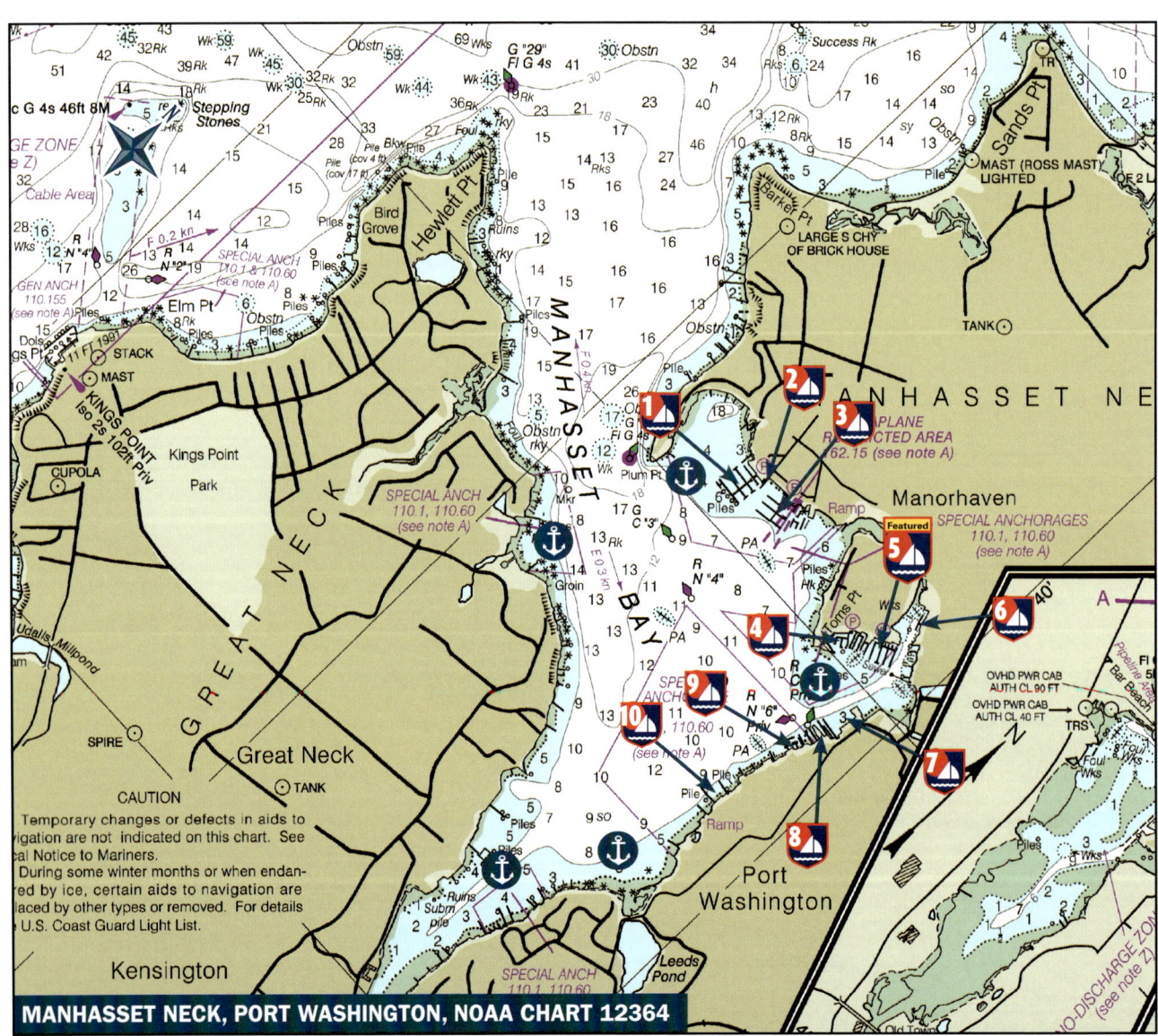

MANHASSET NECK, PORT WASHINGTON, NOAA CHART 12364

MANHASSET BAY MARINA/LaMOTTA'S RESTAURANT

Manorhaven

Plum Point

October. You can bring the dinghy over to take a closer look but you cannot land here.

NAVIGATION: Use NOAA Chart 12364. The straightforward entrance is between Willets Point on the west and Kings Point on the east, which is marked by the 220-foot-high flagpole of the U.S. Merchant Maritime Academy.

Dockage/Moorings: Bayside Marina has seasonal dock space and mooring rentals and provides 24/7 launch service. Call ahead for slip availability.

Anchorage: Little Bay, located between the Throgs Neck Bridge and Willets Point, has 7 to 8 feet MLW in good holding in mud. It is protected from all but the north and northeast but is subject to wakes from boat traffic and noise from highway traffic. Little Neck Bay has 7- to 8-foot MLW depths down the middle with shallows along the banks and in the southeastern corner. Many boats are moored here but there are several good places to anchor, unless the wind is out of the north.

The cove north of Kings Point on the eastern shore has a designated special anchorage with 12 to 14 feet MLW and good holding in mud. It is, however, open and exposed to the northeast.

These are all good spots to wait to time the currents of Hell Gate if headed west and planning a passage through New York City.

Manhasset Bay

Manhasset Bay is one of the most popular and most complete harbors on Long Island Sound. It has deep water throughout, good holding and is easy to enter day or night, making it an ideal stopover whether transiting east or west on Long Island Sound.

Activities in Manhasset Bay during the summer months are so abundant that some boats dock here in the spring and stay through the summer. The waterfront towns of Sands Point, Manorhaven, Port Washington, Plandome, Great Neck and Kings Point surround the Bay. The town of Manhasset is slightly inland and New York City is about 40 miles away by highway or railroad.

NAVIGATION: Use NOAA Charts 12364, 12366 and 12363. From Little Neck Bay the preferred (and safer) route is to pass north of Stepping Stones Lighthouse, keeping it to starboard. Alternately, you can cruise along the eastern shore, keeping about midway between red nun buoys "4" and "2" on the southern edge of Stepping Stones reef and the shoreline.

The wide, unobstructed entrance to Manhasset Bay is between Hewlett Point and Barker Point. Do not cut either point coming in; both have rocks just offshore. About 1 nm inside flashing green "1" marks the crooked finger of Plum Point, which extends out from the eastern shore almost halfway across the bay and protects the inner harbor.

Manhasset Bay

A sizable and strictly enforced No-Wake Zone begins at Plum Point. The inner harbor is also a No-Discharge Zone. Discharge of raw or treated sewage is prohibited.

Dockage/Moorings: The marinas of Manhasset Bay offer complete facilities and services. The yacht clubs are friendly and offer guest moorings to other yacht club members. The shopping, provisioning and restaurants are well within reach of the marinas and anchorages.

The village of Manorhaven boasts that it is the largest boating community in the State of New York. Safe Harbor Capri West and East are located just inside the protective arm of Plum Point. Formerly separate facilities, the two are combined under Safe Harbor management to provide a complete range of integrated marine services. In between Capri's two main piers, the friendly and colorful North Shore Yacht Club maintains a small pier of its own, along with moorings open to transients.

Other facilities are located south of Tom's Point with transient slips and boat maintenance and repairs including the well maintained, 300-slip Manhasset Bay Marina/La Motta's Restaurant. They welcome visitors with 20 reserved transient slips and 40 moorings while also tending to the needs of hundreds of local boats. They can handle most repair or service needs and has a fuel dock, Ship Store and laundry facilities.

Cruisers from other areas often (incorrectly) refer to the entire Manhasset Bay as Port Washington. Port Washington is actually the second largest boating center in Manhasset Bay. The Town of North Hempstead has moorings and a dinghy dock adjacent to the harbormaster's office. There is a second dinghy dock a bit north of the harbormaster's dock. There is no longer a two day grace period for the moorings but launch service is included in the fee. The town offers complimentary pump-out service to boats on the hook or at moorings via its pump-out barge. (Hail on VHF Channel 09.)

Manhasset Bay and Port Washington Yacht Clubs are along this section of the bay, supporting competitive racing programs and a parade of social events. Members of yacht clubs with reciprocity can usually find a mooring with launch service or a slip, along with access to club amenities included in the facility fee.

Anchorage: Manhasset Bay offers protection against most winds for the entirety of its 3.5-nm length and is a snug harbor with room for numerous vessels. The first of five Coast Guard-designated Special Anchorage Areas is Plum Point Cove, which provides a well-protected anchorage area behind Plum Point with excellent holding in mud with 8-foot MLW depths. This is convenient to a beach that can be used for swimming,

Hempstead Harbor, NY

GLEN COVE		Dockage					Supplies		Services					
		Largest Vessel Accommodated	VHF Channel Monitored / Working	Approach / Dockside Depth (reported)	Transient Slips / Total Slips	Floating Docks	Groceries, Ice, Marine Supplies, Snacks	Gas / Diesel	Repairs: Hull, Engine, Propeller	Lift (tonnage) Crane, Rail	Courtesy Car, Laundry, Pool, Showers	Min / Max Amps	Pump-Out Station	Nearby: Grocery Store, Motel, Restaurant
1. Glen Cove Yacht Yard WIFI	(516) 671-5563	75	9/	10/550		15.0/8.0	F	GD	IMS	HEP	L60,C	30/50	LPS	P	GMR
2. Safe Harbor Glen Cove	(516) 759-3129	70	9/	10/550		15.0/6.0		GD	IM	HEP	L50,C	30/50	LPS	P	GM
3. Hempstead Harbour Club	(516) 671-0600	50	72/72	/		8.0/6.0			I				S	P	

🖳 Internet Access   WIFI Wireless Internet Access   onSpot Dockside WiFi Facility

See WaterwayGuide.com for current rates, fuel prices, website addresses, and other up-to-the-minute information. (Information in the table is provided by the facilities.)

GLEN COVE, NOAA CHART 12364

water-skiing and dinghy landings (only accessible by water) no farther than the high tide mark.

The second designated anchorage is at Toms Point but it is shallow (4 to 6 feet MLW) and open and exposed to the southwest. A better option is the designated anchorage at Port Washington with 8 to 12 feet MLW with excellent holding in mud. There is some anchoring room among the moorings and plenty around the perimeter. In the southern end of the bay, Plandome is the most protected designated anchorage to drop the hook in 6 to 8 feet MLW with excellent holding in mud. It is exposed to the north. The final designated anchorage at Kings Point, across from Plum Point, offers good holding in mud with 11- to 12-foot MLW depths. Tuck in far enough to avoid swells/wake from passing traffic on Long Island Sound.

In the southeast corner of Manhasset Bay near Leeds Pond, there is a popular anchorage used on weekends for raft-ups and swimming. This is exposed to the north.

Hempstead Harbor

Glen Cove, surrounded by water on three sides, is a popular part of the North Shore's Gold Coast where J.P. Morgan and F.W. Woolworth had homes. Many mansions remain along the 300-plus acres of nature preserves overlooking Hempstead Harbor.

J.P. Morgan built the 40-acre Morgan Memorial Park in memory of his wife. The park overlooks Long Island Sound and has a picnic area, playground, concession stand, restrooms and a beach. There is also a walkway along the bluff providing panoramic views. Just north of the creek is the 62-acre Garvies Point Museum and Preserve (516-571-8010), which documents the life and culture of Long Island, geology and Native American archaeology. The grounds include nature trails and an abundance of wildlife. Visit www.garviespointmuseum.com to plan your visit.

NAVIGATION: Use NOAA Charts 12364, 12366 and 12363. Boats eastbound from Manhasset Bay should round Barker Point passing north of Gangway Rock. Local boats often cut inside the white and orange can buoy marking Success Rock but this is not advisable unless you really know the area. Run between the lighted buoys off Sands Point to starboard and Execution Rocks to port. The grouping of the lighthouse and small buildings at Execution Rocks constitute a major landmark and one of the most important aids to navigation in western Long Island Sound.

Leave plenty of room around the ledge at Execution Rocks. The name is derived from a local belief that during the Revolutionary War British soldiers chained American patriots to the rocks at low tide and let them drown when the tide rose. This theory has been discounted but it does make a colorful story.

Hempstead Harbor, southeast across Long Island Sound from Mamaroneck and Rye, has a 4-mile-wide entrance between Prospect and Matinecock Points. The harbor is open to the northwest. Note that exiting the harbor against wind and waves from this direction can be a long motor, especially in a sailboat with light auxiliary power.

Glen Cove Creek is the deepest, best-protected, most active yachting port in Hempstead Harbor. The creek, which is north of Sea Cliff, would be almost imperceptible on first-time arrival but for yellow can buoy "A" and yellow nun buoy "B" marking the outer channel. When you are centered between the two buoys, face the creek to the east, and green entrance can buoy "1" and red nun buoy "2" will show the way to the narrow channel between the bulkheads. At low tide, in particular, deeper-draft boats should favor the right side of the channel on entry staying closer to the collapsing bulkhead to starboard. There should be 6.5-foot MLW depths here and substantially more otherwise, given the 8-foot tidal range.

Dockage/Mooring: The 550-slip Safe Harbor Yacht Yard at Glen Cove is immediately to starboard (hard right) beyond the bulkheads with all the amenities a cruiser could desire. The cove is also home to the hospitable Hempstead Harbour Club. Transient vessels are usually able to secure an overnight mooring in this harbor.

Anchorage: One of Long Island Sound's best beaches (unnamed on the chart, but known locally as Half Moon Beach) is the stretch of shore between Barker Point and Sands Point, west of Hempstead Harbor. Boats anchor in the bight just off the beach with excellent holding in 13- to 14-foot MLW depths.

The breakwater at Glen Cove is a protected anchorage that was used by J.P. Morgan's *Corsair* and other vessels of the great steam-yacht period. There is an ample anchorage area beyond the mooring fields; however, cruisers have noted that even behind the breakwater it can be uncomfortable in a northwest or westerly wind. This also applies to any anchorage farther to the south.

Oyster Bay Harbor

Oyster Bay, located east of Hempstead Harbor, has one of most attractive and unspoiled harbors on Long Island Sound. Oyster Bay Harbor is a long horseshoe with Centre Island (not really an island) in the middle and it shares an entrance (Oyster Bay) with Cold Spring Harbor.

Oyster Bay Harbor offers fine beaches, beautiful estates, a well-kept oyster fleet and a choice of generous, sheltered anchorages. The Town of Oyster Bay comprises 18 small hamlet communities that collectively boast over 600 acres of park lands and pristine beaches weaving along both the north and south shores. Even though the village is small, attractions include several well-recommended restaurants and breweries.

Oyster Bay Harbor is the termination point of the Oyster Bay Branch of the Long Island Railroad, making it a convenient spot to tie up and head into New York City for a day trip. See details at www.mta.info/lirr.

On Oak Neck Point on the low-lying shore is the Village of Bayville. This resort community has pretty cottages and fine public beaches replete with the requisite hot dog stands, ice cream parlors and cocktail lounges, as well as amenities for cruising boats. From here it is common to see the labor-intensive activities of Oyster Bay's colorful oyster fleet, working the bottom in the traditional manner.

NAVIGATION: Use NOAA Charts 12364 and 12365. The route around Matinecock Point, past Oak Neck and Rocky Point on Centre Island, follows what was once the most elegant stretch of Long Island. The shore, lined with handsome estates, is also lined with rocks and requires careful navigation. To enter Oyster Bay from the west off Long Island Sound, round green bell buoy "17" north of Centre Island Reef and stay clear of the rocks off hilly Rocky Point.

The preferred course is southeast across the bay, leaving flashing 37-foot Cold Spring Light (where current runs strong) to starboard. Boats drawing under 7 feet usually cut through the light's red sector, running west about halfway between the light and the line from red nun buoys "2" and "4" off Plum Point.

Once inside, the inner bay shoots off southeast to Cold Spring Harbor and southwest to the 4-mile U-turn around Centre Island through Oyster Bay Harbor and into West Harbor. To reach Mill Neck Creek off West Harbor, you will have to negotiate the **Bayville Bridge** (9-foot closed vertical clearance). The bridgetender can be contacted on VHF Channel 13 for an opening any day during the season (May 1 through October 31) from 7:00 a.m. to 11:00 p.m. and from November 1 through April 30 between 7:00 a.m. and 5:00 p.m., Monday through Friday. At all other times the draw will open on signal with at least a 2-hour

Oyster Bay, NY

		Dockage					Supplies		Services					
		Largest Vessel Accommodated	VHF Channel Monitored / Working	Transient Slips / Total Slips	Approach / Dockside Depth (reported)	Floating Docks	Gas / Diesel	Groceries, Ice, Marine Supplies, Snacks	Repairs: Hull, Engine, Propeller	Lift (tonnage), Crane, Rail	Min / Max Amps	Courtesy Car, Laundry, Pool, Showers	Pump-Out Station	Nearby: Grocery Store, Motel, Restaurant
OYSTER BAY HARBOR														
1. Sagamore Yacht Club	(516) 922-0555	50	78/	/	10.0/7.0							S		GR
2. Oyster Bay Marine Center (WiFi)	(516) 624-2400	160	71/	4/32	13.0/22.0	F	GD	IM	HP	C	30/50	S	P	GR
OAK NECK														
3. Bridge Marine Sales & Marina	(516) 628-8686	42	/	/52	7.0/7.0	F		IS	HEP	R	30			GR
COLD SPRING HARBOR														
4. Powles Marina	(631) 367-7670	31	10/	/	20.0/4.0	F	GD	IMS	EP				P	GMR
5. Whalers Cove Yacht Club	(631) 367-9822	44	9/	/50	15.0/25.0	F		I			30	S		GR

▯ Internet Access   WiFi Wireless Internet Access   onSpot Dockside WiFi Facility

See WaterwayGuide.com for current rates, fuel prices, website addresses, and other up-to-the-minute information. (Information in the table is provided by the facilities.)

OYSTER BAY HARBOR, OAK NECK, COLD SPRING HARBOR, NOAA CHART 12364

Oyster Bay

advance notice, given by calling the number posted at the bridge.

Oyster Bay is home to the famous Seawanhaka Corinthian Yacht Club. The sailing fleet here chooses two excellent harbors as home ports: Oyster Bay Harbor and Cold Spring Harbor. Deep, protected anchorages abound throughout both harbors including one of Long Island Sound's best gunkholes, the Sand Hole at Lloyds Neck.

Dockage/Mooring: In the southwest corner of Oyster Bay Harbor, Sagamore Yacht Club and Oyster Bay Marine Center usually have a slip or mooring available for cruising visitors (by reservation only). To approach these facilities, take the branch of the marked channel leading toward the large fuel tanks. The branch channel then makes a hard right just before shore, leading past the fuel dock. From here, it is an easy walk to the town's superb park and the amenities of the Village. The town dock next to the marina does not offer transient space.

Anchorage: South of Centre Island, protection and pleasant surroundings can be found in the big cove between the town of Oyster Bay and the high wooded bluffs of Cove Neck. Two miles long and one mile wide, it has little current and holding is good in 8 to 9 feet MLW. It never seems to be crowded, although there might be a club raft-up or two during summer months. A great variety of waterfowl can be seen in the marshes at the head of the cove, especially during the seasonal migrations.

A popular anchorage with good holding in 7 to 8 feet MLW is in West Harbor, to the northwest of Centre Island. This is a wide, open body of water with good

depth and protection all around with a few moorings and lots of beaches.

A peaceful anchorage area can be found on the southwest shore of Mill Neck Creek near Bridge Marina (yacht brokerage). This is a great place to hunker down in a blow as it provides all-around protection with 7 to 13 feet MLW with good holding in mud and grass. You will likely need to call for an opening of the Bayville Bridge (9-foot closed vertical clearance).

Cold Spring Harbor

Bordered by the 180-foot cliffs of Cooper Bluff, Cold Spring Harbor is an uncluttered bay almost 3 nm long and 1 nm wide. It has several beaches, wooded hills on the east and west sides and the Village of Cold Spring Harbor in the southeast corner. Its wooded surroundings and steep shores make this harbor seem more like a beautiful northern inland lake than a piece of Long Island Sound. Cold Spring Harbor was so named by settlers in 1653 because of the harbor's icy freshwater springs. There are actual piped cold springs where you can fill up water jugs. (Ask a local.)

There are many beaches in the area where you can land without trespassing. When you come upon a private section, law provides that you may walk along the wet sand portion of the beach below the high tide line.

The village of Cold Spring Harbor preserves the maritime history of Long Island in the Whaling Museum and Education Center (631-367-3418), located amid the cluster of 18th-century and 19th-century houses overlooking the narrow harbor. See www. cshwhalingmuseum.org for details. Cold Spring Harbor is also home to the DNA Learning Center (516-367-5170), the world's first Biotechnology Museum (www.dnalc.org) and the Cold Spring Harbor Fish Hatchery & Aquarium (516-692-6768), which raises a variety of species of trout to stock ponds and turtles for release into the wild. It is extremely "kid friendly."

Dockage/Moorings: South of Cold Spring Beach, the harbor is filled with a local mooring field. Keep to the middle of the narrow, deep channel leading in. Inside are good depths along the eastern shore, which will take you to a marine facilities along the southern shore.

Anchorage: Much of the anchorage area at the Village of Cold Spring Harbor is taken up with permanent moorings. You may still be able to anchor with good depths (8 to 12 feet MLW) north of Cold Spring Beach, a skinny stretch of shore with a bulbous tip that almost closes up the inner harbor. You can also anchor in the inner harbor in 14 feet MLW with good holding near Whalers Cove Yacht Club. The approach to the inner harbor is a bit narrow so exercise caution.

Side Trip: The Sand Hole

The Sand Hole is one of the most popular gunkholes on Long Island Sound. It offers an easy anchorage when transiting the Sound in either direction. Surrounded by a state park, it is a hike to get to by land; however, it seems as if every boat on Long Island Sound heads there on summer weekends. It can (understandably) get crowded and noisy.

The Sand Hole was originally dredged for private yachts. There is only one house overlooking it, on long-established private land. The rest of the surrounding land is grassland, beach and some marshland. Should you choose to walk the shoreline be sure to stay away from the house's guarded land and take notice that parts of the barrier beach are often restricted due to nesting birds. Remember: Obey the signs, avoid the fines.

NAVIGATION: Use NOAA Charts 12364 and 12365. To reach The Sand Hole steer about 50° magnetic from green gong buoy "1" at the mouth of Oyster Bay. You will see the jetty (except at high tide) and should give it a wide berth when turning in.

Anchorage: The Sand Hole has two basins. The inner basin almost appears to be barred by shallow water when, in fact, depths over the bar are about 4 feet MLW. Leading just off the spit that divides the basins is a deep, narrow channel leading to the inner basin, where you will find 7- to 14-foot MLW depths. You can opt to anchor directly behind the jetty (outer harbor)

in 9 to 15 feet MLW. You may get some wave action from the west but will be protected from wind from all directions.

◼ HUNTINGTON BAY AREA

The eastern part of the North Shore of Long Island, Huntington Bay to Plum Gut, is the widest part of Long Island Sound. The breezes freshen and the harbors become fewer in number. Huntington Bay sprawls inward from Long Island Sound. It is the largest of the Long Island harbors and marks the beginning of Suffolk County. Nassau County is to the west. The wide entrance to Huntington Bay lays between two high, wooded headlands, each almost an island, connected to the mainland by a narrow, sandy isthmus. To the west is private Lloyd Neck. To the east is the jutting headland of Eatons Neck, with its famous old lighthouse and Coast Guard station.

Huntington Bay narrows as it goes south and then spreads out to the east, west and south into seven separate, sheltered, inner harbors lined by the villages of Huntington, Centerport and Northport. Boating amenities are everywhere. There are many anchorages—some crowded, some isolated—plus good beaches and fine restaurants.

Lloyd Harbor

Lloyd Harbor is the westernmost of the Huntington Bay harbors. It has a wide outer harbor and long, narrow inner harbor. The outer harbor, almost one-half mile long, has a few boats at moorings, attractive houses hidden among the trees and a small summer camp but no docks or marinas. It is cool and thickly wooded but can be crowded on weekends. No motorized vessels are allowed in the narrow inner harbor.

NAVIGATION: Use NOAA Charts 12364 and 12365. To reach Lloyd Harbor enter north of Huntington Harbor Lighthouse. It is a storybook graystone residence that tends to fade into the surroundings and can be difficult to spot from a distance. The narrow channel is clearly buoyed with stakes and poles marking obstructions or shoal spots. Extending westward the inner harbor runs nearly 1.5 nm toward Oyster Bay. It provides an interesting dinghy trip (no motors allowed) and is good for windsurfing but too shallow for deep-keeled boats.

Anchorage: Anchoring and motoring is prohibited in the inner harbor at Lloyd Harbor. Several hundred feet

Huntington Harbor

west of Lloyd Harbor green can buoy "3" and red nun buoy "4" (not Huntington Harbor buoys) you will find spots to anchor both to the north and south. There is 8 to 14 feet MLW with excellent holding in mud. The more southern anchorage area provides good protection from the prevailing southwest wind but it is open to some surge and wakes from the constant stream of boats that use the Huntington Harbor channel. The more northern area gives protection from the north and northeast behind the spit. The speed limit is 5 knots. Stay away from the buoyed water-skiing area. Rafting is allowed but you must maintain a safe distance from other boats.

Huntington Harbor

At the southwestern end of Huntington Bay, just around the lighthouse from Lloyd Harbor, a well-marked channel leads into Huntington Harbor. Although this is one of the best-protected harbors in Long Island Sound, it is also more tightly packed with boats than any eastern Long Island Sound harbor. The waters are usually crowded with racing sailboats or

cruisers so proceed slowly through the fleet and be sure you do not leave a wake.

Compass Rose Marine Supply (15 Mill Dam Rd., 631-673-4144) is nearby with a huge inventory of marine supplies and can order parts for rapid delivery. Provisions and supplies are close at hand and anything the cruising mariner is likely to require is also readily available.

The center of Huntington is about a 20-minute walk from the marinas on the inner harbor. The town is well worth a walking tour. It offers one of the most sophisticated arts communities in the area.

NAVIGATION: Use NOAA Charts 12364 and 12365. The narrow but well-marked entrance to Huntington Harbor runs between a boulder reef extending out from West Neck to starboard and 1 and 2-foot MLW shallows around Wincoma Point to port upon entry. Favor the West Neck shore and allow for the 2-knot current through the narrows. Dominating the entrance from a hill on the southern shore is baronial Château at Coindre Hall, a 40-room, 80,000-square-foot mansion

Huntington Bay, NY

HUNTINGTON HARBOR		Largest Vessel Accomodated	VHF Channel Monitored / Working	Approach / Dockside Depth (reported)	Transient Slips / Total Slips	Floating Docks	Gas / Diesel	Groceries, Ice, Marine Supplies, Snacks	Repairs: Hull, Engine, Propeller	Lift (tonnage), Crane, Rail	Min / Max Amps	Courtesy Car, Laundry, Pool, Showers	Pump-Out Station	Nearby: Grocery Store, Motel, Restaurant
				Dockage				**Supplies**		**Services**				
1. Gold Star Battalion	(631) 421-3366	45	9/	/	15.0/8.0	F		IM	HEP	C	30	S	P	
2. Knutson Marine [WiFi]	(631) 549-7842	68	9/	5/130	10.0/8.0	F		IMS	HEP	L35	50	LS	P	R
3. Huntington Yacht Club ▢ [WiFi]	(631) 427-4949	100	68/68	20/103	/12.0	F	GD	IS			30/100	PS	P	GR
4. Knutson's Yacht Haven Marina Inc. ▢ [WiFi]	(631) 673-0700	100	/	4/38	20.0/20.0	F		GIMS	HEP	L35	20/100	LS	P	GMR
5. Coneys Marine	(631) 421-3366	55	9/	/	15.0/12.0	F		IMS	HEP	L,C	30	LS	P	GR
6. Willis Marine Center	(631) 421-3400	80	9/	12/120	12.0/10.0	F	GD	GIM	HEP	L20,C	30/50	LS	P	GR
7. West Shore Marina [WiFi]	(631) 427-3444	150	9/73	20/300	15.0/18.0	F		IMS	HEP	L35	30/100	LPS	P	GR

▢ Internet Access   [WiFi] Wireless Internet Access   ⬤onSpot Dockside WiFi Facility

See WaterwayGuide.com for current rates, fuel prices, website addresses, and other up-to-the-minute information. (Information in the table is provided by the facilities.)

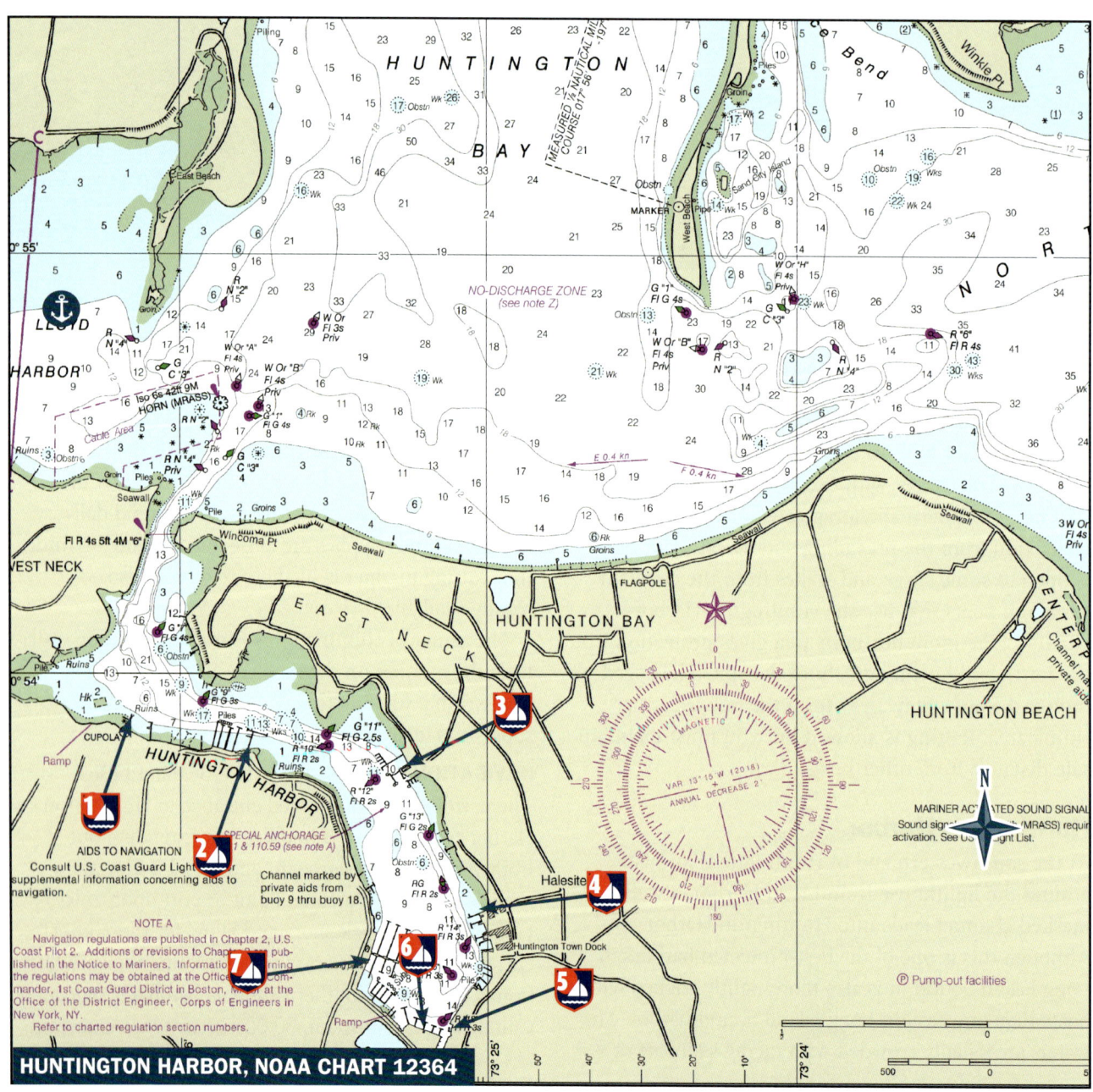

HUNTINGTON HARBOR, NOAA CHART 12364

constructed in 1912 in the style of a medieval French château (open to the public).

After rounding flashing green buoy "7" the channel swings east for about 1,000 yards before turning south into the harbor's lower end. Watch your wake as you navigate the channel as a 5-mph speed limit is strictly enforced. There is no room here to anchor.

Dockage/Moorings: Marinas offer berth space in Huntington Harbor and several independent concerns rent moorings with launch service to the village. Repairs are available at several of these facilities. The long-established Huntington Yacht Club which welcomes visiting yachts on their docks. Or if you prefer, you can rent one of the club's moorings (swift launch service included) for a modest facility fee.

Northport Bay

The eastern arm of Huntington Bay is Northport Bay. It is a body of water with its own complex of harbors, coves, sandy beaches, a neat town on the harbor and a colorful resident shell fishing fleet. Long Island Lighting Company (LILCO) opened the Northport Power Station in 1967. This is the largest oil-fired electric generating station on the East coast. The four stacks are a famous landmark to boaters on the sound. They can be seen as far away as Connecticut and line up close to magnetic north.

Moving counterclockwise from the west around Northport Bay, the first harbor is Centerport Harbor on the southern shore, separated from Northport Harbor to the east by Little Neck. Duck Island Harbor is to the north, almost directly across from Centerport Harbor. Centerport Harbor is easily the quietest harbor in the area and offers some services for shoal-draft boats. You can explore the coves and marshes by dinghy but it is too narrow to anchor here with confidence.

NAVIGATION: Use NOAA Charts 12364 and 12365. The entrance channel begins at flashing green buoy "1" just off West Beach, a 1-mile-long spit extending south from Eatons Neck. Do not cut this light too closely or go inside it as a sandbar comes out from the point. The well-marked channel lines up clearly to the east. Mind the navigational aids. A 2-knot current might put you on shoals and rocks. Be especially mindful of red nun buoy "4," which marks a 3-foot MLW spot in what appears to be the middle of the bay.

GOIN' ASHORE

NORTHPORT, NY

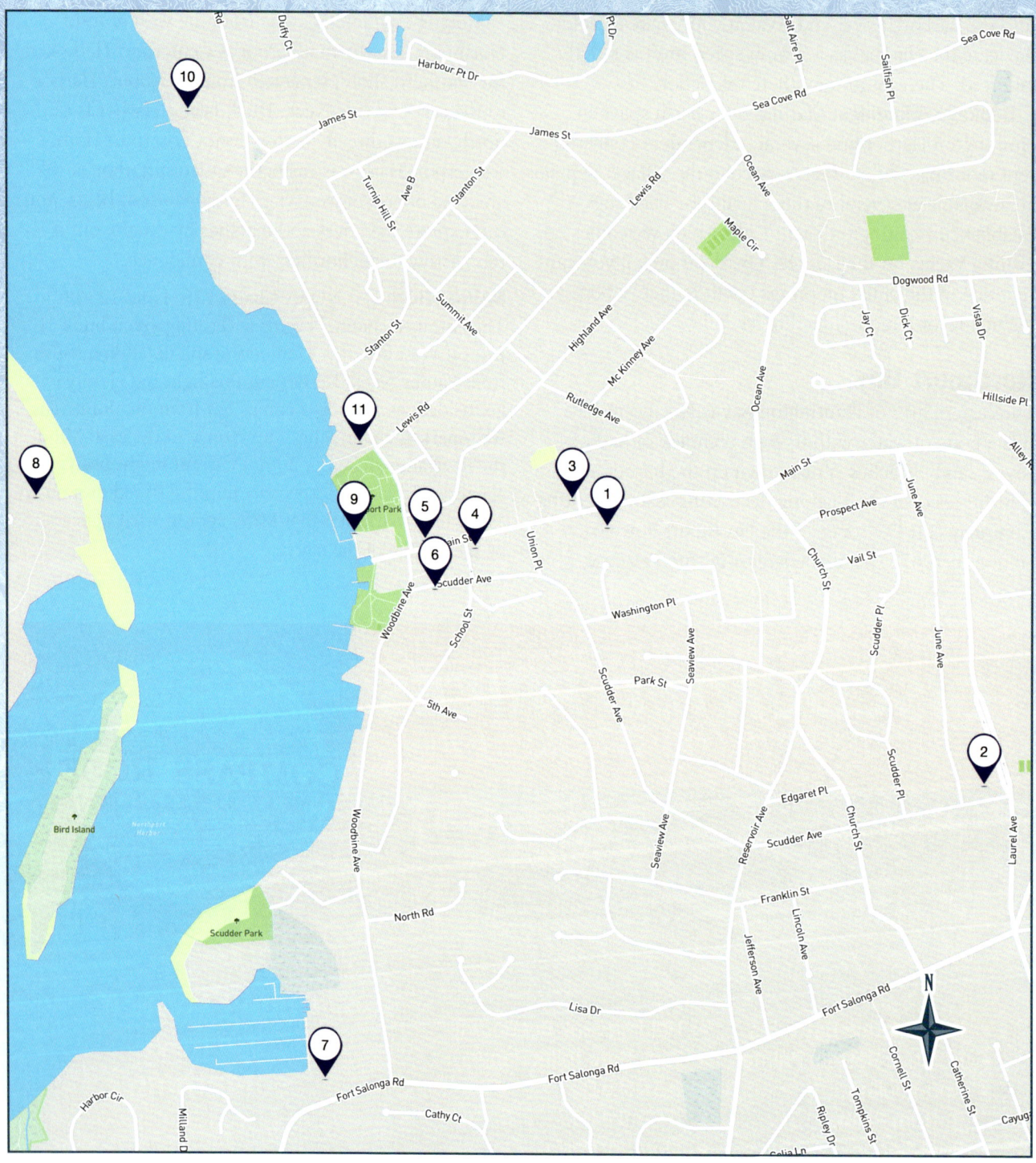

The Matinecocks (one of the 13 Native American tribes of Long Island) were the original inhabitants of the Northport area, which was the called Opcathontyche, meaning "wading place creek." In 1656, Chief Asharoken, head of the tribe, sold the area to three Englishmen who grazed cattle on pastures around the harbor. The harbor became known as Cow Harbor. In 1932, the village of Northport purchased the land along the harbor and created Northport Memorial Park, which remains a strong feature of Northport today.

SERVICES

1. Northport Post Office
240 Main St. (631-261-6941)

2. Northport Public Library
151 Laurel Ave. (631-261-6930)

ATTRACTIONS

3. Northport Historical Society
Located at 215 Main St. with exhibits and a museum shop (631-757-9859).

SHOPPING

4. Jones Drug Store
100 Main St. (631-261-7070)

5. Northport Harbor Deli
Prepares hot and cold sandwiches to go (51 Main St., 631-261-6808).

6. Snug Harbor Marine Supply
16 Scudder Ave. (631-754-0777)

MARINAS

7. Britannia Yachting Center
81 Fort Salonga Rd. (631-261-5600)

8. Centerport Yacht Club
Beach Plum Dr. (631-697-8691)

9. Northport Village Dock
224 Main St. (631-261-7502)

10. Northport Yacht Club
11 Bluff Point Rd. (631-261-7633)

11. Seymour's Boat Yard
63 Bayview Ave. (631-261-6574)

Northport Harbor, NY

NORTHPORT	Phone	Largest Vessel Accomodated	VHF Channel Monitored / Working	Transient Slips / Total Slips	Approach / Dockside Depth (reported)	Floating Docks	Groceries, Ice, Marine Supplies, Snacks	Gas / Diesel	Repairs: Hull, Engine, Propeller	Lift (tonnage), Crane, Rail	Courtesy Car, Laundry, Pool, Showers	Min / Max Amps	Pump-Out Station	Nearby: Grocery Store, Motel, Restaurant
		Dockage					Supplies		Services					
1. Northport Yacht Club	(631) 261-7633	50	71/	/	7.0/4.0		IS				PS			R
2. Centerport Yacht Club WiFi	(631) 697-8691	45	68/	/	8.0/6.0		I				PS	30		GMR
3. Seymour's Boat Yard WiFi	(631) 261-6574	60	68/	4/12	8.0/7.0	F	I	GD	HEP	C,R		30	P	GMR
4. Northport Village Dock	(631) 261-7502	120	/	/	6.0/6.0							30	P	GMR
5. Britannia Yachting Center WiFi	(631) 261-5600	45	9/	15/310	5.0/9.0	F	GIMS	GD	HEP	L55,C	PS	30/100	P	GMR

□ Internet Access   WiFi Wireless Internet Access   onSpot Dockside WiFi Facility

See WaterwayGuide.com for current rates, fuel prices, website addresses, and other up-to-the-minute information. (Information in the table is provided by the facilities.)

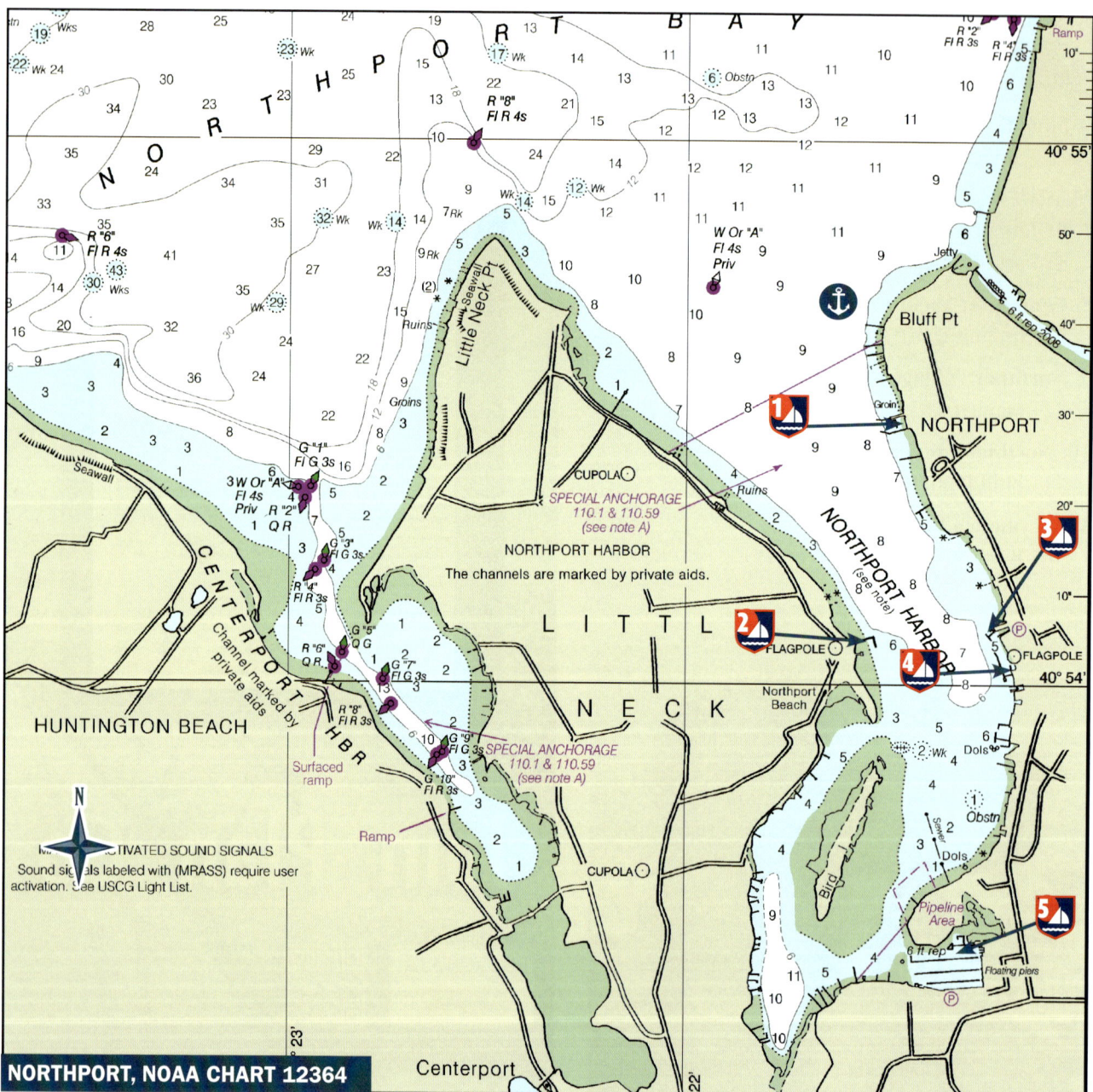

NORTHPORT, NOAA CHART 12364

Dockage/Moorings: Slips or moorings are available here via two yacht clubs (Northport and Centerport), a well-regarded boat yard (Seymour's Boat Yard), a large, full-service marina (Brittania Yachting Center) and the Northport Village Dock. Launch service is available but it is a relatively short run to the dinghy landing just inside the town dock.

The lengthy Northport Village Town Dock is marked by a gazebo on its north end and offers free two-hour tie-ups, possibly longer on less crowded weekdays. It is convenient for shopping in the village. After 8:00 p.m. an overnight fee is charged but a portion of it is refunded if you leave by 11:00 p.m. This accommodates people who want to come in just for the evening. No water or electricity is available and you will want to put out a fender board to stay off the pilings during the 7- to 9-foot tide change.

Anchorage: Anchorage in Northport Harbor is not possible as the whole area is occupied with mooring balls. Anchorage is available just outside the harbor north and northwest of Bluff Point. Holding is good in 9 to 11 feet MLW but you are exposed to north and northwest winds. The dinghy ride to the nearest landing will require strong arms at the oars or, preferably, a motor. All spaces at the dinghy dock in Northport are rented out to locals. There is a $200 fine for violations. Check with the on-site dockmaster about where to tie up your dinghy.

For anchoring with protection from other wind directions, head to Asharoken, Duck Island Harbor or Price Bend. Price Bend is wide open to the south with holding ground that leaves much to be desired so this is a better lunch or swimming spot than an overnight anchorage. Note that rafting is not permitted in the town of Asharoken, which includes Asharoken Bight, Price Bend and Eatons Neck Basin. The "no rafting" law is strictly enforced by the local marine police. Local ordinances also forbid anchoring within 50 feet of the shore and require holding tanks or self-contained heads. Wind protection is from northerly directions but much farther from Northport or the other harbors.

Eatons Neck

Eatons Neck Basin is a convenient overnight spot for those transiting the sound and not wishing to enter any of the larger harbors. Known locally as Coast Guard Cove, this tiny harbor is home of the local Coast Guard station. The 144-foot white stone lighthouse on Eatons Neck is one of the oldest on Long Island. It was established in 1792 on direct orders from George Washington.

NAVIGATION: Use NOAA Charts 12364 and 12365. The flashing green "1" entrance buoy marks the end of a submerged breakwater and must be left to port. At low tide you are likely to see a few clam boats arrive. Note that Coast Guard rescue craft can head out at high speed and throw a heavy wake. Be certain not to anchor in the channel or anywhere that might interfere with their operations.

Heading east from Huntington Bay give Eatons Neck Point a wide berth. Depths are as shallow as 4 feet at MLW for almost 1 mile to the northeast.

Anchorage: This is strictly an anchorage with no amenities. The cove is exempt from the local ordinance against anchoring within 50 feet of shore. Good depths run right up to the western shore but depths become shallower and anchoring spots fewer east of the channel. Going ashore is not permitted.

◼ SMITHTOWN BAY TO MATTITUCK INLET

Smithtown Bay

Another of Long Island's appealing towns, Stony Brook lies in the southeastern corner of Smithtown Bay, south of Crane Neck Point. While the harbor is crowded and difficult to enter, it is a rewarding port of call.

The Stony Brook area dates back to Revolutionary times when George Washington traveled the Heritage Trail (now State Highway 25A). While the British Army provisioned from Stony Brook's gristmill, Washington's spy ring concurrently operated from the town. Stony Brook Village Center is one of the first planned business centers. The Colonial-style center now houses numerous quaint shops and restaurants (www.stonybrookvillage.com)

The historic Stony Brook Grist Mill (c. 1751), where millers are still grinding grain, is a 5-minute walk from the Village Center and is open for tours Wednesday through Sunday, June through August (631-751-2244 or 631-689-3238).

Must see: The mechanical eagle that flaps its wings on the hour while perched atop the Stony Brook Post Office.

Stony Brook Harbor, NY

STONY BROOK		Dockage				Supplies			Services			
	VHF Channel Monitored / Working	Largest Vessel Accomodated	Approach / Dockside Depth (reported)	Transient Slips / Total Slips	Floating Docks	Groceries, Ice, Marine Supplies, Snacks	Gas / Diesel	Repairs: Hull, Engine, Propeller	Lift (tonnage), Crane, Rail	Min / Max Amps	Courtesy Car, Laundry, Pool, Showers	Pump-Out Station	Nearby: Grocery Store, Motel, Restaurant
1. Stony Brook Yacht Club (631) 751-9873	54	9/	2/187	6.0/8.0		GD	I			30	S		GMR

⌨ Internet Access 📶 Wireless Internet Access 🛜onSpot Dockside WiFi Facility
See WaterwayGuide.com for current rates, fuel prices, website addresses, and other up-to-the-minute information. (Information in the table is provided by the facilities.)

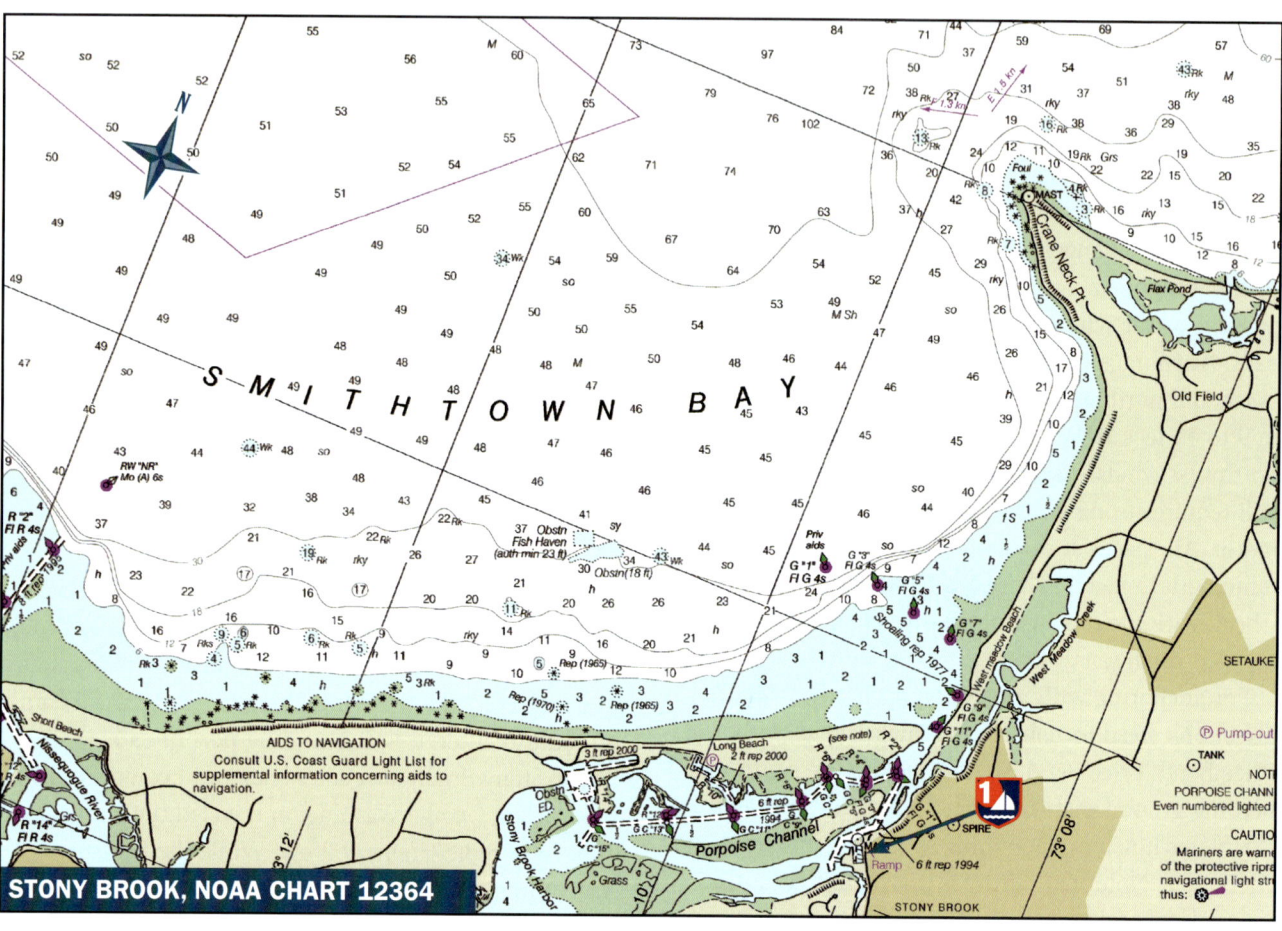

STONY BROOK, NOAA CHART 12364

NAVIGATION: Use NOAA Charts 12364 and 12365. Most cruising boats coming from Northport Bay cut straight across the broad (about 10 miles wide) Smithtown Bay by picking up green can buoy "13" off Eatons Neck and running 100° magnetic to green gong buoy "11A" off Old Field Point (northwest of Port Jefferson) rather than taking the more direct route through Long Island Sound. When you are bucking a foul current, the trip closer to the beach and bluff-lined shore is easier and faster due to a weaker current speed.

Approach to the Stony Brook Harbor is over a bar (less than 2 feet MLW) that extends about 1 mile above the entrance. Minimum channel depth inside is 5 feet MLW. Mean tidal range is more than 6 feet so deeper-draft boats can enter on a rising tide. The privately marked and maintained entrance channel leads east from the charted flashing green buoy "1." Just short of the shoreline of West Meadow Beach the channel turns south to parallel the beach. Strong currents speed through the narrow opening between West Meadow Beach and Long Beach, calling for cautious navigation. Inside Porpoise Cove leads southwest to Stony Brook.

Dockage/Moorings: The Stony Brook Yacht Club has limited transient docking for boaters requiring daily or overnight docking. There is a strong current so care must be taken when maneuvering. There is also a small town dinghy dock available for more than 3-hour tie-ups.

Sunken Meadows State Park

Port Jefferson Harbor

Port Jefferson, a favorite stop of cruising boats, is a deep, 2-mile-long harbor. If you are traveling east, it is the last real harbor until Mattituck, some 26 miles farther on. Port Jefferson is a justly popular harbor. The village is located on the harbor and has boating amenities and beaches where you can swim and picnic.

The hilly streets in town leading to the harbor are bursting with museums, historic homes, shops, restaurants and varied architectural styles. You can take the railroad to New York City, a ferry to Bridgeport, CT, or make convenient connections by air via MacArthur Airport at Islip. Most amenities, including the library and Post Office, are situated on Main and East Main Streets, which run south from the waterfront.

Located on the west side of Port Jefferson Harbor, the remote little 17th-century town of Setauket offers a fascinating side trip for dinghies or small, shoal-draft boats. Setauket has a small, private marina at the head of the inlet surrounded by well-kept, Colonial-style homes. The entrance to the Setauket Harbor is suitable for a 5-foot draft but the harbor is fully occupied with mooring balls and anchoring is not possible. There is a good dinghy dock adjacent to the private marina, which will allow you to tie up. The village center is about 1.5 mile away with a shopping center (Three Village Plaza) with cafés, a laundry and limited shopping.

NAVIGATION: Use NOAA Charts 12364 and 12362. Port Jefferson is best approached from the red and white sea buoy "PJ" Morse (A), located about 1 mile northwest of the entrance to the harbor. Coming from Connecticut the 100-foot-high bluff of Mount Misery Point offers a prominent landmark. Once inside the entrance buoys head for the church spire in the center of town. You can see it situated between the large hospital to the east and the Port Jefferson power plant stacks to the west. The narrow cut between Mount Misery Point and the lighted end ("flashing red "2A") of Old Field Beach can be crowded with traffic, and when wind and tide are opposed it can be quite turbulent. Currents average 2.5 knots on the flood and 2 knots on the ebb. Be alert for barge and ferry traffic but otherwise there are few obstructions or dangers on the bay.

Stretching north from the head of the harbor below the high-banked eastern shore much of Port Jefferson's recreational fleet lies tethered at moorings. The well-marked harbor channel leads directly to a hub centering on the municipal marina, ferry dock and the unmistakable power station. Keep clear of this area to allow for the passage of commercial traffic and be aware of the frequent, swift-traveling car-carrying ferries, which back toward the power station on each return to Bridgeport. Be watchful and always be prepared to give way to the ferries.

Dockage/Moorings: The municipal Port Jefferson Marina west of the ferry landing may have transient space available on an hourly or daily basis. The marina monitors VHF Channel 09. Free pump-out service is available at the courtesy dock.

Smithtown Bay, NY

		Largest Vessel Accommodated	VHF Channel Monitored / Working	**Dockage** Transient Slips / Total Slips	Approach / Dockside Depth (reported)	Floating Docks	**Supplies** Gas / Diesel	Groceries, Ice, Marine Supplies, Snacks	Repairs: Hull, Engine, Propeller	**Services** Lift (tonnage), Crane, Rail	Min / Max Amps	Courtesy Car, Laundry, Pool, Showers	Pump-Out Station	Nearby: Grocery Store, Motel, Restaurant
PORT JEFFERSON														
1. Port Jefferson Marina [WiFi]	(631) 331-3567	50	16/9	10/120	20.0/		GD	I	HEP		30/50	LS	P	MR
2. Danfords Hotel & Marina [Internet][WiFi]	(631) 928-5200	200	9/8	75/75	25.0/15.0	F	GD	GIS			30/100	LS	P	GMR
3. Port Jefferson Yacht Club [Internet][WiFi]	(631) 473-9650	60	68/68	/	12.0/6.0	F		I			30	S	P	GMR
MOUNT SINAI														
4. Ralph's Fishing Station & Marina	(631) 473-6655	50	67/	5/50	15.0/15.0	F	GD	IMS	HEP	L	30			GR
5. Mt. Sinai Yacht Club	(631) 473-2993	45	9/71	10/99	17.0/12.0	F	GD	GIMS			30/50	S	P	GR
6. Old Man's Boat Yard	(631) 473-7330	50	/	3/60	12.0/12.0	F		IM	HEP	L25,C	30			GR

□ Internet Access   [WiFi] Wireless Internet Access   onSpot Dockside WiFi Facility

See WaterwayGuide.com for current rates, fuel prices, website addresses, and other up-to-the-minute information. (Information in the table is provided by the facilities.)

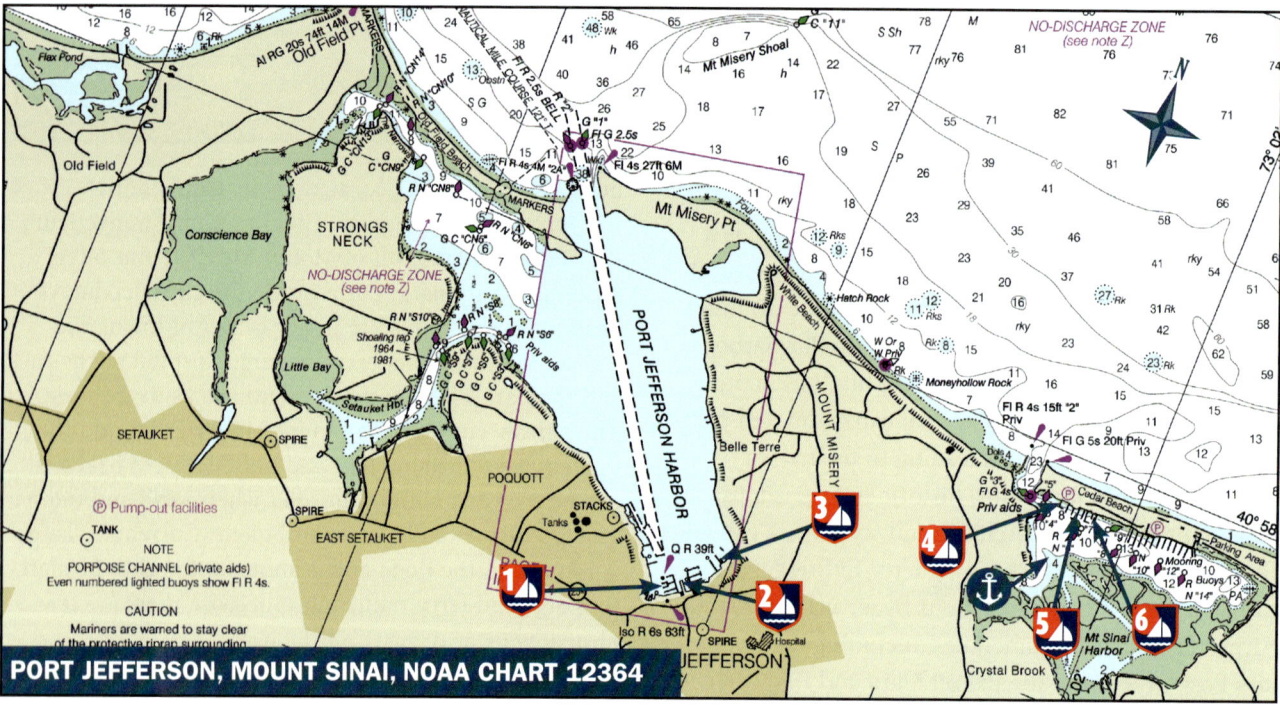

PORT JEFFERSON, MOUNT SINAI, NOAA CHART 12364

Danfords Hotel & Marina, just east of the ferry dock, offers the protection of its wooden sea barrier and can accommodate vessels up to 200 feet in deep water (15-foot at MLW) slips on floating docks. They also sell all fuels and have an on-site restaurant and a spa. This is a great place to get off the boat for the night or meet up with new crew, family and friends.

Port Jefferson Yacht Club has guest moorings and slips available to overnight cruisers and short-term day visitors. The largest mooring operation in the harbor is run by Port Jefferson Launch, which rents its 40 moorings (bright red balls) and provides launch service to and from its location adjacent to the ferry dock. Hail "Port Jefferson Launch Service" on VHF Channel 68. A mooring can be very uncomfortable during a blow from the north since the harbor's considerable fetch will permit a buildup of 2- to 3-foot seas.

Anchorage: Just to the east of the entrance, Mount Misery Cove (locally known as the Sand Pit or Pirate's Cove), is almost completely occupied by mooring balls and anchoring inside the cove is prohibited. (You may anchor outside the cove.) To the west of the main channel just inside the harbor entrance a seasonal channel leads to the cove behind Old Field Beach and Conscience Bay. Several shallow spots (3- to 6-foot MLW mounds) require deep-draft vessels to proceed with some care at less than half-tide. Once inside this is a secure and quiet anchorage in depths ranging from 10 to 14 feet MLW. There are numerous private moorings here but there's still room to anchor.

North of the main mooring field in Post Jefferson Harbor there is good holding and room for anchorage within a reasonable distance from shore. Port Jefferson Launch offers launch service in the harbor. Call "Port Jefferson Launch" on VHF Channel 68 or you can dinghy to Danford's dock, which has a 10-foot limit and is available for a fee.

Mount Sinai Harbor

After leaving Port Jefferson, travel east for about 3 miles beyond high Mount Misery to Mount Sinai Harbor. Once an uncharted marshy gunkhole inhabited mainly by ducks and mosquitoes, the Mount Sinai Harbor was dredged and converted to a boat-packed, well-protected port with good anchorages, a fine beach (dedicated to the residents of the Village of Brookhaven) and pleasant surroundings. Much of the extensive marsh area is set aside as a nature reserve and is an important nesting area for a number of birds. Ralph's Fishing Station & Marina rents sturdy two-seat kayaks for explorations of the tidal estuary.

NAVIGATION: Use NOAA Chart 12364. Mount Sinai Harbor is clearly marked, first by an offshore

red-and-white "M" buoy, then by the unnumbered flashing green light at the end of the east breakwater and a flashing red light to the west. The harbor entrance hooks to port on entry but is wide enough for comfortable ingress with at least 12-foot MLW depths throughout the harbor's well-marked main channel. Locals advise that when entering the harbor you should give a wide berth to the sandy beach (easily visible to port inside the entry jetties) when making the left turn into the harbor mooring area. The shoal extending from the beach into the channel is not marked.

Dockage/Moorings: A marina, yacht club and boat yard host the immense number of boats here. When you enter the harbor, the fuel dock and facilities of Ralph's Fishing Station & Marina are immediately evident to port.

Immediately past the marina, the friendly Mt. Sinai Yacht Club has moorings available to visitors for a modest facility fee. About 0.25 mile east along the harbor channel, Old Man's Boat Yard has slips on floating docks and full-service repair operations.

Anchorage: Anchoring space may be difficult to find due to the great number of moorings in Mount Sinai Harbor but holding in the far west end of the harbor is good in mud and grass. This offers protection from all but easterly winds. The extension of the harbor to the southwest after the entrance may have a little space to swing on the hook. You may also find a spot in the east corner of the harbor.

Mattituck Inlet

The 40 miles between Mount Sinai and Plum Gut can be long ones for slow boats. Mattituck Inlet is the only stopover between the two. Mattituck is a well-protected, quiet, relaxed village typical of eastern Long Island. The entry into Mattituck Creek can be very challenging when the winds are out of the north and the water depth is a challenge at low tide. The 2-mile-long creek is winding at first then straightens with sand, marshes, trees and many lovely houses flanking its banks.

The Mattituck Creek was dammed in 1812 and a tidal gristmill turned both night and day. The old mill can still be seen on your right about one-third of the way into the creek. Kayaking is a popular activity in the protected waters of the Mattituck Inlet, which is home to many wading birds. It also boasts a large population of osprey nests on many of the daybeacons and the platforms set up for them.

Long Island Sound, NY

MATTITUCK INLET		VHF Channel Monitored / Working	Largest Vessel Accomodated	Approach / Dockside Depth (reported)	Transient Slips / Total Slips	Floating Docks	Gas / Diesel	Groceries, Ice, Marine Supplies, Snacks	Repairs: Hull, Engine, Propeller	Lift (tonnage), Crane, Rail	Min / Max Amps	Courtesy Car, Laundry, Pool, Showers	Pump-Out Station	Nearby: Grocery Store, Motel, Restaurant
				Dockage				**Supplies**		**Services**				
1. Strong's Yacht Center	(631) 298-4480	110	/	10/45	/10.0	F	GD	M	HEP	L75	30/50	PS		R
2. Strong's Water Club and Marina (WiFi)	(631) 298-4739	75	9/68	/135	9.0/7.0	F	GD	IM	HEP	L50	30/50	LPS		GMR

Internet Access   WiFi Wireless Internet Access   onSpot Dockside WiFi Facility
See WaterwayGuide.com for current rates, fuel prices, website addresses, and other up-to-the-minute information. (Information in the table is provided by the facilities.)

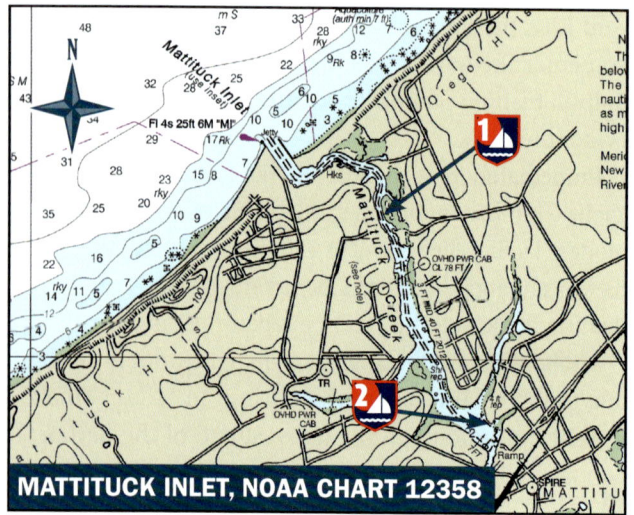

MATTITUCK INLET, NOAA CHART 12358

Some of the famous Long Island vineyards in the area offer retail opportunities, tours and wine tastings. There are many "pour & pedal"-type tours during which you bike to from one vineyard to another throughout the course of a day. Routes, lengths and costs vary.

NAVIGATION: Use NOAA Charts 12358 and 12354. It is difficult to see the entry to Mattituck Inlet from offshore but the dredged and jettied channel creates a deep gap in the shoreline bluffs. The best approach is to take a compass course due south from green gong buoy "3A," 1 mile north of the entrance, and then watch for flashing white "MI" at the end of the western jetty. The entrance channel is well marked and carries 6-foot MLW depths. If your draft is even close to 6 feet, enter on a rising tide.

A heavy sea can build up in the entrance in northerly winds blowing against an ebbing current. Once inside the inlet and past the sharp turn to port, keep in mid-channel but favor the outside edge when the creek turns to avoid shoaling on the inside of the bends. Tidal range is more than 5 feet and currents run as much as 3 knots. Currents diminish as you travel up the creek and depths decrease somewhat. In the upper creek

observe the very small, privately maintained channel buoys, which can appear to be fishing floats. The basin and anchorage at the head of the creek have up to 7-foot MLW depths.

Dockage: This area offers repair yards, waterside restaurants and marinas. Strong's Yacht Center and Strong's Water Club and Marina at the head of the creek have slips and repairs. The town of Mattituck is a 10-minute walk away.

Anchorage: The anchorage at the Federal Basin off of Strong's Yacht Center at the head of the creek is totally protected but can get very crowded on summer weekends. The holding is fair (5 to 7 feet MLW in mud) but the area offers all-around protection. Great Peconic Bay is only 1 mile overland to the south from this point.

There is a town dinghy dock at the end of the basin gives access to Mattituck and famous Love Lane, a 5-minute walk. There is also great shopping, groceries, restaurants and a beach (Veterans Park) within walking distance.

◼ NEXT STOP

From Mattituck the coast stretches on eastward. It is generally bluff, rocky and unbroken by harbors for almost 18 miles to Orient Point. The water is generally deep close to shore as the 10-fathom curve is less than 1 mile offshore at most points. Currents are strong. Landmarks include the light high on Horton Point, tall water tanks at Greenport on the far side of the Long Island land mass and water tanks on Plum Island, well to the east and past Orient Point. The 65-foot Orient Point Light, locally called the Coffee Pot, marks Plum Gut and serves as the turning point into Gardiners Bay.

Long Island Twin Forks, NY

Some of the finest cruising grounds can be found within the Twin Forks of Long Island, NY. The two ends of Long Island surround Great Peconic Bay and Gardiner's Bay and are known as the North and the South Forks.

The eastern end of Long Island splits like two flukes of a fish tail. The deep cleft begins at the town of Riverhead. Known as the Twin Forks, the Forks, or sometimes the Fish Tail, this area comprises deep bays, large islands and big jutting peninsulas that create miles of attractive cruising territory with good harbors and generally deep water. The north fork runs about 30 miles from Riverhead to Orient Point, and the south fork, 40 miles long, stretches from Riverhead to Montauk Point.

Gardiners Bay, situated below Plum Gut and inside of Orient Point, is separated from Block Island Sound and the open ocean by Gardiners Island. Gardiners Bay is the entrance to Shelter Island Sound, the Peconic Bays and an intriguing assortment of small bodies of water extending west to Riverhead. Big, irregularly shaped Shelter Island sits in the middle and nearly joins the

North and South Forks. About 8 miles east of Riverhead on the south fork, the Shinnecock Canal connects Great Peconic Bay with Shinnecock Bay and, through Shinnecock Inlet, the Atlantic Ocean.

■ NORTH FORK: PLUM GUT TO SOUTHOLD BAY

Gardiners Bay

From Gardiners Bay through Little Peconic Bay the water depths are about 20 feet MLW in the main channels and 10 feet MLW or more through Great Peconic Bay. Project depths to the head of navigation at Riverhead are 6 feet MLW. Currents run swiftly in narrow channels but normally do not exceed 2 knots. Marinas and anchorages are plentiful and dredging has opened many once-inaccessible side creeks and small bays to deeper draft boats. (Dredged channels have a habit of silting in so verify depths locally.)

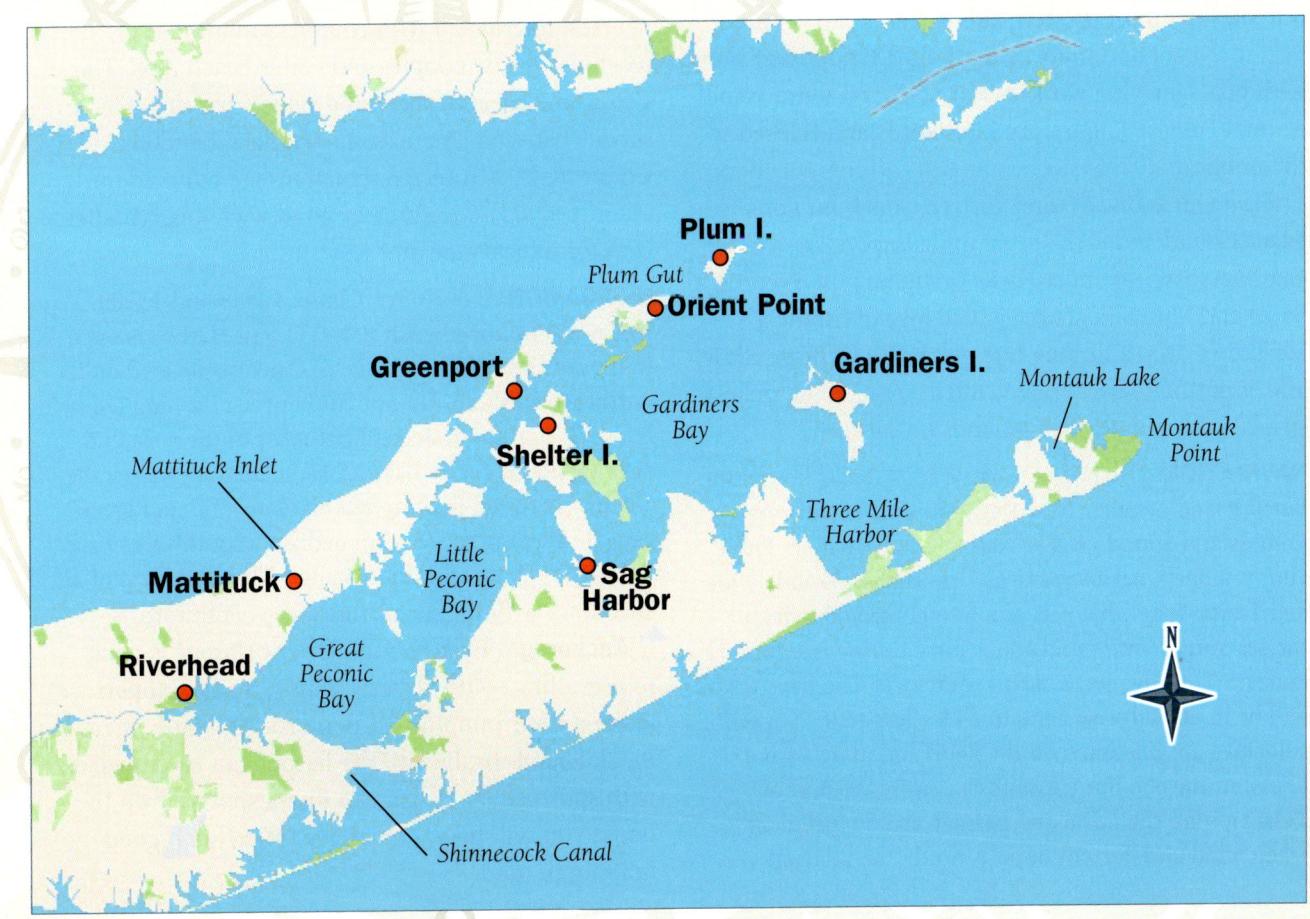

Orient Point Lighthouse

Plum Gut runs between Orient Point and Plum Island and guides you into Gardiners Bay. About 1 mile in you will see the major docks of Orient by the Sea Marina on the western shore. The Cross Sound ferries (New London to Orient Point) tie up here along with boats ferrying workers to the federal Plum Island Animal Disease Laboratory on Plum Island (closed to the public).

Plum Gut is one of three eastern exits from Long Island Sound and is the usual route to ports in Gardiners Bay, the inner Forks (including the Peconic Bays) and Montauk. Those with a love of fishing are advised to drop a trolling lure overboard (if licensed) at any opportunity because you are in some of the richest striped bass and bluefish grounds on earth.

NAVIGATION: Use NOAA Chart 13209. Boats bound for Block Island or other New England ports usually exit Long Island Sound via The Race. The alternative, Plum Gut, is a deep, narrow passage (less than 0.75-mile wide and 1-mile long) that acts as a funnel through which the sea surges with tremendous force during maximum current. The advantage of this route over The Race is you will be in any adverse conditions for less time. Normal velocities are 3.5 knots on the flood and more than 4 knots on the ebb but currents can easily top 5 knots. Tidal rips are the norm and passage can be turbulent when wind and current oppose. Study the tide and current tables and try to plan your passage (whether east or west) when a fair current or slack water are expected.

Dockage: The seasonal Duryea's Orient Point on the south side of Orient Point has transient slips (to 50 feet) with few amenities but a great tiki bar. They also sell all fuels.

Anchorage: To the southwest of Orient Point is Orient Beach State Park with good fishing and swimming. The water is deep almost to the beach. This is a fair-weather open roadstead anchorage with deep water and excellent holding in sand.

Orient Harbor

Orient is an excellent place to recapture the unhurried pace of what once typified small town America. Quaint, small houses date back to the 1700s and have seen Indian raids as well as a visit from George Washington. Huge exotic trees and well-loved lawns and gardens adorn the tranquil streets. Orient Beach State Park, located at the east end of North Country Road, offers 10 miles of beaches ideal for shelling, bird watching and nature study.

Walking and shelling along the north side of Long Beach Point is a special treat. The "beach" is an expansive strand of colorful, smooth and rounded pebbles, intermixed with countless thousands of rosehips, yellow poppies and edible beach peas. The Cross Sound Ferry operates a vehicle/passenger ferry service between Orient Point and New London, Connecticut. Advance reservations are required for autos. Call 631-323-2525 or go to www.longislandferry.com for information and reservations.

NAVIGATION: Use NOAA Charts 12358 and 13209. Just north of Long Beach Point, Orient Harbor is open to the southwest. The village of Orient is located on its northeastern shore. Do not cut between flashing red bell buoy "2" and the restored lighthouse at the west end of Long Beach charted as "LT HO." Instead, follow the channel between flashing red bell buoy "2" and green can "3" keeping the area immediately southwest of the lighthouse at a respectful distance. This will prevent an encounter with the shoals that creep southward.

Anchorage: Even though Orient Harbor is open to prevailing southwesterly winds, many skippers make it their jumping-off point for Montauk or Block Island. In the fall, the harbor can be crowded with sportfishers. If you can find a spot to drop the hook, you will have 7 to 20 feet MLW with good holding in mud.

During settled weather good anchorage can also be found in 10-foot to 20-foot MLW depths within easy reach of the shore along the north side of Long Beach Point near the two working fish weirs. If you work your way east above the weir closest to the point, you will notice a decided drop-off from the trough-like 8- to 10-foot MLW depths paralleling the shore. Hard-mud holding is excellent in the deeper trough, while a secure set in the surrounding shallower waters is typically thwarted by extensive areas of hard-packed stones. (You will encounter millions more of these on the stony beach.)

Take care in navigating this area to avoid the additional floating nets that are sometimes stationed here. This is a relatively popular place on weekends, yet the feeling is remote and more reminiscent of Maine than Long Island. You can dinghy further east to a dock that gives access to the State Park.

Greenport Harbor

Greenport, settled in 1682, remains encircled by bucolic landscapes and is a low-key and peaceful seaside village. Because of its deep and protected harbor, Greenport became a major whaling port between 1795 and 1859 when more than 20 whaling ships berthed here. The town was also a very busy shipbuilding center. By the mid-1800s the menhaden fishing industry employed thousands of people. During the first half of the 20th century, Greenport became a huge oystering center. When the oyster industry began to shrink, Greenport turned to tourism and became a destination for global visitors.

Greenport is still the annual site of a tall-ship rendezvous but now they come for fun, not commerce. Greenport is bordered on one side by Shelter Island Sound and by Long Island Sound on the north side.

NAVIGATION: Use NOAA Charts 12358 and 13209. Greenport is almost 8 nm south-southwest of Orient Point across the 1-mile-wide pass north of Shelter Island. The harbor is easily reached via a deep, well-marked channel. Landmarks include a water tank, white church spire and, at night, a television tower with a fixed red light. Flashing red 19-foot "8A" at the south end of the breakwater marks the harbor entrance.

Stirling Basin (known locally as Stirling Harbor) is the primary recreational boating center. The entrance is along the buoyed channel leading northwest from the outer harbor and roughly parallels the jetty. Favor the west shore on entry to avoid the shoal extending southwest of Youngs Point. West of the narrow cut upon entry into the nearly landlocked basin you can see an abstract stone monument honoring sailors lost at sea. The red nun just west of the monument marks the channel's edge.

Dockage/Moorings: Town moorings in Greenport are immediately evident upon entering Stirling Basin. The moorings are white, lobster-style buoys with yellow pick-up toggles. The dinghy dock is located opposite the monument at the harbor entrance. From here it is less than a 10-minute walk to the Greenport business district.

Two Safe Harbor facilities are in the harbor. Safe Harbor Greenport is popular with locals and offers full-service quality repair service, a substantial parts

Greenport Harbor

Shelter Sound, NY

		Largest Vessel Accommodated	VHF Channel Monitored / Working	Transient Slips / Total Slips	Approach / Dockside Depth (reported)	Floating Docks	Gas / Diesel	Groceries, Ice, Marine Supplies, Snacks	Repairs: Hull, Engine, Propeller	Lift (tonnage) Crane, Rail	Min / Max Amps	Courtesy Car, Laundry, Pool, Showers	Pump-Out Station	Nearby: Grocery Store, Motel, Restaurant
PLUM GUT				**Dockage**				**Supplies**			**Services**			
1. Duryea's Orient Point WiFi	(631) 323-2424	50	9/	10/95	6.0/10.0	F	GD	IS	HEP		30	S		8R
GREENPORT														
2. Safe Harbor Greenport 💻 WiFi	(631) 477-9594	60	9/	8/200	7.0/8.0	F		IM	HEP	L70	30/50	CLPS	P	GMR
3. Safe Harbor Stirling 💻 WiFi	(631) 477-0828	100	9/	15/185	12.0/7.0	F	GD	IM	HEP	L50	30/50	LPS	P	GMR
4. Townsend Manor Marina 💻 WiFi	(631) 477-2000	60	9/	25/50	8.0/7.0	F		IS			30/50	LPS		GMR
5. Greenport Yacht and Ship Co.	(631) 477-2277	120	/	6/6	20.0/12.0				HEP		30			GMR
6. Preston's Marine Supply and Docks	(631) 477-1990	65	/	10/10	20.0/8.0			M						GMR
7. Claudio's Marina, Restaurant and Clam Bar 💻 WiFi	(631) 477-0355	240	9/	35/35	45.0/15.0			GIMS		L,R	30/100	S		GMR
8. Mitchell Park Marina WiFi	(631) 477-2200	250	11/	60/60	45.0/10.0	F		IM			30/100	S	P	GMR
9. Brick Cove Marina WiFi	(631) 477-0830	48	16/	30/140	6.0/6.0	F		IMS	HEP	L30	30/50	LPS	P	R
10. Goldsmith's Boat Shop	(631) 765-1600	32	9/68	/109	3.0/5.0	F	G	M	EP		30			R
11. Port of Egypt Marine WiFi	(631) 765-2445	35	/	10/150	5.0/5.0		GD	IMS	HEP	L25	30	PS	P	4R
SHELTER ISLAND														
12. Shelter Island Yacht Club WiFi	(631) 749-0888	75	74/	/	10.0/7.0	F		IS				S		GMR
13. Piccozzi's Dering Harbor Marina WiFi	(631) 749-0045	160	16/9	15/35	12.0/12.0		GD	GIMS			15/100	S	P	GMR
14. The Pridwin Hotel & Cottages	(631) 749-0476	40	/	4/5	5.0/4.0						30	LPS		MR
15. The Island Boatyard and Marina WiFi	(631) 749-3333	60	9/	5/80	6.0/6.0	F	GD	GIMS	HEP	L25,C	30/50	LPS	P	GMR
16. Coecles Harbor Marina & Boatyard WiFi	(631) 749-0700	60	9/	25/40	6.0/6.0	F	GD	IMS	HEP	L	30/50	LPS	P	GMR

💻 Internet Access WiFi Wireless Internet Access onSpot Dockside WiFi Facility

See WaterwayGuide.com for current rates, fuel prices, website addresses, and other up-to-the-minute information. (Information in the table is provided by the facilities.)

department. To the north is Safe Harbor Stirling with excellent amenities that make it a cruising destination for boating clubs as well as individual cruisers. There is usually space available except for on the busiest weekends. The marina provides complimentary shuttle service to and from town, several miles distant by road from this side of the harbor and may be the best hurricane hole you will ever find anywhere.

Across the basin, northwest from the basin entrance, Townsend Manor Marina is a charming, comfortable and quiet transient marina with plenty of space for vessels to 60 feet. They offer resort amenities including an extra-large pool, modern showers/restrooms and an easy walk to town. They also have an on-site hotel, on-site restaurant and a sunken bar with stunning water views.

Outside Stirling Basin, in Greenport's harbor proper, there are additional docking possibilities ranging from a full-service boat yard to a restaurant to a municipal marina protected by an extensive wave suppression system. In addition to slips, Preston's Marine Supply and Docks has nautical gifts and decor and marine supplies. They have been in the same buildings in Greenport Harbor for over 125 years serving boats and their crews.

This area is not so well protected so you will want to rig fender boards for protection against wakes that bounce along unprotected bulkheads.

Anchorage: You can anchor in at least 8 feet MLW inside the jetty (allowing ample room for traffic in the marked channel to Stirling Basin) but this is a restless spot, offering scant protection. Better anchorage is possible in Gull Pond east of the breakwater. This enclosed basin has 6 to 7 feet MLW with good holding in mud and all-around protection.

Southold Bay

Southwest of Greenport, Southold Bay has a small harbor and an attractive village. Mill Creek, the entrance to Hashamomuck Pond, has a few marinas that welcome cruising boats. Southold itself is west of Mill Creek and is a pleasant place to visit in a shoal-draft craft.

Dockage: The full-service, family-owned Brick Cove Marina is in an enclosed basin and can accommodate vessels to 48 feet. Other small-boat facilities are to the west with slips, marine supplies and some boat repairs.

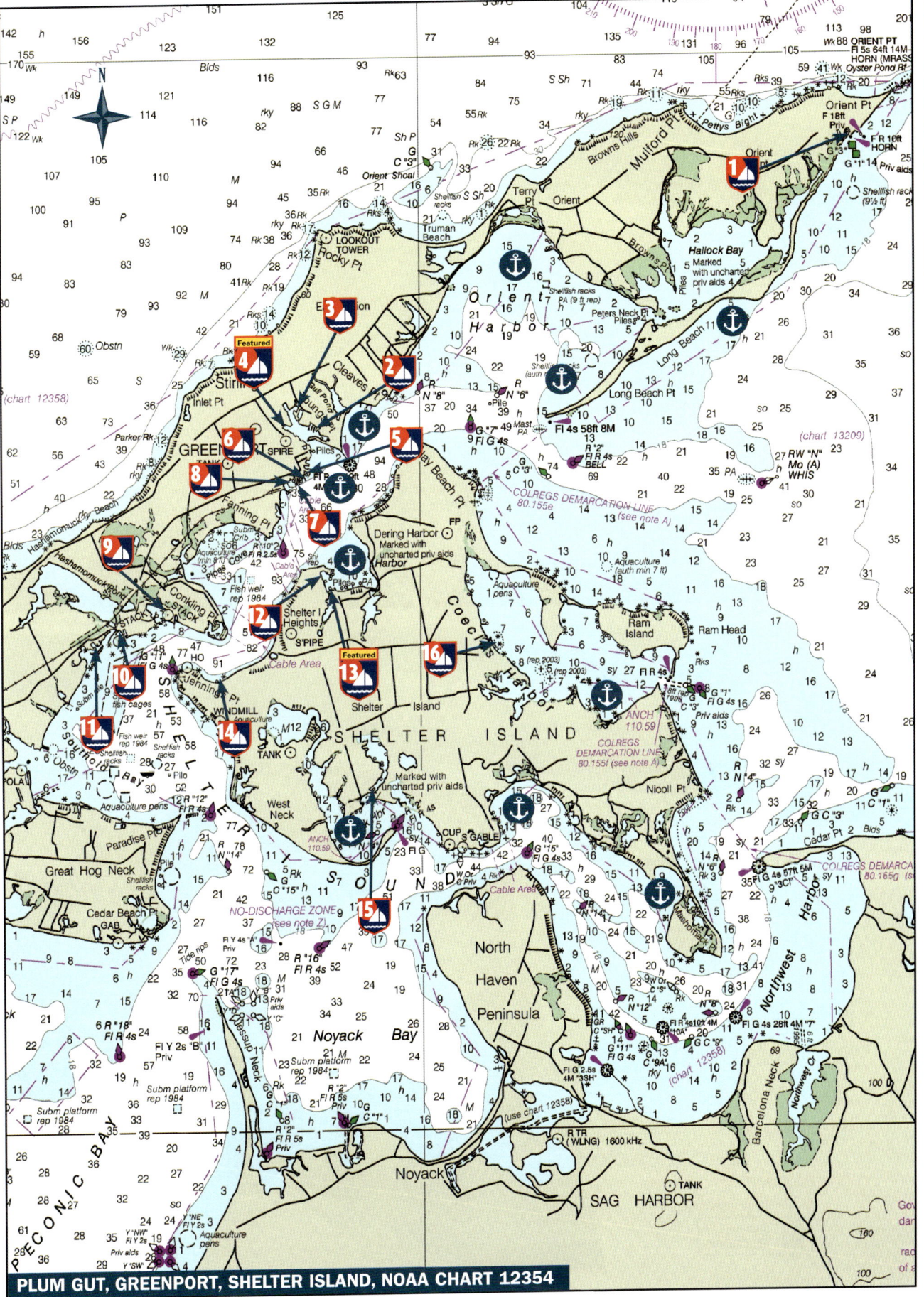

PLUM GUT, GREENPORT, SHELTER ISLAND, NOAA CHART 12354

Youngs Point

TOWNSEND
MANOR MARINA

TOWNSEND MANOR MARINA

For the cruising yachtsman, Townsend Manor has one of the finest marinas in Eastern Long Island. Nestled in the protected waters of the secluded Stirling Basin, yet just a short walk from Greenport's stores and activities, are deep-water slips for transient yachts up to 60 feet and complete resort facilities for living aboard or ashore.

- 50 slips with electric & water (30 floating)
- 31-room Inn with guest suites
- Olympic swimming pool with tiki bar
- Onsite restaurant & sunken bar
- Newly remodeled showers & restrooms
- Laundry room, BBQ area
- Mechanics on call

TOWNSENDINN.COM • VHF CH.9
631-477-2000

Find us on:
facebook.

TOWNSEND MANOR
MARINA
SWIMPOOL
HOTEL·RESTAURANT

■ SHELTER ISLAND

Experience a little slice of small-town New England in the midst of Shelter Island's charm and some of the most enjoyable cruising grounds on the Northeast coast. Shelter Island is an elegant summer enclave with rolling, wooded terrain, sheltered beaches, attractive homes and serpentine roads. The shoreline has protected harbors on all sides and you can circumnavigate the island in a few hours with a lunch stop at either Smith Cove or Majors Harbor.

Two ferries connect Shelter Island with Long Island itself. One goes to Greenport on the North Fork, while the other goes to North Haven Peninsula and Sag Harbor on the South Fork. About 4 miles long by 5 miles wide, the island is entirely surrounded by well-marked channels. Just watch for charted shoals close inshore, especially near Ram Head and Hay Beach Point.

> Note: The town discourages the off-loading of trash on the island. Bottles, cans and paper must be separated for acceptance at each harbor's recycling center. Non-recyclable trash must be placed in Town of Shelter Island disposal bags available for purchase at each center.

Dering Harbor

Cruising counterclockwise from Greenport will bring you to Dering Harbor on the north side of the island, where a mooring in the shadow of Shelter Island Heights offers a peaceful contrast to the bustle of Greenport, 1 mile north across the channel.

NAVIGATION: Use NOAA Charts 12358 and 13209. Entry is straightforward with 8-foot to 14-foot MLW depths into the center of the harbor but be sure to favor Dering Point to the northeast to avoid shoals extending from the south side of the entrance. The charted "Disposal Area" (long-ago discarded oyster shells) presents no hazard to navigation.

Dockage/Moorings: Dering Harbor is a good place for a secure mooring when the wind is up from any direction other than north. It is popular during the summer so it is best to call ahead to reserve a mooring or slip. Anchoring space is very limited and discouraged. The Shelter Island Yacht Club has moorings available to members of clubs on the reciprocal list for a facility fee, which covers launch service and use of the club amenities.

Piccozzi's Dering Harbor Marina at the head of the harbor has rental moorings, dock space for vessels to 160 feet and a popular fuel dock. Piccozzi's is in close proximity to restaurants, groceries and shopping and has bicycle rentals available for exploring the island. The town dock next door permits a complimentary two-hour tie-up.

On the northwest shore of Shelter Island you will pass Jennings Point on the way to West Neck Harbor to the south, a favorite among cruisers. This harbor is scenic and well protected and home to The Pridwin Hotel & Cottages. This classic resort hotel has been providing guests a unique experience on Shelter Island since 1927. The nearly 10-acre site on Crescent Beach offers a few slips to 40 feet with protected waters, gentle bay breezes and breathtaking water views.

Anchorage: The mooring field at Dering Harbor occupies virtually all of the harbor anchorage space but a small boat might find a spot at the east end of the cove in 10 feet MLW with secure holding in mud.

West Neck Harbor

NAVIGATION: Use NOAA Charts 12358 and 13209. Across Shelter Island Sound from Gleason Point on the North Haven Peninsula, the entry to West Neck Harbor between the bar at the end of Shell Beach and flashing red buoy "2" is daunting on review of the chart and appears challenging at your first on-site observation. The water is actually deep here (even at low tide), allowing reliable access to knowledgeable skippers of large boats with drafts of 5 feet and more. At low tide the deep channel is located midway between the end of Shell Beach and the buoy. At high tide favor flashing red buoy "2" slightly. Thereafter, your chart shows the correct path, hugging the contour at about 100 yards off the north side of Shell Beach. Keep an eye to the depth sounder for chart-matching numbers and avoid straying to starboard. It is best to pick a rising tide for a first attempt but the serenity beyond is well worth a little anxiety at the entrance.

Dockage: At West Harbor, the Island Boatyard and Marina has 80 slips that can accommodate power or sailboats to 60 feet with resort facilities They also offer a free shuttle van for exploring the Islands. There is a restaurant on the premises as well as a retired twin-mast vessel once used in the Great South Bay

GOIN' ASHORE

SHELTER ISLAND, NY

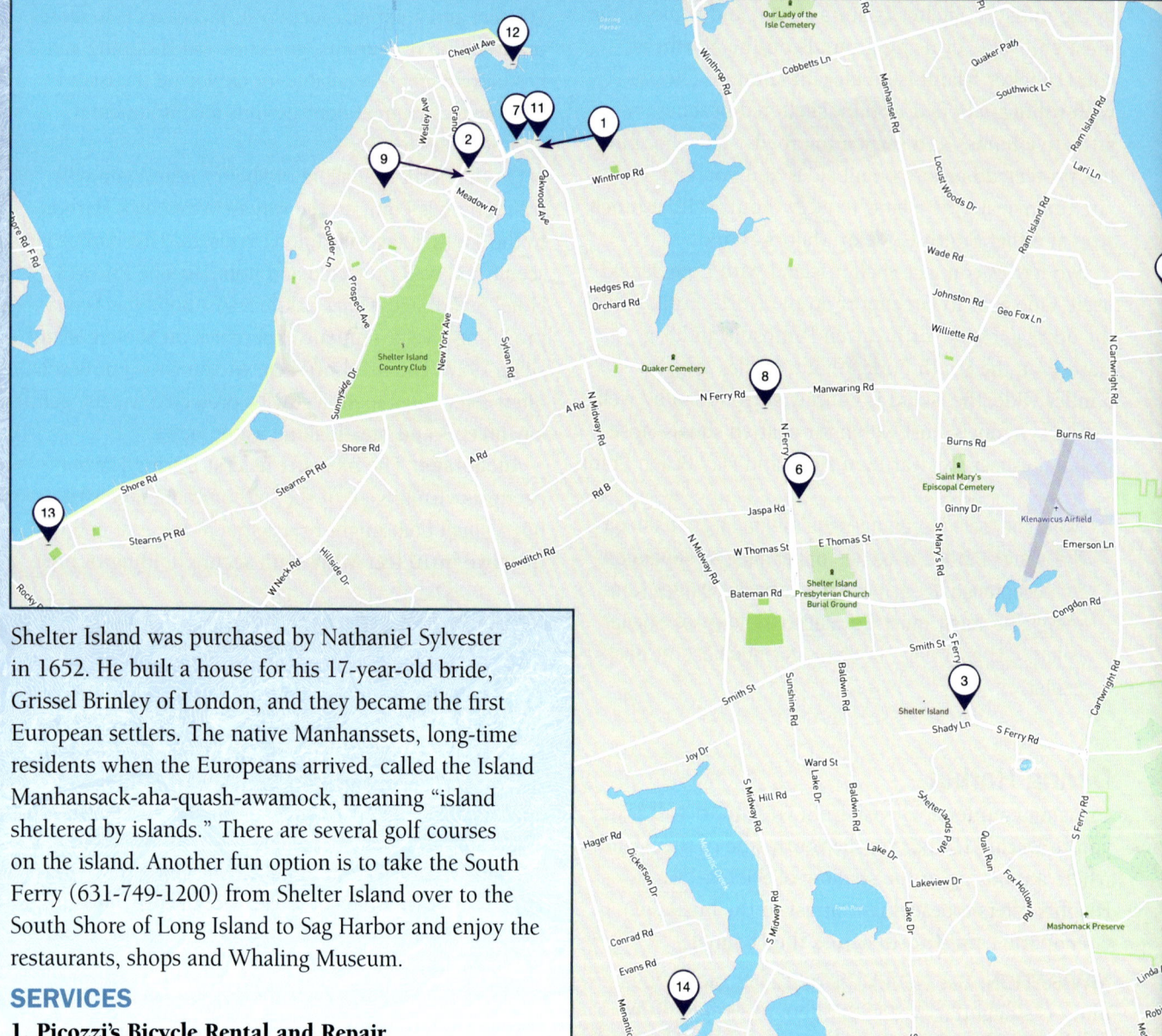

Shelter Island was purchased by Nathaniel Sylvester in 1652. He built a house for his 17-year-old bride, Grissel Brinley of London, and they became the first European settlers. The native Manhanssets, long-time residents when the Europeans arrived, called the Island Manhansack-aha-quash-awamock, meaning "island sheltered by islands." There are several golf courses on the island. Another fun option is to take the South Ferry (631-749-1200) from Shelter Island over to the South Shore of Long Island to Sag Harbor and enjoy the restaurants, shops and Whaling Museum.

SERVICES

1. Picozzi's Bicycle Rental and Repair
Bike rentals available at 177 N. Ferry Rd. (631-749-0045).

2. Shelter Island Post Office
6 Grand Ave. (631-749-0486)

ATTRACTIONS

3. Havens House Museum and Store
Museum and store are open Monday, Wednesday, Friday and Saturday from 10:00 a.m. until 2:00 p.m. through the summer and fall. The Shelter Island Historic Society hosts many programs and events in this historic (circa 1743) home at 16 S. Ferry Rd., (631-749-0025).

4. Mashomack Preserve
Four well-marked interconnected trails range from 1.5 to 11 miles long on 2,100-acre Nature Conservancy's Preserve. Visitors' Center is open Wednesday through Monday from 9:00 a.m. to 5:00 p.m. (March through September) with maps, programs and guided hikes (79 S. Ferry Rd., 631-749-1001).

5. Shelter Island Kayak Tours
Rent a kayak and explore the 12-station Coecles Harbor Marine Trail at 80 Burns Rd. (631-749-1990).

SHOPPING

6. Black Cat Books
54 N. Ferry Rd. (631-725-8654)

7. Jack's True Value Hardware & Marine
188 N. Ferry Rd. (631-749-0114)

8. Shelter Island IGA
Supermarket that will deliver to your boat (75 N. Ferry Rd., 631-749-0382).

9. Shelter Island Hardware
4 Grand Ave. (631-749-0097)

MARINAS

10. Coecles Harbor Marina & Boatyard
18 Hudson Ave. (631-749-0700)

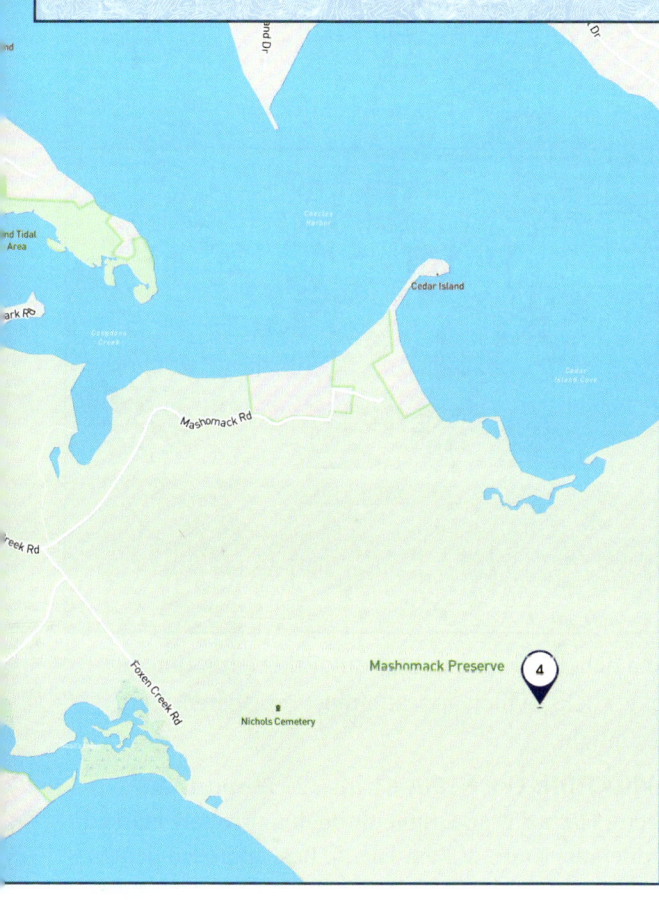

11. Piccozzi's Dering Harbor Marina
177 N. Ferry Rd. (631-749-0045)

12. Shelter Island Yacht Club
12 Chequit Ave. (631-749-0888)

13. The Pridwin Hotel & Cottages
81 Shore Rd. (631-749-0476)

14. The Island Boatyard and Marina
63 S. Menantic Rd. (631-749-3333)

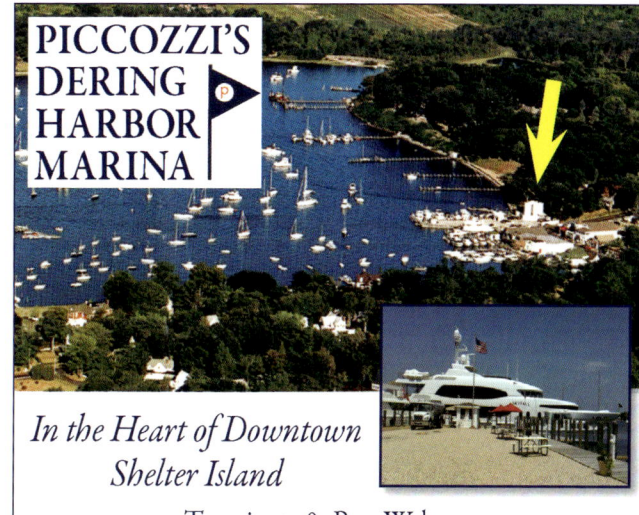
for harvesting oysters and clams that now serves as a full bar.

Anchorage: Non-residents are limited to a 48-hour stay and must anchor in the southern end of the harbor in the area designated by several marker buoys. There has been shoaling along the channel to West Neck Bay and, therefore, depths are somewhat less than those indicated on the chart. Nevertheless, there is good holding in mud and protection in 10 to 12 feet MLW from all but the northeast.

Smith Cove & Majors Harbor

These two unspoiled coves on the southern shore of Shelter Island are pretty, quiet and easy to enter. There are high green banks, good beaches, clean water and ample depths with good protection (except in southerly winds). Smith Cove, the westernmost of the two, is larger and deeper. The western end of the cove serves as the ferry landing to North Haven and Sag Harbor. If the strong current and an opposing wind combine, the passage from West Neck Harbor to Smith Cove can be challenging.

Great & Little Peconic Bays, NY

		Largest Vessel Accomodated	VHF Channel Monitored / Working	Approach / Dockside Depth (reported)	Transient Slips / Total Slips	Floating Docks	Gas / Diesel	Groceries, Ice, Marine Supplies, Snacks	Repairs: Hull, Engine, Propeller	Lift (tonnage), Crane, Rail	Min / Max Amps	Courtesy Car, Laundry, Pool, Showers	Pump-Out Station	Nearby: Grocery Store, Motel, Restaurant
CUTCHOGUE				**Dockage**				**Supplies**			**Services**			
1. Cutchogue Harbor Marina Inc.	(631) 734-6993	50	9/	2/120	6.0/9.0	F	GD	IMS	HEP	L30	30/50	LS	P	GMR
2. New Suffolk Shipyard	(631) 734-6311	40	9/	5/70	5.0/6.0	F	G	GM	HEP	L25,C	30	S	P	GMR
MATTITUCK														
3. Strong's Marine Mattituck Bay 🛜	(631) 298-4770	47	68/	/100	4.0/5.0	F	GD	IM	HEP	L	30/50	S	P	GMR

🖥 Internet Access   🛜 Wireless Internet Access   ⚓onSpot Dockside WiFi Facility

See WaterwayGuide.com for current rates, fuel prices, website addresses, and other up-to-the-minute information. (Information in the table is provided by the facilities.)

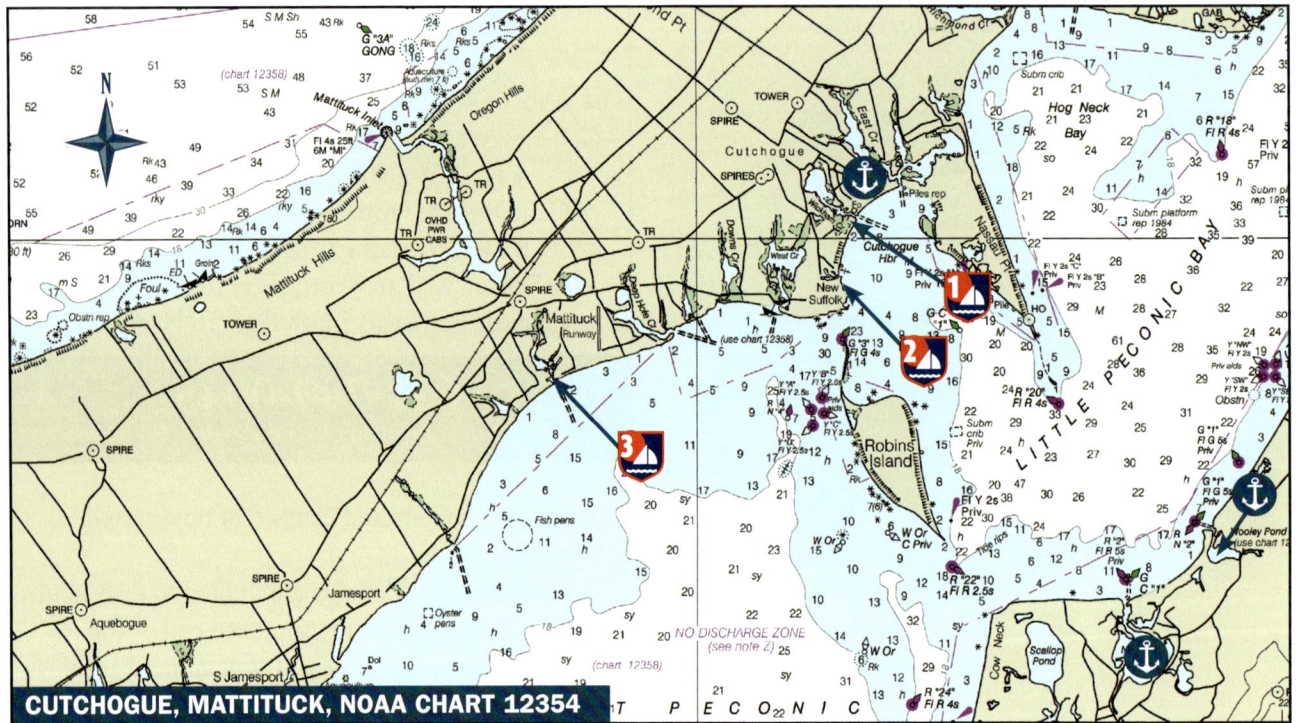

CUTCHOGUE, MATTITUCK, NOAA CHART 12354

Anchorage: Smith Cove offers good anchorage close to a long stretch of undeveloped beach (open to the south) and is reported to have good fishing. You can drop the hook here in 15- to 20-foot MLW depths with good holding in soft mud. Majors Harbor to the southeast is an attractive bight with no services and no shore access. When entering give Majors Point and its off-lying rocks a clear berth. Inside you will find 6 to 9 feet MLW with good holding in sand.

Coecles Harbor

Continuing the circle around southern Shelter Island, Coecles (pronounced "cockles") Harbor is located on the eastern shore about 6 miles southwest of Orient Point. This large, tree-lined harbor offers an idyllic setting, excellent anchorage, a traditional full-service marina and a choice of well-regarded restaurants. It is

also a delightful spot to find tiny yellow and orange cockle shells, which appear almost transparent in the sunlight.

NAVIGATION: Use NOAA Charts 12358 and 13209. Coecles Harbor is accessible through a privately marked channel just south of Ram Island. Best approach depths will be found at about 30 yards off flashing green buoy "1" and green can "3," which is followed by green can buoy "5" to port. Boats drawing 6 feet or more will want to wait for a rising tide (3-foot tidal range) before attempting an entry. Dredging has widened the opening between Reel Point (flashing red 4-sec light) and Sungic Point green can buoy "5."

Dockage: The full-service Coecles Harbor Marina & Boatyard, located at the west end of the harbor, may be easily reached on any tide by vessels with drafts less than 5 feet. The only significant shallow spot consists of a narrow 5-foot MLW mud "hump" extending southwest of red nun buoy "10" off Little Ram Island. Otherwise, the center harbor areas carry 6- to 8-foot MLW depths with substantially better depths at high tide. The marina has slips (to 60 feet), all fuels and an on-site restaurant.

Anchorage: The designated anchorage in Coecles Harbor is just to port after entry and is clearly marked by orange and white markers. If you plan to anchor you are required to anchor here. Be sure to turn to port well before reaching green can buoy "7" and the rocks that lie just beyond that buoy. There is good holding in soft mud in 9 to 11 feet MLW. This area is a No-Discharge Zone and from May 15 to September 15 anchorage is limited to a 48-hour stay with a posted $250 fine and towing fees assessed against violators. This protects local shellfishing, which is available to anyone who secures a town permit. For a small fee, Coecles Harbor Marina offers use of its dinghy dock and facilities to those at anchor.

■ LITTLE & GREAT PECONIC BAYS

Little Peconic Bay

Little Peconic Bay, about 5 miles long, is full of interesting coves and creeks. It is southwest of the circumnavigation of Shelter Island and it is large and deep but can be airless in the summer. Hog Neck Bay, with two pretty streams (Corey Creek and Richmond Creek), is located in the northwest corner of Little Peconic Bay. Both streams have good beaches, narrow-dredged channels and no services. Charted depth is 7 feet MLW but both creeks are better for dinghies than big boats.

Jessup Neck and Great Hog Neck mark the eastern edge of the Peconic Bays. The waters around the sand spit of Jessup Neck, a wildlife preserve with picnic grounds, provide good fishing, especially for blues and weakfish. Farther around Nassau Point is Cutchogue Harbor. Half a dozen gunkholes, fine beaches and a charming town with one of the country's oldest houses characterize this side bay. Off Cutchogue Harbor are several dredged basins for local boats but most are shoal. All offer interesting exploration by dinghy. New Suffolk is the port for Cutchogue, 1 mile inland. The village has a commercial fishing fleet, a restaurant, rowboat rentals and bait sales. Boating amenities are on Cutchogue Harbor and up Schoolhouse Creek (unnamed on the chart). Check depths with locals.

Dockage: New Suffolk Shipyard welcomes transients at two facilities here. Cutchogue Harbor Marina on Wickham Creek offers gas and diesel sales, a Ship Store, and full boat service and refinishing. Stay to mid-channel as shoals are to port. The flagship New Suffolk Shipyard is a short distance with similar amenities.

Anchorage: A cove that is unnamed on the chart but known locally as The Horseshoe offers a protected anchorage north of Nassau Point in Cutchogue Harbor. Here you will find 9 to 11 feet MLW with good holding in mud. This is somewhat exposed to the north.

Great Peconic Bay

NAVIGATION: Use NOAA Chart 12358. Dividing Little Peconic Bay and Great Peconic Bay is Robins Island, which is privately owned. The 435-acre island is home to rare animal and plant species. Landing on the island is forbidden. Two marked channels go past Robins Island. North Race is more protected but spotted with shoals. South Race is the preferred passage for deeper-draft boats and is better marked but is subject to tide rips when current and wind oppose.

Dockage: Around the harbor are a number of marinas that will accommodate small boats. On the north shore of Great Peconic Bay is the Village of Mattituck, discussed in the previous chapter. While most of the cruising amenities are located on Mattituck Creek off the inlet from Long Island Sound, you can access the town and Strong's Marine Mattituck Bay from this side by way of James Creek. Approach depths are listed as 4 feet MLW so call ahead for exact depths.

Flanders Bay

Flanders Bay is the gateway to the Peconic River and Riverhead. Settled in 1690, Riverhead has good shops, restaurants and an inn but few transient boat amenities. Much like the North Fork, this area is famous for farm stands and wineries. Riverhead has more than 20,000 acres involved in crops or vineyards and local produce abounds (in season).

NAVIGATION: Use NOAA Chart 12358. Large, full of shoals and with a twisting channel, Flanders Bay is the

Flanders Bay, NY

RIVERHEAD AREA		Largest Vessel Accomodated	VHF Channel Monitored / Working	Approach / Dockside Depth (reported)	Transient Slips / Total Slips	Floating Docks	Gas / Diesel	Groceries, Ice, Marine Supplies, Snacks	Repairs: Hull, Engine, Propeller	Lift (tonnage), Crane, Rail	Min / Max Amps	Courtesy Car, Laundry, Pool, Showers	Pump-Out Station	Nearby: Grocery Store, Motel, Restaurant
			Dockage					**Supplies**			**Services**			
1. Treasure Cove Resort Marina 🖥 📶	(631) 727-8386	65	11/11	25/120	5.0/8.0	F	GD	IMS	HEP	R	30/50	LPS	P	GMR
2. Lighthouse Marina, Inc. 🖥 📶	(631) 722-3400	70	10/	6/150	6.0/8.0	F	GD	IMS	HEP	L35	30/50	CLPS	P	GR
3. Great Peconic Bay Marina 🖥 📶	(631) 722-3565	65	/	10/175	6.0/6.0	F	GD	IMS	HEP	L50	30/50	S	P	4MR

🖥 Internet Access   📶 Wireless Internet Access   🔵onSpot Dockside WiFi Facility

See WaterwayGuide.com for current rates, fuel prices, website addresses, and other up-to-the-minute information. (Information in the table is provided by the facilities.)

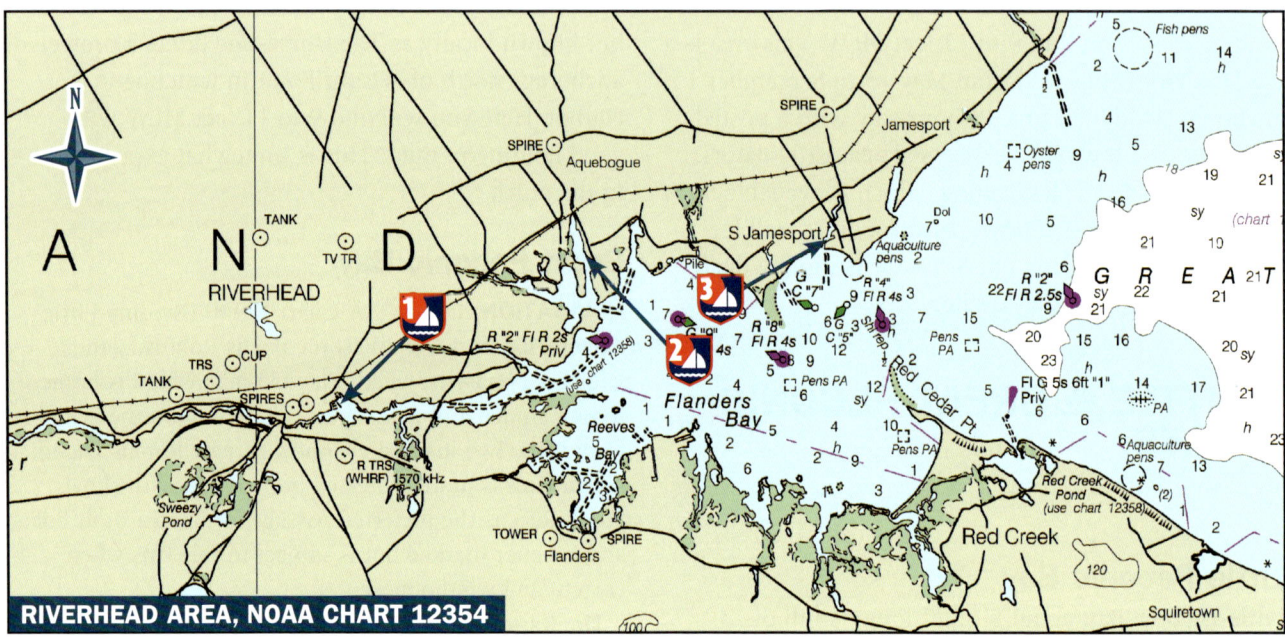

RIVERHEAD AREA, NOAA CHART 12354

last link in the Peconic chain. Enter between Miamogue and Red Cedar Points, follow all aids to navigation carefully and keep a close eye on your depth sounder. The bay has nice creeks, some deep enough for larger boats, but most are more suited for dinghy navigation.

You can get to Riverhead via the Peconic River's narrow, marsh-bordered channel with 6-foot MLW depths. Buoys lead you to the head of navigation, 2 miles from Flanders Bay. The fixed **CR 105 Bridge** (25-foot vertical clearance) crosses the Peconic River about 1 mile downstream of the village so most sailboats cannot make it all the way.

Dockage: East Creek Marina in Riverhead is for town residents only. Boaters are permitted to tie up at the town waterfront all day without a permit. Boaters who would like to spend an evening must come to the Recreation Department and purchase a permit.

■ SOUTH FORK: SHINNECOCK CANAL TO LAKE MONTAUK

Shinnecock Canal

NAVIGATION: Use NOAA Chart 12358. This easy-to-use canal runs between Peconic and Shinnecock Bays, joining Long Island's interior waters with its southern shore. A single jetty leads into the well-marked and lighted canal entrance from Great Peconic Bay, about 8 miles east of Riverhead. Fixed bridges set controlling vertical clearance at 22 feet. The canal is regularly dredged and its banks are lined with marinas, boatyards, restaurants and fishing stations. At each end of the canal is a DIY gin pole, which you can use to un-step or step your sailboat's mast at no charge. Shinnecock Bay is described in detail in Chapter 4: "Long Island South Shore."

Noyack Bay

Heading east and back toward Shelter Island and North Haven Peninsula, the quiet Noyack Bay has accommodations for shallow-draft boats and a few stores and restaurants that are within walking distance of the harbor. Fishing is good in the rips off high, needle-sharp Jessup Neck, which is part of a nature preserve with paths and picnic tables. Jessup Neck Basin is just barely navigable because of shallow depths. Boats do moor here, however, and it is quiet since it is surrounded by the nature preserve. There is a sandy beach at the south end of the bay (Long Beach) where you can rent small sailboards and other watercraft.

Dockage: Mill Creek is a snug harbor with dockage to 45 feet. The marinas are also an easy walk to Trout Pond, which is excellent for freshwater swimming.

Anchorage: There is limited room for anchoring in the snug basin of Mill Creek. Anchoring outside on the southern shore of Noyack Bay can be pleasant in settled weather.

Sag Harbor

Sag Harbor is one of the major cruising ports on eastern Long Island. Two important harbors provide extensive services for most any need. The town is close to both harbors and is brimming with shops, Colonial houses, restaurants and monuments to Sag Harbor's history as a whaling port.

NAVIGATION: Use NOAA Charts 12358 and 13209. Sag Harbor is about 10 miles south of Plum Gut, 12 miles northeast of Shinnecock Canal and is easily approached from the east or west. A long breakwater extends most of the width of the harbor, but it is easy to enter the deep channel between the western end and North Haven. If you are approaching Sag Harbor from the east do not cut any of the buoys to avoid a large rock field. Make sure you pass very close to or west of green-and-red can "SH." Every year a good number of boats visit the rocks and some end up with serious damage.

Heading east from Sag Harbor, stick to the well-marked channel, favor the Shelter Island side and stay north of the numerous rocks marked by flashing green buoy "11." Charted Sand Spit is a large shoal partly bare at half-tide north of the channel and marked by a small, 10-foot tower.

Dockage/Moorings: At the eastern end of the harbor inside the Sag Harbor breakwater are several facilities including Sag Harbor Yacht Yard & Marina

with a full-service mechanic's shop that can handle engine, transmission, electrical, plumbing and welding work. They also provide rigging and mast work as well as prop and shaft repairs. They have the only fully-stocked ship chandlery in the area. Nearby Sag Harbor Yacht Club offers slips with many amenities (no club affiliation required). Advance reservations are recommended, especially for peak weekends. The Yacht Club is conveniently located close to Sag Harbor's Main Street (5-minute walk) plus many historic sites, vineyards, farms, mansions, scenic vistas and some of the world's best beaches.

Long or short-term tie-ups may be possible at the 311-slip Village of Sag Harbor Dock. Reservations are required. Some of the numerous moorings here are available as transient rentals from Sag Harbor Launch & Mooring Rentals (25-foot minimum).

The completely protected inner harbor, Sag Harbor Cove, lies just beyond the fixed **Ferry Road Bridge** (21-foot fixed vertical clearance). Inside the cove are several more marine facilities with space for transients with various amenities. All fuels are also available here.

Anchorage: Boats are seen anchored in 10- to 15-foot MLW depths outside the breakwater to the east. Exercise extreme caution threading the shoals marked by flashing green buoy "11" and the green can "1" just west of the shoal's rocky outcrop. There is good holding in soft mud, although this anchorage is somewhat exposed to the northeast and northwest. From here you can dinghy through the gap in the breakwater to the town dinghy dock to visit the shopping and dining district.

Three Mile Harbor

Back out on the south shore of Gardiners Bay (beyond Shelter Island and Sag Harbor) is Three Mile Harbor, shown as Threemile Harbor on some charts. The scenic harbor has fine beaches, all manner of marine services, good anchorages and restaurants. A short bike or taxi ride away brings you to the Historic Village of East Hampton with soft sand beaches, shopping and nightlife. There is also local bus service (www.sct-bus.org) for details.

NAVIGATION: Use NOAA Chart 13209. Three Mile Harbor is 15 miles west of Montauk Point, 8 miles south of Plum Gut and 6 miles east of Sag Harbor. The entrance between Sammy's Beach and Maidstone Park Beach is plainly announced by the red-and-white Morse (A) "TM"

GOIN' ASHORE

SAG HARBOR, NY

Much of Sag Harbor is a National Historic Site. Its history centers heavily on its days as a whaling port, although it was inhabited well before Europeans settled here. In the mid-1800s, almost half the total population of Sag Harbor served on whaling ships. Today the town swells with vacationers in the summer drawn by the two beaches (Foster Memorial and Havens Beach), an assortment of restaurants and easy provisioning options. The Sag Harbor Yacht Club hosts a spectacular 4th of July fireworks celebration, which has become a major attraction on the East End of Long Island, annually drawing 20,000 plus spectators.

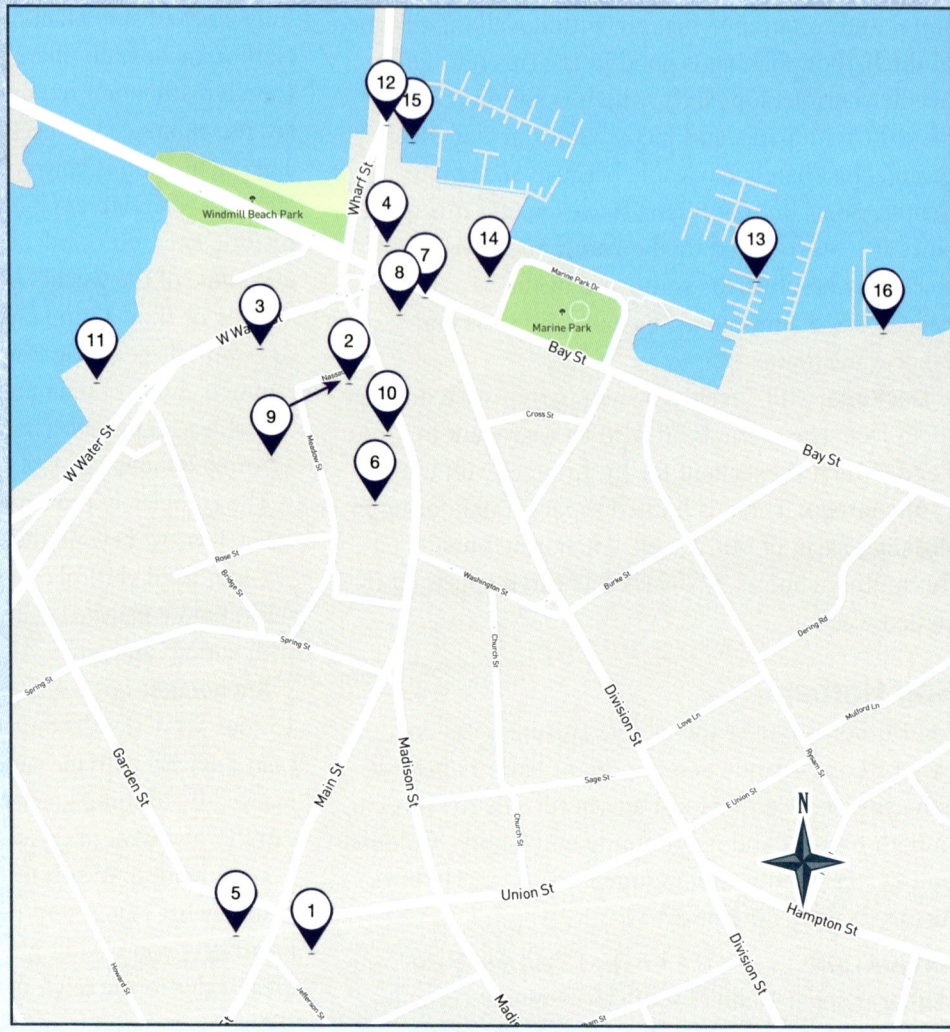

SERVICES

1. John Jermain Memorial Library
   201 Main St. (631-725-0049)

2. Sag Harbor Launderette
   20 Main St. (631-725-7257)

3. Sag Harbor Post Office
   21 Long Island Ave. (631-725-8968)

ATTRACTIONS

4. Bay Street Theater
   Features small productions with Broadway casts at 1 Bay St. (631-725-9500).

5. Sag Harbor Whaling Museum
   Greek-revival mansion built in 1845 for a whaling tycoon that displays exhibit artifacts of whaling and the whaling era (200 Main St., 631-725-0770).

Sag Harbor Whaling Museum

SHOPPING

6. Emporium True Value Hardware
Chain retailer carrying household tools and supplies at 72 Main St. (631-725-0103).

7. Provisions Natural Food Market and Cafe
Natural food market at 7 Main St. (631-725-3636).

8. Sag Harbor Books
Sells books, games and stationery at 7 Main St. (631-725-8425).

9. Sag Harbor Liquor
52 Main St. (631-725-0054)

10. Schiavoni's Market
Carries a wide selection of groceries, fresh meats, produce and deli specialties (48 Main St., 631-725-0366).

MARINAS

11. Sag Harbor Cove Yacht Club
8 West Water St. (631-725-1605)

12. Sag Harbor Launch & Mooring Rentals
Long Wharf (631-466-8180)

13. Sag Harbor Yacht Club
27 Bay St. (631-725-0567)

14. Village of Sag Harbor Dock
7 Bay St. (631-725-2368)

15. Waterfront Marina
1A Bay St. (631-725-3886)

16. Sag Harbor Yacht Yard & Marina
53 Bay St. (631-725-3838)

Noyack Bay, NY

W
G

		VHF Channel Monitored / Working	Approach / Dockside Depth (reported)	Transient Slips / Total Slips	Floating Docks	Largest Vessel Accomodated	Gas / Diesel	Groceries, Ice, Marine Supplies, Snacks	Repairs: Hull, Engine, Propeller	Lift (tonnage), Crane, Rail	Min / Max Amps	Courtesy Car, Laundry, Pool, Showers	Pump-Out Station	Nearby: Grocery Store, Motel, Restaurant
NOYACK				**Dockage**				**Supplies**			**Services**			
1. Mill Creek Marina	(631) 725-1351	45	/	5/145	4.0/4.0	F		G	I	HEP	L25	30	S	P	GR
2. Hidden Cove Marina Inc.	(631) 725-3333	40	9/	/56	6.0/6.0	F		G	GIMS	HP					GMR
SAG HARBOR														
3. Sag Harbor Yacht Yard & Marina 🖥 WiFi	(631) 725-3838	118	10/	5/31	13.0/10.0	F			GIM	HEP	L35	30/50	S	P	GMR
4. Sag Harbor Yacht Club 🖥 WiFi	(631) 725-0567	200	9/	/62	11.0/10.0		GD		IM			30/200+	S	P	GMR
5. Waterfront Marina WiFi	(631) 725-3886	210	9/11	1/77	10.0/10.0				I			30/200+	S	P	GMR
6. Sag Harbor Launch & Mooring Rentals	(631) 466-8180	120	73/	/	10.0/12.0							C			GMR
7. Village of Sag Harbor Dock WiFi	(631) 725-2368	175	9/10	25/311	10.0/10.0	F						30/100	S	P	GMR
8. Sag Harbor Cove Yacht Club WiFi	(631) 725-1605	80	9/	20/160	8.0/7.0	F		GD	I			50	LS		MR
9. Ship Ashore Marina	(631) 725-3755	45	9/9	/45	5.0/5.0	F		G			HEP	L35	30			GMR

🖥 Internet Access   WiFi Wireless Internet Access   onSpot Dockside WiFi Facility

See WaterwayGuide.com for current rates, fuel prices, website addresses, and other up-to-the-minute information. (Information in the table is provided by the facilities.)

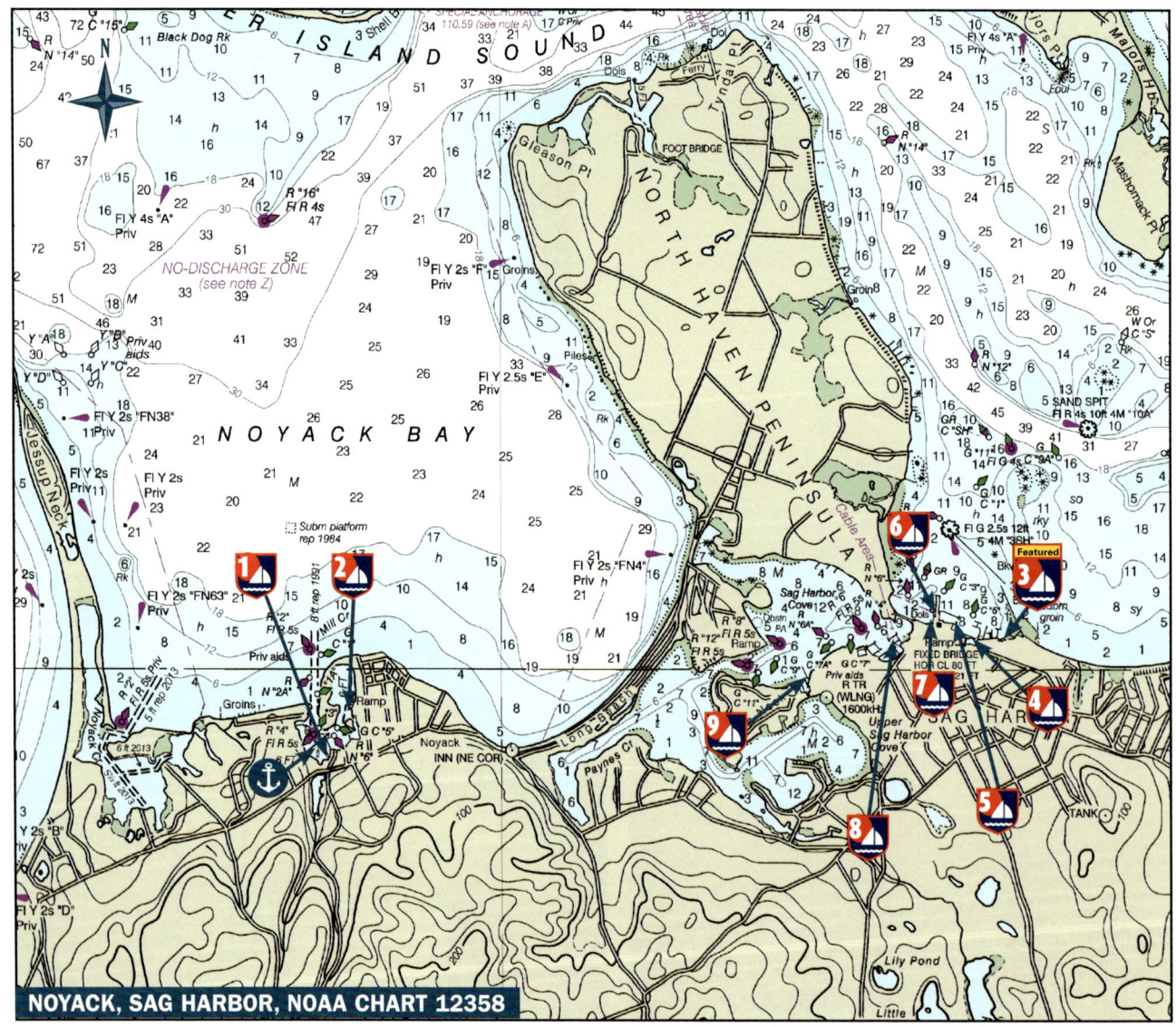

NOYACK, SAG HARBOR, NOAA CHART 12358

SAG HARBOR
YACHT YARD & MARINA

GOIN' ASHORE

East Hampton, NY

The Village of East Hampton was founded in 1648 as a farming community with ties to whaling and fishing. The governors of Connecticut Colony and New Haven Colony purchased the land from the Montauk Indians in exchange for small drill bits used to make "Wampum," a traditional shell bead of the local Indian tribes. The village is located within the Town of East Hampton, the easternmost town in the state of New York.

ATTRACTIONS

Regarded as one of the most beautiful areas in the United States, East Hampton is a world-famous, oceanside town with miles of white sandy beach located approximately 100 miles from New York City. The village of East Hampton offers a wide selection of dining options, art galleries, boutiques and outdoor activities including five village beaches–Georgica, Main Beach, Wiborg Beach, Egypt Lane Beach and Two Mile Hollow. Georgica Beach, like most village beaches, is a locals beach popular with surfers that requires a vehicle parking permit. Main Beach is one of the most popular beaches in the Hamptons with lifeguards, a snack bar, restrooms and public parking. Wilborg Beach is located next to the Maidstone Club (private) and does not have a lifeguard on duty. Egypt Beach, although rocky, is a great beach to swim and sunbathe. Two Mile Hollow Beach is less crowded than the others with wide sandy beaches.

SHOPPING

East Hampton is a shopper's paradise. Visitors (and locals) can enjoy everything from one-of-a-kind boutiques to big name stores such as Lululemon, Vineyard Vines, J Crew, Tahari and Ralph Lauren. Three streets comprise most of the shopping–Main Street, Newtown Lane and Park Place. Stop into Kirna Zabete (66 Newtown Ln., 631-527-5792) for a great selection of high-end, designer brands. Looking for a local boutique with international recognition? Check out AERIN (7 Newtown Ln., 631-527-5517) owned by Aerin Lauder, the granddaughter of Estee Lauder.

AERIN carries her own branded items as well as items from her favorite designers. For sunglasses, beach items, bicycles and more, don't miss Khanh Sports (60 Park Pl., 631-324-0703). For foodies, Citarella Gourmet Market (2 Pantigo Rd., 631-283-6600) has a signature selection of fresh, world-class seafood, prime aged meats, artisanal cheese, caviar and other delicacies. The closest grocery market to Three Mile Harbor is Damark's Market (331 Country Rd. 40, 631-324-0691).

DINING

In addition to the waterside restaurants along the Eastern Shores of Three Mile Harbor, the East Hampton Village offers fine dining at East Hampton Grill (99 Main St., 631-329-6666), which is the go-to for American standards such as steak and ribs in an airy bistro with an open kitchen and bustling bar. Other hot spots include village eateries of Nick and Toni's (136 N. Main St., 631-324-3550), The Maidstone Hotel (207 Main St., 631-324-5006), Fresno (11 Fresno Pl., 631-324-8700) and Carissa's (221 Pantigo Rd., 631-604-5911). If you're in the mood for local seafood, check out Bostwick's Chowder House (277 Pantigo Rd., 631-324-1111), a hopping seasonal fish house in casual beachy digs with patio tables. For a slice of world-famous New York pizza, head to Sam's Restaurant (36 Newtown Ln., 631-324-5900). This long-standing Italian spot serves thin-crust pizza and red sauce pasta in a local tavern setting.

Cedar Point Lighthouse

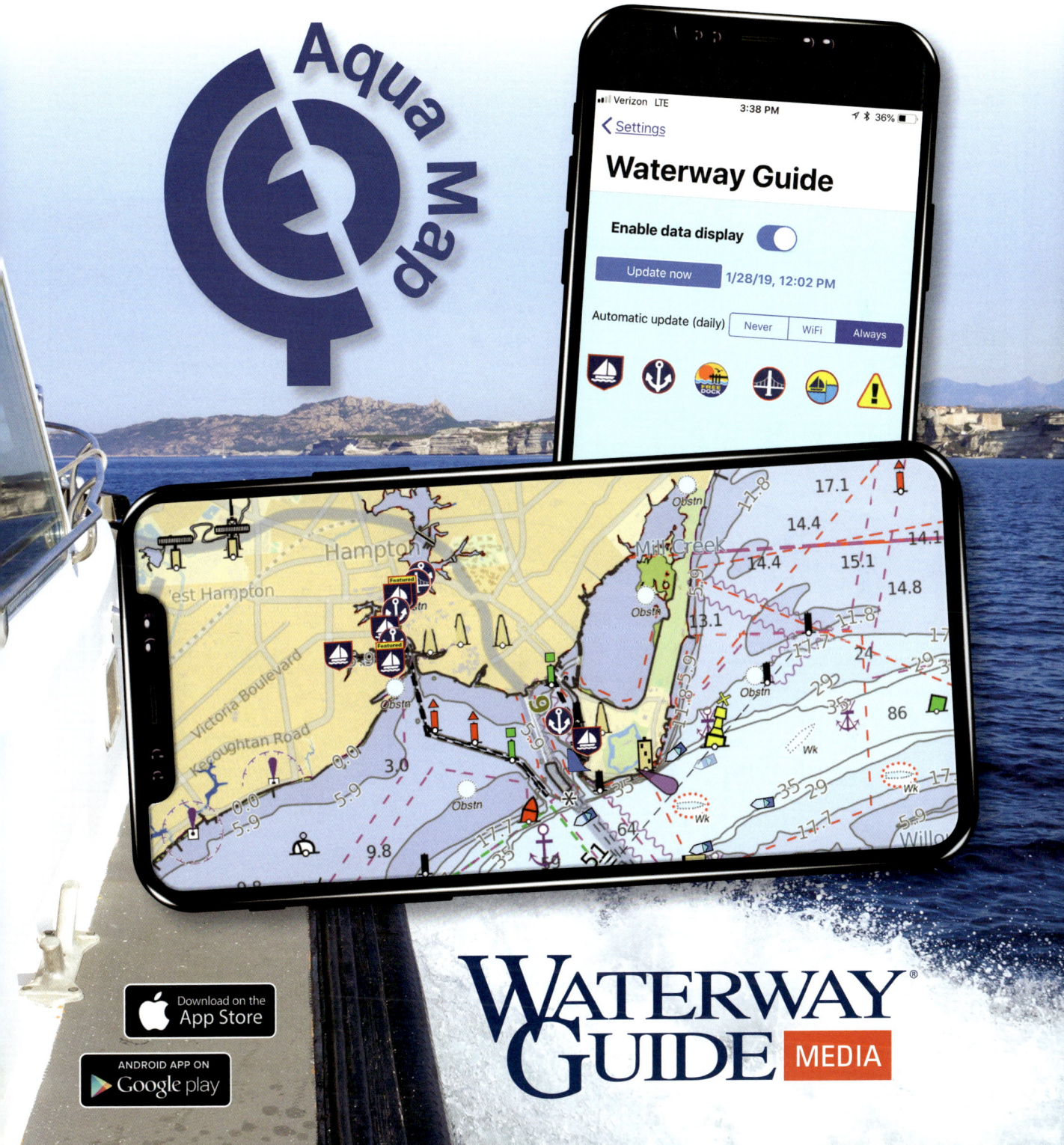

Three Mile Harbor, NY

THREE MILE HARBOR AREA		Largest Vessel Accommodated	VHF Channel Monitored / Working	Transient Slips / Total Slips	Approach / Dockside Depth (reported)	Floating Docks	Gas / Diesel	Groceries, Ice Marine Supplies, Snacks	Repairs: Hull, Engine, Propeller	Lift (tonnage), Crane, Rail	Min / Max Amps	Courtesy Car, Laundry, Pool, Showers	Pump-Out Station	Nearby: Grocery Store, Motel, Restaurant
				Dockage				Supplies	Services					
1. Harbor Marina of East Hampton 💻 WiFi	(631) 324-5666	65	9/	7/95	10.0/8.0	F	GD	IMS	HEP	L25	30/50	S	P	GR
2. Maidstone Harbor Marina	(631) 324-2651	75	/	/95	9.0/8.0	F		GI	HE		30/100	LPS	P	GMR
3. East Hampton Point Marina & Boatyard 💻 WiFi	(631) 324-8400	90	9/	10/55	8.0/7.0		GD	GIMS	HEP	L35,C	30/100	LPS	P	GMR
4. Shagwong Marina	(631) 324-8400	90	9/	3/40	7.0/6.0	F		I			30/100	LPS	P	GMR
5. Halsey's Marina 💻 WiFi	(631) 324-5666	75	9/	5/44	10.0/7.5			IM	HEP		30/50	LS	P	GMR
6. Gardiner's Marina 💻 WiFi	(631) 324-5666	110	9/	5/45	9.0/6.5	F		IMS	HEP		30/50	LS	P	GMR
7. East Hampton Town Dock	(631) 537-7575	36	/	/	8.0/6.0			GIM						GR
8. Three Mile Harbor Marina 💻 WiFi	(631) 324-1320	65	9/	7/63	10.0/8.5	F		GIMS	HEP	L40	30/50	LS	P	GMR
9. East Hampton Marina	(631) 324-4042	26	16/10	/	5.0/6.0		G	IM	HEP		30			R

💻 Internet Access WiFi Wireless Internet Access onSpot Dockside WiFi Facility
See WaterwayGuide.com for current rates, fuel prices, website addresses, and other up-to-the-minute information. (Information in the table is provided by the facilities.)

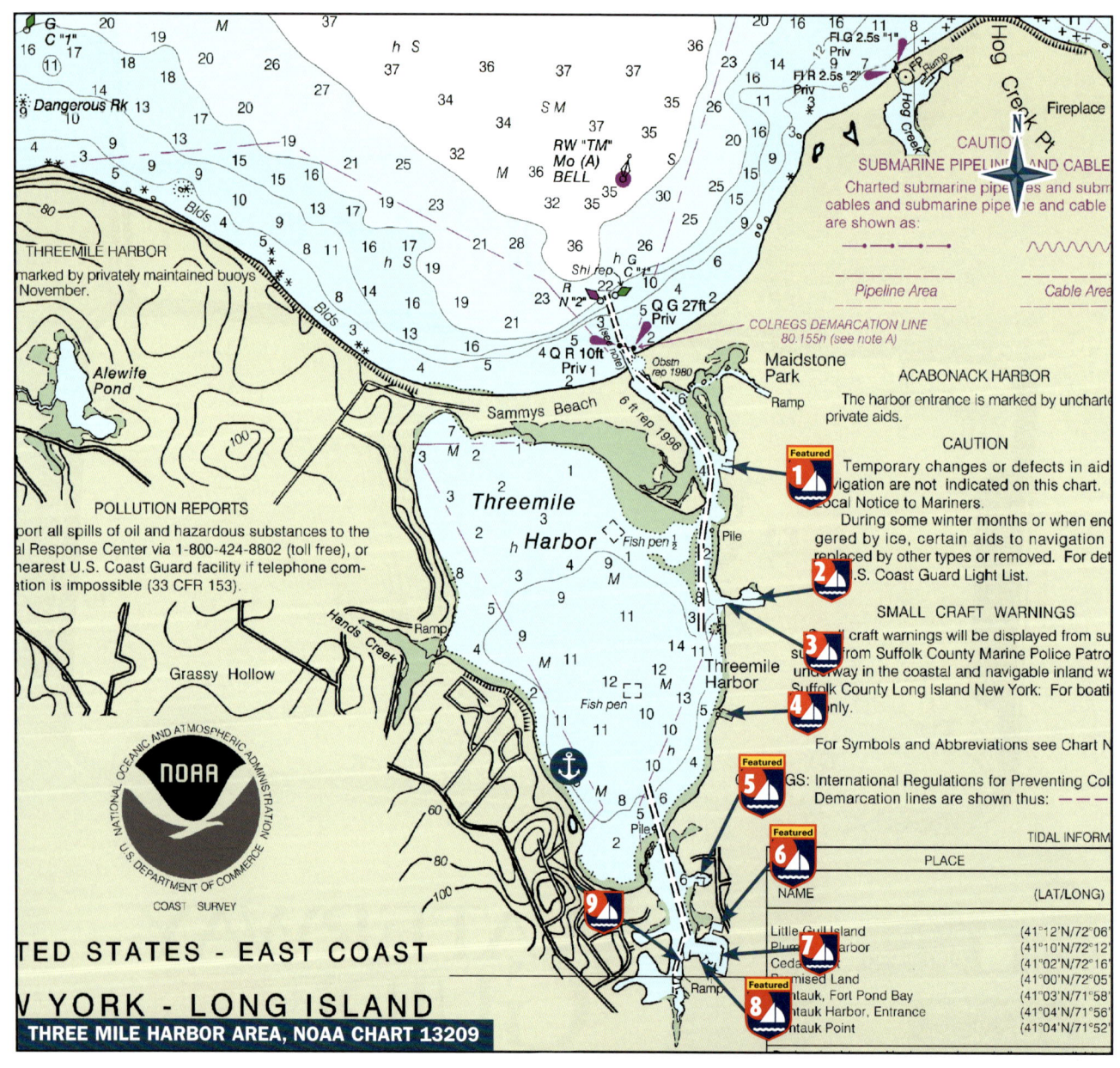

THREE MILE HARBOR AREA, NOAA CHART 13209

Three Mile Harbor

THREE MILE HARBOR
EAST HAMPTON · NY

MARINAS OPERATED BY SEACOAST ENTERPRISES ASSOCIATES, inc.

Fuel · Service · Slips · Storage
Ship's Stores · Restaurant

631.324.5666 | SEAincorp.com

   WESTERBEKE YANMAR YAMAHA

bell buoy and marked by green can "1" and red nun "2" at the beginning of the entrance channel.

Dockage/Moorings: Docking and marine service opportunities are extensive along the eastern shore of Three Mile Harbor. (See our marina table for details.) East Hampton Point Marina & Boatyard has a hotel as well as a restaurant (seasonal) that is housed in an attractive lighthouse-like structure. At its centerpiece is a classic, fully rigged Olympic racing contender.

First along the marked channel leading to the head of the harbor, Halsey's Marina of East Hampton has the presence of the small, highly exclusive yacht club it once was. There are usually well-protected transient slips available here. At the head of the harbor, Gardiner's Marina has transient slips available in a protected, park-like setting. They can accommodate vessels to 110 feet.

For those desiring the security of a fixed mooring, Seacoast Enterprises has four (marked "T") just inside the channel. Boaters must call ahead for a reservation. Do not pick up a pennant without a reservation. Seacoast Enterprises also operates four of the marine facilities in the area: Harbor Marina of East Hampton, Halsey's Marina, Gardiner's Marina and Three-Mile Harbor Marina & Boatyard. Boaters can call one number (631-324-5666) to make a reservation at any of these facilities or reserve a mooring.

The town's free pump-out service can be contacted on VHF Channel 73 ("Pump-out Boat"). East Hampton Town Dock at the head of the harbor serves as a dinghy dock for the anchorage, as does the dinghy dock at Gann Rd. near Harbor Marina of East Hampton.

Anchorage: Inside the breakwater-protected entrance at Three Mile Harbor, the dredged channel runs between shores for 0.5 mile before opening up to the vistas of a large and scenic harbor. The eastern shore is well developed with marinas, boatyards and restaurants. In contrast, the western side remains wild, rimmed with high green hills and dense forest along the shoreline, which occasionally parts to reveal the existence of a cloistered summer home. Marsh grass and sandy patches of beach are visible off to the north.

Although the number of private moorings have been increasing in the harbor, most of the south and west areas of the harbor are still open for excellent anchorage options in 10- to 12-foot MLW depths with excellent holding in mud. It is rarely too crowded, even on busy summer weekends.

On approaching the anchorage be sure to honor the second red marker off (and fully past) the wood

GURNEY'S WORLD CLASS MARINAS IN MONTAUK AND NEWPORT

GURNEY'S STAR ISLAND
MONTAUK, NY

· Craft capacity of 220 feet with a maximum 12 foot draft
· Access to resort amenities, wellness activations and lifestyle programming
· Upscale and casual dining
· Dock-side room service
· Private beach
· Two outdoor heated pools and one indoor heated pool
· Casual and fine dining including The Pool Club and award-winning Showfish

GURNEY'S NEWPORT
NEWPORT, RI

· 22 slips accommodating up to 125 feet
· Fully operational for transient dockage
· Full-service spa
· Fitness center and branded wellness
· Indoor and outdoor pools
· Dock-side room service
· Private sailing lessons, sunset cruises and water sports available

**GURNEY'S STAR ISLAND
RESORT & MARINA**

GURNEYSRESORTS.COM/STAR-ISLAND
833-235-8500

**GURNEY'S NEWPORT
RESORT & MARINA**

GURNEYSRESORTS.COM/NEWPORT
833-235-7500

barricaded docks of East Hampton Point Marina before turning to starboard. This will avoid a shallow, but nearly invisible bar that extends along the west side of the channel. The town has free pump-out service can be summoned on VHF Channel 73 (call for pump-out boat).

Lake Montauk

Montauk is only 17 nm from Block Island, 14 nm from Plum Gut, 13 nm from Three Mile Harbor and 11 nm from The Race. Montauk is famous for tuna, marlin, swordfish and shark fishing in its offshore waters and for outstanding sportfishing and yachting facilities ashore. The surf around Montauk Point serves as one of the East Coast's premier striped bass fisheries and the area has become a hotbed of saltwater fly fishing.

Excellent marinas cater to sportfishing and cruising vessels of all descriptions. The place buzzes with activity during the summer, yet it is easy to escape to a quiet spot with a near-empty seascape. The beaches are superb both on the Block Island Sound side and Atlantic Ocean side. The classic Montauk Lighthouse beckons and the picturesque nearby village has all the necessary amenities.

NAVIGATION: Use NOAA Chart 13209. From Three Mile Harbor the route curves around Hog Creek Point, southwest of Gardiners Island, past Acabonack Harbor, Napeague Harbor and Fort Pond Bay to Lake Montauk. Montauk Point itself is farther east. Harbors along the route tend to be shoal, wild and interesting but safer for dinghy exploration (in good weather) than for anchorages. Several of the dredged harbors are protected but prone to shoaling.

Enter Montauk Harbor, located in the northern part of Lake Montauk, via a channel protected by lighted jetties. Favor the western jetty, allow for the 2.5-knot current and keep clear of off-channel rocks inside the breakwaters. The current chart indicates 12-foot MLW depths. Along the western shore and in the bight west of Star Island are Montauk's headquarters for charter and head boats and the ferry to Block Island. The well-marked channel to the east takes you to Lake Montauk and several opportunities for dockage and other facilities in less hectic surroundings.

Dockage: Montauk Harbor (turn to starboard on entering the channel) is crowded and active. See the marina table for details on docking options. Dockage on the west side of the inner harbor is within easy walking distance of urban-style amenities and

the Gosman's Dock complex (500 W. Lake Dr.) of restaurants and shops.

Westlake Marina claims to be "Montauk's friendliest marina" and offers dockage to 45 feet. Call ahead for dockside depths. The 100-slip Snug Harbor Motel & Marina is a great place to change crew or just take a room and get off the boat for a while. The marina offers all the usual amenities plus a pool and easy access to shopping and dining.

On the west side of Star Island, the Star Island Yacht Club & Marina is a "hardcore" fishing center, where virtually all boats sprout outriggers in their floating slips. Major fishing tournaments regularly run from here and services, equipment and baits for saltwater anglers are complete.

Gurney's Star Island Resort & Marina next comes into view. A perennial favorite among the boating community and a haven for cruisers, sportfishers and megayachts, Gurney's can accommodate vessels to 280 feet on floating docks. Two restaurants and a bar are on site, as well as indoor/outdoor pools, and the delightful private Gin Beach (memorializing Prohibition days) is only a short walk to the north with water that is a little warmer than the ocean. This is the only beach with a

Lake Montauk, NY

MONTAUK HARBOR		Dockage					Supplies		Services					
		Largest Vessel Accommodated	VHF Channel Monitored / Working	Transient Slips / Total Slips	Approach / Dockside Depth (reported)	Floating Docks	Groceries, Ice Marine Supplies, Snacks	Gas / Diesel	Repairs: Hull, Engine, Propeller	Lift (tonnage), Crane, Rail	Min / Max Amps	Courtesy Car, Laundry, Pool, Showers	Pump-Out Station	Nearby: Grocery Store, Motel, Restaurant
1. Uihlein Marina and Boat Rentals	(631) 668-3799	40	14/	5/18	9.0/9.0	F	G	GIMS	HEP	L25	30	S		GMR
2. Montauk Marine Basin ⌨ WiFi	(631) 668-5900	100	19/	75/150	7.0/8.0	F	GD	GIMS	HEP	L70	30/50	LS		GMR
3. Diamond Cove Marina	(631) 668-6592	50	/	12/50	6.0/6.0	F		I	HP	L40	30/50	S		GMR
4. Westlake Marina WiFi	(631) 668-5600	45	19/	15/100	5.0/3.0	F		I			20/50	S		GMR
5. Snug Harbor Motel & Marina WiFi	(631) 668-2860	50	9/	25/80	6.0/6.0	F					30/50	LPS		MR
6. Star Island Yacht Club and Marina ⌨ WiFi onSpot	(631) 668-5052	165	9/10	75/170	10.0/6.0	F	GD	GIMS	HEP	L100	30/100	LPS	P	GMR
7. Gone Fishing Marina WiFi	(631) 668-3232	50	19/	30/170	6.0/6.0	F	GD	GIMS	HEP	L35	30/50	LS		GMR
8. Gurney's Star Island Resort & Marina ⌨ WiFi	(631) 668-3100	280	9/11	90/232	/12.0	F		IS			30/200+	LPS	P	GMR
9. Montauk Lake Club and Marina ⌨ WiFi	(631) 668-5705	200	12/	20/104	9.0/9.0	F	GD	IS			30/100	LPS	P	MR

⌨ Internet Access   WiFi Wireless Internet Access   onSpot Dockside WiFi Facility

See WaterwayGuide.com for current rates, fuel prices, website addresses, and other up-to-the-minute information. (Information in the table is provided by the facilities.)

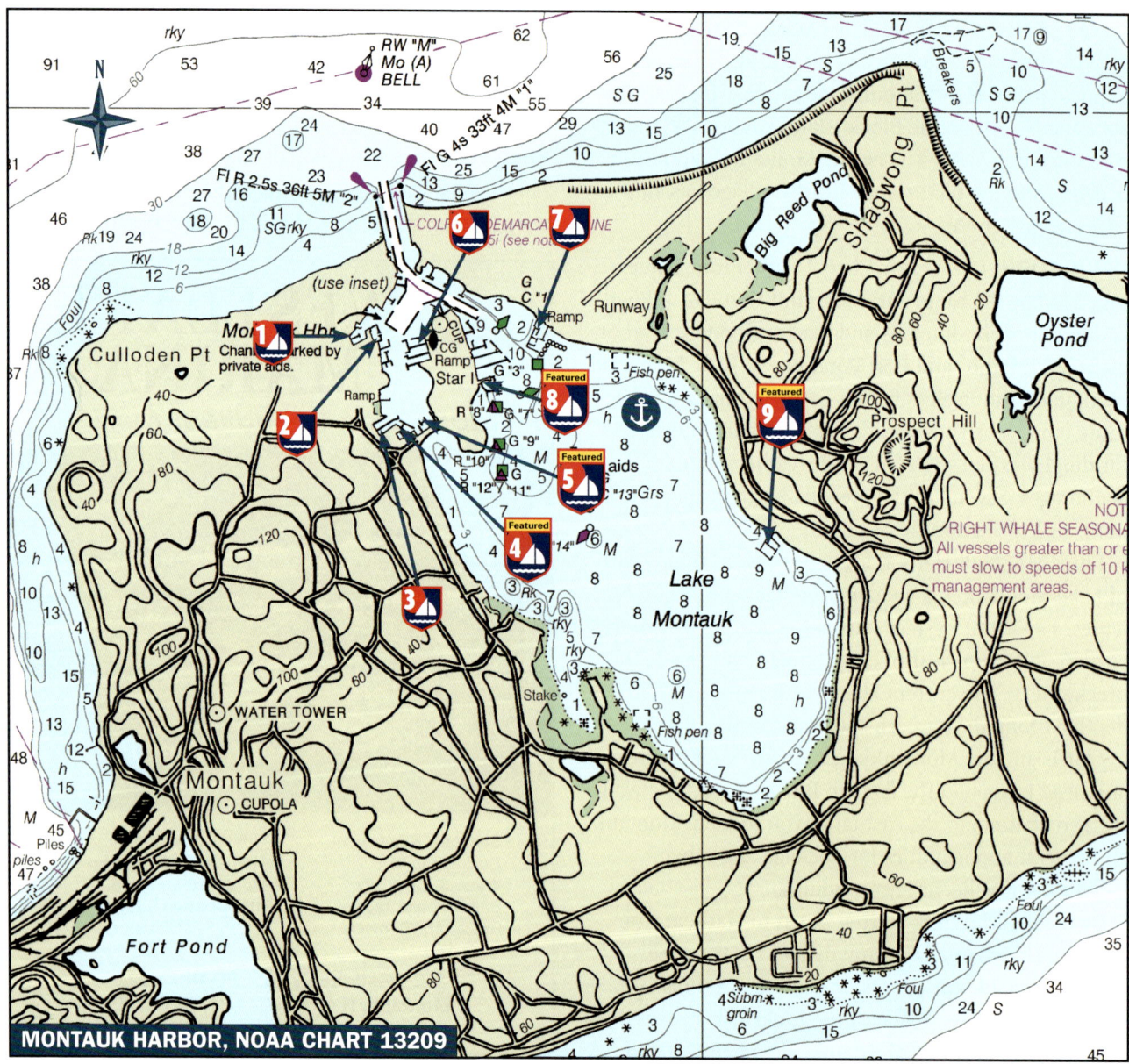

MONTAUK HARBOR, NOAA CHART 13209

GURNEY'S STAR ISLAND RESORT & MARINA

WESTLAKE MARINA

SNUG HARBOR MOTEL & MARINA

Star Island

Lake Montauk Inlet

MONTAUK LAKE CLUB
& Marina

Guest Rooms   Spa   Bar & Restaurant   Heated Pool   Fitness Club

www.montauklakeclub.com   Latitude: 41.061255   Longitude: 71.91221   Tel: 631.668.5705   © Aerial Pros

GOIN' ASHORE

MONTAUK, NY

The main town of Montauk is a couple of miles away from the marinas on the Atlantic Ocean side. Montauk's landmark lighthouse (1797), one of the oldest and most important on the coast, is a couple of miles in the opposite direction. Towering 168 feet over Montauk Point, the light is still serving as an active aid to navigation and can be seen 19 miles out to sea. The area around Montauk Light is considered a haven for avid birdwatchers, especially during the off-season. Tours can be arranged through the Montauk Point Lighthouse Museum & Gift Shop (2000 Montauk Hwy., 631-668-2544) near the lighthouse. There is a seasonal bus you can catch on the highway outside Ditch Plains to take you to the lighthouse or to town. Go to www.sct-bus.org for schedules and routes.

SERVICES

1. Montauk Library
871 Montauk Hwy. (631-668-3377)

2. Montauk Post Office
73 S. Euclid Ave. (631-668-7043)

ATTRACTIONS

3. Ditch Plains Beach
A popular spot for surfing and swimming with seasonal lifeguards and scenic views. Locals say the Ditch Witch food truck serves the best beach food around (23 Ditch Plains Rd., 631-377-8270).

4. Kirk Park Beach
White-sand beach with seasonal lifeguards plus toilet and shower facilities (95 S. Emerson Ave.).

5. Montauk Cycle Company
For advice on the best trails and routes, trail maps, organized rides and other helpful information at 463 West Lake Dr. (631-668-8975).

6. Montauk Manor Hotel
In 1926, visionary developer Carl Graham Fisher implemented plans to make Montauk the "Miami Beach of the North" complete with the imposing Montauk Manor Hotel (an American castle) overlooking the lake. It was his vision that transformed the East End's windswept landscape into a polished summer yachting and fishing resort.

7. Second House Museum
Operated by the Montauk Historical Society and housed in a 1700s farmhouse once built for East Hampton shepherds. Features the Montauk Indian Museum providing an intimate space in which to imagine the deep roots of the past. Open daily (seasonally) except Wednesday. Hosts numerous events throughout the year such as craft fairs and outdoor movies on the lawn.

SHOPPING

8. Montauk IGA
Large grocery store (654 Montauk Hwy., 631-668-4929)

MARINAS

9. Diamond Cove Marina
364 W. Lake Dr. (631-668-6592)

10. Gone Fishing Marina
467 E. Lake Dr. (631-668-3232)

11. Gurney's Star Island Resort & Marina
32 Star Island Rd. (631-668-3100)

12. Montauk Lake Club & Marina
211 E. Lake Dr. (631-668-5705)

13. Montauk Marine Basin
426 W. Lake Dr. (631-668-5900)

14. Snug Harbor Motel & Marina
3 Star Island Rd. (631-668-2860)

15. Star Island Yacht Club and Marina
59 Star Island Rd. (631-668-5052)

16. Uihlein Marina and Boat Rentals
444 W. Lake Dr. (631-668-3799)

17. Westlake Marina
352 W. Lake Dr. (631-668-5600)

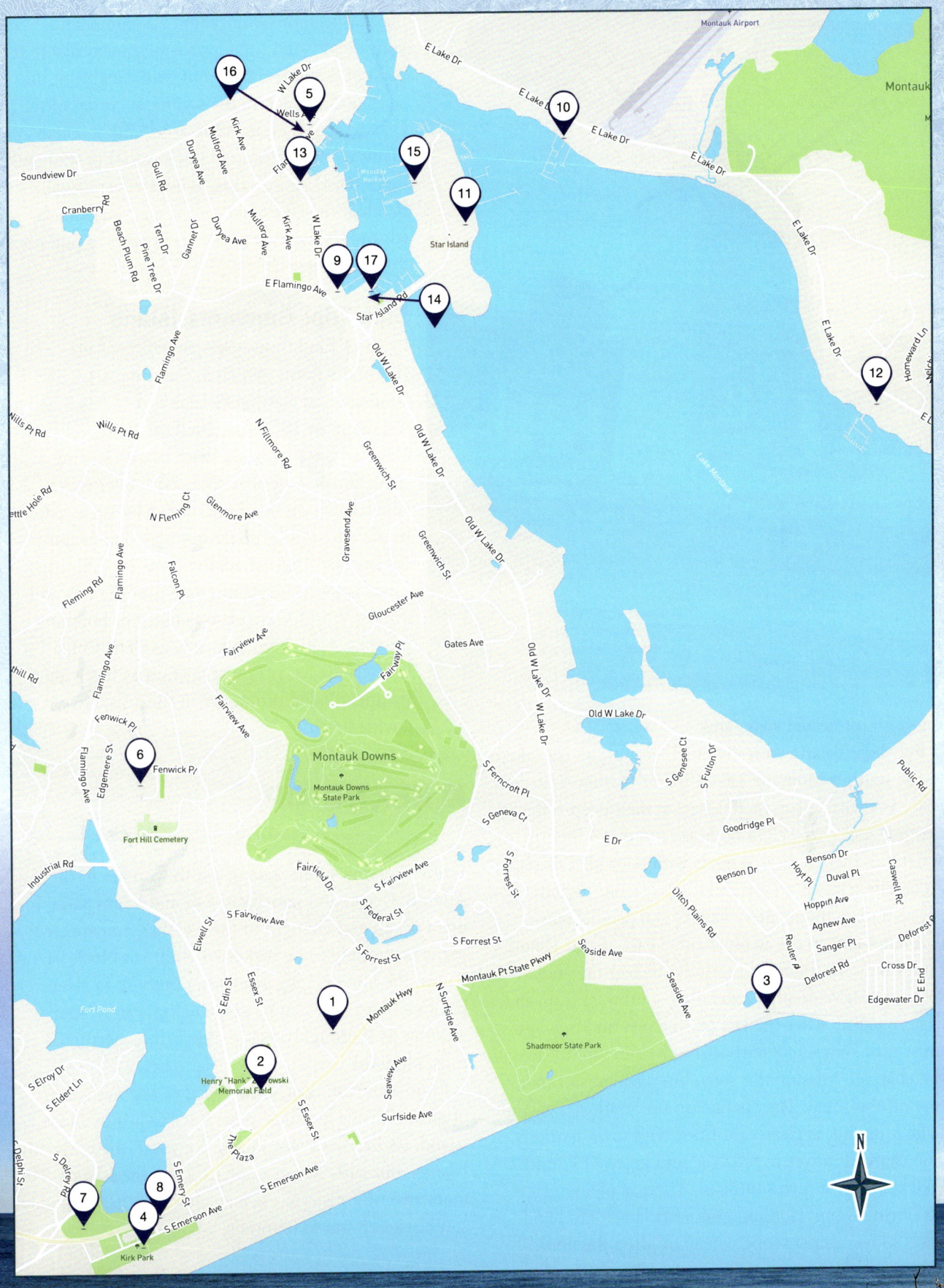

Gardiners Island

marinas usually do not mind accommodating your dinghy and some provisions are available at most of them. You may pull your dinghy on the sides of the beach in the southeast corner of the Lake to access basic heads or to walk to Ditch Plains or the bus stop to town (west) or Montauk Light (east). Some cruisers use the very small beach at the Gosman's complex at the inside edge of the west entrance breakwater to pull up their dinghies.

Side Trip: Gardiners Island

In 1855 a lighthouse was constructed on Gardiners Point, which at that time was connected to Gardiner's Island. A March nor'easter in 1888 destroyed the light and changed the peninsula to an island. During the Spanish-American War, Fort Tyler was constructed on Gardiner's Point Island as part of the chain of fortifications aimed at keeping the Spanish from attacking New York. Shifting sands caused the abandonment of the fort and during World War II it was used for bombing practice. Now known locally as "The Ruins," it is a serious hazard to navigation as there may be unexploded ordinance in the area. Give it a wide berth.

roped off, protected swim area.

For those desiring a really quiet location on the lake, to the south is Montauk Lake Club & Marina. Transient space is available (up to 200 feet) at their deep-water floating docks, as well as both gas and diesel fuel. Amenities include heated pools with poolside cabanas, an on-site restaurant, spa and fitness facility, beach access and complimentary kayaks and paddleboats.

Anchorage: In the main channel east of Star Island buoys must be followed carefully to clear the shoal (2- to 6-foot MLW depths) extending southwest from the eastern shore. After the last marina pier and pile you must turn sharply to starboard to be sure not to miss the channel. Missing the green buoy may result in a tow off the shoal. The channel to the southeast part of Lake Montauk is clearly outlined with town markers. The channel moves to red "14" and green "13" mid-lake before you turn southeast. There is plenty of anchoring room. Holding ground is fair in mud and grass so use ample scope when you drop the hook.

If you do choose to anchor in the lake, the local

■ NEXT STOP

From Montauk Point, east or south, you are in the Atlantic Ocean and your vessel should be prepared for open ocean and changes in the weather. Unexpected fog is something to be reckoned with. On Block Island Sound the famous long swells can put you to sleep but in a blow, they can be challenging. Know your weather as thoroughly as possible before starting from Montauk.

From Montauk boaters can head to any number of great cruising grounds, most notably nearby Block Island. Or head to Point Judith, Newport, the Elisabeth Islands, Buzzards Bay or Cape Cod and the Islands. The more adventurous cruisers may choose to head roughly southeast 628 nm to Bermuda.

Block Island to Nantucket Sound

■ Rhode Island Sound   ■ Buzzards Bay, MA   ■ Nantucket Sound, MA

Rhode Island Sound

■ NAVIGATING RHODE ISLAND WATERS

After exiting the eastern end of Long Island Sound through The Race or Fishers Island Sound's Watch Hill Passage, mariners enter the exciting cruising grounds of southern New England: Block Island Sound, Rhode Island Sound and Narragansett Bay, including the world-famous destination of Newport, RI.

Rhode Island waters can often be challenging. To reach Block Island is to venture into open ocean, out of sight of land on hazy days. You should review your boat's safety and navigational gear and the crew's preparedness before you set out to Block Island.

While Rhode Island has much industry, the State is completely water-oriented. Narragansett Bay, cutting 25 miles inland, gives the state a lot more shoreline than you would think, considering the state's small size. Rhode Island's seafaring tradition dates back more than 300 years and survives today up and down the shores of Narragansett Bay. Fishermen still make a living from the sea, yachts from around the world constantly converge on Newport and visiting mariners tie up on moorings or at docks in one of the many marinas in the maze of harbors.

Our coverage continues on towards Buzzards Bay and Vineyard Sound, where small, deep water harbors, such as Falmouth on Cape Cod or Oak Bluffs on Martha's Vineyard, are thick with boats and are much different than the sprawling harbors of Nantucket and Edgartown. Cruisers will also find secluded hideaways such as Katama Bay inside the south shore of Martha's Vineyard next to Edgartown. The variety of nautical scenery is part of what draws us to Buzzards Bay, Cape Cod and the Islands.

The commercial harbors of New Bedford, with a huge fishing fleet, and Woods Hole, with an oceanographic fleet, contrast with the elegant yacht harbors of Quissett with its local small-boat fleet and Padanaram, on Buzzards Bay, with its traditional wooden boat fleet. There is something for every mariner and harbors for every family. There is bountiful, fresh seafood, beautiful waterfront scenery and the thrill of venturing east to Cape Cod.

Cruising Conditions

These waters are among the most beautiful on the East Coast of the United States but with a change of tide or wind they can suddenly become quite choppy and can be dangerous. A watchful eye on the chart, the compass and the weather is always necessary. NOAA Weather Radio is an essential tool and many VHF radios can notify you in case of severe weather alerts. Sudden blows are a possibility but the other major hazard is the chop set up by a current running counter to the wind.

Chop can make a skipper and their crew uncomfortable and impatient and it can also make it harder to locate buoys leading into harbors or even small boats. Constant attention and cultivated patience are necessities. Do not hesitate to stay comfortably tied

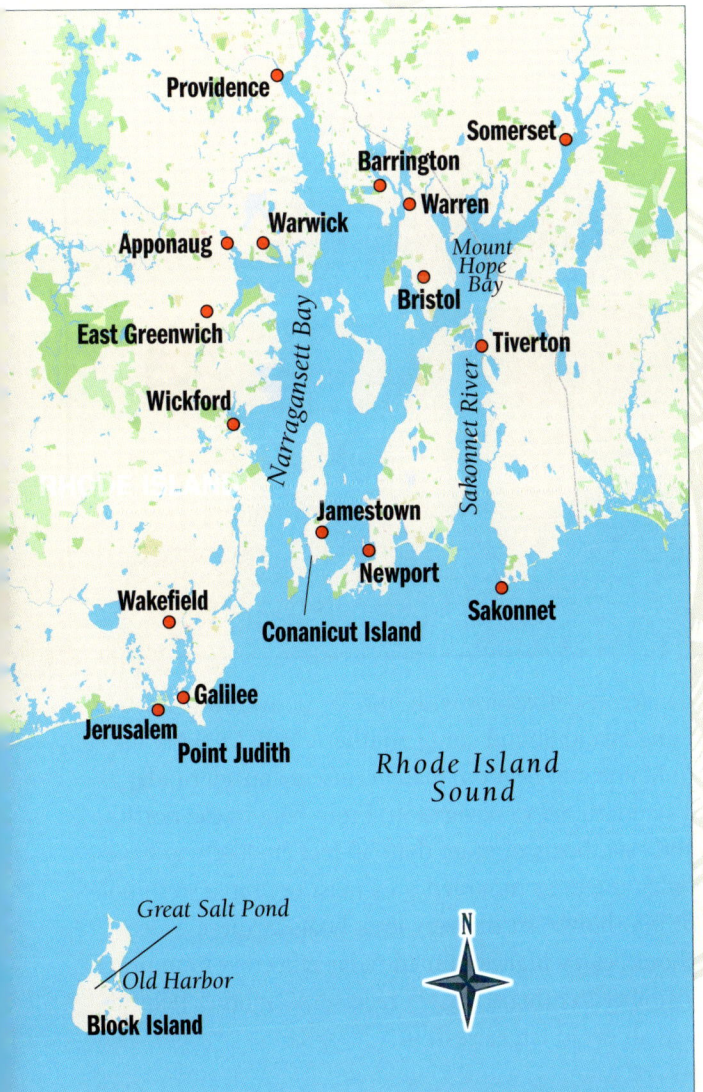

Block Island, RI

BLOCK ISLAND		Largest Vessel Accomodated	VHF Channel Monitored / Working	Transient Slips / Total Slips	Approach / Dockside Depth (reported)	Floating Docks	Gas / Diesel	Groceries, Ice, Marine Supplies, Snacks	Repairs: Hull, Engine, Propeller	Lift (tonnage), Crane, Rail	Min / Max Amps	Courtesy Car, Laundry, Pool, Showers	Pump-Out Station	Nearby: Grocery Store, Motel, Restaurant
				Dockage				**Supplies**			**Services**			
1. Champlin's Hotel, Marina & Resort ☐ WiFi	(401) 466-7777	300	68/68	/225	25.0/30.0	F	GD	GIMS	EP		30/50	LPS	P	GMR
2. New Harbor Boat Basin	(401) 480-1429	110	9/10	85/100	14.0/10.0	F		GIMS	E		30/50	S	P	GMR
3. Payne's Dock	(401) 466-5572	300	/	50/50	21.0/16.0	F	GD	GIS			30/50	S	P	GMR
4. Old Harbor	(401) 466-3235		12/	30/30	/								P	MR

☐ Internet Access WiFi Wireless Internet Access onSpot Dockside WiFi Facility
See WaterwayGuide.com for current rates, fuel prices, website addresses, and other up-to-the-minute information. (Information in the table is provided by the facilities.)

BLOCK ISLAND, NOAA CHART 13217

up in port if weather conditions are not to your liking.

Ferry boats crisscross Block Island Sound, Rhode Island Sound, Vineyard Sound and both Narragansett and Buzzard's Bays constantly throughout the day. Be watchful at all times. Tugs with barges far astern, freighters, stealthy submarines and seemingly endless, random recreational boat traffic should warn the skipper and crew to be alert and watchful at all times. You will encounter strong currents and big tidal ranges and need to keep an eye out for lobster pots, rocks and ledges.

Fog is always a possibility and can create very dangerous situations with little or no warning. From Long Island Sound along Southern New England up to Maine and beyond, many cruisers consider radar as a standard aid to navigation. From here to the north and east, boats of more than 30 feet are likely to have radar antennas mounted on a mast or atop a stern pole or pilothouse. At the very least boats in these waters should carry high-mounted radar reflectors to improve visibility to others. An AIS receiver is another helpful way to avoid larger vessels.

Great Salt Pond

Block Island

Harbor Neck

Dockage

There are hundreds of marinas in the area covered by this chapter but transients may not be their priority. They are often nearly full with their local customers. Finding a dockside slip for an overnight stay could prove difficult in the peak season of July and August. Skippers accustomed to tying up every night and plugging into shore power might have a challenge finding that kind of dockage. Reserve a slip where possible but some marinas will not take reservations in advance. Their rule is generally first-come, first-served. You should call the marina of your choice on VHF radio as you come within range or try calling them early in the day via cell phone if you did not get a reservation. If slips are not available, ask for a mooring of suitable size. If that fails, be prepared to anchor or, at worst, move on to the next harbor.

To avoid end-of-day disappointment try to arrive early in the afternoon of the day you need accommodations or anchoring space.

Every destination in this corner of the Eastern seaboard is well worth any effort and, fortunately, there are many places to set your anchor safely. There is nothing like a sunrise or sunset over Block Island, Nantucket, Martha's Vineyard or Cape Cod. Not much compares to this beautiful cruising area.

◾ BLOCK ISLAND

Navigating Block Island

Block Island, 12 miles south of the mainland, has tall hills and bluffs that make it visible on the horizon during clear weather. It appears a tempting challenge to cruisers transiting between the Long Island Sound and the Narraganset or Buzzards Bay but offshore voyagers often greet it with happiness and sometimes with relief, since it provides a haven and a staging spot to make the most of the raging currents of those neighboring bodies of water. It is only 6 miles long and 3 miles wide but the Great Salt Pond is welcoming during rough weather on the sound.

The beautiful, sun-washed beaches, cliff-side views, fresh air and island mystique draw boaters and non-boaters, young and old alike. The pork chop-shaped island has 20 miles of shoreline, high clay bluffs and lonely beaches known mainly to seabirds and the occasional seal.

Often called the "Bermuda of the North," the temperatures on Block Island are often 10 degrees cooler than the mainland in summer and warmer than the mainland in winter. It might be foggy, cool and damp during the early morning and evening but

GOIN' ASHORE
NEW SHOREHAM (BLOCK ISLAND), RI

New Shoreham, RI, is the smallest town in the smallest state in the U.S. It was incorporated in 1672 and only encompasses Block Island, although people rarely say they are going to (or are from) New Shoreham; they say they are going to Block Island. The Island has approximately 1,000 year-round residents and 15,000 to 20,000 seasonal visitors at a time. On Block Island, there are some 400 miles of stonewalls and 32 miles of trails, and 43 percent of the Island is preserved open space. The lighthouse at Sandy Point in the northwest corner of the island is the fourth near this location.

SERVICES

1. Block Island Post Office
32T Water St. (401-466-7733)

2. Island Free Library
9 Dodge St. (401-466-3233)

3. Island Moped & Bike
Rents moped, bicycles and beach chairs on Water St. (401-466-2700).

ATTRACTIONS

4. Block Island Historical Society
Historical society exhibiting regional artifacts, such as arrowheads, plus maps and memorabilia (18 Old Town Rd. & 1 Bridgegate Square, 401-466-2481).

SHOPPING

5. Block Island Grocery
242 Ocean Ave. (401-466-2949)

6. Island True Value Hardware
Chain retailer carrying household tools and some boating supplies at 102 Ocean Ave. (401-466-5831).

sometimes when fog is heavy outside the breakwaters, the sun is shining on the island proper. The island can develop its own wind, often from the southwest, which cools the island in the summer but can create problems for the anchored fleet in Great Salt Pond. At the same time, just beyond the breakwaters, calms can prevail and sailboats that reduced sail area in expectation of a rough passage to Rhode Island or Connecticut find themselves wallowing without wind in the rolling swells from the southwest. The opposite can also occur.

The long, lazy ocean swells that are characteristic of Block Island Sound heave gently, even in good weather. Submarines heading for New London can appear unexpectedly (especially stimulating in the fog), and ferries, freighters, naval vessels and barge traffic crisscross the waters continuously.

Block Island is often quite crowded on high-season weekends and holidays. As many as 2,000 boats encamp here over the Fourth of July week, when a festive, carnival-like atmosphere overtakes the island, and its unique Americana parade expands contemporary understandings of patriotism. Holiday sunsets here are often celebrated with impromptu boat horn symphonies followed by revelries far into the night.

Over a normal summer weekend, the island easily accommodates some 1,200 to 1,300 boats, although latecomers should expect all moorings to be taken, many with raft-ups, and shallow-depth anchorage space long gone or quite crowded. Block Island requests a small landing fee ($0.50) from every adult who arrives by private boat or ferry. The fee is collected on the honor system via collection boxes at marinas and town docks.

NAVIGATION: Use NOAA Charts 13215 and 13217. Boats converge on Block Island from many directions: east from Connecticut via The Race, about 21 nm; southeast from Watch Hill Passage, about 13 nm; southwest from Newport, about 26nm; northeast from Montauk Harbor, about 17 nm; and south from Point Judith, some 10 nm across Block Island Sound.

While the odds are good for a trouble-free crossing, Block Island Sound should always be accorded proper respect. Easy swells can become seas in minutes. Fog is frequent, sometimes patchy and at other times all-encompassing and unnerving. Big ship traffic will show AIS signatures and significant radar returns but sportfishers don't stay home for a little fog and are often harder to see and avoid! Current pours through The Race and Watch Hill Passage and can significantly affect

Block Island

entry channel is not natural. It was cut through from Block Island Sound to the natural salt pond in 1895 after several failed attempts.

Great Salt Pond offers all the attributes of a cruising mecca: easy access, plenty of water, good marinas with repair capabilities, dining options, excellent beaches and room to anchor, although holding varies with location. Ferries from Point Judith and Montauk tie up regularly at marina docks in the Great Salt Pond.

NAVIGATION: Use NOAA Charts 13217 and 13205. The Great Salt Pond channel is well marked and easy to enter. The 49-foot-high 4-second flashing red beacon "4" will attract your attention from a distance but it is somewhat southwest of the channel itself. Red bell buoy "2" is a better place to start if you don't have local knowledge because it gets you lined up to run the channel straight ahead. It is unlighted but has a bell.

The first lighted channel markers are flashing green buoy "7" and flashing red buoy "8," both of which are stationed well within the shallow zone. Keep an eye on your set between red bell buoy "2" and the lighted buoys when the current is running. The channel heads straight past the former Coast Guard station (also on the west shore) and into Great Salt Pond itself. Prevailing sou'westerlies and local racing traditions seem to encourage sailing vessels to enter and exit under canvas, which causes no particular difficulty. Sailing traffic with wide ranges of speed and maneuverability, along with power cruisers at various levels of skills and determination, can make the short passage interesting and colorful. In Great Salt Pond, the water is deep almost to the banks with few rocks or obstructions except at the southwestern corner.

Dockage/Moorings: The cost of a rental mooring when the anchorage is full is a relaxing investment in this harbor, when safety and convenience are top concerns. The town's ever-increasing moorings are light green with black lettering and are located along the southern edge of Great Salt Pond in front of the marinas. They are first-come, first-served. Early

your navigation efforts in or out bound.

If you make your approach in clear weather from the west, you may think you are looking at two islands. Great Salt Pond almost bisects the island and the shore on both sides of the pond is low. The land in between will appear as you get closer with higher ground to the south. If coming from points east or heading to Old Harbor from the west, do not cut the corner at flashing green "1BI" at the northern end of the island. That treacherous bar has caught many skippers who thought they were in deep water and the summer westerlies complicate the sailor's path. Even crossing safely north, breakers complicate the passage when ocean rollers pile up on the suddenly shallow sea bottom.

Many boats travel close to shore on the southern and western sides of the island but unmarked rocks are all around. There is a five-turbine wind farm a little less than 4 miles southeast of Block Island. They are in deep water and the blades are above all but the very tallest vessels. Numerous small fishing boats collect near them and prudence is advised. Currents run strong all around the island, southeasterly on the ebb and westerly on the flood.

New Harbor (Great Salt Pond)

The Great Salt Pond is more than 1 nm long and almost as wide. New Harbor is in the southeastern corner but the whole of Great Salt Pond is often (erroneously) called New Harbor. The 11.5-foot MLW

arrivals should simply pick up the pennant of an available green buoy. The harbormaster's launch will drop by to collect the fee. Rafting of up to two boats is permitted (with permission) but not required. Other moorings are private but the harbormaster may know of ones that are available. Skippers of larger boats (40-foot lengths or more) or late arrivals who can't locate an available mooring should contact the harbormaster on VHF Channel 12 for directions to an appropriate tie-up. The town has a number of heavier moorings for larger vessels.

Four marinas line the southern shore of Great Salt Pond. The 225-slip Champlin's Resort & Marina is first on entry and the largest in the harbor. Champlin's has a movie theater, a hotel, a huge swimming pool and a private beach on the saltwater pond. Other facilities here offer deep-water slips and services for large (to 300 feet) yachts.

Anchorage: Unlike other popular harbors, Great Salt Pond almost always has adequate room to anchor, although the open space is reduced by an area set aside for undisturbed shellfish beds. This area (roughly the northwestern half of the harbor) is a well-marked "No Anchorage" zone with faded pinkish red buoys set at perhaps 50-yard increments running east-west. Don't be seduced by the 16-foot spots because moving farther south quickly nets you 25 to 30 feet MLW.

The standard rule of anchoring at Block Island is to dig in deeply and keep an eye on the weather, particularly when rafted. Only those with sufficient rode aboard should anchor in the 30- to 50-foot MLW areas. Chain is especially appropriate here. It's not uncommon for boats without sufficient rode to drag in strong winds. Stick to the standard rules of thumb (minimum of 5:1 with chain, 7:1 on rope) and avoid the embarrassment of dragging. Holding is only fair in the gravel to the northwest. Holding is generally better to the east and northeast as this area is shallower and has less gravel. If any high winds are predicted, it's better to leave more space and use greater scope than to try packing in among other boats. Old Port Launch (VHF Channel 68) runs in most weather and late into the night. The launches are based at the New Harbor Boat Basin, where there is also ice available at the dock house.

In 2018, a dinghy dock, "around the corner," in New Harbor between Payne's Dock and Dead Eye Dick's was built and donated by the Wronoski family who owns the Cross Sound Ferry and Dead Eye Dick's. It is removed

at the end of each season and stored in New London. There is room for about 100 dinghies (12-foot max.) If these dinghy docks are full, it's best to go to the beach between New Harbor Boat Basin and Payne's Dock.

Dinghy dockage is also available at floats located at Champlin's Resort and Marina and New Harbor Boat Basin. Both accept separated trash and recycling. At New Harbor Boat Basin you must not tie up in the well-marked areas reserved for the launches. Your dinghy will be cut free. If the dinghy docks are full, it's best to go to the beach between New Harbor Boat Basin and Payne's Dock.

It is important to note that showers are not available for moored or anchored vessels at any of the marinas. Showers in the Great Salt Pond marinas are for vessels in slips only. The Frederick Benson Town Beach pavilion, housing the town's showers, is reached by beaching your dinghy on the east side of the pond. A wooden walkway over the marsh grass puts you on a busy roadway for a very short walk to the north. Turn right into the first small parking lot and head east towards the beach. From there, it is a 0.5-mile trek south to the pavilion. Showers are available but rather expensive as each token provides only 4 minutes of water. The surf is cool and refreshing on even the hottest day. Chairs, umbrellas and windscreens may be rented at the pavilion.

> The Great Salt Pond is a No-Discharge Zone, one of the first anywhere. Even treated effluent cannot be discharged overboard. The town of New Shoreham makes it easy to comply with this law by providing free pump-out service for any boat in the harbor. Simply call "Pump-out Boat" on VHF Channel 73. Although service is fast and efficient, they are busy and it is best to call early in the day to be put on the list.

Old Harbor

This small harbor of refuge, protected from the ocean by breakwaters, is on the island's eastern side (not accessible by boat from New Harbor). Old Harbor is the center of town and the larger commercial ferry landing location, which means that it is the more modern, tourist-centric side of the island. New Harbor, strangely, is the more traditional, recreational port in atmosphere.

The town of New Shoreham (Old Harbor) ordinances require yachts to stand clear of the marked channel

Point Judith
Pond, RI

SNUG HARBOR		Dockage					Supplies		Services						
		Largest Vessel Accomodated	VHF Channel Monitored / Working	Transient Slips / Total Slips	Approach / Dockside Depth (reported)	Floating Docks	Gas / Diesel	Groceries, Ice, Marine Supplies, Snacks	Repairs: Hull, Engine, Propeller	Lift (tonnage), Crane, Rail	Min / Max Amps	Courtesy Car, Laundry, Pool, Showers	Pump-Out Station	Nearby: Grocery Store, Motel, Restaurant	
1. Snug Harbor Marina Inc.	(401) 783-7766	70	66/	1/11	6.0/6.0	F	GD	GIS			50			GR	
2. Point Judith Marina WiFi	(401) 789-7189	110	9/	7/294	10.0/12.0	F	GD	I	EP	L50	30/100	LPS	P	GR	

⌨ Internet Access 📶 Wireless Internet Access onSpot Dockside WiFi Facility

See WaterwayGuide.com for current rates, fuel prices, website addresses, and other up-to-the-minute information. (Information in the table is provided by the facilities.)

SNUG HARBOR, NOAA CHART 13219

Sand Hill Cove

Galilee

Jerusalem

Point Judith Pond

Snug Harbor

area between the harbor entrance and the pier marked "Ferry" at the southeastern end of the harbor. Ferries leave from here for Point Judith, RI, and New London, CT, about 11 times a day in peak season (early June through Labor Day) and less frequently off season.

NAVIGATION: Use NOAA Chart 13217. The straight entry to Old Harbor is easy to navigate except in strong easterlies when seas are heavy. Jetty lights and a foghorn help in bad weather. A small inner harbor in the southeastern corner has a town dock and offers excellent protection from all but extreme weather.

Dockage: There is a town dock in Old Harbor with 30 slips on fixed docks with limited services. Showers are available in the dockmaster's building.

Anchorage: Anchoring anywhere in Old Harbor can be a problem. It has very limited space for anchoring, which is restricted to a total of 7 days in a 14-day period. Commercial boats, fishing and charter boats use Old Harbor extensively and Med-moor to walls or anchor fore-and-aft with their sterns to the breakwater. Depths are about 10 to 15 feet MLW. You can land your dinghy on the sandy beach of the outer harbor or anchor inside and use the showers in the dockmaster's building. Outside the breakwater, there may be some protection from big waves but it is shallow far from the beach and many rocks make it a bad bet.

■ POINT JUDITH POND

West of Point Judith, the Rhode Island shore to Watch Hill Passage is 18 miles of beach with occasional rocky projections and a few "inlets" navigable only by very small boats and then mainly at high tide. For the mariner this section of coast between Watch Hill and Point Judith has little to offer but coastal scenery and a strong current, and the trip can be very long indeed if the current is foul. Perhaps on a calm day you can anchor off the beach for a dinghy ride ashore to swim. East of Point Judith are the compact cruising grounds of Narragansett Bay.

The Point Judith Harbor of Refuge is a V-shaped, slowly deteriorating sea barrier nearly 3 miles long that provides one of the few easy-access shelters in a long stretch of deceptively difficult water. Granite sea arms stretching from the mainland provide a protective shield with marked openings to the east and west. Passage through either opening is easy in good visibility and fair weather.

You will find better protection and more interesting scenery in Point Judith Pond. Its shores and islands are lined with fishing villages, community docks and well-equipped marinas. Mean low water depths for 3.5

miles to the head of the pond are usually enough for boats with drafts of up to 6 feet. Refer to the Waterway Explorer (www.waterwayguide.com) and NOAA online charts for the most up-to-date information. The channels, dredged out of shoal and marsh, can silt up quickly after a storm.

NAVIGATION: Use NOAA Chart 13217. In planning a transit from Block Island to the Rhode Island mainland, keep in mind that you will encounter strong currents, lots of boat traffic, frequent fog and significant shipping lanes. When coming from Great Salt Pond, around the north side of Block Island, you should set your course from the vicinity of flashing green bell buoy "1BI." The waters between Sandy Point and the bell buoy will show breakers in all weather and they break up the swell in a confusing fashion. From that mark, it is about 7 nm to the western entrance of the Point Judith Harbor. From Old Harbor take departure from green can "5." A course of about 020° magnetic will take you to the west entrance, a little over 9 miles away.

Be alert for the strong currents flowing in or out of Rhode Island Sound and Narragansett Bay. This area can be quite choppy and confused, particularly when strong currents and winds are in opposition. If your destination from Block Island is Narragansett Bay, chart a course to Breton Reef, well east of Point Judith. Under all conditions, keep an eye on the mouth of Narragansett Bay for departing cruise ships and other large commercial traffic. High speed ferries operate between Block Island and Point Judith. Mariners are cautioned that these craft move rapidly and at angles to the normal direction of traffic. An AIS receiver is especially helpful in such places. If a close encounter is expected, contact the ship on VHF Channel 13. Outbound ships might be headed east into the Atlantic Ocean, up Buzzards Bay, or west towards Long Island Sound.

Take special care upon entering the harbor from the busier western entrance. The breakwater obscures outbound boats from the Breachway in the channel directly inside the wall. Point Judith is the home of one of the largest commercial fishing fleets on the North Atlantic seaboard and is a terminus for the Block Island Ferry so an approaching skipper who cuts close to the port side of the western opening of the refuge can get a sudden and dangerous surprise. The eastern entrance has far less traffic.

If approaching from Narragansett Bay, give Point

Judith the respectable sea room it deserves. A warning light has been at this location for nearly 200 years for good reason. It has swift currents, unexpectedly strong winds and submerged boulders marking the memory of countless ships lost in this area over the centuries. Be cautious also of the thicket of lobster buoys and fish traps you will find in the region east of the refuge.

The passage into the harbor at the eastern breakwaters west of Point Judith itself are first marked by flashing red buoy "2" followed by the 39-foot flashing green "3" on the west breakwater. The western entrance of the harbor is marked on the northern breakwater by the 35-foot flashing green horn "3" and its southern neighbor, 40-foot flashing red "2." Each entrance carries 18- to 30-foot MLW depths.

⚠️ The breakwater seawall in the Point Judith Harbor of Refuge is degraded in various areas through natural erosion to below the water line at high tide. The sea wall still performs its intended function to break waves and prevent heavy seas from entering Point Judith Harbor but certain environmental conditions may cause segments of the structure to become awash and not detectable by eye or radar. Mariners are advised to maintain a safe distance from the breakwater at all times. Navigational lights on the east and west end of the breakwater mark entry into the Harbor of Refuge.

Anchorage: The V-shaped breakwater that protects the Point Judith Harbor provides good anchorage when sea conditions are calm but large seas will come right over the breakwater, especially at high tide and from the west where the wall is more broken down. Good holding takes work due to heavy patches of kelp that foul the bottom. In addition to double-checking for a secure set, choose a spot well within the "V" to be clear of vessels traveling between the eastern entrance and the channel leading into Point Judith Pond.

Summer evening squalls can create sudden wind shifts so avoid locations overly close to the breakwater. Sand from the Pond is piling up inside the V of the breakwater, especially on the southwestern side, forming a substantial shoal. When northerly winds interrupt the prevailing summer southwesterlies, it is best to anchor in the lee of Galilee off the beach at Sand Hill Cove, although wakes will keep the boat dancing day and night. Under these conditions, secure anchorage in sand and mud can be found in depths of 7 to 12 feet MLW.

Whatever your location in the Point Judith Harbor, the surge attending Block Island Sound's characteristic ground swells seems to find its way through the breakwater. Moderate to heavy conditions outside will provide plenty of movement inside the harbor.

Note: Point Judith is a No-Discharge Zone. Sealed heads, holding tanks and using a pump-out station are required.

Galilee & Jerusalem

There are no real accommodations for cruisers at either Galilee or Jerusalem, which flank the entrance to Point Judith Pond. Visiting boats may tie up at the state pier at Galilee for as long as 2 hours to explore or dine at several fine restaurants. Galilee's sea-oriented commerce is located along a single street paralleling Point Judith Pond. There is no shortage of fresh fish and prepared seafood to go.

NAVIGATION: Use NOAA Chart 13219. Enter Point Judith Pond by running the strong currents between the rock jetties of The Breachway in the northwest corner of the harbor. Currents at full tidal flow run 3 to 4 knots through this narrow passage where commercial and recreational traffic can be intense. Weaving, leaping and capsizing jet skiers contribute another dimension to the already turbulent waters. You can't count on having the full width of the channel due to large commercial fishing boats rushing to market with tackle extended. They will crowd and pass a slow boat attempting to sail or power against the current. Meanwhile, fishermen and sightseers line the jetty in all weather. Returning a friendly wave to the onlookers, although a pleasure, can be a dangerous distraction.

Once through The Breachway, the channel almost immediately divides at a prominent red and green bell buoy "N." Galilee is to the west with its big state piers berthing the commercial fishing fleet and the Block Island ferry. Jerusalem, a village of cottages, is to the east. Off the piers, a fair-sized area has been dredged, but the current remains strong here and larger vessels need all the maneuvering room available.

Anchorage: Cruising facilities are scarce at both Galilee and Jerusalem. Those wishing a more extensive visit might do well to remain outside the pond, taking the dinghy in for shore activities or a swim. There is a small dinghy dock just to starboard inside the Breachway at Galilee to accommodate cruisers wishing to shop or dine ashore.

Upper Pond, RI

WAKEFIELD		Largest Vessel Accomodated	VHF Channel Monitored / Working	Transient Slips / Total Slips	Approach / Dockside Depth (reported)	Floating Docks	Gas / Diesel	Groceries, Ice, Marine Supplies, Snacks	Repairs: Hull, Engine, Propeller	Lift (tonnage), Crane, Rail	Min / Max Amps	Courtesy Car, Laundry, Pool, Showers	Pump-Out Station	Nearby: Grocery Store, Motel, Restaurant
				Dockage			**Supplies**		**Services**					
1. Silver Spring Marine 🖥 WiFi	(401) 783-0783	35	7/	12/85	5.0/5.0	F		IM	HEP	L35	30/50	PS		GMR
2. Ram Point Marina 🖥 WiFi	(401) 783-4535	60	9/66	2/200	6.0/6.0	F	GD	IM	HEP	C,R	30/50	LS	P	GMR
3. Marina Bay Docking 🖥	(401) 789-4050	50	9/	2/65	6.0/5.0	F		I	E		30/50	S		GR
4. Stone Cove Marina 🖥 WiFi	(401) 783-8990	50	/	4/165	6.0/6.0	F	G	IMS			30	S	P	GMR
5. Long Cove Marina Campground	(401) 783-4902	24	/	3/45	6.0/4.0	F						S		GMR

🖥 Internet Access   WiFi Wireless Internet Access   onSpot Dockside WiFi Facility

See WaterwayGuide.com for current rates, fuel prices, website addresses, and other up-to-the-minute information. (Information in the table is provided by the facilities.)

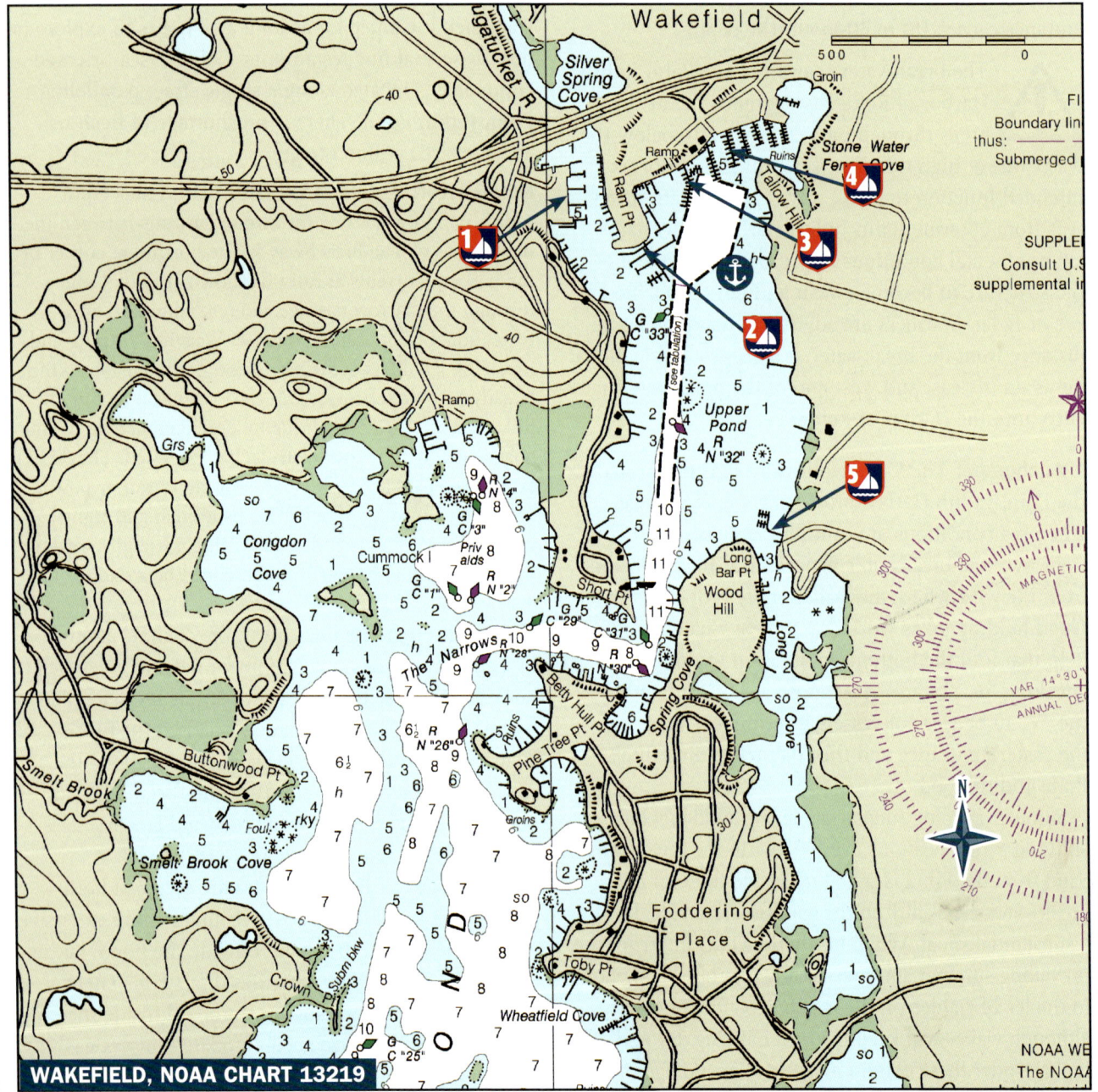

WAKEFIELD, NOAA CHART 13219

Snug Harbor

Quiet Snug Harbor, on the western shore just north of the Breachway, offers easy-access dockage, marine facilities, fuel and casual restaurants as well as fresh caught seafood.

NAVIGATION: Use NOAA Chart 13219. A marked channel, carrying at least 6-foot MLW depths, leads north on the west side of the pond to Snug Harbor, almost 1 mile above the entrance. Note that there has been significant shoaling reported between red nun buoy "6" (just north of the State Pier on the Jerusalem side) and green can buoy "7." Just past the large wooden piling north of red nun buoy "6," begin to trace the westward-curving crescent of the shoreline at a distance of approximately 150 to 200 feet off the beach, leaving green can buoy "7" about 100 feet off to port. You will notice deep-draft commercial vessels taking this course, where there are 8- to 10-foot MLW depths.

Be cautious farther upstream and observe all channel markers. Boats drawing much over 5 feet may touch bottom (in soft mud) at low water, even in the center of the channel. Locals advise hugging the west side between green can buoys "17" and "19." After that, depths increase to 9 feet MLW until reaching the 5- to 6-foot shoal preceding green can buoy "25" just north of the passage between Gardner Island and Beach Island. As with all such channels, try to make the passage on a rising tide if you have a deep-draft vessel. At red nun buoy "28" just north of Pine Tree Point, the channel takes a sharp turn east into The Narrows and then another turn north to head for the Upper Pond. Give the point a healthy respect.

Dockage: Several marinas here have floating docks with all fuels and slips for transients. (See marina table for details.) From any of these locations in Snug Harbor it is easy to arrange a rental car or call a taxi for provisioning in nearby Wakefield or inland sightseeing.

Anchorage: Anchorage-intent cruisers should round Gardner Island and take the Gardner Island-Beach Island passage south (following the chart closely) to drop a hook northeast of Plato Island. Holding is excellent here in firm mud but shoaling extends from the east tip of Plato Island so check with a depth sounder to be sure you have adequate swinging room in 5 to 7 feet MLW. This is a duly-marked no wake zone but, unfortunately, enforcement is spotty at best. Plato Island is inhabited. Respect the owner's privacy.

The adjacent islands, Gardner and Beach, are also private, yet you may explore with appropriate respect for their natural settings. On a summer's morning, you can watch the quahog fishermen muscle their clam rakes for hours, pulling this delicacy from the now-clean pond waters. Good fishing has returned here as well. Flounder, stripers and blues are all said to be susceptible to the right rig in season.

Wakefield

Originally a mill town, Wakefield is centrally located close to all of Rhode Island's beaches and offers a provisioning opportunity. The interstate highway and its ramps make it a difficult walk, but a major shopping mall with a variety of stores and chain restaurants can be accessed by walking under the U.S. Rt. 1 overpass, north one long block and then going right about 0.2 miles to the plaza on the right.

Dockage: Several Wakefield marinas offer slips on floating docks and repairs. Ram Point Marina is the only area marina with laundry. The University of Rhode Island Sailing Center is to the west.

Anchorage: The Upper Pond is almost entirely filled with private moorings, making anchoring difficult but not impossible. You can drop the hook south of Tallow Point in 5 to 6 feet MLW with good holding in mud. This provides all-around protection.

◼ WEST PASSAGE: NARRAGANSETT BAY TO GREENWICH BAY

Although Newport is a world-class yachting center and a high point of Narragansett Bay, the Bay has much, much more to offer. Narragansett Bay stretches 18 nm from Block Island Sound to the Providence River and was named for the original inhabitants of Rhode Island. The bay is also an estuary of national significance and a spawning ground and habitat for winter flounder, lobster, hard shell clams, seals and eel grass.

Rolling hills, green fields, woods and houses surround Narragansett Bay. It offers protected waters, well-marked waterways, sheltered coves and attractive ports of call. You can anchor nearly anywhere you find a lee or a cove and in many places you can go ashore to swim, picnic or hike.

Modern marinas, excellent marine repairs, services,

West Passage, RI

		Largest Vessel Accomodated	VHF Channel Monitored / Working	Transient Slips / Total Slips	Approach / Dockside Depth (reported)	Floating Docks	Gas / Diesel	Groceries, Ice, Marine Supplies, Snacks	Repairs: Hull, Engine, Propeller	Lift (tonnage), Crane, Rail	Min / Max Amps	Courtesy Car, Laundry, Pool, Showers	Pump-Out Station	Nearby: Grocery Store, Motel, Restaurant
DUTCH HARBOR				**Dockage**			**Supplies**		**Services**					
1. Dutch Harbor Boat Yard 🖥 📶	(401) 423-0630	75	69/	/	15.0/12.0			I	HEP	R		LS	P	GMR
WICKFORD														
2. Wickford Shipyard	(401) 884-1725	60	/	10/137	9.0/9.0	F	GD	IM	HEP	L50,C	30/50	LPS		GMR
3. Safe Harbor Wickford Cove 📶	(401) 884-7014	74	9/	6/155	9.0/10.0	F	GD	IMS	HEP	L70	30/50	LS	P	GMR
4. Wickford Yacht Club	(401) 294-9010	50	9/	/	7.0/7.0			I			30	S		GR
5. Pleasant Street Wharf Inc.	(401) 294-2791	35	/	2/42	13.0/10.0	F	GD	IM	EP	L15	30	S		GMR
6. Wickford Marina 🖥 📶	(401) 294-8160	100	10/	6/65	12.0/7.0	F		I			30/50	CLS	P	GR
7. Northwick Boatyard	(401) 932-3613	33	/	/50	/							S		
ALLEN HARBOR														
8. The Marina at Rhode Island Mooring Services	(401) 295-2502	60	/	/69	8.0/8.0	F		M	HEP	L25,C	30		P	MR
9. Allen Harbor Marina	(401) 294-1212	40	16/	2/115	8.0/9.0	F		IS			30	S	P	MR
10. Mill Creek Marine 📶	(401) 294-3700	50	/	6/	6.0/6.0	F	GD	M	HEP	L20	30	LS	P	GMR

🖥 Internet Access   📶 Wireless Internet Access   onSpot Dockside WiFi Facility

See WaterwayGuide.com for current rates, fuel prices, website addresses, and other up-to-the-minute information. (Information in the table is provided by the facilities.)

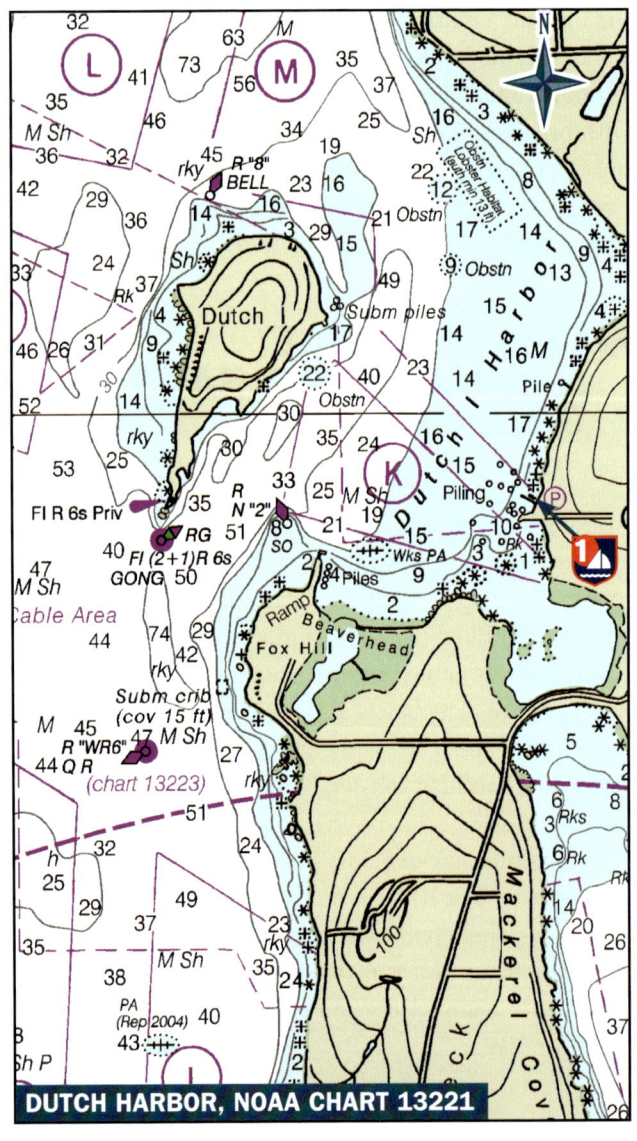

DUTCH HARBOR, NOAA CHART 13221

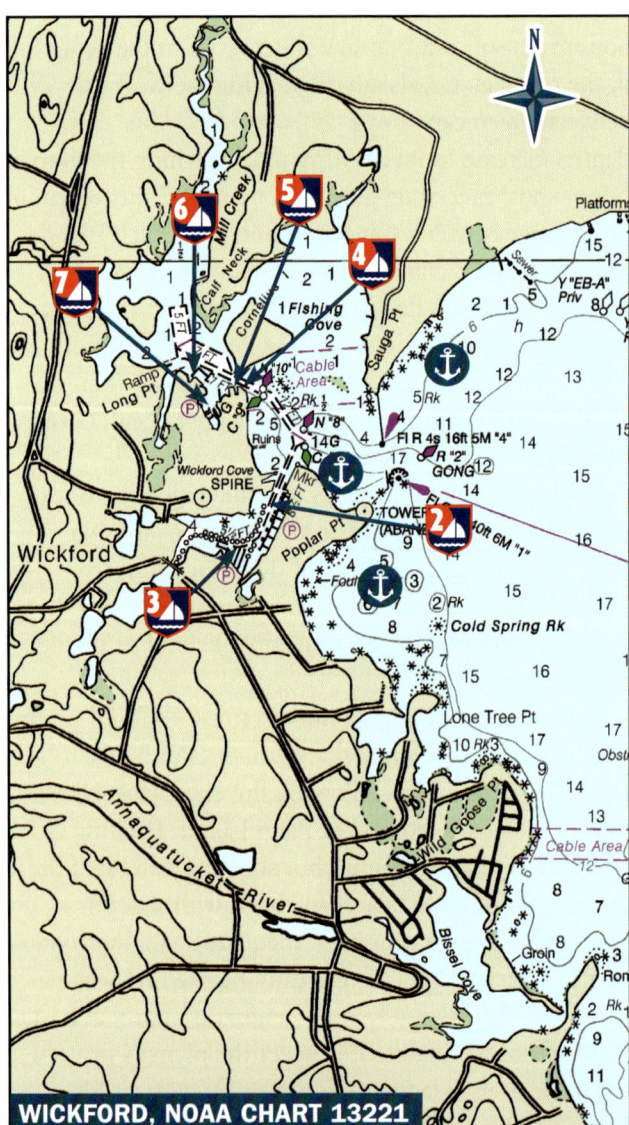

WICKFORD, NOAA CHART 13221

ALLEN HARBOR, NOAA CHART 13221

suppliers, pump-out stations, restaurants, shore transportation and accommodations are easy to locate throughout the bay. However, the popularity of this "Jewel of Rhode Island" continues to outpace the availability of slip space and moorings. Those wanting the convenience of dockage or moorings should reserve them in advance.

A tour of the Narragansett from west to east could take in quite a few excellent harbors, anchorages and shore trips. Heading north up the West Passage, Dutch Harbor and its fascinating island can be followed by Wickford or Allen Harbor and then some of the pleasures of Greenwich Bay. The narrow channel between Warwick Point and Patience Island provides access to the Providence River, Warren and Bristol. These ports set up the trip south via the East Passage with very popular stops at Prudence Island, Jamestown and Newport. Some will choose to use the less-traveled path and round Aquidneck Island's northern end in Mount Hope Bay before heading south through Tiverton (which involves a fixed bridge with 65-foot vertical clearance) and down the Sakonnet River, where Sachuest Point's Third Beach is a back door to Newport.

Villages with small, popular harbors, excellent sailing conditions and fun excursions characterize the West Passage. It is easier on this passage to anchor somewhere that feels somewhat wild while still being able to access necessities like groceries and fuel. Whether desiring a hike in Goddard Memorial

State Park or a ramble through the ruins on Dutch Island, visiting the village shops in Wickford or East Greenwich, or stopping at one of the full-service marinas, the West Passage will provide what you're after.

> Beavertail Point Light, which marks the southern point of Narragansett Bay, is on the National Historic Register. The original stone base was uncovered during the hurricane of 1938. The lighthouse was built in 1749, making it the third oldest lighthouse in America. The present granite tower, built in 1856, is just north of the original light. During any significant storm hundreds of people visit Beavertail State Park to watch the waves and surf.

NAVIGATION: Use NOAA Chart 13221. Conanicut Island's Beavertail Point Light is an easy landmark. Its 64-foot-tall tower flashes white every 9 seconds with a horn blast every 30 seconds in fog. The Western Passage is wide and deep at the entrance. The dangers are seaward of the point, marked by green and red bell buoy "NR," and westward where Whale Rock is marked by flashing green gong buoy "8."

To head into the Bay via the West Passage, the Beavertail Point Light should be left well to the east. To head north via the East Passage it is left well to the west.

Dutch Harbor

The large cove of Dutch Harbor is on the west side of Conanicut Island, 2.5 miles north of Beavertail Point. It is easy to enter from either north or south. Dutch Island protects it on the west and provides excellent scenery. Northerly winds can whip up a chop. Turning and anchor room are ample with good holding in 9- to 20-foot MLW depths. Scenic paths and abandoned bunkers make for good exploring on Dutch Island (part of the Rhode Island Park System). You must take great care exploring if you go beyond the ruins on the north end of the island. The island paths have become overgrown and even though the park system has installed fencing and rails, there are still sharp drop-offs to watch for. (All that overgrowth attracts ticks, which are a major concern for humans and pets).

Moorings: Guest moorings are available from Dutch Harbor Boat Yard for overnight or afternoon stopovers. Fees include launch service from the mooring field. Hail NOVA on VHF Channel 69. From this tranquil and mostly protected location, the excellent restaurants and amenities of Jamestown are an easy and pleasant 0.5-mile walk to the east.

Anchorage: Uncomplicated anchorage in mud is located just outside the mooring field along the northeast side of Dutch Harbor in 13- to 17-foot MLW depths. If there is a chance of a northerly wind, the small bight at the southern side of the Dutch Island is an anchoring possibility. There is no launch service available to anchored boats but there is a public dinghy dock next to the town pier (immediately south of the boatyard dock). You can off-load your trash at the town-maintained dumpster just above the dinghy dock and use the DIY pump-out station at the town's easy-access, deep-draft dock, accommodating boats to about 40 feet. Signs limit dinghy tie-ups to 30 minutes but this is not typically enforced unless it is very crowded.

Wickford Harbor

On the west mainland shore of the West Passage, Wickford is one of the most charming cruising destinations on Narragansett Bay. From a berth in either cove be prepared for about a 0.5-mile trek to the commercial facilities along Brown Street, running parallel to the inner harbor. It may be more convenient, particularly from a mooring or Wickford Cove dock, to take your dinghy or your boat for a short-term tie-up alongside the town dock (7-foot MLW depths) at the head of Wickford Cove.

NAVIGATION: Use NOAA Chart 13221. Wickford's twin harbors are located 3 nm northwest of the double-spanned **Jamestown Verrazano Bridge** (135-foot fixed vertical clearance) connecting Conanicut Island to the mainland at North Kingstown.

Fox Island forms the southeastern end of Wickford's large entrance cove. Don't let local fishing boats lead you between it and Rome Point. While there is plenty of water in this area, there are also plenty of rocks. Wickford's outer harbor is easily entered due west of red gong buoy "2" between the well-marked, lighted ends of the jetties (flashing green 40-foot "1" and flashing red 16-foot "4") guarding the mooring field within. Green can buoy "7" identifies the split between Wickford Cove to the south and Mill Cove to the west. The channels and coves of Wickford Harbor (but not the full outer harbor) are dredged to a 7-foot MLW depth throughout. You can count on 8-foot MLW depths in Wickford Cove (despite the charted 5.5 feet) but take care to stay in the channel.

Dockage/Moorings: Wickford Cove is a tight and busy channel lined with marinas. Wickford Shipyard is to the east in Wickford Cove and well-protected Safe Harbor Wickford Cove is to the south in Wickford Cove with slips and 44 moorings. Safe Harbor Wickford Cove also maintains five heavy-duty, short-term rental moorings outside the breakwater, but this can be a restless spot when the wind picks up. Their launch (also monitoring VHF Channel 09) provides on-call water taxi service throughout the harbor. This service is complimentary, although a tip to the launch driver is much appreciated. This is the closest base for a walking or dinghy excursion to the village.

Mill Cove has a dredged, 7-foot (MLW) marked channel to starboard after entering the breakwater. Several marinas and a yacht club are located here with various amenities. From Mill Cove, it is a pleasant 0.4-mile walk to the center of Wickford's historic village.

The Wickford Town Dock lies immediately parallel to Brown Street, which is the town's primary shopping row. There are four slips available for transients on a first-come, first-served basis with a three-night maximum. The dock is substantial in size, carries 7-foot MLW depths and is convenient for shopping and provisioning. Dinghy docks are provided in town.

Anchorage: Anchoring is prohibited inside the harbor and a patrol boat will roust you, even if sufficient room is found. Visiting skippers frequently take advantage of settled summer weather to anchor in the bight south of the abandoned tower (preceding the port-side jetty of the harbor entrance) off Wickford's town beach. Holding is excellent in 7-to 8-foot MLW depths with a sand and mud bottom and protection is good from prevailing winds, although it is somewhat exposed from northeast through southeast with a long fetch. You will want both a chart and a rising tide to help you pick your way in past two shallow (2- to 3-feet at MLW) spots on the open path to the best beachside anchorage.

Additional anchoring room is north of the harbor entrance, outside the small mooring field. Holding is secure in 10- to 12-foot MLW depths but the fetch for prevailing southwesterly winds and front-driven northerlies is substantial. It can get rocky in these conditions.

Allen Harbor

Allen Harbor is 2.5 miles north of Wickford. Both Wickford Harbor and Allen Harbor, originally maintained by the Navy as part of the Seabee's training center, are now under the jurisdiction of the North Kingstown harbormaster. It's a bit tricky to identify because of the distracting industrial installations just south but the masts of the recreational harbor resolve themselves as you approach.

NAVIGATION: Use NOAA Chart 13221. Head northwest from flashing red buoy "14" or southwest from green can buoy "3" for the harbor entrance. Green can buoy "1" and flashing red buoy "2" provide the starting point and there are no further markers. Aim straight down the throat and keep an eye on the depth sounder; shoals are on either side. If you draw more than 5 feet enter on a rising tide. Once inside you will find depths of 10 to 11 feet MLW. When you continue north stay outside of green can buoy "3" marking the outer limit of Calf Pasture Point.

Dockage/Moorings: Moorings are more likely to be available than slips here. Contact the harbormaster on VHF Channel 16. The Marina at Rhode Island Mooring Service has slips, even though their primary service is mooring repair and placement. The town of North Kingston has a pump-out station at Allen Harbor.

Greenwich Bay

Greenwich Bay is a 3-mile-long arm of Narragansett Bay with three good harbors. Ashore are parks, beaches, amusements, transportation and boating amenities. Shoals and rocks are usually well marked, although some buoy numbers may not match older charts.

NAVIGATION: Use NOAA Chart 13221. In all but the clearest weather follow at least a rough compass or specific GPS course for the entire section between Quonset Point and Warwick Point. This precaution will not only keep you clear of Calf Pasture Point but also the buoyed rocks 1 mile east of Potowomut Neck. Shoal water extends well to the east of Sandy Point. Pass well east of Round Rock off Potowomut Neck (flashing green buoy "1") and do not cut across the shoal east of Sandy Point. Follow the chart and buoys through the deep channel south of Warwick Point's lighthouse. Once inside you have a choice of several good harbors: Warwick Cove, Apponaug Cove and Greenwich Cove.

In the northeastern sector of the bay, Warwick is convenient to the T.F. Green (Providence) Airport, as is East Greenwich and other some other Narragansett Bay marinas. A major transportation center provides access to commuter trains into Boston and Amtrak trains to New York City and the Connecticut towns on the way. Entering Greenwich Bay heading northwest

Oakland Beach

Warwick Neck

Greenwich Bay, RI

Table columns (under groups **Dockage**, **Supplies**, **Services**):
Largest Vessel Accommodated · VHF Channel Monitored/Working · Transient Slips/Total Slips · Approach/Dockside Depth (reported) · Floating Docks · | · Gas/Diesel · Groceries, Ice, Marine Supplies, Snacks · | · Repairs: Hull, Engine, Propeller · Lift (tonnage), Crane, Rail · Min/Max Amps · Courtesy Car, Laundry, Pool, Showers · Pump-Out Station · Nearby: Grocery Store, Motel, Restaurant

	Phone	Largest Vessel	VHF Mon/Work	Transient/Total Slips	Approach/Dockside Depth	Floating Docks	Gas/Diesel	Groceries, Ice, Marine Supplies, Snacks	Repairs	Lift/Crane/Rail	Min/Max Amps	Courtesy Car/Laundry/Pool/Showers	Pump-Out	Nearby
WARWICK COVE														
1. Harbor Lights Marina 🖥 WiFi onSpot	(401) 737-6353	50	9/8	2/225	8.0/6.0	F	GD	IS	HEP	L70,C	50	LPS	P	GMR
2. Bay Marina Inc. WiFi	(401) 739-6435	50	/	5/200	6.0/6.0	F		M	HEP	L,C	30	S	P	GR
3. Safe Harbor Greenwich Bay East Yard WiFi	(401) 884-1810	60	/	5/210	10.0/7.0	F	GD	IS	HEP	L35,C	30/50	LPS	P	R
4. Safe Harbor Greenwich Bay (North Yard) WiFi	(401) 884-1810	60	/	10/380	10.0/7.0	F	GD	IS	HEP	L35,C	30/50	LPS	P	GR
5. Fairwinds Marina (formerly Warwick Cove Marina) 🖥	(401) 921-1955	45	71/	/90	7.0/6.0	F		IM	HEP		30	S		GMR
6. Angel's Marina	(401) 737-9805	40	/	/75	6.0/6.0	F		I	P					R
APPONAUG COVE														
7. Ponaug Marina 🖥 WiFi	(401) 884-1976	40	14/	2/150	5.0/4.0	F	G	I	HP		30	S	P	GMR
8. Apponaug Harbor Marina WiFi	(401) 739-5005	50	/	2/348	8.0/6.0	F	D	GIM	HE	L35,C	30	S	P	GR
COWESETT														
9. Safe Harbor Cowesett North 🖥 WiFi	(401) 884-0544	60	9/	20/380	12.0/6.0	F	GD	IMS	HEP	L35	30/200+	LPS	P	GMR
10. Safe Harbor Cowesett South 🖥 WiFi	(401) 884-0544	150	9/	20/750	8.0/10.0	F	G	IM	HP	L50,C	30/50	LPS	P	GMR
GREENWICH														
11. Prime Marina East Greenwich 🖥 WiFi	(401) 884-8828	300	9/	30/186	8.0/10.0	F		IM	HEP	L35,C	30/100	S	P	GR
12. East Greenwich Yacht Club 🖥 WiFi	(401) 884-7700	75	9/8	/120	12.0/10.0	F	GD	I			30/50	LS	P	R
13. Greenwich Cove Marina	(401) 885-6611	40	/	/	10.0/8.0						30	S		R

🖥 Internet Access   WiFi Wireless Internet Access   onSpot Dockside WiFi Facility

See WaterwayGuide.com for current rates, fuel prices, website addresses, and other up-to-the-minute information. (Information in the table is provided by the facilities.)

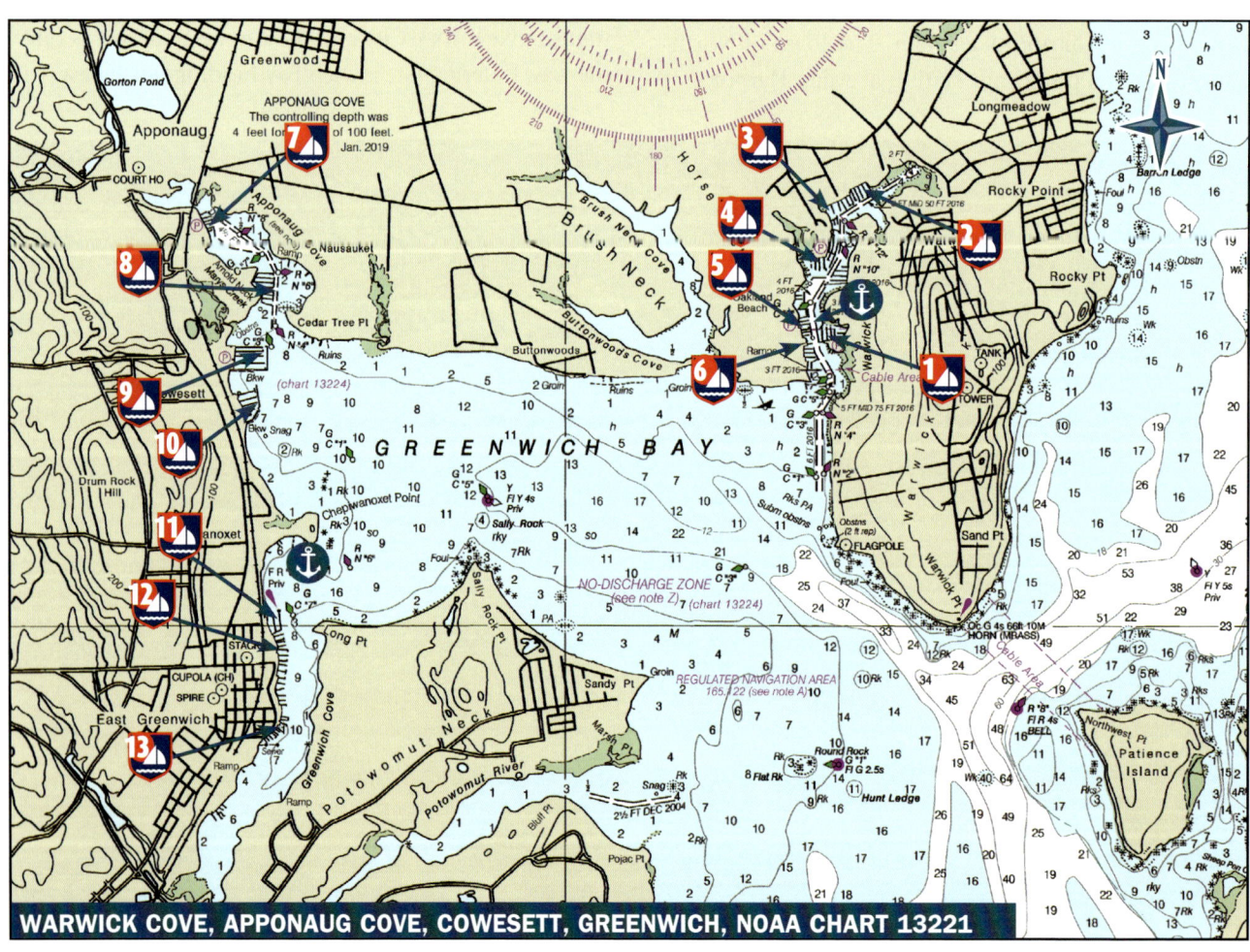

WARWICK COVE, APPONAUG COVE, COWESETT, GREENWICH, NOAA CHART 13221

then turn north after the charted flagpole without hugging Warwick Neck because of the charted rocks. If approaching from the west, don't cut green can buoy "1." Local small fishing boats can lead you astray in this area. The channel proceeds along Warwick Neck into the harbor.

In the northwest corner of Greenwich Bay is Apponaug Cove with a direct, easy entrance between Arnold Neck to the west and Cedar Tree Point to the east. This cove ensures good protection from the nor'easters but is open to southeast breezes at the entrance. Shores of the cove are attractive. The pleasant little town of Apponaug is near the harbor and within easy reach are shore accommodations, provisions and beaches. From point east head for the highly visible Safe Harbor Cowesett North and South marina bulkheads before turning north for green can buoy "3." The well-buoyed, 8- to 10-foot MLW depth channel extends about 1 mile to a fixed railroad bridge (22-foot vertical clearance). Check locally for latest depths; the edges of the channel shoal up periodically.

The long, finger-like Greenwich Cove is fully protected from all but strong northerlies. It is also one of the most popular stops on Narragansett Bay and boasts a fair mix of marine facilities and amenities along the western edge with a backdrop of unspoiled greenery on the eastern side. There is no shortage of slips and moorings in Greenwich Cove. Some have on-site chandleries, some have restaurants and some have both.

East Greenwich, the village, is a 0.25-mile walk uphill and north of the dinghy dock/boat launch on the west shore. The provisioning possibilities here are quite good. Even though approach and entry to the cove is relatively easy, this is no place to cut buoys. Stay well north of green can "5" (marking Sally Rock) in starting your path to green can "7." Watch the shoal east of red nun "6" and poking slightly south of it as well but don't miss green can buoy "7" marking the shoaling north and east of Long Point. The mooring fields use all available space so don't expect good depths everywhere you see a mooring.

When leaving Greenwich Bay turn north between Warwick Neck and Patience Island, a state park and estuarine sanctuary. Narragansett Bay becomes the deep and well-marked Providence River (described later in this chapter) at Conimicut Point. If wind and tide are in opposition you might experience a riptide in the passage between Warwick Point and Northwest Point on Patience Island.

Dockage/Moorings: Busy Warwick Cove is loaded with fishing stations and marinas. Some marinas may be filled to capacity with local boats. Call ahead.

Safe Harbor Greenwich Bay Marina at Cowesett to the south of Apponaug Cove offers boaters a choice of two marinas (A and B) with over 500 combined slips with full amenities. Grocery stores, chandleries and fine dining are all nearby.

Town moorings are located well inside the harbor at Apponaug Cove and deep-water transient berths are almost certain to be at your disposal here, along with the usual amenities. Greenwich Cove has transient slips and moorings and can do haul-outs and service and have a well-stocked ship's store. East Greenwich Yacht Club sells all fuels and Greenwich Cove Marina has moorings for boats to 40 feet.

Anchorage/Moorings: The narrow, dredged entrance to Warwick Cove is well marked around a shoal that is exposed at low water off the southeastern end of Horse Neck. Between here and the harbor head are moorings and an anchorage basin. Make contact with the harbormaster through Warwick Town Hall. He will direct you to a mooring or a spot to anchor for the night. There are a number of small areas to anchor and locals use the upper reaches to seek protection from serious storms.

There is very little room to anchor outside the multiple mooring fields in Apponaug Cove. You can, however, anchor in 6 to 9 feet MLW in Cowesett in prevailing southwest summer breezes.

It is possible to anchor in East Greenwich but we don't recommend it as the inner harbor is chock full of moorings. It can be hard to anchor there without swinging into the channel. You may find a spot southwest of Chepiwanoxet Point's long shoal just outside the mooring field. The better anchorage for both swing room and scenery is off the beach between Sally Rock and Long Point in 7-feet MLW. Goddard State Park is popular and the anchorage tends to attract day-trippers so it gets quieter at night. The trip into the dinghy dock in East Greenwich is long and can be wet in a west wind. Big northerlies create big chop and a lee shore.

Two ramps face each other across Greenwich Cove past the marinas. The one to the west provides a good dinghy tie-up and quick access to the village's shopping. The eastern one is part of the Goddard State Park and is an excellent place to begin a moderate hike and shoot a picture of your boat at anchor off the beach.

Newport Harbor, RI

		Largest Vessel Accommodated	VHF Channel Monitored / Working	Transient Slips / Total Slips	Approach / Dockside Depth (reported)	Floating Docks	Gas / Diesel	Groceries, Ice, Marine Supplies, Snacks	Repairs: Hull, Engine, Propeller	Lift (tonnage), Crane, Rail	Min / Max Amps	Courtesy Car, Laundry, Pool, Showers	Pump-Out Station	Nearby: Grocery Store, Motel, Restaurant
				Dockage			**Supplies**			**Services**				
BRENTON COVE														
1. Brenton Cove Moorings	(401) 474-6061	50	9/	/	14.0/	F	GD	S			50	S	P	GMR
2. Ida Lewis Yacht Club	(401) 846-1969	50	/	/	12.0/8.0	F		I			30/50	S	P	GR
NEWPORT														
3. West Wind Marina	(401) 849-4300	200	9/	50/60	/13.0	F	D	I		E	30/100	LS	P	GMR
4. Casey's Marina	(401) 849-0281	250	9/	/35	16.0/12.0	F	D	I		C	30/100	LS	P	GMR
5. Newport Marina	(401) 849-2293	140	9/	15/45	17.0/12.0	F		I			30/200+	LPS	P	GMR
6. The Marina at Brown & Howard Wharf	(401) 846-5100	250	9/	/	14.0/14.0	F					30/100			MR
7. Newport On-Shore Marina	(401) 849-0480	100	9/	8/65	12.0/5.0	F		I			30/100	LS		MR
8. City of Newport Maritime Center	(401) 845-5870	40	/9	/	11.0/4.0			I				LS	P	GMR
9. Forty 1 degree North	(401) 846-8018	250	9/	25/29	40.0/12.0	F		I			30/200+	LS	P	GMR
10. Newport Yachting Center	(800) 653-3625	180	9/	150/200	22.0/18.0	F	GD	I	HEP		30/100	LS	P	GMR
11. Oldport Marine Services	(401) 847-9109	65	68/68	/	30.0/	F		IM	EP				P	GMR
12. Bannister's Wharf Marina	(401) 846-4556	280	9/	24/30	20.0/16.0	F	GD	GI			30/100	LS	P	GMR
13. Bowen's Wharf	(401) 640-4104	180	9/	/	20.0/	F		IMS			30/100	LS	P	GMR
14. Newport Harbor Hotel & Marina	(401) 848-3310	150	9/	60/60	17.0/8.0	F		I			30/100	LPS	P	GMR
15. Newport Yacht Club	(401) 846-9410	140	78/78	10/64	20.0/15.0			IS			30/50	LS	P	GMR
16. Safe Harbor Newport Shipyard	(401) 846-6000	315	9/	60/60	20.0/20.0	F	D	IMS	HEP	L500,C	20/100	CLS	P	GMR
GOAT ISLAND														
17. Goat Island Marina	(401) 849-5655	250	9/	25/175	19.0/17.0	F	GD	GIS		E	30/100	LS	P	GMR
18. Gurney's Newport Resort & Marina	(401) 849-2600	220	9/	22/22	20.0/20.0	F		IS			30/200+	PS	P	GMR

☐ Internet Access   (WiFi) Wireless Internet Access   ⚓onSpot Dockside WiFi Facility

See WaterwayGuide.com for current rates, fuel prices, website addresses, and other up-to-the-minute information. (Information in the table is provided by the facilities.)

◼ NEWPORT AREA

Cruisers focused on visiting Newport or Jamestown and moving on will use the East Passage. The trip past Newport Neck often feels like accidentally joining a parade. Keep a camera handy because whatever your taste in boats you'll most likely see one or more of your favorites underway here in season.

NAVIGATION: Use NOAA Chart 13221. When bound for Newport enter the deep, well-buoyed passage between Beavertail Point and the 40-foot-tall Castle Hill Lighthouse. You'll pass magnificent waterfront estates including the 28-room Hammersmith Farm, the childhood home of Jackie Kennedy Onassis. If entering from the east honor quick flashing red whistle buoy "2" off Brenton Reef because the 20-foot MLW depths are less important than the fishing gear that comes all the way up to the surface during some seasons. Red gong buoy "4" and red bell buoy "6" mark the last two significant reefs. The pre-Civil War Fort Adams marks the entrance to Newport Harbor, where the water is deep right up to its banks.

Brenton Cove

Tucked inside the protective arm dominated by Fort Adams, Brenton Cove is filled with private and rental moorings. This spot is removed from the churn of activity in the center harbor and, as such, it is a quieter place to review the ongoing passing spectacle. You will, consequently, spend more time waiting for and riding the launch to town.

Forget the prospect of serenity during mid-June of every even-numbered year, however, when the cove becomes a rendezvous center for the finest and best equipped ocean-racing yachts in the world. Crews make last-moment preparations for the biennial Newport-to-Bermuda race. The shore of Brenton Cove is home to Harbor Court, the Newport base of the New York Yacht Club (NYYC). This impressive structure was previously the home of John Nicholas Brown of Brown University fame and was purchased and converted by the NYYC in the 1990s.

Dockage/Moorings: You can rent a transient mooring from Brenton Cove Moorings that includes launch service (VHF Channel 09). They also sell all

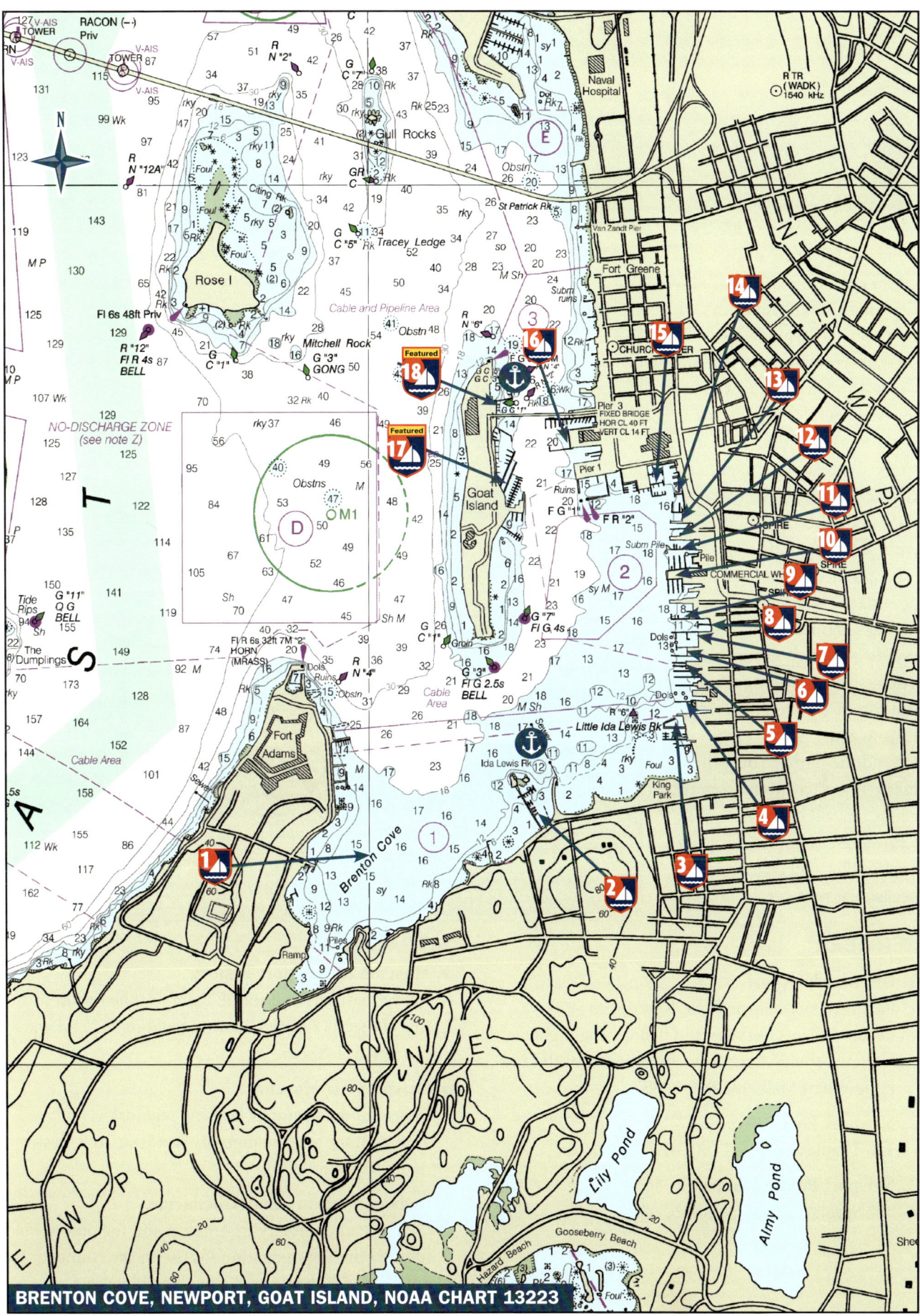

BRENTON COVE, NEWPORT, GOAT ISLAND, NOAA CHART 13223

GOIN' ASHORE

NEWPORT, RI

Newport abounds in maxi-yachts, 70-knot powerboats, cruise ships, round-the-world racers and luxurious cruising palaces. These waters are a terminus for many of the world's great races, such as the Cruising Club of America's Newport-to-Bermuda Race on even years and the OSTAR single-handed race, as well as the Maxi Series. The Classic Yacht Regatta, Admiral's Cup trials, the New York Yacht Club Cruise and the Volvo Ocean Race and other special events with some regularity. The America's Cup trials and races dominated Newport for many decades and the legacy of those events is evident everywhere. The main street along the waterfront is called America's Cup Avenue. At moorings around the harbor you will see many 12-meter racers from the classic period of the America's Cup. These refurbished racers are used for day charters and occasional regattas..

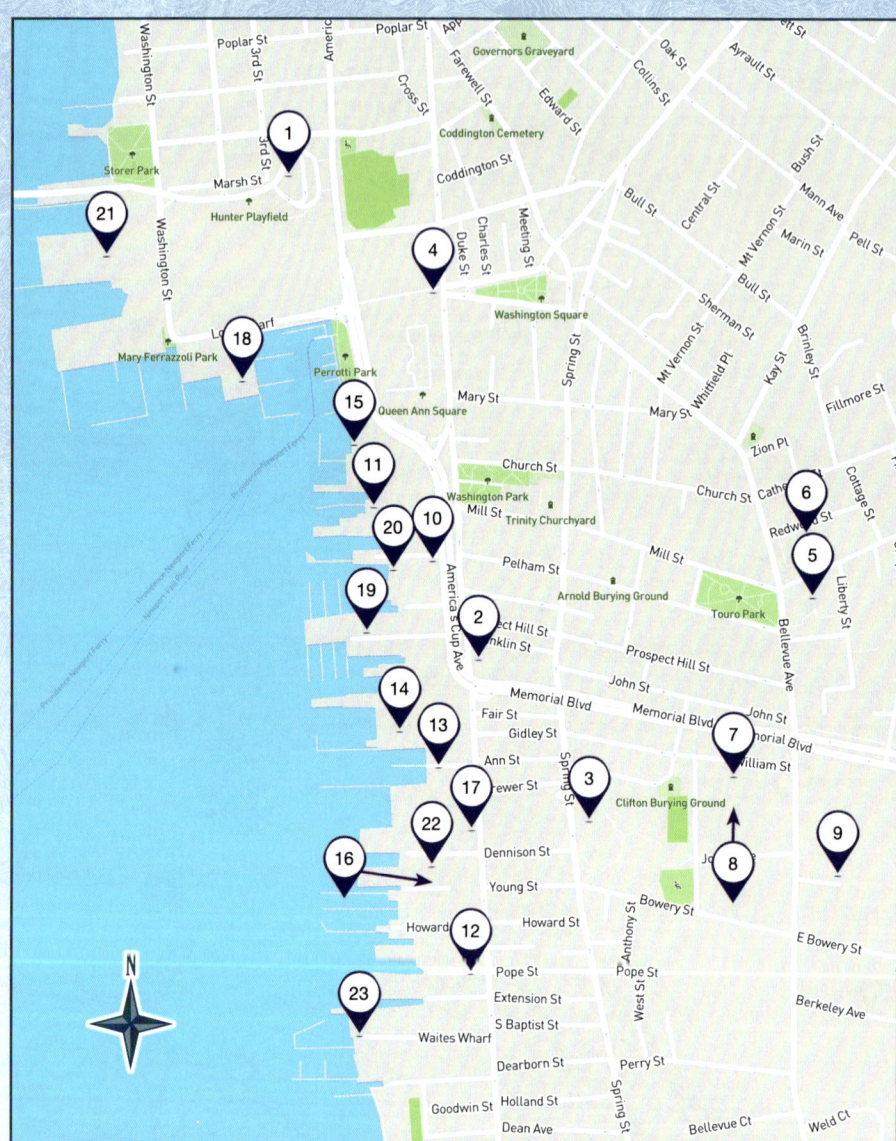

SERVICES

1. Discover Newport
Pick up a city map and find a complete guide to shore events, services and historic highlights. Narrated trolley tours leave from here as well (44 Long Wharf Mall, 401-849-8048).

2. Newport Post Office
320 Thames St., Ste. 1 (401-847-9835)

3. Newport Public Library
300 Spring St. (401-847-8720)

ATTRACTIONS

4. Museum of Newport History
Relive maritime and social history of the region in this classic 1772 Brick Market building (127 Thames St., 401-841-8770).

5. Newport Art Museum
Multi-building campus housing regional 19th-century to contemporary works at 76 Bellevue Ave. (401-848-8200).

6. Redwood Library and Athenaeum
Oldest lending library in America and the oldest library building in continuous use in the country, with beautiful books and superb exhibits (50 Bellevue Ave., 401-841-5680).

SHOPPING

7. A Market
Health food store at 181 Bellevue Ave. #1 (401-846-8137).

8. CVS
Drugstore chain at 181 Bellevue Ave. (401-846-7800).

9. Newport Ace Hardware
Chain hardware store with tools and home supplies at 1 Casino Terrace (401-849-9442).

MARINAS

10. Bannister's Wharf Marina
1 Bannister's Wharf (401-846-4500)

11. Bowen's Wharf
Bowen's Wharf (401-849-2243)

12. Casey's Marina
10 Spring Wharf (401-849-0281)

13. City of Newport Maritime Center
365 Thames Rd. (401-845-5870)

14. Forty 1° North
351 Thames St. (401-846-8018)

15. Newport Harbor Hotel & Marina
49 America's Cup Ave. (401-847-9000)

16. Newport Marina
26 Lee's Wharf (401-849-2293)

17. Newport On-Shore Marina
405 Thames St. (401-849-0480)

18. Newport Yacht Club
110 Long Wharf Ave. (401-846-9410)

19. Newport Yachting Center
20 Commercial Wharf (800-653-3625)

20. Oldport Marine Services
1 Sayers Wharf (401-847-9109)

21. Safe Harbor Newport Shipyard
1 Washington St. (401-846-6000)

22. The Marina at Brown & Howard Wharf
21 Brown & Howard Wharf (401-751-0700)

23. West Wind Marina
26 Waites Wharf (401-849-4300)

GURNEY'S NEWPORT
RESORT & MARINA

GOAT ISLAND MARINA

Newport Harbor

Goat Island Marina

An island oasis in the heart of Newport Harbor.

NewportExperience.com

5 Marina Plaza   Newport, RI 02840   401-849-5655   VHF 09

fuels. Rental moorings also may be available from the Ida Lewis Yacht Club (VHF Channel 78A).

Anchorage: Anchoring is not permitted in Brenton Cove proper, where moorings have triumphed fully in the battle for available space. You can anchor to the east in the area fanning out north of Ida Lewis Yacht Club (conspicuous on the rocky island of the same name) and the long pier from shore just a bit more to the east. The holding is good in mud with 18 to 23 feet MLW but you will need substantial swing room with the ebb and flood of the tidal currents. Skippers are warned to stay to the shore side of the cable area marked on the harbor chart and delineated with buoys in the water.

Dockage is limited to 14 days with at least 4 days between visits according to Newport ordinance. Note that cannons are fired from the clubhouse lawn at 8:00 a.m. and sundown, alerting crews to raise and lower the standards of many nations throughout the harbor.

The east side of the pier east of Ida Lewis Rock (and Yacht Club) provides short-term dinghy access, as does Fort Adams. Launch service is available from Oldport Marine Service but be prepared to wait because it takes time for launches to circumnavigate the harbor.

Newport Harbor

Newport is a world-class yachting center. Just about every boat traveling the coast or coming from international ports makes a stop at Newport. Big yachts, sail and power, lay over at one of several major yards, putting in for crew changes, provisioning or refurbishing. Yachts and tourists stop in Newport for the spectacle of the incredible collection of vessels from all over the world and the interesting people who travel on them. It is possibly the most sophisticated yachting center in the U.S. and maybe the world. Varnish work, fiberglass and wood hull repairs, onboard catering, custom rigging services, new keel designs, maritime history, fine dining and galleries...Newport is where to find it all.

NAVIGATION: Use NOAA Chart 13223. Although wide at the mouth, Newport Harbor is well protected, easy to enter and deep throughout. The only cautionary advice for first-time skippers rounding the 32-foot-tall flashing red "2" and red nun "4" off the point north of Fort Adams is to be aware that large, unusual and otherwise distracting vessels ply these busy waters in profusion. They are often under full sail and occasionally at speeds that mock known safety limits. Take more than ordinary

caution and concentrate on the navigational and tie-up tasks at hand.

Dockage: Despite Newport's popularity, transient space on floating docks is usually available. The City of Newport Maritime Center has free transient dockage for vessels up to 40 feet on a first-come, first-served basis with coin-operated showers and laundry but no electric.

Newport Yachting Center, home of the annual Newport International Boat Show in September, is easy to spot on entering Center Harbor.

A bit farther north the Newport Harbor Hotel & Marina is a prime location with resort amenities. They have 60 transient slips, a heated saltwater pool and an on-site restaurant. This is also home to four classic 12-Meter America's Cup Yachts that have been meticulously restored and maintained.

Across the harbor on Goat Island, Goat Island Marina is a full-service operation that can accommodate vessels to 250 feet. Here you can enjoy breathtaking harbor views while relaxing at your slip or take a quick shuttle ride into town to experience Newport's revered shopping and exciting nightlife. Also on Goat Island is Gurney's Newport Resort & Marina with ample amenities, including a spa, fitness center, indoor and outdoor pool and complimentary launch service to town. They have 22 slips for vessels to 250 feet. They also offer sunset cruises and water sports.

Moorings: Commercially run mooring areas operate at several locations. Oldport Marine Services (VHF Channel 68) maintains moorings in Center Harbor. Choices for mooring your vessel include single-ball moorings, helix moorings and bow-to-stern tie-ups. Launch service is available for a fee. Rental moorings are also available from Newport Mooring Service in Center Harbor or Newport Yacht Club (VHF Channel 09) on the north side of the harbor. Otherwise, it is best to call the Newport Harbormaster (VHF Channel 09 or 401-845-5815) for advice. This is not the place to assume that a vacant mooring may simply be borrowed for the evening. In fact, temporary guest use of a private mooring is limited to 7 consecutive nights and only with written permission from the mooring owner.

Launch service is available throughout the harbor from Oldport Marine Service but be prepared to wait due to the time it takes to circumnavigate the harbor and make frequent stops. The large harbor can make the launch a good option for anyone uncomfortable negotiating heavy traffic in a dinghy.

GURNEY'S WORLD CLASS MARINAS IN MONTAUK AND NEWPORT

GURNEY'S STAR ISLAND
MONTAUK, NY

· Craft capacity of 220 feet with a
  maximum 12 foot draft
· Access to resort amenities, wellness
  activations and lifestyle programming
· Upscale and casual dining
· Dock-side room service
· Private beach
· Two outdoor heated pools and
  one indoor heated pool
· Casual and fine dining including The
  Pool Club and award-winning Showfish

GURNEY'S NEWPORT
NEWPORT, RI

· 22 slips accommodating up to 125 feet
· Fully operational for transient dockage
· Full-service spa
· Fitness center and branded wellness
· Indoor and outdoor pools
· Dock-side room service
· Private sailing lessons, sunset
  cruises and water sports available

GURNEY'S STAR ISLAND
RESORT & MARINA

GURNEYSRESORTS.COM/STAR-ISLAND
833-235-8500

GURNEY'S NEWPORT
RESORT & MARINA

GURNEYSRESORTS.COM/NEWPORT
833-235-7500

A mobile pump-out station services the entire harbor. Simply call "pump-out boat" on VHF Channel 09. The pump-out boat will also pick up your trash for a small fee.

Anchorage: Because of Newport's popularity anchoring is limited to 14 days with at least 4 days between visits, according to Newport ordinance. The harbormaster maintains tight control of the anchorage and mooring fields to insure compliance with local regulations.

There are eight dinghy docks in the harbor including one on the Ann Street Pier with direct access to the Newport Maritime Center. This former armory, built in 1894, offers coin-operated showers, laundry and ice and vending machines for boaters. The social area is an excellent place to meet fellow-boaters and the building's history is on display there. Step back and face the water, then look up. The room was used for target practice and the heavy beams retain the scarring from many a bad aim. Dockage is complimentary for vessels less than 14 feet.

Two blocks north of Oldport Marine's launch dock is the Seaman's Church Institute (www.seamensnewport.org) where you will find clean showers with soap and fresh towels for a small fee from 7:00 a.m. to 9:00 a.m. The Institute also has coin-operated laundry machines. This venerable institution has been looking out for the special needs of seafarers for generations and deserves the kind words and donations it receives from the yachting community.

A tighter dinghy dock at the foot of Extension St. is slightly closer to the anchorage area but the same distance from groceries and other supplies, all of which are uphill from the waterfront. Some of the marinas near the bridge to Goat Island provide short-term dinghy access.

Jamestown, Conanicut Island

Two miles across East Passage from Newport on Conanicut Island is the summer resort and residential town of Jamestown, a popular stop for the cruising boater. There are excellent restaurants and shops in an idyllic village setting, full-service marine facilities and good places to walk or cycle amid vistas of crashing surf, sheer cliffs, rolling pastures and woodlands. From the docks and mooring field, the view across The Dumplings toward Newport is glorious, and nearby Fort Wetherill State Park is great for walks, picnics and exploration of the World War II fortifications. The Fort area is also a popular diving spot.

The Jamestown-Newport ferry leaves from Conanicut Marine Services Inc. and takes passengers and bicycles to Newport and back with stops at Rose Island, Fort Adams, Waites Wharf, Bowens Wharf and Perrotti Park. It runs Memorial Day to Labor Day with a reduced schedule in September (www.conanicutmarina.com/jamestown-newport-ferry-tours-cruises/overview).

Dockage/Moorings: On entering East Passage from Block Island Sound, Jamestown Boat Yard is the first yacht facility you will encounter. It is sheltered from prevailing southerlies by Bull Point at the southeastern tip of Conanicut Island. Clark Boat Yard & Marine Works is nearby as well with mooring service.

Conanicut Marine Services Inc. (VHF Channel 71) operates the recreational waterfront at the village center, supervising seasonal and transient moorings. The launch service to the mooring field is fast and the drivers are deserving of a gratuity for their careful and courteous work. All fuels are available (including propane and compressed natural gas) and kayaks can be rented here.

East Passage, RI

JAMESTOWN		Largest Vessel Accomodated	VHF Channel Monitored / Working	Transient Slips / Total Slips	Approach / Dockside Depth (reported)	Floating Docks	Groceries, Ice, Marine Supplies, Snacks	Repairs: Hull, Engine, Propeller	Gas / Diesel	Lift (tonnage) Crane, Rail	Min / Max Amps	Courtesy Car, Laundry, Pool, Showers	Pump-Out Station	Nearby: Grocery Store, Motel, Restaurant
				Dockage			**Supplies**			**Services**				
1. Jamestown Boat Yard	(401) 423-0600	70	72/	/	12.0/7.0			IM	HEP	L35,C,R	50	S		
2. Clark Boat Yard & Marine Works, LLC 📶	(401) 423-3625	65	69/69	/	/			I	HEP	R	30	S	P	GMR
3. Conanicut Marine Services Inc. 🖥 📶	(401) 423-1556	175	71/	20/100	35.0/15.0	F	GD	IMS	HEP	L30,C	30/100	LS	P	GM

🖥 Internet Access 📶 Wireless Internet Access 📡 onSpot Dockside WiFi Facility

See WaterwayGuide.com for current rates, fuel prices, website addresses, and other up-to-the-minute information. (Information in the table is provided by the facilities.)

JAMESTOWN, NOAA CHART 13223

◼ EAST PASSAGE: NARRAGANSETT BAY TO PROVIDENCE

Less than 2 miles wide at most points, Narragansett Bay runs deep to the Providence River to the north and lies between the bay's three large islands: Conanicut Island and Prudence Island on the west and 12-mile-long Aquidneck Island on the east.

Melville

If you want to avoid the hubbub of Newport and Jamestown but still take advantage of the area's many attractions, Melville is a great alternative. During World War II Melville was the site of a PT boat officer training center. Among the officers trained there was future U.S. President John F. Kennedy.

NAVIGATION: Use NOAA Charts 13221 and 13223. Melville is 7 miles north of Newport, on the east side of East Passage just above Dyer Island.

Dockage: Hinckley Yacht Services Portsmouth has slips and is also home to an array of top-flight specialty marine shops and fabricators. Hunt Yachts/Hunt Marine Services is located nearby, as is Safe Harbor New England Boatworks at East Passage Yachting Center, in a protected basin to the north. All of these facilities sell gas and diesel, have some transient space reserved and offer repairs.

Potter Cove, Prudence Island

Near the north end of Prudence Island, Potter Cove (not to be confused with the Potter Cove charted just north of the Newport Bridge on Conanicut Island) offers good shelter but no amenities. This natural basin is almost landlocked by the elbow of the curving sand spit. The entrance is well buoyed, although it will not look that way on approach from the main channel. You must locate and honor all three nun buoys: red nuns "2," "4" and "6" to starboard, lest you snare your keel on the shoals off Gull Point. The beach is a popular place for gatherings and will sometimes have a dozen dinghies pulled up nice and high.

Anchorage: There are a large number of private moorings in Potter Cove but no public ones. Anchoring is allowed but be sure to keep a reasonable distance from moorings and other boats. Note that the cove runs shallow to the north, punctuated by minuscule Shell Island, which is just visible at low tide, and by a wreck marked by a Coast Guard buoy.

Mooring floats have been dropped in by frequent visitors from local ports. On weekday evenings, when many of their owners are likely to be elsewhere, you are free to take one if you trust whatever may lie below holding it. Should the owner arrive, you must (of course) move along. The small spit of land that extends along the northeast edge of the cove is a great place to land a dinghy for exploration.

On busy summer weekends, a better bet may be to set a hook in 10 to 11 feet MLW off the pebbled beach running to the southeast between the cove and Mount Tom Rock. Note that frequent swells from boat traffic in the channel will find their way into this anchorage.

From here you can dinghy in for exploration of the Narragansett Bay Estuarine Sanctuary surrounding the cove.

Bristol Harbor

Cupped securely between the arms of Popasquash and Bristol Necks, Bristol Harbor is one of Narragansett Bay's most important for recreational boating history and maritime scenery. The Herreshoff Marine Museum is here and houses the America's Cup Hall of Fame (www.herreshoff.org). For museum information, admission and hours, call 401-253-5000. Although an excellent stop for boating culture, there is no fuel in the harbor so plan ahead.

NAVIGATION: Use NOAA Chart 13221. Bristol Harbor is 2 miles long and over 1 mile wide. Although open to the south except where Hog Island breaks up the wind and waves, it is protected to the north, east and west. The well-marked channels on either side of Hog Island make for a painless entry. Nonetheless, take care to honor the channel buoys marking the shoal extending northward of Hog Island and the rocky ledge on the southeast of Popasquash Neck.

Dockage/Moorings: Bristol Yacht Club rents moorings to visitors for a facilities fee that includes launch service, access to the club's dinghy dock and use of the facilities in the clubhouse annex. From here, it is a pleasant 1-mile walk to town, although you can often find a ride. The Herreshoff Marine Museum has moorings and dockside slips available for transients to 200 feet. Dinghy docks are available throughout the town.

The Bristol Maritime Center (www.bristolri.gov/departments/harbor/maritime-center) located in the

East Passage, RI

MELVILLE		Largest Vessel Accomodated	VHF Channel Monitored / Working	Dockage					Supplies			Services					
				Transient Slips / Total Slips	Approach / Dockside Depth (reported)	Floating Docks	Gas / Diesel		Groceries, Ice, Marine Supplies, Snacks	Repairs: Hull, Engine, Propeller	Lift (tonnage), Crane, Rail	Min / Max Amps	Courtesy Car, Laundry, Pool, Showers	Pump-Out Station	Nearby: Grocery Store, Motel, Restaurant		
1. Hinckley Yacht Services Portsmouth 🖥 📶	(401) 683-7100	220	9/9	30/101	20.0/15.0	F	GD		IMS	HEP	L160,C,R	30/200+	CLS	P	4.4R		
2. Hunt Yachts/Hunt Marine Services	(401) 324-4201	150	9/7	20/30	17.0/17.0	F	GD		IMS	HEP	L100,C	30/100		P	GMR		
3. Safe Harbor New England Boatworks	(401) 683-4000	150	9/	20/360	15.0/15.0	F	GD		GIMS	HP	L	30/100	LPS	P	GR		

🖥 Internet Access 📶 Wireless Internet Access 📶 onSpot Dockside WiFi Facility

See WaterwayGuide.com for current rates, fuel prices, website addresses, and other up-to-the-minute information. (Information in the table is provided by the facilities.)

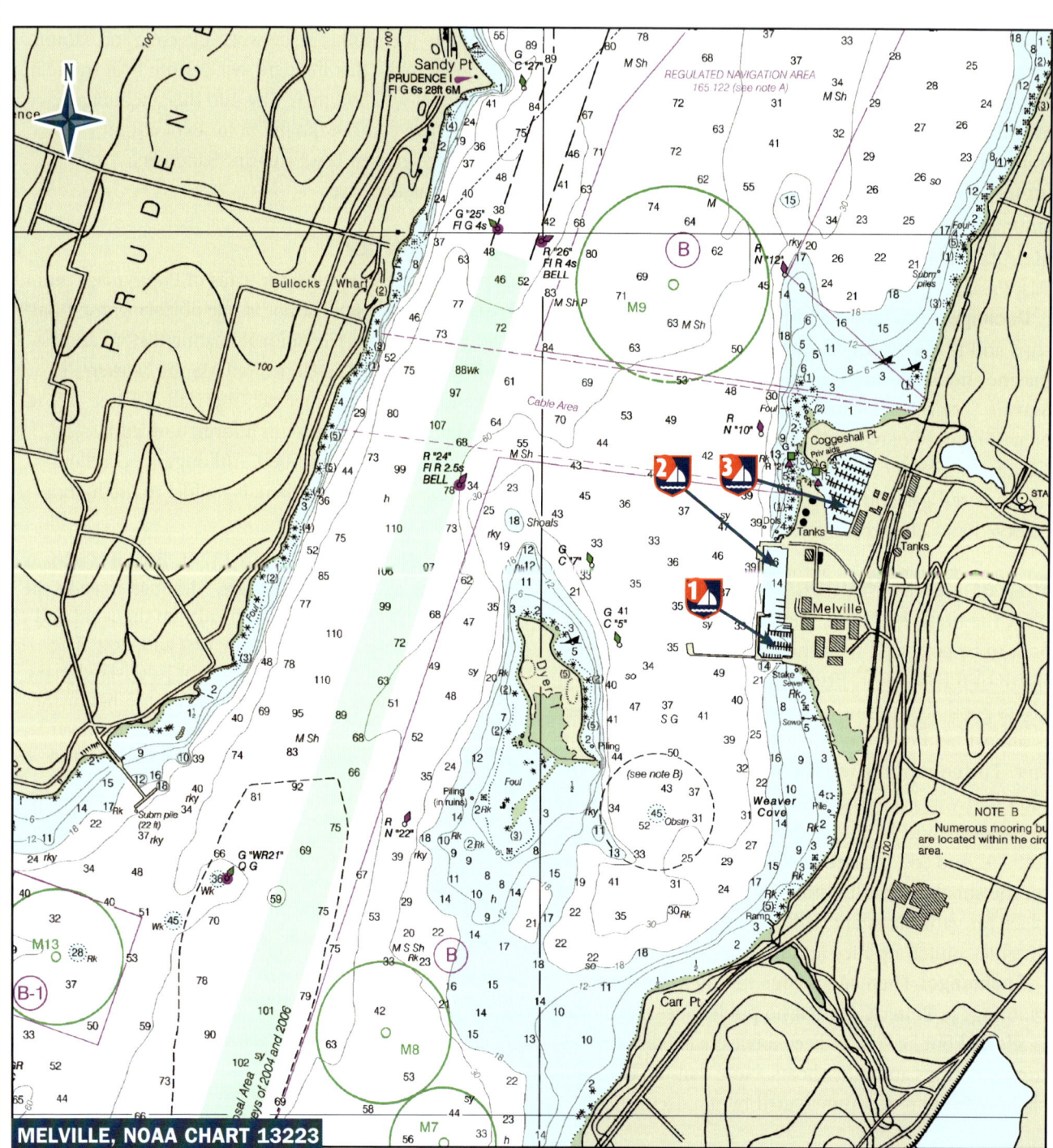

MELVILLE, NOAA CHART 13223

historic naval reserve armory building on the east side of Bristol's harbor, offers services for boaters that include restrooms and showers, laundry facilities and an area to relax and meet with other visiting boaters. Contact the Bristol Harbor Master's Office at 401-253-1700 for more information.

Anchorage: Bristol Harbor is big enough and generally deep enough to accommodate a large local fleet with anchorage room to spare. It would be advisable for cruisers to call the Bristol Harbormaster (401-253-1700) for suggestions on anchoring. When the prevailing southwesterlies stiffen up, the harbor can develop a noticeable chop. In most other conditions it is pleasant and comfortable. It is a bit of a pull into town from the anchorage. You can tie up your dinghy just north of the old stone armory in front of Rockwell Park.

Cruisers who are not visiting the town can anchor east of Hog Island, south of Bristol Harbor proper. Good holding in mud can be found north of green can "3" in 17- to 25-foot MLW depths.

Warren & Barrington

Barrington was originally a part of Warren, which was famous for the fine vessels launched from its yards in the middle of the 19th century. These vessels engaged in whaling, merchant service and the West India trade. Three notable ships were built in Warren by Chase & Davis: the 1853 clipper *Lookout*, the 1853 clipper bark *Gem of the Sea* and the 1854 clipper bark *Mary Ogden*. Today it is the homeport of a (relatively) small cruise liner that travels to New England, Canada, Florida and the Bahamas.

NAVIGATION: Use NOAA Chart 13221. A bit before the start of the Providence River at the most northern part of Narragansett Bay, a narrow channel winds its way north on the Warren River, eastward of Rumstick Neck. The channel threads through shoals with ample aids to navigation. At Tyler Point, about 2 miles upstream, the Barrington River flows in from the northwest. To the east is the industrial boatbuilding town of Warren. To the west is Barrington, the main recreational boat center for the area. Fixed bridges with 10- and 5-foot vertical clearances, respectively, will restrict many boats from traveling upriver.

Dockage/Moorings: Barrington Harbor has extremely strong currents but protection from all winds. Even though there is a large local fleet, marinas do welcome transients with slips and/or moorings.

The harbormaster in Barrington makes a real effort

to assign moorings by making efficient use of the space available in this popular harbor. (Call 401-437-3930, police dispatch, for a mooring assignment). Moorings are for 40-foot maximum length vessels with no on-shore amenities. There are two pump-out stations in the area, as well as all fuels. It would be difficult to find a place to anchor here due to the proliferation of moorings.

Providence River

West of Warren at Conimicut Point, Narragansett Bay becomes the deep and well-marked Providence River. The other point on the 1-mile-wide mouth is Nayatt Point, on the eastern shore. A 58-foot-high, rip-rap lined lighthouse 0.5 mile off Conimicut Point leads traffic (mostly oceangoing and other commercial craft) into the river. The Nayatt Point Lighthouse opposite Conimicut Point at Barrington also guides vessels along the Providence River. Nyatt Point Lighthouse was built in 1856 but is now a private residence and is on the National Register of Historic Places but is not open to the public.

A concentration of marinas stands between the northern end of Pawtuxet Neck and Fields Point on the outskirts of the City of Providence. These are on the river itself but well off the main channel. Close by are shore accommodations and transportation.

Less than 1 mile to the west is Roger Williams Park Zoo, which houses over 100 species from around the world. Call 401-785-3510 or visit www.rwpzoo.org.

The Seekonk River is a tidal extension of the Providence River that flows 5 miles from Providence and East Providence to the Blackstone River and Pawtucket Falls. The river is home to the Brown University rowing team as well as the Narragansett Boat Club (the oldest rowing club in the country).

NAVIGATION: Use NOAA Chart 13221. Nearly landlocked Bullock Cove on the eastern shore is the first harbor heading north on the Providence River. A well-marked channel from Bullock Point leads into Bullock Cove, beginning at flashing green buoy "1." At mean high water expect 10-foot depths, but with a 6-foot tidal range skippers of deep-draft boats will want to check the local tide table or call ahead to the marina before entering.

Narrow, dredged Pawtuxet Cove is a little farther upriver and on the western shore behind Pawtuxet Neck. The village of Pawtuxet was founded in 1638

Bristol Harbor, RI

		VHF Channel Monitored / Working	Largest Vessel Accomodated	Approach / Dockside Depth (reported)	Transient Slips / Total Slips	Floating Docks	Groceries, Ice, Marine Supplies, Snacks	Gas / Diesel	Repairs: Hull, Engine, Propeller	Lift (tonnage), Crane, Rail	Courtesy Car, Laundry, Pool, Showers	Min / Max Amps	Pump-Out Station	Nearby: Grocery Store, Motel, Restaurant
BRISTOL				**Dockage**				**Supplies**			**Services**			
1. Bristol Yacht Club	(401) 253-2922	45	68/	/	12.0/6.0					I			S	MR
2. Bristol Marine WiFi	(401) 253-2200	100	69/	6/20	12.0/8.0	F			IMS	HEP L50	50	S	P	G
3. Herreshoff Marine Museum 💻 WiFi	(401) 253-5000	200	68/	8/12	16.0/7.0	F			S		30/50	S		GR
BARRINGTON														
4. Stanley's Boat Yard Inc.	(401) 245-5090	55	16/	3/130	10.0/5.0	F			IM	HEP L35	30/50	S	P	GR
5. Barrington Yacht Club WiFi	(401) 245-1181	43	68/	/	/7.5		GD		IMS		30/50	PS	P	GR
6. Striper Marina Inc.	(401) 245-6121	45	65/	4/125	8.0/6.0	F	G		IM	EP R	30			GR

💻 Internet Access WiFi Wireless Internet Access onSpot Dockside WiFi Facility

See WaterwayGuide.com for current rates, fuel prices, website addresses, and other up-to-the-minute information. (Information in the table is provided by the facilities.)

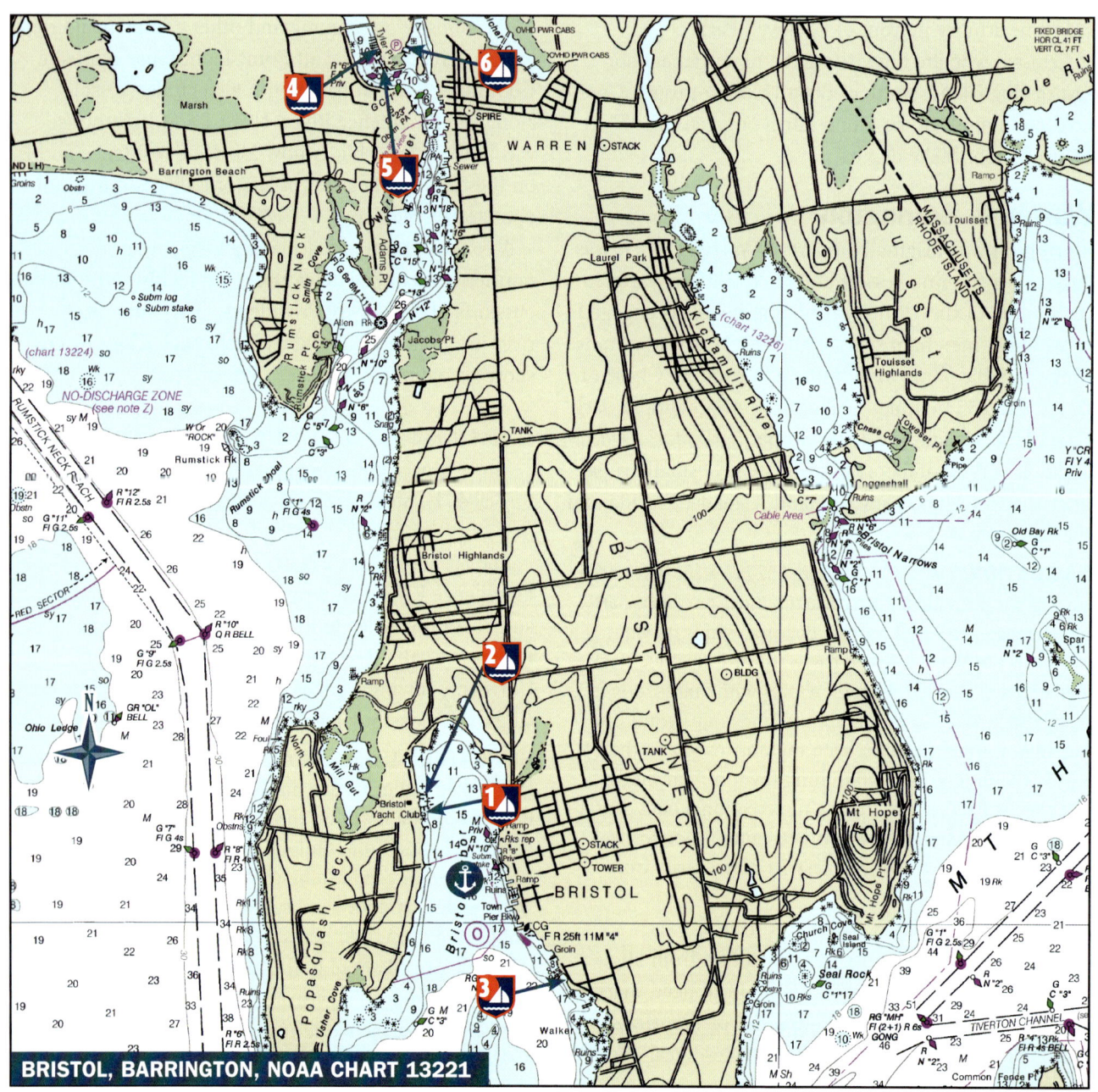

BRISTOL, BARRINGTON, NOAA CHART 13221

Mount Hope Bay

and is an interesting historic location to visit. Enter Pawtuxet Cove from the main river channel through a straight cut lined by rocks and shoals. Private range lights help you through the opening between the point and the end of the dike. At the opening turn north for the harbor and marinas but turn south for the anchorage. In recent years the entrance channel has shoaled to less than 6 feet MLW. Refer to the Waterway Explorer (www.waterwayguide.com) and the latest NOAA print-on-demand charts for latest depths in the channel.

Edgewood is as close to Providence as most boats get. Only a short ride from the center of town, it makes an ideal layover spot from which to visit the historic city. The river from here north is heavily commercial and the waterborne traffic is fearsome. A hurricane barrier just past the **IWAY (I-195) Bridge** (35-foot fixed vertical clearance) blocks navigation further up the Providence River.

Dockage/Moorings: The City of East Providence on Bullock Cove maintains rental moorings in the relatively narrow harbor. Call the harbormaster on VHF Channel 09 (or 401-639-8437) for availability. The full-service Safe Harbor Cove Haven dominates the eastern shore with its floating dock complex. This is a major repair center with and on-site marine metal fabrication and a canvas shop. There is a dinghy landing at the town dock but there is no room to anchor here.

Dockage options at Pawtuxet Cove include a marina and a yacht club. A second yacht club is at Edgewood. There is a small-boat facility at Providence but you must navigate the three river gates of the hurricane barrier with a restricted vertical clearance of 21 feet to reach it.

Anchorage: The only anchorage basin on this part of the Providence River is in a diked area south of the entrance to Pawtucket Cove. Here you will find 6 to 8 feet MLW with good holding in mud.

■ MOUNT HOPE BAY TO SAKONETT

Mount Hope Bay

The Rhode Island/Massachusetts border divides Mount Hope Bay. Mount Hope itself is high on Bristol Neck. The bay is easy to reach from busier nearby waters and offers safe and scenic cruising. Its upper eastern shore is the waterfront for Fall River, a mill town with heavy commercial boat traffic plying well-marked channels.

At Fall River you can visit the famous battleship *Massachusetts*, the star attraction of the Battleship Cove and Maritime Museum (508-678-1100, www. battleshipcove.org). Besides "Big Mamie," you can explore the submarine *Lionfish*, the destroyer *Joseph P. Kennedy Jr.*, plus a helicopter, gunboats and P.T. Boats.

Providence River, RI

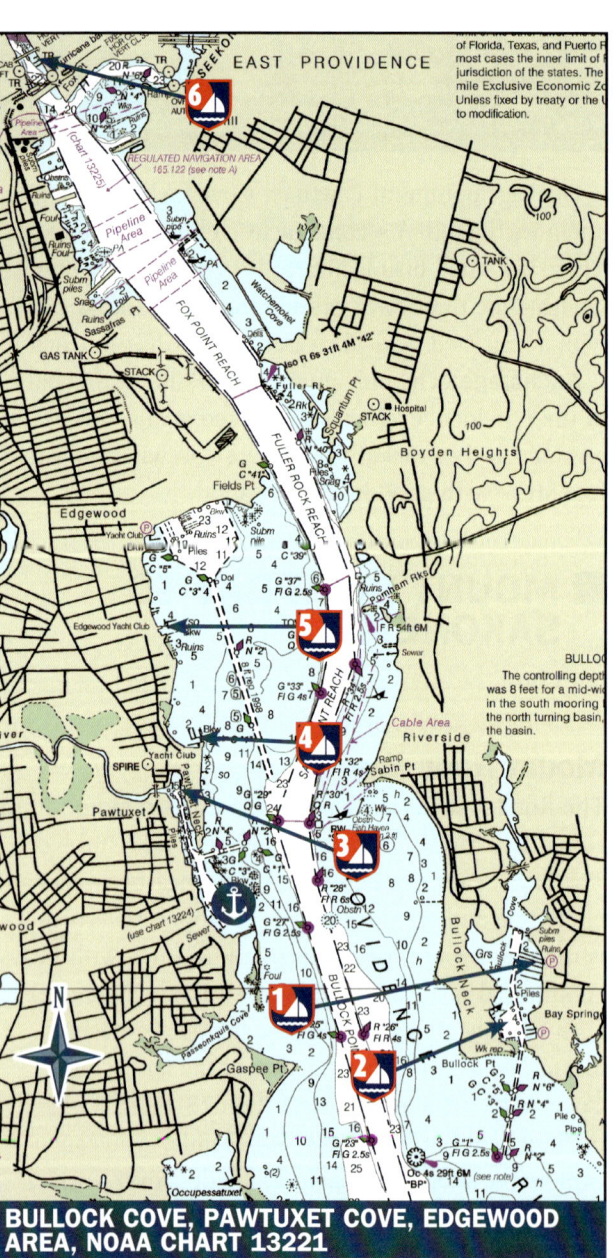

		Dockage					Supplies		Services					
		Largest Vessel Accommodated	VHF Channel Monitored / Working	Transient Slips / Total Slips	Approach / Dockside Depth (reported)	Floating Docks	Gas / Diesel	Groceries, Ice, Marine Supplies, Snacks	Repairs: Hull, Engine, Propeller	Lift (tonnage), Crane, Rail	Min / Max Amps	Courtesy Car, Laundry, Pool, Showers	Pump-Out Station	Nearby: Grocery Store, Motel, Restaurant
BULLOCK COVE														
1. Safe Harbor Cove Haven ☐ WiFi	(401) 246-1600	100	9/	10/348	13.0/12.0	F	GD	IM	HEP	L150	30/50	CPS	P	GR
2. East Providence Harbor Master	(401) 639-8437		9/	/	9.0/9.0								P	GR
PAWTUXET COVE														
3. Pawtuxet Cove Marina	(401) 941-2000	60	/	4/98	5.0/4.5	F		I	HEP	L25	30	LS	P	GMR
EDGEWOOD AREA														
4. Rhode Island Yacht Club	(401) 941-0220	70	78/	/90	8.0/6.0	F		I		L2	50	S	P	R
5. Edgewood Yacht Club ☐	(401) 781-9626	50	14/	6/55	6.0/5.0	F		I			20/30	LS	P	
6. Providence Marina WiFi	(401) 369-7547		/68	/56	/						30	S		R

☐ Internet Access WiFi Wireless Internet Access onSpot Dockside WiFi Facility

See WaterwayGuide.com for current rates, fuel prices, website addresses, and other up-to-the-minute information. (Information in the table is provided by the facilities.)

BULLOCK COVE, PAWTUXET COVE, EDGEWOOD AREA, NOAA CHART 13221

The on-site maritime museum has nautical history exhibits. Boating visitors can dinghy ashore.

NAVIGATION: Use NOAA Chart 13221. Mount Hope Bay can be accessed by proceeding east from Providence River and passing under the high-level **Mount Hope Bridge**. It can also be reached from the Sakoneet River to the south, as described below. It is 6.5 miles to the next bridge, the high-rise **Charles M. Braga Jr. Bridge**. Next is the restricted **Brightman Street Bridge** (27-foot-closed vertical clearance). Visit Waterway Explorer (www.waterwayguide.com) for the opening schedule.

Dockage: The 260-slip Borden Light Marina Inc. at Fall River may have space for you. Call ahead. They also sell all fuels. More marine facilities are located up the Taunton River past the Brightman Street Bridge. See our marina table for details.

Anchorage: Coves at the entrance to each of three small rivers along the northern shore of Mount Hope Bay offer potential anchorages and opportunities for dinghy exploration beyond navigable depths.

To the west, the Kickamuit River offers all-around protection in a soft mud bottom with depths from 7 to 17 feet MLW. Take care on entry to thread the buoys precisely through aptly named Bristol Narrows. In the event of an approaching storm this is a good choice for shelter but arrive early as many local boats use the Kickamuit as a hurricane hole.

During most summer weather, there is good anchorage along the western shore of a cove at the mouth of the Cole River in 9 to 12 feet MLW with good holding in mud. It is also possible to anchor off Swansea Marina on the Cole River just beyond the mooring field in 9-to 14-foot MLW depths. This is somewhat exposed to the south. The Cole River itself, beyond the cove, is not navigable (despite the several deep-footed vessels that have somehow found the way to a protected berth beyond the breakwater). However, it is a good place to explore by dinghy. The best time to enter is at slack water just before the ebb. Otherwise, an unfavorable current can present quite a challenge.

The Lee River to the east has no amenities but it also presents no obstructions and is closest to the marked channel to Fall River. In a pinch, you can drop the hook in Fox Hill Cove in soft mud with 8 to 11 feet MLW in the shadow of a massive electric plant.

South to Sakonnet Harbor

The Sakonnet River, lying between Aquidneck Island and the mainland, is easternmost of the Narragansett north–south waterways. Many fishermen and recreational boats use the 13-mile-long river, named *Saughkonet* by the Wampanoag people for "black goose place." Its waters and anchorages seem dramatically quiet, particularly in comparison to the crowded waters of Newport, located not far to the west.

The Sakonnet Passage is deep, the main channel is close to midstream and all shoals and obstructions are clearly marked. A scattering of towns and harbors along the river offer recreational boating amenities. Tiverton is just south of Mount Hope Bay and north of small, wooded Gould Island, which sits dead center in the Sakonnet River.

During the Revolutionary War, Tiverton gained acclaim for a particularly daring act by one of its parishioners, Col. William Barton, who led a raiding party to capture a British general. Today, only a tower remains of the historic Fort Barton and there is little else around to attract tourists. For boaters, however, it is a protected and attractive spot with ample facilities on both sides of the river.

On the eastern side of the Sakonnet River near its mouth, Sakonnet Harbor is well protected from the south and east behind Sakonnet Point and from the west by an 800-foot breakwater extending northward from Breakwater Point. This is the boating center for the resort area of Little Compton, located 3 miles inland.

Sakonnet Vineyard, about 5 miles from the harbor, produces about 10,000 cases of wine a year in its solar-heated winery. They named a wine after the state bird, which is a chicken called the Rhode Island Red.

NAVIGATION: Use NOAA Chart 13221. Enter the river from Mount Hope Bay by going eastward around Common Fence Point, Aquidneck's northernmost tip. Continuing south, pass between the bare pilings that formerly supported a swing bridge and under the 65-foot fixed vertical clearance **Rt. 24/138 Bridge**. This marks where the river narrows into picturesque Tiverton Basin, the Sakonnet's most active boating center. Be prepared for swift currents at the bridge except at slack water. At the bottom of the pinch, the rustic remains of the 1810 stone bridge that linked Tiverton to Aquidneck for 150 years is here, restricting the flow of water in an already tight passage. Expect swift currents here on either tide.

It is easy to exit the river between Sakonnet and Sachuest Points but be alert for often-inconspicuous floating fishnets, traps, weirs and lobster buoys. Stay close to the navigation buoys. Rocks, reefs and islets surround the prominent abandoned lighthouse off Sakonnet Point. The same precautions apply when entering the river, though even in poor visibility, these impediments may be far less daunting than the boisterous seas that can squall up suddenly in Rhode Island Sound to the south.

Dockage/Moorings: About 0.5 mile south of Common Fence Point, just south and west of green can "17," head west to Cedar Island Pond to starboard to reach the well-protected Safe Harbor Sakonnet. They have a spacious 6-acre spread between the North and South Yards to offer plenty of service accommodation and storage space. Just south of the bridges on the eastern shore Tiverton Yacht Club welcomes visitors from other clubs with a vacant mooring or even a slip at the club's dock. A small grocery store is located near the clubhouse. Standish Boatyard to the south at Tiverton has slips and moorings and offer repair services.

Facilities at Sakonnet include a marina and a yacht club. You can also take advantage of one of the two town-owned guest moorings. Call the Harbormaster at 401-835-4474. A nearby beach offers good swimming. This harbor is quite small and there is no room for anchoring.

Anchorage: Significant depths, swift currents and commercial traffic make anchoring unwise at Tiverton. It is far better to locate a mooring or slip. However, for boats drawing 4 feet or less and having vertical clearance requirements of less than 25 feet (due to a fixed bridge), The Cove, located west of Tiverton Basin at Hummock Point, is a favorite gunkholing spot. Most cruisers will have to reserve this spot for dinghy exploration.

Mount Hope Bay, MA

WG

		Largest Vessel Accomodated	VHF Channel Monitored / Working	Transient Slips / Total Slips	Approach / Dockside Depth (reported)	Floating Docks	Gas / Diesel	Groceries, Ice, Marine Supplies, Snacks	Repairs: Hull, Engine, Propeller	Lift (tonnage), Crane, Rail	Min / Max Amps	Courtesy Car, Laundry, Pool, Showers	Pump-Out Station	Nearby: Grocery Store, Motel, Restaurant
				Dockage				**Supplies**		**Services**				
COLE RIVER														
1. Swansea Marina	(508) 672-8633	34	/	/	13.0/6.0			G						
2. Borden Light Marina, Inc. 🖥 WIFI	(508) 678-7547	65	/	/260	/	F	GD	IS	HEP	L35,C	30/50	CLPS	P	GR
TAUNTON RIVER (SOUTH)														
3. Captain O'Connell Co.	(508) 672-6303	75	/	4/25	7.0/5.0	F	G	M	HEP	L60	30/50			
4. Bristol Marine, Somerset WIFI	(508) 678-1234	100	/	10/25	21.0/6.0				HEP	L80	30/50		P	GR
TAUNTON RIVER (NORTH)														
5. Taunton Yacht Club	(508) 669-6007	40	68/	2/40	5.0/8.0		GD	I				S		GR
6. Shaw's Boat Yard Inc.	(508) 669-5714	60	/	2/60	7.0/6.0	F		IM	HEP	C	30/50	S		G

🖥 Internet Access WIFI Wireless Internet Access onSpot Dockside WiFi Facility

See WaterwayGuide.com for current rates, fuel prices, website addresses, and other up-to-the-minute information. (Information in the table is provided by the facilities.)

About halfway down the river from Tiverton, Fogland Point juts out from the eastern shore to create a large bight. Fogland Point anchorage is easy to enter, roomy and has good holding in 11 feet MLW but is wide open to the north. Plenty of water can be found at the mouth but don't go too far in as depths tend to shoal.

Below High Hill Point on the eastern side of the river is an unnamed cove, which has been known to serve as a good anchorage. Here you will find 9 to 15 feet MLW with good holding in mud and shell. This is somewhat exposed from the northwest through the southwest. Watch for the large spread of aquaculture floats, where oysters for Newport's best restaurants are grown.

On the west side of the mouth of the Sakonnet River, behind Flint Point, is Sachuest Cove. Give plenty of room to unmarked rocks charted off Flint Point. The cove is open to the northeast but is seldom crowded and makes a welcome change from the Newport scene. You might experience a slight surge from the bay but it is usually comfortable for an overnight stay and has at least 8 feet MLW. No amenities are available directly off the beach except when the ice cream truck is present, but Second Beach and Easton's Beach provide excellent views.

Entering Sakonnet Harbor from Rhode Island Sound

Quite a few mariners on the trek between Cape Cod Canal or the Islands and Newport are forced to take an unintended turn into the river when conditions in the sound deteriorate. Once inside they are amazed to find that the angry 10-foot waves, powered by 35-to 40-knot gusts outside, fall away almost immediately to placid waters and gentle breezes in the protection of the river's banks. The Sakonnet River is an excellent refuge to keep in mind when planning an outside passage south of Narragansett Bay.

NAVIGATION: Use NOAA Chart 13221. Coming from the Rhode Island Sound, you can identify the entrance to Sakonnet Harbor by four-second flashing red light "2" at the breakwater's end. After the first week of June, the best route of entry is that used by the fishing boats–upriver from the south, below the numerous fish traps, standing off the breakwater at about 50 yards, then turning abruptly southeast at the entrance. Before early June, however, the fish trap line is strung at right angles from the breakwater, making the southern approach impossible. Barrels and high-standing radar reflectors at each end mark the traps but spotting them can be quite difficult in fog or when the wind is up. Additional traps, similarly marked, are to the southwest of red bell buoy "2A," near the center of the river.

■ NEXT STOP

From here, many boaters will elect to head towards the Elizabeth Island chain (anchored by Cuttyhunk), Cape Cod or the islands of Martha's Vineyard and Nantucket. But do not forget the less crowded and equally charming smaller ports along the Massachusetts mainland on Buzzard's Bay, covered in the next chapter.

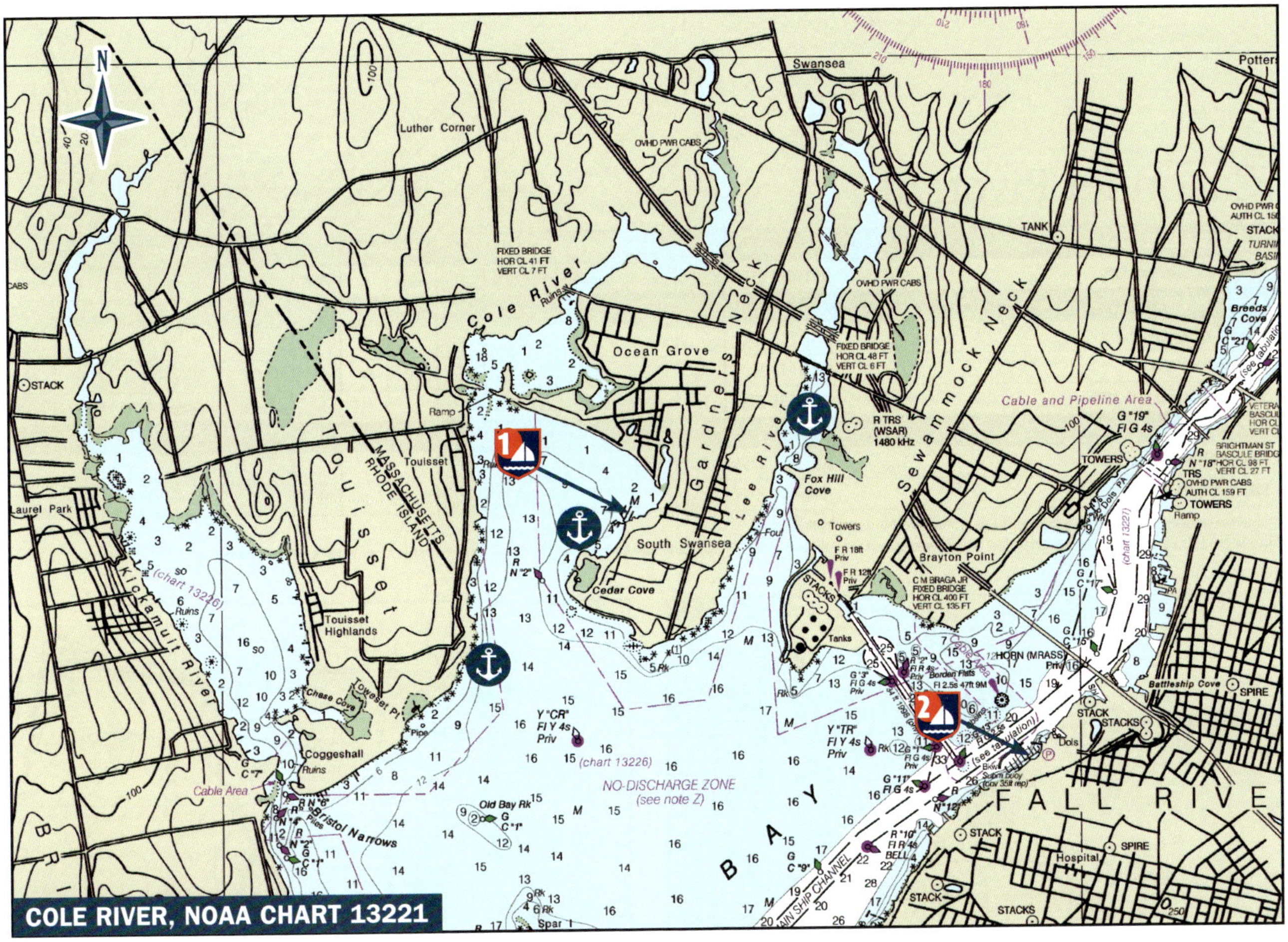

COLE RIVER, NOAA CHART 13221

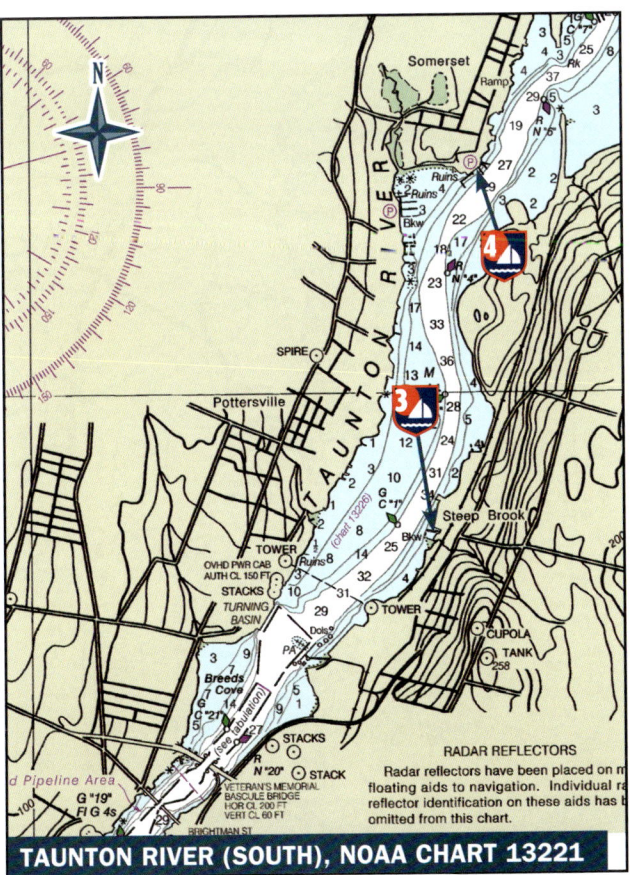

TAUNTON RIVER (SOUTH), NOAA CHART 13221

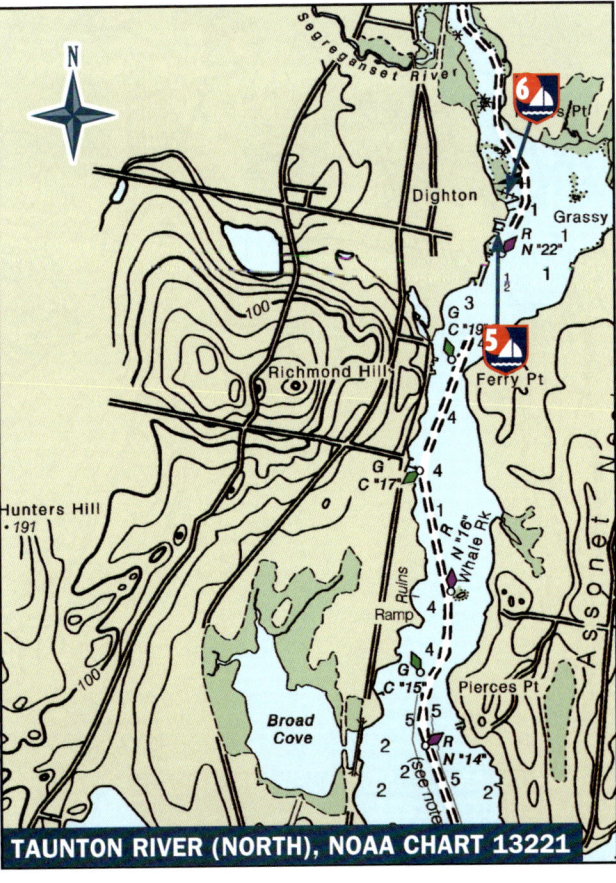

TAUNTON RIVER (NORTH), NOAA CHART 13221

Sakonnet River, RI

		Largest Vessel Accomodated	VHF Channel Monitored / Working	Approach / Dockside Depth (reported)	Transient Slips / Total Slips	Floating Docks	Gas / Diesel	Groceries, Ice, Marine Supplies, Snacks	Repairs: Hull, Engine, Propeller	Lift (tonnage), Crane, Rail	Courtesy Car, Laundry, Pool, Showers	Min / Max Amps	Pump-Out Station	Nearby: Grocery Store, Motel, Restaurant
CEDAR ISLAND POND						**Dockage**		**Supplies**			**Services**			
1. Safe Harbor Sakonnet WiFi	(401) 683-3551	50	9/	1/314	6.0/10.0	F	GD	I	HEP	L35,C	30/50	LPS	P	GMR
TIVERTON AREA														
2. Tiverton Yacht Club	(401) 816-0811		/	/21	35.0/8.0	F		IS				PS		GMR
3. Standish Boat Yard	(401) 624-4075	70	16/69	4/24	35.0/10.0	F	GD	IM	HEP	C	30/50	S	P	3R
4. Safe Harbor Island Park WiFi	(401) 683-3030	70	9/	25/76	25.0/7.0	F		IMS	HP	L60,C	30/50	S	P	GMR
SAKONNET														
5. Sakonnet Point Marina WiFi	(401) 635-4753	75	6/	3/31	8.0/8.0			I			30/50	C		
6. Sakonnet Yacht Club	(508) 994-2075		/	/	8.0/6.5			I				S		R

🖥 Internet Access   WiFi Wireless Internet Access   onSpot Dockside WiFi Facility

See WaterwayGuide.com for current rates, fuel prices, website addresses, and other up-to-the-minute information. (Information in the table is provided by the facilities.)

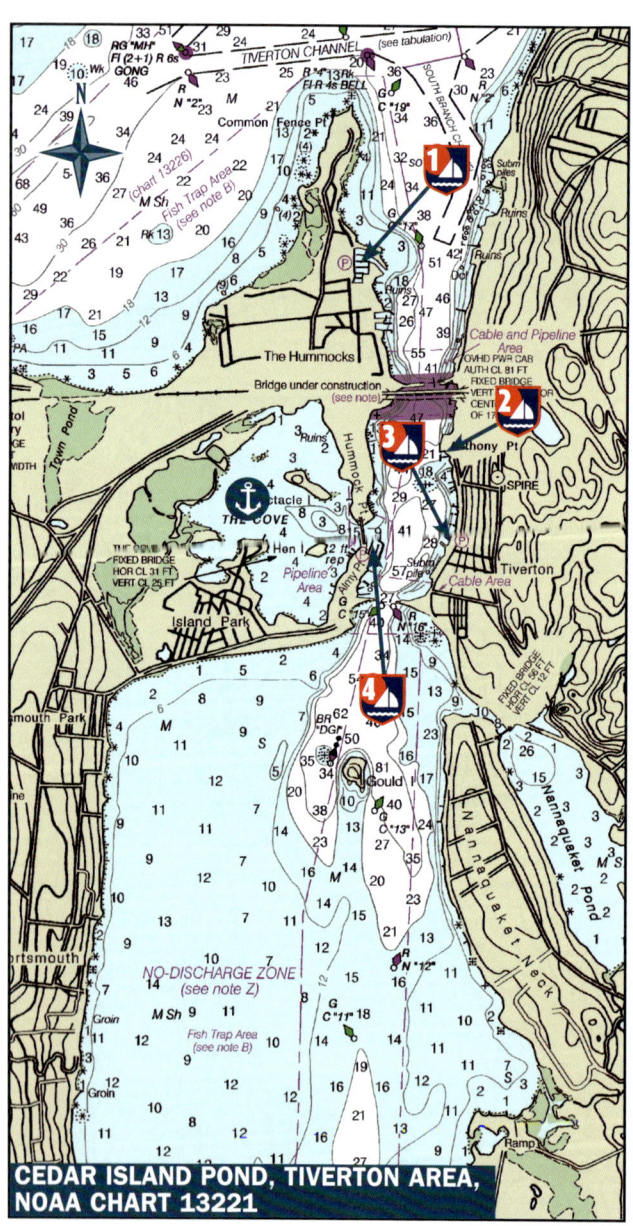

CEDAR ISLAND POND, TIVERTON AREA, NOAA CHART 13221

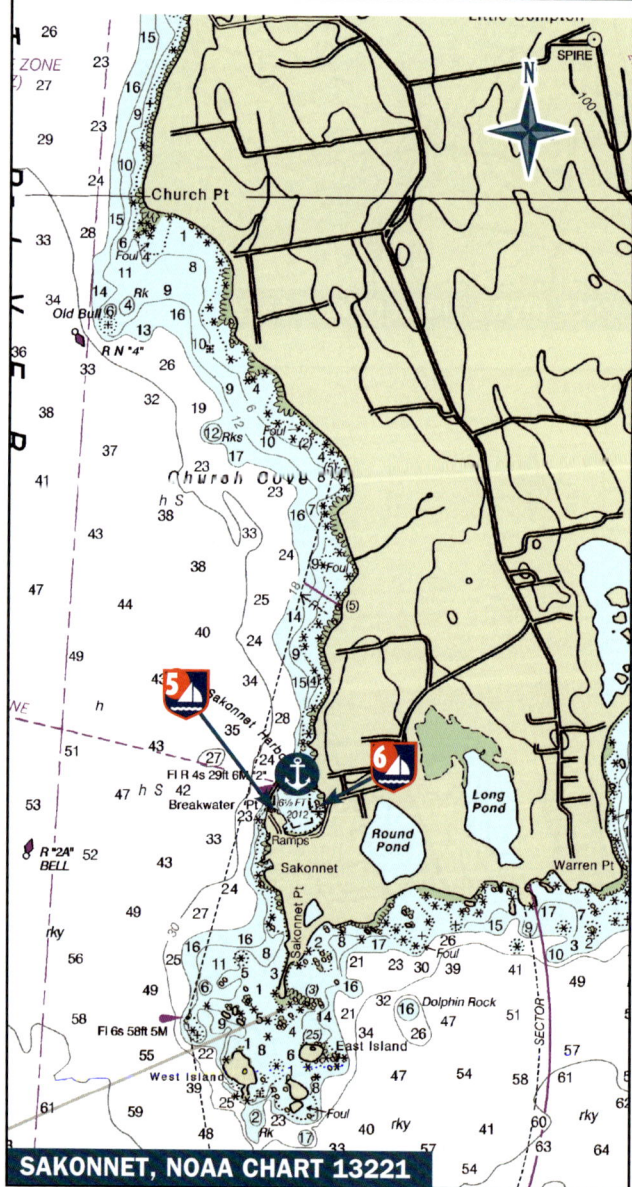

SAKONNET, NOAA CHART 13221

Buzzards Bay, MA

Had the colonists known their birds, this body of water might have been called Osprey Bay. Instead, Buzzards Bay is one of many examples of home-spun naming by early colonists. Gooseberry Neck's Hen and Chickens islands are nearly 5 miles from Cuttyhunk Island's Sow and Pigs Reef at the bay's western mouth, which begins just east of the border between Rhode Island and Massachusetts. Even though rocks, reefs and shoals extend from the shorelines, the bay runs broad and open almost 30 miles northeasterly. It bulges in the middle then bends and narrows at the top, a funnel for the western entrance to the Cape Cod Canal.

Prevailing southwesterly winds blow 15 to 20 knots on summer afternoons. The winds funnel up the narrowing bay to create short, steep seas. A 4- to 5-foot sea state is not unusual, especially on an ebb tide, which opposes the southwesterly winds creating the characteristic Buzzards Bay chop.

Riding the end of the flood north provides the most settled conditions in a southwesterly wind but take care not to get caught in the turnaround: Heading into the Cape Cod Canal against the current is a difficult proposition for slow boats. Lucky for cruisers, both sides of the bay have multiple excellent stops where boaters can wait out the tide and enjoy

a waterfront small town at the same time.

The ship channel is busy enough that smaller boats do well to run outside of it. Most will be able to stay north of the channel and cut the corner heading around Sconticut Neck and West Island (south of Fairhaven) but study the chart for hazardous ledges and rocks. Refer to the Waterway Explorer (www.waterwayguide.com) and NOAA online charts for the most up-to-date information.

The fog on Buzzards Bay tends to burn off by late morning but a haze might linger. Despite its reputation as a rough body of water, the bay provides fine sailing and snug, picturesque harbors. Many sailors, especially racers, consider Buzzards Bay to be some of the finest sailing in New England with reliable winds and charming natural harbors on both shores.

The complex shoreline of Buzzards Bay and most of New England is due to the rise in sea level after the last ice age. The remnants of this can still be seen along Buzzards Bay Moraine, which runs north to south in Bourne and Falmouth, then curves to become the Elizabeth Islands. Also left behind were a sandy ridge on the eastern shore of the bay and a slowly rising shoreline to the west.

◼ WESTERN SHORE TO CAPE COD CANAL

Westport Harbor

Westport was originally formed as part of Old Dartmouth and was incorporated in 1878. The one-time whaling center of Westport Point is now a recreational boating and commercial fishing port. Virtually landlocked behind the overlapping points of The Knubble with its lighthouse on a granite mound and Horseneck Point, Westport Harbor is well protected in all but near-hurricane conditions. Despite the formidable approach shown on the chart, sailboats routinely traverse the relatively shallow entrance and flats-strewn channel to the amenities within. The low-lying but lush

Westport Harbor, MA

WESTPORT		Dockage				Supplies		Services					
		VHF Channel Monitored / Working	Largest Vessel Accomodated	Approach / Dockside Depth (reported)	Transient Slips / Total Slips	Floating Docks	Gas / Diesel	Groceries, Ice, Marine Supplies, Snacks	Repairs: Hull, Engine, Propeller	Lift (tonnage), Crane, Rail	Min / Max Amps	Courtesy Car, Laundry, Pool, Showers	Pump-Out Station	Nearby: Grocery Store, Motel, Restaurant

WESTPORT				Dockage			Supplies	Services				
1. F.L. Tripp & Sons Inc. 🖥 WiFi	(508) 636-4058	65	9/8	4/178	10.0/12.0		GD	IM	HEP	L20,C	30/50	LS	P	5MR
2. Westport Yacht Club WiFi	(508) 636-8885	60	/	/	8.0/12.0			I				S		R

🖥 Internet Access   WiFi Wireless Internet Access   onSpot Dockside WiFi Facility

See WaterwayGuide.com for current rates, fuel prices, website addresses, and other up-to-the-minute information. (Information in the table is provided by the facilities.)

WESTPORT, NOAA CHART 13228

scenery is characteristic of what was once typical in southern New England harbors with their low stone walls girding narrow fields leading to the sea, rushing streams, green marshes and sandy beaches, all prefacing the weathered-shingle houses and 19th-century commercial structures of a picturesque uphill village, crowded with active watermen and recreational boaters.

Several miles from the harbor, the 100-acre Westport Rivers Vineyard and Winery (www.westportrivers.com, 508-636-3423) welcomes visitors to its award-winning winery for free 20-minute tours, wine tasting and review of the vineyard's art gallery. The well-preserved 19th-century homes in this unspoiled fishing village are, alone, worth a launch or dinghy ride across the river but there is so much more to see.

NAVIGATION: Use NOAA Chart 13228. The narrow entry at the mouth of the Westport River between The Knubble and Horseneck Point is visible only from close inshore. The shallow bar at the entrance (controlling depth of 6 feet MLW) is dynamic and constricted currents from the estuary's two branches can reach 4 knots at full ebb. Those who know the area advise not to try the entrance during poor visibility or in a southerly blow.

From flashing white Morse (A) red and white bell buoy "WH" near Two Mile Rock head toward the 35-foot (flashing green every 6 seconds) beacon at the eastern tip of The Knubble, being sure to honor green daybeacon "3" marking Two Mile Rock itself on approach. When the green can buoy "5" (marking Dogfish Ledge) is abeam to the southwest, red nun

Westport Harbor

buoy "6" will be northeast. The channel then jogs to the northeast, marked by green can buoys "5A" and "5B" off of Halfmile Rock. Red nun buoy "8" marks the northeast side of the channel off Horseneck Point. The opening into the harbor should now be visible. After rounding The Knubble follow the channel buoys carefully around Horseneck Point and into Westport Harbor along the northeast shore of Acoaxet and the Lions Tongue into the snug cove about 1 mile west of the village of Westport Point.

⚠ Shoaling exists in Westport Harbor in the vicinity of red nun buoy "14" and green can buoy "17." There are other areas of shoaling throughout the Westport Harbor Channel reducing the available depth of water. Mariners are advised to use caution while navigating this area.

When you leave Westport stand well offshore and clear south of the cluster of ledges at Hen and Chickens, Old Cock and The Wildcat, the last marked by green can buoy "1" and a prominent wreck marked by a slanting pipe that sticks 20 or more feet out of the water. The next harbor east of Slocums Neck is the unnamed divot leading to Little and Slocum Rivers (between Barneys Joy and Mishaum Points), which is too shoal for transit. The entrance bar is nearly bare at low tide and the channel is unmarked.

Note: Westport Harbor and the east and west branches of the Westport River are No-Discharge Zones. Pump-out service is available at F.L. Tripp & Sons.

Dockage/Moorings: To the south on entry into Westport Harbor, less than 0.5 mile west of the village landing, F.L. Tripp & Sons usually has transient moorings available as well as a few slips. Rental moorings are marked with a small yellow float. Hail the launch service on VHF Channel 09 and ask their hours. Launch service is generally available from Memorial Day to Labor Day.

On the surf side of the access road to Tripp's, the town's parking lot shows the way to the sandy beach path across gorgeous, wind-swept dunes to unspoiled Horseneck Beach (popular with surfers because of its open-ocean frontage) and to the Cherry and Webb Conservation Area on Horseneck Point.

Next door to F.L. Tripp & Sons, the Westport Yacht Club's unpretentious, weathered clubhouse matches the friendly attitude of its members. The club cannot offer dock space but may have a mooring for visitors from other clubs.

Anchorage: You can anchor overnight at Westport but be aware that the swift current scours the bottom and holding is poor in 6 to 13 feet MLW in a rocky bottom. If you plan ahead, you will find better protection up the East Branch of the Westport River

Buzzards Bay, MA

		Dockage					Supplies		Services					
		Largest Vessel Accommodated	VHF Channel Monitored / Working	Transient Slips / Total Slips	Approach / Dockside Depth (reported)	Floating Docks	Gas / Diesel	Groceries, Ice, Marine Supplies, Snacks	Repairs: Hull, Engine, Propeller	Lift (tonnage), Crane, Rail	Min / Max Amps	Courtesy Car, Laundry, Pool, Showers	Pump-Out Station	Nearby: Grocery Store, Motel, Restaurant
SOUTH DARTMOUTH														
1. New Bedford Yacht Club 🖥 WiFi	(508) 997-0762	70	68/	/100	10.0/9.0		GD	I			30	S	P	GR
2. South Wharf Yacht Yard 🖥 WiFi	(508) 990-1011	135	9/10	15/101	10.0/15.0	F		IM	HEP	L55,C	30/100	LS	P	MR
3. Davis & Tripp Inc.	(508) 993-9232	50	9/	1/80	15.0/7.0			IM	HEP	L60,C	50			GR
FAIRHAVEN AREA														
4. Fairhaven Shipyard Companies South Yard 🖥 WiFi	(508) 999-1600	200	9/10	20/165	18.0/18.0	F	GD	IMS	HEP	L440,C,R	30/100	LS		GMR
5. Fairhaven Shipyard Companies North Yard 🖥 WiFi	(508) 999-6266	200	16/9	/20	20.0/18.0	F		MS	HEP	L150,R	30/100		P	GMR
6. Seaport Inn & Marina 🖥 WiFi	(508) 997-1281	85	/	8/104	7.5/	F	GD	MS			30/50	LPS	P	GMR
7. Pope's Island Marina WiFi	(508) 979-1456	150	9/16	10/204	10.0/10.0	F		IS			30/100	LS		GMR
8. Niemiec Marine	(508) 997-7390	100	/	/	10.0/10.0			M	HEP	L150				
9. Sea Fuels Marine	(508) 992-2323	230	11/11		13.0/13.0		GD	IM					P	R
WEST ISLAND														
10. West Island Marina WiFi	(508) 993-0008	50	18/	3/115	4.5/4.5	F	GD	IMS	HEP	C	30	LS	P	R

🖥 Internet Access   WiFi Wireless Internet Access   onSpot Dockside WiFi Facility

See WaterwayGuide.com for current rates, fuel prices, website addresses, and other up-to-the-minute information. (Information in the table is provided by the facilities.)

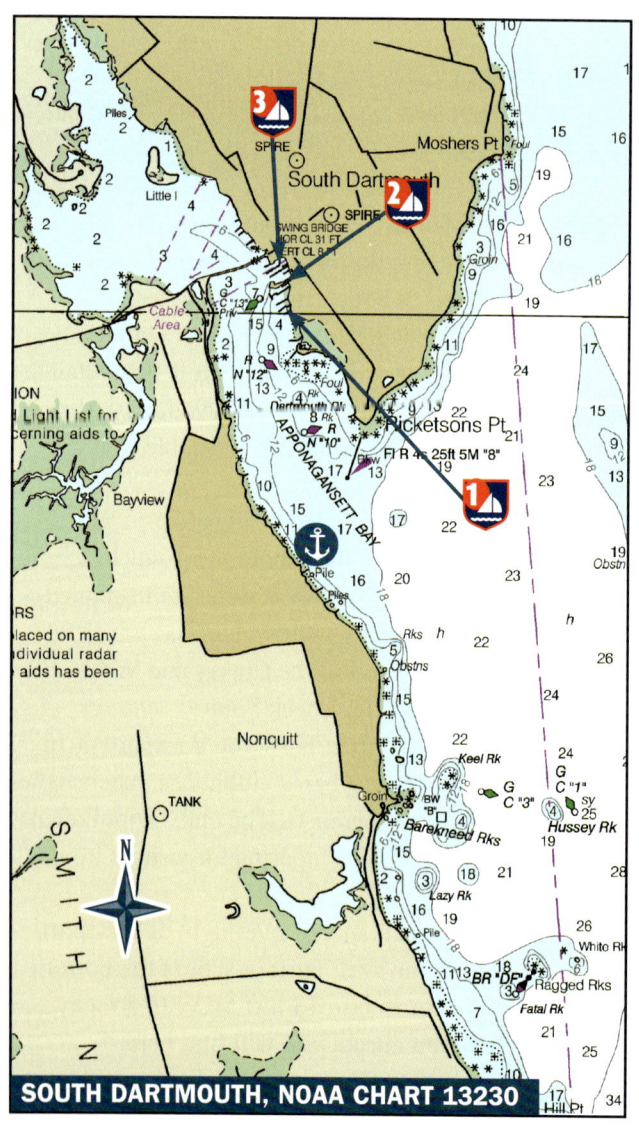

SOUTH DARTMOUTH, NOAA CHART 13230

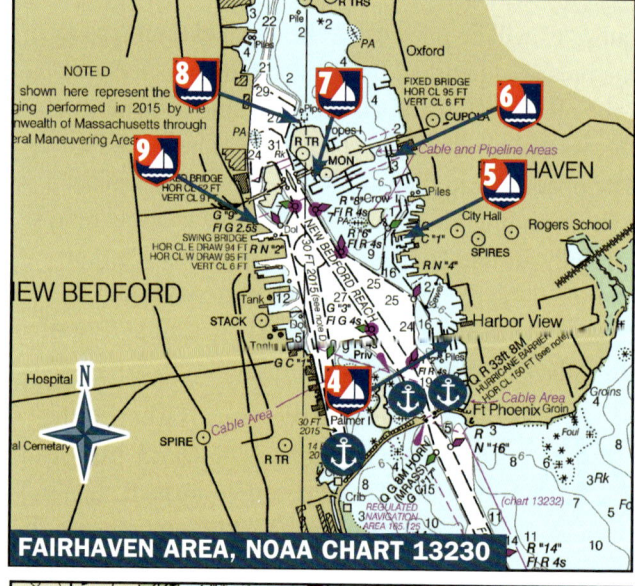

FAIRHAVEN AREA, NOAA CHART 13230

WEST ISLAND, NOAA CHART 13230

New Bedford Harbor

through the **Westport Point Bridge** (21-foot closed vertical clearance), which opens on signal with a 24-hour notice. Here you will find good protection east of Great Island in 6- to 12-foot MLW depths with good holding in mud. Watch for Sunk Rock, which is charted but unmarked, in the center of the channel upriver from the bridge.

The privately marked East Branch of Westport River makes a worthwhile dinghy trip. On a rising tide you can explore all the way to the fixed (7-foot vertical clearance) **Hix Bridge** but note that this trip in depths of 1 to 2 feet MLW requires a very shallow-draft boat. The shores are lovely and rolling hills with summer cottages are sprinkled among the working farms with fields that stretch down to the water's edge. The islands in the river are privately owned.

Apponagansett Bay

Beyond Mishaum Point off Smith Neck and north 2 miles beyond Round Hill Point, Apponagansett Bay forms an open harbor that has been famous to sailors for generations. Invariably known as Padanaram (pronounced "pay-dan-air-am") despite its designation as "South Dartmouth" on the charts, this is the home of the large and active New Bedford Yacht Club and the South Wharf Yacht Yard (known locally as Concordia Yard), once builders of the graceful wooden yawl of the same name. This busy and colorful harbor is the mooring ground and point of departure for

thousands of Buzzards Bay cruisers and racers. It is a favorite destination port for many others. Contact the Dartmouth Natural Resources Trust (508-991-2289) for a guide to walking trails around the village.

You will find many lovely shops and galleries along Elm St. and Bridge St. This compact village is a good place to enjoy the nautical ambiance, poke in the shops, dine and restock the lockers. Immediately across Bridge St. is Sail Loft (774-328-9871) on the harbor, which is a favorite dining spot with the cruising community, as is Little Moss (508-994-1162). Nearby Farm and Coast Market (7 Bridge St., 774-992-7093) has both a deli-grocery and a café. They sell beer and wine, meats, produce and breads and cheeses and have an excellent breakfast.

NAVIGATION: Use NOAA Charts 13229 and 13230. The harbor approach is rock-strewn but straightforward once you are on course. Enter the passage north of Dumpling Rocks slowly until you sort out the buoys. Refer to the Waterway Explorer (www.waterwayguide.com) and NOAA online charts for the most up-to-date information. Honoring green gong buoy "5" and 52-foot flashing green "7" marking Dumpling Rocks, take a course of 031 degrees magnetic to flashing red (2+1) red-over-green gong buoy "AB" and then take a course of 331 degrees magnetic to avoid Hussey Rock on the western shore. The entrance to Apponagansett Bay is marked by the 25-foot-tall flashing red "8."

Mattapoisett Harbor, MA

MATTAPOISETT		Largest Vessel Accomodated	VHF Channel Monitored / Working	Approach / Dockside Depth (reported)	Transient Slips / Total Slips	Floating Docks	Groceries, Ice, Marine Supplies, Snacks	Gas / Diesel	Repairs: Hull, Engine, Propeller	Lift (tonnage) Crane, Rail	Min / Max Amps	Courtesy Car, Laundry, Pool, Showers	Pump-Out Station	Nearby: Grocery Store, Motel, Restaurant
	Dockage						Supplies			Services				
1. Mattapoisett Boatyard	(508) 758-3812	50	68/	/	12.0/6.0		GD	IMS		HE	L35,C	30	S	P

💻 Internet Access 📶 Wireless Internet Access 📡 onSpot Dockside WiFi Facility

See WaterwayGuide.com for current rates, fuel prices, website addresses, and other up-to-the-minute information. (Information in the table is provided by the facilities.)

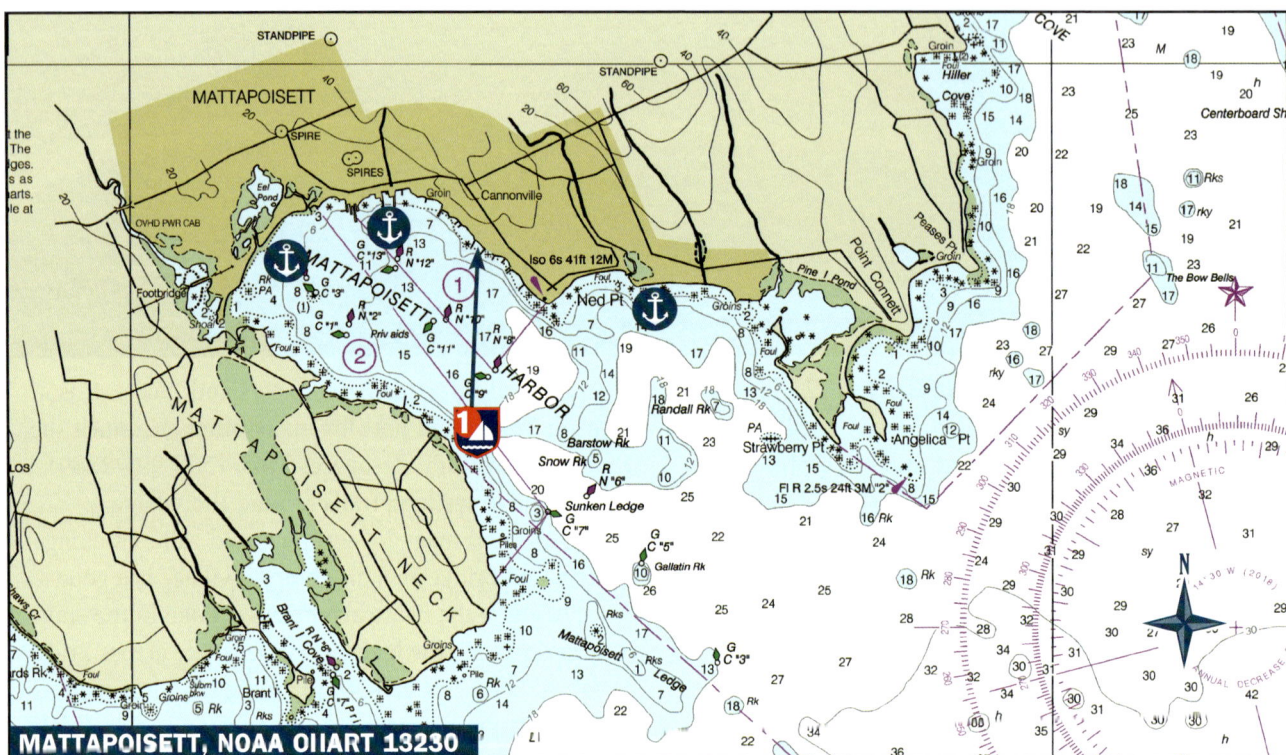

MATTAPOISETT, NOAA CHART 13230

Dockage/Mooring: The red-roofed New Bedford Yacht Club (NBYC) and its vast mooring field dominate Padanaram and Apponagansett Bay. Even though dock space is in very short supply, a slip may be available; call the dockmaster for availability. South Wharf Yacht Yard and Davis & Tripp Inc. south of the swing bridge (usually open) both operate large and active repair facilities. South Wharf has some reserved transient space. There are additional moorings on the west side of the channel with plenty of availability and great protection during a strong northeasterly blow.

Anchorage: You will find plenty of anchorage space beyond the mooring field outside the harbor channel and southwest of red nun buoy "10." There is good holding here in 10- to 12-foot MLW depths quite close to the west shore of the bay. This area, however, is exposed to the east and southeast and boats on moorings will chase away those who anchor close

enough to make them nervous. Clarks Cove to the east has no services but good holding. This provides excellent protection in a fall northerly.

New Bedford Harbor

New Bedford Harbor at the mouth of the Acushnet River is busy, commercial, colorful and imbued with a historic seafaring flavor. Two towns line the harbor head and river–New Bedford on the west and Fairhaven to the east–connected by Route 6, which makes both accessible to the area's major recreational boating center on Popes Island.

New Bedford was once the hub of the American whaling industry, and it retains many a reminder of the days when its fleet was larger than all others combined. During the height of whaling in 1857, there were a total of 329 whaling vessels packed in New Bedford's protected harbor employing well over 10,000 people.

The New Bedford Whaling Museum (18 Johnny Cake Hill, 508-997-0046), open all year, and the Seamen's Bethel Church (15 Johnny Cake Hill, 508-992-3295), with the pew once occupied by *Moby Dick* author Herman Melville, are easy to visit on foot. Today the harbor is an active commercial and fishing port, still boasting a fleet of trawlers, draggers, scallopers and lobster boats.

A massive stone hurricane barrier has made New Bedford/Fairhaven a snug harbor of refuge. The near 1-mile-long barrier encloses the harbor except for a 150-foot channel passage. If a major storm threatens, gates are closed across the opening.

Fairhaven and Popes Island are increasingly important bases for repairs and supplies with marine specialists for engines, machinery and fabrication, rigging, propellers, electronics, canvas and sails. Standard Marine Outfitters (137 Popes Island, 508-990-7917), across the street from the Pope's Island Marina, has a full selection of marine hardware and clothing plus a parts department and commercial fishing counter in the building behind. West Marine (114 Huttleson Ave., 508-994-1122) is about 1 mile from Pope's Island and 1.5 miles from the Fairhaven Shipyard locations.

NAVIGATION: Use NOAA Charts 13229 and 13230. From the Buzzards Bay fairway buoy to the hurricane barrier (approximately 8 nm) the Fort Phoenix Reach approach channel is clearly marked with few obstructions. All but a couple of the odd-numbered channel buoys now carry flashing green lights. Current through the narrow barrier opening runs up to 2.5 knots, with a slight easterly set.

Dockage/Moorings: Fairhaven Shipyard Companies North and South Yards are first on entry to the harbor on the eastern shore in a cluster of nautical support companies. They have deep-water floating and fixed slips for vessels to 200 feet. They also offer all fuels and comprehensive repairs. They can handle any repair, large or small.

The 204-slip Pope's Island Marina can accommodate most recreational boats entering the harbor. They are well-known for their customer service and convenience to New Bedford amenities. The marina manages all moorings in New Bedford Harbor and keeps 35 to 40 available for transient boaters.

On the western shore of the river at New Bedford is Sea Fuels Marine, which operates a 250-foot fuel dock with wholesale fuel pricing and marine supplies.

Anchorage: Anchoring is restricted to 14 days at a time. Upon entering the hurricane barrier you can anchor to either side in 8 to 16 feet MLW. Vessels also work their way around to anchor west of Palmer Island in 6-to 7-foot MLW depths with good holding in sand. This is exposed to the north. There are city dinghy docks at Pope's Island Marina, the Gifford Street boat ramp, south of the State Pier next to the schooner *Ernestina* and at Tonneson Park, next to the Visitors Center. There is launch service between New Bedford and Fairhaven (seasonal). To schedule a pickup, call on VHF Channel 09 or 508-989-1328.

Mattapoisett Harbor

Mattapoisett Harbor is beautiful and easy to enter. The village is postcard New England–clapboard, picturesque and historic. Some of the finest whaling ships in the world were built here during the heyday of the whaling industry. Shipyard Park at the village center commemorates a time when some 400 men worked the yards and the bowsprits of mighty vessels shrouded the roadways.

The harbor itself is an inverted "U" from the southeast, funneling in the prevailing southerlies and is quite pleasant on a hot, light air day but is rolly when the wind pipes up across the diagonal-width fetch of Buzzards Bay.

The excellent Inn on Shipyard Park (13 Water St., 508-758-4922) is the first restaurant off the boat and offers both a bar and sit-down dining with a raw bar, shareable plates, burgers and seafood. County Rd. curves in a mirror of the shoreline and puts many fine shops less than 1 mile from Shipyard Park.

NAVIGATION: Use NOAA Chart 13230. Although the approach is straightforward, numerous submerged obstructions lie adjacent to the buoys marking the generous channel access. Snow Rock, for example, will find the bottom of a 5-foot-draft vessel straying beyond the channel marked by red nun buoys "6" and "8." It is best to remain carefully within the channel buoys until well past red nun buoy "8" at Barstow Rock.

Dockage/Mooring: Mattapoisett Boatyard (on the east side of the harbor and north of Ned Point) maintains transient moorings; the most obvious ones are painted international orange and anchored directly in front of the yard's landing. If those are occupied or you would rather be closer to the village, call the yard on VHF Channel 68 for directions. The boatyard

GOIN' ASHORE

NEW BEDFORD, MA

New Bedford was once the hub of the American whaling industry, and it retains many a reminder of the days when its fleet was larger than all others combined. During the height of whaling in 1857, there were a total of 329 whaling vessels packed in New Bedford's protected harbor, employing well over 10,000 people. Though we now understand this to be the reason these incredible animals were brought to the brink of extinction, the whale oil industry inspired the city motto "The City that Lit the World." Ferries to Cuttyhunk, Martha's Vineyard and Nantucket are all available from New Bedford.

SERVICES

1. New Bedford Post Office
695 Pleasant St. (508-979-7420)

2. New Bedford Public Library
613 Pleasant St. (508-991-6275)

ATTRACTIONS

3. New Bedford Art Museum
Showcases local talent at 608 Pleasant Rd. (508-961-3072).

4. New Bedford Whaling Museum
Exhibits on the history of whaling. Open year round at 18 Johnny Cake Hill (508-997-0046).

SHOPPING

5. New Bedford Ship Supply Co.
Marine Supply Store at 108 Front St. (508-994-2961).

6. Price Rite
Discount supermarket chain at 39 South St. (508-990-0317).

MARINAS

7. Sea Fuels Marina
101 Co-op Wharf (508-992-2323)

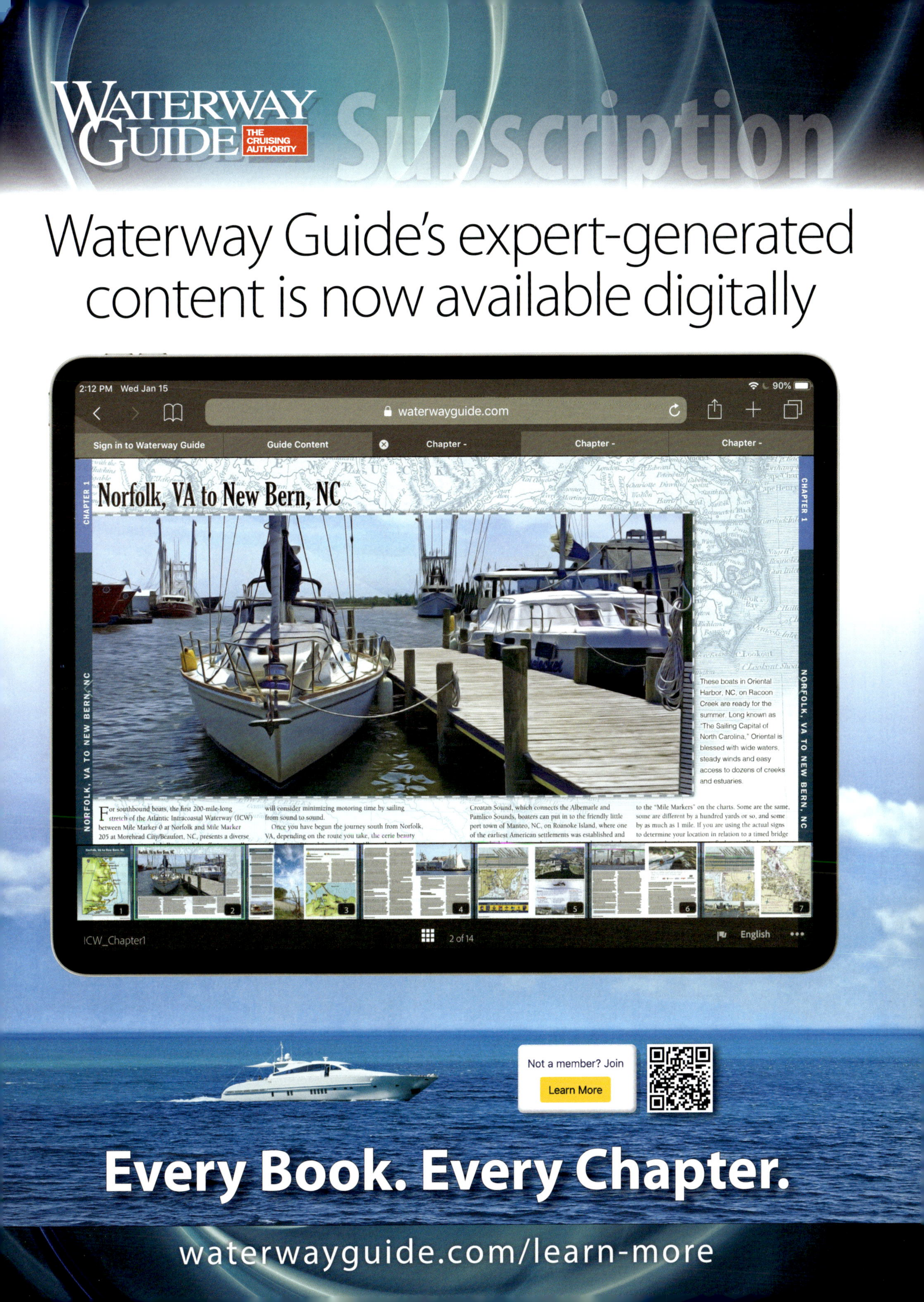

Buzzards Bay, MA

SIPPICAN HARBOR		Largest Vessel Accomodated	VHF Channel Monitored / Working	Approach / Dockside Depth (reported)	Transient Slips / Total Slips	Floating Docks	Gas / Diesel	Groceries, Ice, Marine Supplies, Snacks	Repairs: Hull, Engine, Propeller	Lift (tonnage), Crane, Rail	Min / Max Amps	Courtesy Car, Laundry, Pool, Showers	Pump-Out Station	Nearby: Grocery Store, Motel, Restaurant
				Dockage				Supplies				Services		
1. Beverly Yacht Club WIFI	(508) 748-0540	50	68/68	/	/7.0				IS			S	P	GR
2. Marion Town Landing	(508) 748-3515		/9	/	6.0/7.0	F						S	P	MR
3. Barden's Boat Yard Inc. WIFI	(508) 748-0250		68/	/	/	F	GD	IM	HEP	L35,C	30/50	S	P	GR
4. Burr Bros. Boats Inc. ▯ WIFI	(508) 748-0541	69	68/	5/43	6.0/7.5	F	GD	IM	HEP	L55,C	30/50	LS	P	GMR
WAREHAM RIVER														
5. Zecco Marina ▯	(508) 295-0022	55	16/9	10/120	8.0/6.0	F	GD	IMS	HEP	L35,C,R	30	S	P	GMR
6. Cape Cod Shipbuilding Co.	(508) 295-3550	44	/	/	12.0/9.0	F			H	L	30			R

▯ Internet Access WIFI Wireless Internet Access ☐onSpot Dockside WiFi Facility
See WaterwayGuide.com for current rates, fuel prices, website addresses, and other up-to-the-minute information. (Information in the table is provided by the facilities.)

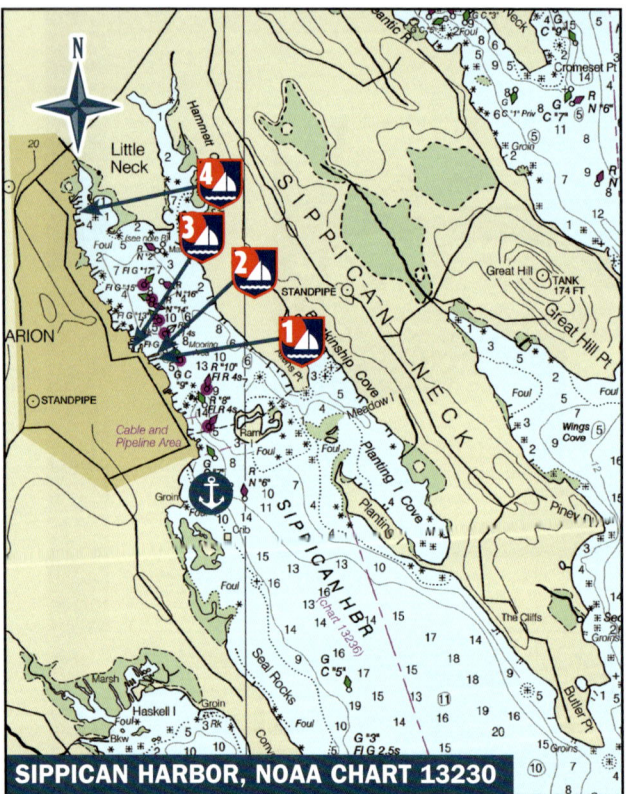

SIPPICAN HARBOR, NOAA CHART 13230

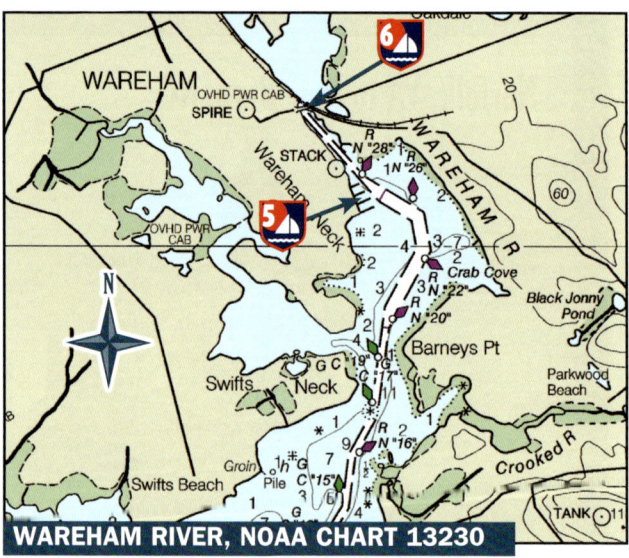

WAREHAM RIVER, NOAA CHART 13230

operates a launch service to and from town or its own dock, which is included in the mooring fee. Next door, the Mattapoisett Yacht Club has an active sailing program and is friendly to visitors (often offering hot coffee at the door) but offers few reciprocal privileges.

At the head of the harbor, three substantial town piers provide space for transient tie-ups but fender your vessel thoroughly against damage from the rough timbers and pilings. There is a self-service pump-out facility at the town wharf, open 24 hours a day and the harbormaster (508-758-4191) operates a pump-out boat Sunday through Thursday.

Anchorage: There may be limited anchorage space near the town piers in the two designated (east and west) anchorage areas. Avoid blocking the roundabout channel circling the harbor's center mooring area. You will find at least 8 feet MLW and protection from all but the southeast.

Additional anchorage room is along the north side of the substantial bight just inside Ned Point. You can drop the hook here in at least 12-foot MLW depths. As in many New England harbors, there are more moorings and fewer anchorage areas each year. Plan accordingly and reserve ahead.

Sippican Harbor (Marion)

Sippican Harbor, the route to the beautiful town of Marion, is tranquil and easy to enter. Tradition has it that as many as 87 ship captains lived in Marion in the mid-1800s. Of the beautiful captain's homes, many were bought by "summer people" once tourism brought visitors in the last 1800s and some of those historic homes remain today. The town has ancient trees shading narrow, cottage-lined streets and the harbor offers protected moorings, marinas and shops that offer all you are likely to need, making this a favorite layover port for cruising boats.

The town has a natural history museum, a historic society, art center and the Tabor Academy, an independent secondary school, easily recognized by its extensive red roofs. Tabor Academy understandably includes sailing in its curriculum and maintains a fleet of launches, day sailors, rowing shells and the 92-foot schooner, *Tabor Boy*.

Virtually all shopping is within two blocks (to the left) of Island Wharf on Front St. Marion General Store (140 Front St., 508-748-0340) has basic provisions, cheeses, wine and beer, ice and baked goods made on the premises.

NAVIGATION: Use NOAA Charts 13229 and 13230. Bird Island to the east recognizable by its lighthouse and Converse Point to the west with a flagpole and large summerhouse, clearly mark the entry to Marion. Keep clear of the Converse Point rocks by leaving flashing green buoy "3" and green can buoy "5" to the west and then laying a course for red nun buoy "6." Simply follow the well-marked, 6-foot MLW

channel to the harbor head. Even though the channel is dredged periodically, it shoals quickly beyond the buoys and turning room can be at a premium during the busy summer season.

Dockage/Mooring: The distinguished Beverly Yacht Club becomes visible to the northwest as you pass green can buoy "9." Members of other recognized clubs may be able to secure a mooring there for a facility fee. Next door, the Marion Town Landing has dock space to accommodate tie-ups to take on drinking water or to use the town's free mobile pump-out service. Call the Marion harbormaster on VHF Channel 09 or by phone (508-748-3535) for this service. Barden's Boat Yard, immediately beyond, is a complete repair facility that rents moorings and operates a public launch service. There is a dinghy dock at Barden's and gas and diesel fuel but no slips.

At the head of the harbor, Burr Bros. Boats Inc. offers a complete range of marina and marine repair facilities in a pastoral setting. Burr Bros. and the Beverley Yacht Club offer launch service on weekends.

Anchorage: Although there is no anchorage in Marion proper, boats can anchor in outer Sippican Harbor in settled weather in 9 to 11 feet MLW in sand. This is open and exposed to the southeast.

Sippican Harbor

Wareham River

Wareham is about 2 nm up the Wareham River and 5 nm from Cleveland Ledge Channel. This resort territory offers good beaches, busy protected coves, crowded anchorages and wonderful scenery and makes an attractive base for exploring.

NAVIGATION: Use NOAA Charts 13229 and 13230. The Wareham River channel is winding but well marked with a depth of 8 feet MLW. Shallow water lies outside the channel on either side; watch buoys carefully to stay in deep water. Near Wareham the river narrows and currents of up to 3 knots can be expected.

When a southwester meets a strong current flowing westward out of the canal, the head of Buzzards Bay can become rough with short, steep seas. The eastbound skipper should lay over at Marion under these circumstances. The westbound skipper, anticipating these conditions, can seek the shelter of Onset Harbor (described below) to wait for more favorable weather.

Dockage: Zecco Marina and Cape Cod Shipbuilding Co. on Wareham Neck both offer repairs. Zecco has also maintains some transient slips and sells all fuels. Call ahead.

Anchorage: A popular anchorage is north of Long Beach Point in 7 to 9 feet MLW with good holding in sand. (Note that Long Beach Point might be completely submerged at high tide.) Anchor west of the line between red nun buoy "12" and green can buoy "13."

Onset

Whatever the weather, Onset makes an attractive cruising stop and a good place to await favorable wind and tide for a trip across the bay or north through the Cape Cod Canal. This Victorian seaside village offers protection from most winds, has attractive white sand beaches, easy accessible facilities and a sizable anchorage area not carpeted with moorings.

Onset Village is just uphill from the town docks. The Onset Village Market (231 Onset Ave., 508-291-1440) combines a grocery and meat market with a substantial liquor store and will provide return-trip transportation and/or grocery delivery for a small fee. The Onset Scenic Trail is a relaxing route for pedestrians, bicyclists and motorists.

NAVIGATION: Use NOAA Charts 13229 and 13230. Examine the chart carefully so that the course is clearly fixed in your mind before making the sharp turn to

Onset from Hog Island Channel. The turning point for the channel leading to Onset Bay off Hog Island Channel is just south of the 35-foot tower presenting quick flashing green "21," which marks the canal channel, not the Onset Channel. Green can buoy "1," immediately east of Hog Neck, begins the sequential marks of the Onset Channel.

While it may feel strange to pass between two green markers, red nun buoy "2" follows closely after to confirm the northeast side of the Onset channel. Allow for swift current, which may attempt to push your boat into a buoy out of the channel. The current diminishes beyond Burgess Point. Be wary of possible shoaling on the west side between green can buoys "3" and "5." Refer to the Waterway Explorer (www.waterwayguide.com) and NOAA online charts for the most up-to-date information.

Dockage/Mooring: Once you have passed red nun "10" on the Onset Channel turn north toward the small private aids (green can buoy "1" and red nun buoy "2") to approach Safe Harbor Onset Bay, which maintains a large mooring field and substantial transient dockage (to 120 feet). They have all the usual amenities plus hauling and storage facilities.

Just west of Safe Harbor Onset Bay, the friendly Point Independence Yacht Club will rent slips to visiting boaters for a reasonable facility fee. Even though the club is oriented primarily to powerboats, its 8-foot MLW dockside depths can accommodate almost any recreational vessel.

Back in the Onset Channel, continue west then north around Wickets Island to reach the docks at Onset Town Pier, which provides plenty of dinghy space and a few slips with easy access to shops and restaurants.

Heading south on the Cape Cod Canal

The town also rents transient moorings. Call ahead on VHF Channel 09 for availability. There are no public showers, although public restrooms are on the pier, and dumpsters in the parking area will accommodate your trash and single-stream recycling.

Anchorage: Holding is good between Wickets Island and Onset Island outside the mooring field in at least 8-foot MLW depths and the dinghy ride to the town pier is a pleasant ride in most weather. The dinghy dock comprises the entire backside of the floating portion and is still often packed. Leave plenty of slack in your painter so others can approach the dock or get out around you.

For skippers of boats drawing 6 feet or less, there is also space with good holding in dense mud west of the Onset Channel between Hog Neck and Burgess Point. Be alert for swirling currents in this location. You may also anchor north of Hog Island near the south end of the Cape Cod Canal in 10 to 20 feet MLW with good holding in sand and mud.

Cape Cod Canal

The Cape Cod Canal cuts across the neck of Cape Cod to points north and east, saving boats from the long, tricky trip through Nantucket Shoals and around Cape Cod to reach Boston or Maine. The Canal is heavily traveled, well marked and offers an attractive trip. In some seasons schooners traverse the canal heading to and from various festivals, giving other boaters close-up views of historic ships.

When the canal opened in 1914, it was 15 feet deep and 100 feet wide. During both World Wars the canal was heavily used to avoid attack by German U-boats, which lurked in offshore waters. The modern day version is the world's widest sea-level canal with a channel width of 540 feet and average depth of 32 feet. Recreational vessels use the canal extensively and service roads on either side provide trails for skateboarding, bicycling and hiking, along with access for fishing.

Anyone who transits the Cape Cod Canal will likely recognize the campus of the Massachusetts Maritime Academy on Taylor Point. The 540-foot training ship of the Academy, *USTS Kennedy*, dominates the west end of the canal. Both the academy and ship are available for tours at no charge (508-830-5000).

NAVIGATION: Use NOAA Chart 13229. The canal is able to handle vessels up to 825 feet long but all vessels larger than 65 feet must contact the Marine Traffic Controller on VHF Channel 13 before entering the canal. The 7-mile-long land cut can be almost clear of fog when both Buzzards and Cape Cod bays are thick with it.

⚠️ Mariners are advised that all vessels 65 feet and over shall not enter the Cape Cod Canal until clearance has been obtained from the Marine Traffic Controller by radio. Vessels shall request clearance at least 15 minutes prior to entering the Cape Cod Canal at any point.

The Cape Cod Canal, including approaches, extends from 1.6 miles seaward of the Canal Breakwater Light (East Entrance Cape Cod Bay) through the land cut to Cleveland Ledge Light in Buzzards Bay approximately

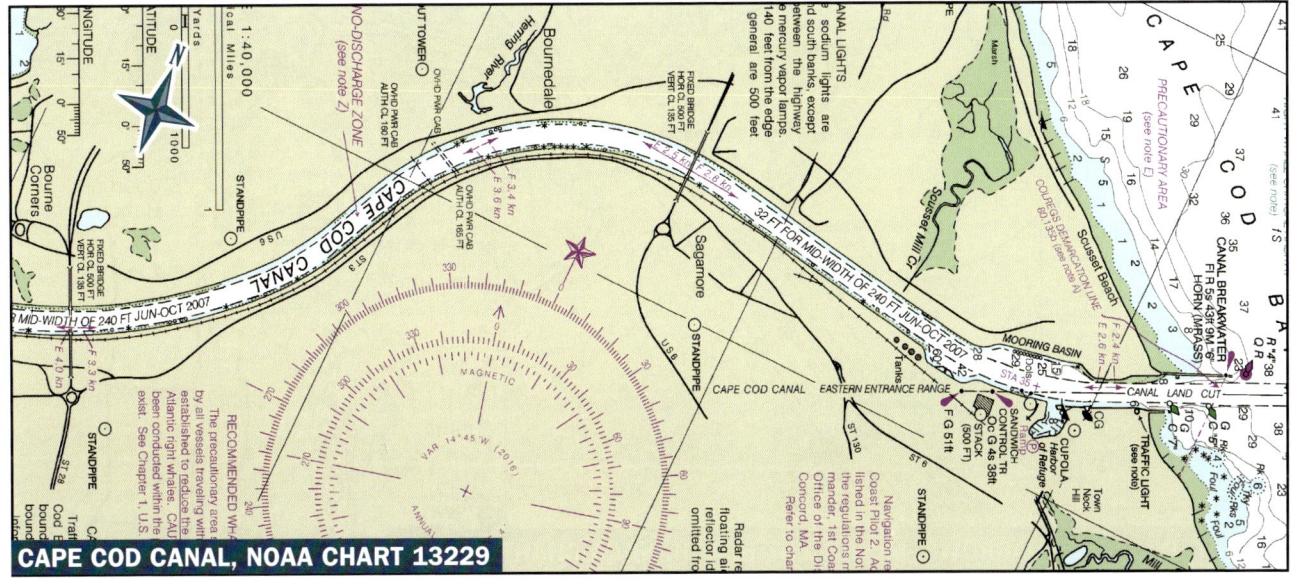

CAPE COD CANAL, NOAA CHART 13229

Onset Harbor Area, MA

ONSET		Largest Vessel Accommodated	VHF Channel Monitored / Working	Approach / Dockside Depth (reported)	Transient Slips / Total Slips	Floating Docks	Gas / Diesel	Groceries, Ice, Marine Supplies, Snacks	Repairs: Hull, Engine, Propeller	Lift (tonnage), Crane, Rail	Courtesy Car, Laundry, Pool, Showers	Min / Max Amps	Pump-Out Station	Nearby: Grocery Store, Motel, Restaurant
				Dockage			**Supplies**		**Services**					
1. Safe Harbor Onset Bay 🖥 WiFi	(508) 295-0338	120	9/	6/100	8.0/6.0	F	GD	IMS	HEP	L50	30/50	LS	P	GMR
2. Point Independence Yacht Club WiFi	(508) 295-3972	70	9/	15/65	8.0/7.0	F	GD	IS			30/50	LS	P	GMR
3. Stonebridge Marina WiFi	(508) 295-8003	35	/	4/60	8.0/7.0	F	G	GIS	HEP		30	LS	P	GR
4. Wareham Harbormaster / Onset Town Pier	(508) 291-3100	100	9/6	6/6	12.0/7.0	F		I				L	P	GMR
PACASSET NARROWS														
5. Taylor's Point Marina 🖥 WiFi	(508) 759-2512	50	9/9	2/148	6.0/9.0	F	GD	IMS			50	LS	P	MR
MONUMENT BEACH														
6. Monument Beach Marina	(508) 759-3105	40	16/	2/61	9.0/6.0		G	I			30	S		

🖥 Internet Access   WiFi Wireless Internet Access   onSpot Dockside WiFi Facility

See WaterwayGuide.com for current rates, fuel prices, website addresses, and other up-to-the-minute information. (Information in the table is provided by the facilities.)

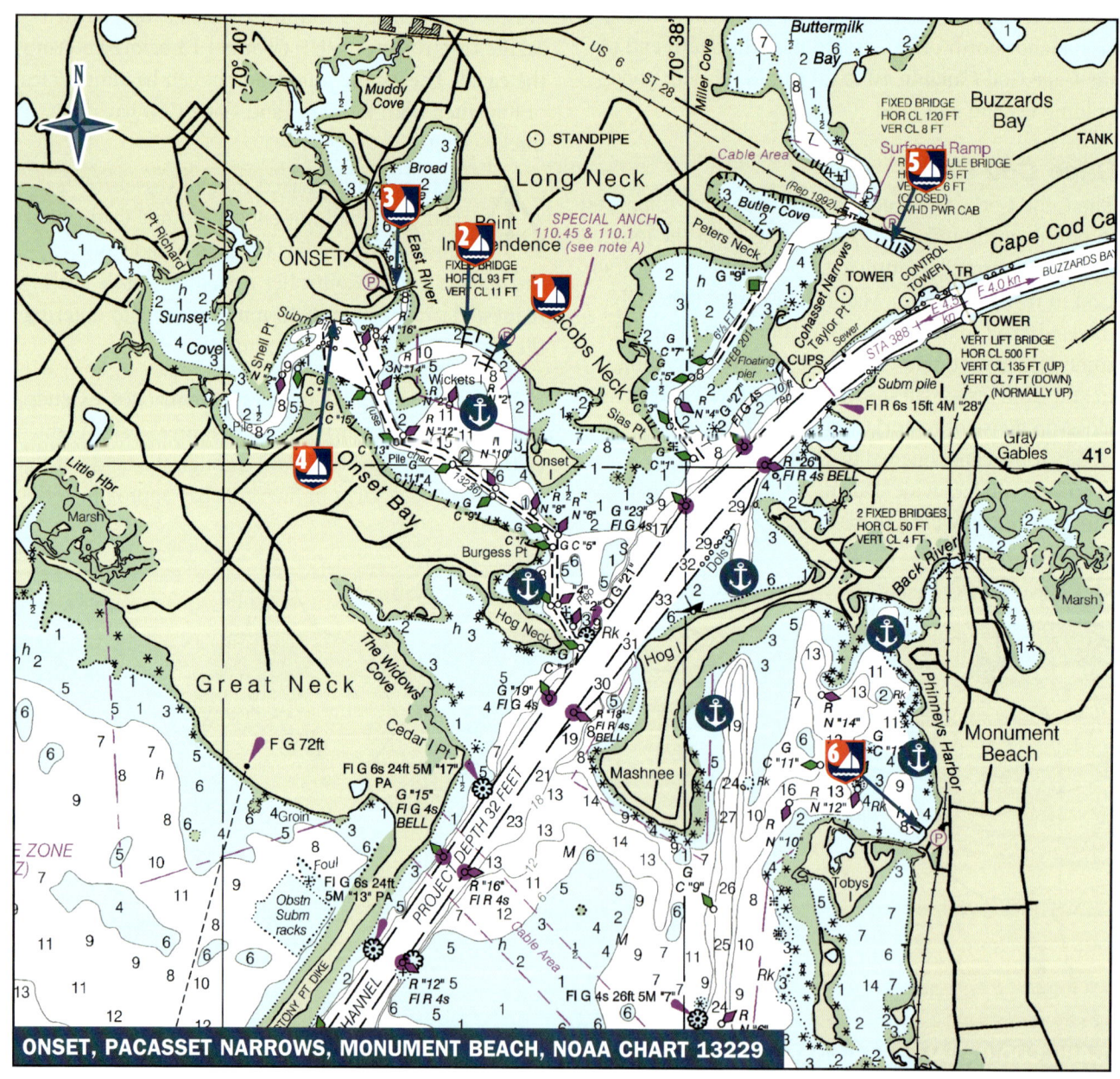

ONSET, PACASSET NARROWS, MONUMENT BEACH, NOAA CHART 13229

4 miles southwest of Wings Neck. Vessels should contact with Cape Cod Canal Marine Traffic Control on VHF Channel 13. All vessels are required to maintain a radio guard on channel 13 during the entire passage. Speed limit is 10 mph.

Despite the width and depth of the canal, tidal range conflict between the Cape Cod Bay end (9 feet) and the Buzzards Bay side (4 feet) remains fierce creating currents of about 3.5 knots on the eastward-setting flood and 4 knots to 6 knots on the ebb. Give careful attention to the tide and tidal current charts and make a very conservative estimate of the time you will need to pass both through the canal and beyond in order to allow for the effects of a foul-setting tide.

A westbound cruiser who chooses to power through against the flood will be sad to see that struggle continue down Buzzards Bay, whereas heading into the canal early in the ebb provides a boost all the way down the bay. The flood provides the eastbound cruiser a quick trip through the canal but turns foul on the other side. This is less problematic than in Buzzards Bay since the current is not as concentrated in Cape Cod Bay and many post-canal destinations don't require heading straight into it.

Even though commercial traffic is heavy on the canal, you should have no difficulties if you pick tide and weather carefully, proceed cautiously and stick to the right side of the channel (as if driving on a highway). The U.S. Army Corps of Engineers cautions that the canal is a No-Wake Zone; boaters must observe a 10-mph speed limit, yet complete their transit within 2.5 hours. If you are unable to complete the transit in that time, you may be required to hire a helper tug at your expense. This last requirement makes it particularly important to calculate your speed-versus-tide requirements with some care. All boats must be under power. Sailing through the canal is not permitted; neither are turning around, fishing or anchoring. Finally, as you transit the canal monitor VHF Channel 13 for communications from the Army Corps of Engineers and be ready to alert them to emergency situations.

The ConRail Railroad Bridge crossing the canal is usually open except during the occasional passage of a train to or from Cape Cod. Closed vertical clearance is a mere 7 feet so very few vessels will clear the bridge during a closure. Monitor VHF Channel 13 for alerts to any closings. If running with a strong, favorable current, look well ahead to assure passage under the bridge as turning at the last minute may not be an option. The bridge operator sounds two long blasts before lowering the bridge. It takes approximately 2.5 minutes to raise or lower it. If the bridge

is lowered during periods of decreased visibility, the bridge operator will signal four short blasts every two minutes. Two highway bridges cross the canal beyond the railroad bridge–the **Bourne Bridge** and the **Sagamore Bridge**–both with 135-foot fixed vertical clearances.

■ EASTERN SHORE TO WOODS HOLE

The eastern shore of Buzzards Bay is generally high and handsome, with fine old trees and houses. Water is comparatively deep close to the banks, and the shore is indented by wide, open bays and protected harbors.

Phinneys Harbor

Working south from the Cape Cod Canal the first of the harbors is big, open and shoal-dotted Phinneys Harbor with a marked entrance and the town of Monument Beach on its eastern shore. Mashnee Island forms its western boundary and Tobys Island forms its eastern boundary. It is 0.70 mile to the village of Monument Beach from the marina, where you will find a Post Office, limited groceries and wholesale seafood.

NAVIGATION: Use NOAA Chart 13229. To avoid the shoal area south of Mashnee Island, an eastbound or westbound boat in Hog Island Channel should use the markers abeam of Phinneys Harbor as a turning point. Estimate the midway point and then turn directly toward the entrance to Phinneys Harbor. Sailors making short tacks should be wary of ledges close to the southern end of Mashnee Island. The route to an anchorage and small marina at Monument Beach is well marked to the east, north of Tobys Island. Keep a mid channel course to avoid rocks to the east and south of the channel.

Dockage: Monument Beach Marina is located in a beautiful setting with a fine public beach to either side of its main pier. The marina offers slips and gas.

Anchorage: The conspicuous rock pile off the eastern side of Mashnee Island serves as a guide to the deepwater gully that leads to a secure anchorage, protected from the north but open to the south. Here you will find 7 to 14 feet MLW with good holding in sand. The most protected anchorage in the area lies in the northeastern corner of Phinneys Harbor near the entrance to Back River, which is very shoal; do not venture upstream. Here you can drop the hook in 9 to 11 feet MLW with good holding in sand and mud. To the south you can anchor right off Monument Beach in 12 to 14 feet MLW with good holding in hard sand.

Upper Buzzards Bay, MA

RED BROOK		VHF Channel Monitored / Working	Largest Vessel Accomodated	Approach / Dockside Depth (reported)	Transient Slips / Total Slips	Dockage	Floating Docks	Gas / Diesel	Groceries, Ice, Marine Supplies, Snacks	Supplies	Repairs: Hull, Engine, Propeller	Lift (tonnage), Crane, Rail	Courtesy Car, Laundry, Pool, Showers	Min / Max Amps	Pump-Out Station	Services	Nearby: Grocery Store, Motel, Restaurant

RED BROOK				Dockage					Supplies		Services						
1. Kingman Yacht Center [WiFi]	(508) 563-7136	120	71/71	20/235	8.0/10.0	F		GD	IMS	HEP	L60,C	30/50	LS	P	GMR
2. Parker's Boatyard Inc. [☐][WiFi]	(508) 563-9366	50	69/69	4/9	6.0/8.0	F		GD	IM	HEP	L35,C	30	S	P	GR
MEGANSETT HARBOR															
3. Safe Harbor Fiddler's Cove [☐][WiFi]	(508) 564-6327	65	9/	1/130	7.0/7.0	F		GD	IMS	HEP	L35	30/50	LS	P	GMR

☐ Internet Access [WiFi] Wireless Internet Access ⊙onSpot Dockside WiFi Facility

See WaterwayGuide.com for current rates, fuel prices, website addresses, and other up-to-the-minute information. (Information in the table is provided by the facilities.)

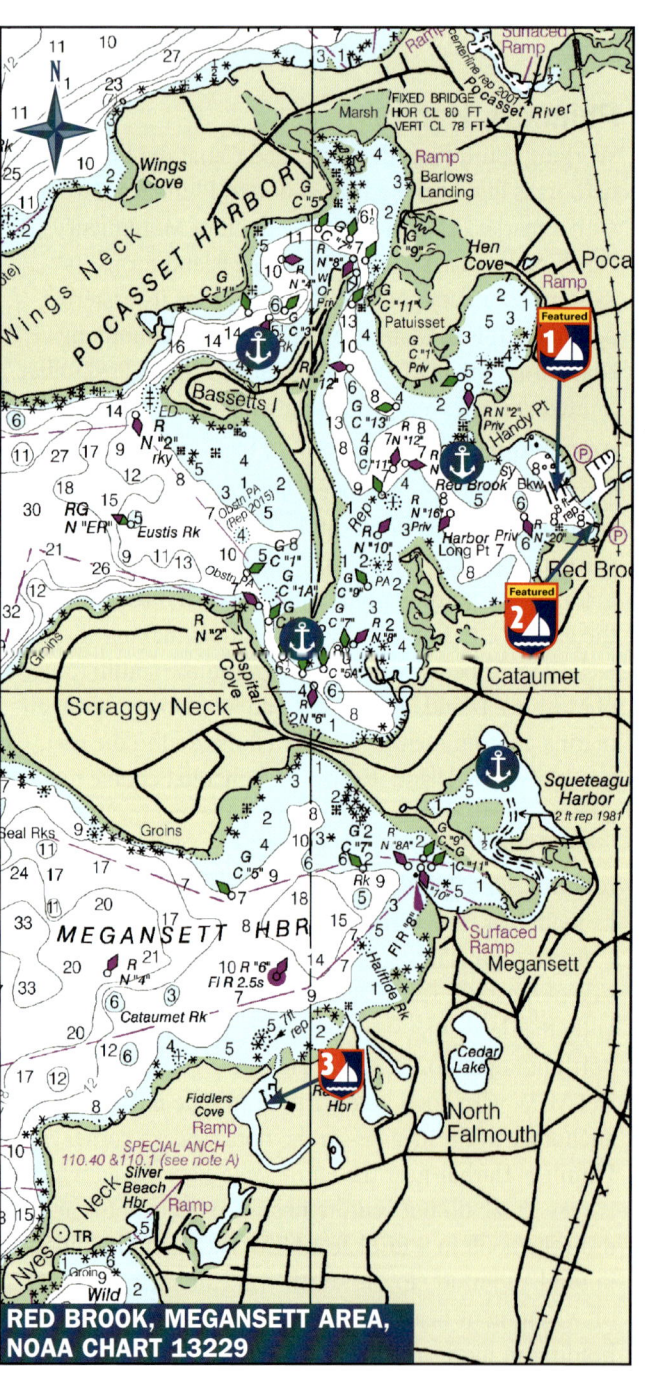

RED BROOK, MEGANSETT AREA, NOAA CHART 13229

Pocasset & Red Brook Harbors

Three-pronged Bassetts Island subdivides the water here. Most of Bassetts Island is privately owned; however, the town owns the south end of the island and it is open to the public. It is a half-mile walk up a gentle grade from Barlows Landing to the village where you will find a hardware store, a market and restaurants.

Large, well-protected Red Brook Harbor is to the southeast at the village of Cataumet. Ample boating amenities, good anchorage and pleasant surroundings define this active harbor. The Chart Room (1 Shipyard Ln., 508-563-5350) has been feeding people aboard a converted barge since 1966 and offers live, nightly entertainment at the piano bar as well as seafood entrées and sandwiches. The seasonal restaurant recommends dinner reservations.

The final harbor in this big semicircle of harbors is Hospital Cove at Cataumet. Handsome and scenic, the shores of this harbor are dotted with greenery and pleasant houses.

On exiting this circuit of harbors give full respect to the buoys marking Southwest Ledge just to the west of Scraggy Neck. A charted rock, exposed at high water, is located just to the north of red nun buoy "10," which marks the northwestern side of the ledge. A forbidding area of rocks also lies just south of red nun buoy "2."

NAVIGATION: Use NOAA Charts 13229 and 13230. You can enter Bassetts Island through either of two narrow, twisting, shoal-prone passages. The northern one inside Wings Neck is a little deeper and more popular but quite unmanageable when the tide ebbs against a southwester. The southern entrance, along Scraggy Neck, has 6.5-foot MLW charted depths.

KINGMAN YACHT CENTER

PARKER'S BOATYARD INC.

Red Brook Harbor

You can reach Hospital Cove either from Red Brook Harbor or via the southern entrance around Scraggy Neck from Buzzards Bay.

Dockage/Moorings: In this harbor you'll find two facilities for consideration, Kingman Yacht Center and Parker's Boatyard. Kingman Yacht Center has an extensive dock complex and massive sheds. This is Cape Cod's largest full-service marina and boatyard with 10-foot MLW dockside depths, 235 slips and 130 moorings. They can accommodate vessels to 120 feet. They also complete marine repairs and maintenance, have a fully stocked chandlery and offer full cruiser amenities.

Family-owned Parker's Boatyard is a classic New England facility rich in history. This full-service yard offers 130 moorings with launch service and a dinghy dock plus dockside accommodations for boats to 50 feet. They sell gas and diesel fuel and provide all types of maintenance and repairs. Provisioning is available from this location within a short driving distance and taxis are available to provide the wheels.

Anchorage: Around the western point of Bassetts Island, there is a secure anchorage in 9 to 14 feet MLW in the sweeping bight along the northern side of the island. Holding is good in soft mud but it is somewhat exposed to the northeast. Barlows Landing, north of the island's northern arm, permits dinghy tie-ups at the floating dock in front of the small pier next to the town beach.

You can drop the hook behind Long Point in Red Brook Harbor in 8 feet MLW with good holding in sand

and rock. This is somewhat exposed to the north.

The final harbor in this big semicircle of harbors is Hospital Cove at Cataumet. Handsome and scenic, the shores of this harbor are dotted with greenery and pleasant houses. You can reach Hospital Cove either from Red Brook Harbor or via the southern entrance around Scraggy Neck from Buzzards Bay.

On exiting this circuit of harbors give full respect to the buoys marking Southwest Ledge just to the west of Scraggy Neck. A charted rock, exposed at high water, is located just to the north of red nun buoy "10," which marks the northwestern side of the ledge. A forbidding area of rocks also lies just south of red nun buoy "2."

While Hospital Cove provides good holding in a relatively secluded spot, the gradual increase of moorings here has limited the anchorage to a comparatively small area near the channel. Make allowance for swing room, both in relation to the channel and to the moored boats toward land. There are no public landings and no marinas, just peace and quiet, except in strong northwesterly winds. Piping southwesterlies can also be quite noticeable here because they blow across the narrow isthmus leading from Cataumet to Scraggy Neck but, fortunately, the short fetch prevents significant wave action from building.

Megansett Harbor

Megansett Harbor to the south lies between Scraggy Neck and Nyes Neck and is wide open to the west. It has three well-protected inner harbors and a large bight, protected only from the north, in the outer harbor east of the bulge of Scraggy Neck.

Dockage: On the southern side of outer Megansett Harbor, southeast of Cataumet Rock (at red nun buoy "4"), the 9-foot MLW channel to Fiddlers Cove is dredged frequently and well marked. Inside this virtual hurricane hole of protection is Safe Harbor Fiddler's Cove. A courteous staff tends to floating docks and mechanics are on call 7 days a week.

Anchorage: Inner Megansett Harbor has a narrow, marked entry with a bar that shoots out from the breakwater. Beyond are a launching ramp, hospitable yacht club and town dock. It is possible to anchor here in 5- to 7-foot MLW depths.

At its eastern end, around a projecting point of land, is Squeteague Harbor, a cove with less than 3-foot MLW depths at its difficult entry but 6 feet MLW once inside. There is very limited space to drop the hook, though, as moorings take up most of the available space. It is well worth exploring, if only by dinghy or shoal-draft boat.

South of Nyes Neck, you may find secure anchorage and protection from a northerly in Wild Harbor. The entry is marked by flashing green buoy "1" and red nun buoy "4" and has adequate depth for most cruisers (9 to 12 feet MLW). Avoid this harbor if there is a prediction of wind shift to the prevailing southwest as it is completely exposed.

Woods Hole

The Village of Woods Hole is the most important oceanographic center on the east coast. Major research facilities firmly settled here are NOAA's NorthEast Fisheries Center, the Marine Biological Laboratory (whose summer labs have produced more than 50 Nobel Laureates) and the Woods Hole Oceanographic Institution. It was researchers from Woods Hole who discovered the *Titanic* in 1985. The Exhibit Center of Woods Hole Oceanographic Institution (15 School St., 508-289-2663) is open daily from Memorial Day to Labor Day and on a more limited schedule beyond those dates.

About 6 miles south of West Falmouth, Quissett Harbor has generally deep-water, high, wooded shores with handsome houses, good protection and easy entrance but no provisions. The small peninsula enclosing the northern side of the harbor is now a nature preserve that is well worth a trip ashore for a walking tour. During the summer season the WHOOSH Trolley (800-352-7155) stops here with service to Woods Hole and Falmouth.

NAVIGATION: Use NOAA Charts 13229 and 13230. Woods Hole marks the difficult and sometimes dangerous passage between Buzzards Bay and Vineyard Sound at the southwestern tip of Cape Cod. Woods Hole consists of three unique harbors: Great Harbor, wide, deep and open to the south; Eel Pond, a hurricane hole in the center of the village; and Little Harbor, given over to U.S. Coast Guard government operations. Nobska Light is an active aid to navigation located at the division between Buzzards Bay and Vineyard Sound in Woods Hole on the southwestern tip of Cape Cod. You will pass it as you travel from Woods Hole to Martha's Vineyard.

The well-marked entrance to Woods Hole is located between The Knob, a prominent hillock on the northern point, and Gansett Point. Follow the channel carefully to avoid the rocks beyond its confines. A course outside red nun buoys "4," "6" or "8" will result in contact with a very hard bottom.

Woods Hole

Dockage/Moorings: Quissett Harbor Boatyard, Inc. usually has an open rental mooring. Simply attach to a vacant one, and the yard's skiff will eventually appear in the evening to collect the fee. There is no launch service but the pump-out boat will respond to a hoisted orange flag (the locally understood signal) or a request of the yard's launch driver or dockmaster. The proliferation of local boats and boatyard moorings has all but eliminated swing room in both the inner and outer harbors. Dropping a hook in either location is discouraged.

Woods Hole Passage

NAVIGATION: Use NOAA Charts 13229 and 13235. Refer to the Waterway Explorer (www.waterwayguide.com) and NOAA online charts for the most up-to-date information. NOAA Chart 13235 of Woods Hole is easier to read but not absolutely necessary if you have NOAA Chart 13229, showing the present buoys.

Tidal currents of 5 knots or more make Woods Hole Passage a strait to be entered with respect if the current is running at its maximum. Even with your boat under control, the short distance is inevitably an interesting piloting experience. A less taxing approach is to plan for the passage at slack tide, just as it is turning in your favor. Consult your tide tables and be sure to study a large-scale chart before you enter the passage.

Note that buoy numbers run from Vineyard Sound (between Nonamesset Shoal's green gong buoy "1" and Great Ledge's flashing red bell buoy "2") to Great Harbor's red nun buoy "8." If heading right through via The Strait, you can cut across south of Red Ledge

using the Broadway by turning northwest at flashing green buoy "5" and making for the southern green can buoy "1" and red nun buoy "2" pair. Alternatively, or if coming from Great Harbor itself, use the northern green can buoy "1" across from red nun buoy "8" to mark the turn west out to Buzzards Bay. Although the numbers reset at The Strait, the proper orientation of your course to the reds and greens does not change. In the language of "red-right-return," you are "returning" to Buzzards Bay throughout the passage.

The current rarely drags under the oversized buoys so laying a course is relatively simple. Keep in mind, however, that the current does not exactly follow the channel. At full flow you may find yourself pushed off course and straining to correct in an underpowered vessel. Except at slack water you will also encounter tidal swirls that require a firm hand at the helm to stay in mid-channel. Unless you have radar avoid this passage when visibility is poor. The northern channel is the better choice for low-powered craft. It takes plenty of thrust to negotiate the sharp turn in Broadway, the southern channel.

If passing from Buzzards Bay to Vineyard Sound in a strong favorable current, be very aware of red nun buoy "2" (in the area denoted as Broadway on NOAA Chart 13235), which marks the edge of the shoals extending from Red Ledge. It is not unusual to see vessels pushed east toward these shoals. The exit from Woods Hole to Vineyard Sound is wide and clearly marked. Great Ledge lays almost dead center. It is well marked and you can pass it on either side. The route west of Great

West Falmouth, Woods Hole, MA

WOODS HOLE AREA		Dockage				Supplies		Services					
		Largest Vessel Accomodated	VHF Channel Monitored / Working	Approach / Dockside Depth (reported)	Transient Slips / Total Slips	Floating Docks	Gas / Diesel	Groceries, Ice Marine Supplies, Snacks	Repairs: Hull, Engine, Propeller	Lift (tonnage), Crane, Rail	Courtesy Car, Laundry, Pool, Showers	Min / Max Amps	Pump-Out Station	Nearby: Grocery Store, Motel, Restaurant
1. Quissett Harbor Boatyard, Inc. 🖥 📶	(508) 548-0506	70	/	/	11.0/16.0	F		I	HEP	R			P	GMR
2. Woods Hole Yacht Club-PRIVATE	(508) 548-9205	65	/	/	6.0/6.0							S		
3. Woods Hole Marine	(508) 540-2402	50	9/	1/26	7.0/15.0			GIMS			30	S		GMR

🖥 Internet Access 📶 Wireless Internet Access onSpot Dockside WiFi Facility

See WaterwayGuide.com for current rates, fuel prices, website addresses, and other up-to-the-minute information. (Information in the table is provided by the facilities.)

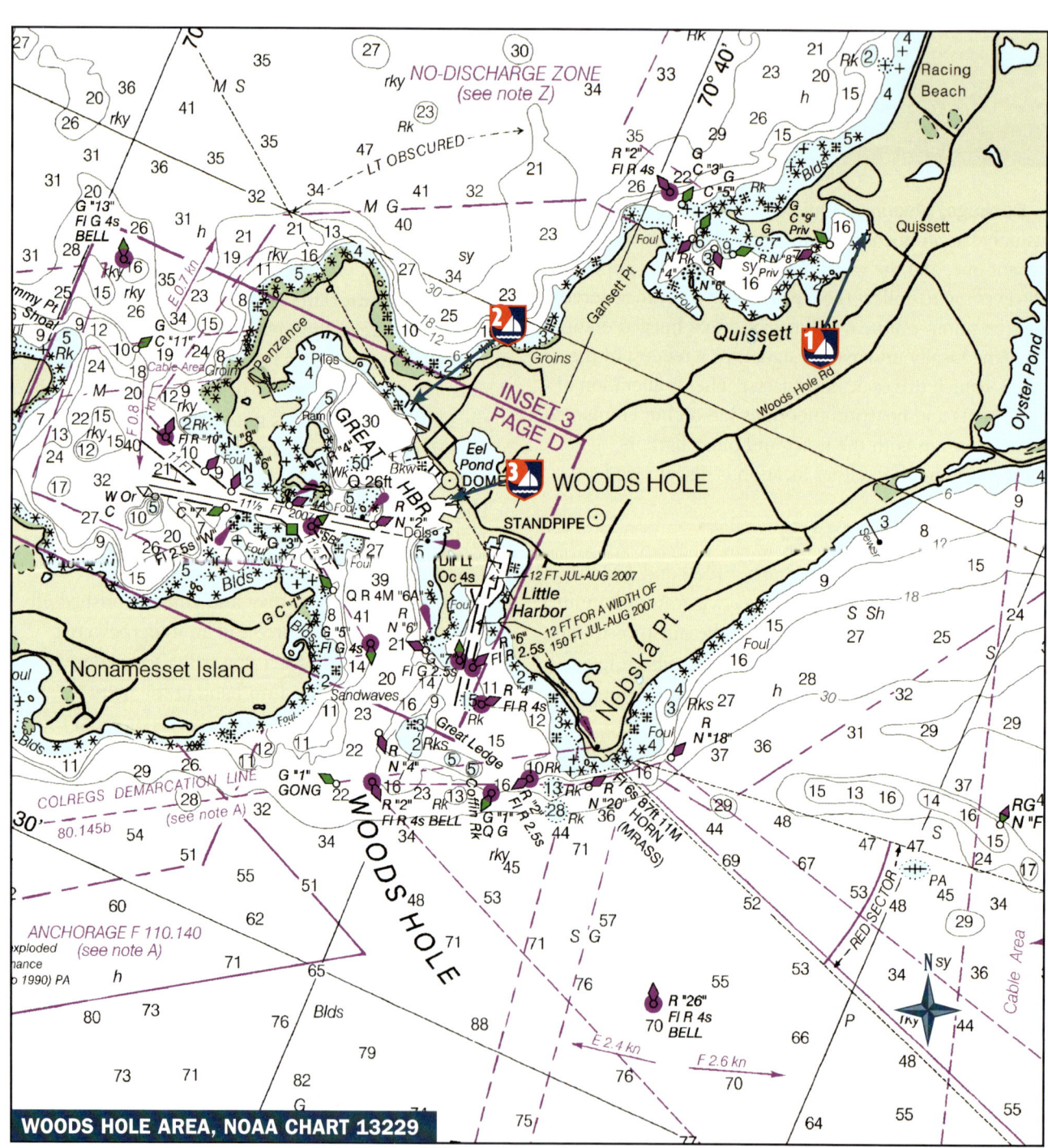

WOODS HOLE AREA, NOAA CHART 13229

Ledge, however, between flashing green buoy "1" and flashing red bell buoy "2" is less confined and easier to follow.

Dockage: To the west in Great Harbor, the private but friendly Woods Hole Yacht Club may accommodate visitors from other clubs; call ahead. This area is exposed to the south, however, with a considerable fetch for wave buildup. The most secure transient berth is at Woods Hole Marine in Eel Pond. Enter the pond through the channel leading under the **Eel Pond (Water Street) Bridge** (5-foot closed vertical clearance) in the center of the village. The bridge will open on signal from May 15 through June 14 and from September 16 through October 14, from 7:00 a.m. to 7:00 p.m. and from June 15 through September 15, from 6:00 a.m. to 9:00 p.m. on the hour and half-hour.

The marina docks are immediately to the west past the bridge. A slip is usually available but given the diminutive size of this facility (26 slips) and the limits to maneuverability in this pinched harbor, you should make a reservation and ask for specific directions. There may be transient moorings with a dinghy landing at the restaurant. A trolley bus leaves from out front for Falmouth every 30 minutes.

Anchorage: Great Harbor has limited anchorage space due to shoaling. Water depths as low as 5 feet MLW have been observed. Because of the southern exposure here, a spot as far as draft will permit into the cove at the northwest corner of the harbor is best. This area is about 1 mile from the village center but a motorized dinghy makes the ride under the Eel Pond Bridge (5-foot closed vertical clearance) to the dinghy landing reasonably convenient.

■ THE ELIZABETH ISLANDS

Four passages from Buzzards Bay into Vineyard Sound are located between the islands: Canapitsit Channel, Quicks Hole, Robinsons Hole and Woods Hole. Canapitsit Channel and Robinsons Hole can be used in calm weather with caution. Uncharted rocks and strong currents can make these areas unsafe for all but local mariners. Quicks Hole and Woods Hole are the safest, deepest and best-marked passages. When making a passage through Quicks Hole, consider a lunch or swim stop in an excellent anchorage on the southern side of the passage. There is good holding out of the channel and a sandy beach nearby.

The Elizabeth Islands extend about 14 nm off the southwestern end of Cape Cod and separate Vineyard Sound from Buzzards Bay. The islands are of varying sizes and–with the exception of Cuttyhunk and Penikese–are privately owned by the Forbes family. Mariners are permitted to land in certain areas if they observe the rules: leave dogs aboard, build fires only below the high-water mark, keep to the trails, do not try to bushwhack and clean up after your visit.

Cuttyhunk & Nashawena Islands

Westernmost of the island chain is Cuttyhunk, located within easy reach of South Shore and Cape Cod ports and offering a particularly attractive stopover en route to Martha's Vineyard and Nantucket heading east or Newport heading west. Nashawena Island is located between Cuttyhunk Island (to the west) and Quicks Hole (to the east).

Cuttyhunk Island is 2 miles long and less than 0.5 mile wide. There are about 50 official residents but most of them aren't year-round. Summer visitors are served by a population swollen to maybe 400. There are a few trucks for hauling but most people walk or ride golf carts. Walking along the paved road west leads to a dead end at the island's highest point with spectacular views of this eastward-running archipelago, its surrounding waters and the distinctive cliffs of Martha's Vineyard to the southeast.

Cuttyhunk Fishing Club (508-997-0858), which was founded in 1894, is almost exactly as it was when William Howard Taft accompanied President Theodore Roosevelt for a fishing trip here. Breakfast on the porch (or inside) comes with breathtaking views of the Elizabeth Islands to the east and Martha's Vineyard to the southeast. The Cuttyhunk Historical Society and Museum (508-984-4611) combines historical exhibits with displays of local art. Most of the island's other amenities are found in the weathered shacks along Fisherman's Dock.

M/V Cuttyhunk, the island's dependable ferry to and from New Bedford, is run by Cuttyhunk Ferry Company (508-992-0200) and is the lifeblood of the island. The Cuttyhunk Water Taxi Seahorse (508-789-3250) also runs between New Bedford and Cuttyhunk. All trips are scheduled by appointment.

Cuttyhunk Harbor, MA

WG

CUTTYHUNK POND		Dockage				Supplies		Services		
	Largest Vessel Accomodated	VHF Channel Monitored / Working	Approach / Dockside Depth (reported)	Transient Slips / Total Slips	Floating Docks	Gas / Diesel	Groceries, Ice Marine Supplies, Snacks	Repairs: Hull, Engine, Propeller	Lift (tonnage), Crane, Rail	Courtesy Car, Laundry, Pool, Showers	Min / Max Amps	Pump-Out Station	Nearby: Grocery Store, Motel, Restaurant

CUTTYHUNK POND		Dockage				Supplies		Services		
1. Cuttyhunk Marina	(508) 990-7578	110	9/10	50/85	10.0/8.0	GD	GIS		30/50	GMR

🖥 Internet Access 📶 Wireless Internet Access 📶onSpot Dockside WiFi Facility

See WaterwayGuide.com for current rates, fuel prices, website addresses, and other up-to-the-minute information. (Information in the table is provided by the facilities.)

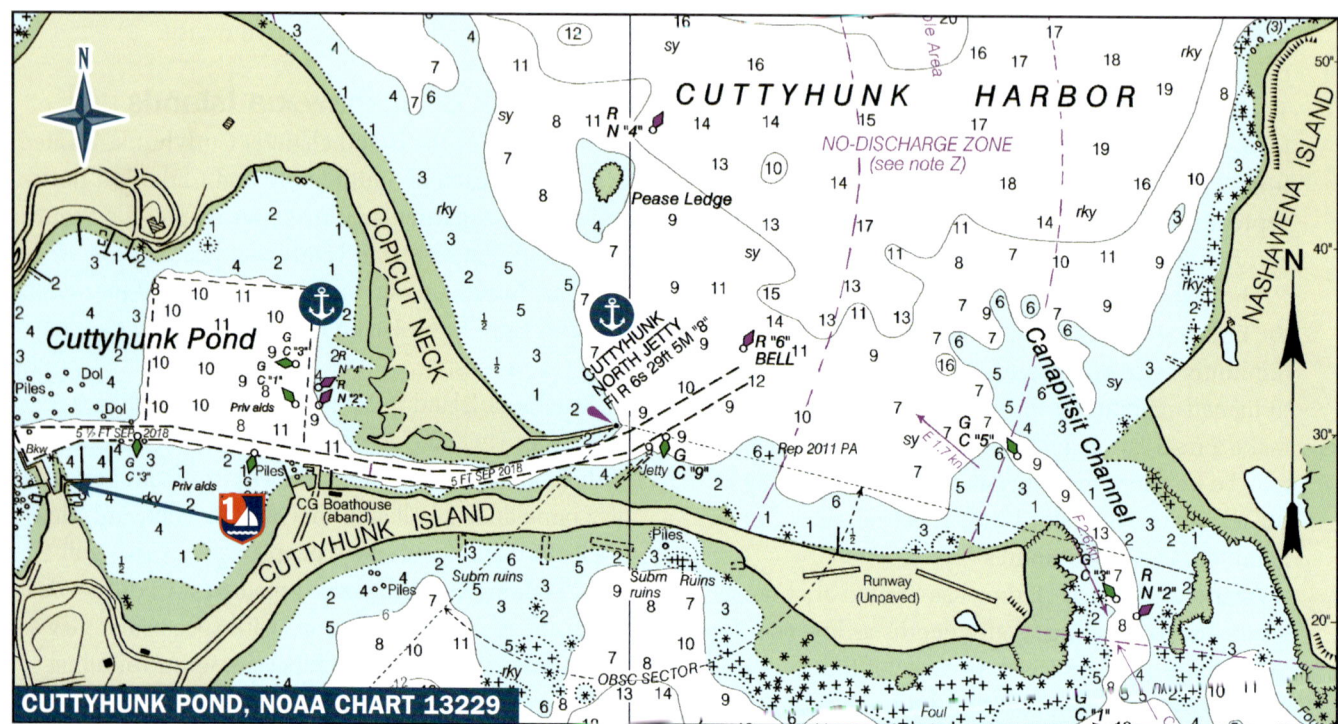

CUTTYHUNK POND, NOAA CHART 13229

NAVIGATION: Use NOAA Chart 13229. The Middle Ground red-and-green nun buoy "MG" marks the entrance to Cuttyhunk Harbor from the west. Leave red nun buoys "2W" and "4" well to your west on approach to avoid Whale Rock, marked by a white-and-orange obstruction buoy, and Pease Ledge, southwest of red nun buoy "4." Red bell buoy "6" is posted to the northwest of the entrance to the inner harbor channel jetty, which is marked by a 29-foot-high tower with a red flashing "8" to the north and green can buoy "9" to the south.

The approach from the east is marked red-and-white Morse (A) bell buoy "CH." On entering the outer harbor from the east leave red nun buoy "2E" to the north to avoid shoals that extend southward from Gull Island and leave green can buoy "1E" to the south to avoid the shoal working out from Knox Point. The channel into Cuttyhunk Pond was dredged in winter 2019-2020 to alleviate the encroaching shallows on each side. It is no longer nerve-wracking to pass another boat in the channel on the way into the Pond.

Cuttyhunk's recycling center accepts separated clear, green and brown glass, plastics, aluminum and other metals. Mixed trash can also be deposited here for a small fee. Public restrooms are next to the recycling trailers but there are no shower facilities. Token-operated laundry machines may be found at Pete's Place Rentals, just a short walk away. Cuttyhunk's fuel facility (both gasoline and diesel) is next to the abandoned red-roofed Coast Guard building.

Dockage/Moorings: Depths in the Cuttyhunk Pond are good but if both your keel and your fear of shoaling run deep, phone or radio ahead to the Cuttyhunk Harbormaster for specific advice. Those desiring a slip or fuel from the Cuttyhunk Marina should also call ahead to the Harbormaster (VHF Channel 09, 508-990-7578).

In the inner harbor, 50 closely spaced rental moorings (marked Town of Gosnold) fill the dredged anchorage north of the town marina. They are available on a first-come, first-served basis and you must supply your own bridle and chafing gear. An agile hand forward will be required to thread the eye of the unusual stand-up pennant on these moorings. A relatively short tether is advised in view of the limited swing room. (No more than two boats are permitted to raft.) The town launch will come by early in the evening to collect the mooring fee. All the mooring fields are likely to be filled to capacity on summer weekends and holidays.

Anchorage: Just inside Cuttyhunk Pond, a dredged, square mooring area is clearly charted and well marked. Anchorage inside the white corner markers, north of the town moorings, may be possible for early arrivals, although a thin grass cover makes holding less than ideal. Nevertheless, it does provide all-around protection in 7 to 10 feet MLW. The area outside the white buoys is not dredged and it shallows rapidly. The dinghy landing in the marina does get crowded so be prepared to clamber from dinghy to dinghy holding your long painter.

The outer harbor is a better bet with potentially good holding in a hard sand-mud mix and 12 to 17 feet MLW. Patches of grass can frustrate a clean anchor set in this area; however, and considering Buzzards Bay's well-earned reputation for strong onshore afternoon winds, be certain you are firmly secured before going ashore or retiring below. Anchoring throughout the outer harbor is possible but be aware that current becomes an issue closer to the Canapitsit Channel.

If you want to get away from the crowds at Cuttyhunk, it is possible to anchor on the northeast side of Nashawena Island adjacent to Quicks Hole Passage. Here you will find at least 8 feet MLW with excellent holding in sand. This is open to the north and southeast and should only be attempted in settled weather. There are no services here.

Naushon Island

Naushon Trust owns Naushon Island and most of the land is clearly posted against trespassing but cruising boats are welcome in peaceful Hadley Harbor, a totally protected natural refuge, easily accessible from Buzzards Bay and located directly across from Woods Hole.

NAVIGATION: Use NOAA Chart 13229. Naushon Island is located between Cuttyhunk to the south and Woods Hole to the north. To reach Hadley Harbor eschew the open-looking but unmarked northern side for the narrow passage just off the northwestern corner of Nonamesset Island. The red nun buoy "2" and green can buoy "3" lead you well south of the privately maintained white-and-brown daybeacon marking an uncovering shoal. Follow Nonamesset Island as it curves south through the pinch as it passes eastward of Bull Island. The Inner Harbor widens as it turns west, then south, around Goats Neck.

Moorings/Anchorage: As you cruise the Vineyard Sound side of Naushon Island, you can anchor in

Tarpaulin Cove when weather permits. The cove has wooded shores and a fine beach but it is open to the south and east. The best protection is in the southwestern corner, due north of the 78-foot-high lighthouse, in about 11 feet MLW (about 150 to 200 yards south-southwest of green can buoy "1"). The scene ashore is reminiscent of 18th-century America–a classic seaside farmhouse with various outbuildings, rambling stonewalls and deserted beaches. Tarpaulin Cove can easily accommodate 75 large boats without crowding and is often used by rallies and associations traveling together.

On the Buzzards Bay side of Naushon Island, Kettle Cove makes a good daytime stop. It is open to wind from the west through the north but on a fine day with a southwesterly breeze, you can drop the hook, have lunch and swim from the beach. Here you will find 7 to 12 feet MLW with good holding in sand.

The far end of the Hadley Harbor is crowded with moorings (complimentary on a first-come, first-served basis) but excellent anchorage is available north of the private landing and boathouses between Bull Island and Goats Neck. There is at least 11 feet MLW and excellent holding in soft mud with all-around protection. Some shoals and rocks are located close to the shore so skippers should feel their way cautiously and make anchoring allowances for shifting winds during the evening. The harbor is so popular that those planning to stay overnight should arrive early in the afternoon. Keep a lookout for latecomers who might anchor indiscriminately.

Anchorage should be avoided in any place where the channel is constricted. The Naushon Ferry, bringing freight and passengers from Woods Hole, needs plenty of room to maneuver.

Public access is permitted on tiny Bull Island, where picnic grounds are maintained during the season. Just take your dinghy to the small landing on the southeast corner of the island. Dogs should be kept on leashes and barbecue fires tended responsibly. Signs warn of ticks and danger of Lyme disease; be sure to apply your insect repellent liberally.

East of Hadley Harbor proper and north of Nonamesset Island is a large area suitable for anchorage in southwesterly breezes but it is untenable in northerlies of 20 knots or more. Seas build in the long fetch down the Cape Cod shore and make this area uncomfortable and unsafe. There is at least 7 feet MLW fairly close to shore and good holding in sand and mud.

■ NEXT STOP

Coming up next is the southern shore of Cape Cod, long a popular summer resort for its good beaches and pleasing towns. It is the easternmost point of Massachusetts.

Nantucket Sound, MA

■ FALMOUTH TO STAGE HARBOR

Nantucket Sound is an exciting and tempestuous body of water, due to its well-marked shoals, and it is a fabulous destination that can be traveled as though it's a very, very large bay. A circular voyage through its ports and anchorages begins with the natural beauty of the Elizabeth Islands, slips along Cape Cod's south shore harbors with plenty of marinas, and turns for Nantucket at Hyannis Port, the last of the deep-draft harbors on the southern coast. Heading farther east is for shoal-draft boats only. The prevailing southwesterlies give a close reach from Hyannis Port to the fabulous island of Nantucket and then a beam reach back northwest to Martha's Vineyard. These islands are a favored cruising grounds for thousands of recreational boaters. The best-known harbors grow ever more congested each season, while lesser-known ports are continually being "discovered" by those who seek refuge from the crowds. The discovery of hidden coves and harbors is one of the many joys of cruising these waters.

Falmouth

Falmouth is not only a good base for cruising the islands, it also has one of Cape Cod's best harbors with at least 8-foot MLW depths and every conceivable amenity. It is thoroughly protected and easy to enter. At the head of the harbor on the eastern side the *Island Queen* passenger ferry will take you to Oak Bluffs on Martha's Vineyard. Band concerts in Falmouth are on the western side of the marine park and provide entertainment on Thursday evenings during the summer. In town, the seasonal bustle of a seaside resort village awaits you. Houses built by ship owners and sea captains in the 18th and 19th centuries surround the traditional village green. Accommodations and dining possibilities are almost unlimited.

Although the town of Falmouth is located about 1 mile away, most of the essentials for provisioning and reviving water-weary crews are close to the marinas. A market, West Marine and liquor store are all on the west side of Scranton Ave., across from the Town Marina harbormaster's office. A self-service laundry is a 5-minute walk north. Farther along, at the end of Scranton Ave. and to the right, a fair-sized mall boasts chain stores and fast-food restaurants.

NAVIGATION: Use NOAA Chart 13229. Flashing red bell buoy "16," about 0.50 mile offshore, marks the approach to the breakwater entrance. The entrance is straightforward, although narrow, with 6-foot MLW depths that are relatively consistent in the channel and throughout the dredged harbor. Past the entrance the harbor broadens slightly and both banks are lined with marine facilities and amenities. This is a No-Discharge Zone and a pump-out station is located at the town dock. There is no room for anchoring here.

W G

Falmouth Harbor, MA

FALMOUTH		Largest Vessel Accommodated	VHF Channel Monitored / Working	Transient Slips / Total Slips	Approach / Dockside Depth (reported)	Floating Docks	Gas / Diesel	Groceries, Ice, Marine Supplies, Snacks	Repairs: Hull, Engine, Propeller	Lift (tonnage) Crane, Rail	Min / Max Amps	Courtesy Car, Laundry, Pool, Showers	Pump-Out Station	Nearby: Grocery Store, Motel, Restaurant
				Dockage			**Supplies**		**Services**					
1. Falmouth Marine & Yachting Center	(508) 548-4600	70	9/	23/23	10.0/10.0	F	GD	I	HEP	L70	30/50	S	P	G
2. Falmouth Town Marina	(508) 457-2550	200	16/9	20/100	9.0/6.0	F					30/100	S	P	GMR
3. Pier 37	(508) 388-7573	32	9/	/	10.0/6.0	F	G	IM	HEP					GMR
4. North Marine	(508) 457-7000	50	/	/	8.0/6.0	F	GD	IM	HEP	L,C,R				GMR
5. East Marine	(508) 540-3611	50	16/9	/15	10.0/10.0		GD	IM		L35	30/100	S		GMR
6. MacDougalls' Cape Cod Marine Service ☐ WiFi	(508) 548-3146	120	9/71	10/110	10.0/10.0	F	GD	IM	HEP	L75,C	30/100	LS	P	GMR

☐ Internet Access   WiFi Wireless Internet Access   onSpot Dockside WiFi Facility

See WaterwayGuide.com for current rates, fuel prices, website addresses, and other up-to-the-minute information. (Information in the table is provided by the facilities.)

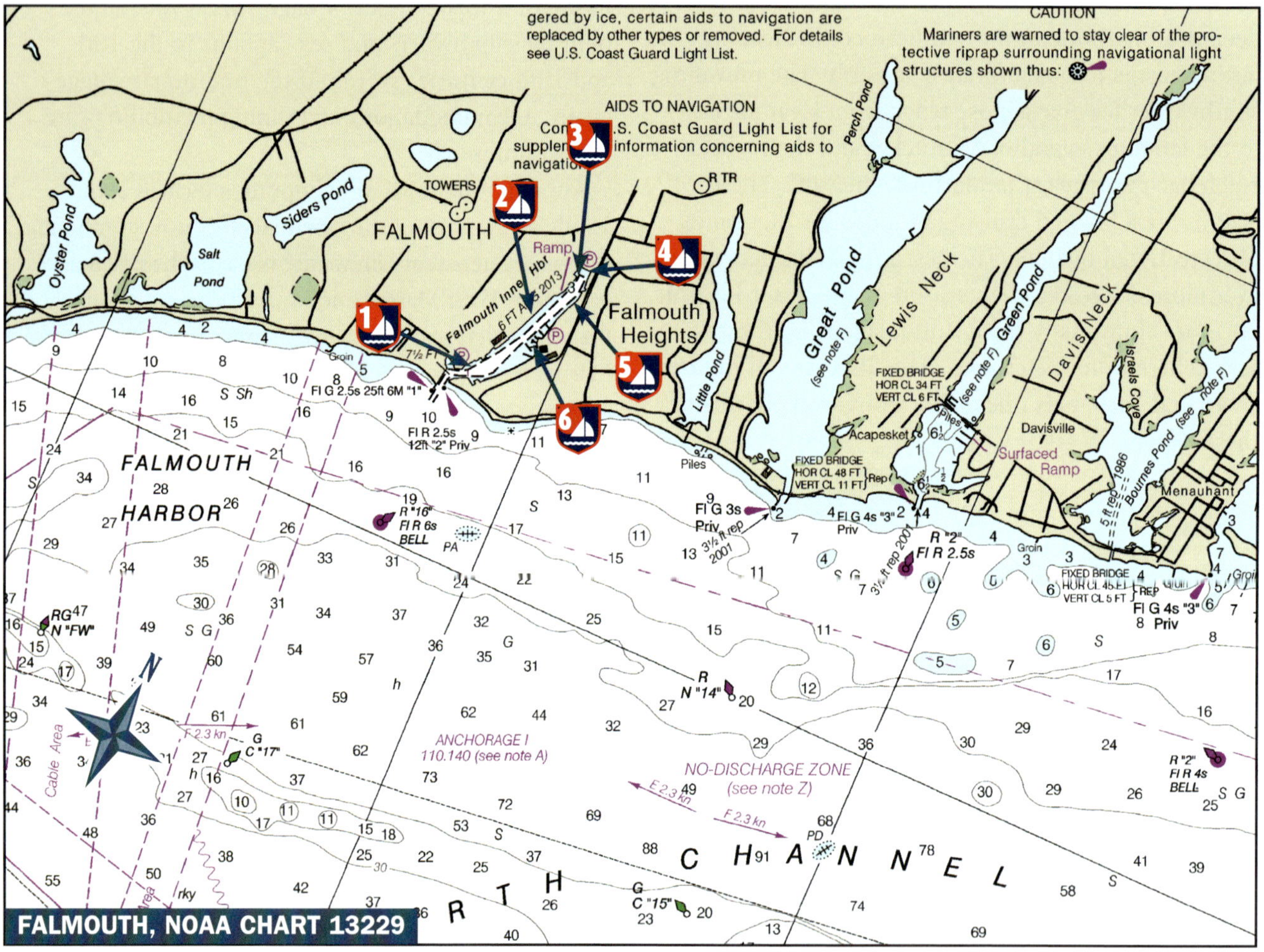

gered by ice, certain aids to navigation are replaced by other types or removed. For details see U.S. Coast Guard Light List.

AIDS TO NAVIGATION
Con... U.S. Coast Guard Light List for suppl... information concerning aids to navigation

CAUTION
Mariners are warned to stay clear of the protective riprap surrounding navigational light structures shown thus:

FALMOUTH

FALMOUTH HARBOR

Oyster Pond · Siders Pond · Salt Pond · TOWERS · Falmouth Inner Hbr · Falmouth Heights · Perch Pond · Great Pond · Lewis Neck · Green Pond · Davis Neck · Little Pond · Acapesket · Davisville · Surfaced Ramp · Bournes Pond · Menauhant

ANCHORAGE I
110.140 (see note A)

NO-DISCHARGE ZONE
(see note Z)

CHANNEL

Cable Area

FALMOUTH, NOAA CHART 13229

Falmouth Harbor

Dockage/Moorings: Marine facilities line the Falmouth Inner Harbor with slips and moorings. The Flying Bridge Restaurant (508-548-2700) has an easy-access fuel dock (at the Mobil sign) and several small finger piers for restaurant patrons. Falmouth Town Marina has berths perpendicular to the seawall and space for transients.

MacDougalls' Cape Cod Marine Service on the western shore of the harbor has extensive marine amenities. They offer both moorings and slips and have a large on-site chandlery and retail supply store, as well as specialty shops for installations, custom fabrications, sailmaking and canvas repairs. They rebuild and re-power gas and diesel engines and have the largest paint booth facility on Cape Cod.

Waquoit Bay

Green Pond, 2 nm east of Falmouth (past Great Pond), is a quiet and peaceful little harbor with a marina (private), town dock and boats at private moorings. Anchoring is not allowed. About 3 miles east of Green Pond is the narrow entrance to Waquoit Bay, which

is home to hundreds of boats and a better bet for accommodations and amenities.

NAVIGATION: Use NOAA Chart 13229. The well-marked entrance to Waquoit Bay is between Washburn Island and Dead Neck (South Cape Beach). Controlling depth in Waquoit Bay is 4 feet MLW, and you can leave the marked channel to make a side trip to the mouths of the Great and Little Rivers on the eastern shore. Approach the southwestern tip of Seconsett Island with caution as there are shoals extending from this point into Waquoit Bay.

When returning to Nantucket Sound you can try an alternate route, if you have shallow draft. Head southwest down the Seapit and Childs Rivers to Eel Pond and through the Menauhant jetties. Depths at the jetties can be as shallow as 2 feet MLW so go on a rising tide. Any aids to navigation are privately set and maintained; use caution.

Dockage: Off the northernmost tip of Washburn Island is a channel marker for the Seapit River. Head to the southwest on the river to Seapit Point, then round the point and head north for Bosun's East Falmouth

Falmouth Harbor, MA

		Largest Vessel Accommodated	VHF Channel Monitored / Working	Transient Slips / Total Slips	Approach / Dockside Depth (reported)	Floating Docks	Gas / Diesel	Groceries, Ice, Marine Supplies, Snacks	Repairs: Hull, Engine, Propeller	Lift (tonnage), Crane, Rail	Min / Max Amps	Courtesy Car, Laundry, Pool, Showers	Pump-Out Station	Nearby: Grocery Store, Motel, Restaurant
GREEN POND					**Dockage**			**Supplies**			**Services**			
1. Green Pond Marina - PRIVATE	(508) 457-9283		/	/67	4.0/4.0						30		P	
WAQUOIT BAY														
2. Bosun's East Falmouth Marina [WiFi]	(508) 548-2216	45	16/9	1/36	4.0/4.0		GD	IM	HE	R	30	S	P	R
POPPONESSET BAY, COTUIT BAY														
3. Bosun's Mashpee Neck Marina	(508) 477-4626		/	/	/	F	G	M	HEP	L				
4. Cotuit Town Dock	(508) 790-6245	50	/	/	5.0/5.0		G	G			30			G
OSTERVILLE														
5. Corey Yacht Docks	(617) 633-1151	80	9/	4/4	8.0/9.0						30/100	S		GMR
6. Oyster Harbors Marine	(508) 428-2017	110	9/79	5/110	6.0/6.0	F	GD	IMS	HEP	L75	30/50	S	P	GR
7. Nauticus Marina	(508) 428-4537	120	16/9	/5	7.0/8.0	F					30/100	S		GR
8. Crosby Yacht Yard Inc. [Internet] [WiFi]	(508) 428-6900	95	9/	10/125	6.0/5.0	F	GD	IMS	HEP	L70,R	30/50	S	P	R

☐ Internet Access   [WiFi] Wireless Internet Access   onSpot Dockside WiFi Facility

See WaterwayGuide.com for current rates, fuel prices, website addresses, and other up-to-the-minute information. (Information in the table is provided by the facilities.)

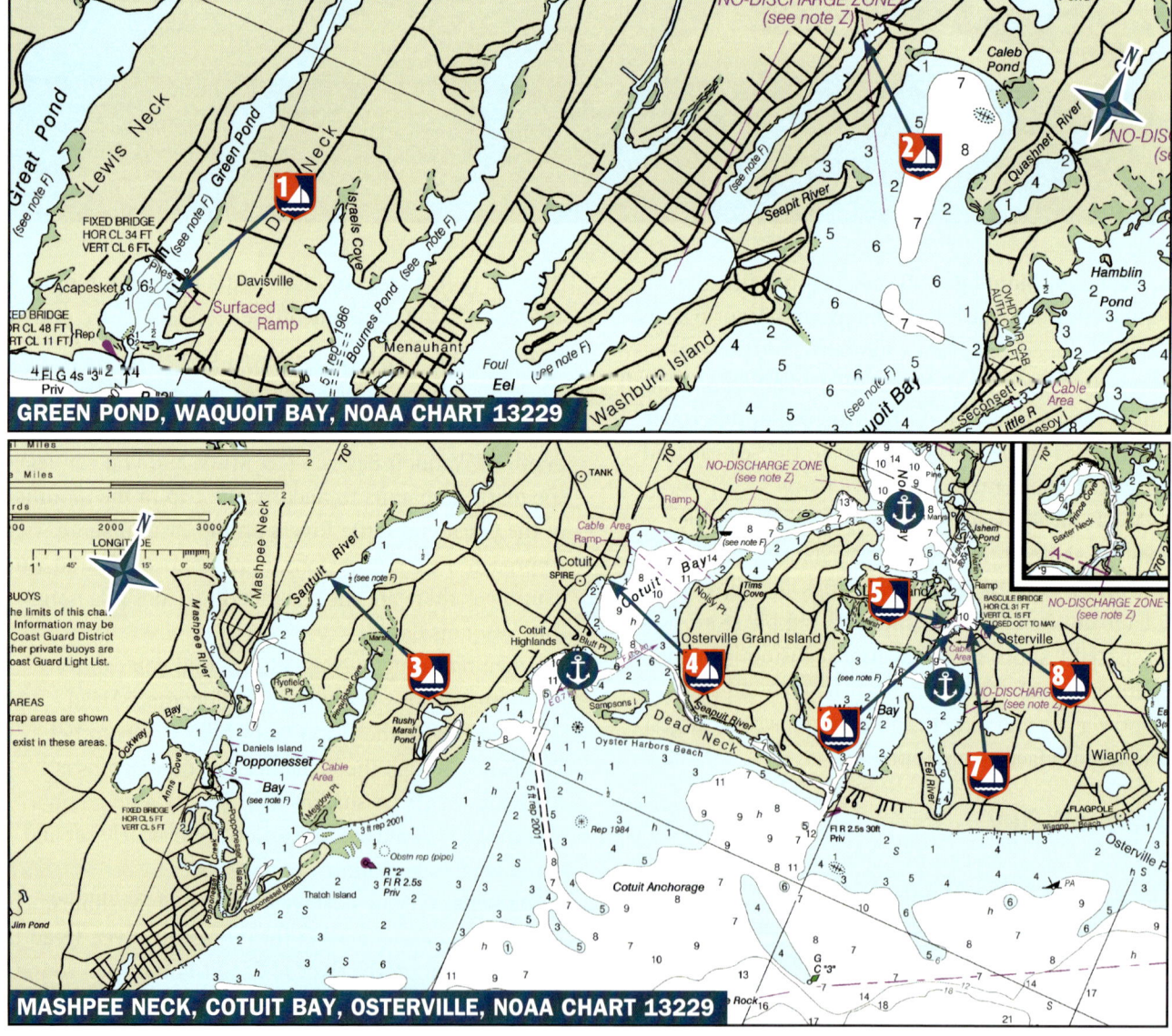

GREEN POND, WAQUOIT BAY, NOAA CHART 13229

MASHPEE NECK, COTUIT BAY, OSTERVILLE, NOAA CHART 13229

Quissett Harbor

Marina on the western shore. They sell all fuels and have transient space. They report 4-foot MLW approach and dockside depths.

Cotuit Bay

The Village of Cotuit is within walking distance of the town dock. The east side of Cotuit Bay is all Osterville Grand Island. Inside Cotuit Bay is a big, almost circular area with a well-buoyed, continuous waterway leading through three bays and a narrow river. Each offers coves and creeks for gunkholing, good beaches, fine anchorages, ample yacht amenities and charming towns. The complete landlocked circuit can be made without leaving sheltered water, although a boat drawing 5 feet or less has a better chance of a successful circuit of Osterville Island. The Eel River, in the southeastern corner of West Bay, is also worth a dinghy trip but it shoals at the entrance.

NAVIGATION: Use NOAA Chart 13229. Between Popponesset Beach and Wianno Beach on Nantucket Sound, two buoyed channels lead inland to one of the most beautiful harbor complexes on the south shore. Westernmost is the 4-foot MLW channel to Cotuit and Cotuit Bay. To reach Cotuit follow the long, dredged channel that leads for more than 1 mile through 1- and 2-foot MLW shoals that encroach closely on either side.

The channel makes an S-curve around the pointing finger of Sampsons Island and then around Bluff Point. Stay well off the point. The narrow channel lies close to the shore of Sampsons Island and is somewhat parallel to it until the small black buoy (privately maintained). Most vessels will need to enter Cotuit on a rising tide.

North Bay is the connecting link between Cotuit and West Bays and the entrance to delightful Prince Cove. From Cotuit Bay follow the buoyed passage from the deeper northern end (7 to 10 feet MLW) that leads past Point Isabella into North Bay. According to local authorities, this channel is good for 5 feet MLW. From North Bay pass through the **West Bay Bridge** (15-foot closed vertical clearance), which connects Osterville on the east shore with Little Island and Osterville. The bridge opens on signal from May 1 through June 15 and from October 1 through October 31, from 8:00 a.m. to 6:00 p.m.; and from June 16 through September 30, from 7:00 a.m. to 9:00

GOIN' ASHORE

HYANNIS, MA

Hyannis grew into a busy fishing and trade port in the 1800s and Congress authorized building of a lighthouse at South Hyannis in 1848. (The light was discontinued in 1929.) Today, Hyannis is the largest community on Cape Cod. For cruisers, the town's attractions are close at hand, just a little more than 1 mile away from the waterfront. The beaches are very plentiful and popular. Kalmus Beach has great wind and surf for windsurfers, while Veterans Beach is a great family beach and is the home of historical shrines honoring John F. Kennedy and the Korean War Memorial. Keyes Beach is known for beautiful sand and has a snack bar and picnic tables.

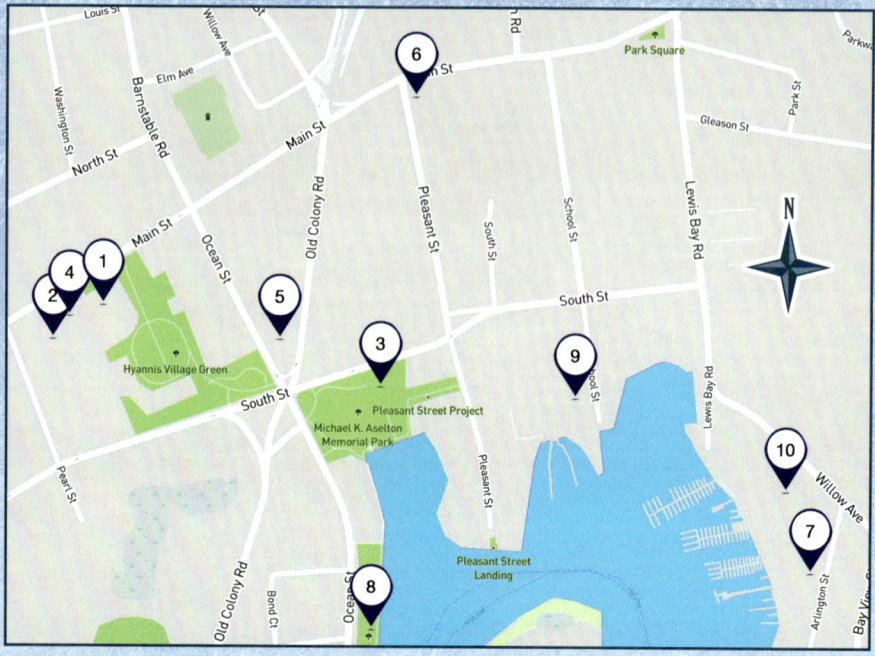

SERVICES

1. Hyannis Post Office
385 Main St. (508-775-7344)

2. Hyannis Public Library
401 Main St. (508-775-2280)

ATTRACTIONS

3. Cape Cod Maritime Museum
Open mid-March to mid-December with displays and programs for "celebrating, preserving and interpreting Cape Cod's maritime past, present and future" at 135 South St. (508-775-1723).

4. John F. Kennedy Hyannis Museum
Showcases the life of John F. Kennedy with a focus on his time spent in the Hyannis area (397 Main St., 508-790-3077).

SHOPPING

5. Ocean St. Market
Limited groceries and provisions (50 Ocean St., 774-552-3912).

6. Bradford's Ace Hardware
Chain hardware store with home supplies and tools at 231 Main St. (508-775-0620).

7. Marina Parts Plus
Discounted marine parts at 21 Arlington St. (online only/no local pickup).

MARINAS

8. Bismore Park Marina
1189 Phinney Ln. (508-790-6273)

9. Dockside Marina
145 School St. (508-680-3293)

10. Hyannis Marina
1 Willow St. (508-790-4000)

p.m. At all other times from May 1 through October 31, the draw shall open on signal if at least a 4-hour advance notice is given by calling the number posted at the bridge.

The final link in the Cotuit–North–West Bays circuit is Seapuit River, west of the entrance to West Bay from Nantucket Sound. From West Bay it leads between the dunes of Dead Neck (landing is prohibited) and the southern shore of Osterville Grand Island. The NOAA chart shows a shoal area for quite a distance behind Dead Neck but locals claim that the controlling depth is 4 feet MLW. Refer to the Waterway Explorer (www.waterwayguide.com) and NOAA online charts for the most up-to-date information.

An alternate route into this area is through West Bay. The narrow, dredged approach to West Bay from Nantucket Sound is deep, well-marked and has a breakwater on both sides. Once inside, the first opening to the west leads to Cotuit Bay via Seapuit River and the main 6-foot MLW channel runs northward up West Bay between shoals.

Dockage/Moorings: On the west shore of Cotuit Bay, you can tie up at the Cotuit Town Dock for 30 minutes or rent a mooring and dinghy ashore. Marinas, fuel docks and boat yards are clustered north of the West Bay Bridge between Oysterville and Little Island. Most of the West Bay activity is around the bridge providing easy provisioning, a library, shopping and restaurants.

The well-regarded Crosby Yacht Yard Inc. has been in business since 1850 and offer a full range of boat and marine services as well as seasonal and transient dockage and moorings, repairs, restoration and maintenance.

Anchorage: You can drop the hook in the northeastern corner of West Bay in at least 8 feet MLW with good holding in mud and all-around protection. One of the best anchorages around is in North Bay, where you will find 7 to 10 feet MLW with excellent holding in mud and all-around protection. (Prince Cove is best investigated by dinghy due to its narrow, hard-to-negotiate entry.)

At the Cotuit Bay entrance, tuck behind Sampsons Island in at least 7 feet MLW with good holding in sand and mud. This is somewhat exposed to the northeast. Cotuit Town Dock has a dinghy landing.

Hyannis

Hyannis was settled by a handful of Puritans well over 400 years ago and their surnames still figure prominently in the town's grand list. But not all of the area's famous residents came early. The Kennedys are an example, having arrived in 1926.

For cruisers the town's attractions are close at hand, just a little more than 1 mile away from the waterfront. (Guests in a hurry can use the Hyannis Marina courtesy vans or ride the Cape Cod Trolley.) At the harbor, the Cape Cod Maritime Museum (135 South St., 508-775-1723) is open mid-March to mid-December with displays and programs for "celebrating, preserving and interpreting Cape Cod's maritime past, present and future." History buffs will enjoy a visit to the JFK Museum (397 Main St., 508-790-3077), showcasing the life of John F. Kennedy, with a focus on his time spent in the Hyannis area.

Hyannis Harbor is one of the most popular areas with boaters on Cape Cod. The harbor is deep and easy to enter with summer traffic of all sorts–yachts under sail, commercial vessels, charter fishing and "head boats," ferries from Martha's Vineyard and Nantucket, as well as recreational boats of all kinds. Hyannis acts as the hub of Cape Cod offering cruisers a wide range of services from health (Cape Cod Hospital) and retail (Cape Cod Mall) to cultural (Cape Cod Maritime Museum) and transportation (Barnstable Municipal Airport, Cape Cod Regional Transit Authority and ferry service to the islands).

NAVIGATION: Use NOAA Chart 13229. The most straightforward approach to Hyannis from the west is through the buoyed channel (respecting the buoys marking numerous rocks and ledges on approach from east or west). Following the lead of the red and white Morse (A) "HH" bell buoy, head north toward the Hyannis breakwater. Once inside you can see the Kennedy compound, which faces the harbor and Nantucket Sound. From the breakwater east, the marked channel begins its long sweep through Lewis Bay toward Harbor Bluff. On approach the channel angles northeast on a direct course to Hyannis' busy inner harbor, where access to marine services and town amenities is assured. This harbor routinely services large megayachts with drafts exceeding 10 feet.

Hyannis Harbor, MA

HYANNIS		Dockage					Supplies		Services					
		Largest Vessel Accomodated	VHF Channel Monitored / Working	Transient Slips / Total Slips	Approach / Dockside Depth (reported)	Floating Docks	Gas / Diesel	Groceries, Ice, Marine Supplies, Snacks	Repairs: Hull, Engine, Propeller	Lift (tonnage), Crane, Rail	Min / Max Amps	Courtesy Car, Laundry, Pool, Showers	Pump-Out Station	Nearby: Grocery Store, Motel, Restaurant
1. Hyannis Yacht Club	(508) 778-6100	140	69/	/24	10.0/8.0			GIM			30	S		GR
2. Bismore Park Marina	(508) 790-6273	75	16/9	2/24	12.0/8.0						50		P	GMR
3. Dockside Marina WiFi	(508) 680-3293	150	9/72	/23	15.0/14.0	F		I		L50	30/50	LS		R
4. Hyannis Marina □ WiFi	**(508) 790-4000**	200	9/72	25/180	16.0/16.0	F	GD	GIMS	HEP	L,C	30/100	CLPS	P	GMR

□ Internet Access WiFi Wireless Internet Access onSpot Dockside WiFi Facility

See WaterwayGuide.com for current rates, fuel prices, website addresses, and other up-to-the-minute information. (Information in the table is provided by the facilities.)

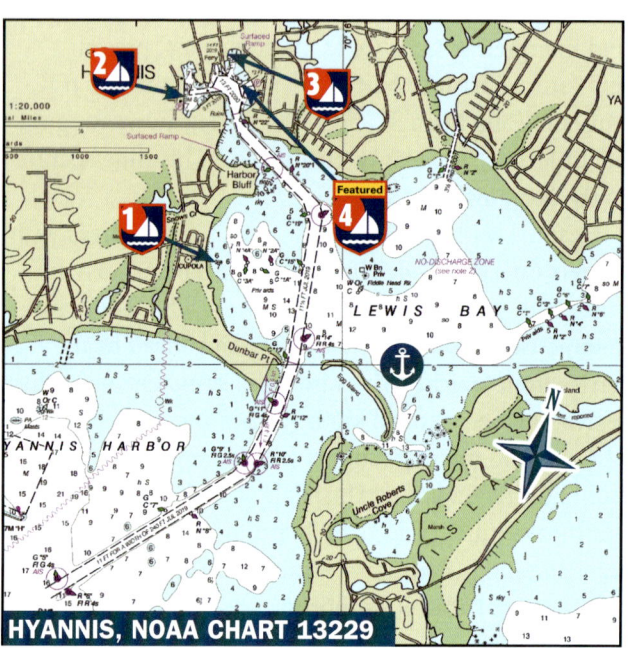

HYANNIS, NOAA CHART 13229

Winter Snow Tip

Even if your boat is self-bailing, fresh snow won't drain out of the scuppers and can sink a moored boat. Dry, fluffy snow can weigh more than 5 pounds per cubic foot while a wet snow can weigh 15 pounds or more. Plan to shovel after a snow fall so drains and through-hull fittings are not submerged and your boat stays afloat. Monitor winter storms as you would hurricanes and, if practical, arrange to haul out if a severe snowstorm threatens your area. If your boat is on land already, move it from under any roof that might be questionable, as roof collapses in covered slips are also responsible for sinkings.

Lewis Bay

Harbor Bluff

Hyannis Marina

Hyannis

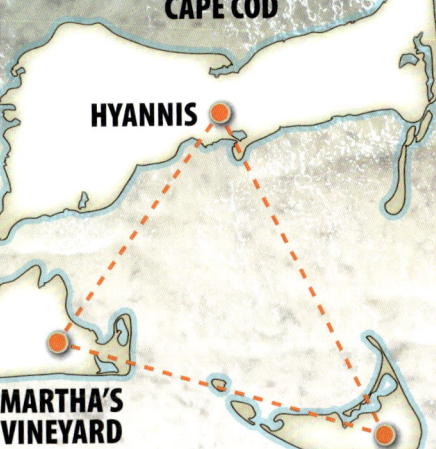

Harwich Port, MA

			Dockage				Supplies				Services			
		Largest Vessel Accommodated	VHF Channel Monitored / Working	Transient Slips / Total Slips	Approach / Dockside Depth (reported)	Floating Docks	Gas / Diesel	Groceries, Ice, Marine Supplies, Snacks	Repairs: Hull, Engine, Propeller	Lift (tonnage), Crane, Rail	Min / Max Amps	Courtesy Car, Laundry, Pool, Showers	Pump-Out Station	Nearby: Grocery Store, Motel, Restaurant
HARWICH PORT AREA														
1. Allen Harbor Marine Service, Inc.	(508) 430-6008	50	68/	3/52	6.0/6.0	F	GD	IMS	HEP	L9	30/50		P	GR
2. Allen Harbor Yacht Club-PRIVATE	(508) 432-9774	55	9/	/	6.0/4.0	F	GD	I				S	P	R
3. Saquatucket Municipal Marina	(508) 430-7532	55	68/66	10/195	6.0/8.0	F	GD	I			30/50	LS	P	GMR
BASS RIVER														
4. Ship Shops Inc. ☐	(508) 398-2256	50	/	1/40	6.0/6.0		GD	IM	EP	L7	30			GMR
5. Bass River Marina ☐ WiFi	(508) 394-8341	40	71/	20/160	10.0/10.0	F	G	IMS	HEP	L15,C	30/50	S	P	R

☐ Internet Access   WiFi Wireless Internet Access   onSpot Dockside WiFi Facility
See WaterwayGuide.com for current rates, fuel prices, website addresses, and other up-to-the-minute information. (Information in the table is provided by the facilities.)

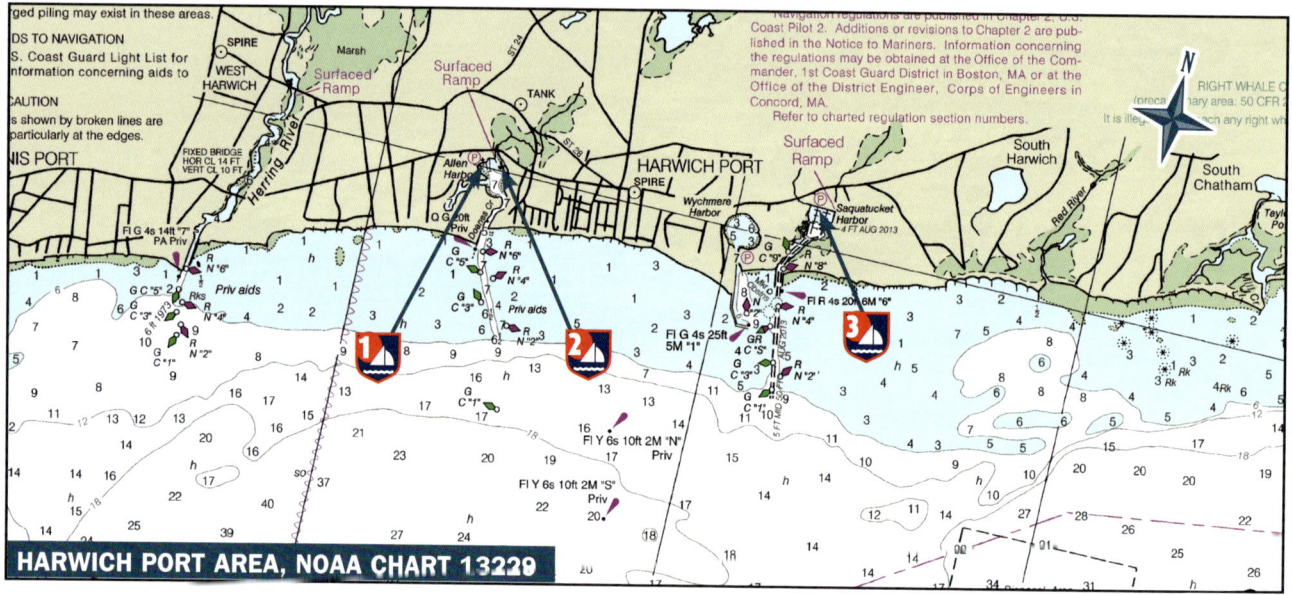

HARWICH PORT AREA, NOAA CHART 13229

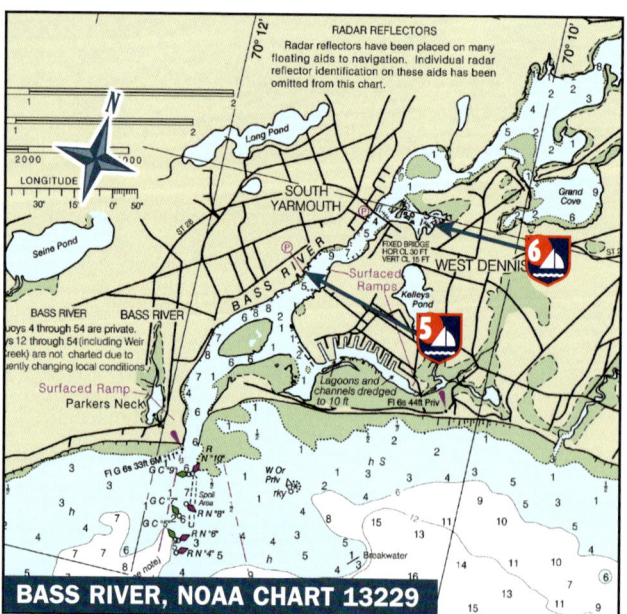

BASS RIVER, NOAA CHART 13229

Dockage: On entering Lewis Bay, you will first see the Hyannis Yacht Club, west of the channel behind Dunbar Point. They may be able to accommodate you; call ahead. At the inner harbor, and within the protection of Harbor Bluff, are three facilities: Bismore Park Marina is west, Dockside Marina is north and Hyannis Marina is on the eastern side of the bay.

Your best bet for a slip is at the large and modern Hyannis Marina, which can accommodate everything from small motorboats to deep-draft sailboats and megayachts up to 200 feet in length. Hyannis is beautiful, well-protected and a natural deep-water harbor. The marina is a gorgeous resort in a club-like setting with a full-capability service and repair yard. There are floating docks with all the usual amenities, a harborside pool (with a poolside cabana), a full-menu restaurant and a marine store and gift shop.

Anchorage: Cruisers that prefer anchoring will find 7 to 8 feet MLW with good holding in mud northeast of crescent-shaped Egg Island in Lewis Bay. The remainder of Lewis Bay is suitable in settled weather but open to the southwest. This isn't on the "main drag" but provides protection and its quiet.

East to Stage Harbor

One of Cape Cod's prettiest rivers and a popular cruising area for small boats, the long, winding Bass River loops lazily inland toward the towns of South Yarmouth and West Dennis. Attractive houses, old windmills, several restaurants, hotels, motels, good-looking yachts and fine marinas are above and below the fixed 15-foot bridge between South Yarmouth and West Dennis.

Continuing east, Harwich Port has a colorful 300-year history as a shipbuilding, whaling and cod fishing center. The three good harbors (Allen, Wychmere and Saquatucket) are maintained to 6 feet MLW. Fine beaches remain and have been joined by good restaurants and full-service amenities.

Large, protected Stage Harbor is the last port on the south side of Cape Cod and the logical starting point for boats making the outside run around the hook to Provincetown. As much a fishing port as a yacht harbor, Stage Harbor has appealing creeks and coves and good boating amenities and anchorages.

NAVIGATION: Use NOAA Chart 13229. If you plan to stop in the Bass River, flashing red bell buoy "2"

marks the beginning of the approach. The approach to the jettied entrance across Dogfish Bar is narrow and depths fluctuate from about 7 to 3.5 feet MLW, depending on when it was last dredged and the amount of silting since. Enter only on a rising tide. A 15-foot fixed vertical clearance bridge connects West Dennis and South Yarmouth north of red nun "22."

Allen Harbor, to the west of Harwich Port, is so well protected that the entrance is hard to find, and you will not see the harbor until the last turn of Doanes Creek. Privately maintained buoys lead you to the 20-foot tall, quick-flashing unnumbered green at the end of the breakwater and into Doanes Creek, which has 6-foot MLW depths.

When approaching Chatham Roads, watch for fish weirs on the northwestern side and along the edge of shallows on the Martha's Vineyard side of Monomoy Island. Very shoal-draft boats, aided by local knowledge, use the cut between Morris Island and Monomoy Island to reach Chatham Harbor. Otherwise, you must circumnavigate Monomoy Island to reach this shoaling passage inside the barrier beach. Even this route, however, calls for caution and local knowledge of the shoals.

The Army Corps of Engineers advises that this is a very dynamic area that is subject to constantly shifting shoals and that boaters should seek local knowledge before using the channel. The Outermost Harbor area was last dredged in June of 2019 but the northern harbor channel dredging is tied up in legal challenges

Bass River

Stage Harbor, MA

CHATHAM		VHF Channel Monitored / Working / Largest Vessel Accommodated	Dockage				Supplies		Services					
		Largest Vessel Accommodated	VHF Channel Monitored / Working	Transient Slips / Total Slips	Approach / Dockside Depth (reported)	Floating Docks	Gas / Diesel	Groceries, Ice, Marine Supplies, Snacks	Repairs: Hull, Engine, Propeller	Lift (tonnage), Crane, Rail	Courtesy Car, Laundry, Pool, Showers	Min / Max Amps	Pump-Out Station	Nearby: Grocery Store, Motel, Restaurant
1. Oyster River Boat Yard	(508) 945-0736	34	9/10	/26	3.0/5.0	F	G	IMS	HEP			30		MR
2. Stage Harbor Marine	(508) 945-1860	114	9/	1/30	10.0/6.0	F	GD	IMS	HEP	C		30	P	GM
3. First Light Boatworks	(508) 945-7800	50	/	/	7.0/8.0	F		M	HEP	R		30		
4. Outermost Harbor Marine	(508) 945-2030	36	80/	/80	3.0/3.0	F	G	IMS	HEP	L		30	P	GMR
5. Ryders Cove Boat Yard	(508) 945-1064	30	9/	/32	4.0/4.0	F	G	IMS	HE	L				

☐ Internet Access   (WiFi) Wireless Internet Access   onSpot Dockside WiFi Facility

See WaterwayGuide.com for current rates, fuel prices, website addresses, and other up-to-the-minute information. (Information in the table is provided by the facilities.)

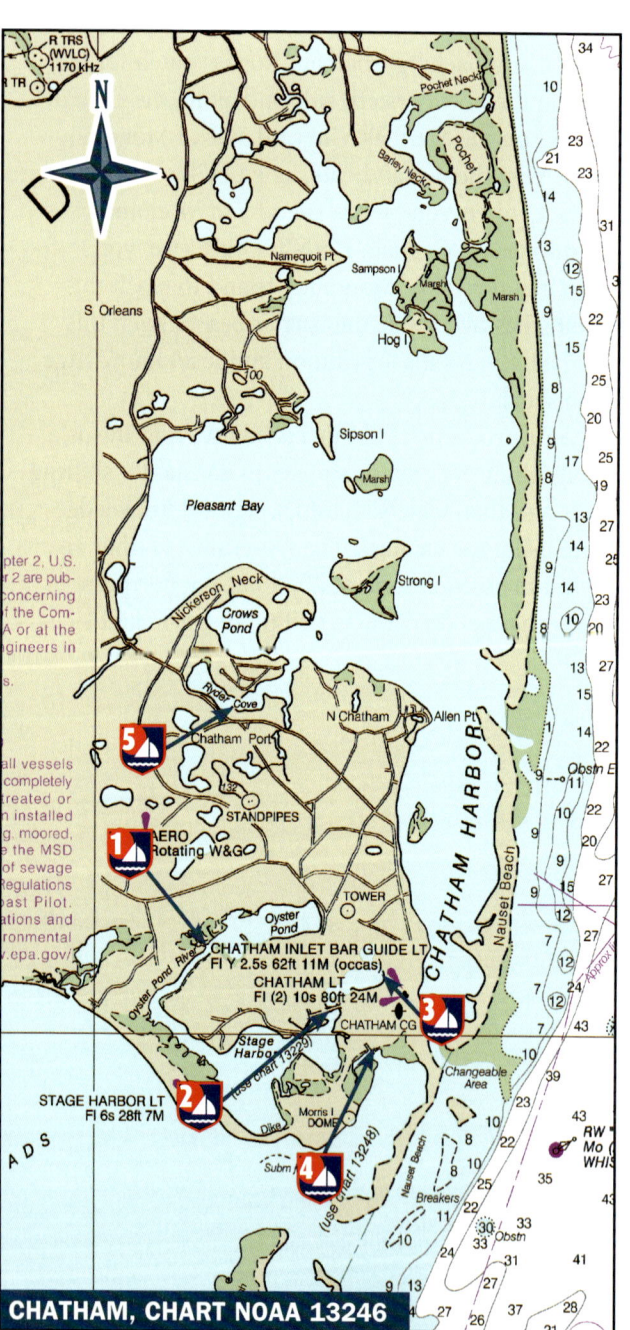

CHATHAM, CHART NOAA 13246

and even the commercial fishing and U.S. Coast Guard vessels are having a tough time.

You can reach Stage Harbor via a land cut through Harding Beach. Follow the main channel buoys to reach the inner harbor. The **Chatham Highway Bridge** (8-foot closed vertical clearance) will open on signal from May 1 to October 31 from 8:00 a.m. to 5:00 p.m. if at least a 1-hour notice is given by calling the Town of Chatham Harbormasters Department (508-945-1213). From 5:00 p.m. to 8:00 a.m. the draw will open on signal if at least a 12-hour notice is given. At all other times, the bridge will only open with a 24-hour advance notice. Local boats mostly occupy the area above the bridge.

Dockage/Moorings: Gas and diesel fuel, transient slips and repairs can be found on the Bass River, at Allen Harbor and at Saquatucket Harbor, which shares a common entrance with Wychmere Harbor. The Saquatucket waterfront has been redeveloped in recent years and slips added to the town marina. Call the Saquatucket Municipal Marina on VHF Channel 16 or 68. Harwich Port's stores, restaurants and art gallery are 1 mile from Allen Harbor and 2 miles from Saquatucket. The round, nearly landlocked Wychmere Harbor is jammed with moorings. The crowded harbor does not have dockage available for transients but if you ask at the town dock, someone might be able to point out a mooring or an available slip.

There are numerous docking and mooring options near Stage Harbor, including Oyster River Boat Yard on Oyster Pond River, Stage Harbor Marine (at the foot of the Chatham Highway Bridge), Pease Boat Works & Marine Railway (in Mill Pond) and Outermost Harbor Marine, accessed via a channel between Morris Island and Nauset Beach. Slips, moorings, fuel and repairs can be found here; see the marina table for details. Note that Outermost Harbor Marine reports 3-foot MLW approach depths so call ahead for exact depths and directions. To the north of Chatham, Ryders Cove Boat Yard has moorings with 4-foot MLW approach depths.

Anchorage: You can anchor behind Harding Beach Point south-southeast of red nun "10" in 12 to 15 feet MLW with excellent holding in sand or just off the channel in Stage Harbor northeast of green can "13" in 13 feet MLW with good holding in mud and grass. If you and your dinghy are up to it, there are public landings on both the Oyster River and the Mitchell River, close to Main Street.

■ NANTUCKET ISLAND

Nantucket, one of the most beautiful islands on the east coast, is 14 miles long, 3.5 miles wide and 27 miles out to sea. It is by far one of the most popular vacation spots for cruisers. When you first step ashore, you will be overwhelmed by the feeling you are stepping back in history when whaling ships filled the port and sea captains walked the gas-lit cobblestone streets. The entire island of Nantucket is a historic district designated as a National Historic Landmark. Don't miss an opportunity to visit and spend time on this island out of time; your experience will be memorable.

NAVIGATION: Use NOAA Charts 13244, 13242, 13241, and 13237. A passage to Nantucket crosses some 30 miles of open water and may call for navigation in fog. The journey to Nantucket from the west is between shoals: south of Horseshoe Shoal; north of Hawes, Norton and Cross Rip shoals; and then east of Tuckernuck Shoal. The closer to the shoals your course, the more noticeable the tidal rips.

Aids to navigation are widely spaced. Frequent dead reckoning and GPS fixes should be considered mandatory as is a keen lookout (with radar if possible) for other recreational boats, fishing vessels and ferries that frequent these much-traveled waters. If the sky is clear and the water sparkling, the island stands out in spectacular fashion, even though its highest point is only 108 feet above sea level.

The red-and-white Morse (A) bell buoy "NB" marks the entrance to the buoyed 1.5-mile channel leading to Brant Point. Semi-submerged breakwaters to either side reveal the danger of straying beyond the channel's confines. A navigational range (two towers: the first a quick-flashing light and the second a constant light) will come into view directly down the center of the channel, just west of the Brant Point Lighthouse. Follow the channel buoys while rounding the 26-foot occulting red 4-second lighthouse with a watchful eye for ferryboats and other vessels that must also negotiate this relatively narrow passage.

Dockage/Moorings: Once beyond Brant Point, the Nantucket Boat Basin becomes immediately evident ahead and just to the south of the boat basin enclosure, the town pier usually has a raft of fishing vessels tied to its T-shaped end. To the east of the wide inner-harbor channel upon entry, a large mooring field also should be visible.

Nantucket Boat Basin, to the south in the large, protected basin, sets an industry standard for service for transients. You will find slips to accommodate boats to 200 feet as well as dockside electricity, water and fuels (including propane refills) with individualized pump-out stations designed to reach virtually every slip. Ashore are restroom and shower facilities, a large 24-hour coin-operated laundry, rental cottages and lofts along the wharves and even a pet-friendly park. The concierge at the Boat Basin, located on the fuel dock, will arrange restaurant reservations, sightseeing trips, car rentals and such. The management recommends early reservations (before March) for this popular, end-destination marina; many peak-season weekends are booked as much as a year in advance.

Nantucket Moorings holds the exclusive town franchise for 125 transient moorings and maintains a field of round white floats secured by heavy tackle. Expect to pay daily rates for these (without other services) that are among the highest in New England. Even at this premium, the popularity of this destination harbor is such that an advance reservation is highly recommended.

Anchorage: The space shown as "General Anchorage" on NOAA Chart 13242 is almost completely filled with moorings. Some limited anchor room still remains to the north and east of the moorings. To the north there is 15 to 20 feet MLW with excellent holding.

Somewhat quieter ground may be found east of the extensive shoaling area in east center harbor. There you will find more sand (and some grass) in 10- to 12-foot MLW depths. Since the shoal is unmarked,

Nantucket Sound, MA

NANTUCKET		Largest Vessel Accomodated	VHF Channel Monitored / Working	Approach / Dockside Depth (reported)	Transient Slips / Total Slips	Floating Docks	Groceries, Ice, Marine Supplies, Snacks	Repairs: Hull, Engine, Propeller	Gas / Diesel	Lift (tonnage), Crane, Rail	Courtesy Car, Laundry, Pool, Showers	Min / Max Amps	Pump-Out Station	Nearby: Grocery Store, Motel, Restaurant
				Dockage				**Supplies**			**Services**			
1. Nantucket Yacht Club-PRIVATE	(508) 228-1400	110	/	/	15.0/15.0			I			L		S	GR
2. **Nantucket Boat Basin** 💻 📶 onSpot	**(508) 325-1350**	200	9/11	/240	12.0/12.0	GD		I				30/100	LS	P	GR
3. Nantucket Moorings	(508) 228-4472	85	68/	/	11.0/			I					LS	P	GMR
4. Grey Lady Marine	(508) 228-6525	50	9/69	/	6.0/8.0			M	HEP	L27				GMR

💻 Internet Access 📶 Wireless Internet Access onSpot Dockside WiFi Facility

See WaterwayGuide.com for current rates, fuel prices, website addresses, and other up-to-the-minute information. (Information in the table is provided by the facilities.)

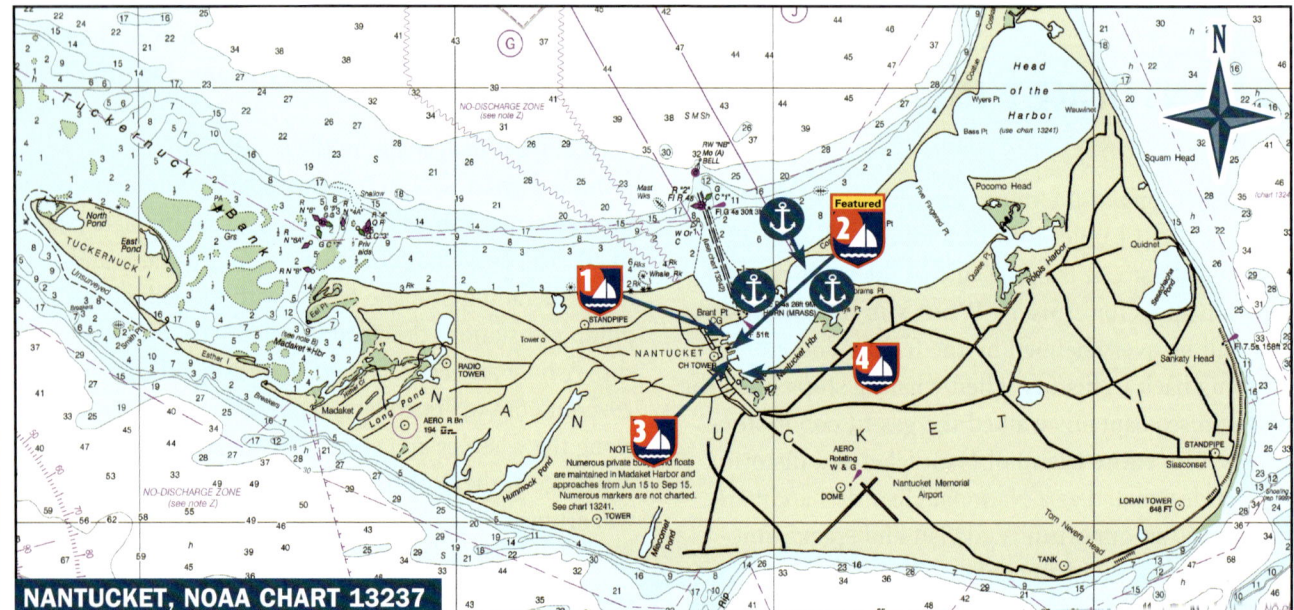

NANTUCKET, NOAA CHART 13237

NANTUCKET BOAT BASIN

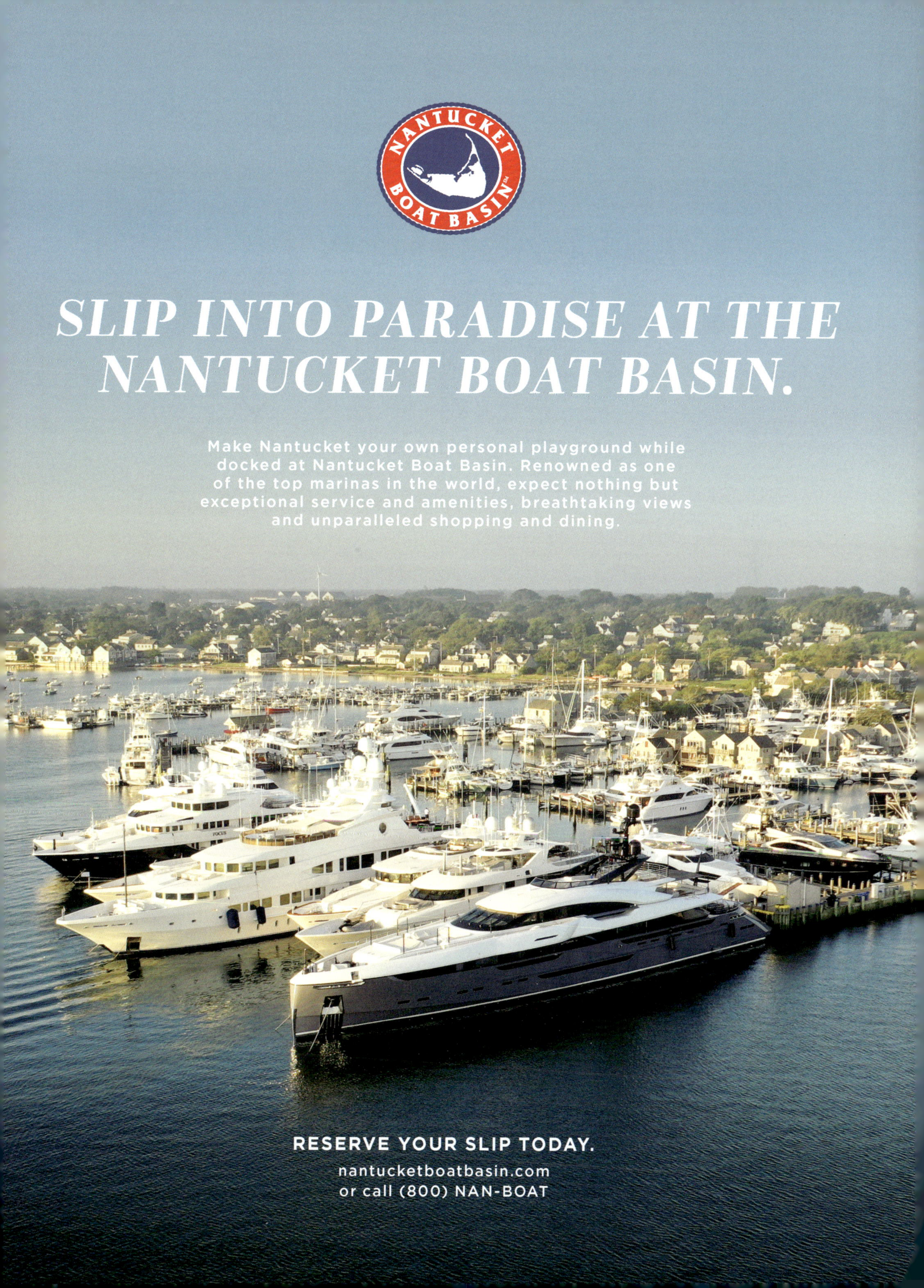

SLIP INTO PARADISE AT THE NANTUCKET BOAT BASIN.

Make Nantucket your own personal playground while docked at Nantucket Boat Basin. Renowned as one of the top marinas in the world, expect nothing but exceptional service and amenities, breathtaking views and unparalleled shopping and dining.

RESERVE YOUR SLIP TODAY.
nantucketboatbasin.com
or call (800) NAN-BOAT

GOIN' ASHORE

NANTUCKET, MA

Nantucket is adapted from an ancient Algonquian name for the island, perhaps meaning "land far at sea." Whaling dominates both the history and current mystique of this far-flung and naturally barren sea island. By 1700, islanders–Europeans and Wampanoag alike–had already begun the serious pursuit of whales in long boats from the shore. Half a century later, Nantucket was known as the whaling capitol of the world. Until the economic basis for whaling collapsed with the efficient recovery of petroleum in the late 19th century, whaling dominated almost every aspect of Nantucket life and was the sole basis of island wealth. Moby Dick was published in 1851 after Melville came to Nantucket before the whaling boom in 1830. Hundreds of people from all walks of life worked the rope walks, candle factories, chandleries and sail lofts of this tiny Industrial island. The entire town was a constant bustle with many shops, three newspapers and four banks.

All of that changed in 1849 when 14 ships commanded and crewed by Nantucket seamen left for the Golden Gate. The last whaling ship left Nantucket in 1869 and the whaling days of the island were over. Local author Nathanial Philbrick's In the Heart of the Sea summed up the history and intensity of the whaling industry quite poetically and is a must read. It didn't take long for tourism to thrive on this wind-swept island where today it is the principal source of income for island residents.

ATTRACTIONS

1. Nantucket Atheneum
Worth a visit on architectural merit alone but you will also find current newspapers and periodicals, as well as some solitude (1 India St., 508-228-1110).

2. Nantucket Lightship Basket Museum
Small museum dedicated to baskets crafted by local men stationed on offshore lightships (49 Union St., 508-228-1177).

3. Nantucket Whaling Museum
World-class collection of whaling artifacts, exhibits and tours at 13 Broad St. (508-228-1894). A "must see" is a fully reconstructed 46-foot-long sperm whale skeleton that is now on display at the museum.

4. Sea Nantucket Paddle Sports
Try your hand at kayaking, paddle boarding or sailing on one of the 10 beaches on the island, all with free access (76 Washington St., 508-228-7499).

SHOPPING

5. Brant Point Marine
Located next to the town dock with marine hardware, electronics and gear (32 Washington St., 508-228-6244).

6. Nantucket Harbor Stop & Shop
Carries some food items and provisions (9 Salem St., 508-825-8833).

MARINAS

7. Grey Lady Marina
96 Washington St. (508-228-6525)

8. Nantucket Boat Basin
Swains Wharf (508-325-1350)

9. Nantucket Moorings
34 Washington St. (508-228-7261)

10. Nantucket Yacht Club
1 S. Beach St. (508-228-1400)

nose your way in carefully to avoid grounding. Refer to the Waterway Explorer (www.waterwayguide.com) and NOAA online charts for the most up-to-date information.

If you do not mind a considerable dinghy ride to town, there is plenty of swing room and 10- to 12-foot MLW depths in the second harbor to the east beyond First Point. Holding is spotty (due to grass) but the scenery is splendid.

Wherever you anchor in Nantucket Harbor, the protection afforded by a nearby "landmass" seen on the chart is deceptive: Low-lying dunes do not block the wind. The fetch is considerable, particularly from the east and northwest, portending wet dinghy (even launch) rides and rock-and-roll evenings during all but the most settled weather.

For an extra fee, Harbor Launch (VHF Channel 68) will provide reliable service (on a mooring or at anchor) and their dock personnel will dispose of your trash. A dinghy dock is found just inside the southern side of the town's T-shaped pier. A second, larger dinghy float complex is on the north side of the pier closer to shore. Water is available at the T-end of the town pier, where you will also find a free pump-out station. (Note that a raft of commercial fishing boats often blocks access to these facilities.) Restrooms and showers are located at the head of the dock just behind the Harbormaster's office. Recycling bins and a dumpster are located on the right side of the Harbormaster's office and bags of cube ice are available for purchase inside. The center of town is a pleasant two-block walk to the right from here.

Nantucket is a federal No-Discharge Zone: no dumping of sewage–treated or untreated–is permitted, holding tanks must be used and heads must be sealed. In addition to the town's pump-out station at the end of the town dock, Nantucket Boat Basin offers courtesy pump-out service at its fuel dock, immediately north of the municipal pier. For boats on moorings or at anchor, the town operates a free pump-out boat: call "Headhunter" (get it?) on VHF Channel 09 or contact the Nantucket Harbormaster (also Channel 09 or 508-228-7260) for pump-out boat hours and availability.

Martha's Vineyard, MA

		Largest Vessel Accomodated	VHF Channel Monitored / Working	Transient Slips / Total Slips	Approach / Dockside Depth (reported)	Floating Docks	Gas / Diesel	Groceries Ice Marine Supplies Snacks	Repairs: Hull, Engine, Propeller	Lift (tonnage), Crane, Rail	Min / Max Amps	Courtesy Car, Laundry, Pool, Showers	Pump-Out Station	Nearby: Grocery Store, Motel, Restaurant
EDGARTOWN HARBOR				**Dockage**			**Supplies**			**Services**				
1. Edgartown Harbor	(508) 627-4746	90	74/	3/3	20.0/25.0	F	GD	IMS	HP		50		S	P	GMR
2. Prime Marina Edgartown	(508) 627-6500		/	/	/			GIMS	HEP	L25			S	P	GMR
3. Mad Max Marina	(508) 627-7400	165	71/9	4/8	15.0/15.0							30/50			R
4. Martha's Vineyard Shipyard, Edgartown	(508) 627-6000	50	9/73	/	15.0/15.0			GM	HEP	L35					GMR
5. Edgartown Yacht Club-PRIVATE	(508) 627-4746		72/	/	/	F		I							GMR
OAK BLUFFS HARBOR														
6. Dockside Marina	(508) 693-3392	70	9/71	8/8	12.0/7.0		GD	I				30/50	LS	P	G
7. **Oak Bluffs Marina**	**(508) 693-4355**	110	71/71	75/81	9.0/11.0		**GD**	I				30/50	LS	P	**GMR**
VINEYARD HAVEN HARBOR														
8. Town Dock at Owen Park	(508) 696-4249	60	9/69	/	7.0/6.0								LS	P	GMR
9. The Black Dog Wharf	(508) 693-3854	190	72/72	15/15	14.0/11.0			IS				30/100	LS	P	GMR
10. Vineyard Haven Marina	(508) 693-0720	200	9/10	52/52	12.0/12.0		D	GIMS				50/200+	LS	P	GMR
11. Tisbury Wharf Company	(508) 693-9300	300	9/74	15/15	16.0/14.0		GD	I				30/100	S		GMR
12. Martha's Vineyard Shipyard	(508) 693-0400	50	9/73	/	12.0/10.0			IM	HEP	L20					GMR
LAGOON POND														
13. Prime Marina Vineyard Haven	(508) 693-4174	38	/	4/65	4.0/6.0	F	G	IM	HEP		30	LS		GMR
MENEMSHA														
14. Menemsha Texaco Service	(508) 645-2641	120	9/88	/17	11.0/11.0		GD	IMS				30/50			GR
15. Menemsha Harbor, Town of Chilmark	(508) 645-2846	70	16/9	17/	8.0/10.0	F	GD	GIM	HEP		30/50	S	P	GR

⌨ Internet Access (WiFi) Wireless Internet Access 📶 onSpot Dockside WiFi Facility

See WaterwayGuide.com for current rates, fuel prices, website addresses, and other up-to-the-minute information. (Information in the table is provided by the facilities.)

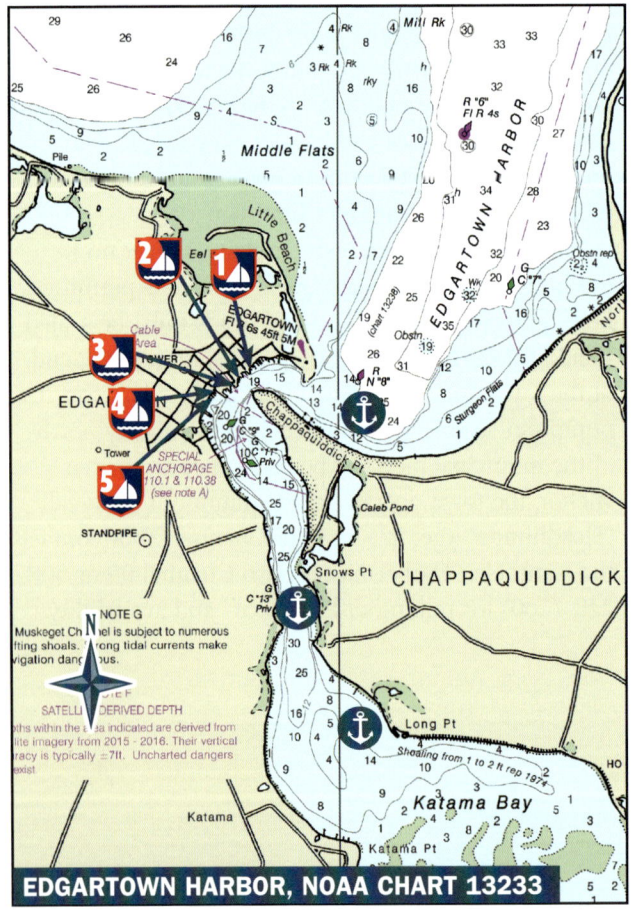

EDGARTOWN HARBOR, NOAA CHART 13233

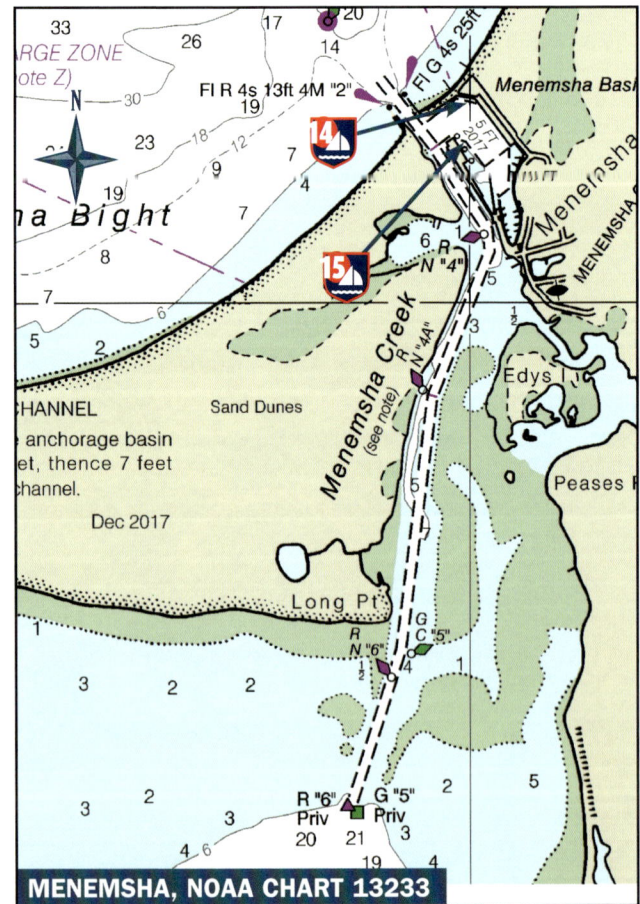

MENEMSHA, NOAA CHART 13233

OAK BLUFFS HARBOR, VINEYARD HAVEN HARBOR, LAGOON POND, NOAA CHART 13233

■ MARTHA'S VINEYARD

A distance of less than 4 nm divides Martha's Vineyard from the southern shore of Cape Cod. A relaxed summer resort, the Vineyard has four distinctively different harbors (Menemsha, Vineyard Haven, Oak Bluffs and Edgartown), high land, wooded bluffs, historic towns and handsome houses. The southern and western shores consist of ocean beach, salt marsh and the multicolored cliffs of Gay Head towering high above the sea. Colored veins of earth-hued clay (white, yellow, tan, sienna, rust, brown) make the cliffs a muted rainbow. Remember that many of the towns on The Vineyard are "dry" so bring your own (brown bagging) is the rule when it comes to alcohol. This method is permitted at most restaurants. Martha's Bike Rentals (833-362-7842) will deliver and pick up bikes anywhere on the island.

Edgartown Harbor

Edgartown is one of the world's great yachting centers. An elegant town that takes itself and its yachting seriously, old Edgartown is beautiful and not to be missed. This is a wonderful walking town with lovely boutiques, small cafés and galleries. Many impressive yachts are moored here in season. Particularly striking are the classic wooden power vessels, kept in peak condition by ever-polishing, multi-member crews. Elegant antique, New England houses, all meticulously restored, line the streets ashore. With the help of prevailing sea breezes, grand shade trees provide natural air-conditioning and flowers abound.

Katama Bay continues to be a naturalist's delight. Ospreys, terns, whippoorwills and a variety of gulls all seem to thrive here. Near-deserted South Beach, one of the most unspoiled and beautiful in the islands, is a relatively easy motorized dinghy ride from almost any spot in the bay.

GOIN' ASHORE

EDGARTOWN, MA

King James II of England had a son named Edgar, Duke of Cambridge, while still the Duke of York. This distant community, originally named Great Harbor, did not have the 24-hour news cycle that we either live on or flee from in this day and age, and their attempt to flatter the future monarch went a bit awry. Exactly a month before they changed their town's name, the three-year-old heir died, most likely of the same weaknesses that killed five of his siblings. Only two of his sisters lived to adulthood, Mary and Anne, and their adulthoods were spectacular: those two reigned as Queens, one after another. Edgartown was named for the son of English King James II, who bore the title of Edgar, Duke of Cambridge.

The seaport village was the first colonial settlement on Martha's Vineyard and has been the county seat since 1642. In the late 1700s, Martha's Vineyard developed a booming whaling industry and by the 1800s, more than 100 Edgartown men were captains of whaling ships. Between Nantucket and Martha's Vineyard together, they owned one-quarter of America's whaling fleet. By the beginning of the 20th century, the influence of Edgartown in the whaling industry began to decline. Today, Edgartown is known more for summer tourism.

Lining the harbor, gracious Greek Revival homes of long-ago sea captains suggest tales of whale oil, mutinous crews and wooden ships lost in frigid seas while anxious wives paced the widow's walks above. Many of these restored houses along the tree-lined streets are now elegant shops with goods and services to match almost any desire. A huge pagoda tree brought from China as a seedling by Captain Thomas Milton in the early days of the 20th century dominates South Water St.

ATTRACTIONS

At the corner of Cooke St. and School St. is the Martha's Vineyard Museum (59 School St., 508-627-4441), which is housed in the Thomas Cooke House (circa 1740). The friendly and knowledgeable staff can direct you on a walking tour of Edgartown that will take you past many other historic locations, including the Vincent House Museum (508-627-8619), built in 1672, and the Old Whaling Church (99 Main St., 508-627-8017) with its six massive columns, which is now a performing arts center.

Don't miss an opportunity to visit the Edgartown Lighthouse (121 N. Water St.), open daily from late June to early September and weekends on the shoulder season starting late May and then again until mid-October. There is a small charge for admission.

The building housing the U.S. Post Office (Church St., just east of Main St.) doubles as the municipal

transportation center. You can catch a bus for South Beach (every 15 minutes between 10:00 a.m. and 6:30 p.m.). Frequently scheduled buses also depart for Oak Bluffs and Vineyard Haven, less frequently for Gay Head (Aquinnah).

Head for South Beach on Katama Rd. for an afternoon on beautiful, white fluffy sand where you can now walk from South Beach to Chappaquiddick, which was originally an island but has recently merged with the barrier beach. If you prefer, the Chappaquiddick ferry landing (immediately east of the town wharf) is where the On Time ferries (both of them) make short but frequent transits between Edgartown and Chappaquiddick (7:30 a.m. to midnight). Naturalists will enjoy a guided kayak tour of the Felix Neck Wildlife Sanctuary (508-627-4850).

SHOPPING

Within just a few blocks of the harbor, you will encounter a near endless variety of nautical, surf and gift shops. A Stop and Shop supermarket (225 Upper Main St., 508-627-9522) is less than a mile from the dinghy dock near Edgartown Yacht Club, as is Edgartown Hardware (61 Edgartown Rd., 508-627-4338). Visit the Edgartown Paper Store (25 Main St., 508-627-9599) for current newspapers and sundries, and Edgartown Books (44 Main St., 508-627-8463), which has author signings all summer, taking advantage of the great number of writers who make their home on Martha's Vineyard. Edgartown also offers an almost overwhelming variety of restaurants, ranging from open-air casual to the most elegant.

NAVIGATION: Use NOAA Chart 13233. Entry to Edgartown Harbor is relatively simple; however, the rocks and shallows known as the Middle Flats are marked by red nuns at roughly 1-mile increments, west of safe water. A few green cans along the eastern side of the entrance make sure you don't stray too close to the Cape Poge Elbow. Although the inner harbor is deep and well-marked, currents of several knots at the height of the tidal flow are further complicated by frequent and rapid cross-channel transits by the Chappaquiddick ferry, *On Time*. On entering the inner basin it's safest to round green can buoy "9" even though the mooring field beyond it gives the illusion of safe passage. The sandbar between the green can buoy "9" and Chappaquiddick Point has snagged many a keel.

Dockage/Moorings: The Edgartown Harbormaster controls some 700 moorings in the harbor, about 100 of which are reserved for transients on a first-come, first-served basis. Launch service is available; call VHF Channel 68 or 401-847-9109.

Although moorings in Edgartown Harbor are numerous, actual dockage is in short supply. Several marinas, a private yacht club and a full-service shipyard are among the offerings. (See our marina table.) Marina Edgartown has a small general store and will deliver block and cube ice to your vessel upon request (via the launch service). These are all within walking distance to restaurants and shopping.

Edgartown is in a no-discharge zone; boats are forbidden to discharge sewage of any kind (even treated) into harbor waters. A free pump-out station, operating from 9:00 a.m. to 5:00 p.m., is stationed on Memorial Wharf (next to the ferry landing). In addition,

Photo courtesy of Oak Bluffs Division of Tourism.

OAK BLUFFS MARINA

Oak Bluffs Marina

N

*A*s the largest marina on Martha's Vineyard, Oak Bluffs Marina is a long-time favorite of many boaters, and offers unrivaled access to the rest of the Island.

- 81 slips, 45 moorings, and can med-moor yachts up to 110'
- Large-capacity launch vessel (hail "Oak Bluffs Launch" on VHF 77)
- On-site pump-out facility for vessels up to 40'; pump-out boat available for larger craft
- New fuel dock–fastest pumps on the island!
- Variety of activities for families, couples, groups
- Nearby restaurants, grocery stores, liquor stores, bars and shops
- Taxis, buses, and car and bike rentals nearby

Phone: 508-693-4355
Fax: 508-693-7402 • VHF Channel 71

Email: obmarina@comcast.net
www.oakbluffsmarina.com
41° 27' 39" N • 70° 33' 22" W

the town pump-out boat is on call (VHF Channel 74) with free service to all those anchored or on moorings.

Anchorage: Anchoring is not permitted in the crowded mooring field inside the harbor, east of the harbor channel, but ample swinging room and good holding usually await cruising visitors south of the mooring area along the Chappaquiddick shore at Snows Point in at least 10 feet MLW with good holding in mud. Good holding can also be found in upper Katama Bay in soft mud. Keep an eye on the harbor chart and your depth sounder when approaching an appealing spot, particularly as you head south, farther into the bay. Katama Bay is reasonably well protected from all but strong southerly winds. The town dinghy dock is located next to the Edgartown Yacht Club. An additional landing area is at North Wharf.

Shortly before entering the Edgartown inner harbor, you will find ample anchorage space (increasingly popular with large charter vessels and schooners) off Sturgeon Flats on the northerly side of Chappaquiddick Island in deep water (17 to 20 feet MLW) with good holding in mud. This area is exposed to the north, however, and likely will challenge your comfort levels in all but the calmest weather. The town of Edgartown does not permit overnight anchorage in Cape Poge Bay.

Oak Bluffs Harbor

Just to the south of the high bluffs of East Chop lies Oak Bluffs, known in the 19th century as "Cottage City." Tiny houses with small front porches, gaily painted and festooned with gingerbread and scrollwork can still be seen here at the Martha's Vineyard Camp Meeting Grounds, a Methodist camp that dates back to 1835. Today, Oak Bluffs is the resort harbor of Martha's Vineyard.

The harbor is crowded and hectic and there is much to enjoy here. Some skippers will actually pass on Oak Bluffs Harbor because it always looks full. In fact, because of the careful organization of this harbor, far more mooring and slip space is available than in either Vineyard Haven or Edgartown (but there's no room for anchoring). There's good eating along Circuit Ave. Just stroll up and back until the right scent hits you.

NAVIGATION: Use NOAA Chart 13233. The landlocked harbor has a dredged, breakwater entry good for 7-foot MLW depths. Access is straightforward, marked by a red 4-second flashing light atop a 30-foot-high tower at the end of the breakwater to the north. Be careful

during the arrival or departure of the passenger ferry. Sharing space in the harbor channel with this vessel is not advisable.

Dockage/Moorings: Oak Bluffs Marina is the largest marina on Martha's Vineyard with 81 berths and 45 moorings. Their unusual, pear-shaped floats are marked "Town of Oak Bluffs." You will need your own bridle. The marina offers launch service, a pump-out facility, showers and easy access to nearby amenities. Their fuel dock has the fastest pumps on the island.

Two Texaco fuel docks are located just beyond the harbormaster's office, south after entry. Note that it is not possible to take on water while refueling at either of these docks. To replenish water tanks, you will need to contact the Oak Bluffs Marina manager who will direct you to an available town slip. Bags of ice are available at the fast-food stand at the harbor head.

Vineyard Haven Harbor

In 1845, most coastal shipping traveled through Vineyard Sound with 13,814 vessels counted in that year alone. This was due to Vineyard Haven's premiere location on the sailing routes. The island's chief port, Vineyard Haven, still has a busy harbor that serves as the primary ferry terminal and the foremost commercial and recreational marine center. The harbor is wide and open to the northeast but a rock breakwater protects the inner harbor beach and recreational beach from all but the worst of the incoming swells.

The beach is the big attraction on the Vineyard and many beaches can easily be reached from the marinas by bike. Beyond the numerous marine facilities, Vineyard Haven has just about any recreational and provisioning opportunity you might want, set in the ambiance of an old New England village.

NAVIGATION: Use NOAA Chart 13233. Enter Vineyard Haven Harbor between the lighthouses on the headlands of West Chop and East Chop. The harbor mouth is more than 1 mile wide at its outermost extremity, narrowing gradually upon approaching the inner harbor breakwater and the ferry wharf at harbor's head. Buoys on entry are gauged to deep-draft vessels; however, due respect must be paid the rocky ledges along the eastern shore of West Chop, which begin at Allegheny Rock, marked by green can "25" and west of red nun buoy "4."

Vineyard Hiking & Biking

Martha's Vineyard is home to dozens of hiking trails through the woods, along the oceanfront and high over the bluffs. A few of the very accessible trails include:

1. Great Rock Bight–located off North Road in Chilmark with a few miles of easy hiking and views of Vineyard Sound. Trails are dog friendly.

2. Long Point Wildlife Refuge–offers miles of trails with broad vistas and lots of island vegetation on the south shore. Trail leads right to the beach.

3. Caroline Tuthill Preserve–easy to access off of Edgartown-Vineyard Haven Road and leads over hills and through the woods. Water views are of Sengekontacket Pond. Trail is dog friendly.

4. Menemsha Hills–a 211-acre preserve where you can climb the second-highest point on Martha's Vineyard for awesome ocean views. Three miles of trails transit wetlands, woodland groves, coastal plains and a rocky ocean edge. Dogs are not allowed.

5. John Presbury Norton Farm to Womesket Preserve–easy hiking trails that eventually lead to Blackwater Pond. Trail is dog friendly.

6. Chappaquiddick Island–offers several trails.

    Trail maps for most of these hikes are available at www.thetrustees.org.

One of the least known pleasures of Martha's Vineyard is the beautiful, ample and well-protected harbor of Lagoon Pond, just southeast of Vineyard Haven Harbor and securely nestled beneath the bluffs of East Chop. The **Lagoon Pond Bridge** (closed vertical clearance of 15 feet) is a replacement for the 1935 original, which left only a small gap for masts to pass through. From May 15 through September 15, the draw opens on signal from 8:15 a.m. to 8:45 a.m., from 10:15 a.m. to 11:00 a.m., from 3:15 p.m. to 4:00 p.m., from 5:00 p.m. to 5:45 p.m. and from 7:30 p.m. to 8:00 p.m. At all other times the draw will open for the passage of vessels if at least a 4-hour advance notice is given by calling the number posted at the bridge. From September 16 through May 14 the draw will only open on signal if at least a 24-hour advance notice is given by calling the number posted at the bridge.

Lagoon Pond is navigable (controlling depth 6.5 feet MLW) and well-marked throughout its 1.75-mile length. Be sure to go south around the white private buoy at Robbins Rock, about 1 mile past the bridge.

Dockage/Moorings: The Town Dock at Owen Park offers protected tie-ups (tucked behind the breakwater), whether hitched to the pier or tethered to a town mooring. Short-term tie-ups are possible in 8- to 10-foot MLW depths alongside the municipal pier and an overnight stay may be arranged as well. Call the Harbormaster (VHF Channel 09) for availability and directions. A dinghy dock is available on the north side of the pier. The Black Dog Wharf to the south has been a fixture here since 1964 and offers hourly tie-ups and long-term transient slips.

Additional facilities that may have space for you include Vineyard Haven Marina and Tisbury Wharf Company. Martha's Vineyard Shipyard has built hundreds of local boats and has full repair capabilities. The free town pump-out boat (on call, VHF Channel 09) serves boats at marinas, on moorings or anchored.

Prime Marina Vineyard Haven maintains the rental moorings along the western side of Lagoon Pond.

Anchorage: Substantial anchorage room is still available outside the mooring field along the easterly side of West Chop, south of the rocky outcrop marked by a warning buoy and inside a line between red nun buoys "4" and "6." Holding is good here on a firm bottom in 7 to 15 feet MLW, but the area is fully exposed to the northeast and to the wakes of frequently arriving and departing ferries. The harbormaster's office has free hot showers.

Powerful blows from the northeast can easily be ridden out beneath the highest of Lagoon Pond's tan-and-white cliffs on the eastern shore. There is 7 to 9 feet at MLW. There is a three-day anchoring limit. There is a dinghy dock at the boat ramp just north of Cedar Neck.

It is possible to anchor in 6 to 10 feet MLW with good holding in sand and mud in Lake Tashmoo on the north side of Martha's Vineyard. There is a 6-foot channel leading into this protected anchorage and a dinghy dock at the foot of Lake Street. There is a three-day anchoring limit here.

Menemsha Basin

Consciously quaint Menemsha, about 3 nm east of Aquinnah (Gay Head) on the Vineyard Sound side, is a fishing port working at staying unspoiled. You can hike along vacant dunes, watch the long liners unload, socialize with local artists and get a well-prepared meal or deli sandwich here. The Menemsha Basin is homeport to lobster boats, trawlers, sportfishers and charter and party boats. Shanties used by fishers line the picturesque but crowded harbor head. A couple of fish markets, several fine restaurants, a market and a

wide variety of shops can be found in this picturesque town. Fish markets will cook your purchase if requested and you can go behind the market and eat at one of their picnic tables.

Menemsha is the closest harbor to Aquinnah, the westernmost town on Martha's Vineyard, which is not easily accessible by boat. The Wampanoag Tribe runs the Aquinnah Cultural Center (508-645-7900) and gift shop. Other gift and craft shops, as well as restaurants and snack shops, are nearby. You can also walk to 1844 Gay Head Light, which was moved 129 feet farther from the eroding cliff in 2015 and offers a magnificent view of the Elizabeth Islands.

> Note that many long-time residents and visitors will still refer to Aquinnah as Gay Head but all road signs have been changed.

NAVIGATION: Use NOAA Chart 13233. Access to the Menemsha Basin is straightforward and can handle commercial drafts of up to 18 feet. The entrance is marked by green bell buoy "1," which is located approximately 300 yards off the channel's mouth. The 25-foot-high, 4-second flashing green "3" indicates the end of the seawall to the northeast and a stone jetty is

prominent to the southwest. The currents in this passage are straightforward and swift. It is best to pick a slack tide for entry.

Just past the entrance to Menemsha Harbor the channel continues up to Menemsha Pond. This pond is shallow and overnight stays are not allowed even if you have a shallow draft boat. There is, however, good clam and mussel digging in the pond. Be sure to get a shellfish license if you decide to dinghy in and dig around.

Dockage/Moorings: Transients can be accommodated along the western side of Menemsha Harbor at the town dock (with limited space for sailboats due to shallow depths). These slips have no finger piers so boats with swim platforms will have an easier time than those without. Two heavy town moorings (and other moorings off the beach) are offered but expect to raft up (50-foot maximum boat length). There are six additional moorings

in the outer harbor. There are showers but few other amenities and no launch service. Contact the Chilmark Harbormaster on VHF Channel 16. Fuel can be acquired from the town dock or Menemsha Texaco Service, which also sells ice.

 Menemsha is a No-Discharge Zone with $1,000 cash fine for violators (treated effluent included). A pump-out station is available.

■ NEXT STOP

Mariners who choose to leave the Islands to head for Cape Cod Bay will not be disappointed by the charming ports of Plymouth, Marblehead and Gloucester, among others.

Above Cape Cod

■ Cape Cod Bay to Salem Sound, MA ■ Gloucester Harbor, MA to Cape Elizabeth, ME ■ Casco Bay & the Mid-Coast of Maine
■ Penobscot Bay & Down East Maine

Eastport

Bangor

Bucks Harbor

Belfast

Bar Harbor

Camden

Southwest
Harbor

Frenchman Bay

Rockport

Mt. Desert Island

Rockland

Isle au Haut

Penobscot Bay

Bath

Muscongus Bay

Freeport

Yarmouth

Falmouth

Portland

Casco Bay

Saco

Cape Elizabeth

Boothbay Harbor

Kennebunkport

York Village

Kittery

Portsmouth

Isles of Shoals

Gulf of Maine

Hampton

Newburyport

Cape Ann

Atlantic Ocean

Gloucester

Marblehead

Massachusetts Bay

Boston

Weymouth

Provincetown

N

Plymouth

Cape Cod Bay

Visit Waterway Explorer at www.waterwayguide.com

Boston Harbor Sailing Club

Cape Cod Bay to Salem Sound, MA

■ NAVIGATING ABOVE CAPE COD

Maritime Heritage

The cold waters north and east of Cape Cod are the birthplace of much of America's maritime heritage. Every harbor and almost every ledge carries a piece of American history or a legend of the sea. Cruising these waters gives the modern-day sailor a strong feeling of sea tradition. The fastest traditional sailing ships the world has ever known sailed out of these ports including the great clipper ships *Flying Cloud*, *Sovereign of the Seas* and *Lightning* among others. Often considered the most seaworthy and able sailing vessels ever built, the huge Gloucester fishing schooners made their fame and fortune fishing the Grand Banks in the dead of winter. They were designed and built along the river banks near Cape Ann.

Cruising Conditions

Cape Cod is shaped like a great sandy arm–the upper arm extending easterly 31 miles from the mainland, the forearm heading 25 miles northward, and then the fist angling 7 miles back west. From the eastern end of Cape Cod Canal, many boats choose the short offshore run to Gloucester on Cape Ann, then another run for Portland Harbor's large navigational buoy (which replaced an old lightship), from which all of Casco Bay, the Mid-Coast and Penobscot Bay are easily accessible. Others bide a while in Provincetown before the long offshore run directly to Isle au Haut or Mount Desert Island and Acadia National Park. These routes take you through Stellwagen Bank, a prolific whale-watching area. Most boats, though, make the leisurely cruise up the coast to explore the historical ports from Plymouth to Boston, Marblehead, Salem and Gloucester, and then on to Portsmouth, Kittery and the beginning of the Down East coast.

The passage through or around the crooked elbow of Cape Cod may not win you an earring like crossing the equator, but it marks a major step for most coastal cruising plans and the entrance into an endless mariner's paradise.

To cruise "above the Cape" is to venture farther away from civilization and the recreational boating crowds. Self-sufficiency and competent seamanship become more important. The water is colder, weather changes quickly, the fog is thicker and the ledges are crueler in the swells of the open ocean. The sea here can be less forgiving to carelessness

Salem Sound

Boston — Boston Harbor

Massachusetts Bay

Cohasset

Scituate

Provincetown

Race Pt.

N

Plymouth

Wellfleet

Cape Cod Canal

Cape Cod Bay

Barnstable

Cape Cod

Distances—Down East

This table provides point-to-point mileage for the Maine coast. All distances are given in approximate nautical miles.

LOCATION	MILES
SAND COAST	
Kittery	0
York Harbor	11
Wells Harbor	14
Kennebunk River	5
Cape Porpoise Harbor	5
Biddeford/Saco	15
CASCO BAY	
Portland Head Light	19
Falmouth Foreside	7
Yarmouth	8
South Freeport	8
Potts Harbor, Harpswell Neck (from Portland Light)	11
Mackerel Cove, Bailey Island	6
SEGUIN ISLAND TO MUSCONGUS BAY	
Seguin Island	15
Bath, Kennebec River	12
Ebencock Harbor, Sheepscot River (from Seguin Island)	8
Boothbay Harbor (from Seguin Island)	10
Christmas Cove, Damariscotta River	6
Pemaquid Point	4
Monhegan Island	9
Friendship (from Pemaquid Point)	12
PENOBSCOT BAY	
Rockland (from Pemaquid Point)	31
Rockport	6
Camden	5
Dark Harbor, Isleboro Island	7
Belfast	11
Castine (from Rockland)	22
Stonington, Deer Isle (from Rockland)	20
Carvers Harbor, Vinalhaven (from Rockland)	13
Isle au Haut	11
MOUNT DESERT/FRENCHMAN BAY	
Southwest/Northeast Harbors	28
Bar Harbor	12
Winter Harbor	6
EAST OF SCHOODIC POINT	
Petit Manan Island (from Bar Harbor)	17
Jonesport	17
Machiasport	20
Cutler	13
West Quoddy Head	15
Lubec	3
Eastport	3

Distances—MA Waters

This table provides both point-to-point and cumulative distances from the Cape Cod Canal and from Boston. All measurements are given in approximate nautical miles.

LOCATION	BETWEEN POINTS	CUMULATIVE
EAST FROM CAPE COD CANAL		
Cape Cod Canal	0	0
Barnstable	10	10
Sesuit Harbor	7	17
Wellfleet	12	29
Provincetown	25	54
NORTH FROM CAPE COD CANAL		
Cape Cod Canal	0	0
Plymouth	20	20
Duxbury	2	22
Scituate	18	40
Cohasset	6	46
Boston	15	61
NORTH FROM BOSTON		
Boston	0	0
Marblehead	19	19
Salem	5	24
Beverly	1	25
Manchester	6	31
Gloucester	5	36
Rockport	17	53
Essex	8	61
Newburyport	16	77
Rye	15	92
Portsmouth	6	98
Isles of Shoals (offshore)	7	105

PROVINCETOWN MARINA

and inexperience than any other waters we cover. There are no barrier islands offering an "inside passage" and protection from the sweep of the sea, except in small cross-cuts between rivers and deep in the bigger bays.

A voyage in these waters warrants considerable preparation and flexibility. A journey from one harbor to another will probably involve a stretch of open water so skipper, crew and vessel must be prepared for the challenge. The water is markedly colder than the water below the Cape and the vessel's water supply and hull will feel much cooler as a result. Most locals and cruising boats that tackle this area have a heating source to warm up the cabin on cool mornings. Swimming is a more venturesome exercise than in more southern climes, and an accidental swim must be considered a matter of life or death because hypothermia is a risk, even in the summer.

Fog can be a factor on any day (especially in June and July), although it might burn off by mid-morning and leave a clear, warm day. A wind from a southerly or easterly direction may bring in unannounced fog at any time. The skipper making his way through "a pea-souper" for the first time is likely to take his navigational skills more seriously thereafter. Fog is usually accompanied by calm waters and light winds but beware the "smoky sou'wester." During this condition a stiff breeze builds up rough seas that break on the ledges and obscure the sounds of bells and gongs. And if the fog remains heavy, obscuring islands, buoys and other boats, it is advisable to stay put in the harbor.

The rise and fall of the tide is an important factor in each day's plans, especially as you voyage farther east. Tides of 10 to 13 feet are not unusual in these parts. Keep in mind that many harbors are available to even the deepest-draft vessels at high tide, but that same tide can put you high and dry where hours earlier there was plenty of water underneath the keel. Conversely, anchoring for low-tide depths will be dangerously short scope at high water. Furthermore, that ledge at the mouth of the harbor that is clearly visible as you enter at low water might be submerged and dangerous when you leave. Tidal currents are less predictable than they are below Cape Cod and may unexpectedly flow even after predicted high and low tides.

W G

Cape Cod Bay, MA

Column groups: **Dockage**, **Supplies**, **Services**

Marina	Phone	Largest Vessel Accommodated	VHF Channel Monitored/Working	Transient Slips/Total Slips	Approach/Dockside Depth (reported)	Floating Docks	Gas/Diesel	Groceries, Ice, Marine Supplies, Snacks	Repairs: Hull, Engine, Propeller	Lift (tonnage), Crane, Rail	Min/Max Amps	Courtesy Car, Laundry, Pool, Showers	Pump-Out Station	Nearby: Grocery Store, Motel, Restaurant
PROVINCETOWN														
1. Long Point Marina ▫ (WiFi)	(774) 593-5120	140	14/	6/14	20.0/11.0	F	D		E		30/100			GMR
2. Provincetown Marina ▫ (WiFi)	(508) 487-0571	400	16/9	80/100	13.0/13.0	F	GD	I			30/200+	LS	P	GMR
3. Flyer's Boat Shop & Rentals ▫ (WiFi)	(508) 487-0898	95	11/	/	25.0/12.0	F		IM	E	L3,R		S	P	GMR
WELLFLEET														
4. Town of Wellfleet Marina (WiFi)	(508) 349-0320	55	16/9	6/200	10.0/6.0	F	GD	IMS			30	S	P	GMR
SESUIT HARBOR														
5. Dennis Yacht Club-PRIVATE	(508) 385-3741	30	/	/	5.0/5.0			I				S		
6. Northside Marina	(508) 385-3936	85	/	/120	6.0/6.0	F	GD	IS	HEP	L	30	S	P	GMR
7. Dennis Municipal Marina	(508) 385-5555	60	9/66	5/268	6.0/8.0	F					30	S		GMR
BARNSTABLE														
8. Millway Marina	(508) 362-4904	32	9/78	/50	5.0/5.0	F	G	IM	HEP					GR
9. Barnstable Marine Services	(508) 362-3811	45	/	/45	3.0/5.0	F	GD	IMS	HEP	L20	30/50	S		GMR
10. Barnstable Harbor Master	(508) 790-6273	40	16/9	/	4.0/5.0	F		M			30	S	P	GMR
CAPE COD CANAL														
11. Sandwich Marina/East Boat Basin (WiFi)	(508) 833-0808	160	9/8	22/198	11.0/11.0	F	GD	I			30/100	LS	P	GMR

▫ Internet Access   (WiFi) Wireless Internet Access   onSpot Dockside WiFi Facility

See WaterwayGuide.com for current rates, fuel prices, website addresses, and other up-to-the-minute information. (Information in the table is provided by the facilities.)

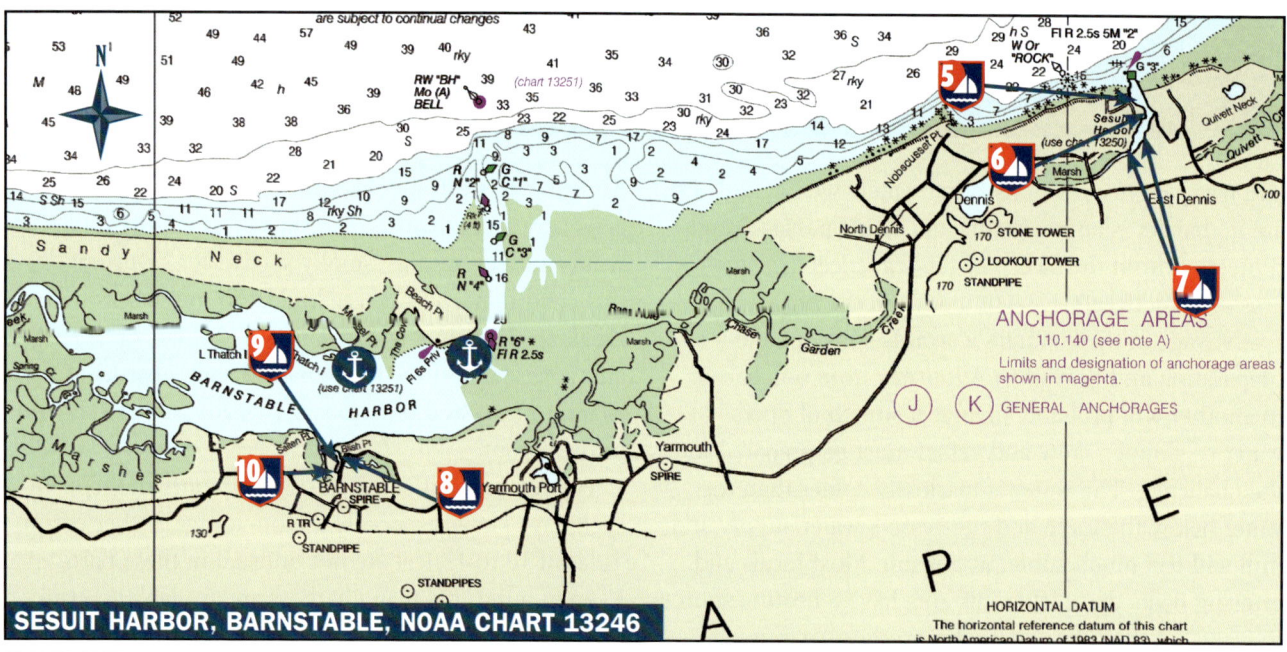

SESUIT HARBOR, BARNSTABLE, NOAA CHART 13246

CAPE COD CANAL, NOAA CHART 13246

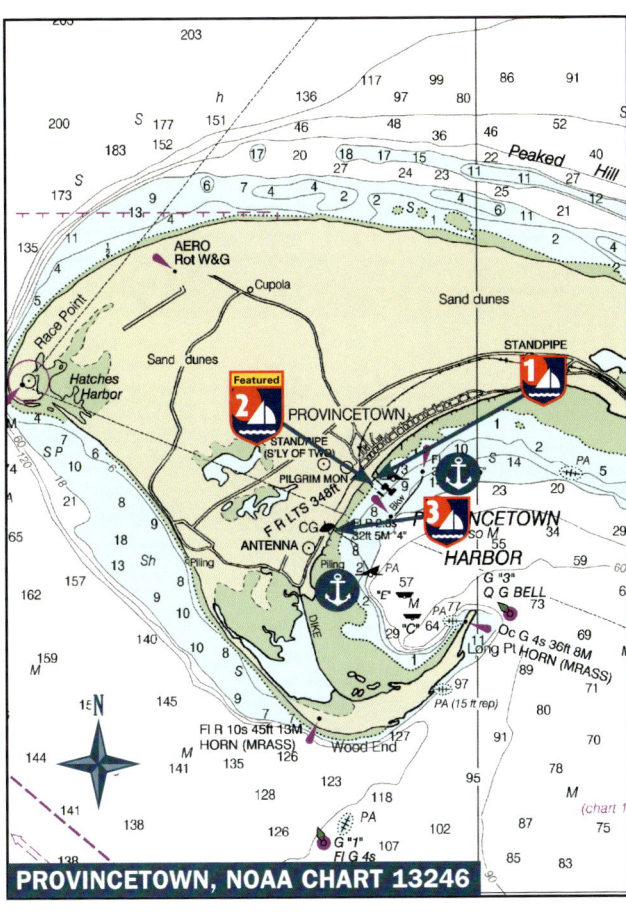

PROVINCETOWN, NOAA CHART 13246

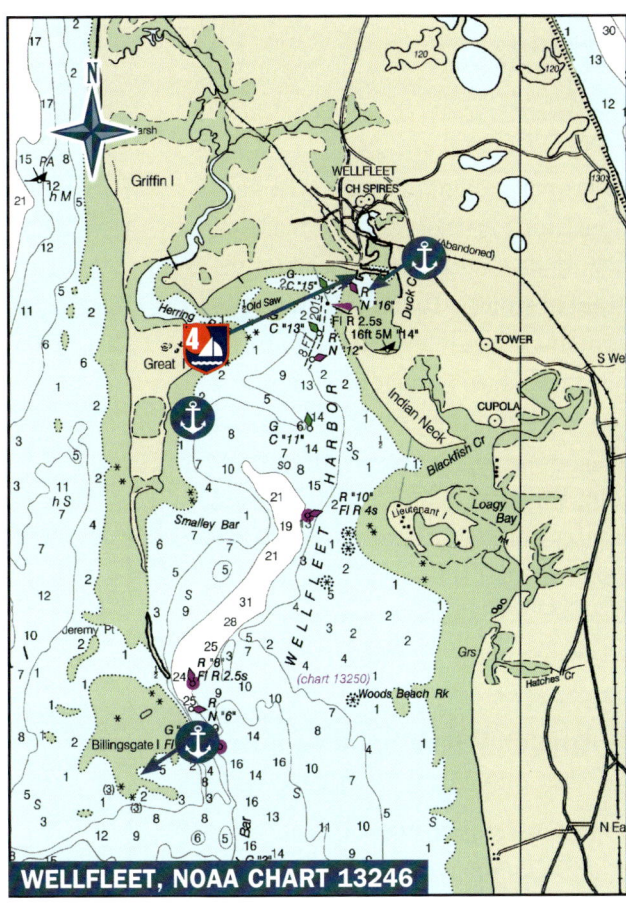

WELLFLEET, NOAA CHART 13246

DISCOVER PROVINCETOWN

New dockage. Upgraded facilities. Slips that can accommodate larger vessels – even mega yachts.
All nearby to the restaurants, galleries, shopping, and fishing of picturesque Provincetown, MA.

- 100 slips accommodating vessels up to 300'
- 85 moorings
- Outdoor Captain's Lounge with flat screen TV's and fire pits
- 725 feet new mega yacht dock
- Electrical services up to 480 volt 3 phase
- Fuel dock and pumpout services
- On-site parking and security
- New showers, bathrooms and laundry
- Complimentary Wi-Fi

ptownmarina.com   9 Ryder Street Ext. • Provincetown, MA 02657 • 508-487-0571 • info@ptownmarina.com

LOCATION • CONVENIENCE • NEW DOCKS

GOIN' ASHORE

PROVINCETOWN, MA

In Provincetown, mariners will find a flourishing artists' colony, a working fishing fleet and, in summer months, an army of smiling tourists. Provincetown contains a heady mixture of cultures – sidewalk artists, actors, summer residents and the people who live here year-round, most notably, the fisher folk. While old elm trees and Colonial houses still have the traditional Cape Cod look, art schools and gallery shows, book shops and tourist attractions now fill the narrow streets.

SERVICES

1. Arnold's Where You Rent Bikes
329 Commercial St. (508-487-0844)

2. Provincetown Post Office
219 Commercial St. (508-487-0368)

3. Provincetown Public Library
Town library in an airy former church built in 1860 with a half-scale model of a 1905 schooner at 356 Commercial St. (508-487-7094).

ATTRACTIONS

4. Expedition Whydah Museum
Displays of artifacts and treasures from a 1717 pirate shipwreck at 16 MacMillan Pier (508-487-8899).

5. Pilgrim Monument
The 252-foot monument is the tallest all-granite structure in the country and commemorates the Mayflower Pilgrims' first landing in the New World in Provincetown in November 1620. The walk to the top includes 116 steps and 60 ramps and takes about 10 minutes at a leisurely pace. Provides great views of the harbor.

6. Provincetown Art Association and Museum
Permanent collection and special exhibitions in six gallery spaces plus three landscaped sculpture gardens at 460 Commercial St. (508-487-1750).

7. Provincetown Museum
Cozy local museum featuring exhibits focused on the region's cultural and maritime history at 1 High Pole Hill Rd. (508-487-1310).

SHOPPING

8. CVS Pharmacy
Chain drug store at 132 Bradford St. (508-487-0019).

9. Far Land Provisions
Deli/bakery offering sandwiches and light fare plus specialty grocery items (150 Bradford St., 508-487-0045).

10. Lands' End Marine Supply
Chain hardware store with home tools and some boat supplies (337 Commercial St., 508-487-0784).

11. Provincetown Bookshop
A local treasure since 1932 at 246 Commercial St. (508-487-0964).

MARINAS

12. Flyers Boat Rentals
131 Commercial St. (508-487-0898)

13. Long Point Marina
16 MacMillan Pier (774-593-5120)

14. Provincetown Marina
9 Ryder St. Ext. (508-487-0571)

■ PROVINCETOWN TO CAPE COD CANAL

In contrast to the resort atmosphere on the south side of the Cape Cod arm, the ambiance inside the curve of Cape Cod Bay is quiet and relaxed. Even the weather cooperates. The boisterous southwester that creates heavy seas in Buzzards Bay can become a pleasant offshore breeze on Cape Cod Bay. Beyond Plymouth, flats, shoals, ledges and rocks appear, big headlands and capes thrust outward, and harbors are spaced far apart. Yet, inside the welcoming harbors of Provincetown and Wellfleet, sand dunes and sea grass mark your way and make for relaxed beachcombing.

Provincetown Harbor

Located at the extreme northern tip of Cape Cod, Provincetown has one of the most popular large harbors on the Atlantic coast. The marinas and some moorings are tucked behind an extended seawall, and all of the anchorages are lovely and give access either to the highly entertaining town or the beaches wrapping around to protect the harbor against ocean surge.

In Provincetown (popularly called P-town) makes a wonderful stop because of its vibrant arts scene, performance street artists, a variety of restaurants and the delightful nightlife. Much like Key West, it has a salty, edge of the world feel. If the busy town overwhelms, rent a bicycle, horse, car or beach buggy to get away to the fine beaches.

A visit to the Pilgrim Monument and Provincetown Museum (508-487-1310) provides great views of the harbor and one fee covers both attractions. The 252-foot monument is the tallest all-granite structure in the country and commemorates the first landing of the *Mayflower* in the New World in Provincetown in November 1620. The walk to the top includes 116 steps and 60 ramps and takes about 10 minutes at a leisurely pace.

NAVIGATION: Use NOAA Chart 13249. The big, wide Provincetown Harbor is over 1 mile from Long Point to the town dock and is easy to enter under almost any condition. Situational awareness is important, nonetheless. Quite a few schooners, whale-watching tours and fishing charter boats operate in the area and it's a popular place to show off one's tacking prowess.

Whether coming in from offshore, the Boston area or the canal, the rounded edges of Race Point and Wood End can be approached very closely unless weather dictates otherwise. Race Point's 41-foot flashing light is also a radio beacon while 45-foot Wood End Light is a flashing red with a horn that is quite useful in seasonal fog. The end of Long Point is less approachable. Make for quick-flashing green bell buoy "3" rather than for the 36-foot occulting green light on shore.

Dockage/Moorings: A cluster of facilities on Provincetown Harbor offer slips and moorings. Long Point Marina is situated just seaward of the town landing and offers dockage, diesel and launch service to both moored and anchored boats (VHF Channel 09). The Provincetown Harbormaster may be reached at 508-487-7030 and VHF Channel 12 is monitored for pump-out service.

Provincetown Marina has a 650-foot wave attenuator dock that provides a calm boat basin for its 100 slips and 85 moorings. They sell gas and diesel and allow boaters to fill their water tanks or wash their boats for a fixed fee. Amenities include showers, lockers, laundry and an outdoor Captain's Lounge with large-screen TVs and fire pits. Just a short walk down the pier is the downtown and Commercial St. with an incredible array of restaurants and shops. Reserve as early as March if looking to visit on peak weekends.

Anchorage: The mooring field now completely fills the area behind the breakwater at Provincetown and extends to the southwest past the breakwater and the Coast Guard station. After new floating docks were added, even more moorings were placed southwest of the breakwater so formerly acceptable anchoring areas have been overtaken.

You may be able to find room to anchor northeast of the breakwater in 6 to 12 feet MLW, keeping in mind the 9-foot tides. This area puts you as close as possible to the dinghy dock on the first dock out from shore on the northeast side of the pier, but it is exposed to big fetch from the east to the south.

The anchorage 1 mile south of the Provincetown breakwall has better protection from the prevailing southwesterly winds. Get as close to the ledge as your draft permits and be cautious of a sunken fishing boat marked with a small red buoy located towards the east side of the anchorage. Chop can create a long, wet ride back from town in any real southwesterly. Anchoring is prohibited around the piers and between the breakwall and the mooring field on the southwest side.

Wellfleet Harbor

The next viable harbor for shallow draft boats is Wellfleet Harbor. Once second only to Gloucester as a cod and mackerel fishing port, Wellfleet is a quiet summer resort nestled among dunes, ocean and moors. Located about halfway down the "hook," the town has high green hills, sleepy rural streets, lovely old houses and a tidy village straight out of Colonial America. It was here that Marconi built his first wireless station in 1901 and sent the first trans-Atlantic telegram in 1903.

Wellfleet is adjacent to the Cape Cod National Seashore, which offers excellent birding, hiking, swimming and surfing. Groceries, restaurants and shopping range up Commercial Street. Fresh seafood is available from a number of markets in this seaside town.

NAVIGATION: Use NOAA Charts 13250 and 13246. The protected harbor, about 26 miles east of the Cape Cod Canal, has a 5-mile-long, shoal-littered entry east of Billingsgate Shoal and Island. The latter qualifies as an island only at low water. The channel and harbor were partially dredged to 10 feet MLW in the fall/winter of 2020 and more dredging is scheduled to resume in fall 2021. Updates can be obtained from the Wellfleet Dredging Task Force (508-349-0300).

Flashing green buoy "3" sets up the boater for the turn north. Lieutenant Island Bar is well marked with red buoys, but Smalley Bar (on the west side of the channel) has no greens. A straight line from flashing red buoy "8" and flashing red buoy "10" is safe, and a ribbon of deep water leads past green can buoy "11" to the narrow, dredged channel that begins with red nun buoy "12." Looking toward Wellfleet Harbor you will see a couple of church spires and the fire lookout tower located in South Wellfleet. The Wellfleet breakwater light, flashing red "14," sits upon a skeleton-like tower to the east as you enter.

Dockage/Moorings: The Town of Wellfleet Marina and mooring basin is located behind Shirttail Point. There are patches of 1 to 2 feet MLW and an average of 2 to 3 feet MLW in the mooring field, making this a "no go" for deep-draft boats. The Wellfleet Harbormaster may be reached at 508-349-0320 for exact depths and updates on whether any dredging has been completed. On the public wharf is a well-placed launching ramp. VHF Channels 09 and 16 are monitored for pump-out service.

Anchorage: If your draft permits, the best overall anchorage is in the inner harbor off the town wharf in

4 to 7 feet MLW. Pay attention in the channel between the inner and outer harbors as it can get narrow in spots. There are shoals on both sides so keep an eye on the buoys.

In settled weather, there is good mud bottom north of Smalley Bar. Watch for the shoal marked by green can buoy "11" and keep the 10-foot tidal range in mind. The depths will range from 7 to 10 feet MLW. To the south of Billingsgate Shoal there is a good anchorage in 8 to 13 feet MLW. The shoal serves as a natural breakwater from north winds and seas.

Sesuit Harbor

Sesuit Harbor has the easiest entry on Cape Cod Bay's southern shore. The breakwater-protected entry channel is short and comparatively straight but does have a tendency to shoal. It is periodically dredged to 6-foot MLW depth but exercise proper caution and watch the depth sounder. This is a good place to seek local knowledge before entering. Note that there is a 4-mph speed limit, and anchoring is not allowed in the harbor.

Dockage: Sesuit Harbor is home to Northside Marina and Dennis Municipal Marina and is an excellent base from which to do some sightseeing in the nearby villages. Both marinas have slips, and Northside Marina sells all fuels. Nearby Dennis Yacht Club is private. The town of East Dennis provides provisioning possibilities, restaurants and other services. The Sesuit Harbormaster may be reached on VHF Channel 09 for pump-out service.

Barnstable Harbor

Barnstable is the largest community on Cape Cod. It is made up of seven villages: Barnstable, Centerville, Cotuit, Hyannis (including Hyannis Port), Marston Mills, Osterville and West Barnstable. The town was named after a village in Devon, England. The first settlers were farmers but fishing and salt soon became major industries. Before the arrival of the railroads towards the end of the 1800s, there were as many as 800 ships harbored there.

Barnstable is about 70 miles southeast of Boston, which made it a popular summer location for prominent 19th-century Bostonians. Some of the most famous people to have summered in Barnstable included Presidents Ulysses S. Grant, Grover Cleveland and, of course, the Kennedys. Given its location, beaches and wide variety of shops, it is no wonder that tourists come in droves to the Barnstable area.

NAVIGATION: Use NOAA Charts 13246 and 13250. Entry to Barnstable Harbor should not be attempted in periods of high winds or seas. The constantly shifting channel is tricky and the prevailing currents tend to set a vessel outside the channel. From a distance, you will be able to see a lighted radio tower in Barnstable, the tower of a former lighthouse on the south side of Beach Point and, farther in the distance, a spire from a Yarmouth church.

So much of the entrance is marsh that the surroundings change completely between high and low tide. Followed the buoyed channel from red-and-white bell buoy "BH" to just south of Beach Point and take

Sandwich Harbor

Bourne Bridge

care to pass north of Horseshoe Shoal by leaving green can buoy "9" and flashing green buoy "11" to the south.

Once west of green can buoy "13" the channel west to the yacht club is buoyed with green cans and red nuns and shouldn't be mistaken for the buoys marking the channel south to Maraspin Creek after flashing green buoy "1." The harbor is small and charts indicate an approach depth of 7 feet MLW but lows as shallow as 5 feet have been seen. Refer to the Harbormaster, Waterway Explorer (www.waterwayguide.com) and NOAA online charts for the most up-to-date information.

Dockage/Moorings: Facilities in Barnstable Harbor offers slips, all fuels and repairs. Barnstable's municipal marina has an occasional slip for transients and report 4-foot MLW approach depths. Call the Barnstable Harbormaster on VHF Channel 16 for slip availability and local knowledge on channel depths. Availability is always an issue in the summer months as there are long waiting lists to use the marinas and moorings.

Anchorage: The channel approaching Barnstable widens after rounding flashing red buoy "8" and good holding can be found south of the channel in at least 7 feet MLW. Be aware of the shoal between the channel and the anchorage. If you poke in south of Horseshoe Shoal, watch out for the charted cable area extending southward from Beach Point. This is badly exposed to the northeast at high tide. If you anchor between flashing red buoy "8" and flashing green buoy "9," get as far out of the channel as possible and be prepared for close encounters with fishing and whale-watching boats speeding through. Be aware of the tide status and your swinging radius and remember that the mean tide range is 9.5 feet. Tides flood southward and ebb northward at an average of 1.3 knots.

Note that the entire Nantucket Sound is designated as a No-Discharge Zone so it's helpful to take full advantage of Barnstable's ample number of pump-out stations before traveling on.

Cape Cod Canal (East End)

Heavily traveled, well marked and attractive, the Cape Cod Canal passage cuts across the neck of Cape Cod from Buzzards Bay to Cape Cod Bay, saving boats from the 135-mile trip through Nantucket Shoals and around Cape Cod to reach Boston or Maine. Over 14,000 commercial and recreational vessels transit the 17.5-mile waterway each year.

Sandwich is the site of the Cape Cod Bay entrance to the Cape Cod Canal. Sandwich, established in 1637, is the oldest town on Cape Cod and is rich in history and New England charm. It is surrounded by beautiful walking and biking trails, bird sanctuaries, saltwater estuaries, fresh water ponds and the seashore to tempt cruisers into a longer stay. The Sandwich Boardwalk is a favorite for visitors and residents alike. The Cape Cod Canal Visitor Center in Sandwich (508-833-9678) lays out the current features and operation of the Cape Cod Canal as well as providing historical objects and stories.

NAVIGATION: Use NOAA Chart 13229. The canal is able to handle vessels up to 825 feet long and has a 32-foot MLW controlling depth but all vessels with lengths greater than 65 feet must contact the Marine Traffic Controller on VHF Channel 13 before entering the canal and any delay on your part requires a second clearance to continue.

Other restrictions include:

- Vessels must be adequately powered, properly equipped and seaworthy.

- Sailboats must use auxiliary power during canal passage. Use of sails while motoring is permitted. However, large course changes and/or tacking are strictly prohibited in the land cut and approach channels.

- A 10-mph speed limit and "no excessive wake" is in effect for Cleveland Ledge and Hog Island channels and the land cut of the canal. The wake restrictions and speed limit are strictly enforced.

- Stopping, anchoring, fishing, unnecessarily idling at a low speed or otherwise obstructing navigation within the limits of the canal is prohibited. Low-powered vessels not making adequate headway are an obstruction to navigation. Vessels must stay to the right-hand side of the channel while transiting.

- Personal watercraft, kayaks, canoes, windsurfers or other non-motorized craft are not permitted to operate within or pass through the canal.

Despite the width and depth of the canal, the current within the canal can reach a velocity of 6 knots. Vessels of low power should not attempt to transit the canal against the current. Give careful attention to the tide and tidal current charts and make a very conservative estimate of the time you will need to pass both through the canal and beyond in order to allow for the effects of a foul-setting tide.

The Army Corps of Engineers also cautions that boaters must complete their transit within 2.5 hours. If you are unable to complete the transit in that time, you may be required to hire a helper tug at your expense. This last requirement makes it particularly important to calculate your speed-versus-tide requirements with some care. See more at www.nae.usace.army.mil.

Prominent on the east end of the canal is the stack from the power plant on the southern bank near the boat basin where larger vessels must wait for permission to transit the canal. Boats over 65 feet long must obey the two traffic lights–one on the eastward approach from Cape Cod Bay and the other at Wing's Neck on the westward approach from Buzzard's Bay. The red/amber/green configuration of these lights will indicate if any traffic emergencies have occurred in the canal potentially affecting your passage. The 7-mile-long land cut can be almost clear of fog when both Buzzards and Cape Cod Bays are thick with it.

Two highway bridges cross the canal before the low railroad bridge (**Bourne and Sagamore Bridge**s), both with 135-foot fixed vertical clearances. **ConRail Railroad Bridge** is normally open except during the very rare passage of a train to or from Cape Cod. If the draw is not in the fully open position, the opening signal is one prolonged and one short blast. Closed vertical clearance is a mere 7 feet so very few

IMPORTANT INFORMATION

- An online telecam is updated every 30 minutes from sunrise to sunset at: www.telecamsystems.com/capecodcanal
- Weather for the canal: 508-759-5991 or www.weather.gov/forecasts/graphical/sectors/massachusetts.php#tabs
- Navigational Regulations at: www.nae.usace.army.mil/recreati/ccc/navigation/navreg.htm

Cape Cod Bay, MA

		Dockage					Supplies		Services					
		Largest Vessel Accomodated	Transient Slips / Total Slips	VHF Channel Monitored / Working	Approach / Dockside Depth (reported)	Floating Docks	Gas / Diesel	Groceries, Ice, Marine Supplies, Snacks	Repairs: Hull, Engine, Propeller	Lift (tonnage), Crane, Rail	Min / Max Amps	Courtesy Car, Laundry, Pool, Showers	Pump-Out Station	Nearby: Grocery Store, Motel, Restaurant
PLYMOUTH														
1. Plymouth Yacht Club	(508) 747-0473	45	8/	/	12.0/12.0			I				LS		GMR
2. Safe Harbor Plymouth 💻 📶	(508) 746-4500	150	9/72	15/105	10.0/8.0	F	GD	IM	HEP	L80,C	30/50	LS	P	GMR
3. Plymouth Town Wharf	(508) 830-4182	110	16/	/	7.0/11.0		GD	I						GMR
DUXBURY														
4. Bayside Marine	(781) 934-0561		8/8	/	8.0/6.0		G	IM	HEP					
5. Duxbury Town Pier	(781) 934-2866	50	16/	/	8.0/8.0			IS	HEP				P	GR
6. Long Point Marine	(781) 934-5302	60	16/78	/	/			M	HEP	L35,C	30			
GREEN HARBOR RIVER														
7. Taylor Marine	(781) 837-9617	45	/	4/130	6.0/6.0	F	GD	I	E	L10,C	30	S	P	GR
8. Safe Harbor Green Harbor	(781) 837-1181	60	65/	20/180	8.0/8.0	F	GD	IM	HEP	L25	30/50	S		GR

💻 Internet Access 📶 Wireless Internet Access 🔵 onSpot Dockside WiFi Facility

See WaterwayGuide.com for current rates, fuel prices, website addresses, and other up-to-the-minute information. (Information in the table is provided by the facilities.)

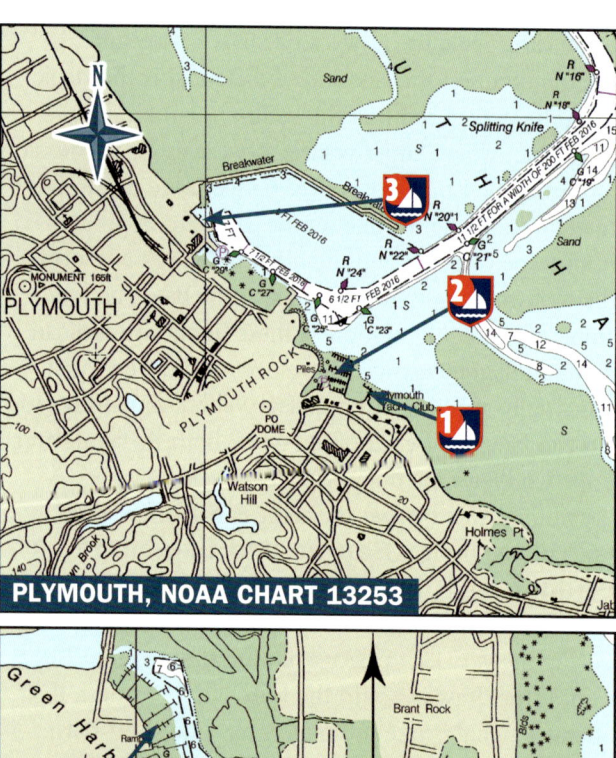

PLYMOUTH, NOAA CHART 13253

GREEN HARBOR RIVER, NOAA CHART 13253

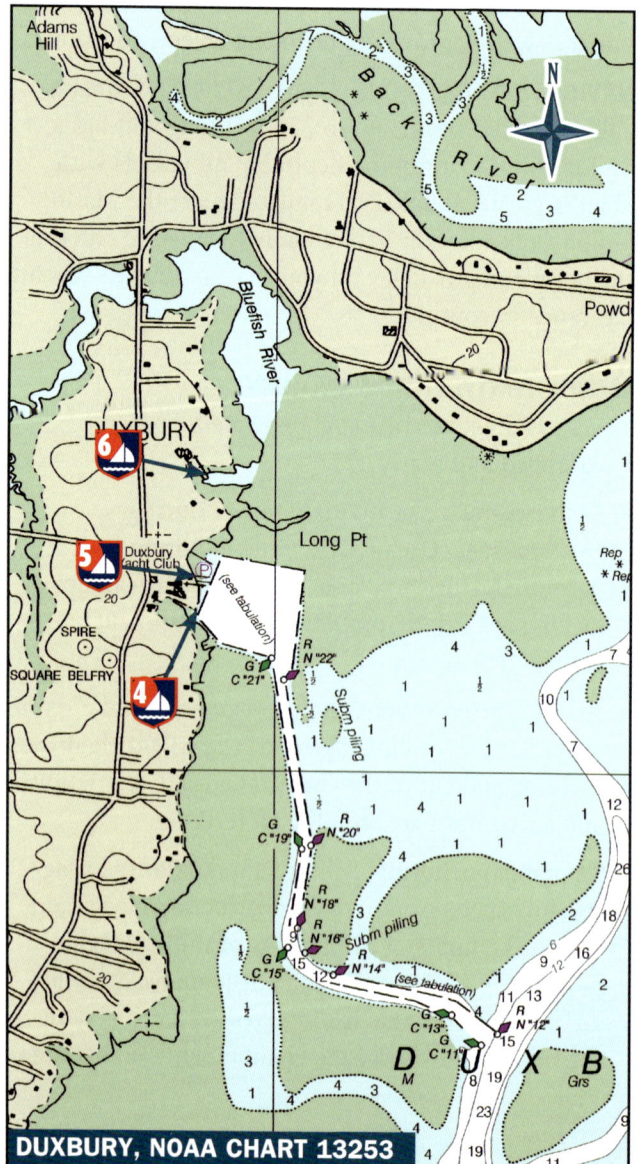

DUXBURY, NOAA CHART 13253

vessels will clear the bridge during a closure. Monitor VHF Channel 13 for alerts to any closings. If running with a strong, favorable current, look well ahead to assure passage under the lift span as turning at the last minute may not be an option. The bridge operator sounds two long blasts before lowering the bridge. It takes approximately 2.5 minutes to raise or lower it. If the bridge is lowered during periods of decreased visibility, the bridge operator will signal four short blasts every 2 minutes.

Even though commercial traffic is heavy on the canal, you should have no difficulties if you pick tide and weather carefully, proceed cautiously and stick to the right side of the channel as if driving on a highway.

Dockage: The Sandwich Marina/East Boat Basin, operated by the Town of Sandwich, has floating piers throughout the harbor with transient slips, an immaculate laundry and full fuel service. Arrange in advance to rent slip space from the marina if you wish to lie over at the eastern end of the canal. They offer slips for 2- to 4-hour stays as well as overnight. The Sandwich Harbormaster's office monitors VHF Channels 08 and 09 for pump-out service.

The charted commercial pilings opposite the entrance to the harbor of refuge are reserved for barge traffic, which can arrive at any time and recreational boats are banned from using these pilings. Video monitors will pick you up immediately and a Coast Guard boat will arrive quickly to ask you, in no uncertain terms, to move along. Additionally, cruisers may not anchor in the tiny harbor of refuge, a dredged pocket of deep water at the eastern (Cape Cod Bay) end of the canal.

◼ TO COHASSET HARBOR

Plymouth Harbor

About 20 miles northwest from the east end of the Cape Cod Canal is the historic town of Plymouth, nestled deep behind Plymouth Beach. In the northern segment, the Cowyard leads to Duxbury Bay.

Plymouth, known as "America's Hometown," was the site of the first enduring colony in New England, founded in 1620 by the passengers of the *Mayflower*, establishing New England. In the Plymouth Village Historic District you will find many restored 18th-century houses including half a dozen you may visit. The Pilgrim Hall Museum (508-746-1620) is one of the very oldest in the country and contains an impressive collection of Pilgrim lore and possessions including Miles Standish's swords.

Plimoth Plantation (508-746-1622) is a re-enactment town demonstrating the colonists' 17th-century lifestyle and the ship that brought them, although the spelling is changed to differentiate it from the town and original locations. Inside the plantation's 1622 fort "villagers" reenact the daily lives of their original counterparts as they tend gardens, cook food over open fires and make their own furniture, baskets and pottery. The reproduction *Mayflower II*, which was built in Plymouth, England, using 17th century tools and sailed to Plymouth, MA, in 1957 to great acclaim. After receiving a four-year, 11-million-dollar Mystic Seaport "spa treatment," the ship is back in Plymouth.

NAVIGATION: Use NOAA Chart 13253. Entry to the bays between Plymouth and Duxbury begins inside the long finger of Gurnet Point's high, bare cliff with its white, 102-foot-tall lighthouse, the oldest freestanding wooden light-house in the country. From the outset you will have to navigate around lobster buoys and fishers in skiffs.

The navigational aids down the wide channel keep cruisers off Browns Bank and a generous distance from Saquish Head. However, the outgoing tidal rip across the channel can present quite a challenge to inbound craft under sail. Duxbury Pier Light (locally known as "Bug Light" as are so many squat lighthouses) sits at the confluence of the Plymouth channel and the Cowyard, which leads north to Duxbury. The light was turned over to a non-profit in 2019 with the understanding that they would care for it in perpetuity so it will remain a photogenic staple of every visit.

The flashing green bell buoy "9" and red-over-green buoy "NC" located southwest of Duxbury Pier mark the entrance to Plymouth Harbor Channel. The red-over-green denotes that the southerly channel to Plymouth is primary while the westerly channel into Kingston Bay is secondary. The Plymouth Harbor channel parallels the beach in a southeasterly direction for about 1 mile between two 16-foot flashing lights: quick-flashing red "12" and flashing green "17." There the channel takes a sharp turn southwest for another well-marked run past the breakwater to the inner harbor. Refer to the Waterway Explorer (www.waterwayguide.com) and NOAA online charts for the most up-to-date information as the buoys are changed as needed.

Scituate Harbor, MA

SCITUATE		Dockage					Supplies		Services					
		Largest Vessel Accommodated	VHF Channel Monitored/Working	Transient Slips/Total Slips	Approach/Dockside Depth (reported)	Floating Docks	Gas/Diesel	Groceries, Ice, Marine Supplies, Snacks	Repairs: Hull, Engine, Propeller	Lift (tonnage) Crane, Rail	Min/Max Amps	Courtesy Car, Laundry, Pool, Showers	Pump-Out Station	Nearby: Grocery Store, Motel, Restaurant
1. Scituate Harbor Yacht Club WiFi	(781) 545-0372	38	9/	5/97	10.0/10.0	F	GD	IS			50	S		GMR
2. Satuit Boat Club ☐ WiFi	(781) 545-9752	58	9/9	/	8.0/8.0	F	GD	I	HEP	L,R		S	P	GMR
3. Scituate Harbor Marina ☐ WiFi	(781) 545-2165	75	9/11	5/85	11.0/9.0	F	GD	I			30/50	S		GMR
4. Mill Wharf Marina ☐ WiFi	(781) 545-3333	55	9/	2/89	11.0/8.0	F	GD	IMS			30/50	S		MR
5. Cole Parkway Marina	(781) 545-2130	50	16/9	10/180	10.0/8.0			I			30/50	S	P	GR
6. Scituate Launch/Waterline Moorings ☐ WiFi	(781) 545-4154	50	9/9	/	10.0/8.0			I	HEP			LS	P	GMR
7. Scituate Boat Works	(781) 545-0487	45	9/	/	12.0/10.0	F		IM	HEP	L35	30/50	S		GMR
8. Scituate Marine Park & Maritime Center	(781) 545-8724	45	/9	/78	12.0/10.0	F		IM	HEP	L		S		GMR

☐ Internet Access WiFi Wireless Internet Access onSpot Dockside WiFi Facility

See WaterwayGuide.com for current rates, fuel prices, website addresses, and other up-to-the-minute information. (Information in the table is provided by the facilities.)

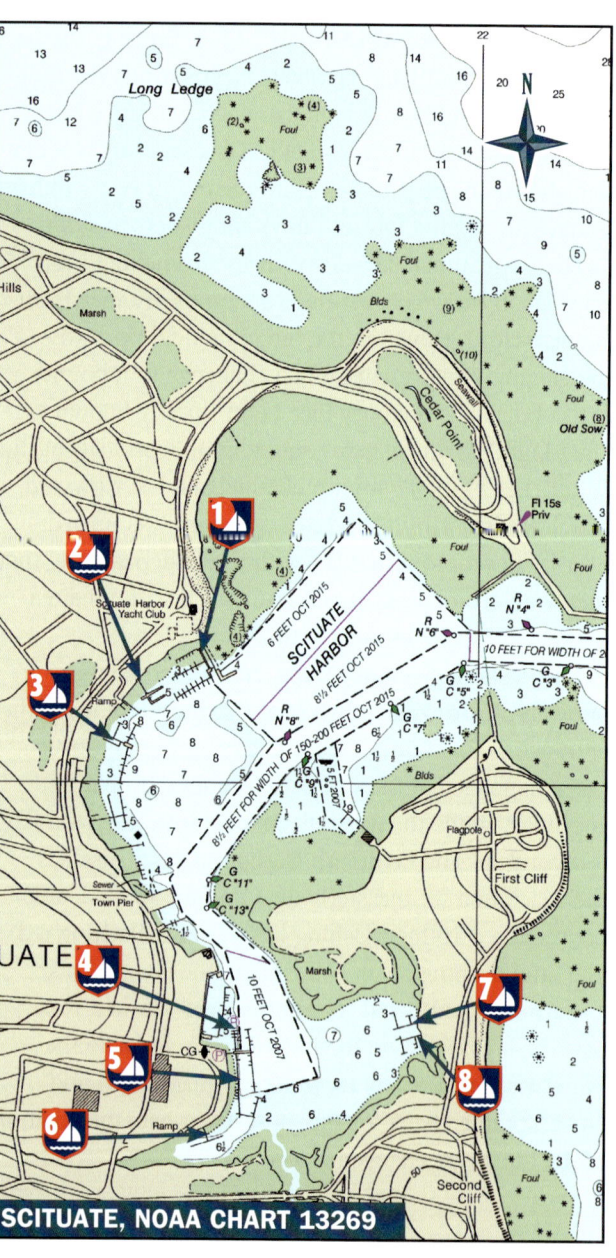

SCITUATE, NOAA CHART 13269

Dockage/Moorings: Upon entering the inner harbor, the Greek Revival monument protecting what remains of Plymouth Rock lies dead ahead. Plymouth Yacht Club offers transient moorings and is prominently located on the knoll south of green can buoy "23," followed immediately by the extensive facilities of Safe Harbor Plymouth, a full-service boatyard and marina with deep-draft transient slips. The yard has complete repair and fabrication shops and easy access to both gasoline and diesel fuel.

The Plymouth Town Wharf is located at the end of the buoyed channel. It has diesel and gasoline and a dinghy dock. Call the Plymouth Harbormaster for slip availability at 508 830 4182 and VHF Channels 09 and 16 are monitored for pump-out service.

Anchorage: Anchoring is prohibited in the Plymouth inner harbor, which is filled with commercial craft and private moorings. Moorings also fill other reasonably close areas with reasonable depths so a mooring will be required if you plan to stay in Plymouth.

Duxbury Bay

Miles Standish founded the Colonial town of Duxbury early in Massachusetts' history. Even though traditional clapboard housing stock of the period remains, today Duxbury bustles with summer resort and tourist traffic flocking to the contemporary shops and restaurants. The harbor is well protected and visiting cruisers are welcomed but available space is tight.

NAVIGATION: Use NOAA Chart 13253. Duxbury Bay is a big, shallow body of water. After rounding Duxbury Pier Lighthouse, a 35-foot tall flashing red, mind the

Scituate Harbor

buoys and watch the chart while the Cowyard is to the east and the eroded remains of Saquish Head's long point stretch to the west. The channel divides west of privately owned Clarks Island. The privately marked eastern branch follows the west side of Clarks Island to a fixed bridge (5-foot vertical clearance) three miles north, which connects Duxbury to Powder Point. The main channel turns to the northwest and leads into Duxbury Harbor.

The Duxbury channel and harbor are shoal-prone, reducing the optimal depth significantly between dredging projects. Minimum depths of 7 feet MLW were experienced by our Cruising Editor in 2020. Call ahead or check with locals for current depths. Privately maintained channel buoys mark the encroaching shoal at the southern tip of the Cowyard's long bar and 0.5 mile west at the mouth of the Jones River, north of The Nummet.

Dockage/Moorings: There are few reserved transient slips here but the Town of Duxbury offers moorings. Contact the Duxbury Harbormaster on VHF Channel 16. While there is no pump-out service offered by boat, you can use the shoreside pump-out station, which monitors VHF Channel 16. You may land your dinghy at the Harbormaster's dock and there is a bakery, fish market, wine store and Post Office all within walking distance.

Anchorage: Red nun buoys "4" and "6" lead to an anchorage off Goose Point in Kingston Bay in 10 to 15 feet MLW with some protection from the north. Duxbury's harbormaster allows dinghy landing at their dock but it's a long trip from here. Farther north in Duxbury Bay you can drop the hook to the west of Clarks Island in 10 to 18 feet MLW, where the Pilgrims first anchored, or just north of it for some protection

from the north through south. The closest anchorage to Duxbury is north of red nun buoy "12" in 9 to 13 feet MLW.

Depths are highly variable in the Cowyard. Check specific locations carefully against charted depths and actual soundings. The current is strong so swim with care.

Green Harbor

Just 5 miles north of Gurnet Point, Green Harbor River is home to many charter and recreational fishing boats. Green Harbor Lobster Pound (781-834-4571) is on the western shore at Marshfield with lobsters, clams, scallops, fish and shrimp and is open daily from Memorial Day to Labor Day (781-834-4571). There is no room for anchoring in this harbor.

NAVIGATION: Use NOAA Chart 13253. Flashing green bell buoy "3" has been set 600 yards southeast of the jettied entrance at the north end of long curving Duxbury Beach. The Army Corps of Engineers dredges here most years to maintain project depths of 6 feet MLW but shoaling is swift since a jetty breach worsened the situation. The local harbormaster needs Congressional approval and funding to fix not only the breach but a misalignment of the jetties, which exacerbates the problem. Project depths and widths were accomplished in May 2020 but be prepared for decreasing depths and a narrowing of the 100-foot nominal channel over time, exercise caution and obtain local knowledge. Another full dredging is planned for 2021.

Many local fishermen do not enter or leave Green Harbor within 90 minutes either side of low tide. Do not

Cohasset
Harbor, MA

COHASSET		Largest Vessel Accommodated	VHF Channel Monitored / Working	Transient Slips / Total Slips	Dockside Depth (reported)	Floating Docks	Gas / Diesel	Groceries, Ice, Marine Supplies, Snacks	Repairs: Hull, Engine, Propeller	Lift (tonnage), Crane, Rail	Min / Max Amps	Courtesy Car, Laundry, Pool, Showers	Pump-Out Station	Nearby: Grocery Store, Motel, Restaurant
				Dockage				**Supplies**			**Services**			
1. Cohasset Yacht Club	(781) 383-9633	45	10/	/	6.0/6.0			I			30			
2. Mill River Marine Railways	(781) 383-1207	70	/	2/2	6.0/10.0	F		M	HEP	R	30/50			MR
3. Cohasset Harbormaster	(781) 383-0863	55	9/10	/	/			IS	HE	R			P	GMR
4. Cohasset Harbor Marina	(781) 383-1504	42	/	75/75	7.0/6.0	F			HP		20/50		P	GMR

□ Internet Access 📶 Wireless Internet Access ⊙ onSpot Dockside WiFi Facility

See WaterwayGuide.com for current rates, fuel prices, website addresses, and other up-to-the-minute information. (Information in the table is provided by the facilities.)

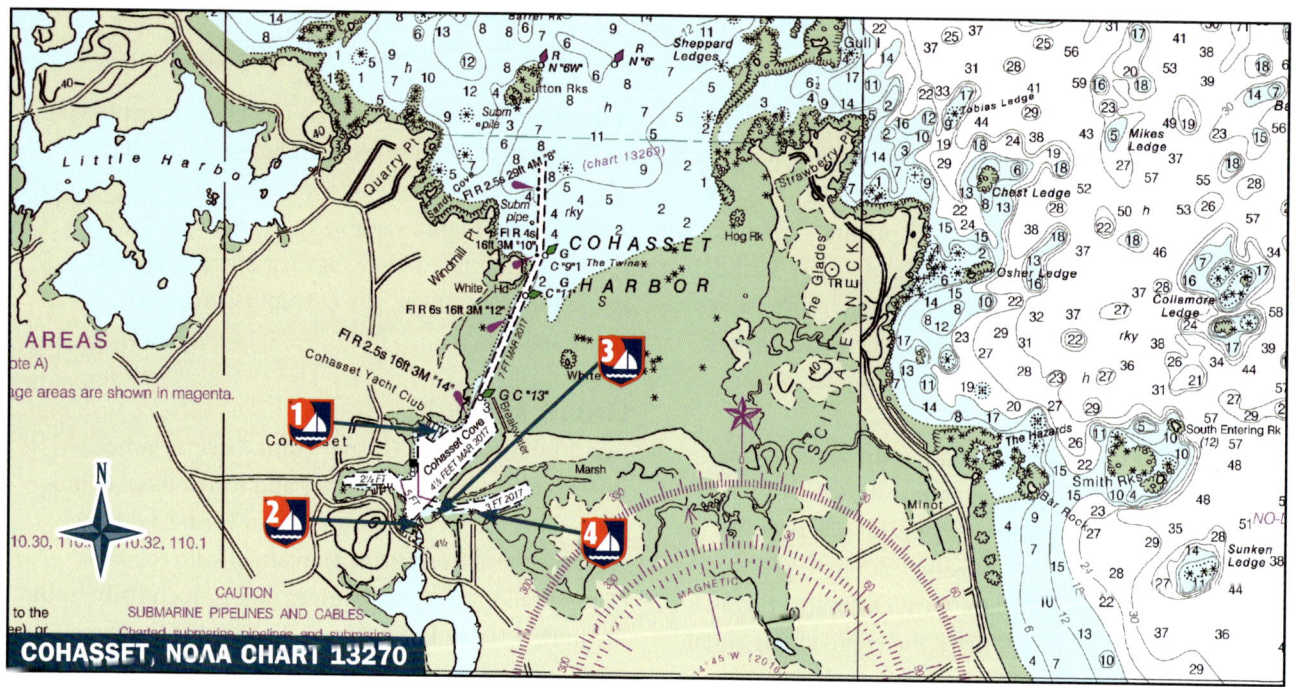

COHASSET, NOAA CHART 13270

attempt to enter on an ebb tide with easterly winds and be cautious of submerged boulders on the south side of the channel. On the way in watch out for Bartlett Rock and pick up the channel at red nun buoy "2GH" if in doubt. After leaving red nun buoy "6" to the east, find flashing red "8" sited on the end of a jetty off Blackmans Point. Center up between the western jetty and the flashing red "8" then head straight along the western jetty (without straying toward it). Center up between that jetty and the point as you enter the narrowest part of the channel. Watch for moored boats that may make this narrow passage even smaller.

Dockage: Taylor Marine offer slips and all fuels. Supplies and an excellent beach are a short walk away. To the north and across the harbor is the 180-slip Safe Harbor Green Harbor, which welcomes transients with reserved slips, a fuel dock, a restaurant with an outdoor deck overlooking the marina, a bait shop and a marine safety school. The marina is located within walking distance to shops and groceries.

Scituate Harbor

Scituate (pronounced "SIT-you-it" from the Wampanoag word *satuit* or "cold brook") rings a small, snug harbor, one of the most accommodating on the East Coast for recreational boats. The town harbor surrounds Scituate and offers a variety of fine restaurants to satisfy any body's appetite, a supermarket, hardware stores and a theater company/playhouse.

Although it is a crowded harbor and anchoring is prohibited, the harbor and town are well worth a stop for a day or two. The Scituate Lighthouse, built in 1810, provides a good view of the harbor and surrounding areas. Other sites of historical interest are the Cudworth House, Lawson Tower and the Stockbridge Mill, which are all easily visited. The Scituate Chamber of Commerce provides up to date information on their web site at www.scituatechamber.org.

Speed limit in the harbor is 6 mph and is strictly enforced as is the No-Discharge law. A seasonal Coast Guard station is located inside the channel entrance.

NAVIGATION: Use NOAA Chart 13267. Scituate Harbor is easily entered between Cedar Point to the north, marked on the chart by ABAND LT HO and First Cliff to the south. From the red-and-white Morse (A) gong buoy "SA," follow a course of 289° magnetic to the mouth of the channel. A breakwater protects the well-marked basin and its many lobster buoys. Scituate Harbor's entrance channel is well marked but stay to the center until well past the jetties. If unfamiliar with this port, do not attempt the approach after dark. Channel depth is charted at 10 to 12 feet MLW but shoals are present on the outside edges.

Dockage/Moorings: Private marinas, yacht clubs and a town-operated marina may have slips available by reservation or on a first-come, first-served basis. The Scituate Marine Park & Maritime Center has a public kayak ramp and public bathrooms and showers. There is a walking trail around the perimeter of the park, as well as two historical buildings preserving Scituate's maritime history.

The Scituate Boat Club is a favorite stop among cruisers looking for transient moorings with launch service to local restaurants and pet-friendly access to the beach. Satuit Harbor Yacht Club, Scituate Harbor Marina, Mill Wharf Marina, Cole Parkway Marina (managed by the Town of Scituate's Harbormaster) and Scituate Boat Works all have transient slips. Scituate Launch/Waterline Moorings supervises a large number of rental moorings and can often accommodate transients. Rental includes showers and launch service into town or to the many restaurants on the harbor. Call the launch on VHF Channel 09 for hours of operation and pump-out boat status.

Cohasset Harbor
On the fringes of Boston, Cohasset is a popular, crowded harbor with a large local fleet and good anchorage. Ashore you will find plenty of restaurants and beaches.

NAVIGATION: Use NOAA Charts 13269 or 13270. Cohasset Harbor was dredged in 2016 and surveyed in 2017. The entrance channel is charted as 7 feet MLW and most of the cove has 6 to 9 feet MLW. It shallows badly deeper in and there are barely shoal-draft depths to and past the town landing. Contact the Cohasset Harbormaster on VHF Channel 10 for approach depths.

Dockage/Moorings: The hospitable Cohasset Yacht Club may have a space for you; call ahead. Mill River Marine Railways is a working yard with a railway and limited transient space. The 75-slip Cohasset Harbor Marina may be a better bet for a transient slip (to 42 feet). Contact the Cohasset Harbormaster on VHF Channel 10 for slip, mooring and pump-out service requests. What used to be an anchorage is filled with mooring balls. The cove no longer has space for anchoring, even in the incredibly shallow Bailey Creek.

◼ BOSTON HARBOR AREA

Boston's attractions, historic landmarks and amenities are so numerous that they deserve a guidebook of their own. Fortunately, several are widely available in tourist shops around the harbor.

Unlike most big cities, Boston and its environs has dozens of friendly yacht clubs, protected marinas, secluded anchorages, boatyards and facilities for recreational craft, many of which welcome cruising boats. Fascinating sightseeing is within easy distance of almost anywhere you dock. Nearby are historic towns and notable shore resorts to visit as well as dozens of islands to investigate by dinghy.

Entering Boston Harbor
Like all big-city harbors, Boston is crowded with commercial and recreational boats of all types. Freighters, tankers, cruise ships, high-speed ferries and excursion boats vie with pleasure craft of all descriptions. The Harbor hums with activity and nautical history.

NAVIGATION: Use NOAA Charts 13270 and 13272. Red-and-white Morse (A) buoy "B," located 8 miles east-northeast of Deer Island, guides you into Boston Harbor. Note that the Coast Guard has received reports of periodic GPS reception problems near buoy B and ask that mariners use caution in this area and

WG

Nantasket Roads Area, MA

		Largest Vessel Accommodated	VHF Channel Monitored / Working	Transient Slips / Total Slips	Approach / Dockside Depth (reported)	Floating Docks	Gas / Diesel	Groceries, Ice, Marine Supplies, Snacks	Repairs: Hull, Engine, Propeller	Lift (tonnage), Crane Rail	Min / Max Amps	Courtesy Car, Laundry, Pool, Showers	Pump-Out Station	Nearby: Grocery Store, Motel, Restaurant
HULL BAY					Dockage			Supplies		Services				
1. Hull Yacht Club WiFi	(781) 925-9739	45	71/71	/	6.0/9.0			I		L2		S		GR
2. Sunset Bay Marina 💻 WiFi	(781) 925-2828	80	7/7	10/170	12.0/12.0	F	G	I	HEP	C	30/50	LS	P	GMR
3. Steamboat Wharf Marina WiFi	(781) 925-0044	120	7/7	/87	14.0/12.0	F		I	HEP		30/50	S		GMR
4. Hingham Yacht Club	(781) 749-3806	30	71/	/	15.0/9.0		GD	IS				S	P	
WEYMOUTH BACK RIVER														
5. Hingham Shipyard Marinas 💻 WiFi	(781) 749-2222	135	9/	15/500	15.0/12.0		GD	GIS	H		30/100	LS	P	GMR
6. Tern Harbor Marina 💻 WiFi	(781) 337-1964	110	9/	10/150	15.0/10.0	F		IM	HEP	L35	15/50	LS	P	R
WEYMOUTH FORE RIVER														
7. MarineMax Boston at Bay Pointe Marina 💻 WiFi	(617) 326-3294	150	9/	/247	45.0/8.0	F	GD	IMS	HEP	L50	30/50	LS	P	GMR
8. Captain's Cove Marina 💻 WiFi	(617) 328-3331	60	69/69	22/180	40.0/20.0	F		I			30/50	S	P	GMR

💻 Internet Access   WiFi Wireless Internet Access   📶 onSpot Dockside WiFi Facility

See WaterwayGuide.com for current rates, fuel prices, website addresses, and other up-to-the-minute information. (Information in the table is provided by the facilities.)

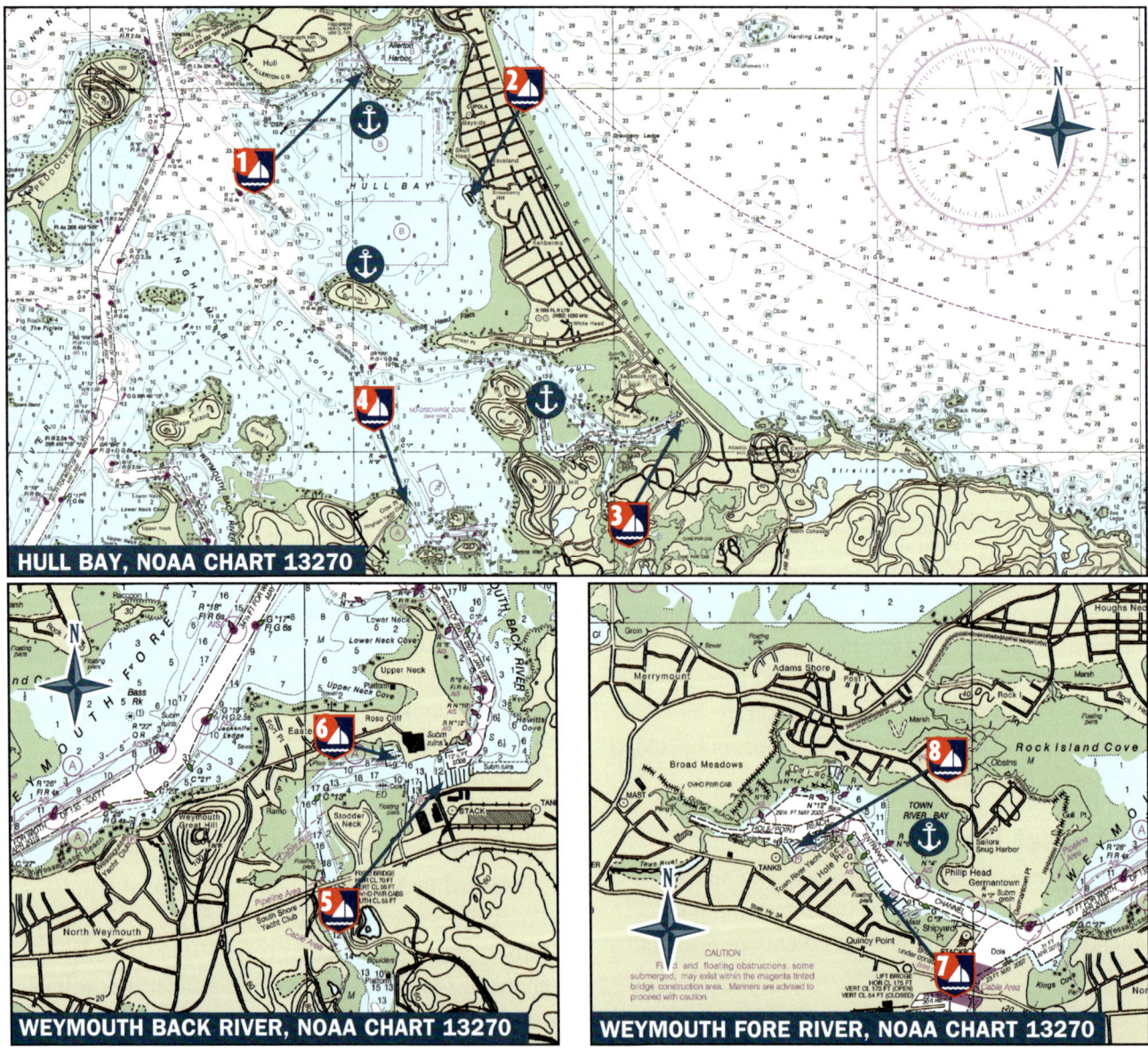

HULL BAY, NOAA CHART 13270

WEYMOUTH BACK RIVER, NOAA CHART 13270

WEYMOUTH FORE RIVER, NOAA CHART 13270

report any reception issues by calling 703-313-5900 or emailing tis-pf-nisws@uscg.mil.

The Deer Island Light fog signal has been changed to a Mariner Radio Activated Sound Signal (MRASS). During times of reduced visibility, mariners are requested to turn their VHF-FM radio to Channel 83A/157.175Mhz and key their microphone 5 times consecutively to activate the fog signal for 45 minutes.

Boston Harbor requires an attentive navigator. Hazards include crisscrossing wakes and ferry routes, numerous buoys and channels, shipping traffic, and unmarked shoals, rocks and ledges in apparently good water. Many side waters, notably Quincy and Dorchester Bays, are relatively unmarked. Even the numerous islands rarely look as you would expect from the charts. The plethora of lights and buoys can be confusing; be sure to keep them sorted out in your mind and on your chart. Keep an eye astern for two reasons: ferries traveling up to and over 30 knots for one and for another the currents, which can run to 2.5 knots or more and set you off course into very shallow, dangerously rocky, waters.

Marking the entry on Massachusetts Bay is the 114-foot Minots Light, famous up and down the coast as the "I Love You Light," for its "one-four-three" flashing light pattern. From here the approach is via any of three natural channels: Eastern Channel, The Gangway and Western Channel. All are marked and well charted, threading between outlying rocks and ledges. These passages, like those found in Maine and on the northern shore of Long Island Sound, are somewhat difficult but present no problem in clear weather.

Local boaters like the wider Gangway Channel despite its unmarked rocks. The *Coast Pilot* prefers the narrower but deeper and clearer Eastern Channel. The Western Channel between Brush Ledge and Chittenden Rock is the shallowest with depths less than 6 feet MLW and all agree that the best time to enter, especially if you draw more than 5 feet, is on a rising tide.

Both main entrances to the harbor have numerous, well-marked side channels feeding off in all directions. If entering the harbor from the south, the more southerly and frequently used by recreational craft is Nantasket Roads, giving direct access to a vast circle of bays, anchorages and rivers in the harbor's southern sector. The other entrance, President Roads, is the main ship channel leading to the inner harbor and to northern parts of the outer harbor. Connecting the two are The Narrows and Nubble Channel.

With all its smaller bays and rivers, the Boston area has many viable anchorages. Only a small handful will be noted in the text below. You must keep the tidal range in mind when setting an anchor. The average rise and fall in the Boston Harbor area is 9.5 feet and some

Boston Financial District

BOSTON WATERBOAT MARINA

BOSTON YACHT HAVEN INN & MARINA

Boston

CONSTITUTION MARINA

CHARLESTOWN MARINA

high tides can be almost 12 feet MLW. An anchor rode of 50 feet in 10 feet of water (5:1 scope) is woefully inadequate at high tide of 20 or 21 feet. Do not fail to consult the Boston tide tables when setting the anchor.

Nantasket Roads

Wide Hull Bay is perhaps the easiest of any Boston harbor to enter from Massachusetts Bay. The buoyed channel of the Weir River to the south passes around Worlds End, a 251-acre park maintained by The Trustees of the Reservation with sweeping views of Boston and 4.5 miles of carriage paths and footpaths, perfect for moderate hiking. The channel then leads to Nantasket Beach, a favorite Boston retreat with over a mile of fine beach. To the west a channel leads past Crow Point's range lights into Hingham Harbor.

Continuing in a clockwise direction, the long, deep Weymouth Back River is midway between Hingham Harbor and Weymouth Fore River. Wide and open to Germantown Point, the Weymouth Fore River has protected reaches that extend to East Braintree and Weymouth on the south.

Big and generally shallow, Quincy Bay has a number of yacht clubs along its shores. The town of Quincy (pronounced "KWIN-zee") is the birthplace of U.S. presidents John Adams and John Quincy Adams, a story that is well documented at the fascinating Adams National Historic Park, accessible by conducted van tour only. Information and tickets may be found at the National Park Service Visitor Center (1250 Hancock St., 617-770-1175). The United States Naval Shipbuilding Museum is here, housed in the *U.S.S. Salem*, a heavy cruiser docked at the former Fore River Shipyard. Call 617-479-7900 for more information on tours and times.

NAVIGATION: Use NOAA Chart 13270. Enter Nantasket Roads between Point Allerton at the northern end of Nantasket Reach and Little Brewster Island, the site of the 102-foot-tall Boston Lighthouse. A short 2 miles west, turn south into Hull Gut (with a 2- to 3-knot current) to pass between Windmill Point and Peddocks Island into Hingham Bay with its various arms and islands.

Well-marked Hingham Bay has few obstructions all the way to the Weymouth Back and Fore Rivers. Upriver from the deep-draft channel on the Weymouth Fore River, depths are uncertain. **The SR3A (Fore River) Bridge** (with 60-foot closed vertical clearance) opens on signal except from 6:30 a.m. to 9:00 a.m. and from 4:30 p.m. to 6:30 p.m., Monday through Friday,

excluding holidays. In a bit of excellent charity, a portion of the old temporary bridge here is now a short bridge over a formerly dangerous river in Perches, Haiti.

Dockage/Moorings: The Hingham Harbormaster manages four moorings located on the east side of Worlds End and two moorings at Langlee Island in Hingham Harbor (available with online reservation at www.bostonharborislands.org/boating).

The Hull Yacht Club welcomes transient boats on moorings in Allerton Harbor in the northeast corner of Hull Bay. To the south, Hingham Yacht Club at Crow Point on Hingham Harbor has moorings and sells all fuels. The public landing has pump-out service.

The Weymouth Back River offers both protection and a range of marine and other facilities including Hingham Shipyard Marinas, which is conveniently adjacent to the commuter ferry to downtown Boston as well as a ferry to the Boston Harbor Islands. A dozen restaurants are within easy walking distance of Stodders Neck in the big strolling outdoor mall, which also has a movie theater and shopping. The Weymouth Harbormaster may be reached at 781-682-6109 and VHF Channel 9 is monitored for pump-out service.

In Weymouth Fore River is your destination, turn northwest at Germantown Point and follow the entrance channel into Town River Bay. Bay Pointe Marina has slips for vessels to 150 feet, a fuel dock and an on-site service center. Captain's Cove Marina is located up the river past Hole Point in a protected inlet in which boaters often take shelter during storms. Restaurants and grocery stores are nearby.

Anchorage: Directly off Nantasket Roads to the south is Perty Cove on the northwest side of Peddocks Island. This has fair holding in 11 to 16 feet MLW with mud and rock and is open and exposed from north through southwest.

Protected from all but westerlies, Hull Bay has several good anchorages. Designated Special Anchorage Areas are located at Spinnaker Island (which protects Allerton Harbor) and Bumkin Island in 6 to 10 feet MLW. On approach to Bumkin Island take care to avoid the submerged rock that's 2 feet below the surface at low tide. It is marked by a red barrel used as a privately maintained buoy and located about 400 yards north-northeast of the western tip of the island. Slim anchorage is available at Worlds End to the southeast, where you will find 7 to 9 feet MLW with excellent holding in mud and all-around protection.

Good holding can be found on the east side of the

Boston Harbor Area, MA

WG

Facility	Phone	Largest Vessel Accommodated	VHF Channel Monitored/Working	Transient/Total Slips	Approach/Dockside Depth (reported)	Floating Docks	Gas/Diesel	Groceries, Ice, Marine Supplies, Snacks	Repairs: Hull, Engine, Propeller	Lift (tonnage), Crane, Rail	Min/Max Amps	Courtesy Car, Laundry, Pool, Showers	Pump-Out Station	Nearby: Grocery Store, Motel, Restaurant
		Dockage					**Supplies**		**Services**					
BOSTON HARBOR ISLANDS NATIONAL PARK														
1. Spectacle Island Marina	(857) 452-7221	60	/	40/40	12.0/10.0	F		MS						
PRESIDENT ROADS														
2. Safe Harbor Marina Bay [Internet][WiFi]	(617) 847-1800	300	10/	25/686	14.0/13.0	F	GD	GIMS	HEP	L35,C	30/50	LS	P	GMR
3. Old Colony Yacht Club	(617) 436-0513	46	/	6/	6.0/4.0			I				S		
4. MarineMax Russo [Internet][WiFi]	(617) 288-1000	60	/	20/150	17.0/17.0	F	GD	IM	HEP	L60	50			R
5. Dorchester Yacht Club [WiFi]	(617) 436-1002	40	/	/	6.0/6.0	F	G					PS	P	R
6. Savin Hill Yacht Club	(617) 288-9293		/68	/	/		G	IS				S		GMR
7. South Boston Yacht Club	(617) 268-6132	30	/	/	6.0/6.0	F	G	I				S		
WINTHROP														
8. Crystal Cove Marina	(617) 846-SAIL	70	10/	10/118	6.0/6.0	F	GD	GI	HEP	C	30	LS	P	GMR
BOSTON'S INNER HARBOR														
9. Boston Harbor Shipyard and Marina [WiFi]	(617) 561-1400	65	/9	/180	25.0/25.0	F	GD	IMS	HEP	L50	30/50	LS	P	GR
10. Fan Pier Marina Boston [WiFi]	**(617) 865-5757**	400	9/	25/100	25.0/25.0	F	D	IS			30/100	CS	P	GMR
11. Marina at Rowes Wharf [WiFi]	(617) 748-5013	200	9/	19/38	30.0/25.0	F		IS		R	30/100	LPS	P	GMR
12. Boston Waterboat Marina [Internet][WiFi]	**(617) 523-1027**	200	9/8	20/45	32.0/14.0	F		IM			30/100	LS	P	GMR
13. Boston Yacht Haven Inn & Marina [Internet][WiFi]	**(617) 367-5050**	400	9/	30/100	25.0/25.0	F	GD	I			30/200+	CLS	P	GMR
14. Constitution Marina [Internet][WiFi]	**(617) 241-9640**	165	69/69	100/300	35.0/10.8	F		IS	HEP		30/200+	CLPS	P	GMR
15. Charlestown Marina [WiFi]	**(617) 242-2020**	500	71/	50/250	45.0/35.0	F	GD	I			30/200+	LS	P	GMR
16. Marina at Admirals Hill [WiFi]	(617) 889-4002	60	9/	5/136	6.0/6.0	F		IMS	HEP	L50	30/50	LS	P	GR
MYSTIC RIVER														
17. The Mystic Wellington Yacht Club Inc.- PRIVATE	(781) 396-2367		/	/128	/			S			30			MR

[Internet icon] Internet Access   [WiFi icon] Wireless Internet Access   [onSpot] Dockside WiFi Facility

See WaterwayGuide.com for current rates, fuel prices, website addresses, and other up-to-the-minute information. (Information in the table is provided by the facilities.)

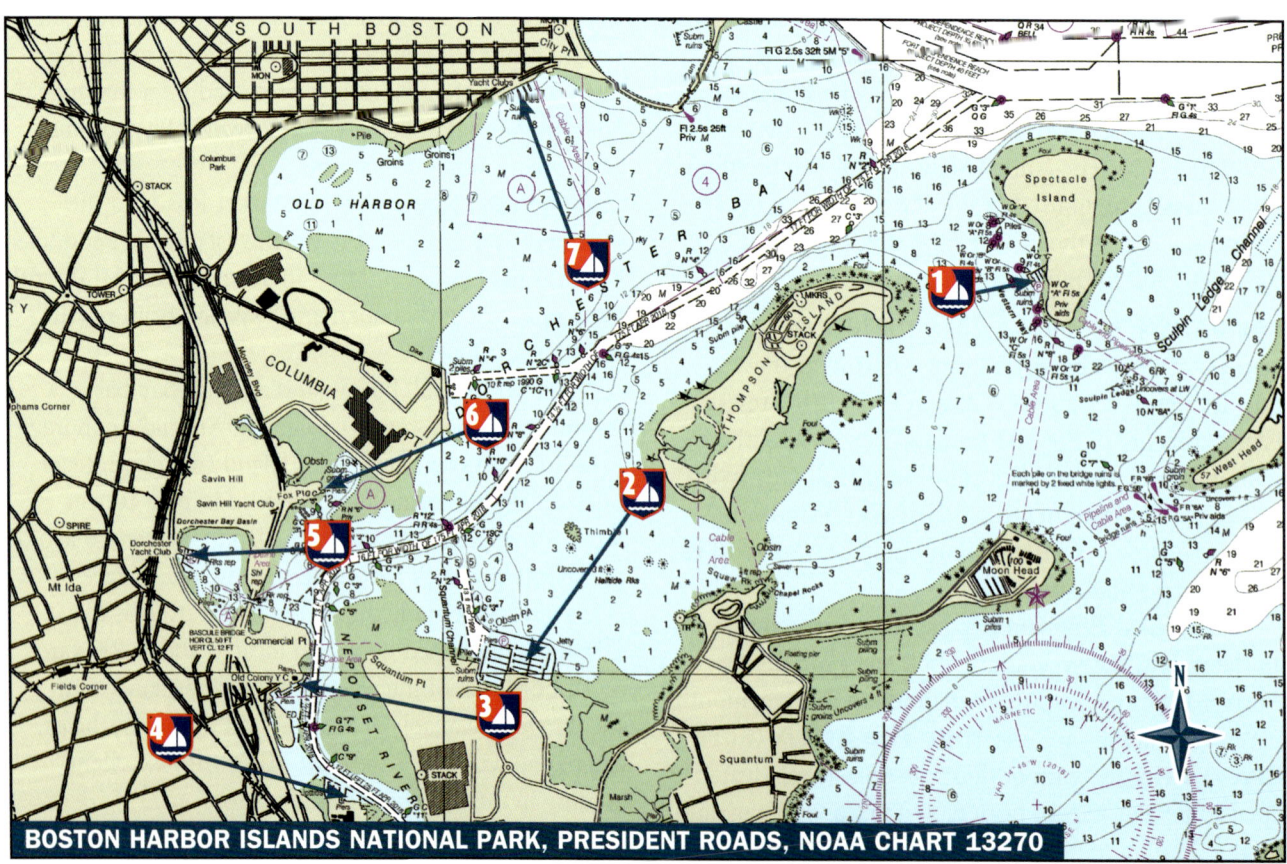

BOSTON HARBOR ISLANDS NATIONAL PARK, PRESIDENT ROADS, NOAA CHART 13270

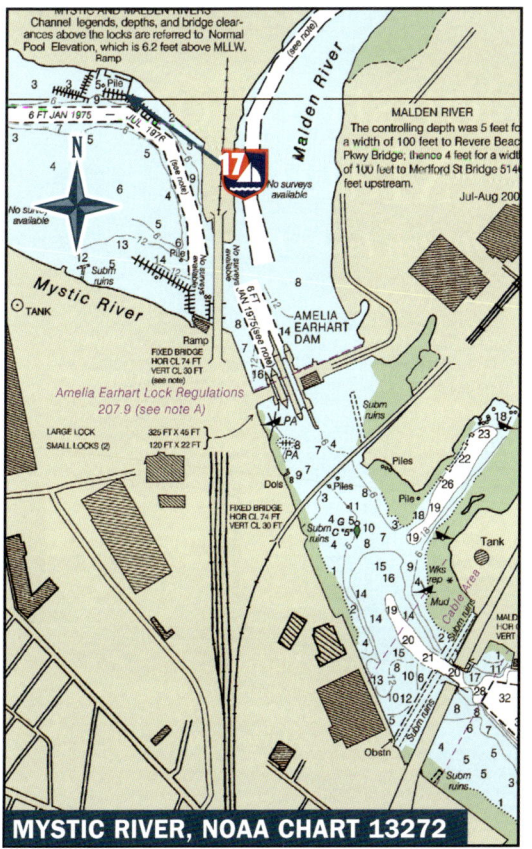

WINTRHOP, BOSTON'S INNER HARBOR, NOAA CHART 13270

MYSTIC RIVER, NOAA CHART 13272

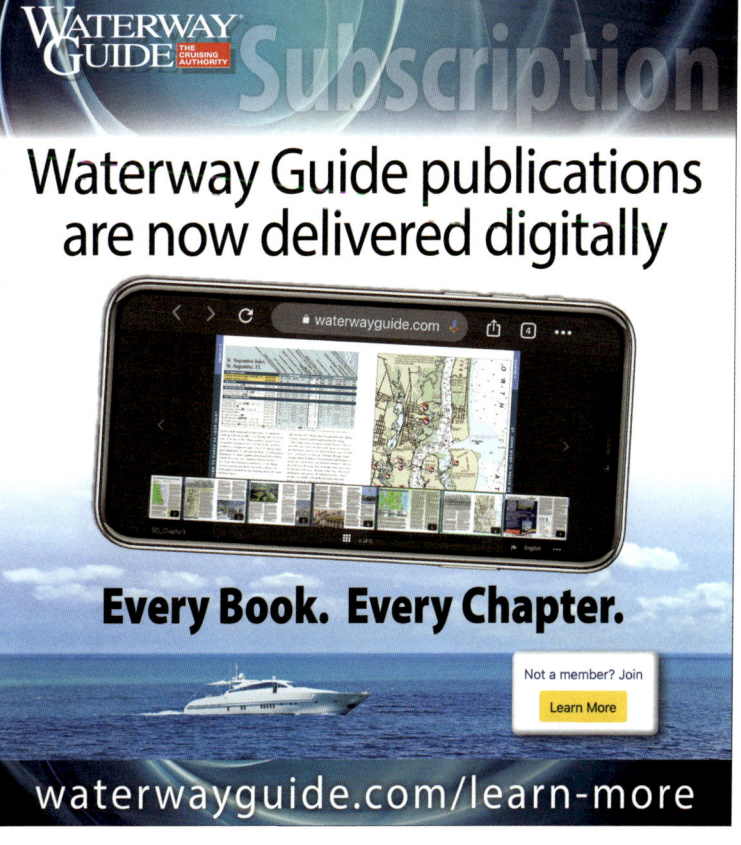

CONSTITUTION MARINA

Charles River

entrance channel of the Weymouth Back River after making the turn south (past Grape Island) but the ferry and other traffic keep the waters roiling. Anchor anywhere out of the channel to the east of flashing red buoy "4" and north of green can buoy "7" in 16 to 19 feet MLW. The previous anchorage in Town River Bay in the Weymouth Fore River is completely filled with mooring balls.

Boston Harbor Islands National Park

The islands of outer Boston Harbor have long been a wonderful cruising ground. These islands offer history, hiking and geocaching, picnic trails and camping, all within a stone's throw of downtown Boston (also accessible by ferry). The ferry docks are mostly reserved for off-loading people and supplies with limited space to land a dinghy; however, the beach area on most islands is ample and fair game. It is important to know that private boaters may not land on Thompson, Moon, Long, or Gallops Islands.

Pets are restricted from specific islands. Check out the Boston Harbor Islands online trip planner at www.bostonharborislands.org for pet policies and a calendar of festivals, concerts and other special events. All the National Parks have a carry in, carry out policy when it comes to trash.

On the northern edge of Nantasket Roads, Georges Island is a hub of the Boston Harbor Islands. Historic Fort Warren, a Civil War-era fort known for its graceful granite archways and reputed ghost "the Lady in Black," offers an afternoon of exploration and a panoramic view of Boston Harbor. Visitors can take a guided tour of the fort or explore the island on their own. Restrooms, picnic areas with grills and a snack bar are here. In addition, Georges Island is a frequent stop for the island ferries and a jump off point to other islands.

Little Brewster Island, east of Nantasket Roads, is home to the Boston Light, which is located on the site of the first lighthouse in the U.S. Although boaters can view the light from offshore, it is not recommended to attempt a landing on the dock. Tours of the island and light begin at Fan Pier in South Boston and include a narrated history of Boston harbor and its lights, as well as viewing of two other lighthouses.

Dockage/Moorings: The Boston Harbor Islands National and State Park maintains public moorings on Spectacle, Peddocks, Georges and Gallops Islands (with no island access at Gallops), and there is a marina on Spectacle Island. The calmest, most sheltered moorings are found on the west side of Peddocks Island (71 total moorings). Moorings and slips are available for reservation online at www.bostonharborislands.org/boating.

Spectacle Island Marina offers docking with day or overnight slips. The marina is staffed by Massachusetts Maritime Academy. There is free dockage for smaller vessels on a first-come, first-served basis on the western side of Georges Island.

Three moorings are located off of Thompson Island, closer to Boston. These are available for free on a first-come, first-served basis. Note that there is no public access to Thompson Island from these moorings.

Anchorage: At Georges Island, the best anchorage is north of the dock but substantial weekend traffic and eddying currents through and around the islands keep the waters disturbed. The superb view of the Boston skyline at sunset makes a little rocking well worthwhile. The south side of nearby Gallops Island is another option. The east side of Long Island with 8- to 12-foot MLW depths doesn't have a skyline view but the lighthouses are spectacular from here.

President Roads to Boston Inner Harbor

President Roads leads into Boston Harbor to the north and Dorchester Bay to the south. The inner coves of Dorchester Bay and tidal reaches of the Neponset River are home to a number of yacht clubs as well as large, full-service marinas. Winthrop, to the northeast of President Roads, has numerous beaches due to its geographic location.

As you enter the Inner Harbor, downtown Boston's historical buildings and skyscrapers dominate the view to port. The huge and distinctive federal courthouse on the northeast elbow of South Boston serves as a sentinel beacon to the first of several excellent marinas that will take your lines for a berth in the center of the city's historic district. You will sure to notice the planes taking off and landing at Logan Airport as you approach.

From the Inner Harbor, just beyond the Coast Guard base, a turn west takes you into the mouth of the Charles River. The adjacent water shuttle leaves every 15 minutes for Faneuil Hall Marketplace and downtown.

Immediately east of Constitution Marina, its namesake, the *U.S.S. Constitution* ("Old Ironsides"), famed frigate of the War of 1812, has found its final berth in the Charlestown Navy Yard (also known as Boston Navy Yard and Boston Naval Shipyard) and is now maintained as a historic site by the National Park Service (617-426-1812/617-242-5601). The yard is also home to the *U.S.S. Cassin Young*, a 250-foot long destroyer commissioned in 1902 and serving the Navy until the mid-1950s.

Getting around is not a problem. Boston Water Taxi (617-227-4320) can transport you and your guests on a short trip across the harbor to Logan International Airport, among other destinations. Train stations are easy walks from marinas and the historical downtown is a pleasure to walk.

⚠️ Dredging began in Boston Inner Harbor in 2018 and will continue until 2021. Mariners are requested to pass at their slowest safe speed.

Dockage/Moorings: Safe Harbor Marina Bay is more of a self-contained yachting community than a marina. With some 685 berths, it is one of the largest marinas in the northeast. Transient slips are usually available and easily approached in at least 13-foot MLW depths. In addition to coin-operated laundry machines and

ice, you can access ATM and express mailing services. Restaurants and a supermarket are nearby or call a cab (Marina Bay Taxi, 617-472-4111) for rapid access to a pharmacy and complete provisioning possibilities in downtown Boston, which is a 15-minute ride.

West of Squantum Point, a number of mooring/dockage possibilities are located across the Neponset River in Dorchester Bay and moorings are available east of Squantum Point from the yacht clubs there.

There are also facilities in Old Harbor to the northeast and at Winthrop (east of Logan Airport). On the west side of Logan Airport is Boston's Inner Harbor with more slips, moorings and repairs. A large fleet of daysailers may be out and about here. They belong to the Boston Harbor Sailing Club, a major organization that promotes interest in boating.

Just past the distinctive New England Aquarium on Central Wharf, Faneuil Hall Marketplace, Quincy Market and the best Italian food on this continent await you on the North End, easily accessible from several marine facilities. Boston Waterboat Marina is tucked behind the north side of Long Wharf. Along with dockage and moorings, they offer a fairly protected dinghy landing as well as on-site marine supply and maintenance. The marina traces its heritage to the days when Boston's actual waterboat, which was tasked to tend oceangoing vessels moored in the harbor, once berthed here. It is the city's oldest continually operating yachting facility and has been family owned for over 150 years.

On the next wharf is Boston Yacht Haven Inn & Marina. This full-service marina offers slips that can accommodate vessels up to 400 feet with dockside electricity, water and in-slip, pump-out stations. On shore the 10-room boutique hotel has amenities for both yacht owners and crew in addition to the usual marina amenities. The concierge will assist you in making reservations for dinner, attending the theater or touring around Boston. Make your reservations as early as March if planning a visit on peak weekends.

On the north side of the Charles River, Constitution Marina offers protected floating berths and moorings in the scenic outer harbor. It is located right on the Freedom Trail in the Charlestown neighborhood of Boston and has a year-round liveaboard community. There is usually ample transient space, although reservations are advised. Laundry facilities and a heated swimming pool are available at Constitution

Broad Sound, MA

LYNN HARBOR		Largest Vessel Accomodated	VHF Channel Monitored / Working	Approach / Dockside Depth (reported)	Transient Slips / Total Slips	Floating Docks	Groceries, Ice, Marine Supplies, Snacks	Gas / Diesel	Repairs: Hull, Engine, Propeller	Lift (tonnage), Crane, Rail	Min / Max Amps	Courtesy Car, Laundry, Pool, Showers	Pump-Out Station	Nearby: Grocery Store, Motel, Restaurant
				Dockage				**Supplies**			**Services**			
1. Lynn Yacht Club	(781) 595-9825	50	9/	2/50	12.0/8.0	F			I		L	30	S	R
2. Seaport Landing Marina	(781) 592-5821	65	16/9	20/165	20.0/15.0	F	GD	GIMS	HEP	L25	50	LS	P	GR

🖥 Internet Access   [WIFI] Wireless Internet Access   ◉onSpot Dockside WiFi Facility
See WaterwayGuide.com for current rates, fuel prices, website addresses, and other up-to-the-minute information. (Information in the table is provided by the facilities.)

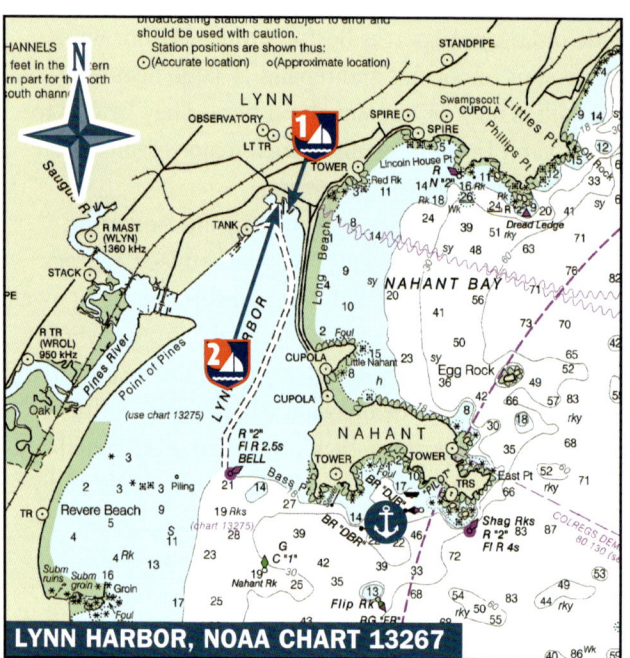

LYNN HARBOR, NOAA CHART 13267

Marina's main building and restaurants are within easy walking distance.

With a full range of dockside services, Charlestown Marina (to the north) offers single- and doubled-loaded slips with 600-foot wave attenuator that creates a calm boat basin. Facilities include dockside electricity, water and in-slip pump-out stations and a coin-operated laundry.

Chelsea is across the Mystic and Chelsea Rivers from Boston, straight ahead while heading up the harbor. It is the second most densely populated city in Massachusetts and the smallest by area. Marina at Admiral's Hill is past the high-rise bridge and a park, then north up a side channel with slips (to 60 feet) and repairs.

Broad Sound

NAVIGATION: Use NOAA Chart 13270. From Boston Harbor, North Channel (preferred) and South Channel both lead from President Roads into big Broad Sound.

Wide North Channel, marked by large, lighted sea buoys, is the primary thoroughfare for both big ships and recreational craft. South Channel is narrower, aids are smaller and ledges encroach. From Finns Ledge at the northern end of North Channel, it is 3 miles to Bass Point on the southwestern tip of Nahant. Beyond Nahant are two narrow channels—one leading to Lynn Harbor and the other to Point of Pines and Pines River.

Dockage: Dockage may be found at Lynn Yacht Club or Seaport Landing Marina, which also sells gas and diesel fuel and offers repairs and services.

Anchorage: Nahant Harbor off Broad Sound has 17 to 23 feet MLW with good holding in sand. It is protected from the northeast through northwest.

■ SALEM SOUND

Four historic harbors—Marblehead, Salem, Beverly and Manchester—line Salem Sound, a 4-mile-wide break in the shore located to the northeast of Boston Harbor's entrance. Although all four began as commercial fishing villages, they have evolved into popular recreational harbors with dockage, moorings, marine suppliers and a wealth of shoreside attractions.

Salem Sound's mouth is littered with islands, rocks and ledges with three main channels threading through them. Strangers should be wary of trying to enter or leave in heavy weather or poor visibility, but keep the camera handy on a clear day. Good landmarks are on both sides of the sound including the tall lights on Bakers Island and Marblehead Neck, the looming red brick steeple of Abbot Hall, the three stacks of Salem's power plant and the observation tower on Gales Point.

The historical tendency here was to go easy on boats by leaving them on moorings rather than beating them up on rough piers. That trend has been carried to the

SALEM, MA

For a period of 20 years around the turn of the 18th century during the "Golden Age of Sail," Salem was truly America's trading capital and crossroads of the world. Daring sea captains and undaunted investors launched voyages that would open up the lucrative eastern trade to New England. Vessels laden with cod, rum, molasses, shingles and other products plied angry waters around Cape Horn and Cape of Good Hope to exchange their goods for exotic spices and other luxuries, returning to reap vast profits. By 1800, Salem was the sixth largest city in America and the richest per capita. Although those days are gone, the aura of that time persists in the grand homes and government houses that marked the era and, in a few remaining wharves, memorializing the many that once stretched their arms toward returning ships from the Orient.

SERVICES

1. **Salem Post Office**
   2 Margin St. (978-744-4671)

ATTRACTIONS

2. **New England Pirate Museum**
   Historic presentations on pirates with wax figures, some artifacts and a souvenir shop (274 Derby St., 978-741-2800).

3. **Peabody Essex Museum**
   Modern museum featuring regional American/Asian art and artifacts plus an atrium and garden restaurant (161 Essex St., 978-745-9500).

4. **Salem Maritime National Historic Site**
   Historic buildings, wharves and a tall ship on a 9-acre park exploring the age of sailing ships (160 Derby St., 978-740-1650).

5. **Salem Witch Museum**
   Life-size stage sets, exhibits and tours exploring the 1692 Salem witch trials through modern-day witchcraft at 19 1/2 N. Washington Square (978-744-1692).

6. **The House of the Seven Gables**
   Tours of the restored 1668 home that inspired Hawthorne's novel plus verdant seaside gardens at 15 Derby St. (978-744-0991)

MARINAS

7. **Fred J. Dion Yacht Yard**
   23 Glendale St. (978-744-0844)

8. **Palmer Cove Yacht Club**
   74 Leavitt St. (978-744-9722)

9. **Pickering Wharf Marina**
   23 Congress St. (978-744-2727)

10. **Safe Harbor Hawthorne Cove**
    10 White St. (978-740-9890)

Marblehead Harbor, MA

WG

MARBLEHEAD		Largest Vessel Accommodated	VHF Channel Monitored / Working	Transient Slips / Total Slips	Approach / Dockside Depth (reported)	Floating Docks	Groceries, Ice, Marine Supplies, Snacks	Gas / Diesel	Repairs: Hull, Engine Propeller	Lift (tonnage), Crane, Rail	Courtesy Car, Laundry, Pool, Showers	Min / Max Amps	Pump-Out Station	Nearby: Grocery Store, Motel, Restaurant
		Dockage					**Supplies**			**Services**				
1. Corinthian Yacht Club □ WiFi	(781) 631-0005	100	9/9	/	10.0/7.0						LS			
2. Eastern Yacht Club-PRIVATE	(781) 631-4059		/9	/			IS			C	PS			MR
3. Marblehead Yacht Club	(781) 631-9771		/71	/	8.0/6.0	F	IS				S	30	P	MR
4. Dolphin Yacht Club	(781) 631-8000		68/	/	20.0/8.0		IS				S			R
5. Boston Yacht Club	(781) 631-3100	80	68/	/	20.0/20.0	F		GD		I	S		P	GMR
6. Marblehead Harbormaster	(781) 631-2386	100	16/14	/	22.0/15.0	F					LS	30/100	P	GR
7. Marblehead Trading Co.	(781) 639-0029	100	/	4/	30.0/17.0	F	IM	GD	HEP	C,R		30/100		GMR

□ Internet Access   (WiFi) Wireless Internet Access   onSpot Dockside WiFi Facility
See WaterwayGuide.com for current rates, fuel prices, website addresses, and other up-to-the-minute information. (Information in the table is provided by the facilities.)

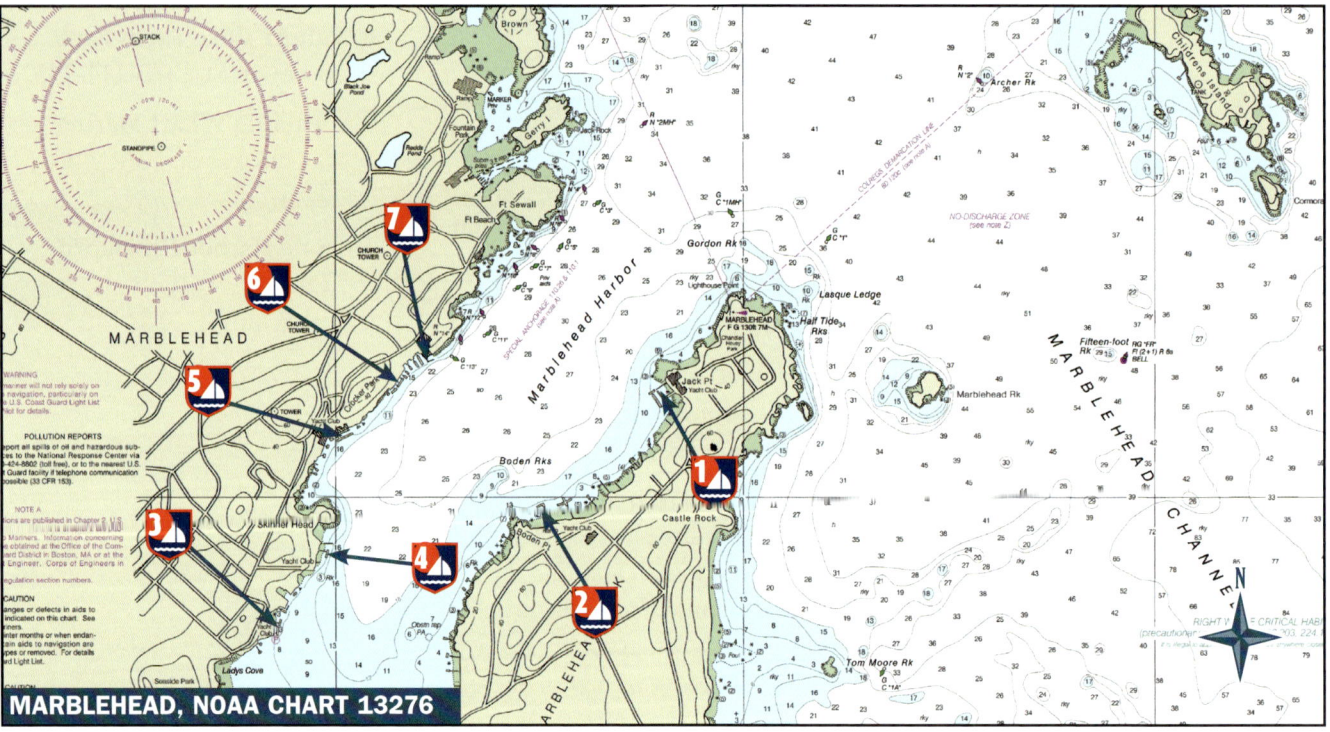

MARBLEHEAD, NOAA CHART 13276

as it is famous. Visiting yachtsmen, as guests of the club, may request a rental mooring on a first-come, first-served basis that includes launch service but be sure to pack your navy-blue blazer for dinner.

The Marblehead Town Landing is also on the northern side of the harbor with a large dinghy dock and additional docks for loading and unloading (30-minute limit). Public restrooms, phones, trash barrels and limited parking are provided. Contact the Marblehead Harbormaster (VHF Channel 16) for availability of transient dock space and for assistance on your approach.

The Marblehead Trading Company, the first facility on the northern shore, is a compact, but complete boatyard with major lift capacity and a marine supply store, The Forepeak Ship's Chandlery (781-631-7184).

Salem Harbor

Peabody Essex Museum and numerous other intriguing museums, fashionable period homes, points of interest, restaurants and boating amenities are all within easy walking distance of this premier harbor.

Salem Harbor itself is homeport to a multi-million-dollar replica of the 171-foot *Friendship of Salem*, a world-ranging square-rigged trading ship, originally launched in 1797, on which daily tours are given. Visit Salem during the month-long Haunted Happenings

extreme and every bit of water that's not actively set aside as a channel has been filled with moorings. In high summer, the carpet of boats swinging together on their pennants is quite the sight to behold.

Marblehead Harbor

Famous throughout the yachting world as the "Yachting Capital of America," Marblehead was historically a fishing village. Even today, the harbor maintains a small fleet of lobster and fishing vessels. But now more than ever, this is a key layover port for cruising and racing boats from the world's most serious yachting circles. Hansen Marine Engineering (32 Tioga Way, 781-631-3282) is a thoroughly outfitted marine engine parts supply, should a DIY project beckon you.

NAVIGATION: Use NOAA Charts 13274 and 13276. Salem Channel, the northernmost entrance to Salem Sound, is the deep-draft passage used by commercial craft heading for Salem's terminals. It runs between Bakers Island and Great Misery Island, through Salem Sound and then turns to the southeast to Salem Harbor. In the middle is Children's Island Channel, which leads between Childrens Island and Eagle Island.

Marblehead Channel, to the west, runs between Children's Island and Marblehead Neck, then along the peninsula past mid-sound rocks and shoals to Salem Harbor.

Tidal range here averages 9 feet but the tidal current has little force except in Beverly Harbor, where it sets across the channel in several places.

The Marblehead Harbor is well protected in all directions except the northeast. Indeed, many vessels have fetched up on the causeway beach at the head of the harbor during a 3-day nor'easter. If the wind veers toward that direction, seek shelter on the Beverly side.

Dockage/Moorings: While anchoring in this busy harbor is not an option, several yacht clubs and the town of Marblehead are likely to have moorings available to visitors. Most of the 2,300 or so remaining moorings in the harbor are privately owned (there's a 15-year waiting list to get one) and you must call ahead to one of the several listed facilities to arrange for a mooring, based upon availability.

The yacht clubs here include Corinthian Yacht Club, Eastern Yacht Club, Marblehead Yacht Club and Dolphin Yacht Club. Moorings and launch service is available at all of these, except Eastern Yacht Club, which is private. The Boston Yacht Club is as elegant

Marblehead Harbor

Salem Harbor

Salem Sound, MA

SALEM		Largest Vessel Accomodated	VHF Channel Monitored / Working	Approach / Dockside Depth (reported)	Transient Slips / Total Slips	Floating Docks	Groceries, Ice, Marine Supplies, Snacks	Gas / Diesel	Repairs: Hull, Engine, Propeller	Lift (tonnage), Crane, Rail	Courtesy Car, Laundry, Pool, Showers	Min / Max Amps	Pump-Out Station	Nearby: Grocery Store, Motel, Restaurant
			Dockage				**Supplies**			**Services**				
1. Safe Harbor Hawthorne Cove 🛜	(978) 740-9890	65	8/	1/110	15.0/6.0	F			IM	HEP	L35	30/50	LS	GMR
2. Pickering Wharf Marina ⌨	(978) 744-2727	55	9/	10/100	8.0/8.0	F			IS			30/50	LS	GMR
3. Palmer's Cove Yacht Club 🛜	(978) 223-7527	40	78/	/162	/						L	30	S	GMR
4. Fred J. Dion Yacht Yard Inc. ⌨	**(978) 744-0844**	**100**	**9/**	**/20**	**10.0/8.0**	**F**			**M**	**HEP**	**L50,C**	**30**	**S**	**GMR**
BEVERLY														
5. Jubilee Yacht Club ⌨	(978) 922-9611	50	78/	/	35.0/7.0	F	GD		I				S	R
6. Tuck Point Marina	(978) 922-4631	35	7/68	6/53	35.0/25.0				I		L	30/50	LPS	GMR
7. Beverly Port Marina Inc. 🛜	(978) 232-3300	200	79/	50/350	28.0/28.0	F	GD		IMS	HEP	L35	30/100	LS	R
DANVERS														
8. Liberty Marina	(978) 774-5105	50	9/	12/180	12.0/8.0	F			I	HEP	L35	30/50	LS	MR
9. Danversport Marina 🛜	(978) 774-8644	55	9/	5/304	8.0/8.0	F	G		IMS	HEP	L50,C	50	LPS	P	GMR

⌨ Internet Access 🛜 Wireless Internet Access 🛜 onSpot Dockside WiFi Facility

See WaterwayGuide.com for current rates, fuel prices, website addresses, and other up-to-the-minute information. (Information in the table is provided by the facilities.)

celebration in October and you'll see an entirely different side of the original "witch" city.

NAVIGATION: Use NOAA Charts 13274 and 13275. From Marblehead follow the South Channel (Marblehead Channel) leaving Grays Rock to the northeast and pass directly between green daybeacon "1" and red nun buoy "2." As you continue, pass between green can buoy "3" and red nun buoy "4" marking the underwater Triangle Rocks to the north. Next leave red nun buoy "6" and the submerged Aquavitae rocks to the north. Enter Salem Channel between Baker and Great Misery Island and then follow the well-marked, deep-water ship channel into Salem Harbor. The lighted stacks (aptly charted "STACKS") of the Salem Harbor power plant on Salem Neck can be seen for many miles out to sea.

Dockage/Moorings: Salem is the U.S. Customs Port of Entry for the region, and Customs maintains a dock for incoming vessels. The Salem Harbormaster (978-741-0098 or VHF Channel 09) can assist with mooring requests.

Safe Harbor Hawthorne Cove has the first transient docks encountered on entry, to the northwest just past the power plant's huge stacks. The marina offers 110 slips to 65 feet and 270 moorings for seasonal customers and transient boaters. They also offer repairs. The marina is conveniently located next to the famed House of Seven Gables and in close proximity to some of the most historic and reportedly haunted sites in the U.S. Be sure to call Safe Harbor (VHF Channel 78) for

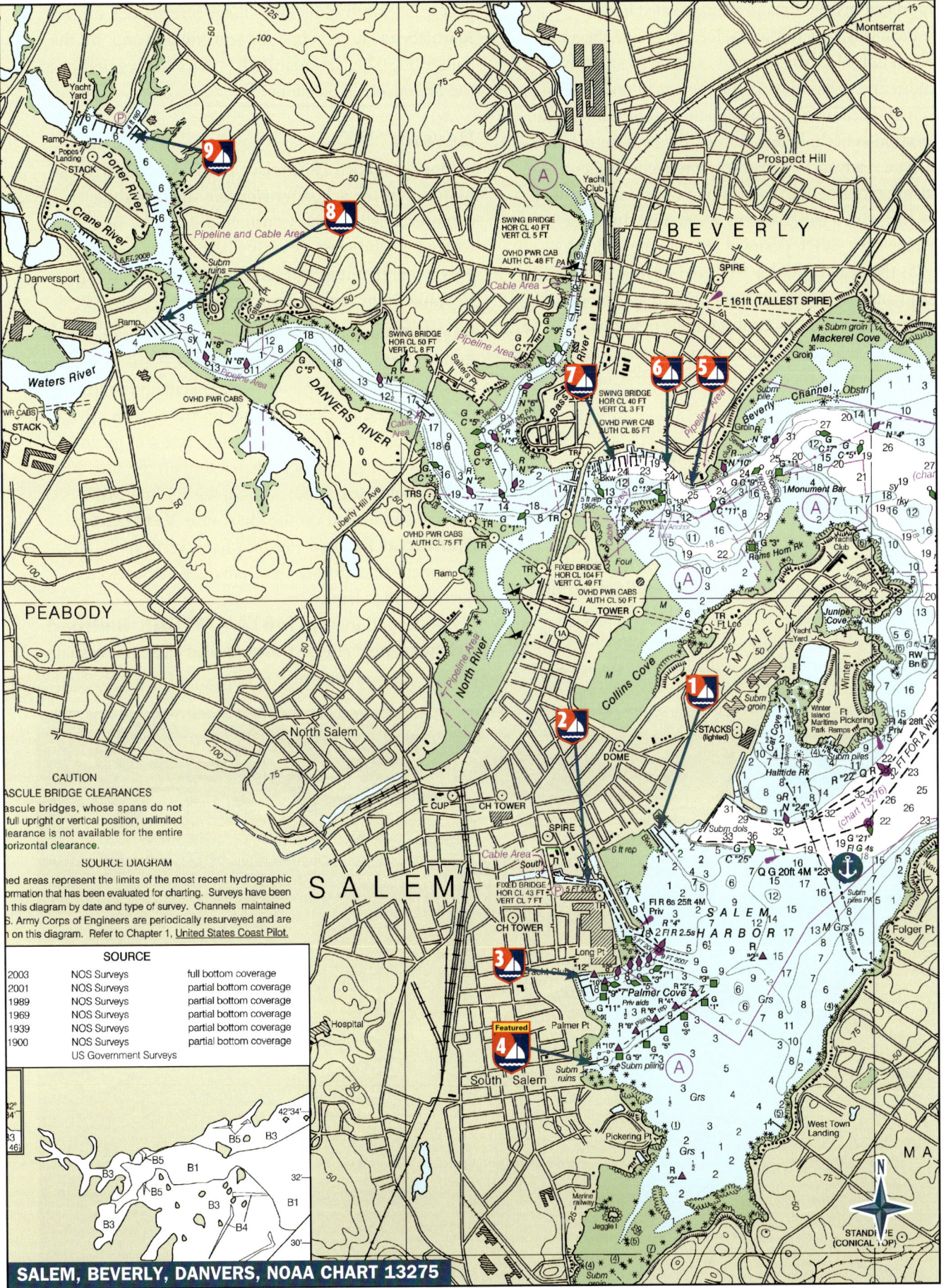

CAUTION

...ASCULE BRIDGE CLEARANCES

...ascule bridges, whose spans do not
...full upright or vertical position, unlimited
...learance is not available for the entire
...orizontal clearance.

SOURCE DIAGRAM

...ed areas represent the limits of the most recent hydrographic
...ormation that has been evaluated for charting. Surveys have been
... this diagram by date and type of survey. Channels maintained
...S. Army Corps of Engineers are periodically resurveyed and are
...n on this diagram. Refer to Chapter 1, United States Coast Pilot.

SOURCE		
2003	NOS Surveys	full bottom coverage
2001	NOS Surveys	partial bottom coverage
1989	NOS Surveys	partial bottom coverage
1969	NOS Surveys	partial bottom coverage
1939	NOS Surveys	partial bottom coverage
1900	NOS Surveys	partial bottom coverage
	US Government Surveys	

SALEM, BEVERLY, DANVERS, NOAA CHART 13275

approach instructions to their private channel.

Pickering Wharf Marina, located inside the ample protection of Derby Wharf, is central to an array of shops and restaurants in the mini-mall on Pickering Wharf. Because of its convenient access and central location, a berth here is in high demand during the summer; advance reservations are recommended. A secure mooring for vessels up to 65 feet in length can be had with a call to Salem Water Taxi. Just hail "Salem Water Taxi" (VHF Channel 68) on approach.

At the head of the harbor, Fred J. Dion Yacht Yard can handle virtually any yacht refitting or rebuilding requirement and has a substantial stock room. The yard is a third-generation family business with a tradition of quality service since 1914. Call on VHF Channel 09 for availability and directions.

> The town of Salem requires a closed head (No-Discharge) and offers free pump-out services only on weekends. Call Salem Pump-out on VHF Channel 09.

Anchorage: A few boats can anchor outside the Salem Harbor mooring area to the south of flashing green "22" in 7 to 17 feet MLW. Holding is good in mud and grass, although it is exposed to the northeast. Most boats honor the no-wake buoy by inches so it is

best to be south of it. The Village Street Dock on the Marblehead shore is free for your dinghy and, on the Salem side, the National Park Service allows tie-ups at the *Friendship of Salem* dock.

Beverly

Although dubbed "Birthplace of the American Navy" in honor of the schooner *Hannah*, the first ship commissioned for the Continental Navy by Gen. George Washington, Beverly's harbor area today has only a few reminders of its historic past including Hospital Point Lighthouse (circa 1801).

NAVIGATION: Use NOAA Chart 13275. Entrance into Beverly Harbor is easily made at Tuck Point by keeping Hospital Point Lighthouse to the north and following the deep, well-marked channel up the Danvers River. Be mindful of the rocks to the southwest of green daybeacon "13A," which, depending on the tide, may or may not be exposed. A shoal with 5-foot MLW depths is indicated on the chart near **Veterans Memorial Bridge** (49-foot fixed vertical clearance) that crosses the Danvers River between Beverly and Salem.

Just beyond that is a **MBTA/AMTRAK Railroad Bridge** with a closed 3-foot vertical clearance (usually

FRED J. DION YACHT YARD INC.

Salem

Beverly Harbor

open). The swing bridge opens on signal from 5:00 a.m. to midnight daily. On Christmas Day and New Years Day, the draw will open as soon as possible but not more than 1 hour after notice is given by calling the number posted at the bridge. You can contact the Beverly Harbormaster for more details at 978-921-6059.

Beyond the bridge, the Bass River (carrying depths to 5 feet MLW) branches off to the north. Severe shoaling has been reported on the Bass River from the **Hall Whitaker Bridge** (5-foot closed vertical clearance) to Bass Haven Yacht Club. The draw for the bridge will open on signal if at least a 24-hour notice is given. Mariners are advised to use caution while transiting the area.

The Danvers River continues to the west with good depths beyond the **Kernwood Avenue Bridge** (8-foot closed vertical clearance). The draw will open on signal from May 1 through September 30, midnight to 5:00 a.m., and from October 1 through April 30, from 7:00 p.m. to 5:00 a.m., only after at least a 1-hour advance notice is given by calling the number posted at the bridge.

Further travel up the Danvers River is somewhat problematic for deep-drafted vessels as the channel is winding and sometimes narrow. You are well advised to keep an eye on the depth sounder. The entire Danvers River is a No-Wake Zone.

Dockage: Jubilee Yacht Club has moorings for members of clubs with reciprocal arrangements and also maintains a launch service and fuel dock. Nearby Beverly Port Marina Inc. has slips to 200 feet. A good selection of fine restaurants and a movie theatre are within a healthy walking distance up Cabot Street.

Liberty Marina is located on the Danvers River at the split where the Crone River branches to west and Danversport Marina is located where the Danvers becomes the Porter River. Both of these reserve space for transients.

Side Trip: Great Misery & Little Misery Islands

Originally inhabited by the Masconomet people and named by the European arrivals for the three miserable winter days that shipbuilder Captain Robert Moulton spent on the island in the 1620s, these islands sport the ruins of an early-20th-century resort built to leverage the stunning views of Salem Sound, which tragically burned to the ground in the 1920s. Located at the mouth of Manchester Bay, these nearly joined scenic gems offer quiet refuge from the crowded harbors of the Salem Sound area, although weekend day-trippers are numerous. These islands are maintained by the Trustees of the Reservation and offer 2.5 miles of moderate hiking trails but no services.

Anchorage/Mooring: The City of Beverly maintains eight moorings between Great & Little Misery Islands. A number of private or local yacht club moorings are often available at either location and the locals take their chances with them for the night, knowing that they must move if the owners arrive.

Manchester Harbor, MA

MANCHESTER		Largest Vessel Accommodated	VHF Channel Monitored / Working	Transient Slips / Total Slips	Approach / Dockside Depth (reported)	Floating Docks	Groceries, Ice, Marine Supplies, Snacks	Gas / Diesel	Repairs: Hull, Engine, Propeller	Lift (tonnage), Crane, Rail	Courtesy Car, Laundry, Pool, Showers	Min / Max Amps	Pump-Out Station	Nearby: Grocery Store, Motel, Restaurant
				Dockage			**Supplies**				**Services**			
1. Manchester Yacht Club	(978) 526-4595		78/	/	/		I				S			GR
2. Crocker's Boat Yard	(978) 526-1971	60	78/	2/16	7.0/7.0	F	M		HEP	L30,C		30		GR
3. Manchester Marine Corp. WIFI	(978) 526-7911	45	72/	6/40	9.0/7.0	F	I	GD	HEP	L35,C	S	30/50	P	GR

📖 Internet Access   WIFI Wireless Internet Access   onSpot Dockside WiFi Facility
See WaterwayGuide.com for current rates, fuel prices, website addresses, and other up-to-the-minute information. (Information in the table is provided by the facilities.)

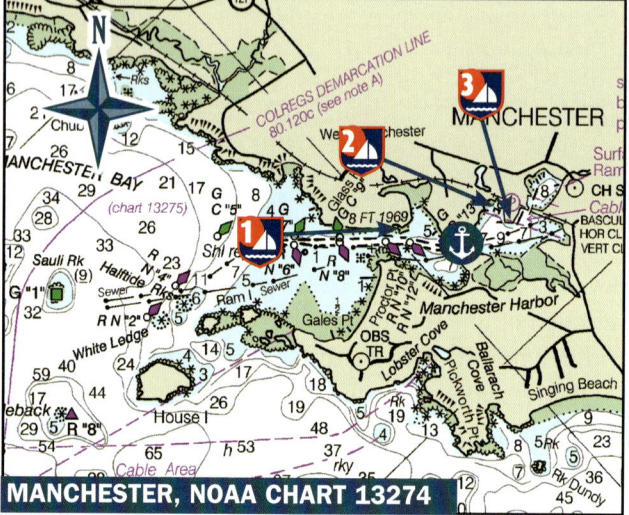

MANCHESTER, NOAA CHART 13274

Anchorage is available at "Cocktail Cove," the small bight on the north side of Great Misery Island, and at the tiny bay leading to the unnavigable cut between the two islands. The islands are largely open and their accessible beaches invite exploration by dinghy.

Manchester Harbor

Beautifully kept clapboard homes quietly line the narrow, shaded streets in the well-known New England village of Manchester. Commercial establishments are sprinkled along the road tracing the head of the harbor. Crosby's Marketplace (978-526-4444) is stocked with all the supermarket basics and many specialty items. There is a cleaner, a sizable hardware store, gift shops and restaurants. A large public library is just up the hill overlooking the harbor. Visitors can use the Internet access at the library one time for up to 1 hour. Singing Beach, an excellent swimming spot, is just a 1-mile walk from the boatyards.

NAVIGATION: Use NOAA Charts 13274 and 13275. Cruising the 6 miles from Beverly to Manchester, you will find good water close to shore for a waterside view of the elegant estate and summer homes of Boston's Gold Coast. The entrance to Manchester is crowded but the unhurried harbor is graced by the Manchester Yacht Club's beautiful Victorian gazebo perched on a promontory near the entrance in front of its refined clubhouse. The channel is straight and well marked but a bit shallow. Boats drawing more than 5 feet are advised to arrive on a rising tide.

The harbor, above Proctor Point, is virtually landlocked affording excellent protection and the village, although small and picturesque, is surprisingly accommodating to cruising visitors.

Dockage: In the inner harbor at the top of the bight north of green can buoy "13" Crocker's Boat Yard is a family-owned and -operated traditional working yard. A few transient moorings are likely to be open here. Next door, Manchester Marine Corp. is a full-service operation that has some transient floating dock space, as well as guest moorings with launch service. Manchester Yacht Club has moorings but does not have transient space. Short-term tie-ups (15 minutes) are possible at the nearby Manchester Town Dock (6-foot MLW depths).

Anchorage: There is room to anchor in the inner basins in 6 feet MLW; however, anchoring is restricted to vessels 45 feet and under and is strictly enforced. Reed Park, at the northeastern end of the harbor, allows short-time tie-ups.

◼ NEXT STOP

Gloucester marks another change in the tenor of the coastline and a new set of leaps up the coast. Long hops bring the boater to the small stretch of New Hampshire coastline and the beginning of Maine's.

Gloucester, MA to Cape Elizabeth, ME

■ GLOUCESTER TO NEWBURYPORT, MA

Sandy beaches, culturally vibrant villages, and boat-loads of history await between the Queen's capes. Cape Anne to Cape Elizabeth can be taken in a leap, but that discounts temptations like the offshore Isles of Shoals and rewarding river towns like Newburyport, Portsmouth, Kittery and Kennebunkport. The ambiance from Gloucester north reflects a growing distance from the more recreational-focused ports further south and cruisers feel a shift in the balance of services. Working waterfronts slot maritime businesses and visitors' pleasures neatly together to the benefit of both.

Gloucester Harbor

For three centuries, the name Gloucester has been synonymous with fishermen and their boats. The remaining fishing fleet has been joined by busy schooner cruise business and both of those are wonderful foreground against the green hills dotted with wind towers, lighthouses and the old town's spires. Photographers will rejoice. On the western shore near the entrance of Gloucester is Normans Woe Rock of Longfellow's famous poem "Wreck of the Hesperus."

Poems and memorials aside, Gloucester is also a highly practical stop. The harbor offers different anchorages for whichever wind threatens, repairs for any size boat, restaurants with docks and an active summer community. Grocery stores are short walks from either side of the inner harbor and marine hardware can be obtained at the end.

NAVIGATION: Use NOAA Chart 13274. Serious ledges litter the coast between Manchester and Magnolia Harbor. Stay at least 1 mile offshore to avoid the navigational difficulty. Do not be tempted to follow the lobster boats working closer inshore; they work the ledges in ways that would be unsafe for most recreational boats.

Magnolia Harbor, a summer resort village with a landing and an anchorage, offers poor holding ground and southerly exposure. At low tide, there are areas with 6-foot MLW depths (charted but unmarked) that narrow the entrances to Magnolia Harbor. The approach from the west has fewer obstructions. Most boaters stay south of Kettle Island.

Approaching Gloucester Harbor is made easier by a pair of large, bright lights. A former home of painter Winslow Homer (in 1880), the Eastern Point Lighthouse flashes its big white light every 5 seconds from a height of 57 feet. It's rated as visible to 24 nm so use it to get near enough to find the Dog Bar Light, but don't approach too close to the ledges just south of the lighthouse. Dog Bar Light is a tower on a platform anchored to the rock of the breakwater and is charted as the Gloucester Breakwater Light. It is 45 feet tall and has an occulting red light at 4 seconds. (Occulting means it is regularly lighted and clicks off briefly every 4 seconds as opposed to the more usual flashing light that is regularly off and clicks on briefly.)

Gloucester Harbor, MA

		Largest Vessel Accommodated	VHF Channel Monitored / Working	Transient Slips / Total Slips	Approach / Dockside Depth (reported)	Floating Docks	Gas / Diesel	Groceries, Ice, Marine Supplies, Snacks	Repairs: Hull, Engine, Propeller	Lift (tonnage), Crane, Rail	Min / Max Amps	Courtesy Car, Laundry, Pool, Showers	Pump-Out Station	Nearby: Grocery Store, Motel, Restaurant
GLOUCESTER				**Dockage**			**Supplies**		**Services**					
1. Gloucester Harbormaster	(978) 282-3012		16/15	/	/									GMR
2. Cruiseport Gloucester Marine Terminal ☐ WiFi MM 2.1	(978) 282-9700	500	/	2/6	26.0/20.0	F	D	M	HEP	L,C,R	50/200+		P	GMR
3. Rose's Marine	(978) 283-0280		/	/	/		D	M	HP	L70,C				GMR
4. Pier 7 Marina ☐ WiFi	(781) 858-5279	70	7/16	4/30	25.0/15.0	F		IM			30/100	S		GMR
5. Brown's Yacht Yard WiFi	(978) 281-3200	55	9/19	6/20	12.0/12.0	F	GD	IM	HEP	L35	30/50	S	P	GR
6. Beacon Marine Basin Inc.	(978) 283-2380	100	/	1/50	15.0/15.0	F	GD	M	HEP		30			GMR
7. North Shore Sport Fishing Dock	(978) 283-6880	46	/	2/16	12.0/8.0	F	GD	IM			30	S		GR
8. Eastern Point Yacht Club WiFi	(978) 283-3520		/71	/	25.0/6.0	F		IS				PS		MR
ANNISQUAM RIVER														
9. Cape Ann's Marina Resort ☐ WiFi MM 1.0	(978) 283-2116	150	10/10	22/278	10.0/8.0	F	GD	IMS	HEP	L75,C	30/100	LPS	P	GMR
10. Gloucester Marina	(978) 283-2828	40	/	1/100	10.0/20.0	F		IM	HP	C	30	S		GR
11. Annisquam Yacht Club	(978) 283-4507	40	68/	/	6.0/6.0			I				S		GR
ROCKPORT														
12. Sandy Bay Yacht Club WiFi	(978) 546-9433		9/		6.5/6.5	F		IS				S	P	GMR
13. Rockport Harbormaster	(978) 546-9589	143	9/16	/	6.5/6.5	F							P	GMR

☐ Internet Access WiFi Wireless Internet Access onSpot Dockside WiFi Facility

See WaterwayGuide.com for current rates, fuel prices, website addresses, and other up-to-the-minute information. (Information in the table is provided by the facilities.)

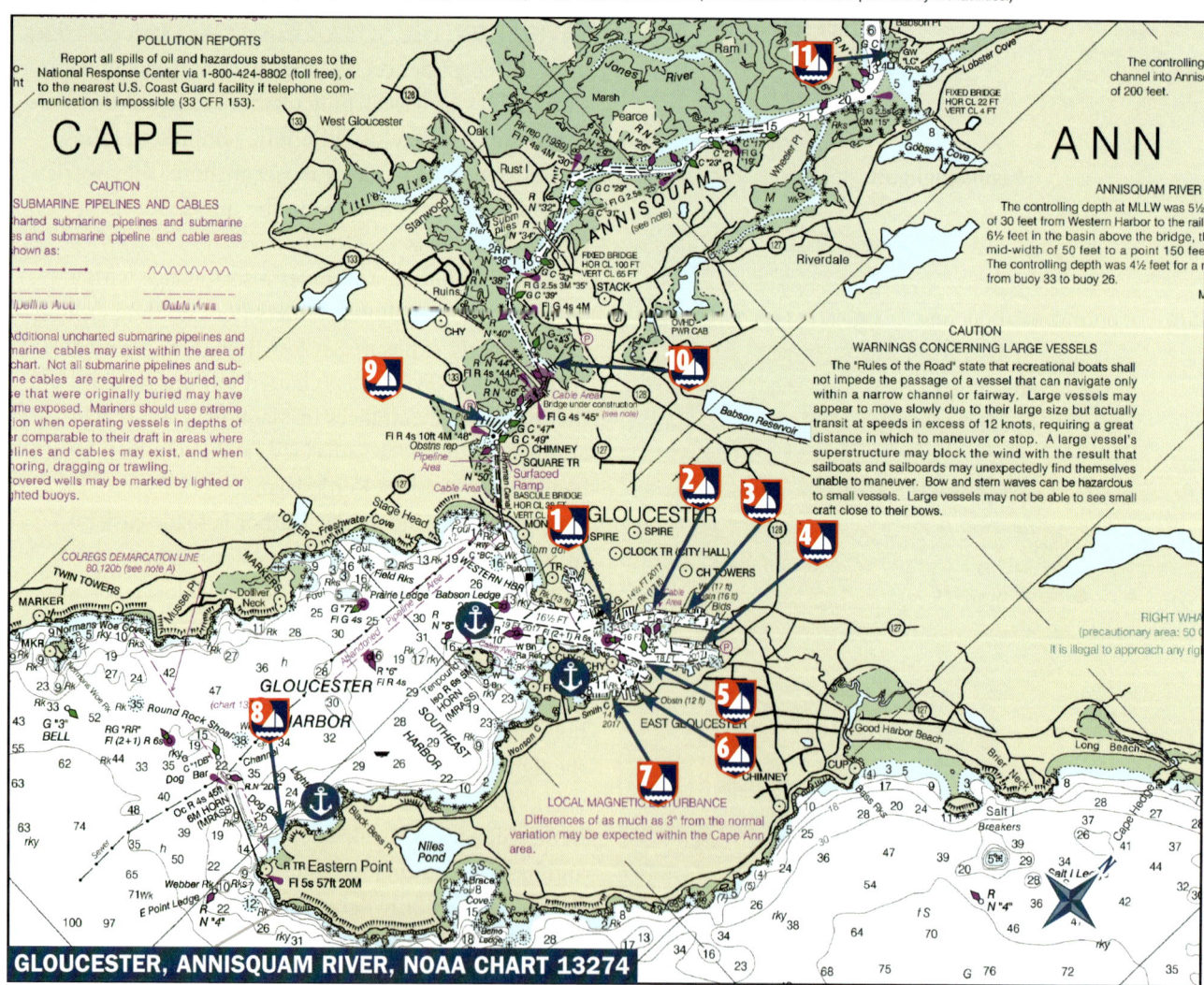

GLOUCESTER, ANNISQUAM RIVER, NOAA CHART 13274

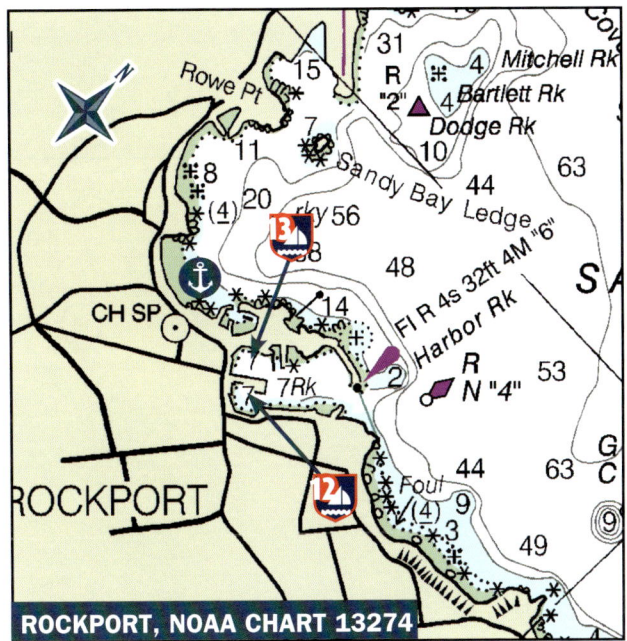

ROCKPORT, NOAA CHART 13274

Most recreational boats can take advantage of the full width of the Gloucester Harbor entrance rather than squeezing between green can buoy "1DB" and red nun buoy "2DB." Round Rock Shoal only shallows to 15 feet MLW and is, therefore, of little danger to most cruising vessels.

Dockage/Moorings: For a harbor of the size and historic seafaring renown of Gloucester, surprisingly few marine facilities are open to cruising visitors. The town maintains 28 transient moorings for vessels to 60 feet in three areas. The Inner Harbor moorings are well protected and close to shore. The Western Harbor moorings provide protection from the west through northeast and excellent views of the town. The Southeast Harbor moorings are farthest from shore access and the most exposed to wake and wind chop, but don't discount the entertainment value of watching the informal sunset schooner parade against a fiery sky. Launch service is complimentary if renting a town mooring.

The large Cruiseport Gloucester Marine Terminal is west of the state fishing pier. They have diesel and can accommodate vessels up to 500 feet (20-foot dockside MLW depths). To the southeast, Brown's Yacht Yard has transient slips and moorings. There is no launch service included, but dinghy tie-ups are permitted at the yard's full-service dock. Several other facilities here offer slips on their floating docks for vessels both large and small.

The Eastern Point Yacht Club–at the mouth of the river, southwest of Lighthouse Cove–will provide reciprocal amenities to cruisers with a yacht club affiliation. There is no dockage but rental moorings here include launch service to and from the restaurant and bar at the cove's edge. The town launch also serves this area.

Anchorage: There is plenty of deep water for anchoring in Gloucester Harbor. The harbor's considerable fetch and openness to prevailing southwesterlies makes a spot behind the breakwater at Eastern Point the most chop-protected choice in summer. Even so, you are almost certain to roll with the wrap-around ocean surge in this otherwise attractive location.

Farther up the harbor, it is also possible to anchor in the lee of Tenpound Island in 16 to 21 feet MLW with good holding in soft mud. The farther south you set your hook, the more wake you'll get from the fishing fleet and the less you'll benefit from the northerly wind break of Tenpound Island. In a shoulder-season nor'easter, snugging up close to the few moorings in Wonson Cove provides the most protection outside the inner harbor in 14 to 22 feet MLW with a mud bottom. (Don't forget the 9-foot tidal range and the scope that goes along with high tides.)

If you like being in the middle of everything, there's a special inner harbor area north of Rocky Neck that is kept clear of moorings. It spans a triangle between red-over-green pillar-shaped buoy "GH" and the red nun buoy "2"/green can buoy "3" pair. Use sufficient scope and stay clear of the neighboring boats. If the harbormaster thinks you are anchored in an unsafe place or manner, you will hear about it.

A dinghy dock is in the inner harbor's North Channel, behind the harbormaster's water taxi stop. Proceed to the space between the floating dock and the rock wall from either side of the docks.

Side Trip: Blynman Canal, Annisquam River

From the northwestern end of the Gloucester outer harbor, Blynman Canal leads into the Annisquam River and makes a good foul-weather (and picturesque fair-weather) alternative to the offshore run around Cape Ann. It is an easy run for small, maneuverable boats but offers a tricky blind curve that can create trouble for full-keel sailboats and others that don't back well. The route is frequently narrow and lined with boats on moorings. This can be helpful as it forms a sort of curb to drifting outside

GOIN' ASHORE

GLOUCESTER, MA

From the shelter of the Inner Harbor marinas, there is plenty to see and do in Gloucester. The area's history is long for an American town: Gloucester was first settled only 3 years after the pilgrims landed in Plymouth. These folks didn't find the soil to be friendly and moved to the then-brand-new settlement at Salem, even disassembling and transporting their meetinghouse. When people started to move back only a couple years later, they did so on a subsistence basis until the Gloucestermen began to command the Georges and Grand Banks fisheries. The largest and best-known seafood business there gave us the iconic fisherman image of a man in slickers and a sou'wester hat: Gorton's. Gloucester was one of the land-based settings for Sebastian Junger's book "The Perfect Storm" about the sad demise of a local fishing boat, the *Andrea Gail*. While you're there, tip a cold one at the Crow's Nest (334 Main St., 978-281-2965) in honor of the crew of the *Andrea Gale*.

SERVICES

1. Cape Ann Chamber of Commerce
Great resource with a walking map and information on the Saltwater Trolley at 33 Commercial St. (978-283-1601).

2. Gloucester Post Office
15 Dale Ave. (978-283-2361)

3. Isabel Babson Memorial Library
69 Main St. (978-283-5624)

ATTRACTIONS

4. The Fisherman's Memorial
A natural destination for any mariner, the 8-foot-tall statue looks out to sea just east of the entrance to Blynman Canal on Stacy Blvd. Each Memorial Day wreaths and flowers are thrown from the base of the statue in honor of the fishermen who never returned. The 94-year-old memorial was added to the National Register of Historic Places in 1996.

5. Cape Ann Museum

Houses collections celebrating the rich history of Cape Ann's evolving artistic and cultural history. The fine arts collection spans the full range of art created on and about Cape Ann (27 Pleasant St., 978-283-0455).

6. Gloucester Harborwalk

A total of 42 granite story posts define this self-guided walking tour, each highlighting an aspect of Gloucester's history as a seaport, the rich culture and people, and how the town has evolved in response to a modern, sustainable fishing industry.

7. Maritime Gloucester

Restored industrial harbor buildings with education and visitor centers, aquariums and exhibitions (23 Harbor Loop, 978-281-0470).

SHOPPING

8. Shaw's

Supermarket chain at 7 Railroad Ave. (978-283-2601).

9. Walgreens

Drugstore chain at 201 Main St. (978-283-7361).

MARINAS

10. Beacon Marine Basin

211 E. Main St. #19 (978-283-2380)

11. Brown's Yacht Yard

139 E. Main St. (978-281-3200)

12. Cruiseport Gloucester Terminal

6 Rowe Sq. (978-282-9700)

13. Gloucester Harbormaster

19 Harbor Loop (978-282-3012)

14. North Shore Sport Fishing Dock

211 E. Main St. (978-283-6880)

15. Ocean Alliance Docks–Gloucester

32 Horton St. (978-281-2814)

16. Pier 7 Marina

6 Cripple Cove Ln. (781-858-5279)

the channel. Regardless, due to shoaling, boats with drafts deeper than 5 feet will do well to pass when the 8-foot tide is at or near high.

NAVIGATION: Use NOAA Chart 13274. If entering from Gloucester Harbor, the canal's entrance at the fast-operating **Blynman (SR 127) Bridge** (8-foot closed vertical clearance) is all but invisible until you are lined up with it. The bridge opens on signal except on holidays. See details at Waterway Explorer (www.waterwayguide.com). It is not uncommon to wait up to 10 minutes after signaling for an opening. Be sure to stand well off until you are sure the opening is clear. The current runs fast as do the commercial fishing boats you'll share this passage with, and the narrow confines of the draw provide no room for passing. Boats leaving the canal have the right-of-way.

Beyond the bridge, the route turns north at green can buoy "49" and is straight for 0.3 mile to the **MBTA Bridge** with a 16-foot closed vertical clearance (usually open unless a train is approaching). Just north of the bridge, a 90-degree turn in the channel creates a serious traffic hazard as it is impossible for southbound boats to see northbound boats until they are within 50 feet of the very narrow bridge. In this spot, the southbound cruiser should swing wide to the north for as much advance warning as possible and proceed at steerage speed until the opening is confirmed to be clear.

One-half mile farther, the channel turns sharply north and goes under the **SR 128 (Yankee Division) Bridge** (65-foot fixed vertical clearance) into the Annisquam River. When last surveyed in March 2017, the controlling depth was 6 feet MLW from Western Harbor to the railroad bridge. Between the railroad bridge and red nun buoy "26" the depths were surveyed at 4.3 feet MLW and between there and green can buoy "21" they were 4.8 feet. The remainder of the river carries 7 feet or better MLW. In 2020, observed mid-channel depths did not go below 7 feet throughout but shoaling was heavy in places along the sides of the channel.

The northern end's heavy shoaling and narrow channel create difficult circumstances in a heavy sea but the route is well buoyed. Though avoiding bad weather off Cape Ann is one reason to take this route, consider carefully how you will power into open water beyond the long western shoal.

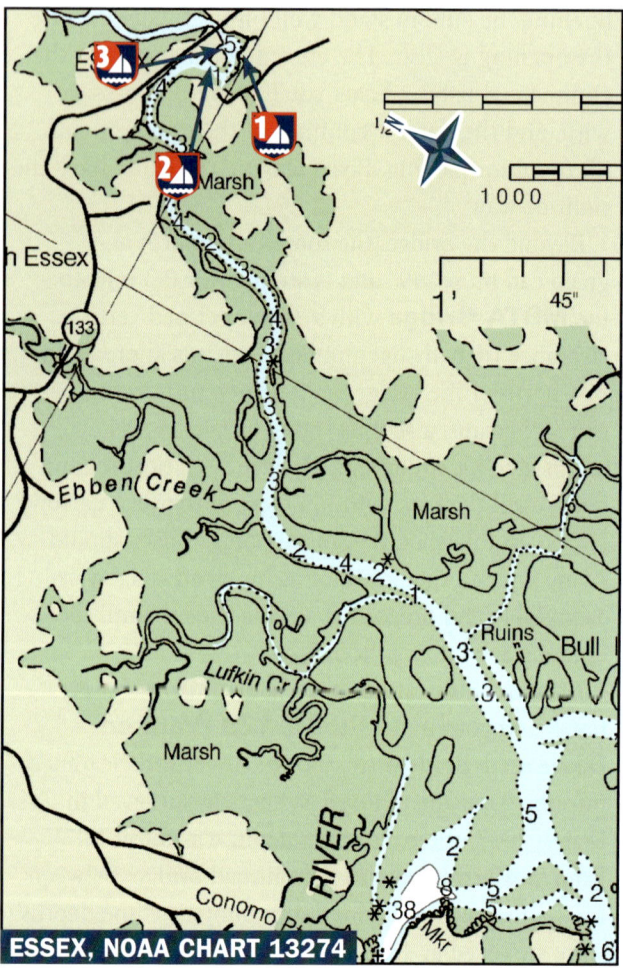

Essex River, MA

ESSEX		Largest Vessel Accomodated	VHF Channel Monitored / Working	Approach / Dockside Depth (reported)	Transient Slips / Total Slips	Floating Docks	Gas / Diesel	Groceries, Ice, Marine Supplies, Snacks	Repairs: Hull, Engine, Propeller	Lift (tonnage), Crane, Rail	Min / Max Amps	Courtesy Car, Laundry, Pool, Showers	Pump-Out Station	Nearby: Grocery Store, Motel, Restaurant
				Dockage				**Supplies**			**Services**			
1. Essex Marina	(978) 768-6833	34	16/	/80	4.0/4.0	F			IMS	EP		30	S	GMR
2. Perkins Marine	(978) 768-7145	24	/	/96	4.0/4.0	F	G	IM	HEP	L25	30/50			MR
3. Pike Marine	(978) 768-7161	32	/	/70	1.0/4.0	F		M	HEP	L10,C				3MR

☐ Internet Access   **WIFI** Wireless Internet Access   📶 onSpot Dockside WiFi Facility

See WaterwayGuide.com for current rates, fuel prices, website addresses, and other up-to-the-minute information. (Information in the table is provided by the facilities.)

ESSEX, NOAA CHART 13274

Dockage: Between the bridges on the Blynman Canal lies Cape Ann's Marina Resort, a full-service marina, hotel and service yard. The Annisquam Yacht Club is also here with some mooring space reserved; call ahead. From this point, bird watching and picnicking at beautiful Wingaersheek Beach is a short dinghy ride away.

Side Trip: Thacher Island

Thacher Island (south of Rockport) affords a unique view of lighthouse history. The north and south towers on Thacher Island are the only operating twin lighthouses in America. The Thacher Island Association maintains three moorings for visiting boats. Call the keeper in advance at 508-284-0144. Once moored, you may row ashore to the ramp but expect a small per-person landing fee. Ashore you can climb the North Tower for views from Maine to Boston, hike and explore the trails covering the 50-acre island and visit the various buildings of the light station. There are no amenities or services offered on the island.

Rockport Harbor

Several small harbors break the coastline of Cape Ann, but Rockport stands out as one of the foremost art centers on the East Coast. The fisherman's shack here has been the subject of so many paintings that it is known throughout the art world as "Motif No. 1." The lobster buoys that adorn the shack honor local lobstermen who have passed away.

Wander out on Bearskin Neck and you will find restaurants, a fish market, craft and gift shops and historic sites. Cruise up Main St. and, in addition to a great selection of art studios, find the Rockport Art Association (12 Main St., 978-546-6604), home base to some of the best-known professional artists in the country who live, work and teach here in Rockport. Art courses of a few days to several weeks are offered all summer and there are open studios on designated weekends.

History buffs will enjoy a visit to the Sandy Bay Historical Society (40 King St., 978-546-9533) for an overview of North Shore history and to hear the colorful tale as to how Rockport became a "dry" town. Be sure to call for their limited hours.

Rockport Harbor

It's a bit of a hike to Halibut Point State Park at the tip of Cape Ann but well worth the trip when you see the breathtaking views of the ocean from this former Babson Farm granite quarry.

NAVIGATION: Use NOAA Chart 13274. Located at the southwestern end of Sandy Bay, Rockport is protected by two outer and two inner breakwaters but is still open to strong northeasterly and easterly winds. The bay's southern entrance, between Straitsmouth Island and Avery Ledge, is narrow and rocky but the northern entrance is wide, deep and easy to navigate. Rockport Harbor itself consists of an outer basin and two inner basins divided by the town wharf. Controlling depth is 7 feet MLW. Larger boats stop at Gloucester and visit overland.

Anchorage/Moorings: The harbor is not large and has only a few moorings available by reservation. In summer, especially on weekends, call the Rockport Harbormaster (VHF Channels 09 or 16) to arrange for a mooring or berth.

When you contact the harbormaster, you will likely be directed outside to an anchorage off the church (charted as "CH SP") in the cove north of town and south of Sandy Bay Ledge. Here you will find 11- to 22-foot MLW depths with good holding in mud and rock. In less than ideal conditions, it is not the most comfortable anchorage but you can easily dinghy ashore to visit the town.

Ipswich Bay (Essex)

North of Cape Ann is where the Annisquam River enters Ipswich Bay. The bay and surrounding areas are famous for their clam beds. You will encounter a few attractive harbors along this sandy coast but enter all of them carefully as shoals constantly change the channels. Again, note that using the canal and river as a "short cut" south to Gloucester Harbor in lieu of going around Cape Ann is not advisable.

In the southwest corner of Ipswich Bay is the entrance to Colonial Essex with well-preserved houses, excellent seafood restaurants (many dockside) and facilities for shallow-draft boats up to 40 feet. The village is a short walk from the waterfront. Many of the great Gloucester schooners were built here and the Story Shipyard that built them still stands at the head of the shallow, winding river.

The Essex Shipbuilding Museum (978-768-7541) is located in an old schoolhouse at 66 Main St. and contains photographs and artifacts from the great days of Essex shipbuilding. The extensive history includes the *Evelina M. Goulart*, originally built in 1927 and now on display at the museum.

Merrimack River, MA

W G

NEWBURYPORT		Largest Vessel Accommodated	VHF Channel Monitored / Working	Transient Slips / Total Slips	Approach / Dockside Depth (reported)	Floating Docks	Gas / Diesel	Groceries, Ice, Marine Supplies, Snacks	Repairs: Hull, Engine, Propeller	Lift (tonnage), Crane, Rail	Min / Max Amps	Courtesy Car, Laundry, Pool, Showers	Pump-Out Station	Nearby: Grocery Store, Motel, Restaurant
				Dockage			**Supplies**		**Services**					
1. Newburyport Harbor Marina 🖥 Wifi onSpot	(978) 462-3990	125	74/74	20/70	12.0/12.0	F	GD	GIMS	HEP	L85,C	30/100	LS	P	GMR
2. Newburyport Central Waterfront Park	(978) 462-3746	140	12/12	/	12.0/22.0	F		IS			30/50	LS	P	GR
3. Hilton's Marina 🖥 Wifi onSpot	(978) 462-3990	100	74/74	5/65	12.0/12.0	F		I	HEP	L85,C	30/50	LS	P	MR
4. Windward Yacht Yard 🖥 Wifi onSpot	(978) 462-6500	80	74/74	6/160	15.0/15.0	F		IMS	HEP	L85,C	30/50	LS	P	GMR
5. Newburyport Yacht Club 🖥 Wifi	(978) 463-9911	55	71/71	5/192	30.0/10.0	F		IS		L,C	30	PS	P	GMR
6. Newburyport Boat Basin 🖥 Wifi onSpot	(978) 465-9110	60	74/74	10/225	12.0/12.0	F		IMS	HEP	L35	30/50	LS	P	GMR
7. Merri-Mar Yacht Basin Inc. Wifi	(978) 465-3022	100	16/9	10/50	20.0/15.0	F		IM	HEP	L50,C	30/50	LS	P	GMR
8. Yankee Landing Marina	(978) 463-0805	80	/	/60	20.0/15.0	F				L50	30			GMR
9. Cove Marina Wifi 3	(978) 462-4998	60	10/	2/142	15.0/15.0	F		I	HEP	L	30/50	LS		GMR
10. Bridge Marina	(978) 465-1153	60	/	/110	/		GD	IMS	H	L40			P	R
11. Rings Island Marina Wifi	(978) 465-0307	60	/	/120	15.0/12.0	F		IM	HEP		30/50	S	P	MR

🖥 Internet Access　Wifi Wireless Internet Access　onSpot Dockside WiFi Facility

See WaterwayGuide.com for current rates, fuel prices, website addresses, and other up-to-the-minute information. (Information in the table is provided by the facilities.)

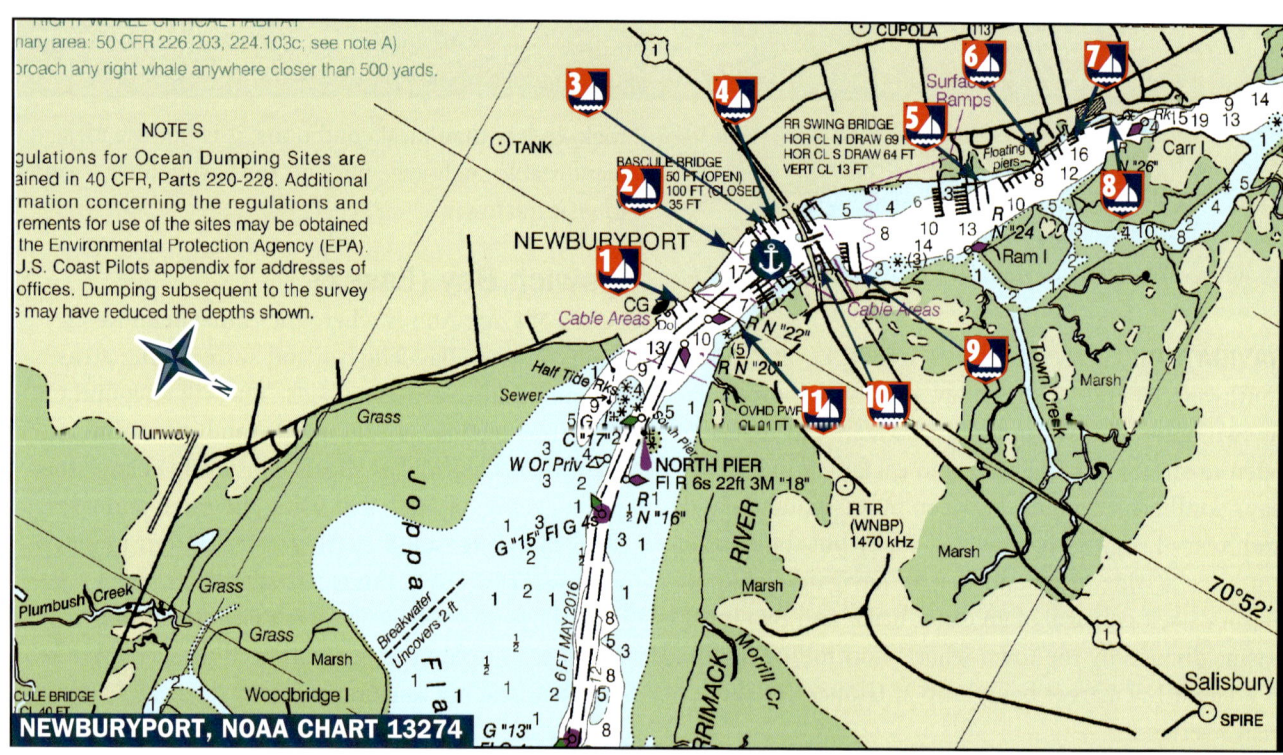

NEWBURYPORT, NOAA CHART 13274

NAVIGATION: Use NOAA Chart 13274. The entrance from Ipswich Bay shifts constantly and the aids to navigation (not charted) shift to match. In heavy weather seas across the bar might make the entry impassable. Controlling depth to the town, about 4 narrow, shallow, meandering miles upriver, is 4 feet MLW and the river bottom is all (forgiving) mud.

   Dockage: The small boat marinas here can only be accessed by shallow-draft boats. See our marina table in this chapter for details. Call ahead for exact depths.

   Anchorage: Entry and passage of Essex River are best made at half-tide or better; the mean tidal range is about 9 feet. If, after exploring the river, conditions for leaving Essex Bay are bad, head for the protected anchorage in the lee of Castle Neck. While there are no amenities, this is a comfortable place to wait out the weather before crossing the bar back into Ipswich Bay. Be careful, though, as depths shallow quickly (ranging from 3 to 7 feet MLW) as you move west into the anchorage.

Side Trip: Plum Island Sound

Plum Island Sound is the juncture for the gentle rivers and streams flowing from the west and north between Castle Neck and Newburyport creating a superb kayaking area. It lies behind Plum Island's barrier strip, home to the Parker Island National Wildlife Refuge, where you might see native and migrating wildfowl. This area is a beachcomber's paradise, favored by shell collectors who find whelks, periwinkles, slipper shells and blue mussels along the narrow sandy beach. The sound and its northern extension, Plum Island River, make a 10-mile link between Ipswich and Newburyport, but the river is suitable only for dinghies.

Newburyport Harbor

Newburyport on the Merrimack River is the smallest city in the state and one of the oldest, having been founded in 1635. The city boasts some finest examples of Colonial and Federal-era architecture in the nation, reminders of the days when its ships sailed around the world. Some of the most famous clipper ships in history were built here. This classic New England coastal village offers historical interest, shopping and dining adventures. The Custom House Maritime Museum (25 Water St., 978-462-8681) and the Cushing House Museum & Garden (98 High St., 978-462-2681) are both well worth an afternoon visit.

NAVIGATION: Use NOAA Chart 13274. Newburyport Harbor has a well marked and jettied inlet entrance via the Merrimack River, well known for its strong currents

Newburyport waterfront

Hampton River, MA

HAMPTON BEACH			Dockage				Supplies		Services			
		VHF Channel Monitored / Working	Largest Vessel Accomodated	Approach / Dockside Depth (reported)	Transient Slips / Total Slips	Floating Docks	Groceries, Ice, Marine Supplies, Snacks	Gas / Diesel	Repairs: Hull, Engine, Propeller	Lift (tonnage), Crane, Rail	Courtesy Car, Laundry, Pool, Showers	Min / Max Amps	Pump-Out Station	Nearby: Grocery Store, Motel, Restaurant
1. Hampton River Marina WiFi	(603) 929-1422	65	/	/134	11.0/	F				L25	30/50	S		MR

☐ Internet Access   WiFi Wireless Internet Access   ⊙ onSpot Dockside WiFi Facility

See WaterwayGuide.com for current rates, fuel prices, website addresses, and other up-to-the-minute information. (Information in the table is provided by the facilities.)

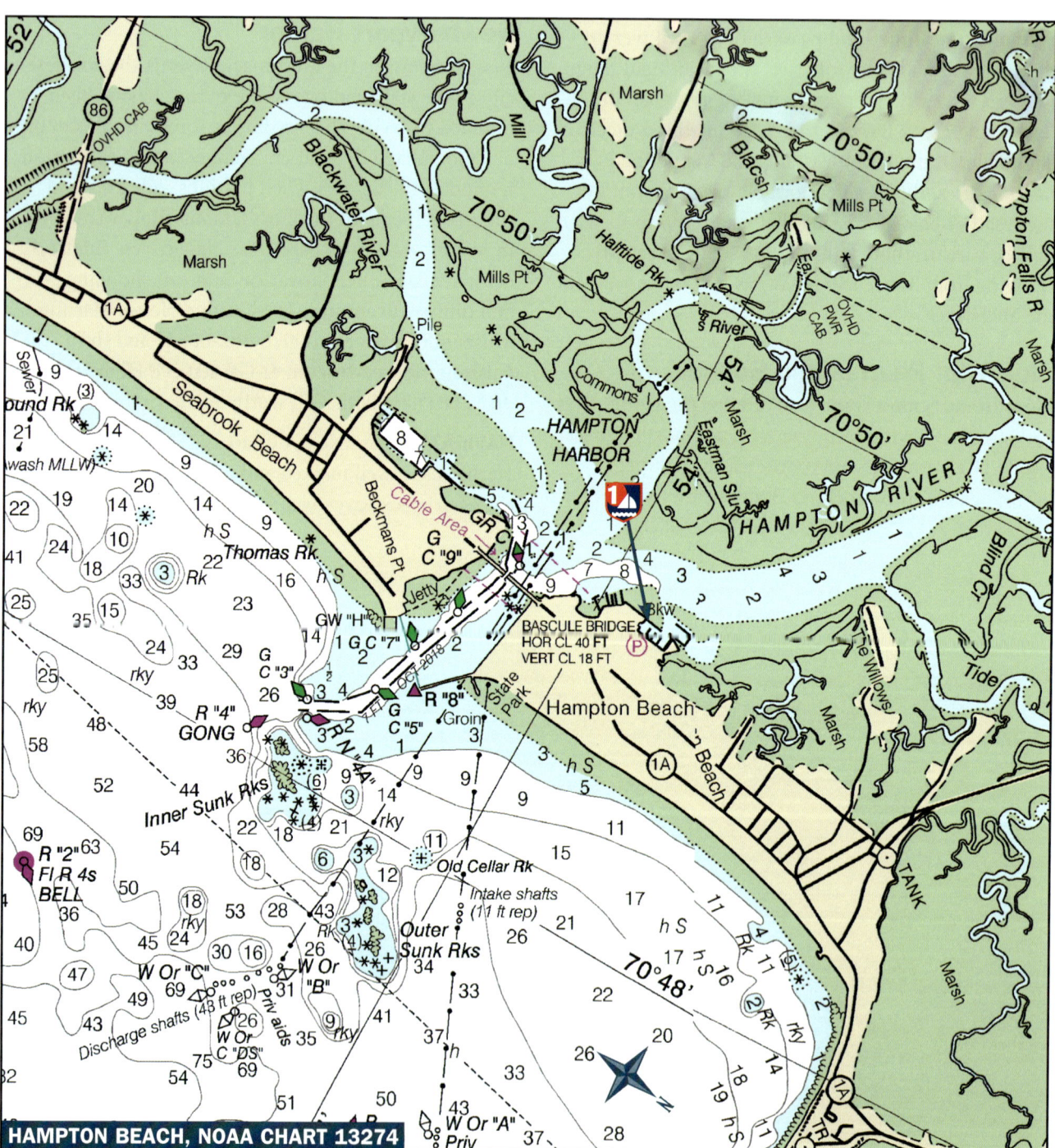

HAMPTON BEACH, NOAA CHART 13274

and regular shoaling. There were only 3.5-foot MLW approach depths in a May 2018 survey just outside the jetties and no dredging has been undertaken since then. As you approach the Merrimack River entrance, call the Coast Guard for the latest information. Alternatively, plan your entry with the tide, which is significant enough to be quite helpful at roughly 9 feet. Currents run around 2 knots on the ebb and 3 or more on the flood.

Bar Guide Light, a quick-flashing yellow 47-foot-tall light, is just inside the entrance on the beach end of the jetty. When the light is flashing, it means the river entrance is not safe to enter or exit. The Coast Guard does not promise that the bar is safe when the light is not flashing, but does warn that only experienced skippers should try to cross the bar when it is flashing. A white sign reading "Rough Bar" is maintained through the boating season from April 1 to October 31. The sign is not readily apparent when you are entering the Merrimack River; it is much more visible when you are leaving. Once inside the water is smooth, although the current is strong for some distance upriver.

The first of two bridges is the **Newburyport (US 1) Bridge** (35-foot closed vertical clearance), which opens on signal from May 1 through November 15, from 6:00 a.m. to 10:00 p.m., except from Memorial Day through Labor Day, when the draw opens on signal only on the hour and half-hour. At all other times the draw will open on signal after at least a 1-hour advance notice is given by calling the number posted at the bridge. Just beyond the highway bridge is the **Boston and Maine Railroad Bridge** with 13-foot closed vertical clearance. It is usually left in the open position. No-Wake speed limits are strictly enforced here.

Dockage/Moorings: The city's municipal harbor is an amenable host to both cruising boats and a sportfishing fleet. Transient vessels may tie up for an afternoon or overnight (for a fee) and have easy access to downtown restaurants, museums, shops and galleries, and even a local theatre.

Full-service boat yards, marinas and yacht clubs are above and below the bridges with space for transients and varying amenities including all fuels. Newburyport Harbor Marina welcomes transients on the west side of the river before the bridge and nearby Newburyport Central Waterfront Park lets transient mariners tie up overnight or rent a mooring.

Anchorage: You can drop the hook north of red nun buoy "20" in 10 to 12 feet MLW but be aware of the charted cable area.

■ SIDE TRIP: ISLE OF SHOALS

The Isles of Shoals straddle the state line between New Hampshire and Maine well out into Bigelow Bight. Capt. John Smith charted this group of islets and ledges in 1614. Taken by their wind-swept beauty, he also attempted to name them in his honor, but the earlier name given the isles by itinerant fishermen is the one that stuck. There are currently nine islands included in the Isles of Shoals: Appledore Island, Star Island, Seavey Island, Malaga Island, Cedar Island, Smuttynose Island, Lunging Island, White Island and Duck Island. Despite their popularity with weekenders out of Portsmouth and distance cruisers stopping over during the trek to or from Maine, all of them are privately owned and only one, Smuttynose Island (technically across the Maine line), is open to visitors.

At Smuttynose Island negotiate dinghy passage into Haley Cove and land on an obliging rock adjacent to the island's two evident fishing cottages. During the summer months you will likely be met by a volunteer "ranger" who will lend you a booklet describing a self-guided walking tour of this pleasant and historic spot. On a clear day, the views are gorgeous from almost every aspect of this easily traversed ocean jewel. At less than high tide Smuttynose Island is connected to tiny Malaga Island, the one place around where seagoing pets can find a relief station. Smuttynose Island is also connected via a rock breakwater to barren Cedar Island, immediately to the south.

Star Island on the south (New Hampshire) side of Gosport Harbor provides the green but treeless setting for what was once the Star Island Hotel. Now owned by the non-profit Star Island Corporation (603-430-6272), the island hosts conferences and retreats. They offer a complimentary tender service rather than allowing dinghies to land on their docks so cruisers can access the island for self-guided tours, a snack bar and family-style meals with reservations. Check in at the reception desk for a copy of the corporation's map and guidelines.

Appledore Island (north of Smuttynose Island) also tolerates visits from the general public (no pets), although most of the island's acres (also Duck Island farther north) have been designated Critical Natural Areas of the State of Maine and are off-limits. This includes all buildings.

WENTWORTH BY THE SEA MARINA

New Castle Island

NAVIGATION: Use NOAA Charts 13278 and 13274. When approaching from the south, red nun buoy "2" south of Anderson Ledge provides the first guidance. Steer between it and Isles of Shoals Light, a 82-foot lighthouse with a 15-second light located on the eastern end of White Island. In any difficult weather or visibility stay west of red nun buoy "4" and use red-and-white bell buoy "IS" as the safe vector for entering Gosport Harbor. From the north stay well to the west of Duck Island and its surrounding rocks and ledges. A course from red nun buoy "2" off the western side of Appledore Island to red-and-white bell buoy "IS" provides safe entry to the harbor. From the Piscataqua a heading of 140 degrees will bring you to the red-and-white bell buoy "IS." On the chart it will look as though you are following the New Hampshire/Maine line.

Moorings/Anchorage: Gosport Harbor has served visiting mariners for almost 400 years, but it has done so with a sustained reputation for poor holding and scant protection. To offset this difficulty, private parties from the mainland have established moorings of convenience here. Local tradition has it that they are yours for the taking on a first-come, first-served basis. There are no guarantees on their condition, and if the owner shows up you will be asked to vacate the mooring. There are plenty of moorings, except on peak summer weekends.

If the wind is up from the northwest, Gosport Harbor is not the place to be. If this is the case cruisers either avoid the Isles of Shoals altogether or take shelter in the cove formed by the southwestern side of Smuttynose Island and the causeway leading from there to Cedar Island. Here you can drop the hook in at least 7 feet MLW with good holding and some protection from all but the east.

■ PORTSMOUTH, NH TO CAPE ELIZABETH, ME

Portsmouth

New Hampshire meets Maine on the Piscataqua (pronounced "pis-KA-tuh-quah") River. The Abenaki name was used by Capt. John Smith in 1614 but the spelling wasn't regularized until 1623, the same year that the very first colonial saw mill was completed on this river's banks. History didn't leave this area alone, and WWII saw four captured German submarines towed to the Portsmouth Naval Shipyard for study. The biggest prize contained a disassembled Messerschmitt Me 262 jet fighter and a top secret bonus: 1,232 pounds of uranium oxide. That nuclear material was provided to the Manhattan Project and became part of the atomic bomb dropped on Hiroshima.

The border between the states is a matter of much history as well, and what may or may not be the final word was laid down by the U.S. Supreme Court in 2002 giving Seavey Island to Maine.

Cruisers won't need to worry about borders. The Portsmouth/New Castle and Kittery sides are certainly different, but an enjoyable walk across the **Memorial (U.S. 1) Bridge** and Badger Island brings the two together. Portsmouth is a lovely old town with lots to do and see, while Kittery's charms are quieter and more spread out.

Among New England seaports, Portsmouth probably has more of its historic architecture intact than any other. Dozens of 17th-, 18th- and 19th-century homes, churches, shops and pubs were spared the city fire of 1813 and the wrecking crews of more recent times. The town is laced with historic houses inviting inspection. There is a collection of more than 30 such structures saved from urban renewal in the Puddle Dock area and recreated in their exact look and feel during specific periods of the past four centuries.

Named after the earliest Portsmouth settlement, the Strawberry Banke Museum (Marcy St., 603-433-1100) sits on 9.5 acres of museum grounds with each building showing a slice of living history from a bygone era, along with serious archaeological and crafts work that continues by staff and artisans. The museum office is located just west of the waterfront behind Prescott Park and the Public Gardens. A visit to the *U.S.S. Albacore* (600 Market St., 603-436-3860) provides a fascinating self-guided tour of the 1953 retired submarine.

Within a few blocks' walk from the waterfront, you will encounter several banks, a supermarket, multiple bookstores and lots of interesting shops. A dozen different dining out options may be found within an 8-block area of the waterfront, along Market, Ceres and Congress Streets.

West of New Castle Island, the Piscataqua River leaves Portsmouth Harbor to start its winding northward course up into rural New Hampshire. Pleasant communities with considerable yachting activity line the banks.

Portsmouth Harbor, NH

	Phone	Largest Vessel Accommodated	VHF Channel Monitored / Working	Transient Slips / Total Slips	Approach / Dockside Depth (reported)	Floating Docks	Gas / Diesel	Groceries, Ice, Marine Supplies, Snacks	Repairs: Hull, Engine, Propeller	Lift (tonnage), Crane, Rail	Min / Max Amps	Courtesy Car, Laundry, Pool, Showers	Pump-Out Station	Nearby: Grocery Store, Motel, Restaurant
NEW CASTLE ISLAND				Dockage			Supplies		Services					
1. Wentworth by the Sea Marina WiFi onSpot	(603) 433-5050	250	16/71	100/170	10.0/10.0	F	GD	IS			30/200+	CLPS	P	3R
2. Portsmouth Yacht Club	(603) 436-9877	40	9/78	/	20.0/15.0		GD	I			30	S	P	GMR
PORTSMOUTH														
3. Prescott Park Municipal Dock	(603) 498-6816	55	9/	8/10	40.0/18.0	F					30			R
4. Marina at Harbour Place WiFi	(888) 802-5871	175	/		35.0/18.0	F					30/100	LS		GMR
ELIOT														
5. Kittery Point Yacht Yard - Eliot	(207) 439-3967	85	71/	/	/	F		M	HEP	C	30/50			GR
NEWINGTON														
6. Great Bay Marine Inc. □ WiFi	(603) 436-5299	90	68/68	15/128	30.0/8.0	F	GD	IM	HEP	L35,C	30/50	LS	P	4MR
KITTERY AREA														
7. Piscataqua Marina □ WiFi	(207) 439-3810	125	/	1/34	65.0/6.0	F		I	HEP	L20,C,R	30/50	LS	P	GMR
8. Kittery Point Yacht Yard □ WiFi	(207) 439-9582	60	71/	5/10	35.0/22.0	F		IM	HEP	L50,C	30/50	S	P	GR
9. Pepperell Cove WiFi	(207) 332-2656	90	16/9	6/6	15.0/11.0	F		IS		L40	30/50			7R

□ Internet Access   WiFi Wireless Internet Access   onSpot Dockside WiFi Facility

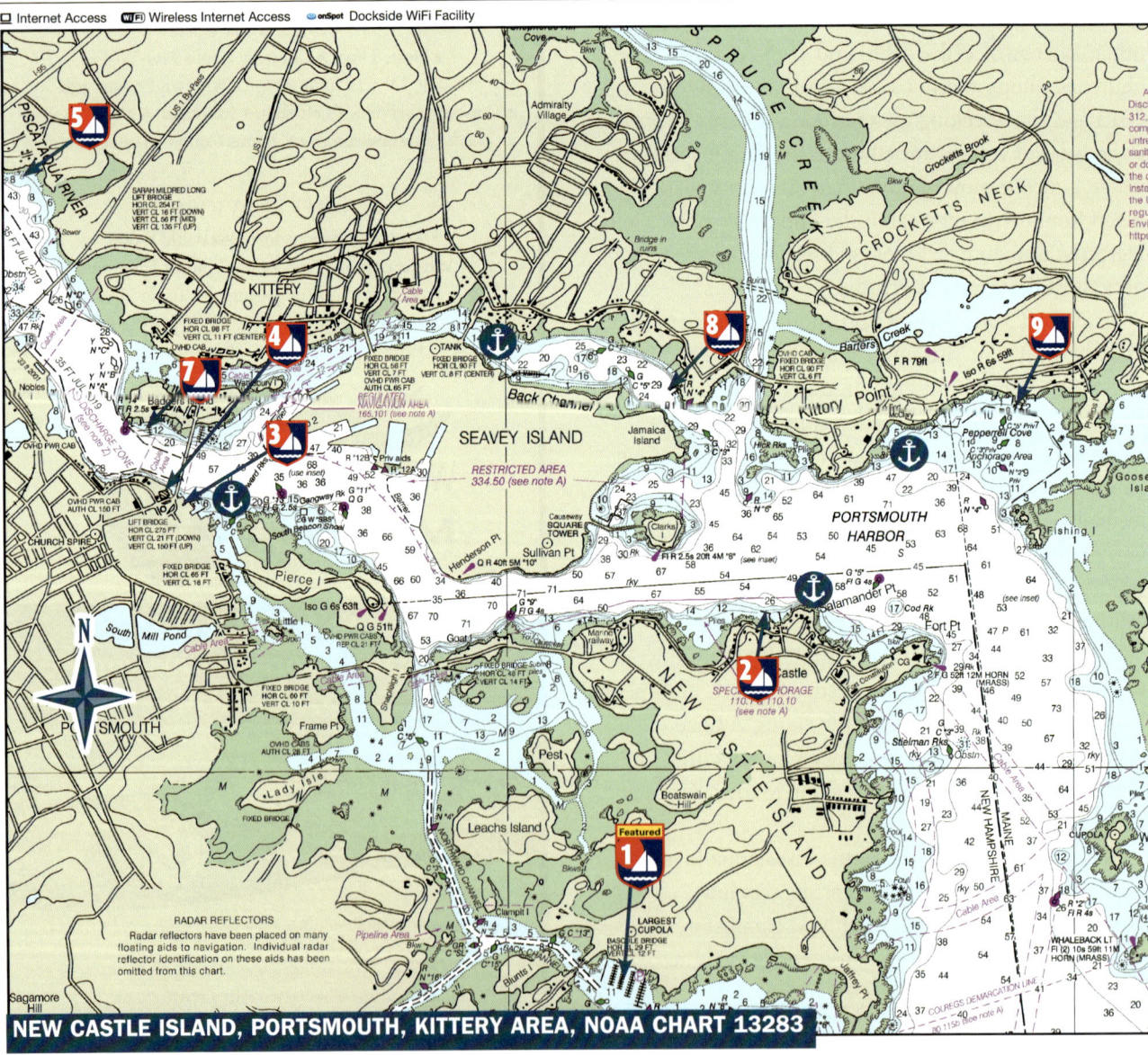

NEW CASTLE ISLAND, PORTSMOUTH, KITTERY AREA, NOAA CHART 13283

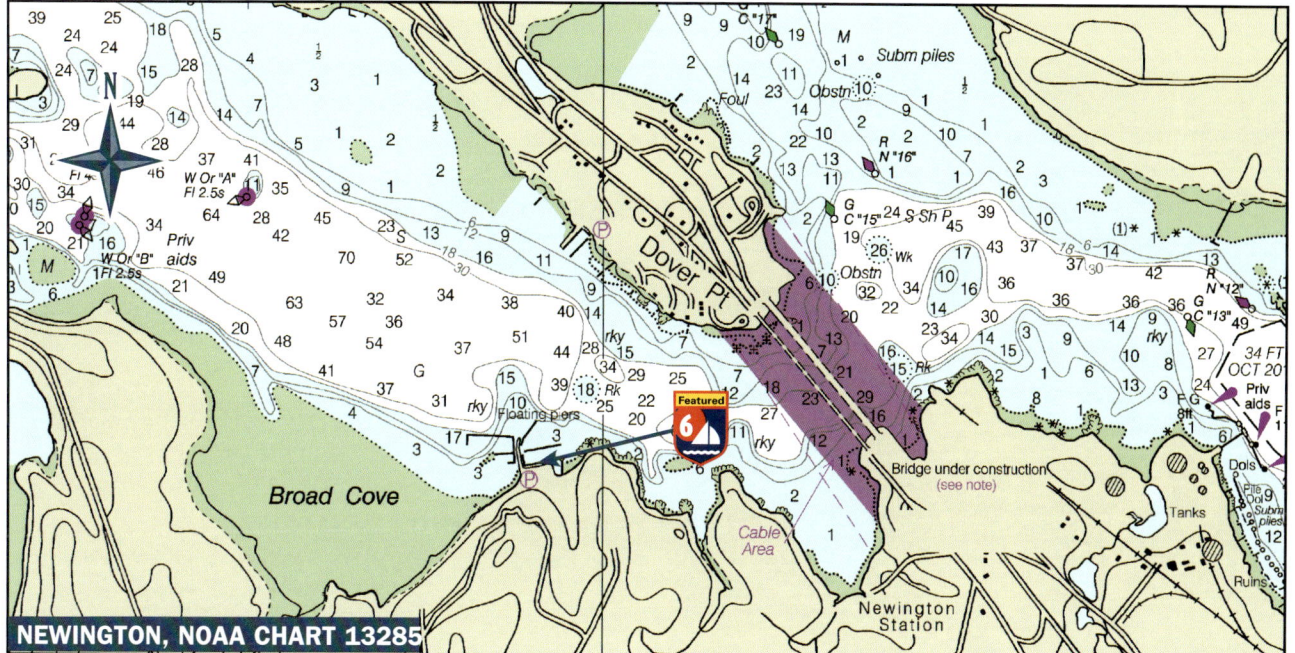

NEWINGTON, NOAA CHART 13285

NAVIGATION: Use NOAA Charts 13283 and 13274. The well-marked, deep-water entry was designed and is maintained for the passage of large naval ships, making it easy for smaller vessels to navigate under the right conditions. At full flow the river develops fierce currents whistling along at 4 knots under the **I-95 Bridge** (3 miles upriver) on an average tide.

This is where you get your first taste of Down East tides. The tidal range of 10 feet creates currents that drag buoys under. Locals profess that theirs are the most brutal currents on this stretch of coast. To minimize excitement, check the tide and current tables to coordinate comings and goings with slack water and minimal flows. Its best to time your arrival for slack water, about 1.5 hours behind the turnaround of the tide, to avoid the 3-knot currents through tricky stretches of navigation. Allow extra scope when anchoring as if expecting high winds.

Whaleback Light provides a dramatic welcome on entry and should be left well to the east. The main channel turns west at flashing green buoy "5" to head south of Seavey Island, which cannot be circumnavigated due to low fixed bridges on the Kittery side.

There are numerous bridges in this harbor. Refer to Waterway Explorer (www.waterwayguide.com) for restrictions and schedules. None are located between the river entrance and downtown Portsmouth. About 5 miles upstream the river forks and fixed bridges (46-foot vertical clearance) cross from Dover Point to Newington Station.

Currents run strong, almost 4 knots on the ebb upriver on the Piscataqua. About 5 miles upstream, **Little Bay Bridge** (46-foot fixed vertical clearance) crosses from Dover Point to Newington Station. The river forks here. On the western branch, Little Bay and its tributary streams including scenic Great Bay offer good anchorages and fascinating exploration.

Dockage/Moorings: Wentworth by the Sea Marina is a resort property offering full amenities surrounding its floating docks in Little Harbor. The marina provides impeccable service and the ultimate in convenience for guests arriving by sea. Transients have access to the marina's heated pool, tennis courts and concierge services, in addition to laundry facilities, fuel and on-site restaurants. Some additional amenities include courtesy vehicles and trolley service to historic Portsmouth.

Portsmouth Yacht Club on New Castle Island welcomes transients at their moorings, which include access to the club's showers and restrooms. Launch service usually operates until sundown, or you can use the club's dinghy landing. For a trip to town, a ride or taxi will be needed.

Portsmouth operates a municipal dock in Prescott Park, right on the waterfront and seaward of the **Memorial U.S. 1 Bridge** (19-foot closed vertical clearance) on entry. Transient stays are limited to 72 hours and are no longer complimentary but 30- and 50-amp power is now available. The swift currents

and high wakes require careful approach and tie-up, but the location in the heart of downtown, is a true pleasure.

Marina at Harbour Place, on the opposite side of the bridge, offers deep-water transient dockage for yachts to 175 feet and is located in the heart of downtown Portsmouth. Note the current is strong here. Call ahead for approach advice.

Numerous state moorings are maintained in Little Harbor (adjacent to the Wentworth By the Sea docks) for lease to local residents. At any given time, half a dozen of these moorings are likely to be vacant and may be picked up by overnight visitors but with the caveat that an uninvited guest should be prepared to leave if the rightful lease-holder returns.

Great Bay Marine Inc. is a year-round, full-service facility with 128 slips, 72 moorings and fuel. It boasts one of the largest dry storage yards in the region and has experienced technicians on site as well as a well-stocked chandlery.

Kittery

Kittery is Maine's first port and you may be lucky enough to see the historic gundalow (cargo barge) *Piscataqua* plying a 21st-century cargo trade up and down its namesake river. Settled and established as a fishery in 1623, Kittery turned to boatbuilding early. *Ranger*, the first vessel to fly the Stars and Stripes, was launched from here in 1777. Although Portsmouth receives a lot of deserved attention, there's plenty to explore on the Maine side of the river. Many colonial homes are open to the public, old Fort McClary (now a memorial park) makes a great stop and the Portsmouth Naval Shipyard and several friendly marinas bring a rich maritime history into the present.

NAVIGATION: Use NOAA Charts 13283 and 13286. Back Channel splits off the Piscataque River to the north but has several low bridges (7-foot controlling vertical clearance) connecting Kittery to the Portsmouth Naval Shipyard on Seavey Island. If continuing up the Piscataqua stay south of Seavey Island. The **Memorial (U.S. 1) Bridge** (19-foot closed vertical clearance) opens on signal except from May 15 through October 31, from 7:00 a.m. to 7:00 p.m., when the draw need open only on the hour and half hour for recreational vessels

Dockage/Moorings: Pepperell Cove is the first mooring field and is northeast on Portsmouth Harbor.

Portsmouth Harbor

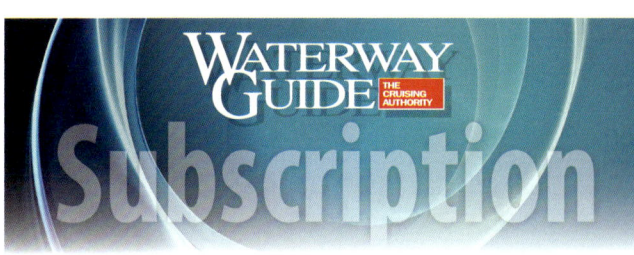

York River Area, ME

YORK RIVER			Dockage				Supplies			Services			
		Largest Vessel Accomodated	VHF Channel Monitored / Working	Transient Slips / Total Slips	Approach / Dockside Depth (reported)	Floating Docks	Gas / Diesel	Groceries, Ice, Marine Supplies, Snacks	Repairs: Hull, Engine, Propeller	Lift (tonnage), Crane, Rail	Min / Max Amps	Courtesy Car, Laundry, Pool, Showers	Nearby: Grocery Store, Motel, Restaurant / Pump-Out Station
1. York Harbor Marine Service (WiFi)	(207) 363-3602	100	16/	/50	8.0/8.0	F	GD	IM	HEP		30	LS	R
2. York Harbor-Town of York	(207) 363-0433		/	/	8.0/8.0								R
3. Donnell's Marina	(207) 363-4308	80	/	3/6	10.0/10.0	F					30/100	C	R

🖵 Internet Access   (WiFi) Wireless Internet Access   ⊙ onSpot Dockside WiFi Facility
See WaterwayGuide.com for current rates, fuel prices, website addresses, and other up-to-the-minute information. (Information in the table is provided by the facilities.)

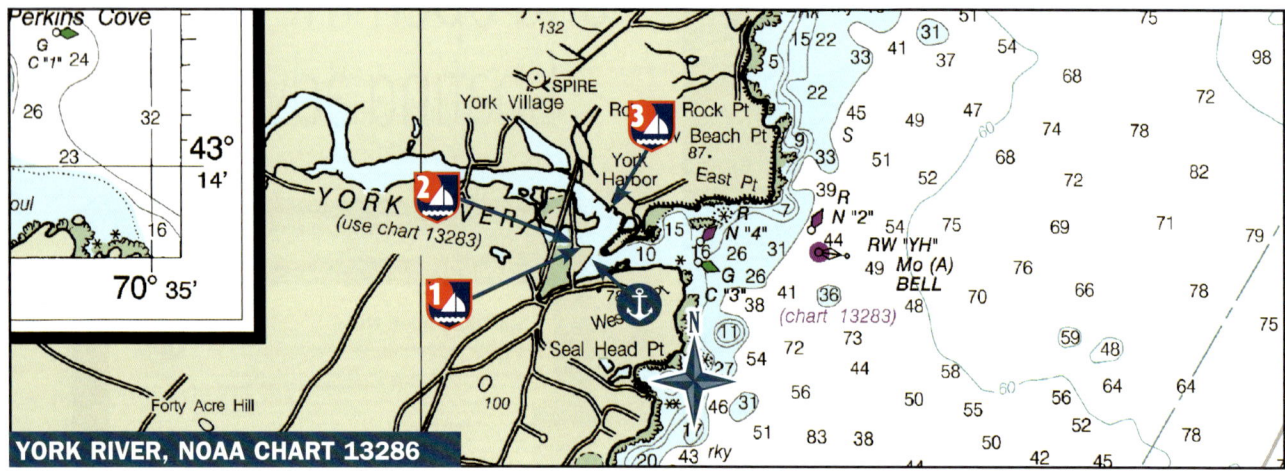

YORK RIVER, NOAA CHART 13286

The harbormaster is willing to pick up transients on moorings in his workboat and a restaurant and general store at the dock are open seasonally. The full-service Kittery Point Yacht Yard, at the entrance of the Back Channel, has transient slips at Kittery Point and at Eliot. They offer major repairs and full services at both locations.

Badger's Island Marina offers two locations, east and west of the Memorial Bridge and can accommodate boats up to 125 feet. Being right on the river, the marina community turns out to handle lines for fellow-boaters navigating the swift current, and the marina management may put you on the T-head temporarily until slack allows easier maneuvering. It's best to call ahead with your ETA.

Anchorage: Pepperell Cove is comfortable unless the wind pipes up from the south. Patience may allow you to find a spot among the lobster buoys west of the mooring field in front of Fort McClary in 7 to 14 feet MLW. The Kittery Point Wharf dinghy docks are usually full, but those at anchor can use them if you limit your stay to a few days. Back Channel, behind

Seavey Island, has a grass-over-granite bottom and the current runs swiftly, making this a poor anchorage.

York Harbor

York is a secure harbor and noted hurricane hole with a busy summer resort community. Museums of Old York is here, which is a Maine Colonial village (207 York St., 207-363-4974). Its best-known attraction is the Old Gaol, built in 1719 and the last English public building in the infant nation. Near the Old Gaol is the Emerson-Wilcox House, used alternately as a general store, Post Office and tavern where Post Road travelers stopped for rest, food and drink. These are within easy walking distance to York Village shops, restaurants and art galleries, plus a convenience store and laundromat. A walking tour through the historic district leads a 17-acre nature preserve.

As a practical matter, be sure to arrive with enough room in your holding tank for the duration as there is no pump-out service in the harbor.

NAVIGATION: Use NOAA Chart 13283. It is about 6 miles north from Kitts Rock outside Portsmouth Harbor to popular, landlocked York Harbor. Currents run strong in the narrow, winding channel, causing surges and boils. It's inadvisable to enter at night or in fog without local knowledge. From the south, lighted red-and-white bell buoy "YH" is farther offshore than any shallow ledges but green can buoy "3" is quite close to depths as low as 5 feet MLW off Argo and Western Points. Splitting the difference can be efficient while staying safe. From the north, the position of red nun buoy "2" incorporates a healthy safety margin for rounding East Point.

Enter at slack or against the ebb for best steerage. If entering on the flood, the turn slightly south after green can buoy "7" is where the current becomes a problem. A heading at or even just south of red nun buoy "8" may not accommodate the sweep toward Stage Neck. Stay south of the straight line between those two buoys until abeam of red nun buoy "8" then take care not to be swept too close to green daybeacon "9." The current eases in the inner harbor. The river is crossed by the fixed **Lilac Lane Bridge** above Bragdon Island, with a 15-foot vertical clearance.

Dockage/Moorings: York Harbor Marine Service is just inside Stage Neck on the protected side of Harris Island with slips, gas, diesel and laundry. The York Harbor-Town of York dock located next to the bridge has no transient space but they do rent moorings. The northern of the two town docks is less than 1 mile from the historical attractions but 2 miles from the nearest supermarket. Dinghy to the landing at the Hancock Warehouse (no longer operating as a museum) to save a half-mile of walking while loaded down with groceries. It is on the north side of the York River just before the **Sewall Bridge** (3-foot vertical clearance). With the expansion of the mooring field above and below Bragdon Island, anchorage is now prohibited in the harbor.

Cape Neddick Harbor

Cape Neddick is best known for the very picturesque Nubble Light (officially the Cape Neddick Light Station), which was built in 1879 and has a beacon that reaches 13 miles offshore. North and slightly west of the cape, small Cape Neddick Harbor offers emergency shelter for small boats.

NAVIGATION: Use NOAA Chart 13283. If approaching from the south, pass the light and continue 0.75 mile to the unnamed cove south of Barn Point or a bit more than 1 mile into Cape Neddick Harbor at the entrance of the Cape Neddick River. Barn Point has shoals leading both north and south with unmarked but charted rocks.

York River

Webhannet River, ME

WELLS HARBOR		Largest Vessel Accomodated	VHF Channel Monitored / Working	Approach / Dockside Depth (reported)	Transient Slips / Total Slips	Floating Docks	Gas / Diesel	Groceries, Ice, Marine Supplies, Snacks	Repairs: Hull, Engine, Propeller	Lift (tonnage), Crane, Rail	Courtesy Car, Laundry, Pool, Showers	Min / Max Amps	Pump-Out Station	Nearby: Grocery Store, Motel, Restaurant
				Dockage					**Supplies**		**Services**			
1. Wells Harbor Town Dock	(207) 646-3236	44	9/16	/	5.0/7.0	F		I						R

☐ Internet Access   WIFI Wireless Internet Access   ⬤ onSpot Dockside WiFi Facility

See WaterwayGuide.com for current rates, fuel prices, website addresses, and other up-to-the-minute information. (Information in the table is provided by the facilities.)

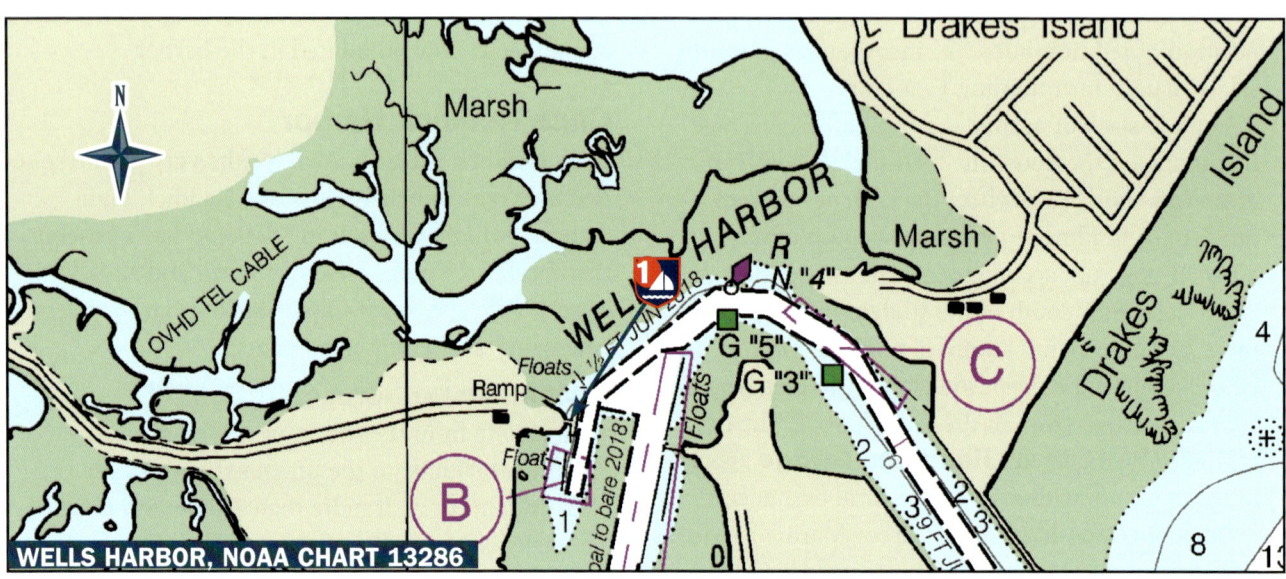

WELLS HARBOR, NOAA CHART 13286

Perkins Cove

Anchorage: In settled weather, deep-water anchorage can be made long enough to enjoy the view in the bight just north of the Cape Neddick Light. In a prevailing southwesterly seek shelter in the unnamed cove between Cape Neddick proper and Barn Point. Just north of Barn Point is Cape Neddick Harbor with depths of 10 to 12 feet MLW well into the cove and fair holding in rock and sand. Watch the chart carefully through the area as there are rocks and shoals but no aids to navigation.

Wells Harbor

Ten miles north of Cape Neddick is Wells Harbor, a less-traveled road for cruisers. The Rachel Carson Wildlife Refuge (321 Port Rd., 207-646-9226) offers nature hikes, photography and bird watching several miles away for those willing to rent a car.

NAVIGATION: Use NOAA Chart 13286. Two jetties marked by lights protect Wells Harbor's entrance. Favor the south jetty on the way in then proceed straight in 8-foot MLW depths around green can buoy "5." The channel shallows to 4 feet MLW from here to the town landing.

Dockage/Moorings: Wells Harbor has limited accommodations for transient boats less than 44 feet with very shoal draft at the town dock, where crew can be picked up and dropped off. Moorings are also available. There is no place to anchor.

Kennebunk River

Kennebunkport has become one of Maine's most popular tourist magnets. Its maritime heritage and extraordinary 19th-century architecture, a veritable treasure trove of Colonial- and Federal-era sea captain's homes, are worth the short journey up the Kennebunk River.

The amazingly ornate and intricate Wedding Cake House (104 Summer St.) was built in 1825 and is one of the most photographed Gothic Revival Style buildings in the U.S. White Columns (8 Main St.) sports its original furnishings and decor. No visit to Kennebunkport is complete without stopping at the Seashore Trolley Museum (195 Log Cabin Rd., 207-967-2712), started in 1939, and currently the largest railroad museum in the world.

Kennebunkport is an excellent place to provision. The Dock Square area just east of the swing bridge and about

Kennebunk River, ME

KENNEBUNKPORT		Largest Vessel Accomodated	VHF Channel Monitored / Working	Approach / Dockside Depth (reported)	Transient Slips / Total Slips	Floating Docks	Gas / Diesel	Groceries, Ice, Marine Supplies, Snacks	Repairs: Hull, Engine Propeller	Lift (tonnage), Crane, Rail	Min / Max Amps	Courtesy Car Laundry, Pool, Showers	Pump-Out Station	Nearby: Grocery Store, Motel, Restaurant
		Dockage						**Supplies**			**Services**			
1. Chicks Marina ⬚ WiFi	(207) 967-2782	165	9/9	30/40	7.0/7.0	F	GD	IMS			30/100	LS		10MR
2. Kennebunkport Marina	(207) 967-3411	80	9/	8/41	6.0/6.0	F		IM	HEP		30/50	S		GMR
3. Yachtsman Lodge & Marina	(207) 967-2511	120	9/	5/64	7.0/7.0	F		IS			30/100	S		MR
4. DiMillo's Kennebunk Marina WiFi	(207) 318-0628	85	9/71	8/28	8.0/8.0	F		G			30/50	S		GMR
5. Performance Marine	(207) 967-7	70	9/7	/20	6.0/6.0	F	GD	GIM	HEP	L10	30/50	LS		GMR

⬚ Internet Access   WiFi Wireless Internet Access   onSpot Dockside WiFi Facility
See WaterwayGuide.com for current rates, fuel prices, website addresses, and other up-to-the-minute information. (Information in the table is provided by the facilities.)

0.5 mile north of the marinas has a general market, gourmet shop, pharmacy, well-stocked bookstore and several interesting galleries.

NAVIGATION: Use NOAA Chart 13286. The entrance to Kennebunk River is well protected by substantial breakwaters and the east one is lighted. The preferred approach is east of flashing green bell buoy "1" and green can buoy "3" then favor the eastern jetty. An approach can also be made from the southwest between black-and-white "F" and green-and-white "O" located approximately in the middle of the fairly extensive rocky ledge charted as Fishing Rock.

The river is best negotiated just after low tide so the mud flats are revealed and wave action over the bar at the mouth is subdued. Entrance during peak ebb can be downright nasty when the river's tidal current meets ocean swells driven by prevailing southwesterlies, all to the tune of powerful craft of all descriptions muscling their way out before being trapped by low water.

At dead low water, particularly when there is a less than average tide, several spots upstream will challenge keels of over 3 feet. The river is well marked but moored boats may obscure buoys. New visitors should stay to mid-channel, especially giving room to red nun buoy "8." If your vessel is large, a security call on VHF Channels 16 and 13 is recommended prior to entering the channel. Navigate river bends carefully to avoid being swept outside the channel. Even though it still stands on its 1896 granite abutments, the **Highway 9 Swing Bridge** (5-foot closed vertical clearance) is structurally deficient and does not open for boat traffic. (Shown on the latest NOAA chart as "under construction.") Be aware of the large security area off

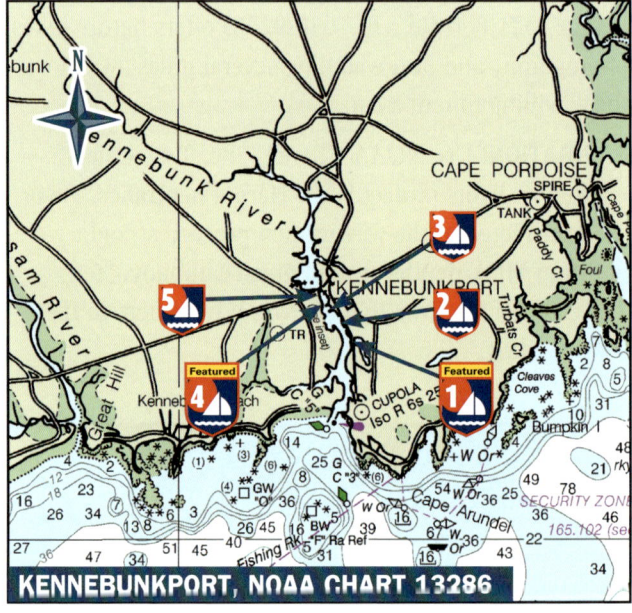

KENNEBUNKPORT, NOAA CHART 13286

Walkers Point, which is closed to navigation.

Dockage: Slips are plentiful in Kennebunkport. Chicks Marina, a full-service facility with a hospitable welcome for visiting yachts, has dockage to 165 feet, sells all fuels and offers concierge service. They also have low-speed electric vehicles available for shopping and dining. The same family has operated the marina for over 25 years.

The gated DiMillo's Kennebunk Marina has slips for vessels to 90 feet with all the usual amenities in a secure, quiet setting. This is the closest transient marina to the sites of Kennebunkport. Performance Marine is the last marina before the bridge and offers repair work and a quiet, comfortable setting with a pastoral scene across the narrow river. Anchoring is not permitted anywhere on the river.

DiMillo's Kennebunk Marina

Chicks Marina

Kennebunk River

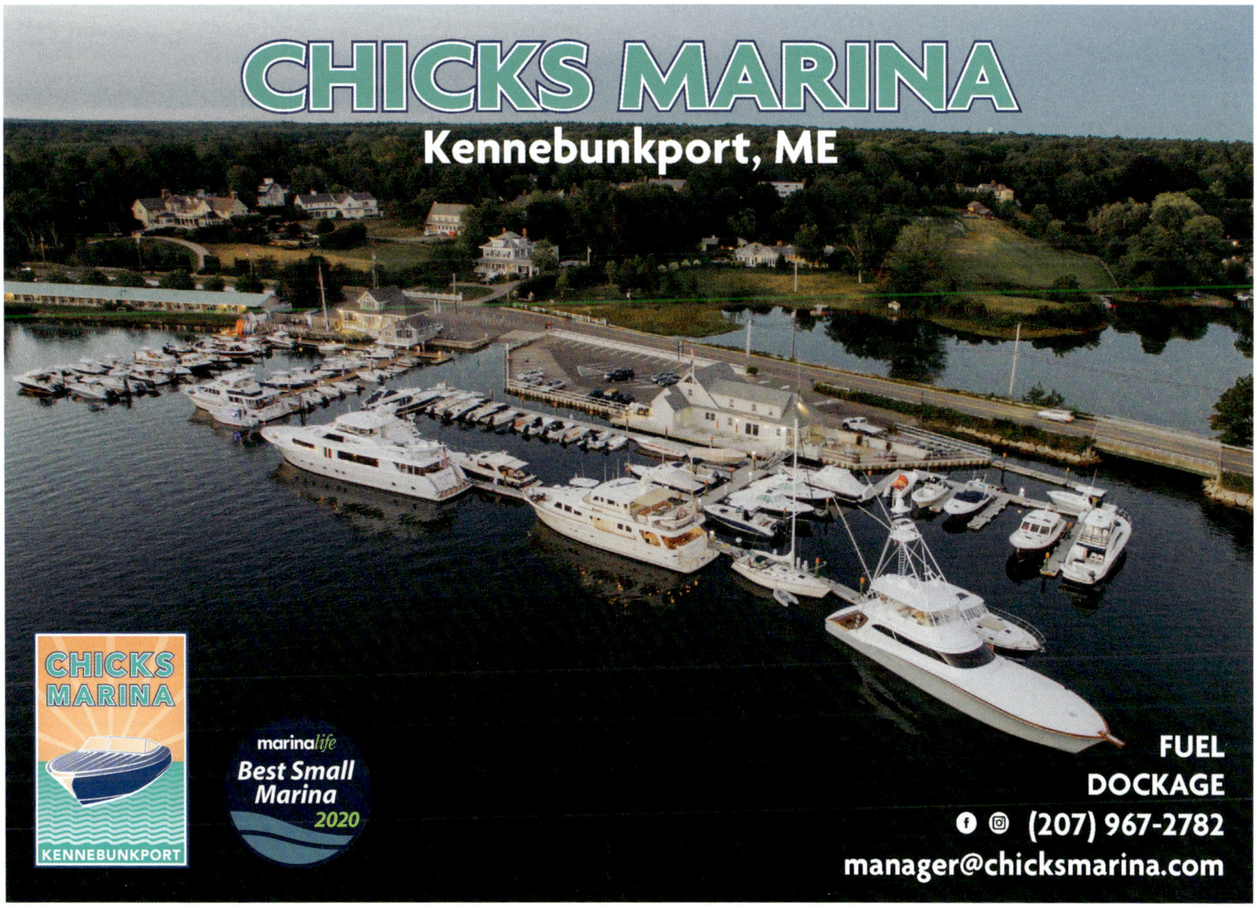

CHICKS MARINA
Kennebunkport, ME

CHICKS MARINA
KENNEBUNKPORT

marinalife
Best Small Marina
2020

FUEL
DOCKAGE
(207) 967-2782
manager@chicksmarina.com

Saco River, ME

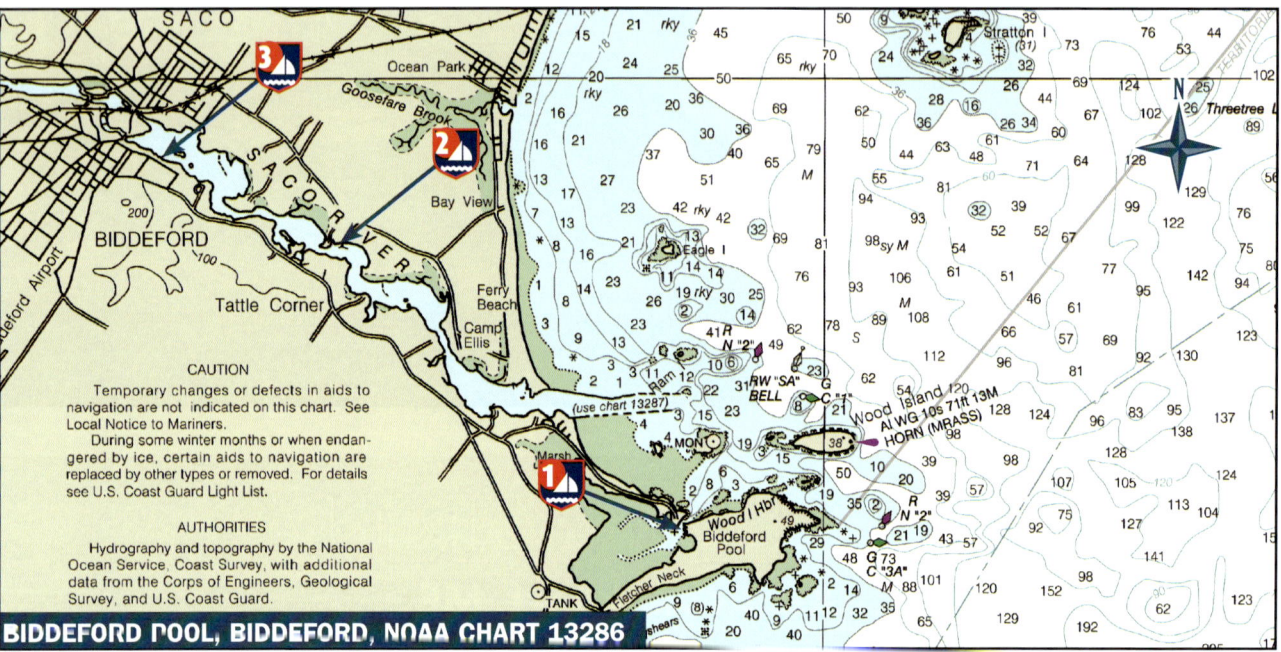

BIDDEFORD POOL		VHF Channel Monitored / Working	Largest Vessel Accomodated	Approach / Dockside Depth (reported)	Transient Slips / Total Slips	Floating Docks	Groceries, Ice, Marine Supplies, Snacks	Gas / Diesel	Repairs: Hull, Engine, Propeller	Lift (tonnage), Crane, Rail	Courtesy Car, Laundry, Pool, Showers	Min / Max Amps	Pump-Out Station	Nearby: Grocery Store, Motel, Restaurant
		Dockage					**Supplies**			**Services**				
1. Biddeford Pool Yacht Club (WiFi)	(207) 282-0485	68/9		/		8.0/		GD	I				S	R
BIDDEFORD														
2. Marston's Marina (WiFi)	(207) 283-3727			/	/120	/	F		G	IS			30	S	P	R
3. Rumery's Boatyard	(207) 282-0408	50		/	/22	6.0/6.0	F			GMS	HEP	L25,C	15/30	S		GR

☐ Internet Access　(WiFi) Wireless Internet Access　(onSpot) Dockside WiFi Facility

See WaterwayGuide.com for current rates, fuel prices, website addresses, and other up-to-the-minute information. (Information in the table is provided by the facilities.)

BIDDEFORD POOL, BIDDEFORD, NOAA CHART 13286

Note: We have received reports that pump-out service is scarce in this area. Hopefully this situation has been remedied as we do not encourage offshore pumping.

Cape Porpoise Harbor

A deep-water commercial lobster boat harbor with an easy, straight entrance, Cape Porpoise is seldom visited by recreational boats, even though it offers the only full protection between Portsmouth and Portland for boats drawing up to 8 feet and makes a reasonable midway stop. Few services are available here and those that are cater to the lobster fleet. If you allow the working folk first crack at fuel and loading at the town dock, tie your dinghy with a long line and observe other working harbor etiquette, you may find it to be a wonderful stop.

NAVIGATION: Use NOAA Chart 13286. Bell and whistle buoys and a horn and light on Goat Island make the harbor easy to find, even in fog. The drying ledges on each side of the entrance channel should not be crossed without local knowledge. If the seas are breaking on the outer ledges, reconsider stopping.

Dockage: A public dock on Bickford Island offers dinghy floats, a phone, a dumpster and a take-out chowder house where you can get ice. Water, gasoline and diesel fuel are available but tie-ups at the dock can be difficult and require fender boards or resignation to grimy pilings. There are no slips or moorings, although the harbormaster at the public dock may know of someone away from theirs.

Anchorage: Anchor in mud with good holding anywhere off the channel in 10-foot MLW depths.

Saco River

Saco River

About 8 nm from Cape Porpoise Harbor is Wood Island Harbor, just north of Biddeford Pool. This is a pretty spot with ample space to walk along rock-bound coastal scenery and to watch the tidal workings of the pool. The twin towns of Biddeford and Saco (which were curiously ignored during southern Maine's coastal revival of the 1980s) lie on either side of the Saco River about 4 miles upstream.

NAVIGATION: Use NOAA Charts 13286 and 13287. If you require more than 5-foot MLW depths, call ahead for local information before attempting passage upriver. The current runs swiftly the entire length of the Saco River and causes significant shoaling. Look for a smooth sea and rising tide before entering the river. The entrance jetties are covered for their first 0.5 mile at high water.

Dockage/Moorings: Call the Biddeford Pool Yacht Club (VHF Channel 68) to see if guest moorings and launch services are available in Wood Island Harbor. They also sell all fuels.

Marston's Marina has moorings and slips and sells gas. If you need repairs, Rumery's Boatyard in Biddeford can likely handle them. The town of Saco has a few moorings on a first-come, first-served basis. The moorings are free; however, the town appreciates donations to help with the cost.

Anchorage: Wood Island Harbor is protected by Wood Island and surrounding ledges in most weather conditions but its grassy bottom makes for poor holding. The anchorage is best approached from the north, leaving both Wood Island and green can buoy "1" (marking the entrance to the Saco River) to the south and passing between the westernmost ledge of Wood Island and the distinctive stone monument on Stage Island. Watching your depths, skirt the large mooring field while looking for anchorage in 8 to 15 feet MLW. The pool itself is almost entirely landlocked and tiny at low water and not an anchorage option.

There is room for several boats to anchor on the north side of the channel northwest of Chandler Pt. in 5 to 8 feet MLW. Note that the current runs swift here.

Richmond Island Area

⚠ A research buoy is anchored in Saco Bay, 400 yards off Scarborough Beach at N 43° 32.913'/W 070° 17.092'. The buoy's structure is white in color with reflective bands and a yellow strobe light mounted to it. The structure is anchored in 43 feet at MLW by three mooring balls with approximately 275 feet of anchor line each. Mariners are advised that this buoy is NOT for navigational use and that vessels transiting this area should do so with caution.

Anchorage A breakwater connecting Cape Elizabeth and Richmond Island creates two anchorages. The western one is Richmond Island Harbor with protection from the northwest through the southeast. Here you will find 11 to 15 feet MLW with good holding in sand.

During summer's prevailing southwesterlies, go around to Seal Cove on the eastern side of the breakwater. Note that there are charted but unmarked rocks in Seal Cove that require you stay close to Richmond Island upon entry. You can drop the hook in 9 to 14 feet MLW with good holding in sand. Neither anchorage is free of surge and the breakwater doesn't provide much protection.

■ NEXT STOP

Beyond Cape Elizabeth is Casco Bay and the larger port of Portland. The scenic Casco Bay Islands lie beyond that, like stepping stones to the inland cruising grounds of the Kennebec River, Damariscotta River and St. John River. Here you will find miles and miles of protected tidal exploration.

Casco Bay & the Mid-Coast of Maine

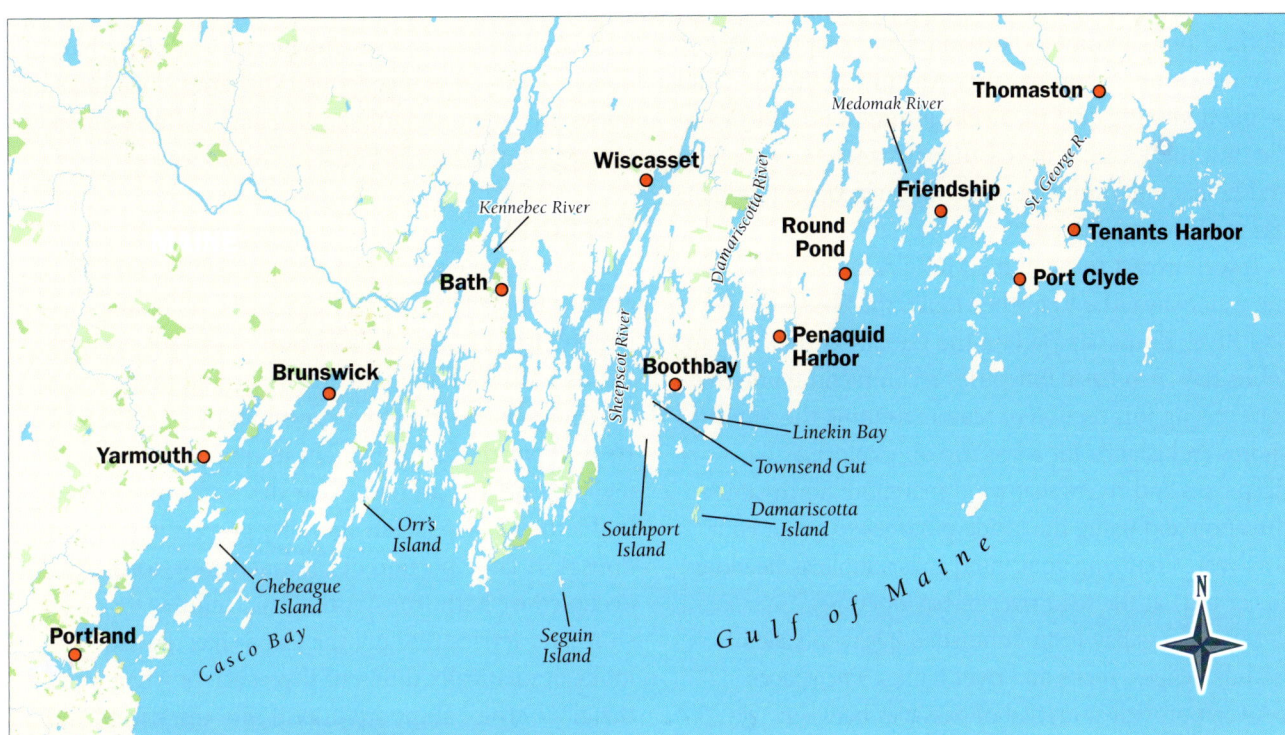

NAVIGATING MID-COAST MAINE

Maine stands in glorious company as a fabled summer cruising ground featuring dramatic tides and currents, underwater rocks, isolated anchorages surrounded by thick green wooded hills and small seaports bustling with industries that respect traditions going back hundreds of years. It's the Puget Sound with less rain; the Hebrides with less wind; Norway with less ice. Those joys, plus helpful southwestern prevailing winds, make Maine an Eastern Seaboard favorite.

The Gulf of Maine measures 250 miles across between Kittery and Eastport, which is the easternmost town in the U.S. By land, it's a 293-mile trip. The space between them, though, is crenellated by 4,568 miles of breath-taking coastline. Added to that, there's another 2,000-plus miles inscribing island after beautiful island, a stunning 4,627 of them. Adventurers heading "Down East" (as it's called due to those aforementioned winds and the northeastern slope of the continent) often choose a zigzag path that allows them to explore the thousands of islands, many navigable rivers, tributaries, inlets, bights and bays.

Of the many wonderful and picturesque lighthouses in Maine, two are worth an extra mention. The highest lighthouse in the country at an elevation of 186 feet is on Seguin Island. And Casco Bay's Great Diamond Island has Pocohontas Light, the smallest lighthouse registered with the U.S. Coast Guard at 6 feet tall.

The cruising ambiance shifts heading north as the sweeping beaches become rare and the shoreline becomes rocky. Areas near mudflats can offer great holding but tide- and sea-scoured rock bottoms can be treacherous, even with modern ground tackle. The 10- to 15-foot tidal range often doubles the low-water safe scope while creating currents that put a dangerous strain on under-scoped ground tackle. While the rule of thumb is 7-to-1 scope, 10-to-1 dramatically increases the chances of a good night's sleep, even in the many deep-water harbors.

No matter where you go in Maine, the name of the game is "Dodge the Lobster Buoy." Those lucky (or well-prepared) people with their prop in an aperture or protected by a cable from keel to skeg may not worry much, but any unprotected prop can easily pick up a line. If you suspect you've run over a buoy line, put your engine in neutral immediately. In areas with greater tide heights, an additional float (called a leader and usually white) is attached on a fairly short line that can trip up everyone but those with prop cages such as the lobster boats are fitted with.

Casco Bay's urban/rural divide allows boaters to get all the city they want in Portland while keeping quiet islands within a short day trip. An entire summer could be filled investigating the necks jutting south into Casco Bay, but the 17 miles of coastline between Cape Small and Pemaquid Point epitomize the rugged scenery that has made Maine famous.

Traveling east through the Mid-Coast, there are five big waterways: the Kennebec River, the Sheepscot Bay and River, Boothbay Harbor, the Damariscotta River and Johns Bay. Two basic itineraries recommend themselves for cruising this section of Maine: running the outer shores and islands for a fast trip, or exploring the deep bays and rivers that wind in a more north/south direction and using the inside passages to make your way east. Changing your mind is as simple as heading in (or out) at the next river or bay opening.

Muscongus Bay is an unfinished jigsaw puzzle of islands, ledges, rocks and river banks. The spaces between provide a myriad of passages between copious safe harbors. Some boaters sail directly to the famed cruising of Penobscot Bay to avoid the careful navigation required but the small towns are pure Maine, focused on going about their business rather than serving cruisers, an atmosphere with its own rewards.

> If you plan to stay awhile, Maine has some strenuous registration and tax laws pertaining to watercraft of all sorts. Go to www.maine.gov/ifw or check with a local marina for details.

■ CASCO BAY & ISLANDS

Casco Bay is the beginning of the famously rocky coast of Maine. Long necks (as peninsulas are known hereabouts) divide the 12-mile width of the bay in generally northeast-to-southwest directions, with cross cuts breaking the 20-mile length into islands. Rock ledges require careful navigation at all times, but the water is deep enough in most of the channels and the ledges are well-enough marked that it's easy to stay out of trouble with some attention. Charted but unmarked hazards are fairly common so take navigation seriously. Shallows around the islands provide a wealth of

unofficial anchorages for the weather-savvy.

Though nicknamed the "Bay of Pigs" in the 1980s for the outrageous number of tangled and mangled lobster traps and their accompanying buoys, Casco Bay has done a good job of managing its fisheries since then and buoys are only ordinarily bothersome in these waters. Heading farther north, you'll see much worse.

Portland

Portland has a long, colorful history and is still an active seaport for oceangoing vessels. As Maine's largest city, it is also a major port of call for cruising yachts with well-appointed marinas and pretty much anything you need before continuing Down East. It's well worth the investment in time to spend a few days poking around. Near the waterfront, you'll find a food co-op, small specialty grocers and coffee houses. A large portion of the waterfront, formerly occupied by Bath Iron Works, has facilities for cruise ships and ferries that ply the Casco Bay. The town looks dramatically different if you arrive when one of the giant cruise ships are in port and the streets and restaurants are full.

NAVIGATION: Use NOAA Chart 13288. Portland is announced well to seaward by the red-and-white "P" light buoy (5 miles east-southeast of Cape Elizabeth) with horn, Morse (A), whistle and RACON (- -), and the ship channel leading into the harbor is clearly marked. Nevertheless, monitor a continuous position as keel-grinding obstructions abound outside the channel, which first slants north and then hooks sharply east. Keep a sharp lookout for commercial traffic in this busy channel.

Portland Harbor can be easily visualized in a clockwise circle that begins in South Portland. A 54-foot, 6-second flashing light with a horn marks the end of the jetty extending from Spring Point in South Portland. Most of Portland's amenities are on the Fore River, where flashing green buoy "5" marks the turn southeast. Docks and moorings make it very easy to stay in deep water as far as the **Casco Bay Bridge** (55-foot closed vertical clearance, opens on signal), but above the bridge it becomes important to stay to the center of the channel or keep an eye on the depth sounder.

Dockage/Moorings: Just around the jetty is the 275-slip Spring Point Marina, which has dockage for vessels up to 200 feet and sells all fuels. Leave the

GOIN' ASHORE

PORTLAND, ME

In a state with the lowest population density east of the Mississippi, Portland is where the people are, and it's a modern city in the midst of battling stakeholders. Managing growth has meant that the town has built fabulous parks and waterfront trails but lost some of the practical boating and fishing businesses on the waterfront in favor of mixed-use storefront, office, and residential development. Portland's maritime heritage and vital lobster fishery have begun to triumph recently, so the town may keep its best features, such as the incredible Harbor Fish Market where boats pull up to the water side and buyers walk in from the wharf side. A side trip down the sketchy-looking alley just before the market provides a behind-the-scenes look at the boats and a bit of stone walkway that is both lovely and mysterious.

Annual events such as the Tall Ship Parade and the Peaks to Portland Swim (sponsored by the local YMCA) keep local non-boaters involved in their thriving waterfront. A narrow-gauge railway offers short trips along the water and into the past. The many fine dining establishments in and around Commercial St. have developed the reputation as being some of Maine's finest culinary offerings.

ATTRACTIONS

Portland Museum of Art (7 Congress Sq., 207-775-6148) is Maine's largest, where works of Homer and Wyeth share space with the Impressionist masters. Portland Symphony Orchestra (20 Myrtle St., 207-842-0800) performs at Merrill Auditorium and plays pops as well as classical. A performance of the Portland Players (420 Cottage Rd., South Portland, 207-799-7337) may be just the ticket. The Portland Observatory (138 Congress St., 207-774-5561) is an impressive building built in 1807 and has spectacular views of Casco Bay from the top.

SHOPPING

A walk along Commercial St. (the waterfront boulevard), through the preserved and restored downtown grid, reveals interesting shops, pubs and restaurants. Getting even one block away from Commercial St. brings you to a warren of small, locally owned options for shopping. The Chart Room at Chase Leavitt & Co. (207-772-6383) is nearby and has an impressive array of major marine appliances, equipment and hardware, and one of the most complete retail offerings of U.S. and Canadian charts anywhere. West on Commercial St., Adams Marine Center (14 Ocean St., 207-772-2781) offers marine products at somewhat less than full list price. Hamilton Marine, the largest marine supply store north of Boston, was pushed off the waterfront by the development craze and is now a good 3 to 4 miles from the downtown marinas.

The Public Market House (28 Monument Square on Congress St., 207-228-2056) is a historic building repurposed to hold a variety of vendors selling cheeses from Maine farms, fresh cut flowers, sandwiches on fresh baked breads and beer from several microbreweries in a historic location. Up and over the hill that divides Portland, West Marine (127 Marginal Way, 207-761-7620) is about 1 mile away. In the same area, Trader Joe's and Whole Foods Market should cover most of your grocery needs, all within a healthy walk. Hannaford's is a bit farther on.

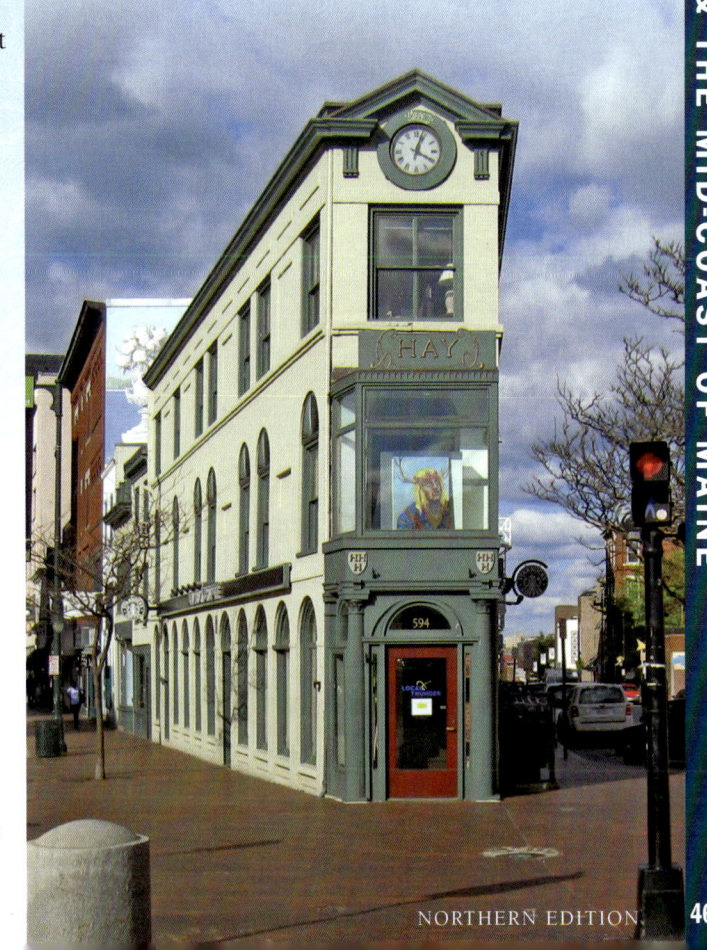

Portland Harbor, ME

PORTLAND AREA		Largest Vessel Accommodated	VHF Channel Monitored / Working	Transient Slips / Total Slips	Approach / Dockside Depth (reported)	Floating Docks	Gas / Diesel	Groceries, Ice, Marine Supplies, Snacks	Repairs: Hull, Engine, Propeller	Lift (tonnage), Crane, Rail	Min / Max Amps	Courtesy Car, Laundry, Pool, Showers	Pump-Out Station	Nearby: Grocery Store, Motel, Restaurant
				Dockage			**Supplies**		**Services**					
1. **Spring Point Marina** WiFi	(207) 767-3213	200	9/	20/275	10.0/8.0	F	GD	IMS	HEP	L50	30/100	CLS	P	GMR
2. Breakwater Marina	(207) 799-2817	45	9/	/125	7.0/7.0	F	GD	GIMS	HEP		30/50	LS	P	GR
3. **Sunset Marina** ⌨ WiFi	(207) 767-4729	250	9/12	20/160	30.0/15.0	F	GD	GIMS	HEP		30/50	LS	P	GMR
4. Centerboard Yacht Club WiFi	(207) 799-7084	36	/68	/	8.0/4.0	F		I				LS		GR
5. **South Port Marine** ⌨ WiFi	(207) 799-8191	160	16/78	30/170	8.0/13.0	F	GD	GIMS	HEP	L35,C	30/200+	LS	P	GMR
6. Thomas Knight Park & Knightville Landing	(207) 767-7650	35	13/	/	8.0/6.0	F							P	GR
7. Portland Yacht Services ⌨ WiFi	(207) 774-1067	175	9/	8/65	35.0/22.0	F	D	IM	HEP	L150	30/100	LS	P	GMR
8. Portland Yacht Services at Commercial St.	(207) 774-1067	120	/	/	27.0/27.0			M	HEP	L150	30/50			R
9. Vessel Services, Inc.	(207) 772-5718	125	16/19	1/1	/15.0		D	IM						G
10. **DiMillo's Marina & Yacht Sales** ⌨ WiFi	(207) 773-7632	250	9/71	/125	40.0/35.0	F	GD	IMS	EP		30/100	LS	P	GMR
11. **Fore Points Marina** ⌨ WiFi	(207) 517-4860	630	10/10	60/150	24.0/24.0	F	GD	IS			30/200+	LS		GMR
12. Maine Yacht Center WiFi onSpot	(207) 842-9000	150	16/9	/80	12.0/16.0	F	GD	IMS	HEP	L80,C	30/100	LS	P	3
FALMOUTH FORESIDE														
13. Handy Boat Service ⌨ WiFi	(207) 781-5110	125	9/	/	20.0/10.0	F	GD	IMS	HEP	L35,C	30/50	LS	P	GMR
14. Portland Yacht Club ⌨ WiFi	(207) 781-9820	64	68/68	/	25.0/8.0	F		I			20	LS		GR

⌨ Internet Access WiFi Wireless Internet Access onSpot Dockside WiFi Facility

See WaterwayGuide.com for current rates, fuel prices, website addresses, and other up-to-the-minute information. (Information in the table is provided by the facilities.)

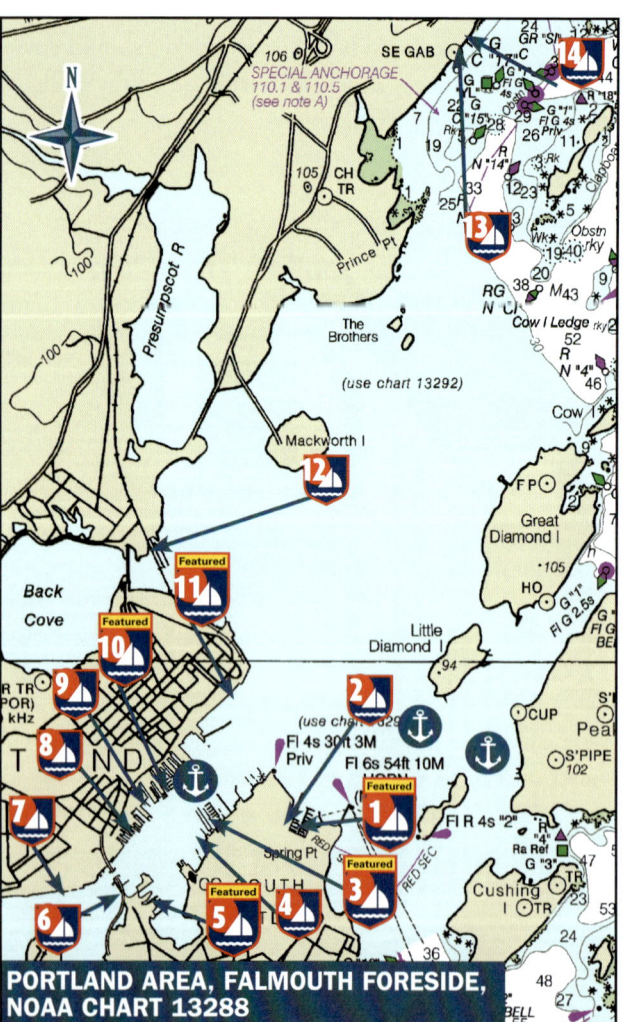

PORTLAND AREA, FALMOUTH FORESIDE, NOAA CHART 13288

SOUTH PORT MARINE

SUNSET MARINA MAINE

DiMILLO'S MAIRNA & YACHT SALES

FORE POINTS MARINA

SPRING POINT MARINA

Photo courtesy of SouthPortland.org

Casco Bay

mooring field to the south and call VHF Channel 09 for docking instructions. The marina has a well-stocked marine store and service department.

Beyond Spring Point, the Fore River divides South Portland from Portland proper. Past the abandoned lighthouse tower (Bug Light), the family-owned and -operated Sunset Marina Maine has 20 slips reserved for transients and can accommodate vessels to 250 feet with full amenities including laundry facilities. They also sell all fuels and offer repairs. Centerboard Yacht Club will accommodate visiting yachts on moorings with 4-foot MLW depths for a facilities fee. Water-taxi service to the Portland side via the club's launch is possible when a lull in ordinary business permits.

Continuing south, South Port Marine has 170 slips and dockage for boats up to 160 feet and with 8-foot

draft. They also sell all fuels and marine supplies and offer repairs, from re-powers to complete refurbishing and including 24-hour emergency hauling.

The Thomas Knight Park & Knightville Landing just past the Casco Bay Bridge is a town dock with complimentary 4-hour dockage (and overnight for a reasonable rate) but this is strictly small and shallow-draft boat territory.

Crossing the river to the Portland side, there are several service facilities and DiMillo's Floating Restaurant (25 Long Wharf, 207-772-2216) makes the marina easy to spot. It's a huge and handsomely re-outfitted ferryboat, which serves well-prepared food at moderate prices. Ferries and water taxis create significant wake in the area. DiMillo's Marina can accommodate yachts to 250 feet in their deep-water

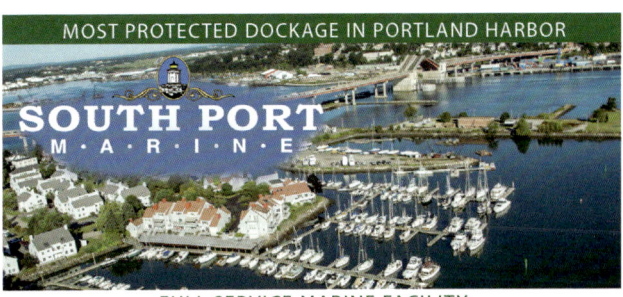

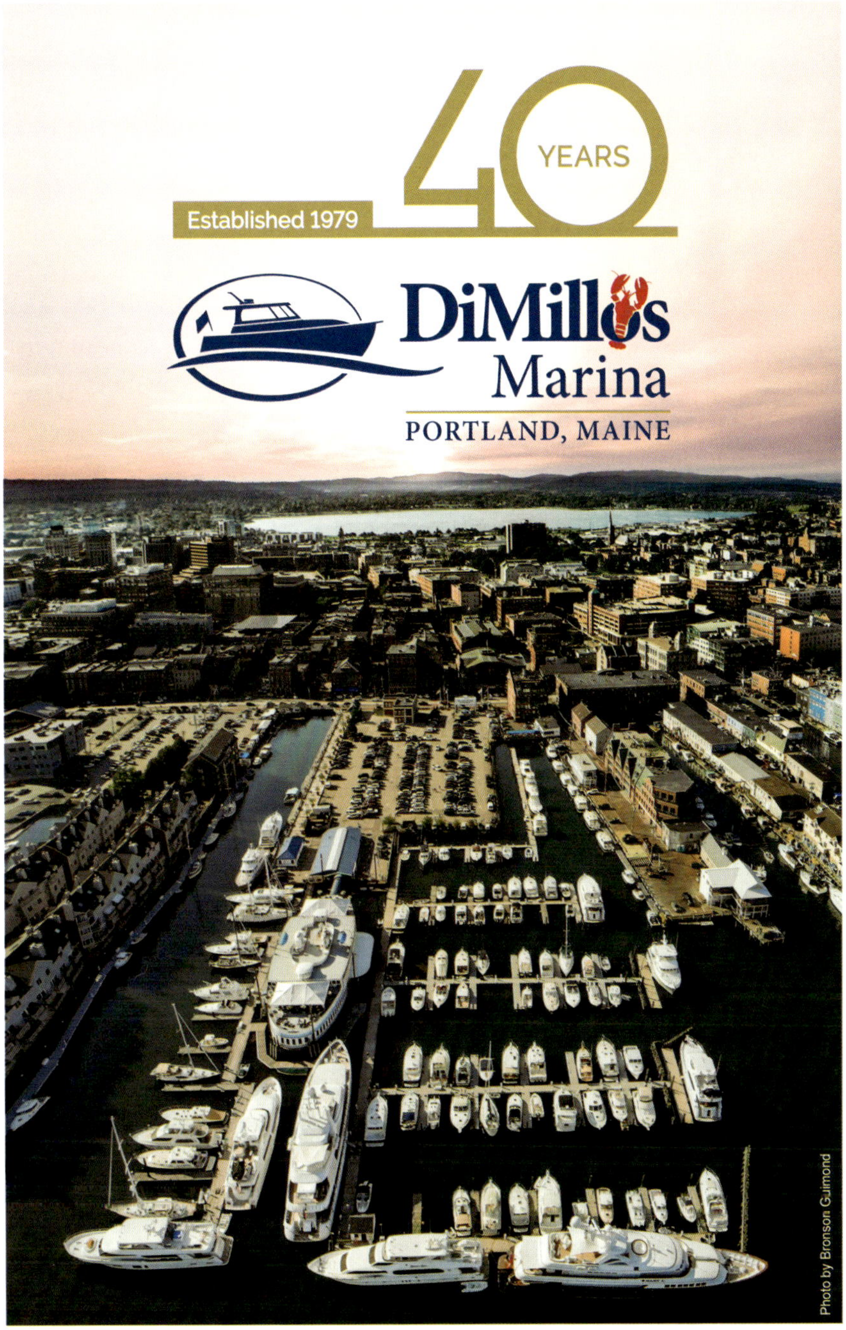

slips with full amenities and on-site service technicians. They also offer a well-stocked Ship Store, provisioning service and a rental car.

Designed for megayachts, Fore Points Marina welcomes boats of all sizes (no restrictions) with full-service amenities and modern utilities. A full-service concierge and professional dock staff, hi-speed in-slip fueling and a marina bar round out the offerings. The scenic and well-protected harbor is convenient to Old Port for shopping and dining.

Anchorage: Because this is a deep-water port with 10 to 12 foot tides and a lot of moorings, anchoring requires quite a bit of rode. The most scenic anchorage is in the mouth of the Presumpscot River, although the currents can be strong. Feel your way in north of red nun buoy "6" for 10 to 15 feet MLW in mud and sand. One formerly popular anchorage off the Eastern Promenade has been buoyed as an entrance channel for a commercial ferry that runs from the park and is no longer available. Several other charted anchorages are full of moorings.

A public boat ramp, just north of a breakwater at Portland, is a good place to leave the dinghy for a jaunt around town but being considerate to others using the launch is key to a good relationship with the park rangers. Fore Points Marina and DiMillo's each offer dinghy dockage for a fee.

Falmouth Foreside

NAVIGATION: Use NOAA Charts 13290 and 13288. About 5 miles north of Portland, the suburb of Falmouth Foreside is the yachting center of Casco Bay, even though Clapboard Island to the east provides the only protection and the south chop can get fierce. Falmouth Foreside is easily accessible from Bigelow Bight via the well-marked channel through Hussey Sound or north from Portland through a wide, unobstructed passage. The thicket of masts between Clapboard Island and the mainland guides the way. A couple of miles from the waterfront a market and hardware store are among the provisioning possibilities. Sailing visitors arriving in mid-August can see, or participate in, the Monhegan Island Race, which has been run annually for most of the 20th century.

Moorings: As you approach the mooring field, Handy Boat Service can guide you to an affordable mooring (with launch service) and take care of your

fuel needs and repair work. On site is a chandlery and nautical clothing store. Next door, Portland Yacht Club, the second oldest yacht club in the U.S., has moorings (with launch service) available on a reciprocal basis to members of recognized clubs and for a facilities fee for others.

Anchorage: Squeezing in on the shore side of the moorings isn't a good idea due to shoaling and seriously packed-in moorings, plus the whole area is exposed from northeast through south. If dedicated to going ashore here, your best bet may be anchoring just past the northernmost moorings. The southern end of the mooring field is better protected and more peaceful but it's a long ride to the marina dock. Another (faraway) option is to anchor off Clapboard Island's western shore in 7 to 11 feet MLW. Dinghy tie-ups are not permitted under the pier at the town landing and folks on moorings for the season have assigned spaces.

Side Trip: Yarmouth

A side trip up the Royal River to Yarmouth is well worth the 2-mile dogleg passage through the tidal flats to visit the fishing village at the head of navigation. In the age of sail, wooden boat-building shipyards lined the river and many of the historic homes belonged to ship captains or owners. The town comes alive for the Yarmouth Clam Festival in mid-July, where all vendors are volunteer organizations raising funds.

Landing Boat Supply (207-846-3777), a well-stocked chandlery in an old sardine cannery, lies between Yarmouth Boat Yard and Yankee Marina and Boatyard. The nearest supermarket and a hardware store are one mile away from the marinas.

NAVIGATION: Use NOAA Charts 13290 and 13288. The channel is typically less than 50 feet wide and shoals fast enough that the buoys are less trustworthy than your depth sounder. It is routinely dredged and carries 7-foot MLW depths. Unlike much of Maine, the Royal River has a forgiving mud bottom. A dinghy ride under the fixed bridge at the head (at Grist Mill Park) reveals an old mill and the falls that powered it.

Dockage: On the southerly side of the river, within walking distance of village amenities, are Yankee Marina and Boatyard and Yarmouth Boat Yard. Both offer transient slips and some repairs. Call ahead. There is no room for anchoring here.

Bailey Island

South Freeport

One of the most accommodating yacht harbors in Maine, South Freeport, on the Harraseeket River, is large, completely protected and relatively easy to enter. For most, going ashore at South Freeport means a courtesy car ride to the outlet shopping and other temptations of Freeport proper, several miles away. *De rigueur* in this harbor is a tour of L.L. Bean's flagship store (95 Main St., 877-755-2326) and a photo with the giant boot. The L.L. Bean Outlet (207-552-7772) is just a few blocks away at Freeport Village Station.

NAVIGATION: Use NOAA Charts 13290 and 13288. Given the number of small islands, rock outcrops and ledges in upper Casco Bay, the best approach for first-timers to the harbor is via Broad Sound, east of Jewell Island. From the west end of Whaleboat Island, follow the series of nun and can buoys leading to the opening of the Harraseeket River. In poor visibility, check your depths to maintain 25 feet of water so as to skirt the east edge of Crab Ledge and Crab Island on approach. The harbor entry is made between Stockbridge Point to the west of the channel and Pound of Tea Island, the islet southwest of Moore Point. Depths drop quickly north of green can buoy "7" so it is best to keep the can relatively close on the west side while rounding Pound of Tea Island into the deep harbor beyond.

Dockage/Moorings: South Freeport Harbor has many full-service marinas and moorings to serve the visiting yachtsman. Strout's Point Wharf Co. is the first marina to the west on entering the mooring field. In addition to moorings, you may find a vacant slip on their floating docks and they sell fuels and offer repairs. Farther along, also to port, Brewer South Freeport Marina offers 15 moorings and 110 slips at its modern docks, gasoline and diesel at the fuel dock and the capability to handle nearly any marine repair need.

Despite the harbor's large size, anchoring is not permitted. On particularly busy weekends, when accommodations are tight, you may want to call the Freeport harbormaster for assistance on VHF Channel 09 or 16 or 207-865-4546.

Casco Bay Islands

The islands of this area were once known as the Calendar Islands, one for every day of the year. Two ferry services provide transportation to the island. The Chebeague Transportation Company makes the 15-minute run from Cousins Island, which is connected by the fixed **Drinkwater Point Bridge** (25-foot vertical clearance) to Yarmouth. Casco Bay Lines provides service on all mail-boat and other "down-bay" trips that travel beyond Long Island.

Casco Bay, ME

		Largest Vessel Accommodated	VHF Channel Monitored / Working	Transient Slips / Total Slips	Approach / Dockside Depth (reported)	Floating Docks	Groceries, Ice, Marine Supplies, Snacks	Gas / Diesel	Repairs: Hull, Engine, Propeller	Lift (tonnage), Crane, Rail	Min / Max Amps	Courtesy Car, Laundry, Pool, Showers	Pump-Out Station	Nearby: Grocery Store, Motel, Restaurant
ROYAL RIVER				**Dockage**			**Supplies**				**Services**			
1. Yankee Marina and Boatyard ▭ WiFi	(207) 846-4326	65	/9	2/100	8.0/8.0	F	GIMS		HEP	L60,R	30/50	LS	P	GR
2. Yarmouth Boat Yard WiFi	(207) 846-9050	46	73/	2/125	6.0/6.0	F	IM		HEP	L	30/50	S		GMR
3. Royal River Boat WiFi	(207) 846-9577		9/	/75	7.0/7.0	F	IM	GD	HEP	L75	30	CLS	P	GMR
HARRASEEKET RIVER														
4. Harraseeket Yacht Club-PRIVATE	(207) 865-4949	30	/	/	20.0/10.0							S		
5. Strouts Point Wharf Co. ▭ WiFi	(207) 865-3899	120	16/9	2/120	20.0/18.0	F	IMS	GD	HEP	L25,C	30/200+	S	P	GM
6. Brewer South Freeport Marine ▭ WiFi	(207) 865-3181	150	9/10	8/110	16.0/14.0	F	IMS	GD	HEP	L35	30/50	LS	P	GMR
GREAT CHEBEAGUE														
7. Chebeague Island Boat Yard	(207) 846-4146	40	/	/	19.0/4.0		IMS	GD	HEP	L30	30	S	P	GMR

▭ Internet Access WiFi Wireless Internet Access onSpot Dockside WiFi Facility

See WaterwayGuide.com for current rates, fuel prices, website addresses, and other up-to-the-minute information. (Information in the table is provided by the facilities.)

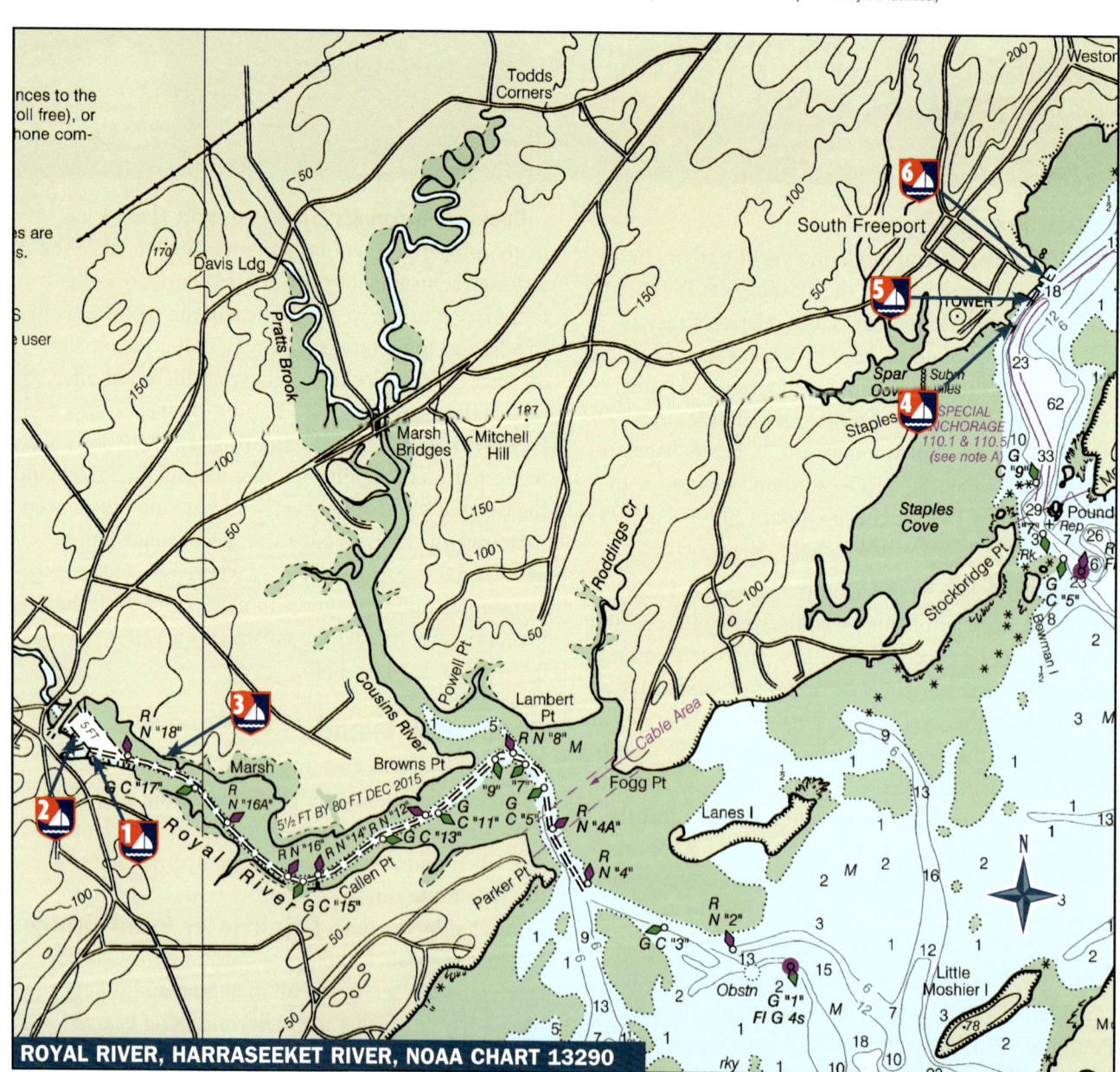

ROYAL RIVER, HARRASEEKET RIVER, NOAA CHART 13290

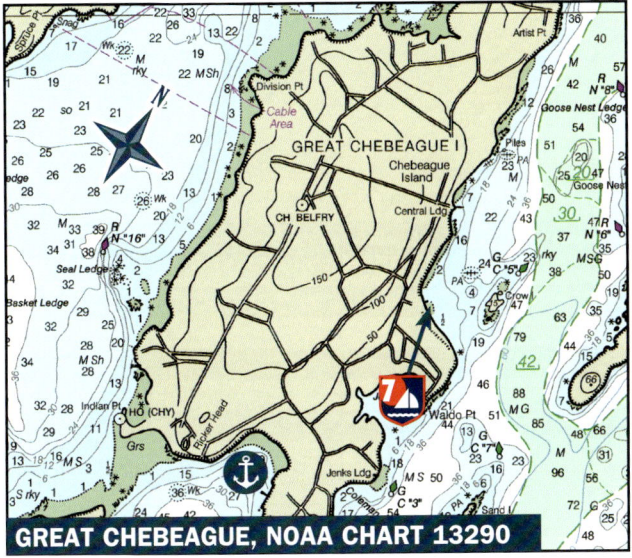

GREAT CHEBEAGUE, NOAA CHART 13290

Great Chebeague Island

Ten miles northeast of Portland is Great Chebeague Island, the biggest of the Calendar Islands, which has a population of less than 350. Ashore are a market, phones and a take-out restaurant where you can buy ice.

NAVIGATION: Use NOAA Chart 13288. If transiting the northwest side of Great Chebeague Island, keep well over toward Littlejohn Island leaving flashing red buoy "18" to the southeast before turning toward Great Chebeague. You can use the big, yellow Chebeague Island Inn building as a range. Simply head right for it. On the southeast side of the island, the depths are good, but the slots between Great Chebeague and Hope and Rogues Islands are carpeted with lobster buoys.

Moorings: Chebeague Island Boat Yard, on the southeast shore, offers moorings and fuel. If heading here from the south, rounding Crow Island's green can buoy "5" is a safer bet than following the locals in between Crow and Chebeague.

Anchorage: The best anchorage is in Chandler Cove on the south side of the island off the stone pier in about 10 feet MLW. Keep outside the moorings because it gets shallow as you get close to the pier. Holding is good in mud. You can dinghy to the ferry float and tie up there to go into town. Getting there means transiting the narrow hooked channel created by Long Island's north point poking up between Little and Great Chebeague. If there's even a hint of fog outside, this channel will be thick with it.

Jewell Island

Deserted except by boaters and maintained by Maine State Parks, Jewell Island is a prime example of what mariners hope to find in Maine. Jewel Island was a World War II outpost for submarine spotting. The tower is open for climbing and offers a breathtaking view of the Gulf of Maine. Local tales put both Captain Kidd and bootleggers ashore with their different treasures.

NAVIGATION: Use NOAA Charts 13288 and 13290. Approaching from the west, use red bell buoy "6" off of the southwestern tip of Cliff Island as a target. Follow the western contour of Jewell Island and avoid the ledges to the south of the charted old wharf. Continue until north of red nun buoy "4" as you leave it south so that you can look straight into the protected harbor between Jewell Island and Little Jewell Island before starting in.

Approaching from the east, head south of red nun buoy "2" off Drunkers Ledges then west toward West Brown Cow. Leave red-and-white bell buoy "BS" well to the north and keep Cliff Island dead ahead until you are abeam the northern tip of Jewell Island.

Anchorage: A secure anchorage on the western side of Jewel Island, affectionately known as Cocktail Cove, provides a lovely spot to stay aboard and a safe spot to leave the boat while going ashore. If you plan to stay overnight, get in by early afternoon because the harbor is always popular, especially on weekends. This encourages short scope, so be friendly and ask nearby boaters how much chain/rode they have out. Favor Jewell Island's western shore slightly, with an eye to needed swinging room with the turn of the tide. Little Jewell Island is ideal, though boats with substantial keels anchor as far down as the pilings near the head of the harbor in 10- to 17-foot MLW depths. Beach the dinghy on gravel or mud to get ashore.

If Cocktail Cove is full or you'd rather have more space, you can also drop the hook in Luckse Sound on Cliff Island in 8 to 16 feet MLW with good holding. This is exposed to the southwest but protected from the ocean swell. Of the two scallops on the southeastern side, the eastern one is within an easy row of Cocktail Cove and clear of mooring balls.

Middle Bay, ME

	Phone	Largest Vessel Accommodated	VHF Channel Monitored/Working	Transient Slips/Total Slips	Approach/Dockside Depth (reported)	Floating Docks	Gas/Diesel	Groceries, Ice, Marine Supplies, Snacks	Repairs: Hull, Engine, Propeller	Lift (tonnage), Crane, Rail	Min/Max Amps	Courtesy Car, Laundry, Pool, Showers	Pump-Out Station	Nearby: Grocery Store, Motel, Restaurant
				Dockage			**Supplies**		**Services**					
MEREPOINT BAY														
1. Paul's Marina	(207) 729-3067	40	9/	/	6.0/6.0		GD	GIMS	EP	C	30		P	G
POTTS HARBOR														
2. Dolphin Marina & Restaurant 🖥 wifi	(207) 833-5343	200	9/9	20/40	40.0/12.0	F	GD	GIMS	HEP	L20,C	30/50	CLS	P	GMR
ORRS ISLAND														
3. Orr's Bailey Yacht Club	(207) 833-7312	47	/	/	9.0/9.0	F	G							GMR
SEBASCODEGAN ISLAND AREA														
4. Safe Harbor Great Island wifi	(207) 729-1639	70	9/10	6/65	12.0/10.0	F	GD	IMS	HEP	C,R	30/50	LS	P	10
5. New Meadows Marina wifi	(207) 443-6277	40	/	6/60	7.0/6.0	F	G	GM	HEP	C	30	S		GM
6. Sebasco Harbor Resort	(800) 225-3819	90	9/	35/35	20.0/6.0	F	G	IS				LPS	P	GMR

🖥 Internet Access wifi Wireless Internet Access onSpot Dockside WiFi Facility

See WaterwayGuide.com for current rates, fuel prices, website addresses, and other up-to-the-minute information. (Information in the table is provided by the facilities.)

Eagle Island

Admiral Robert Peary, who led the sometimes-disputed first expedition to the North Pole, retired on Eagle Island with his wife and two children. Eventually, the 17-acre island was gifted to the State of Maine and their house is now a National Historic Landmark. In a wonderful private/public partnership, the State maintains the house and grounds with help from and improvements funded by the Friends of Peary's Eagle Island. A video at the Welcome Center and audio wands for self-guided tours help visitors get to know this amazing family. The player piano that accompanied Peary's sea-voyage to Greenland is in the parlor and the knowledgeable and welcoming docents are happy to allow visitors to work the pedals after donning protective booties.

Moorings: Complimentary moorings maintained by Maine State Parks are first-come, first served. The 2-hour limit is flexible if they are not full and the island is a nice spot for a picnic lunch.

Potts Harbor

Located in a bight at the south end of Harpswell Neck, Potts Harbor has long been favored by cruising skippers, but its history goes back farther. In the 1830s, at the dawn of the lobster craze, smacks (wooden sailboats with holes drilled through the hull to circulate seawater through built-in tanks) made regular trips from the fishing hamlets at the end of Harpswell all the way to New York City with live lobsters.

NAVIGATION: Use NOAA Charts 13288 and 13290. The preferred approach to Potts Harbor is from the southwest through Broad Sound, taking the north side of red nun buoy "4" to negotiate the channel between Upper Flag Island and Horse Island. In good light the crooked, though well-marked channel leading in from Merriconeag Sound is also usable and, for some sailors, an enjoyable challenge with its sharp turn between Haskell Island and Potts Point. From whichever direction you enter, keep an eye on the seaweedy uncovering edges of Thrumcap Island and proceed north past green can buoy "13" before turning to pass the tiny island.

Dockage/Moorings: Dolphin Marina & Restaurant offers transient slips and ample moorings. There is an on-site restaurant and excellent provisioning is possible in Brunswick but the distance is greater (about 20 minutes by car) than may appear on your chart.

Anchorage: Potts Harbor is well protected by surrounding islets and ledges yet offers matchless long-distance views of Casco Bay's archipelago scattered to the southwest. The designated anchorage basin is full of moorings but there is room to anchor just south in 16 to 22 feet MLW in good holding. Ash Point Cove is farther from the marina but has less traffic and also offers 16 to 22 feet MLW in mud. There is usually ample dinghy room inside the marina's inner float (paralleling the shore), although it's a shock to see all the rocks and ledges out of the water at low tide if you arrived at high tide.

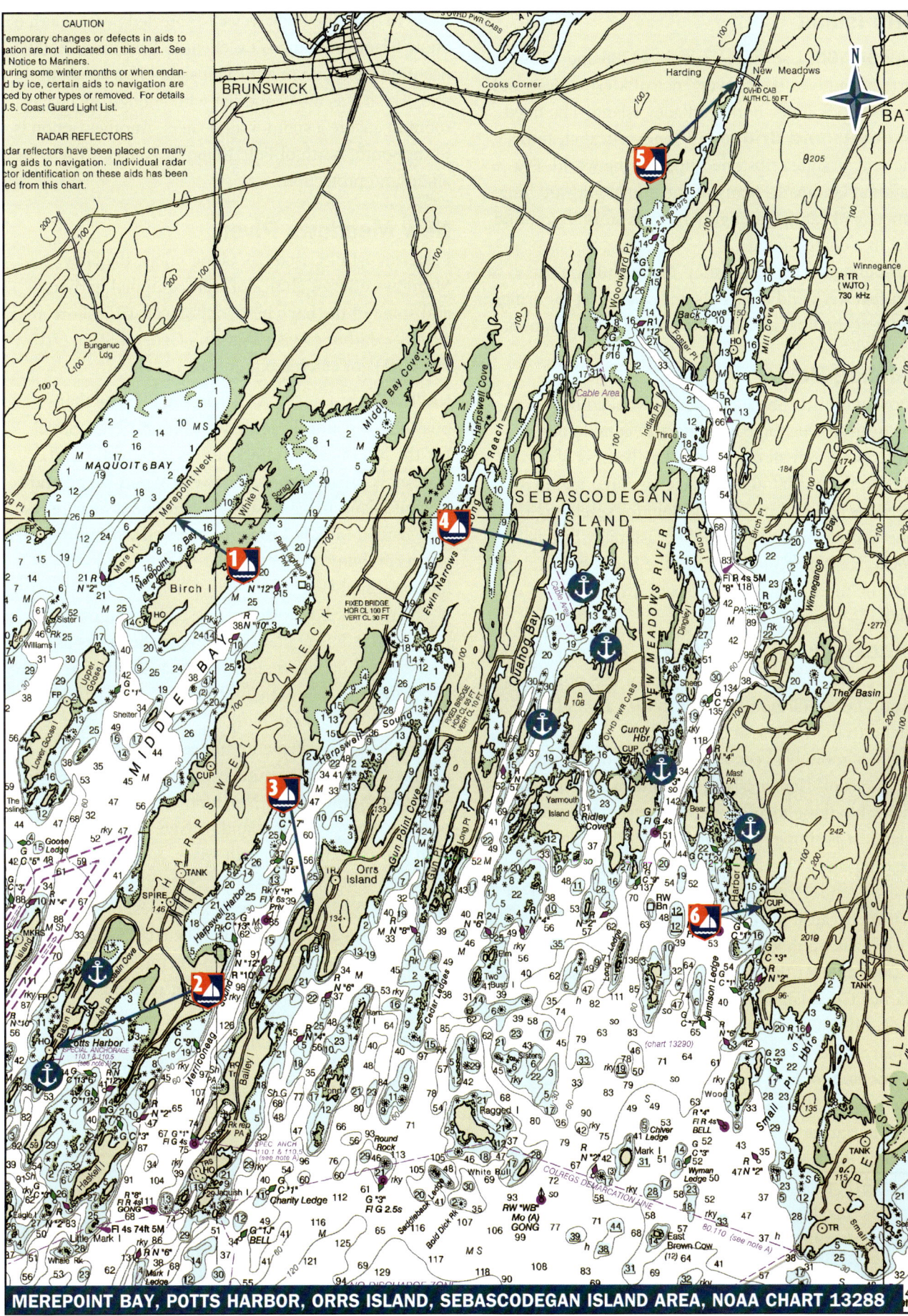

MEREPOINT BAY, POTTS HARBOR, ORRS ISLAND, SEBASCODEGAN ISLAND AREA, NOAA CHART 13288

Orrs Island

NAVIGATION: Use NOAA Charts 13288 and 13290. Orrs Island is at the convergence of Merriconeag and Harpswell Sounds, north of Bailey Island. The fixed **Bailey Island Bridge** (13-foot vertical clearance), the only granite cribstone bridge in the world, is a national landmark. Many of the inhabitants are long-timers and can tell a mighty fine sea story if you find one in a chatty mood.

Moorings: The Orr's Bailey Yacht Club, on the southwestern end of Orrs Island, has guest moorings, water at the float and a dumpster for trash disposal.

Quahog Bay

Snow and Little Snow Island add wooded beauty to the head of Quahog Bay, while also completing the protection from all directions. The flatness of the bottom is unusual in this glacier-scoured region and provides copious amount of room for spreading out. This ordinarily peaceful spot occasionally brings noisier visitors on jet skis, but the bay is big enough that the more courteous ones stay away. Snow Island is private.

NAVIGATION: Use NOAA Chart 13288. Keep an eye on the many ledges running more or less north and south. Leave Yarmouth Island to the east and Pole Island to the west with Center Island ahead on entry. There is room between Pole Island's North Ledge and the rocks off Center Island to allow passage between them if looking to anchor south or southeast of Snow Island. It is simpler to leave Center Island to the east if heading up to Orrs Cove or looking to anchor north of Snow Island. Orrs Cove is easy to navigate as far as the marina because the central channel is bordered thickly with boats on moorings.

Dockage: At the upper reaches of Quahog Bay, Safe Harbor Great Island is a tidy, full-service marina and boatyard in Orrs Cove. They sell fuel and offer some repairs in addition to transient slips.

Anchorage: If in need of boat supplies, anchor at the entrance to Mill Cove in 9 to 14 feet MLW and dinghy to Safe Harbor Great Island. Between Snow and Ben Islands to the south and Mill and Brickyard Cove to the north, a 14-foot MLW area spreads in welcome for groups traveling together or simply for the pleasure of being far from neighbors.

For peace and quiet, turn to the east before Center Island and you will still be in 14-foot MLW depths and ready to drop the hook in well-protected peace south of Snow Island. Holding is excellent in hard mud. In this beautiful spot, you might catch sight of an acrobatic seal. The bay is broad and flat with enough anchoring room to ensure a spot for all boaters. Another option is to the south, north of Pole Island in 16 feet MLW with all-around protection.

New Meadows River

Easternmost of Casco Bay's long inlets, the New Meadows offers a choice of well-equipped harbors and some of the bay's best anchorages. Go ashore at Cundys Harbor to visit Watson's General Store (207-725-7794) or catch a bite to eat.

NAVIGATION: Use NOAA Chart 13288. The first possible stop after heading west around Cape Small (or the last one if heading east) is the Small Point Harbor. A broad entrance between Wood Island and Hermit Island make entering a breeze but beware the well-named Middle Ledge. It's marked with unlighted green can buoy "3" so take care if traversing the harbor at night.

The next harbor north is Sebasco Harbor, east of Harbor Island. Stay midway between the buoys to avoid rocky ledges on either side. Note that flashing red buoy "8" marks the New Meadows River. It can be used to line up with green can buoy "1" to the east but it will be left to the north when entering Sebasco Harbor. The Dry Ledges will be to the south.

Dockage/Moorings: North on New Meadows River, beyond Sebascodegan Island, is New Meadows Marina with gas and some transient space. At the south end of the river at Cape Small, the Sebasco Harbor Resort offers dockage and full resort amenities, including on-site suites and restaurants. The CUP symbol on current charts is the cupola on the top of the resort hotel. Hail on VHF Channel 09 for docking assistance or mooring assignment.

Anchorage: Open to the south but protected from northwest to east winds, Small Point Harbor does good duty as an anchorage in sand in 12 to 15 feet MLW. Across the New Meadows River is the quintessential Maine fishing village of Cundys Harbor (Cundy Harbor on the chart) with anchoring in 20 feet MLW.

An idyllic hurricane hole called The Basin is a favored anchorage of many Casco Bay cruisers and will be crowded when severe weather is forecast. To get inside head northward up the New Meadows River about 2 miles beyond Sebasco Harbor. Watch for the house on

Sequin Island

the northern shore and head for it once it is in view. Stay in mid-channel until you are inside the basin. As you round the southern tip of the peninsula, you may encounter 7-foot MLW depths.

You can also anchor at Sebasco Harbor by the resort in 5 to 25 feet MLW with good holding in mud. This is somewhat exposed to the southwest.

Seguin Island

Sequin Island Light shines steadily, day and night, 180 feet above the water, the highest focal point of all the operational lighthouses in Maine. This unmistakable light beams from a 53-foot tower set atop a 145-foot hill. Yachts heading east and westbound craft returning from Down East are usually glad to see the turtle shape of Seguin Island on the horizon. The island defines the two approaches to the Kennebec River and the strong tidal currents plus an opposing wind can help a thoughtful skipper decide which direction to take or whether to wait out the chop by visiting Seguin Island.

George Washington commissioned the Sequin Island Light in 1795. It was originally built with a wooden tower but the constant battering required a granite brick tower to be built in 1857. This provided an opportunity to install a First Order Fresnel lens, the largest and brightest class of lens. The lighthouse was automated in 1985 and, even though the Coast Guard still maintains the condition of the light and foghorn, the property was transferred outright to the non-profit group, Friends of Seguin Light.

The maintenance and major construction work on the island is mostly done by volunteers with Friends of Seguin Light and during the summer months the lighthouse is tended by a volunteer Keeper Couple. The Lighthouse Keepers maintain the residence and the immediate lighthouse grounds, tell stories, give tours and give the place that warm lived-in feeling.

NAVIGATION: Use NOAA Chart 13293. Heading east, a south approach to Seguin Island is safest for cruisers, since the only ledge in that direction has depths of 20 feet MLW, while its north side presents hazards. Ellingwood Rock creates a local magnetic disturbance of up to 8° for a 1-mile radius. If fixing your position with GPS, this is not as much of an issue but be aware and pay close attention to possible differences between GPS readings and a magnetic compass. The light's horn will help your dead reckoning, especially in fog. Once east and barely north of the island point your bow at the northern tip until the house at the head of the bight is clearly in view. Turn south and favor the western shore as you enter.

Moorings: One large metal Coast Guard mooring might be available but it will beat your boat in any surge. Six small mooring floats are available of all shapes and sizes compliments of the Friends of Seguin Island. No one monitors use and they are first-come, first-served. Be prepared to turn and head back out if all the moorings are taken. Midday is the best time to attempt to pick one up, after boaters have taken a morning walk on the island and before the rest of

Kennebec River, ME

BATH		Dockage					Supplies		Services				
		VHF Channel Monitored / Working	Largest Vessel Accommodated	Transient Slips / Total Slips	Approach / Dockside Depth (reported)	Floating Docks	Groceries, Ice, Marine Supplies, Snacks	Gas / Diesel	Repairs: Hull, Engine, Propeller / Lift (tonnage) Crane, Rail	Courtesy Car, Laundry, Pool, Showers	Min / Max Amps	Pump-Out Station	Nearby: Grocery Store, Motel, Restaurant
1. Maine Maritime Museum 🖥 WiFi	(207) 443-1316	300	/	/	25.0/14.0	F					S		GMR
2. Kennebec Tavern & Marina 🖥 WiFi	(207) 442-9636	32	/	12/65	40.0/40.0	F	G	GIS		30			GMR

🖥 Internet Access   WiFi Wireless Internet Access   ⊙onSpot Dockside WiFi Facility

See WaterwayGuide.com for current rates, fuel prices, website addresses, and other up-to-the-minute information. (Information in the table is provided by the facilities.)

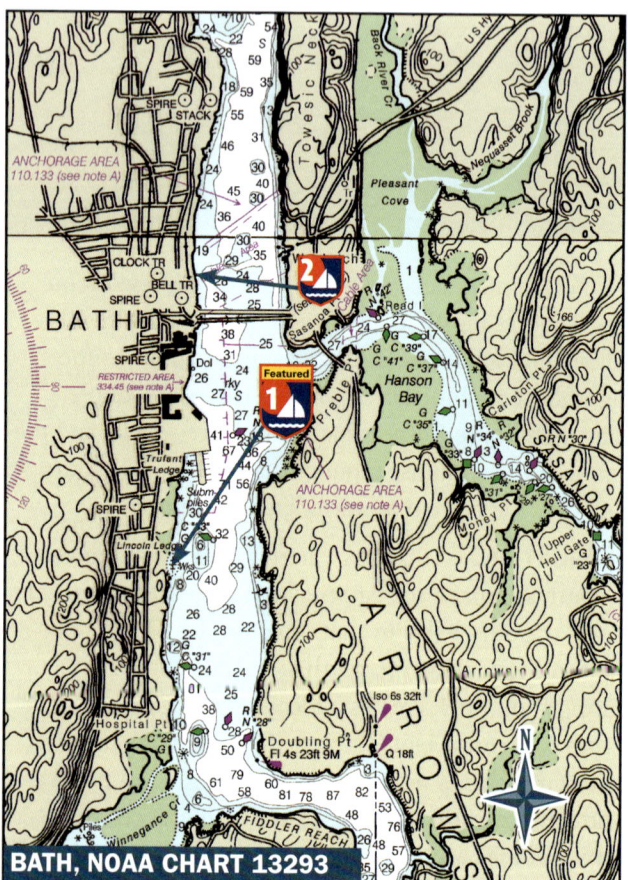

BATH, NOAA CHART 13293

the travelers arrive. Anchoring is prohibited due to the power cable for the island, which runs right up the sand and pebble beach where you can leave your dinghy while walking the island's trails or climbing the lighthouse tower. This spot is a dangerous one if the winds kick up from the east.

■ KENNEBEC & SHEEPSCOT RIVERS

The very first attempt at planting an English colony in New England took place at Fort Popham in 1607, only a few months after Jamestown, VA, was settled. Though loss of life wasn't nearly as devastating as that experienced down south, leadership problems plagued the settlement, which was originally named Sagadahoc. The first leader died in the middle of a power struggle and the next one inherited a title and estate in Devon, providing him with strong reasons to give up on the infant settlement. The most successful project undertaken by the erstwhile colonists was the demonstration that the trees in the New World could be used for shipbuilding. They construction the pinnace *Virginia* and promptly sailed her back to England, abandoning the settlement. Deserted Fort Popham on Hunnewell Point at Atkins Bay is a semi-circular granite fort built in 1861 and used during the Civil War, the Spanish-American War and World War I. Popham Beach State Park provides an excellent recreational swimming area for an energetic crew.

From Popham, yachts often follow a fair tide past the hills on the Phippsburg side to the west and the salt marshes to the east. If you have a line with lure or bait on board, you might find it worthwhile to try for a bluefish. These lonely marshes and grassy meadows supplied salt hay used by early settlers. The expanse of waving meadow grass gives the impression that little has changed ecologically for several centuries. As the Kennebec River twists north, groups of houses introduce signs of civilization. North of Lee Island the river narrows but beyond the dogleg at Winnegance Creek, the channel widens again as you approach Bath. Depending on wind and tide, you may see boats anchored in the creek.

The upper Kennebec River is more placid than at its mouth and provides ample opportunity for explorations; however, currents run swiftly its entire length. It is navigable for 40 miles to Maine's capital, Augusta. Bath, one of the country's leading shipbuilding centers, is 10 miles up the river. If entering the Kennebec heading north to Bath, enter on the slack before the flood and ride the current up.

Bath is an energetic "big town, small city" kind of place. The famous Bath Iron Works builds commercial ships and state-of-the-art naval vessels. Back in 1938, Bath Iron Works turned out the America's Cup defender *Ranger,* still considered the fastest sloop ever built.

Wooden shipbuilding lives on, as well, at the Maine Maritime Museum (243 Washington St., 207-443-1316). The museum offers an active wooden boat-building shop, vintage boat collection, seven major exhibits, as well as tours of the Bath Iron Works and lighthouse river cruises in season with reservations. A replica of the pinnace *Virginia of Sagadahoc* (which was the first ship built in what became the U.S.) is being built by the organization Maine's First Ship (Bath Freight Shed, 2 Commercial St.). This huge undertaking is a volunteer effort and visitors can take part in the work.

Waterfront Park (Commercial St.) is the focal point for visiting boaters and a complimentary transient dock is the park's centerpiece. Leave the inside of the northern section free for the harbormaster's patrol vessel. A public launch ramp is at the northern end of the town near Waterfront Park.

NAVIGATION: Use NOAA Charts 13288, 13293 and 13295. The mouth of the Kennebec River is 1 long mile north of Seguin Island and invites you to explore the lower reaches of this historically famous and splendid waterway. A strong southwesterly wind against an ebbing tide might produce confused sea conditions as you approach the mouth of the river but with sufficient power, careful navigation will soon bring the well-found yacht into calmer water off Fort Popham. As usual, the best time to enter the river is at slack water or on a rising tide.

Be aware that green can buoy "17," just north of Squirrel Point Light and south of Goat Island, was reported to be sinking in June 2019. This is a bad one to miss, being just after a turn in the river for those heading north.

Pass east of Pond Island and west of Jack Rock. Although there is good depth east of Jack Rock and it is marked with green daybeacon "5A," the tidal rips make the main channel (using green can buoy "5" and red nun buoy "6") the safer bet. A long shoal south of Perkins Island pushes the deep water channel far to the west at red nun buoy "12" though locals rarely bother to round that red. Just west of Perkins Island's lighthouse green can buoy "13" marks a sudden 5-foot MLW spot. Goat Island and the Pettis Rocks (off Lee Island) should be passed on the east. North of those, the mid-river islands, rocks and ledges disappear and navigation is straightforward as far as Bath.

Note that the **Carleton Bridge** crossing the Kennebec River between Bath and Woolwich (10-foot closed vertical clearance) opens on signal during the day, but you must call the phone number posted on the bridge 2 hours prior to a requested opening falling between 5:00 p.m. and 8:00 a.m. from May 15 through September 30 and 24-hour notice is required outside that season. Usually, however, the span is often left in the raised position making it possible to pass without signaling for an opening. Downtown Bath is north beyond the adjacent fixed **Carlton (U.S. 1) Bridge** (70-foot vertical clearance).

Dockage/Moorings: Dockage is usually available at the Maine Maritime Museum to the south of the bridges. From late-May to mid-October, the Museum offers 10 moorings and floating dock space for vessels to 300 feet. To ensure availability of suitable accommodations for your vessel, advanced reservations are highly recommended. The City of Bath (207-443-5563) provides free dockage for a limited stay on the long concrete dock running parallel to the city park. Tie up where available and call to check in.

Anchorage: Tuck into Atkins Bay to the north in 7 to 10 feet MLW with good holding in mud. This is somewhat exposed from the northeast and southwest. Two miles south of Bath and on the west side of the river, Winnegance Creek offers good holding in mud at 8 to 16 feet MLW and, being situated in a bend in the river, the north and slight east exposure is less important than the protection from the fierce currents.

W/G

Sheepscot Bay, ME

		Largest Vessel Accommodated	VHF Channel Monitored / Working	Transient Slips / Total Slips	Approach / Dockside Depth (reported)	Floating Docks	Gas / Diesel	Groceries, Ice, Marine Supplies, Snacks	Repairs: Hull, Engine, Propeller	Lift (tonnage), Crane, Rail	Min / Max Amps	Courtesy Car, Laundry, Pool, Showers	Pump-Out Station	Nearby: Grocery Store, Motel, Restaurant
				Dockage			**Supplies**		**Services**					
SHEEPSCOT RIVER														
1. Sheepscot Bay Boat Co.	(207) 371-2442	30	9/	/	10.0/9.0	F	GD	M	HEP	C	30			R
2. Derecktor Robinhood ▢ WiFi	(207) 371-2525	110	9/	15/135	70.0/20.0	F	GD	IMS	HEP	L50,C	30/100	CLS	P	10R
WISCASSET														
3. Wiscasset Yacht Club	(207) 882-4058	30	/	/	20.0/6.0							S		
4. Wiscasset Town Dock ▢ WiFi	(207) 380-3502	250	9/	/	20.0/20.0	F				L20		S		5MR
EBENECOOK HARBOR														
5. Hodgdon Yacht Services - Southport Boatyard ▢ WiFi	(207) 633-2970	80	9/	5/40	15.0/8.0	F	GD	IMS	HEP	L50	30/50	LS	P	GMR

▢ Internet Access WiFi Wireless Internet Access onSpot Dockside WiFi Facility

See WaterwayGuide.com for current rates, fuel prices, website addresses, and other up-to-the-minute information. (Information in the table is provided by the facilities.)

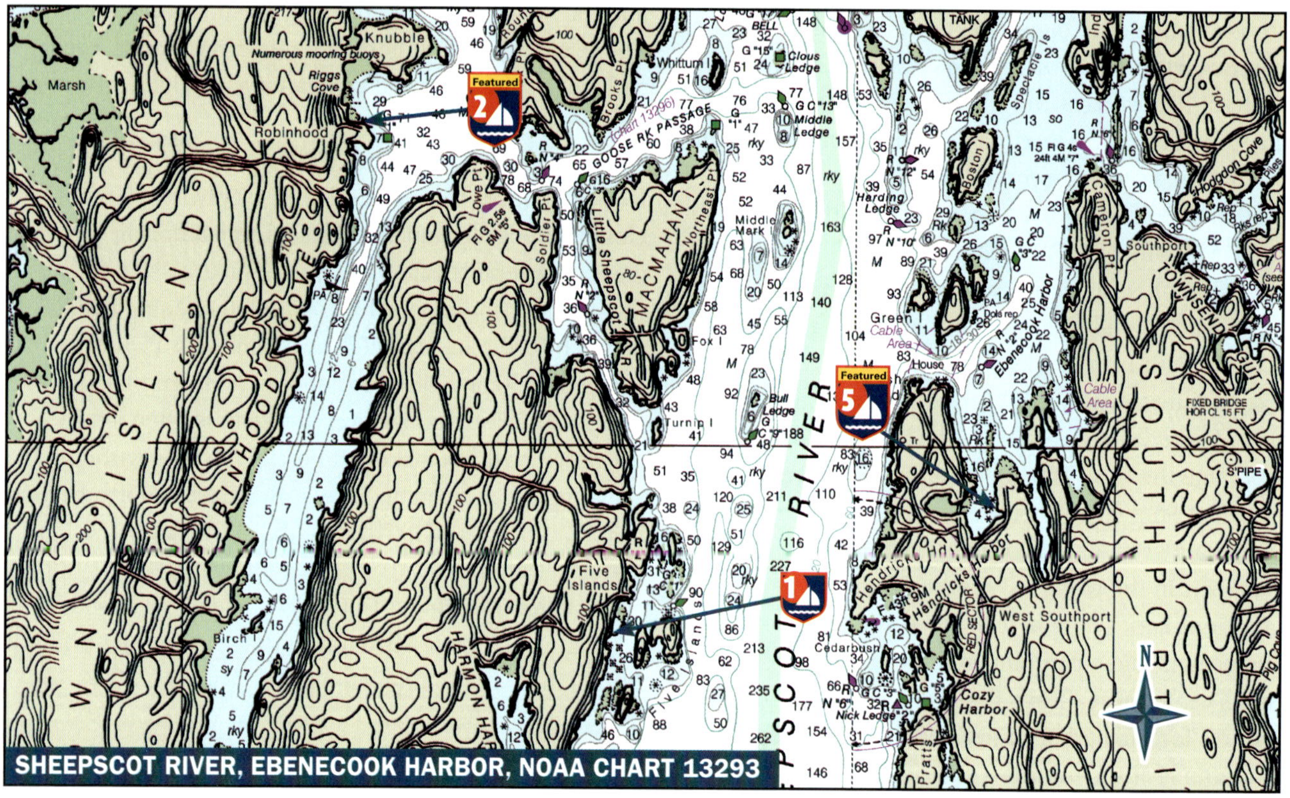

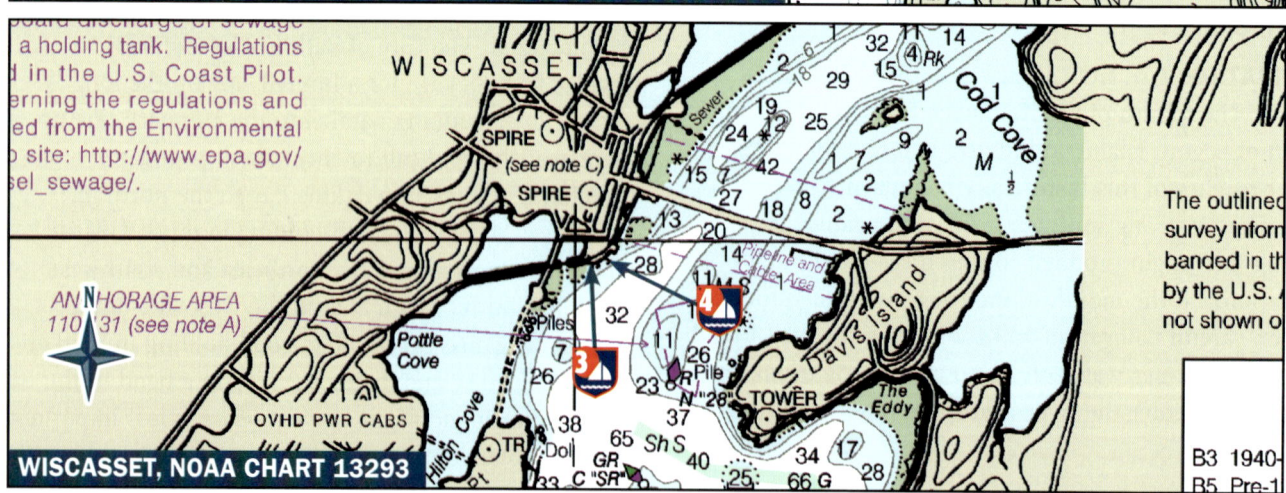

SHEEPSCOT RIVER, EBENECOOK HARBOR, NOAA CHART 13293

...board discharge of sewage
a holding tank. Regulations
...d in the U.S. Coast Pilot.
...erning the regulations and
...ed from the Environmental
...b site: http://www.epa.gov/
...sel_sewage/.

The outlined
survey inform
banded in th
by the U.S. ...
not shown o

WISCASSET, NOAA CHART 13293

B3 1940-
B5 Pre-1

Inside Passage: Bath to Boothbay Harbor

The inside passage between Bath and Boothbay Harbor is truly the wilds of Maine. When Champlain explored the Sasanoa River, they had to pull his boats up the river from Boothbay to Bath. That's not one of the "delights" in store for modern cruisers, but the seaweed-strewn rocks and wooded shores provide excitement and scenery in abundance. To run this 11-mile winding passage is a delight for boats drawing less than 7 feet and able to negotiate the fixed **Wilder Memorial Bridge** (51-foot vertical clearance) over the Sasanoa River. However, several important cautions should be kept in mind:

- Before you pass under the Wilder Memorial Bridge be sure you have NOAA Chart 13293. Refer to Waterway Explorer (www.waterwayguide.com) and NOAA online charts for the most up-to-date information.

- While the state of the tide is not easily predicted, plan to start an eastward trip when the tide at Boothbay is at low water and a westward trip on the Boothbay high water.

- On the westward trip Hockomock Bay between Phipps Point and Hockomock Head, out of the main current, is a good place to anchor in 12 to 14 feet MLW to wait on the tide if a sailboat's auxiliary isn't powerful enough to buck the current.

- Keep close watch on the series of channel buoys between Mill Point and Castle Island, south along the main body of Hockomock Bay to avoid being swept into the shallows.

- Upper Hell Gate (south of Money Point) and–even more so–Lower Hell Gate (between Westport Island and Beal Island) require motoring hard if a boater misjudges the tides.

- Expect strong currents and swirling rips through Lower Hell Gate regardless of the state of the tide. A strong hand on the tiller or wheel is necessary. Three knots on the flood and 3.5 knots on the ebb are common in this area but up to 9 knots have been observed at The Boilers east of red nun buoy "2."

- An alternate route for the side trip-enthused cruiser stretches north from Hockomock Bay, through idyllic Montsweag Bay's camps and nature preserves to the Cowseagan Narrows' fixed bridge (48-foot vertical clearance) and then to the Sheepscot River at charming Wiscasset. This semi-circumnavigation of Westport Island has the scenic pleasure of the inside route in extended format.

NAVIGATION: Use NOAA Chart 13293. The channel between Bath and Knubble Bay is marked from southeast to northwest so the numbers will descend if beginning the trip in Bath. Past the Wilder Memorial Bridge (51-foot fixed vertical clearance), the buoys lead a curved path around the mudflats of Hanson Bay and down to Upper Hell Gate at green daybeacon "23." Upper Hell Gate is followed immediately by Lime Rock, which appears in the middle of the river. Red daybeacon "22" shows the straight-line safe course east of the rock. The route west of Lime Rock is wider and deeper but the curves are more difficult to handle when the Sasanoa Rover is in full flow. Between Tibbett and Swett Points, the river narrows dramatically again but without the swirls and rips of the Hell Gates.

The wide open space of Hockomock Bay will allow time for a deep and relaxing breath but watch the boat's motion because the current can pull you out of the channel. Diving south at green can buoy "5" you will be back on the narrow rocky way and the waters near red nun buoy "2" rarely stop roiling. Knubble Bay brings you to Robinhood Cove, a good place to bide a while, or to Goose Rock Passage and the remainder of the trip to Boothbay Harbor. Heading east, pass MacMahan Island and cross the Sheepscot River to find the buoys that lead to Ebenecook Harbor and on to Townsend Gut and Boothbay.

■ NAVIGATING THE SHEEPSCOT RIVER

Big, easy-to-enter Sheepscot Bay leads into the Sheepscot River, with deep channels, tree-lined shores, craggy rocks and small towns. In the early 17th century, Champlain mistook the Sheepscot for the St. Lawrence River. Cape Harbor, at the eastern entrance to the bay between Cape Island and Cape Newagen, is attractive, convenient to open water and easily entered from the west via a marked channel. You can approach from the east but the passage is shallow and calls for local knowledge.

To Robinhood Cove

Accessible either through the Little Sheepscot River (easiest from Five Islands) or from the east through Goose Rock Passage, Robinhood Cove is both a perfectly sheltered retreat from the elements and part of an intricate connective system between the Sheepscot and Kennebec Rivers. In this area, many large land masses are actually islands created by the interweaving rivers. The driving distances between points can be significant, which has allowed much of the land here to remain less-settled than many more easily-accessed parts of the Maine coast. Robinhood Cove is a good example of a type: no services down in the cove but excellent food and services at an easily accessed waterway crossing.

South of Robinhood Cove on the east side of the Sheepscot River is large Ebenecook Harbor, on the northwestern shoulder of Southport Island. Ebenecook Harbor is large, protected and easy to enter in any weather. Many local small-boat sailors enjoy their time tacking between the islands and the open area west of Cameron Point is frequently an energizing scene. Three coves at the south end offer lovely scenery and protected stops. The Southport General Store (443 Hendricks Hill Rd., 207-633-6666) is well stocked and has a popular deli.

NAVIGATION: Use NOAA Chart 13293. Easiest and safest transit is made during slack water to avoid the considerable effects of ripping tidal currents. Goose Rock Passage's trickiest turn is marked by red nun "4," which seems impossibly far south at high tide but is crucial to honor. The current gets tricky in the vicinity of Riggs Cove and the Derecktor Robinhood mooring field and then reverses in the narrowing just south. No navigation aids mark the cove because it is deep and open down the middle with no hazards except at the edges.

Approaching Southport Island from the south, turn east at the top of Dogfish Head and proceed south to the marina or anchorage areas. For a trickier but less-trafficked route from the north, turn northeast once south of Ram Island and make for green day-beacon "1." Continue on the northeasterly course until Spectacle Island is visible 0.5 mile southeast. Follow

Isle of Springs and leave Spectacle Island to the west. A 4-foot MLW spot makes it important not to bend your course toward Sawyer Island, but it is deep quite close to Indiantown Island. Once between Spectacle and Indiantown Islands, green can buoy "3" shows the way to the southern coves. Red nun buoy "2" marks the north end of the shoals separating Maddock Cove and Pierce Cove. The three coves have no aids to navigation so go carefully to avoid the rocks and shoals. Love Cove's entrance is also bordered by rocks submerged through most of the tide and can be difficult to line up properly without a chartplotter.

Dockage/Moorings: As you reach the western mouth of Goose Rock Passage or coming around the Nubble, Derecktor Robinhood will be visible immediately ahead. At this full-service facility you will find ample slips and moorings for transients as well as a fully capable shipyard. On-site amenities include showers, laundry facilities and a well-stocked chandlery. A courtesy car is available should you need more supplies. The Brunswick sprawl starts with Bath on the west side of the Kennebec.

More accessible than it appears on the chart, Five Island Harbor to the south on the Sheepscot River may be entered with plenty of depth from the east or north. Sheepscot Bay Boat Company permits short-term dinghy tie-ups for loading and unloading at its substantial dinghy landing and, although this is primarily a small-boat facility, there is turning room and ample depth (10 feet MLW) for craft in the 30- to 40-foot range to take on gas or diesel at its fuel dock. Several complimentary moorings are available courtesy of the Five Islands Yacht Club (with no clubhouse, just good-spirited members).

Hodgdon Yacht Services-Southport Boatyard is at the southwest corner of Ebenecook Harbor. They have been building boats for 200 years and are the nation's oldest boat builders. With easily accessible facilities and in-house expertise in specialty trades, Hodgdon can accommodate varying scopes of work to meet boaters' needs. They offer full amenities and sells all fuels. This is one of their three locations in Maine.

Anchorage: Moorings fill Riggs Cove but travel farther south into Robinhood Cove for 7 to 15 feet MLW and good holding in mud and rock. The center of the cove is very deep and the entrance is thick with lobster buoys, but there is quite a bit of space along the sides on the north end for easier access to shore via the marina. If you prefer to be farther from the crowds, the south end is a gorgeous combination of rock outcroppings and forested hills. North of Birch Island, the shallow area (6 to 9 feet MLW) is wide and the traffic is mostly lobster boats. Shallow, secure anchorage is rare enough in Maine that it might be a relief to put out less chain than usual. Anchoring is less attractive between Birch Island and Phebe Island as the bottom becomes rocky and holding is trickier.

You can anchor in Five Island Harbor just north of Malden Island in 8 to 10 feet MLW with good holding in mud and rock and protection from the prevailing southwesterlies. Keep an eye on the weather, though, as it is open to the northeast. You can dinghy in next to the town dock.

Ebenecook Harbor offers good anchorage in a choice of sheltered coves. You can drop the hook east of Dogfish Head in 15 feet at MLW but watch your depth, be aware of the tide state and check the chart for cable crossing areas before setting the anchor. Pierce Cove and Love Cove to the east are good anchorages with many moorings. In either of these, you will find at least 7 feet at MLW, excellent holding in mud and protection from all but the north. The large quantity of unoccupied moorings makes this a popular spot to borrow one, as long as you remain ready to move if the owner appears.

To Wiscasset

A major port of entry for goods from England until the War of 1812, Wiscasset is still a thriving village, today more given to tourism than trade. Buildings and gardens from the town's heyday are now major attractions for history buffs. Locals refer to Wiscasset as the prettiest village in Maine, where you can take a delightful, self-guided walking tour of several historic buildings including: Kingsbury House (1763, oldest in the town) at Federal and Washington St.; Lilac Cottage (c. 1789) at Washington and Main St.; Castle Tucker (1807) at High and Lee St. (an authentic Victorian house containing no reproductions); the Nickels-Sortwell House (1807) at Main and Federal St.; the Wiscasset Academy (1807) at Hodge and Warren St. (now home to the Maine Art Gallery); the 1869 Customs House (c. 1869-1870) at Water, Fore and Middle St. and a variety of classic gardens that are open to the public. Many of the town's private homes are also well restored.

NAVIGATION: Use NOAA Chart 13293. For the 9 island-studded miles to the **U.S. Route 1 Bridge** at Wiscasset (4 miles south of the limit to navigation at

Sheepscot), the Sheepscot River is deep, well marked and attractive with lobster buoys covering every square foot of water. Look for the measured mile with shore ranges on the eastern bank at Barters Island to the east.

Dockage/Moorings: Friendly Wiscasset Yacht Club just south of the Town Landing has overnight dockage to accommodate members of reciprocating clubs and welcomes guests on two courtesy moorings available on a first-come, first-served basis. The Town of Wiscasset has two deep water moorings and some dockage space but overnight tie-up to either requires harbormaster permission and payment. Water is available for refills and there are restrooms on the wharf, open during the day.

Anchorage: Even though slips and moorings are few in number, there is ample anchorage in 12 to 20 feet MLW with secure holding east of the town's mooring field in Wicasset. Tidal currents run swiftly on both ebb and flow, which should encourage setting a secure hook (tested in both directions) with adequate scope. There is a 7-day limit on anchoring without a permit, which is available from the harbormaster for a fee and extends the limit to 14 days in a calendar year.

Townsend Gut

To avoid going the long way around Southport Island between the Sheepscot River and Boothbay Harbor, take the lovely channel called Townsend Gut. This is also the continuation of the inside passage from Bath.

NAVIGATION: Use NOAA Chart 13293. Head north from Ebenecook Harbor and pass 24-foot flashing green "7" on Cameron Point, leaving room for the rocks that are awash at low tide. Turn toward and then favor red nun buoy "6" marking Indiantown Island Ledge, one of the tightest squeezes on the cruise. Stay in the middle to pass through the next narrowing. Hodgdon Cove opens up to the north and is good hangout area while waiting for the bridge opening. The fast-operating **Townsend Gut (Southport/SR 7) Bridge** (10-foot closed vertical clearance) opens on signal except from April 29 through September 30, between 6:00 a.m. and 6:00 p.m., when the draw will open on the hour and half hour only. Currents run swiftly through here. Hug the bold western shore and stay south of red nun buoy "2." Leaving Townsend Gut heading east, Boothbay Harbor is northeast and Burnt Island is southwest.

BOOTHBAY HARBOR TO LINEKIN BAY

Boothbay Harbor

A summer resort with natural beauty, an easy entrance and many shore attractions, Boothbay (pronounced "BOOTH-bay") Harbor has ample yachting amenities available on all but the busiest of holiday weekends. This harbor can be crowded both on the water and ashore. An unusual wooden pedestrian footbridge built in 1900 spans the inner harbor, saving visitors and residents from the long walk around. It is occasionally washed out by ice but is always rebuilt, and it protects a small-boat area that is heavily used by kayaks, dinghies and other low-profile vessels.

This easily approached and scenic bay has a well-documented maritime history dating from the 15th century. During the summer, sloops and a host of other classic hulls and rigs add interest to a harbor already bursting with boating color. Although the center of activity is Boothbay Harbor, all the significant islands protecting this classic bay are populated during the summer months. This has been an enduring truth since 1837, when legions of "invalids" breathed the pure air and bathed in the clear water, resources hard to come by in densely populated Boston and New York.

NAVIGATION: Use NOAA Chart 13293. Boothbay Harbor is deep and access is easy from any direction in any weather. The popular entrances are protected Townsend Gut from the west and the somewhat-protected Fisherman Island Passage from the east. From Fisherman Island Passage head from Dictator Ledge's red nun "6" across Linekin Bay's mouth for Spruce Point. From offshore Damariscove Island is the first protection from eastern swells and the Cuckolds' 59-foot-tall lighthouse's flashing white light and horn simplify entrance in thick weather or at night. Head west of Squirrel Island and east of Burnt Island, then flashing red buoy "8" shows the safe water west of Tumbler Island. From there the harbor blooms and your heading will depend on your plans.

Dockage/Moorings: The easiest access to shoreside fun in this resort town is found in the northeastern cove (or inner harbor) of Boothbay Harbor. Excellent full-service marinas crowd along the eastern and western edges of the inner harbor. Most offer both moorings

CASCO BAY & THE MID-COAST OF MAINE

Boothbay Harbor, ME

WG

		Dockage				Supplies		Services						
BOOTHBAY HARBOR AREA	Largest Vessel Accomodated	VHF Channel Monitored / Working	Transient Slips / Total Slips	Approach / Dockside Depth (reported)	Floating Docks	Gas / Diesel	Groceries, Ice, Marine Supplies, Snacks	Repairs: Hull, Engine, Propeller	Lift (tonnage), Crane, Rail	Min / Max Amps	Courtesy Car, Laundry, Pool, Showers	Pump-Out Station	Nearby: Grocery Store, Motel, Restaurant
1. Carousel Marina ⌨ WiFi (207) 633-2922	180	9/	15/50	30.0/22.0	F	GD	GIMS	EP		30/100	CLS	P	GMR
2. Brown's Wharf Marina, Inn & Restaurant ⌨ WiFi (207) 633-5440	170	9/8	15/40	25.0/25.0	F		I			30/50	CLS	P	GMR
3. Cap'n Fish's Waterfront Inn & Marina ⌨ WiFi (207) 633-6605	100	16/	5/5	15.0/10.0	F		IS						MR
4. Oceanside Marina-Boothbay Harbor Oceanside Golf Resort ⌨ WiFi (207) 633-4455	80	9/9	/15	18.0/8.0	F		I			50		P	GMR
5. Boothbay Harbor Marina WiFi (207) 633-6003	150	9/68	20/40	20.0/12.0	F		I			30/50	CLS		R
6. Tugboat Inn & Marina ⌨ WiFi (207) 633-4435	100	9/9	11/30	15.0/10.0	F		IS			30/50	LPS	P	GMR
7. Boothbay Harbor Shipyard (207) 633-3171	200	9/	/	25.0/9.0			M	H	R				MR
8. Hodgdon Marina ⌨ WiFi (207) 633-2970	200	9/	5/30	16.0/16.0	F	GD	IM	HEP	L,C	30/100	LS		GMR
9. Signal Point Marina (207) 633-6920	60	9/	20/48	25.0/15.0	F		GI			30/50	LS	P	GR
10. Boothbay Harbor Yacht Club ⌨ WiFi (207) 633-5750	60	9/	/	20.0/14.0	F		I				LS		GMR
LINEKIN BAY													
11. Linekin Bay Resort WiFi (207) 633-2494		9/9	/	32.0/18.0	F		IS				LPS		3MR

⌨ Internet Access   WiFi Wireless Internet Access   onSpot Dockside WiFi Facility

See WaterwayGuide.com for current rates, fuel prices, website addresses, and other up-to-the-minute information. (Information in the table is provided by the facilities.)

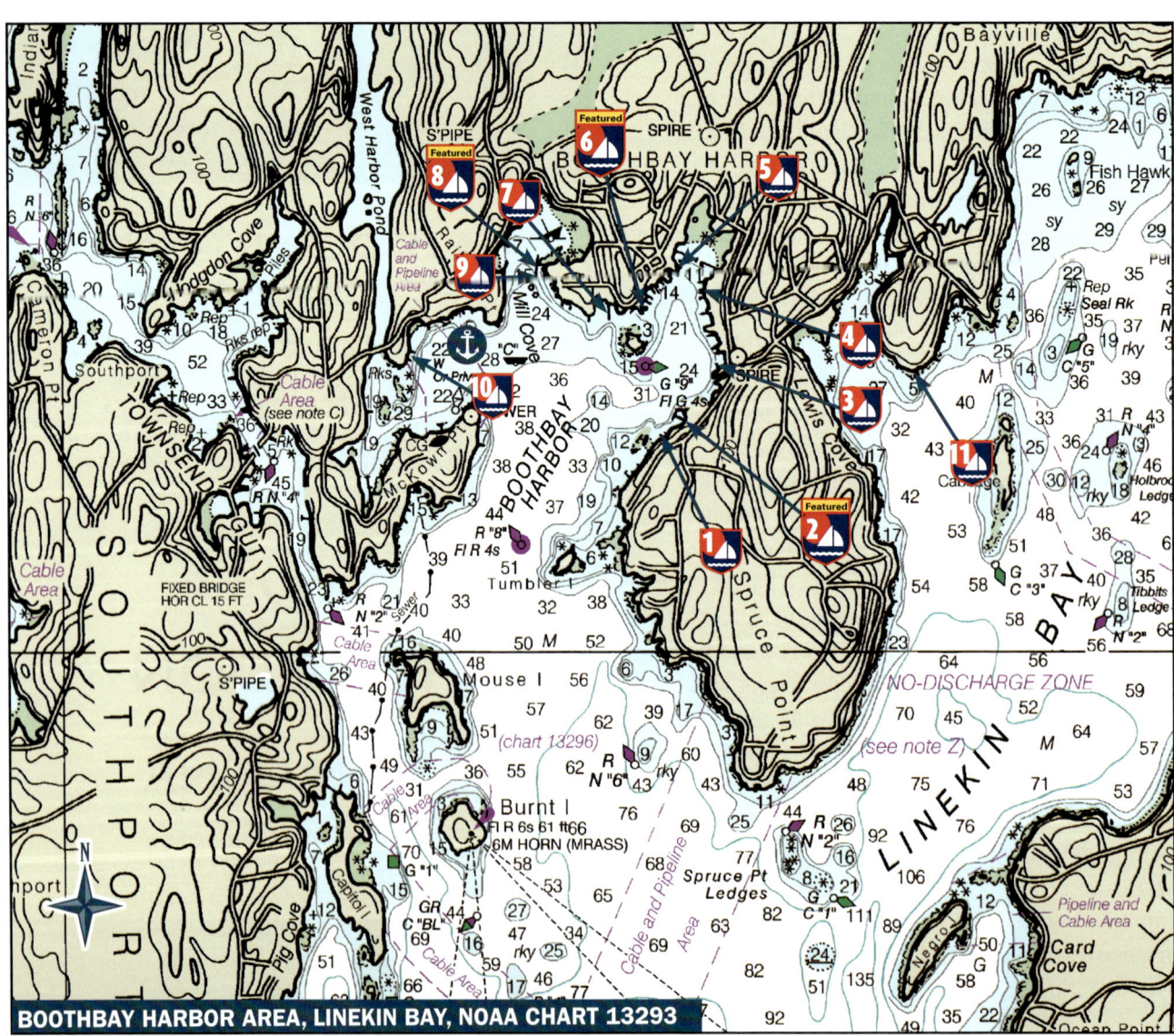

BOOTHBAY HARBOR AREA, LINEKIN BAY, NOAA CHART 13293

and transient slips but it is best to call ahead (VHF Channel 09 or by phone) for a reservation.

The family-run Brown's Wharf Marina, Inn & Restaurant has been in business for more than 70 years. Flowers run riot at Brown's (even the pilings sprout them in season) and there are 40 slips with water, electricity and cable TV in clear view of the boating action but beyond the traffic noise from town. Two shopping trolleys leave from this location on a regular basis. Directly to the north on the harbor the Tugboat Inn & Marina offers slips on floating docks and moorings and a marina lounge. This is a great place for a crew change or to just get off the boat for a while.

West of McFarland Island in Mill Cove is Hodgdon Marina, which caters to transient boaters of all types including megayachts. This is one of three locations in Maine. This facility provides dockside depths from 8 to 18 feet MLW, 750-linear feet of dockage space, gas and diesel fuel and full marina amenities. Hodgdon is located on the quiet side of the harbor, yet still within walking distance of downtown's restaurants, galleries and shops. West of Mill Cove, Boothbay Harbor Yacht Club maintains a large number of moorings, some of which may be available for visiting yachtsmen. The club is identifiable by the BHYC sign on its roof.

Anchorage: Mill Cove, between Farland Point and Railway Point, offers a designated anchorage with good holding in 15 to 25 feet MLW outside the mooring field. The shallows north of McKown Pt. are a long dinghy ride from town but have 17- to 26-feet MLW depths and good holding in mud and rock.

Side Trip: Damariscove Island

If year-round fishing villages count, Damariscove Island was unquestionably the earliest permanent European colony in the New World. It was permanent, that is, until the last resident family moved to the mainland in 1939. The *Mayflower* stopped at the island to barter for provisions en route to Massachusetts Bay in 1620, returning early the following year to beg additional supplies from the hearty Damariscove fishers for the beleaguered Plymouth Colony settlers. Now all that remains are abandoned farmsteads, the boarded-up former Coast Guard station and a rustic Boothbay Region Land Trust hut.

Damariscove's 209 acres look to be separated into two islands but they are connected by a narrow, low neck, 0.25-mile wide and 1.7 miles long. This windswept island echoes the austere beauty of the Hebrides and of lost Viking outposts. The largest eider-duck colonies in the U.S. reportedly nest here, along with their nemesis, the great black-backed gull. Common yellow throats, yellow warblers, catbirds and Savannah sparrows also nest here in abundance.

The 1.5-mile walk along the Pond Loop Trail traverses rocky shore, coastal tundra, salt marsh, freshwater pond and upland meadow. Passage here during mid-summer's wildflower profusion is certain to leave a lasting memory. The delicate natural beauty of the island argues for strict observance of the Conservancy's rules: no fires or camping and the northern end of the island is off limits for the protection of nesting eider ducks until mid-August. Pets are not allowed at any time.

NAVIGATION: Use NOAA Chart 13293. South of Boothbay Harbor in Booth Bay, the approach to Damariscove Island is more straightforward than it might appear, especially when you look at waves broken by the reef known as The Motions. The reef is located to the west of an entrance barely revealed

HODGDON MARINA

TUGBOAT INN & MARINA

BROWN'S WHARF MARINA,
INN & RESTAURANT

Ebenecook Harbor

GOIN' ASHORE

BOOTHBAY HARBOR, ME

This easily approached and scenic bay has a well-documented maritime history dating from the 15th century, but authenticated Viking relics push the first dates of European exploration and fishing expeditions back centuries earlier. Permanent settlement failed until a group of feisty Scotch-Irish borderlanders, descendants of the Braveheart Scots, combined bullheadedness and friendliness to the local Wabanaki people. While maritime traditions are honored here, it is the more modern attractions and cool seaside summer weather that draw thousands of vacationers, both by land and by sea, each season. Though the center of activity is in Boothbay Harbor, all the significant islands protecting this classic bay are populated during the summer months. This has been an enduring truth since 1837, when legions of "invalids" breathed the pure air and bathed in the clear water, resources hard to come by in densely populated Boston and New York.

ATTRACTIONS

Daily during the summer, sloops and a host of other classic hulls and rigs add interest to a harbor already bursting with boating color. The locally favored Coastal Maine Botanical Garden (207-633-8000) features a constantly changing seasonal landscape among 248 waterfront acres. The Boothbay Opera House (86 Townsend Ave., 207-633-5159), built in 1894, hosts over 100 events and performances each year. Windjammer Days, a 50-plus-year-old festival in late June, culminates with the unforgettable parade of majestic, fully rigged windjammers sailing into the harbor. Harborfest is the first week in September and features music, an art show, photo workshop, food tastings, a cocktail competition and a "fishing for fashion" show. The Claw Down, a lobster cooking competition, is held the third week in September. Visit the Boothbay Harbor Information Center (17 Commercial St.) for more information.

SHOPPING

On the western side of the footbridge, Boothbay Harbor's resort village has numerous shops, offering fudge and cotton candy, souvenirs, curios and antiques. A bank (with weather-protected, 24-hour ATM) is located at center harbor on McKown St. WiFi and public use computers are available at the Boothbay Harbor Library (207-633-3112). North of the town dock (Fisherman's Wharf), you will find the well-stocked Grovers' Hardware (47 Townsend Ave., 207-633-2694). Complete provisioning requires a visit to the shopping center about one-half mile north of town, home to a large Hannaford Supermarket (180 Townsend Ave., 207-633-6465) and a coin-operated laundry.

CASCO BAY & THE MID-COAST OF MAINE

by the sharp cliffs cascading into the narrow slot of a harbor. Several warnings are in order:

- Stay well inside Bantam Rock, which is actually a cluster of rocks extending toward the island from red bell buoy "2BR" located about 1 mile to the south-southwest of the harbor entrance.

- When passing east of red-and-white gong buoy "TM" (The Motions), set a course for the center of the harbor opening and maintain enough speed to retain steerageway in following seas.

- Once abeam of the western tip of the harbor entrance, correct course to favor that side slightly as there is a submerged boulder off the eastern shore very nearly even with the tip of the western point.

Moorings/Anchorage: The Boothbay Region Land Trust maintains two complimentary moorings available for 24 hours. There are even courtesy dinghies on the stone pier if you don't have one or don't want to launch it. Simply land at the pier long enough to tie one on and head over to the mooring. If both moorings are taken, you can anchor in soft mud just past the abandoned Coast Guard Station (now privately owned) at the south end of the island. In this long, narrow bight, fore and aft anchors will allow adequate scope for the 10-foot tides while preventing grounding at low tide. It is also possible for a boat or two to set a careful hook in the inner harbor beyond the channel's choke point and abeam of the Nature Conservancy's hut, also to the west. Since swing room is quite limited, and there is almost always a lobster car and boat nearby, nighttime fenders are in order.

During settled weather, it is possible to anchor at the north end of the island at Bar Cove Beach then row in for a landing on the pebbled beach below the island's freshwater pond. The cove is sheltered from the surge produced by prevailing southwesterlies but is open to the northeast. Wherever you anchor, the Boothbay Region Land Trust asks that you check in with them before hiking ashore.

Linekin Bay

In contrast to Boothbay Harbor, Linekin Bay, just east of Spruce Point, is quiet, non-commercial and nearly deserted. The original Scotch-Irish settlers and their descendants fought development so obstinately that even the man it's named after, Benjamin Linekin, couldn't have his way without a fight. The Montgomery clan had been farming the neck for

decades when the newcomer Linekin arrived and built a house, causing friction. When he retreated to Boston for the harsh winter, they disassembled Linekin's house and carried it and his possessions away completely. Linekin took the Montgomerys to court but a sympathetic jury found them not guilty.

The highlight of Linekin Bay, in addition to excellent protection in an easterly or southeasterly blow, is the renowned P.E. Luke Yard (207-633-4971) on the southeastern coast. Marine engineering buffs will relish a free tour of Luke's private museum of the company's colorful history in the world of traditional boatbuilding and ocean yacht racing. Luke's has an extensive repair trade and manufactures heavy three-piece storm anchors and ingenious automatic feathering props.

NAVIGATION: Use NOAA Chart 13293. If continuing east from Boothbay, note that the best course in good weather is to pass well to the east of Squirrel Island then continue through the Fisherman Island Passage to the red-and-white Morse (A) bell buoy "HL" off the mouth of the Damariscotta River. Entrance to Linekin Bay is an easy matter through the wide, deep passage between bold and wooded Negro Island (off the west side of Ocean Point) and green can buoy "1."

Moorings: The Linekin Bay Resort dominates the northern edge of the cove and the remainder of the shore is dotted by homes. The resort offers mooring rental that include use of the pool and shower.

Anchorage: An often-overlooked anchorage is Lewis Cove, on the western side of Linekin Bay. There is excellent holding and good protection in 14 to 22 feet MLW with excellent holding in mud outside the mooring field.

◼ DAMARISCOTTA RIVER TO GEORGES ISLANDS

Damariscotta River

Around Linekin Neck from Boothbay Harbor via the well-marked Fisherman Island Passage, the Damariscotta River is about a century removed from its more active neighbor to the west. One of Maine's most beautiful rivers, it flows past 15 miles of wooded islands, hidden coves, jagged rock outcroppings and high, green bluffs.

Damariscotta River

NAVIGATION: Use NOAA Chart 13293. Once plied by commercial schooners, the Damariscotta River's lazily winding channel is easy to navigate. You will pass harbors with sophisticated attractions, good food and two small, but important shipbuilding villages. At the head of the river are two Colonial cities that once served as ports of entry. The tidal range here is 9 feet so it is advisable to travel on a fair tide.

Close to the river entrance, about 1 mile north of thickly wooded Inner Heron Island, Christmas Cove at Rutherford Island has an easy entrance, perfect protection, a handsome shoreline and magnificent views. While the rocks that form an informal breakwater look intimidating upon entry, careful navigation will provide safe entry. After passing red nun buoy "4" north of Inner Heron Island, head for the center of the harbor entrance leaving Foster Point (and red-over-green nun buoy "FP") to the north. Inside the outer harbor look for red daybeacon "2," which is on rocks and then green daybeacon "3" further in, and pass between them without getting close to either.

Until the river reaches the twin villages of Damariscotta and Newcastle, 13 miles from the open ocean, it offers only beautiful scenery and an unlimited choice of peaceful anchorages. River currents run rapidly (up to 5 knots on the ebb) and the upper 2 miles of the river are winding and narrow, although reasonably well marked. Those with limited cruising experience in such waters should seek local knowledge before making the trip. Cruising upriver to Damariscotta is a nice day trip when fog on the outside limits your options.

Dockage/Moorings: Dockage is usually available from Coveside Marina & Restaurant at the south end of Rutherford. Hail them on VHF Channel 16 or 09 for slip or moorings assignment. There is no room for anchoring in Christmas Cove due to the proliferation of moorings. At the north end of Rutherford Island, the historic Gamage Shipyard is located on the west side of **The Gut Bridge** (4-foot closed vertical clearance), which opens on signal. The shipyard has slips and moorings as well as fuel and repairs.

The small boatbuilding village of East Boothbay is located on the west side of the Damariscotta River with a mooring-filled cove. Ocean Point Marina is easily spotted because of its prominent sheds and long fuel dock paralleling the river's western shore. East Boothbay's Post Office is central to the waterfront. At

Johns Bay, ME

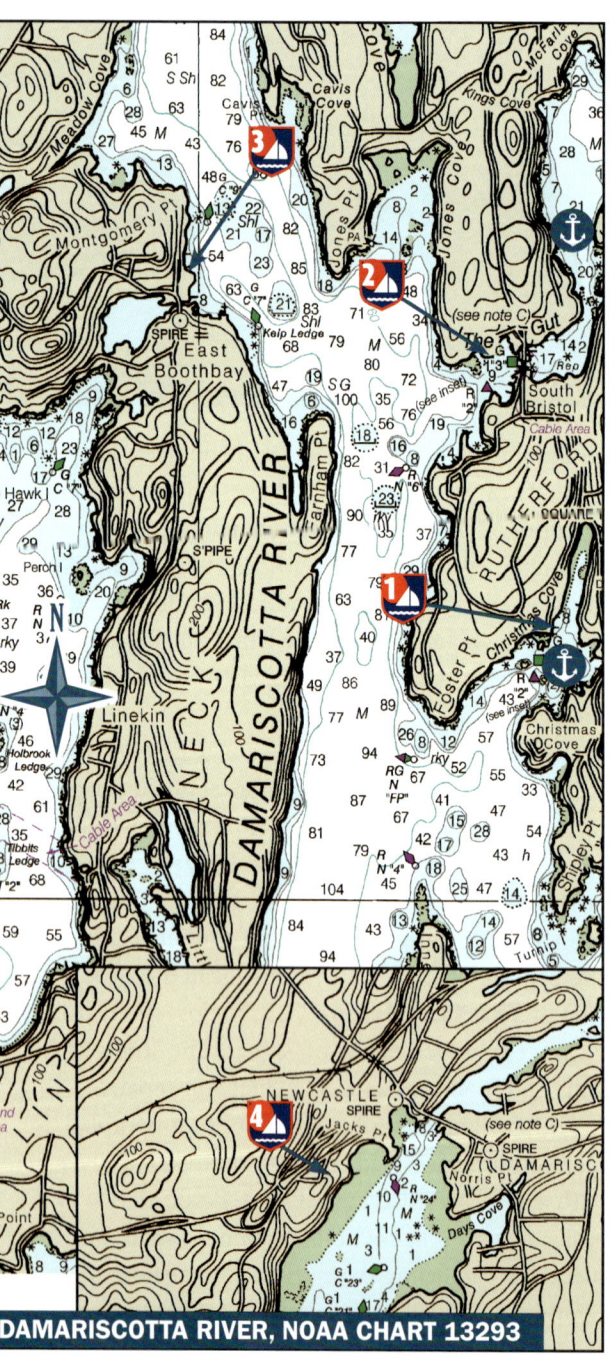

DAMARISCOTTA RIVER		VHF Channel Monitored / Working	Largest Vessel Accomodated	Approach / Dockside Depth (reported)	Transient Slips / Total Slips	Floating Docks	Gas / Diesel	Groceries, Ice, Marine Supplies, Snacks	Repairs: Hull, Engine, Propeller	Lift (tonnage), Crane, Rail	Min / Max Amps	Courtesy Car, Laundry, Pool, Showers	Pump-Out Station	Nearby: Grocery Store, Motel, Restaurant
				Dockage				**Supplies**		**Services**				
1. Coveside Marina & Restaurant	(207) 644-8282	60	/9	12/12	10.0/10.0	F					30	S		R
2. Gamage Shipyard 🖳	(207) 644-8181	100	9/	3/44	10.0/10.0	F	GD	IM	HEP	L25	50	LS	P	GMR
3. Ocean Point Marina 🖳 WIFI	(207) 633-0773	150	16/9	8/70	35.0/15.0	F	GD	IMS	HEP	L35	30/50	LS	P	GMR
4. Riverside Boat Co.	(207) 563-3398	40	/	/	/			IS	H	R		L	P	R

🖳 Internet Access WIFI Wireless Internet Access onSpot Dockside WiFi Facility
See WaterwayGuide.com for current rates, fuel prices, website addresses, and other up-to-the-minute information. (Information in the table is provided by the facilities.)

DAMARISCOTTA RIVER, NOAA CHART 13293

the East Boothbay General Store (255 Ocean Point Rd., 207-633-7800), two blocks south of the harbor on the road to Ocean Point, fresh pastries, newspapers and coffee draw an early bird crowd. The store also stocks some dry goods, dairy and deli items and a limited variety of sodas, beers and wines.

Ask the Newcastle and Damariscotta volunteer harbormaster if a mooring is available (207-563-3398). On the Newcastle (west) side of the river, front floats of the town dock are reserved for short-term, courtesy dockage (up to 2 hours) and there is an ample dinghy dock. At the head of navigation, before the fixed 5-foot vertical clearance **Damariscotta Bridge**, Riverside Boat Co. has moorings for vessels to 40 feet. On the Damariscotta side, Schooner Landing Restaurant & Marina (207-563-7447), built over the water at the main channel, has facing docks with 7-foot MLW alongside depths on the channel for diners. The current is pushed to high velocity here due to the restriction of the channel just south of the bridge, making docking a challenge. Damariscotta offers a range of services on Main St., half a block off the harbor front. There is a full-service grocery store 1 mile east of the town dock.

Anchorage: Once past Fort Island there is a small anchorage with excellent protection in Seal Cove on the east side of the river. The bar going into the anchorage carries 5 feet MLW with 12 to 17 feet MLW once inside the inner basin. For those who don't want to cross the bar at Seal Cove, another option is Long Cove also on the east side of the river approximately 0.5 mile north. Here you will find at least 10 feet MLW and good holding. Watch for the charted rocks on your way in. Once past Miller Island there is a good anchorage to the west in Pleasant Cove with 13 to 16 feet MLW and good holding in sand and mud.

At Newcastle and Damariscott there is usually ample anchorage room in front of the a town dock (out of the intense current) in 11 feet MLW.

Johns Bay

Circular Pemaquid Harbor is a pleasant stopover 3 miles up Johns Bay on the eastern shore. Ashore, you can get a fine dinner at the Pemaquid Seafood Restaurant (32 Co-op Rd., 207-677-2642) and possibly a slip with 4-foot MLW dockside depths. Visit reconstructed Colonial Pemaquid State Historic Site Fort William Henry (2 Colonial Pemaquid Dr., 207-677-2423), open April through October, and from its parapets, gaze at a splendid view of the bay, Pemaquid River and Johns Island. On a warm day, the swimming is excellent on crescent-shaped Pemaquid Beach. Limited day dockage may be available.

NAVIGATION: Use NOAA Chart 13293. A number of routes lead into deep and open Johns Bay. You can sail around Thrumcap Island, then to the north between it and Pemaquid Point; or you can follow the deep, narrow Thread of Life, a fascinating buoyed thoroughfare northwest of Thrumcap Island, which runs between Thread of Life ledges and Turnip Island. Or, for perhaps the most interesting route of all, travel The Gut, a shortcut from the Damariscotta River, running through the lift bridge at South Bristol (4-foot closed vertical clearance), which opens on signal. The wooded, rocky shores make this an especially beautiful trip. Keep a sharp eye out for lobster buoys here.

Anchorage: Northwest of Witch Island you can drop the hook in 21 to 28 feet MLW with good holding in mud. This is somewhat exposed to the north. Watch for possible lobster buoys when you swing with the tide. Diving in the Thread of Life provides and up close and personal assurance that this is prolific lobster bottom.

You can anchor in Pemaquid Harbor to the north in 10 to 18 feet MLW with excellent holding in soft mud and all-around protection.

Muscongus Sound

Once an active shipbuilding, quarrying and cargo port, Round Pond on Muscongus Sound is now most active in the lobster trade and home to a considerable number of cruising vessels. The Post Office is about 0.5 mile south of the village center.

The Historic Gamage Shipyard

The Gamage Shipyard rests on storied ground. The A & M Gamage Shipyard was born when Albion and Menzies Gamage bought a tract of land from local fishers in 1871. They had been building large wooden sailing vessels together since the early 1850s and built at least 88 sail and steam-powered boats over the next 50 years. The last three boats to leave the A & M Gamage Shipyard were the Damariscotta Steamboat Company's original fleet of of *Anodyne* (1895), *Bristol* (1901) and *Newcastle* (1902).

The yard lay fallow for more than 20 years before Harvey F. Gamage left his apprenticeship to build a new boat shed on the family land. He built 288 vessels in an array of styles–sailboats, powerboats, lobsterboats, draggers, scallopers, and windjammers–between 1924 and 1976. He leaned toward John Alden's designs at first but specialized in the heavily framed, powerful wooden fishing boats that gave the Gloucester and New Bedford, MA, fishing fleets their opportunity to hit the Grand Banks as hard as it hit them.

In 1959, the yard built the 83-foot *Mary Day* for Captain Havilah Hawkins. The yard built 43 more vessels before Gamage's death in 1976. These include famous schooners still in the passenger trade today, as well as the 106-foot gaff-rigged sloop *Clearwater*, commissioned by singer Pete Seeger. The vessel is known as "America's Environmental Flagship" and remains a Hudson River force for cleaning up the heavily polluted waterway.

Toward the end of Gamage's life, the schooner *Harvey F Gamage* was launched for educational and charter trips. The 2016-2017 season took her far from her Maine birthplace, all the way down to the southern coast of Cuba and back for a journey through the Canadian Maritimes.

The yard stopped building new boats in 1981 but found a new life in 2000 as a marina and repair yard.

Muscongus Sound, ME

ROUND POND	Largest Vessel Accommodated	VHF Channel Monitored / Working	Dockage				Supplies		Services				
			Approach / Dockside Depth (reported)	Transient Slips / Total Slips	Floating Docks	Groceries, Ice, Marine Supplies, Snacks	Gas / Diesel	Repairs: Hull, Engine, Propeller	Lift (tonnage), Crane, Rail	Min / Max Amps	Courtesy Car, Laundry, Pool, Showers	Pump-Out Station	Nearby: Grocery Store, Motel, Restaurant
1. Padebco Full Service Boatyard & Custom Boat Builders (207) 529-5106	50	/	/	9.0/3.0	F	GD	IMS	HEP	L20,C				GMR
HOCKOMOCK CHANNEL													
2. Broad Cove Marine Service 💻 WiFi (207) 529-5186	42	9/	4/16	6.0/6.0	F	GD	GIM	HE			L	P	G

💻 Internet Access   WiFi Wireless Internet Access   🛰onSpot Dockside WiFi Facility
See WaterwayGuide.com for current rates, fuel prices, website addresses, and other up-to-the-minute information. (Information in the table is provided by the facilities.)

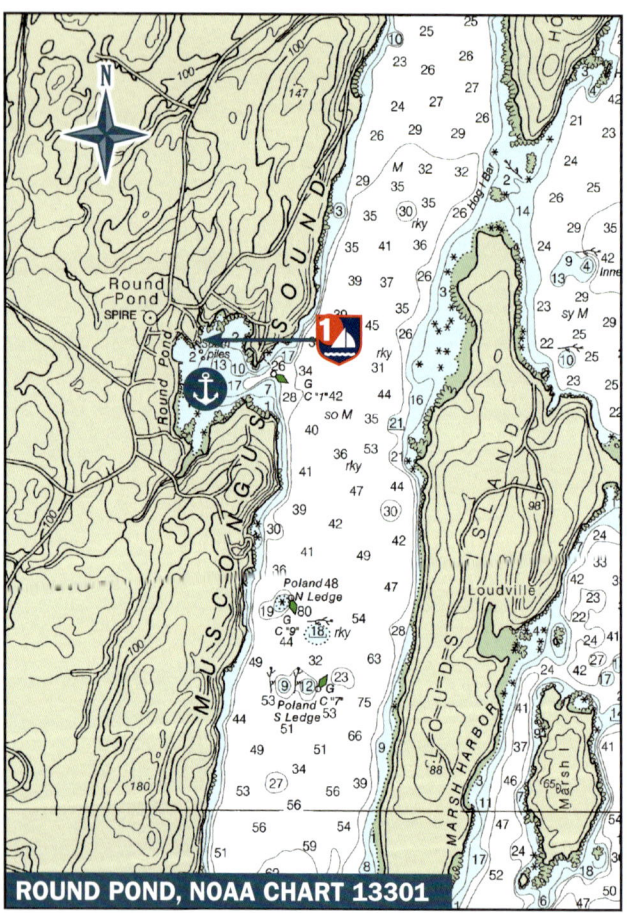

ROUND POND, NOAA CHART 13301

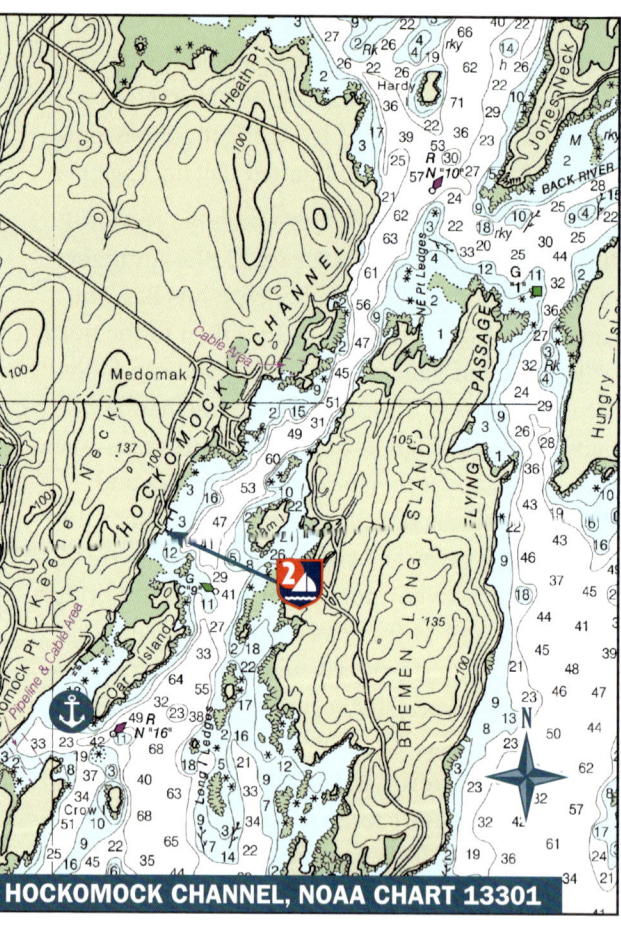

HOCKOMOCK CHANNEL, NOAA CHART 13301

Muscongus Bay Lobster (28 Landing Rd., 207-529-5528) has gasoline, diesel and fresh lobsters at the head of the dock.

NAVIGATION: Use NOAA Charts 13288 and 13301. When heading north in Muscongus Sound, honor the marks precisely. On approaching Round Pond strictly observe green can buoy "9" southeast of Poland North Ledge (just awash at low tide). Look for the small red house as a landmark for the Round Pond entry channel. Lobster pots are thickly placed throughout this area in both the harbor channel and the sound itself.

Dockage/Moorings: There are mooring balls in Round Pond's harbor. Simply tie up and await the Round Pond harbormaster to collect the fee, or call the Harbormaster (207-529-5123) to assist you in finding a vacant mooring. The town dock, with some dinghy space, is just to the right of the paved boat ramp. Use a long painter and tie up loosely so others can maneuver around you. Padebco Full Service Boatyard & Custom Boat Builders is located at the floating wharf farthest north of the town dock and offers moorings, fuel and repairs. They are also helpful with acquiring supplies.

Just 1.5 miles farther north of Muscongus Harbor on

Round Pond

the west side of Hockomock Channel is Broad Cove Marine Services. Located inside the northwest end of Oar Island, they offer fuel, as well as lobsters and clams, either live or cooked. Transient space is usually available and can be reserved on VHF Channel 09.

Anchorage: There is room for anchoring in Round Pond in 9 to 17 feet MLW with all-around protection. You can also anchor behind Oar Island on Hockomock Channel in 8 to 14 feet MLW with good holding in mud and rock. This is somewhat exposed to the southeast.

Friendship Island

About midway across Muscongus Bay on the Meduncook River is Friendship Island, birthplace of the Friendship sloop. Originally designed for fishing and lobstering, these elegant sailboats are now in demand as a recreational craft on the U.S. East and West Coasts among wooden boat aficionados. Friendship is a busy fishing and lobstering town and appreciates cruisers who respect the work being done.

NAVIGATION: Use NOAA Charts 13288 and 13301. The entrance to Friendship Harbor is north of Friendship Long Island and south of Hatchet Cove. It has a good, easy-to-enter harbor that is protected in all but southwesterly winds. The center is deep but don't stray toward Friendship Long Island while approaching green daybeacon "9." The town dock is north of green can "7."

Anchorage: After passing through Friendship Harbor turn due south after green can buoy "7" (but be ready for locals to cut it thereby cutting you off) and proceed through the channel between Friendship Long Island and Garrison Island. Turn west after red nun buoy "6" and anchor in 7 to 12 feet MLW in mud and sand. This is well protected from all directions but the southeast and you're likely to be alone here except for the lobster boats zooming by all day. It's the anchorage closest to the town dock, which has a dinghy dock that is an education on how to tie up properly when sharing space with many other boats. Walk straight uphill then turn right on the first major road for supplies at Wallace's Market (11 Harbor Rd., 207-832-2200), which stocks an impressive array of canned and boxed goods for such a small store. Their real strengths are produce, meats, cheeses, deli salads and sandwiches.

Hatchet Cove is northwest of Friendship and has at least 11 feet MLW but it's a long row to get to the dinghy dock. Anchoring is also possible a little farther south among boats in the cove lying between Friendship Island and Cranberry Island. There is 9 to 14 feet MLW with good holding in mud and rock. Harbor Island to the south is private property but you can anchor in the cove in at least 7 feet MLW with good holding in mud and grass.

Working outward from Friendship, you will discover several secure anchorages and a number of picturesque

St. George River, ME

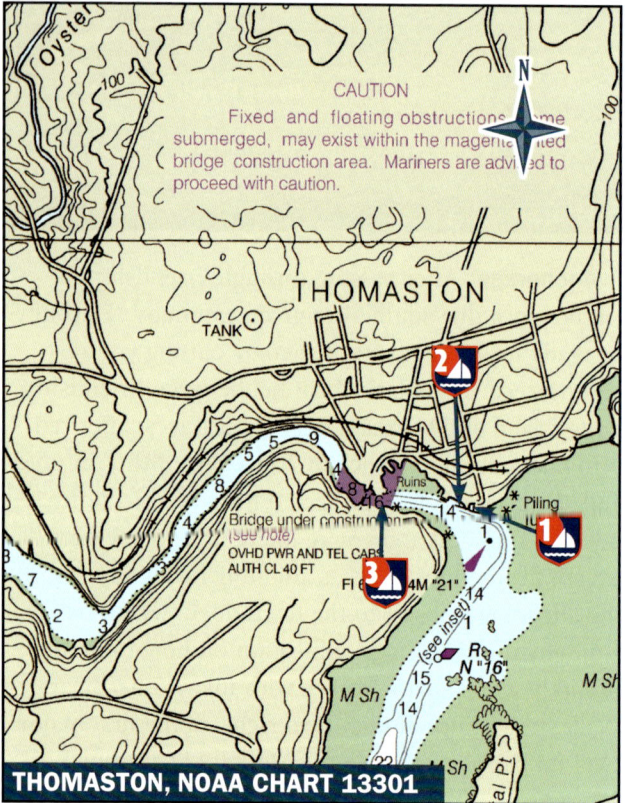

THOMASTON		Dockage					Supplies		Services				
1. Lyman-Morse Boatbuilding	(207) 354-6904	150	16/	6/10	12.0/10.0	F	GD	M	HEP	L110,C	30/100	CLS	P	GR
2. Thomaston Town Landing	(207) 354-6107	70	/	/3	7.0/8.0			IM					GR
3. Jeff's Marine Service	(207) 354-8777	35	/	5/20	8.0/9.0			M	HEP		30		GMR
PORT CLYDE													
4. Port Clyde General Store	(207) 372-6543	50	9/	/	/		GD	GIMS					GR

⌨ Internet Access 🛜 Wireless Internet Access ⌨onSpot Dockside WiFi Facility

See WaterwayGuide.com for current rates, fuel prices, website addresses, and other up-to-the-minute information. (Information in the table is provided by the facilities.)

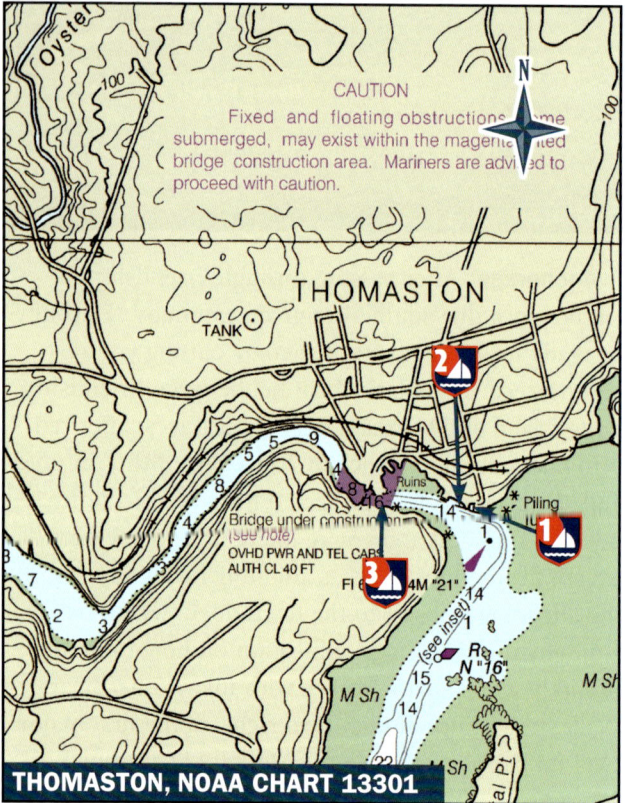

THOMASTON, NOAA CHART 13301

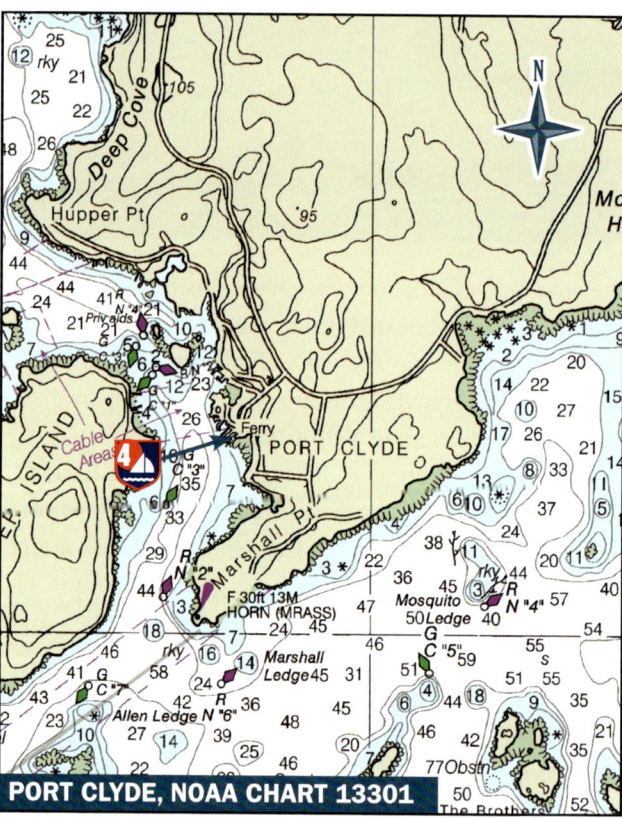

PORT CLYDE, NOAA CHART 13301

offshore island communities seldom visited except by the boats that come to pick up herring and lobsters. Remote and peaceful, these spots have and few visitors and nothing set up for cruisers to do or buy.

St. George River

NAVIGATION: Use NOAA Charts 13288 and 13301. Heading east from Friendship starting south of Garrison Island, honor red nun buoy "4" and turn east to miss the long shoal extending northeast from Morse Island. Make a 290-degree turn around green can buoy "3" and head southwest for red nun buoy

"2" off the end of Gay Island, favoring Morse Island to the northeast. Discussing lobster buoys can become monotonous in Maine, but this passage contains an incredible concentration of them with the additional complication of secondary buoys on short lines in case the primaries are dragged under by the mix of extreme tides and currents. Continue past Gay Island, leave the southern tip well to the north and then look for green can buoy "1" marking Goose Rock Ledge. Steer northeast leaving that mark well to your north and then work your way up the St. George River.

Several easy, attractive miles upriver at the head of navigation on the St. George River is historic

Port Clyde

Hupper Island

Thomaston, where large, beautiful vessels are still built as they have been for decades. The major tourist attraction at Thomaston on the St. George River is the restored Montpelier, home of Gen. Henry Knox, fellow campaigner of George Washington and the nation's first Secretary of War. The General Henry Knox Museum (corner of U.S. Rte. 1 and Maine Rte. 131, 207-354-8062) offers a window into real lives of the past. Within a few blocks are several churches, banks and a public library. Epifanes North America (70 Water St., 207-354-0804) has a beautiful office with a spectacular view and welcomes visitors curious about these high-quality paints and varnishes.

Dockage: Up the river at Thomaston, you will find several established boat yards but few transient slips. Thomaston Town Landing has just three slips so call ahead.

Anchorage: Maple Juice Cove, about halfway up on the west side of the river, has excellent protection and good holding in mud with 8 to 14 feet MLW. Turkey Cove on the east side of the river is more exposed and can be bumpy in southwest winds. Both provide protection and easy entrance but have no facilities. Point Pleasant Gut to the south has 12 to 16 feet MLW and good holding. It is somewhat exposed to the east.

Port Clyde

Once called Herring Gut, Port Clyde lies between Marshall Point and Hupper Island, close to the west-east route, east of the entrance to the St. George River. Widely used by fishers and boaters as a harbor of refuge, it is the home port of the Monhegan Boat Line passenger ferry and always busy with lobster boats. A general store, restaurants and ice cream provide for the body while the many art galleries fill more esoteric needs.

NAVIGATION: Use NOAA Charts 13288 and 13301. Port Clyde's northern entrance between Hupper Island and a ledge off Hupper Point is tricky and the chart shows 5- to 6-foot MLW depths at points. Reports of 8-foot MLW depths where the chart calls for 2 feet MLW might tempt a boater but ease in unless the tide is high. The southern entrance is easier, well marked and wide open.

Moorings: Ask about moorings at the Port Clyde General Store wharf, where you can also get fuel but not a shower. A convenient launch ramp is nearby.

Anchorage: North of Hupper Island there is a deep-water anchorage with protection from the southern rollers. It is open to the northwest but the holding is deep mud in 21 feet MLW. The anchorage right

GOIN' ASHORE

MONHEGAN ISLAND, ME

Monhegan is the most famous island in Maine, due to the art of George Bellows, Edward Hopper, Rockwell Kent, Jamie Wyeth and many others who have been drawn to paint its dramatic cliffs, which are the highest on the New England coast. However, Mainers know the island as a fiercely independent yet strongly communal place, where crucial decisions are made at the Stanley's fish house just as they have been since the 1780s. One case in point was the unusual, perhaps even unique, decision taken by the island's lobstermen to adopt a 600-trap limit voluntarily when most folks were fishing 1200 or more. The year was 1974, and this wasn't the first sustainability initiative from the islanders. In the 1940s, Dwight Stanley used the power of his fish house to convince the others to free undersized lobsters and the proprietors of the island store, Doug and Harry Odom, refused to sell to the only islander who

balked. Their demonstrated ability to work together for the greater good, plus a whole lot of stubborn persistence with the state legislature, won them the legal right to be a "locally managed subzone" of the lobster fishery.

ATTRACTIONS

Monhegan is imminently walkable: 1.4 miles long and 0.7 miles wide. It's only 10 miles off the coast of Maine and naturalists, birdwatchers, and hikers flock to the island just like the 200 species of birds passing along the North Atlantic flyway who stop to feast on the more than 600 varieties of wildflowers. Over 350 acres of the island are privately owned by a non-profit organization first developed in 1954 by the two biggest landowners of the day: Sherman Stanley (yes, another Stanley) and Ted Edison, son of Thomas Edison. Monhegan Associates has protected the famous cliffs from development, while also building community and opportunity for the year-round islanders. Around 9 miles of official trails fan out from the village, and there is around 17 miles of walking area total. No wheels

Monhegan Island

of any sort are allowed past the fire trails, so be prepared carry children if they get tuckered out.

Awe-inspiring walks, inns, shopping, an artists' colony, museum and swimming beach that provide much to do. Aside from exceptional hiking, views of rustic fishing sheds and studio-browsing ashore, few amenities are available. The Monhegan Associates Trail Map, available for a small charge at the inns and most shops, is invaluable for those hoping to sort out the island's maze of marked and highly scenic trails. If you decide to use the online version, download it to your phone so you don't lose it along with your signal.

"Main Street" on Monhegan is actually a dirt road that connects most of the inns, restaurants, galleries and other businesses on the island. After leaving the studio-dotted main road, a walk along the island's rocky perimeter will almost as inevitably turn up flocks of eiders as it will breathtaking seascapes. The Monhegan Museum (Light House Hill Rd., 207-596-7003), preserving artifacts and memorabilia from the island's unique history, is located in the lightkeeper's house overlooking the harbor. The light tower is open for weekly tours. The museum houses a tremendous art collection including works by Rockwell Kent, George Bellows, Robert Henri, Andrew Wyeth and many more.

SHOPPING
L. Brackett & Son is the local grocery store that also sells breakfast and lunch, donuts, beer and wine, plus locally grown produce. Black Duck Emporium (5 Oceanside Dr., 207-596-7672), located at village center next to the Post Office, is known for its daily baked goods, espresso, cappuccino and teas. Fish House Fish Market, on Fish Beach just off Main St., has fresh fish, lobster, stews, chowders and lobster rolls.

> **Note:** Monhegan Island residents are dedicated to the preservation of their island environment and are especially concerned about the hazard of fire. As a result, most areas outside the village, including the rocks and cliffs, are off-limits to both smoking and outdoor fires.
>
>

off Port Clyde is even deeper at 25 feet MLW and is both open to southern weather and somewhat rolly. Remember, these low-water depths mean 30 to 40 feet at high tide. Use appropriate scope for your tackle and the weather.

Georges Islands
In this seemingly remote fishing outpost, you can feel like you have truly arrived Down East. The few structures are ramshackle but businesslike, and the docks are mounted on stripped fir tree poles at an impressive height. The tidal currents are fierce here.

Allen Island is privately owned and is developed only to the extent of an attractive house, barn and outbuilding complex for an experimental sheep ranching operation. Dogs are not allowed on Allen Island. Lobstering activity starts well before dawn on Benner Island with harrumphing engines joining the bleating of the lambs in this otherwise idyllic setting. Directly to the east, Burnt Island has a scallop-shaped harbor fashioned by Burnt Island's northern beach and Little Burnt Island to the northwest.

Anchorage: Between Benner and Allen Islands, you can anchor in the protected Georges Harbor, following the tradition set by English explorer George Waymouth in 1605 aboard the *Archangel* He hit Monhegan first but moved to this spot for a calmer, more secure anchorage. There is at least 7 feet MLW with good holding in sand and rock. Burnt Island provides good protection from the prevailing southwesterlies. The holding is good here in at least 7 feet MLW with a sand bottom but this location is quite exposed to winds shifting east and north.

Side Trip: Monhegan Island
Long a favorite retreat for artists and writers, Monhegan Island is far enough off the beaten path to remain relatively undisturbed by tourism and commercial development. Though it is only 9 miles southwest of the ferry landing in Port Clyde and little more than a dozen miles from the moorings at Tenants Harbor, the island never seems to attract more than a few sailors and a scattering of rough-clad day hikers who quickly blend in with the island's fishers and summer resident painters. They disappear along the island's 17 miles of mapped trails to imposing outlooks and quiet glens, or they are off to visit the rustic studios of some 20 professional artists who regularly display their works here.

Penobscot Bay, ME

		Largest Vessel Accomodated	VHF Channel Monitored / Working	Approach / Dockside Depth (reported)	Transient Slips / Total Slips	Floating Docks	Groceries, Ice, Marine Supplies, Snacks	Gas / Diesel	Repairs: Hull, Engine, Propeller	Lift (tonnage), Crane, Rail	Min / Max Amps	Courtesy Car, Laundry, Pool, Showers	Pump-Out Station	Nearby: Grocery Store, Motel, Restaurant
TENANTS HARBOR				**Dockage**				**Supplies**			**Services**			
1. Tenants Harbor Town Dock	(207) 372-6363	40	16/11	/	15.0/3.0									GMR
2. Tenants Harbor Boat Yard 🖥 📶	(207) 372-8063	170	9/68	/	7.0/7.0	F	GD	IM	HEP	L25,R	30/50	S	P	GMR
SPRUCE HEAD														
3. Spruce Head Marine	(207) 594-7545	38	16/	/	/			GM	HEP	L20,C				GMR

🖥 Internet Access   📶 Wireless Internet Access   🔵onSpot Dockside WiFi Facility

See WaterwayGuide.com for current rates, fuel prices, website addresses, and other up-to-the-minute information. (Information in the table is provided by the facilities.)

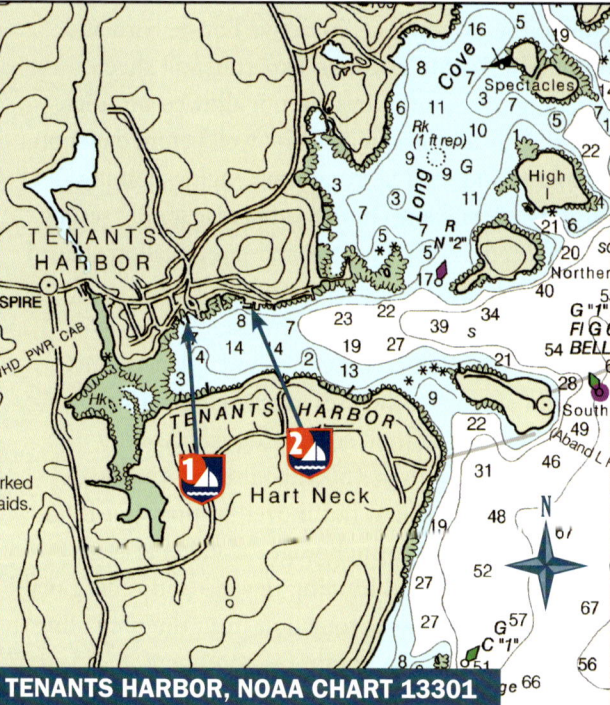

TENANTS HARBOR, NOAA CHART 13301

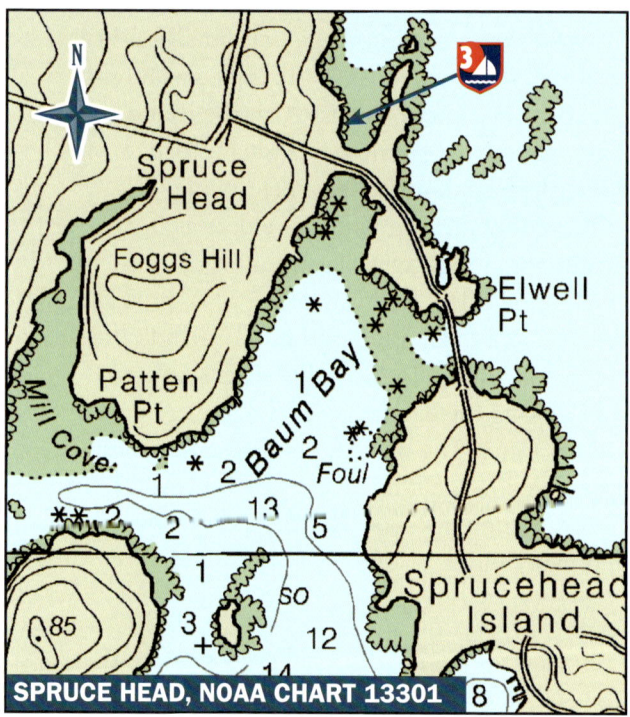

SPRUCE HEAD, NOAA CHART 13301   8

The tranquil beauty of the place, both natural and manmade, has a haunting quality that begs an early return. A passion for nature is so intrinsic to the island itself that the sign over a local store's newspaper rack reads: "If You Cannot Enjoy the Natural Beauty of this Place Without the New York Times, the Boat Leaves at 12:30 p.m. and 4:30 p.m. Have a Happy Crossing." One might add that if you need to drive in order to get around…well, you know when the boat leaves.

If you happen to be making the trip in June, stop by Eastern Egg Rock to (respectfully) see the Atlantic Puffins who breed there on the west side.

NAVIGATION: Use NOAA Charts 13288 and 13301. The island is easily approached from any direction with relatively few obstructions. From sea, Monhegan's powerful light (flashing every 15 seconds, 178 feet

above sea level) is visible for many miles and is an important landmark for those making overnight crossings from southern New England or farther south. Monhegan Light, supplemented by the horn on immediately adjacent Manana Island, will guide you directly into the open entrance of Monhegan Harbor. From Sheepscot Bay to the west or from Muscongus Bay to the north, care must be taken to avoid the shallow ledges surrounding Duck Rocks (south of flashing green bell buoy "5"). Harbor entry can be made from the south between Monhegan and Manana Islands.

Dockage/Moorings: Tie-ups are possible for up to 30 minutes at the town dock but your vessel must remain attended. Stand clear for the arrival or departure of the daily ferries. (Typically, they arrive late morning and depart in the afternoon.) For an overnight stay, it is best to arrange for a mooring from the Monhegan harbormaster, who is usually available at the fish shack next to Fish Beach (second beach down from the town dock). You can try to hail him on VHF Channel 19A or call 207-594-9342. One of the limited private moorings off the town beach may be available without charge or at a small fee. Otherwise, after the ferryboats have left for the day, visitors may tie up on any of their four heavy-tackle mooring balls (north of the town dock) until the next day's ferry arrivals.

Anchorage: Anchoring is not recommended in the harbor's deceptive mix of sand and rocks. It looks secure but is not. Anchored boats regularly are dragged away by swift tidal currents. In settled weather locals suggest that a hook can be set securely in Deadman Cove. This location requires deep water scope and a strong pulling arm for the dinghy, but it offers fair holding in grass and rock.

It is possible to tether a dinghy to the town pier next to the vertical ladder but the rapid rise and fall of a substantial tide makes landing here undesirable for a visit of more than a few minutes. The better alternative is at Fish Beach. Even here, a long dinghy tether secured to a location above the high-water mark will be required.

■ MUSCLE RIDGE CHANNEL TO PENOBSCOT BAY

North and east of Monhegan Island, the mouth of Penobscot Bay welcomes waterborne pilgrims to this sailor's mecca. Although exposed to an easterly blow, Tenants Harbor is the first of several fine shelters on the course ascending the bay. Much as pleasure-boaters enjoy the area, it's also crucial to the commercial fishing industry. Give a friendly wave to the folks feeding us all.

Northeast of Tenants Harbor, Muscle Ridge Channel offers an inside passage to Rockland. Protected from the open sea by a string of outlying islands, it is studded with well-marked rocks and ledges that should present no problem in good visibility, and numerous bights and coves provide shelter when needed.

Tenants Harbor

Tenants Harbor

NAVIGATION: Use NOAA Charts 13301 and 13302. About 4 miles up the coast, Tenants Harbor is a good refuge in fog or heavy weather and its approach is well marked and unobstructed. An unusual-looking abandoned lighthouse and attendant buildings mark the approach at the end of Southern Island. If approaching after dark, look for the illuminated flag on the tall flagpole. The nearby flashing green bell buoy "1" should be left to the south as you enter the wide mouth of the harbor. The harbor entrance is deep with no obstructions on the straight course down the center of the harbor channel. Nevertheless, watch carefully to negotiate the minefield of brightly colored and closely spaced lobster buoys and toggles throughout the channel.

Muscle Ridge Channel begins with Whitehead Light, a gray tower with a green occulting light (4 seconds on and a blink off) but take care with South Breaker, which is marked with bell buoy "SB." After green can buoy "3" turn west if visiting the large, well-marked Seal Harbor between Whitehead Island and Sprucehead Island. The green-red-green Burnt Island Ledge buoy shows green for the main channel (Muscle Ridge) and red for the Seal Harbor entrance. The channel is well provided with reds and greens but two sets stand out that require extra care. South of Ash Island, an un-numbered red-green-red nun marks the Upper Gangway Ledge, while green can buoy "15" shows rocks off Ash Island. Grindstone Ledge is marked by green can buoy "21" and red nun buoy "22" to keep cruisers off shallow rocks to either side.

Dockage/Moorings: The Tenants Harbor town dock is a U-shaped affair with plenty of dinghy room inside the "U" leaving the face dock for larger vessels. Expect 3 feet MLW here with a 9-foot tidal range. The town moorings in the inner harbor are round and white with a blue band marked "Rental" and a helpful pick-up wand. The public landing and dinghy dock are at the head of the harbor to the north. Ice and other supplies are available adjacent to the public wharf and a motel and restaurants are right nearby. The town services trash barrels placed at the head of the dock ramp.

Tenants Harbor Boat Yard has moorings available to transient boaters. The actual rental moorings may be difficult to distinguish from lobster buoys. Colors change somewhat with the seasons so look closely to distinguish the rental moorings from the lobster buoys. At the top of the gentle rise above the public landing, turn right on Tenants Harbor's Main Street for a one-block walk to Tenants Harbor General Store (16 Main St., 207-372-6311). This old-fashioned country store offers a good selection of fresh fruits, veggies and meats, general groceries, ice, beer, wine, fresh lobster rolls and seafood. The Post Office and a laundry are just up the street.

Anchorage: Anchoring is no longer allowed in Tenants Harbor. Boats may anchor in the outer harbor, however, in the charted 13-foot MLW area on the south side, inshore from Southern Island. Another anchorage is found in Long Cove, just north of red nun buoy "2" marking the channel west of Northern Island, although it is open to the southwest and has a ledge at the entrance. Long Cove can accommodate vessels but is a distance from village amenities.

On the eastern side of Muscle Ridge Channel, High Island and Dix Island are the largest of a group of islands providing good anchorage and shelter. The entrance going east is straightforward. Stay well north of red nun buoy "10" and well south of red daybeacon "12." Pilot a center course between Oak Island to the south and Little Green Island to the north. Snug up to a windward shoreline to find protection from all but northwesterly winds. The anchorage has 8- to 20-foot

MLW depths but be mindful of the charted 3-foot MLW shoal between High and Little Green Islands.

> In the late 19th century, as many as 2,000 quarrymen worked at Dix Island. Today their houses and the opera house are gone. The private association that now owns Dix Island permits cruising visitors ashore but prohibits littering, fires or camping and swimming in the quarries.

Side Trip: Matinicus Island

Remote Matinicus Island is accessible by ferry from Rockland, located 20 miles away. Matinicus shares with Vinalhaven some of the richest lobstering bottom in the world and has been taking full advantage of them for ages. In the mid-1800s, there were 15 families living on the island and 22 individual lobster boat owners.

The quintessential offshore Maine fishing and farming community, Matinicus Island is not well organized for tourists and visiting cruisers. It is perhaps because of this that the island is such a special place to visit. Here, the stylistic Down East tall-timbered waterfront is matched by classic New England farmsteads, some still delivering summer produce to the semi-weekly Farmers' Markets (check signs ashore for times and locations). On a clear day, a leisurely walk around the island's level roadways offers 19th-century vistas and profound seascapes at every turn.

NAVIGATION: Use NOAA Charts 13302 and 13303. Because of numerous islets and ledges surrounding the entrance, Matinicus Harbor is best approached in fair weather and good visibility. From the north stand east of Zypher Rock, marked by flashing green buoy "5," are No Mans Land, The Barrel (just awash and charted but not marked by a navigational aid) and Harbor Ledge (immediately north of the red-and-green entrance bell buoy). From the south leave Ragged Island and its surrounding islets to the west, making passage toward the entrance bell just west of West Black Ledge. Leave the south end of Wheaton Island well to south to avoid the submerged rocks there. When entering the harbor, simply keep to the Matinicus shore on entry to avoid the shallows on the Wheaton side and the center harbor reef.

Moorings/Anchorage: As you enter the harbor limited anchorage (room for only a few boats) is located just inside the lee of Wheaton Island to the south in 10 to 20 feet MLW. The moorings situated farther to the south in the area between Wheaton Island and Matinicus Island are attached to the bottom via a series of underwater cables, which will foul an anchor. Reportedly, one or two of these moorings may be available for overnight rental; ask around at the wharf. Do not attempt to claim the apparently empty area in the center of the harbor. It's empty because Indian Ledge looms menacingly near the surface at low water.

Additional calm-weather anchorage is available in Old Cove, just south of the main harbor. Entrance to Old Cove is unencumbered (except for the rocky ledge stringing southward of Wheaton Island) and holding is secure in sand with 15 feet MLW. Enter the cove at dead center making certain to clear the cut between Wheaton and Matinicus Islands with enough distance to accommodate adequate rode scope without blocking the channel.

Intrepid (and substantial) lobster boats blast through the narrow and not altogether deep passage between the main harbor and Old Cove frequently, often at night, on any tide. This and the ocean swells will make certain that you are rocked asleep (or awake). Nevertheless, the cut is convenient for a dinghy trip to the town wharf inside the main harbor. Tie the dinghy up to the side of the steel ladder on the town wharf, allowing enough painter length for the 9-foot tidal range and space for transport boats that also make the ladder their destination.

■ NEXT STOP

The last leg of this Down East journey takes the adventuresome boater from Rockland in Penobscot Bay to the Canadian border and includes some of the most pristine and breathtaking scenery in the U.S. In the case of the Maine cruise, the best is yet to come.

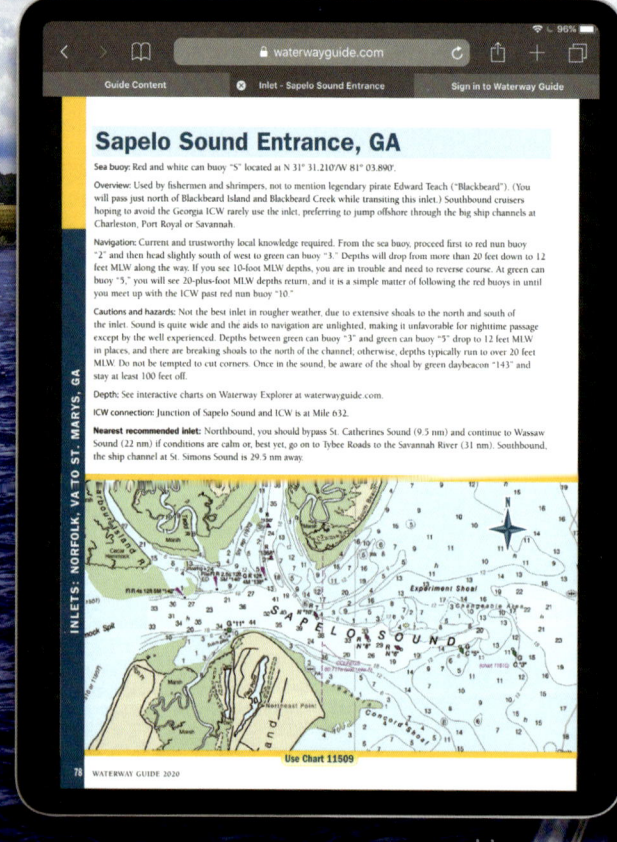

Penobscot Bay & Down East Maine

Fifteen miles south of Vinalhaven Island, the imposing 90-foot lighthouse on Matinicus Rock guides offshore mariners into Penobscot Bay. The largest of Maine's coastal indentations, Penobscot Bay is 20 miles wide and nearly 30 miles long. This watery basin of flooded mountain range is rimmed by Camden Hills and Mount Battie to the west and Blue Hill and Cadillac Mountain to the east. Large and small islands–dominated by Islesboro to the north with North Haven Island and Vinalhaven Island to the south–separates East and West Penobscot Bays and those two bays are subdivided into a welter of smaller bodies of water with their own characters. Deer Isle and Isle au Haut mark Penobscot Bay's eastern boundary. Justifiably, Penobscot Bay is the most popular cruising destination in Maine.

■ PENOBSCOT BAY & RIVER

West Penobscot Bay, lying between the mainland and the islands, has few offshore rocks and ledges and is easy to navigate in the absence of fog. As fog descends, bring to bear all your navigational skills and equipment: GPS, radar, AIS, compass, charts, fog horn and bell. Navigation must be precise and buoys must be strictly followed but shoaling isn't a serious factor

Rockland Harbor, ME

ROCKLAND		Dockage					Supplies			Services			
		Largest Vessel Accomodated	VHF Channel Monitored / Working	Transient Slips / Total Slips	Approach / Dockside Depth (reported)	Floating Docks	Gas / Diesel	Groceries, Ice, Marine Supplies, Snacks	Repairs: Hull, Engine, Propeller	Lift (tonnage), Crane, Rail	Courtesy Car, Laundry, Pool, Showers	Min / Max Amps	Pump-Out Station	Nearby: Grocery Store, Motel, Restaurant
1. Rockland Public Landing ⌨ WiFi	(207) 594-0312	95	16/11	15/15	12.0/10.0	F		I			50	LS	P	GMR
2. Safe Harbor Rockland ⌨ WiFi	(207) 596-0082	200	16/	20/34	12.0/12.0	F		IM	HEP		15/100	CLS	P	GMR
3. Landings Restaurant & Marina ⌨ WiFi	(207) 596-6573	200	9/11	12/72	25.0/12.0	F	GD	IM			30/100	LS	P	GMR
4. Journey's End Marina ⌨ WiFi	(207) 594-0400	275	16/9	10/85	20.0/14.0		GD	IM	HEP	L75,C	30/100	LS	P.	GMR
5. Knight Marine Service WiFi	(207) 594-4068	82	9/	8/10	12.0/12.0	F	GD	IMS	HEP	L35,C	30	LS		GMR

⌨ Internet Access   WiFi Wireless Internet Access   ⬤onSpot Dockside WiFi Facility

See WaterwayGuide.com for current rates, fuel prices, website addresses, and other up-to-the-minute information. (Information in the table is provided by the facilities.)

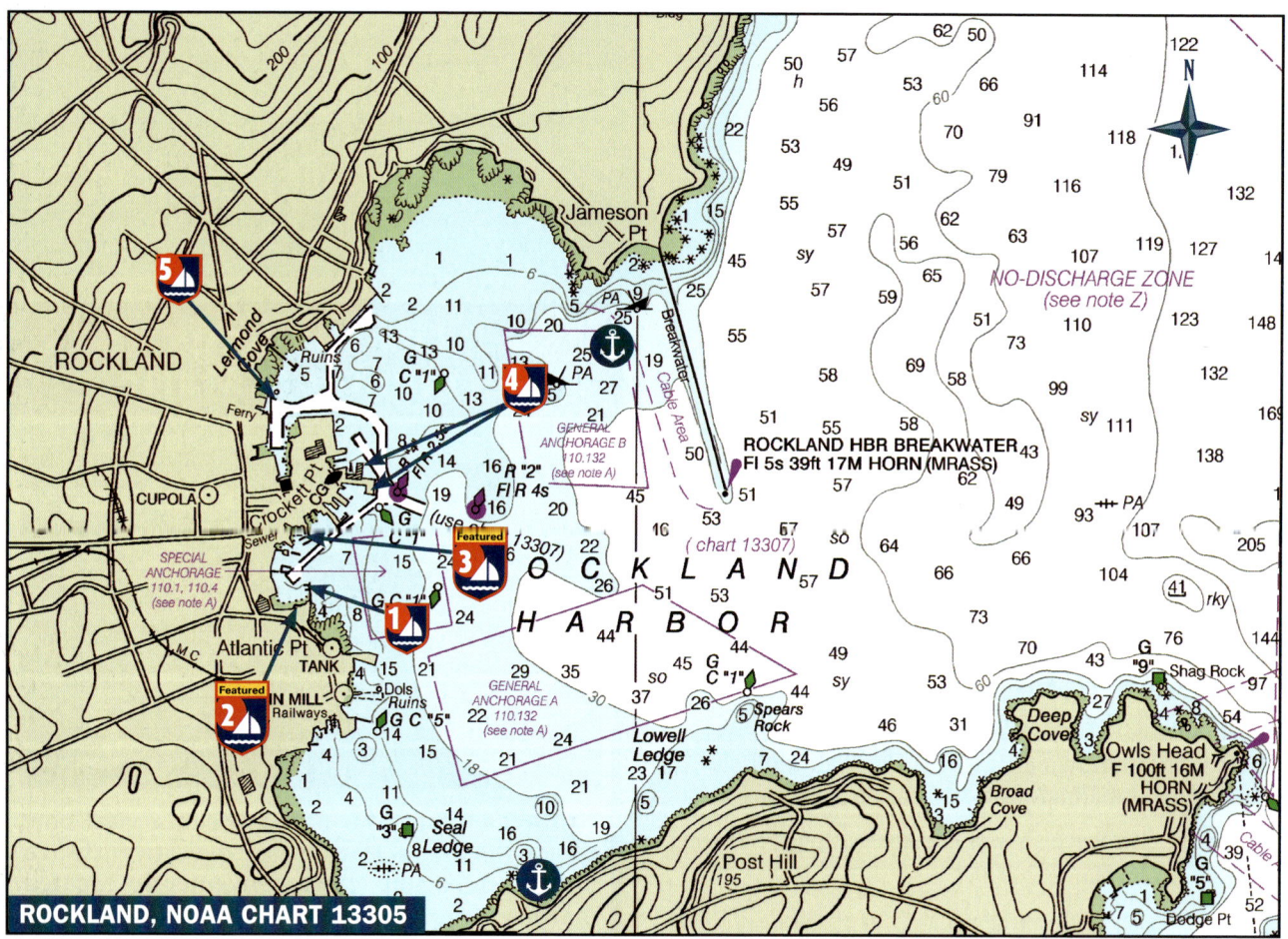

ROCKLAND, NOAA CHART 13305

and charts change slowly. Sand- and mud-accustomed mariners will find the stakes of a grounding higher than in southern cruising grounds but visitors from the Puget Sound or northeastern Europe will find themselves right at home.

Rockland Harbor

Rockland's large, open, easy-access harbor is ringed by all the services one would expect from a major recreational boating center including marinas with slips and moorings. Still, if there is a serious blow rolling in, cruisers and any nearby commercial vessels head for more protected waters at the northern end of the bay or out to the numerous island coves and harbors. In the absence of fog, superb views of the Camden Hills to the north are guaranteed. Rockland is famous for having a wonderful selection of fine restaurants representing a globally eclectic array of choices within a walk of the dinghy dock.

Small Owls Head Harbor south of Rockland is home

Rockport & Camden Harbors, ME

		Largest Vessel Accomodated	VHF Channel Monitored/ Working	Approach / Dockside Depth (reported)	Transient Slips / Total Slips	Floating Docks	Groceries, Ice, Marine Supplies, Snacks	Gas / Diesel	Repairs: Hull, Engine, Propeller	Lift (tonnage), Crane, Rail	Courtesy Car, Laundry, Pool, Showers	Min / Max Amps	Pump-Out Station	Nearby: Grocery Store, Motel, Restaurant
ROCKPORT				**Dockage**				**Supplies**			**Services**			
1. Rockport Marine Inc. WiFi	(207) 236-9651	105	/	5/5	20.0/10.0	F	GD	I		HEP	L50,C	50		R
CAMDEN														
2. Camden Yacht Club	(207) 236-3014	42	68/68	/3	12.0/9.0			I						GMR
3. Camden Harbormaster	(207) 236-7969	160	16/	10/	10.0/10.0	F						30/100		GMR
4. Lyman-Morse at Wayfarer ▭ WiFi	(207) 236-4378	200	71/	37/37	12.0/14.0	F	GD	GIMS		HEP	L110,C	30/100	CLS	P	GMR

▭ Internet Access   WiFi Wireless Internet Access   ☀onSpot Dockside WiFi Facility
See WaterwayGuide.com for current rates, fuel prices, website addresses, and other up-to-the-minute information. (Information in the table is provided by the facilities.)

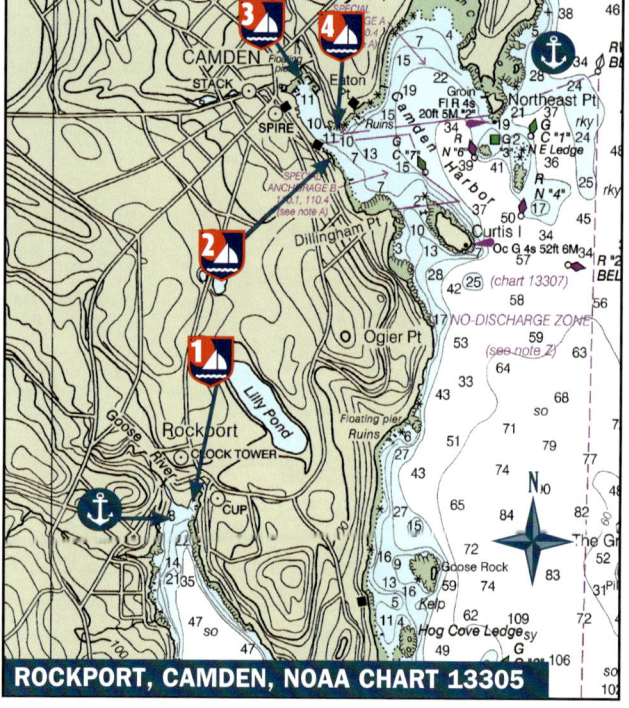

ROCKPORT, CAMDEN, NOAA CHART 13305

to a substantial lobstering fleet. Owls Head Lighthouse, an active aid to navigation at the entrance of Rockland Harbor, is worth a visit.

NAVIGATION: Use NOAA Charts 13302, 13305 and 13307. After Muscle Ridge Channel passes between Ash Island and Fisherman Island, it jogs east. If your destination is Owls Head, the northern route begins at the green-red-green can over Emery Ledge. There is no need to deflect west toward green daybeacon "1" if continuing. Red nun buoy "4" is the better navigational aid to aim for.

Around the bold, jutting headland of Owls Head with its picturesque lighthouse is Rockland Harbor. Easily approached from any direction, the harbor is protected from northeasterly weather by a 4,346-foot granite

breakwater. The southern half of the harbor is wide open to a severe easterly blow but quite comfortable in summer's prevailing southerwesterlies. A 5-second flashing light marks the end of the breakwater, which should be left to the north, with a horn mounted on a 39-foot tower. Fully 0.5 mile south, green can buoy "1" marks Spears Rock off the north tip of Battery Point.

Dockage/Moorings: For a town mooring (almost always available), call the Rockland harbormaster on VHF Channel 09 or 11. The harbormaster's office is at the end of the pier left of the Coast Guard station.

The private, gated facility of Yachting Solutions Boat Basin (Safe Harbor Rockland) offers friendly service and full amenities for boats to 250 feet. From brokerage to restorations and customizations, full yard services and an ever-expanding marina, this facility offers a comprehensive experience. From here you can enjoy a few leisurely hours at a private sandy beach or take an easy stroll along the boardwalk to downtown Rockland, where you will find a plethora of shops, galleries, restaurants and museums. Courtesy vehicles are available for touring nearby Rockport and Camden.

Landings Restaurant & Marina, just east of the public landing, has slips and moorings and a gas and diesel fuel barge with high-speed pumps. Boater-friendly amenities include laundry and an on-site chandlery. Several dinghy docks are available for the convenience of mooring tenants and visitors. Be sure to stop in the office when you make landfall.

Anchorage: As in many popular harbors, the number of moorings has increased dramatically over the past decade but ample anchorage room and depth is generally available in any of the designated anchorage areas. These areas, however, put the boater a healthy row from the town pier's dinghy dock, which sometimes

GOIN' ASHORE

ROCKLAND, ME

A jaunt along Harbor Walk, a public footpath hugging Rockland's historic waterfront, provides beautiful harbor vistas. Visit the Chamber of Commerce (1 Park Dr., 207-596-0376) to net a map and a story or two, since you'll want to stop there anyway. It's located just off Main Street in the info-packed home of the Maine Discovery Center, a first-class visitor center with museum exhibits and travel information, and the Maine Lighthouse Museum.

SERVICES

1. Rockland Chamber of Commerce/Maine Lighthouse Museum

Building that houses both a first-class visitor center and two museums at 1 Park Dr. The Maine Lighthouse Museum (207-594-3301) is home to the largest collection of Fresnel lighthouse lenses in the U.S., among other fascinating artifacts. The lower level of the building houses the Rockland Historical Society with a wonderful museum of items from the lime industry, the shipbuilding industry, the fishing industry and other exciting aspects of the history of Rockland, including Civil War memorabilia. Before you leave the Chamber of Commerce building, pick up a map for the Harbor Walk, a public footpath hugging Rockland's historic waterfront (207-596-0376).

2. Rockland Post Office
21 Limerock St., Ste. 9998 (207-596-6461)

3. Rockland Public Library
80 Union St. #2925 (207-594-0310)

ATTRACTIONS

4. Farnsworth Art Museum
Paintings and sculptures by renowned American artists with Maine connections, most notably the Wyeths at 16 Museum St. (207-596-6457).

SHOPPING

5. Hamilton Marine
Largest marine retailer north of Boston with an extensive selection of hardware at 20 Park Dr. (207-594-8181). Stock includes some iconic Mainer items you may have begun to envy on your travels, such as a canvas gunwale guard for your dinghy.

MARINAS

6. Journey's End Marina
120 Tillson Ave. #100 (207-594-0400)

7. Landings Marina
5 Park Dr. (207-594-4899)

8. Rockland Yacht Club
1 Harbor Park (207-233-2800)

9. Safe Harbor Rockland
60 Ocean St. (207-596-0082)

Islesboro Island, ME

DARK HARBOR		VHF Channel Monitored / Working	Largest Vessel Accomodated	Dockage				Supplies				Services			
				Approach / Dockside Depth (reported)	Transient Slips / Total Slips	Floating Docks	Gas / Diesel	Groceries, Ice, Marine Supplies, Snacks	Repairs: Hull, Engine, Propeller	Lift (tonnage), Crane, Rail	Courtesy Car, Laundry, Pool, Showers	Min / Max Amps	Pump-Out Station	Nearby: Grocery Store, Motel, Restaurant	
1. Dark Harbor Boat Yard	(207) 734-2246	100	9/11	/	14.0/6.0		GD	IMS	HE	L,C,R			LS		
2. Pendleton Yacht Yard	(207) 734-6728		9/	/	5.0/5.0		GD	IM	HEP	L15,C					

🖳 Internet Access 📶 Wireless Internet Access 📶onSpot Dockside WiFi Facility
See WaterwayGuide.com for current rates, fuel prices, website addresses, and other up-to-the-minute information. (Information in the table is provided by the facilities.)

DARK HARBOR, NOAA CHART 13302

It is difficult not to notice the lime kilns here that were commercially critical to the area a century ago. You may also see the diminutive wood-fired loco-motive that hauled lime and cordwood to the kilns.

NAVIGATION: Use NOAA Charts 13302, 13305 and 13307. Rockport Harbor is easy to enter, deep almost to the shore and free of ledges and boulders. The exception is Porterfield Ledge at the center of the entrance, marked by a great pillar of granite blocks topped by a green-and-white daybeacon. Note that the ledge extends farther west than might appear on the large-scale chart. Take care when entering from the north and east not to cut corners when rounding Indian Island. A submerged reef extends to the south of the island. Leave the 25-foot-high, flashing red six-second light "2" at Lowell Rock to the east.

Dockage/Moorings: Rockport Marine Inc. usually has slips and moorings available and sells gas and diesel fuel. The marina does not monitor the radio or provide launch service so pick up a mooring pennant from one of the numbered white buoys then dinghy in to complete your arrangements. The Rockport Marine Park on the northwestern side of the inner harbor, just west of the boat club, has two large floats with 6 feet MLW to accommodate crew changes, trips to replenish the larder and refilling of water tanks. If space permits, overnight tie-ups are sometimes possible. Contact the Rockport Harbormaster on VHF Channel 16 for availability.

Anchorage: You can anchor in 17 to 25 feet MLW in the outer Rockport Harbor if space is available but this location will require long dinghy rides ashore. The inner harbor has 9 to 11 feet MLW with good holding in mud, if you can find a space. There is dinghy space behind the fuel dock in the harbor.

has a fee. The most secure anchorages for heavy weather (especially from the east) are located in the extreme northern or southern ends of the harbor. Note that there is a cable area immediately behind the breakwater. Avoid anchoring in this area and be mindful that portions of the breakwater may be submerged at high tide. Watch for shallows and always consider the 10-foot tides in your scoping equations.

Anchoring is possible outside the mooring field at Owls Head Harbor to the south in 15 to 25 feet MLW with good holding and protection

Rockport Harbor

Built on the hills surrounding this harbor 5 miles north of Rockland, protected yet commodious Rockport has become a cruising favorite. The harbor is protected by all but southerly winds and has a full-service marina, public landing and an attractive and busy restaurant serving all your Mainer favorites.

Camden Harbor

At the foot of Mount Battie, Camden is one of Maine's busiest and best-equipped harbors. Camden Harbor is full of boats including the largest coastal schooner fleet in the country, offering week-long and hourly cruises of the spectacular Maine coast.

> This is where the 3-mile-long Megunticook River drops approximately 142 feet and ends in a 25-foot waterfall, which may be rushing or not, depending on the water in the river. The fall can best be seen from Harbor Park or the Camden Public Landing.

NAVIGATION: Use NOAA Charts 13302 and 13305. As you approach from the south, The Graves is marked on its eastern edge by flashing green gong buoy "13" and may be left to either side. If taking the shore side, however, stay well away from the buoy. Camden Harbor is marked by red bell buoy "2" located about 600 yards from the accessible southeastern entrance. Leave Curtis Island, identified by an occulting 53-foot-high green light, to the south and west while honoring the straight line between red nun buoys "4" and "6."

The northeastern approach is far narrower, although quite well marked by the red-and-white bell buoy "CH" located just less than 0.5 mile east-northeast off Northeast Point then by a 20-foot-high flashing red "2" on the point. The channel's south edge, created by the Northeast Ledge, is marked by green can buoy "1" then green daybeacon "3."

Dockage/Moorings: Transients are welcome at the Camden Yacht Club's dock for short (20-minute) tie-ups for crew changes and to take on water or drop off trash. The club also provides harbor launch services. Willey Wharf has 80 feet of dock space and one guest float in the inner harbor. The Camden Harbormaster can help you find a slip as well. Across the harbor, on Eaton Point, the Camden Town Dock has 10-foot MLW dockside depths. Lyman-Morse at Wayfarer has slips and moorings. They sell gasoline and diesel at the fuel dock and have a well-stocked chandlery. During July and August, cruisers are advised to call in advance to reserve dockage.

Anchorage: The only anchorage available in Camden is outside the mooring field to the west of the Inner Ledges in 20 to 30 feet MLW. There is usually plenty of room to anchor here but a long anchor rode is recommended to accommodate a 10-foot tidal range and southern swell.

A visit to nearby Curtis Island to see the lighthouse and walk the island is possible by docking your dinghy on the small beach located on the eastern side of the island; mid-tide is the best time to visit.

Side Trip: Islesboro

A fashionable resort, with grand old estates at Dark Harbor and a busy yachting community, large Islesboro is the heart of a group of islands cutting across Penobscot at mid-bay. The island has regular ferry service to Lincolnville on the mainland north of Camden. A convenient launching ramp is adjacent to the ferry dock.

NAVIGATION: Use NOAA Chart 13302. Gilkey Harbor is easily approached from either north or south. The lovely town of Dark Harbor, on the northeastern side of Seven Hundred Acre Island, is the hub of the most scenic route to northern Penobscot Bay: a rocky through-passage along Islesboro's southern half. Make note that the nuns and cans switch sides after Spruce Island. Do not attempt Bracketts Channel, a privately marked southeastern channel between Islesboro and Job Island. The ledges and current make this narrow channel hazardous unless you know it well.

Moorings: Off the east side of Seven Hundred Acre Island in Cradle Cove, moorings are available from Dark Harbor Boat Yard, which offers water, all fuels and repairs at its floating dock. Pendleton Yacht Yard in Ames Cove (Dark Harbor) has moorings with a dinghy dock that is available 2 hours either side of high tide. They also sell gas and diesel fuel and offer repairs.

At the northern end of the through-passage, opposite Grindel Point, a mariner's park encompasses all of wild, remote Warren Island. Accessible only by boat, uncrowded and a regular port of call for cruising schooners, Warren Island State Park has 10 free moorings for cruising boats. The inner moorings are 150-pound mushrooms, while the two outermost are 1-ton blocks. A dock and float with 4-foot MLW depths and picnic tables are available.

Anchorage: On entry into Cradle Cove mind the private stake-markers identifying the ledges on either side of the wide channel. There is still plenty of room to turn and maneuver. Shielded by northerly necks of Seven Hundred Acre Island, this anchorage affords excellent protection and good holding in 9- to 16-foot

Penobscot Bay & River, ME

WG

	Largest Vessel Accommodated	VHF Channel Monitored / Working	Approach / Dockside Depth (reported)	Transient Slips / Total Slips	Floating Docks	Gas / Diesel	Groceries, Ice, Marine Supplies, Snacks	Repairs: Hull, Engine, Propeller	Lift (tonnage), Crane, Rail	Min / Max Amps	Courtesy Car, Laundry, Pool, Showers	Pump-Out Station	Nearby: Grocery Store, Motel, Restaurant
BELFAST			**Dockage**			**Supplies**			**Services**				
1. Belfast City Landing 💻 WiFi (207) 338-1142	200	16/9	25/25	15.0/13.0	F	GD	I			30/100	S	P	GMR
2. Belfast Boatyard (207) 338-5098	75	9/	2/20	16.0/10.0			M	HEP		30			GMR
3. Belfast Marina & Yacht Club (207) 323-9040		/	/	/			IS				LS		GMR
4. Front Street Shipyard 💻 WiFi (207) 930-3740	200	9/16	15/48	20.0/14.0	F		IMS	HEP	L485,C	30/100	CLS	P	GMR
SEARSPORT HARBOR													
5. Searsport Public Landing (207) 548-2722	60	9/16	/3	11.0/4.5	F								GMR
BUCKSPORT													
6. Bucksport Public Dock / Municipal Marina WiFi (207) 469-5902	300	9/9	4/9	16.0/15.0	F	GD	IMS			30/50	CS	P	GMR
7. Bucksport Marina WiFi (207) 469-5902	40	9/9	/48	19.0/6.0	F	G	IMS			30/50	S	P	GMR
BANGOR													
8. Hamlin's Marina 💻 (207) 907-4385	55	9/	4/20	30.0/8.0	F		IM	HEP	R			P	GR
9. Bangor Landing Waterfront Park (207) 992-4490	165	16/9	/30	16.0/15.0						50	S	P	GMR

💻 Internet Access   WiFi Wireless Internet Access   onSpot Dockside WiFi Facility

See WaterwayGuide.com for current rates, fuel prices, website addresses, and other up-to-the-minute information. (Information in the table is provided by the facilities.)

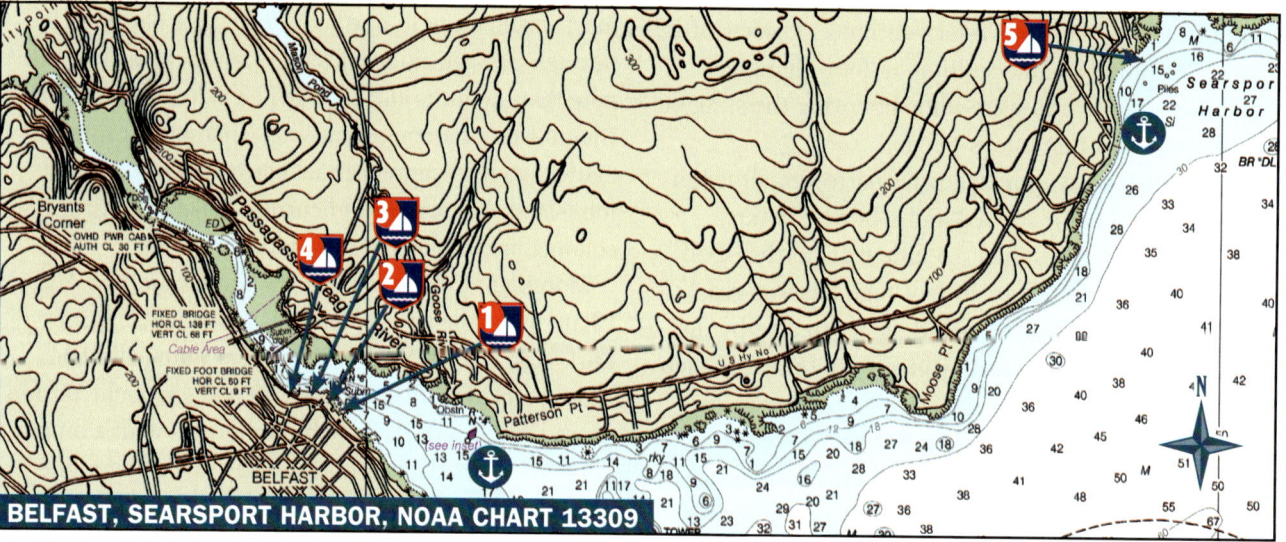

BELFAST, SEARSPORT HARBOR, NOAA CHART 13309

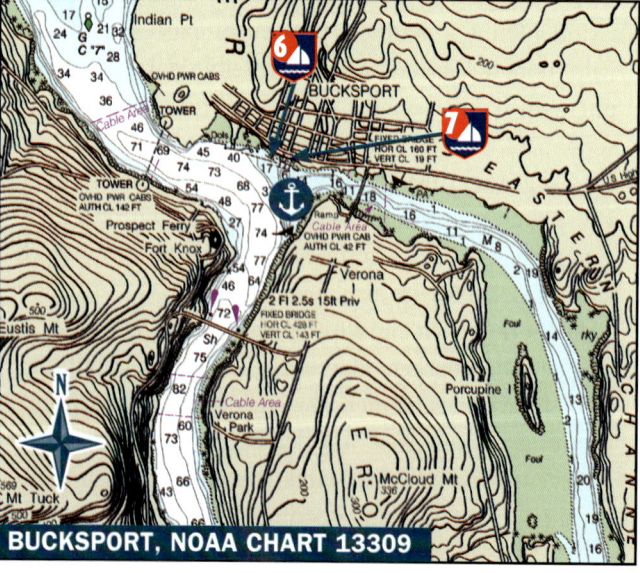

BUCKSPORT, NOAA CHART 13309

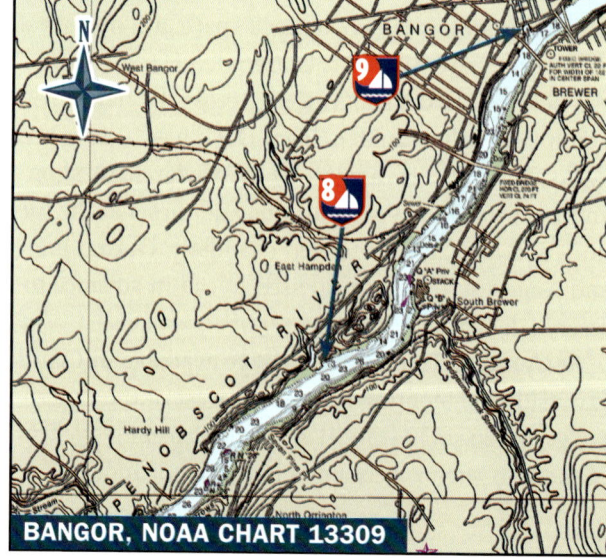

BANGOR, NOAA CHART 13309

MLW depths. Large yachts will anchor there alongside small travelers, making for an amusing line-up at times. To the north, you will find 8 to 24 feet MLW between Warren Island and Spruce Island.

Ames Cove is home to the Tarratine Yacht Club. Moorings may be available here but if not, there is good holding in the cove and the nearly 100-year-old clubhouse offers a pleasant view from the anchorage. Good anchorage in 17- to 28-foot MLW depths may be had to the north in the cove just above Thrumcap Island with good holding in mud. This is somewhat exposed to the north. Sabbathday Harbor on the east side of Islesboro has good holding in 10 to 15 feet MLW with protection from all directions but south.

Belfast Harbor

NAVIGATION: Use NOAA Charts 13302 and 13309. North of Camden, the steep shore is broken by few harbors. Heading north along the coast, the entrance to the Passagassawakeag River is a broad-mouthed funnel. The entrance is marked by Steels Ledge Monument Light, which makes a good radar target and has no other hazards. Belfast Harbor spans the river from bank to bank before the **Belfast Foot Bridge** with 9-foot fixed vertical clearance. Custom boat builder French

& Webb (21 Front St., 207-338-6706), known for their precision joinery, welcomes visitors to their shop bordering the waterfront park.

Dockage/Moorings: Belfast City Landing offers slips for transients, as well as rental moorings. Contact the harbormaster on VHF Channel 09 for a slip or mooring assignment. The WiFi is strong on the docks but still requires a booster to be received at the moorings.

Belfast Boatyard has transient space for boats and is under the management of the nearby Front Street Shipyard, which has slips and moorings. Front Street is also a builder of custom boats and is capable of handling megayachts. Even boaters who don't stay with them should take the short walk down the waterfront to see the enormous lift and the equally enormous boats that require so much hauling power.

Anchorage: Even though the name Belfast means "good anchorage," moorings fill the inner portion of the harbor. You can anchor off the entrance to the river west of Steels Ledge in 11- to 21-foot MLW depths with good holding in mud and rock. Be sure to leave the main channel open for the small cruise ships that dock in town. You can also anchor to the south at Belfast Dam (Browns Head) in 7 to 23 feet MLW.

Belfast Harbor

Searsport

Searsport's Main St. (U.S. Route 1) is about 0.25 mile due north from the docks. Within a few blocks, you'll see a Post Office, a grocery store and a couple of banks. The Penobscot Marine Museum (5 Church St., 207-548-2529), where "Maine and the Sea Make History," is farther along to the east at the end of the business district. The museum's evolving collection of marine paintings, treasures brought home from abroad by local ships years ago, restored 19th-century buildings and re-creations of Searsport life in a bygone era are almost certain to appeal.

About 1 mile farther east on U.S. 1, Hamilton Marine (155 E. Main St., 207-548-6302), the largest marine supplier north of Boston, has marine supplies, gear, equipment, books and charts. This large, family-run operation will special-order parts for rapid delivery but their local-pro selection is vast and worth a look.

NAVIGATION: Use NOAA Chart 13309. Four miles northeast of Belfast the expansive, wide-open harbor of Searsport offers no obstructions on approach and easy shore access. This ancient home to ship captains and flourishing maritime industries is today dominated by a recreational small boat fleet including some very serious anglers.

Dockage/Moorings: The anchorage and mooring field for recreational boats is to the northwest on approaching the wide, scalloped harbor at Searsport. As you approach the recreational fleet, check in with the Searsport Harbormaster (monitoring VHF Channels 09, 10, 71 and 78A) to inquire about the availability of a mooring or for current anchoring instructions. The town mooring (#1, attached to a large granite block) may be available or possibly the museum's large mooring ball (#55, hooked to a 10-ton block) will be unclaimed.

The town dock complex (periodically dredged to 4.5 feet MLW) makes it possible for smaller vessels and those working with the tide to tie up for 2- to 4-hour periods on one of the inner docks. For most visitors it will be more convenient to pull a tender up to one of the floating dinghy landings inside the L-shaped outer dock for the walk to town. (Be sure to note signs with rules for each dock.)

Anchorage: You will most likely be anchoring outside the mooring field in 23- to 32-foot MLW depths with a 9-foot tidal range. Prevailing southwesterlies are tempered by Islesboro Island, yet it is often quite breezy in the afternoon. The accompanying seesaw action of waves over a long fetch regularly sends boats on insufficient scope drifting into the mooring field even though the holding is good. Make sure your anchor is well set and consider being generous with the scope, remembering to factor in the additional depth at high tide. Oil tankers, potato reefers and other large commercial ships dominate the more protected Long Cove beyond Mack Point east of the village.

Bucksport

The Penobscot River is navigable for 25 miles to Bangor but the current flows swiftly at its mouth and must be entered on a rising tide. Expect significant currents. If you made it this far Down East you'll be rewarded with some of the most remarkable scenery and cruising grounds a boater may experience. Slow down and savor every moment as few get to experience the treasures offered by this incredibly diverse bio-region.

The neighboring towns of Bangor and Hampden worked together to develop 11 acres as a boating center with marina, restaurant, motel and chandlery. Bangor is perhaps best known by the general public as the home of best-selling American author Stephen King.

NAVIGATION: Use NOAA Charts 13302 and 13309. Past Fort Point Cove, the river narrows over the 4 miles to Bucksport (past the high-rise **Penobscot Narrows Bridge**) and then widens out at Frankfort Flats, another 2 miles up the river. Heavy commercial traffic makes night running tricky. Bangor is about 12 miles upstream from Winterport.

Dockage: Shops are handy in downtown Bucksport and the old railroad station has been converted into a historical museum. Bucksport has a walkway along much of the town's waterfront and several park areas. The 9-slip Bucksport Public Dock/Municipal Marina or the larger Bucksport Marina may have space for you and gas and diesel fuel are available.

Across from Bucksport is Fort Knox Park, with its granite fortress and picnic grounds. Fort Knox was built in the 1840s to defend against a feared third British invasion (following the Revolutionary War and the War of 1812), which never occurred. The Penobscot Narrows Observatory (711 Fort Knox Rd., 207-469-6553) in the western tower of the high-rise highway bridge near Fort Knox is the highest bridge observatory in the world and offers a tremendous view of Penobscot

Silver Lake

Bucksport

Bay and the surrounding area. For boaters, this will involve anchoring or mooring in Bucksport and walking or getting a taxi to the bridge. A combined trip to the bridge and Fort Knox Park makes a great outing.

The 30-slip Bangor Landing Waterfront Park offers deep-water slips for vessels to 165 feet near the village center.

Anchorage: If you anchor at Bucksport, make sure you are solidly hooked as the current runs swift. Much of the bottom is covered with sawdust from lumbering days and offers poor holding. It would be best to anchor south of town in the cove to the north of Fort Point in 7 to 16 feet MLW with good holding and much less current.

Castine Harbor

Pre-dating the colonial settlement at Plymouth by 7 years, Castine is one of the oldest towns in New England, originally a fur trading post that still remains well worth a visit. During its highly contested early colonialist days, Castine changed hands 25 times among the English, French, Dutch, Spanish and American colonists. The town is rich with reminders of

its exciting past. Paul Revere ruined his military career in an ill-fated attempt to capture Fort George from the British in 1779. The fort is open to the public but the entire town is on the National Historic Register.

Castine is an active summer resort, although it is more reserved and far less hectic than Camden. Your best bet is to pick up a copy of A Walking Tour of Castine from any local merchant. The Castine Historical Society (13 School St., 207-326-4118) houses a permanent exhibit on the ill-fated Penobscot expedition of 1779 and seasonal exhibits on various aspects of Castine's rich history. Admission is free. Dominating the harbor is the State of Maine, the 13,000-ton, 500-foot-long training ship of the Maine Maritime Academy (54 Pleasant St., 800-464-6565), which offers undergraduate and graduate degrees in engineering, transportation and management. Both the vessel and the Academy are open to visitors.

NAVIGATION: Use NOAA Charts 13302 and 13309. The bluffs of Dice Head guard the entrance to the Bagaduce River and Castine Harbor at the head of East Penobscot Bay off the northern end of Islesboro. The

East
Penobscot Bay, ME

CASTINE		Dockage				Supplies		Services				
	VHF Channel Monitored / Working	Largest Vessel Accomodated	Approach / Dockside Depth (reported)	Transient Slips / Total Slips	Floating Docks	Groceries, Ice, Marine Supplies, Snacks	Gas / Diesel	Repairs: Hull, Engine, Propeller	Lift (tonnage), Crane, Rail	Min / Max Amps	Courtesy Car, Laundry, Pool, Showers	Pump-Out Station	Nearby: Grocery Store, Motel, Restaurant
1. Castine Town Dock	(207) 266-7711	80	9/16	3/3	60.0/25.0	F				30/100		P	GMR
2. Eaton's Boat Yard	(207) 326-8579	200	9/	8/8	12.0/11.0	F	GD	IM	HEP	L20	30/100	S	GMR

💻 Internet Access   📶 Wireless Internet Access   onSpot Dockside WiFi Facility
See WaterwayGuide.com for current rates, fuel prices, website addresses, and other up-to-the-minute information. (Information in the table is provided by the facilities.)

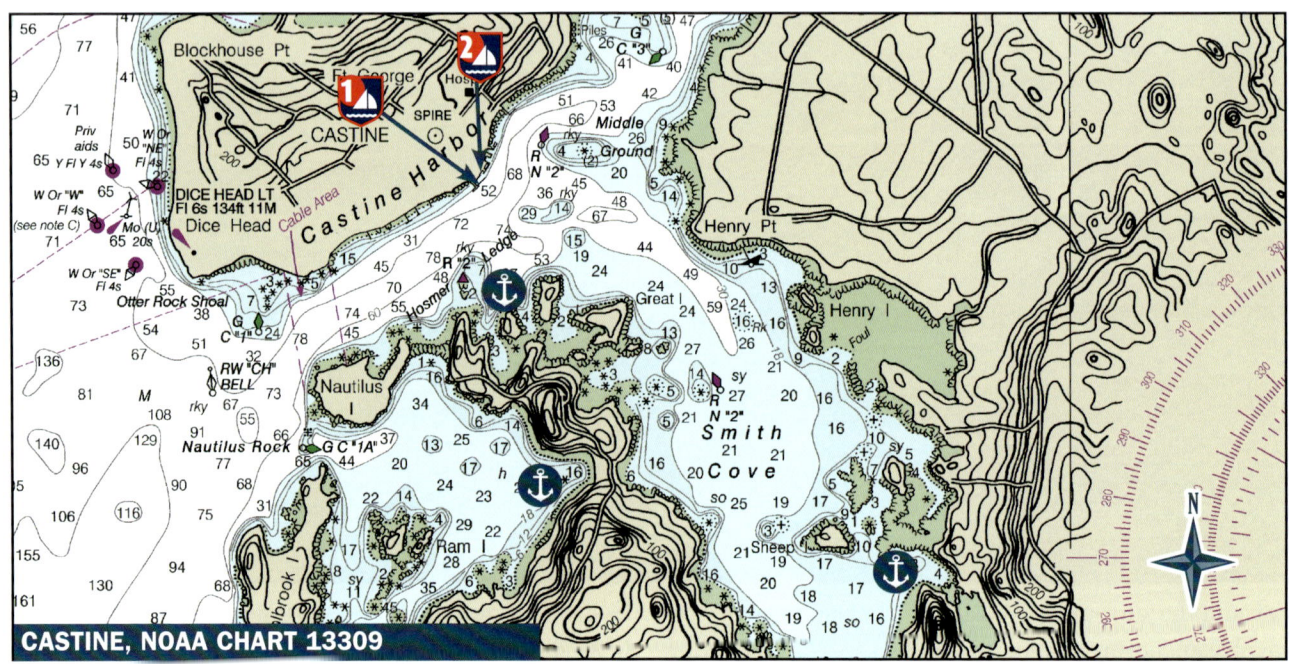

CASTINE, NOAA CHART 13309

red-and-white bell buoy "CH" assists those entering during a fog but there is no red marker off Nautilus Island. If in doubt, tend toward green can buoy "1" then stay toward the north side of the channel.

Dockage/Moorings: The Castine Town Dock has just three total slips. Eaton's Boatyard is more likely to have space for an overnight stay alongside their docks or on a rental mooring.

Anchorage: The holding ground is poor off Castine, where depths of the Bagaduce River run to 72 feet (12 fathoms) and swift tidal currents scour the bottom. A secure anchorage can be found, however, to the south. The closest anchorage to town, out of the main current, is the area just south of Hosmer Ledge (e.g., off Hospital Island).

The most attractive gunkhole in Castine is well inside the protection of Smith Cove to the south, southeast of Sheep Island. When heading for this anchorage be careful of the buoyed Middle Ground rock in

mid-harbor to the west of Sheep Island. It comes clear out of the water with spring tides.

One of the most interesting of Castine's anchorages is Holbrook Harbor (unnamed on the chart) and entered from East Penobscot Bay between Nautilus Island and Holbrook Island. Stay clear of the buoyed mid-channel rock in the entrance marked by green can buoy "1A." An alternate entrance to Holbrook Harbor is between Cape Rosier on the south and Holbrook and Ram Island (known locally as "Rain") on the north side. Holbrook Island is a state park with hiking trails; a float on the east side is available to tie up a dinghy and one complimentary mooring is maintained.

If anchoring between Holbrook and Ram Island, use the center of the channel or risk ending up on the copious rocks and ledges to either side. A larger anchorage extends throughout the rest of the harbor with weather perhaps determining which shore would be most comfortable to huddle behind.

Side Trip: The Barred Islands

Approximately 4 nm south of Cape Rosier, the Barred Islands combine to form an anchorage surrounded by unspoiled, spruce-capped islets between Great Spruce Head Island to the west and Butter Island to the east.

NAVIGATION: Use NOAA Charts 13302 and 13305. If you are entering the lagoon-like bay formed by these islands for the first time, it is best to enter from the northwest at below half-tide after running southeasterly past green can buoy "3" off Great Spruce Head Island. Favor the northernmost of the islands, Escargot, since it is bold, while a reef extends to the north from Little Barred Island on the southern side of the harbor entrance.

Anchorage: The anchorage to the southeast of Little Barred Island affords good holding with protection offered by a sandbar and rocks that block the prevailing southwesterlies. The ospreys provide constant entertainment as they fish for their dinner. The anchorage between the small islands between Great Spruce Island and Butter Island is good in fair weather with outstanding scenery.

◼ NORTH HAVEN ISLAND

The northern cap of the archipelago is known as the Fox Islands (for the abundant silver foxes seen by the first European explorers here). North Haven Island with its various channels, coves and islets offers exciting and scenic cruising for the rugged-at-heart. Excellent, uncluttered harbors are abundant and a non-stop variety of "one-off" and classic cruising boats ply these waters. No doubt you will contend with obstructions, dense fog, swift currents and extreme tidal ranges, but for the most part the area is well charted and marked and no problem for the seasoned cruiser.

Pulpit Harbor

NAVIGATION: Use NOAA Chart 13305. On the northwestern shore of North Haven Island, guarded by pointed Pulpit Rock, is popular Pulpit Harbor. Do not be dismayed if you see a line of boats ahead of you turning in; there is plenty of room. Narrow coves fanning outward from the entrance provide abundant space. Entry is easy, although you might not

Castine Harbor

Penobscot Bay
Islands, ME

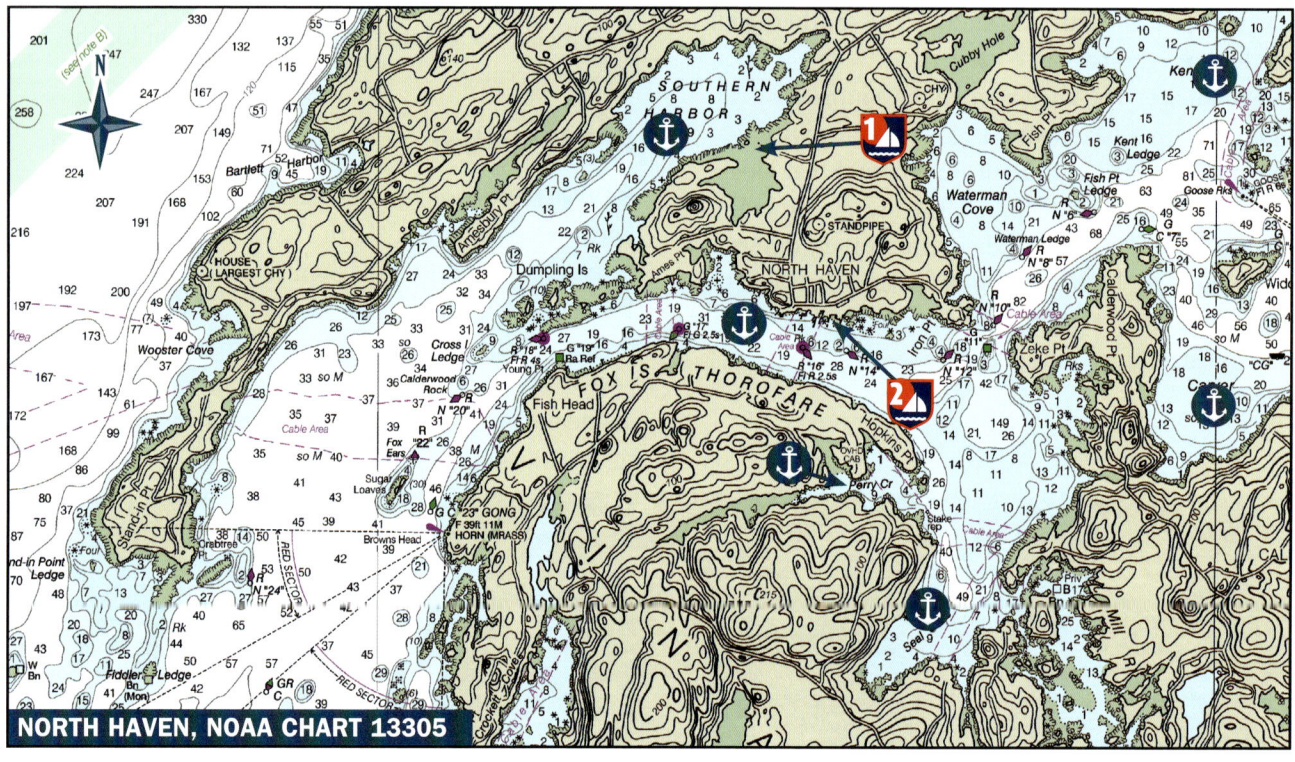

		Largest Vessel Accomodated	VHF Channel Monitored/ Working	Approach / Dockside Depth (reported)	Transient Slips / Total Slips	Floating Docks	Groceries, Ice, Marine Supplies, Snacks	Gas / Diesel	Repairs: Hull, Engine, Propeller	Lift (tonnage), Crane, Rail	Courtesy Car, Laundry, Pool, Showers	Min / Max Amps	Pump-Out Station	Nearby: Grocery Store, Motel, Restaurant
NORTH HAVEN						**Dockage**			**Supplies**		**Services**			
1. Thayer's Y-Knot Boatyard	(207) 867-4701	50	16/9	/	4.0/4.0			M	HEP	L,C,R		S		GR
2. Browns Boatyard 🖥 WiFi	(207) 867-4621	60	16/9	/	15.0/5.0	F	GD	IM	HEP	L30	30	LS		2.5R
VINALHAVEN														
3. Hopkins Boat Yard	(207) 863-2551		/	/	16.0/8.0			M	HEP	L35	30/100			GMR

🖥 Internet Access   WiFi Wireless Internet Access   onSpot Dockside WiFi Facility

See WaterwayGuide.com for current rates, fuel prices, website addresses, and other up-to-the-minute information. (Information in the table is provided by the facilities.)

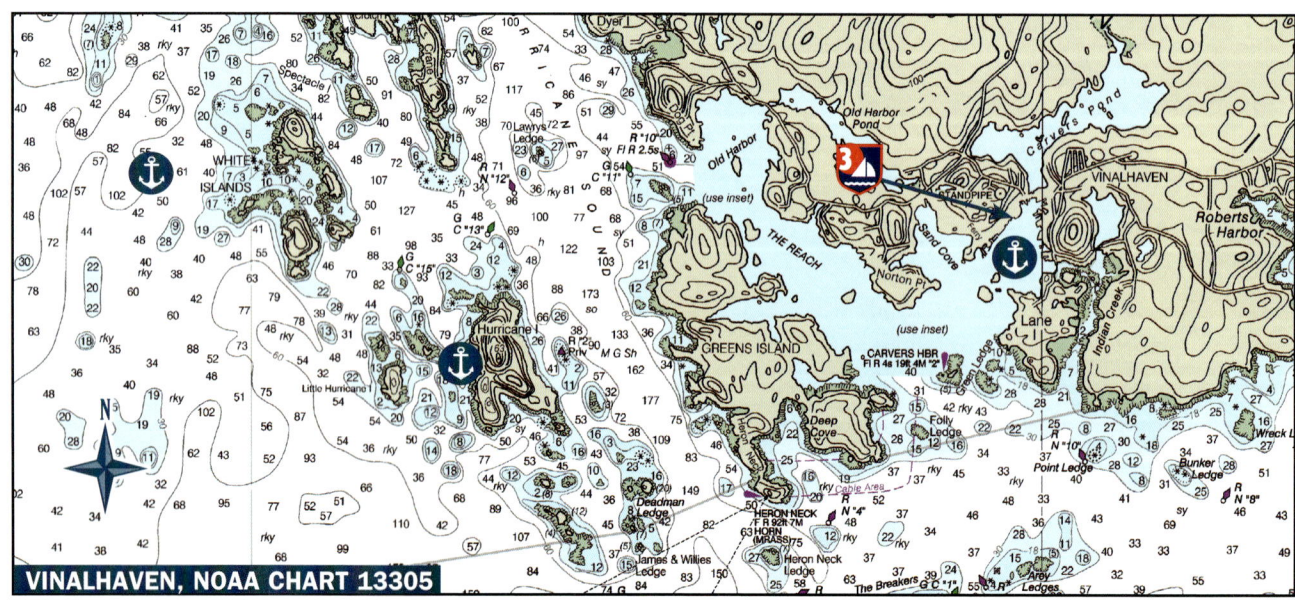

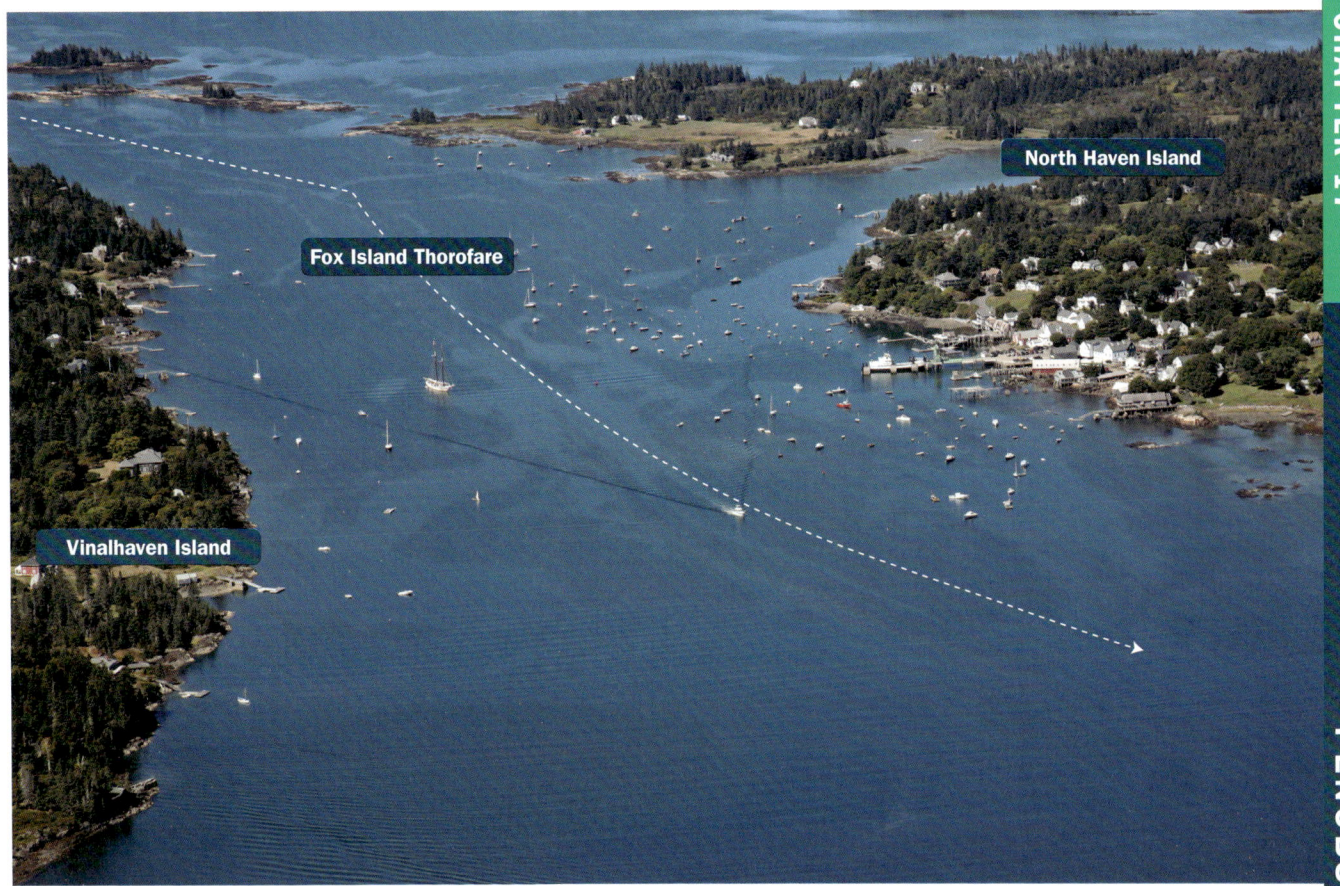

Fox Island Thorofare · North Haven Island · Vinalhaven Island

think so until you get close enough to see the rock with the osprey nest. Enter between the rock and the western shore.

Anchorage: The harbor is well protected, and anchorage is secure in mud but you will have to cope with some kelp here. Latecomers will be obliged to anchor in more than 20 feet MLW toward the center of the harbor at low tide. At the northeastern end of the harbor, a public float provides a dinghy dock. From the dock it's a short walk to North Haven Grocery (124 Pulpit Harbor Rd., 207-867-2233), a small grocery store that is well stocked. Exploring the upper reaches of the channel past the dock with a dinghy is rewarding in every way.

Southern Harbor

NAVIGATION: Use NOAA Chart 13305. During clear weather entrance to the nearly 2-mile-long bight of Southern Harbor is straightforward in the relatively wide channel between Amesbury Point and the Dumpling Islands. The Fox Island Thorofare is the narrower opening but also the one marked by buoys. After passing the Sugar Loaves and Calderwood Rock on the north side steer a course straight down the

center of the channel between Amesbury Point and the easternmost outcropping of the Dumpling Islands. The northeastern shore has fewer dangerous rocks for the first third, but don't favor it too hard as Seal Ledge provides an invisible danger before the easy-to-see Lobster Island.

Moorings: Moorings are available from Thayer's Y-Knot Boatyard, which reports 4-foot MLW approach and dockside depths with a 10-foot tidal range. They also offer repairs.

Anchorage: You can anchor in 9- to 15-foot MLW depths with relatively secure holding in a soft mud bottom. Southern Harbor is exposed to the prevailing southwesterlies, which can kick up some wave action at times.

Village of North Haven

NAVIGATION: Use NOAA Chart 13305. The quiet village of North Haven is about halfway through Fox Islands Thorofare and is centered on the ferry landing. The village and surrounding island countryside have long been a summer refuge for families from among the leading names of American industry, law and politics. Provisioning is no longer possible in the village but you can call North Haven Grocery (124 Pulpit Harbor Rd., 207-867-2233) for a ride. The North Haven village store has been reborn as Waterman's Community Center (12 Main St., 207-867-2100) with a coffee shop and activities for all ages including plays and films.

Moorings: Browns Boatyard (rental buoys marked "JOB") own all moorings east of the ferry landing. Pick one up and pay the fee in the antique yard office ashore. Brown's has an amazing assortment of spares and odd-lot parts and can order equipment and supplies from the mainland. You also can purchase live lobsters from Brown's tank. You cannot dispose of trash here or anywhere else on the island.

While it is possible to anchor outside the mooring field adjacent to the village waterfront, it is not recommended because of uncertain holding and rapid, bi-directional currents that scour this area. This is also the ferry approach. Fortunately, vacant rental moorings are almost always available at a competitive fee. The public landing has generous dinghy space and 2-hour tie-ups for larger boats.

Kent Cove Anchorage

Fully exposed to the south, Kent Cove is less favored than other harbors in this region; nevertheless, it is easily accessible and anchorage is secure in the northeastern bight of the cove between Indian Point and the island off the western shore in 8 to 12 feet MLW.

■ VINALHAVEN ISLAND

Vinalhaven Island to the south is the southernmost of Penobscot Bay's large islands and a very popular local haunt with its rugged shoreline, satellite islands, scores of coves and anchorages and one major harbor with a remote but rugged village. The eastern shore is full of gunkholes for exploring and even in high season there's plenty of room to go hook-down for days on end.

Fox Island Thorofare to Carver Cove

The most popular passage across Penobscot Bay, Fox Islands Thorofare runs between North Haven Island and Vinalhaven Island. It is about 7 miles long and is well marked with all obstructions clearly charted and buoyed. Note that the buoys lead from east

to west. It has several snug anchorages, although holding can be poor with a thin layer of mud over a slick layer of Maine's world-famous granite. A little extra chain on the bottom is helpful in staying put. You will find excellent harbors for a rustic but secure anchorage both to the north and south of this breathtaking channel.

NAVIGATION: Use NOAA Chart 13305. Proceeding south from the Fox Island Thorofare enter at the center of the channel between the small island off the tip of Hopkins Point and the southern shore. At high tide submerged ledges extending from both north and south will not be visible; centering on the channel is critical. Once fully past the small island at the entrance favor the southern shore, heading at the first small point inside to avoid a 4-foot MLW spot.

Anchorage: Just south of Fox Islands Thorofare, tucked behind Hopkins Point (less than 1 mile southwest of North Haven as the crow flies), Perry Creek offers a series of small, pastoral and well-protected anchorages. Houses hug the shoreline and their private moorings riddle the harbor close in. Anchor west of the cable area marked on the chart in 8- to 12-foot MLW depths. The holding is good in mud, but keep to the center of the creek when anchoring at high tide to avoid ending up with more than an anchor on the bottom. A falling tide reveals muddy banks gradually sloping toward the center.

Carver Cove is easily entered from either west or east of Widow Island, which straddles the Fox Islands Thorofare and is popular with the windjammer fleet. Best anchorage is found at the mouth of the cove's extension at its south end in 8- to 13-foot MLW depths. Holding is good in mud with good protection from the prevailing summer southerlies. When the wind backs to the northeast or north, however, this is not the place to be. Wildlife–of the aquatic, land based and aviary variety–is abundant here.

Winter Harbor & Seal Bay

NAVIGATION: Use NOAA Chart 13305. Enter south of Calderwood Neck, north of Bluff Head and the Hen Islands. Steer a center channel course to avoid the entrance's 2-foot MLW spot near the Calderwood Neck side. Otherwise, passage is unencumbered and the scenery is unsurpassed. Winter Haven is the smaller and more western of the two Winter Harbors of the State

Vinalhaven Island

Carvers Harbor

of Maine, the other being the town on the Schoodic Peninsula and part of Acadia National Park.

Entering from East Penobscot Bay on the same course as taken to Winter Harbor, steer center channel just past the westernmost of the two Hen Islands and then take an abrupt turn to the southeast along the bold shore of the western Hen Island. Obstructions along the eastern end of Penobscot Island will not be visible at high water. On a clear day you can work your way around the east end of Penobscot and Davids Islands then around to the north of Hay Island.

Anchorage: Winter Harbor is one of the most rustic and unspoiled anchorages on Vinalhaven Island and is relatively easy to enter and is well protected from every direction except northeast. During the height of the summer cruising season, there are likely to be several boats anchored in the center of this beautiful sea finger, yet anchorage is less than certain here. More secure holding is reported on the Penobscot Island side of the harbor in 8 to 10 feet MLW just northeast of the two small islets and immediately across from the unmistakable 163-foot sheer rock bluff on the Calderwood Neck side of the harbor. The harbor is passable by small boat for almost 2 miles into the interior of Vinalhaven where it becomes the Mill River.

To some cruisers the anchorages of Seal Bay surpass even those of Winter Harbor in their unspoiled dramatic beauty and silent seclusion. If you are seeking an anchorage to ride out severe weather there is none better. The best holding is between the northern ends of Burnt Island and Hay Island in 7 to 10 feet MLW. There is also good holding past Burnt Island in 6 to 10 feet MLW.

If the Hay Island anchorage looks too challenging, additional good anchoring can be found in about 10 feet MLW at the southeast end of Seal Bay near Coombs Neck. Approach on a mid-tide or better to avoid several low spots reported on the path to this location. Thick-blooded locals favor the sandy beach on Hay Island for swimming and sunbathing (but southern cruisers should be advised that the water is cold year-round).

Carvers Harbor

Carvers Harbor is on the south shore of Vinalhaven Island, protected by Greens Island and numerous islets and ledges and is the island's most important commercial port. Although seemingly ample in size, the harbor is teeming with lobster boats, draggers, seiners, floats and tenders. The village is a good place to provision, dine out or arrange an emergency repair.

Carvers Harbor is a great place to stretch the legs. The classic municipal watering troughs, hitching posts and other remnants of the granite quarrying days of old are evident. A visit to the Nature Conservancy preserve on Lane Island at the southernmost head of the harbor is a good way to walk off the sea-legs on a cool summer morning. The seasonal Vinalhaven Historical Society (41 High St., 207-863-4410) up the hill from the central village is well worth a visit. Across Main Street from the town landing, Carver's Harbor Market (36 Main St., 207-863-4319) has fresh locally grown vegetables, fruits, meats, live lobsters, beer, wine and all kinds of dry goods. They also have an ATM and the Post Office is right next door.

NAVIGATION: Use NOAA Chart 13305. Carvers Harbor may be approached via marked channels from either south or west. Both channels enter the south end of Carvers Harbor Inlet. The southern approach is marked by 19-foot-high flashing red "2." The western approached is via The Reach from Hurricane Sound north of Greens Island by entering the northeastern end of The Reach between green can buoy "11" and red nun buoy "10." Despite well-placed navigation aids, these winding, rock- and ledge-strewn passages are no place to be in dense fog.

Dockage/Moorings: Hopkins Boat Yard may have a slip but note they only take cash. They are also a good contact for emergency repairs. There will likely be a few moorings available for visiting cruisers in the harbor but they are hard to spot. It is best to call Hopkins for availability and location. The town-maintained dock at the extreme head of the harbor has ample space for a dinghy tie-up (2-hour limit). Trash barrels are located just above the landing at the town's breakwater.

Anchorage: There may be anchorage space in the southeastern end of the harbor in 9 to 18 feet MLW but swing room will be at a premium.

Long Cove

At the northeastern end of Hurricane Sound, due east of Leadbetter Island, Long Cove forms a remote mini-fjord stretching for the better part of 1 mile into the interior of Vinalhaven Island. American eagles nest here and their aerial presence offers a rare treat but ospreys, too, are here in abundance and the two species constantly battle for fishing rights. Their acrobatics at the far end of the inner cove are a daily event for cruisers from all over the globe.

NAVIGATION: Use NOAA Chart 13305. The entrance to Long Cove is marked by a great pile of granite tailings on the hill to the right of the channel and visible for some distance from the west. Enter the channel just north of Fiddlehead Island. The channel then turns left and narrows as it enters the inner anchorage, which will most likely be overcrowded on a summer weekend.

Anchorage: The cove is filled with private moorings. Still, there is usually room to set a hook with good holding by proceeding east to somewhat deeper water (25- to 30-foot MLW depths). Near the top of a rising tide, it is possible to cross the reef that cuts off access to the far reaches of the cove during low tide. The water deepens appreciably beyond the reef with numerous pools of 20 to 30 feet MLW, making good anchorage spots amid rustic surroundings as well as being a perfect hurricane hole. If it's too crowded in the inner cove, the outer cove has good holding in 16 to 25 feet MLW with fewer mosquitoes.

Side Trip: Hurricane Sound Islands

Southwest of Vinalhaven, parallel strings of classic Maine islands form a delightful passage with remote harbors and scenic vistas. You can enter Hurricane Sound from the south between Greens Island and

Hurricane Island, keeping well clear of charted but unmarked Deadman Ledge and the northerly running reefs to the east of Hurricane Island.

Hurricane Island was once the site of a thriving granite quarry business with a local population in excess of 1,000. The industry had a short life, lasting only from the mid-1870s until 1915, but in its heyday island granite was used in the bridges and buildings of major cities throughout the country including the Metropolitan Museum of Art in New York City.

The 2.5-mile path around the island winds through woods loaded with raspberry and blueberry bushes and field-pea vines to an ocean side granite ledge offering a magnificent view of island-dotted seascapes. The path continues past a summerhouse, cantilevered from a sheer cliff over a breathtaking view of the southern approach to Penobscot Bay. Smoking and campfires are strictly prohibited.

Moorings: The Hurricane Island Foundation (207-867-6050) welcomes visiting mariners. On approach look out for the spindle-marked ledge fronting the east side of the island, which will block a straightforward run at the moorings. Four moorings (marked by bright orange floats with pick-up toggles) are located on the east side of the island on a first-come, first-served basis (overnight or as a day stop with fees).

Anchorage: It is possible to anchor to the north of Hurricane Island among either the White Islands or between Lawry and Cedar Islands.

Side Trip: Brimstone Island

Off the southeastern tip of Vinalhaven Island is Brimstone Island. All pure volcanic rock, the island has beaches of round black stones; on calm days you can land on the beaches on the north side. Brimstone Island is privately owned so respect the property: no fires, no smoking and no litter. It is not suitable for an overnight anchorage but it's a breathtaking hike.

Isle au Haut

This heavily wooded island, named in 1604 by Samuel de Champlain, is pronounced "eye-la-HO." The majority of the wild 550-foot high island is part of Acadia National Park, with miles of trails to explore. There is one main road in town and the only connection to the outside world is the privately run Stonington mail/passenger boat and private vessels. The 45 year-round residents, however, generously share the island with a considerable number of summer people.

The Village of Isle au Haut on the east side of the Isle au Haut Thorofare opposite Kimball Island has a store, small school, church, community center and town wharf. At the northern end of the Thorofare is the summer community of Point Lookout. The Island Store (3 Main St., 207-335-5211) offers an excellent variety of goods for provisioning, featuring fish and produce, beer, wine and ice. Call for hours and to place advance orders.

Anchorage: Duck Harbor, on the southwest shore of the island and north of Duck Harbor Mountain is a gunkhole for one or two boats, more if all agree to anchor fore-and-aft. If the wind is more south than west, it is a protected spot with good holding in 8 to 10 feet MLW but it shoals quickly beyond the ferry dock. The ferry dock offers shore access to the excellent National Park trails including one rated "difficult" (due to a couple of short scrambles over rock requiring hands) that leads to the mountaintop from which it may be possible to get a bird's eye view of your own boat, at anchor, more than 300 feet below.

In settled weather the anchorage in Marsh Cove at the west end of the Thorofare is an attractive option. Moores Harbor on the western shore and Head Harbor on the southern both look inviting on the chart but are wide open to the prevailing southwesterly winds.

◼ EGGEMOGGIN REACH

The broad and well-marked Eggemoggin Reach route is northernmost of the sheltered inside passages that join Penobscot Bay to Jericho Bay. It runs southeast between the mainland and the Deer Isles. The passage offers dozens of enticing islets and coves, some with yacht facilities and boatbuilding establishments. It is called a reach because the prevailing southwesterlies usually blow across the length of the channel allowing wind-driven vessels to sail on a reach, whether eastbound or westbound. The **Deer Island Bridge** has a vertical clearance of 85 feet. Horseshoe Cove at the western entrance to Eggemoggin Reach may be a little difficult to find and enter but it's well worth a night on a mooring.

Not to be missed is a tidal float trip by dinghy up the winding, 2-mile "river" that makes up this cove to the

Eggemoggin Reach, ME

HORSESHOE COVE			Dockage				Supplies		Services			
		Largest Vessel Accomodated	VHF Channel Monitored / Working	Transient Slips / Total Slips	Approach / Dockside Depth (reported)	Floating Docks	Groceries, Ice, Marine Supplies, Snacks	Gas / Diesel	Repairs: Hull Engine, Propeller	Lift (tonnage), Crane, Rail	Min / Max Amps	Courtesy Car, Laundry, Pool, Showers	Pump-Out Station	Nearby: Grocery Store, Motel, Restaurant
1. Seal Cove Boatyard Inc.	(207) 326-4422	57	9/16	/	8.0/8.0			M	HEP	L35,C,R	30			
BUCKS HARBOR														
2. Bucks Harbor Yacht Club	(207) 326-0556		/9	/	28.0/20.0	F		I						GR
3. Buck's Harbor Marine | Yacht Charters and Marina 🖥 📶	(207) 326-8839	70	9/10	/	28.0/20.0	F	GD	IMS			30/50	LS	P	10.5R

🖥 Internet Access 📶 Wireless Internet Access ⊙ onSpot Dockside WiFi Facility

See WaterwayGuide.com for current rates, fuel prices, website addresses, and other up-to-the-minute information. (Information in the table is provided by the facilities.)

HORSESHOE COVE, BUCKS HARBOR, NOAA CHART 13309

shallow tidal basin at its head. The trip should begin with the tapering of the flood, about 1 hour before slack tide. Returning on the ebb and waiting for the tide change will come more slowly than your ascent on the rapids of the flood so count on needing at least 3 hours for this adventure.

Horseshoe Cove

NAVIGATION: Use NOAA Chart 13309. A critical find for a stranger to the area is privately maintained red daybeacon "2" northwest of Thrumcap Island, about 0.25 mile off the point marked "Horseshoe Cove" on the chart. It marks the end of a shoal extending from the point. Do not cut it off or you may end up at low water on the exposed ledges with the seals. Follow a course centering between the red daybeacon to the northeast and the small island off the shore to the southwest. Immediately after entry a slight turn north

will align your passage directly down the center of the relatively narrow channel ahead. About 0.5 miles from the entrance two closely spaced green spar buoys ("3" and "5") indicate an otherwise tricky twist in the channel. Favor these buoys and leave them close to the west. Shortly after, small red daybeacon "6" indicates a rounded rock exposed at low tide.

Moorings/Anchorage: Seal Cove Boatyard Inc. maintains several moorings in this area and immediately to the north. Visit the boatyard in your dinghy not your boat. Passage above the moorings looks easy but most boats will not successfully negotiate the submerged boulders without a pilot.

There's no swing room in the mooring area but anchorage is possible south of the green spar buoys in more than 20 feet MLW. This spot is well protected and extraordinarily beautiful.

Orcutt Harbor

Over Long Mountain, directly to the east of Horseshoe Cove, Orcutt Harbor is easy to enter and reasonably well protected at its far reaches. Its character is somewhat suburban with many well-trimmed lawns reaching its edges. Favor the eastern shore upon entry to avoid a 5-foot MLW spot off the western shore. Another 5-foot-deep rock, about two-thirds of the way along the bight, is identified on the chart. There are no shoreside amenities for 7 miles.

Anchorage: There is good holding in mud in 7 to 20 feet MLW in upper Orcutt Harbor.

Bucks Harbor

Bucks Harbor has been a special favorite of cruisers for many years. Located at the western mouth of Eggemoggin Reach and protected by tiny Harbor Island, are an active yacht club, marina and other facilities that welcome visiting yachts. Provisions can be obtained at the top of the rise (from the yacht club) at Buck's Harbor Market (6 Cornfield Hill Rd., 207-326-8683), stocking all the basics and fresh baked breads, specialty meats, gourmet cheeses, fine wines, beer and local produce.

NAVIGATION: Use NOAA Chart 13309. The inner harbor is easily approached on either side of Harbor Island from red-and-white Morse (A) bell buoy "EG" at the mouth of Eggemoggin Reach to the south, the inner harbor is unobstructed (save for submerged Harbor Ledge, marked by green can buoy "1").

Dockage/Moorings: Except when a visit coincides with a touring yacht club or power squadron, a mooring is almost always available in Buck's Harbor. Buck's Harbor Yacht Club maintains two guest moorings (marked BHYC), and it is possible to tie up briefly at the club's floating dock in 12-foot MLW depths. Bucks Harbor Marine/Yacht Charters and Marina has a dinghy landing behind the docks. They also sell gas and diesel. The marina sits on a granite dock that dates back to the days when schooners lay alongside to load the giant stones that built many of New York City's skyscrapers and bridges.

Anchorage: Bucks Harbor affords some anchorage at 23-foot MLW depths with secure holding at the eastern end (outside the mooring fields), making it a favorite spot for touring schooners.

Benjamin River

In the pastoral stretch of green fields, gently rolling land, tiny towns and awesome "pine orchards," Benjamin River enters the Eggemoggin Reach from the north at the village of West Brooklin.

NAVIGATION: Use NOAA Chart 13316. Entry is easiest at low tide, when it is possible to see the channel ledge extending from the eastern shore and all but blocking access to the inner harbor of the Benjamin River. Incoming yachts must favor the western shore as it curves to the northwest until reaching the 50-foot MLW pool inside.

Moorings/Anchorage: Moorings may be available from Benjamin River Marine but do call ahead. Anchoring is possible along the eastern side of the Benjamin River in mud with 7 to 18 feet MLW. Fuel is not available and services are very limited.

Center Harbor

NAVIGATION: Use NOAA Chart 13316. Farther down Eggemoggin Reach, tucked in behind Chatto Island, Center Harbor (self-proclaimed "wooden boat capital of the world") is dominated by Brooklin Boat Yard at its eastern end, specializing in the construction and reconstruction of wooden boats of all sizes. In 1998, the yard launched the traditional 76-foot W-class cutter *Wild Horses*, designed by the late Joel White. Because of this wooden boat orientation and the specialized maintenance services provided here, many owners of traditional boats make Center Harbor their homeport. Classic lines, shapes and styles (flawlessly restored) encourage a stop for closer review. *WoodenBoat* magazine and its associated boat school is headquartered in Brooklin.

Dockage/Moorings: Brooklin Boat Yard has lobster-buoy-shaped moorings. You can tie up a dinghy behind the marina's float for a walk to town. It is also possible to dock briefly here (with 4 to 5 feet MLW) to take on water or off-load trash. The Village of Brooklin is about 0.2 mile up the rise from the docks to the main road, then to the right about 1 mile farther.

Naskeag Harbor Anchorage

Just behind Hog Island, near the eastern end of Eggemoggin Reach, Naskeag Harbor provides adequate protection in most conditions. Best anchorage is found close to the north of Hog Island, avoiding The Triangles, a rocky ledge north of the island. Here you will find 14 to 16 feet MLW in thick mud.

Eggemoggin Reach, ME

		Largest Vessel Accomodated	VHF Channel Monitored / Working	Approach / Dockside Depth (reported)	Transient Slips / Total Slips	Floating Docks	Groceries, Ice, Marine Supplies, Snacks	Gas / Diesel	Repairs: Hull, Engine, Propeller	Lift (tonnage), Crane, Rail	Min / Max Amps	Courtesy Car, Laundry, Pool, Showers	Pump-Out Station	Nearby: Grocery Store, Motel, Restaurant
BENJAMIN RIVER				**Dockage**			**Supplies**		**Services**					
1. Benjamin River Marine	(207) 359-2244			/	/	/		M						
CENTER HARBOR														
2. Brooklin Boat Yard	(207) 359-2236	120	/	/	7.0/5.0	F		M	HEP	L80,C				GMR
STONINGTON														
3. Billings Diesel & Marine ☐ Wifi	(207) 367-2328	75	16/	20/25	20.0/10.0	F	GD	GIM	HEP	L75,C,R	30/200+	LS	P	GMR

☐ Internet Access   Wifi Wireless Internet Access   onSpot Dockside WiFi Facility

See WaterwayGuide.com for current rates, fuel prices, website addresses, and other up-to-the-minute information. (Information in the table is provided by the facilities.)

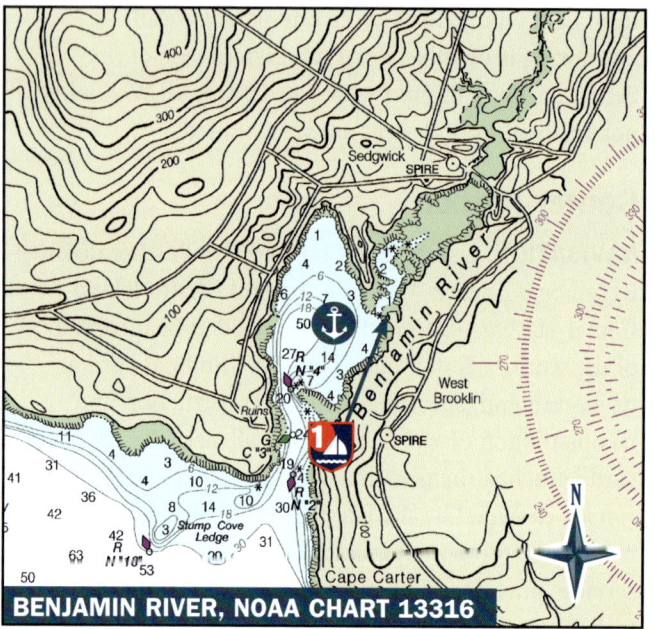

BENJAMIN RIVER, NOAA CHART 13316

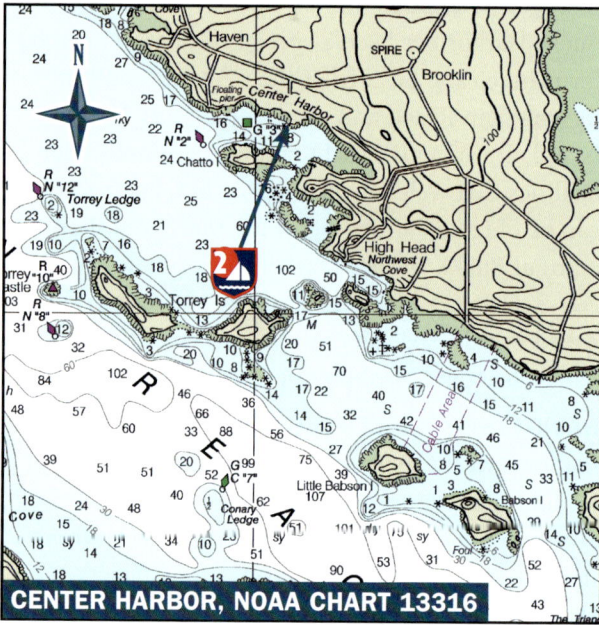

CENTER HARBOR, NOAA CHART 13316

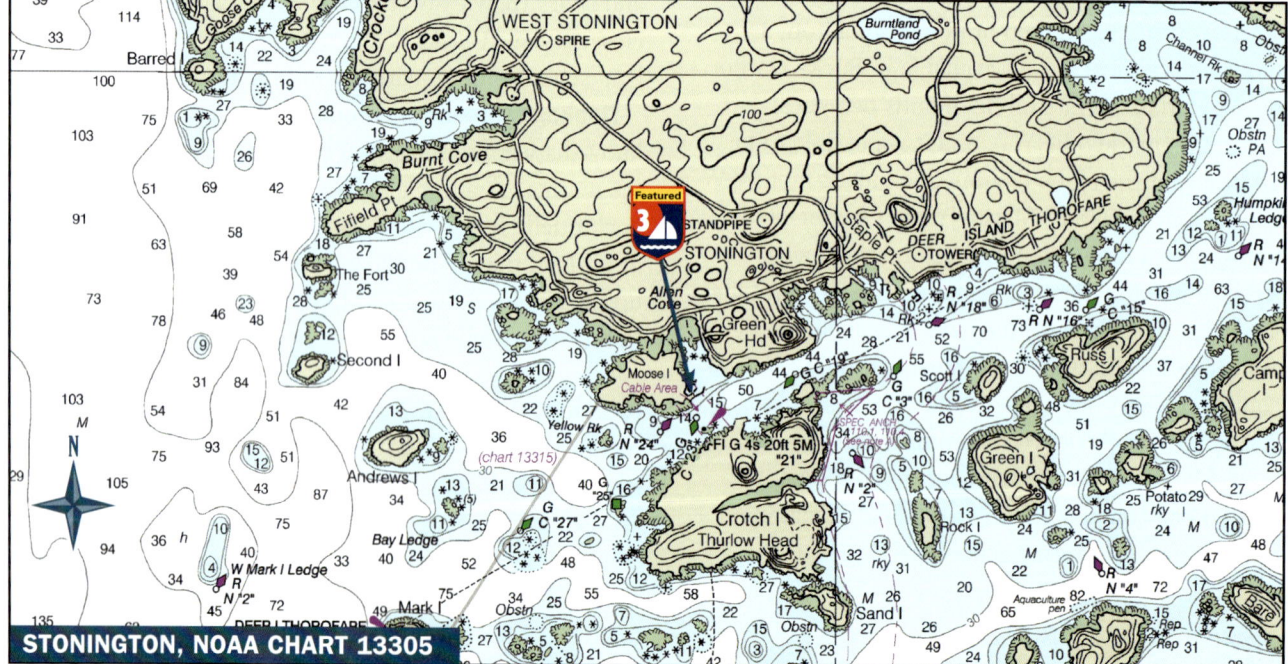

STONINGTON, NOAA CHART 13305

Penobscot Bay

Billings Diesel & Marine

Stonington

Deer Island Thorofare

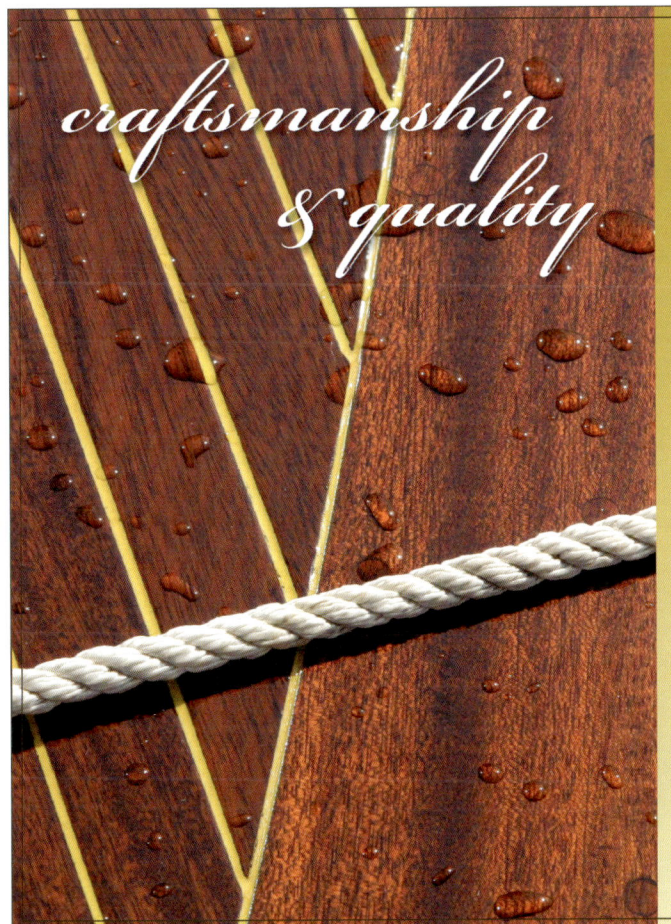

■ DEER ISLE

The working waterfront town of Stonington sits on the side of a hill sloping down to the harbor on the south shore of Deer Isle. The inhabitants of Stonington once depended on granite quarries and sardine canneries but now derive their living mainly from lobster pounds and summer visitors. Draggers, fishing smacks, yachts, an excursion boat, a ferry and fishers all make Stonington their home port, giving harbor and town an appealing blend of these diverse elements. Proclaimed the lobster capital of Maine (measured by shear poundage of lobster meat delivered to the world from this port).

The Stonington Chamber of Commerce offers a downtown walking trail map that features pictures of the buildings from far back in their histories. The Deer Isle Granite Museum (51 Main St., 207-367-6331) is open in July and August only and charges no admission. It features a working model of the local granite quarry as it was operated in the early 1900s, when they supplied granite for such enduring works as the Kennedy Memorial, the Brooklyn Bridge and the Rockefeller Center.

NAVIGATION: Use NOAA Charts 13305 and 13313. The large summer resort island of Deer Isle is the southern edge of Eggemoggin Reach. The fixed **Rainbow Bridge** joins Little Deer Island to the mainland. Bridge lovers will seriously enjoy passing under this 85-foot vertical clearance bridge.

At the southern end of Deer Island the narrow but well marked Deer Island Thorofare threads between rocky outcroppings and tiny islands and past protected coves and scenic anchorages. Consider carefully before entering in fog and use sound signals to communicate your presence to the professional mariners who use the area in all weather. When traveling through the Thorofare, expect to encounter very dense concentrations of lobster buoys.

> Crotch Island on the western end of the Deer Island Thorofare is the source of famous Deer Island granite and still is an active quarry. Here you can see the gantry used to lift granite blocks for loading on a barge.

Dockage/Moorings: A town dock and a dinghy dock sit between the commercial fishing piers in Stonington. The town also has floats and a shoreside walkway. Nearly 1 mile west of the village center, full-service

Stonington

Billings Diesel & Marine on Moose Island has well-equipped shops dedicated to every phase of boat maintenance, along with three marine railways, a lift and a crane. They also have a fully-stocked marine store and sell gas and diesel fuel.

Anchorage: Harbors on the western shore of Deer Isle include Sylvester Cove, which has a hospitable yacht club with guest moorings and an anchorage south of Dunham Point. The long, narrow Northwest Harbor, north of Dunham Point, is another potential anchorage. The best spot is in the center of the harbor where you will find 11 to 15 feet MLW with good holding in mud. The head of the harbor dries at low tide and is open to northwest winds.

You can anchor out of the Deer Island Thorofare south of Deer Island in 15 to 24 feet MLW. This only provides protection from the north; try to anchor out of the fast-moving current. Burnt Cove at the village of West Stonington is another option if you want to be close to Stonington.

There are several scenic summer anchorages south of the Deer Island Thorofare. One fine anchorage is due east of the northern end of Camp Island in 11 to 17 feet MLW and another is west of the southern end of Bold Island next door. The lengthy slot east of

Hells Half Acre between Bold Island and Devil Island is also a gorgeous anchorage with good holding in depths from 11 to 22 feet MLW. A dinghy trip to state-owned and uninhabited Hell's Half Acre is a must for a walk around this diminutive but beautiful spot. Camping is permitted here but build fires below the high-water mark.

Merchant Row Passage

The southernmost passage between East Penobscot Bay and Jericho Bay lies between the south end of Deer Island (Stonington area) and Isle au Haut. Merchant Row Passage is wider and deeper than Deer Island Thorofare, easy to navigate (all major obstructions are buoyed) and hemmed in by islands ranging in size from a single big rock to 1-mile-long Merchant Island.

Anchorage: Merchant Row consists of protected, uninhabited islands providing many anchorages. Opportunities abound to go ashore for beachcombing or blueberry picking, and it is never too crowded to find a private anchorage.

McGlathery Island is a particularly favored spot. Best anchorages are in the cove on the north side of the island in 21-foot MLW depths or in the slot between

McGlathery and Round Island just to the west in 8 to 10 feet MLW. McGlathery Island is a nature preserve and its beaches, cliffs and woods beg to be explored. On Wreck Island just west of McGlathery you may see evidence of grazing sheep brought to the island from the mainland for the summer season.

■ SWANS ISLAND

NAVIGATION: Use NOAA Chart 13313. Remote Swans Island lies directly in the path of the Eggemoggin Reach, southwest of Mount Desert Island. A year-round ferry serves the year-round population of about 350 from Bass Harbor. There are three villages: Atlantic in Mackerel Cove on the north coast and Swans Island and Minturn in Burnt Coat Harbor to the south.

North Shore: Mackerel Cove

Mackerel Cove on the north shore of Swans Island is entered from York Narrows between Orono and Round Islands to the north and Swans Island shore on the south.

⚠ Midway between the tip of Roderick Head and green can "3" (off the ferry landing), an enormous ledge presents a considerable hazard to navigation since it is submerged at high tide. During high water give this visible ledge a very wide berth at slow speed, watching the depth sounder.

Moorings/Anchorage: Mackerel Cove is large enough to accommodate a Spanish armada. Two favored anchorage spots are on either side of Roderick Head (East and West) in 8 to 15 feet MLW. Protection from the prevailing southwesterlies is excellent. The only improved landing in Mackerel Cove is found near the ferry dock on the east side of the cove. Should you choose to set a hook here, stay well south of the ferry's comings and goings from Bass Harbor on Mount Desert Island.

There are also private moorings in Mackerel Cove and it is possible to pick up a vacant one, if you are prepared to move should the owner appear. The views of Mt. Desert Island are impressive from this well protected anchorage.

North Shore: Buckle Harbor

A tour of the island paths is a must from Buckle Harbor on the northwest side of the island. Wild strawberries growing atop granite boulders, seascape cameos through mossy vistas, the door of a long-vanished cabin framing a nearly hidden pathway in the mist, the scolding of an invisible squirrel or a doe venturing out to a seaside meadow as your dinghy departs....You get the picture.

Anchorage: An anchorage is located between Swans Island and Buckle Island just south of York Narrows. Enter Buckle Harbor noting the charted 6-foot MLW spot between green can buoys "7" and "5" in the York Narrows Channel. This is a secure anchorage that can accommodate a dozen boats with good holding in 7 to 10 feet MLW.

South Shore: Burnt Coat Harbor

Burnt Coat Harbor on the southwest side of the island is long, narrow, well protected and serves as home port for the small villages of Swans Island and Minturn. Enter south of green can buoy "3" off Gooseberry Island and pass between green gong buoy "5" off the tip of Hockamock Head and red daybeacon "4" north of Harbor Island.

Although not recommended, vessels do enter and exit through the narrow but well-marked channel between Harbor Island and Stanley Point. Follow a local boat with similar underwater characteristics for greater peace of mind. The last 100 yards after green can buoy "5" are nerve-wracking without local knowledge.

Moorings/Anchorage: Closer to the village of Swans Island on the western shore, heavy-tackle rental moorings (brightly painted lobster buoys) are available from the Fishermen's Cooperative (382 Harbor Rd., 207-526-4327), along with diesel fuel and engine oil. (Recreational boats are asked to fuel up before 1:00 p.m. to make room for returning lobster boats.) Approximately 0.5 mile north of the Fishermen's Co-Op, the harbor shallows appreciably, making even a grocery run by dinghy tide dependent.

Turn north for anchorage outside the mooring field in 20 to 35 feet MLW. The amount of scope necessary and the lobster boats passing in the early morning restrict the number of boats that can safely anchor here. Anchorage is also possible on the north side of Harbor Point but can be uncomfortable due to its greater vulnerability to ocean swells and constant traffic from lobster boats using the narrow channel just south.

There is no public transportation on the island but locals will often offer a ride, and the Island Market & Supply (40 North St., 207-526-4043) sells groceries and take-out and may deliver. There is no alcohol on this dry island; even brown bags are out of bounds at the restaurant. You can have a freshwater swim at Quarry Pond at Minturn. If a sandy, secluded ocean beach is your preference, ask for directions. Three are within walking distance of the harbor.

Side Trip: Long Island

Southeast of Swans Island is the former pirate's hideout of Long Island, which is high, wooded and round and not "long" at all. Long Island is popular both as an end-of-the-line stop and as a great place to work out some of those cruising kinks on a trip farther east.

Roads on both sides of the harbor are paved but intriguing dirt roads and trails lead off in several directions and can be picked up from the harbor or by beaching a dinghy in Eastern Cove. One interesting walk begins at the head of the harbor where a narrow dirt road departs the pavement southward, undulating pleasantly to the granite-bound south shore. A walk east along the rocks picks up a well-worn path with a circle back through an ancient fir-fringed bog, where orchids bloom every July and white-winged crossbills trill throughout the summer. Before exploring you should wisely invest in an island trail map at the museum.

Perched on a side hill at the head of the harbor (beyond a variety of precarious lobstering sheds and docks), the island's small museum captures the spirit of a seafaring past. It is run by the Frenchboro Historical Society (Schoolhouse Hill, 207-334-2924). The attached lending library will lend books to visitors on the promise to mail them back. Also, there is the tiny Frenchboro Post Office, attached to a local lobsterman's house.

The Long Island Store (262 Island Ave., 207-766-2512) is alive and well as a part of the community for 100 years and serves prepared food and ice cream and sells various sundries. They also carry beer and wine, as does Boathouse Beverage & Variety (55 Wharf St., 207-766-5709), which has some groceries as well.

NAVIGATION: Use NOAA Charts 13312 and 13313. Frenchboro, the tiny hamlet at Lunt Harbor, is the vision of what a classic out-island Maine fishing village should look like. The harbor is fortified against all winds but the strongest northeasterlies and even those are partially blocked by Harbor Island at its mouth. Easily accessible, Lunt Harbor may be approached from the west using

green bell buoy "1" as a guide to the channel between Harbor Island and the northwestern shoulder of Long Island. About one-third of the way along Harbor Island a hard turn to the south will take you into the open mouth of the harbor. From the east the red-and-white Morse (A) gong buoy "LI" aids the passage south-southwest below Crow Island and Harbor Island for an almost straight course into the harbor.

Moorings: Pick up one of Lunt's Dockside Deli moorings in the outer harbor and row in for a tie-up behind the face dock and pay the fee at the deli take-out window. The rental comes with free WiFi. Rental moorings available on a first-come, first-served basis and are marked with large white mooring balls with white pickup buoys.

Anchorage: On the east side of Long Island, Eastern Cove is as remote and unspoiled as it is beautiful. The cove is protected from the south and east by Richs Head and the main island to the north and west. Holding is good and exploration of the long-abandoned farmsteads ashore is well worthwhile, although the rubble on the beach can be hard on a dinghy. Lunt Harbor is about a one-hour woodland walk away. Southwest Point provides the dramatic feeling of being at land's end when staring south over open water.

■ BLUE HILL BAY

About 14 miles long, Blue Hill Bay has few obstructions, numerous coves, wooded islands and dramatic scenery on all sides. This mostly uninhabited area derives its name from the rounded mountain that towers over it to the northwest. The evergreen trees on the mountain take on a bluish cast from a distance.

Pond Island & Herrick Bay

North of Casco Passage, there is a wonderful anchorage on the southeastern side of Pond Island. The anchorage is well protected from the prevailing southwesterlies and you can anchor off the rocky beach in 13 to 18 feet MLW. (Remember, the tidal range in this area is 9 to 12 feet so scope accordingly.)

Farther north the Pond Island Passage connects Blue Hill Bay with Herrick Bay, a wide, deep area with anchorages west of Flye Point. Herrick Bay is not buoyed but it is accurately charted and unless the wind is from the southeast safe to enter and anchor in 7 to 11 feet MLW.

East
Penobscot Bay, ME

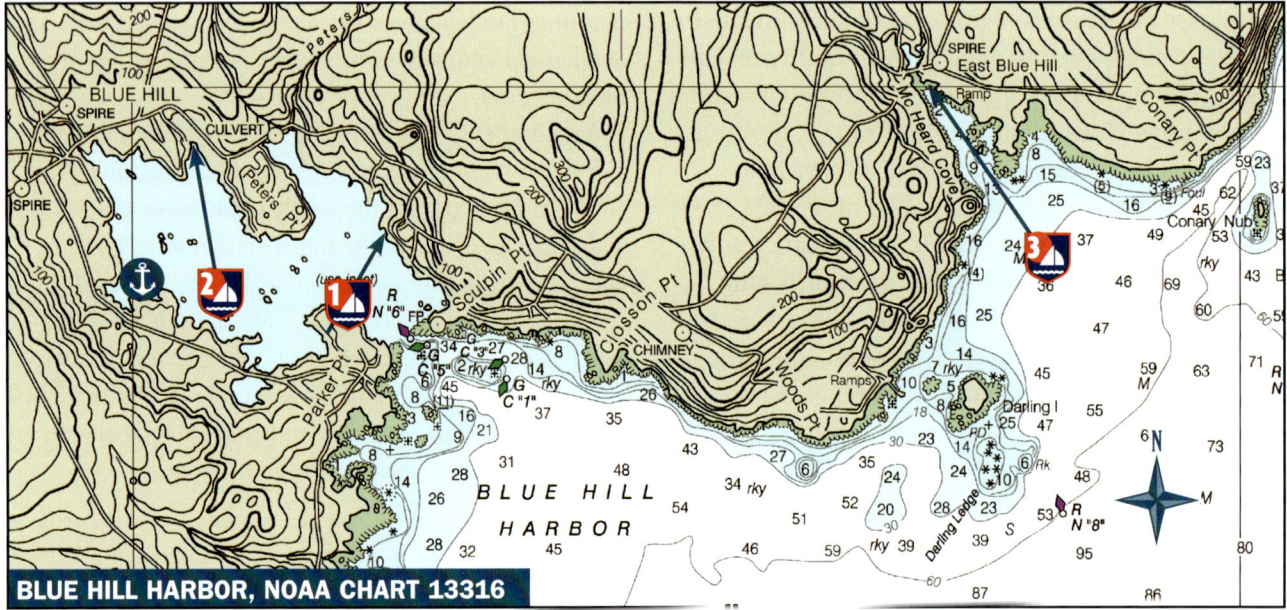

BLUE HILL HARBOR		Dockage					Supplies		Services				
		VHF Channel Monitored / Working	Largest Vessel Accomodated	Approach / Dockside Depth (reported)	Transient Slips / Total Slips	Floating Docks	Gas / Diesel	Groceries, Ice, Marine Supplies, Snacks	Repairs: Hull Engine, Propeller	Lift (tonnage), Crane, Rail	Min / Max Amps	Courtesy Car, Laundry, Pool, Showers	Pump-Out Station	Nearby: Grocery Store, Motel, Restaurant
1. Kollegewidgwok Yacht Club 🖥 WIFI	(207) 374-5581	50	9/68	/	20.0/12.0	F	GD	GI			30		P	GMR
2. Raynes Marine 🖥	(207) 374-2877	50	/	/	/			M	HEP				P	GMR
3. Webbers Cove Boatyard	(207) 374-2841	48	/	/	14.0/3.0	F		M	HP	L25				

🖥 Internet Access   WIFI Wireless Internet Access   onSpot Dockside WiFi Facility

See WaterwayGuide.com for current rates, fuel prices, website addresses, and other up-to-the-minute information. (Information in the table is provided by the facilities.)

BLUE HILL HARBOR, NOAA CHART 13316

Blue Hill Harbor

To the north on the western shore is Blue Hill Harbor. Nestled in a rustic setting, the harbor is fully protected against winds from any quarter yet convenient to provisioning, shopping and good restaurants. In short, Blue Hill Harbor is everything a cruising destination should be.

NAVIGATION: Use NOAA Charts 13312 and 13316. Blue Hill's inner harbor is most easily approached on a due-north course from a position off Sand Point on Blue Hill Neck (across Blue Hill Bay from a second Long Island). Shallow ledges guard the entrance making it necessary to carefully observe the entrance buoys. The second flagpole (west of Sculpin Point and identified on the Blue Hill Harbor chart) will be visible long before the channel cans come into view and should be used for a bearing on approach.

Dockage/Moorings: On the east side of the inner harbor moorings are usually available for a modest

facilities fee from the Kollegewidgwok (pronounced "College-widge'-wok") Yacht Club. Look for KYC markings on the floats or call the club's launch tender (VHF Channel 09) for assistance. The club provides tie-up space for your dinghy and a comfortable clubhouse with a harbor view. There is ample depth at the club's fuel dock to refill both fuel (gas and diesel) and water tanks and to buy ice but overnight dockage is not allowed. From the club, it is a scenic 1.7-mile walk to the village. Raynes Marine is farther up in the harbor (closer to the village) with rental moorings.

Anchorage: The inner harbor's combination of an 11-foot-plus tidal range and a densely packed mooring field makes an attempt to anchor on the easterly side of the harbor ill advised. Above half-tide you can take your dinghy west across the inner harbor to the town dock and dinghy dock at the harbor's northwestern head, just across from the Blue Hill Memorial Hospital. Below half-tide, the dock is left high and dry for some distance.

The west side of the inner harbor also has plenty of

anchorage space in 10 to 20 feet MLW. If setting the hook, it is best to wait for low tide when the limits to safe anchorage will be more apparent. There is good holding here in a mud bottom.

Side Trip: Union River Bay

Cruising sailors seldom use Union River Bay because its narrow north–south orientation makes sailing difficult in the prevailing summer southerlies, but this spot is very inviting for travelers who value their privacy. Ellsworth, north on the Union River, has a delightful Main Street that is accessible by dinghy at low tide. Be aware of possible strong currents, especially in rainy weather. A dam above Ellsworth controls the river current and level.

Anchorage: There are two well-protected anchorages: Mill Cove (8- to 13-foot MLW depths) and Patten Bay (14- to 20-foot MLW depths). The latter is within walking distance of the grocery store in Surry.

■ MOUNT DESERT ISLAND

Samuel de Champlain named this large magnificent island L'Isle de Monts Desert when he visited in 1604. Even though some visitors pronounce the name like "dessert," locals place the accent on the first syllable for the bare, "desert-like" mountaintops.

The free, propane-powered Island Explorer shuttle bus service (207-667-5796) is sponsored by Friends of Acadia and L.L. Bean and connects all the Acadia National Park destinations, villages and cruising harbors of Mount Desert: Bar Harbor, Northeast Harbor, Somes Sound, Southwest Harbor and Bass Harbor, as well as the airport. It's a great way to explore the entire island.

NAVIGATION: Use NOAA Charts 13312, 13316, 13318 and 13321. The shallow Mount Desert Narrows and a fixed 25-foot vertical clearance bridge on the northwest side of the island connecting it to the mainland prevent the circumnavigation of Mount Desert. Our coverage of the island moves counterclockwise from the bridge.

Northwest Cove to Seal Cove

Western Bay on the northwest side of Mount Desert Island has two good anchorages: Northwest Cove (with 7 to 10 feet MLW) and Goose Cove (with 7 to 13 feet MLW); however, both experience surge when southwesterlies are blowing.

Galley Cove to the south is a nice anchorage with a small beach off the northeast side of Bartlett Island. There is good protection from the southerlies and nice views of the "quiet side" of Mt. Desert Island. There is a municipal landing at Bartlett Narrows but there are no services ashore except for a trash dumpster. Pretty Marsh Harbor to the south on Mount Desert Island's western shore is easy to enter. The harbor is well protected and scenic and provides good holding in 8 to 13 feet MLW. Nearby Hardwood Island is privately owned. Seal Cove to the south has at least 14 feet MLW but is open to westerlies.

Bass Harbor

Bass Harbor, in the southwestern corner of the island, just off Blue Hill Bay, is southernmost of the fabulous isle's yacht harbors. A lovely port in the shadow of Mount Desert's hills, Bass Harbor has a substantial lobster fleet, a ferry to Swans Island and facilities in the inner and outer harbors.

In recent years, Bass Harbor has become popular with cruisers seeking serenity and scenery. Restaurants and bed and breakfasts dot the shore of the harbor, which is flanked by the cozy communities of Bass Harbor on the east and Bernard on the west.

NAVIGATION: Use NOAA Charts 13312 and 13318. The entrance is easy. Pass either side of Weaver Ledge (marked by two buoys) into the outer harbor (open to the south). On the eastern shore are the ferry slips, a full-service boatyard, the town dock and the village of Bass Harbor. When approaching the innermost area of the harbor be alert for red nun buoy "6," which can be obscured by moored boats and is deceptively close to the shore. Leave it to the east on entering the inner harbor and then turn into the mooring pool.

Dockage: There is a fuel dock (and wholesale seafood) near the entry to the well-buoyed inner harbor at F.W. Thurston Co. (207-244-3320). The Tremont Harbormaster (207-244-4564) oversees all activities in the harbor. On the western shore is the charming old community of Bernard, where the yellow roof of Thurston's Lobster Pound (207-244-7600) is prominent. Thurston's has short-term tie-ups (two boats at a time) and is a great place for a real Maine lobster dinner. The inner harbor is completely filled with private moorings making anchoring impossible.

Southwest Harbor

Southwest Harbor is a good stop for provisioning and playing "tourist." There are hiking possibilities (including Flying Mountain Hiking Trail and Wonderland Trail) and birders and wood carvers will want to visit the Wendell Gilley Museum (4 Herrick Rd., 207-244-7555) with a distinctive collection of bird and waterfowl carvings, demonstrations and workshops on wooden decoy carving.

Hamilton Marine (165 Clark Pt. Rd., 207-244-7870) has an extensive marine parts selection and is located on the north side of the harbor. A West Marine (11 Apple Ln., 207-244-0300) is located on the south side of the harbor.

In the village at the harbor head, you will find Sawyer's Market (344 Main St., 207-244-3315) selling groceries, meats, fresh vegetables and fresh breads. A close relative, Sawyer's Specialties, is a purveyor of fine wines, beer, liquor and other delicacies. They also deliver. A mile up the road, the Food Mart IGA (101 Main St., 207-244-5601) is a supermarket with reasonable prices for a destination island.

NAVIGATION: Use NOAA Charts 13312 and 13318. If approaching from the west, the pinch between the Bass Harbor Head Lighthouse and Great Gott Island creates a confluence of forces that must be respected. Most of the water between those landmasses washes over an 8-foot ledge. The 14-foot MLW channel between gong buoy "WB" to the west and gong buoy "EB" to the east rushes with fast currents and whistles with compressed and directed winds. Gong buoy "EB" periodically comes off station so you may need to keep checking the bearing to "WB" as you pass through the channel if you don't have an up-to-date chartplotter. If sailing, keep an eye on other boats to catch a glimpse of the wind sheer and plan your sheet-easing accordingly. Enter Western Way between Great Cranberry Island and the mainland of Mount Desert. Southwest Harbor opens up to the east and is frequently used by large commercial vessels and recreational boats.

Dockage/Moorings: Southwest Harbor has a large mooring field; contact the Southwest Harbor Harbormaster (207-244-7913 or VHF Channel 09) to reserve a mooring. The town maintains a public dinghy dock on the north side of the harbor.

The Hinckley Company's well-known yacht yard and ship store are on the south shore at Manset. What began in 1928 as a small service yard today ranks as a world-class builder of power and sailing yachts. Hinckley Yacht Services Southwest Harbor has 70 moorings and can accommodate vessels to 150 feet.

Dysart's Great Harbor Marina at the head of the harbor has 135 floating slips with 50 reserved for transients behind a breakwater and numerous amenities including a West Marine, a sail loft, bakery, provisioning service and a restaurant. They also sell gas and diesel fuel.

Southwest Boat Marine Services can facilitate repairs for recreational and commercial vessels and may have transient space for you; call ahead. Beal's Lobster Pier, next to the Coast Guard station, has moorings, a does the Claremont Hotel. Call ahead for availability.

Anchorage: Anchoring is no longer allowed in Southwest Harbor but good holding can be found between the Southwest Harbor shore and Greening Island, north of the harbor proper and east of the Coast Guard station. Holding is best closer to Greening Island in 12 to 17 feet MLW. This does, however, create a lengthy dinghy ride to shore access at the town dock.

Somes Sound

Considered the only true fjord on the North American east coast, Somes Sound begins its dramatic 6-mile cleavage into the heart of Mount Desert Island at the busy channel off Clark Point, the tip of the peninsula that separates Southwest Harbor from the sound. Throughout most of the sound's length, 600 to 800-foot hills ease down to the water's edge and beyond. In the background, mountains of substantially greater size add grandeur to an awe-inspiring landscape and seascape.

Outside the prevailing southwesterly winds, those under sail will find the sound reminiscent of lake sailing–whistling winds abating almost instantly to a dead calm, rapid wind shifts and reversals of 180 degrees. Part way along, Valley Cove attracts adventuresome crews with the promise of accessible paths to the summits of the sheer cliffs above for stunning views. The water is deep in the cove (up to 90 feet) within a short distance of the shore.

A short walk from the landing is the Village of Somesville, the oldest settlement on Mount Desert Island. The town's white-washed clapboard houses and vintage public buildings are bordered by garlands of brilliant flowers, encouraging visitors to stretch their legs in search of the perfect photo from the head of the harbor. The Mount Desert Historical Society Museum (373 Sound Rd., 207-276-9323) is tucked behind a flower-ringed pond crossed by the **Thaddeus Shepley Somes Bow Bridge**, which fairly begs to be photographed. It crosses

DYSART'S GREAT HAR-
BOR MARINA

Southwest Harbor

a lake created by a dam that was originally built by the island's first permanent settler, Abraham Somes. The museum offers year-round entertaining and informative educational programs.

Turn north on the highway from the harbor road then cross the street to use the sidewalk for less than a mile walk to basic commercial amenities. On the Run (1052 Hwy. 102, 207-244-5504), also known as Circle K, stocks some groceries and various deli items and prepared sandwiches among other sundries. You can have your propane tank filled here and there are FedEx and UPS drop stations. The Mount Desert Post Office is right across the street.

NAVIGATION: Use NOAA Charts 13312 and 13318. Somes Harbor is entered west of Myrtle Ledge through the deep but narrow passage between green can buoy "7" and Bar Island (owned by the State of Maine and open for exploration).

Moorings: Several moorings are likely to be vacant in Somes Harbor, although no one manages their use while their owners are away. To the south on the west side of the sound, John Williams Boat Company rents a few transient moorings and can facilitate engine, hull and rigging repairs.

Anchorage: Valley Cove on the southwestern side of Somes Sound is a good anchorage. Make sure you have sufficient scope for 30- to 40-foot MLW depths. Sargent Cove on the east side of the sound is a good anchorage with depths from 7 to 15 feet MLW. At the head of

DYSART'S GREAT HARBOR MARINA
Full service marina in the heart of Acadia National Park

West Marine • Ethanol Free Gas
Maine Point Embroidery • Free Internet WiFi
Hinckley Yacht Service • Little Notch Bakery
Diesel • Mail and FedEx • Yacht Provisioning
Alongside Floating Docks • Breakfast Restaurant
Upper Deck Seafood Restaurant • New Breakwater •
Recently Dredged to 16' MLW

Tel: (207) 224 0117 • www.dysartsmarina.com
VHF Channel 9
No. 11 Apple Lane • PO Box 1503
Southwest Harbor • Maine • 04679

Find us on Facebook

NORTHERN EDITION 535

Mount Desert Island, ME

		Largest Vessel Accomodated	VHF Channel Monitored / Working	Approach / Dockside Depth (reported)	Transient Slips / Total Slips	Floating Docks	Groceries, Ice, Marine Supplies, Snacks	Gas / Diesel	Repairs: Hull, Engine, Propeller	Lift (tonnage), Crane, Rail	Min / Max Amps	Courtesy Car, Laundry, Pool, Showers	Pump-Out Station	Nearby: Grocery Store, Motel, Restaurant
SOUTHWEST HARBOR				**Dockage**				**Supplies**			**Services**			
1. Hinckley Yacht Services Southwest Harbor	(207) 244-5531	150	10/	/	30.0/25.0		D		IS	HEP	L160,C		LS	P	GMR
2. Dysart's Great Harbor Marina 🖥 WiFi	**(207) 244-0117**	200	9/8	50/135	15.0/15.1	F	GD	IMS	HEP		30/200+	CLS	P	GMR
3. Southwest Boat Marine Services	(207) 244-5525	120	/	5/24	25.0/14.0	F					C,R	50		P	GMR
4. Beal's Lobster Pier	(207) 244-3202	100	16/88	/	15.0/10.0	F	GD								GR
5. Claremont Hotel	(800) 244-5036	40	/	/	30.0/7.0			I							GMR
SOMES SOUND															
6. John Williams Boat Company	(207) 244-7854	60	/	/	/38.0					HEP	L50,C				
NORTHEAST HARBOR															
7. Morris Service Northeast Harbor WiFi	(207) 276-5301	60	9/	12/18	6.0/6.0	F		GIMS	HEP	L25,C	50	LS		GMR
8. Northeast Harbor Marina 🖥 WiFi	(207) 276-5737	180	9/68	15/60	12.0/12.0	F		I			30/100	LS	P	GMR
9. Clifton Dock Corporation	(207) 276-5308	100	9/	/	30.0/20.0	F	GD	IMS					P	GMR
BAR HARBOR															
10. Bar Harbor Municipal Pier 🖥 WiFi	(207) 288-5571	185	9/68	8/8	16.0/11.0	F					30/100	LS	P	GMR
11. Harborside Hotel, Spa & Marina 🖥 WiFi	(207) 801-3904	200	1/	8/8	7.0/8.0	F	D	I			30/200+	LPS	P	MR
12. Bar Harbor Regency Oceanfront Resort & Marina	(207) 288-9723	150	/	10/	15.0/12.0	F	GD	I			30/100	LPS		GMR

🖥 Internet Access   WiFi Wireless Internet Access   ⦿onSpot Dockside WiFi Facility

See WaterwayGuide.com for current rates, fuel prices, website addresses, and other up-to-the-minute information. (Information in the table is provided by the facilities.)

Southwest Harbor

Mount Desert Island

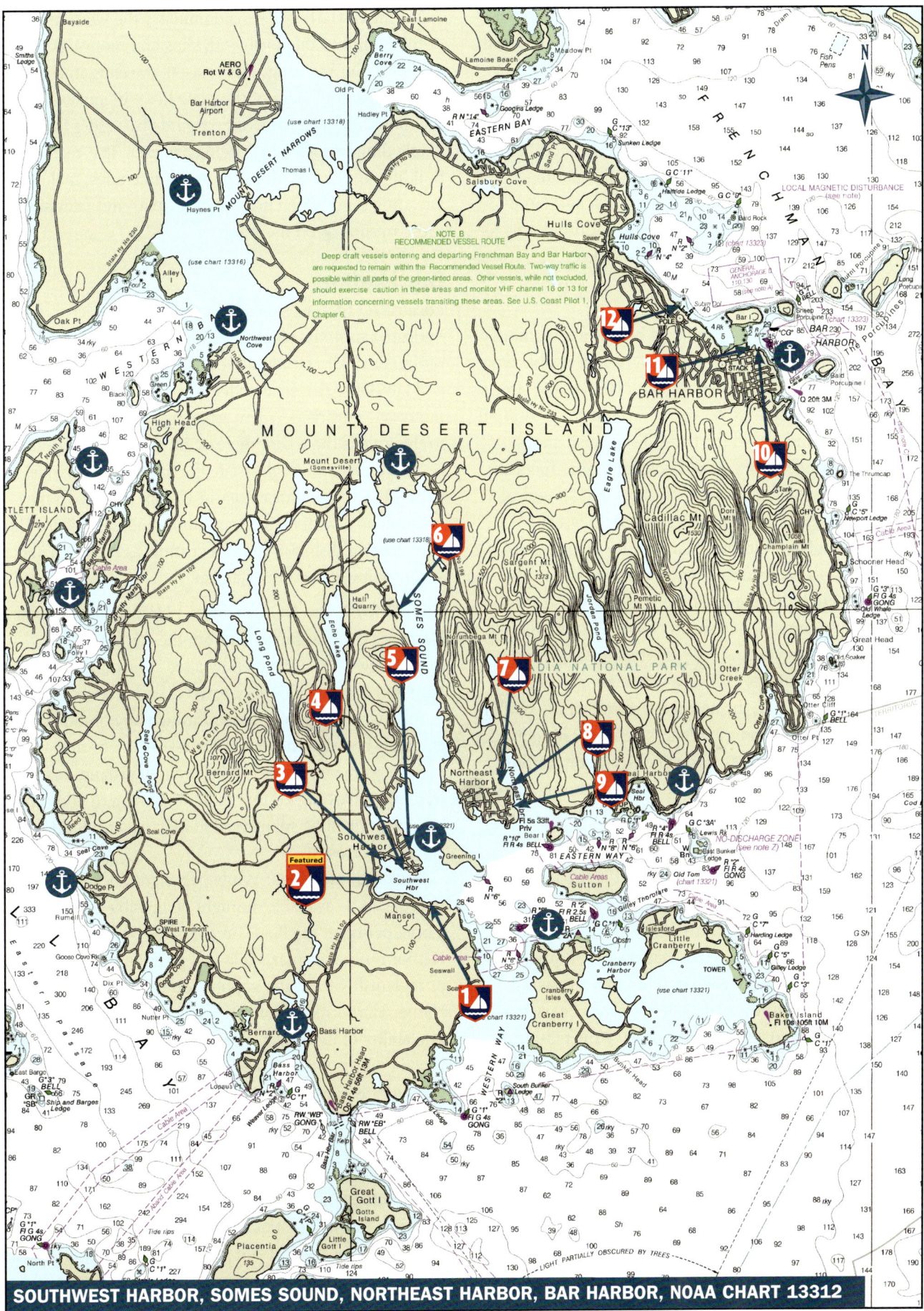

SOUTHWEST HARBOR, SOMES SOUND, NORTHEAST HARBOR, BAR HARBOR, NOAA CHART 13312

head of the sound to the east of Squatum Pt. is another nice anchorage (unless the wind is out of the south) with 6-foot MLW depths.

Numerous private moorings dot the Somes Harbor, yet you will still find adequate swing room northeast of Mason Point with 15-foot MLW depths and good holding. On the west side of the harbor, Somesville Landing Corp. maintains a substantial floating dock and ramp to accommodate dinghies (transients to the south, locals to the north). They request donations for upkeep.

Northeast Harbor

Northeast Harbor is well-organized but always seemingly filled to capacity and hosts nearly every conceivable type of recreational vessel. As in Southwest Harbor, the streets of the town are thronged by visitors who enjoy a meal off the boat and finding hidden treasures in small shops. A gift and wine specialties shop, bookstore, coin-operated laundry, newspaper and stationery store and several attractive galleries and boutiques line Main Street.

F.T. Brown Hardware and Marine (106 Main St., 207-276-3329) is a well-stocked hardware store with some foul-weather clothing and fishing gear. They also carry basic marine supplies in a shed behind the store. Bicycle rentals are just beyond.

The Thuya Gardens (207-276-5130) are permanently moored to the hill on the northeastern side of the harbor and are a botanist's and a gardener's delight. This gorgeous flowering garden features an open observation pavilion that sits at the top of a slight incline on the north end overlooking the main garden that cascades down to a shallow reflecting pool below.

NAVIGATION: Use NOAA Charts 13312 and 13318. Northeast Harbor is a landlocked bight, easily entered from the south. Its only obstruction is a rock located about 500 yards directly off the center of the harbor's mouth marked by green can buoy "1" to the east and red bell buoy "2" to the west. The rock may be passed on either side, if you take care to observe the red-right-returning rule for the eastern passage around the rock, west of Bear Island and red nun buoys "2A" and "4."

Dockage/Moorings: Northeast Harbor maintains a complimentary 2-hour-max floating dock with water and power just south of the looming concrete municipal pier. The dock is in high demand and waiting for a spot can encourage a visitor to request a spot at a paid dock. There are also moorings available for a fee. Anchoring is not permitted in the harbor.

Northeast Harbor Marina dominates the western cove of the harbor to the north with slips and moorings. Some are two-point moorings and cruisers traveling in company can request both sides of the same float. In any event, the moorings are a relatively easy ride by tender from the ample dinghy dock at the municipal pier. The Yachtsmen's Building on the waterfront provides amenities, including a reading room with current newspapers and television to those in slips or on moorings.

Bar Harbor

Located on the east side of Mount Desert, under the imposing summits of Cadillac, Dorr and Champlain Mountains, Bar Harbor attracts throngs of hikers, climbers and kayakers, as well as sedentary vacationers and motorists. Surprisingly few arrive by water. An exception to this rule is the recent increase in visits by cruise ships. Be aware that you might share the harbor and channel with a 1,000-foot cruise liner or two and the town may be inundated with their several thousand passengers. But don't let that dismay you from visiting, as the town and surrounding area are spectacular.

NAVIGATION: Use NOAA Charts 13312 and 13318. Bar Harbor is easily approached from the south on either side of Egg Rock, identified by a red 5-second flashing light and horn on a 64-foot tower. The harbor is open to the east and can be entered through any of the deep channels between the Porcupine Islands. A breakwater extends to the west from Bald Porcupine Island, marked by a quick flashing 20-foot light at its western end. The breakwater will be submerged at high water but do not attempt to cross it.

Dockage/Moorings: While overnight dockage is unlikely to be available, it might be possible to tie up for a brief period at the floats on the eastern side of the Bar Harbor municipal pier while you provision, change crews or replenish your water supply. You can reach the Bar Harbor Harbormaster on VHF Channel 09 to check on availability of moorings. The town's large dinghy dock is located on the western side of the pier.

Nearby is Harborside Hotel, Spa & Marina, which offers transient dockage that includes access to resort amenities. Access to the village center will require about a 1-mile walk or taxi ride.

Anchorage: While it is possible to anchor outside the mooring area just east of the municipal pier, the holding ground is poor in sand and grass and the relatively open harbor can become quite rough. Leaving an anchored boat unattended here is not recommended.

Side Trip: Great Cranberry Island

Just two to three miles southwest of Mt. Desert's Southwest Harbor, the Cranberry Islands seem remote yet accessible and familiar. Combining a mix of working lobstermen, long-term summer residents, artists and artisans, these islands are both interesting and friendly places to visit. Even though the namesake cranberry bogs have long been drained, these islands still excel for pleasant walks with seascape backdrops of Mount Desert.

Great Cranberry Island, the largest of the group, is home to some 50 families year-round and a much expanded summer population. Great Cranberry Island Historical Society (251 Great Cranberry Rd., 207-244-7800) details the history and sense of community of the islands in its arts center. Behind the museum is a lovely public trail (about 1 mile) through the woods to Whistlers Cove on the Western Way.

Cranberry Road is lined with views of water on both sides and lovely old ship captains' homes. One-half mile away is Cranberry House (163 Cranberry Rd.), which hosts the Preble-Marr Historical Museum (207-244-7800). The museum documents the island's varied history from Penobscot rule, European settlement, shipbuilding and the influx of wealthy "Rusticators" to the present. The front deck of the Cranberry House is the location of Hitty's Café (207-244-7845), serving lunch and ice cream treats. You can also check your email using their WiFi. Along the parking lot next to the town dock is the Cranberry General Store (138 Shore Front Rd., 207-244-0622).

NAVIGATION: Use NOAA Chart 13318. The approach to Spurling Cove on the north side of Great Cranberry Island is open and straightforward. The few outlying obstructions are well marked.

Anchorage: Although wide open to the north and northwest, anchorage is possible outside Spurling Cove's mooring field in 10- to 15-foot MLW depths and there is a dinghy float at the (west) public dock. If weather conditions preclude anchoring off Great Cranberry, consider taking a mooring in Northeast Harbor and riding one of the regular ferries to the island.

Side Trip: Little Cranberry Island

Little Cranberry Island is smaller, yet attracts a greater number of visitors by boat. Perhaps this is because the number of shoreside attractions is greater and the woodsy walks, though just as appealing, are shorter. The vibrant community of Islesford–some 400 in the summer, although it pares down to about 80 in the winter–seems to instill those who visit with a yen to return for years to come.

The Islesford Dock is a local gathering place and something of a destination point for locals "in the know" from Mount Desert. Just inland of the dock and to the left, the National Park Service maintains the tiny but fascinating Islesford Museum, which displays well-presented artifacts and pictures of traditional Maine island life. The Neighborhood House and Library has a remarkable children's collection and houses Julia's Garden, a sculpted cedar fencing enclosing a must-see collection of local mosses, plants and flowers.

Bar Harbor

Frenchman Bay, ME

			Dockage			Supplies		Services					
	VHF Channel Monitored / Working	Largest Vessel Accomodated	Approach / Dockside Depth (reported)	Transient Slips / Total Slips	Floating Docks	Gas / Diesel	Groceries, Ice, Marine Supplies Snacks	Repairs: Hull, Engine Propeller	Lift (tonnage), Crane, Rail	Courtesy Car Laundry, Pool, Showers	Min / Max Amps	Pump-Out Station	Nearby: Grocery Store, Motel, Restaurant
SORRENTO													
1. Sorrento Town Dock	(207) 266-5706	80	9/	/	/4.0								18
HANCOCK POINT													
2. Hancock Point Dock	(207) 422-3393		/	/	/								MR

🖳 Internet Access   **WIFI** Wireless Internet Access   **onSpot** Dockside WiFi Facility

See WaterwayGuide.com for current rates, fuel prices, website addresses, and other up-to-the-minute information. (Information in the table is provided by the facilities.)

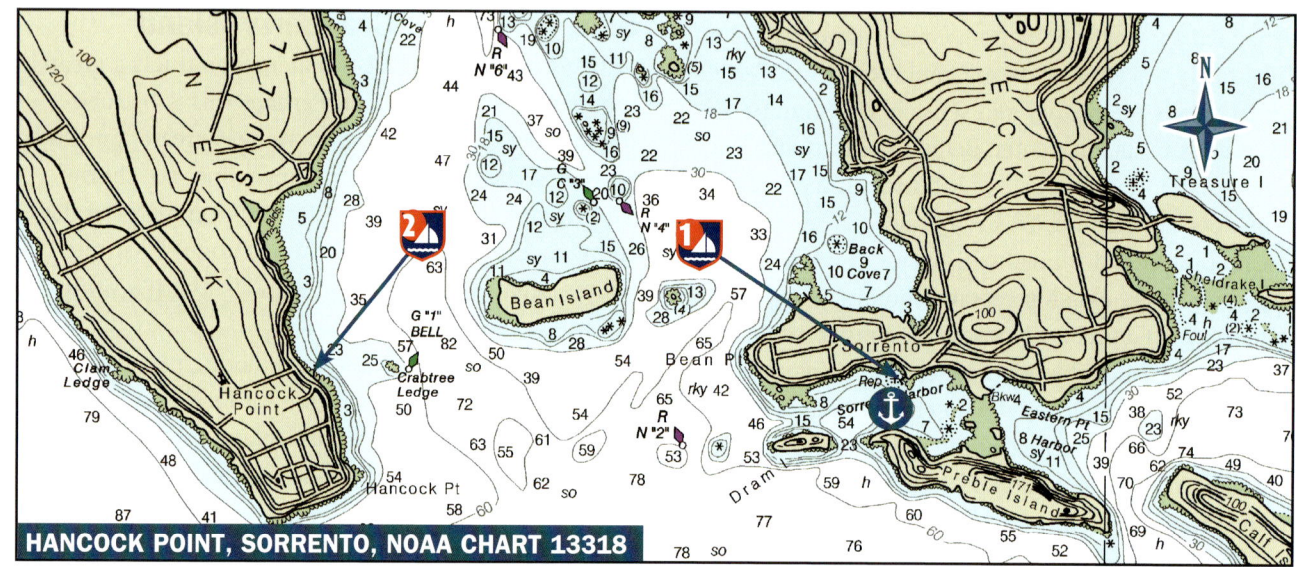

HANCOCK POINT, SORRENTO, NOAA CHART 13318

Frenchman Bay

Islesford Dock Restaurant is a hopping destination that can provide small plates and drinks or full meals with equal ease. Keep your eyes peeled for the seafood stew in a copper tureen and consider how hungry you really are. In addition to serving great food, they also sell fuel. Left of the ferry dock, the Lobstermen's Co-op sells fresh live lobsters.

NAVIGATION: Use NOAA Chart 13318. Little Cranberry Island is as easily accessed as its sister island to the west. Simply steer north of red bell buoy "2," marking Spurling Rock and an unnamed 6-foot MLW hump and enter Hadlock Cove, west and then south of green can buoys "1" and "3."

Moorings/Anchorage: The town of Islesford maintains three moorings marked GUEST, which are complimentary for up to two nights. Cruise the outer southwestern edge of the mooring field to find them.

Anchoring is possible outside the mooring area in Hadlock Cove but the bottom here is covered with thick grass and often kelp. (Even more so toward the head of the harbor.) Setting a hook securely enough to handle relatively swift currents of reversing tides may require several tries.

Tie up loosely at the crowded dinghy dock alongside the ferry landing so each dinghy can make its way to the dock for loading and unloading. Stay clear of the face dock, which is regularly taken over by the inter-island ferry from Northeast Harbor.

◼ FRENCHMAN BAY

Frenchman Bay offers a few harbors on its eastern side, but most of the services (and they are significant) are offered in the well-established and visitor-centric harbors of Mount Desert Island.

Frenchman Bay is 4 miles wide, 10 miles long and easy to navigate, and it offers dramatic views of Mount Desert and the bluffs of the Schoodic Peninsula to the east. A group of islands with deep channels between them cuts across the bay about halfway up, creating shelter for the upper bay. It is a spectacular run up the bay along sea-washed cliffs past Thunder Hole (where you can hear the surf crashing against the rocks at the right tidal stage), Sand Beach (behind Old Soaker) and great inland mountains.

Sorrento Harbor & Hancock Point

NAVIGATION: Use NOAA Chart 13318. Sorrento is at the tip of Waukeeg Neck and it resembles its namesake, Sorrento, Italy, which is another city by the sea with spectacular mountain vistas.

Dockage/Moorings: The Sorrento Town Dock has limited space (no amenities). There are guest moorings maintained by the Sorrento Yacht Club. Across the bay from Sorrento Harbor is Hancock Point Dock, which has just one transient mooring.

Anchorage: Protection is excellent throughout the Sorrento Harbor in at least 8-foot MLW depths.

Winter Harbor

Three harbors make up Winter Harbor, which is unobstructed and easy to enter from the south, even in fog. Each harbor has a landing with a floating dock but ease of access to the village varies. The Post Office is about 0.5 mile east on Main Street and the Winter Harbor IGA (254 Main St., 207-963-2256) is across the street.

The Channing Chapel (18 Chapel Ln., 207-963-7556), home to an excellent public library, was built of beach and field stones in 1888. The owner established a free library of the classics in the upper rooms and that tradition was continued except for a long period after the chapel was sold in 1958. The library returned in 1996 under the auspices of the Channing Chapel Preservation Society.

NAVIGATION: Use NOAA Chart 13318. From the north the option to head around the islands off the Grindstone Neck may seem troublesome compared to cutting between Spectacle and Turtle Islands, but the ledges between the island are unmarked and are better attempted with local knowledge. Taking the route south of Turtle and Mark Islands has the additional benefit of providing a good view of an abandoned lighthouse on Mark Island's hillside.

Continuing due north from the green-over-red gong buoy "MI," the wooded shores of Grindstone Neck will eventually retreat west and reveal the distinctive clubhouse of the Winter Harbor Yacht Club on the west shore of Sand Cove. Harbor Point will be directly ahead with Inner Winter Harbor and Henry Cove north and east, respectively.

Moorings: Protection is only fair in Sand Cove. Your boat will pitch a bit here when the wind is up but the Winter Harbor Yacht Club's moorings are up to the task.

Winter Harbor, ME

		Largest Vessel Accomodated	VHF Channel Monitored / Working	Transient Slips / Total Slips	Approach / Dockside Depth (reported)	Floating Docks	Gas / Diesel	Groceries, Ice, Marine Supplies, Snacks	Repairs: Hull, Engine, Propeller	Lift (tonnage), Crane, Rail	Courtesy Car, Laundry, Pool, Showers	Min / Max Amps	Pump-Out Station	Nearby: Grocery Store, Motel, Restaurant
		Dockage						**Supplies**		**Services**			
SAND COVE													
1. Winter Harbor Yacht Club	(207) 963-2346	55	9/9	/	50.0/20.0			IS			S		
HENRY COVE													
2. Winter Harbor Marine Inc.	(207) 963-7449	100	16/9	/	35.0/25.0	GD		GIMS	HEP		LS	P	GMR

⬚ Internet Access **WiFi** Wireless Internet Access **onSpot** Dockside WiFi Facility

See WaterwayGuide.com for current rates, fuel prices, website addresses, and other up-to-the-minute information. (Information in the table is provided by the facilities.)

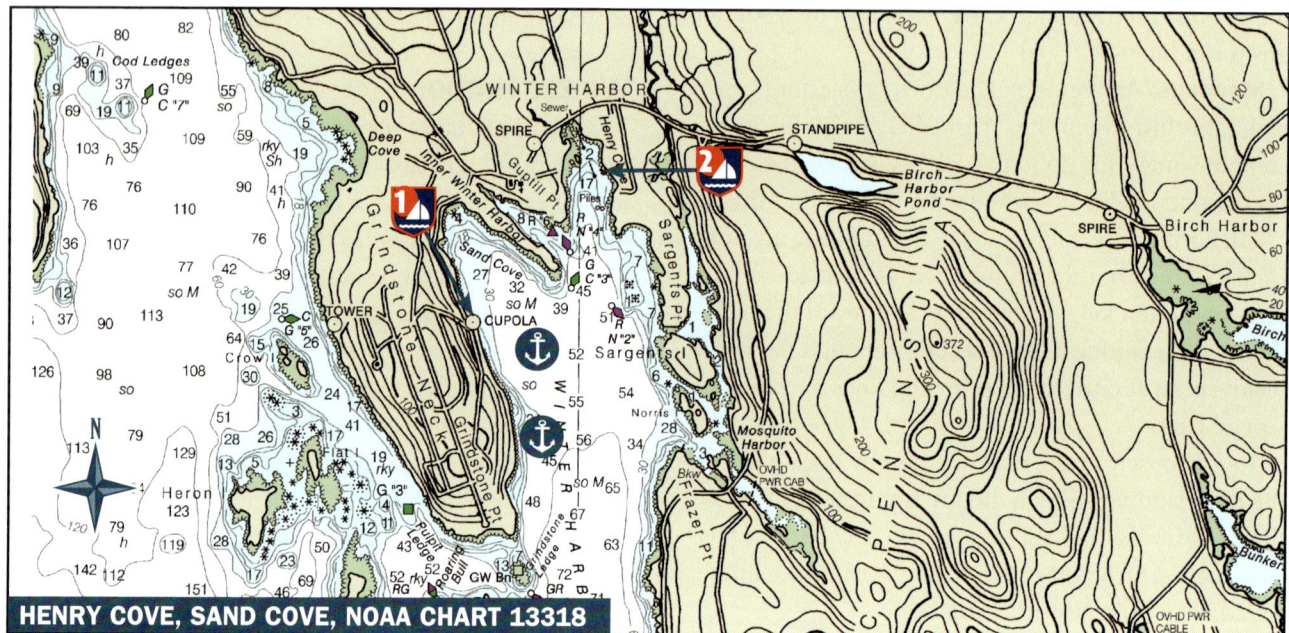

HENRY COVE, SAND COVE, NOAA CHART 13318

Launch and trash disposal services are included with the mooring fee, and showers are available in the clubhouse basement for a small fee.

There are no other facilities on Sand Cove and the village is about a 1-mile walk north. Another mile or so trek on the dirt road east from the clubhouse will take you to pleasant outlooks over the pink granite shore at the southern tip of Grindstone Neck.

Local fishers have wisely claimed virtually the entire Inner Harbor, which offers the harbor's overall best protection. There is no room to anchor but it may be possible to secure a vacant mooring; ask a lobsterman. Winter Harbor Co-Op has a dock and float with both gasoline and diesel fuel (207-963-5857). It may be possible to rent dock space with electricity here. The village is but a few blocks away from the landing.

Henry Cove, a straight shot in from the outer harbor, is the most exposed of the three coves but is relatively convenient to groceries and restaurants. Winter Harbor Marine on the east side of the cove sell all fuels and may be able to make room for you. Call ahead.

Anchorage: There is plenty of deep water and anchorage room in 25 to 35 feet MLW with excellent holding in mud on either end of the Sand Cove mooring field in the outer harbor. Continuing past the mooring field to the end of the cove might reveal room to anchor off the pebble beach in 7 to 10 feet MLW, cutting out a good deal of the walk into town after beaching the dinghy. Henry Cove has anchorage in 17 to 22 feet MLW with excellent holding in mud but more exposure to the south.

■ EAST FROM SCHOODIC POINT

Beyond Mount Desert and Schoodic Point lies a green, lonesome land of ragged islands, rocky reaches, swift Bay of Fundy currents and ever-increasing tidal stages.

An exciting, even dangerous coast, this is an area for the experienced captain or the wary neophyte not the afternoon sailor in a small powerboat or low-powered auxiliary. The currents along this stretch of coast often create strong "whirlpool" eddies, which the prudent navigator should avoid, especially during peak ebb flow.

From Schoodic Point east, tidal range increases rapidly. Sixteen feet is normal for U.S. waters (easterly storms add a fathom) and in the Bay of Fundy, the tidal difference reaches 60 feet. Obviously, such tidal changes produce powerful currents of widely varying set. No graphs or sets of tables help much and current predictions are impossible.

For the last swath of Maine coast the best guidebook is experience and vigilance. You will need excellent planning and routing skills, practical navigational know-how, a thorough oceangoing knowledge of your boat and how she responds under all weather conditions and enough mechanical ability to make repairs as needed. Between Winter Harbor and Eastport, more than 60 miles away, there are no lifts and few mechanics.

All vessels should be equipped with a depth sounder, a VHF radio, GPS, radar and a stable dinghy. A cabin heater is often welcome to dry out during foggy spells and to warm up on chilly evenings. The best time for cruising extends from mid-July to late August, although some cruisers enjoy the clear, cool weather of early September.

Between Schoodic Point and the U.S./Canadian border (which bisects Quoddy Roads) lie a few dozen islands and ports where fuel is available. Few have fresh water in quantity; fewer still have dockside electricity; however, most offer excellent mechanical services. In general, fuel ports lie well up the reaches so allow for a fairly lengthy inshore run when fuel gets low.

These are working ports, not yachting centers but cruising folks are welcomed with a smile. Most Down East towns have no facilities other than small lobster boat docks so be prepared to make touch-and-go dockside stops, if any at all, and get out on a mooring or anchor for the night. The exception is Eastport, which is described later in this section.

Despite such daunting observations, the ragged island outposts to the east bear silent witness to an increasing parade of recreational craft under sail and power each summer, as intrepid voyagers seek the solitude and pleasure of a near-wilderness experience.

Inshore or Offshore Route

NAVIGATION: Use NOAA Charts 13324 and 13326. The 39-foot fixed vertical clearance Bridge Street (Beals Island) Bridge on Moosabec Reach usually dictates the choice between going offshore or running the coast. The cruiser who runs outside the islands and headlands and works the sea buoys has a comparatively easy but less interesting run than the vessel cruising the reaches and thoroughfares. The former faces the usual blue water sea and weather problems, while the latter follows stretches of coast where carpets of lobster buoys intermingle with small islands and ledges crowded with sunbathing seals. The route has hazards that make piloting a challenge even to the experienced cruising mariner, but the payoff of breathtaking scenery makes the adventure well worth the effort.

When Schoodic Head and the island disappear into the fog astern, some harbors of a different stripe lie ahead. As long as the wind is fair and seas are moderate, do not let fog interfere with your cruising plans. Fog is simply a fact of life here so having the proper tools to deal with it is essential.

Jonesport

This small fishing Village of Jonesport, with less than 1,500 residents, has a state pier, launching ramp, fuel, ice and some provisions (at a small convenience store). Jonesport Pizza Shop (187 Main St., 207-497-2187) is the town's breakfast spot in addition to selling pizza, beer and some groceries.

If you can handle the 39-foot fixed vertical clearance **Bridge Street (Beals Island) Bridge**, sail through Moosabec Reach to Jonesport. Otherwise, you must use the eastern approach around Head Harbor Island. The tidal range at Jonesport is impressive as is the speed of ebb and flood currents.

Moorings: Jonesport Shipyard is located here with a few moorings. Do not try to dock at the Look Wharf. An orange mooring ball is in the narrow channel just in front of the co-op's dock, which you can use for a short transaction, but vessels of more than 30 feet will have to move to make room for unloading lobster boats when they arrive. Ask about the availability of a mooring in the inner harbor for a longer stay.

Anchorage: East of Petit Manan there are many islands in Narraguagus Bay and Pleasant Bay that are highly regarded as secure anchorages. In Narraguagus

Moosabec Reach, ME

JONESPORT				Dockage				Supplies		Services			
	VHF Channel Monitored / Working	Largest Vessel Accomodated	Approach / Dockside Depth (reported)	Transient Slips / Total Slips	Floating Docks	Gas / Diesel	Groceries, Ice, Marine Supplies, Snacks	Repairs: Hull, Engine, Propeller	Lift (tonnage), Crane, Rail	Courtesy Car, Laundry, Pool, Showers	Min / Max Amps	Pump-Out Station	Nearby: Grocery Store, Motel, Restaurant
1. Jonesport Shipyard 💻	(207) 497-2701	45	9/9	/	6.0/6.0	F		M	HEP	L30,C		LS	GR

💻 Internet Access 📶 Wireless Internet Access 🌐onSpot Dockside WiFi Facility

See WaterwayGuide.com for current rates, fuel prices, website addresses, and other up-to-the-minute information. (Information in the table is provided by the facilities.)

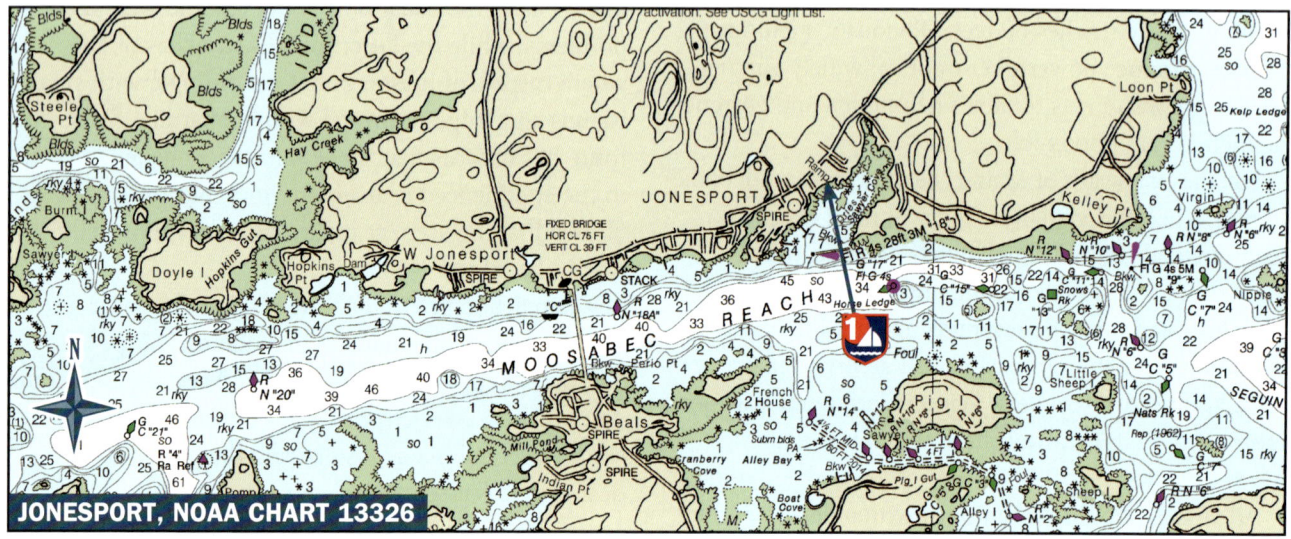

JONESPORT, NOAA CHART 13326

Bay, anchor north of Trafton Island in 8 to 14 feet MLW with fair holding in soft mud and rock. This is exposed to the north. From here you can pass through deep Flint Island Narrows to an anchorage northeast of Flint Island, where you will find at least 22 feet MLW with good holding in sand and rock. This is exposed to the north.

If you need protection from the north, Eastern Harbor behind Moose Neck has at least 7 feet MLW and good holding in mud and rock. There are also good anchorages scattered throughout the islands of Western Bay. Just pick through the islands carefully and watch for ledges and uncharted rocks.

Eastern Bay

This island-studded Eastern Bay lies partly enclosed between Great Wass Island on the west side and Head Harbor Island and Steele Harbor Island on the east. In clear weather Eastern Bay is an intricate but generally well-buoyed puzzle. In fog it becomes a worrisome place when landmarks and navigational aids are obscured. Fortunately, a reliable foghorn is mounted on the lighthouse (flashing 30-second light at 72 feet in elevation) at what is known as Moose

Peak, showing the way into the deep passage of Main Channel Way east of Mistake and Knight Islands. Do not attempt to enter the false channel between these two islands. While high tide gives the appearance of a channel here, a barely submerged rock ledge bars the way.

Anchorage: Having entered Main Channel Way, west of Steel Harbor Island, make a turn south around the northern end of Knight Island, which will lead to a well-protected anchorage between Mistake Island and Water Island in 10 to 15 feet MLW. There is room for half a dozen boats here, but be wary of kelp that can foul your anchor and of shoaling that occurs on the western side of Mistake Island. From here a short dinghy ride into the cut between Knight and Mistake Islands will bring you to an abandoned Coast Guard boathouse and ramp. A wooden boardwalk leads through the scrub and the abundant blueberry and raspberry bushes on the way to the lighthouse on Moose Peak. (Be ready for a piercing blast from the foghorn if light conditions weaken.) The lightkeeper's house is long gone but the scenery and views on a clear day make the trip well worth the effort.

Eastern Bay has numerous other anchorages, particularly along the east and north shores of Great

Wass Island. The most important of these, both for the beauty of its setting and hurricane hole protection, is in Mud Hole. This 1-mile-long cleft in the east side of Great Wass Island is northwest of the northern tip of Knight Island. Entry and departure are most safely made on a rising tide, half tide or higher, skirting the south side of the harbor entrance to avoid a grass-covered shoal that blocks the north side. Reports are that the submerged remains of an old weir obstruct the area about 0.125 mile outside the entrance to the south (on entry). You will want to skirt that location before heading toward the south side of the harbor entry to work your way in, where you will find depths of 16 feet MLW and excellent holding in mud.

In settled weather good anchorage can be made outside Mud Hole in at least 14 feet MLW to permit exploration by dinghy. Most of Great Wass Island is owned by the Nature Conservancy, which maintains hiking trails. Park your dinghy at a likely landing spot on the south side of Mud Hole (keeping in mind the 10-foot tidal range when tying off the painter) and scramble up the bank for about 50 yards to reach the unmistakable trail above. In a 2-hour summer walk through the spruce forests, along the boreal bogs and out to the granite beaches, you will undoubtedly observe dozens of types of mosses and lichens, a variety of mushrooms, bell flowers, beach irises and possibly unusual plants such as the baked-apple berry and dragon's mouth orchid. American eagles are frequent visitors, as are numerous songbirds including the palm warbler, which nests here.

Roque Island

Privately owned Roque Island has a large outer harbor with a deservedly famous beach. The entire island is posted as a wildlife stronghold and a sign prominently posted by the Roque Island Gardner Homestead Corp. denies access beyond the beach itself except to those with written permission from the island's owners. The owners request that you do not enter the southern half of the 1-mile-long beach, which is reserved for the Gardner family. Despite these restrictions, the area is worth a stop because of its extraordinary beauty. Bald eagles are almost inevitably sighted here and Seal Ledge on the eastern side of the harbor is still appropriately named.

Anchorage: Pick your spot at Rogue Island according to wind. Secure anchorage is easy in sand or mud and located only a short ride from a dinghy landing on the beach. Lakeman Harbor, formed by Marsh, Bar and Lakeman Islands at the southeastern end of Roque Island, offers a protected inner harbor with secure holding in 7 to 8 feet MLW. Chandler Bay to the north in Roque Harbor has 10 to 15 feet MLW and excellent holding in hard sand.

On the northern side of Roque Island, Shorey Cove is protected from the prevailing southwesterlies and offers good holding in 7 to 11 feet MLW with pleasant views of the Gardner houses, barns and docks. Public use of the dock is prohibited. The rock "Rep" in the center of the channel west of Great Spruce Island is reportedly not to be found by either depth sounder or keel.

Cutler

Beyond Cross Island and northwest of Grand Manan Channel is Cutler, marked by the 56-foot Little River Island light and horn. Cutler is closer to open water than many of the villages along this coast, yet is a secure anchorage except in a piping nor'easter. It is also a good point of departure for the Canadian Maritime Provinces and is frequently a gathering place for club cruises rallying for an international passage. It has little to offer in the way of amenities but there is WiFi available at the town library. Cutler is the home of the U.S. Navy's very low frequency (VLF) transmitter station, which provides one-way communication to U.S. strategic submarine forces.

Moorings/Anchorage: A few moorings might be available but most boats anchor in soft mud. Dragging anchors are commonplace in a blow. You can land a dinghy on the dark beach in front of the village's cluster of houses, although you should make provision for the Fundy-influenced 13-foot tides. You can also make landing farther down the harbor at the float at the end of the Little River Lobster Co. dock. Just tie your dinghy to the dock and carefully climb the wooden ladder marked with a sign that says, "Pass at Your Own Risk."

Lubec Narrows

A day's sail east of Cutler will bring you to West Quoddy Head, the easternmost point of land in the United States. Around the corner from the barber-pole lighthouse, Lubec Channel leads to the town of Lubec and eventually to Eastport. Lubec is located on the narrows of the same name, separating Maine from Canada. You can take a taxi to Campobello Island, where the former home of Franklin and Eleanor Roosevelt is open to the public.

Friar Roads, ME

		Largest Vessel Accomodated	VHF Channel Monitored / Working	Transient Slips / Total Slips	Approach / Dockside Depth (reported)	Floating Docks	Gas / Diesel	Groceries, Ice, Marine Supplies, Snacks	Repairs: Hull, Engine, Propeller	Lift (tonnage), Crane, Rail	Min / Max Amps	Courtesy Car, Laundry, Pool, Showers	Pump-Out Station	Nearby: Grocery Store, Motel, Restaurant
				Dockage			**Supplies**			**Services**				
LUBEC														
1. Lubec Municipal Marina	(207) 733-8999		9/16	10/10	/	F	D	I			L	30/50	LS	GMR
EASTPORT														
2. Moose Island Marine	(207) 853-6058	60	11/11	/	/	F		IM	HE	L60,C				GMR
3. Eastport Breakwater/City Dock	(207) 853-4614	180	16/9	20/50	40.0/8.0	F	GD	GIMS		L50			L	GMR

☐ Internet Access   [WiFi] Wireless Internet Access   ⊙onSpot Dockside WiFi Facility

See WaterwayGuide.com for current rates, fuel prices, website addresses, and other up-to-the-minute information. (Information in the table is provided by the facilities.)

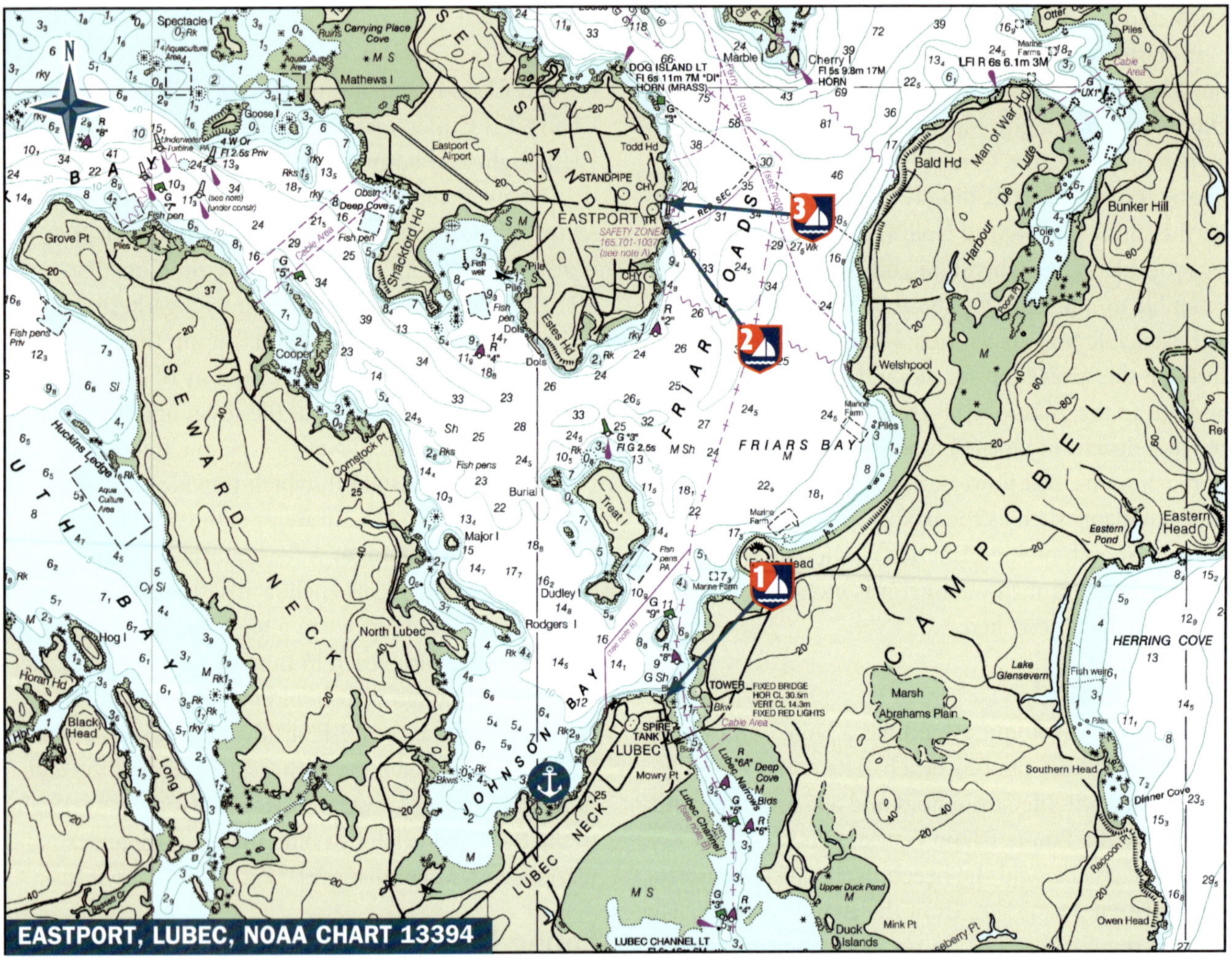

EASTPORT, LUBEC, NOAA CHART 13394

The town of Lubec is located beyond the fixed **FDR International Memorial Bridge** at the narrows (with a vertical clearance of 47 feet). If you are determined to take this route, plan to reach the bridge at low slack water (which lasts 5 to 15 minutes) or at the early stage of the flood. Incoming currents become swift here (up to 6 knots) and the outgoing even more so (as swiftly as 8 knots). The passage is quite narrow and long-tethered Coast Guard buoys might appear to be off-station at low water. (As a result, many locals advise in favor of the longer passage around East Quoddy Head on Campobello Island through Head Harbor Passage and Friar Roads.)

Dockage: The 10-slip Lubec Municipal Marina may have space for you and sells diesel fuel.

Anchorage: Johnson Bay has 9 foot MLW and good holding in mud and rock. This is open to the north so choose wisely.

Eastport, Moose Island

NAVIGATION: Use NOAA Charts 13325, 13394 and 13396. Forty miles by highway from Lubec but only 3 miles by water, Eastport is a better layover choice. The large gray stone building just to the left of the harbor houses the Post Office on the upper level and the U.S. Customs office below. (This is by far the easiest place in these waters to check back into the United States after a trip to Canada.)

The R&M IGA Foodliner (88 Washington St., 207-853-4050) provides all items necessary for major provisioning. East of the harbor, the Eastport Chowder House (167 Water St., 207-853-4700) offers an alternative both for dockage (in a quieter and less crowded setting) and for dining, as well as a diesel fuel depot.

Dockage/Moorings: Eastport's Harbormaster (VHF Channel 16, 207-853-4614) assigns space at the breakwater/wharf and on moorings with price breaks for week- and month-long stays.

Moose Island Marine has slips and moorings and offers repairs. Their ship store is located immediately at the end of the short road leading from the breakwater to Water Street. An impressive array of parts and supplies is available there and specialty items can be ordered quickly.

Waco Diner (207-853-9226) has a pier with floats and offers transient dockage that is complimentary for stays of less than 24 hours. The Eastport Chowder House welcomes transients on their docks and is the only place that offers showers (207-853-4700).

■ NEXT STOP

At the Canadian border mariners may choose to head for superb cruising opportunities in the Maritime Provinces or to retrace steps homeward. A third alternative before heading south and without checking in and out of Canada is to experience the beauty and extraordinary riptides (6-foot dancing waters and dinghy-sized whirlpools) of a day cruise along the international border in Passamaquoddy Bay and up the lower reaches of the St. Croix River.

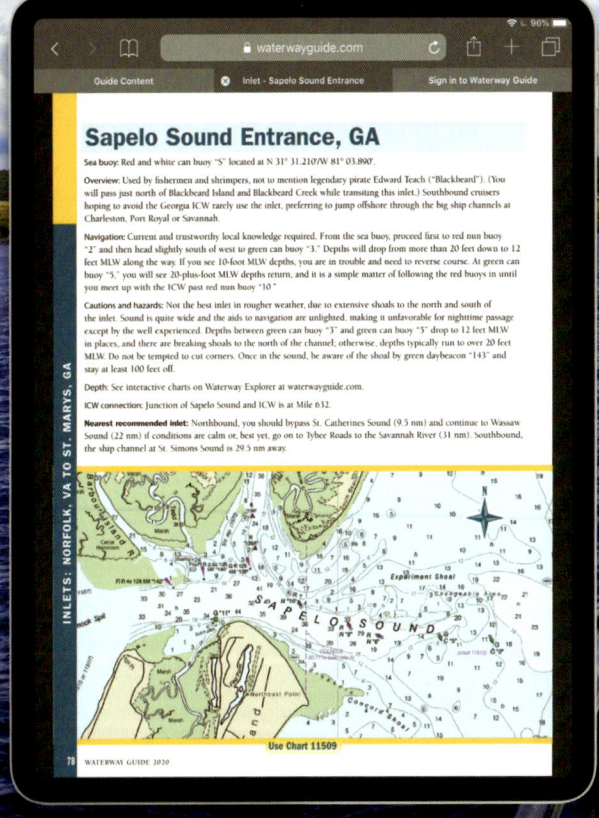

Marina/Sponsor Index   Sponsors are listed in **BOLD**.

MARINA/SPONSOR INDEX

Subject Index

Most relevant pages are listed in **BOLD**.

Goin' Ashore Index